D1023609

📖 Let's Go writers travel on your budget.

"Guides that penetrate the veneer of the holiday brochures and mine the grit of real life."

—*The Economist*

"The writers seem to have experienced every rooster-packed bus and lunar-surfaced mattress about which they write."

—*The New York Times*

"All the dirt, dirt cheap."

—*People*

📖 Great for independent travelers.

"The guides are aimed not only at young budget travelers but at the independent traveler; a sort of streetwise cookbook for traveling alone."

—*The New York Times*

"Flush with candor and irreverence, chock full of budget travel advice."

—*The Des Moines Register*

"An indispensible resource, *Let's Go*'s practical information can be used by every traveler."

—*The Chattanooga Free Press*

📖 Let's Go is completely revised each year.

"Only *Let's Go* has the zeal to annually update every title on its list."

—*The Boston Globe*

"Unbeatable: good sightseeing advice; up-to-date info on restaurants, hotels, and inns; a commitment to money-saving travel; and a wry style that brightens nearly every page."

—*The Washington Post*

📖 All the important information you need.

"*Let's Go* authors provide a comedic element while still providing concise information and thorough coverage of the country. Anything you need to know about budget traveling is detailed in this book."

—*The Chicago Sun-Times*

"Value-packed, unbeatable, accurate, and comprehensive."

—*Los Angeles Times*

Let's Go Publications

Let's Go: Alaska & the Pacific Northwest 2000
Let's Go: Australia 2000
Let's Go: Austria & Switzerland 2000
Let's Go: Britain & Ireland 2000
Let's Go: California 2000
Let's Go: Central America 2000
Let's Go: China 2000 **New Title!**
Let's Go: Eastern Europe 2000
Let's Go: Europe 2000
Let's Go: France 2000
Let's Go: Germany 2000
Let's Go: Greece 2000
Let's Go: India & Nepal 2000
Let's Go: Ireland 2000
Let's Go: Israel 2000 **New Title!**
Let's Go: Italy 2000
Let's Go: Mexico 2000
Let's Go: Middle East 2000 **New Title!**
Let's Go: New York City 2000
Let's Go: New Zealand 2000
Let's Go: Paris 2000
Let's Go: Perú & Ecuador 2000 **New Title!**
Let's Go: Rome 2000
Let's Go: South Africa 2000
Let's Go: Southeast Asia 2000
Let's Go: Spain & Portugal 2000
Let's Go: Turkey 2000
Let's Go: USA 2000
Let's Go: Washington, D.C. 2000

Let's Go Map Guides

Amsterdam	New Orleans
Berlin	New York City
Boston	Paris
Chicago	Prague
Florence	Rome
London	San Francisco
Los Angeles	Seattle
Madrid	Washington, D.C.

Coming Soon: Sydney and Hong Kong

Let's Go

2000

INDIA & NEPAL

Christiana E. King

Editor

Brendan T. Daly

Associate Editor

Sharmila Surianarain

Associate Editor

Researcher-Writers:

Andrew Berry

Andrew D. Boch

Jon Finer

Sumeet Garg

Samidha Ghosh

Jennifer Gootman

Ona M. Hahs

Risha Kim Lee

Leeore Schnairsohn

Alex Travelli

Honza Vihan

Paul Warham

St. Martin's Press ≋ New York

HELPING LET'S GO If you want to share your discoveries, suggestions, or corrections, please drop us a line. We read every piece of correspondence, whether a postcard, a 10-page email, or a coconut. Please note that mail received after May 2000 may be too late for the 2001 book, but will be kept for future editions. **Address mail to:**

> Let's Go: India & Nepal
> 67 Mount Auburn Street
> Cambridge, MA 02138
> USA

Visit Let's Go at **http://www.letsgo.com,** or send email to:

> **feedback@letsgo.com**
> **Subject: "Let's Go: India & Nepal"**

In addition to the invaluable travel advice our readers share with us, many are kind enough to offer their services as researchers or editors. Unfortunately, our charter enables us to employ only currently enrolled Harvard students.

ABOUT LET'S GO

FORTY YEARS OF WISDOM

As a new millennium arrives, *Let's Go: Europe*, now in its 40th edition and translated into seven languages, reigns as the world's bestselling international travel guide. For four decades, travelers criss-crossing the Continent have relied on *Let's Go* for inside information on the hippest backstreet cafes, the most pristine secluded beaches, and the best routes from border to border. In the last 20 years, our rugged researchers have stretched the frontiers of backpacking and expanded our coverage into Asia, Africa, Australia, and the Americas. We're celebrating our 40th birthday with the release of *Let's Go: China*, blazing the traveler's trail from the Forbidden City to the Tibetan frontier; *Let's Go: Perú & Ecuador*, spanning the lands of the ancient Inca Empire; *Let's Go: Middle East*, with coverage from Istanbul to the Persian Gulf; and the maiden edition of *Let's Go: Israel*.

It all started in 1960 when a handful of well-traveled students at Harvard University handed out a 20-page mimeographed pamphlet offering a collection of their tips on budget travel to passengers on student charter flights to Europe. The following year, in response to the instant popularity of the first volume, students traveling to Europe researched the first full-fledged edition of *Let's Go: Europe*, a pocket-sized book featuring honest, practical advice, witty writing, and a decidedly youthful slant on the world. Throughout the 60s and 70s, our guides reflected the times. In 1969 we taught travelers how to get from Paris to Prague on "no dollars a day" by singing in the street. In the 80s and 90s, we looked beyond Europe and North America and set off to all corners of the earth. Meanwhile, we focused in on the world's most exciting urban areas to produce in-depth, fold-out map guides. Our new guides bring the total number of titles to 48, each infused with the spirit of adventure and voice of opinion that travelers around the world have come to count on. But some things never change: our guides are still researched, written, and produced entirely by students who know first-hand how to see the world on the cheap.

HOW WE DO IT

Each guide is completely revised and thoroughly updated every year by a well-traveled set of over 250 students. Every spring, we recruit over 180 researchers and 70 editors to overhaul every book. After several months of training, researcher-writers hit the road for seven weeks of exploration, from Anchorage to Adelaide, Estonia to El Salvador, Iceland to Indonesia. Hired for their rare combination of budget travel sense, writing ability, stamina, and courage, these adventurous travelers know that train strikes, stolen luggage, food poisoning, and marriage proposals are all part of a day's work. Back at our offices, editors work from spring to fall, massaging copy written on Himalayan bus rides into witty, informative prose. A student staff of typesetters, cartographers, publicists, and managers keeps our lively team together. In September, the collected efforts of the summer are delivered to our printer, which turns them into books in record time, so that you have the most up-to-date information available for your vacation. Even as you read this, work on next year's editions is well underway.

WHY WE DO IT

We don't think of budget travel as the last recourse of the destitute; we believe that it's the only way to travel. Living cheaply and simply brings you closer to the people and places you've been saving up to visit. Our books will ease your anxieties and answer your questions about the basics—so you can get off the beaten track and explore. Once you learn the ropes, we encourage you to put *Let's Go* down now and then to strike out on your own. You know as well as we that the best discoveries are often those you make yourself. When you find something worth sharing, please drop us a line. We're Let's Go Publications, 67 Mount Auburn St., Cambridge, MA 02138, USA (email: feedback@letsgo.com). For more info, visit our website, http://www.letsgo.com.

HOW TO USE THIS BOOK

DISCOVER INDIA AND NEPAL. The subcontinent is *big*. Use the **Discover** chapter (p. 1) in conjunction with **Let's Go Picks** (p. xviii) and the **Highlights of the Region** boxes at the beginning of each chapter.

BEFORE YOU GO. Traveling to India and Nepal, even on a budget, is a costly undertaking that requires a lot of preparation: vaccinations, visas, choosing the right color backpack, and so on. The **Essentials** section (p. 7) contains all that and more, explaining the logistics of getting there and, once there, the particulars of staying fed, sheltered, clothed, and healthy as you travel. It also contains helpful information on **Customs and Etiquette** (p. 56) and **Trekking** (p. 36).

CULTURAL INFORMATION. Chapters on **India** (p. 65) and **Nepal** (p. 705) trace the two countries' history from ancient civilizations to this year's elections, and provide background on the religious and artistic traditions of South Asia. At the end of the book, there's a **glossary** (p. 807) of terms used commonly in this book.

LANGUAGES भाषा. Most of the city and town names in this book are translated into some **local script**. Although English and a lot of patience are all the communication tools you really need for most travel in India and Nepal, it never hurts to have the Hindi (or Kannada or Tamil) city name ready to show your bus driver. The appendix contains **phrasebooks** (p. 811) for the Hindi, Bengali, Tamil, Marathi, Nepali, Gujurati, Kannada, Malayam, and Telegu languages. Learning even a few words will ease communication and gain you a lot of new friends.

 WARNING. This is a warning box. Read these for information on how to avoid getting ripped off by jewelry smugglers. Or trampled by angry rhinos. Or both.

INDIA. Our coverage of India is organized geographically, moving in a roughly counter-clockwise direction from **Delhi** (p. 102) and **Uttar Pradesh** (p. 129) to the **Northeast States** (p. 673). With a few exceptions, each state is treated in its own chapter, with coverage radiating out from a major city.

NEPAL. Coverage begins in the **Kathmandu Valley** (p. 719) and moves to the **Western Hills** (p. 759), the lowland **Terai** (p. 772), the **Eastern Hills** (p. 785) and culminates with our section on **Trekking in Nepal** (p. 787), which includes detailed information on planning, packing, and health concerns for trekkers.

CITY BY CITY. Within each city or town, information is presented in the following order: **Transportation**, **Orientation and Practical Information**, **Accommodations**, **Food**, and **Sights**. When applicable, you'll also see **Nightlife**, **Entertainment**, and **Shopping** sections. **Let's Go Picks** are those restaurants and hotels which our researchers found stellar, but pick or no pick, our discriminating experts picked their favorites and listed those first.

A NOTE TO OUR READERS The information for this book was gathered by *Let's Go*'s researchers from May through August. Each listing is derived from the assigned researcher's opinion based upon his or her visit at a particular time. The opinions are expressed in a candid and forthright manner. Those traveling at a different time may have different experiences since prices, dates, hours, and conditions are always subject to change. You are urged to check beforehand to avoid inconvenience and surprises. Travel always involves a certain degree of risk, especially in low-cost areas. When traveling, especially on a budget, always take particular care to ensure your safety.

CONTENTS

MAPS

RESEARCHER-WRITERS

Andrew Berry   *Western Nepal, Kerala*

Nice researcher, this. Turning in ream after ream of painstakingly detailed copy and "picturesque" maps, he reported on the shape, smell, and savor of each sandwich he swallowed on his way from Kollam to Kathmandu. After roaming the beach in search of every undiscovered local joint, Andrew drew on his fifteen years of Himalayan trekking know-how to comb the hills of Nepal in search of yet another beautiful hike. We liked him so much we brought him back for more.

Andrew D. Boch   *Kathmandu Valley, Eastern Nepal*

Our Drugstore Cowboy in Nepal, Andrew penned a poem or two in Patan's square, unfazed by the twelve bus accidents he witnessed in one week on his way there. Kathmandu's nightlife was the better for his wild research, while Bungamati left him feeling the intruder—no "one pen, one rupee" here, just stares. He hobnobbed with local tea farmers in Nepal's terraced fields and downed a *tong-ba* or two in celebration of each completed batch.

Jon Finer   *Sikkim, West Bengal, Northeast States, Orissa*

He had a nose for nature, sniffing it out of the national parks of the Northeast—West Bengal's Jaldapara remained a secret until Finer caught the scent. With cultural savvy and a creative style, he crafted page after page of charming copy, delighting us with his creative graybox coverage/contributions. Though the Northeast denied him access, he followed his nose elsewhere, landing on India's eastern shore and riding astride the chariots of Orissa's temples.

Sumeet Garg   *U.P. Hills, Kolkata, Andaman Islands*

With several trips to the subcontinent already under his belt, Sumeet rediscovered his roots in the hills of Uttar Pradesh. He weathered the hardships of navigating the rustic country, but city-boy-at-heart Sumeet couldn't wait to settle down in the subway metropolis of Kolkata. In the streets of India's most densely populated city, he found his niche among the urban comforts of (almost) home. Reluctant to leave this haven of civilization, he nevertheless trudged on with exemplary *Let's Go* sticktoitiveness, braving the storm yet again in the Andamans and promising to return someday under clearer skies.

Samidha Ghosh   *Madhya Pradesh, Karnataka*

Cyber-cafe-hopping her way across the subcontinent, Samidha still had a hard time keeping in touch, but at least her regular copy kept us informed of her most recent exploits. She fell in love with Mandu and found herself at home in Aihole, but Bijapur, Gokarna, and Jog Falls will have to wait until next time. Bottoms up!

Jennifer Gootman   *Rajasthan, Gujarat*

With exuberance and charm, Jenny trooped across the deserts of Rajasthan, braving the sweltering heat with her polished *Lets Go* skills of summers past. Armed with a no-nonsense approach and plenty of attitude, Jenny fended off would-be suitors and scammers. Her copy streamed in with details of thrilling escapades and photographs to prove 'em.

Ona M. Hahs   *Maharashtra*

After foraging for nuts and berries in the ghost town of Matheran, Ona explored the legendary cave temples of Ajanta and Ellora. She waded ankle-deep through the floodwaters of Mahabaleshwar, learning new ways to keep the bugs at bay...until Bombay. In spite of sailing into some rough seas, Ona made us proud with her resilience and positive attitude, and we hope that her adventurous spirit takes her back to India someday.

Risha Kim Lee *Tamil Nadu, Andhra Pradesh*

Risha?!?! A year in Israel was still not enough to prepare her for her amazing tour of South India. Loving every minute of it, from the sublime to the utterly chaotic, Risha frequently found herself muttering "the goal of the day is not to die"—her writing was always full of life. Tales of her daily adventures—snorkeling in a *salwar kameez* and seeing more of the locals than she had bargained for in Kurtrallam—had us in hysterics. A budding cartoonist and in every way a stellar researcher, Risha surprised us with her inexhaustible enthusiasm and unflagging endurance as she plowed through "just another state" before leaving her heart behind in India.

Leeore Schnairsohn *Goa, National Parks*

Surrounded by techno/rave/trance junkies in Goa, Leeore managed to keep his wry wits about him throughout his trip. Undaunted by illness and political instability, he slyly charmed his way through India, leading a tough life hanging out on the beach, lying out on the beach, visiting national parks (we're sure it was a chore), and hanging out on the beach. After a previous stint as an R-W in the urban jungle of New York, this *Let's Go* vet braved the wilds of southern India, never losing his cool and his perspective through some wild adventures.

Alex Travelli *Mumbai*

Alex Travelli called us from Delhi, and asked if we needed some aid. We thought we'd be fine. In the end we were lyin', so we asked him to start right away. It took him some time to finally get online, but the sights came out great anyway.

Honza Vihan *Punjab, Haryana, Himachal Pradesh, Ladakh*

Our hirsute Honza put off shaving for weeks hoping to blend right in with the Sikhs, before continuing his cultural quest in Ladakh and Himachal. Determined to follow his investigative instinct into mountain art galleries, Honza was unhindered even by the stick-wielding old lady (really an ex–concentration camp guard) who shooed him out the door. His coverage of the Lesser Himalayas delighted us, with each new copybatch topping the last. We wish him the very best as he stays behind to further acclimatize to Indian culture. If he *does* get any marriage proposals, we hope he'll let us know.

Paul Warham *Delhi, Uttar Pradesh, Bihar*

Paul dished the dirt on every creeping, crawling, nooky, crooked, low-roofed, little knot of rooms he could find, but "squeezing an elephant through a toilet roll" was surely his best trick yet. He dodged obstacles with a dashing skill and didn't blink an eye when his research asked him to step over a dead body face-down in a puddle of muck. His witty and fluid prose amused and informed us and helped us through the late nights.

ACKNOWLEDGMENTS

These books don't just put themselves together, you know. They are assembled by machine.

TEAM I&N THANKS: Sonesh for staying awake with us down to the last. Alex for humor and life-saving. Christian for linguistic savvy. SEAS for playing ABBA 24-7. Bede (for all his help) and the Pod Down Under for having such juicy conversations. Matt and Melissa for iconic vision. The Map Master, Dan. RL for beggin' for more. HV for being a superstar. Anne for her authoritative voice. Ankur for his Indian accent. Aarup, Anup, Esti, Josh, Karin, Keith, Nadia, Rocket, Yi, Zahr, and Will Vogel.

CHRISTIANA THANKS: Sharmi and Brendan alike for working so hard—S for showing up with a smile day after day, and B for catching, all my, mistakes. Sara, Kevin, and Mario for accompanying me on a fateful journey; Aaron and Sara for meeting me in Rajasthan for another :). Bill and Jula for bringing India home in the first place ✌. Nana for her wanderlust. Stephani, Susan, and Shannon for being there. And Joshua for being the best damn baby that I've ever seen.

BRENDAN THANKS: Christiana and Sharmi, for being so nice to a meat-eater. My parents, for love and patience, and their other progeny: Andrew, for keeping me young, and Kevin, for making me act my age. J.S. Bach, Trevor Pinnock, Philippe Herreweghe, Christopher Hogwood, musica ficta, hemiola, and the fugue. Kit, for always listening, and Nadia, for trying something different. Michael, Evan, and Samuel Adams. And Yosemite, for lessons on the purity of simple, honest feelings.

SHARMI THANKS: Christiana for being an inspiring editor. Brendan for his bizarre sense of humor. Manju, Humayun, and Thangamma Mami for fonts and phrases. Yi, Sonia, and the Posses. Isaac and Rocket. Alex and Ankur for the warm clothing and hugs. Ella, Brahms, Smashmouth, and Sting—*thankas* for the music. Salman Rushdie and Waterman. Tealuxe. My sister Charu. And finally, Amma and Appa for being the most amazing parental units that operated long distance.

Editor
Christiana E. King
Associate Editors
Brendan T. Daly, Sharmila Surianarain
Managing Editor
Sonesh Chainani

Publishing Director
Benjamin Wilkinson
Editor-in-Chief
Bentsion Harder
Production Manager
Christian Lorentzen
Cartography Manager
Daniel J. Luskin
Design Managers
Matthew Daniels, Melissa Rudolph
Editorial Managers
Brendan Gibbon, Benjamin Paloff,
Kaya Stone, Taya Weiss
Financial Manager
Kathy Lu
Personnel Manager
Adam Stein
Publicity & Marketing Managers
Sonesh Chainani,
Alexandra Leichtman
New Media Manager
Maryanthe Malliaris
Map Editors
Kurt Mueller, Jon Stein
Production Associates
Steven Aponte, John Fiore
Office Coordinators
Elena Schneider, Vanessa Bertozzi,
Monica Henderson

Director of Advertising Sales
Marta Szabo
Associate Sales Executives
Tamas Eisenberger, Li Ran

President
Noble M. Hansen III
General Managers
Blair Brown, Robert B. Rombauer
Assistant General Manager
Anne E. Chisholm

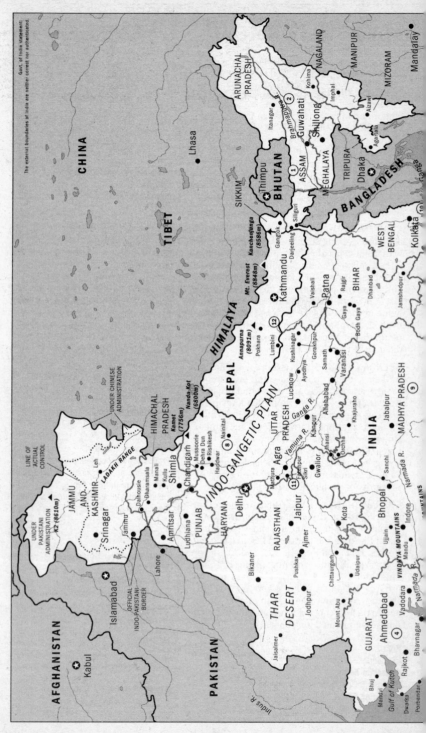

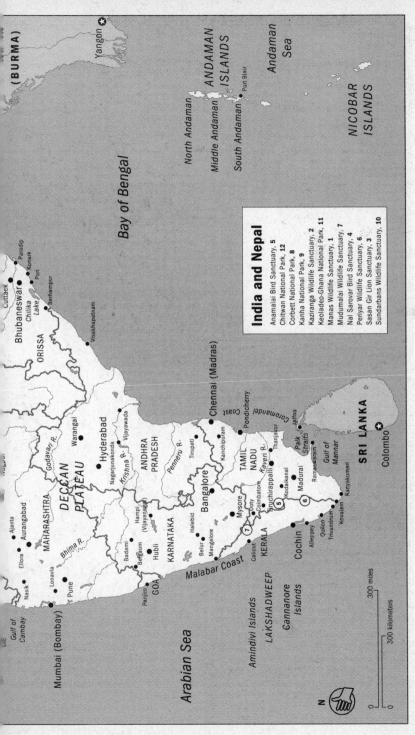

India and Nepal

Anamalai Bird Sanctuary, 5
Chitwan National Park, 12
Corbett National Park, 8
Kanha National Park, 9
Kaziranga Wildlife Sanctuary, 2
Keoladeo-Ghana National Park, 11
Manas Wildlife Sanctuary, 1
Mudumalai Wildlife Sanctuary, 7
Nal Sarovar Bird Sanctuary, 4
Periyar Wildlife Sanctuary, 6
Sasan Gir Lion Sanctuary, 3
Sundarbans Wildlife Sanctuary, 10

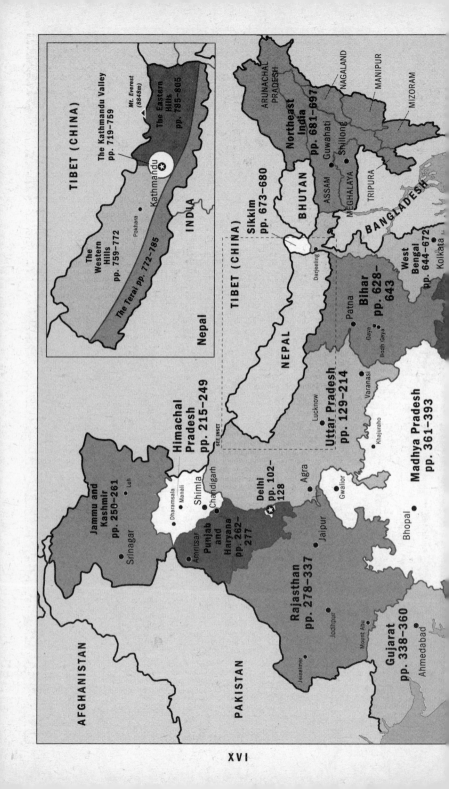

AFGHANISTAN

PAKISTAN

Jammu and
Kashmir
pp. 250–261

• Srinagar

• Leh

Himachal
Pradesh
pp. 215–249

• Dharamsala • Manali

Shimla •

Amritsar •

Punjab
and
Haryana
pp. 262–
277

Chandigarh •

Delhi
pp. 102–
128

SEE INSET

Agra •

Jaipur •

Rajasthan
pp. 278–337

Jodhpur •

Jaisalmer •

Mount Abu •

Gujarat
pp. 338–360

Ahmedabad •

Bhopal •

Gwalior •

Madhya Pradesh
pp. 361–393

Khajuraho •

TIBET (CHINA)

NEPAL

Lucknow •

Uttar Pradesh
pp. 129–214

Varanasi •

Patna •

Bihar
pp. 628–
643

Gaya •
Bodh Gaya •

Darjeeling •

Sikkim
pp. 673–680

BHUTAN

ARUNACHAL
PRADESH

NAGALAND

MANIPUR

MIZORAM

Northeast
India
pp. 681–697

ASSAM

Guwahati •

Shillong •

MEGHALAYA

TRIPURA

BANGLADESH

West
Bengal
pp. 644–672

Kolkata •

INSET:

TIBET (CHINA)

The Western
Hills
pp. 759–772

Pokhara •

The Terai pp. 772–785

Nepal

INDIA

Kathmandu ✈

The Kathmandu Valley
pp. 719–759

Mt. Everest
(8848m) ▲

The Eastern
Hills
pp. 785–805

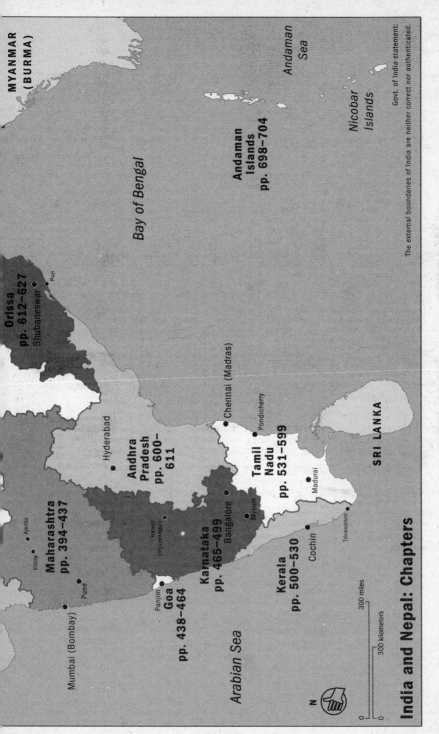

India and Nepal: Chapters

MYANMAR (BURMA)

Orissa pp. 612–627
Bhubaneswar
Puri

Maharashtra pp. 394–437
Ajanta
Ellora
Pune
Mumbai (Bombay)

Hyderabad

Andhra Pradesh pp. 600–611

Hampi (Vijayanagar)

Panjim
Goa pp. 438–464

Karnataka pp. 465–499
Bangalore
Mysore

Chennai (Madras)
Pondicherry

Tamil Nadu pp. 531–599
Madurai

Kerala pp. 500–530
Cochin
Trivandrum

SRI LANKA

Bay of Bengal

Andaman Sea

Andaman Islands pp. 698–704

Nicobar Islands

Arabian Sea

N

0 _____ 300 miles
0 _____ 300 kilometers

The external boundaries of India are neither correct nor authenticated.

Govt. of India statement:

LET'S GO PICKS

THE BEST OF HINDUISM: Hindu holy cities abound in India, but none are holier than **Varanasi** (p. 197). Other Hindu religious centers and temple towns include **Madurai** (p. 577), **Khajuraho** (p. 379), **Nasik** (p. 418), **Pushkar** (p. 297), **Tirumala** (p. 610), **Kanchipuram** (p. 547), **Chidambaram** (p. 564), **Bhubaneswar** (p. 612), and **Konark** (p. 619).

THE BEST OF BUDDHISM: The ancient ruins at **Sanchi** (p. 366), **Sarnath** (p. 208), **Lumbini** (p. 774), **Vaishali** (p. 642), and **Bodh Gaya** (p. 637) provide glimpses of Buddhism past. Modern Tibetan Buddhism thrives in **Dharamsala** (p. 223), where the Dalai Lama lives, the **Kathmandu Valley** (p. 719), **Ladakh** (p. 252), **Darjeeling** (p. 663), and **Sikkim** (p. 673).

THE BEST OF THE REST: Sikkism revolves around Amritsar's **Golden Temple** (p. 272). India's greatest Jain temples are at **Sravanabelagola** (p. 485), and **Mount Abu** (p. 313); **Ajmer** (p. 295), **Lucknow** (p. 185), and **Hyderabad** (p. 600) are centers of Indian Muslim culture. Christian structures include the colonial and pre-colonial churches of **Old Goa** (p. 446), **Chennai** (p. 532), and **Velankanni** (p. 570), while **Cochin's** (p. 516) Jewish synagogue is the fifth-oldest in the world. Finally, the **Baha'i Temple** in Delhi (p. 124) is one of India's most beautiful modern structures.

MONUMENTS AND FORT: Among the must-sees are Agra's **Taj Mahal** (p. 176), Delhi's **Jama Masjid** (p. 121) and **Red Fort** (p. 120), Jaipur's **Pink City** (p. 279), Patan's **Durbar Square** (p. 747), Hyderabad's **Golconda Fort** (p. 606), Kolkata's **Victoria Memorial** (p. 655), the **Jaisalmer Fort** (p. 324), and the abandoned capitals of **Fatehpur Sikri** (p. 179), and **Hampi** (p. 493).

TREKKING: Nepal is where trekking was invented and perfected. The **Annapurna** (p. 792) and **Everest Treks** (p. 802) are most popular, but Nepal's **Langtang Region** (p. 799) is also incredible. India's **Himachal Pradesh** (p. 215), **Ladakh** (p. 252), and **Western Sikkim** (p. 677) also have good trekking.

NATIONAL PARKS: A few tigers and a whole lot more inhabit South Asia's parks and reserves, including Nepal's **Chitwan** (p. 777) and India's **Corbett** (p. 156), **Kanha** (p. 377), **Keoladeo Ghana** (p. 293), **Kaziranga** (p. 687), **Jadalpara** (p. 662), **Mahatma Gandhi Marine** (p. 703), and **Sassam Gir** (p. 354).

ASHRAMS, MONASTERIES, AND GURUDWARAS: Those interested in studying the faith head to **Rishikesh** (p. 147), **Haridwar** (p. 142), **Pune** (p. 420), **Pondicherry** (p. 557), **Bangalore** (p. 477), **Dharamsala** (p. 223), **Bodh Gaya** (p. 637), **Amritsar** (p. 268), and **Chandigarh** (p. 262).

CAVES AND CAVE TEMPLES: Bring a flashlight to these ancient places of worship, hidden deep in the bowels of a mountain. **Ajanta** (p. 434), **Ellora** (p. 432), **Elephanta** (p. 416), **Udaigiri and Khandagiri** (p. 618), and **Badami** (p. 497).

HILL STATIONS: Built by the British as retreats to flee the heat of the plains, these hill stations are blessed with cool climes and lush tea plantations. **Dharamsala** (p. 223), **Darjeeling** (p. 663), **Ooty** (p. 594), **Kodaikanal** (p. 589), **Shimla** (p. 215), **Manali** (p. 238), **Munnar** (p. 525), **Mahabaleshwar** (p. 427), **Kullu** (p. 235), **Ilam** (p. 787), and **Mount Abu** (p. 313).

DISCOVER
INDIA & NEPAL

With a population that has just topped one billion, India bursts at the seams with a melange of cultures to match the magnitude of its sheer numbers. Birthplace of three of the world's oldest religions—Hinduism, Buddhism, and Jainism—the nation today accommodates countless others and struggles to maintain its secular facade. For the traveler venturing forth into this grandest of cultural confluences, India is both challenging—at times even threatening—and rewarding. This is not a country simply to observe; India demands reaction. From the moment you deplane, your senses will be assaulted by the myriad sights, sounds, and smells that characterize India. The sublime beauty of its natural vistas and towering temples are as likely to overwhelm as the ubiquitous smells of dirt, dust, and dung. *Paan* stains the city streets, *tilak* powder dusts the temple walls, the odor of freshly caught fish permeates the seaside air, and traffic horns could honk you out of your senses. But the magical mosques and minarets, the quick and spicy meal in a roadside *dhaba*, and the early morning chiming of temple bells make the journey into the subcontinent well worth it.

From the world's highest peaks to some of its greenest valleys, Nepal is a country that has been shaped by its geography. Ridges and rivers split the land into small pockets of tillable earth, networked by roads that connect its Indian-influenced Hindu lowlands to its Tibetan-influenced Buddhist highlands—a cultural transition marked by the geographical barriers that separate the regions. Every romantic ideal you ever envisioned about the Himalayan kingdom is fulfilled in the country's political and social center, the Kathmandu Valley. While a milder version of India in many ways, Nepal also presents challenges to the traveler— harrowing bus rides, persistent touts, and cow-dung obstructed streets. A closed kingdom isolated from the world until 1951, Nepal now greets both hippies and hikers with open arms and a lot of style.

An open mind and a healthy dose of patience are your best innoculations against the travails of travel in the subcontinent. So, don a pair of non-leather sandals, brush up on those non-verbal communication skills, grab some anti-diarrhea medication, and get ready to roll.

INDIA	NEPAL
■ **Official Name:** Republic of India	■ **Official Name:** Kingdom of Nepal
■ **Capital:** New Delhi (10.1 million)	■ **Capital:** Kathmandu (700,000)
■ **Population:** 1 billion	■ **Population:** 23 million
■ **Land Area:** 3,287,590 sq. km	■ **Land Area:** 147,181 sq. km
■ **Highest Point:** Kanchenjunga, 8598m	■ **Highest Point:** Everest, 8848m
■ **Languages:** Hindi & English, plus 14 official languages and over 700 dialects	■ **Languages:** Nepali, plus 20 other major languages and numerous dialects
■ **Religions:** 80% Hindu, 14% Muslim	■ **Religions:** 90% Hindu, 5% Buddhist
■ **Average Income Per Capita:** US$350	■ **Average Income Per Capita:** US$165
■ **Literacy:** 66% male, 38% female	■ **Literacy:** 41% male, 14% female

DISCOVER

THINGS TO DO

From scaling the world's tallest mountains to jostling worshippers at a local temple, from raving by the beach to wandering through a medieval fort, you can do it all in India and Nepal. For a more detailed list of the best things to see and do, refer to **Let's Go Picks** (p. xviii) and the **Highlights of the Region** box at the beginning of each chapter.

HOLIER THAN THOU

Visit some of the subcontinent's most sacred sites to witness the rituals and traditions that have remained intact for thousands of years. Hinduism's holiest city, **Varanasi** (p. 197) is the stomping-ground of Lord Shiva himself and the city where pious Hindus come to live out their last moments of earthly existence. Walk in the footsteps of the 9th-century saint, Shankara, who established India's four major *dhams* (sacred sites) in each of the cardinal directions: **Badrinath** (p. 155) in the north, **Dwarka** (p. 355) in the west, **Rameswaram** (p. 584) in the south, **Puri** (p. 621) in the east. The holiest city for Sikhs, **Amritsar** (p. 268) houses the blindingly beautiful Golden Temple. Free yourself from worldly desire in **Bodh Gaya** (p. 637), where the Buddha attained nirvana, or dip into the sacred pond where Lord Krishna pleasured his divine consort Radha in **Vrindaban** (p. 184). Holy Jains head to **Mount Abu** (p. 313) for its gorgeous Dilwara temples; other religious crowd-pullers are the Sun Temple in **Konark** (p. 619), the Meenakshi Amman Temple in **Madurai** (p. 577), and the Har-ki-Pairi *ghat* in **Haridwar** (p. 142).

THE GREAT OUTDOORS

The Himalayas crown North India and Nepal, boasting superb trekking among the world's highest mountains. Journey past **Mt. Everest,** the **Annapurna massif** and the **Langtang Valley** to experience the transition from Nepali villages to Tibetan hamlets (p. 787). The **Kinnaur-Spiti Road** in Himachal Pradesh passes through some of the most remote and resplendent regions of India, with great hikes along the way, particularly near **Kalpa** (p. 246). Challenge yourself on a trek in **Western Sikkim** (p. 679), in the desert plateaus near **Leh** (p. 258), or in Kashmir's **Nubra Valley** (p. 259). Catch a glimpse of a rhino or two in Assam's **Kaziranga National Park** (p. 687) or Nepal's **Chitwan National Park** (p. 777). Elephants abound at **Jaldapara Wildlife Sanctuary** (p. 662), and a brood of birdies and beasties in **Sariska Tiger Reserve** (p. 292), **Corbett National Park** (p. 156), and **Keoladeo Ghana National Park** (p. 294).

ALL THINGS BOLD AND BEAUTIFUL

The abandoned capital of **Fatehpur Sikri** (p. 179) typifies the Mughal style of architecture, while the erotic sculptures of **Khajuraho** (p. 382) attract visitors interested in more than just intricate stonework. Delhi's **Red Fort** and **Jama Masjid** (p. 120) command tourist attention, as does the impressive tribute to the Raj, the **Victoria Memorial** (p. 655) in Calcutta. Patan's temple-packed **Durbar Square** (p. 752) is worth a wander, and the **great stupa** at Boudha (p. 747) is well worth the hype. The **Vijayanagar ruins** in Hampi (p. 496) are overrun with hippies, while the **Lake Palace** in Udaipur (p. 310) captures the romantic allure of Rajasthan. Among the biggest and best of India's forts and palaces are the **Gwalior Fort** (p. 392), Jaipur's **City Palace** (p. 289), the windswept **Jaisalmer Fort** (p. 328), Hyderabad's **Golconda Fort** (p. 606), and the **Maharaja's Palace** (p. 481) in Mysore. Tomb of a beloved wife and India's most famous attraction is, of course, the **Taj Mahal** (p. 176) in Agra.

BEACH BUMS

Washed by the Arabian Sea, the Bay of Bengal, and the Indian Ocean, peninsular India has hip and happenin' beaches for the party animal as well as serene, palm-fringed shores for the more meditative. For some serious beach action, head to Goa: from the tourist-trafficked shores of **Anjuna** (p. 452) to its less-frequented beach brethren **Benaulim** (p. 462) and **Palolem** (p. 463), Goa has it all. Further north, **Dwarka's** (p. 355) shores are lapped by the waves of a salty Arabian sea. The white sands of **Kovalam** (p. 506) and **Puri** (p. 625) are outdone only by the pristine shores of **Varkala** (p. 511) and the popular strand of temple-studded **Mahabalipuram** (p. 557). The fisherman of **Calangute** and **Baga** cast their nets, while the coves and coconuts of **Port Blair** (p. 698), Andaman Islands cast a spell.

THE BACKPACKER SCENE

Love 'em or hate 'em, these Bohemian hang-outs are great places to pick up travel tips and make necessary arrangements for the next leg of your journey. Among the backpacker meccas of India and Nepal are: **Manali** (p. 238) and **Dharamsala** (p. 223) in Himachal Pradesh, **Pushkar** (p. 297) in Rajasthan, **Anjuna** (p. 452) in Goa, **Kovalam** (p. 506) in Kerala, **Mahabalipuram** (p. 552) in Tamil Nadu, **Puri** (p. 621) in Orissa, **Darjeeling** (p. 663) in West Bengal, **Pokhara** (p. 765) in Nepal's Western Hills, and **Kathmandu's** (p. 719) Thamel district, to name a select few.

HIDDEN GEMS

Traveling during the off season is a great way to dodge the crowds, but there are fascinating regions which see surprisingly little backpacker traffic regardless of the season: **Kausani** (p. 168) in the U.P. Hills, **Chamba** (p. 233) in Himachal Pradesh, **Bikaner** (p. 331) in Rajasthan, **Mandvi** (p. 359) and **Dwarka** (p. 355) in Gujarat, **Mandu** (p. 372) and **Orchha** (p. 386) in Madhya Pradesh, **Kodaikanal** (p. 589) and **Rameswaram** (p. 584) in Tamil Nadu, **Kirtipur** (p. 744) and **Manakamana** (p. 761) in Nepal, and **Jaldapara Wildlife Sanctuary** (p. 662) in West Bengal.

WHO KNEW?

And then there are the exceptions. Jaisalmer's **camel safaris** (p. 330) whisk you away to desert destinations, while Srinagar's Dal Lake is sprinkled with **houseboats** (p. 261), and **backwater cruises** (p. 524) send you coasting along the Malabar sea-shore. Gape at the fierce **kathakali dancers** in Cochin (p. 522) or, for another kind of dance, check out the **border ballet** (p. 276) at Tarn Taran. Hop on a **toy train** (p. 663) to Darjeeling or spend the night in a converted palace among Orchha's 17th-century **ruins** (p. 386). The city of Bhuj offers **village tours** (p. 359) to nearby hamlets of handicrafts fame, while Dakshinkali in Nepal dishes up a different deal, with bi-weekly **sacrifices** (p. 758) to the bloodthirsty goddess Kali. Share a room with a Buddhist monk in one of Bodh Gaya's **monestaries** (p. 640) or brush up on single-point **meditation** (p. 231) in Dharamsala. If the **ashrams** (p. 150) of Rishikesh were good enough for the Beatles, they're good enough for you.

SUGGESTED ITINERARIES

HOLY COW! THE BEST OF INDIA & NEPAL (6-8 WEEKS) Capital of the Republic, **Delhi** (p. 102) begins and ends this epic journey through the subcontinent. Transcend the physical realm in **Rishikesh** (p. 147), the spiritual retreat center made famous by the Beatles, or at hippie hang-out **Manali** (p. 238). Visit the mountain home of Tibetan Buddhism in exile in **Dharamsala** (p. 223), continuing the pilgrimage to **Amritsar** (p. 268), focal point of the Sikh faith. Head over to the desert capital of Rajasthan, **Jaipur** (p. 279), with a quick stop in the oases of **Pushkar** (p. 297) and **Udaipur** (p. 305). Halfway down the Malabar coast, the clubs of India's largest and most western-ized city, **Mumbai** (p. 394), try to prepare you for **Goa** (p. 438), host to the funkiest rave scene in India; follow the hippie highway to **Hampi's** (p. 493) extensive ruins. **Mysore** (p. 477) boasts a magnificent Maharaja's Palace in an idyllic natural setting. Continue your coastal jaunt, stopping by wealthy port **Cochin** (p. 516), where you can cruise through the backwaters of the Arabian Sea. **Madurai** (p. 577), capital of the Pandya kingdom, is the most dazzling of Tamil Nadu's temple cities. Pay tribute to Muslim stronghold **Hyderabad** (p. 600) before hitting temple-packed **Bhubaneswar** (p. 612). Visit one of India's biggest cultural powerhouses, **Calcutta** (p. 644), before sipping tea in mountain getaway **Darjeeling** (p. 663) and crossing the border into the lush greenery of the Hindu-Buddhist **Kathmandu Valley** (p. 719). For even more

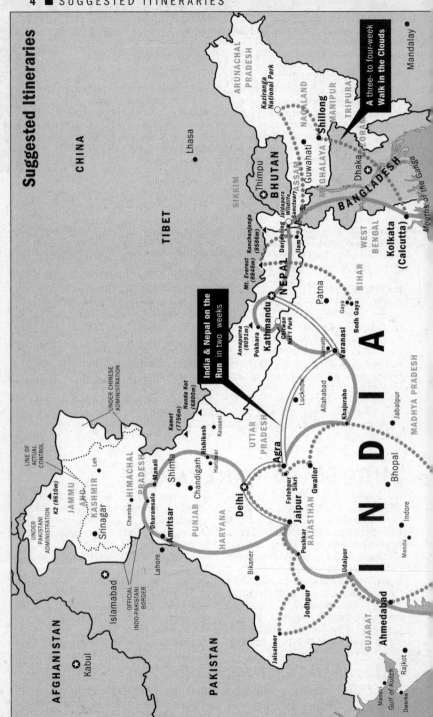

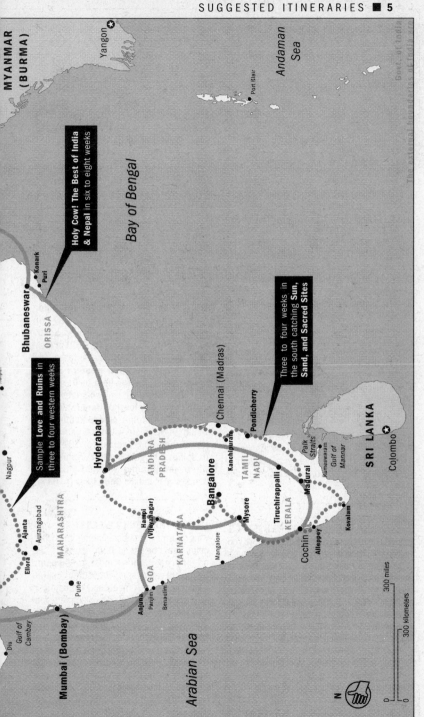

MYANMAR (BURMA)

Yangon ✪

Andaman Sea

Bay of Bengal

Port Blair

Holy Cow! The Best of India & Nepal in six to eight weeks

Nagpur

Bhubaneswar

● Konark
Puri

ORISSA

Sample **Love and Ruins** in three to four western weeks

Three to four weeks in the south catching **Sun, Sand, and Sacred Sites**

Chennai (Madras)

Hyderabad

Pondicherry

ANDHRA PRADESH

Kanchipuram

Ajanta

Ellora

Aurangabad

MAHARASHTRA

Bangalore

TAMIL NADI

Diu

Gulf of Cambay

Pune

Hampi (Vijayanagar)

KARNATAKA

Mysore

Tiruchirappalli

Madurai

KERALA

Rameswaram
Gulf of Mannar

Palk Straits

SRI LANKA

Colombo ✪

Mumbai (Bombay)

Anjuna
Panjim
Benaulim

GOA

Mangalore

Cochin
Alleppey

Kovalam

Arabian Sea

N

0 ___ 300 miles
0 ___ 300 kilometers

spectacular views of Himalayan peaks, spend some time in **Pokhara** (p. 765) before trekking through the mountains of the **Annapurna Region** (p. 792). Swing by **Chitwan National Park** (p. 777) for that up-close-and-personal encounter with a rhino before cruising by the burning *ghats* in **Varanasi** (p. 197) and gawking at the sexy stonework in **Khajuraho** (p. 379). This subcontinental sweep fittingly culminates in **Agra** (p. 169), home to India's crown jewel and ultimate mustsee, the Taj Mahal.

LOVE AND RUINS: WEST INDIA (3-4 WEEKS) Begin with India's "Golden Triangle" of **Delhi, Agra,** and **Jaipur** (see above). 50,000 camels converge in **Pushkar's** (p. 297) annual camel fair; continue your tour of Rajasthan in the vibrant "Blue City" of **Jodhpur** (p. 317), with its impressive palace complex. Wander the winding streets and intricately carved *havelis* inside **Jaisalmer's** (p. 324) fort, the golden prize at the end of a journey to India's western border. Rooftop restaurants and lakeside views make the "White City" of **Udaipur** (p. 305) an idyllic desert oasis. Visit Maharashtra's famous cave temples at **Ellora** (p. 432) and **Ajanta** (p. 434) and **Khajuraho's** (p. 379) racy temple sculptures, the pride of neighboring Madhya Pradesh. The impressive ancient fort of **Gwalior's** (p. 389) has seen centuries go by, while time stands still in the abandoned city of **Fatehpur Sikri** (p. 179).

SUN, SAND, AND SACRED SITES: SOUTH INDIA (3-4 WEEKS) Start your tour of India's southern tip by taking in the remnants of India's 16th century majesty in **Hyderabad's** (p. 600) Golconda Fort. Hang with the hippies among **Hampi's** (p. 493) ruins or rub elbows with the country's hi-tech elite in **Bangalore** (p. 466) and visit the ashrams of an internationally-loved spiritual leader all in one day. Tour the grounds of the stunning Maharaja's Palace on the back of an elephant in **Mysore** (p. 477), Karnataka. In the port of **Cochin** (p. 516), sit back for a performance of *kathakali* dance, then journey through Kerala's backwaters, where you can see Indian village life up close on your way to **Alleppey** (p. 512). Bask in the sun at the mellow beach town of **Kovalam** (p. 506) before bargaining for batiks in the bazaars of **Madurai** (p. 577), where the Meenakshi Amman Temple towers. Echoes of French colonialist history greet you in **Pondicherry** (p. 557), where you can eat French food while overlooking the Indian Ocean's rocky coast. Finish off your South Indian adventure in **Kanchipuram** (p. 547), and shop for silk *saris* amid the sound of temple bells in this sacred city.

A WALK IN THE CLOUDS: NORTHEAST INDIA & NEPAL (3-4 WEEKS) Bastion of Bengali culture **Kolkata** (p. 644) is a natural introduction to the hidden treasures of the northeast. Breathe in the mountain air in cloud-filled **Shillong** (p. 691), tripping to Assam's fauna-filled **Kaziranga National Park** (p. 687) on your way to the other rhino haven, **Jaldapara Wildlife Sanctuary** (p. 662) in West Bengal. Trek through tea estates and Tibetan monasteries in **Western Sikkim** before taking the toy train to **Darjeeling** (p. 663). If trekking isn't your cup of tea, head to the tiny town of **Ilam** (p. 787) in Nepal's Eastern Hills. No trip to the region would be complete without a peak at the top of the world: **Everest** (p. 802). Soar to spiritual heights under the pipal tree, where the Buddha attained enlightenment back in India's **Bodh Gaya** (p. 637).

I&N ON THE RUN (2 WEEKS) This whirlwind tour of the subcontinent's most precious gems begins in **Delhi** (p. 102), the nation's capital for almost a millenium. Savor the richness of Rajasthani culture (and maybe even meet the Maharaja!) in **Jaipur's** (p. 279) Pink City. Complete your exploration of India's "Golden Triangle" in **Agra** (p. 169), home to the Taj Mahal. The holiest of the Hindu cities, **Varanasi** (p. 197) presents a fascinating spectacle of ritual bathing in the holy waters of the Ganga. Spend your last few days in the temple-packed **Kathmandu Valley** (p. 739), basking in the beauty of the world's highest peaks.

ESSENTIALS

FACTS FOR THE TRAVELER

WHEN TO GO

Both India and Nepal have high and low periods for tourism, which correspond with changes in the weather as well as the timing of vacations and festivals. High season brings inflated prices and a flood of people; low season (which coincides with the monsoon in most of the subcontinent) means reduced services and reduced traffic at reduced prices, and certain tourist towns close down altogether during this time. Specific peak seasons vary by location. It might also be worth timing your trip to enjoy some of the festivals that take place every year in India or Nepal; for more information, see **Holidays and Festivals for 2000-2001,** p. 806.

INDIA

Temperatures and climate in India range from the temperate regions of the North to the tropical monsoon of the South. The country's geography is so diverse that different regions have vastly different weather, even at the same time of year.

The mountain valleys in the Himalayan foothills have extremely cold winters but are reasonably warm in the summertime. Some mountain roads are only accessible during the summer, generally the best time to visit the hills. Northern reaches in Himachal Pradesh and Ladakh are also in rainshadow and get none of the monsoonal torrents. The rest of India, however, relies heavily on the mighty **monsoon.** During the monsoon—which refers not to a single event, but to a series of storms—it downpours most days, although the afternoon sun will emerge occasionally and steam things up—mountain views, however, remain perpetually obscured. The monsoons can be extremely destructive, inducing mudslides and flooding, cutting communications and transportation lines, and causing power outages. The mountains of Northeast India are especially hard hit in July and August, and deadly landslides are not uncommon. The two major monsoons hit the southwest and northeast coasts in late May or early June. They advance inward over the next two months, dumping water on most of India except the Himalayan foothills and the deep South—Tamil Nadu, southern Andhra Pradesh, and the Andaman Islands get monsoon lashing in mid-October.

The monsoon wanes in September, beginning India's **cool season,** although it takes a few more months for the Deccan plateau to dry up. December and January are cool, even cold, at night. Tropical ovens like Mumbai and Chennai go from being almost intolerably hot to being merely hot, and many travelers head south to beach haunts like Goa. **Winter** is the best time to visit India, although some find the Indian hills too chilly—spring and autumn are the most popular times to go. Few good things last forever, though, and by February, heat begins building up across the plains. April, May, and June can be suicidally hot, with temperatures of over 45°C(110°F). After a few weeks of downright unbearable weather (dust and lightening storms are commonplace) the rains come again, and the cycle repeats.

NEPAL

Most tourists visit Nepal in the **autumn** (Oct.-Nov.), when the countryside is fresh, the temperatures are mild, the air is clear, and the mountains are visible. The dry, clean air also makes autumn a great time for trekking. **Spring** is also a good time to visit: flowers are in bloom in the hills, the days are longer, and temperatures are a little warmer than in the autumn. **Winter** is probably the worst time to go to Nepal:

snow covers ground over 2000-3000m, and even Kathmandu gets damp and cold. April to June **(pre-monsoon)** gets hot and dusty, especially in the Terai, although temperatures at higher elevations are more bearable, but the haze eclipses the mountains. The **monsoon** descends from late June to September. While most of the country is cloud-cast and beset with downpours, western Nepal, largely in rain-shadow, is drier. Although the land greens visibly during the monsoon, there are some drawbacks: roads wash out, flights get cancelled, and leeches become your closest companions on trekking routes.

Destinations	High/Low Temp. (°C)				Average	Best Months
	Jan.	Apr.	July	Oct.	Monsoon	to Visit
Calcutta	26/12	35/23	32/25	29/23	June-Sept.	Nov.-Mar.
Chennai (Madras)	29/20	34/23	36/25	32/24	Oct.-Dec.	Dec.-Mar.
Cochin	31/23	31/26	29/24	29/24	May-Aug.	Dec.-Mar.
Delhi	21/7	32/17	39/26	35/16	June-Sept.	Nov.-Mar.
Darjeeling	9/3	17/9	19/15	19/11	June-Sept.	Apr.-June, Oct.-Nov.
Hyderabad	29/16	36/24	31/22	30/19	June-Sept.	Nov.-Feb.
Guwahati, Assam	23/10	32/18	32/25	27/22	Apr.-Sept.	Oct.-Mar.
Jaipur	22/8	33/19	35/26	31/15	July-Aug.	Nov.-Mar.
Kathmandu	18/2	28/12	29/20	27/13	June-Aug.	Oct.-Nov.
Mumbai (Bombay)	31/16	32/23	29/25	32/23	June-Aug.	Nov.-Mar.
Panjim, Goa	31/19	32/23	28/24	32/21	June-Aug.	Dec.-Mar.
Shimla	9/3	17/10	21/15	19/8	July-Sept.	Apr.-July, Oct.-Nov.
Srinagar, Kashmir	4/-3	20/7	31/17	22/6	None	Mar.-Sept.

DOCUMENTS AND FORMALITIES

ENTRANCE REQUIREMENTS.
Passport (p. 9). Required for all citizens traveling to India and Nepal.
Visa (p. 11). Required for all travelers, except citizen of India traveling to Nepal and vice versa.
Inoculations (p. 26). Visitors who have been in Africa, South America or Trinidad and Tobago within six days prior to their arrival in India must have a certificate of vaccination against yellow fever.
Work Permit (p. 14). Required for foreigners planning to work in India or Nepal.

EMBASSIES AND CONSULATES

INDIA

U.S.: Embassy of India, including visa and passport division for the southeastern U.S.: 2536 Massachusetts Ave. NW, Washington, D.C. 20008 (tel. (202) 939-9839; www.indianembassy.org); for visas, submit applications M-F 9:30am-12:30pm and pick up visa on the same day, 4-5pm. Applications submitted by mail take at least 10 working days to process and must be paid by cash or money order. **Consulates:** Northeast: Consulate of India, 3 East 64th St., **New York,** NY 10021 (tel. (212) 774-0600; www.Indiacgny.org); submit application M-F 9:30am-noon, pick up visa 4:30-5:15pm. West: Consulate General of India, 540 Arguello Blvd., **San Francisco,** CA 94118 (tel. (415) 668-0683; fax 668-9764; www.indianconsulate-sf.org); submit visa application 9am-1pm; U.S. passport-holders can pick up visa same day 2-4:30pm. Midwest: Consulate General of India, 455 North City Front Plaza Drive, NBC Tower Building, Suite 850, **Chicago,** IL 60611 (tel. (312) 595-0405; chicago.indianconsulate.com); submit applications 9am-noon and pick up visa 3:30-4:30pm.

Canada: 10 Springfield Rd., **Ottawa,** Ontario K1M 1C9 (tel. (613) 744-3751); submit application M-F 9:30am-12:30pm and pick up visa 3:30-5:15pm. **Consulates:** 2 Bloor St., West, 5th fl., **Toronto,** Ontario M4W 3E2 (tel. (416) 960-0751); submit application 9:30am-12:00pm and pick up 2:30-4pm; 325 House St., Suite 201, **Vancouver,** B.C.

V6C 1Z7 (tel. (604) 662-8811); submit application M-F 9:30am-12:30pm and pick up visa next working day 3:30-5pm.

U.K.: India House, Aldwych, **London,** WC2 B4NA (tel. (0171) 836 8484). **Consulates:** 20 Augusta St., Jewellery Quarter, Hockley, **Birmingham** B18 6JL (tel. (0121) 212 2778); submit visa application 9:30am-12:30pm, pick up visa the same day 3-4:30pm. Fleming House, 134 Renfrew St., **Glasgow** G3 6ST (tel. (0141) 331 0777); submit application M-F 9:30am-12:30pm, pick up visa 4-5pm.

Ireland: 6 Leeson Park, Dublin 6 (tel. (01) 497 0843; fax 497 8074); visa services open 9:30am-12:15pm; Irish citizens should allow 2 working days for processing.

Australia: 3 Moonah Place, Yarralumla, **Canberra,** ACT 2600 (tel. (02) 6273 3999; fax 6273 1308). **Consulates:** 25, Bligh St., Level 27, **Syndey,** NSW 2000 (tel. (02) 9223 9500); open M-F 9am-1pm; visa takes 2-3 days in person. 195 Adelaide Terrace, 1st Fl., **East Perth,** Western Australia 6004 (tel. (08) 9221 1485); open M-F 9am-12:30pm; visa takes 5 working days. 15 Munro St., **Coburg,** Victoria 3058 (tel. (03) 9384 0141); open M-F 9am-1pm; visa takes five working days.

New Zealand: 180 Molesworth St., FAI House, Level 10, P.O. Box 4045, Wellington 4045 (tel. (04) 473 6390). Open M-F 9am-5:30pm; visa takes min. 10 days.

South Africa: 852 Schoaman St., Arcadia, Pretoria 0083; P.O. Box 40216, Arcadia, Pretoria 0007 (tel. 12 342 5392).

NEPAL

Would-be wanderers from Ireland should contact the embassy in London, while New Zealanders are served via the Sydney office. There is no embassy in South Africa. For more information, see **Visas,** p. 6.

U.S.: 2131 Leroy Place NW, Washington, D.C. 20008 (tel. (202) 667-4550; fax 667-5534); accepts visa applications 10am-12pm and 2-4pm. Allow a few days for processing. **Consulate:** Royal Nepalese Consulate General, 820 Second Ave., 17th floor, New York, NY 10017 (tel. (212) 370-3988; fax 953-2038; www.undp.org/missions/nepal/consulate.htm); accepts applications 10am-1pm for return the next day. Tourist visas available upon entry into Nepal.

Canada: Royal Nepalese Consulate, 200 Bay St., Toronto, Ontario M5J 2J9 (tel. (416) 865-0210; fax 865-0904). Open for walk-in visa service Th 9am-3pm.

U.K.: 12a Kensington Palace Gardens, London W8 4QU (tel. (0171) 229 1594). Submit visa application M-F 10am-12pm; allow 1 day for processing.

Australia: 48 Mitchell St., McMahons Point, Sydney, NSW 2060 (tel. (02) 956 8815).

EMBASSIES AND CONSULATES IN INDIA AND NEPAL

Most countries have embassies and consulates in **Delhi** (see p. 112). Many have offices in **Mumbai** (see p. 405), and a few in **Chennai** (see p. 405) and **Calcutta** (see p. 651). In Nepal, all foreign diplomatic missions are in **Kathmandu** (see p. 726).

PASSPORTS

REQUIREMENTS. Citizens of Australia, Canada, Ireland, New Zealand, South Africa, the U.K., and the U.S. need valid passports to enter India and Nepal and to re-enter their own country. India and Nepal do not allow entrance if the holder's passport expires in under six months; returning home with an expired passport is illegal and may result in a fine.

PHOTOCOPIES. Photocopy the page of your passport that contains your photograph, passport number, and other identifying information, along with other important documents such as visas, travel insurance policies, airplane tickets, and traveler's check serial numbers, in case you lose anything. Carry one set of copies in a safe place apart from the originals and leave another set at home.

LOST PASSPORTS. Immediately notify the local police and the nearest embassy or consulate of your home government. To expedite its replacement, you will need to know all information previously recorded and show identification and proof of citizenship. In some cases, a replacement may take weeks to process, and it may be valid only for a limited time. Any visas stamped in your old passport will be irretrievably lost. In an emergency, ask for immediate temporary traveling papers that will permit you to re-enter your home country. Your passport is a public document belonging to your nation's government. You may have to surrender it to a foreign government official, but if you don't get it back shortly, inform the nearest mission of your home country.

NEW PASSPORTS. All applications for new passports or renewals should be filed several weeks or months in advance of your planned departure date—remember that you are relying on government agencies. Most passport offices offer emergency services for an extra charge. Citizens residing abroad who need a passport or renewal should contact their nearest embassy or consulate.

Australia: Citizens must apply for a passport in person at a post office, a passport office, or an Australian diplomatic mission overseas. Passport offices are located in Adelaide, Brisbane, Canberra, Darwin, Hobart, Melbourne, Newcastle, Perth, and Sydney. New adult passports cost AUS$126 (for a 32-page passport) or AUS$188 (64-page), and a child's is AUS$63 (32-page) or AUS$94 (64-page). Adult passports are valid for 10 years and child passports for 5 years. For more info, call toll-free (in Australia) 13 12 32, or visit www.dfat.gov.au/passports.

Canada: Application forms are available at all passport offices, Canadian missions, many travel agencies, and Northern Stores in northern communities. Passports cost CDN$60, plus a CDN$25 consular fee, are valid for 5 years, and are not renewable. For additional info, contact the Canadian Passport Office, Department of Foreign Affairs and International Trade, Ottawa, ON, K1A 0G3 (tel. (613) 994-3500; www.dfait-maeci.gc.ca/passport). Travelers may also call 800-567-6868 (24hr.); in Toronto, (416) 973-3251; in Vancouver, (604) 586-2500; in Montreal, (514) 283-2152.

Ireland: Citizens can apply for a passport by mail to either the Department of Foreign Affairs, Passport Office, Setanta Centre, Molesworth St., Dublin 2 (tel. (01) 671 16 33; fax 671 1092; www.irlgov.ie/iveagh), or the Passport Office, Irish Life Building, 1A South Mall, Cork (tel. (021) 27 25 25). Obtain an application at a local Garda station or post office, or request one from a passport office. Passports cost IR£45 and are valid for 10 years. Citizens under 18 or over 65 can request a 3-year passport that (IR£10).

New Zealand: Application forms for passports are available in New Zealand from most travel agents. Applications may be forwarded to the Passport Office, P.O. Box 10526, Wellington, New Zealand (tel. 0800 22 50 50; www.govt.nz/agency_info/forms.shtml). Standard processing time in New Zealand is 10 working days for correct applications. The fees are adult NZ$80, and child NZ$40. Children's names can no longer be endorsed on a parent's passport—they must apply for their own, which are valid for up to 5 years. An adult's passport is valid for up to 10 years.

South Africa: South African passports are issued only in Pretoria. However, all applications must still be submitted or forwarded to the applicable office of a South African consulate. Tourist passports, valid for 10 years, cost SAR80. Children under 16 must be issued their own passports, valid for 5 years, which cost SAR60. Time for the completion of an application is normally 3 months or more from the time of submission. For further information, contact the nearest Department of Home Affairs Office (www.southafrica-newyork.net/passport.htm).

U.K.: Full passports are valid for 10 years (5 years if under 16). Application forms available at passport offices, main post offices, and many travel agents. Apply by mail or in person to one of the passport offices, located in London, Liverpool, Newport, Peterborough, Glasgow, or Belfast. The fee is UK£31, UK£11 for children under 16. The process takes about four weeks, but the London office offers a 5-day, walk-in rush service; arrive early. The U.K. Passport Agency can be reached by phone at (0870) 521 04 10, and more information is available at www.open.gov.uk/ukpass/ukpass.htm.

U.S.: Citizens may apply for a passport at any federal or state courthouse or post office authorized to accept passport applications, or at a U.S. Passport Agency, located in most major cities. Refer to the "U.S. Government, State Department" section of the telephone directory or the local post office for addresses. Passports are valid for 10 years (5 years if under 18) and cost US$60 (under 18 US$40). Passports may be renewed by mail or in person for US$40. Processing takes 3-4 weeks. For more info, contact the U.S. Passport Information's 24hr. recorded message (tel. (202) 647-0518) or look on the web at travel.state.gov/passportservices.html.

VISAS, INVITATIONS, AND WORK PERMITS

VISAS. All travelers to India and Nepal (except citizens of India going to Nepal, and vice versa) need a visa to enter. U.S. Citizens can take advantage of the **Center for International Business and Travel (CIBT)** (tel. 800-925-2428), which will secure visas for travel to almost all countries for a variable service charge. For more information on visa services, see p. 8.

INDIA

Tourist visas are available for six months or one year and normally allow for multiple entries (important for side-trips to Nepal and other countries). Other options include a one-year visa for students, journalists, or business travelers, or a five-year visa for Indian nationals living abroad. When applying for a visa, make sure your passport is valid six months beyond the date of intended return.

It is always faster to apply through the embassy in your home country where you are a citizen. You'll need to fill out an application form and provide your current passport, as well as at least two passport photographs. **Australia:** AUS$55 for six months. **Canada:** CDN$47 for six months. **Ireland:** IR£23 for six months; non-Irish citizens add IR£10. Irish passport holders should send a stamped, self-addressed envelope to the embassy to get an application. **New Zealand:** NZ$50 for six months. **South Africa:** Three- to six-month visa is free. Contact the embassy for more information. **U.K.:** UK£19for six months. Processing takes about three weeks except in the busy tourist season (Nov.-Jan.) when it will take about six weeks. **U.S.:** US$50 for six months, US$70 for one year. Residents should contact the Indian Embassy in Washington or the consulate appropriate for their area (see **Embassies and Consulates,** p. 9).

SPECIAL PERMITS. Certain areas of India require a special permit in addition to an Indian visa. Permits can be issued by Indian diplomatic missions abroad, by Foreigners' Registration Offices in various Indian cities, or by the Ministry of Home Affairs in Delhi, Lok Nayak Bhawan, Khan Market New Delhi (open M-F 10am-5pm). Regional instability is often the reason for the extra requirements.

Northeast India: Under the Government of India's policy, many areas like Assam, Meghalaya, and Tripura are now open for tourists. A permit is no longer needed for these three states, but it is still a good idea to consult your embassy about the political situation there, especially in Assam, before visiting. Due to tribal insurgencies and fears of a conflict with China, the other four states of the northeast—**Arunachal Pradesh, Nagaland, Manipur,** and **Mizoram** require restricted area permits. Almost all requests are granted, but travelers must plan in advance. A minimum of 4 people are required to travel together, and the group must be sponsored by a government-approved travel agency, which generally charges Rs300-400. The permits, themselves, are free and allow 5-15 days of travel, depending on the state. **Restricted area permits are only available at the Ministry of Home Affairs in New Delhi.** Permits take 2 to 50 days to process.

West Bengal: Some areas around Darjeeling require a 15-day permit available to individuals or tourists traveling in groups. Permits can also be obtained through the Home Department of West Bengal.

Sikkim: Sikkim borders China and is treated by the Indian government as a military buffer. Foreigners need a permit to enter Sikkim and can only remain there 15 days per year. Permits are free and available in the major Indian cities; the red tape is thickest in Darjeeling, where the process takes an hour; elsewhere it takes only a few moments. Permits allow travel as far north as Phodang and Yuksam. Permits can be extended at the Commissioner's Office in Gangtok in special circumstances, but then only for three to five days, and only once. For North Sikkim, an inner line permit is required. It is only issued through tour companies to groups of four or more. A guide must accompany the group and the minimum charge is US$30-50 per day, including guide. It takes a solid work day to procure such a permit, available only in Gangtok. **See Sikkim,** p. 673.

Andaman and Nicobar Islands: If traveling by air to the Andaman Islands, a permit will be granted upon arrival in Port Blair (valid for 15 days). If traveling by sea to the islands, a permit must be obtained in advance from the Ministry of Home Affairs. The Nicobar Islands are off-limits to non-Indian citizens. **See The Andaman Islands,** p. 698.

Lakshadweep: The islands of Bangaran, Suheli, and Tilkam are open to tourists traveling in groups for up to a week. The necessary permit can only be obtained through the Ministry of Foreign Affairs and the Administrator of Lakshadweep.

Bhutan: Though officially an independent country, Bhutan's foreign policy and immigration procedures are controlled by India. The number of visas to Bhutan is limited by a quota system and, though visas are granted to individuals traveling alone, those who travel in group tours are much more likely to receive one. Those traveling alone are required by the Government of Bhutan to spend *at least US$240 per day*—this fee decreases slightly with larger groups. To apply for a visa, contact the Director of Tourism, Ministry of Finance, Tachichho Dzong, Thimpu, Bhutan or the Bhutan Foreign Mission, Chandra Gupta Marg, New Delhi 110021 (tel. 91 (11) 609217).

NEPAL

Anybody with a passport and a photo can get a Nepalese visa upon arrival at the airport in Kathmandu or at any of the land border crossings from India; it's really not worth fussing over ahead of time unless you're looking for something to fuss over, the fee is the same either way; at the border it must be paid in U.S. dollars. Any Nepalese consulate or embassy can issue visas for up to 60 days, although this time can be extended once you're in Nepal. The Department of Immigration, Tridevi Marg, Thamel, Kathmandu (tel. (1) 470650 or 494273), grants extensions for up to four months. Apply for a visa extension a day or two before you really need it. Extensions are no longer granted on a daily basis. Keep this in mind when scheduling flights, if your plane leaves even a day after your visa expires you'll end up paying for a full months extension. **Australia/New Zealand:** AUS$40 for 15 days (single entry), AUS$50 for 30 days (single entry), AUS$70 for 30 days (multiple entry), and AUS$100 for 60 days (multiple entry). Submit three passport photos, a passport, and three application forms (available from travel agents) by mail or in person. Visas are processed on the spot for applicants who come in person, or mailed the same day for those who apply by post. **South Africa:** There is no Nepalese embassy in South Africa, which makes getting visa information a little trickier. Contact the Department of Immigration in Kathmandu, Tridevi Marg (tel. 412337, 418573) for more information on how to proceed. **U.K./Ireland:** UK£20 for 30 days (single entry), UK£45 for 60 days (multiple entry). Passport holders from either country should contact the Royal Nepalese Embassy in London for an application. **U.S.:** US$30 (single entry) and $US60 (multiple entry) for 60 days; extensions US$50 per month. Payment should be a money order, cashier's check, or cash. **Canada:** CDN$24 for 15 days (single entry), CDN$40 for 30 days (single entry), CDN$64 for a 30 days (double entry), and CDN$96 for 60 days (multiple entry). Send a stamped, addressed envelope if applying by mail. The Consulate is open for walk-in visa service Thursday 9am-3pm. **Trekking permits** are required for some trekking areas in Nepal. For more information, see **Trekking,** p. 36.

SURROUNDING COUNTRIES

It's not easy to travel to many of the countries that surround India and Nepal, nor is it always wise. Myanmar (Burma) and China, in particular, present massive amounts of red tape and restrictions. Also, a few of these countries are politically unstable; it's important to check for up-to-date information before embarking. The following info is meant as a starting point. (See **Border Crossings**, p. 55.)

Bangladesh: All citizens should contact a Bangladeshi embassy or high commission; visa rules change frequently. In any event, 72-hour permits to cross the border are easy to obtain, and they can be validated and upgraded at the Department of Immigration Office in Dhaka. Single-entry visas are valid for 15 days. The High Commission's address is 56 Ring Rd., Lajpat Nagar III, Delhi (tel. 91 (11) 683 4668); 9 Circus Ave., Park Circus, Calcutta (tel. (33) 247 5208); and in Nepal it's located on Chakrapath, Maharajgunj, Kathmandu (tel. (1) 372843; fax 373265). Tourist visas cost US$45 for up to 6 months.

China: To travel into Tibet from Nepal, a Chinese travel visa is required. Such visas are almost impossible to get at the embassy in Kathmandu. Visas are valid for 30 days and can be extended twice by 15 days per extension. Some travelers have also entered China by signing up for short "mini-tours" advertised all over Thamel, semi-legal group tours of a few days' duration that disband soon after crossing the border. Some travelers may, however, get hassled by Chinese police when traveling without the tour. Many travel agents in Kathmandu can arrange mini-tours. The Chinese Embassy in India is at 50-D Shantipath, Chanakyapuri, Delhi (tel. 91 (11) 600328) and in Nepal, Baluwatar, Kathmandu (tel. (1) 413916 or 414045.

Myanmar (Burma): For a Burmese visa, be prepared to fill out forms, write letters, and show proof that you have already set up a place to stay. Tourist visas last 3 months and barely get you into the country. To go very far beyond Rangoon or Mandalay, more permits or a licensed guide are required. The Burmese embassy in India is located at 3/50-F Nyaya Marg, Chanakyapuri, Delhi (tel. (11) 600 251/2; fax 6877942) and in Nepal at Chakupat, Patan City Gate, Kathmandu (P.O. Box 2437; tel. (1) 521788 or 524788; fax 523402). Note that border crossings into Burma are only in Thailand and China.

Pakistan: The U.S., British, and Australian Departments of State warn their citizens to defer all nonessential travel to Pakistan. Those who do decide to travel to Pakistan need a visa prior to entry. The single-entry tourist visa costs $US45 and is valid for three months after date of issue, but foreign visitors must register after 30 days at the Foreigners' Registration Office, which has branches in all major cities and towns. In Delhi, 2/50-G Shantipath, Chanakyapuri (tel. (11) 600603), and in Kathmandu, Pani Pokhari (tel. (1) 441421; visa services 415806).

Sri Lanka: A passport and onward/return ticket, as well as proof of sufficient funding (US$15/day), are required to travel to Sri Lanka. Visas are valid for a maximum of 90 days. Visitors staying in private households must register with the local police.

Thailand: Citizens from most European countries and the U.S., Canada, and Australia need not obtain visas if they plan to be in Thailand for less than 30 days and if they have a confirmed ticket as proof of departure. For travelers who wish to spend more time in the country, Thailand issues two main types of visas: **tourist visas** (up to 60 days, US$15) and **non-immigrant visas** for business or employment (up to 90 days; single entry US$20, multiple entry US$40). Single entry visas are valid for entry up to 90 days from date of issue; multiple entry visas must be used within 60 days. For those on tourist visas who want to pop back to Thailand repeatedly, a **reentry permit.** Applications should be made at the main Immigration Office well before departure. Make sure to get an exit stamp when you leave Thailand, or face deportation upon your next visit. The Thai embassy in India's address is 56-N Nyaya Marg, Chanakyapuri, Delhi (tel. (11) 6118103; fax 6872029) and in Nepal, Bansbari, Kathmandu (tel. (1) 420411).

WORK PERMITS. Admission as a visitor does not include the right to work, which is authorized only by a work permit, and entering India and Nepal to study requires a special visa. For more information, see **Alternatives to Tourism,** p. 60.

IDENTIFICATION

When you travel, always carry two or more forms of identification, including at least one photo ID. A passport combined with a driver's license or birth certificate is usually adequate proof of your identity and citizenship. Never carry all your ID together; you risk being left entirely without ID or funds in case of theft or loss.

STUDENT AND TEACHER IDENTIFICATION. The **International Student Identity Card (ISIC)** is useful only for the medical insurance it provides. However, it still may be worth getting for a discount fare on your plane ticket (most travel agencies require an ISIC for student fares). For U.S. cardholders traveling abroad, the ISIC also provides insurance benefits, including US$100 per day of in-hospital sickness for a maximum of 60 days, and US$3000 accident-related medical reimbursement for each accident (see **Insurance,** p. 33). In addition, cardholders have access to a toll-free 24-hour ISIC helpline with multilingual staff (tel. 800-626-2427 in the U.S. and Canada; elsewhere call collect 44 181 666 90 25).

Many student travel agencies around the world issue ISICs, including STA Travel in Australia and New Zealand; Travel CUTS in Canada; USIT in Ireland and Northern Ireland; SASTS in South Africa; Campus Travel and STA Travel in the U.K.; Council Travel, STA Travel, and via the web (www.istc.org) in the U.S.; and any other travel agency with a student focus. When you apply for the card, request a copy of the International Student Identity Card Handbook. However, beyond flight discounts at Indian Airlines and discounts on rail passes and tour packages from STIC Travels, this card is only good for a handful of commercial establishments in Delhi. The card costs AUS$15, CDN$15, or US$20. Applicants must be degree-seeking students of a secondary or post-secondary school. Because of the proliferation of phony ISICs, many airlines and some other services require additional proof of student identity, such as a signed, stamped letter from the registrar.

YOUTH IDENTIFICATION. The International Student Travel Confederation also issues a discount card to travelers who are 25 years old or younger but not students. Known as the International Youth Travel Card (IYTC) (formerly the GO25 Card), this one-year card offers many of the same benefits as the ISIC, and most organizations that sell the ISIC also sell the IYTC. To apply, you will need either a passport, valid driver's license, or copy of a birth certificate, and a passport-sized photo with your name printed on the back. The fee is US$20.

CUSTOMS

Upon returning home, you must declare all articles acquired abroad and pay a **duty** on the value of articles that exceed the allowance established by your country's customs service. Goods and gifts purchased at **duty-free** shops abroad are not exempt from duty or sales tax at your point of return; you must declare these items. "Duty-free" merely means that you need not pay a tax in the country of purchase. For specific information on customs requirements, contact the following:

Australia: Customs National Information Line 1 300 363 263; www.customs.gov.au.

Canada: Canadian Customs, 2265 St. Laurent Blvd., Ottawa, ON K1G 4K3 (tel. (613) 993-0534 or 24hr. automated service 800-461-9999; www.revcan.ca).

Ireland: The Collector of Customs and Excise, The Custom House, Dublin 1 (tel. (01) 679 27 77; fax 671 20 21; email taxes@revenue.iol.ie; www.revenue.ie/customs.htm).

New Zealand: New Zealand Customhouse, 17-21 Whitmore St., Box 2218, Wellington (tel. (04) 473 60 99; fax 473 73 70; www.customs.govt.nz).

South Africa: Commissioner for Customs and Excise, Private Bag X47, Pretoria 0001 (tel. 12 314 99 11; fax 328 64 78).

United Kingdom: Her Majesty's Customs and Excise, Custom House, Nettleton Road, Heathrow Airport, Hounslow, Middlesex TW6 2LA (tel. (0181) 910 36 02/35 66; fax 910 37 65; www.hmce.gov.uk).

United States: U.S. Customs Service, Box 7407, Washington D.C. 20044 (tel. (202) 927-6724; www.customs.ustreas.gov).

MONEY

Once you get there, travel in India or Nepal is unvelievably cheap. Depending on your traveling style and the area in which you find yourself, you can expect to spend anywhere from $5-20 per person per day. As a general rule, smaller, less-touristed towns are cheaper than the major hubs. A little bit goes a long way in India and Nepal, and spending a few dollars more on **accommodations** amounts to huge gains in comfort. Accommodations start at about $2-3 per night for a single or double, but you can find a much nicer place if you're willing to spend closer to $10. While it's not unusual for a basic sit-down meal to cost as little $1, your chances of consuming good, clean food are much greater if your willing to double that amount. Carrying cash with you, even in a money belt, is risky but necessary; personal checks are useless and even traveler's checks may not be accepted in some of the more remote locations.

CURRENCY AND EXCHANGE

The currency chart below is based on published exchange rates from August 1999. Although changes in India's economy could cause prices in this book to go up by about 8%, the exchange rate is likely to change as well, meaning that prices will probably stay the same in hard currency terms. Check all bank notes carefully; ripped bills will be refused by many merchants (although banks will exchange them for new ones). It is common practice for banks to staple bundles of notes together.

THE INDIAN RUPEE
Currency is measured in rupees (Rs) which are divided into 100 paise (p.). Rupees come in Rs1, 2, and 5 coins and bills worth Rs1, 2, 5, 10, 20, 50, 100, and 500.

US$1 = Rs43.45	Rs100 = US$2.30
CDN$1 = Rs29.15	Rs100 = CDN$3.42
UK£1 = Rs69.85	Rs100 = UK£1.43
IR£1 = Rs58.41	Rs100 = IR£1.71
AUS$1 = Rs28.03	Rs100 = AUS$3.57
NZ$1 = Rs22.71	Rs100 = NZ$4.40
SAR1= Rs7.20	Rs100 = SAR13.85

THE NEPALESE RUPEE
Currency is measured in rupees (Rs) which are divided into 100 paise (p.). Rupees appear in one and ten-rupee coins and 1, 2, 5, 10, 20, 25, 50, 100, 500, and 1000 rupee notes.

IRs100 = Rs157.93	Rs100 = IRs63.22
US$1 = Rs68.73	Rs100 = US$1.45
CDN$1 = Rs46.11	Rs100 = CDN$2.17
UK£1 = Rs110.49	Rs100 = UK£0.91
IR£1 = Rs92.40	Rs100 = IR£1.08
AUS$1 = Rs44.33	Rs100= AUS$2.26
NZ$1 = Rs35.93	Rs100 = NZ$2.79
SAR1= Rs11.38	Rs100 = SAR8.77

As a general rule, it's cheaper to convert money in India or Nepal. It's good to bring enough foreign currency to last for the first 24-72 hours of a trip to avoid being penniless after banking hours or on a holiday. Travelers living in the U.S. can get foreign currency from the comfort of their home; **Capital Foreign Exchange** (tel. 888-842-0880) or **International Currency Express** (tel. 888-278-6628) will deliver foreign currency (for over 120 countries) or traveler's checks overnight (US$15) or second-day (US$12) at competitive exchange rates. Avoid changing money at luxury hotels and restaurants, which will likely gouge you on both exchange rates and commission rates; the best deal is usually found at major banks. The national **State Bank of India** and the **Nepal Bank Ltd.** are the most common places to change money. In major cities, currency exchange booths controlled by major banks are common. Although commission rates at the booths may be slightly higher, they are convenient and keep longer hours than the banks. Foreign banks, like ANZ Grindlays and Hong Kong Bank, can be more efficient. **Bank of Baroda** (in India) offers cash advances on Visa and Mastercard at most of its many locations. Banking hours are short (M-F 10am-2pm, Sa 10am-noon). A good rule is only to go to banks that have at most a 5% margin between their buy and sell prices. ATMs are only available in major cities. Also, get an **encashment certificate** as proof. This is sometimes demanded when paying for plane and train tickets or large bills in rupees.

Since you lose money with each transaction, convert in large sums (unless the currency is depreciating rapidly). If you use traveler's checks or bills, also carry small denominations (US$50 or less) for when you are forced to exchange money at disadvantageous rates. It may be a good idea to keep some U.S. dollars or pounds sterling on hand in case smaller banks and exchange booths refuse to accept other currencies.

Both India and Nepal have recently made their currencies fully convertible and subject to market rates, so there's not much to be gained from changing money on the **black market.** Those who are still willing to risk confiscation of their money for the small premium (and speedier service) must change their money discreetly, with shopkeepers, out of public view, rather than with touts in the street. It is also worth remembering that changing money on the black market contributes to a cycle of illegal transactions, especially the smuggling of gold, gems, and electronic goods, and impedes the government's ability to regulate the economy.

In India and Nepal, Western currency will actually be preferred to local, but avoid using Western money when you can. Throwing dollars around for preferential treatment may be offensive, and it can attract thieves. It also marks you as a foreigner and invites many locals to jack prices up as much as tenfold or more.

TRAVELER'S CHECKS

Traveler's checks are one of the safest and least troublesome means of carrying funds; they can be refunded if stolen. Several agencies and banks sell them, usually for face value plus a small percentage commission. (Members of the American Automobile Association, and some banks and credit unions, can get American Express checks commission-free). If you're ordering checks, do so well in advance, especially if you are requesting large sums. **American Express** and **Thomas Cook** are the most widely recognized in India and Nepal. Banks in small towns are less likely to accept traveler's checks than banks in touristed cities. Each agency provides refunds if your checks are lost or stolen, and many provide services, such as toll-free hotlines in the countries you're visiting, emergency message services, and stolen card assistance.

In order to collect a **refund for lost or stolen checks,** keep your check receipts separate from your checks and store them in a safe place or with a traveling companion. Record check numbers when you cash them, leave a list of check numbers with someone at home, and ask for a list of refund centers when you buy your checks. Never countersign your checks until you are ready to cash them, and always bring your passport with you when you plan to use the checks.

American Express: Call 800-251 902 in Australia; in New Zealand 0800 441 068; in the U.K. (0800) 52 13 13; in the U.S. and Canada 800-221-7282. Elsewhere, call U.S. collect 1-801-964-6665; www.aexp.com. Checks can be purchased for a small fee (1-4%) at American Express Travel Service Offices, banks, and American Automobile Association offices. AAA members (see p. 49) can buy the checks commission-free. American Express offices cash their checks commission-free (except where prohibited by national governments), but often at slightly worse rates than banks. *Cheques for Two* can be signed by either of two people traveling together.

Thomas Cook MasterCard: From the U.S., Canada, or Caribbean call 800-223-7373; from the U.K. call (0800) 622 101; from elsewhere, call 44 1733 318 950 collect. Checks in 13 currencies. Commission 2%. Cook offices cash checks commission-free.

Visa: Call 800-227-6811 in the U.S.; in the U.K. (0800) 895 078; from elsewhere, call 44 1733 318 949 and reverse the charges. Any of the above numbers can tell you the location of their nearest office.

CREDIT CARDS

Credit cards are gaining wider acceptance in South Asia, but plastic is by no means the only kind of money you'll need. Cards can, however, be a useful backup to your traveler's checks and are invaluable in an emergency. Credit cards often offer an array of other services, from insurance to emergency assistance. Check with your company to find out what is covered. Additionally, you can use credit cards to purchase domestic airline tickets and train tickets in India.

There is still a great deal of variation in credit card acceptance. A high-class restaurant may refuse credit cards while a home-owned trinket stall accepts every credit card under the sun. Generally, plastic is accepted at major hotels, expensive boutiques, and fine restaurants. **American Express, MasterCard,** and **Visa** are welcomed most often. Credit card companies get the wholesale exchange rate, which is generally 5% better than the retail rate used by banks and other currency exchange establishments. Teller machines are located only in big cities and, even then, they're few and far between. **American Express** cards also work in some ATMs, as well as at AmEx offices and major airports. All such machines require a **Personal Identification Number (PIN).** Ask your credit card company for a PIN before you leave; without it, you will be unable to withdraw cash with your card. If you have a PIN, check with the company to make sure it will work in India or Nepal. **Credit card scams** of various sorts are extremely common in India and Nepal. Be very cautious when purchasing items with a credit card. Make sure that the card remains within view at all times, to ensure that the vendor does not make extra imprints. Also, if you're planning to ship purchased goods through a shop owner, don't believe him when he says he won't forward the credit slip for payment until you've received the goods. For more information on credit card scams, see **Warning,** p. 21.

CREDIT CARD COMPANIES. Visa (U.S. tel. 800-336-8472) and **MasterCard** (U.S. tel. 800-307-7309) are issued in cooperation with individual banks and some other organizations. **American Express** (tel. 800-843-2273) has an annual fee of up to US$55, depending on the card. Cardholder services include the option of cashing personal checks at AmEx offices, a 24-hour hotline with medical and legal assistance in emergencies (tel. 800-554-2639 in U.S. and Canada; from abroad call U.S. collect 1-202-554-2639), and the American Express Travel Service. Benefits include assistance in changing airline, hotel, and car rental reservations, baggage loss and flight insurance, sending mailgrams and international cables, and holding your mail at one of the more than 1700 AmEx offices around the world.

CASH CARDS. Cash cards—called ATM (Automated Teller Machine) cards—are not widespread in India and Nepal. Major cities such as Delhi, Mumbai, Chennai, and Calcutta, have scattered ATMS, but that's about all. ATMs, though, do get the same wholesale exchange rate as credit cards. If you're traveling from the U.S. or

Money From Home In Minutes.

If you're stuck for cash on your travels, don't panic. Millions of people trust Western Union to transfer money in minutes to 165 countries and over 50,000 locations worldwide. Our record of safety and reliability is second to none. For more information, call Western Union: USA 1-800-325-6000, Canada 1-800-235-0000. Wherever you are, you're never far from home.

www.westernunion.com

WESTERN UNION | MONEY TRANSFER®

The fastest way to send money worldwide.

Canada, memorize your PIN code in numeral form; machines elsewhere often don't have letters. If your PIN is longer than four digits, ask your bank whether the first four digits will work, or whether you need a new number. The two major international money networks are **Cirrus** (U.S. tel. 800-4-CIRRUS (424-7787)) and **PLUS** (U.S. tel. 800-843-7587 for the "Voice Response Unit Locator"). To locate ATMs around the world, use www.visa.com/pd/atm or www.mastercard.com/atm.

GETTING MONEY FROM HOME

Having money wired to India and Nepal can be a bureaucratic fuss, subject to long delays; most travelers wisely avoid it. If you really need money, it should take about two to three working days. Foreign banks such as CitiBank and ANZ Grindlays are the most reliable; be precise about the branch you want the money sent to.

AMERICAN EXPRESS. Cardholders can withdraw cash from their checking accounts at any of AmEx's major offices and many of its representatives' offices, up to US$1000 every 21 days (no charge, no interest). Green card holders may withdraw up to US$1000 in a 7-day period. 2% transaction fee for each cash withdrawal, with a US$2.50 min./$20 max. To enroll in Express Cash, Cardmembers may call 800-CASH NOW (227-4669) in the U.S.; outside the U.S. call collect 1-336-668-5041. You can call AmEx in India at 11-371-2513; in Nepal 01-226172.

WESTERN UNION. Travelers from the U.S., Canada, and the U.K. can wire money abroad through Western Union's international money transfer services. In the U.S., call 800-325-6000; in the U.K., call (0800) 833 833; in Canada, call 800-235-0000; in India, call 17-270-4279; in Nepal, call 141-8738. To cable money within the U.S. using a credit card (Visa, MasterCard, Discover), call 800-CALL-CASH (225-5227). The rates for sending cash are generally US$10-11 cheaper than with a credit card, and the money is usually available within an hour.

U.S. STATE DEPARTMENT (U.S. CITIZENS ONLY). In emergencies, U.S. citizens can have money sent via the State Department. For US$15, they will forward money within hours to the nearest consular office, which will disburse it according to instructions. The office serves only Americans in the direst of straits abroad; non-American travelers should contact their embassies for information on wiring cash. Contact the Overseas Citizens Service, American Citizens Services, Consular Affairs, Room 4811, U.S. Department of State, Washington, D.C. 20520 (tel. (202) 647-5225; nights, Sundays, and holidays 647-4000.

ECONOMICS AND ETHICS

For foreigners, the shock of entering a new culture in India or Nepal is often compounded by an equal shock caused by the poverty of those around them. Due to their relative wealth, foreigners are mobbed by **touts** (see p. 20), assailed by armies of **beggars** (see p. 22), accosted by slippery **con men** (see **Warning,** p. 21), and often charged more than locals. For budget travelers, these shenanigans can be exhausting and infuriating, and you may find yourself arguing over small differences in money simply as a matter of principle. However, Western travelers trying to pinch paise should remember how much their money really means to the people they deal with. Foreigners are wealthy compared to most Indians and Nepalis—no budget travel excuses are acceptable here. Even the most austere budget travelers frequently spend as much in a day as their hotel watchman or rickshaw-*wallah* earns in a month. Budget travelers have also paid for a round-trip plane ticket to India and Nepal, an unimaginable sum of money for most Indians and Nepalis. It is important to accept your status as a privileged outsider and to be prepared to pay more sometimes. The following sections describe some of the issues foreign travelers in India and Nepal face when they deal with money.

BARGAINING: THE ART OF THE DEAL

Bargaining represents a pricing system—indeed a true art form—prevalent all over India and Nepal. One of the biggest cultural gaps to bridge may be overcoming the disparity between tourist and local price. All it takes is a little persistent haggling; keep the following tips in mind.

1. Bargaining needn't be a fierce struggle laced with barbs. *Au contraire:* good-natured wrangling with a cheerful face may prove your biggest weapon.

2. Don't leave your poker face at home—the less your face betrays your interest in the item the better. Covetous eyes are the cat's meow to sellers and the kiss of death to buyers, but on the other hand, outward displays of anger rarely speed desired results.

3. Know when to bargain. In most cases, it's quite clear when it's appropriate to pull out your guns. Bargaining ability can also earn respect; some vendors, in fact, may take offense at acceptance of the first price. When in doubt, it's advised to ask tactfully, "Is that your lowest price?" or whether discounts are given.

4. Never underestimate the power of peer pressure. A buyer's market, with hordes of sellers and one buyer, does not prove advantageous. Bargaining with more than one person at a time—particularly auto-rickshaw drivers—almost always yields higher prices.

5. A highly desirable purchase merits stringent comparison shopping to gain a sense of profit margins and mark-ups. However, to start bargaining without an intention to buy constitutes a major *faux pas.* Agreeing on a price and declining it is poor form. One effective strategy is to turn away slowly with a smile and "thank you" upon hearing a ridiculous price. Turn around with the same nonchalance and the price may plummet.

TIPPING AND BARGAINING

Small **tips** are expected for restaurant service, train "coolie" porter service, and unofficial tour guides. There is no need to tip taxi drivers, who often overcharge as is. Tips depend on your level of satisfaction or gratitude, and usually run between Rs1 and Rs20, not following any particular percentage rule. Alternatively, a pack of cigarettes or some other small gift is often appreciated. In restaurants, leave a few extra rupees in change on the table. Most Indians and Nepalis expect great tips from foreigners, but don't be swayed by groans. The word **baksheesh** is usually translated as a "tip," but the concept really includes exchanges from gifts to outright bribes. For more information, see **Unusual Laws and Regulations,** p. 25.

India and Nepal are wonderful places to practice your **bargaining** skills. Taxi and auto-rickshaw fares (when not metered) and items in outdoor markets are fair game for haggling. Don't bargain on prepared or packaged foods (on the street or in restaurants) or on items marked with a price tag. But in smaller, family-run stores you might actually offend if you don't try to bargain. Be prepared to pay what you offer; it is considered outrageous to refuse to purchase something after settling on a price. Start by offering a quarter of the stated price and let your charisma do the rest. Never feel awkward or guilty offering what seems to you like a ridiculously low price; once the purchase has been made, and the shopkeeper breaks out in a satisfied grin, you'll realize that you've made him very happy. When metered taxi and rickshaws are not available, you must rely on your bargaining skills. Drivers will automatically quote you a price which is several times too high; it's up to you to get them down to a reasonable rate. If they won't cooperate, simply move on to the next; there won't be any shortage of drivers wanting your business. Feel free to refuse any vendor or rickshaw-*wallah* who bargains rudely.

TOUTS, MIDDLEMEN, AND SCAMS

Touts are the scruffy-looking men who surround travelers at bus stands and train stations, or accost them in streets of tourist ghettos, offering deals on transportation, currency exchange, drugs, or any service rupees can buy. If you have trouble finding something, a tout will probably be able to help you for a little *baksheesh*, but what really distinguishes touts is their *un*helpfulness. They are pushy and will try to trap you into paying for something you don't want; they count on foreigners to be naive enough. When ignored, many touts are equipped with a guilt-trip line, tailored to your demographic group, for example: "Excuse me, sir, one question: Why don't you white Americans like to talk to us Indians?" Don't let these guilt trips get to you—they're only interested in your money.

It is hard to **find a hotel** without a tout getting involved; you'll usually be approached as soon as you get off the bus or train. Touts (and taxi drivers and rickshaw-*wallahs* too) are paid commissions by hotels to gather tourists, and these commissions are usually added to the hotel bill. The best policy is to be firm. Decide where you want to go and have someone take you there. If the hotel isn't paying commissions, touts will tell you it's full or closed; don't believe it. If no one will take you there, have a driver take you to a general area from where you can hunt for a good place to stay on foot.

In major tourist centers you'll often meet people who want you to visit their home or their workplace or to take you for tours. Unless you have asked to go somewhere, you are under no obligation to follow them or to pay them for being taken to a place in which you have no interest. Don't give them money when they ask you for it, regardless of what they say they will do for you.

Some **travel agents** in the major tourist centers are basically touts with desks and telephones. They are known to give false information, charge hefty commissions, and they even sometimes sell bogus tickets. Unless they have a peon to do it for them, most Indians buy train tickets directly from the station. It's best to do this yourself too. **Eliminating the middleman** will give you control and save you money.

Another hassle at many monuments and temples are the unofficial **guides** who spew uninformed drivel, later demanding *baksheesh*. Be forceful with these people and they will usually back off—don't hesitate to push your way through. It is usually better to book a guide through a tourist office or other government organization than to wait to be approached.

Be very cautious about accepting **food or drinks** from a stranger. There have been reports of con men who drug travelers by putting sleeping pills in their tea and rob or even rape them. However, remember that offers of food and drink are also one of the primary forms of Indian hospitality. A gracious "Doctor told me I shouldn't have that" is a good way to turn down food or drink without offending.

WARNING: Travelers in the biggest tourist centers of the subcontinent, i.e., Delhi, Jaipur, Agra, Kathmandu, etc., are frequently accosted by locals interested in chatting about tourism, education, the city, and life abroad. Having thus established themselves as "friends," they offer travelers their hospitality: "You're a guest in my country. The least I can do is invite you to my place for some food." Nine times out of ten, their "place" is a **jewelry, gems, or rug shop.** Eventually, travelers are offered the opportunity to carry anywhere from US$500 to US$10,000 worth of jewelry abroad to be handed over to an "overseas partner." In return, these dealers offer a 100% commission. The rationale is straightforward. Export laws impose a 250% tariff on gems and jewelry. Foreigners with tourist visas are allowed to carry a certain amount of gems and jewelry out of the country. So, by having tourists do their exporting for them at 100% commission, gem dealers save a lot of money. But first, they'll insist you give them your **credit card** number for "insurance purposes," since valuables are often appropriated by corrupt customs officials. The gem dealers call it "couriering," and insist that it's done all the time. Of course, as soon as you hand over your card, they will charge hundreds of dollars to your account. **Export schemes** sound too good to be true because they are—stay away from them. If you ever feel uncomfortable in a store, just leave, even if it seems rude or awkward. (Also see **Credit Cards**, p. 17.)

ESSENTIALS

BEGGING

From lines of beggars outside temples to children weaving through traffic to beg at car windows, the sad phenomenon of begging is impossible to ignore in India and Nepal. While giving may temporarily ease your conscience, it is not always the best choice. Giving can encourage a cycle of poverty—it is said that some children are maimed by family members in order to increase sympathy and hence charity. But many beggars (lepers, amputees, emaciated mothers) have very obvious needs. When giving to beggars, remember that Rs30 is more than many Indian working people see in a week. **Carry coins and one- or two-rupee bills**—in most cases, these make appropriate donations. For children, offer food instead of money—a gift of biscuits will more likely benefit the child than a cash donation, which often goes immediately into the hands of their ringleader. It is customary to give a little to beggars at pilgrimage sites and to *sadhus*, wandering Hindu holy men who survive by begging (as well as to transvestites on trains; see **The Third Sex,** p. 410). **Don't give** to cute, healthy kids who cheerfully approach tourists with requests for rupees, coins, or pens. These are not beggars, but regular schoolchildren having fun trying their luck to see what they can get from foreigners. This encourages a begging mentality, and their parents usually find this behavior embarrassing. A quick "Begging is bad" is a more appropriate response.

SAFETY AND SECURITY

India and Nepal are generally safe countries in which to travel; rates of crime, especially violent crime, are extremely low. The sheer mass of population in India means that you will almost always be surrounded by people, and most Indians and Nepalis are well-meaning and will go out of their way to help a foreigner in trouble if they can. What goes on in public is everyone's business, for better or worse.

BLENDING IN

Any would-be attacker knows that tourists carry large amounts of cash and are not as street-savvy as locals, so foreigners are particularly vulnerable to crime. Even if you look South Asian, most people will be able to recognize that you're a foreigner. You won't ever blend in completely, but it is wise to try not to stand out. **Dress modestly,** ideally in local clothes. Try to look like you know what you're doing; the gawking camera-toter is a more obvious target than the low-profile traveler. Do not flaunt your money, or nationality, in public. Try to memorize your map and organize your pack while you're still in your hotel room and if you must do one of these things while outside, step into a shop or restaurant to get your bearings. Watch out for people who grope in crowds—that goes for both men and women! If you are traveling alone, be sure that someone at home knows your itinerary and **never admit that you're traveling alone.**

If you are able to speak even a few words of the **local language,** this may help you seem confident, and it can gain the confidence of someone who might not help you otherwise. Even if you're communicating only in English, it takes some effort to understand many Indians. Be aware of how others are behaving and follow their lead. If no one else has their feet on the table or is jaywalking in a mini-skirt, you shouldn't be either. For more information, see **Customs and Etiquette,** p. 67.

EXPLORING

Find out about unsafe neighborhoods from tourist offices, from the manager of your hotel, or from a local whom you trust. Whenever possible, *Let's Go* warns of unsafe areas, but only your eyes can tell you for sure if you've wandered into one. General desertedness is a bad sign. If you feel uncomfortable, leave as quickly and directly as you can, but don't allow fear to close off whole worlds to you. Careful, persistent exploration will build confidence and make your stay in an area much more rewarding. India and Nepal can be more dangerous **at night** simply because crowds of people will not be around. When walking at night, stick to main roads and avoid dark alleyways. Unless you are in a neighborhood that is very active at night, it is best not to go out alone. Don't let rickshaws or auto-rickshaws take you down roads you don't know, and don't attempt to cross through parks or any other large, deserted areas. A blissful beach can become unsafe as soon as night falls.

GETTING AROUND

Despite the occasional fatal accident, **trains** are definitely the safest way to travel; theft is probably the greatest risk involved in train travel. Although the railways are quite extensive in India, they don't run to some of the smaller towns, and they don't exist in Nepal. **Buses** are the most viable options in these situations, and they can be particularly convenient for shorter trips. However, as you'll soon discover, road rules are virtually nonexistent in India and Nepal, and bus accidents are quite common, particularly in hilly or mountainous regions. The sobriety of bus drivers is also never certain, making road travel even more dangerous. Although **cabs** are forced to drive on the same crazy roads amidst the same crazy drivers, they are ultimately safer than buses. You can insist that your driver slow down, and the size of the vehicle makes it less likely to topple over the side of a mountain. Having said this, buses are usually fine for local travel and in non-mountainous areas. When **on foot**, be very careful of Indian and Nepalese traffic, which is very chaotic; rickshaws and buses will not stop. *Let's Go* does not recommend hitchhiking, particularly for women. For more information on **Getting Around**, see p. 48.

SELF-DEFENSE

A good self-defense course will give you more concrete ways to react to different types of aggression. **Impact, Prepare, and Model Mugging** can refer you to local self-defense courses in the United States (tel. 800-345-5425) and Vancouver, Canada (tel. (604) 878-3838). Workshops (2-3 hours) start at US$50 and full courses run US$350-500. Both women and men are welcome.

ANIMALS

Watch out for stray animals in India and Nepal; rabies is much more prevalent here than in Western countries. The rhesus **monkeys** that hover in the treetops above temples are sometimes aggressive, and they will snatch food and bite. If a stray **dog** growls at you, pick up a stone and act like you're about to throw it—it is truly amazing how often dogs fall for this trick. Even if you can't find a stone, just pretending to pick one up usually scares dogs away. Also be wary of **rats,** which can be a problem in sketchier hotels. Since rats are often attracted to crumbs, keep food away from your bed if you think your hotel is infested. Poisonous **snakes** such as cobras also present a slight danger, even in urban areas. If you've left your shoes outdoors, it never hurts to shake them out before putting them on. Finally, India's larger wildlife, from innocuous **buffalo** to gargantuan **elephants** to (of course) Bengal **tigers** can gore, maul, and trample people.

POLITICAL INSTABILITY

Political violence is another problem in parts of India and Nepal. Punjab, which was a big problem in the 1980s and early 1990s, appears to have calmed down for now, but the Assam has also has since become unstable. Kashmir is particularly unstable at the moment. Threats to foreigners are usually incidental, but in 1995 five western tourists were taken hostage by a militant group in Kashmir. One, a Norwegian, was beheaded. Only that state's eastern regions of Ladakh and Zanskar are completely safe for tourists. Despite the political instability, a small number of tourists opt for package tours of Srinagar in Western Kashmir. **These tours are the only remotely safe way to travel through Srinagar.** For more information, see **Srinagar,** p. 260. Even when there's not war for secession going on, law and order can be sketchy in remote parts of India and Nepal where political parties or organized thugs rule the countryside. Bihar, eastern Orissa, and some of the northeastern states are the areas of which to be most wary. The best place to get advice about unsafe areas is your country's embassy or high commission, and read the newspapers while you're in India or Nepal to keep abreast of what's going on.

FURTHER INFORMATION. The following government offices provide travel information and advisories by telephone or on their websites:

Australian Department of Foreign Affairs and Trade. Tel. (02) 6261 1111. www.dfat.gov.au.

Canadian Department of Foreign Affairs and International Trade (DFAIT). Tel. 800-267-8376 or (613) 944-4000 from Ottawa. www.dfait-maeci.gc.ca. Call for their free booklet, *Bon Voyage... But.*

United Kingdom Foreign and Commonwealth Office. Tel. (0171) 238 4503. www.fco.gov.uk.

United States Department of State. Tel. (202) 647-5225. travel.state.gov. For their publication *A Safe Trip Abroad,* call (202) 512-1800.

FINANCIAL SECURITY

PROTECTING YOUR VALUABLES

To prevent easy theft, don't keep all your valuables (money, important documents) in one place. You should carry your **passport, traveler's checks,** and **plane ticket** on you at all times. **Photocopies** of important documents allow you to recover them in case they are lost or filched. Carry one copy separate from the documents and leave another copy at home. **Don't put a wallet with money in your back pocket.** Never count your money in public and carry as little as possible. If you carry a purse, buy a sturdy one with a secure clasp, and carry it crosswise on the side, away from the street with the clasp against you. Secure packs with small combination padlocks which slip through the two zippers. A **money belt** is the best way to carry cash; a nylon, zippered pouch with a belt that sits inside the waist of your pants or skirt combines convenience and security. A **neck pouch** is equally safe, although less accessible. Keep a small amount of money in your pockets so you don't need to sift through a stack of cash every time you buy a snack. For information on **Touts, Middlemen, and Scams,** p. 20.

ACCOMMODATIONS AND TRANSPORTATION

Most **hotels** have locks on the doors, but this doesn't mean you'll be the only one with access to your room. Hotel staff can probably get into your room if they want to, and though uncommon, it's not unheard of for theft to occur in this way. Never leave valuables in your hotel room, even if it's locked. You might want to leave your luggage at a guest house while you are trekking, but don't leave your valuables there, and make sure what you do leave is locked.

Be particularly careful on **buses,** carry your backpack in front of you where you can see it, and don't trust anyone to "watch your bag for a second." If your bag is going on a bus roof rack, make sure it's tied down securely so someone couldn't jump off with it in a hurry. Thieves thrive on **trains;** professionals wait for tourists to fall asleep and then carry off everything they can. When traveling in pairs, sleep in alternating shifts; when alone, use a lock to secure your pack to the bunk. Keep important documents and other valuables on your person and try to sleep on top bunks with your luggage stored above you (if not in bed with you).

If your belongings are stolen in India or Nepal, you should go to the police. While there is virtually no chance you'll ever see your camera again, you can at least get an official **police report** which you'll need for an insurance claim. **Travel Assistance International by Worldwide Assistance Services, Inc.** provides its members with a 24-hour hotline for assistance. Their year-long frequent traveler package ($235-305) includes insurance, financial assistance, and help in replacing lost documents. Call (800) 821-2828, fax (202) 828-5896, or write them at 1133 15th St. NW, Ste. 400, Washington, D.C. 20005-2710. The **American Society of Travel Agents** provides extensive informational resources, both at their website (www.astanet.com) and in their free brochure, *Travel Safety.* You can obtain a copy by sending a request and self-addressed, stamped envelope to them at ASTA Fulfillment, 1101 King St., Suite 200, Alexandria, VA 22314. Be sure to indicate which brochure you want.

DRUGS AND ALCOHOL

While marijuana (*ganja*) and hashish (*charas*) are grown throughout the Himalaya and are extremely cheap everywhere in India and Nepal, travelers should understand that these **drugs are illegal** and considered socially unacceptable by most Indians and Nepalis. An exception is made for *sadhus* (Hindu holy men), since *ganja* is associated with Shiva, and a few ethnic groups in the Himalaya openly use *ganja* and *charas* with no stigma. This does not extend to tourists, however, and penalties are sometimes harsher when it comes to foreigners.

India has a 10-year minimum sentence for drug possession or trafficking, but those caught with only a minute amount of *ganja* may get off lighter. If charged with drug possession, you are likely to find yourself required to prove your innocence in an often-corrupt justice system whose rules you don't understand. Those who attempt to "influence" a police officer must do so discreetly and euphemistically. Drug law enforcement in Nepal is a bit more lax, but sentences are still stiff. If you get into trouble with the law, contact your country's diplomatic mission. Bear in mind that if you are arrested, diplomats can visit you, provide a list of lawyers, inform family, and lend you a shoulder to cry on, but they can't get you out of jail.

The more touristy places in India and Nepal, like Kathmandu, Pokhara, and Goa, have an abundance of **alcohol.** Beer is popular, but India and Nepal also produce drinkable vodka, gin, rum, whisky and other liquors; in India these are classified as IMFL (Indian-Made Foreign Liquor). Beware of home-brewed concoctions in India and Nepal, however; every year dozens of revelers are killed by bad batches of toddy. The Indian state of Gujarat has been officially dry since 1947, and its prohibitive efforts have recently been copied by Haryana and Manipur. But illegal, boot-legged alcohol can still be found in so-called "dry" states. Other areas, like Tamil Nadu, Mumbai, and Delhi, have dry days. Liquor permits, available at embassies, consulates, and tourist offices in Delhi, Chennai, Mumbai, and Calcutta, aren't essential but may help you get booze with less difficulty in dry areas. There is no drinking age in India or Nepal.

UNUSUAL LAWS AND REGULATIONS

Common throughout India and Nepal is the practice of informal bribery, informally known as **baksheesh.** Those who find themselves in trouble with some aspect of the law may be able to get out of it with some money and a little bit of finesse, depending on the nature of the offense. Contrary to western notions of legality, "smoothing over" problems with a little cash is not only common but even expected in India and Nepal. For such incursions as a traffic offense or a minor customs violation, some find that an offer of money or goods may suddenly shed new light on the situation. While bribery is common, and sometimes expected, there are risks involved, as with anything illegal. Honest officials may take offense, which would only aggravate problems. Those who attempt to bribe officials must do so discreetly, with plenty of excuses. It is never wise to call a bribe a bribe.

Visitors to Nepal (especially those who plan to drive) should also be aware that **killing a cow** is a major offense, punishable by long prison terms. It is also illegal to actively proselytize on behalf of any religion in Nepal, with both the convert and converter eligible for long prison terms. It is perfectly acceptable, however, to tell others about what you believe and to ask others about their faith.

HEALTH

Common sense is the simplest prescription for good health while you travel. Travelers complain most often about their feet and their gut, so take precautionary measures. Drink lots of fluids to prevent dehydration and wear sturdy, broken-in shoes. During the hot season, take extra precautions against heatstroke and sunburn. To minimize the effects of jet lag, "reset" your body's clock by adopting the time of your destination as soon as you board the plane.

BEFORE YOU GO

For minor health problems, bring a compact **first-aid kit,** including bandages, aspirin or other pain killer, antibiotic cream, a thermometer, a Swiss army knife with tweezers, moleskin, decongestant for colds, motion sickness remedy, medicine for diarrhea (Pepto Bismol and Immodium), sunscreen, insect repellent, burn ointment, and a syringe for emergency medical purposes (get a letter of explanation from your doctor). **Contact lens** wearers should bring an extra pair, a copy of the prescription, a pair of glasses, extra solution, and eyedrops.

In your **passport,** write the names of any people you wish to be contacted in case of a medical emergency, and also write down your blood type and any **allergies,** medical conditions, or prescriptions you would want doctors to be aware of. Allergy sufferers might want to obtain a full supply of any necessary medication before the trip. Matching a prescription to a foreign equivalent is not always easy, safe, or possible. Carry up-to-date, legible prescriptions or a statement from your doctor stating the medication's name, manufacturer, chemical name, and dosage. While traveling, be sure to keep all medication with you in your carry-on luggage.

IMMUNIZATIONS

Take a look at your immunization records before you go. Travelers over two years old should be sure that the following vaccines are up to date: MMR (for measles, mumps, and rubella); DTaP or Td (for diptheria, tetanus, and pertussis); OPV (for polio); HbCV (for haemophilus influenza B); and HBV (for hepatitus B).

Some travelers to India and Nepal also take mefloquine, an oral inoculation, to guard against the relatively low risk of malaria (see p. 29). Check with a doctor for guidance through this maze of injections.

 INOCULATION REQUIREMENTS AND RECOMMENDATIONS. In most cases, no inoculations are *required* for entry into India or Nepal, but that doesn't mean no inoculations are necessary. Additionally, visitors who have been in Africa, South America, or Trinidad and Tobago within six days prior to their arrival in India must have a certificate of vaccination against yellow fever.

The Center for Disease Control recommends the following inoculations:
• Hepatitis A or immune globulin (IG).
• Hepatitis B, if you might be exposed to blood, have sexual contact, stay longer than 6 months, or be exposed through medical treatment.
• Rabies, if you might be exposed to animals at all.
• Typhoid vaccination is particularly important because of the presence of S. Typhi strains resistant to multiple antibiotics in this region.
• As needed, booster doses for tetanus-diphtheria and measles, and a one-time dose of polio for adults. Hepatitis B vaccine is now recommended for all infants and for children ages 11–12 years who did not receive the series as infants.

USEFUL ORGANIZATIONS

The U.S. **Center for Disease Control and Prevention (CDC)** (tel. 888-232-3299; www.cdc.gov) is an excellent source of information for travelers around the world and maintains an international fax information service for travelers. The CDC also publishes the booklet *Health Information for International Travelers* (US$20), an annual global rundown of disease, immunization, and general health advice, including risks in particular countries. This book may be purchased by sending a check or money order to the Superintendent of Documents, U.S. Government Printing Office, P.O. Box 371954, Pittsburgh, PA, 15250-7954. Orders can be made by phone (tel. (202) 512-1800) with a major credit card (Visa, MasterCard, or Discover).

The **United States State Department** (travel.state.gov) compiles Consular Information Sheets on health, entry requirements, and other issues for all countries of the world. For quick information on travel warnings, call the **Overseas Citizens' Services** (tel. (202) 647-5225; after-hours 647-4000). The State Department's regional passport agencies in the U.S., field offices of the U.S. Chamber of Commerce, and U.S. embassies and consulates abroad provide the same data, or send a self-addressed, stamped envelope to the Overseas Citizens' Services, Bureau of Consular Affairs, #4811, U.S. Department of State, Washington, D.C. 20520.

MEDICAL ASSISTANCE ON THE ROAD

Tourist centers are full of **pharmacies,** and many pharmacists (called "chemists" in India) speak enough English to understand what medication you need. Most pharmacies sell prescription meds as over-the-counter drugs. Few are open 24 hours. In an emergency, head to the nearest major hospital, which is open all night and will have an in-house pharmacy. Outside the major tourist centers, the going is a bit rougher, although every major town should have at least one pharmacy.

Both India and Nepal suffer from a lack of doctors and medical equipment. In India, there is only one doctor for every 2440 people; in Nepal, only one for every 16,829 people. **Public hospitals** are overcrowded, short on staff and supplies, and rarely have English-speaking staff. In many places in India, "hospitals" function essentially as hospices—homes for the dying. In cases of serious medical problems most foreign visitors to India go to more expensive **private hospitals.** These are mainly located in the big cities; elsewhere, they are usually known as **nursing homes.** The best are often run by medical schools or Christian missionary organizations. Small private **clinics,** usually operated by a single physician, are also widely available. In Kathmandu, a number of tourist-oriented clinics offer care up to Western standards. For serious medical problems, however, those who can afford it have themselves evacuated to better facilities in Singapore or Europe.

You can also contact your **diplomatic mission** upon arrival and inquire as to their suggested **list of doctors.** Carry these names around with other medical documents. To be admitted to many hospitals or nursing homes one must have a doctor who will take your case. If a **blood transfusion** is necessary, inquire as to whether someone from your diplomatic mission can donate blood, or whether family members at home can send blood by air. Also ask whether your diplomatic mission can help arrange emergency evacuation. Often, hospital syringes haven't been properly sanitized, so it's also a good idea to carry a few unused syringes with you in case you need some sort of injection. Make sure you also carry a doctor's note explaining that they are for medicinal purposes, lest anyone get the wrong idea.

Travel insurance (such as that offered with the ISIC and ITIC cards) is enough to cover most **medical expenses** in India or Nepal. Even for long-term stays and major surgery at top hospitals, costs are exponentially lower than what they would be in developed countries. Nevertheless, it is a good idea to carry a credit card for immediate payment. Westerners do not have good reputations for paying their bills fairly and squarely; many hospitals are hesitant to trust them with late payments.

Two services offer access to medical support for travelers: **Global Emergency Medical Services (GEMS)** has products called *MedPass* that provide 24-hour medical assistance and support coordinated through registered nurses who have online access to your medical information, your physician, and a worldwide network of screened, English-speaking doctors and hospitals. Subscribers also receive a personal medical record that contains vital information in case of emergencies, and GEMS will pay for medical evacuation if necessary. Prices start at about US$35 for a 30-day trip and run up to about $100 for annual services. For more information contact them at 2001 Westside Dr. #120, Alpharetta, GA 30004 (tel. 800-860-1111; fax (770) 475-0058; www.globalems.com). The **International Association for Medical Assistance to Travelers (IAMAT)** has free membership and offers a directory of English-speaking doctors around the world and detailed charts on immunization requirements, various tropical diseases, climate, and sanitation. Chapters include: **U.S.,** 417 Center St., Lewiston, NY 14092 (tel. (716) 754-4883, 8am-4pm; fax (519) 836-3412; email iamat@sentex.net; www.sentex.net/~iamat); **Canada,** 40 Regal

Road, Guelph, ON, N1K 1B5 (tel. (519) 836-0102) or 1287 St. Clair Avenue West, Toronto, ON M6E 1B8 (tel. (416) 652-0137; fax (519) 836-3412); **New Zealand,** P.O. Box 5049, Christchurch 5 (fax (03) 352 4630; email iamat@chch.planet.org.nz).

If your regular **insurance** policy does not cover travel abroad, you may wish to purchase additional coverage. With the exception of Medicare, most health insurance plans cover members' medical emergencies during trips abroad; check with your insurance carrier to be sure. For more information on, see **Insurance,** p. 33).

MEDICAL CONDITIONS

Those with medical conditions (e.g., diabetes, allergies to antibiotics, epilepsy, heart conditions) may want to obtain a stainless steel **Medic Alert** identification tag (US$35 the first year, and $15 annually thereafter), which identifies the condition and gives a 24-hour collect-call information number. Contact the Medic Alert Foundation, 2323 Colorado Ave., Turlock, CA 95382 (tel. 800-825-3785; www.medicalert.org). Diabetics can contact the **American Diabetes Association,** 1660 Duke St., Alexandria, VA 22314 (tel. 800-232-3472), to receive copies of the article "Travel and Diabetes" and a diabetic ID card, which carries messages in 18 languages explaining the carrier's diabetic status.

ENVIRONMENTAL HAZARDS

Heat exhaustion and dehydration: Heat exhaustion, characterized by dehydration and salt deficiency, can lead to fatigue, headaches, and wooziness. Avoid heat exhaustion by drinking plenty of clear fluids and eating salty foods, like crackers. Always drink enough liquids to keep your urine clear. Alcoholic beverages are dehydrating, as are coffee, strong tea, and caffeinated sodas. Wear a hat, sunglasses, and a lightweight longsleeve shirt in hot sun, and take time to acclimate to a hot destination before seriously exerting yourself. Continuous heat stress can eventually lead to **heatstroke.** Heatstroke is rare but serious, and victims must be cooled off with wet towels and taken to a doctor as soon as possible.

Sunburn: If you're prone to sunburn, bring sunscreen with you (it's often more expensive and hard to find when traveling), and apply it liberally and often to avoid burns and risk of skin cancer. If you are planning on spending time near water, in the desert, or in the snow, you are at risk of getting burned, even through clouds. Protect your eyes with good sunglasses, since ultraviolet rays can damage the retina of the eye after too much exposure. If you get sunburned, drink more fluids than usual and apply Calamine or an aloe-based lotion.

Hypothermia and frostbite: A rapid drop in body temperature is the clearest warning sign of overexposure to cold. Victims may also shiver, have poor coordination or slurred speech, hallucinate, or suffer amnesia. Seek medical help, and *do not let hypothermia victims fall asleep*—their body temperature will continue to drop and they may die. To avoid hypothermia, keep dry, wear layers, and stay out of the wind. In wet weather, wool and synthetics such as pile retain heat. Most other fabric, especially cotton, will make you colder. When the temperature is below freezing, watch for **frostbite.** If a region of skin turns white, waxy, and cold, do not rub the area. Drink warm beverages, get dry, and slowly warm the area with dry fabric or steady body contact, until a doctor can be found.

High altitude: Travelers to high altitudes must allow their bodies a couple of days to adjust to lower oxygen levels in the air. Alcohol is more potent at high elevations, and many foreign brews pack more punch than U.S. equivalents. High altitudes mean that ultraviolet rays are stronger and the risk of sunburn is therefore greater, even in cold weather.

Heat rashes: For some travelers, a visit to India and Nepal will mean an introduction to **prickly heat,** a rash that develops when sweat is trapped under the skin. Men are particularly susceptible to developing this rash in the groin area. To alleviate itch, try showering with mango *neem* soap or sprinkle talcum powder on the affected area just after bathing. Moist, hot weather can irritate the skin in other ways as well. Various **fungal infections** (athlete's foot, jock itch, etc.) can be prevented by washing often and drying thoroughly. Wear loose-fitting clothes made of absorbent fibers like cotton.

PREVENTING DISEASE

INSECT-BORNE DISEASES

Many diseases are transmitted by insects—mainly mosquitoes, fleas, ticks, and lice. Be aware of insects in wet or forested areas, while hiking, and especially while camping. **Mosquitoes** are most active from dusk to dawn. Use insect repellents, such as DEET. Wear long pants and long sleeves (fabric need not be thick or warm; tropic-weight cottons can keep you comfortable in the heat) and buy a mosquito net. Wear shoes and socks, and tuck long pants into socks. Soak or spray your gear with permethrin, which is licensed in the U.S. for use on clothing. Natural repellents can be useful supplements: taking vitamin B-12 pills regularly can eventually make you smell bad to insects, as can garlic pills. Calamine lotion or topical cortisones (like Cortaid) may stop insect bites from itching, as can a bath with a half-cup of baking soda. Tiger balm, a favorite Chinese method, is readily available in pharmacies or from street vendors. **Ticks**—responsible for Lyme and other diseases—can be particularly dangerous in rural and forested regions. Pause periodically to brush off ticks using a fine-toothed comb on your neck and scalp. Do not try to remove ticks by burning them or coating them with nail polish remover or petroleum jelly.

Malaria is the most serious disease that travelers to India and Nepal are likely to contract. It is transmitted by *Anopheles* mosquitoes that bite at night. It can take months for an infected person to show symptoms. Early symptoms include fever, chills, aches, and fatigue, followed by fever and sweating, sometimes with vomiting and diarrhea. See a doctor for any flu-like sickness that occurs after travel in a risk area. Left untreated, malaria can cause a death. The least danger exists in more urbanized areas. The best way to combat malaria is to wear insect repellent, sleep under bed nets, and stay away from uninhabited jungle areas. There are a number of oral prophylactics for the disease. Western Doctors typically prescribe **mefloquine** (sold under the name Lariam) or **doxycycline.** Both these drugs and other malaria treatments can have very serious side effects, including slowed heart rate and nightmares, which your physician can explain.

Dengue fever is an "urban viral infection" transmitted by *Aedes* mosquitoes, which bite during the day rather than at night. Dengue is often indicated by a rash 3-4 days after the onset of fever. Symptoms for the first 2-4 days include chills, high fever, headaches, swollen lymph nodes, and muscle aches. Then the fever disappears, and profuse sweating follows. For 24 hours there is no fever, but a rash appears all over the body. If you think you have contracted dengue, see a doctor, drink liquids, and take fever-reducing medication such as acetaminophen (Tylenol). *Never take aspirin to treat dengue fever.*

Japanese encephalitis is transmitted by the *Culex* mosquito and is prevalent during the rainy season in rural areas near rice fields and livestock pens. Symptoms are flu-like—chills, headache, fever, vomiting, muscle fatigue—and include delirium; it's vital to go to a hospital as soon as symptoms appear. A vaccine, JE-VAX, is effective for a year. The CDC claims that there is little chance that a traveler will be infected if proper precautions are taken (using mosquito repellents containing DEET, sleeping under nets, etc.).

Other insect-borne diseases: Filariasis is a roundworm infestation transmitted by mosquitoes. Infection causes enlargement of extremities and has no vaccine. **Leishmaniasis,** a parasite transmitted by sand flies, can occur in the Indian subcontinent. Common symptoms are fever, weakness, and swelling of the spleen. In parts of Asia, the **plague** and **relapsing fever,** which are transmitted through fleas and ticks, still occur. Treatment is available for both, and a vaccine can prevent the plague.

ESSENTIALS

FOOD- AND WATER-BORNE DISEASES

Food- and water-borne diseases are the number one cause of illness in travelers to India and Nepal. In India and Nepal, where the risk of contracting traveler's diarrhea or other diseases is high, you should never drink unbottled water which you have not treated yourself. **Drink only boiled, filtered or otherwise purified water and avoid ice.** To purify your own water, bring it to a rolling boil or treat it with **iodine tablets,** available at any camping goods store. An easy alternative to boiling and chemical treatments is to buy **mineral water,** which is available almost everywhere in India and Nepal. Beware of unsealed bottles—these have been refilled with tap water—add iodine drops to a bottle if it seems suspect. Don't brush your teeth with tap water or rinse your toothbrush under the faucet, and keep your mouth closed in the shower. Ice cubes are just as dangerous as impure liquid water.

Carbonated drinks ("cold drinks") are also safe—they must be carbonated in factories which use clean water, and they are sealed to keep in the fizz. If a carbonated drink is flat, don't drink it. There have been incidents of "fake" Coca-Cola in India, but if you taste it, you'll know. Remember, however, that caffeine (contained in cola drinks) is a diuretic, and therefore can be bad for rehydration. Fresh lime soda, a mixture of club soda, lime juice, and sugar, is a refreshing, mineral-rich alternative. **Coconut water,** or tender coconut water, sold on street corners all over India, is excellent for replacing fluids and minerals. **Coffee** and **tea,** which are boiled in preparation, are also usually safe, although some of the toughest parasites are not killed by simple boiling. Avoid drinks such as *lassis* or *nimbu pani* (lemonade) except in the best restaurants; these are made with ice-water, and it often isn't purified. **Insist on beverages without ice,** even if that means desert temperatures can only be combatted with lukewarm Thums-Up Cola. The water used to make ice is rarely clean, though many restaurants use "Aquaguard" filters, which make their water safe to drink. Water safety is also seasonal, and it's riskier to drink the water during the **monsoon,** when all the year's crud seeps into the water supply, than during the dry season.

Any food that is cooked immediately before serving is probably safe. To be extra sure, however, avoid food cooked by street vendors, tempting as *chaat* is. Street vendors are rarely sanitary, and their equipment is open to disease-carrying flies. The same is true of juice stands. If possible, eat in restaurants that serve local food and are popular with locals. Tourist restaurants that serve shoddy imitations of Western food are often less sanitary than *dhabas* that dish out *dal bhat* to truckers all day. Everything will be much easier, in fact, if you eat at regular times and eat the same sort of foods regularly every day.

The biggest risk to travelers usually comes from **fruit, vegetables, and dairy products.** With fruit, if you can peel it, you can eat it, and beware of watermelon, which is often injected with impure water. If you crave a salad, make sure the restaurant soaks its vegetables in iodine. Take dairy products only from clean-looking establishments. Other than that, the spiciness of the food and the variation in ingredients can also put a strain on your stomach. Adjust to the region's cooking slowly. Have high-energy, non-sugary foods with you to keep your strength up; you'll need plenty of protein and carbohydrates. **Washing your hands before you eat** is a sensible rule that you should not forget while you travel. Bring a few packs of handi-wipes or diaper wipes (or even alcohol pads), or a quick-drying purifying liquid hand cleaner; sinks and soap may not always be available.

Traveler's diarrhea results from drinking untreated water or eating uncooked foods. Few travelers to India and Nepal get away without at least one bout of **diarrhea.** It is usually an indication of your body's temporary reaction to the bacteria in unfamiliar food ingredients. It can last three to seven days. Symptoms include nausea, bloating, urgency, and malaise. If the nasties hit you, have quick-energy, non-sugary foods with protein and carbohydrates to keep your strength up. Over-the-counter remedies (such as Pepto-Bismol or Immodium) may counteract the problems, but they can complicate serious infections. Avoid anti-diarrheals if you suspect that you are risk for other diseases. **The**

most dangerous side effect of diarrhea is dehydration; the simplest and most effective anti-dehydration formula is 8 oz. of (clean) water with a ½ tsp. of sugar or honey and a pinch of salt. Soft drinks without caffeine or salted crackers are also good. If you develop a fever or symptoms don't go away after four or five days, consult a doctor. You may have dysentery (see below). If children develop traveler's diarrhea, consult a doctor; treatment is different.

Dysentery results from a serious intestinal infection caused by bacteria. The most common type is bacillary dysentery, also called shigellosis. Symptoms include bloody stools mixed with mucus, fever, and abdominal pain. Bacillary dysentery generally only lasts a week but is highly contagious. Amoebic dysentery develops more slowly, and may cause long-term damage if left untreated. A stool test can determine which have; you should seek medical help immediately. In an emergency, norfloxacin or ciprofloxacin (commonly known as Cipro) can be used. If you are traveling in high-risk regions (especially rural areas) consider obtaining a prescription before you leave home.

Cholera is an intestinal disease caused by a bacteria found in contaminated food. Cholera is still a perennial problem in India and Nepal. The first severe symptoms of cholera are diarrhea, dehydration, vomiting, and cramps. Untreated cholera can cause death quickly. See a doctor immediately. Antibiotics are available, but the most important treatment is rehydration. Consider getting a (50% effective) vaccine if you have stomach problems (e.g. ulcers) or if you will be camping or living where water is not reliable.

Hepatitis A (distinct from B and C, see below) is a high risk in India and Nepal. Hep A is a viral infection of the liver acquired primarily through contaminated water, ice, shellfish, or unpeeled fruits, and vegetables, but also from sexual contact. Symptoms include fatigue, fever, loss of appetite, nausea, dark urine, jaundice, vomiting, aches and pains, and light stools. Ask your doctor about the vaccine called Havrix, or ask to get an injection of immune globulin (IG; formerly called gamma globulin).

Parasites such as microbes and tapeworms hide in unsafe water and food, particularly undercooked meat and dirty vegetables. **Giardia,** for example, is acquired by drinking untreated water from streams or lakes all over the world. Symptoms in general include swollen glands or lymph nodes, fever, rashes, digestive problems, eye problems, and anemia. Drink purified water, wear shoes, avoid bugs, and eat only cooked food.

Schistosomiasis is another parasitic disease, caused when the larvae of the flatworm penetrates unbroken skin. Swimming in fresh water, especially in rural areas, should be avoided. If your skin is exposed to untreated water, the CDC recommends immediate and vigorous rubbing with a towel and/or the application of rubbing alcohol. If infected, you may notice an itchy localized rash; later symptoms include fever, fatigue, etc. Schistosomiasis can be treated with prescription drugs once symptoms appear.

Typhoid fever is common in villages and rural areas in South Asia. While mostly transmitted through contaminated food and water, it may also be acquired by direct personal contact. Symptoms include fever, fatigue, loss of appetite, constipation, and a rash. Antibiotics can treat typhoid, but the CDC recommends vaccinations (70-90% effective) if you will be hiking, camping, or staying in small cities or rural areas.

OTHER INFECTIOUS DISEASES

Rabies, common in India and Nepal, is transmitted through the saliva of infected animals. It is fatal if untreated. Avoid contact with animals. If you are bitten, wash the wound thoroughly and seek immediate medical care. Once you begin to show symptoms (thirst and muscle spasms), the disease is in its terminal stage. If possible, try to locate the animal that bit you to determine whether it does have rabies. A rabies vaccine is available but is only semi-effective. Three shots must be administered over one year.

Hepatitis B is a viral infection of the liver transmitted through the transfer of bodily fluids, by sharing needles, or by having unprotected sex. Its incubation period varies and can be much longer than the 30-day incubation period of Hepatitis A. A person may not begin to show symptoms until many years after infection. The CDC recommends the Hepatitis B vaccination for health-care workers, sexually active travelers, and anyone planning to seek medical treatment abroad. Vaccination consists of a 3-shot series given over a period of time, and should begin 6 months before traveling.

Hepatitis C is like Hepatitis B, but the modes of transmission are different. Intravenous drug users, hemodialysis patients, or recipients of blood transfusions are at the highest risk, but the disease can also be spread through sexual contact and sharing of items like razors and toothbrushes, which may have traces of blood on them.

Meningococcal meningitis is an inflammation of the lining surrounding the brain and spinal cord. The bacteria are carried in the nose and throat and are often spread through coughs and sneezes. Meningitis is less common in India than in Nepal. The first symptom of meningitis is a rash, then fever, sensitivity to light, stiffness of the neck, and headache. Consult a doctor immediately if you have these symptoms; meningitis can kill in hours. Fortunately a vaccine exists (see **Inoculations,** p. 26).

AIDS, HIV, STDS

Acquired Immune Deficiency Syndrome (AIDS) is a growing problem around the world. Because of an active prostitution industry and drug subculture, HIV and AIDS are proliferating at a frightening rate in India and Nepal. The World Health Organization estimates that there are over four million people living with HIV/AIDS in India and over 25,000 in Nepal. The governments of India and Nepal are beginning to recognize AIDS as a problem. If you need an injection, make sure the needle has been sterilized; to be extra safe, carry your own **syringes** with you and insist these be used. Bring a letter from your doctor stating that the syringes are for medicinal purposes. If you get a shave from a barber make sure he uses a new blade. The most common mode of transmission is sexual intercourse. Health professionals recommend the use of latex condoms. For more information on AIDS, call the **U.S. Center for Disease Control's** 24-hour hotline at 800-342-2437. In Europe, contact the **World Health Organization,** Attn: Global Program on AIDS, Avenue Appia 20, 1211 Geneva 27, Switzerland (tel. (44 22) 791 21 11; fax 791 31 11), for statistical material on AIDS internationally. Council's brochure, *Travel Safe: AIDS and International Travel*, is available at all Council Travel offices and at their website (www.ciee.org/study/safety/travelsafe.htm).

Sexually transmitted diseases (STDs) such as gonorrhea, chlamydia, genital warts, syphilis, and herpes are easier to catch than HIV, and some can be just as deadly. **Hepatitis B** and **C** are also serious sexually-transmitted diseases (see **Other Infectious Diseases,** above). Warning signs for STDs include: swelling, sores on sex organs, rectum, or mouth; burning and pain during urination and bowel movements; itching around sex organs; swelling or redness in the throat, flu-like symptoms. If these symptoms develop, see a doctor immediately. Condoms may protect you from certain STDs, but oral or even tactile contact can lead to transmission.

WOMEN'S HEALTH

Women traveling in unsanitary conditions are vulnerable to **urinary tract** and **bladder infections,** common and severely uncomfortable bacterial diseases that cause a burning sensation and painful and sometimes frequent urination. To avoid these infections, drink plenty of vitamin-C-rich juice and plenty of clean water, and urinate frequently, especially right after intercourse. If symptoms persist, see a doctor.

Women are also susceptible to **vaginal yeast infections,** a treatable but uncomfortable illness likely to flare up in hot and humid climates. Wearing loosely fitting trousers or a skirt and cotton underwear will help. Yeast infections can be treated with an over-the-counter remedy like Monostat or Gynelotrimin. **Tampons** and **pads** are sometimes hard to find when traveling, and your preferred brands may not be available, so it may be advisable to take supplies along. **Reliable contraceptive devices** may also be difficult to find.

Women who need an **abortion** while abroad should contact the **International Planned Parenthood Federation,** European Regional Office, Regent's College Inner Circle, Regent's Park, London NW1 4NS (tel. (171) 487 7900; fax 487 7950).

INSURANCE

Travel insurance generally covers four basic areas: medical/health problems, property loss, trip cancellation/interruption, and emergency evacuation. Although your regular insurance policies may extend to travel-related accidents, you may consider purchasing travel insurance if the cost of potential trip cancellation/interruption or emergency medical evacuation is greater than you can absorb. **Medical insurance** (especially university policies) often covers costs incurred abroad; check with your provider. **Medicare does not cover foreign travel.** Canadians are protected by their home province's health insurance plan for up to 90 days after leaving the country; check with the provincial Ministry of Health or Health Plan Headquarters for details. **Homeowners' insurance** (or your family's coverage) often covers theft during travel and loss of travel documents (passport, plane ticket, railpass, etc.) up to US$500. **ISIC** provides basic insurance benefits, including US$100 per day of in-hospital sickness, US$3000 of accident-related medical reimbursement, and US$25,000 for emergency medical transport (see **Identification,** p. 14). **American Express** (tel. 800-528-4800) grants most cardholders automatic car rental insurance (collision and theft, but not liability) and ground travel accident coverage. Prices for travel insurance purchased separately generally run about US$50 per week for full coverage, while trip cancellation/interruption may be purchased separately at a rate of about US$5.50 per US$100 of coverage.

INSURANCE PROVIDERS. Council and **STA** (see p. 46 for complete listings) offer a range of plans that can supplement your basic insurance coverage. Other private insurance providers in the **U.S. and Canada** include: **Access America** (tel. 800-284-8300; fax 804-673-1491); **Berkely Group/Carefree Travel Insurance** (tel. 800-323-3149 or (516) 294-0220; fax 294-1095; info@berkely.com; www.berkely.com); **Globalcare Travel Insurance** (tel. 800-821-2488; fax (781) 592-7720; www.globalcare-cocco.com); and **Travel Assistance International** (tel. 800-821-2828 or (202) 828-5894; fax 828-5896; email wassist@aol.com; www.worldwide-assistance.com). Providers in the **U.K.** include **Campus Travel** (tel. (01865) 258 000; fax 792 378) and **Columbus Travel Insurance** (tel. (0171) 375 0011; fax 375 0022). In **Australia** try **CIC Insurance** (tel. (02) 9202 8000; fax 9202 8220).

PACKING

Pack according to the extremes of climate you may experience and the type of travel you'll be doing. **Pack light**—a good rule is to lay out only what you absolutely need, then take half the clothes and twice the money. The less you have, the less you have to lose (or store, or carry on your back).

CLOTHING. Bring lightweight and layerable clothing; avoid jeans in favor of cotton/linen pants. Female travelers should wear **modest clothing** which cover their legs and arms; many find long, lightweight skirts indispensable. Shorts are a bad idea, even for men, unless you'll be spending all of your time in a major city. Even if you're in the middle of a trek, shorts are still a bad idea—you don't want to make it easy for insects and leeches to bite. Generally, the best clothes you can wear in India and Nepal are the ones you can buy there. Comfortable walking shoes are essential. For heavy-duty trekking, a pair of study lace-up **hiking boots** will help out. A double pair of socks—light polypropylene inside and thick wool outside—will cushion feet and keep them dry. **Rain gear** is essential in cooler climates. A good rain jacket (Gore-Tex® is a miracle fabric that's both waterproof and breathable) and backpack cover will take care of you and your stuff at a moment's notice, which is often all you'll get. If you plan to be doing any **Trekking,** see p. 36.

LUGGAGE. If you plan to cover most of your itinerary by foot, a sturdy frame backpack is unbeatable. **Internal-frame packs** mold better to your back, keep a lower center of gravity, and can flex adequately on difficult hikes that require a lot of bending and maneuvering. **External-frame packs** are more comfortable for long hikes over even terrain—like city streets—since they keep the weight higher and distribute it more evenly. Look for a pack with a strong, padded hip belt to transfer weight from your shoulders to your hips. Good packs cost anywhere from US$150 to US$500. Organizations that sell packs through mail-order are listed on p. 39.

Toting a **light suitcase** is fine if you plan to live in one or two cities and explore from there, but a very bad idea if you're going to be moving around a lot. Make sure suitcases have wheels and consider how much they weigh even when empty.

In addition to your pack, a small backpack, rucksack, or courier bag may be useful for sight-seeing expeditions; it doubles as an airplane **carry-on.** An empty, lightweight **duffel bag** packed inside your pack may be useful. Once abroad you can fill your luggage with purchases and keep your dirty clothes in the duffel.

TOILETRIES. Deodorant, tampons, razors, and contraceptives are difficult to find, especially in rural areas (see **AIDS, HIV, and STDs,** p. 32). Most other hygiene items are available in pharmacies and shops. Keep in mind that fragrant deodorants, shampoos, and soaps attract insects and other unwelcome forest creatures. Be sure to bring more than enough of any prescription drugs that you will need. Bring a small supply of **toilet paper,** enough for the day or two it takes you to find one of the many pharmacies that sell it (most Indians and Nepalis don't use toilet paper; they simply rinse with water and their left hands). Machines which heat-disinfect **contact lenses** will require a small converter. Consider switching temporarily to a chemical disinfection system for contacts, but check with your lens dispenser to see if it's safe to switch. Contact lens supplies are difficult to find; bring enough saline and cleaner for your entire vacation.

WASHING CLOTHES. Many hotels in India and Nepal provide laundry service for their guests for a small, per-item fee (or can direct you to a local *dhobi,* "launderer"). It may be cheaper and easier to use a sink, so bring a small bar or tube of detergent soap, a small rubber ball to stop up the sink, and a travel clothes line.

ELECTRIC CURRENT. In India, electricity is 220 volts AC, enough to fry any 110V North American appliance. 220V Electrical appliances don't like 110V current, either. Visit a hardware store for an adapter (which changes the shape of the plug) and a converter (which changes the voltage; US$20). Don't make the mistake of using only an adapter (unless appliance instructions state otherwise). Power cuts and surges are quite common, so don't count on electricity, especially in rural areas.

FILM. Film in India and Nepal generally costs $3-4 for a roll of 24 color exposures, and the quality is *usually* pretty good. Developing can cost under $1, but you might not be thrilled with the results. If you're not a serious photographer, you might want to consider bringing a **disposable camera** or two rather than an expensive permanent one. Always pack it in your carry-on luggage, since higher-intensity X-rays are used on checked luggage.

OTHER USEFUL ITEMS. Carry your own towel and sheets for very cheap hotels and overnight train rides. Also bring a strong **padlock** (some hotels don't have locks on room doors, and it's a good idea to lock your backpack to something on the train if you're planning on sleeping). No matter how you're traveling, it's always a good idea to carry a first-aid kit including sunscreen, insect repellent, and vitamins (see **Health,** p. 25). Other useful items include: sealable plastic bags (for damp clothes, soap, food, shampoo, and other spillables); alarm clock; waterproof matches; sun hat; moleskin (for blisters); needle and thread; safety pins; sunglasses; pocketknife; compass; string; **flashlight** (for during power cuts); cold-water soap; earplugs (for loud bus rides and hotels); electrical tape (for patching tears); tweezers; garbage bags; a rubber squash ball for plugging hotel sinks to hand-wash your clothes; and a small calculator for currency conversion.

ACCOMMODATIONS

Cheap accommodations in India and Nepal are plentiful. You can easily stay here without spending more than US$2 or US$3 per night, as long as you don't mind life sans air-conditioning. Even posh hotels are much cheaper here than they would be at home. Rates often vary according to the season, however, and in cheaper hotels they're often negotiable. The prices listed in this book represent our best research efforts, but often we cannot predict the frequent ups and downs of Indian and Nepali hotel prices—all prices listed in this book are subject to change.

BUDGET HOTELS

The main travel centers nurture **tourist districts** of shabby built hotels containing bare concrete cells with hard beds and a ceiling fan on overdrive. These hotels often have restaurants, and managers are usually happy to arrange to provide any service rupees can buy. Where tourist districts have developed and most of the clientele is foreign, competition has made hotels much cheaper, cleaner, and more comfortable. It is rarely necessary to make **reservations** at such hotels, except at major peak times (such as festivals). However, it can be difficult to get accommodation in big cities that see few foreign tourists—the hotels may be full of businessmen, or they may lack the paperwork to accept foreigners. On a positive note, budget hotels frequently have **restaurants** attached, and even Star TV and air-conditioning in some of the nicer places. One attractive feature of budget hotels in India is **room service,** which usually costs no more than food in the restaurant. If you are a lazy **launderer,** you can surrender your clothes to the local *dhobi* (most hotels have their own, and store-front laundries are pervasive in most places).

One thing to look out for when choosing a hotel is the **check-out time**—many cheap hotels have a 24-hour rule, which means if you arrive in town in the morning after an overnight train you'll be expected to leave as early when you check out. Above all, don't let touts or rickshaw-*wallahs* make your lodging plans. These shady characters often cart tourists off to whichever hotel offers the biggest **commission,** which you'll end up paying for, whether you realize it or not. Touts will fervently insist that the hotel where you wanted to stay is "closed" or "full." (For more information, see **Touts, Middlemen, and Scams,** p. 20.)

Many budget travelers prefer to bring their own **padlock** for budget hotels, since the locally made padlocks they provide are often suspect. Sheets, towels, soap, and **toilet paper** (available at most pharmacies) also need to be carried. It is good to ask about utilities before choosing a hotel. Many have **hot water** only at certain hours of the day, or only in buckets (and for a fee). Since the power supply is erratic everywhere in India, **generators** provide a very noisy solution. **Air-cooling,** a system by which air is blown by a fan over the surface of water, is common.

Prices fluctuate wildly according to the season, and seasons fluctuate wildly according to the destination in question. Most foreign tourists come to India during the winter months (Nov.-Feb.), so places that draw mostly foreigners have "high season" and correspondingly high prices. Indian tourists head for the hill stations during the sweltering pre-monsoon months (May-July), causing rates to head higher as well.

Some hotels in various towns have built reputations as places for foreign travelers to hang out and share stories. In a particularly sad twist, many of these in India have even instituted discriminatory **no-Indians policies** in order to create sanitized, foreigners-only environments for their clients.

Nepal's budget lodge scene differs from India's in that it is the result of a very recent boom, and foreign tourists are its main targets. Major tourist districts, unlike anything in India, have grown up in Pokhara and Kathmandu, where fierce competition between neighboring guest houses has led to rock-bottom prices and generally better and friendlier hotels than in India.

ESSENTIALS

HOSTELS

Youth **hostels** are scattered throughout India, especially in the far north and south. They are extremely cheap and tend to be popular with foreign visitors. **YMCAs and YWCAs** are only found in the big cities and are usually quite expensive, although YWCA's women-only policy makes them safer for lone women travelers. Hostels in India rarely exclude nonmembers of hosteling organizations or charge them extra. Hostels in Nepal are nonexistent. In India, the state tourism development corporations have set up large **tourist bungalows** in both popular and less-touristed areas. Combining hotel with tourist office, these places may be convenient, but the slight improvement over budget hotels is seldom worth the price.

UPSCALE HOTELS

Nicer hotels offer an escape from the sometimes harsh realities of Indian and Nepalese life; sometimes such an escape is necessary to maintain one's sanity. Pricier accommodations are certainly available almost anywhere in India, offering such amenities as air conditioning, 24-hour hot water, and televisions, which you won't find in budget hotels. Although these hotels' rates seem exorbitant when compared to those of budget hotels, they are really nothing compared to hotel rates at home. But many mid-range hotels are all show, and upstairs from a spacious, carpeted lobby decorated with hotel logos, the rooms are only marginally better than those in budget hotels. Across western and central India, many former **palaces of rajas and maharajas** have now been turned into middle-range hotels, offering travelers the decadence of a bygone era at an affordable price. Sections of these palace hotels are sometimes still inhabited by the royal families themselves. Large, expensive hotels such as the Taj, Sheraton, and Oberoi chains and the ITDC's line of Ashoks are also present in the main cities and tourist centers. In Nepal, more expensive hotels are only available in Kathmandu and Pokhara. If a night's stay is beyond your budget, the bookstores, restaurants, and pools at these places are often a great resource. Larger hotels usually require payment in **foreign exchange;** this rule extends even farther down the price scale in Nepal.

RELIGIOUS REST HOUSES

Traditional rest houses for Hindu pilgrims known as *dharamshalas* are sometimes open to foreign guests as well, providing the most spartan accommodations free of charge, although it is kind to give a donation. Sikh *gurudwaras* also have a tradition of hospitality. Be on your best behavior if you stay in such religious places. Remember, these places aren't hotels; many have curfews or other restrictions and usually smoking and drinking are not allowed.

HOMESTAYS

Homestays with Indian families provides the paying guest with the opportunity to experience the people, country, and traditions first-hand, and the Government of India Tourist Department is aggressively promoting this concept. The **Paying Guest Scheme** is a relatively new phenomenon in India but is gaining momentum in a number of states, particularly Tamil Nadu and Rajasthan. The Government of India Tourist Offices publish a list of host families and information about the rooms, facilities, and meals that will be provided. Homestays are more expensive than budget hotels but cheaper than starred hotels. Homestays are rare in Nepal.

TREKKING

The siren call of South Asia's mountains is being answered by ever more people. In 1986, some 25,000 people went trekking in Nepal's Annapurna region—that figure has doubled by 1996. Plenty come to trek and spend a great deal of money to do so, but there are also plenty of opportunities for non-mountain jocks to experience the mountains and life on the trail in a low key, low cost and low impact way. Trekking has become a flourishing industry in Nepal and India, and mountain tourism provides jobs to skilled guides, porters, cooks, village lodgers, and shop owners.

Trekking is neither mountaineering nor backpacking. It is simply a journey on foot through the hills that can take a day, a week, a month, or if it suits you, a lifetime. You may well be walking from village to village along ancient highways, or you may be striking off into more remote (and higher) areas where local accommodation is sparse and a tent necessary. However you do it, and wherever you do it, though, you'll be living off the land—eating local food and meeting local people. Typically, however, a "day" involves 5-6 hours on the trail with frequent stops for tea and photography. Most treks go through heavily populated country, but some also venture over high passes and along trails previously only used by herders en route to summer high altitude pastures. Having chosen some "easy" low-altitude trek, don't kid yourself that it's going to be a pushover: the Himalayas are the biggest mountains in the world and even the foothills—what you'll probably be scrambling over—make for plenty of tough walking. At the end of the day, while you're putting Band-Aids on your blisters, admire the magnificent views. A few aching muscles are a small price to pay.

WHEN TO GO

The post-monsoon reprieve (Oct.-Nov.) is the favored trekking season for **Nepal's** treks (see p. 787), and things can get kind-of crowded on the more popular routes. March-May is Nepal's not-quite-so-crowded secondary trekking season. In India, the two main trekking seasons are pre-monsoon (May-June) and post-monsoon (Sept.-Nov.) in the monsoonal hill regions of **Kangra, Kullu** (see p. 235), **Shimla** (see p. 215), **Garhwal** and **Kumaon** (see p. 129). The areas of **Upper Kinnaur** (see p. 243), **Lahaul** (see p. 238), **Spiti** (see p. 247), and **Ladakh** (see p. 258) are in rain shadow and get none of the monsoon rains. From December to February, it is be too cold for trekking at high altitudes. The temperatures rise in March and April, making trekking more feasible. The air is usually dusty and dry, but rhododendrons, magnolias, and orchids compensate magnificently. In May—the hottest and least predictable of months—the monsoon is just around the corner and most trekking activities taper off, or trekkers retreat to higher regions. Few trekkers choose to endure the cloud-bound, slippery, and leech-beleaguered trail conditions of the monsoon. But for the persistent and enterprising, trekking during the summer season has the benefit of the virtual absence of Western tourists. Remember, however, that extreme weather conditions can arise unexpectedly.

PLANNING A TREK

There are two ways of organizing a trek in the Indian or Nepalese Himalayas. Trekking independently saves money and allows you to tailor your trek to suit your interests. You set the pace, choose your companions, and plan rest days and side trips of personal interest. There is a downside to such freedom, however. Arranging your own trek also entails obtaining permits, renting equipment, buying supplies, and hiring porters and guides. If you are blessed with the virtue of patience and the asset of time, then planning an independent trek may be the way to go. Otherwise, a trekking agency can take care of all the preparations for you, and their expertise may make it possible to trek through more remote back country. The ease and comfort come, of course, with a price tag. (For more detailed information on planning a trek in Nepal, also see **Trekking in Nepal,** p. 787.)

TREKKING PERMITS AND OTHER FEES

Permits are no longer required for the Everest, Langtang, and Annapurna trekking areas in Nepal. Permit for other areas can be obtained at the Immigration offices in Kathmandu. You can complete the process in one day, but at the height of the season, long lines can extend the process to two or even three days. **Your permit will be checked regularly (and stamped) at police check-posts.** If your trek enters a national park, you may have to pay a fee (for more information see **Kathmandu, Practical Information: Immigration Office,** p. 727). Except in **North Sikkim** (see p. 679), trekking permits are not required in India. Area permits give access to all trekking areas as well, but no overnight camping is allowed in mountain national parks.

PRACTICAL INFORMATION

Trekking in India requires far more self-sufficiency than does trekking in Nepal. India has no equivalent of Nepal's tea houses; in certain areas, there may be the occasional rest house, but they are often out of the way and food supplies en route are unreliable. Tents are essential for shelter, and the stock of supplies and equipment you'll have to carry is considerably greater. Because of the heavier load, porters or horsemen are needed more often than in Nepal—backpacks become a weighty burden on treks longer than a few days. Furthermore, population densities tend to be a lot lower in the Indian Himalaya than in Nepal, and often trekkers see no one but their own partners for three or four days at a time. Beginner and expert trekkers alike should be accompanied by someone who knows the specific trails. For more information, see **Packing and Equipment,** p. 39. For practical information on trekking in **Nepal,** see (p. 789).

PORTERS AND GUIDES

One variation on individual trekking is to hire your own porters and guides. You'll have a knowledgeable local with you, you won't have to carry as much, and you'll boost the local economy. **Porters** carry most of your gear, allowing you the comfort of walking with only a small pack with the items you'll need during the day. You will have to constantly make sure that your porter understands what you want him to do and where you want to go. There is a small chance that your porter will disappear, leaving you with just that pair of sunglasses that was in your daypack. Choose your porter carefully; in general the extra expense entailed in hiring a porter through a recognized trekking agency is a sound investment.

  Guides, who usually speak English, are not necessary on the better-known routes, where it's easy to find your way. Having someone who knows English and who is educated might prove helpful in negotiations and pre-trek planning, however. A guide can color your experience with his knowledge, and often, guides will take trekkers on unusual side trips to visit friends and family. Guides are generally reluctant to carry anything (that's what porters are for).

  In Nepal, porters can often be hired on the spot, even in the most unlikely of places. The trekking service industry in the Indian Himalaya is not as developed, but you can arrange your own equipment, food, and staff at most hill stations or trailheads. Although porters and guides are easy to find, you'll want to investigate their honesty and experience. Spending some time in choosing a good guide is well worth the effort. Ask to see letters of recommendation from previous employer-trekkers. You can be almost certain to get reputable workers through a guest house or trekking agency. Guides and porters hired through companies are slightly more expensive but are, in most cases, more reliable and better qualified. In the unlikely but possible event that your guide or porter disappears, you have a company to hold responsible—an insurance that is worth the extra couple of dollars per day. If you do hire your own guides and porters, make sure you know exactly what services are covered, where you will go, and what supplies you will be obliged to provide along the way. Most agreements stipulate that guides and porters pay for their own food and housing. As a responsible employer, you should make sure that porters and guides are adequately clothed when trekking at high altitudes by outfitting them with good shoes, a parka, sunglasses, mittens, and a sleeping bag. Establish beforehand if you expect them to return anything. The standard salary for a porter carrying 20 kilos is about US$10 per day Nepal, US$5 per day in India; the salary for guides is higher (US$12-20 per day in India). In addition to these fees, you are expected to tip your staff generously at the end of a trek.

ORGANIZED TREKKING

Many tourists do not want to spend their precious vacation time planning their trek, buying equipment, and hiring a porters and guides. You can book through a big international adventure travel company from your home country, in which case everything is organized and arranged before you even touch down in South Asia. If you wait until you arrive, you can book through a local trekking agency, which usually requires one week's advance notice. The agent makes reservations for hotels and transportation well in advance and provides a complete staff—a guide, porters, and cooks—for the trek. While you don't need to worry about arrangements, you must commit to the prearranged itinerary. You may also be trekking alongside people you have never met before. Organized treks can usually veer off from the crowded routes into more remote areas, however. The group carries its own food, which is prepared by cooks skilled in the art of kerosene cuisine. Porters carry tents for the group. Although tents can be colder and more cramped, they do offer a quiet night and the convenience of setting your own bedtime. The comforts of trekking through an agency may also include tables, chairs, dining tents, toilet tents, and other modern luxuries. For all this comfort and convenience, there is a price, which can range from US$15 to US$150 (usually US$40-50) per person per day, and almost none of this money ever reaches the people who live in the trekking region; instead it pads the wallet of the middleman in the city.

PACKING AND EQUIPMENT

What you carry with you on your trek will depend greatly on where you go, the style of trekking you choose, and, if you have arranged a trek through an agency, what they provide. In Nepal, tea house trekking relieves you of having to carry food, cooking supplies, and tents unless you're going to high altitudes beyond the reach of tea-house culture. Because there's a chance that others will have exhausted a village's supply of blankets and because those blankets are not always spotlessly clean, bringing a sleeping bag is definitely a good idea.

In Nepal, with its plethora of trekking stores, you could show up naked in Kathmandu and be equipped for the most arduous trek within hours (see Nepal Treks, p. 787), but in India it's largely a matter of bringing your own gear with you.

Because it is particularly important to have **footwear that fits** and is comfortable, break in shoes or boots before you leave. For low-altitude treks, running shoes are adequate. However, boots provide ankle protection and are more comfortable in the long run over rough ground. Boots are necessary wherever there is snow. Clothing should be lightweight and versatile to accommodate the variations in temperature. You should also carry a bare minimum of equipment to keep you alive should disaster befall. This includes raingear, multiple warm layers (not cotton), hat and mittens, a first-aid kit, high energy food, and water.

Clothing	Equipment
boots or running shoes	sleeping bag
camp shoes or thongs	water bottle
lots of socks (polypropylene and wool)	flashlight, batteries
down jacket	insulated mat, if camping
wool shirt	backpack and some kind of daypack
shorts/skirt	toilet paper and hand trowel
long pants	lighter
rainwear and umbrella	sunblock and lip balm
cotton t-shirts or blouses	towel
thermal underwear	laundry soap
gloves	sewing kit with safety pins
sun hat and wool hat	small knife
snow gaiters	first aid kit
water purification system	zip-loc bags
snow goggles/sunglasses	tons of film and camera batteries

ESSENTIALS

HEALTH AND SAFETY

Trekking is hard work, but don't overdo it. Go at a comfortable pace and take rest days when necessary. Make sure your water is safe; boiling is often impractical (and ineffective at high altitudes where water boils at a lower temperature), so some kind of chemical treatment is probably the best option. Either iodine solution of iodine-water purification tablets will do the job. Use Tang or chewable vitamin C tablets to mask the iodine flavor. And consider modifying your diet. If you're eating in local inns, become a vegetarian and stick to fried food—a good dose of hot oil does for even the most resilient of nasties, and given the rate at which calories burn as you toil uphill, the normally forbidden delights of the frying pan can be seen, when trekking, as a means of preventing yourself from fading away. Whatever you choose to eat, it's unlikely you'll get too much vitamin C; many trekkers take a supplement. Be careful what you eat. Just because you've forsaken the grime of the city doesn't mean to say that bacteria have given up their pursuit of you: the popular Nepalese trekking routes witness a lot of diarrhea and nausea-induced misery. For more information, see **Health,** p. 20.

Individuals, particularly **women,** are not advised to trek alone. It is better to find a group, either on your own, through notice boards, or through a trekking agency. For women trekking alone, it might be better to have a porter than a guide. Some agencies now specialize in providing female porters/guides for women.

Knee and ankle strains are common trekking injuries. Knees can become painfully inflamed. If you think you're susceptible to knee injuries, bind them with an ace bandage as a preventive measure. Sprained ankles can be serious and keep you from walking for hours or days. Good footwear with ankle support is the best prevention. A bad **blister** will ruin your trek. If you feel a "hot-spot" coming on, cover it with moleskin immediately. Keep your feet as dry as possible. Take your boots and socks off at a rest stop. Change your socks regularly. Once you've got a blister, you can either live with it, or drain the fluid using a sterilized (in a metal flame) needle and then dress it.

Carry a first-aid kit for minor injuries (see **Health,** p. 25). Cuts to the skin should be cleaned with Dettol, clean water, or Betadine solutions, and covered with a firm bandage. Clean and dress the wound daily. If the wound becomes infected, apply an antibiotic ointment. Although trekkers do not often need serious medical attention, trekking mishaps do happen. In non-urgent cases, find some kind of transport (porters, pony, yak) to help get a sick or injured trekker to the nearest hospital or airstrip. If urgent medical attention is needed, **emergency rescue** request messages can be sent by radio at police, army, national park, and other official offices. Helicopter rescue is very expensive (usually US$1000-2000). In Nepal, money must be deposited or guaranteed in Kathmandu before the helicopter will fly. For people on agency treks, the agency will advance the money. This process is often made easier if you are registered with your national embassy.

ACUTE MOUNTAIN SICKNESS (AMS). If you are trekking to altitudes above 3500m, you will probably experience mild symptoms of altitude sickness, which can worsen into **Acute Mountain Sickness (AMS).** AMS can be fatal if left untreated. At high altitudes, there is less oxygen and lower atmospheric pressure, which can take their toll on the body—even the Sherpas aren't immune to elevation changes. It is important to allow time for acclimatization. Most people are capable of adjusting to very high elevations, but the process must be done slowly. Trekkers who fly directly to high altitudes are more likely to be affected by AMS than those that walk up gradually. AMS is highly unpredictable: some people have no problems acclimatizing rapidly, while others take a long time. Despite what you read, there are no prescriptions for avoiding AMS. In practice, you should see how you're going, make sure that you're well informed, and make your plans accordingly.

Take it slowly. Once you're about 3000m, try to sleep no more than about 300m higher than the previous night. Going to higher altitudes, however, during the day seems to aid acclimatization. **Take in lots of fluids.** It's always sensible to be well hydrated, but take it further at altitude—drink as much as 5 or 6 liters of water a day. Note that alcohol is not a good idea at altitude and impedes acclimatization. **Watch for symptoms.** Typically the first symptom is a mild headache, but there's a whole suite of other symptoms: dizziness, nausea, insomnia, racing heart, fatigue. If you are experiencing these symptoms, do not sleep higher. Don't ascend and they'll probably pass within 24 hours. If, however, you continue to deteriorate, you must descend. Even a modest descent of a few hundred vertical meters can make all the difference. Build up of fluids in the brain (oedema) and lungs can rapidly be lethal. Descent—don't even wait for helicopter rescue. **Most AMS fatalities occur in groups.** A badly affected trekker doesn't want to hold the others up and presses on regardless. If you're trekking in a group, you must gain altitude at a rate suited to the slowest acclimatizer. **Sleep low, go high.** If, say, you have to cross a high pass, sleep at the bottom and make it a long day up and over. In the early days of the trekking industry, people regularly died in the Everest region simply because they didn't know about AMS. Now that organizations like the Himalayan Rescue Association have done much to raise awareness about the problem, people suffering seriously from AMS are few and far between. Because the rate of acclimatization is so variable and unpredictable, be sure to budget plenty of time for high altitude portions of your trek. If you're trekking in Nepal, having a trekking permit valid for a week longer than you think you'll need is a good idea.

FROSTBITE AND HYPOTHERMIA. Frostbite and **hypothermia** might seem a long way away when you're sweating in sunny valleys, but they're an ever-present danger at altitude. To prevent exposure, dress warmly and in layers, keep dry, cover any extremities (wear a hat and mittens), eat well, and drink warm liquids. Make for shelter if conditions become severe. All too often people run into problems because they are determined to press on through bad conditions. If the weather turns against you, get to shelter ASAP, even if it means retracing your steps. A good pair of sunglasses can protect you from **snow blindness,** a condition caused by ultraviolet light reflected from snow or ice. Ultraviolet light is stronger at higher altitudes, so it necessary to protect against sunburn with sunblock and a hat. Note that sunburn can be particularly severe from reflected UV if you're on snow or ice, and that it can show up in the strangest places, like under your chin, because of the angle of reflected light. You can't, in these conditions, overdo the sunblock.

LEECHES. Leeches are rampant during monsoon season. Trekkers often get them on their legs or in their boots. Carry salt with you in a small container for chemical attack on them. Carefully applying a burning cigarette is another effective way of removing them. Unlike ticks, they do not leave any part of themselves behind, so it is safe to pull them off; be careful to disinfect the bite afterwards. A leech bite isn't painful and leeches do not transmit diseases. The effect is more psychological.

RESPONSIBLE TREKKING

Trekking can enhance the local economy, but it can also burden and degrade the environment. Cultivate a respectful relationship with the land on which you tread. The delicate ecological balance in the Himalaya is at risk due to overgrazing, landslides, pollution, and, perhaps most importantly, **deforestation.** When at all possible, eat at teahouses that cook with kerosene or electricity instead of wood. Treat your water with iodine instead of asking innkeepers for boiled water. If trekking with an agency, request that kerosene or gas be used for cooking and heating water; blazing campfire hearths are taboo where deforestation is a problem. Limit hot showers to those heated by electricity, solar energy, or back-boilers. Such industrious and innovative shower suppliers deserve encouragement. Flora and fauna are also threatened in the Himalaya. Trekkers should never cut vegetation or clear new campsites. Loss of vegetation is the beginning of an ecological spiral culminating in **erosion** and **landslides.**

Trekkers and their waste also contribute to litter, sanitation, and water pollution problems. The rule to follow is: burn it, bury it, or carry it out. Toilet paper is generally burned, biodegradables such as food wastes are buried, and non-disposables (plastics, aluminum foil, batteries, glass, cans, etc.) are packed up and carried to a suitable waste treatment site. All excrement should be buried in 40cm-deep holes in a spot far away from water sources, religious sites, village compounds, and crop fields. Use biodegradable soap and shampoo, and don't rinse directly in streams. If you can't leave the area clean, don't go. On organized treks, make sure that a person from your team is the last to leave camp; guided tour operators seldom do what they promise about camp garbage disposal. If you hear of a clean trek being organized, jump at the opportunity. Trekkers don't only have an impact on the environment they're travelling through, but also can have profound effects on the local people they encounter. Observe basic social rules: the right hand, no unduly revealing attire, no skinny dipping (even when you think nobody's watching). And don't encourage the "Give me school pen" routine among children. A school pen might seem a worthy gift but you're merely condoning and encouraging begging. The same applies to the distribution of medicine: by all means do what you can in an emergency, but leave doctoring to doctors. If you're moved by the plight of the villagers you meet, make a donation at the end of your trip to a charity or aid program involved in education and health care.

FURTHER SOURCES

Himalayan Rescue Association (HRA) is located just off Jyatha just south of Thamel (tel. 262746; email hra@aidpost.mos.com.np; www.nepalonline.net/hra). A voluntary non-profit organization providing information for trekkers on where and how to trek, trekking hazards, altitude sickness, and how to protect the environment. They also have in-season clinics with volunteer Western doctors during the trekking season in Pheriche on the Everest trek and in Marang on the Annapurna Circuit. Open Su-F 10am-5pm.

Kathmandu Environmental Education Project (KEEP), also off Jyatha, close to the HRA (tel. 250070 or 250646). A non-profit organization that promotes "soft trekking," which minimizes impact on the environment and culture. They offer free advice to trekkers and trekking staff. During the trekking season (Oct.-Dec. and Feb.-May) they have a free talk on eco-tourism at their office at 4pm every Friday. A good place to find trekking companies and a good source of up-to-date information and rates. Open Su-F 10am-5pm.

Annapurna Conservation Area Project, c/o King Mahendra Trust, P.O. Box 3712, Kathmandu (tel. 977 (1) 526571; fax 526570). ACAP is located in the King Mahendra Trust Office, near Grindlay's bank in Jawalakhel or in the Natural History Museum on Pokhara's Prithvi Narayan campus. The most authoritative source of information on the Annapurna region of Nepal, ACAP promotes environmentally sound practices among trekkers. Open M-F 9am-5pm.

Nepal Mountaineering Association (NMA) is located just south of Nag Pokhari in Naxal, in Kathmandu (tel. 977 (1) 411525; fax 416278). The NMA issues permits necessary for climbing Nepal's Himalayan peaks.

Indian Mountaineering Foundation, Benito Juarez Marg, Anand Niketan (tel. 91 (11) 602245 or 671211). Information on treks, especially climbs over 6000m.

KEEPING IN TOUCH

MAIL

SENDING MAIL TO AND RECEIVING MAIL IN INDIA AND NEPAL

Airmail letters under 1 oz. take two to three weeks to go between North America and India and Nepal and cost about US$1. Envelopes should be marked "air mail" or "par avion" to avoid having letters sent by sea. There are several ways to arrange pick-up of letters sent to you while you are abroad.

General Delivery: Mail can be sent to India and Nepal through **Poste Restante** (the international phrase for General Delivery) to almost any city or town with a post office. Address *Poste Restante* letters to: Jane DOE, *Poste Restante*, GPO, Mumbai, 400001, India. The mail will go to a special desk in the central post office. As a rule, it is best to use the largest post office in the area, and mail may be sent there regardless of what is written on the envelope. When possible, it is usually safer and quicker to send mail express or registered. If the clerks insist that there is nothing for you, have them check under your first name as well. *Let's Go* lists post offices in the **Practical Information** section for each city and most towns.

American Express: AmEx's travel offices throughout the world will act as a mail service for cardholders if you contact them in advance. Under this free **Client Letter Service,** they will hold mail for up to 30 days and forward upon request. Address the letter in the same way shown above. Some offices will offer these services to non-cardholders (especially those who have purchased AmEx Travellers Cheques), but call ahead to make sure. Check the **Practical Information** section of the countries you plan to visit; Let's Go lists AmEx locations for most large cities. A complete list is available free (tel. 800-528-4800).

If regular airmail is too slow, **Federal Express** (U.S. tel. for international operator 800-247-4747) can get a letter from New York to New Delhi in five days for a whopping US$41, rates among non-U.S. locations are prohibitively expensive (London to New Delhi, for example, costs upwards of $27.80). By **U.S. Express Mail,** a letter from New York would arrive within four days and would cost US$21.50. **DHL** (tel. (800) 225 5345) operates throughout South Asia; it costs about US$75.20 to India or Nepal. Delivery takes three to five business days. DHL packages sent from India or Kathmandu to the U.S. cost US$30-40 and take three business days.

SENDING MAIL HOME FROM INDIA AND NEPAL

Aerogrammes, printed sheets that fold into envelopes and travel via airmail, are available at post offices. It helps to mark "airmail" in the appropriate language if possible, though "par avion" is universally understood. Most post offices will charge exorbitant fees or refuse to send aerogrammes with enclosures. Allow *at least* two weeks for mail delivery to or from South Asia. Much depends on the national post office involved. Sending a **package** home will involve getting it cleared by customs, taking it to get it wrapped in cloth and wax-sealed, going to the post office to fill out the customs forms, buying stamps, and finally, seeing it processed and on its way. It may take a couple of months or even a couple of years to get home if you send your booty surface mail—and all packages run the risk of getting x-rayed or searched. If you need to receive a package from abroad, have it registered—this will lessen the great likelihood that your goods will get stolen.

TELEPHONES

CALLING INDIA OR NEPAL FROM HOME

INDIA PHONE CODES		Jaipur	0141
Agra	0562	Khajuraho:	07686
Ahmedabad	029	Leh	01982
Amritsar	0183	Manali	01902
Bangalore	080	Mumbai	022
Bhopal	0755	Patna	0612
Bhubaneswar	0674	Panjim	0832
Calcutta	033	Shimla	0177
Chandigarh	0172	Trivandrum	0471
Chennai	044	Varanasi	0542
Delhi	011	NEPAL PHONE CODES	
Dharamsala	01892	Kathmandu	01
Guwahati	0361	Chitwan	056
Hyderabad	040	Pokhara	061

1. The international access code of your home country. Country codes and city codes are sometimes listed with a zero in front (e.g., 033), but after dialing the international access code, drop successive zeros (with an access code of 011, e.g., 011 33).

2. India or Nepal's country code.

3. The city code and local number. In the listings for this book, city codes are preceded by a zero; when calling internationally, don't dial the 0 in the city code.

CALLING HOME FROM INDIA OR NEPAL

COUNTRY CODES		Nepal	977
Australia	61	New Zealand	64
Canada	1	South Africa	27
India	91	U.K.	44
Ireland	353	USA	1

Phones are widespread in India and Nepal, and fairly easy to use. The **STD/ISD** sign (Standard Trunk Dialing/International Subscriber Dialing) means that there's a phone nearby. Many towns have 24-hour **Central Telegraph Offices,** which allow free local calls. Many STD/ISD booths are open 24 hours a day and offer fax services. Calling home from an STD/ISD booth, dial the international access code (00), the country code, the city or area code, and then the number. Incoming calls are usually the cost of a local call, if not free, so it's a good idea to place your call and then have someone call you back. Discuss this with the booth operator before you try it; they may refuse to allow this since they don't make any money this way. Rates for international calls from India are the same around the clock.

A **calling card** is another (often futile) alternative. Calls are billed either collect or to your account. Though calling cards work in the major tourist centers of India and Nepal, the STD/ISD booths in many smaller cities and villages do not have access to international operators. And even those cards that potentially work are often disallowed by booth owners, who don't profit on calling card calls. **MCI WorldPhone** also provides access to MCI's Traveler's Assist, which gives advice, exchange rate information, and translation services. Other phone companies provide similar services. **To obtain a calling card,** contact a national telecommunications service before you leave. International **collect calls** cannot be made from India or Nepal to some countries, and booth owners often won't let you try.

TIME ZONES. India is 5½ hours ahead of GMT, 4½ hours behind Australian Eastern Standard Time, and 10½ hours ahead of North America's Eastern Standard Time. Summer time puts the northern countries an hour closer to India. India is 15 minutes behind Nepal.

CALLING WITHIN INDIA AND NEPAL
To call within India or Nepal, dial the city code and then the number. Long-distance calls are either full price (M-Sa 8am-7pm); half-price (M-Sa 7-8am and 7-8:30pm, Su 7am-8:30pm); one-third price (daily 6-7am and 8:30-11pm); or one-quarter price (daily 11pm-6am).

EMAIL AND INTERNET

Hundreds of so-called **cyber-cafes** can be found all over India, allowing Internet access from most major cities and quite a few small towns for a fixed hourly rate. The easiest way to send email from these places is via free, web-based email providers such as Hotmail (www.hotmail.com). Almost every internet search engine has free email service. In Nepal and in some of India's more mountainous regions it is often possible to send email from some local entrepreneur's account.

GETTING THERE
BY PLANE

When it comes to airfare, a little effort can save you a bundle. If your plans are flexible enough to deal with the restrictions, courier fares are the cheapest. Tickets bought from consolidators and standby seating are also good deals, but last-minute specials, airfare wars, and charter flights often beat these fares. The key is to hunt around, to be flexible, and to persistently ask about discounts. Students, seniors, and those under 26 should never pay full price for a ticket.

DETAILS AND TIPS
Timing: Airfares to India and Nepal peak between mid-June and early September, and holidays are also expensive periods in which to travel. Midweek (M-Th morning) round-trip flights run US$40-50 cheaper than weekend flights, but the latter are generally less crowded and more likely to permit frequent-flier upgrades. Return-date flexibility is usually not an option for the budget traveler; traveling with an "open return" ticket can be pricier than fixing a return date when buying the ticket and paying later to change it.

Route: Round-trip flights are by far the cheapest; "open-jaw" (arriving in and departing from different cities) and round-the-world, or RTW, flights are pricier but reasonable alternatives. Flights between capital cities or hubs will offer the most competitive fares.

Boarding: Whenever flying internationally, pick up tickets for international flights well in advance of the departure date, and confirm by phone within 72 hours of departure. One carry-on item and two pieces of checked baggage is the norm for non-courier flights. Consult the airline for weight allowances.

Fares: From **North America:** Round-trip fares to India from the U.S. range from US$900-1200 during the low season, to US$1200-1700 during the summer. Many U.S. and European carriers offer free stops in Europe. Low season flights from **London** to Delhi/Mumbai run between UK£450-750; flights are slightly more expensive to Kathmandu. High-season flights to Delhi/Mumbai run UK£500-900. Fares to Chennai and other Indian cities cost UK£40-100 more. From **Australia** and **New Zealand** peak season fare (between late Nov. and late Jan.) runs between AUS$2000 to AUS$3000 round-trip from the east coast of Australia to Delhi/Calcutta/Kathmandu. Low season fares are AUS$1500 to AUS$2200. Flying from Perth is usually about AUS$150 cheaper than flying from the east coast, but not as many airlines fly out of Perth. Many agents also offer free stopovers in either Bangkok or Singapore, depending on the airline, and most tickets are valid for three months. A one-year ticket is usually AUS$100 extra.

BUDGET AND STUDENT TRAVEL AGENCIES

A knowledgeable agent specializing in flights to India and Nepal can make your life easy and help you save, too, but agents may not spend the time to find you the lowest possible fare—they get paid on commission. Students and under-26ers holding **ISIC** and **IYTC cards** (see **Identification,** p. 14), respectively, qualify for big discounts from student travel agencies.

Campus/Usit Youth and Student Travel, 52 Grosvenor Gardens, **London** SW1W 0AG (in U.K. call (0870) 240 1010, in North America call 44 171 730 21 01, worldwide call 44 171 730 81 11; www.usitcampus.co.uk). Other offices include: 19-21 Aston Quay, O'Connell Bridge, **Dublin** 2 (tel. (01) 677 8117; fax 679 8833); New York Student Center, 895 Amsterdam Ave., **New York,** NY, 10025 (tel. (212) 663-5435; email usitny@aol.com).

Council Travel (www.counciltravel.com). U.S. offices include: Emory Village, 1561 N. Decatur Rd., **Atlanta,** GA 30307 (tel. (404) 377-9997); 273 Newbury St., **Boston,** MA 02116 (tel. (617) 266-1926); 1160 N. State St., **Chicago,** IL 60610 (tel. (312) 951-0585); 10904 Lindbrook Dr., **Los Angeles,** CA 90024 (tel. (310) 208-3551); 205 E. 42nd St., **New York,** NY 10017 (tel. (212) 822-2700); 530 Bush St., **San Francisco,** CA 94108 (tel. (415) 421-3473); 1314 NE 43rd St. #210, **Seattle,** WA 98105 (tel. (206) 632-2448); 3300 M St. NW, **Washington, D.C.** 20007 (tel. (202) 337-6464). **For U.S. cities not listed,** call 800-2-COUNCIL (226-8624).

STA Travel, 6560 Scottsdale Rd. #F100, Scottsdale, AZ 85253 (tel. 800-777-0112 fax (602) 922-0793; www.sta-travel.com). A student and youth travel organization with over 150 offices worldwide. Ticket booking, travel insurance, railpasses, and more. U.S. offices include: 297 Newbury Street, **Boston,** MA 02115 (tel. (617) 266-6014); 429 S. Dearborn St., **Chicago,** IL 60605 (tel. (312) 786-9050); 7202 Melrose Ave., **Los Angeles,** CA 90046 (tel. (323) 934-8722); 10 Downing St., **New York,** NY 10014 (tel. (212) 627-3111); 4341 University Way NE, **Seattle,** WA 98105 (tel. (206) 633-5000); 2401 Pennsylvania Ave., Ste. G, **Washington, D.C.** 20037 (tel. (202) 887-0912); 51 Grant Ave., **San Francisco,** CA 94108 (tel. (415) 391-8407). In the U.K., 6 Wrights Ln., **London** W8 6TA (tel. (0171) 938 47 11 for North American travel). In New Zealand, 10 High St., **Auckland** (tel. (09) 309 04 58). In Australia, 222 Faraday St., **Melbourne** VIC 3053 (tel. (03) 9349 2411).

Travel CUTS (Canadian Universities Travel Services Limited), 187 College St., Toronto, Ont. M5T 1P7 (tel. (416) 979-2406; fax 979-8167; www.travelcuts.com). 40 offices across Canada. Also in the U.K., 295-A Regent St., **London** W1R 7YA (tel. (0171) 255 19 44).

Other organizations that specialize in finding cheap fares include:

IN NORTH AMERICA
Hariworld Travel (www.hariworld.com) has offices in New York, NY (tel. 800-957-3299) and Atlanta, GA (tel. (404) 233-5005) and offers flights to most destinations in India.

Air Brokers International, San Francisco, CA (tel. 800-883-3273, www.airbrokers.com) will fly you from the West Coast to all over India, with free stops in Southeast Asia. They also offer Round the World tickets.

Cheap Tickets (tel. 800-377-1000) flies worldwide to and from the U.S.

IN BRITAIN AND IRELAND
Trailfinders (www.Trailfinders.com) offers discounted tickets to all over India and to Kathmandu with offices in London (42-50 Earls Court Rd. (tel. 0171 938 3366) and 194 Kensington High St. (tel. 0171 938 3939), Manchester (58 Deansgate (tel. 0161 839 6969), Birmingham (22-24 Priory Queens Way (tel. 0121 236 1234), and Bristol (48 Corn St. (tel. 0117 929 9000). Trailfinders also has an office in Dublin at 4/5 Dawson St., Dublin 2 (tel. 1 677 7888).

COMMERCIAL AIRLINES

The commercial airlines' lowest regular offer is the **APEX** (Advance Purchase Excursion) fare, which provides confirmed reservations and allows "open-jaw" tickets. Generally, reservations must be made 7 to 21 days in advance, with 7- to 14-day minimum and up to 90-day maximum-stay limits, and hefty cancellation and change penalties (fees rise in summer). Book peak-season APEX fares early, since by May you will have a hard time getting the departure date you want. Although APEX fares are probably not the cheapest possible fares, they will give you a sense of the average commercial price, from which to measure other bargains. Specials advertised in newspapers may be cheaper but have more restrictions and fewer available seats. Most major U.S. and European airlines (Delta, United, KLM, British Airways, Lufthansa) offer flights to major cities in India and Nepal. Other popular carriers include:

Aeroflot (NY office tel. (212) 332-1050), with connecting service through Moscow, is usually cheapest, but their service records are close to abysmal.

Air India (NY office tel. (212) 407-1300, www.airindia.com) has direct service from London and connecting service from New York and Chicago to Bombay.

Malaysia Airlines (tel. (800) 552-9264, www.malaysia-airlines.com) offers connecting service to Delhi and Chennai from New York and Los Angeles.

Royal Nepal Airlines (tel. (1) 220757; fax (1) 225348; London office tel. (0171) 757 2525; www.catmando.com/com/machold/mac) operates regular flights to Kathmandu from London, Paris and Frankfurt.

OTHER CHEAP ALTERNATIVES

AIR COURIER FLIGHTS
Couriers help transport cargo on international flights by guaranteeing delivery of the baggage claim slips from the company to a representative overseas. Generally, couriers must travel light (carry-ons only) and deal with complex restrictions on their flight. Most of these flights also operate only out of the biggest cities, like New York. Generally, you must be over 21 (in some cases 18), have a valid passport, and procure your own visa, if necessary. Groups such as the **Air Courier Association** (tel. 800-282-1202; www.aircourier.org) and the **International Association of Air Travel Couriers**, 220 South Dixie Hwy., P.O. Box 1349, Lake Worth, FL 33460 (tel. (561) 582-8320; email iaatc@courier.org; www.courier.org) provide their members with lists of opportunities and courier brokers worldwide for an annual fee.

TICKET CONSOLIDATORS

Ticket consolidators, or **"bucket shops,"** buy unsold tickets in bulk from commercial airlines and sell them at discounted rates. The best place to look is in the Sunday travel section of any major newspaper, where many bucket shops place tiny ads. Call quickly, as availability is typically extremely limited. Not all bucket shops are reliable establishments, so insist on a receipt that gives full details of restrictions, refunds, and tickets, and pay by credit card. For more information, check the website **Consolidators FAQ** (www.travel-library.com/air-travel/consolidators.html).

SPECIALTY CONSOLIDATORS. A limited number of travel agencies deal in unconventional arrangements of flights. Round-the-World (RTW) and Circle Asia tickets string together one-way flights. These tickets are best for extended trips; most have flexible dates, good up to one year from commencement of travel. For itineraries more complicated than a simple round-trip, RTW and other unconventional tickets are often a better deal. Try **High Adventure Travel** (tel. 800-428-8735 or (415) 912-5600; www.airtreks.com) or **Ticket Planet** (tel. 800-799-888; www.ticketplanet.com), and leave at least a month to book and confirm tickets.

BY SEA

If you really have travel time to spare, **Ford's Travel Guides,** 19448 Londelius St., Northridge, CA 91324 (tel. (818) 701-7414; fax 701-7415) lists **freighter companies** that will take passengers from all over the world to all over the world, including to ports in India. Ask for their *Freighter Travel Guide and Waterways of the World* (US$15.95, plus $2.50 postage if mailed outside the U.S.).

GETTING AROUND

BY CAR

Driving a car (or better yet a VW Microbus) across Asia was a classic 1960s hippie expedition. Now, it's a nightmare. The only border crossing open from Pakistan to India is between Lahore and Amritsar. There are no borders open between India and China. Selling your car in India or Nepal was once a good way to finance a trip, but car import duties have now stolen that hopes. You must have a *carnet,* an automotive passport, to prove that you'll take your car out with you and not sell it on the black market. Unleaded gas and foreign parts are rare in India.

Driving a car in India or Nepal is not for the faint of heart. Besides swerving to avoid cars, motorcycles, rickshaws, people, and cows, there is also a general disregard for anything resembling traffic regulations. Drivers are reckless and aggressive, constrained only by the general dilapidation of the roads and their vehicles. Many pedestrians who have just arrived from villages lack a basic traffic sense. Not surprisingly, India and Nepal have high rates of road accidents—although these seem to result in remarkably few fatalities. If you get into a traffic accident in India or Nepal, **leave the scene of the accident immediately and go to the nearest police station.** Also keep in mind that killing one of those omnipresent cows, even by accident, is punishable in Nepal by up to 20 years imprisonment.

A car is entirely unnecessary in a large city where buses, rickshaws, and taxis can get you anywhere you want to go, cheaply. Also, some rental companies do not offer insurance; a serious accident may mean spending some time in jail or the hospital, and shelling out a large sum of money to cover damages. If you absolutely must have a car, keep your **international driving permit** (see below) handy, as well as a substantial amount of money.

The cost of renting a four-door sedan is many times the cost of a night's stay at a guest house. It is more common to hire a car with a **driver,** who looks after petrol costs and repairs, and who will take responsibility. It is cheaper to hire a taxi for the day or for a specific journey; fares vary by distance. With enough passengers to split the costs, this is usually within the budget traveler's price range.

Hitchhiking is practically unheard of and unnecessary in most parts of India and Nepal, since public transportation networks are extensive and cheap. In mountain areas like Kumaon and Himachal Pradesh, where traffic is sparse, jeeps and cargo trucks sometimes take on passengers for a small charge. *Let's Go* does not recommend hitchhiking, and women should never hitchhike alone.

DRIVING PERMITS AND CAR INSURANCE

INTERNATIONAL DRIVING PERMIT (IDP). Renting a car, **motor-scooter,** or **motorcycle** in India and Nepal usually requires an IDP. Your IDP, valid for one year, must be issued in your own country before you depart; AAA affiliates cannot issue IDPs valid in their own country. You must be 18 years old to receive the IDP. A valid driver's license from your home country must always accompany the IDP. Applications for IDPs usually need to include one or two photos, a current local license, an additional form of identification, and a fee.

CAR INSURANCE. Most credit cards cover standard insurance. If you rent, lease, or borrow a car, you will need a **green card,** or **International Insurance Certificate,** to prove that you have liability insurance. Obtain it through the car rental agency; most include coverage in their prices. If you lease a car, you can obtain a green card from the dealer. If you have a collision abroad, the accident will show up on your domestic records if you report it to your insurance company. Rental agencies may require you to purchase theft insurance in countries that they consider to have a high risk of auto theft. Ask your rental agency about India and Nepal.

BY AIR

AIRCRAFT SAFETY. The airlines of third-world nations do not always meet safety standards. The *Official Airline Guide* (www.oag.com) and many travel agencies can tell you the type and age of aircraft on a particular route. This can be especially useful in the subcontinent, where less reliable equipment is often used for inter-city travel. The **International Airline Passengers Association** (U.S. tel. (972) 404-9980, safety office open M-F 9-11am; U.K. tel. (181) 681 6555) provides region-specific safety information. The Federal Aviation Administration (www.faa.gov) reviews the airline authorities for countries whose airlines enter the U.S. Travel advisories made by the **U.S. State Department** (tel. (202) 647-5225; travel.state.gov/travel_warnings.html) sometimes involve foreign carriers, especially when terrorist bombings may be a threat.

India and Nepal both have extensive air networks serving every corner of their countries. In the last few years both countries have opened up the skies to private companies, but the government-run **Indian Airlines** and **Royal Nepal Airlines Corporation (RNAC),** which had monopolies, still have the most extensive schedules and fly subsidized routes to less popular destinations. However, air travel is much more expensive than surface travel, and it will not always save you time. Waiting in airport-office queues, traveling to and from airports (which are often far from town), and checking in can slow you down, but most of all, Indian and Nepalese airports love to subject passengers to purgatorial delays. It is best to fly only to escape unbearable cross-country bus or train rides. In Nepal, where the roads are so bad—and bus rides therefore dangerous and interminable—the balance might be shifted slightly in favor of air travel. Air travel is generally safe even though the planes are usually hand-me-downs from European or East Asian airlines, and flights are often bumpy (see **Aircraft Safety,** below).

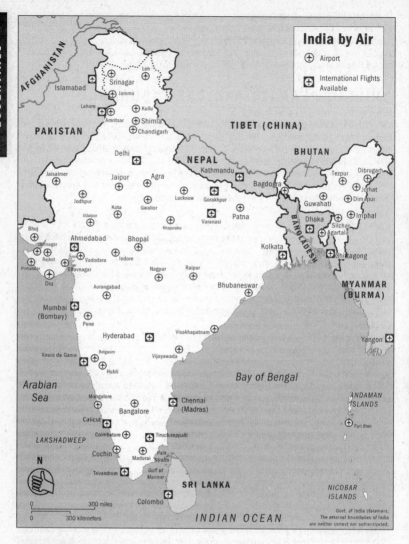

India by Air

⊕ Airport

⊕ International Flights Available

AFGHANISTAN

Islamabad

Srinagar
Leh
Jammu
Lahore
Kullu
Amritsar
Shimla
Chandigarh

PAKISTAN

TIBET (CHINA)

Delhi

NEPAL
Kathmandu

BHUTAN

Jaisalmer
Jaipur
Agra
Lucknow
Gorakhpur
Bagdogra
Tezpur
Dibrugarh
Jorhat
Dimapur
Jodhpur
Kota
Gwalior
Patna
Guwahati
Imphal
Udaipur
Khajuraho
Varanasi
Silchar
Agartala
Bhuj
Ahmedabad
Bhopal
Dhaka
Jamnagar
Kolkata
Chittagong
Rajkot
Vadodara
Indore
BANGLADESH
Porbandar
Bhavnagar
Nagpur
Raipur
Diu
Aurangabad
Bhubaneswar
MYANMAR (BURMA)

Mumbai (Bombay)
Pune

Hyderabad
Visakhapatnam

Vasco da Gama
Belgaum
Vijayawada
Yangon
Hubli

Arabian Sea

Bay of Bengal

ANDAMAN ISLANDS

Mangalore
Chennai (Madras)
Calicut
Bangalore
Port Blair

LAKSHADWEEP
Coimbatore
Tiruchirappalli

Cochin
Madurai
Palk Straits

N

Trivandrum
Gulf of Mannar

SRI LANKA

NICOBAR ISLANDS

0   300 miles
0   300 kilometers

Colombo

INDIAN OCEAN

Govt. of India statement:
The external boundaries of India
are neither correct nor authenticated.

IN INDIA. Though several small private airlines (officially called ATOs, "air taxi operators") such as Jet Airways and Modiluft flies to most destinations, Indian Airlines still has the largest fleet and handles about 75% of the traffic. **Reservations** are essential on almost all flights and must be made well in advance, especially during the peak seasons, as flights almost always sell out. Go to one of the airlines' offices to make a booking, or use a travel agent. If you don't get a seat, put your name on the waiting list and show up at the airport early; miracles can happen. Guard your airline ticket well—if you lose it, airlines and travel agents will accept no responsibility. Check-in time for domestic flights is one hour before departure.

Indian Airlines offers **youth fares** at a 25% discount off Economy Class fares (in $US) for passengers ages 12 to 30. Children under 12 pay 50%, and infants under two pay 10%. Indian Airlines offers a traveling package for foreign tourists called **"Discover India"** that provides for 21 days of unlimited air travel for US$750, or 15 days for US$500, provided that no destinations are repeated except the first and last points; only a limited number of seats on each flight are allotted to "Discover India" subscribers.

IN NEPAL. Air travel is essential to Nepal's economy, providing access to northern mountainous regions where there are no roads. Travelers will find that air travel is just as important to avoid long, hellish bus rides. RNAC operates flights to about 35 airports and airstrips in Nepal, though it is suffering financially and its planes are constantly filled to capacity. Privatization has recently given birth to three new airlines: **Everest Air, Necon Air,** and **Nepal Airways.** All airlines' prices are the same, but the new private companies are said to have better service. All foreigners must pay for flights with foreign exchange, and prices range from US$50-160 for domestic flights. On the whole, air travel in Nepal is unpredictable. Bad weather prevents take-offs and landings, so long delays at the airport are the norm. During the high trekking season it might be difficult to get tickets for popular destinations. It is best to book plane tickets through travel agents.

BY TRAIN

The Indian rail network, one of the few things Indians will readily thank their British colonial masters for, is incredibly extensive. For budget travelers rail is the best way to get around India. Due to its mountains and freedom from colonization, Nepal has no trains except for one that runs across the Indian border to Janakpur.

With over 1.6 million workers on its payroll, **Indian Railways** is the world's largest employer, and trains are generally the best way to cover long distances in India at a reasonable cost. Eleven million passengers are carried over its vast network daily; you're bound to get a glimpse of Indian India on the train, or at least a glimpse of how India travels. You'll meet locals eager to chat about your country and theirs. The Indian Railways might not get you there on time, but they will get you there—and "there" is just about anywhere in the country. The only exceptions are the hilly areas, mainly in the North. A few hill stations, such as Darjeeling, Ooty, and Shimla, are reached by **"toy trains,"** narrow-gauge machines that run at a snail's pace. **Express** or **mail** trains are the fast, convenient ones that rush between cities. The *Shatabdi Express*, *Rajdhani Express*, and *Taj Express* are the fastest trains that cover the main lines (e.g., Delhi-Mumbai and Delhi-Calcutta) and even some smaller ones (e.g., Delhi-Bhopal or Chennai-Mysore). These trains come with full air conditioning and meals, stop only at big cities, and cost at least four times as much as standard second class fares. Below these is a hierarchy of superfast, mail, and express trains, which cost the same but vary in speed. Unless you are headed to a remote village it is probably best to avoid local **passenger** trains, which slowly stop at every small-town station. **The trains listed in each city of this guide often represent only a select few of the many trains going to a given destination.**

Various classes of comfort are available, from air-conditioned first class, to non-A/C first, to the many avatars of second class. **First class** on an Indian train is three or four times the price of second class, though still not very expensive by Western standards. In first class, you won't be squeezed to your bench by an excessive crowd and your view of the countryside will often be through scratched, amber-tinted windows. Air conditioning is usually unnecessary on trains, even during the summer, because once the train gets moving you'll be cooled off anyway. First-class **sleeper cars** are divided into compartments, offering more privacy than second-class sleepers, which have rows of berths in the open. Though sometimes crowded and dirty, second-class will give you more contact with fellow passengers, and it is easy to get a good night's sleep in second-class sleepers (you're guaranteed a vaguely padded berth to yourself). During the day, and for shorter trips, regular second class is something of a free-for-all, but once you've gotten a seat, it's yours. Women traveling on their own or with children should enquire about **ladies' compartments,** available on most overnight mail and express trains.

For long trips, especially overnight ones, it's necessary to make **reservations** (usually a day or two in advance). It is safest to do this right at the station or booking office; **travel agents** frequently charge hefty commissions and have been known to give false information. **Computers** in most stations have made bookings systematic, but there are still long, anarchic queues. A **tourist quota** is often set aside those with foreign passports, and a few major stations even have separate lines for tourists. Many stations have ladies' queues or allow women to jump to the front of the line to avoid pushing and shoving. Get a reservation slip from the window, and scribble down the train you want. Each route has a name and a number; for route information, arm yourself with a copy of *Trains at a Glance* (Rs25), which contains **schedules** for all express and mail trains, though the timetable can be difficult to decipher and does not list every stop each train makes. The fares on Indian Railways correspond to distance and class. The staff at most train station **enquiry counters** are generally well-informed and English-speaking.

Foreign passport holders can buy **Indrail Passes,** which are available for anywhere from half a day to three months in a variety of classes (paid for in US dollars or pounds sterling). They include all fares, reservation charges, and any supplementary charges, but prices are very high and it's tough to get your money's worth. Indrail Passes can save you some hassle—on super-fast trains, pass holders are exempt from reservation fees and extra charges and, on shorter journeys, don't need tickets—but reservations are still necessary for longer trips.

If you fail to get a reservation, you can still get on the **waiting list** and hope. In an emergency, try to find the **station master.** He will probably be busy and not thrilled, but if anyone can find a seat for you on a "full" train, it's he and you might be able to persuade him. As a last resort, *baksheesh* to porters has been known to turn up unreserved berths. If you cancel your reservation more than 24 hours before your trip, you can still get a refund but you'll be charged Rs10-50 depending on the class; up to four hours before, you'll get 75% back, and after that (even sometimes 12 hours after the train has left), you can get still get 50%.

If you have a reservation, you'll be fine getting to the station just a few minutes before the train arrives. If you're leaving from a major station, check the computer-printed list (usually on the platform or attached to the side of each train car) for your name and seat and listen for announcements. If your train is delayed, the **waiting rooms** can be a good place to pass time. It's usually not difficult for foreigners to assume a place in the first class waiting room, regardless of what class they're traveling. Railway **retiring rooms,** usually cheaper than budget hotels, are available to anyone with a valid ticket or Indrail pass. They operate on a 24-hour basis, and most also rent for 12 hours at a stretch.

BY BUS

 WARNING. Poor road conditions and aggressive driving make road travel in India and Nepal dangerous, **particularly in hilly or mountainous regions.**

Extensive networks of bus routes cover all of India and Nepal. In train-less Nepal, buses are the most popular mode of long-distance transportation. In India they finish a close second to trains. Generally buses are as fast as, or faster than, trains. Buses also go to the hilly areas of India where trains cannot go, and they involve less pre-departure hassle. For short trips, advance bookings are rarely necessary—just show up at the bus stand and climb aboard; you can pay the conductor somewhere along the way. For longer trips (over 10hr.) it might be necessary to book a day ahead. Do this directly at the bus stand rather than through an agent.

The main drawback to most bus travel in India and Nepal is its discomfort. Seats are usually narrow, with very little cushioning and allow almost no legroom. There are often more passengers than seats, and many make the trip standing up. Buses also tend to make frequent, albeit brief, stops for snacks and *chai*, which slow down the journey, but offer much-needed chances to stretch—however, you may lose your seat if you get up. At scheduled rest stops, women might have a hard time finding a place to use a toilet; they should ask the conductor to wait longer for them as they search. There is also some risk involved in bus travel, as in all road travel in South Asia (see **Getting Around: By Car,** p. 48). Road conditions are usually poor and traffic unpredictable—expect to hear gears grinding and horns blaring, and to feel sudden lurches. **Never ride on the roof of a bus,** no matter how cool the breeze or how gorgeous the scenery. This is illegal and terribly dangerous.

Among the different of types of buses available, **tourist buses** or **"superdeluxe" buses** have cushioned seats and more space than others; although they are certainly not luxurious by Western standards, they usually seat four passengers abreast rather than five. Tourist buses often have fans and sometimes air conditioning, are usually only available on popular tourist routes. For other journeys, **express buses** are the norm. Express buses still have padded seats, but they are much more crowded, they stop for anyone who wants to get on, and they don't get there any faster. Nepal and some places in India have special **night buses,** which have reclining seats and a bit more legroom, but you shouldn't count on getting any sleep. They stop for *chai* endlessly (just be glad the driver is getting his caffeine). At all costs, **avoid video coaches** unless you like watching old black-and-white Hindi films for five hours (or more) at ear-splitting levels.

Luggage on the roof rack of a bus is usually safe, but bags have been known to disappear at intermediate stops in a flurry of untraceable movement. Make sure your pack is tied down, or ask if you can put it elsewhere—in a compartment at the back, or at the front where you can keep an eye on it. If your luggage goes on the roof, give *baksheesh* to the person who put it up there.

Local buses in big cities have their destinations inscribed in the local language. In a hurry to wedge themselves into city traffic, bus drivers tend to roll-stop, so you may want to learn the skill of leaping on and off the back stairs. Once safely in, sit or stand until the bus-*wallah*, with his little bus satchel, comes by and clicks a small metal contraption in your face. That means pay-up—ask how many rupees it is to your destination, since prices vary by distance. Women on city buses tend to get preferential seating; male passengers may be expected to give up their seats.

IN INDIA. Bus travel in India is slightly complicated by the existence of both state and private bus companies. In this guide, **bus stands** and **bus stations** are where state (and sometimes private) buses roll in and out; private buses often leave from the particular company's office. State government buses are often crowded, so get to the bus stand at least half an hour before departure. Some private bus companies offer excellent service, while others should not be licensed; there are so many private bus companies that it is difficult to know the quality of an operation until you're already screaming down the highway. As with train tickets, it is generally unwise to buy bus tickets from random travel agencies.

IN NEPAL. Bus travel is widely used in Nepal, although road conditions are poor and the hilly terrain multiplies travel time. Almost all buses are privately owned, but look out for the government **Sajha** buses which are safer and much more comfortable. For these you'll probably have to book tickets from the bus stand a day in advance. Booking bus tickets from Kathmandu or Pokhara can be a hassle because the bus stands are far from the tourist center; it might be easier to book through a travel agent. Avoid package deals for complex bus journeys as these often turn out to be scams. It's best to buy your second ticket once you arrive.

LOCAL TRANSPORTATION

AUTO-RICKSHAWS AND TEMPOS

To some, these podlike three-wheelers are a symbol of the South Asian experience; to others, they are diesel fume-belching beasts. Fans argue that they are cheap compared to taxis, more convenient than buses, and small enough to dart through heavy traffic. Much of this, of course, depends upon the driver. Detractors criticize them for the damage they do to the environment and human ears. Auto-rickshaws seat one to three adults (but often up to 10 schoolchildren). Low ceilings, minimal legroom, and narrow seats are part of the adventure. While the auto-rickshaw-*wallah* will often insist that it's "broken," try to insist that they use the **meter.** Avoid pushy drivers, and always scoff at the first price demanded—try to bring him down to at least 30-40% of his original price. **In most cities, it is illegal for rickshaw-wallahs to overcharge for local, daytime service.** A threat to report them to the police can often do wonders to eke out a fair fare. Depending on the town, some drivers may add a surcharge to the meter or display a price increase card, because the meters are outdated and the price of fuel has risen. **Nighttime fares** can be up to two times the standard meter rate.

Rickshaw-*wallahs*, who have a habit of getting in **commission** cahoots with hotels, may inform you that your choice has been shut down or that its staff is on strike. Chances are that the "insider info" is incorrect. If a driver taking you home asks if you need a ride the next day, know that if you flippantly agree he will probably sleep in his rickshaw that night waiting for you.

Tempos seat about six, follow fixed routes, and have fixed fees; they are of limited use to foreigners, however, because their destinations are never marked.

CYCLE-RICKSHAWS

There are two other kinds of rickshaws in India and Nepal. Calcutta is home to the India's only fleet of **hand-pulled rickshaws,** though even these are rumored to near extinction. Far more common are **cycle-rickshaws,** where the driver pedals in front while his trusting passengers sit on a cushioned box above the rear axle. They are not always found in metropolitan areas, such as Mumbai, but they are found in the countryside wherever there is flat terrain. In Nepal rickshaws are limited to the Terai and to parts of Kathmandu, where they mainly cater to tourists. In addition to the fresh breeze and open views, the benefits of riding in a cycle-rickshaw means you won't be contributing to the already suffocating city smog; negatives include the longer traveling time and the sorrow of seeing an old man labor away (although he definitely wants your business). If he jumps out and starts pushing you up a hill that's too steep to pedal, it's polite to lend a hand. **Make sure your rickshaw-wallah is not intoxicated.** The worst part about a rickshaw ride is settling the **price,** which is highly negotiable. Foreigners usually pay about Rs10 per kilometer in India—more in touristy places, less in villages—but feel free to haggle.

TAXIS

Taxis are found in the larger cities of India and Nepal; in some cities, such as Mumbai, only taxis and not rickshaws or auto-rickshaws are allowed within the metropolitan limits. India's international airports offer reliable **pre-paid taxi services**—you pay at the official office, and give your receipt to a driver in the waiting queue, who takes you where you need to go. Taxis are supposed to have meters, but these are sometimes out of date, so the driver will add a percentage or wield an official-looking "fare adjustment card" with up-to-date prices. All this varies from city to city; there are no hard-and-fast rules, but in general you should insist on using the meter rather than negotiating a price. Private companies exist to rent out taxis and drivers for longer hours, short trips, or even days; enquire at train stations, airports, or tourist offices. In mountainous regions, **jeeps** (sometimes called Gypsies or Mahindras) function as taxis or mini-buses.

MOTORCYCLES, MOPEDS, AND SCOOTERS

A **motorcycle** can liberate you to explore rural roads not accessible by public transportation, although they can be very dangerous in India and Nepal. Helmets are rarely provided, but you should not get on a motorcycle or motorbike without one—traffic fatalities on motorcycles are frighteningly high. Motorcycle rental shops are abundant near major tourist stops. An **International Driving Permit** (see p. 49) is legally required for you to rent a scooter or motorcycle but is rarely checked. Motorcycle and scooter engines in India and Nepal are usually only 100cc, so they are not very good for long trips. **Mopeds** are easy to operate but dangerous to take into any sort of traffic. **Scooters** have a high center of gravity and small wheels, which make them very dangerous; most scooters are also very difficult to operate and must be manually shifted from gear to gear. A popular alternative for tourists in some areas is to rent Kinetic-Hondas, automatic shifting scooters that are easy to operate and a bit safer on the road.

BICYCLES

Because of the over-congested streets, trying to ride a bicycle in the big Indian cities is often an exercise in futility, worse, but on back roads through rural towns, and in much of Nepal, bicycles are a great alternative to motorcycles or scooters. Most bikes in India and Nepal don't have gears, so hills are hellish. In many tourist centers like Kathmandu and Pokhara, bikes can be rented very cheaply, usually on a daily basis. Clunky Indian bikes are also cheap to buy and resell.

BOATS

Ferries run between Mumbai and Goa, and ships travel regularly from Calcutta and Chennai to Port Blair. During monsoon, ferries are often the only way to cross certain rivers. White-water rafting the only type of boat travel in Nepal.

BORDER CROSSINGS

India-Nepal: There are six overland border crossings between India and Nepal: Mahendranagar, Dhangadi, Nepalganj, Sunauli, Raxaul/Birganj, and Kakarbhitta. Sunauli is a 3hr. bus ride from Gorakhpur in Uttar Pradesh; from there you can catch a 10hr. bus to Pokhara or a 11hr. bus to Kathmandu. Raxaul is a 6hr. bus ride from Patna in Bihar; from Birganj, across the border, it's a 10-12hr. bus ride to Kathmandu. The Kakarbhitta crossing, at the eastern end of Nepal, is easily accessible from Siliguri, which is a transit point for Darjeeling. It is not necessary to get a Nepalese visa before you arrive at the border, but you must get your Indian visa ahead of time if you're going from Nepal to India. Visitors are also allowed to drive across the border if they possess an international *carnet*. For more information see **Raxaul,** p. 643; **Birganj,** p. 781; **Sunauli,** p. 773; and **Kakarbhitta,** p. 785.

India-Bangladesh: Flights depart Kolkata for Dhaka (1hr.). Trains and buses run from Calcutta to Bangaon in West Bengal. From there it is a rickshaw ride across the border to Benapol, Bangladesh, with connections via Khulna or Jessore to Dhaka. The northern border, near Darjeeling, from Jalpaiguri to Haldibari, is only periodically open and requires an exit permit.

India-Burma: No land frontier open.

India-Bhutan: If you are lucky enough to get a Bhutanese visa, you must cross the border at Puntsholing, a 3-4hr. bus ride from Siliguri in West Bengal. Make sure you also have a "transit permit" from the Indian ministry of External Affairs.

India-China: No land frontier open.

India-Pakistan: Due to the Kashmiri-cool relations between India and Pakistan, only one crossing is open along the entire length of the countries' 2000km border. A daily train runs from Amritsar in the Indian Punjab through Attari, the border town, to Lahore, in the Pakistani Punjab. There is also direct bus service between Delhi and Lahore. For more information see **Pakistan Border,** p. 277.

India-Sri Lanka: The boat service from Rameswaram in Tamil Nadu to Talaimannar in Sri Lanka has been indefinitely suspended due to the war in northern Sri Lanka. Travelers must fly to Colombo, Sri Lanka.

Nepal-China: The Arniko Rajmarg (Kathmandu-Kodari Highway) links Kathmandu with the Tibet Autonomous Region of China via the exit point of Kodari. The border is currently open only to travelers on organized tours. Before crossing into Tibet, check in with your embassy in Kathmandu to make sure that the border situation is stable, as there have occasionally been difficulties for tourists crossing overland into Tibet.

ESSENTIALS

WHEN IN INDIA AND NEPAL...

CUSTOMS AND ETIQUETTE

CLOTHING. Dress modestly. In some areas, a man sporting shorts will be giggled at, since panthood is synonymous with manhood. Similarly, but for different reasons, women should try to keep legs covered, at least to the knee. Bare shoulders are another sure sign of immorality (and a quick way to sunburn). Ragged clothes will also draw attention to you. In India, many women will find they are treated more respectfully when they wear a *salwar kameez*. While men's clothing in India is typically more Westernized, men might want to buy a thin cotton *kurta pajama*—these garments will cover you up while keeping you cool. If you are well-dressed, this will certainly affect the way that people respond to you as a foreigner. Of course, these rules vary by region. Clothing taboos are looser in Nepal and throughout the Himalaya, and also in big cities like Mumbai and Bangalore.

FOOD. Most Indian and Nepalis eat with their hands. While restaurants usually give cutlery to foreigners, you may have to eat with your hands if you are invited to someone's home. The most important thing is to **eat with your right hand only.** The left hand is used for cleaning after defecation; so it is seen as polluted. You can use your left hand to hold a fork or to pass a dish but it should never touch food or your lips directly. Any food that comes into contact with one person's saliva is unclean for anyone else. Indians and Nepalis will not usually take bites of each other's food, or drink from the same cup; watch how locals drink from water bottles, pouring the drink in without touching their lips. In Hindu houses, the family **hearth** is sacred, so if food is cooked before you on a fire (as it frequently is in trekking lodges) never play with the fire or throw trash in it.

Meals in India or Nepal begin with a staple dish: usually rice in southern and eastern India, wheat bread in the north. For many people it is the only food they eat on a regular basis. Almost all Jains and many Hindus (especially in South India) are **vegetarian,** and besides, for many non-vegetarians, meat is an expensive luxury. Due to the cow's sacred status in Hinduism, beef is scarce. Muslims do not eat pork and are supposed to shun alcohol, although the latter restriction is not always observed. Only the most modernized women of any religion drink alcohol.

HYGIENE. All **bodily secretions** and products are considered polluting. The people who come into contact with them—laundrymen, barbers, latrine cleaners—have historically formed the lowest ranks of the caste system. The **head** is the most sacred part of the body, and purity decreases all the way to the toes. To **touch**

SQUAT TOILETS: A BILLION PEOPLE CAN'T BE WRONG...
Indian toilets appear to be simple holes in the ground, which can be an unpleasant first surprise. Even worse is discovering that there is no toilet paper. Wait! Don't panic! Placing your feet on either side of the orifice, you squat and push—an elegant process. Many Indian toilets feature painted footprints for the uninitiated; also, the squatting position is less likely to strain your back or give you a hernia than sitting. Next to the hole, there is generally a cup and a spigot. To clean yourself in the time-honored Indian fashion, fill the cup and—holding it with your RIGHT hand—pour it near the base of your spine while wiping with your LEFT hand. It is remarkably effective and environmentally friendly; think of how much toilet paper you use and multiply that by 950 million—it's a lot of trees. Two warnings, however: (1) wash both hands carefully afterwards and (2) never, NEVER use the right hand to wipe; this practice is one reason for the stigma associated with the left hand in Indian society. Flushing is usually accomplished by pouring a cup or two of water down the hole.

something with your feet is a grave insult; you should never touch a person with your feet, step over a seated person's outstretched legs, or even point at someone with your foot. Never put your feet on a table, or any other surface used for eating or studying. To touch someone else's feet, on the other hand, is an act of veneration. If you accidentally touch someone else with your foot, touch your eyes and then their knee or foot, whichever is more accessible. The **left hand** is also polluted. Always use your right hand to eat, give, take, or point.

COMMUNICATION AND BODY LANGUAGE. A quick **sideways tilt of the head,** similar to shaking one's head but more like a sideways nod, means "OK," or "I understand." Many foreigners are baffled by this gesture, thinking their hosts are answering their most innocent comments and requests with a firm "no." **Indian English,** especially when written, is full of colorful and antique-sounding phrases. You may be surprised to hear people address you as "madame" or "good gentleman," or to read letters asking you to "kindly do the needful" and signed "your most humble servant."

Many foreigners have trouble adjusting to the constant **stares** they get in India and Nepal. There's no taboo against staring in South Asian culture, and no harm is intended, but be sure not to send mixed signals. Meeting someone's gaze is often tantamount to expressing a desire for further contact. At the same time, realize that it can both acceptable and appropriate to ignore attempts at conversation.

WOMEN AND MEN. Displays of physical affection between women and men are rare. Some affection is considered completely natural and acceptable, such as that between the same sex. Everywhere, men walk comfortably down the street clasping hands. Most Indian and Nepali women appear quite meek and quiet in public, and it is difficult and unusual for strange men to talk to them. Women travelers may have a hard time meeting Indian and Nepali women, although women should try to find other women to help out in emergencies (see **Women Travelers,** p. 57).

PLACES OF WORSHIP. Be especially sensitive about etiquette in places of worship. **Dress conservatively,** keeping legs and shoulders covered, and **take off your shoes** before entering any mosque, *gurudwara,* or Hindu, Jain, or Buddhist temple. Visitors to Sikh *gurudwaras* must cover their heads as well—handkerchiefs are usually provided. At the entrance to popular temples, shoe-*wallahs* will guard your shoes for a few rupees. Ask before taking **photographs** in places of worship. It is normally forbidden to take pictures of images of deities in Hindu temples. Many Hindu temples, especially those in Kerala, but also in Nepal and in pilgrimage sites such as Puri and Varanasi, ban **non-Hindus** from entering. In practice this rule excludes anyone who doesn't look sufficiently South Asian. Purity laws dictate that **menstruating women** are forbidden to enter some Hindu and Jain temples.

It is common practice in Hindu temples to partake of offerings of consecrated fruit and/or water called **prasad,** which is received with the right hand over the left (and no one takes seconds). It is protocol to leave a small donation at the entrance to the temple sanctuary, though this can cause some dilemmas when temple priests aggressively force *prasad* into your hands, expecting large amounts of cash in return. Usually a donation of one or two rupees will suffice. Hinduism and Buddhism consider the right-hand side auspicious and the left-hand side inauspicious; thus it is customary to walk around Hindu temples and Buddhist *stupas* **clockwise** with your right side toward the shrine. In fact, any circular motion, such as the turning of Tibetan Buddhist prayer wheels, goes in a clockwise direction.

WOMEN TRAVELERS

Incidents of **sexual harassment** are very common, especially in northern India, but seldom more serious than verbal advances or groping. Too many Indian and Nepali men are under the impression that white women are promiscuous. This belief is partly due to the stereotypes from American television and movies, and partly because Western women do certain things that "good" Indian and Nepali women do not. The less you look like a tourist, the better off you'll be. Look as if you know where you're going (even when you don't) and approach other women (or couples) if you need help or directions. **Dress conservatively, covering legs and shoulders, and always wear a bra.** Don't jump to the conclusion that since Indian women wearing saris may reveal their lower backs and stomachs, it's OK to wear shorts—it's definitely not. And don't automatically assume that a t-shirt, which appears to cover the same vital areas as a sari, if not more, is appropriate. The shape of the breast should be left a mystery—most women's chests are covered by more than one layer of clothing. Consider wearing a *salwar kameez*, Indian baggy pants with a loose long-sleeved shirt. Wearing a conspicuous **wedding band** may also help prevent unwanted overtures. Some travelers report that carrying pictures of a "husband" or "children" is extremely useful to help document marriage status. Even a mention of a husband waiting back at the hotel may be enough in some places to discount your potentially vulnerable, unattached appearance. Also realize that **non-verbal communication** is quite different than in the West. Behavior that would be polite back home (making eye contact, responding when asked a question) can easily be seen as a come-on by South Asian men.

Invest in secure accommodations, particularly family-run guest houses with doors that lock from the inside. Stay in central locations and avoid late-night walks. **Hitching** is never safe for solo women, or even for two or more women traveling together. On trains, try to get into a **ladies' compartment.** Train stations often have **ladies' waiting rooms.** On buses, you should be allowed to sit near the front.

South India is said to be safer for women than the north. Bihar and eastern Uttar Pradesh, where law and order are lax, are some of the most dangerous areas; there have even been cases of foreign women being raped. The Himalayan regions, however, from Himachal Pradesh to Nepal to Sikkim, are among the safest areas; attitudes toward women are much more liberal among many mountain ethnic groups. And in the cosmopolitan circles in major cities (especially in Mumbai) women can usually feel as comfortable as they would in any other big city.

The slightest bit of resistance usually stops most harassers who have encountered few foreign women before and are unsure of themselves. Your best answer to verbal harassment is no answer at all; feigned deafness, sitting motionless and staring straight ahead at nothing in particular will do a world of good that reactions usually don't achieve. The extremely persistent can sometimes be dissuaded by a firm, loud, and very public "Mujhe chod dho!" ("Go away!" in Hindi). If need be, **turn to an older woman** for help in an uncomfortable situation; her stern rebukes will usually be enough to embarrass the most persistent jerk. Don't hesitate to get the attention of **passersby** if you are being harassed, as people have a strong sense of public morality, and don't hesitate to seek out a policeman. Keep in mind, however, that they, like other men, may assume that a women traveling alone is looking for sex; don't place all your trust in them, particularly in untouristed areas. Emergency numbers (uniform across India and Nepal) are listed on the inside back cover of this book, as well as in the **Practical Information** listings of cities. An **IMPACT Model Mugging** (see **Self Defense,** p. 23) self-defense course will not only prepare you for a potential attack, but will also raise your level of awareness as well as your confidence For information on specifics see **Women's Health,** p. 32).

SPECIFIC CONCERNS

SENIOR CITIZENS. Senior citizens are rarely offered special discounts in India or Nepal. Agencies for senior group travel are growing in enrollment and popularity. **Elderhostel,** 75 Federal St., Boston, MA 02110-1941 (tel. 617-426-7788 or 877-426-8056; email registration@elderhostel.org; www.elderhostel.org). Programs at colleges, universities, and other learning centers in India on varied subjects lasting 1-4 weeks. Must be 55 or over (spouse can be of any age).

GAY AND LESBIAN TRAVELERS. Homosexuality is a taboo topic in India and Nepal, and in India, male homosexual sex is illegal. *Hijras* (male eunuchs) form a subculture of prostitutes in the big cites, especially Mumbai and Hyderabad, but this scene is not open to foreigners (see **The Third Sex,** p. 410). Most gays and lesbians in India and Nepal stay closeted. Heterosexual marriage is expected of just about everyone, so occasional sexual encounters are much more common than long-term relationships. While male friends may hold hands or hug in public, these gestures are not considered sexual. There are only a handful of specifically gay clubs or cruising areas in India and Nepal, although solo male travelers can expect to be propositioned in public places now and then. Gay organizations tend to stay underground. The following organizations offer materials addressing some specific concerns: Aero Travel, Inc., 4001 N. 9th St., Ste. 217, Arlington, VA 22203 (tel. (800) 356-1109, (703) 807-1172), is a travel agency specializing in travel to India *and* travel for gay couples. **Trikone,** P.O. Box 21354, San Jose, CA 95151 (tel. (408) 270-8776), is a U.S.-based organization for gay and lesbian South Asians. They provide a list of gay and lesbian centers in India at www.trikone.org.

DISABLED TRAVELERS. Most of South Asia is ill-equipped to deal with disabled travelers. Hospitals, even those in major cities, cannot be relied upon to replace broken braces or prostheses successfully. Public transportation (trains, buses, rickshaws, etc.) is completely inaccessible, and most cities have no sidewalks or ramps, and large cities are packed with steps. Many sights require climbing long staircases or hiking.

MINORITY TRAVELERS. India's caste system unofficially associates dark skin with inferiority; such associations are sometimes applied to foreigners as well. But more often than not the worst most non-white travelers experience is a lot of benignly curious, if unceasing, stares and comments. In many cases, South Asians of the diaspora may find themselves the targets of contemptuous glares, insulting wisecracks, or even handicapping discrimination in lines at the bank and post office. While many Indians and Nepalis have somewhat mixed feelings concerning fair-skinned tourists, often regarding them with a combination of reverence and resentment, they frequently perceive South Asians who act like foreigners as having "sold out." Women may have an even tougher time, as they are often viewed as having succumbed to depraved Western moral standards.

TRAVELERS WITH CHILDREN. If you are traveling with small children, it is particularly crucial to follow the health advice and protect them from sunburn, excessive heat, insect bites, and especially diarrhea, which can cause severe dehydration and is extremely dangerous for children. Older children should carry some sort of ID in case of an emergency, and arrange a reunion spot in case of separation when sight-seeing. Children under two generally fly for 10% of the adult airfare on international flights (this does not necessarily include a seat). International fares are usually discounted 25% for children from two to 11. Finding a private place for **breast feeding** is often a problem while traveling, so pack accordingly.

DIETARY CONCERNS. India and Nepal are a paradise for vegetarians. the staple foods of a budget-minded connoisseur (rice and *dal*) will meet the most stringent vegetarian standards. Vegans, however, should be warned that *ghee* (clarified butter) is widely used in Indian cooking, and that cheese often appears in otherwise vegetarian entrees. While the Muslim presence makes halal food a large part of the cuisine, kosher meals are next to nonexistent in India and Nepal.

ENVIRONMENTALLY RESPONSIBLE TOURISM. A visit to India or Nepal can be quite a shock for even not-so-environmentally-conscious travelers. From the smog-choked sprawl of Delhi to trailside heaps of trash in Nepal, garbage and pollution are a fact of life in these countries. Fortunately, there's a lot you can do to minimize your own environmental impact as you travel. The two biggest and often least obvious ways that tourists are prone to **waste** are the overuse of **water** and **electricity.** Most of the trash you generate will end up on the street whether you throw it there or not, so the key is to generate less garbage, period. Heavily touristed areas, whether large cities or small towns, often have water shortages. Squat toilets and bucket showers may be tough to get used to, but they consume far less water than their Western counterparts. Sending your laundry to a *dhobi* may seem like a luxury, but they use less water than one would in your hotel sink. However, the detergents which they use usually end up in a nearby river. Turn off the lights and A/C when you leave a room, and make sure that doors and windows are shut while the A/C is on; or don't use it at all.

Avoid excess packaging when you're shopping, particularly styrofoam boxes which are not biodegradable. Use refillable ballpoint pens, glass soda bottles over drinking boxes, or marginally recyclable aluminum cans. In cities with good tap water, use purifying tablets and your own canteen to avoid having to throw out countless plastic water bottles. Try to reuse plastic bags, though it might be hard to convince market vendors not to give you three bags where one would suffice. One option to relieve yourself of some guilt is to volunteer for one of the many environmental organizations there (see **Alternatives to Tourism,** p. 60). Should you happen to uncover a great "ecotourism" operator or have other ideas of how to be a low-impact tourist, we at *Let's Go* would love to hear of them.

ALTERNATIVES TO TOURISM

What follows is a list of organized study and work programs and resources for finding out more information, but a surprising number of alternatives can be arranged informally. If you're willing to work for room and board, you will find many possibilities open to you (just make sure you have the correct documentation—valid visas, work permits, etc.). We list such out-of-the-way opportunities in the specific city sections when we can, but the best advice is to look and ask around.

UNIVERSITIES AND LANGUAGE SCHOOLS

Foreign study programs vary tremendously in expense, academic quality, living conditions, degree of contact with local students, and exposure to local culture and languages. There is a plethora of exchange programs for high school students, especially during the summer. Most undergraduates enroll in semester- or year-long programs sponsored by universities, and many colleges have offices that give advice and information on studying abroad. Most American undergraduates enroll in programs sponsored by U.S. universities. However, if you already know an Indian language, local universities can be much cheaper, though you may not be able to receive academic credit. Some schools that offer study abroad programs to foreigners are listed below.

Association of Commonwealth Universities, John Foster House, 36 Gordon Square, London WC1H OPF, England (tel. (0171) 387 8572; fax (0170) 387 2655; email info@acu.ac.uk; www.acu.ac.uk). Administers scholarship programs such as the British Marshall scholarships and publishes information about Commonwealth universities.

College Semester Abroad, School for International Training, Admissions, Kipling Rd., P.O. Box 676, Brattleboro, VT 05302 (tel. (800) 336-1616 or (802) 258-3267; fax 258-3500). Offers extensive semester- and year-long Study Abroad programs with homestays, intensive language classes, courses in history, politics, arts and humanities, anthropology with field study, etc.: in India and Nepal (US$10,300) and Tibetan Studies (US$11,500). Program costs include international airfare, tuition, room and board, and health insurance. Scholarships are available and federal financial aid is usually transferable from home college or university. Many colleges will transfer credit for work done abroad.

Friends World Program, 239 Montauk Highway, Southampton, NY 11968 (tel. (516) 287-8466; fax 287-8463). Offers a semester- or year-long program in Bangalore that includes language training (in either Hindi, Kannada, or Tamil) and cultural training (approx. US$12,725 per semester, including international airfare, tuition, room and board, and other program costs).

Naropa Institute, 2130 Arapahoe Ave., Boulder, CO 80302 (tel. (303) 444 0202; fax 444 0410; www.naropa.edu/conted/sjourney.html). Runs a program in Boudha, Nepal; students take classes in art and culture, Buddhist civilization, Nepali, as well as a required meditation class. Open to both undergraduate and graduate students (US$9350 for tuition, room, and board; does not include international airfare).

International Partnership for Service Learning, 815 Second Ave., Ste. 315, New York, NY 10017 (tel. (212) 986-0989; fax 986-5039; www.studyabroad.com), offers a 3-week program in Jan. or Aug., with the option of extending each into a 9-week semester. Both combine volunteer social work (with terminally ill patients in Missionaries of Charity hospices and in children's rehabilitation centers) with intensive study of language (Bengali) and culture. The cost of the 3-week program is US$4700 (airfare included); the semester-long program is US$8300 (including airfare and intercession). Study is done in Calcutta (in small hotels during 3-week program, homestays during the semester), with trips to Agra and Delhi.

Peterson's Guides, P.O. Box 2123, Princeton, NJ 08543-2123 (tel. (800) 338-3282; fax (609) 243-9150; www.petersons.com). Their comprehensive Study Abroad (US$26) annual guide lists programs in countries all over the world and provides essential information on the study abroad experience in general. Purchase a copy at your local bookstore or call their toll-free number in the U.S. You get 20% off the list price when you order through their online bookstore.

Pitzer College, External Studies, 1050 N. Mills Ave., Claremont, CA 91711-6110 (tel. (909) 621-8104; fax 621-0518; www.pitzer.edu/academics/ilcenter/external_studies). Semester-long program (fall and spring) on Nepali language and culture. Different family homestays just outside Kathmandu, with treks in Annapurna Conservation Area and Chitwan National Park. US$15,168 includes airfare, tuition, room and board, and field trip. Financial aid usually transferable.

University of Wisconsin-Madison, 500 Lincoln Dr., 252 Bascom Hall, Madison, WI 53706 (tel. (608) 265-6329; fax 262-6998; www.wisc.edu/studyabroad). Has college-year programs in Hyderabad, Madurai, and Varanasi, and a summer performing arts program in Kerala. The college-year programs concentrate on field work, with a year-long local language class and independently-chosen tutorial as well. One year of local language is required; for an extra US$2750, the program offers a 10-week summer intensive language program (mid-June to mid-Aug.) Fees for the college-year program cover academic expenses, administrative costs, a one-way West Coast to India plane ticket, room, meals, and pocket expenses: US$12,500 for India, US$13,000 for Nepal. Transferable financial aid and travel grants are open to students from other schools.

Visva Bharati University, Shantiniketan, West Bengal 731235 (tel. (03463) 52751, ext. 362; fax (03463) 52672; email pritam@vbharat.ernet.in). Offers a one-year Foreigner Casual Course, which can be taken in any subject: painting, Indian philosophy, music or Indian languages. Direct inquiries to Pritam Ray, advisor to foreign students.

WORK

Although it's easy to find a temporary job in India and Nepal—native speakers of English often find that their skills are in high demand—it will rarely be lucrative or glamorous, and it may not even pay for your airfare. It is also very difficult to get permission to work at all (both India and Nepal are exporters of labor, with many going to earn a living in the Middle East). Officially, you can hold a job in most countries only with a **work permit.** Your employer must obtain this document, usually by demonstrating that you have skills that locals lack—not the easiest of tasks. Friends in your destination country can help expedite work permits or arrange work-for-accommodations swaps. Many permit-less agricultural workers go untroubled by local authorities. Students can check with their universities' foreign language departments, which may have connections to job openings abroad. Call the Consulate or Embassy of the country in which you wish to work to get more information about work permits (see **Embasssies and Consulates,** p. 8).

Many books exist which list work-abroad opportunities. Note especially the excellent guides put out by **Vacation Work.** In order to avoid scams from fraudulent employment agencies which demand large fees and provide no results, educate yourself using publications from the following sources.

Council, publishes *International and Volunteer Projects Directory* (US$20) and *Volunteer! The Comprehensive Guide to Voluntary Service in the U.S. and Abroad* (US$12.95). Write to Council, Marketing Services Dept., 205 E. 42nd St., New York, NY 10017-5706 (tel. (888) 268-6245; fax (212) 822-2699; www.ciee.org).

Uniworld Business Publications, Inc., 257 Central Park West, New York, NY 10024-4110 (tel. (212) 496-2448; fax 769-0413; email uniworld@aol.com; www.uniworldbp.com). Check your local library for their The Directory of American Firms Operating in Foreign Countries (1996; US$220). They also publish regional and country editions of the two Directories (US$29 and up).

International Schools Services, Educational Staffing Program, P.O. Box 5910, Princeton, NJ 08543 (tel. (609) 452-0990; fax 452-2690; email edustaffing@iss.edu; www.iss.edu). Recruits teachers and administrators for American and English schools in India and Nepal. All instruction in English. Applicants must have a bachelor's degree and two years of relevant experience. Nonrefundable US$100 application fee. Publishes *The ISS Directory of Overas Schools* (US$34.95).

Office of Overseas Schools, A/OS Room 245, SA-29, Dept. of State, Washington, D.C. 20522-2902 (tel. (703) 875-7800; fax 875-7979; email overseas.school@state.gov; state.gov/www/about_state/schools/). Keeps a list of schools abroad and agencies that arrange placement for Americans to teach abroad.

Archaeological Institute of America, 656 Beacon St., Boston, MA 02215-2010 (tel. (617) 353-9361; fax 353-6550; email aia@bu.edu; www.archaeological.org), puts out the *Archaeological Fieldwork Opportunities Bulletin* (US$16 for non-members), which occasionally lists field sites in India. This can be purchased from Kendall/Hunt Publishing, 4050 Westmark Dr., Dubuque, Iowa 52002 (tel. 800-228-0810).

VOLUNTEER

Volunteer jobs are readily available almost everywhere, and the cost of living in India and Nepal is low enough that volunteering is not a great financial setback. You may receive room and board in exchange for your labor. You can sometimes avoid the high application fees charged by the organizations that arrange placement by contacting the individual workcamps directly; check with the organizations. Listings in Vacation Work Publications's *International Directory of Voluntary Work* (UK£11; £9 if purchased online at www.vacationwork.co.uk) can be helpful.

New College of California, 741 Valencia St., San Francisco, CA 94110 (tel. (800) 335-6262 ext. 406, (415) 437-3406; fax 776 7190). Offers volunteer programs in Nepal and India. Contact Jerry Dekker of the World Studies Project.

Peace Corps, 1111 20th St. NW, Washington, D.C. 20526 (tel. 800-424-8580; www.peacecorps.gov). Write for their "blue" brochure, which details application requirements. Opportunities in a variety of fields in India and Nepal. Volunteers must be U.S. citizens, age 18 and over, and willing to make a 2-year commitment. A bachelor's degree is usually required.

Volunteers for Peace, 1034 Tiffany Rd., Belmont, VT 05730 (tel. (802) 259-2759; fax 259-2922; email vfp@vfp.org; www.vfp.org). A nonprofit organization that arranges speedy placement in 2-3 week workcamps in Nepal comprising 10-15 people. Their website also lists organizations that place volunteers in India. Most complete and up-to-date listings provided in the annual *International Workcamp Directory* (US$15). Registration fee US$195. Free newsletter.

The Joint Assistance Center, Attn: Prof. P.L. Govil G17/3 DLF Qutab Enclave Phase I, Gurgaon 122022, Haryana INDIA (tel. 011 91 124 352141) places volunteers directly in India. Friends of JAC in the Americas, POB 14481 Santa Rosa, CA 95402 (tel: 707-573-1740, fax: 528-8917, email: jacusa@juno.com, www.members.aol.com/jacusa/index.html) assists with placement.

Dakshinayan, Attn: Siddarth Sanyal F-1169 2nd Fl. Chittaranjan Park New Delhi 110019 (tel./fax 011 91 11 648 4468, email sid@linkindia.com, www.linkindia.com/dax), places volunteers in short or long-term work projects in India.

SPIRITUAL INTERESTS

The birthplace of several major world religions (Hinduism, Buddhism, Jainism, and Sikhism), South Asia remains a land of strong religious beliefs and spirituality. It is no wonder that India and Nepal attract many travelers wishing to throw off their old assumptions and try out other approaches to life's questions. Aside from the mainstream traditions in India and Nepal (see **India: Religion,** p. 81, and **Nepal: Religion,** p. 712), certain religious communities are open to initiates from abroad.

For **Hinduism,** these mostly take the form of ashrams (retreats), many of which are under the leadership of a modern-day guru—those who have attracted many foreign devotees are often referred to as "export gurus." Some of the most famous ashrams in India include that of the late **Sri Aurobindo** in Pondicherry (see p. 557), the **Osho Commune** in Pune (see p. 420), and **Sai Baba's** ashrams in Andhra Pradesh and Karnataka (see p. 477). **Rishikesh** is a major center for gurus and students of yoga (see p. 147). Those who stay in an ashram are usually required to stay clean and quiet and to avoid meat, alcohol, tobacco, *paan* (betel), and any drugs.

Since the 1959 Chinese crackdown in Tibet, India and Nepal have become the most accessible places in the world to study **Tibetan Buddhism. Dharamsala** (p. 223) in India, the home of the Dalai Lama and the Tibetan government-in-exile, is a popular place to study Tibetan Buddhism and learn about Tibetan culture. In Nepal (the Buddha's birthplace), the foremost Tibetan Buddhist center is located at **Boudha** (see p. 746), just outside of Kathmandu. Unlike lamas (monks), Western students of Tibetan Buddhism do not usually live in monasteries, although they are expected to live austerely. Public lectures (sometimes in English) and meditation courses are offered at the major Tibetan Buddhist centers. The most thoroughly connected source for information on Tibet is the International Campaign for Tibet, based in Washington, D.C., which provides information about Tibetan organizations worldwide in the International Tibet Resources Directory (US$7). Contact the International Campaign for Tibet, 1820 K St. NW, Ste. 520, Washington, D.C. 20006 (tel. (202) 785-1515; fax 785-4343; www.savetibet.org).

Christianity is India's third largest religion, after Hinduism and Islam. There are long traditions of indigenous faith (Christianity arrived in India in the first century AD) and missionary work. Many hospitals, schools, and Non-Government Organizations are run or supported by local or international Christian organizations.

OTHER RESOURCES

USEFUL PUBLICATIONS

Specialty Travel Index, 305 San Anselmo Ave., #313, San Anselmo, CA 94960 (tel. (415) 455-1643 or 888-624-4030; email spectrav@ix.netcom.com; www.spectrav.com). Published twice yearly, this is an extensive listing of "off the beaten track" and specialty travel opportunities. One copy US$6, one-year subscription (2 copies) US$10.

Hippocrene Books, Inc., 171 Madison Ave., New York, NY 10016 (tel. (212) 685-4371; orders (718) 454-2366; fax 454-1391; email contact@hippocrenebooks.com; www.netcom.com/~hippocre). Free catalog. Publishes travel reference books, travel guides, foreign language dictionaries, and language guides which cover over 100 languages.

Adventurous Traveler Bookstore, 245 S. Champlain St., Burlington, VT 05401 (tel. 800-282-3963; 802-860-6776; fax 860-6667; www.adventuroustraveler.com).

THE WORLD WIDE WEB

Numerous web sites can provide general information on travel as well as provide a brief cultural and historical overview. You can use the web to search for plane tickets and to plan a rough itinerary through the subcontinent. However, few businesses in India and Nepal have websites, so you won't be able to use the web to plan the specifics of your trip. You can search a large database of India-only web sites at **www.123india.com.** The Indian and Nepali governments offer collections of cultural, business, and tourism resources at **www.indiagov.org** and **www.info-nepal.com.** Those in search of the latest current events and culture can read online versions of most of India's major English-language newspapers, including the *Times of India* **(www.timesofindia.com)** and the *Hindu* **(www.webpage.com/hindu/today).** Let's Go (www.letsgo.com) is where you can find our newsletter, information about our books, up-to-the-minute links, and more.

INDIA भारत

LAND AND BIODIVERSITY

The landscape of India has often been likened to the colors of its flag: green jungles, white Himalayan snows, orange-red Deccan earth. Poetic as the description may be, it does not begin to capture the diversity and complexity of the country's natural features. The great range of the **Himalayas** (literally, "abode of snow") crowns the country, forming a historical barrier between India and Central Asia, Tibet, and China. Highest and youngest of the world's mountain ranges, they extend over 2000km in a series of mountain chains rather than a single range. Here also lie the watersheds of the subcontinent's three major river systems, the **Indus, Ganga,** and **Brahmaputra.** Fed by rain and glacial run-off, the rivers' networks of tributaries nourish the vast, densely-populated **Indo-Gangetic Plain,** stretching from Rajasthan in the west to West Bengal in the east.

The **Vindhyas**, a belt of stepped hills, divide the Indo-Gangetic Plain from the **Deccan Plateau,** India's oldest surface, on which rest present-day Maharashtra, Karnataka, and Andhra Pradesh. The Archean rocks of the Deccan Plateau, are some 300 to 500 million years old. Washed by the **Arabian Sea** to the west and the **Bay of Bengal** to the east, peninsular India tapers to the south, dipping into the **Indian Ocean** at its tip, Kanyakumari. Flanking the **Malabar Coast** of Kerala, Karnataka, and Goa, the **Western Ghats** (a north-south chain of hills) are separated from the coast by a narrow strip of richly forested plain. The **Eastern Ghats** are farther inland, giving the **Coromandel Coast** a broader swath of coastal plain. The Ghats converge at the **Nilgiri Hills** of Kerala and Tamil Nadu, the southernmost tip of the Deccan Plateau. The **Lakshadweep Islands,** just off the Malabar Coast in the Arabian Sea, and the **Andaman and Nicobar Islands** in the Bay of Bengal, are also Indian territories.

From the pine-clad slopes of the Himalayas to the scrub and thorn forests of northwest and peninsular India and from the semi-arid central forests to the evergreen deciduous groves of Kerala, Bengal, the northeast hills, and the Andaman and Nicobar Islands, India's vegetation is tailored to its diverse topography. The Gangetic delta in West Bengal is home to tidal mangrove forests, where there roam the fast disappearing Bengal tiger and a small population of crocodiles. Other Indian animals include the monkeys, elephants, foxes, jackals, mongoose, dromedary camels, and the occasional lion of the Gir National Park, Gujarat. The Indian crocodile, the *gharial,* and lizards and snakes—including the cobra— comprise the indigenous reptile population. The Indian national bird, the peacock, joins the ranks of birds from cranes, storks, ibises, hawks, hornbills, parrots, and the (all too) common crow.

PEOPLE AND LANGUAGES

The 940 million who inhabit India represent such diversity that India might seem like a dozen nations packed into one. Six major religions, 18 major languages, and numerous racial and ethnic groups coexist in India, often harmoniously but sometimes not. In this nation whose economy remains primarily agricultural, fully 75% of the population lives in rural areas largely unaffected by the changes that industrialization has brought to India's huge cities. Population is densest in the valley and delta of the Ganga river and in the extreme south (Tamil Nadu and Kerala). India's four largest cities—Bombay (13 million), Calcutta (12 million), Delhi (9 million), and Madras (6 million)—hold only 4% of the population. The ethnic origins of Indians reflect a mix between the light-skinned **Aryan** people, who still reside mostly in the north, and the darker-skinned **Dravidian** peoples of the south. Numerous "tribal" groups or *adivasis* (aboriginal peoples), whose ethnic origins are

INDIA

SCRIPTS OF INDIA Devanagari भारत is the most common script in South Asia, used for the Hindi, Marathi, Konkani, Rajasthani, and Nepali languages. Sanskrit also uses Devanagari, and several other languages derive their alphabets from it, including **Gurmukhi** ਪੰਜਾਬ, used for Punjabi, **Gujarati** ગુજરાત, **Bengali** পশ্চিম বঙ্গ, and **Oriya** ଓଡ଼ିଶା. In the south, Dravidian languages are spoken, and their scripts are distinctive from those of the Sanskrit-based tongues. **Tamil** தமிழ் நாடு and **Malayalam** കേരളം share similar scripts, as do **Kannada** ಕರ್ನಾಟಕ and **Telugu** ఆంధ్ర చదు. **Urdu** کشمیر, uses the Persian alphabet and is the state language of Kashmir.

Tibeto-Burmese or Proto-Australoid, are concentrated in the northeastern states of Madhya Pradesh, Orissa, and Gujarat. Eighty percent of Indians are Hindu, and the rest of the country's religious demographic is filled out by Muslims (11%), Christians, Sikhs, Jains, Parsis, Buddhists, and Jews.

India is home to an astounding 1600 dialects, varying from state to state and even between villages. North Indian languages such as **Hindi** and **Bengali** descended from Sanskrit, the language spoken by the Aryan invaders who entered the subcontinent around 1500 BC. They are part of the greater Indo-European family, and it is not unusual to find North Indian words that resemble their counterparts in English or other European languages. **Urdu,** spoken among Muslims in India, sounds very similar to Hindi but borrows heavily from Persian. The major **South Indian languages**—Kannada, Telugu, Malayalam, and Tamil—all belong to the Dravidian family and are unrelated to the North Indian languages. Indo-Aryan and Dravidian languages have influenced one another, and they share some features, like retroflex consonants, where the tongue curls back to touch the palate.

The 1950s territorial reorganization of India along linguistic lines recognized 18 official languages—Assamese, Bengali, Gujarati, Hindi, Kannada, Kashmiri, Konkani, Malayalam, Manipuri, Marathi, Nepali, Oriya, Punjabi, Sanskrit, Sindhi, Tamil, Telugu, and Urdu. The Indian constitution (written in English) planned for Hindi to be the national language, as it is the most widely-spoken language, used by about 30% of the people. Attempts to spread Hindi have met with resentment; don't be surprised to find some Indians willing to speak anything *but* Hindi, particularly in South India. The nation's lingua franca, particularly in commerce, English is an ironic vestige of British imperialism. English is the first language of many upper-class Indians, and millions more learn English in school. It is easy to get around India with English, although this might make it difficult to have more than simple conversations. For basic Hindi, Bengali, Tamil, Marathi, Gujarati, Telugu, Kannada, Malayalam, and Nepali vocabularies, see the **Phrasebook,** p. 811.

GOVERNMENT AND POLITICS

India's **parliamentary system** is modeled after Britain's but adapted to suit Indian needs. Adopted in 1950, the Indian **constitution** is the world's longest, with 395 articles. The framers of the constitution endeavored to create a **federal system** that would reflect India's diversity, but they also wanted a strong central government to handle poverty and religious conflicts. The result has been a highly centralized form of federalism.

At the head of India's government are the president, vice president, and a council of ministers, headed by the prime minister. The president is essentially a figurehead. The prime minister, chosen by the majority party in the **Lok Sabha,** the lower house, holds the real executive power. The Lok Sabha ("House of the People") and the **Rajya Sabha** ("Council of States") together make up the Indian parliament. All but two of the Lok Sabha's 545 seats are elected by general suffrage; members of the Rajya Sabha are chosen by state governments. India's **Supreme Court** is remarkably independent, often asserting its right to make bold decisions on controversial issues the other branches of government would rather avoid.

Each of India's 26 states has a similar governmental structure. **Governors,** chosen by the prime minister's cabinet, act as figureheads, while the real power lies with the **chief minister,** the leader of the party in control of state parliaments. Each state also has a legislative assembly, or *Vidhan Sabha,* whose members are elected for a term of up to five years. Although the state governments depend on the national government for financial support, they have jurisdiction over education, agriculture, welfare, and the police. State governments are divided into local administrations, with the **panchayat** or village council at the lowest level. The central government has the power to dismiss state governments in cases of emergency, and this option of **"President's Rule"** has been abused by central government administrations—most notoriously by Indira Gandhi's—to attack their opponents.

The Congress (I) party, which grew out of the Congress that led India to independence, has dominated Indian politics since 1947. Despite the Congress' tradition of inclusiveness, it has had difficulty incorporating all the disparate interests of ideology, caste, region, and religion. As a result, politics have become more and more regionalized, with parties such as the **DMK** (in Tamil Nadu), the **Communist Party of India** (in Bengal), and the **Akali Dal** (in Punjab) earning more votes. In the 1996 elections, no single party won a majority of seats in the Lok Sabha, so a piece-meal left-wing coalition including populist, lower-caste parties such as the Janata Dal and parties like the Communist Party of India ruled with the support of Congress (I). Last year's mid-term elections shifted the balance, with the Hindu Nationalist **Bharatiya Janata Party (BJP)** emerging as the leader of a shaky coalition which eventually collapsed because of the withdrawal of regional support.

Politics in India are often marred by **corruption** (numerous state and national governments have been brought down by corruption scandals), and violence is used in some regions to intimidate voters, but India's democracy does work smoothly on the whole. India's Election Commission, which has controlled and supervised polling at the past two elections, was made autonomous by Chief Election Commissioner T.N. Seshan in 1996.

ECONOMICS

India's economy is overwhelmingly **agricultural,** with about 70% of the people earning a living from some sort of farming. Staple foods like wheat and rice are the major crops. Cash crops such as tea and cotton are important exports. At the same time, India is a technologically advanced nation. Nuclear reactors, satellites, television sets, and oil rigs are all built in India, although these industries have not yet produced top-quality items for international markets.

The current situation was brought about by government planning during the 1950s and 60s. A series of **Five Year Plans,** modeled on those of the Soviet Union, created huge state-owned industries. Private industries were restricted by licensing, and foreign investment was almost nonexistent. The aim was for India to attain self-sufficiency, in the tradition of the *swadeshi* movement (in which Indians boycotted British imports).

A lack of exports meant that India had to borrow in order to buy from abroad, and in 1991 a **financial crisis** almost forced the country to default on its foreign debt. Under pressure from reformers within India and also from the World Bank and the International Monetary Fund, India made dramatic changes in its economic policies, liberalizing its economy to encourage private investment. The government eliminated licensing and scrapped quotas on imports. As a result, the economy has experienced rapid industrial development in the past few years. Foreign investment has been pouring in, especially in the areas of communication, electricity, and computer technology. The government has delayed the sale of its money-losing public sector industries, however, for fear of massive layoffs.

Big economic reforms have done little so far for the vast majority of Indian people. While there is no way to calculate average incomes in a country where so many people live off the land and pay no taxes, it is painfully obvious that poverty is widespread. In addition, although food production has increased dramatically since Independence (in fact, in many years, India has a grain surplus), as much as 30% of the population suffers from malnutrition.

HISTORY

PRE-HISTORY AND THE INDUS VALLEY CIVILIZATION (400,000-1500 BC)

Primitive tools and weapons found scattered through the region of the Soan River in modern-day Pakistan have provided the first bits of evidence of human existence on the subcontinent. The discovery of these remnants of Paleolithic settlement indicate that humans migrated to South Asia between 200,000 and 400,000 years ago. While the majestic Himalayan mountain range to the north and the surrounding seas and oceans have been credited with keeping the subcontinent rather isolated through the millennia, the mountain passes at the northwest frontier did provide a point of entry for migrants and foreign invaders, and the first known civilization in the Indian subcontinent arose precisely in this region. The Indus River Valley civilization emerged around 2500 BC in what is now Pakistan and flourished for nearly a thousand years. When the Indus civilization was discovered in the 1920s at the archaeological sites of **Harappa** and **Mohenjo-Daro,** India's urban history was expanded by at least a thousand years.

The over 100 cities of the Indus civilization, spanning an area of almost half a million square miles, were planned according to rigid patterns that apparently changed little over their 1000-year history, thus indicating the presence of a strong central organization. The streets were laid out in grids incorporating elaborately engineered drainage systems and a large central bath which probably served some ritual function. The Indus dwellers were skilled farmers and had highly developed systems of irrigation, which allowed them to harvest and keep huge stores of wheat and barley. Artifacts indicate that the Indus people traded by land and sea with the civilizations on the Nile, Tigris, and Euphrates Rivers. Despite all of this, little is known about this ancient culture; their script, found on numerous **steatite seals,** remains undecipherable. The seals depict humans, gods, and animals, and they suggest that the people worshipped a mother-goddess and a deity who may have been a precursor to the Hindu god **Shiva.** Around 1800 BC the Indus River changed its course, causing catastrophic flooding which spelled disaster for the civilization that had thrived on the subcontinent for a millennium.

THE ARYANS (1500-300 BC)

As the Indus civilization went into decline, a new group entered the subcontinent. The **Aryans,** a branch of the Indo-European tribes of central Asia, were a light-skinned, nomadic people who came across the northwest frontier, establishing themselves in India around 1500 BC. A loose band of tribes, each of which was ruled by a *raja* (chieftain or king), the Aryans spread from the Punjab and the northern Indus Valley across all of northern India. These warrior people, with their horses and spoke-wheeled chariots, brought with them a technology and culture that permanently altered the civilizations they encountered.

The Aryans' spoken language was **Sanskrit** (in which *arya* means "noble one"), a member of the family of Indo-European languages which also spawned Latin and Greek and the root of all the North Indian languages. Their early religion was characterized by a ritual orientation—they performed fire-sacrifices, making oblations to a pantheon of various deities. These rites were performed by the *brahmins,* sages of the priestly caste who chanted the hymns of the **Rig Veda,** a collection of

Sanskrit hymns which were transmitted orally for several centuries until they were written down between 1200 and 400 BC (see **Vedic Literature,** p. 82).

The Aryans brought to the subcontinent not only their language and religion but also a new social order. Aryan society had three classes or *varnas,* literally meaning "colors," thought to have been loosely based on race. The social hierarchy, consisting of *brahmins* (priests), *kshatriyas* (warriors), and *vaishyas* (merchants), formed the basis for what later became the **caste system** (see below, p. 67). As they pressed farther on into new territory, the Aryans met with indigenous peoples whom they called *dasas.* The *dasas* are now thought to be the ancestors of South India's Dravidian people and the remaining survivors of the once-great Indus civilization who fled south during its decline. Taken as slaves by the Aryans, the *dasas* were incorporated into society as a servant class known as *shudras.*

The environment of India altered many of the cultural practices of the Aryans. As they moved into the Doab, the fertile plain of the Ganga and Yamuna rivers, the Aryan tribes clumped into kingdoms and the people settled in villages. By the time they reached what is now Bihar around 1000 BC, they had abandoned bronze for iron. They were superb metallurgists, and the discovery of iron allowed them (for better or for worse) to clear the great forests that then covered the region. The changes wrought by Aryan culture increasingly alienated the peoples in the lands they had conquered. Many thinkers became dissatisfied with the old Brahmanic religion and its corps of elite priests. A highly philosophical reexamination of the meaning behind the sacrifice and vision of the Vedic hymns developed during this time; the reformative spirit was expressed most profoundly in the **Upanishads,** which criticized the performance of ritual as superfluous to the religious quest. In the 6th century there emerged two new faiths, Jainism and Buddhism, which also provided alternatives to Brahminical religion (also see **Religion,** p. 19).

Centuries later, as the Aryans ceased to be a nomadic people, the great Sanskrit epics, the **Ramayana** and the **Mahabharata,** emerged (see **Epic Literature and Dharma Texts,** p. 82). Chronicling royal rivalries and a deteriorating world order, the epics reflect the political and religious climate of the epoch of Aryan settlement into towns and cities, where they subdued the indigenous peoples they encountered.

THE MAURYAS (300-200 BC)

Although communications and trade had improved in North India by the 6th century BC, the land of the Aryans remained divided into 16 separate kingdoms. In 326 BC, Alexander the Great showed up at India's northwest frontier intent on plundering the land's riches for himself, but his troops resisted the march to the east, and he consented to turn back. The Greek invasion seems to have provided both the inspiration and the instability that allowed another conqueror to take control of India. Shortly thereafter, **Chandragupta Maurya,** an adventurer from eastern India, took control of the kingdom of Magadha, the most powerful Aryan state, located in present-day Bihar. Advised by his brilliant minister Chanakya, alleged author of the *Arthashastra,* Chandragupta consolidated his grip over all of North India. Over the next 100 years, however, the Mauryan Empire seated at Pataliputra, the site of modern **Patna** (see p. 628), would come to control the whole of the subcontinent save the southern tip.

At the height of the empire's power, its policies of violent military expansion were abandoned after its ruthless invasion of the Kalinga Kingdom (present-day Orissa). The Mauryan emperor **Ashoka** (r. 269-232 BC) was so affected by this battle, the bloodiest of his era, that he renounced violence and became an ardent Buddhist. His edicts propagating the message of Buddhism were inscribed on pillars and stones, contributing greatly to growth of Buddhism in India, but he also preached universal values of mutual respect and tolerance. Although the Mauryan empire collapsed after Ashoka's death, his edict-inscribed **pillars** still stand as reminders of India's first imperial unification.

TRADE AND THE GROWTH OF BUDDHISM (200 BC-AD 300)

After the disintegration of the Mauryan Empire around 200 BC, India found itself politically divided once again. New settlers, such as the **Shakas** and **Kushanas,** established powerful kingdoms in the north, and indigenous kingdoms, like the **Andhras,** rose up in the peninsula, but none of these ever expanded beyond their regional domains. Despite this political disarray, however, the subcontinent experienced a time of great economic prosperity and cultural ferment. A system of caste-based craft guilds advanced Indian technology, and trade became India's main cohesive force. At the southern tip of the peninsula, it ended the isolation of the **Cheras, Pandyas,** and **Cholas,** three Dravidian kingdoms that had never been part of the Mauryan sphere, giving India commercial links to China and the West, where Roman traders paid richly for Indian cloth, spices, wood, and gems.

This period also witnessed the zenith of **Buddhism** in South Asia, which had continued to grow after Emperor Ashoka's death. Mahayana Buddhism, a sect that de-emphasized monastic life and made Buddhism accessible to the layperson, proved attractive to those dissatisfied with Brahminic dominance. Many Hindus, however, were also turning away from the old Brahminic rituals, and a new devotional movement which emphasized personal, unmediated worship emerged. Competing with Buddhism, **bhakti** (literally "devotion") spread in the south, gradually bringing most of India back into the Hindu fold. (see Hindu Practice, p. 83).

Buddhism inspired many artistic and intellectual pursuits, hosted by monasteries and paid for by wealthy guilds. **Sculpture,** in particular, reached new aesthetic heights with stone carvings of the Buddha produced for use in worship. At the same time, Indian **medicine** and **astronomy** began a phase of rapid advancement with a push from the Greeks, who had settled down on the northwest frontier after Alexander's campaigns. India's **linguistics** and **mathematics** were already far ahead of those in the West, however—a scientific system for Sanskrit grammar had been developed by Panini as early as the 4th century BC, and Indian mathematicians invented the concept of zero as well as the system of numerals called "Arabic" by Europeans who learned of it from Arab merchants.

THE GUPTAS: A GOLDEN AGE (300-500)

In AD 319 another Chandragupta came to power in the eastern kingdom of Magadha. Though he was not related to his namesake (the founder of the Maurya dynasty), **Chandragupta** sought to emulate the earlier ruler and launched an empire of his own. From their base in Pataliputra (Patna), Chandragupta and his son **Samudragupta** after him expanded up and down the Ganga Valley. At its peak under **Chandragupta II** (r. 375-415), the Gupta Empire encompassed all of North India.

The Guptas are most renowned for the cultural refinement and religious tolerance of India's "Golden Age." They were great patrons of the arts and sciences, financing them with the proceeds of overseas trade and wealthy craft guilds. India's first stone dams and temples were built, and the cave-sculptures at **Ajanta** were painstakingly carved out of a sheer cliff face (see p. 434). **Kalidasa,** the greatest literary poet of this time, was a member of the court of Chandragupta II. Though they sponsored the activities of all religions, the Guptas themselves were Hindu, and they lavished resources on Hindu theological studies and on the building of Hindu temples. Their laws and institutions also reflected an adherence to orthodox Hinduism and, in this respect, the Guptas become something of a prototype for future Hindu monarchs. (also see **Hinduism,** p. 81).

Although **South India** lay outside of the Gupta Empire, it was an active participant in Guptan culture. Northern traders and *brahmin* priests had by this point brought the south into the Hindu world, and even though that region remained politically divided, southern kings were modeling their realms on Aryan political structures. Despite this **Aryanization**, distinct South Indian architectural styles emerged, and Tamil poet-saints (the Vaishnava Alvars and Shaiva Nayanars) and thinkers joined the ranks of the holiest Hindus, leading the *bhakti* devotional movement that eventually overtook the North.

REGIONALISM (500-1192)

The Gupta Empire slowly disintegrated in the 5th century under attacks from **Huns** of Central Asia. North India broke into small kingdoms once again and remained divided for 700 years—except for the years from 606 to 647, when the young conqueror and poet-king **Harsha** built an empire from his capital at **Kannauj** in the Ganga plain. The emergence of strong regional identities and the development of a feudal system measuring wealth in land rather than money only furthered the process of increasing fragmentation.

The strongest kingdom in India at this time was the **Chola** dynasty from **Tamil Nadu,** which conquered most of the southern peninsula and even sent forces to the Maldives, Sri Lanka, and Malaysia. The **Rajputs,** a group of warrior clans who probably originated outside of India but claimed the noble status of *kshatriyas* in the Hindu caste system, became the major force in northwest India after the 8th century. They set up several small kingdoms from their base in the Thar Desert of **Rajasthan** and developed a distinct culture of chivalric values, a proud literary tradition, and a grand architectural legacy. The clans warred with one another, however, and they never unified under a single empire. The Rajputs would eventually have to contend with the most serious foreign challenge of the age: people from the west with new ideas and the potential to change India. The divided kingdoms were ill-equipped to face the coming assault.

THE ARRIVAL OF ISLAM (1192-1526)

After its founding in the 7th century (see p. 86), **Islam** spread from Arabia right up to Sindh on the western frontier of India. Muslims traded with India by sea, and a few settled down on the west coast, but Islam made few inroads on the subcontinent during its first 300 years. This changed with the raids of **Mahmud of Ghazni,** the king of a Turkish dynasty in Afghanistan. Between 997 and 1030 Mahmud's armies swarmed in to loot North India on an almost annual basis. Content to carry the land's wealth back into the hills, Mahmud never actually settled in India.

By the end of the 12th century, another Turko-Afghan king moved in on India. In 1192 **Muhammad of Ghur** conquered the Ganga Valley and defeated a loose coalition of Rajputs. Though he quickly returned to his home in Afghanistan, he left behind his general, the slave **Qutb-ud-din Aibak,** to govern the conquered lands from Delhi (see **Qutb Minar,** p. 122). When Muhammad died in 1206, Qutb-ud-din succeeded him, proclaiming the birth of the **Delhi Sultanate,** India's first Muslim kingdom. The Sultanate ruled most of North India for 300 years, and by the early 15th century, independent Muslim kingdoms had emerged in Bengal, Gujarat, and central India. Still, the Delhi Sultanate's hold on power was always precarious. The palace was in constant turmoil, chewing up five dynasties in three centuries, and the sultans' financing their hedonistic court life with taxes paid by Hindus inflamed frequent revolts. In another major setback, the city of Delhi was obliterated by the Central Asian conqueror **Timur** in 1398.

India produced many converts to Islam during this period, many of whom sought to gain favor with those in power or else were Untouchables who had nothing to lose. Hindus did enjoy the protected status Islam usually reserved for Christians and Jews, so it was possible to resist conversion. But the fact that the new faith accepted members of all castes as equals worked in its favor, tarnishing its image only in the eyes of higher-caste Hindus. In parts of India, Hindu monarchs tried to resist the impact of the Muslim sultans. The Hindu **Vijayanagar kingdom** ruled major portions of South India from 1336 to 1565, building temples vigorously until it was defeated by a coalition of Muslim sultanates from the Deccan.

Many movements which attempted to mediate between the two faiths arose at this time. In the Punjab, **Guru Nanak** was attracting adherents to **Sikhism,** a new religion that synthesized Hinduism and Islam (see p. 88). Islam became popular among the masses thanks to wandering **Sufi mystics** and saints, whose religion was similar to devotional movements in Hinduism. Ultimately, religious fragmentation served to undermine the centralized political authority of the **Lodis,** the last of the Delhi sultanate's dynasties. Provincial governors seceded in Bihar, Portuguese ships landed in Goa, and in central India the one-eyed, one-armed Rajput leader **Rana Sanaga** called for foreign intervention to vanquish the Delhi Sultanate.

THE MUGHALS (1526-1700)

Rana Sanaga's call was heeded by the Central Asian warlord **Babur** (1483-1530). Babur, descended from both Timur and **Genghis Khan,** was endowed with a warrior's pedigree, conquering Samarkand at age 13 and Kabul eight years later. Recounting his attack on the Delhi Sultanate, Babur wrote, "I placed my foot in the stirrup of resolution, and my palms I placed on the reins of confidence in Allah." In the **Battle of Panipat,** fought outside of Delhi in the spring of 1526, the overmatched Babur prevailed, crushing the Lodi dynasty. In 1530 when Babur's son **Humayun** became sick, Babur prayed that the sickness which afflicted his son would be transferred to him. Within weeks, Babur was buried in Kabul, and Humayun was proclaimed emperor over territories which stretched from Bihar in the east to Kabul in the west. Sporadic raiding had given way to the Mughal Dynasty.

Addicted to opium and dependent on the capricious predictions of his astrologers, Emperor Humayun had difficulty leading his ethnically diverse army, and within a decade the ranks became rife with disloyalty. In 1540, Humayun was deposed by the Afghan warlord **Sher Shah,** who had carved out a kingdom for himself in eastern India. Humayun was driven into the Sindh desert, while Sher Shah secured his position, laying the groundwork for a sophisticated administration and fortifying key cities. When he was killed during a siege of a Rajput stronghold in 1545, however, Humayun acted aggressively, gaining Persian backing and recapturing Delhi. Only months after his glorious triumphs, Humayun was killed from a fall down his library stairs, and in 1555, **Akbar,** who had been born in the Sindh desert during Humayun's wanderings, became emperor.

Though Akbar was only 13 when he succeeded his father, he quickly proved his military mettle, quashing rebellions and advancing Mughal hegemony with successful campaigns in Rajasthan, Gujarat, Orissa, Kashmir, and Bengal. As Akbar consolidated his empire through battle, he formulated policies rooted in the assumption that the Mughals' long-term future lay in the south, rather than Central Asia. Akbar created a centralized imperial bureaucracy in order to lend Mughal governance an aura of permanence. Moreover, the emperor and his inner circle devised an efficient revenue collection system so that new territories would not need to be conquered in order to keep the existing empire financially solvent. Most importantly, Akbar concluded that for the Mughals to dominate South Asia they could not rely on brute force and repression indefinitely—the Muslim Mughals would need to earn the trust of Hindus. To give Hindu elites a stake in the success of the Mughal regime, Akbar married a Rajput princess and appointed well-educated Hindus to important government posts. To ingratiate himself with the masses, Akbar denounced the destruction of Hindu temples and eliminated the **jizya,** a widely despised tax levied on non-Muslims.

Akbar's policies and generous patronage encouraged the mingling of Hindu and Muslim sensibilities. **North Indian music** began to assimilate Persian influences, and Hindu painters began to experiment with **miniature painting,** a genre favored by the Mughals. The **Urdu** language, with its Persian vocabulary and Hindi grammatical structure, gained popularity, and Muslims began the (Hindu) practice of making pilgrimages to the tombs of holy figures. Akbar invited Hindus, Jains, Christians, and Zoroastrians to discuss their faiths in his court and later attempted to found a new religion based upon ideas from all the major religious systems of the region.

Akbar's successors **Jahangir** (r. 1605-27) and **Shah Jahan** (r. 1628-57) were content to build on Akbar's work, and their reigns were a golden era for the Mughals; the populace was well-fed, the empire's frontiers were relatively secure, and a series of staggeringly beautiful landmarks—the marble **Taj Mahal** (see p. 176) and the sandstone **Red Fort** (see p. 120)—were erected in Agra and Delhi. When Shah Jahan fell ill in 1657, however, his sons began to war with each other over who would succeed him. The bloody familial fighting left the empire in the hands of **Aurangzeb,** who had murdered his older brother during the succession struggle and who imprisoned Shah Jahan lest his health improve.

For 48 years, Aurangzeb ruled South Asia as the new Mughal emperor. Aurangzeb's reign was successful in that his armies were able to conquer massive tracts of fertile land in southern and eastern India. Deeply pious, Aurangzeb zealously rolled back a century of tolerant social policy, making it difficult for Hindus to advance through the civil service bureaucracy, forbidding the repair of Hindu temples, and re-introducing the discriminatory *jizya* (tax). Aurangzeb's short-sighted radicalism lead ordinary Hindus to turn on the Mughals, and by the time the 88-year-old Aurangzeb died, the Mughal empire had frayed irreparably. Over the next half century, the Mughals would rule in name only, as Delhi was sacked and looted by Persians in 1738 and by Afghans in 1757.

As Mughal control over northern India slipped, others sought to step into the vacuum; the Maratha leader **Shivaji Bhonsle** (see p. 425) posed a serious threat to the Mughals during the reign of Aurangzeb, and the **Maratha Confederacy,** comprised of Maharashtrian "nationalists," stood the best chance of taking the Mughals' place in the 18th century. The Marathas were dealt a decisive defeat in 1761 by an invading Afghan army, and the Confederacy splintered. The way was cleared for another empire to play a politically dominant role in South Asia.

EARLY BRITISH RULE (1700-57)

Lured by the famed riches of the Orient, European ships sailed the oceans throughout the 15th and 16th centuries, though India did not witness the arrival of substantial numbers of Europeans until the 17th century, when the English, Portuguese, Dutch, and French came as agents of government-chartered trading companies. The gradual decline of Portuguese sea power together with the Netherlands' decision to concentrate commercial energies elsewhere opened the way for the **English East India Company** to assert monopolistic control over South Asian resources. From its Indian bases in the south and east—two of which would grow into **Kolkata** (see p. 644) and **Madras** (see **Chennai,** p. 532)—the Company engaged in highly profitable trade, exchanging gold and silver for Indian finished goods, especially hand-crafted textiles.

The Company recruited small Indian armies, equipping them with powerful European-made weapons, to defend their warehouses from banditry. These mercenary armies allowed the Company to became a powerful controlling force in Bengal during the mid-18th century, whence it extended its sphere of domination. Led by the iron-willed **Robert Clive,** it aligned itself with a coalition of Muslims and Hindus and, after a series of battles (which culminated with the **Battle of Plassey** in 1757), established unrivalled authority over vast areas of Eastern India.

EAST INDIA COMPANY GOVERNMENT (1757-1857)

During the late 18th century, the Company, led first by **Warren Hastings** and then by **Lord Cornwallis,** was divided into separate political and commercial units. It soon developed a British-dominated bureaucracy to administer the Indian territory, which had become a much more important resource than trade. In accord with the **Permanent Settlement of 1793,** land was distributed such that the Mughal *zamindars* (tax collectors) became owners of the lands they had administered. The Settlement created an elite class of moneyed Indians who became the buffer between the Company and the peasants, who, forced to work the land they once owned, generated the revenue needed by *zamindars* to pay off the Company.

The Settlement was the Company's excuse to seize more land, and by the 1820s, most of India had become a post of the British Empire. In Britain, three camps had formed: the **conservatives** supported exploiting India only economically; the **evangelicals** sought to convert "idolatrous" India; and the **liberals** believed that progress in India was hampered by "irrational" practices. British policy became less conservative in the 1820s and 1830s as evangelicals and liberals held sway.

Between the late 1820s and 1857, the Company was guided by two complementary concerns: eliminating practices they deemed immoral and pressing Indian society into a European mold. Thus, **railways, textile mills,** and **telegraphs** were introduced into South Asia; **sati,** the Hindu custom by which widows were burned on their husbands' funeral pyres, and **thugi,** ritual robbery and murder practiced by devotees of the goddess **Kali,** were banned. In keeping with their goal to infuse Indian culture with civilized Western ideals, British authorities changed the official state language from **Persian** to **English** and funded the development of secondary schools, medical colleges, and universities where the language of instruction was English and Western curricula were used. India was administered by men like **Lord Macaulay,** who claimed that "One shelf of a good English library has more worth than native [Indian] literature in its entirety."

As British imperialism undermined traditional institutions, millions of Indians grew resentful that the new rulers didn't care about the severe and persistent poverty afflicting their people. In the face of seething discontent, British officials extended their authority, inventing an absurd legal fiction, the **Doctrine of Lapse,** which allowed the British to annex any Indian kingdom whose ruler died without a direct male heir. By the 1850s, Indian discontent had grown extremely volatile, and it was not long before the explosive situation would turn violent.

MUTINY AND AFTERMATH (1857-58)

In 1857, the Company introduced a new weapon for use by its 200,000 sepoys (hired Indian soldiers). The **Lee-Enfield** rifle used ammunition cartridges that were rumored to be lubricated with a mixture of pig and cow fat. Hindus (for whom cows are sacred) and Muslims (for whom pigs are impure) were incensed, especially when they learned that soldiers had to bite the tip off the cartridges with their teeth before loading them. What followed in May of 1857 became known as the **Sepoy Mutiny,** in which Indian soldiers raised the Mughal flag over Delhi, indiscriminately massacring Europeans as they reclaimed the city. **Lucknow** (see p. 185) also fell to forces eager to restore the Mughal Empire. Backed by Sikh regiments, British troops retaliated four months later, recapturing Delhi at the cost of great numbers of Indian lives. By March of 1858, the **Mutiny of 1857**—or the **War of Independence,** as Indian nationalists prefer to call it—had been fully suppressed.

After the gory events of the revolt, British attitudes changed radically. An 1858 act of the British Parliament eliminated the governing authority of the Company; within a year, the British crown was directly administering India as a full-fledged colony of the **British Empire.** The Raj had begun. To ensure tight control over India, Crown authorities increased the ratio of British to Indian soldiers stationed in South Asia, forbade Indians from becoming officers of the army, and staffed the upper echelons of the burgeoning **Indian Civil Service** with bureaucrats of British birth. Assuming an attitude marked by increasingly explicit racism, the British also withdrew from Indian society, setting up hill stations remote from major Indian population centers and abandoning their quest to Westernize South Asia.

CROWN RULE AND INDIAN RENEWAL (1858-1915)

As imperial authority grew more invasive, a century-long period of religious revitalization gained momentum with Hindu groups such as the mystical **Ramakrishna**

Mission and the reform-minded **Arya Samaj** at the helm. Muslims underwent a renewal of a different nature. Prominent leaders like **Sir Sayyid Ahmed Khan,** sharing the British liberals' contempt for Indian backwardness, worked to reverse the anti-Muslim sentiment that the Mutiny had left with India's British rulers. Khan sought to remedy the situation through Western-style education, founding a college at **Aligarh** which would become the center for Muslim intellectuals instrumental in the creation of Pakistan. The reorganizing of Hindu and Muslim faiths on this reactionary basis determined the outcome of each during India's **Partition.**

Demanding reforms for more control over their country's affairs, a group of 70 wealthy Indians met in Bombay in 1885 to form a political association, the **Indian National Congress.** As it grew, Congress split into two wings: the **moderates,** who advocated reform within the context of the British Empire, and the **extremists,** who sought to oust the British government. The views of the extremists rose to the fore after 1905, when the British viceroy, seeking to simplify administration and also to create divisions among Indians, partitioned Bengal into two provinces, one with a Hindu majority, the other with a Muslim majority. The anger and resentment felt by millions of Indians was articulated in 1905 by the President of Congress **Gopal Krishna Gokhale.** "A cruel wrong has been inflicted on our Bengali brethren," Gokhale proclaimed. "The scheme of partition . . . will always stand as a complete illustration of the worst features of the present system of bureaucratic rule." The ground had shifted, and self-rule or *Swaraj* became the ultimate objective. In the decade following the partition of Bengal, Indians from a wide variety of backgrounds did what they could to resist British rule. Muslims concerned about Hindu domination of Congress founded the **All-India Muslim League** in 1906. All Indians boycotted British-made textiles, opting instead for the rougher, homespun *swadeshi* cloth, worn proudly as a symbol of national self-sufficiency.

Indian nationalist leaders cooperated with the British during the **First World War,** hoping that their loyalty in the British Empire's time of need would be rewarded by greater freedoms after the war. Instead, the British introduced more oppressive measures in 1919, suspending civil liberties and placing India under martial law. When a group of unarmed Indians assembled in **Amritsar** for a peaceful protest, 400 of them were massacred by the British Indian army (see **Jallianwala Bagh,** p. 275).

It was into this atmosphere of unrest that **Mohandas Karamchand Gandhi** (later proclaimed the Mahatma or "Great Soul" by Bengali poet Rabindranath Tagore) returned from England in 1915. Born into a Gujarati *vaishya* family in 1869, Gandhi had gone abroad to study law. After completing his education in Britain, Gandhi spent 20 years in South Africa, where he devoted himself to ending the racist discrimination experienced by Indian South Africans and, in the process, developed the idea of **satyagraha.** A kind of non-violent resistance defined by Gandhi as "soul force," the ideal of *satyagraha* would lend the Independence movement moral credibility in the world's eyes for the next three decades.

TOWARD INDEPENDENCE (1915-47)

Gandhi enjoyed amazing popularity throughout the 1920s and 1930s, earning support from both Hindus and Muslims, largely due to his religious tolerance. He became much loved by the peasant masses by renouncing Western products in favor of *swadeshi* goods. Gandhi's popularity meant that the leadership of Congress was his; in turn, the once-elite Congress was remade under Gandhi's leadership into a mass party supported by millions of ordinary Indians.

Encouraged by Gandhi's Congress party, millions of Indians participated in nonviolent civil disobedience throughout the 1920s. In 1930, however, Gandhi's power appeared to have been stolen by **Jawaharlal Nehru,** the young leader of the Congress party's radical wing, who had audaciously declared January 26, 1930 to be **Indian Independence Day.** Gandhi embarked on his famous **Salt March** seven weeks after Nehru's declaration. Imperial authorities had declared it illegal for salt to be sold or manufactured except under the auspices of the heavily taxed official monopoly. Gandhi and his supporters marched 380km through present-day

Gujarat in defiance of the law, from his **Sabarmati Ashram** in Ahmedabad (see p. 344) to the sea, attracting crowds of supporters and media coverage along the way. Staff in hand and clothing fraying, Gandhi reached the coastal town of **Dandi** on April 6. Wading into the water, Gandhi proceeded to make salt by taking a handful of sea-water and pouring it on dry ground, breaking the salt law. British authorities responded by arresting over 60,000 Indians, but they could not control the rising nationalism. In 1932, the army began granting commissions to Indian officers; in 1935, the **Government of India Act,** which granted authority over provincial government to elected Indian representatives, was passed.

Meanwhile, the tensions between Congress and the Muslim League escalated. In 1940, leaders of Congress charged that the Muslim League had taken advantage of relocations of families during the war to gain power for itself. Claiming to speak for India's Muslim communities, leaders such as Muhammad Ali Jinnah retorted that aggressively seizing power was necessary, for Muslim rights could not be guaranteed in the independent, Hindu-dominated India which seemed about to materialize. In 1940, the League declared that the Muslims of India were a separate nation and demanded the creation of an independent Muslim state. The state, the League declared, should be named **Pakistan.**

Weakened by its fight against Nazi Germany, Britain concluded soon after World War II ended that India could no longer be held as a colony. The vicious religious conflicts which bloodied Kolkata, the Punjab, and the Ganga Valley in 1946 made the division of India into two sovereign states—one Hindu-dominated, the other Muslim-dominated—the only reasonable option. Defying geography, the new state of Pakistan was carved out of Muslim-majority areas in both east and west India. Bengal and the Punjab were both rent in two. Independence for India officially arrived when the vast territory which had been the "the jewel in the crown" of the British Empire was **partitioned.** The nation of Pakistan sprang into existence on August 14, 1947, and India followed suit 24 hours later. The last British viceroy, **Lord Mountbatten,** stayed in India voluntarily to help in the exchange of power, but the British Raj was over. Hours before Independence, Nehru addressed the Constituent Assembly in New Delhi: "At the stroke of the midnight hour, when the world sleeps, India will awaken to life and freedom. A moment comes, which comes but rarely in history, when we step from the old to the new, when an age ends, and when the soul of a nation, long suppressed, finds utterance."

AFTER INDEPENDENCE (1947-64)

Midnight struck, and on **August 15** a nation was born, and a host of high expectations and pressing problems lay before it. As countries were created, so were refugees: millions of Sikhs and Hindus streamed into India while millions of Muslims headed for Pakistan. These simultaneous, massive migrations (probably the largest population movement in human history) touched off stampedes and religious violence on a horrific scale, and more than 500,000 people were killed. Five months later, Mahatma Gandhi was assassinated on his way to evening prayers by **Nathuram Godse,** a Hindu extremist angered by Gandhi's attempts to appease the Muslim League (see **Raj Ghat,** p. 122).

The immediate tasks before **Nehru's government**—forging democratic institutions and establishing a functional administrative structure—were straightforward. It was quickly decided that India would be ruled as a **federation,** with power split between state and national authorities. In fulfillment of a pledge Congress had made long before Independence, Nehru's government passed the **States Reorganization Act** (1956), which re-drew India's internal boundaries along linguistic lines.

On the economic front, Nehru's India had many difficulties, the most serious of which were massive poverty and the substantial economic disparity between the urban middle class and village-dwelling farmers. While the socialist Nehru labored heroically to make India a more prosperous nation, embarking on **five year plans** and successfully soliciting foreign aid, poor economic growth could not match the needs of a rapidly growing population.

Nehru was constantly dogged by foreign policy trouble. At Independence, Kashmir, a former kingdom in the Himalayas with a Hindu maharaja and a 75% Muslim population, was faced with the choice of joining either India or Pakistan. Border skirmishes with Pakistan led the maharaja to accede to India, with Nehru promising fair elections soon. A brief, undeclared war between India and Pakistan ended in 1949 with a U.N.-brokered cease-fire. While the war established a *de facto*—and still disputed—border between Pakistani Kashmir and Indian Kashmir, it did not solve difficult underlying problems. As a result, Indian Kashmir has been the site of terrible violence since 1989. For more information, see **Jammu and Kashmir** (p. 250). The border troubles of the new nation weren't limited to Pakistan, though. In 1962, a boundary dispute led India to war with **China.**

INDIRA'S INDIA (1964-84)

After Nehru died in 1964, he was succeeded by **Lal Bahadur Shastri,** who died of a heart attack after leading India to victory in a defensive war with Pakistan. Shastri was succeeded by Nehru's daughter, **Indira Gandhi** (see **What's in a Name?,** p. 78). As soon as she came into power, it became evident that Mrs. Gandhi had ambitious plans. She feuded with the Congress "old guard," eventually splitting the party into **Congress (I)**—"I" for Indira—and the remainder of the party, which dissolved by the 1980s. Mrs. Gandhi also began to move India closer to the **USSR.**

In 1971, **East Pakistan** (the future **Bangladesh**) declared independence, and West Pakistan promptly invaded its eastern wing. Millions of refugees fled into India to avoid persecution, inflicting a heavy financial burden on India's treasury. India began to arm and train Bengali guerrillas, and in December, Pakistani planes attacked Indian airfields. The next day, Indira Gandhi sent the Indian army into both Pakistan and Bangladesh. Less than two weeks later, Pakistan surrendered; the result was the creation of the independent nation of Bangladesh. With Pakistan defeated, India emerged as South Asia's dominant power.

Though Gandhi's early years boded well for the nation's agricultural problems—with the **Green Revolution's** introducing high-yield seedings, modern farm machinery, and chemical fertilizers—she was unable to solve the fundamental problems of insufficient production. Also, small farmers who could not afford the modern tools were unable to compete with larger agricultural operations. Later, Prime Minister Gandhi focused on the elimination of poverty, family planning measures, and self-sufficiency strategies, but her methods became increasingly totalitarian.

Due to its autocratic nature (Mrs. Gandhi rarely attended Parliament, surrounded herself with sycophants, and meddled with state governments), her rule was filled with problems. After the oil crisis of 1973, India was faced with runaway inflation and the thread of famine, with millions of Indians slipping toward starvation. Solving economic problems seemed least important on the agenda of a government steeped in corruption and nepotism. In 1975, Mrs. Gandhi was found guilty of election fraud. Rather than step down as the law demanded, she declared a **National Emergency,** "suspending" all civil rights. Imposing sterilization on families with more than two children, aggressively censoring the press, mobilizing India's intelligence agencies as her own special police force, and having her political opponents jailed, Mrs. Gandhi seemed ever more the tyrant.

The state of emergency ended in January 1977, and Mrs. Gandhi believed that she would be re-elected legitimately. She wasn't. The **Janata Dal,** an anti-Indira coalition led by **Morarji Desai,** Mrs. Gandhi's former finance minister, came to power two months later. Unable to hold his party together, however, Desai was toppled and Mrs. Gandhi was re-elected in 1980. Her second term was plagued by regional problems. In 1984 she ordered the dismissal of Kashmir's popular Chief Minister, **Farooq Abdullah,** and soon after gave another such order to the governor of Andhra Pradesh to remove its popular Chief Minister, N.T. Rama Rao, a former film star and the leader of an opposition party. She also confronted separatist **Sikh militants** who had launched a campaign of terror in Punjab and Haryana to force the government to create a sovereign Sikh nation. In 1984, when armed militants seized the

WHAT'S IN A NAME? No family in India has sparked as much controversy and as many op-eds as the Gandhis. Between the charismatic **Jawaharlal Nehru,** his daughter **Indira Gandhi,** and her son **Rajiv Gandhi,** the Nehru-Gandhi family has dominated 40 out of 52 years of independent India's government. Rumored to have married her husband Feroze Gandhi in order to use the Mahatma's last name (no relation), Indira Gandhi was a populist tyrant—she called her rule "democracy with discipline." She was assassinated by her Sikh bodyguards in 1984. Her son Sanjay, whom she had been grooming to take over, was killed in a plane crash in 1980, so her other son Rajiv became prime minister after her death. Rajiv also met an untimely death, killed by a Tamil Tiger suicide-bomber while campaigning in 1991. Sanjay's widow **Maneka Gandhi** is a prominent animal rights activist and environmentalist, and Rajiv's widow, the Italian-born **Sonia Gandhi,** catapulted into the limelight when she became president of the Congress (I) and announced her candidacy for prime minister in the October 1999 elections.

Golden Temple in Amritsar (see p. 272), the Sikhs' holiest site, Mrs. Gandhi sent in the army, and tragedy resulted. Thousands of militants died, and hundreds of soldiers and civilians were killed during the four-day battle that ensued. But the worst was still yet to come. By effectively desecrating the temple, Mrs. Gandhi incurred the wrath of the militants, and on October 31, 1984, two of her Sikh bodyguards assassinated her at her home in New Delhi. Her death sparked massive rioting in the capital accompanied by massacres of Sikhs by Hindu thugs.

THE LAST 15 YEARS

A "sympathy vote" in the elections following Indira's assassination swept Rajiv Gandhi's Congress (I) party to an impressive majority position. Many Indians had high hopes that Rajiv's administration would bring about the changes India so badly needed. But Gandhi's term as prime minister began inauspiciously, when a gas leak from the Union Carbide chemical plant in December 1984 killed nearly three thousand people in **Bhopal** (see p. 361). Then there was the government's last-minute withdrawal from an agreement with Sikh leaders that would have improved the Punjab situation by giving the Sikhs the city of Chandigarh. Rajiv's free-enterprise, trickle-down economic policies brought in the imported goods that the rich craved, but they did little for the poor.

Rajiv had mixed success with foreign policy. He improved Indo-U.S. relations without moving away from the Soviet Union, but he made ill-advised decisions in the case of **Sri Lanka.** An island 35km off the coast of southern India, the nation is inhabited by a 70% Buddhist Sinhalese-speaking majority, and a Hindu Tamil minority, who constitute about 15%. Tamils have felt increasingly alienated since 1956 as successive Sri Lankan governments have instituted policies favoring the Sinhalese. Since the early 1980s, the **Liberation Tigers of Tamil Eelam** have fought a guerrilla war for a separate Tamil nation in the north of Sri Lanka. The Tigers had been surreptitiously armed and trained in India during Mrs. Gandhi's administration, and by the time Rajiv came power, the group had become a significant force. Under the mantle of the **South Asian Association for Regional Cooperation (SAARC),** which India had started in 1985 to promote regional amity, Rajiv sent the **Indian Peace Keeping Force (IPKF)** to Sri Lanka, whose government was happy to withdraw its own troops from the fray. The Tigers routed the government forces, and by the time the IPKF withdrew, there were 100 Indian soldiers dead for every Tiger killed.

The 1989 elections transferred power to a fragile coalition of parties, including the Hindu Nationalist Bharatiya Janata Party (BJP), led by Prime Minister **V.P. Singh** of the Janata Dal. Even as Singh tried to settle the Punjab crisis, the Kashmir situation worsened. Muslim militants in Kashmir, allegedly trained and armed in Pakistan, started campaigning against Indian authorities. The state capital of Srinagar, once a popular tourist destination, became a war zone (for more information, see p. 250). Other problems, such as the Mandal Commission's endorsement of the policy that 60% of university admissions and civil service jobs be reserved for lower castes and former Untouchables, posed threats to the Singh government. Young high-caste Hindus took to the streets, and a few even publicly immolated themselves in protest. The arrest of L.K. Advani, the leader of the BJP who was trying to rally support for the building of a Hindu temple on a controversial site in **Ayodhya**, Uttar Pradesh (for more information, see below; for the full story, see p. 192), caused the BJP to withdraw its support, and the government fell. A new government formed under Prime Minister **Chandra Shekhar** lasted only a few months.

The elections of 1991 brought Congress (I) back to power, largely because of a sympathy vote soon after Rajiv Gandhi was assassinated by a Tamil Tiger suicide bomber while campaigning in Tamil Nadu. The new prime minister, **P.V. Narasimha Rao**, an aging disciple of Nehru, was seen by the party as a compromise candidate, but he surprised everyone with his political acumen. A 1991 financial crisis necessitated the initiation of unpopular **economic reforms** which included cutting government spending and opening India to foreign investment.

Late 1991 brought renewed rumblings of the dispute over the Babri Masjid in Ayodhya. In December 1992, with a BJP government ruling the state of Uttar Pradesh, where Ayodhya is located, Hindu nationalist leaders called for volunteers to build a temple on Rama's birthplace. From all over India devotees converged on Ayodhya, bricks in hand, and proceeded to tear down the mosque. **Hindu-Muslim violence** erupted across South Asia, especially in major cities like Bombay. Rao's government banned the Hindu nationalist parties, dismissing the government of Uttar Pradesh and three other states ruled by the BJP.

Though visibly weakened, the Rao government clung to power and continued with its program of economic liberalization. By 1994 the **Hindu nationalists** (see below) had made a complete comeback, winning elections in several states. In 1995 the state of Maharashtra, which includes the industrial powerhouse of Bombay, came under the control of a particularly radical nationalist party, the **Shiv Sena**. Problems in Kashmir continued as well, with the government's handling of the insurgency bringing international condemnation for human rights violations.

The BJP won more seats than any other party in the May 1996 Lok Sabha elections, but it still had a minority, and the government it formed fell to a vote of no-confidence two weeks later. Power passed in June to a loose coalition of low-caste, populist, and socialist parties called the **United Front**, which chose **H. D. Deve Gowda** as its candidate for prime minister.

Elections were held in the troubled state of **Kashmir** in May and September 1996, and although there were some reports of military coercion, most Kashmiris were able to vote freely. The 1996 parliamentary elections left no clear majority, leading India to a succession of teetering **coalition governments.** The 1998 elections did little to consolidate the center, but the Hindu Nationalist BJP came out on top. A series of five **nuclear tests** conducted in May shoved Prime Minister Atal Behari Vajpayee into the international spotlight and intensified the regional arms race. Later that year, Indian and Pakistani troops exchanged heavy shelling across the disputed border of Kashmir, and more than 90 soldiers and civilians were killed.

THIS YEAR'S NEWS

In December 1998, Amartya Sen, a professor at Harvard University, received the Nobel Prize for Economics, the first ever awarded to an Asian. January 1999 saw an Australian missionary and his two sons burned to death by Hindu activists in Manoharpur, Orissa. Just two days later, the Ranbir Sena, an army of upper-class landlords in Bihar, gunned down 22 lower-class Dalits, prompting a swift response—34 upper-class Biharis were killed in March. In April, the ruling BJP government fell, losing a parliamentary vote of confidence by one vote as its coalition partner, the southern **AIADMK** party led by J. Jayalalitha, withdrew support. The opposition Congress (I) President Sonia Gandhi, the Italian-born wife of the deceased Rajiv Gandhi, was unable to piece together a majority, so the struggle for

THE HINDU JUGGERNAUT What it means to be "Indian" eludes historians and ordinary citizens alike, but a chosen few don't share this doubt. Hindu nationalism has its roots in the 19th century, when religious reformers resisted British attempts to Westernize India. The freedom fighter **V.D. Savarkar** coined the term **Hindutva,** asserting that all Indians, regardless of religion, are bound to a "Hinduness" out of loyalty to the nation's ancient culture. The paramilitary **Rashtriya Swayamsevak Sangh** (National Volunteer Corps or RSS) was founded in 1925, aiming to expunge Hinduism of any other influences. A former RSS member, **Nathuram Godse** assassinated Mahatma Gandhi because of Gandhi's concessions to Muslims. Since then, the number of Hindu Nationalist parties has multiplied. Founded in 1980, the most successful of these has been the **Bharatiya Janata Party (BJP),** under L.K. Advani. Others prominent nationalist parties are the quasi-fascist **Shiv Sena** of Maharashtra, led by Bal Thackeray, and the **Vishwa Hindu Parishad (VHP),** which spearheaded the December 1992 destruction of the Babri Masjid in Ayodhya, U.P. Since that event, the BJP has parlayed this more populist platform into greater success at the polls.

a majority in Parliament remains unresolved pending the outcome of elections in October. In late May, Indian jets attacked Muslim guerilla forces that had advanced beyond the Line of Control marking the disputed border with Pakistan. The battle that ensued killed and injured hundreds and forced thousands to flee their homes. On August 2, nearly 400 people were killed when two trains collided near Gaisal, West Bengal in one of the worst railway accident in India's history.

CASTE

The ancient codes of *dharma* divided Hindu society into four ranks, each emerging from a different part of the primordial Person, *Purusha*: the *brahmins*, the priestly and scholarly caste, came from his mouth; the *kshatriyas*, the warrior-ruler caste, from his arms; the *vaishyas*, merchants, from his thighs; and finally the *shudras*, laborers, came from Purusha's feet. These four *varnas* (colors), form the ideological basis of the Hindu caste system. Principles of *karma* and reincarnation offer an explanation of one's relative fortune (or misfortune) in this life and a hope for improvement in the next. The practical rules of conduct which have solidified and preserved the caste system mostly concern notions of "substance" and "purity." Any transaction mixes the "essences" of different people and creates "pollution" between members of different castes. *Brahmins* must be exceptionally pure to perform religious ceremonies, so they do not mix with other castes or accept food cooked by non-*brahmins*. The group formerly known as "Untouchables" included people of such highly-polluting occupations (usually toilet-cleaners, leather tanners, and undertakers) that they were considered to be outside of the caste system altogether.

In practice, however, the hierarchy of the caste system has never been clear-cut. More socially important than the *varnas* are **jatis,** subdivisions linked by kinship and usually sharing a very specific occupation (farming, pottery, etc.). There are thousands of these *jatis* in India, some very small and peculiar to a few villages, others numbering in the tens of millions and spread across huge regions. Due to various political and sociological events, such as famines, wars, mass conversions and reconversions, many of these *jatis* have split, joined, risen in status, or descended, regardless of the *varna* they belong to. Some regions of India have politically dominant castes, such as the **Jats** in Rajasthan and Punjab and the **Reddis** in Andhra Pradesh, who were originally very low castes.

There is no surefire way to tell someone's caste, although after a while in India you'll recognize some common last names or styles of dress and link them to caste. Occupations are also an indicator, but never certain. Efforts at reform and the demands of life in urban areas have gone a long way towards deteriorating the caste system. The notion of untouchability is on the wane and caste in general determines less absolutely one's social position. Former untouchables, now known as "Dalits" (the Oppressed), ride on the same buses and play on the same sports teams as *brahmins*. However, in India's villages (where 70% of the population lives), caste is still extremely important and extremely restrictive (see **This Year's News**, p. 79). And even among educated urbanites, most Hindu marriages still take place within *jatis*, or at least between *jatis* of equal status.

In the realm of politics, however, caste is increasingly important recently. Lower castes have managed to translate their demographic strength into political clout, although the sheer size of the group makes any kind of internal cohesion almost impossible. Internal differentiation has pitted Untouchables against *shudra* OBCs (Other Backward Castes), who are less low-caste. While lower-caste parties are in power in many states, the only party with national appeal is the Janata Party. Affirmative action programs for lower-caste Hindus have recently been implemented, with quite a large proportion of university spaces and civil service jobs reserved for these "scheduled castes." India's President, **K.R. Narayanan,** is a Dalit, the first ever to hold that title. Countervailing these developments is the rise of the BJP, an upper-caste political party, which once was influential only regionally but is now an important national party (although it still has not fully penetrated South India).

RELIGION

HINDUISM

Known to its many practitioners as **Sanatana Dharma** (Eternal Faith), Hinduism is one of the oldest and most versatile of the world's religions, claiming the largest number of followers in Asia. Heavily laden with ritual, this blend of mono- and polytheism is somewhat hard to define and difficult to grasp. "Hinduism" was the name of the religion of the people whom **Alexander the Great** called "Hindus," because they lived across the Indus River. Hinduism actually consists of a multitude of local and regional religions and integrates these many different traditions in a way that accommodates them all. This emphasis on diversity is illustrated in the common definition of Hinduism as *varna-ashrama-dharma*, which loosely translates as "performing the duty accorded to one's stage of life, caste and social situation." While all Hindus acknowledge the truths set forth in the books of the four **Vedas,** there is a great deal of variation within Hinduism itself, with followers worshipping thousands of gods and goddesses in a number of ways.

CENTRAL HINDU BELIEFS

Of the six major schools of Indian philosophy, *Vedanta* is, in many ways, the most important of them, producing most of Hinduism's characteristic features of belief. It is based on the existence of an absolute, unchanging and omnipresent reality called **Brahman,** a universal spirit or essence, and which is present in every individual in the form of **Atman,** the self or soul. While individuals perceive a separation between themselves and Brahman, this is actually **maya,** or illusion. The ultimate purpose of existence is to attain **moksha** (liberation) by realizing the inherent unity and, according to some philosophical schools, identity between *Brahman* and *Atman.* Liberation from **samsara,** the cycle of birth, death, and rebirth, can be achieved through a variety of methods. The *Bhagavad Gita* describes four such paths for reaching *moksha:* action, devotion, knowledge, and psychic exercises. *Karma,* the moral law of cause and effect, teaches that present conditions are the result of past deeds. It is one's *karma* that keeps one bound to the cycle of rebirth; one is continually reborn into this world until one's karmic debt has been paid. *Dharma* has several meanings, but most commonly refers to one's personal duty which maintains social, and ultimately, cosmic order (see **dharma,** p. 82).

INDIA

There are four major **aims of life** in traditional Hindu thought. While *dharma* (duty) and *moksha* (release) remain the ultimate goals in life, there is also room for *kama* (sensual enjoyment) and *artha* (wealth). Hindu thought also divides life into four stages in which to seek these goals. The first 25 or so years should be devoted solely to knowledge; the second 25 to being a householder, fulfilling the duties to raise a family and to future generation; the third stage rounds out the householder life and is a preparatory and slow detachment from worldly connections to enter into the fourth ascetic stage, a complete renunciation of one's life.

Time is cyclical in Hindu thought. Periods called *mahayugas* constitute the world's sojourn from creation to destruction and last approximately 4,320,000 years. Each *mahayuga* is divided into four *yugas*, beginning in a golden era of prosperity during the *krita yuga* and devolving until the *kali yuga*, when *dharma* declines and the world is destroyed to be renewed again in the next *mahayuga*. The world is believed to be near the tail end of a *kali yuga* at the moment.

VEDIC LITERATURE

The earliest existing religious influences in modern Hinduism came from the religion of the Aryans and that of the Indus Valley Civilization (see **History,** p. 68). The origins of Aryan religion are found in books known as the Vedas (meaning "knowledge" or "what is known"), collections of poetic hymns in Sanskrit transmitted orally and then written down between 1200BC-200AD. These oral texts are regarded as unitary, eternal, and without human origin, as they were "heard" by sages, or **rishis** (literally, "those who hear"). The **deities** in the Vedas are usually associated with certain natural phenomena: Indra (the most frequently mentioned god) appears as the god of war; Varuna is the sky god and guardian of *rita* (cosmic order); Agni is the sacred fire; Soma is the moon, as well as a hallucinogenic drink. Shiva and Vishnu are only mentioned in passing.

Vedic religion featured the ritual of **fire-sacrifice,** performed to maintain *rita* (a word replaced in later texts by *dharma*): the Vedas were chanted by the *brahmin* priest who also consumed *soma*, which was then offered to the fire. The sacrifices were performed in order to win the favor of gods in hopes of favorably altering the forces of nature, but the gods also relied upon these rituals to support their function in the cosmos; any lapse in sacrifice would result in the dissolution of *rita*.

Towards the end of the Vedic period, three groups of philosophical texts were written, reforming and reassessing the world-view of the *Vedas*. The **Brahmanas,** the **Aranyakas** and, most importantly, the **Upanishads** began to examine the underlying of power of ritual, declaring it metaphysical in nature. The rituals of the Vedas gave way to an inner quest for transcendence, and teachings, previously restricted to priests, became more openly transmitted. These texts are the first in the Hindu tradition to advocate withdrawal from society and the use of various ascetic techniques in the religious quest. It also from the *Upanishads*, that Hinduism's major philosophical tenets of *dharma, karma, moksha* derive.

EPIC LITERATURE AND DHARMA TEXTS

Similar to *rita*, **dharma** has many different meanings. Most commonly, it simply refers to the continual nature, role, and function of everything that persists in the universe. Thus, the words *sanatana dharma* might also be translated as "the way things eternally are," or "the eternal religion." Another example of *dharma* could be described in the image of a river. Why does a river flow downhill? Because that is its role, its nature, its *dharma*. In the same vein, it is the *dharma* of a *kshatriya* king to eat meat, engage in war, offer food and money to *brahmins*, and rule a kingdom. *Dharma*'s meaning also has connotations of duty. *Dharma* extends to the social order in the form of the *Manusmriti*, the **Laws of Manu**, and in texts called **dharmashastras.** Generally, there are laws one should follow: the first is adherence to cosmic *dharma* through religious observances; the second is adherence to one's caste (*jati*) *dharma*; the third is following one's *svadharma*, or personal moral code. Hindu epics play on themes of conflict between these various duties and portray the tension between adherence to one's *dharma,* with all of its worldly obligations, and striving toward *moksha,* liberation from the world.

One of the most popular and sacred Hindu scriptures, the **Bhagavad Gita,** makes up the sixth chapter of the great Sanskrit epic, the **Mahabharata,** a dialogue between **Krishna,** an *avatar* (incarnation) of Vishnu, and prince **Arjuna.** As Arjuna heads into a great battle, he sees many friends, teachers, and elders whom he will be forced to fight. Growing despondent, he threw down his weapons in refusal. Krishna (as Arjuna's chariot-driver) then gives his disciple a lesson on *dharma,* explaining that He alone is the doer and sustainer of all activity. He explains that Arjuna should not be attached to the fruits of his actions, but should fulfill his *dharma* as a *kshatriya* (a member of the warrior caste) and fight, allowing himself to be an instrument of the Supreme power and not "the doer."

The **Ramayana,** possibly the best-loved epic story in India, chronicles the story of Lord Rama. An incarnation of Vishnu, Rama is revered as an archetype of one who staunchly follows his *dharma* without batting an eyelash. Though Rama is legally the rightful heir to the throne, a series of fateful events hinder his succession, but Rama stoically accepts his fate. (For further details, see **The Ramayana,** p. 586.)

HINDU PRACTICE

Hinduism encompasses a variety of practices from strict asceticism to elaborate rituals, although the most popular today derive from a tradition known as **bhakti.** The *bhakti* movements, which began around the 11th century, were spread by popular poet-saints and characterized by ecstatic religious devotion as a way of realizing the divine. It is said that a true *bhakta* desires not to merge and become one with God, but rather to remain a devotee forever, always praising God. Rebelling against religious orthodoxy and intolerance, *bhakti* worship is filled with songs sung in local dialects and messages delivered to everyone, regardless of caste. *Bhaktas* also perform **puja,** acts of reverence to a god, spirit, or aspect of the divine, in which flowers, sweets, and other foods are offered to the deity. Most often that contact is through an object: an element of nature, a sculpture, or an image of the deity. Contrary to appearances, idols are not what is being worshipped; they are seen as vessels which the deity comes to occupy during worship. The visible form serves as a focus for the believer's devotion; the "seeing" of the god through its image is called **darshan,** during which the god sees the worshipper.

One of the most important leaders of the *bhakti* movement in South India was **Ramanuja,** who established the **Sri-Vaishnava** sect. In North India, **Chaitanya** increased the following of Krishna, who is most often worshipped through *bhakti* devotion. Other prominent *bhakti* figures throughout India were **Mirabai** (p. 310), **Sur Das, Tukaram,** and **Eknath.** A great devotional figure for both Hindus and Muslims was **Kabir** (1440-1518). Born a Muslim weaver in Varanasi, Kabir spread a message of unity between faiths, insisting that Rama and Allah were the same God.

HINDU IMAGERY

- **Brahma:** Four-faced creator. Sits on a lotus growing from Vishnu's navel.
- **Vishnu:** Reclines on a many-headed serpent; travels via man-bird. His incarnations include blue-skinned, heroic **Rama,** and flute-playing, cowherd **Krishna.**
- **Shiva:** Terrifying, yet compassionate. Depicted as a trident-weilding, long-haired **ascetic,** or as **Nataraja,** a many-armed, evil-dwarf-stomping cosmic dancer; worshipped through the *linga.* Popular with ascetic holy men.
- **Kali:** Black-skinned, red-tongued, skull-garlanded bloodthirsty mother goddess. Embodies *shakti,* the feminine life-force. Her forms include **Durga,** a ten-handed, tiger-riding woman warrior.
- **Ganesh:** Elephant-headed remover of obstacles. Travels via mouse.
- **Hanuman:** Monkey-god, Rama's faithful sidekick.

> **SWASTIKAS** Visitors to India with memories of WWII (inherited or otherwise) may be shocked to see the profusion of swastikas painted on walls and windshields or worked into the architecture. However, swastikas go a long way back in South Asia, and *swastika* is actually a Sanskrit word meaning "it is well." The cross with bent arms was a widespread symbol of good luck and power in the ancient world, used by ancient Greeks, Mesopotamians, Chinese, early Christians, Mayans, and Navajos, among others. The ancient Indo-Aryans also used the swastika, and it remains one of the most cherished symbols of Hindus, Jains, and Buddhists. The swastika is associated with good luck and the removal of obstacles. With arms pointing clockwise, it is an auspicious solar symbol, depicting the sun's path from east to south to west across the sky. The counter-clockwise swastika, however, is a symbol of night, and is considered inauspicious. The Hindu swastika may have originated from a wheel, or from the fire sticks in Vedic sacrifices, which were lain on the ground in the form of a cross.

GODS AND GODDESSES

There is general agreement that underlying reality is an impersonal, attributeless, spiritual essence called **Brahman,** which is One, present in each individual in the form of the **Atman,** which can be loosely translated as "soul." But Hindus simultaneously believe that Brahman takes an infinite number of forms. Shiva, Vishnu, and Devi, and their various incarnations, receive the most adulation, but there are countless others—local deities, those described in the Vedic hymns of the Aryans, those from long-lost prehistoric nature cults, and various syntheses of all of these.

No one really knows exactly how many gods and goddesses the Hindu pantheon holds; some put the number at 333 million. From the central trinity of **Brahma** (Creator), **Vishnu** (Preserver), and **Shiva** (Destroyer), many gods and goddesses emerge, each embodying an attribute of the eternal soul. The popularity of individual deities varies from the North to the South, village to village, and family to family. The largest distinction lies between Vaishnava (worshippers of Vishnu) and Shaiva (worshippers of Shiva) devotees. Strangely unbefitting of his role as creator of the human world, Brahma is rarely worshipped, and only a single temple in **Pushkar** (see p. 297) is dedicated to him.

One of the most popular gods, especially in the South, **Shiva** is at once terrifying and compassionate. The Destroyer is most commonly depicted as an uncouth ascetic who wears live cobras and leopard skins, wields a trident, rides his bull Nandi, and lives atop Mount Kailasha in the Himalayas with his consort, Parvati, and their two sons, Ganesh and the six-headed Kartikeya (known as Murugan in Tamil Nadu). Yet, Shiva also represents the creative and spiritual energy of the universe, and he is worshipped through his *linga,* a simple, phallus-shaped stone shaft which symbolizes his creative power. Twelve temples around India are sanctified *jyotirlingas* (*lingas* of light) where Shiva, also known as **Mahadev** (Great God), is said to have burst from the earth. He takes on many forms, including **Ardhinarishwara** (half-male, half-female), **Rudra** (the Howler), and **Nataraja** (the Lord of Dance), whose movements, said to have inspired the cosmos, also possess the power to destroy it. Most **sadhus,** Hindu ascetics, are devotees of Shiva.

Vishnu reclines upon a many-headed snake afloat on a sea of milk. As Preserver of the cosmos, he has repeatedly stepped in to save the universe from calamity, usually in the form of his eleven *avatars,* three of which are very well known. Incarnation number seven is **Rama,** the hero of the *Ramayana.* Rama, a popular deity in North India and the focus of the Ayodhya controversy (see p. 192), represents the ideal son, husband, father, and leader. Vishnu's eighth incarnation is **Krishna,** perhaps the most popular deity in India. Krishna is worshipped as the playful cowherd who cavorts with milkmaids, the philosophical charioteer in the *Bhagavad Gita,* and as a fat little baby stealing butter. Vishnu's ninth incarnation, ironically, is the **Buddha.** Buddhists reject the idea that the Enlightened One is an incarnation of Vishnu; this idea may have evolved by early proselytizing Hindus in attempts to convert them back.

Besides Shiva and Vishnu, many Hindus worship female deities referred to in general as **Devi** (the Goddess). The many goddesses are recognized as aspects of *shakti*, a single female principle that is the dynamic force behind the universe. The Goddess cult probably predates worship of male gods, although specific goddesses have joined the now male-dominated pantheon as consorts. **Kali,** however, remains a force to be reckoned with. Although considered a consort of Shiva, she is an independent goddess of destruction in her own right. Her skin is black, her red tongue lolls, yet she wears a garland of skulls, and she resides in cremation grounds, but she is still worshipped as a "mother goddess." The all-powerful **Durga** was created from the combined power of all of the male deities. When none of the male gods could destroy the demon Mahisha, Durga went forth on her tiger, clutching weapons in each of her ten hands, and emerged victorious. One of the most popular festivals in India is **Navratri** (part of Dussehra, which takes place in September), and consists of nine nights dedicated to Durga. The other major goddesses are largely benevolent. **Parvati,** Shiva's wife, makes Shiva's power accessible to humans. **Lakshmi,** Vishnu's consort, is the goddess of material and spiritual wealth and luck.

Son of Shiva and Parvati, the elephant-headed god **Ganesh** (also known as Ganapati) is very popular in India and Nepal, and all Hindus come to him at some time or another. Worshipped as the "remover of obstacles," he is often positioned at doorways and gateways. Ganesh rides around on a rat, and his huge, fat form is often depicted squashing his poor rodent carrier. Ganesh's unusual physical form is rooted in myth: right after his birth, his mother Parvati told him to guard her bathing spot. When Shiva came along and tried to approach his wife, he was stopped by a boy he did not recognize as his son, and chopped off the boy's head in a blind fury. When Parvati learned of the incident, she demanded that Ganesh be resurrected, and Shiva replaced the boy's head with the head of the next creature he saw—an elephant. **Hanuman,** the monkey god, is another lesser deity with a large popular following. He was Rama's faithful servant during the quest to rescue Rama's wife Sita from Ravana. He is adored for his absolute loyalty; in one story, he tears open his furry chest to reveal the word "Rama" etched millions of times in tiny script across his heart.

MODERN HINDUISM

In the 19th century, Hinduism was reinterpreted by many thinkers, including British and Christian missionaries, who wanted to make it more systematic and "rational." The **Brahmo Samaj,** a group founded by **Raja Ram Mohan Roy** in Bengal in 1828, did away with image-worship and instead held Christian-style services, with readings from the *Upanishads.* Another movement, the **Arya Samaj,** also abandoned caste and images, preaching that the Vedas were sufficient for everything in life. A great figure in the 19th-century Hindu revival was **Sri Ramakrishna** (1836-1886), whose message of religious unity left an indelible impression upon modern Hindu thought. Ramakrishna proclaimed that all religions provide equally valid paths to God, explaining that the best religion for any person was the one in which they were raised. A disciple of Ramakrishna, **Swami Vivekananda** (1863-1902) introduced Hinduism and Ramakrishna's philosophy to the West during the World Parliament of Religions at the University of Chicago in 1893, spreading the lessons of Hindu philosophy to a world-wide audience. Proclaiming that God resides within, he extended his philosophy to a national level, inspiring Indian patriotism and a belief in the nation's indomitable spirit.

Sri Aurobindo was another reformer and Indian nationalist, who, after being imprisoned for sedition by the British in 1908, underwent a series of mystical experiences while practicing yoga in prison. He abandoned his political activities and devoted his life to achieving "Supramental Consciousness" on earth, becoming one of the most prolific 20th-century writers of poetry and Hindu philosophy.

His activities were continued by his associate "The Mother," a French woman named **Mirra Alfassa,** who assisted him in his work. Sri Aurobindo spent the rest of his life in seclusion in Pondicherry, where his ashram remains today (see p. 557).

ISLAM

Approximately 11% of India's population is Muslim, which amounts to about 110 million people, giving India the fourth-largest number of Muslims in the world after Indonesia, Bangladesh, and Pakistan. In fact, India has more Muslims than any two Arab countries put together, and Islam has had a strong influence on Indian culture. Muslims are spread throughout India, forming distinct communities in places like Hyderabad, Lucknow, Kerala, and of course, Kashmir. The questions surrounding their political, religious, and cultural status are the most emotionally charged issues for many Indians today.

HISTORY

Islam was founded by the **Prophet Muhammad,** who lived in Mecca (in what is now Saudi Arabia) during the 7th century AD. Between 610 and 622, Muhammad received revelations from the angel Gabriel concerning the true nature of God. His monotheistic teachings were received coolly in polytheistic Arabia, and finally he and his followers were driven from Mecca in 622; this **Hijra** (flight) to Medina marks the start of the Muslim calendar. The people of Medina embraced the new faith, and after building up an army, Muhammad returned in triumph to Mecca in 630 and established himself as the spiritual leader of a nascent Muslim state. After Muhammad's death, the Muslims conquered Arabia and adjacent lands at an incredible rate, and by 711, less than a hundred years from its quite humble beginnings, Islam had extended its rule from Spain to Sindh in eastern Pakistan.

In 661, however, not long after the Prophet's death, a dispute over Islam's highest office, that of the *caliph*—came to a head in the assassination of Muhammad's son-in-law Ali. This early dissent would deepen to become a real split within Islam, between the **Shi'is,** who recognized only Ali's descendants as legitimate religious leaders, and the **Sunnis,** who accepted the authority of any caliph well-versed in the religion and able to command obedience. Today, Sunnis make up the majority of Muslims in India and in the rest of the Muslim world, except in Iran.

Islam trickled into India over the years; its messengers were Arabian traders, Sufi mystics from Persia, and the armies of Mahmud of Ghazni. Islam's full effect came in after 1192, however, under the **Delhi Sultanate** and then the **Mughal Empire,** and India was ruled by Muslims for over 500 years (see **The Arrival of Islam,** p. 71). A few Hindus converted to Islam in order to join the new elite, and some low-caste Hindus converted to escape the caste system, but the majority of the population remained Hindu. Large-scale conversion took place only on the eastern and western frontiers of South Asia; these areas became Pakistan and Bangladesh upon Independence, when Muslims suddenly became conscious of their minority status in a new and massively Hindu nation. Before departing in 1947, the British carved out the nation of **Pakistan,** a Muslim nation, with one wing on the west and one wing on the east of India. Millions of people suddenly found themselves on the "wrong" side of the **Partition** line at midnight on Independence day, and millions died in the violence following a desperate migration in both directions across the border (see p. 76). However, a sizeable minority of Muslims remained in India.

BELIEFS

All Muslims believe in one supreme god, **Allah,** and worship him by the five "pillars" of Islam: declaring one's faith ("there is no God but God and Muhammad is his prophet"); praying five times daily; giving alms (*zakat*) to the poor; fasting during the month of Ramadan; and making the *haj* (pilgrimage to Mecca) at least once in a lifetime, barring physical or financial hardship. Some Muslims also consider *jihad,* or holy war, a pillar of Islam. Islam's single holy book, the **Qur'an,** is consid-

OF MOSQUES AND MINARETS Whenever you travel in India, you're bound to encounter a *masjid* (mosque) or two, and whether it's the ruins of the Quwwat al-Islam mosque in Delhi—the oldest surviving Islamic building in India—or a modern terro-concrete affair, every *masjid* adheres to a simple design. Because the entire congregation will assemble at the mosque during Friday prayers, each mosque features a large courtyard. While praying, Muslims face towards Mecca (west of India), so the western wall, known as the *qibla*, is often elaborately decorated. A niche in the *qibla*, the *mihrab*, indicates the presence of Allah, and sometimes a light is hung in the niche to represent the Prophet Muhammad. The *minbar*, a kind of raised pulpit, typically with a small staircase attached, may be positioned at the front of the room where everyone can see it. During the Friday service, the *imam* will climb up on the *minbar* and deliver a sermon. Finally, rising into the sky are the mosque's minarets. Traditionally, a *muezzin* would climb these towers to call the faithful to prayer. Today, loudspeakers attached somewhere on the spire often do the job.

ered to be the direct word of God as recorded by the prophet. Second in authority after the Qur'an is the **Hadith,** an assemblage of the words and deeds of Muhammad himself, painstakingly authenticated.

Friday is the Islamic holy day, when a special prayer is given at the mosque. The ninth month of the Islamic calendar marks the celebration of **Ramadan,** a holiday commemorating the Prophet's receiving the holy Qur'an from God, during which all Muslims excepting the very young and the very sick abstain from food and drink during daylight hours. **Muharram** memorializes the death of the Prophet's grandson and is of particular importance to Shi'i Muslims, who observe Muharram with twelve days of song and prayer.

ISLAM IN INDIA

Muslims and Hindus have coexisted in a tense sort of peace for most of their time together, but it is a peace nonetheless. The Mughal Emperor Akbar even tried to bridge the two faiths. Recently, however, **Hindu-Muslim tensions** have flared, as Hindu nationalists grow stronger, claiming that India is a fundamentally Hindu country. Additionally, unfriendly India-Pakistan relations have aggravated India's Hindu-Muslim domestic relations. In recent years the Mughal legacy of temple-breaking has been flung back at Muslims, and many mosques have been destroyed. The **Babri Masjid** in Ayodhya (see p. 194) was destroyed in 1992 by Hindu nationalists. Meanwhile, riots and massacres that began with the 1947 Partition continue.

Islam considers all humans equal and strongly prohibits any discrimination on the basis of race, but Indianized Islam has, to some extent, succumbed to its own, less rigid version of the caste system. Many Muslim women stay secluded in their homes according to the custom of *purdah*, and after centuries of Muslim rule, this practice has spread among groups of Hindu women as well. Muslims are required by the Qur'an to avoid alcohol, pork, and shellfish; Muslims do, however, eat beef, as long as the cow has been slaughtered according to religious prescription and is thus considered *halal*. At noon on Fridays, men gather for communal prayers at the *masjid;* women usually pray at home. Many Indian Muslims also speak Urdu, which, although it uses a Persian script, is very similar to Hindi.

While the Arab practice of Islam is often seen as being marked by doctrinal austerity, Indian Islam is much more devotionally and aesthetically oriented, and it has had an influential impact on Indian culture. While orthodox Islam frowns upon the notion of worship, Indian Muslims have a tradition of *pir* (saint) worship, and both Muslims and Hindus make pilgrimages to *pir* shrines to pray for worldly things like children, good grades, and safe passage.

Art and architecture flourished under the Mughals, who often ignored the Islamic injunction against painting human figures. Sufi mystics introduced the **qawwali,** a melancholy devotional song resembling the Hindu *bhajan*, and the **ghazal,** a poetic song developed by Persian Muslims in India.

SIKHISM

Guru Nanak (1469-1539), a philosopher-poet born into a *kshatriya* Hindu family in what is today eastern Pakistan, is the venerated founder of Sikhism. After traveling to Mecca, Bengal, and many places in between, Guru Nanak proclaimed a religious faith which brought together elements of Hinduism and Islam: he rejected image-worship just as Islam did, borrowed Hinduism's use of music in worship, and rejected Islam's reliance on a holy book. He also rejected caste distinctions, sex discrimination, and ancestor worship, but never actually attacked Hinduism or Islam. Nanak proclaimed that the one God was Truth **(Sat),** and he asserted that liberation from *samsara*, the Hindu cycle of life, death, and rebirth, was possible for those who embraced God, known to people through **gurus.** Nanak contended that bathing, donating alms to charity, and, most importantly, meditating, would erode hubris and would clear the way for individuals to accept God's truth.

After Nanak's death in 1539, spiritual leadership over his *sikhs* (disciples) passed to another guru, **Angad.** Guru Angad wrote his and Guru Nanak's hymns in a new script, called **Gurumukhi** (*gurmukh* means "God"), which is still the written script of the Punjabi language. After Angad's death, guru succeeded guru, each adding new tenets to Sikhism. The third guru, **Amar Das** (1509-74), encouraged Sikhs to worship publicly in temples called **gurudwaras;** the fifth guru, **Arjun Dev** (1563-1606), collected more than 5000 of the previous gurus' hymns into a book called the **Adi Granth** and founded the magnificent **Golden Temple** at Amritsar (see p. 272). After Guru Arjun was executed by the Mughal Emperor Jahangir, an extended period of Mughal repression and Mughal-Sikh fighting ensued. By the time the tenth and final guru, Gobind Singh, was assassinated in 1708, raids and skirmishes had become a sad fact of life throughout Punjab, the Siwalik Hills, and other parts of northern India.

Under the leadership of the tenth guru, **Guru Gobind Singh** (1666-1708), Sikhism underwent a series of radical changes which gave the faith a more cohesive identity. These changes and the military tradition they espoused were an attempt to defend Sikhs against persecution suffered at the hands of the ruling Mughals. In 1699, Gobind Singh founded the Khalsa Brotherhood. Sikh men now had to undergo a kind of "baptism," which included a pledge not to smoke tobacco, not to eat even *halal* meat, not to have sexual relations with Muslim women, and to renounce their caste names; men took the name **Singh** (Lion), and women took the name **Kaur** (Princess). The Khalsa further mandated that members adopt and never go without the **five kakkars:** *kangah* (wooden comb), *kirpan* (sword), *kara* (steel bracelet), *kachch* (short knickers), and *kesh* (uncut hair). Gobind Singh added new hymns to the Adi Granth, re-named it the **Guru Granth Sahib,** and announced that the book was to stand in as the next guru. Since Gobind Singh's death, the Guru Granth Sahib has been Sikhism's spiritual guide and holy book, and Sikhs have become a visible minority, marked by their turbans.

Sikhs have a strong military tradition: the British labeled them one of the "martial races," and there are a disproportionate number of Sikhs in the Indian Army. Yet, they also have equally strong traditions of egalitarianism, hospitality, and community service (*seva*). The religion has no priests, nor are there fixed service times, although congregations often meet in the morning or evenings, and always on the eleventh day of each lunar month, and on the first day of the year. Sikh services include *kirtan* (hymn singing), when verses from the Adi Granth are sung to rhythmic clapping. Following services, Sikhs gather for a communal meal, where all sit at the same level and eat the same food cooked in the *gurudwara's langar* (kitchen). Strong believers in hospitality and kindness, Sikhs offer shelter and food to anyone who comes to their *gurudwaras*. Since Independence, Sikhism has been a rallying cry for Punjabi communalism, and even an independent Sikh homeland (for more information, see **Punjab and Haryana,** p. 262).

CHRISTIANITY

Since Independence, Christianity has become increasingly visible in India, attracting adherents and increasing its political relevance at a pace so rapid that the **Apostle Thomas** would surely be pleased. The apocryphal *Acts of the Apostles According to Thomas* indicate that he was chosen to spread the Gospel to India. While initially averse to the idea of the long trip, Thomas is said to have complied. He arrived on the coast of Kerala as early as AD 52, where he was able to attract some converts. Legend holds that twenty years later, Thomas was killed in Tamil Nadu, his body buried in Mylapore, a suburb of modern Chennai (see p. 532).

Since then, ships carrying missionaries have frequently sailed across the Arabian Sea, here and there seeding India's west coast with Western and Christian ideas. In the 6th century AD, the **Syrian Church** dispatched missionaries to India, introducing Syrian customs—many of which are still alive—to South Asia. In the 16th century, the Portuguese systematically sought to spread Christianity to India, converting without compunction. Soon after the arrival of the Jesuit Saint Francis Xavier in 1542, Portuguese-ruled Goa became a hotbed of **Catholicism** (see **Goa,** p. 446). However, during the early years of the East India Company, Protestant Christian missionary work was actively discouraged. The latter years of British rule were marked by an increase in missionary work which concentrated on building hospitals and schools. Grand churches were built as well, but these were mainly to serve the spiritual needs of the ruling British.

In the post-colonial period, the diffusion of Christianity in India has been marked by the growth of local churches rather than foreign missionary efforts. Today, there are about 25 million Christians in India, 50% more than there were in 1970. Most of India's Christians are Protestant; the largest denominations are the Church of South India and the Church of North India, both members of the worldwide Anglican church. There are also sizeable Catholic populations in several regions of India, particularly in Goa and the South. Christian worship in India varies from congregation to congregation. Even grass-roots churches look to British and American Christianity and welcome that influence, but Indian Christianity, even in missionary-founded churches, is still distinctly Indian—Christians sing devotional songs similar to Hindu *bhajans* and Muslim *qawwalis*, and go to religious retreats at Christian ashrams in the hills.

BUDDHISM

In spite of its origins in the Ganga Valley, only traces of Buddhism remain in India today. **Siddhartha Gautama,** who would come to be called the Buddha (Enlightened One), was born around 560 BC in **Lumbini,** just within the modern borders of Nepal (see p. 774). Gautama was a *kshatriya* prince, as was Mahavira. When Siddhartha was born in miraculous (and quasi-immaculate) fashion by emerging from between his mother's ribs, an astrologer prophesied that Siddhartha would either become a *chakravartin* (universal monarch) or a *buddha* (awakened one). In response, his father denied young Siddhartha his freedom but lavished him with all sorts of comforts in the hope that Siddhartha would appreciate his life in the palace. Finally, however, Siddhartha convinced his charioteer to take him around the outside world. On his famous four outings, he saw a very sick man, a very old man, a corpse, and finally a mendicant. Siddhartha Gautama, unsatisfied with the explanations of worldly suffering given by Hinduism and suddenly taken with the life and attitude of the mendicant, fled his princely life, leaving behind his wife, child, and kingdom at the age of 29. He wandered around the forests of India as an ascetic, joining a band of other ascetics, starving himself, meditating, and practicing other austerities until he was on the brink of death from extreme physical deprivation. He realized that neither abundant wealth nor punishing asceticism were emotionally or philosophically satisfying, and, despite the contempt of other ascetics, he chose a middle path. He sat and meditated under a **bodhi** tree in **Bodh Gaya,** Bihar (see p. 637), achieving **nirvana** (enlightenment) and resisting the temptations offered to him by the demon **Mara.** He set off to preach his discoveries about escaping the suffering of the world by overcoming desire, giving his first sermon in a deer park in **Sarnath** (see p. 208), in what has become known as the first turning of the wheel of Buddhist *dharma* or teachings (a somewhat different meaning attaches to *dharma* for Buddhists than for Hindus).

The Buddha advocated total detachment from the world. Desires arising for physical and mental things, he said, bring suffering, because they cause one to believe in a self and an individual existence, which are impermanent and fleeting illusions. One's goal should be the end of suffering through the end of desires, thus attaining a state of *nirvana* in which the flame of the self is blown out. At some point on the path to *nirvana*, even the desire for *nirvana* must be abandoned. The Buddha named right understanding, thought, speech, action, livelihood, effort, mindfulness, and concentration (the **Eightfold Path**) as the way to *nirvana*. He rejected all of Hinduism's gods and rituals, but preserved Hinduism's doctrine of *karma* and rebirth, although he rejected the concept of an enduring soul. Like a candle flame which lights another candle, an individual's actions give rise to other actions and reactions, but the second candle's flame is not the same flame as that of the first candle, and neither is the second individual (or soul) the same as the first. The Buddha also spoke against the caste system, and, as part of the Noble Eightfold Path, Buddhists became adamant advocates of **ahimsa** (non-violence).

This path of abandoning desires and worldly life seemed to put Buddhism out of the reach of most people, however, and the first Buddhists banded together in monastic communities. Lay people supported and contributed to these communities, although they did not observe the central tenet of renouncing the world; their practices were more devotional and reverential, so that they would gain merit in order to be reborn in a more favorable position for attaining *nirvana*. The Buddhist *dharma*, however, was responsible for the conversion of the Mauryan emperor **Ashoka** in the 3rd century BC, and his state patronage (along with the many edicts regarding proper Buddhist practice he put up on pillars throughout his empire) helped to make Buddhism a mass religion in India, and later, throughout Asia. Although Buddhism more or less died out in India in the first century AD, about seven million Buddhists are left in India. They are found mostly at the fringes of the Hindu world in Ladakh and Sikkim, where Buddhism never let go, and in places that have experienced a huge influx of Tibetan refugees, like Dharamsala, the headquarters of the Tibetan spiritual and political leadership-in-exile (for more information on **Tibetan Buddhism** and the Dalai Lama, see p. 713). In 1956, the leader of the Hindu Untouchables, Dr. B.R. Ambedkar publicly converted to Buddhism as a political protest against caste discrimination; he was followed by another 200,000 Untouchables (mainly in Maharashtra). And in spite of the relative scarcity of Indian Buddhists, sites like Sarnath and Bodh Gaya are active pilgrimage centers, attracting millions of pilgrims yearly from all over Asia.

JAINISM

Jainism began as one of a constellation of alternatives to established Brahmanical authority that came to the fore in a remarkable hundred-year period of religious renewal and regeneration around 500BC. Newly-developing Buddhism was another, and the speculative emphasis of the *Upanishads* was a third. Jainism has, of these three, perhaps the most radical approach. It begins with the belief that all life is sacred, and every living being (whether human, animal, plant, or insect) possesses an immortal soul, or **jiva;** an obligation of **ahimsa** (non-violence) toward all living beings is therefore fundamental in Jainism. They are strict vegetarians, and the most orthodox Jain monks wear a net over their mouths and nostrils to prevent the possibility of killing an insect that might fly in, as well as walking with a broom, sweeping the path before them so as not to crush any crawling creatures. Such behavior is in order to avoid the *karmic* consequences of the taking of life. Monks, nuns, and ambitious laity also undertake **tapas,** severe austerities—the supreme achievement in this line is death by self-starvation.

Jainism was founded by the *kshatriya* prince Vardhamana, or **Mahavira** (Great Hero). At the age of thirty, he renounced the world, plucked out all his hair, and lived from that time forward as a wandering ascetic. He began to gather disciples at the death of his predecessor, the ascetic **Parshavanatha;** these were called **Jains,** meaning "followers of the *jina* (conqueror)." Mahavira is venerated as the 24th and last of a line of **tirthankaras,** or "ford-makers"—those who show the way to another side of existence (Parshavanatha is the 23rd). There are two sects within Jainism: the **Digambara** (Sky-Clad) and the **Shvetambara** (White-Clad). The Digambaras are distinguished from the Shvetambaras by having more austere observances; most importantly, their monks and nuns go unclothed (hence Sky-Clad).

Ornate Jain temples are found throughout India, but most are in Western India, in Gujarat, Rajasthan, and along the west coast. The two most famous sites are at **Mt. Abu** in Rajasthan (p. 313) and **Sravanabelagola** in Karnataka (see p. 485). Today there are an estimated four to five million Jains living in India, mostly in Gujarat.

ZOROASTRIANISM

Founded in Persia between 500 BC and 700 BC by Zarathustra (or Zoroaster), **Zoroastrianism** understands the world as starkly divided between pure good (represented by the god **Ahura Mazda**) and pure evil (represented by the god **Angra Mainyu** and his evil minions, *daevas*). According to Zoroastrian belief, Saoshyant, an immaculately conceived messiah, will one day establish Ahura Mazda's reign of goodness on the earth. Zoroastrians believe that burial and cremation are a pollution of the earth, fire, and air, each of which is sacred for its purity; they leave their dead atop specially-designed Towers of Silence, where vultures have easy access.

Zoroastrianism was introduced to India in the 10th century, when Persian Zoroastrians arrived on the Gujarati coast, fleeing the advance of Islam through Iran and Central Asia. Called **Parsis** because of their ancient roots in Persia, today's dwindling numbers of Indian Zoroastrians—about 95,000 are left—are concentrated in western India, especially Bombay. Though few in number, the Parsis are known for their great wealth. One Parsi family, the Tatas, are renowned throughout India for their manufacturing industries (including India's first steel mill, built in 1908) and for their early financial support for India's independence movement.

THE ARTS
VISUAL ARTS

India has a very old and rich artistic tradition, fed over millennia by contact with other civilizations; yet it remains distinctly Indian. Indian artists have commonly made their works conform to some ideal, rather than show their subjects naturalistically. There are very few individual portraits in Indian art, and temples were often built in the same style regardless of whether wood or stone was used. The idealism of Indian art comes partly from its religious function—for centuries, most art was used to decorate sacred buildings or to illustrate sacred stories.

ARCHITECTURE

Because they used wood and brick as building materials, little is known about the architecture of the ancient Indians. The ruins of the Indus Valley Civilization (c. 2500-1800 BC) found in Pakistan consist of functional buildings arranged in planned cities. However, almost nothing remains from this time until the Maurya period (c. 324-184 BC), when builders began to make sparing use of stone. They built fortified cities and monasteries, but the most lasting structures of this time are *stupas*, huge hemispherical mounds of earth that usually contained Buddhist relics. *Stupas* can be elaborately decorated, with the mound sitting atop a terrace and surrounded by stone railings, and often capped by a stone parasol. The **Great**

Stupa at Sanchi, Madhya Pradesh (built in the first century BC) is the most famous of these structures (see p. 367).

The next few centuries saw the development of the temple in India, a momentous event for architecture. Early temples (Hindu, Jain, and Buddhist) were still built of wood, but in western India some were carved into the rock of the Western Ghats. These Buddhist **cave temples,** or *chaityas*, usually had a projecting apse that led to a long, pillared hall, at the end of which was placed a sacred object. The greatest of these cave-temples is found in **Ajanta** in Maharashtra (see p. 434). Cave-monasteries, with each cell hewn into the rock, were also carved at this time.

Medieval **Hindu temples** consisted only of a small, dark, square sanctum called the *garbhagriha* (womb chamber), which housed the deity. Soon a tall pyramidal spire, or *shikhara*, was added, symbolizing a connection between heaven and earth. Temples gradually became more and more elaborate, with other buildings acting as gateways for the worshipper. In the typical **North Indian** style, a series of up to four rooms leads to the sanctum in a straight line, and each of these outer rooms has its own *shikhara*, growing taller and taller up to the *shikhara* of the sanctum. This row of spires resembles a mountain range, symbolizing the Himalayan peaks inhabited by the gods. Unfortunately, many of the greatest North Indian medieval temples were destroyed by Islamic regimes from the 12th century onwards, but excellent examples remain in **Orissa** (see p. 612) and in **Khajuraho,** Madhya Pradesh (see p. 379). In **South India,** the temple sanctum was expanded to a larger room and surrounded by four rectangular entrance towers, or *gopurams*, which had *shikharas* of their own topped by barrel-vaults. These *gopurams* eventually became so exaggerated that they dwarfed the central shikhara. They marked a sacred area all around, creating great temple-city complexes such as those of **Madurai** (see p. 577) and **Srirangam** (see p. 576) in Tamil Nadu.

The conquest of India by Muslim forces in the 12th century brought the Islamic styles of Persia and Central Asia to India. Since Islam discourages crafting images of human or divine figures, Muslim rulers were glad to put their efforts into architecture, filling India with gorgeous domes, arches, geometric patterns, and calligraphic inscriptions. The most striking monuments to the early years of this Muslim conquest were Delhi's **Quwwat al Islam Masjid** (see p. 123) and **Qutb Minar** (see p. 122), which were built starting in 1199, using the remains of more than 20 Hindu and Jain temples. The most successful mix of Indian Hindu and Muslim architecture occurred in Gujarat, with the construction of such buildings as the **Jami Masjid** at Ahmedabad (see p. 345). Indian Islamic architecture reached its zenith under the patronage of the Mughal emperors. The pink and red post-and-lintel buildings of **Fatehpur Sikri** in Uttar Pradesh (see p. 179), built between 1569 and 1589, are a testament to the elegance of Mughal architecture. The Mughals also built one of the grandest monuments in the world: Agra's **Taj Mahal** (see p. 176), a white marble mausoleum adorned with calligraphy, studded with turquoise, jade, and coral, and surrounded by gardens.

With the decline of the Mughals and the coming of European imperial control, Western architectural forms began to appear in India. The 16th-century Portuguese filled their colony in **Goa** (see p. 438) with Baroque frills and ripples. In the 19th century the British imported their Neoclassical style to the metropolises of Calcutta (now Kolkata), Madras (now Chennai), and Bombay (now Mumbai), where it became fashionable among Indians as well. The British also built in neo-Gothic and neo-Saracenic styles, giving these huge cities a number of massive monuments, such as the **Victoria Memorial** in Kolkata (p. 655). The two great architectural projects of the 20th century in India, the construction of **New Delhi** in the 1920s (see p. 124) and **Chandigarh** (see p. 262) in the 1950s, have both been foreign attempts to find a kind of modern architecture that would suit India.

SCULPTURE

The peoples of the Indus Valley Civilization created many simple terra-cotta figurines and steatite seals with pictures of animals. As with architecture, however, there is a gap in the history of Indian sculpture until the 3rd century BC, when the Mauryan emperor **Ashoka** planted stone columns all over India as a symbol of his rule (see **The Mauryas,** p. 69). Many of the columns were topped with gorgeous animal sculptures, the greatest of which is probably the **Lion Capital** found at **Sarnath** in Uttar Pradesh (see p. 208). With four fierce lions sitting back-to-back on a lotus platform, the sculpture has become one of India's national emblems and appears on all Indian currency. The animals of the Mauryan capitals, which reveal some Persian influence but also bear the marks of an emerging Indian artistic style, are naturalistic and muscular, symbolizing the strength of Ashoka's political power.

The next two centuries saw the rise of two-dimensional **bas-relief sculpture,** which appeared frequently on the railings of **stupas,** telling stories from the life of the Buddha or myths about popular gods and goddesses. The **Great Stupa** at Sanchi in Madhya Pradesh (see p. 367), featuring figures full of energy, emotion, and incredible detail, represents the best of these works. The beginnings of Indian classical sculpture emerged in the first century AD when artists in **Mathura** (Uttar Pradesh) began to carve three-dimensional images of the Buddha (see p. 182). Unlike the earlier relief sculptures, which were primarily educational, these were sacred images used in worship. At around the same time, the **Gandhara** school of art developed in ares of the Punjab. Strongly influenced by Greek and Roman art, Gandhara artists turned out strikingly naturalistic images of the Buddha, emphasizing intricate folds of clothing and other details. Gandharan art looks like nothing else in Indian art, but it gradually evolved to resemble more idealized forms. During the Gupta period (4th-6th centuries AD) the sculptural school that began at Mathura reached its full flowering. Spreading throughout North India, the basic form of the Buddha image was applied to Hindu gods with multiple pairs of arms. The Buddha-figures of this time appear to look inward, toward spiritual contemplation, and they have a more delicate appearance than the Mathura Buddhas. Distinct regional styles spun off from the Mathura style, producing architectural wonders at **Sarnath** (Uttar Pradesh) and in the cave temples of **Ajanta** (see p. 434) and **Elephanta** (see p. 416) in Maharashtra.

Two separate schools of sculpture emerged during the **medieval period.** In North India, the sensuous and voluminous style gave way to a more elegant and rhythmic look. This style reached its apex around the 10th century, when it was used to adorn the exteriors of the great North Indian medieval temples. A distinctively **South Indian style** saw the creation of the great 7th-century bas-reliefs of **Mahabalipuram** (see p. 552), and the many small, light sculptures used to decorate temples in Tamil Nadu in the 9th century. **Bronze sculpture** in South India also reached a peak during the 9th and 10th centuries; the image of Shiva as Nataraja (King of the Dance) surrounded by a ring of fire is one of South India's greatest contributions to Indian art. This image can be found throughout Tamil Nadu, but the one at the **Brihadishwara Temple** in Thanjavur (see p. 570) is the most famous.

Regional traditions also developed at this time in other areas such as Maharashtra, where large, stocky figures were created, conforming to the properties of their material; the best of these are to be found at the **Kailasa Temple** in **Ellora** (see p. 434). Eventually, the Muslim dynasties, with their prohibiting the creation of such images, led to a gradual decline in the production of sculpture in the 12th century.

PAINTING

The art of painting has ancient roots in India, but, due to the humid climate, few examples have survived. The only early paintings that remain are those that were sheltered by rock, such as the **wall paintings** at **Ajanta** in Maharashtra, dating from the 2nd century BC to the 5th century AD (see p. 434). In ancient eastern India, miniature painting on palm leaves was common, though few examples still exist.

The style of Indian painting best known today began in western India during the medieval period. Colorful, cluttered scenes with figures shown in profile were made to illustrate **Jain manuscripts.** The western Indian style gradually spread throughout India and was used for all sorts of religious painting.

The Delhi Sultans and the Mughal Emperors, who began to arrive after the 12th century, brought with them a taste for Persian art, and radically changed the course of Indian painting. **Emperor Akbar** (r. 1556-1605), a great patron of the arts, was almost single-handedly responsible for creating the Mughal school of painting. He supervised his painters closely while they produced beautiful miniature illustrations for written histories, myths, and fables. Among other works, his court artists illuminated a magnificent Persian edition of the *Mahabharata*, which is now kept in the City Palace at Jaipur. As the Mughals settled in India, many began to disregard the Islamic injunction against the representation of human forms, and during the reign of **Jahangir** (1605-27), artistic emphasis shifted to portraiture.

The cool, delicate Mughal style influenced Hindu painting as well. Under the patronage of Hindu Rajput kings in the 16th and 17th centuries, the **Rajasthani School** emerged, combining the abstract forms of the western Indian style with some of the naturalism of the Mughal art. Rajput paintings usually depicted religious subjects, especially myths about Krishna, cavorting with his *gopis* or pining for his number-one maiden, Radha.

Both the Mughal and Rajasthani styles had declined by the 18th and 19th centuries, when European art became a major influence. The first Indian attempts to copy European styles, known collectively as the **Company School,** were lifeless engravings and watercolors. In the late 19th and early 20th centuries, however, artists of the Kolkata-based **Bengal School,** led by Rabindranath Tagore, combined older Indian styles with a touch of modern Western art. In the 20th century a few painters such as Jamini Roy and M. F. Hussain have been quite successful at mixing eastern and western influences. Indian painting has now become prominent in museums and galleries worldwide.

MUSIC

Largely considered a spiritual activity, Indian music is based on two elements, *raga* and *tala*, which form the melodic and rhythmic framework for the musician. Derived from the Sanskrit word which means "to color," *ragas* are the basis of composition and improvisation. Thousands of *ragas* exist, each associated with a particular moment of the day or season of the year. *Ragas* differ from one another according to the scale (which can be different, ascending and descending), and the *rasa* (mood) the composition explores. Each of the 72 parent scales has rules governing its use, but there is no fixed pitch—once the artist establishes the tonic of the *raga*, he is free to improvise as he likes, exploring the *raga's* potential to be created anew with each performance. Likewise, while the rhythmic cycle of the *tala* repeats itself, there are opportunities for improvisation between fixed beats. *Raga* and *tala* interact expressively with one another, with intonation and inflection converging through regular and off-beat emphases of time.

Modern Indian classical music, divisible between the northern **Hindustani** and the southern **Carnatic** styles, traces its origins to ancient chants. Musical form gained full exposition in the *Bharata Natyashastra*, considered the textual source of contemporary music. Classical music styles were also introduced by Persians and Turks, whose courts entertained musicians from around the Perso-Arabic world, presenting the song styles of *qawwali*, *khayal*, and lilting *ghazals*.

Indian classical musicians have gained a worldwide following. **Ravi Shankar,** who introduced Indian music to western ears in the 1960s and attracted the attention of the Beatles, continues to play the *sitar*, a fretted, 20-stringed instrument with a long teak wood neck fixed to a seasoned gourd. **Ali Akbar Khan** has achieved global acclaim for his enrapturing agility on the *sarod*, a fretless stringed instrument similar to a *sitar*). **Allah Rakha** and his son, **Zakir Hussain,** mesmerize audiences with their virtuosity on the *tabla*, a two-sided drum capable of producing many tones. Popular Carnatic musicians include the former prodigy **"Mandolin" U.Srinivasan,** and the legendary singer **M.S. Subbulakshmi.**

Folk music is linked closely to folk dance and varies from region to region. From Punjabi *bhangra* to Rajasthani *langa*, folk tunes remain close to the hearts of

Indians, gaining an even larger audience through the recent international releases of **Ila Arun** and *bhangra*-rap artists in the U.K. A unique genre of Bengali music is *Rabindrasangit*, the poetic words of Rabindranath Tagore set to quasi-classical song, the pride of the state of Bengal.

Popular music ranges from the "filmi" love songs of **Lata Mangeshkar** to the disco-hybrid-pop of divas Made in India to the techno-*bhangra* and *bhangra*-rap played in clubs and blasted from bachelor-filled cars all over India. Subjects run the gamut from the patriotic to the chaotic, from the ecstatic to the erotic, always making for fantastic sing-alongs. Like their voiceless on-screen counterparts, movie singers are elevated to hallowed ground. Popular singers include the playful and prolific **Kishore Kumar,** whose versatile voice has filled in the melodic blanks for countless actors.

DANCE

The cosmic dance of Nataraja, King of the Dance, reaches into every sphere of human activity in India. Born of particular regions and interwoven with music, India's numerous dance forms, including both classical and folk styles, evolved as acts of worship, dramatizing myths and legends. Technique and philosophy, passed down from gurus to students, have carried the "visual poetry" described in the *Natya Shastra* (dating between the 2nd century BC and the 2nd century AD), into modern times. **Bharatnatyam,** the classical dance form, considered India's most ancient, originated in the temples of Tamil Nadu. It is an intricate, fluid combination of eye movements, facial expressions, exacting hand gestures, and strong, rhythmic, ankle-bell-enhanced steps. The art was originally studied as a form of worship and performed by *devadasis*, women who lived in temples and devoted their lives to the temple's deity. *Bharatnatyam* now receives international appreciation. **Kathak,** first performed by *nautch* (dancing courtesans) against the opulent backdrop of North India's Mughal courts, employs dizzying speed and intricacy of footwork and hand gestures. **Kathakali,** an elaborately costumed form of dance-drama unique to Kerala, invents and presents local and mythological stories of heroes, lovers, gods, and battles. Developed from a rigorous system of yoga, the dancers, all male, must study for a minimum of 15 years. A typical study regimen includes strenuous exercise and massage to increase the arch and flexibility of the spine (see p. 522). **Kuchipudi,** a decorative dramatic dance form, originated in southern Andhra Pradesh as a means of worshipping Vishnu and Krishna. The old prohibitions against female dancers have since disappeared, and women have come to master the form. **Odissi,** a devotional dance form originating in Orissa, is both lyrical and sensuous. Regional folk dances are also incredibly popular in India, performed at numerous festivals and private celebrations. Folk dancing has become quite common in contemporary India, and most colleges have a folk dance troupe. **Bhangra,** a Punjabi dance, is one of the most popular and is traditionally performed by males dancing with large sticks in a circle while being accompanied by powerful drumming.

LITERATURE

The oldest known Indian literature is the writings of the Aryans, who brought Sanskrit with them to India around 1500 BC. Since the Aryans did not invent a writing system until about 800 BC, many of their tales were transmitted orally, changing from generation to generation. A remarkable exception is found in the **Vedas,** sacred hymns composed about 1400 BC, which were ritually memorized and passed down verbatim. During the last millennium BC, the greatest of the early Sanskrit stories, the **Mahabharata** (see p. 82) and the **Ramayana,** were composed (see p. 586).

Ancient India also had a secular Sanskrit literary tradition which reached its climax in the work of **Kalidasa,** who probably lived in the 4th century AD. Kalidasa's play *Shakuntala*, about a young girl who becomes the lover of **King Dushyanta,** who, typical male that he is, forgets her when he loses the ring she gave him, has had a tremendous effect on Indian literature.

The South developed its own literature, with annual *sangams*—gatherings of bards, beginning in the first century BC—giving rise to anthologies of poetry. By the 6th century AD, the **Tamil** literary tradition had produced two epics of its own, *Silappadigaram* and *Manimegalai.*

The next major literary trend was started by the Muslim rulers of the 13th century, the Mughals, who patronized the popular Sufi poet **Amir Khusrau** (1253-1325), nicknamed *Tuti-i-Hindi* ("Parrot of India"). Indians began to use Persian as both a literary medium and a *lingua franca.* Amir Khusrau also wrote extensively in Hindi, beginning the fusion of Hindu and Muslim traditions. The broad-minded Mughal emperor Akbar was a great patron of literature; his reign produced **Tulsi Das,** author of the *Ramcharitmanas,* the Hindi version of the *Ramayana,* which is considered a masterpiece in its language. The **Urdu** language (and its literature of *ghazal* poems) also emerged from the Hindu-Muslim synthesis.

The British invasion cast its greatest intellectual spell on Bengal, where English as a medium of instruction exposed them to the influence of Western authors like Shakespeare and Milton. Bankim Chandra Chatterjee combined the European novelistic genre with heady Indian patriotism in *Anandamath* ("The Abbey of Bliss," 1865). The **Bengali Renaissance** also produced **Rabindranath Tagore,** the greatest Indian artistic figure of the 20th century, whose poems, novels, songs, paintings, and plays captured the Bengali spirit. Tagore's English version of his sublime book *Gitanjali* won him the Nobel prize for literature in 1913, making him the first non-European to receive the honor.

British writers in India during the colonial period left a body of work that makes for arguably biased memoirs of the Raj. The "Bard of the Empire," **Rudyard Kipling,** was born in India and returned there after completing school. The author was responsible for a great deal of *sahib* literature, including *Kim,* a perceptive story of a half-white, half-Indian boy growing up in India. **E.M. Forster** presents a far more conflicted view of colonialism, famously depicting the tragedy of cultural misunderstanding in his novel *A Passage to India* (1924).

The most prominent trends in 20th-century Indian literature have been a shift toward humanistic concerns, a wider use of prose, and the adoption of the English language. Among the most influential writers of the early 20th century was **Mulk Raj Anand,** whose small but powerful novels *Untouchable* (1935) and *Coolie* (1936) railed against the cruelty of the caste system and economic exploitation. The South Indian novelist **R.K. Narayan,** perhaps India's greatest English-language writer of the second half of the 20th century, has become well-known in India and worldwide for such books as *The Man-Eater of Malgudi* (1961) and *The Vendor of Sweets* (1967). Proudly distinct literatures written in the various regional languages of India have also thrived in the 20th century. Indian novelists are increasingly breaking into the international literary scene. The only thread that holds them together as a literary "movement," however, is the fact that many of them live outside India and all of them write in English. **Salman Rushdie's** masterpiece *Midnight's Children,* written in 1980, set the stage for the world's new interest in "Post-colonial" literature. The famously reclusive Rushdie may be the best known contemporary Indian author, but a number of other writers, such as Vikram Seth, Anita Desai, Rohinton Mistry, Vikram Chandra, Kiran Desai, Gita Mehta, Amitav Ghosh, and Arundhati Roy, are becoming more and more familiar to an international audience.

FILM

India is home to the most prolific film industry in the world. When, in 1912, Dadasaheb Phalke produced the first Indian feature film, *Raja Harishchandra,* it marked the beginning of the country's obsession. Sound first invaded the frames in 1931 with *Alam Ara,* directed by **Ardeshir Irani.** The first of the "talkies" was very favorably received, but it also fragmented audiences into disparate language

BOLLYWOOD BEAT She emerges onto the scene of a lush landscape, singing a love song, while her sari-clad hips swing in sync with the accompanying beat. Hearing her voice, he rushes in to hold her in a rapturous embrace, yet is rudely interrupted by his evil nemesis, sent by her moral parents to break their love asunder. A brief yet boisterous scuffle ensues, and our hero emerges, unscathed, to return to the passionate embrace. The sun sets on the suddenly mountainous backdrop. This mythical utopia of otherwise unattainable romance and chivalry is available to the common man in the form of the ultimate kitsch, the **masala movie.**

Named after the eclectic spice mixture, these popular films contain a piquant mixture of action, comedy, romance, music, topped with the ridiculously impossible. Marks of this cinematic genre include the favorite gaudy colors, dramatic gestures, and more than a hint of eroticism. Indian pop music, in the form of **filmi** songs, commands the radio waves. Accommodating an average daily audience of 7.5 million, India churns out close to a thousand formula flicks a year in 23 languages. **Bollywood,** the nickname for the largest movie industry in the world, is based in Mumbai, while the thriving South Indian film industry is based in Chennai.

groups, of which Hindi and Tamil have the largest following. The arrival of sound was a milestone in the Indian film industry, and when directors realized that music was the way to overcome linguistic splintering, the Indian musical genre was born. Some films included nearly 70 songs, and hardly any Indian movie today lacks song and dance numbers. In the 1940s, the introduction of pre-recorded songs and playback singing meant that actors no longer had to be singers. The most successful playback singer was **Lata Mangeshkar,** who holds the world record with more than 25,000 recorded songs in her career.

In the 1930s and 1940s, the industry created the **social film** as a more relevant way of addressing the concerns of contemporary life, also introducing the preference for loudness—gaudy costumes, flighty and capricious music, exciting choreography, and implied sex—that has become the hallmark of Bombay film. **Mehboob Khan** (best known for *Mother India*) specialized in Muslim costume dramas and social tragedies, with a sense of the epic and spectacular. **Raj Kapoor,** the "founding father" of popular cinema, introduced a more casual attitude toward sex, against the standard backdrop of melodramatic love.

The decade of the 1950s belonged to the serious filmmaker, with European neo-realism displaying film's potential to function as a searing political and social statement. In the 1950s and 60s, Tamil film emerged as a vehicle to promote Tamil politics. Script writers like Karunanidhi and Anna Durai were key political figures as well. **N.T. Rama Rao** was a leading actor in Telugu cinema for 40 years before becoming the chief minister of the state of Andhra Pradesh.

Neo-realism influenced the emergent **art cinema,** whose leading director, **Satyajit Ray,** is well-known for *Pather Panchali* (1955), in which a diligently composed naturalism focuses on the isolation of rural life. Ray turns his attention to individual relationships in *Charulatha* (1964) and *Pratidwanai* (1970).

Following the tradition of art cinema, **Shyam Benegal** has been awarded the unofficial badge of "India's foremost living filmmaker." His film *Manthan*, about the Gujarat Cooperative Milk Marketing Federation, was funded by donations of two rupees each from 500,000 farmers. Adoor Gopalakrishnan and Aravindan, both directors from Kerala, speak specifically about their own cultures, and the possibility of change. Art films today, however, like **Shekhar Kapur's** *The Bandit Queen* and **Deepa Mehta**'s *Fire,* meet with critical success, their daring themes often leading to censorship or outright bans on their screening. Kapur recently made international news with his acclaimed film, *Elizabeth* (1998).

By the late 70s the classic Bollywood flick had been established—lots of sex, violence and drama. Amitabh Bachchan, with his image of an intelligent and rebellious hero seeking justice, displaced the romantic hero, starring in hit films such as *Sholay* (1975) which ran for five straight years in Bombay.

Contemporary popular films have not relinquished drama, but they have given it a more realistic spin. **Mira Nair's** *Salaam Bombay!* (1988) explores the lives of Bombay's street children, winning the filmmaker international praise and three awards at Cannes. **Mani Ratnam**'s acclaimed *Bombay* (1995), sets an inter-religious love story against the backdrop of religious riots in the big city.

THE MEDIA

Several English-language newspapers are printed in India, though their style tends to be a bit stodgy and archaic. Most newspapers are printed simultaneously in several cities. *The Times of India* is the nation's oldest and grandest newspaper, with good coverage of Indian news and a reputation for being pro-government. The *Times* is most popular in Delhi, Gujarat, Mumbai, and the rest of Maharashtra. The *Indian Express*, another national paper, is a bit less stuffy and more widely read in South India. The most popular paper in South India is *The Hindu*, a conservative paper which covers South Indian news in more detail. The pro-Congress *Hindustan Times* is the best-selling paper in Delhi, while in Kolkata and most of eastern India, *The Statesman* reigns supreme. *India Today* is an excellent fortnightly news magazine with feature articles on Indian politics and society. *Frontline*, published by *The Hindu*, and *Sunday Magazine* are also very good. A number of women's magazines, including *Femina* and *Woman's Era*, are popular in India, although they focus more on glamor than on feminist concerns.

India's national television company, **Doordarshan,** operates two channels. DD1 seems to broadcast endless pictures of hydroelectric projects approaching glorious completion, but it has news in English every night at 7pm. Also ubiquitous is the Hong Kong-based Star TV satellite network, TV tycoon Rupert Murdoch's Indian goldmine. Part of the network is "Channel V," whose music videos mix Indian masala in Western media, producing a brand of raunchiness with a unique Indian flavor. A crop of private channels have also opened in the last few years, relaying Hindi dramas by satellite to India and Indian workers in the Gulf states.

All India Radio has FM stations in Delhi, Mumbai, Kolkata, Chennai, and Panaji, including some English programming and a blend of Indian and Western pop, "composed in a vivacious and contemporary style and therefore highly popular with the urban youth."

SPORTS

Cricket isn't a sport in India—it's a national obsession. Despite the long hours, the long sleeves, and the hot sun, Indians turn out in droves both to watch and to play. Like many other former British colonies, India not only revels in the sport but also regularly beats England at its own game now. One of the few times that India forgets its internal conflicts and bands together as one nation is when the Indian national cricket team plays their arch-rival, **Pakistan.** Test matches are watched avidly by millions of Indians, in upper-middle class homes, and anywhere else that has a TV. Cricket is played on any available street or open ground, usually by young boys wearing little more than a pair of shorts and using sticks for bats and wickets. India reached the semi-finals of the **1996 World Cup** against Sri Lanka (the eventual winners of the World Cup), but the team was disqualified when "fans" began to throw bottles, rocks, and other assorted missiles onto the field.

India is also a consistent Olympic medal-winner in **field hockey.** Involvement with other sports is as much a function of social and regional divisions as anything else in India. Soccer and horse racing are especially popular in the east and in urban areas, while *kabbadi*, an indigenous game of tag, enjoys popularity throughout the north. Tennis, polo, squash, and other games brought to India by British imperialism——except—of course, for cricket—remain the province of the upper classes.

DHABAS If you take a private coach anywhere through India, you're sure to stop at a *dhaba*, the 24-hour truckers' stops. Here, the *parathas* and fried rice drip with grease, the *chai* comes with a kick, and a meal guaranteed to leave you sedentary for a while costs about Rs15. Not just for truckers, these dives also cater to college kids, who come in to refuel after a night at the dance clubs, or for all-night cram sessions. In the wee hours of the morning, truck drivers catch a few winks on the bamboo cots which functioned earlier in the evening as *sambar*-absorbent tables. Because *dhabas* serve a steady stream of hungry diners round the clock, their food is often left to boil and simmer for hours, killing germs and making *dhabas* a generally safe place to eat. Though the truckers' joints originated in Punjab and began serving mainly Punjabi cuisine, truck drivers have disseminated the *dhabas* through all of South Asia.

INDIA

FOOD AND DRINK

In the past, protracted Vedic prose prescribed every dash and pinch, every preparation, even every plate placement to provide the therapeutic and medicinal benefits of sustenance in just the right way. Nowadays, the more casual rules of good taste and great variety have taken over India's victuals. Meals vary regionally in taste, color, and texture but universally tend to smell strong and taste spicy.

A typical meal in many parts of North India consists of a bread, spicy vegetables, rice, and a lentil curry called **dal.** Breads come in different shapes and sizes: *chapati* is a thin whole wheat frisbee; **paratha** is a bi-layered bread, sometimes stuffed with vegetables; **naan** is a thicker, chewy bread made of white flour and baked in a **tandoor,** or a concave clay oven. Some rice dishes come with vegetables such as *biryani* or *pulao*. Meat options consist mostly of chicken and lamb dishes, since beef is off-limits to Hindus and pork is forbidden to Muslims. Appetizers and snacks include **samosa,** a spicy, fried potato turnover, and **bhel puri,** a sweet and sour mixture of fresh sprouts, potatoes, and yogurt. Desserts, often made out of boiled milk, tend to be extremely sweet.

South Indian cuisine employs rice and rice flour much more than the north, with **dosas** (thin pancakes) and **idlis** (thick steamed cakes) taking center stage. These are accompanied by vegetable broths like **sambar** (a thick and spicy lentil soup), **rasam** (thinner, with tomatoes and tamarind), and **kozhambu** (sour), which are poured on the rice and mixed with it. **Dosas** are commonly stuffed with spiced potatoes to make **masala dosas.** Less meat is consumed in the south, but seafood dishes abound in coastal areas. A standard South Indian meal comes in the form of a **thali,** a 40cm steel plate filled with *chapati, papadam*, rice, *sambar*, fresh yogurt, *dal*, and vegetable dishes.

Paan is an after-dinner chew, the cause of much of the crimson-colored spatterings that will surely line every street you traverse. A *paan* leaf can be filled with everything from coconut to sweetened rose petals to fennel seeds to flavored betel nut or tobacco. If you decide to try it, ask for a sweet *paan* with no tobacco, and go easy on the *kath-chuna* (limestone paste).

Sadly, some of India's most delicious drinks have to be avoided because they contain ice cubes made of untreated water. **Lassi,** made with yogurt and sugar, salt or fruit, and the widely sold sugarcane juice are popular to cool off with. Besides its more famous tea, coffee is also popular and delicious, especially in South India.

Drinking **alcohol** is an accepted practice in some parts of the country, while it is frowned upon in other regions and may be hard to find (see **Drugs and Alcohol,** p. 25). Popular brands of beer are Taj Mahal and Kingfisher, while the tasty London Pilsner is not common but worth the search. Be careful when ordering difficult or obscure mixed drinks—what gets called Kahlua could taste a bit like fermented Ovaltine and is probably an example of **Indian-Made Foreign Liquor (IMFL).** Imported brands like Smirnoff are available in big cities, and not-so-good domestic wines are available at nicer restaurants.

OTHER SOURCES

BOOKS

GENERAL

India, by Stanley Wolpert (1991). An easy-to-follow sampler of Indian culture and history by a well-known historian.

An Introduction to South Asia, by B. H. Farmer (1993). A geography-based description of South Asia, its history, politics, and economics.

Culture Shock! India, by Gitanjali Kolanad (1994). A guide to Indian customs and etiquette for those planning to live and work in India, with useful advice for all sorts of social situations and bureaucratic hassles.

TRAVEL/DESCRIPTION

India: A Million Mutinies Now, by V. S. Naipaul (1990). An excellent voyage in prose, this examines the subtle rebellions that characterize Indian life in the 90s.

Arrow of the Blue-Skinned God: Retracing the Ramayana though India, by Jonah Blank (1992). A fabulous book comparing the culture of 1990s India to the *dharmic* ideals of Lord Rama, the hero of the epic *Ramayana.*

The Great Railway Bazaar, by Paul Theroux (1975). A classic, worth reading for descriptions of what it feels like to be a Westerner jammed on a train with hundreds of others.

Tropical Classical, by Pico Iyer (1997). Essays and articles culled from the last ten years of the journalist's career. Always entertaining, and the history of the Raj is solid, as are the pieces set in Bombay and Nepal.

HISTORY

A Traveller's History of India, by Sinharaja Tammita-Delgoda (1995). A clear and readable introduction to Indian history for the beginner, with references to historical sites that can be visited today, and invaluable appendices.

The Discovery of India, by Jawaharlal Nehru (1946). Indian history as seen by the founder of modern India—a classic.

An Autobiography, or, the Story of My Experiments with Truth, by Mohandas K. Gandhi (1927). Gandhi's personal account of the development of his beliefs, with surprisingly little commentary on the political events of the time.

POLITICS AND ECONOMICS

India: Government and Politics in a Developing Nation, by Robert L. Hardgrave, Jr. and Stanley A. Kochanek (1996). The best summary of recent Indian political issues and the government of modern India.

Operation Bluestar: The True Story, by Lt. Gen. K.S. Brar (1993). An in-depth (albeit slanted) account of the Golden Temple's turmoil from an Indian commando.

India: Economic Development and Social Opportunity, by Jean Drèze and Amartya Sen (1995). Analyzes the economic development of India from a social perspective and with empathy for the underprivileged.

RELIGION

Hinduism: A Cultural Perspective, by David R. Kinsley (1993). A comprehensive, thematic introduction to Hindu beliefs, practices and culture.

Banaras: City of Light, by Diana L. Eck (1982). An exploration of the holy city that attempts to "see Kashi through Hindu eyes." A wonderful introduction to the complexities and contradictions of Hinduism in general, and a beautiful description of Varanasi, a city that Eck obviously loves.

What The Buddha Taught, by Walpola Rahula (1959). A Sri Lankan monk's authoritative and comprehensible explanation of Theravada Buddhist philosophy.

WOMEN'S ISSUES

May You Be the Mother of a Hundred Sons, by Elizabeth Bumiller (1990). A British journalist's exploration of *sati,* sex-selective abortion, and dowry deaths, this is a good introduction to Indian society and politics, with a great chapter on Hindi film actresses.

Unveiling India, by Anees Jung (1987). A journalist who grew up in a family practicing strict Muslim *purdah,* Jung examines the lives of Indian women.

FICTION

Midnight's Children, by Salman Rushdie (1980). Rushdie's masterpiece tells the magical tale of children born at midnight on the eve of India's independence, and how the country's life and theirs evolve together.

Such a Long Journey, by Rohinton Mistry (1992). A humanely written tale of Bombay Parsis (Zoroastrians) who inadvertently become involved in Indira Gandhi's government corruption; a great read with an introduction to Parsi culture and India in the 1970s.

Karma Cola, by Gita Mehta (1979). A cynical journalistic satire about Westerners in India, offering insight into dark and comic sides of traveler culture.

The God of Small Things, by Arundhati Roy (1997). An exquisitely woven story of love, betrayal, and tragedy set against the backdrop Kerala's social and political landscape.

A Passage to India, by E.M. Forster (1924). This oft-cited novel tells the story of the friendship of an Englishman and an Indian during the British Raj. An honest, sensitive account whose observations about culture shock still hold true today.

Malgudi Days, R.K. Narayan (1986). Centarian Narayan is one of the few English-language Indian writers who lives in India. No post-colonial angst here, just wry, subtle, charming stories set in a fictional village in Tamil Nadu.

POETRY

Gitanjali, by Rabindranath Tagore (1913). Nobel prize-winning work of the great Bengali poet, it uses images from Indian love poetry to discuss a relationship with God.

The Meghaduta, by Kalidasa (4th century AD). The great Sanskrit poet's account of a cloud's journey across India, surveying the landscape and human activity as it carries a message between separated lovers.

PHOTOGRAPHY

The Ganges, by Raghubir Singh (1992). A compilation of much of the photographer's work, following the course of the Ganga from source to sea, with landscapes and people snapped into amazing configurations.

FILMS

Pather Panchali, by Satyajit Ray (1955). The first film by the late master of Indian cinema. Produced on weekends with a borrowed camera and unpaid actors, its visuals capture the beauty of the Bengali landscape and the isolation of the village in which Apu and Durga, the hero and heroine, live; musical accompaniment by Ravi Shankar.

Gandhi, by Richard Attenborough (1981). A grossly romanticized tale of the Mahatma's life and the Indian Independence movement. Take any history lessons with a grain of salt—watch it only for Ben Kingsley's great portrayal of Gandhi.

Salaam Bombay, by Mira Nair (1988). A disturbing tale of Bombay's street children, This fictional story told in documentary style is somewhat exploitative, and the subtitles aren't always accurate, but it's a moving and well-acted film.

Bandit Queen, Shekhar Kapur (1994). The story of Phoolan Devi, a low-caste bandit-turned-politician. A horrifyingly graphic, true-life portrayal of caste oppression in Uttar Pradesh.

Hello Photo, by Nina Davenport (1994). The next best thing to actually traveling in India, this short, stunning film shows one woman's experience of looking at India and being looked at.

DELHI दिल्ली

India's capital and third-largest city, Delhi offers both sights to stop your heart and the frenetic energy needed to revive it. Unfortunately, the city needs to be coped with before it can be coddled. All of the contrasts familiar to travelers in India are in full force here: rich and poor, old and new, chaos and order. What distinguishes India's capital from other major cities is the polarity between its government and its people. Delhi maintains a dignified front as a national capital, with its official-looking edifices spanning broad green blocks in the city's south-central portion. Nobody sleeps on the lawns between the monuments, and the billboards (in English, of course) fervently promote various welfare campaigns. But belying this facade of control are Delhi's other streets, crammed with the city's legendary slow-churning traffic and threaded by careening auto-rickshaws. It is in these streets that real life happens, where the capital's ballyhooed cosmopolitanism is manufactured and displayed, where Punjabi Sikhs, colorfully dressed Rajasthani women, dreadlocked *sadhus*, and pavement-dwellers all rub shoulders, sharing space, if not conversation. And it is in these streets that North India's heat and humidity (and winter chill) are refracted through layers of polluted air, acting as a relentless social leveler, forcing the climate-controlled few and the shelterless masses to sweat or shiver together—pressed together, layer upon layer, like the city's history itself.

The history of Delhi begins in AD 736, with the founding of Lal Kot by the Tomara clan of Rajputs. Their tumultuous and gory rule was abruptly ended in 1192 by Muhammad Gauri and his slave general Qutb-ud-din Aibak, who swept in from Central Asia and conquered North India, introducing Islam and founding the Delhi Sultanate. For the next 300 years Delhi was wracked by political instability, especially in 1398, when the city was sacked by another Central Asian warlord, Timur. By the early 16th century the Lodi dynasty, the Delhi Sultanate's ruling family, had made its share of enemies in the region. Too meek to challenge the Sultanate on their own, they requested help from Timur's great-grandson, Babur. Babur beat the Lodis into submission and launched the Mughal Empire, which would untie much of South Asia for the next two centuries. The Mughals repeatedly shifted their capital between Delhi and Agra, leaving both cities with monumental tombs, palaces, and forts. Old Delhi's grandest edifices were built during the 17th century by the Mughal emperor Shah Jahan. In the 18th century, however, Mughal strength waned, and the British moved in. In 1911, the British imperial capital was moved to Delhi, and the city began to attract the attention of Indian nationalists, who promised that the flag of an Indian republic would one day fly from the Red Fort. Marking the occasion with a speech by the Prime Minister delivered from the Red Fort and a tremendous parade in front of the city's most important British buildings, today's Delhi celebrates the vindication of the nationalists' predictions every August 15, Independence Day.

HIGHLIGHTS OF DELHI

◼ **Old Delhi** swells with **bazaars** (p. 123) and monuments, including the **Red Fort** (p. 120) and **Jamma Masjid** (p. 121), the largest mosque in India.

◼ South of the city center are the emperor **Humayan's Tomb** (p. 125) and the phenomenal Mughal ruins at the **Qutb Minar complex** (p. 122).

◼ Delhi's lotus shaped, garden-ringed **Baha'i Temple** (p. 124) is one of India's most beautiful modern structures.

◼ The immensely intricate **Jantar Mantar** (p. 125) is an 18th-century astronomical observatory set in stone, complete with massive marble sundials.

Delhi's population is growing rapidly; by some counts it has already topped 10 million. A dramatic influx of modern fortune-seekers, as well as poor and illiterate rural families seeking relief, has caused Delhi to swell and sprawl. South Delhi, which once seemed downright suburban, has been swallowed up and now functions as the center of the city's life.

GETTING THERE AND AWAY

INTERNATIONAL FLIGHTS

 WARNING. You may be tired from your flight, but keep your wits about you, even in the airport. If you don't understand what's going on, or feel pressured or herded in a particular direction, stop to collect yourself—there's really no hurry. When paying at a counter, **count out your cash as you hand it over.** Switch-the-bill schemes are common. **Never** let a cab driver convince you that the hotel you ask for is full or closed. And remember, **the more assertive someone is with their offers of help, the more likely it is that there's something in it for them.** If you need help or have a question, ask someone who hasn't approached you first.

Indira Gandhi International Airport (tel. 565 2011) serves as the main entry and departure point for international flights. There is a 24-hour **State Bank of India** office in the arrivals hall, next to the **Government of India Tourism** and the **Delhi Tourism** information desks. This is the place to pay for a **pre-paid taxi,** the most hassle-free way to get into the city center. Once you pay, you'll receive a receipt with your destination and a taxi number written on it—make sure that the driver takes you where *you* want to go. Delhi Transport Corporation (DTC), the Ex-Servicemen's Shuttle, and EATS (tel. 331 6530) run frequent **buses** to Connaught Place from the airport (Rs30). DTC buses also stop at New Delhi Railway Station and the Interstate Bus Terminal (ISBT) at Kashmiri Gate. To get to the airport (international and domestic terminals), pick up the EATS bus near the middle circle on Janpath. Buses leave daily (4, 5:30, 7:30, 9am, 2, 3:30, 6, 7, 10, and 11:30pm; Rs30). **Auto-rickshaws** shuttle passengers from the airport to downtown at cheaper rates than taxis, but without the security of the pre-payment system.

INTERNATIONAL AIRLINES. Air France, Scindia House, Janpath (tel. 373 8004); **Air India,** Jeevan Bharati Bldg. (tel. 331 3777); **Alitalia,** 16 Barakhamba Rd. (tel. 332 9551); **Biman,** World Trade Center (tel. 335 4401); **British Airways,** DLF Bldg., Sansad Marg (tel. 332 0900); **Cathay Pacific,** Tolstoy House (tel. 332 3332); **Delta,** DLF Centre, Sansad Marg (tel. 373 0197); **El Al,** Prakash Deep Bldg., Tolstoy Marg (tel. 335 7965); **Gulf Air,** G-12, Connaught Pl. (tel. 332 4293); **KLM/Northwest,** Prakash Deep Bldg., Tolstoy Marg (tel. 335 7747); **Kuwait Airlines,** 16 Barakhamba Rd. (tel. 335 4373); **Lufthansa,** 56 Janpath (tel. 332 7268); **Qantas,** Mohan Dev Bldg., Tolstoy Marg (tel. 332 9027); **RNAC (Royal Nepal Airlines),** 44 Janpath (tel. 332 1164); **Singapore Airlines,** Ashoka Estate Bldg., Barakhamba Rd. (tel. 332 9036); **Swissair,** DLF Centre, Sansad Marg (tel. 332 5511); **Thai Airways,** Park Royal Hotel, American Plaza, Nehru Palace (tel. 623 9133); and **United Airlines,** 14 KG Marg (tel. 335 3377).

DOMESTIC FLIGHTS

The airport's **domestic terminal** (tel. 566 5121) is 5km from the international terminal. **Pre-paid taxis, buses,** and **rickshaws** run to and from downtown (see above). Domestic airlines include: **Archana Airways** (tel. 684 2001); **Indian Airlines** (tel. 371 9168); **Jagson** (tel. 372 1594); **Jet Airways** (tel. 685 3700); **Sahara** (tel. 332 6851). Flights to: **Agra** (1 per day, 40min., US$50); **Ahmedabad** (4-6 per day, 1½hr., US$120); **Amritsar** (M, W, and F; 1½hr.; US$90); **Aurangabad** (Tu, Th, and Sa; 3½hr.; US$150); **Bagdogra** (1-2 per day, 2hr., US$185); **Bangalore** (7 per day, 2½hr., US$230); **Bhopal** (1-2 per day, 2hr., US$105); **Bhubaneswar** (1 per day, 2hr., US$195);

DELHI

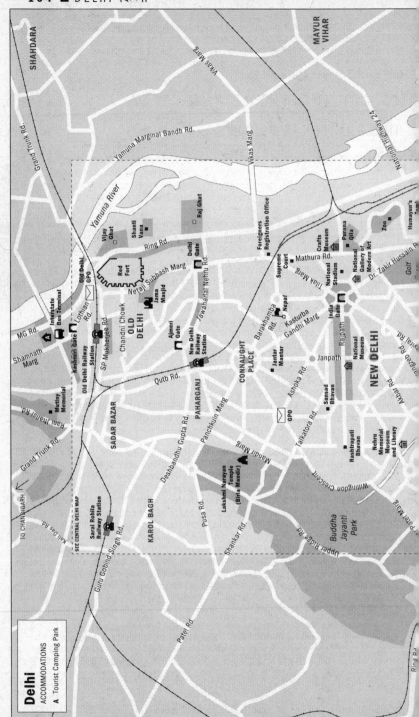

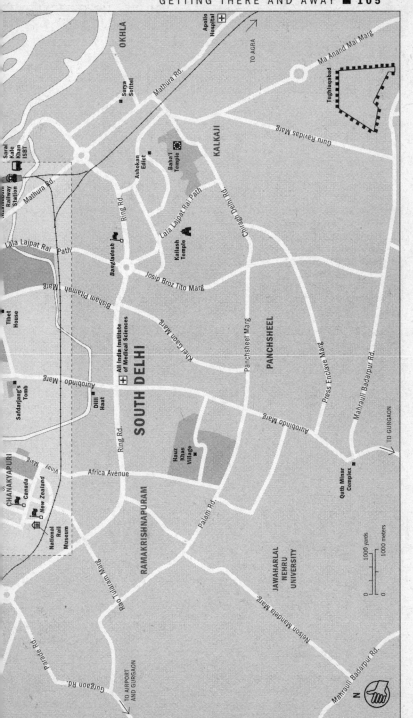

OKHLA

Apollo
Hospital

TO AGRA

Ma Anand Mai Marg

Surya
Sofitel

Mathura Rd.

Tughluqabad

Guru Ravidas Marg

Sarai
Kale
Khan
ISBT

Railway
Station

Mathura rd.

Ashokan
Edict

Baha'i
Temple

KALKAJI

Lala Lajpat Rai Path

Ring Rd.

Lala Lajpat Rai Path

Chirah Delhi Rd.

Bangladesh

Kailash
Temple

Bisham Pitamah Marg

Josip Broz Tito Marg

Tibet
House

All India Institute
of Medical Sciences

Panchsheel Marg

PANCHSHEEL

Press Enclave Marg

Mahrauli Badarpur Rd.

Safdarjang's
Tomb

Aurobindo Marg

Kidai Gaon Marg

SOUTH DELHI

Dilli
Haat

Ring Rd.

Aurobindo Marg

TO GURGAON

CHANAKYAPURI

Canada

New Zealand

Vinay Marg

Africa Avenue

Hauz
Khas
Village

Palam Rd.

Qutb Minar
Complex

National
Rail
Museum

RAMAKRISHNAPURAM

Raj Lallaram Marg

JAWAHARLAL
NEHRU
UNIVERSITY

Nelson Mandela Marg

Parade Rd.

Gurgaon Rd.

TO AIRPORT
AND GURGAON

Mahrauli Badarpur Rd.

N

1000 yards

1000 meters

0

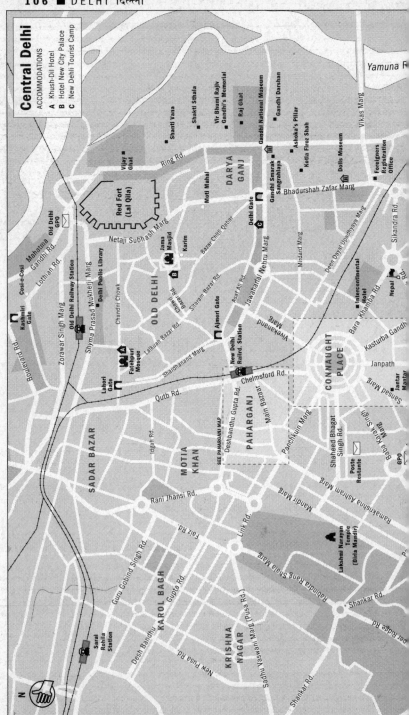

Central Delhi

ACCOMMODATIONS
A Khush-Dil Hotel
B Hotel New City Palace
C New Dehli Tourist Camp

Yamuna R

N

Vijay Ghat

Shanti Vana

Shakti Sthala

Vir Bhumi Rajiv Gandhi's Memorial

Raj Ghat

Gandhi National Museum

Gandhi Darshan

Ashoka's Pillar

Kotla Firoz Shah

Dolls Museum

Foreigners Registration Office

Ring Rd.

DARYA GANJ

Gandhi Smarak Sangrahalaya

Bhadurshah Zafar Marg

Old Delhi GPO

Red Fort (Lal Qila)

Mahatma Gandhi Rd.

Lothian Rd.

Moti Mahal

Delhi Gate

Vikas Marg

Sikandra Rd.

Netaji Subhash Marg

Jama Masjid

Karim

Bazar Chitli Qabar

Mirdard Marg

Deen Dayal Upadhyaya Marg

Zorawar Singh Marg

Shyma Prasad Mukherji Marg

Delhi Public Library

Chandni Chowk

OLD DELHI

Gali

Sitaram Bazar Rd.

Asar Ali Rd.

Jawaharlal Nehru Marg

Nepal

Intercontinental Hotel

Kashmiri Gate

Cosi-e-Cosi

Old Delhi Railway Station

Fatehpuri Mosque

Lalkuan Bazar Rd.

Almeri Gate

Vivekanand Marg

Bara Khamba Rd.

Boulevard Rd.

Lahori Gate

Shardhanand Marg

New Delhi Railrd. Station

CONNAUGHT PLACE

Kasturba Gandh

Qutb Rd.

Chelmsford Rd.

Janpath

Jantar Mantar

Sansad Marg

SADAR BAZAR

Idgah Rd.

SEE PAHARGANJ MAP

Deshbandhu Gupta Rd.

PAHARGANJ

Main Bazaar

Panchkuin Marg

Shaheed Bhagat Singh Rd.

Baba Kharak Singh Marg

Poste Restante

GPO

MOTIA KHAN

Rani Jhansi Rd.

Faiz Rd.

Link Rd.

Ramakrishna Ashram Marg

Mandir Marg

Guru Gobind Singh Rd.

Gupta Rd.

KAROL BAGH

Lakshmi Narayan Temple (Birla Mandir)

Rabindra Rang Shala Marg

Saral Rohila Station

Desh Bandhu Rd.

New Pusa Rd.

KRISHNA NAGAR

Sadhu Vaswani Marg (Pusa Rd.)

Shankar Rd.

Shankar Rd.

per Ridge Rd.

Kolkata (7-10 per day, 2hr., US$180); **Chandigarh** (M, W, and F; 1hr.; US$65); **Chennai** (5-6 per day, 3hr., US$235); **Cochin** (1 per day, 4hr., US$300); **Goa** (2 per day, 2½hr., US$210); **Guwahati** (1 per day, 2½hr., US$210); **Gwalior** (M-Tu, Th, and Sa; 1hr.; US$60); **Hyderabad** (2 per day, 2hr., US$185); **Jaipur** (2-3 per day, 45min., US$58); **Jammu** (2 per day, 1hr., US$105); **Khajuraho** (1 per day, 1½hr., US$90); **Kullu** (4-5 per day, 1½hr., US$150); **Leh** (Tu, Th, Sa, and Su; 1hr.; US$105); **Lucknow** (3-4 per day, 1hr., US$80); **Mumbai** (frequent, 2hr., US$160); **Nagpur** (1 per day, 1½hr., US$135); **Patna** (2-3 per day, 1½hr., US$130); **Ranchi** (1 per day, 3hr., US$170); **Shimla** (1 per day, 1hr., US$105); **Srinagar** (2-3 per day, 1½hr., US$115); **Trivandrum** (1 per day, 4½hr., US$325); **Udaipur** (1-2 per day, 2hr., US$95); and **Varanasi** (2-3 per day, 1-2hr., US$110). Flights to **Dhaka, Bangladesh** (W and Su, 2½hr., US$195) and **Kathmandu, Nepal** (3-5 per day, 3hr., US$142) also depart from the domestic terminal.

TRAINS

> **WARNING.** Delhi's **touts** (young men employed by shop-owners to bring in customers) are the best in the business; they will go to incredible lengths to get you into their employer's office. Although few are actually out to rob or hurt you, touts routinely (and elaborately) lie to tourists, using false identification and guilt trips (e.g., "Why don't you trust me? I'm trying to help you."). For more information, see **Touts, Middlemen, and Scams,** p. 24.

STATIONS. The **New Delhi Railway Station,** the main depot for trains in and out of Delhi, is north of Connaught Pl., at the east end of Paharganj Main Bazaar. It is a chaotic place, so be prepared to push your way around, and beware of theft. Your best bet is to get tickets from the **International Tourist Bureau** (tel. 373 4164), a large room upstairs at Platform 1. The office books reservations on tourist-quota seats and sells Indrail passes. Tickets here must be bought in foreign currency or in rupees with encashment certificates. (Open M-Sa 8am-5pm.) Do not go to the dodgy tourist offices around the railway station. Foreigners can also book train tickets at the usual places: at the windows in the station (for general booking) or the **Computerized Reservation Terminal,** one block south of the station on Chelmsford Rd. Book at least a day or two ahead for some of the more popular trains.

Delhi has three other railway stations: **Delhi Station,** in Old Delhi; **Hazrat Nizamuddin Station,** in the southeast part of the city; and **Sarai Rohilla,** in the northwest. Trains leaving from all stations can be booked at the International Tourist Bureau. Important phone numbers are: **general enquiry** (tel. 331 3535 or 131), **arrivals** (tel. 1331-4), **departures** (tel. 1336-9), and **reservations** (tel. 334 8686 or 334 8787).

DEPARTURES. You can make a train reservation between any two stations in India from Delhi. Clear **timetables** for major destinations are posted in the International Tourist Bureau. The comprehensive *Trains at a Glance* booklet can be bought at the enquiry counter on Platform 1 (Rs25). A/C *Shatabdi Express* trains cost more than standard 2nd-class tickets, but they get you where you're going faster, provide safe food and comfy seats, and feature nice India Tourism posters to make up for the fact that you won't see much out of the tinted windows. The listings that follow represent only the tiniest and fastest selection from among the many trains available from **New Delhi Railway Station.** To: **Ajmer** (#2015, 6:15am, 6½hr., Rs630) via **Jaipur** (4½hr., Rs495); **Amritsar** (#2013, 4:30pm, 6hr., Rs610); **Bhopal** (#2002, 6:15am, 8hr., Rs850) via **Agra** (2hr., Rs390); **Chandigarh** (#2005, 5:15pm, 3hr., Rs435); **Dehra Dun** (#2017, 7:10am, 5hr., Rs495); **Lucknow** (#2004, 6:20am, 6½hr., Rs640) via **Kanpur** (5hr., Rs5850). A/C 3-tier *Rajdhani Express* trains run to **Bangalore,** from H. Nizamuddin (#2430, 9:30am, 34hr., Rs2205); **Chennai,** from H. Nizamuddin (#2634, 3:15pm, 29hr., Rs2045); **Mumbai** (#2952, 4pm, 17hr.; or #2954, 4:50pm, Rs1485); **Varanasi** (#2302, W-Th and Sa-M 5:15pm, 9hr., Rs1130) via **Allahabad** (7hr., Rs975).

BUSES

TERMINALS. There are three **interstate bus terminals (ISBTs)** in Delhi. The new **Anand Vihar ISBT** (tel. 214 8097), east of the Yamuna River, runs buses to Lucknow, Ramnagar (for Corbett National Park), Bareilly, Almora, Nainital, Pithoragarh, and Halwandi. **Sarai Kale Khan ISBT** (tel. 469 8343), two blocks east of the Nizamuddin Railway Station, sends buses to Ajmer, Jaipur, Jodhpur, Ghaziabad, and Udaipur. **ISBT Kashmiri Gate** (tel. 296 0290), north of (Old) Delhi Station, services most other destinations, including Amritsar, Chandigarh, Dehra Dun, Dharamsala, Haridwar, Jammu, Kullu, Manali, Mussoorie, Rishikesh, and Shimla. There is a pre-paid auto-rickshaw stand at Kashmiri Gate (to Paharganj Rs25, Connaught Place Rs32). For enquiries, go to the main information desk. All of the major bus companies have offices on the first floor; if you are led to the third floor to make deluxe bus bookings, something is fishy. **Steer clear of touts offering implausibly low rates.**

DEPARTURES. To obtain bus departure information, it's best to contact the bus company directly. To find out which company serves which destinations, call one of the bus stations (or tel. 296 8836) for general inquiries. Bus companies include: **Himachal Road Transport Company,** 1 Rajpur Rd. (tel. 296 6725); **U.P. Roadways,** Ajmeri Gate (tel. 296 8709 or 214 9089); **Rajasthan Roadways,** Bikaner House (tel. 464 3731); **Punjab Roadways** (tel. 296 7842); and **Haryana Roadways** (tel. 296 1262). Government-run **Delhi Transit Corporation (DTC)** offers deluxe buses to many cities in northern India. Be sure to shop around if you decide to book a seat on a private bus. Hotels usually charge higher rates, so it's better to book directly through a reputable agency (see **Budget Travel,** p. 112).

Ordinary and deluxe buses leave from all three terminals, but Kashmir Gate sees the most traffic. Daily buses from Delhi head to: **Almora** (5 per day 6-9pm, 11hr., Rs160); **Amritsar** (every 30min. 4:30am-10pm, 10hr., Rs150); **Chandigarh** (every 20min. 3:30am-1:30am, 5½hr., Rs80); **Dehra Dun** (every 30min. 5am-10:30pm, 6½hr., Rs95/170); **Dharamsala** (6 per day, 13hr., Rs160/250); **Faizabad** (every hr. 4am-6pm, 18hr., Rs220); **Haldwani** (every hr. 5am-10pm, 8hr., Rs120); **Haridwar** (every 30min. 4am-midnight, 5½hr., Rs77); **Jaipur** (every 30min., 6hr., Rs92); **Jammu** (8, 9pm, and midnight; 12hr.; Rs210); **Jodhpur** (6am, 6, and 11pm; 16hr.; Rs203/346); **Lucknow** (every hr. 7am-9pm, 13hr., Rs160); **Manali** (10 per day, 15hr., Rs215/450); **Mussoorie** (5:30am and 10:30pm, 8hr., Rs145); **Nainital** (6, 7am, 8, and 9:30pm; 9hr.; Rs159); **Pushkar** (every 30min. 7am-midnight, 10½hr., Rs130) via **Ajmer** (10hr., Rs123); **Ramnagar** for Corbett National Park (5, 6, 7, 8am, and every 30min. 5-9pm; 7hr.; Rs95); **Rishikesh** (every hr. 4am-10pm, 7hr., Rs89); **Shimla** (10 per day 4:50-9:25pm, 10hr., Rs125/244); and **Udaipur** (1:30, 5:30, and 6:30pm; 17hr.; Rs223/386).

▐ GETTING AROUND

RICKSHAWS

Auto-rickshaw drivers have a knack for overcharging, driving around in circles and *then* overcharging or changing the agreed fare at the end of the trip. Fluctuating petrol prices have made most meters obsolete, adding a 75% surcharge to the fare. It is usually better to set the auto-rickshaw price in advance if you don't know your way around Delhi—insisting on going by the meter can provoke the auto-*wallahs* to add an extra 1 to 3km to the journey. **Pre-paid autos** are available at the airports, train, and bus stations, and at the Delhi Traffic Police Booth on Janpath, near the Government of India Tourist Office. The maximum reasonable non-pre-paid fares are: Airport to Connaught or Paharganj Rs150-200; Paharganj to Connaught Rs15-20; Paharganj to Old Delhi Railway Rs25-30; Connaught to Old Delhi Rs25-30; Connaught to Chanakyapuri Rs35-40. **Cycle-rickshaws** can't go through parts of New Delhi, but in the narrow streets of Old Delhi, they are ideal. Typical fares: Old Delhi to New Delhi Station (Rs30); Paharganj to Connaught Place (Rs5).

DELHI

BUSES

Buses are certainly cheap, but using them entails long delays and big crowds. Women can sit on specially marked seats to one side. **Delhi Transport Corp (DTC)** is currently struggling with private companies to bring local bus service under government control—in the meantime, things continue to be chaotic and confusing. Many bus lines run sporadically and don't have numbers; for up-to-date information, try the Government of India Tourist Office. (Bus fares are Rs1-15.)

Bus #	Route
101	Chandi Chowk/Red Fort-Bus Station-Connaught Place
425	Connaught Place-Nizamuddin
505	City Center-Qutb Minar
620	Chanakyapuri-Hauz Khas

BICYCLES

Cycling in Delhi can be harrowing but also fun. Old Delhi is congested and slow, New Delhi fast and frantic. Exploring by bike allows you to see places tourists don't usually go, and also gives you a speedy getaway option when the constant attention of touts starts to get tiresome. **Mehta Cycles** (also known as Aadya Shakti Handicrafts), 2 stores east of the Kesri Hotel on Main Bazaar, Paharganj (tel. 354 0370), rents bikes (Rs30 per day, Rs5 per hr., Rs5 overnight charge; Rs600 deposit). Bell and lock are included, but no helmets are available. (Open daily 9am-8pm.)

✈ ORIENTATION

Situated west of the Yamuna River, Delhi runs 30km from north to south and 10km from east to west. The northern two-thirds of the city are circled by the **Ring Road.** Just west of the **New Delhi Railway Station** is **Paharganj,** Delhi's backpacker ghetto, crammed with budget hotels, tie-dye-clad Europeans, and shops full of plastic shoes. The area north of the station is **Old Delhi.** Built by Shah Jahan (and, also called Shahjahanabad), Old Delhi is a delightfully tatty tangle of streets and bazaars. The main road in this part of town is the **Chandni Chowk,** which runs from east to west across the old city.

South of New Delhi Station, the center of **New Delhi** radiates out from **Connaught Place,** a circular hub of two-story colonnaded buildings. Connaught Pl. is the throbbing heart (and capitalist soul) of New Delhi. If you're looking for an AmEx office, a copy of last Tuesday's *USA Today*, or the Kazakhstan Airlines reservation desk, you've come to the right place. Of course, with tourists come touts and tricksters—Connaught Pl.'s hustlers are aggressive and exceptionally savvy; ignore them. Of the streets that break off Connaught Pl., **Sansad Marg** is the most crowded; it leads to the Raj-era parliamentary buildings, 2km west of **India Gate,** straight down **Raj Path.** One kilometer south of the parliamentary buildings is **Chanakyapuri,** home to the embassies of many western countries. **South Delhi** unofficially begins just south of Chanakyapuri. Except for Ring Rd. and **Mehrauli Badarpur Road,** South Delhi's major thoroughfares run north-south. In the center is **Aurobindo Marg,** which connects Safdarjang's tomb with the **Qutb Minar Complex;** in the east is **Mathura Road,** which slices through **Nizamuddin** and turns into **Zakir Hussain Road** as it proceeds southeast from India Gate.

🛈 PRACTICAL INFORMATION

TOURIST AND FINANCIAL SERVICES

Tourist Office: Government of India Tourist Office, 88 Janpath (tel. 332 0005 or 332 0008), between Tolstoy Marg and Connaught Circus Rd. next to Kapoor Lamps and Delhi Photo Company. The perfect place to begin a trip to Delhi or other part of India. Great city map, helpful staff that won't rip you off, and good brochures covering all of

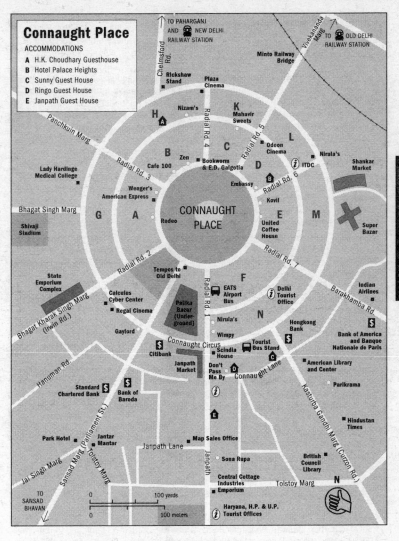

Connaught Place

ACCOMMODATIONS
A H.K. Choudhary Guesthouse
B Hotel Palace Heights
C Sunny Guest House
D Ringo Guest House
E Janpath Guest House

India. Open M-F 9am-6pm, Sa 9am-2pm. Closed major holidays. Two other government-sponsored agencies providing information and bookings are: **India Tourism Development Corporation (ITDC),** also called India Tourism or Ashok Travels, Connaught Pl. (tel. 332 2336; open daily 6:30am-10pm), at the corner of Middle Circle and Radial Rd., and **Delhi Tourism (DTTDC),** not to be confused with IDTC, Connaught Pl., N-block, Middle Circle (tel. 331 4229 or 331 5322; open daily 7am-9pm). All 3 government agencies also have branches in the international terminal at the airport. Delhi has tourist offices for the different states of India. The Chandralok Building, 36 Janpath, south of the government office, is home to the offices for **Uttar Pradesh** (tel. 371 1296 or 332 2251), **Himachal Pradesh** (tel. 332 5320), and **Haryana** (tel. 332 4911). The **Indian Mountaineering Foundation,** Benito Juarez Marg, Anand Niketan (tel. 467 1211), has information on treks. The **Survey of India** (tel. 332 2288) provides maps of the city and a few trekking maps. Open M-F 9am-1pm and 1:30-5pm.

WARNING. Delhi is full of "tourist offices" which claim to provide booking assistance, free maps, and other services. Several of these offices are located near the railway—their bookings are likely to be overpriced, if not fraudulent. Stick to the main government tourist office on Janpath, and for train tickets, to the tourist reservation office in the New Delhi Railway Station and government-approved private travel agencies. **Delhi is a haven for subversive activity.** Con-artists abound, particularly in Paharganj and other tourist hot-beds. If you realize that you've been cheated after the fact, contact the Government of India Tourist Office. They are frequently able to compensate tourists who have been ripped off, even if the exchange in question was ostensibly legal.

Budget Travel: Travel agencies are a dime a dozen; in general, it's best to deal with a government-approved organization. However, there are a few reputable private agencies. For airline reservations and tickets, try **Gagan Travels and Tours,** at the west end of Paharganj Main Bazaar (tel. 751 0061; fax 753 4093), across from the Hotel Amar. This agency has a reputation for honesty. Open daily 9am-6pm. **Bob Tours and Travels** (tel. 355 8788), opposite Sapna Hotel in Paharganj, also provides helpful information.

Diplomatic Missions: Most are in the Chanakyapuri area in south central Delhi and are open all day. Remember, however, that some services are only available at certain times, so call ahead. Most of the listed telephone numbers work 24hr. for emergencies. **Australia,** 1/50-G Shantipath (tel. 688 8223; fax 688 7536). Open M-F 8:30am-noon. **Canada,** 7/8 Shantipath (tel. 687 6500; fax 687 6579). Open M-Th 9am-5pm, F 9am-1pm. **European Union** (tel. 611 9513; fax 687 5731). Open M-F 9am-5:30pm. **Ireland,** 230 Jor Bagh (tel. 462 6733; emergency tel. 688 6775; fax 469 7053). Open M-F 9:30am-5pm; visa services open M-F 10am-noon. **Israel,** 3 Aurangzeb Rd. (tel. 301 3238; fax 301 4298). Open M-Th 9am-5pm, F 9am-3pm. **Nepal,** Barakhamba Rd. (tel. 332 7361 or 332 9218; fax 332 6857). Open M-F 9am-3pm. **New Zealand,** 50-N Nyaya Marg (tel. 688 3170; fax 687 2317). Open M-Th 9am-5pm, F 9am-1pm. **Pakistan,** Shantipath (tel. 600601; fax 687 2339). Open M-Tu and Th-F 8:30am-5pm. **South Africa,** B-18 Vasant Marg, Vasant Vihar (tel. 614 9420; fax 611 3505). **Thailand,** 56-N Nyaya Marg (tel. 611 8103; fax 687 2029). **U.K.,** Shantipath (tel. 687 2161; fax 687 2882). Open M-F 9am-5pm. **U.S.,** Shantipath (tel. 688 9033 or 611 3033). Open M-F 8:30am-5:30pm

Immigration Office: Getting a visa extension is not easy, and the process brings many travelers back to Delhi again and again. For an extension (15 days max.) on a simple **tourist visa** (the extension is not lightly given, so get your story straight ahead of time), first head to the **Ministry of Home Affairs Foreigners Division** (tel. 469 3334 or 461 2543) in Lok Nayak Bhawan, behind Khan Market, off Subramaniya Bharati Marg around Lodi Estate. They're only open M-F 10am-noon, so arrive early with 4 passport photos and a letter stating your grounds for extension. If they process your application, head over to the **Foreigners Regional Registration Office (FRRO)** (tel. 331 9489), located in Hans Bhawan, near Tilak Bridge. Open M-F 9:30am-1:30pm and 2-4pm. The FRRO is also the office for getting **student visas** (with a bona fide student certificate of a recognized school/university, bank remittance certificate, and an extension application in duplicate with 4 photos and proof of stay), as well as **permits** for restricted areas of India. If you need an **exit visa,** the FRRO can process it in about 20min.

Currency Exchange: American Express, A-block, Connaught Pl. (tel. 371 2513 or 332 4119), is probably the best place to change traveler's checks. They sell (for rupees and encashment certificates) and change AmEx checks and cash other brands at 1% commission. There's a counter for lost and stolen cards, though the main office for 24hr. check replacement is at Bhasant Lok (tel. 614 2020). The A-block office issues and receives AmEx moneygrams, and offers usual cardmembers' services, including personal check cashing, card replacement, mail holding, and travel services. Open M-Sa 9:30am-6:30pm. After hours, head to a legitimate money changer, such as **S.G. Securities PVT Ltd.,** M-96, Middle Circle, Connaught (tel. 372 3000 or 331 8000). Open M-Sa 9:30am-8:30pm. **Hotel Grand Regency** (tel. 354 0101), in Paharganj, just a block from the New Delhi Railway Station, changes all major currencies. Open 24hr. **Bank of Baroda,** Sansad Marg (tel. 332 8230), in the big building beyond the outer circle, gives cash advances on Visa and MC. Open M-F 10am-2pm, Sa 10am-noon. **Citibank** (tel. 371 2484), around the corner toward Connaught Pl. from the Bank of Baroda, has a **24hr. ATM** (Cirrus compatible). Open M-F 10am-2pm, Sa 10am-noon. **Bank of America NT&SA,** Hansalaya Bldg., 15 Barakhamba Rd. (tel. 372 2333), has a tightly guarded **24hr. ATM.** The **State Bank of India** branch at Chandni Chowk (tel. 296 0393), 200m from the east end, changes traveler's checks. Open M-F 10am-3:30pm, Sa 10am-12:30pm. The main branch is on Sansad Marg, near Connaught Pl., and there is a 24hr. branch in the international terminal of the airport. In truly desperate situations, some use one of the **illegal money changers** along Main Bazaar in Paharganj. Don't let them go off with your money promising to return with rupees, even if they leave a "friend" of theirs with you while you wait. **Western Union and Money Transfer,** F-12 Connaught Pl. (tel. 331122 or 1-800-325-6000), charges a 5% commission to transfer money from abroad. Open M-F 9:30am-7pm, Sa 9:30am-2pm.

LOCAL SERVICES

Luggage Storage: Many hotels store luggage at no charge. **Ashok Yatra Niwas Hotel** has a safe storage room (Rs4 per day).

Library: The large **American Center Library,** 24 Kasturba Gandhi Marg (tel. 331 6841; fax 332 9499; email libdel@usia.gov), has CD-ROM and Internet databases, and their collection includes the embassy's library. Check out up to 4 books with a Rs200 membership. Admission Rs10 per day. Open M-Tu and Th-Sa 10am-6pm. The **British Council Library,** 17 Kasturba Gandhi Marg (tel. 371140), on the opposite side of the street, lets you check out up to 4 books with a Rs500 membership. Open Tu-Sa 9am-5pm. The **Ramakrishna Mission,** at the west end of Paharganj Main Bazaar, has a library with current periodicals. Rs10 fee, Rs100 deposit. Open Tu-Su 10am-6pm.

Cultural Centers: The American Center and British Council (see above) have regular lectures and film screenings. **Max Mueller Bhavan,** 3 Kasturba Gandhi Marg (tel. 332 9506), has a library and shows films in Siddhartha Hall. Indian cultural centers include **Indian Council for Cultural Relations,** Azad Bhavan, 1P Estate (tel. 331 2274); **India International Centre,** 40 Lodi Estate (tel. 461 9431); **Indira Gandhi National Centre for the Arts,** CV Mess, Janpath (tel. 338 9216); and **Sangeet Natak Akademi,** Rabindra Bhavan (tel. 338 7246), which has information on classical music concerts.

Bookstore: There are several well-stocked bookstores on the inner circle of Connaught Pl., including the **Bookworm** (tel. 332 2260; open M-Sa 10am-7:30pm), the **New Book Depot** (tel. 332 0020; open summer: M-Sa 10:30am-7:30pm), and **E.D. Galgotia and Sons** (tel. 371 3227; open M-Sa 10:30am-7:30pm), next door, all on B-block. Vendors along Paharganj Main Bazaar sell second-hand and new books.

EMERGENCY AND COMMUNICATIONS

Pharmacy: The multi-story **Super Bazaar** (tel. 331 0163-7), outside the M-block of Connaught Pl., has a 24hr. pharmacy. Their **Medical and Surgical Equipment Dept.** (tel. 331476) proffers condoms and sanitary pads around the clock. Several pharmacies along Paharganj Main Bazaar sell tampons and toilet paper.

Hospital/Medical Services: Dr. Sharwan Kumar Gupta's **Care Clinic and Laboratory,** 1468 Sangatrashan (tel. 751 7841; home tel. 623 3088; emergency pager tel. 9632 113979), 2 blocks north of the west end of the Bazaar, is convenient to Paharganj. English-speaking staff is used to dealing with foreign insurance companies. Recommended by IAMAT. Open daily 9am-7:30pm. The **East-West Medical Clinic,** 38 Golf Links Rd., Lodi area (tel. 469 9229 or 469 3865), is recommended by many foreign embassies. Expensive by local standards, the clinic is clean and efficient, run by an American-trained Sikh doctor and his friendly Irish wife. Other hospitals include **Apollo,** Mathura Rd. (tel. 682 1254 or 692 5868; open 24hr.), and the **All-India Institute for Medical Services (AIIMS)** (tel. 656 1123 or 686 4851; emergency tel. 1099 or 102).

DELHI

Police: Branches all over Delhi—look for Delhi Traffic and Tourist Police kiosks at major intersections. Their motto is "for you with you always," but the booths are often deserted. Stations at Chandni Chowk (tel. 233442), next to Bahrandi Mandir, and in Paharganj (tel. 524746).

Emergency: Police, tel. 100. **Fire,** 101. **Ambulance,** 102.

Post Office: There are postal branches in nearly every part of Delhi. The **New Delhi GPO** (tel. 336 4111) is on Ashoka Rd. and Baba Kharak Singh Marg. *Poste Restante* (counter 19) open M-F 10am-5pm, Sa 10am-2pm. Bring a passport to claim mail. *Poste Restante,* GPO, New Delhi, 110001, India. Open M-F 10am-5:30pm. To receive mail at the **Old Delhi GPO,** near the Red Fort and ISBT, use the following address: GPO, Delhi, 110006. Overnight and express couriers, such as **Overnite Express** (tel. 336 8660; open 24hr.) and **Blue Dart** (incorporated with FedEx; tel. 628 8168; open M-Sa 10am-10pm) are located below the state tourist offices in Kanishka Shopping Plaza, next to Ashok Yatri Niwas Hotel. **Belair Travel and Cargo,** 10-B Scindia House (tel. 331 3985), ships bulky luggage and boxes overseas. Open M-F 9:30am-6pm, Sa 10am-2pm. **Postal Code:** 110001.

Internet: Calculus Cyber Center (tel. 373 4007), next to the Regal Cinema, above Khadi Gramadyog; has web access (Rs100 per hr., Rs50 per 30min., Rs25 under 15min.), as does **The Cybercafe,** N-block, Middle Circle (tel. 371 0352; Rs70 per hr.). Both open daily 9:30am-8:30pm.

Telephones: Hotel Anoop and **Divya Telecom,** off Paharganj Main Bazaar at the east end, both have free callbacks. **Eastern Court,** on Janpath, south of the Government of India Tourist Office, has 24hr. STD/ISD, local calls, fax, and postal service.

PHONE CODE	011

ACCOMMODATIONS

Staying in Delhi can be frustratingly expensive. Prices have been driven up so much that it is hard to find anything acceptable for less than Rs100. There are three main budget hotel areas: Paharganj, Connaught Place, and Old Delhi.

Paharganj (Main Bazaar) is Delhi's main tourist enclave. Though it has adapted to travelers' needs, it still retains its legendary squalor and seediness and can be dangerous, especially for women traveling alone. Stories about passport scams, drugged drinks, rapes, and murders in Paharganj are plentiful, and while some of these stories are true, Paharganj has also become the quintessential New Delhi urban legend. Paharganj is packed with STD/ISD booths, Kashmiri "travel agents" with the gift of gab, hash dealers, money changers, and people who cheat tourists for a living—be on your guard. If you've just arrived in India or are simply not into grime, head to **Connaught Place** for its own collection of nicer, though more expensive, guest houses and hotels. On the other hand, if you really want to put your nose in it, there's always **Old Delhi,** the purist's retreat (no banana pancakes here).

PAHARGANJ

Paharganj is one long, messy line of cheap hotels and restaurants. The heart of Paharganj is in the western half of **Main Bazaar** (head here if you crave the constant company of other travelers), but hotels closer to the railway station often have better deals. Most of the better places have rooftop restaurants and generators to keep their guests alive during Delhi's all-too-frequent power outages. All of the following directions (right, left) are given as you walk west on Main Bazaar.

Camran Lodge, Main Bazaar (tel. 352 6053), on the right. Built into an old mosque, this creeping, crawling, nooky, crooked, low-roofed little knot of rooms has more character and atmosphere than you'd expect from a budget hotel. Though not as sterile or modern as other places, this quiet underdog is a good place to dream a few Orientalist dreams before being knocked on the head by real-life Delhi in the morning. Internet access downstairs. Singles Rs80; doubles Rs160, with bath Rs180.

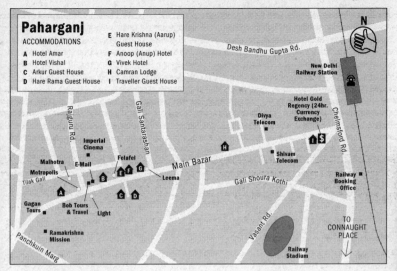

Paharganj
ACCOMMODATIONS

A Hotel Amar
B Hotel Vishal
C Arkur Guest House
D Hare Rama Guest House
E Hare Krishna (Aarup) Guest House
F Anoop (Anup) Hotel
G Vivek Hotel
H Camran Lodge
I Traveller Guest House

DELHI

Vivek Hotel, 1534 Main Bazaar (tel. 351 2900), in the heart of Paharganj. This massive, white backpacker haven is spread over several floors—try to get a room overlooking the courtyard. The attached restaurant, **Leema,** is on the ground floor and the rooftop. Singles with bath and air-cooling Rs200, with TV Rs300, with A/C Rs600; doubles Rs250/400/700.

Traveller Guest House, Main Bazaar (tel. 354 4849), to the left, not far from the railway station. Rooms are small but worth it for the black-and-white TV, "disinfected" toilets, and air-cooling. Doubles Rs200-300.

Anoop (Anup) Hotel, Main Bazaar (tel. 352 1451). Popular, multi-storied backpackers' hotel with strict anti-tout regulations in force. Spacious, well-kept rooms have attached baths. STD/ISD has free callbacks. Bona fide 24hr. Italian rooftop *ristorante*. Singles Rs200; doubles Rs250, with air-cooling Rs270, with A/C Rs400. Extra person Rs50.

Hare Krishna (Aarup) Guest House, Main Bazaar (tel. 753 3017). Less business-oriented than his twin next door, but both are true gems. Quiet, clean-enough rooms have tidy, elevated bathrooms and comfy mattresses. Check-out 24hr. Singles Rs150, with bath Rs180; doubles Rs200/250.

Hare Rama Guest House, 298 Main Bazaar (tel. 351 413), entrance 10m back. Normally packed, often rowdy, sometimes clean. Stay away from the attached travel agency. Singles Rs150; doubles Rs200, with bath Rs250, with A/C Rs350.

Ankur Guest House, opposite Hare Rama Guest House. Soft-spoken in shadow of bigger neighbors, but oh my Ghosh, streetside rooftop restaurant draws a consistent crowd. Decent-sized rooms have working bathrooms. Singles Rs130; doubles Rs180.

Hotel Vishal, Main Bazaar (tel. 753 2079), west end, after the Hare Krishna Guesthouse. More mellow than other popular backpacker hang-outs. The security and safety of his clients is the owner's top priority. Great rooftop for relaxation. Check-out noon. Singles Rs100, with bath Rs150; doubles Rs150/200. Air-cooling Rs25-50 extra.

Hotel Amar, Main Bazaar (tel. 352 4642), on the west end past the Metropolis Hotel. Dimly lit rooms, but most have TV, air-cooling, and telephone. Singles Rs150, with bath Rs250, with TV and A/C Rs500; doubles Rs250/350/600.

CONNAUGHT PLACE

The hotels in and around Connaught Pl. tend to be cleaner and quieter than those in Paharganj—they also tend to cost a lot more, with a few exceptions. The area is less chaotic than Paharganj, though some travelers might find it altogether *too* quiet, especially at night.

🛏 **Hotel Palace Heights,** Radial Rd. 6, D-block (tel. 332 1419), on the top fl. High above the grime and the push of the streets, this is one of the best budget places in Delhi. Quiet, clean, and friendly offers a different sort of rooftop experience and a welcome break from the claustrophobic stuffiness of other cheap hotels. Doubles from Rs325, with A/C Rs630.

🛏 **H.K. Choudhary Guesthouse,** H-35/3, Middle Circle (tel. 332 2043). Excellent service geared toward business travelers. 24hr. STD and email facilities (Rs100 per hr.). Rooms are small but nicely decorated, all with attached baths. Singles Rs400; doubles with air-cooling Rs450, with A/C Rs750.

Ringo Guest House, 17 Scindia House (tel. 331 0605), off Janpath, outside Outer Circle. A little hideaway beneath the waves of cars and people. Staggeringly popular backpackers' retreat is overcrowded and a bit over-priced, but it has a pleasant garden area and a relaxed, safe, and happy atmosphere. Food available 24hr. Check-out noon. Dorm beds Rs90; singles Rs150; doubles Rs250, with bath Rs350, with air-cooling Rs400.

Sunny Guest House, Connaught Ln. (tel. 331 2909), past Ringo Guest House. Standard backpacker grotto. Dorms are significantly more spacious than those at Ringo. Dorm beds Rs90; singles Rs125-170; doubles Rs250, with bath Rs350-400.

Janpath Guest House, 82-84 Janpath (tel. 332 1935), near the Government of India Tourist Office. More upscale place with the usual carpet-and-cable luxuries. Internet cafe. Singles from Rs425; doubles from Rs495.

OLD DELHI AND TOURIST CAMPS

The few who decide to stay the night in **Old Delhi** get a very different experience than do their daytripping neighbors. For better and for worse, Old Delhi doesn't aspire to impress foreign tourists. While prices are cheaper and people are less likely to try to cheat you, it can be hard to find anyone who speaks English. In addition, stereotypes about Westerners—Western women in particular—are stronger here than elsewhere in the city. Many men will assume that solo female travelers are willing to give sexual favors; women should avoid dressing provocatively or going out alone after dark. Nearby, Delhi's **Tourist Camps** offer a much-better-than-it-sounds outdoors experience unlike anything in the rest of the city.

🛏 **Hotel New City Palace** (tel. 327 9548), west of Jama Masjid. Superb views of the mosque, complete with loud prayers. Modern rooms have pencil-thin beds, hot-water showers, and balconies with rooftop access. Shops below cater to late-night mechanics. Check-out 24hr. Singles with bath Rs200; doubles Rs250, with A/C Rs450.

Khush-Dil Hotel, Chandni Chowk (tel. 395 2110), at the west end, just south of the mosque on Fatehpuri Corner. Narrow beds, dank bathrooms, feeble fans, but excellent views of the busy street. Check-out 24hr. Singles Rs90, with bath Rs120; doubles Rs150/180. Air-cooling Rs20 extra.

New Delhi Tourist Camp, Jawaharlal Nehru Marg (tel. 327 2898), near Delhi Gate, opposite J.P. Narayan (Irwin) Hospital. Excellent location—equidistant from Old Delhi, Paharganj, and Connaught Pl. and far enough away from them all to create its own insular, country atmosphere. Camp outside or stay in the rustic buildings around the garden. Currency exchange, free callbacks. Outside restaurant open 7:30am-10pm. Pitch your own tent Rs50; singles Rs125, with bath and air-cooling Rs275; doubles Rs200/390.

Tourist Camping Park, Qudsia Garden (tel. 252 3121 or 252 2597), across the street and to the right of the ISBT at Kashmiri Gate. Great for crashing after a long bus journey. Smaller and less developed than Tourist Camp, they rent tents and have a great restaurant next door. Check-out noon. Rooms have clean common baths. Tents Rs50 per person; singles Rs110, with air-cooling Rs140; doubles Rs140/170.

◖ FOOD

It's worth shelling out a little cash for some of Delhi's excellent meals. There are countless restaurants in all price ranges, respectable Western-style fast food, superb Chinese and Middle Eastern cuisine, a couple of Mexican restaurants, and, of course, knock-out Indian food. For a real splurge (up to Rs300-400 per entree), head to one of the 5-star hotels, like the Maurya Sheraton or the Ashok Frontier.

PAHARGANJ

This backpackers' district has developed several hot spots for hanging out—and all of them are about five stories up. None of these places serves particularly good food (breakfasts are tolerable), but the rooftops are the place to find Paharganj's backpack-rats sipping tea and slurping curd after hours. It's best to get off the Main Bazaar for food—most of the main strip's restaurants cater to the jaded palates and fragile digestive systems of penny-pinching backpackers. The places near the Railway Station have good tea but aren't particularly hygienic. Wander the streets north of Paharganj to see where the locals are eating.

Malhotra Restaurant, 1833 Chuna Mandi. Walk west on Main Bazaar, turn right on Rajguru Rd. at the Metropolis, then take the 1st left. Tucked below street level, it's often packed with locals. Spotless, cool, and hassle-free. Quick, efficient service, and good Indian and Chinese food. The "Continental" menu includes nouvelle cuisine specialties such as...fried eggs and chips. Open daily 8:30am-11pm.

Metropolis Restaurant, Main Bazaar, in the Metropolis Hotel. The best restaurant on the block, with Chinese, Japanese, Indian, and Continental dishes. *Palak paneer* Rs90, Szechuan prawns Rs150, "le poulet sizzling" Rs175. Subdued setting—both inside and on the rooftop. Open daily 8am-11pm.

Leema Restaurant, Main Bazaar, in Hotel Vivek. Probably the best budget-hotel restaurant in Paharganj. A/C, fresh juices, and excellent veg. sandwiches (Rs15), but the service can be painfully slow. Open daily 6am-midnight.

Felafel, Main Bazaar, next to Hotel Vishal and New Lord's Cafe. Surprisingly authentic Middle Eastern food. Fresh pita bread (Rs10) with salad or hummus (Rs30). Open daily 11am-11pm.

Light Restaurant (Sapna Hill Restaurant), Main Bazaar, at the west end. All-veg. *thalis* are only Rs20, and even better, you can look inside the pots and see which 2 vegetables you want with your rice, *dal, chapati,* and *kheer.* Big bowls of rice pudding Rs8.

CONNAUGHT PLACE

Catering to diplomats and executives who long for a taste of home, restaurants in Connaught Pl. offer Indian and international cuisine several times better than that served down the road in backpackers' paradise. In recent years, fast-food joints such as Wimpy and Pizza Hut have also started to muscle their way in.

Gaylord, Outer Circle, next to the Regal Cinema. Large, spacious, chandeliered dining room. Top-notch food and excellent service. Your meal here is likely to be the most expensive you will have in India (Rs150-200 for a main course). It might also be the best. Open daily noon-3pm and 7-11pm.

Nirula's, L-block (tel. 332 2419). Huge multi-restaurant the size of a multi-story car park deck. Head to the ice cream bar for smooth mango scoops and shakes, or try Indian flavors like Zafrani Badaam Pista, 21 Love, or Gulabo (Rs25 per scoop). Hit the Potpourri upstairs for lamburgers (Rs90), an all-you-can-eat salad bar (Rs15), and pizzas (Rs80-120). Eat in their classy "Chinese Room" or sip drinks in one of 2 bars—the popular, pricey, **Pegasus Bar** is open 11am-midnight. Ice cream and fast food branch near Wimpy on N-block. Pastry shop open 9am-9pm. Open daily 10:30am-midnight.

Rodeo, A-block, near the AmEx office. Hitch your pony to a post outside, hand over your pistol at the swinging doors, and sidle up to a saddle stool at the bar, where you might well struggle not to giggle into your bourbon as waiters in Stetsons and spurs play Doc Holliday with the gun-shaped menu they keep in holsters strapped to their sides. Mexican food, beer, and cocktails. Business lunch buffet Rs165. Open daily noon-11pm.

United Coffee House, E-block. High ceilings, ornately carved walls, and an incongruous background soundtrack of 1980's Euro-pop. A firm favorite of the chattering elite. Veg., non-veg. dishes Rs50-100. Last orders at 11:30pm. Open daily 9am-midnight.

Sona Rupa Restaurant, Janpath, past the Government of India Tourist Office. Indian-style McDonald's in marble, with piped-in Hindi muzak. Delicious veg. South Indian food (Rs40-60) and a wide range of ice cream (Rs30). Buffet (Rs95) noon-4pm and 7-10pm. Open M-Sa 11:30am-10pm, Su 12:30-10pm.

Embassy Restaurant, D-block (tel. 332 0480). Classy establishment with tasteful decor and prompt service. Good Indian food at oh-well-what-the-hell prices. Brain curry Rs94, cream of asparagus soup Rs45. Open daily 11am-11pm.

Zen Restaurant, B-block. Quiet and elegant middle-class hang-out. Mostly Chinese food, a Japanese name, and muzak—all in the middle of Delhi. Mysterious sculpture dangles from red, leather-padded walls. Bring a sweater. Veg. dishes Rs75-100, non-veg. Rs105-165. Beer Rs70. Open daily 11am-10:30pm.

Nizam's, H-block, behind Plaza Cinema. Slow service but worth the wait. The tastiest *biryani* (Rs75-80) and kebab eggrolls (Rs45-80) in the city. This meat-lover's paradise also placates the vegetarians—delicious veg. rolls Rs40-60. Mostly an eat-and-run place with a few tables out back by the screaming TV. Open M-Sa 12:30-11pm, Su 5-11pm.

Volgi, Inner Circle. This definitely-not-Russian restaurant rolls out the red carpet for crowds of beer-drinking men who come here to smoke and shout into the cold air. Good Indian dishes Rs100-150. Open daily noon-3:30pm and 7-11pm.

Wenger & Co. Pastry Shop, Inner Circle, A-block, next to the AmEx office. Take-out bakery and patisserie. Doughnuts, strudels, cakes, and tarts galore. Open daily 10am-8pm.

Kovil, near United Coffee House. Popular place serving excellent South Indian veg. meals. Snacks Rs70-30, full meals for Rs100. Open daily 11am-10:45pm.

Parikrama, Kasturba Gandhi Marg. Delhi's revolving rooftop restaurant takes 1½hr. to go around once, and they won't let you finish in less. Good Continental, Chinese, and Indian food. The soft noodles are a delectable melange of Indian and Chinese spices (Rs130). Open daily noon-11pm.

Don't Pass Me By, 79 Scindia House, near Ringo's Guest House (hence the name). Basic, budget eats are nicely prepared. Two tables inside, and more on the outside patio. Cheap, foreigner-friendly breakfasts throughout the day. Open daily 7am-9pm.

OLD DELHI

Old Delhi offers every class of edible fare—from spices to squawking chickens—and boasts a number of renowned restaurants.

Karim, in a small courtyard off Matya Mahal, about 8 shops down from Jama Masjid (not visible from the road). One of the city's most popular and famous restaurants, Karim is run by descendants of the cooks of Mughal royalty. Menu full of rich, meat-heavy dishes. Half dishes (at half-price) fit the bill for the budget traveler. Chicken stew Rs76, mutton *burra* Rs90. Try the paper-thin *roomali roti*. Open daily 7am-midnight.

Moti Mahal Restaurant, Netaji Subhash Marg. Outdoor patio and chandeliered dining rooms serve delicious Indian, particularly *tandoori* cuisine. Live music (usually singing) every night W-M 8-11:30pm. Meaty menu includes chicken entrees Rs60-200. Mineral water Rs30. Open daily 11am-midnight.

Cosi-e-Cosi, opposite Kashmiri Gate ISBT, next to the Tourist Camping Park. Cosi knows how to flavor food. *Dal makhni* (Rs30), mixed veg. (Rs35), and South Indian and Chinese dishes as well.

Shree Delhi Gujarati Samaj, 2 Raj Niwas Marg, past Kashmiri Gate ISBT and the Oberoi Hotel (not visible from the street). Excellent restaurant in the middle of a Gujarati apartment building. Fresh *thalis* Rs17, all-you-can-eat Rs28.

NEW DELHI

Village Bistro, Hauz Khas Village. A complete bazaar of restaurants to treat the South Delhi elite. Le Cafe has Continental fare; Mohalla has spats of live Rajasthani music and an Indian menu; Top of the Village has live jazz nightly.

The Yellow Brick Road, Ambassador Hotel, Sujan Singh Park, 1km south of India Gate. As authentically American as they get in this hemisphere. 1950s photos grace the walls, the decor is bright yellow, and the menu is a bizarre tabloid newspaper. Tiramisu (Rs65), burgers (Rs105-145), Waldorf salad (Rs75), make-your-own sandwiches and pizza (Rs75/125), and Indian fare. Open 24hr.

■ NIGHTLIFE

There's plenty of nightlife in Delhi, but it caters mainly to the city's elite—it seems that every five-star hotel runs a happenin' disco. To the budget traveler, however, the cover charges may seem forbiddingly steep, and the world of jeans-clad bodies writhing to an interminable techno beat under flashing lights may seem less appealing than getting wasted with fellow backpackers in Paharganj. Still, grooving the night away can revive the spirits, and there are bargains to be found.

Mirage (tel. 683 5070), at the Best Western Surya Sofitel. Dance to professionally mixed techno among the sveltest of the svelte. Cover Rs600 per person, Ladies' Night on Wednesdays (women get in free). Open until 4am most nights.

Ghungroo (tel. 611 2233), at the Maurya Sheraton. Reputed to have the best lighting system in South Asia, Ghungroo gives new meaning to "sound and light show." Admission Rs400 per couple. Ladies' Night Sa. Open M-Sa 10pm-3:30am.

Wheels (tel. 463200), at the Hotel Ambassador. Popular with foreigners, who come to hear an eclectic mix of Hindi and Western standards. Rs300 per couple. No single admission. Open daily 10:30pm-3am.

Some Place Else (tel. 373 2477), at the Park Hotel. The familiar sounds of "La Bamba" give way to Bob Marley, rap, and Hindi pop. Cover Rs300. Open 10pm-2am.

CJ's (tel. 371 0101), at Le Meridien. Draws a slightly older crowd. Cover Rs300.

My Kind of Place (tel. 611 0202), at Taj Palace. The place to be seen making a fool of yourself. Has two sections, one featuring a positively sublime dry ice cloud in which to enshroud the dancers. Open 9:30pm-2am.

Annabelle's (tel. 332 0101), at the Intercontinental, formerly the Hilton. Dance competition in August. Drinks Rs150-250. Couples only. Open 9:30pm-2am.

■ ENTERTAINMENT

To find out about weekly musical and cultural events (as well as other relevant contact information for tourists), buy a copy of the *Delhi Diary* (Rs8), which comes out every Friday. **Dances of India** is a nightly performance of Indian dance and music, including *kathak* and *manipuri* (7pm, Parsi, Anjuman Hall, opposite the Ambedkar Football Stadium, Delhi Gate; tel. 331 7831 or 332 0968). There are several **movie theaters** in Delhi which show Hindi movies; some in South Delhi show English films (Rs40). Check daily papers for movie listings. Various cultural centers (see **Cultural Centers,** p. 113) screen foreign films and Indian "art" films that are not shown elsewhere.

The Red Fort's nightly **sound and light show,** focusing on the city's Mughal heritage, is unexpectedly entertaining. The silhouetted sitting halls and mosques invoke the voices of past rulers. A Pink Floyd concert it's not, but it's as good a history lesson as you're likely to get in Delhi (see **Lal Qila,** p. 120). The Old Fort also has a nightly sound and light show on the *Mahabharata* (see **Purana Qila,** p. 126).

◉ SIGHTS

Like any capital city worth its salt, Delhi boasts a vast number of things to see. There are 1376 monuments, two of which are UNESCO World Heritage sites (Qutb Minar and Humayun's Tomb). If you're spending only a couple of days in Delhi, budget your time wisely. The must-sees are the Qutb Minar Complex and the sights of Old Delhi—Lal Qila (Red Fort), Jama Masjid (Friday Mosque), and the bazaars. Round out your time by having a look at Rashtrapati Bhavan, Humayun's Tomb. If you need respite from the midday heat, head to the National Museum. You'll have most of these places to yourself in the early morning. As always, men (and occasionally women) will linger by the entrance to the various tourist attractions, flashing ID cards (often bogus) and offering their services as guides. While they often don't have their facts straight, some are quite knowledgeable. If you hire a guide, be sure to bargain a price in advance. Guides and/or vehicles can be hired for four- to 12-hour stints; contact ITDC or Delhi Tourism (see p. 110). Standard non-A/C taxis cost about Rs350 for 4hr.

Several agencies offer **guided tours** of Delhi (about Rs200). These usually start in New Delhi, stopping at Jantar Mantar, the Lakshmi Narayan Temple, Humayun's Tomb, the Baha'i Temple, driving by the more notable landmarks (such as India Gate), and swinging south of the city to Qutb Minar. Tours of Old Delhi might include the Red Fort, Raj Ghat, Shanti Vana, and a glimpse of Jama Masjid (about Rs100). These tours are rushed, the guides are not always informed, and a full day of bus riding, even in A/C comfort, is never fun, but these tours are helpful if you've only got a short time in Delhi. Book through ITDC, L-block, Connaught Pl. (tel. 332 0331; open daily 6:30am-10pm), or at Delhi Tourism and Transportation (tel. 331 4229; open daily 7am-9pm).

OLD DELHI

RED FORT (LAL QILA)
Enter through Lahore Gate, pass through Chatta Chowk into the palace area. Fort open daily 8am-dusk. Free. Museums open Sa-Th 10am-5pm. Rs2. English sound and light shows Rs20: Nov.-Jan. 7:30-8:30pm.; Feb.-Apr. 8:30-9:30pm; May-Aug. 9-10pm; Sept.-Oct. 8:30-9:30pm.

Shortly after moving the capital from Agra to Delhi in 1639, Mughal emperor Shah Jahan began construction of the Red Fort. Work started on April 16 and was completed nine years later to the day, at a cost of more than 10 million rupees. Soaring to a height of 33.5m, the fort's red sandstone ramparts ring a 2km perimeter and are themselves surrounded by a moat into which the Yamuna once flowed. Some of its more resplendent features are now gone—the famed Peacock Throne was snatched away in 1739, the gems that adorned the palaces have all been removed, and the canals through which the Stream of Paradise once gurgled are now dry. But the Red Fort remains what it has always been—an incredible monument to Mughal power and an architectural marvel.

The entrance to the fort is toward the middle of its west wall, at the three-story **Lahore Gate,** through which the Mughal emperors would leave the fort for the Jama Masjid. Next to the gate is the spot from which the Prime Minister addresses cheering throngs on Independence Day (Aug. 15). Lahore Gate leads to **Chatta Chowk,** the covered passageway filled with shops which today peddles souvenirs, but during the Mughal era provided nobles with top-quality silks, precious jewelry, and fine velvets. Chatta Chowk gives way to the rectangular, three-storied **Naubat Khana** (Drum House); five times a day, music was played from this building in tribute to the emperor and his court. The floral carvings adorning the walls of Naubat Khana were once painted with gold.

Naubat Khana leads into the palace area. Across the mini-courtyard behind the simple, sturdy columns stands **Diwan-i-Am** (Hall of Public Audience), upon which the early Mughal emperors sat (everyone else stood) for two hours a day, receiving visitors, chatting with nobles, deciding criminal cases, and generally conduct-

> **DIVAN DISMEMBERMENT** As Mughal power declined, so did the glory of the Hall of Private Audience. The precious stones once decorating its interior are gone, its silver ceiling was carted off by the Marathas, and the famed **Peacock Throne** was stolen in 1739 by the Turkish raider Nadir Shah. The throne had been commissioned by Shah Jahan upon becoming emperor; it took seven years for laborers to meet the emperor's ostentatious specifications. The throne's feet were of solid gold, its canopy was inlaid with diamonds, gems, and pearls, and a parrot carved from a single emerald was positioned behind the emperor's head.

ing affairs of state. The throne used to sit on top of the canopied white marble platform now on display. To the back of the platform are a series of curious panels adorned with red and green renderings of flowers, birds, trees, and lions. Presiding over the entire scene from the central panel is the Greek god Orpheus. Scholars speculate that the panels, returned from the British Museum in 1903, were crafted in Florence. The low marble platform in front of the emperor's platform was reserved for the prime minister, who would, within earshot of the emperor, entertain grievances.

Beyond Diwan-i-Am were the private palaces of the Mughal emperor. Of the original six palaces, five remain; each was connected to its neighbor by a canal called the **Nahir-i-Bihisht** (Stream of Paradise). The palaces were set in spacious formal *charbagh* gardens. The southernmost of the palaces (the palace farthest to the right, coming from Diwan-i-Am), **Mumtaz Mahal** (Palace of Jewels) originally housed the harem. These days, it houses a museum (see below). North of Mumtaz Mahal is **Rang Mahal** (Palace of Colors), a white marble pavilion where the emperor ate his meals. During the Mughal heyday, the ceilings were decorated with silver; other parts of the ceiling are embedded with tiny mirrors that reflected the light from the emperor's candle-lit banquet tables. Just north of Rang Mahal, **Khas Mahal** (Private Palace) is a sumptuous display of wealth; each of the three apartments was lavishly decorated in silk during the Mughal era. The southernmost of these is **Baithak** (Sitting Room), with a scale of justice carved in marble upon the walls. The emperor used to sleep in the center apartment, known as the **Khwabagh** (Sleeping Chamber). Attached to the outer wall of the Khwabagh is a tower called **Muthamman Burj** (Octagonal Tower), where the emperor would greet his subjects or watch animal fights staged below. King George V and Queen Mary sat on this porch before thousands in 1911, when a *durbar* was held and the announcement was made that the Imperial Capital would be moved to Delhi from Kolkata. North of the Khwabagh is **Tasbih Khana** (Chamber for Telling Beads), where the emperor used to pray.

Just north of Khas-Mahal is the **Diwan-i-Khas** (Hall of Private Audience), constructed entirely of white marble and replete with arches. Here, the emperor would make crucial political decisions, consult privately with advisors, and speak with special visitors. Attempting to rekindle the old spark, Bahadur Shah II, the last Mughal emperor, held court here during the Mutiny of 1857; in retaliation, the British tried him in the Diwan-i-Am, and then exiled him to Burma. North is the **Hammam** (Bath), whose westernmost apartment contained a rosewater fountain. The chambers on either side of its entrance are thought to have been the bathtubs of the emperor's children. West of the Hammam is the delicate **Moti Masjid** (Pearl Mosque), built in 1662 by Emperor Aurangzeb for his personal use. The black marble outlines on the floor were designed to help with the proper placement of the *musallas* (prayer mats). There are two **museums** inside the Red Fort complex. Mumtaz Mahal's is the better of the two, displaying astrolabes, *hookahs*, and weapons. The museum in the Naubat Khana concentrates on military history, and charts the various ways that men have killed each other over the past 200 years.

JAMA MASJID. Built between 1650 and 1656 by Emperor Shah Jahan, the Jama Masjid, 1km west of the Red Fort, is the largest active mosque in India. Set on a high platform on top of a low hill, the Jama Masjid dominates the surrounding streets with its elegant mixture of red sandstone and white marble in its soaring minarets. Its three gateways separate the secular and the sacred. The east gate was once reserved for the Mughal emperor and his family; now it is open to all worshippers on Fridays and Muslim holidays. The 900 sq. meter courtyard packs in nearly 25,000 worshippers during Friday prayers.

As in most South Asian mosques, a *hauz* (tank) at the center of the courtyard is used for cleansing feet and hands before prayer, and each rectangle designates the space for one worshipper. Prayers are sung from the *imam's* platform, under the center arch at the westernmost point of the mosque; before amplification systems, the two small posts between this point and the east gate were used by other *imams* who repeated prayers so that those at the back could hear. Just west of the mosque is the official residence of the *imam*; the Muslim priests have lived here since the time of Shah Jahan, and you can still see them before prayers. It's worth climbing up one of the minarets that rise from the courtyard for the superb views of the city from the top. Women should keep an arm ready to fend off gropers in the stairwell. *(1km west of the Red Fort. Open to tourists 30min. after dawn until 12:20pm (noon on F), 1:45pm until 20min. before prayer call, and again after prayers until 20min. before sunset. Camera fee Rs10. Lungi to wrap around bare legs Rs5-10.)*

RAJ GHAT. Here, a perpetually burning flame and a simple black slab set in a grassy courtyard offer a memorial to Mahatma Gandhi, cremated at this spot after his 1948 assassination by a Hindu extremist. Gandhi's name is notably missing from the monument—the only inscription is of his last words, "Hai Ram" ("Oh God"). Hundreds of visitors come each day to cast flower petals and pray. Just south of the monument is a park full of trees and flowers planted by all kinds of dignitaries: flowers from Eisenhower, a pine from Queen Elizabeth II, and a slanted tree planted by Nasser. *(On the west bank of the Yamuna River, 1km east of Delhi Gate and 2km southeast of the Red Fort. Open dawn-dusk. Free.)*

SHANTI VANA. North of Raj Ghat, this quiet park contains memorials to men and women who have earned a place in India's pantheon of political heroes, including an effusive monument to slain Prime Minister Rajiv Gandhi. An adjacent memorial to his older brother Sanjay, was taken down after critics reminded the government that this Gandhi never served in office or ever accomplished much at all. After it was removed, however, Sanjay's admirers continued to put flowers at the barren spot, and eventually the monument returned. The humble grassy mound that marks the life and death of Jawaharlal Nehru mentions only his wish to have his ashes thrown in the Ganga.

SOUTH DELHI

QUTB MINAR COMPLEX
At the intersection of Aurobindo Marg and Mehrauli Badarpur Rd., 14km southwest of Connaught Pl. Open daily dawn-dusk. Rs5.

Situated in a part of Delhi speckled with crumbling mosques and decaying ramparts, the ruins of the **Qutb Mina**r complex are peerless. The construction of the complex began in 1199 after the Turkish ex-slave Qutb-ud-din Aibak swept into North India and defeated the Rajputs. Qutb-ud-din Aibak installed himself at Lal Kot, the site of an old Rajput city, founding what was to become India's first Islamic Kingdom here in 1706, following the murder of his general, Muhammed Ghuri. The events that led to the building of the complex were epoch-making, and the Qutb Minar serves as a 72.5m-high exclamation point.

The red sandstone Qutb Minar was designed to stand as a celebration of Qutb-ud-din Aibak's triumphs in Northern India and a milestone marking the eastern frontier of the Muslim world. As an inscription on one of the tower notes, "the tower was erected to cast the shadow of God over both East and West." Modeled on the brick victory towers of Central Asia, the Qutb Minar also served as the minaret for the Quwwat-ul-Islam Masjid (see below). Before

OLD DELHI BIZARRE From the Jama Masjid, it's easy to begin an exploration of the busy maze of shops and street vendors that constitute the bazaars of Old Delhi. While the streets surrounding the Jama Masjid are cluttered with overpriced kitsch, walk 200m north, south, or west and you'll be in a part of town rarely visited by tourists. Area vendors peddle wholesale paper, high-quality tools, used car parts, and all sorts of other goodies. To check out one of the smelliest places in the universe, head south from Jama Masjid toward the poultry markets, where chickens trussed together in painfully cramped cages are selected by customers, then butchered on the spot, much to the delight of swarms of flies. Don't be shy about bargaining. Ducking into any of the narrow alleys between the shops on the south side of Chandni Chowk leads to another bazaar-o dream world; follow the labyrinthine "street" any which way and stumble upon the aromatic spice market or snag a deal on gems.

DELHI

dying, Qutb-ud-din Aibak was able to complete only the first three stories of the tower. His son-in-law Iltutmish added a fourth story, and Firoz Shah Tughluq tacked on a fifth after repairing damage caused by a 1368 lightning strike. The fifth-story cupola erected by Firoz was felled by an 1803 earthquake and replaced by British Major Robert Smith; Smith's Mughal-style cupola now sits in the gardens, having been removed from the Qutb Minar because it was so awkward. Visitors have been forbidden from climbing the minaret since 1981, when more than 30 panicked school children were trampled to death during a power outage. While most of the calligraphy carved on the minaret displays Arabic passages from the Qur'an, a few Devanagari inscriptions prove some Indian influence in its design.

Just north of Qutb Minar is the **Quwwat-ul-Islam Masjid** (Might of Islam Mosque), which is the oldest extant mosque in India aside from those in western Gujarat. Begun in 1192 and completed in 1198 (extensions were added over the next two centuries), the mosque was built from the remains of 21 Hindu and Jain temples destroyed by the fanatically iconoclastic Qutb-ud-din Aibak. The pillars from the razed temples support the east end of the mosque and are carved with bells, lotuses, and other Hindu and Jain icons. At the center of the courtyard is the 98% pure iron **Gupta Pillar.** According to the Sanskrit inscription, the pillar was erected in honor of Vishnu and in memory of Chandra, believed to be the Gupta emperor Chandragupta II (r. 375-415 AD). Tradition holds that Anangpal, the founder of Lal Kot, brought the pillar to the area. It is said that anyone who can stand with their back against the pillar and wrap their arms around it is blessed by the gods with superhuman strength.

Just south of Qutb Minar is the domed, red sandstone **Ala'i Darwaza,** built in 1311 to serve as the southern entrance to the mosque. The building boasts India's first true arches. Immediately east of Ala'i Darwaza, the domed octagonal tomb with the *jali* decorative screens holds the body of Imam Zamin, a Sufi saint who came to India from Central Asia in the early 16th century.

North of the Quwwat-ul-Islam Masjid is a massive, unfinished minaret, **Ala'i Minar.** Expansion had doubled the size of the mosque, and Ala'i Minar was to be twice as tall as Qutb Minar. After its first 24.5m-high story was completed, construction was stopped and the wildly ambitious project was abandoned. Just south of Ala'i Minar is the **Tomb of Iltutmish,** which the sultan himself erected in 1235, four years after building his son's tomb, 8km from Qutb Minar. While Iltutmish's red sandstone tomb isn't particularly interesting from the outside, the artfully decorated interior is well worth a look, with its mingling of Hindu and Jain themes (wheels, lotuses, and bells) and Muslim motifs (calligraphic inscriptions, geometric patterns, and the Mecca-facing alcoves built into the west wall). Directly south of Iltutmish's tomb are the ruins of a *madrasa*, an institution of Islamic learning. In keeping with Seljuk Turkish traditions, the tomb of the *madrasa's* founder, Ala-ud-din Khalji, has been placed within it; look for the L-shaped mound of earth and rubble.

TUGHLUQABAD. High up on the top of a lonely, rocky outcrop, is **Tughluqabad,** built as a fortified city by Ghiyas-ud-din Tughluq, who ruled the Delhi Sultanate between 1321 and 1325. These days, the abandoned fort has been invaded and conquered by weeds, monkeys, and a more general pall of desolation. Massive, 10-15m walls run along the 6.5km circumference of the fort. Thirteen separate gates lead through the walls, which are topped with husky stone battlements. The red sandstone and white marble **Tomb of Ghiyas-ud-din Tughluq** employs the first set of sloping walls to grace a Muslim-made building in India. Shortly after Ghiyas-ud-din Tughluq was murdered, Tughluqabad was abandoned, having been occupied for a grand total of five years. (*Mehrauli Badrapur Rd., 9km east of the Qutb Minar Complex and 16km southeast of Connaught Place.*)

BAHA'I TEMPLE. Over the past three decades, members of the Baha'i faith have donated millions of dollars toward the construction of seven Baha'i Temples in locations such as Uganda, Samoa, and the midwestern United States. The latest addition to this series was finished in 1986 and is situated in South Delhi on a 26-acre expanse of cropped grass and elegant pools. The temple, which inevitably draws comparisons to the Sydney Opera House, is built from white marble in the shape of an opening lotus flower. Silence is requested of visitors; there's little to do but settle comfortably onto one of the wood-backed benches, listen to the dull thudding of bare feet, and gaze up at the clean lines of the temple's splendid dome, which soars overhead to a height of 34m. (*4km north of Tughluqabad. Open Tu-Su Apr.-Sept. 9am-7pm; Oct.-Mar. 9:30am-5:30pm. Free.*)

CENTRAL NEW DELHI

SANSAD AND RASHTRAPATI BHAVANS. Of the scores of buildings built by the British when they moved their capital from Kolkata to Delhi in 1911, Rashtrapati Bhavan (President's Residence) and Sansad Bhavan (Parliament House) are the most impressive. Designed by the renowned architect Edwin Lutyens, their massive grandeur—a not-so-subtle display of the vast reserves of British power—was intended to communicate the government's determination that India continue to be the jewel in the imperial crown. The effort backfired—the aesthetic anomaly of European-style buildings in the heart of an Indian city only further angered Indian nationalists, and the buildings became a lightning rod for criticism. In one memorable outburst, Gandhi described them as "architectural piles."

Sansad Bhavan, at the end of Sansad Marg, 1.5km southwest of Connaught Pl., is a massive circular building that resembles a flying saucer. Because India's parliament, the Lok Sabha, meets here (see **Government and Politics,** p. 66), approaching the building can be difficult. To reach **Rashtrapati Bhavan,** head left from the entrance to Parliament and bear right at the statue of Govind Ballabah Pant; or walk due west from India Gate down Rajpath. Once the residence of the viceroy, the pink Rashtrapati Bhavan is now the home of India's president. To get inside the gates of Sansad Bhavan and Rashtrapati Bhavan, you'll need special permission and possibly a letter from your embassy. Enquire at the reception at Rashtrapati Bhavan the day before; you may be allowed to enter if no dignitaries are visiting. Meanwhile, you can get a good view from Raisina Hill, the area between the secretariat buildings. Note the sturdy pillars, the massive copper dome, and the Mughal *chhattris* (kiosks). The 145m-high pillar between the gate and the residence was donated by the Maharaja of Jaipur and is thus known as the **Jaipur Column.** The pillar is capped with a bronze lotus and a six-pointed Star of India.

SECRETARIATS. Flanking Raisina Hill on its north and south sides are the symmetrical Secretariats, which now house government ministries. The buildings are adorned with a variety of slogans singing the praises of enlightened Imperial rule. For some shade (and fresh air), pass under the slogans and into the **Great Hall,** an airy room adorned with medallions and crowned by a baroque dome. Try to visit **Raisina Hill** on a Saturday, when troops march in front of Rashtrapati Bhavan. (*Ceremonial changing of the guard 10:35-11am in the winter; 8:30-9:15am in the summer.*) As you look east from the Secretariats, the arch in the distance is **India Gate,** a memorial to Indian soldiers killed in WWI and the Afghan War of 1919. A memorial beneath the arch commemorates those who were killed in the 1971 Indo-Pakistani War. On Sundays, **Rajpath,** the wide thoroughfare connecting India Gate with Raisina Hill, teems with children frolicking in the fountains; on Republic Day (Jan. 26), it is the scene of a grand military parade.

HUMAYUN'S TOMB. A poem in red sandstone and black-and-white marble, Humayun's Tomb is set amid carefully designed gardens and rows of palm trees, possess a serene grandeur. Humayun was the second Mughal emperor, ruling from 1530 until he was vanquished by Sher Shah in 1540, and again from 1555 until his death one year later. Walking down the stairs of his library, Humayun heard the *azan* and quickly sat himself down on the nearest step; upon rising, the emperor tripped and slid down the stairs. The injuries incurred in his fall proved fatal; it wasn't until 1565, nine years after his death, that his tomb was built. Later, many other prominent Mughals were buried at the site, including Dara Shikoh (Shah Jahan's favorite son) and Bahadur Shah II, the last of the Mughal emperors, who was captured here by the British during the Mutiny of 1857. Humayun's Tomb is located at the center of a rectangular, quartered garden laced with channels and paths (*charbagh*), a type of garden which reached the apex of its development with the building of the Taj Mahal. A pioneering work of Mughal architecture, the octagonal tomb sits on top of a massive pedestal; its double dome rises to a height of nearly 40m and is home to hordes of squealing bats, birds, and bees. *(2.5km southeast of India Gate. Open dawn-dusk. Rs5.)*

HAZRAT NIZAMUDDIN DARGAH. One of Sufism's greatest shrines, Hazrat Nizamuddin Dargah was originally erected in 1325, the year its occupant, the great mystic Sheikh Nizamuddin Aulia, died. The present complex, however, was most recently refurbished in the 16th century by Shah Jahan, one of Nizamuddin's many devotees. Its marble verandahs and delicate latticework are especially radiant at dawn and dusk. Nearby is the grave of the great Urdu poet, Mirza Ghalib. At twilight, bards often gather here to sing *qawwali*, Sufi songs of spiritual ecstasy. *(Southwest of Humayun's tomb, on the western end of Lodi Rd., 6km from Connaught Pl.)*

JANTAR MANTAR. This Mughal astronomical observatory feels like an M.C. Escher lithograph rendered as a red-and-white stone diorama, its rail-less stairs inflecting around tight bends and soaring upward to the heavens. Charged by the Mughal emperor Muhammad Shah with the task of revising the Indian calendar in accordance with modern astronomical knowledge, Maharaja Jai Singh of Jaipur built Jantar Mantar in 1725 after studying European and Asian science and spending years observing the skies of Delhi. The result is as scientifically impressive as it is visually striking: the massive sundials and instruments accurately tell time (in Delhi, London, and Japan), predict eclipses, and chart the movement of the stars. *(Sansad Marg, 750m southwest of Connaught Pl. Open daily sunrise-sunset. Free.)*

LODI GARDENS. Though the sign at the entrance is a bit worrisome—"shooting," it announces, "is forbidden in the park"—the leafy glories of the Lodi Gardens are very pleasant and expertly maintained. A wide variety of trees and birds make their home here—spread around some crushed Magic Masala potato chips, and you're likely to attract hordes of fluorescent green, hyper-aggressive urban parrots. Along with splendid scenery, the gardens boast a jogging trail (crowded on weekends with upper-class masochists), steamy greenhouse, and stone benches. A few ruined buildings scattered throughout the garden rise from the closely cropped grass. Toward the garden's center is the late 15th-century **Bara Gumbad,** a square tomb of gray, red, and black stones topped with a massive dome. Scholars have been unable to determine who is buried here. Attached to the tomb is a mosque, built in 1494, whose interior is embellished with dense floral patterns and Qur'anic inscriptions. The square tomb just north of Bara Gumbad is the early 16th-century **Shish Gumbad** (Glazed Dome), decorated with the remnants of blue tiles that once completely covered it. Nearly 200m north of Shish Gumbad is the badly weathered **Sikandar Lodi's Tomb** (1517-18). For views of the park, climb along the walls that enclose the tomb. Also in the Lodi Gardens, 200m southwest of Bara Gumbad, is **Muhammad Shah's Tomb,** a high-domed octagonal building constructed in the mid-15th century; 75m east of Sikandar Lodi's Tomb is a 16th-century bridge with seven arches. *(Gate 1, Lodi Rd. Gardens open dawn-dusk. Free.)*

SAFDARJANG'S TOMB. West of the Gardens is Safdarjang's Tomb, at the end of Lodi Rd. Built in 1753-54 for the prime minister to the Mughal emperor Muhammad Shah, the tomb is the last great piece of Mughal architecture in Delhi. Built at the center of expansive *charbagh* gardens, the tall, domed edifice was constructed of marble and red sandstone snatched from another local tomb. *(Open dawn-dusk. Rs2.)*

PURANA QILA. The Purana Qila (Old Fort) marks a spot that has been continuously inhabited since the Mauryan period (324-184 BC). The discovery of ceramic shards dating back to 1000 BC vindicated bearers of local tradition, who have long contended that the fort was built atop the site of Indraprastha, the capital city of the Pandava heroes of the *Mahabharata* (commemorated in a nightly sound and light show). There's never been much doubt as to the 16th-century function of Purana Qila—the massive walls, finely preserved mosque, and ruined library that formed the centerpiece of Humayun's (and later Sher Shah's) Delhi are still standing for all to see. Built in 1541 by Sher Shah, **Qila-i-Kuhna Masjid** (Mosque of the Old Fort) is an ornate tangle of calligraphic inscriptions and red sandstone. Less impressive (and less intact) is the **Sher Mandal,** which Humayun used as a library and observatory after seizing Purana Qila from Sher Shah. A small, free museum on the premises showcases some of the artifacts discovered in and around Purana Qila. The Shunga period (184-72 BC) plaques are particularly good. To get a good sense of the incredible height of the fort's walls, walk the **exercise trail,** which begins just left of the entrance to Purana Qila. The trail winds pleasantly around a small lake (dry during the summer) where there are boats for rent. *(Off Mathura Rd., 1km east of India Gate. Mosque open daily dawn-dusk. Rs2. Sound and light show daily Nov.-Jan. 7:30pm; Feb.-Apr. and Sept.-Oct. 8:30pm; May-Aug. 9pm. Rs25.)*

Next to Purana Qila is the **National Zoological Park.** On sunny Sundays, the expansive zoo teems with yelping animal-lovers. Check out the three much-raved-about white tigers. *(Open daily April 15-Oct. 15 9am-4pm, Oct. 16-Mar. 9:30am-4pm.)*

BIRLA MANDIR. Built by the wealthy Birlas in honor of Lakshmi, the goddess of material well-being, the Lakshmi Narayan Temple is a marvel of neo-Orissan temple architecture. The room of mirrors at the back of the temple allows you to see yourself together with the infinite reflections of the Krishna statue in the middle. The surrounding gardens contain ping-pong tables, a brightly colored fountain in the shape of a pile of cobras, gaily painted stone sculptures of tigers and elephants that welcome riders, and a plaster cave entered through a gaping lion's mouth. *(Mandir Marg, 2km west of Connaught Place. Open daily 5am-9pm.)*

MUSEUMS

NATIONAL MUSEUM. The museum's ambitious mission is to provide an overview of Indian life and culture from prehistoric times to the present. Ground-floor galleries showcase some of the museum's most crowd-pleasing items. Other displays trace the international development of Indian scripts, iconography, and coins over the past 16 centuries. (To see the actual coins, head up to the second floor.) An air-conditioned, room-sized vault is the setting for the museum's jewelry collection. Highlights include gaudy gilded earrings, necklaces, and bracelets dating from the first century AD. Another superb gallery on the ground floor hosts beautiful South Asian paintings, the most striking of which are from Tibet, Nepal, and Rajasthan. Also on display is a hefty collection of Neolithic stone tools (3000-1500 BC). On the second floor, the weapons and armor exhibit includes a colorful, brass-reinforced Rajasthani vest, an 18th-century bejeweled rhino-hide shield of Maharana Sangram Singh II, and the grimy curved and serrated weapons of the Pahari. More pacific pleasures can be found among the galleries of colorful masks and clothing associated with the tribal peoples of the northeastern states. The top-notch collection of musical instruments in the Sharan Rani Gallery, donated in 1980 by renowned sarod player Sharan Rani, has unusual breadth, displaying handcrafted Indian instruments including sarangis and sitars. *(Janpath, just south of Rajpath. Tel. 301 9538. Open Tu-Su 10am-5pm. Camera fee Rs10. Guided tours begin at enquiry counter 10:30, 11:30am, noon, 2, and 3:30pm. Films daily at 11:30am and 2:30pm; weekends and holidays also at 10:30am and 12:30pm.)*

CRAFTS MUSEUM. Built in 1991, the mid-sized Crafts Museum is one of the finest in South Asia, and not everything here is stuck in glass cases. The museum is divided into three sections. Entering the museum, you'll pass through an open-air demonstration area where artisans practice their craft, casting metal for sculptures, stringing jewelry, and weaving baskets from straw. Also outdoors is a village complex, filled with life-sized reproductions of rural huts and houses built by craftspeople and brought to Delhi from their native regions. Especially interesting is the vibrantly painted Orissan Gadaha Hut and a spare construction associated with Nagaland's Konyak people, where boys are schooled in preparation for life in the community. Inside, displays showcase the mind-bending diversity of traditional Indian crafts, including 18th-century wood carvings from Karnataka, dazzling storytellers' paintings, and a brightly decorated model of a Bihari wedding chamber. *(Pragati Bhawan, Bharion Marg, off Mathura Rd. Tel. 337 1641. Open Tu-Su 10am-5pm. Outdoor displays closed during the monsoon.)*

NATIONAL GALLERY OF MODERN ART. Once the Delhi mansion of the Maharaja of Jaipur, this gallery houses a culturally enlightening collection of art produced in India over the last 150 years. The collection's highlights are the paintings by artists associated with the turn-of-the-century Bengal School, which was inspired by South Asian folk art and East Asian high art. For excellent examples, see Abanindranath Tagore's searching water colors, Nandalal Bose's small, sensitive paintings, and landscapes by the poet Rabindranath Tagore. Other highlights include Kunhi Raman's cubist-influenced concrete sculpture "Standing Figure" and two 1986 masterpieces by Kapor Wasim that sardonically depict a society withering into bleakness. *(Jaipur House, east of India Gate. Local bus #621 and 622. Tel. 338 2835. Open Tu-Su 10am-5pm. Rs5, students Rs1.)*

NEHRU MUSEUM AND PLANETARIUM. Built inside the home of Jawaharlal Nehru, India's first prime minister, the museum reveals as much about the Independence movement as a whole as it does about Nehru himself. Between voyeuristic peeks into Nehru's study, office, and bathroom, check out the pictures of Nehru as a dour youth (with equally somber-looking relatives), as an ambitious student at Harrow and Cambridge, and as the humble, generous leader of India. Newspaper clippings and photographs lead through the turmoil of India's long struggle for self-rule. Adjacent to the museum is the Nehru Planetarium. *(Teen Murti Bhawan, Teen Murti Rd., north of Chanakyapuri near Murti Marg. Open Tu-Su 9am-5:15pm. Free. Planetarium open 11am-5pm. Rs1. Planetarium showings Tu-Su 11:30am and 3pm. Rs5.)*

OTHER MUSEUMS. The **Indira Gandhi Museum** features exhibits ranging from the blase (gifts the Gandhis received as prime ministers) to the macabre (the bloodstained clothes that Indira and Rajiv were wearing when they were assassinated), all arrayed in Rajiv and Indira's former residence *(1 Safdarjang; open Tu-Su 9:30am-4:45pm)*. The **National Rail Museum** has indoor and outdoor exhibits on the history of Indian Railways and a miniature train for the riding *(Chanakyapuri, near Shantipath; tel. 688 1816 or 688 0939; open Apr.-Sept. Tu-Su 9:30am-7:30pm; Oct.-Mar. 9:30am-5:30pm; Rs5, camera fee Rs100)*. At the Central Bureau of Investigation is the **National Police Museum,** replete with crime pictures, weapons like the Steel Claw, and other kinds of decidedly unpleasant punitive pieces that make you think twice about a life of crime *(Block 4 of the CGO complex, Lodi Rd.; tel. 436 0334; open M-F 10am-1pm and 2:30-5:50pm).*

DELHI

🛍 SHOPPING

Each of **Connaught Place's** blocks is home to booths peddling small curio items, souvenirs, and cold drinks. While prices are better at the **Palika Bazaar** (located beneath the grassy knoll nestled between Radial Rd. 1 and 8), the bazaars of Old Delhi, or even the markets of South Delhi, the Radial Road's stores offer good variety. If you're ready for some bargaining, they can sometimes offer fairly good value as well. Follow the hordes of Western tourists south along **Radial Road,** which becomes **Janpath,** toward the cheapest souvenir shops in Janpath Market, the government tourist offices, and the **Central Cottage Industries Emporium,** Jawahar Vyapar Bhavan, Janpath (tel. 331 2373). The Emporium has pricey furniture, clothes, and high-quality knick-knacks from all over India—a good place to stop for gifts en route to the airport. (Open M-Sa 10am-7pm.) Across the way is a good **Tibetan Market,** priced for tourists, with a wide variety of Kashmiri crafts, *chillums*, jewelry, etc., as well as light-weight travel clothes. **Old Delhi** carries it all, starting on **Chandni Chowk** (where *sari* salesmen pull you into various shops "just for looking") and winding into the maze of alleys off to the sides. **Bina Musical Stores,** 781 Nai Sarak (tel. 326 3595), has tablas and sitars, as does **A. Godin and Co.** on Sansad Marg, though the latter tends to be a bit overpriced.

DELHI

UTTAR PRADESH
उत्तर प्रदेश

Uttar Pradesh, the "Northern State," is the true heartland of India. Its parched plains spring to life at the coming of the monsoon, and from its mountains, the Ganga descends to join her sister river Yamuna in cutting across the earth. Uttar Pradesh, which has been called "U.P." for short ever since the British carved it out as the United Provinces, is India's most populous state, with 138 million residents in all. The eastern half of U.P. is one of India's most economically depressed areas, while western U.P. has shared in the prosperity of neighboring Delhi. The cradle of Indian civilization from the time of the Aryan chieftains to the reign of the great Mughal emperors, U.P. gave India the *Ramayana*, the Hindi language, and since Independence, eight of its 12 prime ministers. It has also been the focus of bitter communal and inter-caste violence. In 1992 the state's BJP government encouraged the destruction of the Babri Masjid in Ayodhya, leading to thousands of deaths in communal riots across India; the state remains a flashpoint for Hindu-Muslim tensions. Radical affirmative action politics for Dalits (former Untouchables) also have a strong base in U.P. Few people visit India without visiting U.P., yet there is nothing here to photograph, slap on a postcard, and declare representative of the state—not its sacred cities of Varanasi, Ayodhya, and Mathura, nor the hill stations and pilgrimage centers in the Himalayas, nor the Taj Mahal in the Mughal capital of Agra, nor the old Muslim city of Lucknow. There is no quintessential U.P. because U.P. is quintessentially Indian.

HIGHLIGHTS OF UTTAR PRADESH

■ **Agra** (p. 169) is home to several of India's most famous and beautiful monuments, including a gem of a royal **fort** (p. 177), the abandoned Mughal capital of **Fatehpur Sikri** (p. 179), and a little marble ditty called the **Taj Mahal** (p. 176).
■ Hinduism's holiest city, **Varanasi** (p. 197) draws the living and the dying to her crowded streets and sacred *ghats*.
■ Ashram towns like **Rishikesh** (p. 147) and **Haridwar** (p. 142), pilgrimage centers like **Gangotri** (p. 154) and **Yamnotri** (p. 153), and national reserves like **Corbett** (p. 156) and the **Valley of Flowers** (p. 155) beckon lovers of the natural and the supernatural alike to northern U.P.'s hill districts.

GARHWAL गढ़वल AND
KUMAON कुमाऊँ

The hills of Uttar Pradesh embody the holy, the hilly, and (at times) the downright helly. The neighboring regions of Garhwal and Kumaon, with their 7000m peaks and *deodar* forests, their chintzy and frenetic hill stations, their austere ashrams and high-rise temples, their sacred rivers and divine mountains, encompass enough to enthrall, enlighten, amuse, and annoy any tourist, trekker, or pilgrim.

In the 9th century the South Indian saint Shankara came to Garhwal, bringing the local population into the Hindu fold and establishing several important temples. The mountains have kept these areas relatively inaccessible for thousands of years, enabling many local customs to survive. In the early 19th century, Garhwal and Kumaon were overrun by the Nepali commander Amar Singh Thapa. In 1816 these areas came under British control and were later made part of the United Provinces. Recently, many Garhwalis and Kumaonis have agitated for a separate state within India to be called Uttarakhand (Land of the North).

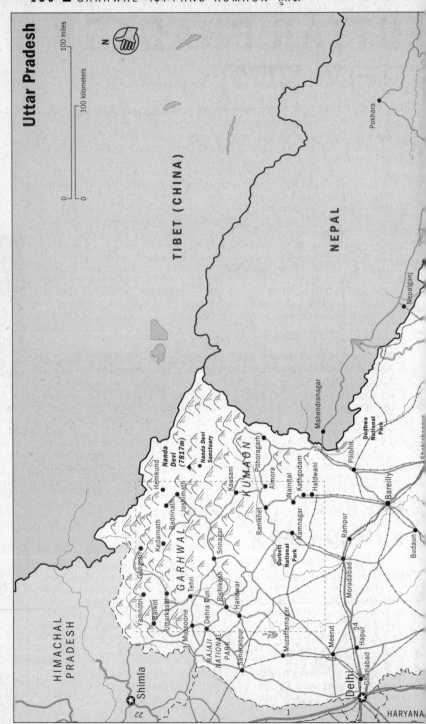

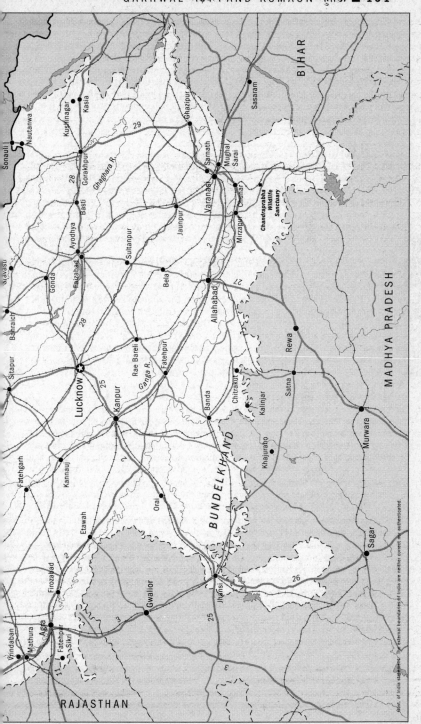

The larger hill stations—Nainital, Almora, Ranikhet, Mussoorie—are more aptly characterized as chaotic Indian cities (with Himalayan views) than as peaceful alpine retreats, and many of the more placid areas, including the major pilgrimage sites, are only open between May and November. Accommodations are provided at dharamshalas as well as at the hotels of the Garhwal Mandal Vikas Nigam (GMVN), and its sister, Kumaon MVN, hilly subsidiaries of U.P. Tourism. GMVN and KMVN hotels are reliable and clean, offering cheap beds in dormitories or expensive room accommodations, and they should be booked as much as a month in advance in peak pilgrimage season (June-Aug.).

DEHRA DUN दहराझ्

That Dehra Dun has two bus stands—one for Delhi, one for Mussoorie—reveals much about the town's polarized character. For its residents, Dehra Dun has grown into a cosmopolitan center with most of the conveniences, and vices, of other modern Indian cities: fuming auto-rickshaws race past rows of shops filled with *saris*, car parts, and English books. Local residents take great pride in education—Dehra Dun is the training ground for much of India's elite, who come to learn at the Indian Military Academy, the prestigious Doon School, or the Indian Forest Research Institute.

But there is also a gentler side to Dehra Dun, with its heart in the laid-back, life-loving ways of the nearby mountain villages. For as much as the buses and auto-rickshaws jockey for room on the congested roadways, their drivers do it with a smile. Residents take pride in their reputation for honesty and are quick to point out how kind-natured Dehra Dun's citizens are relative to their counterparts in Delhi. Most travelers just stop in Dehra Dun for a day or two before going to the Shiwaliks (the Himalayan foothills to the north) or to the hill station of Mussoorie, whose lights are visible from the city at night. There is much to keep a visitor occupied here, including temples, parks, and sulphur springs, but in the end there's too much "city" and not enough "town" to hold Dehra Dun's visitors down.

◪ TRANSPORTATION

Trains: As terminus of the **Northern Railway,** Dehra Dun sends trains all over India. The enquiry office is in the main terminal, the booking office is next door, and the computerized reservation complex is across the way. Open M-Sa 8am-1:30pm and 2:30-8pm, Su 8am-2pm. Fares listed are 2nd/1st class. To: **Delhi** (*Shatabdi Exp.* 2018, daily except Th, 5pm, 5½hr., A/C chair Rs495; *Dehradun-Mumbai Exp.* 9020, 4:45am, 9hr., Rs123/415; *Dehradun-Ujjain Exp.* 4310, 5:55am, 7hr., Rs123/415); **Haridwar** (6 per day 8am-9:30pm, 1½hr., Rs22/173); **Lucknow** (*Doon Exp.* 3010, 8:30pm, 12hr., Rs182/615); **Mumbai** (*Dehradun-Mumbai Exp.* 9020, 4:45am, 30hr., Rs386/1385).

Buses: Several companies run buses from the **Delhi Bus Stand,** next to Hotel Drona. **U.P. Roadways** (tel. 653797) to: **Delhi** (32 per day 5:15am-10:30pm, Rs90/140); **Haridwar** (every 30min. 5am-7pm, Rs18); **Haldwani** (4 per day, 9hr., Rs120); **Rishikesh** (14 per day 5am-7pm, 1½hr., Rs16). **Himachal Bus Lines** (tel. 623435) to: **Shimla** (6 per day, 10hr., Rs110). **Punjab Roadways** (tel. 624410) to: **Amritsar** (5:30 and 7:30am, 14hr., Rs141). U.P. Roadways also leaves from the **Mussoorie Bus Stand** to: **Almora** (6am, 12hr., Rs150); **Mussoorie** (every 30min. 6am-8pm, 1½hr., Rs18); **Nainital** (8am, 11hr., Rs130); **Uttarkashi** (6, 8:30, and 10:30am; 9hr.; Rs89). **Highway Motors,** 69 Gandhi Rd. (tel. 624211), next to the railway station, serves **Hanuman Chatti** (summer 6am, winter 6:30am, 8½hr., Rs78). Signs in town tout speedy, **deluxe van** service to Delhi (Rs150-200). **Taxis,** across from the bus stands, head as far as **Mussoorie** (Rs50 per person shared).

Local Transportation: Local **buses** go to nearby destinations from the City Bus Stand, north of the clock tower. **Tempos** (Rs2 per person) are common and cheap, but they may only get you part of the way to your destination since they only run along fixed routes. **Auto-rickshaws** from the Delhi Bus Stand to the Botanical Gardens are Rs50.

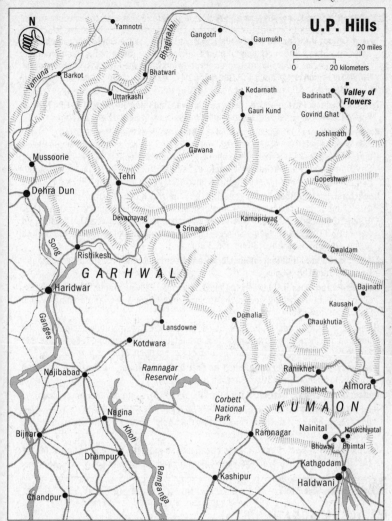

◆ ORIENTATION

Understanding the three main areas in Dehra Dun—the **railway station** area, the **central** area, and the **Astley Hall** area—helps greatly with orientation. The first, the railway station and environs, is to the south; the **Mussoorie Bus Stand** is right next to the railway station, while the **Delhi Bus Stand** (servicing most destinations *not* in the immediate hills) is a five-minute walk north along **Gandhi Road** (a major thoroughfare), just past the hard-to-miss, tan-colored **Hotel Drona**. Following Gandhi Rd. north feeds you on to **Rajpur Road** and into the second main locus of the city, which lies around the tall **clock tower.** Gandhi Park, north of the clock tower, is pretty and peaceful. The **city bus stand** is just north of the clock tower along Rajpur Rd., where many visitor services, high-end hotels, and restaurants lie. This strip is referred to as **Astley Hall** or **Dilaram Bazaar** farther north. The vast web of market streets just south of the clock tower is known as **Paltan Bazaar;** the part of the bazaar nearest to the railway station is called **Darshani Gate.**

⚡ PRACTICAL INFORMATION

Tourist Office: U.P. Tourist Office (tel. 653217), 2nd fl. in the Hotel Drona next to the Delhi Bus Stand. The most helpful tourist office in town. Open M-Sa 10am-5pm. For trekking tips and other information about the Garhwal region, try the government-run **GMVN Headquarters,** Rajpur Rd. (tel. 656817 or 654408), across from Hotel Madhuban. Open M-Sa 10am-5pm.

Trekking Agency: Private agents, such as **Garhwal Tours and Trekking** (tel. 654774), in Rohini Plaza near Hotel Ambassador, plan treks. Open M-Sa 9:15am-1:30pm.

Currency Exchange: The main branch of the **State Bank of India** (tel. 653240), 1 block east of the clock tower, changes cash and AmEx (U.S., U.K., and Canadian currencies) and Thomas Cook (U.S. and U.K. currencies) traveler's checks. Open M-F 10am-2pm, Sa 10am-noon. **Punjab National Bank,** Astley Hall (tel. 656012), on top of Gandhi Park, changes traveler's checks in U.S.$ and U.K.£ for no fee. Open M-F 10am-2pm.

Bookstore: English Book Depot (tel. 655192), next to Kumar Restaurant. Open since 1923, this shop provides a cool and organized browsing environment. Open M-Sa 10am-1:30pm and 2:30-8pm. **The Green Bookshop (Natraj Publishers),** 17 Rajpur Rd. (tel. 653382), has an esteemed nature/ecology section, including maps of the Garhwal region. Open M-Sa 10am-1:30pm and 3-8pm.

Library: Mahatma Khuhiram Public Library and Reading Room, near the Delhi bus stand. Open 8-11am and 5-8pm.

Market: Paltan Bazaar, between the clock tower and railway station, has hundreds of shops, selling everything from sitars to *saris*, and offers a very entertaining evening walk. Open daily 9am-9pm.

Hospital: Dr. Diwan, Kacheri Rd. (tel. 657660), is a well-known and respected physician and pediatrician with his own clinic. He is available 9:30am-2pm and 6-8pm. Consultation Rs80. **Jain Hospital** (tel. 627766 or 621727) is open 24hr.

Pharmacy: Many all over town, such as **Fair Deal Chemists,** 14 Darshani Gate (tel. 625252). Open M-Sa 8:30am-9pm, Su 8:30am-2pm.

Police: Dhara Chowki Station, Rajpur Rd. (tel. 653648), south of Hotel Ambassador.

Post Office: Head Post Office, by the clock tower, has *Poste Restante* (M-Sa 10am-6pm) and EMS speed post services. Parcels M-F 10am-4pm, Sa 10am-3pm; speed post M-Sa 10am-8pm. **Postal Code:** 248001.

Internet: English Book Depot has the cheapest and most reliable connection in the city (Rs50 per 30min.). Many others line Rajpur Rd.; look for the signs.

PHONE CODE	0135

▰ ACCOMMODATIONS

Hotels closer to the bus stands or clock tower tend to be either bland high-end boxes or dingy budget dives, but the noise and stink are tolerable if you're only staying a night. Classier hotels line Rajpur Rd., along Astley Hall and beyond.

Hotel White House, Astley Hall (tel. 652765), 1 block east of Rajpur Rd. While not as palatial as its Washington, D.C. namesake, it's just far enough out of downtown Dehra Dun to be a sound choice for all but those making the briefest of stopovers. Colossal rooms, pleasant gardens, and a kind manager. Check-out noon. Singles Rs180, with bath Rs200; doubles Rs250/275. Air cooling Rs60 extra. AmEx.

Hotel Victoria, 1 block off of Gandhi Rd., near Pashani Circle. Clean rooms, spacious bathrooms, and ceiling fans. Singles Rs90; doubles Rs180.

Hotel Prince, Gandhi Rd. (tel. 627070), 2 blocks south of the Delhi Bus Stand and 2 blocks east of the Mussoorie Bus Stand. A multi-story business hotel without the high-end price and pretension. Basic, stone-wall rooms have fans, comfortable mattresses, desks, and hot water (but no showers). Great top-floor views. A friendly staff adds to the value. Singles Rs150; doubles Rs250; deluxe with color cable TV Rs400; quads Rs450.

Meedo Hotel, 71 Gandhi Rd. (tel. 627088), 1 block from the railway station. Not to be confused with the expensive Meedo Grand out on Rajpur Rd., which shares this Meedo's incongruous neo-Art Deco architecture. Bucket showers, seat toilets, clean rooms. Attached restaurant. Check-out 24hr. Singles Rs150-265; doubles Rs265-285; deluxe Rs350.

Osho Resorts, 111 Rajpur Rd. (tel. 749544), 1km beyond the GMVN Tourist Office. Well-kept rooms, TVs, hot water, and super-guru Osho himself (see p. 424)! Read Osho books, watch Osho TV, or seek enlightenment in the lush meditation center. Rooms range from standard to posh-o "Osho Rajsi" rooms (A/C, carpets, and all the amenities). All rooms have a shower and seat toilet. The attached restaurant, **Heaven's Gate,** serves excellent food in a cool room. Cottage singles Rs390; doubles Rs490. Standard singles Rs490; doubles Rs590. 5% luxury tax added. Off-season rates are Rs100 less.

 FOOD

Restaurants near Astley Hall and on Rajpur Rd. are swanker than those in the grime of the bus stand area. The Paltan Bazaar area has good bakers and sweets vendors, plus a row of fruit stands toward the clock tower side. For those just stopping over, the **Venus** and **Ahuja restaurants** (across from the explosives plant on Gandhi Rd., just east of the railway gate) are open throughout the day. Local specialties include the *kulfi faluda* (Rs18), a luscious log-o'-saffron and pistachio ice cream topped with clear angel-hair noodles, available at the **Kumar Sweet Shop** (next to the clock tower).

Kumar Foods Restaurant, 15B Rajpur Rd., between the post office and Motel Himshri. Together with the **Kumar Vegetarian Restaurant** (½ block to the north) and aforementioned sweets shop, this place rules the food scene in town. Magically delicious renditions of Indian specialties. The *rogan josh* (Rs55) and chicken *tikka masala* (Rs90) are particularly tasty. Great service with a subdued and classy ambience. Open daily 11am-4pm and 7-10:30pm; closed last Tu of the month.

Kasturi Vaishnav Bhojanalama, Gandhi Rd., across from the Venus Restaurant. Extremely popular with locals, this place has a good-natured staff and homey atmosphere. Veg. dishes Rs20-25. Open daily 8am-10pm. Closed last Su of the month.

Motimahal Restaurant, Rajpur Rd., across from the Hotel Ambassador. Quality non-veg. food from a large menu in a dimly-lit, beige dining room with plush drapes and classical Indian prints. No fewer than 18 fans plus A/C make this the coolest duck-away spot in town. Try the chicken curry (Rs60), the mutton *shahi korma* (Rs55), or the *dal makhani* (Rs28). Open daily 9am-10:30pm.

Daddy's, Rajpur Rd., next to the Hotel President. A wanna-be western-style burger joint that comes through on all but interior design. South Indian and Chinese foods accompany a menu of pizza, "thirst aids," fries (Rs25), and theme burgers (Rs40-60) like the "Great Daddy's Twin" (Rs44). Open daily 9:30am-9:30pm.

Baskin Robbins, next to Daddy's. All 31 flavors are represented here in India just like in your local sundae store. Cones Rs50. Open daily 11am-9pm.

👁 SIGHTS

Most of what's to be done in Dehra Dun lies outside the city. Buses and tempos leave for all destinations from the city bus stand; taxis and auto-rickshaws charge Rs40-100 for trips to any of the sights and Rs400-500 for a full day of sightseeing. If you really want to take your time, pick a destination and make it a full day's excursion. If seeing is more important than staying, however, then a good option is the GMVN day-long package bus trip, **Doon Darshan,** which covers the FRI, Tapkeshwar Temple, Malsi Deer Park, and Sahastra Dhara (Rs95). The bus stops for 45 to

90 minutes at each place (leaves daily at 10:30am, returns at 5pm). Contact **Drona Travel,** 45 Gandhi Rd. (tel. 654371), by the Hotel Drona (open daily 7am-10pm). Book one day in advance.

FOREST RESEARCH INSTITUTE (FRI). Established under British auspices in 1906, and residing in its current location since 1924, the FRI has led the country (and the world) toward a better understanding of the uses and abuses of various aspects of forestry, botany, and biodiversity conservation. The long building is beautifully and incorrigibly colonial, and the vast lawn is reminiscent of a European royal palace. Even if you're not into forestry, there's still quite a bit to do here: there are six museums focusing on different aspects of forest life, from the bugs to the trees. The best of the museums is the one devoted to pathology, the cataloguing of plant diseases. The green lawn of the institute's **Botanical Gardens** makes a wonderful picnic spot; feasting in your own nook of the estate is allowed by permission of the director. There is a canteen for afternoon tea or snacks, and at the far corner of the institute there is an information desk with free pamphlets about the institute's many functions. *(Visitors gate on Trevor Rd. Open M-F 9am-5:30pm;. museums open M-F 10am-5:30pm, Su 10am-2pm. Botanical Gardens Rs10.)*

TAPKESHWAR TEMPLE. Dedicated to Shiva, this temple is the most sacred in the immediate area. Because the temple was built into the mountain beside a running stream, the inside is damp, cool, and filled with a curious combination of incense and mist. Note the central *linga* onto which water drips from above. There are several shrines around the temple's entrance, and the nearby stream also serves as a popular swimming hole. The temple is also the site of the **Shivaratri celebration** in the last week of March and the first week of April. *(6km northwest of town. One-way auto-rickshaw Rs60; city bus or tempo from the clock tower Rs2. Open daily 5:30am-9pm.)*

ROBBER'S CAVE. Another natural picnic spot near Dehra Dun is Robber's "Cave," also called **Buchu Pani,** which is actually a 200m long, 15m high chasm. Visitors wade through the stream at the small canyon's bottom, where the water has smoothed the grey rock. At the other end is an opening with large boulders for climbing and even a few little pools for swimming. Wear sandals to Robber's Cave, as the rocks in the stream can be sharp. There's a "real" swimming pool about 100m on the other side from where tour buses stop. *(8km north of town. Transport drops you off 100m from the cave's entrance.)*

MUSSOORIE मसूरी

The mountain hill station of Mussoorie is chintzy, overpriced, and often overcrowded; however, it's also refreshingly cool, in close proximity to tranquil forests, and—because of (*not* in spite of) its touristy, carnival atmosphere—a hell of a lot of fun. The town certainly isn't for everyone—travelers attempting to shun commercialism in favor of spirituality should stay in nearby Haridwar or Rishikesh, and those hoping for mountain tranquility may be better off in Kumaon. But anyone with an interest in the bizarre subculture of Indian tourists could find no better point of observation. A trip to Mussoorie, however brief, will let you timewarp to an era where big hair, clunky roller skates, and the original Nintendo ruled the entertainment scene.

While today it is the focal destination for heat-fleeing tourists from Delhi (it's the closest hill station to the capital), the town was first settled in 1827 by an Englishman, Captain Young. British officials later developed Mussoorie into a Victorian home-away-from-home-away-from-home, complete with an exclusive club, libraries, and an Anglican Church. The central promenade, the mall, was made for afternoon strolls and crusty chit-chat, all in full view of the snow-peaked Himalayas to the northeast and the Doon Valley to the south.

Where once the British rulers ascended the 11km uphill to Mussoorie carried by porters, now Indian throngs pack their Marutis and cruise up the scenic drive from the plains. Peak season is between May and July. Mid-season extends from July to

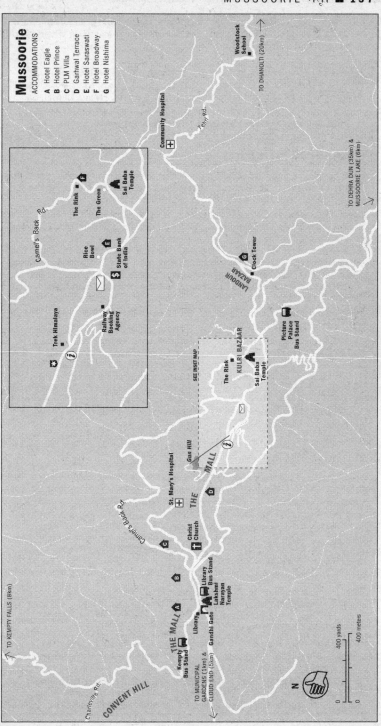

Mussoorie

ACCOMMODATIONS
- **A** Hotel Eagle
- **B** Hotel Prince
- **C** PLM Villa
- **D** Garhwal Terrace
- **E** Hotel Saraswati
- **F** Hotel Broadway
- **G** Hotel Nishima

Woodstock School

TO DHANOLTI (20km)

Community Hospital

Tehri Rd.

The Rink

The Green

Sai Baba Temple

Camel's Back Rd.

Rice Bowl

State Bank of India

Clock Tower

LANDOUR BAZAAR

TO DEHRA DUN (35km) & MUSSOORIE LAKE (6km)

Trek Himalaya

Railway Booking Agency

SEE INSET MAP

The Rink

KULRI BAZAAR

Sai Baba Temple

Picture Palace Bus Stand

Gun Hill

St. Mary's Hospital

THE MALL

Camel's Back Rd.

Christ Church

TO KEMPTY FALLS (8km)

Charleville Rd.

CONVENT HILL

THE MALL

Kempty Bus Stand

Library

Gandhi Gate

Library Bus Stand

Lakshmi Narayan Temple

TO MUNICIPAL GARDENS (1km) & CLOUD END (5km)

400 yards
400 meters

N

October (the foggy monsoon months) and March to May, and prices during these times are mid-range. The off-season, November through March, is when you're more likely to find solitude (and substantial snowfall).

> ⚠ **WARNING.** There is an Indian Army encampment at **Chakrata**, 82km north-west of Mussoorie. No foreigners are allowed north of the east-west road between Yamuna Bridge and Kalsi without a permit from the army. Foreign tourists heading by road for Shimla or eastern Himachal Pradesh must do so via Herbertpur. Foreign tourists have been arrested for traveling north of Kalsi.

⬛ TRANSPORTATION

Trains: No tracks run to Mussoorie, but computerized reservations for trains from Dehra Dun can be made at the **Northern Railways Out Agency,** on the mall below the post office. Open M-F 9am-1pm and 2-4pm, Sa 9-11am and noon-4pm, Su 9am-2pm.

Buses: U.P. Roadways, leaving from the **Kulri** or **Library Bus Stands** (both below the mall) and servicing only **Dehra Dun.** From the Library Bus Stand (tel. 632258; every 30min. 7am-6pm, 1½hr., Rs18). From the Kulri Bus Stand (tel. 632259; every 30min. 6am-7pm, 1½hr., Rs16). Several signs around town advertise daily direct Dehra Dun-Delhi deluxe service, but you have to get to Dehra Dun yourself. Try **Mussoorie Novelty Store** (tel. 632795), opposite the railway booking office. Non-A/C buses (11am and 10pm, Rs150) and A/C buses (8, 11am, and 10pm; Rs250) depart from the clock tower in Dehra Dun.

Taxis: Booking stands next to both bus stands. To: **Dehra Dun** (Rs70 per seat, Rs350 per car); **Haridwar** (Rs750 per car).

✴ ORIENTATION

Mussoorie is 15km long, stretching around the mountain overlooking Dehra Dun, though the town proper is much more compact. The town has two centers, the **Library Bazaar** and **Kulri Bazaar** areas, connected by a 30-minute walk along the **mall,** which is lined with murals and shops of all kinds. Buses from the valley stop near both bazaars. The plaza in front of the library, with a statue of the Mahatma, is called **Gandhi Chowk;** the gate by the library is **Gandhi Gate. Camel's Back Road** runs along the back side of the mountain and connects the two bazaars. **Landour Bazaar,** with its large clock tower, is a 10-minute walk east of Kulri.

⬛ PRACTICAL INFORMATION

Tourist Office: (tel. 632863), near the ropeway, halfway between Kulri and Library Bazaars. Provides handy color brochures about Mussoorie, local sights, and nearby treks. Open daily 9am-7pm, July-Apr. M-Sa 10am-5pm.

Budget Travel: GMVN (tel. 631281), at the Library Bus Stand, offers tours of the northern pilgrimage sites departing from Delhi and Rishikesh. Trips range from a 4-day excursion to Badrinath (Rs2000) to a 12-day voyage to Yamnotri, Gangotri, Kedarnath, and Badrinath (Rs5000). Staff speaks minimal English. Open daily 9am-7pm, Aug.-Apr. 9am-5pm. For sojourns into the hills, **Trek Himalaya** (tel. 30491), on the mall above the ropeway, provides assistance in fluent English for both organized trips and drop-in consultations. Guides available. Tent rental Rs80-100 per day. Fully planned excursions US$50-70 per person for groups of 4 or more. Open daily Mar.-Oct. 10am-8:30pm.

Currency Exchange: State Bank of India, Kulri Bazaar (tel. 632533), cashes AmEx, Thomas Cook, and Citicorp checks in U.S., U.K., and Canadian currencies. Rs4 per check; encashment certificates Rs25. Open M-F 10am-2pm, Sa 10am-noon.

Market: Tibetan Market, along and below the mall near the library. **Kulri Bazaar** has many stores specializing in curios, woolens, and tourist trifles (particularly popular with Indians is the miniature riding whip). Bazaars generally open 9am-9pm.

Library: Tilak Memorial Library, off the mall in Kulri. Open 9am-noon and 4-8pm. The attractive **Mussoorie Library** is better, but it's designed for locals and you can't get in without a week-long application process or an outlandish outpouring of charm.

Bookstore: Several good bookstores along the mall in Kulri have magazines, fiction, and nonfiction. Most open daily 8am-8pm. The **Prabhu Book Depot,** near Banares House Sarees, has a range of popular fiction and Archie comics.

Pharmacies: Ubiquitous along the mall. **P.B. Hamers & Co.** (tel. 632502), up from the Rialto Cinema by President's Restaurant, has a wide selection. Open daily 10am-9pm.

Hospital/Medical Services: The **Community Hospital** (tel. 632541), in Landour 1.5km east of the clock tower, has 24hr. emergency care. **St. Mary's Hospital** (tel. 632144) has branches at Kulri and at Gunhill; both provide ambulance services. For more private treatment, try the **clinic** of Dr. Rana and Dr. Nautiyal (tel. 632594), on the road above the Kulri Mall. Clinic open daily 10am-1pm and 4-7pm.

Police: (tel. 632083), above the mall, just west of the Hotel Mall Queen. Open 24hr. **Landour police** (tel. 632082); chief inspector (tel. 632206).

Post Office: (tel. 632806), near State Bank of India, above the mall in Kulri. Has registered and speed post (via EMS). *Poste Restante* and most services available. Open M-F 9am-1pm and 1:30-5pm, Sa 9am-noon. **Postal Code:** 248179.

Internet: Cyber Corner (tel. 630332), right past Gandhi Gate, offers Mussoorie's only commercial internet access. Rs50 per 30min. Open daily 8am-11pm.

PHONE CODE	0135

ACCOMMODATIONS

Most low-end options are in the **Kulri Bazaar** area. Try to book ahead of time in peak season (May-June), when rates are boosted. Expect discounts mid-season (Mar.-May and July-Oct.), and drastically slashed prices from November to March.

KULRI AND LANDOUR

Garhwal Terrace (tel. 632682 or 632683), on the Mall between Kulri and Library Bazaars. This GMVN-run hotel has dormitories that open up to a lovely veranda with mountain views. Slightly ritzier than at most government hotels. Dorm beds Rs100; rooms Rs1000. Jul. 16-Apr. 15: Rs50/Rs500. Reserve in advance during peak season.

Hotel Saraswati (tel. 631005), up the ramp from the more visible Hotel Amar, past Hotel Mansarovar. Because of its somewhat hidden location, it's likely to have rooms when all else is full. Rooms are immaculate, the staff is gracious, and the surroundings are peaceful in comparison to the activity on Mall Rd. Rooms have mirrors, TVs, seat toilets, and hot water. Doubles Rs250-500. Off-season: 50% discount.

Hotel Broadway, Camel's Back Rd. (tel. 632243), close to the rink near Kulri Bazaar. This converted English guest house retains charm in a peaceful setting, away from all the clamor except that of the roller rink and the nearby mosque. Rooms with balcony have valley view; some have seat toilets. Food available. May 1-July 15: singles Rs200; doubles Rs250, with valley view Rs300, with hot water Rs400. Off-season: 50% discount.

Hotel Nishima, Landour Bazaar (tel. 632227), past the clock tower. Popular among language school students, Nimisha has bright rooms and huge buckets of hot water. Rest easy on thick mattresses behind heavy metal doors. TV in the lobby. Food available, and seat toilets for the lucky few. Rates given are for foreigners—try bargaining with the owners. May-June: doubles Rs150-200.

LIBRARY AREA

Hotel Prince (tel. 632674), off the mall, up the ramp from the horse stand—look for the alley access 30m toward Kulri from the library. A magnificent government-designed site set high above the Mall in a century-old royal summer getaway. Regal halls, huge rooms, high ceilings, and high tea in the drawing room or on the patio. May 15-July 15: doubles Rs600-800. Off-season: 25-50% discount.

PLM Villa (tel. 631090), off Camel's Back Rd., a 5min. walk from the Library. Small garden-fronted place popular with Indian families. Although rooms are small, the views are spectacular. Food available 7am-10pm. Check-out noon. In-season: doubles Rs150, with attached bath Rs200-350. Off-season: 50% discount.

Hotel Eagle (tel. 631446), west of the library, in the bazaar. Clean and simple rooms just inches away from the crazy bazaar (which quiets down at bedtime). Doubles Rs300-400. Off-season: 25-50% discount.

OUTSIDE MUSSOORIE

🏔 **Cloud End Forest Resort** (tel. 632242; fax 625657), west of the library on the road to the municipal gardens; 7km by jeep. Set amid 2000 acres of unadulterated forest on the crest of a ridge overlooking Mussoorie on one side and a lush valley on the other. One of the four oldest buildings in Mussoorie, it was built in 1838 by an East India Company tycoon. The period ambience has been scrupulously preserved with old photographs, plush, upholstered armchairs, and dark wooden beds. At night, guests enjoy tea and snacks beside bonfires under star-filled skies. The restaurant serves unusually fresh and flavorful food—see if they'll make you some *paneer tikka*. The posh doubles are priced accordingly, but spartan dorm bunks get you in cheaply. Camping is also an option (Rs100 per person, Rs50 if you have your own tent). Reserve a day ahead to avoid the Rs150 jeep fee from the library. Dorm bunks Rs200; doubles Rs1000. Off-season: 50% discount. Closed Jan. to mid-Mar. Rs100 fee for MC, Visa, AmEx.

⭕ FOOD

Roasted *masala* corn (Rs5-15) is sold along the Mall, and sweets are scooped up at **Krishna's** in Kulri. Food prices listed are in-season.

The Green, Kulri Bazaar, offers delicious veg. fare at reasonable prices, though a long line of customers makes it impossible to relax in the afterglow of your scrumptious meal. For breakfast, try the lewdly buttered *paratha* (Rs18), stuffed with eggs and topped with raisins and cashews. Open daily 7am-3:30pm and 7-10pm. Off-season: 8am-3:30pm and 7:30-10:30pm.

Rice Bowl, Kulri Bazaar, across from President Restaurant, upstairs. Dining cubicle with street view. Serves Chinese and Tibetan food—a rarity in Mussoorie. Try the garlic chicken (Rs55) or steamed mutton *momos* (Rs20). Noodles and rice available in enormous portions (Rs40-80). Open daily 11am-11:30pm. Off-season: 11am-9:30pm.

Jeet Restaurant, right on Gandhi Chowk, next to the library and Jeet Hotel. The ideal place to plan your trek or your next move since the tables have regional maps built into them. Mostly veg. fare (Rs30-50), nothing fancy-schmancy; chicken curry (Rs65). Cogitate over hot cocoa (Rs20). Attentive service. Open daily 8am-10:30pm.

Le Chef, near the State Bank of India in Kulri. Tries hard to be Western and does a commendable job, with order numbers called over an incomprehensible speaker. French fries (Rs15), pizza (Rs50), hot dogs (Rs35), "gravy items," and fountain drinks. A popular teen hang-out, especially for the after-roller-skating crowd. Open daily 10am-11pm.

Howard Revolving Restaurant, Hotel Howard, on the Mall between Kulri and Library. The small, round restaurant makes one noisy, clunky rotation every 9min.—you may not notice that you're rotating, but you'll wonder why the earth is shaking violently. Good cucumber and tomato salad (Rs15) and lip-smacking *lassis* (Rs15). Last rotation at 11:21pm! Open daily 7:30-11am, 1-3:30pm, and 9:30-11:30pm.

🎵 ENTERTAINMENT

The **Basu Cinema,** in the Library area, and the **Rialto Cinema,** in Kulri across from the President's Restaurant, frequently show Hindi movies (4 daily). There is an abundance of **arcade games** (some dating back to the pre-Pac-Man era—Speed Racer is a local favorite) in the several parlors clustered in Kulri (Rs3 per game). There are several discos in the Mussoorie area, but the nightlife merely duplicates the bazaars' numerous restaurants and opportunities for gawking. **Hotel Rockwood,** Kulri Bazaar (tel. 632850), rocks every night, but only local men seem to go (open daily 8-11pm; Rs150, Rs250 per couple). Outside town, **Residency Manor,** Hotel Jaypee (tel. 631800), has dancing on the weekends (Rs250-375, including dinner).

Mussoorie's true hotspot, **The Rink,** in Kulri, is India's largest roller skating rink. The rink itself dates back 100 years to when British couples experimented with what was all the rage back home. Rent full-shoe skates (Rs50) or strap-ons. Five skating sessions thump to Indian and Western pop music daily. (Beginners 8:30-10am; open skating 11am-1pm, 3-5pm, 6-7:30pm, and 8-9:30pm. Admission with rental Rs40, with your own skates Rs35, "spectators" Rs5.) Those less inclined to roller-derby glory might appreciate the **billiards** here (Rs100 per hr.). Several other rinks can be found below the Mall.

👁 SIGHTS

GUN HILL. Looming directly over the town is Gun Hill, its moniker earned through a pre-Independence ritual of firing guns from the top at midday—the townspeople would adjust their watches accordingly. It's possible to walk (40min.) or to ride rented horses to get to the top, but the best way is via Mussoorie's **ropeway,** a cable car that zips up the 500m mountainside. *(Open daily 8am-10pm; last car up at 8pm. Off-season: 10am-7pm. Rs25 round-trip.)* The top of Gun Hill has several lookout points, small food vendors, a surreal and amusing **Laugh House** with a loud laugh track and bent mirrors to distort your image *(Rs10),* and several photo stands that will photograph you up in glittery local costume. Air-rifle shooting booths are also popular and offer you the chance to win ratty stuffed animals and toys made of decomposing plastic *(Rs5 to play).*

CAMEL'S BACK ROAD. There are several good spots for **walking** around Mussoorie, passing through fragrant pine and *deodar* forests. Camel's Back Road, which winds behind the town (3km total), offers keen views of the Himalayas. Points of interest include the **cemetery** (if the main gate is closed, try the side gate), studded with interesting British tombstones; **Camel's Back Rock** itself, which is shaped like a you-know-what; and **Chatra (Umbrella) Point,** where you can buy *chai* and snacks and look through a telescope, if it isn't broken. The entire walk takes 40 minutes. On a clear day, the sunset view from the road is spectacular.

MUSSOORIE LAKE. The town's newest natural attraction is actually an artificially constructed lake located 6m from town on the road to Dehra Dun. Mussoorie Lake is donut-shaped, with a fountain in the center. Catch a breeze and gaze at the hills while gliding around the lake in a paddle boat (Rs50 per 30min.). Although there's little else here save for a few small shops, this may actually be just what you want after a few days in Mussoorie's bustling Mall area.

DAYTRIPS. To the west lie **Happy Valley** and the nearby **Municipal Garden** *(3km from Mussoorie),* which has a tiny pool for paddle-boats. Two kilometers from the garden are the ruins of the old Mackinnon brewery (see **Strange Brew,** p. 142). A more distant destination to the northwest of town is **Kempty Falls,** a popular "retreat" which has sadly degenerated from an idyllic spot overlooking pristine, rushing falls and peaceful pools to the same old glitz that pervades the rest of town. GMVN runs a three-hour bus trip to Kempty falls *(Apr.-Oct. 9am, noon, and 3pm; off-season 10am and 1pm; Rs50).* They also run combined daytrips to the orchards and dense *deodar* forest of **Dhanolti** *(25km away),* the artificial lake at **Jheel,** which provides boating facilities, and **Surkanda Devi** *(35km from Mussoorie, Rs120).* This temple, atop the highest mountain in the area (3300m), provides great views of snow covered peaks. It's a strenuous 2km walk to the temple from the road head. **Cloud End** (see p. 140), 4km away, is a fairly untouched hiking spot.

LANDOUR LANGUAGE SCHOOL. At the top of the mountain, above Landour Bazaar, is the Landour Language School. Founded in 1870 by British missionaries and grammarians, it launched the international academic study of modern Indian

STRANGE BREW Though an Englishman founded Mussoorie, it took an unruly Scot to set the tone for the revelry that has outlasted the Brits in the hill station. In the 1880s, a fellow named Mackinnon encountered limestone springs—promising for brewing—near present-day Gandhi Chowk. Mackinnon seized the idea and the land and constructed a brewery which soon began producing Garhwal's first fine domestic beer. From the beginning, Mussoorie was a fun-loving town, and the beer-brewing led to a level of bacchanalian debauchery that wrinkled more than a few official brows. Local lore has it that one English lass, well progressed in the appreciation of the Scotch-Indian brew, stood on a chair on Mall Rd. and sold kisses for Rs5. That spelled trouble for Mackinnon. Since an outright ban on Mackinnon's operation would have been illegal, the authorities shrewdly crippled him by refusing him the right to import barley on the government road. Shut down but not broken in spirit(s), Mackinnon would not be snubbed—especially by the English. In a daring scheme, he built his own road, 20km long, fitting it with carts to transport his barley. He even set up a watchtower and tollbooth and ran it as a private highway. Aside from beerstuffs, much of the heavy European furniture in Mussoorie was brought up on "Mr. Buckles' Bullock-Cart Train," as the venture was called. And so, Mussoorie had its beer.

To thank his consumers, Mackinnon threw a massive bash, where he cracked a huge wooden cask of new brew. All present were astonished at how truly excellent it was. The rollicking horde polished off most of the keg, noting repeatedly that it tasted better than any beer in the history of brewing. A scream of horror suddenly broke up the festivities—for in the dregs of the keg lay a decomposing human body. Apparently, an impatient imbiber had slipped into the cellar, helped himself to a few too many, and fallen in with the hops.The brew was through. Mackinnon's ruined brewery looms on the Lynndale Estate 3km west of Mussoorie, but his bullock-cart road now forms 20km of the present road to Rajpur.

languages and now offers credit programs in tandem with the University of Chicago and UC Berkeley, among others. Classes are small, with plenty of individual instruction for the school's 80 or so students. Courses offered range from introductory to graduate classes, and the sensitive administration may be able to tailor instruction to particular circumstances. A 12-week introductory Hindi class costs Rs18,000. Private lessons are Rs75 per hour. Students usually stay in private houses (Rs5000 per month) or in one of the two guest houses near the school (Rs300 per day including food). Contact Principal Chitranjan Datt, Landour Language School, Landour, Mussoorie, U.P., 248179 (tel. 631487; fax 631917).

HARIDWAR हरिद्वार

The city of Haridwar marks the spot where the Ganga emerges from the mountains to carve its tortuous way across India to the Bay of Bengal. Haridwar is a very sacred site, especially for Punjabi Hindus. The city's spiritual preeminence is rooted in three distinct Hindu legends: here, the goddess Ganga was persuaded to descend from the heavens to sanctify 60,000 poor souls burnt to ashes when they disturbed the meditation of Rishi Kapil; Vishnu's footprint is said to mark a stone set in the wall of Har-ki-Pairi (Footstep of God), the main *ghat* to the Ganga; and, most strikingly, Har-ki-Pairi is the site where a divine drop of nectar fell from a pot (*kumbh*) over which the gods and demons had fought for 12 days (see **The Kumbh Mela**, p. 213). The *ghat* became a particularly auspicious spot for a huge communal swim, and during the Kumbh Mela, held in Haridwar once every 12 years, millions rush the Har-ki-Pairi *ghat* at a precisely calculated moment. Often, stampedes during the Mela result in mass killings; at Haridwar's most recent Mela in 1988, 14 devotees were trampled to death. The Har-ki-Pairi also plays host to Haridwar's *aarti* ceremony, a ritual performed every evening at sundown, when pilgrims float candle-lit flower boats down the Ganga.

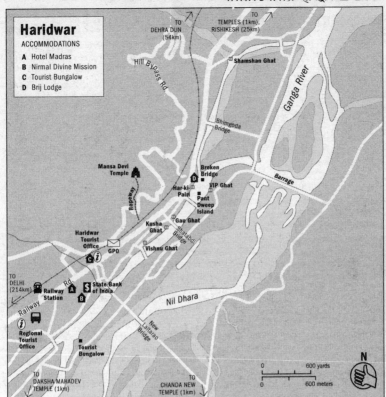

Hindus take holy Haridwar very seriously, and their reverence isn't limited to Mela years. A steady stream of pilgrims courses through the city year-round to worship at the city's many temples. Ancient and modern shrines sit side by side along the Ganga. Although some more modern temples have resorted to gimmicks to draw in visitors, the city's spirit remains sincere in its deep religious devotion.

TRANSPORTATION

Trains: Northern Railway Station, next to the bus stand on Railway Rd. Enquiry on the right-hand side, reservation counter on the other. Buy general tickets at **Northern Railway Booking Office,** Railway Rd. (tel. 427724), north of Laltarao Bridge. Fares listed are for 2nd class sleeper/1st class. To: **Dehra Dun** (9 per day 5:30am-4:55pm, 2hr., Rs84/173); **Delhi** (*Dehradun-Mumbai Exp.* 9020, 1:55pm, 7hr.; *Mussoorie Exp.* 4042, 11:15pm, 8hr., Rs104/352; *Shatabdi Exp.* 2018, 6pm, 4½hr., Rs460 A/C chair car); **Lucknow** (*Dehradun-Howrah Exp.* 3010, 11pm, 11hr,, Rs166/562); **Mumbai** (*Dehradun-Mumbai Exp.* 9020, 1:55pm, 48hr. or more, Rs374/1334); **Rishikesh** (5, 8:45am, and 5:15pm; Rs80/136); **Varanasi** (*Doon Exp.* 3010, 11pm, 20hr., Rs104/352).

Buses: The **bus stand** is across from the railway station at the southwest end of Railway Rd. **U.P. Roadways** (tel. 427037) runs buses to: **Agra** (5 per day 2:30-9pm, 11hr., Rs120; deluxe 7 and 9:15am, Rs196); **Dehra Dun** (every 30min. 5:30am-10:30pm, 1½hr., Rs20); **Delhi** (every 15min. 4:30am-11:30pm, 5hr., Rs73); **Lucknow** (noon, 3:30, and 7:30pm; 14hr.; Rs175); **Rishikesh** (every 30min., 45min., Rs10); **Shimla** (6, 10am, 5, and 10pm; 12hr.; Rs135).

Local Transportation: Tempos cluster on the east bank of the Shatabdi Bridge. From the railway station to Har-ki-Pairi Rs2-3; by **auto-rickshaw** Rs10; by **cycle-rickshaw** Rs5-10.

ORIENTATION AND PRACTICAL INFORMATION

Haridwar runs parallel to and along the River Ganga, which flows from northeast to southwest. Buses and trains arrive at stations near the southwest end of **Railway Road,** the town's main thoroughfare, where most services lie. Walking northeast on Railway Rd., you'll cross **Laltarao Bridge** (over a small stream, not the Ganga) before reaching the post office. Just south of the post office is a barricade that prohibits motor traffic from continuing up Railway Rd. North of this barricade, Railway Rd. becomes **Upper Road.** The main bazaar in town is **Moti Bazaar,** which runs along the streets below Upper Rd., parallel to the river near **Har-ki-Pairi,** which is at the northeast end of Upper Rd. Beyond that is **Broken Bridge**. A strip of land across the river hosts accommodations and the taxi stand. Haridwar's **temples** are spread throughout the city.

Tourist Office: GMVN, Railway Rd. (tel. 424240), at Laltarao Bridge, provides good maps of Haridwar and Rishikesh and has information on local treks. Open M-Sa 10am-5pm. **U.P. Tourism** (tel. 427370), next to Rahi Motel across from the railway station, focuses on the larger Garhwal region rather than Haridwar itself. Open M-Sa 10am-5pm.

Budget Travel: Ashwani Travels, Railway Rd. (tel. 424581), just south of Laltarao Bridge. Open daily 8am-10pm. **Shivalik Travels,** Upper Rd. (tel. 426855), opposite Goraksh Nath Ashram, specializes in transportation to northern pilgrimage sites. Open daily 7am-3pm and 5-10pm. Pilgrimage destinations are open May-Oct.

Currency Exchange: State Bank of India changes U.S. currency at its branch on Sharwan Nath Nagar. Open M-F 10am-2pm, Sa 10am-noon.

Market: Moti Bazaar, 1 block north on Railway Rd. from Laltarao Bridge.

Bookstore: Arjun Singh Bookseller, Bara Bazaar (tel. 421449). Open daily 9am-9:30pm

Pharmacy: Milap Medical Hall, Railway Rd. (tel. 427193), south of and opposite the post office, has drugs, sunscreen, maxi-pads, and toilet paper. Open M-Sa 8:30am-10pm. **Dr. B.C. Hasaram & Sons,** Railway Rd. (tel. 427860), across from the police station, specializes in ayurvedic medicines. Open daily 8am-9pm.

Hospital/Medical Services: Several private clinics are on Railway Rd. **Dr. Kailash Pande** (tel. 426023, emergency tel. 424343), north of Laltarao Bridge, provides **24hr. emergency care;** ask for Dr. O.P. Sharma. Open 11:30am-2:30pm and 6:30-9:30pm. **Ram Krishnan Mission Hospital** (tel. 427141), located east of the river, 1km down MG Rd. from the tourist office, has clean facilities and an English speaking staff.

Police: Main station (tel. 426200 or 425200), Laltarao Bridge.

Post Office: (tel. 427025), on Railway Rd. north of Laltarao Bridge. *Poste Restante,* EMS speed post services. Open M-Sa 10am-4pm. **Postal Code:** 249401.

PHONE CODE	0133

ACCOMMODATIONS

From November to March prices are 25-50% lower. Unless noted, the prices listed below are for high (pilgrimage) season.

Nirmal Divine Mission (tel. 423301), off Railway Rd., 2 blocks north of the railway station. Turn right at Kailash Hotel, go up 3 short blocks, and it's on the left. Look for the large Hindi and small English signs. Good fans, showers (buckets of hot water if showers stop working), and seat toilets. Cooking facilities and mostly Indian guests give a neighborly, homey feel. Small balconies on front rooms. Singles Rs90; doubles Rs120.

Hotel Madras (tel. 426356), off Railway Rd., 2 blocks north of the railway station. Turn right after the Kailash Hotel. A low-end old-timer conveniently close to transport. Rooms built in 1950s have common bath and carpets (also circa 1950). Room service and a highly attentive staff. Singles Rs50; doubles Rs80.

Brij Lodge (tel. 426872), north of Har-ki-Pairi on the right, near the broken bridge (the name is not visible from the road). Watch the nightly *aarti* ritual from the expansive balcony overlooking the Ganga. All rooms have attached bath with seat toilets but no showers. Doubles Rs300; quads Rs650. Off-season: 60-80% discount..

Tourist Bungalow (tel. 426379), across the river from town toward the railway station. Buses pass by on the way in, so keep an eye out and ask the driver to stop. It's pricey and far from most sights, but it's the best place for peace and quiet, with its own little lawn, flower garden, and, strip of riverbank on the holy Ganga. All rooms have air-cooling and attached bath with hot water and seat toilets. Restaurant open 6:30am-10:30pm. Check-out noon. Dorm beds Rs100; air-cooled singles Rs555, with A/C Rs1100; doubles Rs650/1300. Off-season: 25% discount.

FOOD

Purity of diet follows purity of spirit in Haridwar, so alcohol and meat are not available. Most major restaurants are on Railway Rd., midway between the bus stand and Har-ki-Pairi, though some of the little places tucked into the bazaar near Har-ki-Pairi make mean, clean breakfast *puris*.

Ahaar Restaurant, "Asli" Railway Rd., near Laltarao Bridge. The Sikh owner presides from his desk as guests enjoy exceptional South Indian, Chinese, and Punjabi food in a dark, tranquil, subterranean wooden chamber. The hefty Punjabi *thali* (Rs50) is milder than other dishes. Other *thalis* Rs35-65, *dosas* Rs18-30. Open daily 10am-11pm.

New Mysore Kwality Restaurant, Railway Rd., on the west side of Railway Rd. two-thirds of the way to Har-ki-Pairi. South Indian-run restaurant has an unassuming atmosphere, cool air, and great prices. Tomato *utthapam* Rs16, full *thalis* Rs25-40, *dosas* Rs10-20. Open daily 7am-10pm (closes 9pm in winter).

Swagat Restaurant, Railway Rd., in Hotel Mansarovar. Typical business-hotel-restaurant. Entrees Rs40, *thalis* Rs55, veg. chow mein Rs28, rice Rs10. Open daily 6am-11pm.

Chotiwala Restaurant, Upper Rd., near Har-ki-Pairi. Haridwar branch of the Rishikesh institution offers similar food in a less frenetic environment. Veg. *thalis* Rs25-60, and a wide variety of other Indian and Chinese dishes. Open daily 8am-10pm.

SIGHTS

HAR-KI-PAIRI GHAT. The most important spot in Haridwar is the sacred *ghat* of Har-ki-Pairi, site of Vishnu's footprint and point at which the sacred Ganga flows out onto the plains. Water from the pool here is believed by Hindus to be the most sacred on the entire planet. Many pilgrims fill a bottle or two to take home for use in religious ceremonies. Har-ki-Pairi is also the city's most fascinating place, particularly during the *aarti* ceremony. Although most people bathe at sunrise, you'll see devotees there throughout the day; there are chains to keep bathers from getting swept off to Varanasi by the strong undertow. The area is packed with beggars, lepers, *sadhus*, other pilgrims, and several uniformed men who wander the area asking for **donations** for various "trusts." Many of these guys are shysters who pocket their earnings, and you'd do much better to donate via the charity boxes around the area or at the office of Ganga Sabha, above the temple at the *ghat*. Every evening at Har-ki-Pairi is the sublime and spectacular **aarti** ceremony. At sundown, thousands gather to pay tribute to the gods by floating *diyas* (colorful lamps made of cupped leaves filled with flower petals and a lit candle) on the river. Sending a *diya* down the river is believed to fulfill one's wish. Arrive early in the high season. The best places to watch are from the bridge on the south end of Har-ki-Pairi and from the strip by the clock tower. You'll have to check your shoes at the stand if you go down to the *ghat*—avoid the 8pm shoe-return stampede.

FLASHING EYES, FLOATING HAIR, HOLY DREDS

Times were tough for King Bhagiratha: the world had become completely parched, and 60,000 of his ancestors had been burned to a crisp by a disgruntled sage. The King wanted to perform a ceremony to give their souls peace, but to do it he needed holy water, and the parched planet presented no obvious options. A devout man, Bhagiratha took up long ascetic rituals which eventually caught the attention of Brahma, who decided to help him out. Brahma asked the goddess Ganga, who was in the heavens, to descend to earth. However, she was reluctant, for her impact upon landing would pound the earth to bits. Unwilling to turn the proverbial firehose on earth's sand castle, Brahma realized that only Shiva could soften Ganga's landing. So Bhagiratha practiced austerities for many more years until Shiva, Lord of Ascetics (if not of Punctuality), finally arrived. He provided his strands of matted hair as a cushion for Ganga, who then consented to descend. A cascade of water touched ground high up in the Himalayas and flowed down in several streams, directed by Shiva's locks. Today these streams flow together as they approach the plains and emerge at Haridwar. In gratitude, King Bhagiratha prayed to Ganga at Gangotri, the source of one such stream. This river is called Bhagirathi to honor the pious man who saved the world from drought and gave India her great water artery, the Ganga.

MANSA DEVI TEMPLE. Within Haridwar's blessed boundaries, wealthy Hindus have erected a number of recent temples. The two most important have managed to stay immune to the gaudiness that infects many of the other new temples. One of these, just above the city, is the **Mansa Devi Temple.** To visit this shrine to the patron goddess Mansa, stand in line for one of the ropeway trolleys (since 1983, more than 20 million folks have made the trip) that whisk you up and over a garden to the hilltop where views, vendors, and the temple await. You can avoid a potentially long wait in line by making the 30-minute hike up the hill yourself. *(Open in June daily 7:30am-7pm; other months 8am-6pm. Ropeway trolley Rs25 round-trip.)*

OTHER TEMPLES. Chanda Devi temple, the other exceptionally popular temple in Haridwar, honors an avatar of the goddess Adishakti Jagdamba *(3km from Har-ki-Pairi; open 8:30am-6pm).* Also in the area are the **Dakseshwara Temple** (also called Daksha Mahadev) and **Sati Kund,** 4km to the south, in Kankhal. The latter marks the spot where King Daksha Prajaputi, Brahma's son and Sati's father, held a *yagya* (public sacrifice) and invited Sati but not her consort Shiva, whom he thought hung around with a bad—nay—demonic, crowd. Sati was so insulted that she threw herself on her father's sacrificial pyre. (For the end of the story, see **Divine Dismemberment,** p. 687.)

Four kilometers north of town, west of the river, is a small cluster of unusual temples, which are (depending on your viewpoint) either opulent and justly grand, or just chintzy and overdone. Tempo drivers charge Rs200-250 for a three-hour tour of these temples, but it's smarter to let the tempo go once you're at the temples since all are within easy walking distance of each other. The **Pawan Dham Temple,** first along the road from Haridwar, is most representative of the local houses of worship. Its many shrines are made almost entirely of mirrors and stained glass. Shiva and Arjuna ride atop mirror-covered horses while Krishna sees his 100 lovers in 100 different directions. Venture off to the **Sapta Rishi Ashram,** at the north end of the cluster, to pay homage to seven saints in its seven temples.

BHARAT MATA MANDIR AND ENVIRONS. This eight-story shrine to Mother India and its leaders resembles a modern apartment building with colorful temple domes on top. The top story houses the Hindu gods, while the floor below hosts the goddesses, including Ganga and Saraswati, goddess of knowledge. Descending floors honor the saints of India's various religions (from Guru Nanak of the Sikhs to the Buddha and Swami Vivekenanda), saintly sisters (including Gandhi's devotees Annie Besant and Sister Nivedita), and fighters for freedom and independence. The second floor has paintings highlighting characteristic features of India's states (don't miss the stunning panorama for Himachal Pradesh), and the ground floor has a giant relief model of the country. *(At the north end of the temple cluster. Elevator to top story Rs1.)* Near the Bharat Mata Mandir, **Maa Vaishnodevi Mandir** attempts to simulate the experience of visiting a cave in Kashmir—complete with artificial, fruit-bearing mango trees, a giant Ganga Mata with a crocodile, and a tunnel with knee-deep water, through which visitors duck and wade. **Bhuma Niketan,** south of Maa Vaishnodevi Mandir, has the added bonus of automation—pay a rupee to enter a room in which robotic representations of Hindu heroes cavort with a giant devil who looks eerily like T-Rex from *Jurassic Park.*

ASHRAMS

Hindu pilgrims and *sadhus* flock to Haridwar for spiritual enrichment, often staying at one of the numerous ashrams located within or near the city. Western spiritual seekers, on the other hand, often find themselves more at home in **Rishikesh** (see below), which features more yoga centers and open and accepting ashrams. In Haridwar, if you're not Indian you'll have to mightily impress the gurus to gain residence in their ashram. Foreigners aren't totally out of luck, though. The famous **Shantikunj** (tel. 424309; fax 423866; email shantikunj.hardwar@sml.sprint-rpg.ems.vsnl.net.in) offers 9-, 30-, and 90-day courses which use meditation, music, and chanting as a means of attaining higher spiritual states. The 9-day courses begin on the 1st, 11th, and 21st of every month—reserve one month in advance. Single or two-day stays are possible as well. Payment by donation.

RISHIKESH ऋषिकेश

Most travelers come to Rishikesh to find *something*—a cure to some deep-rooted ailment, a spiritual leader, or, most often, themselves. Indeed, something about Rishikesh suggests a power to transform—sages first came here to find a splash of holiness along the crashing Ganga before heading north to the region's pilgrimage sites. Every year, thousands turn up for the International Yoga Week (Feb. 2-7) on the banks of the Ganga. Even the Beatles sought a new path here in 1968, under the guidance of the Maharishi Mahesh Yogi (see **Instant Karma,** p. 152). In the end, what travelers find is almost invariably to their liking. Summer is yoga off-season; winter has fewer Indian tourists. There are fewer temples in Rishikesh than in Haridwar, but more Westerners, more ashrams, and more *sadhus.*

▐▔ TRANSPORTATION

Trains: Railway Station, at the west end of Rishikesh on (surprise!) Railway Rd. Make reservations 8am-2pm. Most connections to major destinations start in Haridwar. To: **Haridwar** (6 per day, 1½hr., Rs18); **Delhi** (6:40am, 10hr., Rs39).

Buses: Rishikesh has 2 bus stands. Smog-snorters heading for the plains leave from the **U.P. Roadways** bus stand, Agarwal and Bengali Rd. (tel. 430066), on the south side of central Rishikesh. To: **Agra** (8am and 6pm, 12hr., Rs165); **Almora** (9am, 12hr., Rs180); **Chandigarh** (9am, 6hr., Rs95); **Dehra Dun** (frequent 5:30am-8pm, 1hr., Rs14); **Delhi** (every hr. 4am-10:30pm, 6½hr., Rs95); **Haldwani** (9am, 10hr., Rs100); **Haridwar** (every 30min. 4am-10:30pm, Rs12); **Nainital** (8am, 12hr., Rs145). For buses to the northern pilgrimage sites, go to the **Yatra Bus Stand** (tel. 430344), on Dehra Dun Rd. at the northwest end of Rishikesh. A rickshaw from the U.P. stand costs Rs10-15. Tickets for Yamnotri, Gangotri, Kedarnath, and Badrinath can be purchased one day in advance. To: **Badrinath** (3:30, 4, and 5am; 12hr.; Rs130); **Chamoli** (7hr., Rs90); **Gangotri** (5:30am, 12hr., Rs130); **Hanuman Chatti** (7am, 12hr., Rs80); **Joshimath** (6am, 10hr., Rs110); **Kedarnath** (5am, 12hr., Rs95); **Srinagar, U.P.** (every 30min. 4am-3pm, 4hr., Rs50); **Tehri** (every 30min. 3:15am-5:15pm, 3½hr., Rs40); **Uttarkashi** (10 per day 3:15am-1pm, 7hr., Rs72). Tehri and Uttarkashi serve as launch

UTTAR PRADESH

points for Yamnotri and Gangotri; Srinagar for Kedarnath and Badrinath. **Shared taxis** to Uttarkashi (5hr.; Rs1200 per cab, up to 5 seats) line up outside the bus stand.

Local Transportation: Getting to and from Ramjhula and Lakshmanjhula from Rishikesh is best done with one of the **tempos** that run along Lakshmanjhula Rd. (Rs2-5). Both bridges must be traversed on foot—no cross-river traffic. But both sides of the river teem with **auto-rickshaws** and **taxis**. A seat in a taxi to Rishikesh from the Ramjhula Bridge costs Rs20; rickshaw fare from the U.P. bus stand to Lakshmanjhula is Rs45.

▚ ORIENTATION

Rishikesh is trisected by the **Ganga** and the **Chandrabhaga Rivers.** Northeast of the dry river bed are **Ramjhula,** and farther northeast, **Lakshmanjhula,** both of which straddle the Ganga and are connected across it by eponymous footbridges. Most travelers head toward the bridges for accommodations. It's a 5km hike into Rishikesh if you're staying in Lakshmanjhula. From the Lakshmanjhula Bridge to the road and taxi stand is itself a surprisingly arduous trek.

The business center of Rishikesh is very small (1 sq. km) and is located on the triangular land mass between the Chandrabhaga and the Ganga Rivers. The river banks are lined with temples, and a grid of paved and unpaved streets covers the remainder of the land. The **railway station** and **main bus stand** are located in the northwest corner of Rishikesh. The **tourist office,** banks, and post office are found in the small city center. **Laksmanjhula Road** anchors the main market and runs northeast through Ramjhula and Lakshmanjhula. **Dehradun Road** runs at the northwest end of Rishikesh along the Chandrabhaga, intersecting at its east end with Laksmanjhula Rd. The eastern part of Ramjhula is known as **Swargashram,** and its western part is called **Muni-ki-Reti** (named for the nearby hill where Lord Hanuman brought herbs to cure Lord Rama's illness). **Kailash Gate,** 1km south of Ramjhula taxi stand, is a major landmark in Rishikesh.

▟ PRACTICAL INFORMATION

Tourist Office: U.P. Tourism, Railway Rd. (tel. 430209), 3 blocks west of the State Bank of India, up an outdoor flight of stairs by a white marble statue. Staff's English is limited. Open M-Sa 10am-5pm, closed second Sa. The helpful staff at the **GMVN Trekking and Mountaineering Office** (tel. 430799), at Kailash Gate, offers detailed information about treks. Open daily May-June and Sept.-Oct. 10am-5pm. Off-season: closed Su. The **Yatra Tourist Office,** on Haridwar Rd. past the post office, is the authority on trips to the northern Hindu pilgrimage sites. Open M-Sa 10am-5pm.

Budget Travel: Several agencies are clustered on Lakshmanjhula Rd., north of the dry river bed on the way to Ramjhula. **Step Himalayan Adventures** (tel. 432581) organizes treks and rafting trips, offers free advice for those planning their own trips, and rents equipment (2-person tents Rs80 per day, sleeping bags Rs25 per day).

Currency Exchange: The **State Bank of India** (tel. 430114) changes foreign currency at its main Rishikesh office, on the north side of Railway Rd., a 5min. walk from Lakshmanjhula Rd. Open M-F 10am-2pm, Sa 10am-noon. **Bank of Baroda,** 74 Dehradun Rd. (tel. 430653), changes AmEx, Thomas Cook, and Visa traveler's checks in U.S.$ and U.K.£. Open M-F 10am-2pm, Sa 10am-noon.

Market: Main Bazaar in Rishikesh, toward the river from the post office. There's a **didgeridoo** shop near the State Bank of India, Hare Krishna tapes and ceramic *linga* ashtrays in Lakshmanjhula, and yoga books and ayurvedic herbs in Ramjhula.

Pharmacy: Dehradun Rd., west of the police office, is peppered with chemists and medical stores who'll help you if they can. Some, such as **Asha Medical Agencies** (tel. 432696), across from the Government Hospital, are open 24hr.

Hospital/Medical Services: Government General Hospital (tel. 430402) and **Ladies' Hospital,** in the same building on Dehradun Rd., are clean, well-staffed, and open 24hr. Several **specialist clinics** crowd the same road. **Dashmesh Hospital** (tel. 431444), between the police station and Yatra Bus Stand, has consultations daily 10am-2pm.

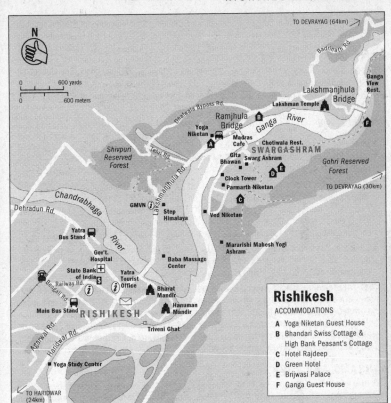

Police: Main Rishikesh Office, Dehradun Rd. (tel. 430100). There's another branch (tel. 430228) on the south end of Lakshmanjhula. Both are open 24hr.

Post Office: Main office (tel. 430340), in the center of town east of Lakshmanjhula Rd. next to the big Hotel Basera, offers EMS and speed post, but only within India. Open M-Sa 10am-5pm. **Ramjhula branch,** Swargashram. Open M-Sa 9am-5pm. **Lakshmanjhula branch,** a 5min. walk south from the bridge. Open M-Sa 9am-5pm. All branches have *Poste Restante.* **Postal Code:** 249201.

Internet: Step Himalayan Adventures, Lakshmanjhula Rd. Web access Rs2 per min. **Blue Hill Travel** (tel. 431865), Swargashram. Web access Rs80 per hr. Open 5am-11pm.

PHONE CODE	0135

■ ACCOMMODATIONS

Searchers for the inner light may want to stay in an ashram. The less spiritually inclined will find their best options on the eastern bank of the Ganga in Lakshmanjhula. Only those needing an early getaway should stay in the loud and congested center of Rishikesh near the railway station and bus stand.

HOTELS AND GUEST HOUSES

Brijwasi Palace (tel. 435181), located behind Gita Bhavan in Swargashram. The recently constructed hotel offers many amenities including laundry (Rs5 per piece), yoga classes (Rs50), and massages (Rs150) to go along with clean rooms and bathrooms. Singles Rs125, with air-cooling Rs225; doubles Rs225, with A/C and TV Rs500.

🔰 **Green Hotel** (tel. 431242), 1 block from the Brijwasi Palace. Well-run place sails in seas of green (green walls, green beds, etc.). Immaculate rooms, seat toilets, hot showers, good attached restaurant. Yoga classes Rs45 per session (8-9:30am). Singles Rs75; doubles Rs150, with air-cooling Rs250.

Ganga Guest House (tel. 433169), 20m south of the Laksmanjhula Bridge. The broad terrace is the hotel's main draw, offering nice views of the valley and river. The tranquility is interrupted, though, by the incessant bell-ringing in the attached shrine, starting at 7am. Showers and seat toilets. Riverside singles Rs125; doubles Rs150.

Hotel Rajdeep (tel. 432826), behind Swargashram in Ramjhula, close to Ramjhula Ashram. This new, upscale facility is pleasantly removed from the noisy main road. All rooms have air-cooling and attached bathrooms with hot showers; most have seat toilets. 24hr. restaurant, great rooftop views, yoga classes (2 per day, Rs50 per hr.), and massage (Rs150 per hr.). Singles Rs160; doubles Rs240; A/C deluxe Rs500-700.

Bhandari Swiss Cottage (tel. 432676), toward Laksmanjhula from Ramjhula (west side). Take Bypass Rd., which branches left; 50m later, turn right at the sign for High Bank Peasant's Cottage and take the gravel path. Rooms offer valley views, seclusion, and a lovely flower garden. Common bath with cold shower and squat toilets. Neat balconies for contemplating the long hike back to town. Singles Rs100-110; doubles Rs150-200.

High Bank Peasant's Cottage (tel. 431167), before the Bhandari on the same trail, on the left side. Same virtues as Bhandari (beautiful garden and views), plus cleaner, bigger rooms, attached baths, and tourist services. Doubles Rs300-350.

Yoga Niketan Guest House, Muni-ki-Reti, before the taxi stand. Has a well-groomed garden and steps leading down to the Ganga. Modern, clean, spacious rooms have high-powered fans, white tile floors, seat toilets, and hot water. Convenient location near the Ramjhula bridge ensures easy access to Rishikesh proper and Swargashram. Free yoga and meditation classes at the nearby Yoga Niketan Ashram. For 3 meals at the ashram add Rs50. Singles Rs200; doubles Rs300.

ASHRAMS AND YOGA

No matter which yoga position you have managed to twist yourself into, an ashram is never far from sight in Rishikesh. Most Westerners head to Ramjhula for ashram stays, which are often combined with yoga and meditation classes. Staying in an ashram is not like bunking up in a hotel—the meditative atmosphere demands that certain rules be followed. These include total avoidance of meat, eggs, smelly food (including onions and garlic), alcohol, tobacco, and drugs of any kind (including *paan*) and adherence to total quiet. Most demand daily bathing and request that menstruating women stay out of the ashram centers, and many have curfews. Some are set up for pilgrims and Hindu worshippers and do not allow foreigners; most ashrams, however, are very welcoming.

Yoga Study Centre (tel. 433837), at the far south end of Lakshmanjhula Rd., nearly outside of town on the river side of the road. Well-known place to learn *iyengar yoga* if you don't want to stay in an ashram, but it lacks the feeling of community. Three classes per day, alternating days. Winter (Feb. 3-25, 2000), summer (April 6-27), and intensive (Sept. 2-24) courses Rs1200 each session. Lodging can be arranged Apr.-Aug. and Oct.-Jan. General yoga classes M-Sa 6:30-8am. Pay on donation basis.

Yoga Niketan (tel. 430227), in the tranquil hills over Ramjhula. 15-night min. stay includes 3 meals, 2 yoga classes, and 2 meditation classes per day. Visible security force keeps the strict rules in this yoga boot camp. Co-ed doubles for married couples only; otherwise, buildings are single-sex. Guard your valuables. Squat toilets, no showers. Kitchen space in all rooms. Guests are expected to help with weekly cleaning. Curfew 9:30pm. Office open 8:30am-noon and 2-5pm. Rs200 per day.

Omkarananda Ganga Sadan (tel. 431473 or 430763), west side of Ramjhula. Big, sterile building just south of the taxi/rickshaw stand. It is the poshest ashram aside from Maharishi Mahesh Yogi's—clean, dazzling white rooms and bathrooms (some attached, all with squat toilets). Try for a river view. Breakfast (Rs15) and lunch (Rs30) daily. 3-

night min. stay (if you bail early, you forfeit a 3-day deposit). Yoga instruction Rs220 per week with one lecture/class each evening Oct.-Apr. only. Rooms Rs65, with balcony Rs75, with attached bath Rs100, with bath and balcony Rs110. Extra bed Rs30. Open summer 6am-10pm, winter 7:30am-9:30pm.

Ved Niketan (tel. 433253), at the south end of Ramjhula's east bank. Caged deities line the entrance to this yellow and orange ashram. The main guru, now 93, still lives here, but others do the teaching. Day-long yoga fee of Rs50 includes 5:30-7:30am meditation, 9-10:30am lecture, and 6:30-8pm yoga. Gates lock at 10pm. Breakfast Rs15, lunch and dinner Rs55. Singles Rs60; doubles with bath Rs100.

◖ FOOD

Restaurants in Rishikesh don't serve meat or alcohol. They abound with yummy vegetarian *thalis*, however, so buck up and *dal* with it.

Ganga View Restaurant, opposite Bombay Kshetra in Lakshmanjhula. This is where the foreign tourists who snapped up rooms in the Kshetra come together to enjoy good conversation, the Ganga view, and comfy *rattan* chairs. Take pictures of the patrons and create your own "White Album." Peanut butter toast with honey (Rs10), spaghetti (Rs30), and porridge with milk, nuts, bananas, raisins, and coconut (Rs20). *Thalis* (Rs25) served 6-8pm, but not June-July. Open daily 7am-9pm.

Ganga Darshan, next to Ganga View, closer to the bridge. Inexpensive *thalis* (Rs15-20) are filling, and some special dishes (like "cheese chow mein") provide respite from the spice of most Indian food. *Dosas* Rs10-18. Balcony tables are awesome, but the service out there is slower. Open daily 5am-8:30pm. Winter: 5am-8pm.

Amrita, in front of Hotel Rajdeep. Offers outstanding fresh-baked raisin bread, jars of pure honey (500g: enough for a pie, Rs75), cheddar cheese, lasagna with homemade noodles (Rs50), banana pancakes (Rs25), and pizza (Rs85). Great ambience inside or on the rooftop. Also has a little library of Western books (deposit Rs100, Rs5 per day).

Chotiwala and Chotiwala Restaurant (tel. 430070), in east Ramjhula near the bridge; impossible to miss. The 2 parts, side by side, were supposedly divided by 2 brothers. Both serve similar, standard Indian fare. Very popular among Indians. Chotiwala *thalis* (Rs25-50), cool and creamy mango custard (Rs10). Open daily 7am-11pm.

Madras Cafe, in the Ramjhula rickshaw stand area. Indian food, California-style—emphasis on sprouts and whole wheat. Indian straws meet their match in viscous *lassis*. Himalayan Health *Pullao,* with sprouts, curd, and ayurvedic herbs (Rs40); hot lemon-ginger-honey tea (Rs15). Open daily 6:30am-10:30pm. Off-season: 8am-9pm.

◉ ♫ SIGHTS AND ENTERTAINMENT

Triveni Ghat, on the south end of Rishikesh, hosts the **aarti** ceremony every evening at sundown and is also a popular site at which to make river offerings at dawn. The ancient **Lakshman Temple** is on the west bank. Make sure to visit the 13-story **Swarga Niwas** ashram and cultural center, which offers a great view from the top. Their exhibits house images and statues of all the major Hindu deities. Please save your donations for the official collection pots inside. **Boats** head across the Ganga at Ramjhula below Sivananda Ashram (one-way Rs5, round-trip Rs7). Another way to go where everything flows is to **shoot the Ganga's rapids.** Outfitters on the north end of Rishikesh, such as Step Himalayan Adventures (tel. 432581), run 15km, 90-minute rafting trips through four "good" and two small rapids (Sept.-May Rs500-900, depending on group size, including transportation). GMVN provides accommodations at its rafting camp in Kaudiyalaj, north of Rishikesh (rooms Rs350, tents Rs100; trips Sept.-May; 3-4hr., Rs400 per person; all-day trip Rs1100).

Many visitors supplement meditation and vegetation with **music lessons. Sivananda Ramesh Music School** will teach you to make the didgeridoo moan, the tabla ring, or the sitar gently weep (left at the sign on the far side of the bridge on

INSTANT KARMA The Beatles came to Rishikesh to study Transcendental Meditation in February, 1968; it was the culmination of several years of Fab Four Indophilia. George Harrison's sitar licks first appeared in "Run For Your Life" (1965), the group attended lectures by the Maharishi Mahesh Yogi in '67, and they recorded tracks for "The Inner Light" just before heading for the Himalayan foothills.

In Rishikesh, George, John, Paul, and Ringo embraced the typical ashram experience—they did fewer drugs, meditated more, and mostly just hung out with other Westerners (including Mia and Prudence Farrow, the Beach Boys' Mike Love, and 60s pop anomaly Donovan). They also wrote profusely. Most of the "White Album" and significant portions of *Abbey Road*, as well as the unreleased "Happy Rishikesh Song," were composed during the group's stay. The most famously Rishikeshan of these is "Dear Prudence," considered an entreaty to the latter Farrow to join in the meditative fun: "The sun is up, the sky is blue/ It's beautiful and so are you/ Dear Prudence won't you come out and play?"

Eventually, though, the blue skies clouded, as the Beatles became disillusioned with the Maharishi. Less than a month after they left Rishikesh, John Lennon and Paul McCartney announced they'd ended their relationship with the guru. The bitterness comes through the thinly veiled lyrics of a song from the *White Album's* second disc: "Sexy Sadie, what have you done/ You made a fool of everyone/.../However big you think you are/Sexy Sadie ooh you'll get yours yet."

Lakshmanjhula Rd. just after Tehri Rd.). Prices vary based on instrument and availability of open time slots. **Hindi lessons** are offered by Mr. Tilak Raj at Ramjhula, Swargasram, behind the Ganga General Store (enquiries daily 9-10am; 10-day advanced course Rs1000, includes 1hr. classes each day; 5-day beginner course Rs500). Settle in for a **massage** at the well-advertised Baba Health and Massage Centre in Rishikesh 100m east of Hotel Shivlok. You can enjoy an ayurvedic, Swedish, Thai, or "general" full-body massage (they even massage your ears) in a dark, cool room with space-age music. (Open daily 8am-8pm. Rs150 per session.) They also teach massage in a month-long course with 4 classes a day (Rs6000, includes lodging). The **Rama Palace cinema,** on Dehradun Rd. in Rishikesh, screens Hindi movies (Rs15).

NEAR RISHIKESH

Wait until the sun is up and the sky is blue before heading to the temple of **Kunjapuri,** which sits atop a nearby mountain and rewards daytrippers with views of the whole region, including Haridwar and the snow-capped Himalayas. The temple itself is disappointingly modern and small, though the priest is friendly to visitors. To get there, take a bus headed for **Tehri** from the Yatra Bus Stand; tell the driver you want to get off at Hindolakhal (1hr., Rs15). From there, it's an hour's walk up the mountain along a paved road and up a surreal, narrow staircase at the top. Hop on a bus coming from Gangotri or Yamnotri to get back (last bus around 7 or 8pm).

Another destination for a day hike is the temple at **Neel Kanth Mahadev,** a place to which so many pilgrims have brought milk, *ghee*, and Ganga water that the *linga* has eroded down to a few inches. This tradition continues every year in mid-July. The temple and nearby bazaar are too modern and hectic be the focal point of the walk—it's the jungle trail along the way, inhabited by wild elephants, that really makes the hike worthwhile. Go early, since it's a four- to five-hour climb with no stops, and the temple is more likely to be peaceful early in the day. Jeeps leave for the trailhead from the Laksmanjhula and Ramjhula taxi stands (12km; Rs40 per person one way, Rs70 round-trip). Regular jeeps return to Rishikesh.

About 10km from Rishikesh lies **Mansa Devi,** a temple providing wall-less shelter for those seeking some distance from town. Camp for free and in relative isolation. Hindu pilgrims flood the site between the 7th and 10th of every month (especially Mar., Sept., and Oct.) for Navratri. Jeeps go to Mansa Devi (Rs25 per seat).

NORTHERN PILGRIMAGES AND TREKS

Until the 1960s, the northern pilgrimage sites could only be reached by foot from the plains, but new roads have now made them accessible to package-tour pilgrims crammed onto buses from Rishikesh. The peaceful isolation of the sites is now only a memory; however, for the true believers, the experience is suffused with a holiness that diesel, mud, and litter cannot spoil.

UTTARKASHI उत्तरकाशी

This busy town on the banks of the Bhagirathi River is the administrative center of the Uttarkashi District, as well as the last place to stock up on supplies or catch a Hindi movie before you head out for a trek. It also serves as a transportation hub for the pilgrimage sites to the north. The **tourist office** at the bus stand provides little help for trekking. Instead, try **Mt. Support Trekking,** BD Nautial Bhawan, Bhatwari Rd. (tel. 2419), about 10 minutes past the bus stand along Gangotri Rd. They also **exchange currency** for a hefty charge. (Open M-Sa 9am-7pm.) **Buses** head to: Barkot (for Yamnotri, in season only, Rs45); Bhatwari (for treks to Sahasratal and Kedarnath, 1hr., Rs14); Gangotri (Rs50); Gaurikund (12hr., Rs97-110); Rishikesh (8hr., Rs65); and Sayana Chatti (for Dodital trek, Rs14). Morning taxis to Rishikesh queue up at the bus stand. The **24-hour emergency District Hospital** lies midway between Gangotri Rd. and the river, near the **post office. Police** roost on Gangotri Rd., 15 minutes from the bus station on the right. **Telephone Code:** 01374.

Overnighting before an early morning departure can be done at **Bhandari Hotel** (tel. 2203), at the bus stand; there's also a restaurant inside (in-season doubles Rs600; off-season Rs300). Another option is **Meghdoot,** Main Market (tel. 2278); some rooms have seat toilets and hot water for Rs5 per bucket (May-June and Sept.: singles Rs100, doubles Rs180; Oct.-Apr. and July: Rs50/90). **GMVN** (tel. 2271) provides clean rooms with hot water and six-bed dorm rooms (in-season dorm beds Rs60, doubles Rs200, with TV and fancy furniture Rs550; off-season Rs60/100/300; May, June, and Sept. book at least one month in advance).

YAMNOTRI यमनोत्री

The source of the Yamuna River and the first stop on the Garhwal pilgrimage circuit, Yamnotri attracts 1500 pilgrims every day during tourist season. Yamnotri essentially consists of a **temple** devoted to the goddess Yamuna surrounded by 10 to 15 concrete structures and numerous *dhabas*. The temple is open from May to November, after which the image from the temple is carried to Kharsoli, a village opposite Janki Chatti. Heavy snows erode the temple so much that it has to be rebuilt every few years, so its architecture is nothing special—a slapdash construction with dressed-up concrete walls and a corrugated metal roof. Yamnotri is accessible only by a 14km trek from the town of Hanuman Chatti. The path angles gently upwards from **Hanuman Chatti** (2134m) for 8km to Janki Chatti (2676m), then turns steeply uphill until it reaches Yamnotri (3235m). Start early in the morning—there is no shade for the first 10km out of Hanuman Chatti, and by then the higher altitudes and steep path will drain any energy you have left. **Horses** with guides can be rented for the 14km trek (Rs200-250). The path is lined with *chai* and cold drink stands. Sleeping arrangements are available at Janki Chatti. The closest **hospital, post office,** and **communications** system (a wireless only for emergencies) are at Janki Chatti. A seasonal **police station** is set up every year at Yamnotri. Hanuman Chatti is well-connected by **buses** from Dehra Dun (163km) and Rishikesh (209km). There are **GMVN lodges** at Sayana Chatti, 6km before Hanuman Chatti (Apr.-Nov.: rooms Rs300; off-season: Rs150); Hanuman Chatti (dorm beds Rs100, rooms Rs500), and Janki Chatti (dorm beds Rs100, rooms Rs300-500). Reservations can be made through the Rishikesh GMVN office. During the pilgrimage season, many of these accommodations are fully booked for package tours operated by GMVN, so it may be a better idea to stay overnight at **Barkot,** 40km south, and take an early morning bus or taxi to Hanuman Chatti. Janki Chatti and Barkot have several private hotels as well.

SNAKE-EATING SADHUS OF GANGOTRI Hash-
ish and tobacco, smoked through a *chillum,* are a big part of the daily intake of most *sadhus,* but really dread-inspiring holy men try something else. A krait (an extremely poisonous snake) is rolled up between two unbaked *rotis* with its tail sticking out, then shoved into the fire. When the *rotis* are fully baked, the *sadhu* removes the deadly sandwich from the fire and pulls at the snake's tail end, ripping off the skin and bones. Then, preparing himself, he puts a jug of water by his side. He takes two to three bites of the snake and immediately goes into a coma. Every eight to ten hours the *sadhu* wakes up to drink some water and take another bite, sending himself back into a poisoned stupor. The whole process lasts three to four days. **Warning: requires 30 years of practice—don't try this at home, or anywhere else!**

GANGOTRI गंगोत्री

After Bhatwari, the road from Uttarkashi narrows and the surrounding mountains become more severe until the shimmering slopes of **Mt. Sudarshan** (6500m) are finally visible, towering above the small town of Gangotri. At an altitude of 3140m and 98km northeast of Uttarkashi (here known as the Bhagirathi), the town is a center for *sadhus* from all over India. The present **temple** at Gangotri was built by the Gorkha commander Amar Singh Thapa in the early 18th century as a replacement for an older structure. The temple is open only from May to November due to heavy winter snowfall. A temporary **police station, post office,** and **health center** are open during the pilgrimage season. Next to the temple is **Bhagiratha Shila,** where King Bhagiratha is said to have prayed for the river to flow (see **Flashing Eyes, Floating Hair, Holy Dreds,** p. 146). Steps here lead down to the *ghat* where pilgrims bathe. A small bridge from the bus stand arches over to Gaurikund, where the Bhagirathi gushes out of the rock into a beautiful pool. **Gaumukh** (Cow's Mouth), an easy 17km trek from Gangotri, is the spot where the Bhagirathi emerges from the Gangotri glacier; there are excellent views of the Bhagirathi peaks along the way.

Recent improvements in transportation mean that nearly 2000 pilgrims can now visit Gangotri every day between May and November, leaving their mark in the form of strewn rubbish and the increased deforestation caused by efforts to accommodate them. To get to Gangotri, take a **bus** or a **shared taxi** from Uttarkashi (see p. 153). Buildings sit on both sides of the **Bhagirathi River.** The main bridge is just next to Dev Ghat, where the Bhagirathi and the **Kedar Ganga** meet. Two parallel paths run on either side of the Bhagirathi, along which all the *dhabas* and hotels are located. In most accommodations, rooms are unpainted, the plaster is crumbling, and beds are dirty—bring a sleeping bag. Accommodations across the river from the temple are quieter and more secluded. **Manisha Cottage,** near the bus stand, provides small two-bedded rooms (with common bath Rs200, deluxe Rs450). The **GMVN Guest House,** next to Gaurikund and away from the crowded bus stand, is spacious and clean, with a garden and a quality restaurant (dorm beds Rs100, rooms Rs300-600 all year). Most ashrams in Gangotri do not accept foreign guests. There are few tourist services in Gangotri.

KEDARNATH केदारनाथ

As one of the 12 *jyotirlingas* of Shiva in India, Kedarnath is considered to be one of Shiva's abodes. According to one account, the Kedarnath **temple** was constructed thousands of years ago when the Pandavas, the heroic brothers of the *Mahabharata,* came here to serve their penance to Shiva. Shiva, who viewed the Pandavas as sinners for having killed their own kin in battle, disguised himself as a bull. When the Pandavas discovered the ruse, Shiva turned to stone and tried to escape into the ground. But as his front half vanished, one of the Pandavas, Bhima, managed to catch Shiva's rocky rear end. Pleased with the Pandavas' diligence, Shiva appeared in his true form and forgave them. The back half of that stone form is now worshiped at Kedarnath. Shiva's front half is said to have disappeared into the ground, broken off, and reemerged in Nepal, where it is venerated at the **Pash-**

upati Temple (see p. 738). Other parts of Shiva turned up at Tungnath (arm), Rudrandath (face), Madhyamaheshwar (navel), and Kapleshwar (locks); together with Kedarnath, they form the **Panch Kedar** (Five Fields) pilgrimage circuit.

Many beautiful treks begin at Kedarnath. The town remains open from May until late October. **Buses** only take pilgrims as far as Gaurikund, 216km from Rishikesh (Rs85). From there, it's a steep 14km, four- to six-hour trek. It's best to start early in the morning or late in the afternoon to avoid the midday sun. **Horses** are also available for hire (Rs250). Many hotel prices are completely negotiable, so bargain hard, especially if you turn up after 7pm. Standard rates are Rs100 for a single and Rs200 for a double in season. **GMVN** has two guest houses in Kedarnath, one immediately on your left as you approach the town (tel. 6210) and a second across the river and below the hillside (tel. 6228). Many ashrams will not accept foreigners, but the **Bharat Seva Ashram** and the **Temple Committee** cave in on occasion.

BADRINATH बद्रीनाथ

The temple town of Badrinath (3133m) is probably the most famous of Garhwal's Hindu pilgrimage sites, attracting the faithful from all across India during its summer season (May-Nov.). Badrinath is the northern *dham* established by the southern saint Shankara in the 8th century. It was once the abode of Lord Vishnu and the site of one of Ganga's 12 water channels. Along with Puri in Orissa, Rameswaram in Tamil Nadu, and Dwarka in Gujarat, it forms the northernmost compass-point in India's sacred geography. Badrinath is located on the Alaknanda River 297km from Rishikesh, not far from the overpowering Nilkanth peak and the Tibetan border. It's accessibility by road attracts growing numbers of pilgrims and secular tourists every year who chose to forego the austerity of a walking pilgrimage (once required) in favor of a harrowing bus ride. Badrinath can be reached by **bus** from Rishikesh via Srinagar, Rudraprayag, and Joshimath (Rs90). Buses also frequently come here directly from Kedarnath (Rs40).

The Badrinath **temple** is colorful, with a long main entrance gate (the Singh Dwara) through which worshippers must pass for *darshan* of the meter-high Badrivishal image inside. The temple's architecture is an unusual mixture of Buddhist and Hindu styles, and there is a large debate over whether it was in ancient times actually a Buddhist temple. Before visiting the temple, worshipper must bathe in the **Tapt Kund** hot spring (45°C/113°F), often in preparation for a dip into the icy waters of the Alaknanda. Very basic **accommodations** are available from numerous *dharamshalas*, at the **Garhwal Hotel,** or at the hotel run by the **GVMN**. There are numerous *dhabas* around the temple site. **Telephone Code:** 01381.

AULI औली

Sometime in the 1970s, the Indian government realized that the mountains south of Joshimath (253km from Rishikesh) could be put to better use as a **ski resort** than as a paramilitary training ground. Chairlifts have replaced airlifts, opening up 550 vertical meters of slopes to skiers. The spectacular scenery, particularly eastward toward Nanda Devi (7800m), keeps Auli open in the summer for sight-seeing rides up the 3km **cable car** from Joshimath. There is a **GMVN lodge** at Auli (Apr.-Nov.: dorm beds Rs60, deluxe rooms Rs750-900; Nov.-Apr.: Rs100/1200-1400). GMVN also rents ski equipment and provides lessons.

VALLEY OF FLOWERS फूलों की घाटी

The floral splendor of this hidden alpine valley high in the Garhwal Himalayas has been attracting botanists, pilgrims, and nature lovers ever since Frank Smith explored the valley in 1937 and publicized his find to the world as the "Valley of Flowers." Ten kilometers long, 2km wide, and enclosed by snow-capped peaks, the valley is bisected by the Pushpawati River. Snow covers the valley floor from November to late May, rendering the area inaccessible to visitors. In late May, the snow begins to melt, and the onset of spring accelerates in June with the first bloomings. The valley usually opens in late June. By late July, the valley is aglow in the shades of *androsace*, marsh orchids, and geraniums. In August, the pinks have faded and the yellow flowers of *pedicularis, grandiflora,* and *potentillas* predominate. There are over 500 species of flower in the valley; many of them, such as the Himalayan blue poppy, are rare and of great interest to ecologists. When the valley was first explored in the late 1930s, the plant species count was 5000. The serious ecological decline of the area has prompted the government to declare it a National Park, so camping and cooking are prohibited within the valley. Visitors must trek in for the day and sleep at **Ghanghria**, 4km away, in either a government rest house, or in one of the private lodges (the Sikh Gurudwara has 1000 beds available). From Rishikesh, take a **bus** to Joshimath (6am, 10hr., Rs100). Govindghat is 19km further by road (buses leave every 30min., Rs10), and from there, one must trek or ride a mule to Ghanghria (13km). To reserve a bed in the dormitory or a room at the tourist rest house, contact the **GMVN Yatra Pilgrimage Tours and Accommodations Office** in Kailash Gate, Rishikesh (tel. 431783).

CORBETT NATIONAL PARK कोरबट

Corbett is India's first national park, founded in 1936 and named in honor of James Corbett (1875-1955), a British gentleman renowned as a hunter of tigers and other large felines. Corbett quit killing tigers for sport in the 1920s, but the hunter-conservationist was still called upon to shoot tigers and leopards when they threatened human lives. He became famous for his photographs of tigers and for the books he wrote, including *The Man-Eaters of Kumaon.*

In 1973, the Indian government, with support from the World Wildlife Fund, launched "Project Tiger" to save the country's dwindling tiger population and its supporting ecosystems. The 1319 sq. km Corbett Tiger Reserve, comprised of the national park and the adjoining Sonandi Wildlife Sanctuary and Reserve Forest, was the first target area of this ambitious preservation project. There are currently 138 tigers in the reserve. Sightings of the Bengal beasts can come several times a day, but, even if you don't catch a glimpse of the largest cat on earth, Corbett's other wildlife will certainly not disappoint. Corbett's other treasures include the endangered gharial crocodile, herds of wild elephants, monkeys, leopards, deer, and over 500 species of birds. The Park's landscape, particularly around Dhikala, is as much a treasure as its wildlife. Mountains thick with *sal* forests bound the Ramganga River and enclose the vast, placid plain and lush jungle.

> **! WARNING.** However you decide to enjoy Corbett, do adhere to the park's rules and regulations about treating nature right. Don't throw burning cigarettes around, don't feed the animals, and keep noise at a minimum. For your own safety (attacks by tigers are not unheard of), never walk outside the camp perimeter, and be careful at night. Driving after dark is forbidden.

 ORIENTATION AND PRACTICAL INFORMATION. Corbett has five **zones** accessible to tourists. These zones are exclusive, which means that one must exit the park and pay another hefty fee in order to enter another zone. **Dhikala** is the most popular among tourists, offering a range of accommodations, two restaurants, film screening facilities, and a library. The other four zones—Bijrani, Jhirna, Lohachavr, and Halduparao—offer greater solitude but fewer services. **Lohachavr** is the best place to go bird-watching; **Bijrani** contains the park's most diverse vegetation and is the zone most frequented by daytripping jeeps; **Jhirna** is an exceptionally beautiful area of the park; and those looking for a more rugged experience and close encounters with wild elephants should head to **Halduparao**. Jhirna is accessible to visitors year-round, but the rest of the park closes during the monsoon (mid-June to mid-Nov.). The wildlife viewing is better in the summer (Mar.-June) than in the winter (Nov.-Mar.), but anytime is great for enjoying the park's overall beauty.

Ramnagar, the town through which all park visitors must pass, is reachable from Delhi by **bus** (12 per day 6am-9pm, 7hr., Rs90) or **train** (11pm, 5½hr., Rs110). The train station is 1.5km south of the bus stand. Ramnagar offers basic services. For last-second currency exchange, the **State Bank of India** (tel. (05945) 85337) has a branch 300m south and a few blocks east of Ramnagar's bus depot. They change US$ and UK£ traveler's checks. (Open M-F 10am-2pm, Sa 10am-noon.)

Visitors must stop at the **Park Office** (tel. 05975 or 85489), across from the Ramnagar bus stand, to secure a **permit** (open daily 8am-1pm and 3-5pm). Overnight visitors may visit any of the park's zones, but daytrippers may only visit Dhikala and Bijrani on guided tours (tour of Dhikala Rs1200, afternoon tour of Bijrani Rs600). The office also books all lodgings inside the park. After securing permits and accommodations, visitors must arrange their own transportation to their site. A **bus** leaves the park office for Dhikala (3:30pm, 2hr., Rs60) and returns from Dhikala at 10am, thus ensuring that your Rs350, three-day fee allows you only one full day in the park. An alternative is to shell out Rs500 (plus Rs130 jeep entry fee) for a one-way **jeep** to Dhikala. Fortunately, it is fairly easy to join up with other visitors and split the cost of the ride. To do so, arrive at the office around 8am; jeeps wait right outside the office.

Each zone has its own gated park entrance. **Dhangarhi Gate,** 16km north of Ramnagar, is the entrance to Dhikala (open 6am-6pm, 6am-5pm in winter; entrance prohibited after dark). Here, you'll pay the fees if you didn't cough them up at Ramnagar (3-day permit Rs350, each additional day Rs175; car or jeep fee Rs100). Before leaving Dhikala, all visitors must obtain a free **clearance certificate,** which should be turned in at Dhangarhi upon leaving. If your next stop is Ranikhet, get off the bus at Dhangarhi and wait by the side of the road for buses headed north (last bus 2pm, 4hr., Rs40).

▛▛ ACCOMMODATIONS AND FOOD. All lodgings within the park must be reserved through the park office in Ramnagar. Log hut dorms, tourist hutments, and cabins are available in **Dhikala.** The **log hut,** one step from the great outdoors, provides austere bunks, stacked three-high and 12 to a room, and lockers (bring your own lock). Squat toilets and showers are in a separate building. **Tourist hutments** (3 beds) and **cabins** (2 or 3 beds) have attached bathrooms. (Check-out 11am. Log hut bunk Rs100, bedding Rs25; tourist hutment Rs500; cabin Rs900.) Be warned that visitors wishing to extend their stay are often told to wait until the evening to see whether space is available, making it possible to be stuck in Dhikala without accommodation, in which case it will be necessary to hire a jeep out (if one is even available) before the night curfew. Calling in advance is especially important if you want to stay in the hutments or cabins. There are no reservations for the log hut, so if there is no space the first night, you are almost guaranteed a bed the next. **Tourist rest houses** in other zones are more expensive, ranging from Rs300 to Rs900, depending on location.

Dhikala provides the only food available inside the park. Its two restaurants both serve Indian, Chinese, and Continental fare for breakfast, lunch, and dinner. The government-run **KMVN Restaurant** is more expensive, but it has indoor seating (veg. *korma* Rs36; open 7:30am-9:30pm). At the other end of the camp, the privately-owned **canteen** serves similar fare for less; it's next to a pleasant pagoda where you can survey the plain while enjoying your vegetable curry (open daily 5am-2pm and 4-10pm). In other zones of the park, visitors must bring their own food, though a kitchen staff is on hand to help prepare it in the rest houses. Note that, in observance of a new policy for all national parks, no alcohol is allowed and only vegetarian food is sold inside the park. A small **kiosk** at Dhangarhi Gate sells bottled water (Rs15) and munchies. Such items are more expensive inside the park, so you may want to stock up before you enter.

If lodgings are not immediately available inside the park, the **Tourist Rest House** (tel. (05945) 85225), next door to the park office in Ramnagar, is more than adequate. It offers well-kept dormitory rooms and super-deluxe suites, with hot water showers, squat toilets, and ceiling fans. (Check-out noon. Dorm beds Rs60; doubles Rs315; deluxe with air cooling Rs420. Extra bed Rs60-80. Extra person Rs30-40.) Accommodations outside the park skyrocket in price and necessitate daily transport into the park. The oasis of package-tour heaven, **Tiger Camp** (tel. 86088 or

MAN BITES CAT Your elephant conductor in Dhikala may be none other than Subradar Ali, the man one man-eater of Kumaon will remember as the one who bit back. While gathering grass for his elephant Gunti on Valentine's Day, 1984, Subradar was attacked from behind by a tiger named Sheroo. The cat leapt nearly 6m for his target, Subradar's head. As he was being dragged away by the neck, Subradar, taking a lesson from his striped assailant, began biting back. Forcing open the jaws of the beast, he yanked on Sheroo's tongue. This put an end to the dragging, and Sheroo pinned him squarely. Another guide appeared on the scene, distracting the tiger long enough for Subradar to roll down a nearby stream bank. With bleeding gashes on his head and arm, Subradar called his elephant to come and kneel so he could crawl on top. Gunti took him the 3km to Dhikala, and not wanting to disturb his family away in Ramnagar, Subradar cleaned his wounds and changed his clothes himself. Both Rajiv and Indira Gandhi later visited him in the hospital. Rajiv asked if he wanted fame and fortune—the event has since been the subject of several movies—but Subradar preferred to return to the elephants and tigers of Corbett. In fact, he views the whole experience as having bolstered his confidence, and he admits with a smile that he is now even more excited to find the tigers than the tourists he guides. His aggressive Valentine's date, Sheroo, has not been seen for years.

87901; fax 85088), 7km from Dhangari Gate towards Ramnagar, proffers two-person tents with mattresses and clean, warm blankets (Rs600, with delicious, all-you-can-eat meals Rs1200). Tiger Camp also arranges bird watching (Rs250), angling (Rs1500), cycling (Rs50 per hour), trekking, and jeep and elephant tours (Rs1200-1500 per day).

For Indian, Chinese, and Continental grub, head to **Govind Restaurant**, one block past the bus station from the rest house. The owner is very friendly and the food is delicious. Their banana pancakes (Rs25) and fruit *lassis* (Rs20) are famous. (Open daily 8am-10pm.) A tramp downhill south of the office leads to good, cheap veg. food at the outdoor **Green Valley** (entrees Rs35; open daily 10am-11pm).

⚑ **THE PARK.** There are ways to get down and dirty in Corbett without breaking the rules. By far the best option is an **elephant ride.** For Rs100, visitors get a two-hour tour across the prairie and through the jungle, all from a pachyderm's perspective. This is the best way to try to see a tiger or to come close to wild elephants and other animals. Sign up for a ride at the station office; during the high season, expect to wait up to several days, but it may be possible to get a ride the same day if you show up early. Tours depart at sunrise and sunset, approximately 6am and 4pm in the summer and 7am and 3pm in the winter. Both tours have their benefits (cooler weather or more sleep, respectively), and sightings are equally likely at either time. From atop your elephant, marvel at what seems to delight tourists most: yes, those are 3m cannabis plants, acres and acres of them.

You can also hire a **jeep**—up to eight may ride with a guide around the Dhikala Station area (best times for jeep tours 5am-11am and 4-7pm; Rs500-600). You cover more ground than you would on the elephants and can get all the way out to the reservoir, where the crocodiles play. While the crocs don't normally encroach on the compound, it's best to heed the sign that warns, "NO SWIMMING: Survivors Will Be Prosecuted." Jeeps are not guaranteed from Dhikala, as they operate from Dhangari and the park office in Ramnagar—it is possible (though not likely) to get stuck in Dhikala waiting for a jeep.

The only excursion **on foot** permitted outside the camp (and then only before sunset) is to the nearby **Gularghati Watchtower,** which offers a good view of the landscape. Free **films** about nature and the park are shown behind the restaurant at around 8pm; check the office for schedules. To pack your brain with even more info about what you've seen and heard, visit the small **library** adjacent to the office (open daily summer 9am-12:30pm and 5:30-8pm; winter 9am-noon and 5:30-7:30pm).

Tiny maps (Rs2) and other information on the park are available at the Ramnagar office, the library at Dhikala, and the office at Dhangarhi Gate.

It is still possible to experience some of the natural beauty and wildlife from outside the park. One such place is **Sitabani,** which has excellent bird-watching opportunities and a nice rest house—enquire at the Ramnagar office for details. There is also a small **museum** at Dhangarhi gate, which consists of one room filled with bizarre and morbid exhibits (Rs10). Beyond the scale model of the park, several stuffed mammal specimens are displayed with signs documenting how they died, along with some preserved artwork and a collection of animal embryos.

NAINITAL नैनीताल

When the body of Shiva's consort Sati was chopped into various pieces (see **Divine Dismemberment,** p. 687), one of her eyes, it is said, fell into the hills, and so the stunning emerald lake of Nainital was formed. Mr. P. Barron of Shahjahanpur, the first of the British colonialists to enjoy and exploit the lake area's beauty, hauled up a yacht and built a "pilgrim cottage," setting in gear what would eventually become a popular British hill station and the summer capital of the United Provinces (which became Uttar Pradesh after Independence). Nainital remains a welcome relief from the scorching heat of the U.P. Plains and is one of the most popular hill resorts for Indians as well as for foreigners. Its temperate climate and low humidity relative to the plains leads to a high season (May-June and October) of inflated prices, bringing smiles to the town's residents who make their livelihood off tourism. The shimmering, eye-shaped Naini Lake is the town's jewel and the center of its activity, but Nainital also offers outstanding views of the Himalayas in autumn after the rains have passed. Nainital in high season is an unparalleled destination for those wishing to trade in the chaos of their daily lives for the cool relief of a peaceful, albeit crowded, lake town.

■ TRANSPORTATION

Trains: The nearest station is in **Kathgodam.** Trains leave Delhi for Kathgodam (*Ranikhet Exp.* 5013, 11pm) and leave Kathgodam for Delhi (*Ranikhet Exp.* 5014, 8:45pm).

Buses: Buses arrive at and depart from the lake front in **Tallital.** Schedules change frequently, so verify times when you arrive. **Haldwani** is the nearest major hub, and nearly every bus goes there first. To: **Almora** (7am, 3hr., Rs37); **Bareilly** (5 per day 7:15am-6:15pm, 4½hr., Rs60); **Bhowali** (every 30min. 6am-6:30pm, Rs6); **Dehra Dun** (regular 5:30, 6, and 7am; deluxe 4:30 and 8pm; 10hr.; Rs150/188); **Delhi** (7 per day 6am-7:30pm, 9hr., Rs116); **Kathgodam and Haldwani** (every 15min. 5am-6:30pm, 2hr., Rs19); **Ramnagar** (5, 5:30, 7, and 7:30pm; 5hr.; Rs45); **Ranikhet** (12:30pm, 3hr., Rs37). Bus tickets to Dehra Dun and Delhi are often sold by the travel agents that line the Mall; many also run deluxe buses to Dehra Dun (Rs300) and Delhi (Rs200).

Local Transportation: Cycle-rickshaws charge Rs4 to drive the length of the Mall. During the high season, traffic is closed to motor vehicles and cycle-rickshaws from 6-9pm.

■ ORIENTATION AND PRACTICAL INFORMATION

The town of Nainital is split into two major parts—**Tallital** and **Mallital**—which are connected by the **Mall,** a road running along the east side of the lake. Buses arrive at Tallital, which hugs the southern tip of the lake. From there, it's a 15-minute walk along either side of the lake to Mallital. Most hotels are found along the Mall, most services at either end. The **Flats,** a common area used for soccer and field hockey, sprawls between Mallital and the water.

Tourist Office: (tel. 35337), about two-thirds of the way to Mallital along the Mall. Provides information for the town and region and arranges transport to nearby sights. Open M-Sa 10am-5pm; May-June and Oct. open M-Sa 8am-8pm, Su 8am-5pm.

Budget Travel: Several tour agents lining the Mall offer comparable tours at similar prices. The tourist office also runs trips. **Darshan Travels** (tel. 37491), towards Mallital on the Mall before the library, offers day tours to nearby resorts and lakes including Bhimtal, Sat Tal, Hanumangarh (Rs80), and Mukteshwar (Rs175). Darshan also runs buses to Delhi (Rs175/300) and Haridwar (Rs250). Open daily 8am-8pm.

Currency Exchange: State Bank of India (tel. 35645), in Mallital just beyond the Flats. Open M-F 10am-2pm, Sa 10am-noon. An "evening branch" on the Mall near Tallital cashes AmEx traveler's checks in US$ and UK£. Open M-F 2-5pm, Sa noon-2pm.

Market: The area west of the Flats in Mallital hosts the **Bera Bazaar.** Scrunched into the west part of this area is a Tibetan market. Open M-Sa 9am-9pm.

Library: Durga Suh Library, lake front along the Mall, lends readers one English book at a time. Rs10 admission, Rs30 deposit. Open M-Sa 7:30-10:30am and 5:30-8:30pm.

Bookstore: Modern Bookstore, on the Mall near the Flats. Open M-Sa 10:30am-9pm, Su 11am-4pm. **Consul Bookstore,** in Mallital across from Green Restaurant. Open M-Sa 9:30am-8pm.

Pharmacy: Indra Pharmacy (tel. 35139), by the bus stand in Tallital, is well stocked and keeps long hours. Open M-Sa 7am-10pm, Su 7am-3pm. Another branch is in Mallital (tel. 35629), in Bara Bazaar. Open M-Sa 9am-10pm, Su 3-10pm.

Hospital/Medical Services: B. D. Pandey Hospital (tel. 35012) is near the State Bank of India in Mallital. Dr. D.P. Gangola (tel. 35039) is a consulting physician at **Indra Pharmacy;** he keeps hours in the Mallital branch (5-8pm) and in Tallital (9am-2pm). Dr. G.P. Shah operates a clinic (tel. 37001) near the entrance to the Flats on the Mall.

Police: Mallital (tel. 35424) and Tallital (tel. 35525), in front of the Hotel Mansarovar at the Tallital end of the Mall.

Post Office: The GPO has its main branch on the north side of Mallital, a few blocks up from the Mall's extension. *Poste Restante* open M-Sa 9am-5pm. The branch in Tallital, facing the bus stop, only sells stamps. Open 10am-5pm. **Postal Codes:** Mallital 263002, Tallital 263001.

PHONE CODE	05942

◤ ACCOMMODATIONS

Prices for lodging in Nainital are higher and more subject to change by season than anywhere else in Kumaon. Listed prices are peak-season rates, except where noted; expect a 25-75% drop outside of May, June, and October. November to March is the cheapest time to come. Those places set higher on the hill have better views and less street noise, though most places along the Mall (where most hotels are) are still pretty sedate and offer views of the lake. Most have 10am check-out.

Hotel City Heart (tel. 35228), near Mallital on the Mall across from the Nainital Club. This gem not only offers spectacular views of the lake from every room but also boasts a courteous staff led by its owner, Pramad Kumar, who happily shares his knowledge of Nainital and the Kumaon region with his guests. Room service (construction is underway for a rooftop restaurant), clean bedding, and spacious rooms, all with attached bath. Doubles Rs600. Off-season: Rs300.

KMVN Tourist Rest House, Tallital (tel. 35570), 200m toward the far side of the lake from the Tallital bus stand; follow signs from the ramp. Set above the road and away from the noise with grand views of the lake and distant hills. 8-bed dorms are often full. Hot water, showers, seat toilets. Suites have TV, telephone, and balcony. Attached restaurant open 7am-10:30pm. In-season (Apr. 1-June 15): Dorm beds Rs75; suites Rs800. Off-season: Rs60/600. Extra person 10%.

Hotel Gauri (tel. 36617), near Tallital, on the road parallel to the Mall, behind the Hotel Mansarovar. Dimly lit hallways lead to cheery rooms with TVs and balconies with views of the lake. Singles and deluxe doubles have seat toilets; regular doubles have squat toilets. Deluxe rooms have showers. Doubles Rs300-700. Off-season: Rs200-350.

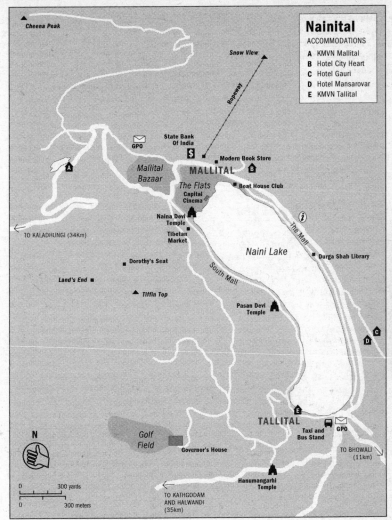

KMVN Mount View Tourist Rest House, Mallital (tel. 35400). The typically clean government-run rest house offers the rare cheap sleep in this hyper-expensive hill station. However, unlike its counterpart in Tallital, this KVMN has no views of the lake and no charming garden. Restaurant open 7:30am-9pm. Dorm beds Rs75; doubles Rs 550. Off-season: Rs60/415.

Hotel Mansarovar (tel. 35581), near Tallital, in front of Hotel Gauri. Spacious rooms with very clean bathrooms (squat and seat toilets in each). Room service, laundry, and TV. Doubles Rs450-750; deluxe suites Rs800-1500.

FOOD

The Mallital end is grounds for gathering grub—restaurants in Tallital are generally not as clean. Roasted *masala* corn and similar delectables can be bought along the Mall, and the **market** west of the Flats has several vendors selling cheap, tasty food (though of questionable quality—eat at your own risk).

Sonam Tibetan Restaurant, next to the Modern Bookstore in Mallital. Meager choices but big servings of Tibetan food. Veg. noodles in broth (Rs25) make for sumptuous sippage—slurp under the Dalai Lama's portait. Open daily 8am-10pm.

Ahar Vihar Restaurant (tel. 35756), upstairs from the well-lit variety stores on the Mall near Mallital. It's a popular low-end restaurant that feels like Mom's kitchen. Large and delicious Gujarati and Rajasthani *thalis* (Rs35-40). Open daily 10am-10pm.

Nanak's Restaurant (tel. 35336), between the library and Mallital on the Mall. A would-be Western restaurant serving fast-food veg. burgers (Rs25), "Jughead's trip in life" (a.k.a pizza), milkshakes, and mango sundaes (Rs80) in a dark room aglow with neon lights. Open daily 9am-11pm.

Green Restaurant (tel. 36522), Bara Bazaar in the heart of Mallital; look for the large banner. The maroon, lamp-lit interior and colorful streamers overhead make up for the uncomfortable chairs and short tables. The Green has *misi roti* (Rs8) and a wide range of Chinese dishes (veg. Rs25-40, non-veg. Rs35-60). Open daily 7:30am-11pm.

👁 SIGHTS AND SCENERY

VIEWPOINTS. Nainital is replete with nearby peaks that offer views of the city and, if the clouds cooperate, Himalayan peaks as far away as the Tibetan border. The best way to see these (according to the touts) is to rent a **horse** from one of Mallital's stables and clip-clop to the top, but the ride, often up steep, loose-stone trails, can be difficult. *(Round-trip Rs125, with the guide jogging alongside your steed. Expect to pay more if you want to stop and see the view for more than an hour.)*

The easiest way to get to the top of **Snow View** is to forsake horse and foot altogether and take the **ropeway,** a cable car that leaves from a clearly marked building a steep 30m up from the Mall in Mallital. The low-effort nature of this excursion makes it incredibly popular during high season, so opening time (8am) is the best bet for ensuring tickets and clear views. The last cable car leaves Mallital at 7pm, but the last car returns from Snow View at 6pm. *(Round-trip Rs50, with a 1hr. stop at the top. Binoculars Rs5. KMVN has a cottage at the top: in-season doubles Rs500.)*

Other viewpoints around Nainital include **Cheena Peak** (2611m), sometimes called China or Naina Peak. The highest thing around, Cheena Peak is 6km away, one hour by horse (Rs100) or three hours by foot. At the top is a snack shop and many nooks where one can sit and contemplate the city below or, if the weather permits, the peaks of Garhwal, including Nanda Devi (7817m). Watch out for leeches in the gravel, though. You can start in Mallital or have a taxi take you to Tonneleay on Kilbury Rd. to shorten the trip. **Land's End,** on the back side of Tiffin Peak (immediately west of the lake), offers views of the sprawling valley to the west. Farther up Tiffin Peak is **Dorothy's Seat,** a flat, green area near the top named after a woman who often sat here after her husband died in a crash.

NAINI LAKE. The town's pride and joy is the lake itself. To really get out in the middle of Sati's emerald eye, **boat rental** is a must *(paddle boats Rs30 per hr. for a 2-seater, Rs60 for a 4-seater; boatman-guided rides Rs50 for full round of the lake, Rs30 for one trip across).* You can rent **yachts** from the Nainital Boat Club, though they will require membership *(yachts Rs60 per hr.; membership Rs150).* There are yacht regattas throughout the year, including the **Kingfisher Regatta** in the third week of June.

OTHER ATTRACTIONS. Wandering up the road heading west of Tallital leads to the remarkably British-looking **Governor's House,** then to **Hanumangarh,** a small temple 3km away. Just beyond the temple is an **observatory** that can be visited independently; call in advance for special night moon viewings *(tel. 35136; free).* In 1880, a landslide killed 151 people and wiped out the city's largest hotel, but the flattened part of the town was turned into the city's best public space. Today the **Flats** are a haunt for snake charmers and musicians and home to tournaments for field hockey and soccer. In October, **Autumn Festival** (see p. 165) sponsors sports competitions by day and cultural programs by night. **Capital Cinema,** near the Flats, runs Hindi movies regularly *(2nd class Rs10, 1st class Rs15, balcony Rs25).* Most under-appreciated is the placid, cool walk along the side opposite the Mall, where there are two small temples and a few ledges near the water. A **stroll along the Mall** becomes more peaceful as darkness enshrouds the piles of chintz in the stores. If the weather's cool, snag one of the quality shawls produced here.

NEAR NAINITAL

Those in search of lake-side solitude will find that Nainital is just the tip of the regional iceberg where peaceful ponds are concerned. These other spots offer not only equally lovely views, but also lower prices. **Bhowali,** 11km east of Nainital (**buses** leave every 30 min. from the Tallital bus station), is the region's transportation hub. Frequent buses depart for all Kumaon destinations and larger hubs outside the region. **Sat-Tal** is a system of seven lakes surrounded by forests of pine and oak trees 21km from Nainital. It is possible to rent boats (Rs100 per hr.) on the lake and buy snacks on the lakefront, but the area surrounding the lake remains undeveloped. The only rest house at Sat-tal is run by KMVN (tel. 47047). Unfortunately, visitors must fork over Rs400-1000 a night in May and June (off-season: 35% discount). Most tour agencies have buses to Sat-Tal and surrounding lakes (Rs80).

Bhimtal, 22km from Nainital, is a smaller and more active version of Nainital which has developed a strong reputation for water sports. As usual, government accommodations are the cheapest. The KMVN tourist bungalow (tel. 47005), on the opposite side of the lake of Bhimtal, is about as quiet and cheap as Bhimtal lake-side hotels come (dorm beds Rs60; tidy doubles with carpets and wood cabinets Rs200). Like treeless Bhimtal, **Naukuchiyatal** offers plenty of solitude but not much shade. The KMVN tourist bungalow at Naukuchiyatal (tel. 47138) has a comfortable lounge and a beautiful garden in front (in-season: dorm beds Rs60; doubles Rs400). The best time to visit the region is in autumn, when the weather has cooled off and the rates have come down. The winter is also beautiful, but make sure to pack warm clothes, gloves, and boots to deal with the cold and snow.

RANIKHET रानीखत

At an altitude of 2000m, Ranikhet is the most alpine of Kumaon's centers. From the town, it's only a short walk up to pine and deodar forests inhabited by *kakar* (barking deer). Those prone to vertigo will undoubtedly note the land's steepness, although the nearby, snow-capped Nanda Devi (7817m) is even steeper. The station was founded in 1869 by the British and served as a relaxation base for soldiers stationed in the U.P. Plains. The military continues to be influential—the Kumaon Regiment is based here. With less traffic noise than the other hill stations, fewer travelers, and much less to do, Ranikhet is a prime spot for hikes and relaxation. It is a quiet town where nary a car horn can be heard after 8pm. This "Queen's Field" is quickly growing, though, with new resorts popping up every year. A local tourist brochure points out: "How long Ranikhet can maintain its virginity is a million dollar question." Maybe that's why you now have to pay a Rs2 toll to enter.

▓ ORIENTATION AND PRACTICAL INFORMATION

Sadar Bazaar, the main road that anchors Ranikhet's meandering topography, is in the town center; most services and numerous hotels and restaurants are found here. **Buses** arrive at either end of the bazaar; **U.P. Roadways** stops at the downhill end, and KMOU buses arrive and depart on the west end. The **Mall** area is located above the bazaar 2km away and features some of the more expensive hotels. To get to the Mall, follow the road next to the **Alka Hotel** (up the mountains and away from the relative chaos). Keep to your left and eventually you will find yourself on the Mall road. There is a mural-sized map of Ranikhet across from the **Rajdeep Hotel** that also gives listings of area attractions. Monday is Ranikhet's **business holiday;** most shops are closed then.

Buses: U.P. Roadways (tel. 20645) runs buses to: **Almora** (5:30am, 2½ hr., Rs28); **Dehra Dun** (8:30am and 3pm, 12hr., Rs150); **Delhi** (4 per day 3-5pm, 12hr., Rs150); **Haldwani/Kathgodam** (every 30min. 5:30am-5pm, 4hr., Rs40); **Kausani** (6am, 12:30, and 2pm; 3hr.; Rs26); **Nainital** (7am, 3½hr., Rs28); **Ramnagar** (8:30am, 1, and 3pm; 5hr.; Rs50). **KMOU** (tel. 20609) has a friendly staff and comfortable buses to: **Almora** (5 per day 6:30am-2:30pm, 2½hr., Rs25); **Haldwani/Kathgodam** (7 per day 7am-2:30pm, 4hr., Rs34); **Kausani** (4 per day 6am-1:30pm, 3hr., Rs27); **Nainital** (11:30am, 3hr., Rs30); **Ramnagar** (5 per day 7am-3pm, 4hr., Rs40).

Tourist Office: (tel. 20227), at the east end of the bazaar, just up from the U.P. Roadways bus stand. The man in charge is very helpful and can provide detailed information about Ranikhet and the Larger Kumaon Area. Open M-Su 10am-5pm. In-season (May-June): open M-Sa 8am-8pm, Su 10am-5pm.

Currency Exchange: The **State Bank of India** (tel. 20262), on the road above and parallel to the bazaar, exchanges US$100 or £50 per day and AmEx and Thomas Cook traveler's checks. Open M-F 10am-2pm, Sa 10am-noon.

Pharmacy: Mayank Medical Hall (tel. 21356), at the U.P. Roadways end of town. English-speaking. Open Tu-Su 8am-8pm and alternate Mondays.

Medical Assistance: The **clinic** of Dr. Prakash Srivastava (tel. 20101) is located on the bazaar uphill from the Mayank pharmacy. Open daily 9am-5pm.

Post Office: The main branch is along the Mall, 2km from town center, and there's another branch near the tourist office. Open M-F 9am-5pm, Sa 9am-noon.

PHONE CODE	05966

ACCOMMODATIONS AND FOOD

Hotels along the bazaar are noisier and less well-kept (but less expensive) than those tucked into the hills along the Mall. In season (April-June) prices are higher and rooms scarcer. Most hotels have a 10am check-out and don't allow alcohol.

Hotel Parwati (tel. 20325), above U.P. Roadways bus stop; look for large signs. The most elevated hotel in Ranikhet, it offers clean rooms and a super view from its lounge. Room service and hot water. Deluxe rooms have TVs. Friendly English-speaking staff. In-season (May-June): singles Rs250; doubles Rs400; deluxe Rs500. No credit cards.

Hotel Everest (tel. 20402), above the bazaar, offers the same basic rooms but rents them at the lowest price. Watch the bazaar from the long balcony. Rooms have mirrors, and common bathrooms are tidy. In-season: singles Rs100, with bath Rs200; doubles Rs125/250. Off-season: 35% discount.

Tribhuwan Hotel (tel. 2524), on the west end of town just before the KMOU bus stand. A mighty beast composed of 3 buildings. Tranquility and higher prices lie farther down the hill from the bazaar. Two-sided balconies offer unobstructed views of the valley. Squat toilets and bucket showers. Carpeted rooms are larger and have small black and white TVs. Basic rooms Rs250; deluxe Rs400. Off-season: Rs400/500.

Moon Hotel, across from Hotel Rajdeep, has the nicest restaurant in town, with prices to match. The long, airy halls are so elegant they seem out of place along the bazaar. The pulled chicken is outstanding (Rs200). The other food is across-the-board spicier than the standard regional fare. Butter *naan* (Rs20). Open daily 8am-11pm.

Sugham Restaurant, in the Hotel Parwati. Although the dimly lit interior is not especially inviting, the attentive staff and good, plain food make this a safe place to eat. Chinese (Rs25-50), Indian (Rs25-40), and Continental dishes. Open daily 8am-9pm.

Tourist Bungalow has a restaurant that isn't worth a trek from town, but it's good if you happen to be along the Mall. Munch down "fingar chips" (Rs18) or vegetable *pakoras* (eight for Rs18) while sipping tea (Rs5) in front of the TV (free). Chinese fare too (chow mein Rs45). Open daily 7-8am (tea only), 8-10am, noon-2:30pm, and 4:30-10:30pm.

👁 🎵 SIGHTS AND ENTERTAINMENT

CHAUBATIA GARDEN. The most renowned attraction in the area, the Chaubatia Garden features many large gardens which are in full technicolor bloom from June to August. It is also a "Fruit Research Centre." Sneaky travelers sometimes do their own "fruit research" while following one of the trails along the mountainside through the forests of fruit trees. Indian vacationers fill the garden in the high season. *(11km away from Ranikhet. 7 buses head to Chaubatia from the U.P. Roadways stand 8am-6pm, 40min., Rs5. Shared taxi Rs20. Garden open daily 24hr.)*

OTHER SIGHTS. Closer to Ranikhet, along the Mall, sits the Hindu temple of **Jhula Devi.** It's small, but the gates around it are covered with bells. Continuing down the Mall, visit the impressive new (1994) **Mankameshwar Temple,** up from the telephone exchange and across from the Nainital Bank.

FESTIVALS. The **Autumn Festival** in late September is Ranikhet's largest. With sports tournaments in field hockey, cricket, and tennis, along with a cultural potpourri from all of Kumaon and India, this 10- to 14-day festival celebrates India's diversity. For 10 days in June, you can stop in at the Nar Singh Stadium (also called the Nar Singh Ground) for the evening **Summer Festival.** A homey country fair, it features a ring toss, magicians, kiddie rides, a mini-zoo, 10-rupee gambling, blaring music, and heartburn-inducing Chinese food.

GOLF COURSE. Fortunately, no metal detectors regulate admission to the **Kumaon Regiment Advanced Training Centre and Golf Course** (also known as "Upat Kalika"), so bring your irons for one of India's most scenic mountain golf courses. It's relatively pricey, but golfers worldwide would fork over a fortune for a chance to see the course's extraordinary views and take their chances at a Himalayan hole-in-one. (6km away. Taxis Rs60. Nine holes for Rs200; club rental Rs100; ball Rs90; caddy Rs50 plus tip. Open Tu, Th, and F 7am-6pm; W and Sa 7am-12:30pm.)

ALMORA अल्मोड़ा

Legend has it that Almora was the city of the gods; it is believed that they left an abundant source of pure water, delivered to this mile-high city from over 120 underground wells, to commemorate the divine presence here. Almora remains the most mystical of Kumaon's hill stations, having drawn peace-seekers from the likes of Gandhi and Nehru (who used to meet here to talk) to Swami Vivekananda and Timothy Leary. The most central hill station in U.P., Almora is also one of the only to have been developed by Indians and not the British—it was created as the seat of the Chanda dynasty 400 years ago. A stroll through the old bazaar evokes those bygone days—the buildings are fading, but colorful facades and cobbled streets echo centuries past. What truly defines the Almora region, though, has not changed in 400 years. The mountains, which offer opportunities for day hikes and exploration, remain oblivious to passing decades and dynasties. Amid the current frenetic activity in the air is also an unmatched quietude. While its neighboring hill stations pursue the Western gods of finance and leisure, Almora is surrounded by modern and ancient Hindu temples and, off in the distance, by the magnificent natural shrines of the cloud-piercing Himalayan peaks.

🛈 ORIENTATION AND PRACTICAL INFORMATION

Almora wraps around its mountain on only four parallel streets. Buses stop at the **town center** on the **Mall,** the major thoroughfare for traffic and the site of most hotels and services; walking in the same direction as arriving buses leads to some restaurants and to the road to Kasar Devi. Most other services lie southwest along the Mall. The **Bazaar** is the first major parallel street up from the Mall. Sunday is Almora's **business holiday;** many businesses are closed then, but you can still find enough open stores and chemists to satisfy your needs.

Buses: Almora's bus stand is on the Mall at the center of town. **KMOU,** before the U.P. Roadways stand along the Mall, serves **Kausani** and **Bageswar** (11 per day 6am-5pm, 2½hr., Rs25); **Kathgodam** and **Haldwani** (6, 6:30, 9:30am, and 1pm; 4½hr.; Rs40); **Nainital** and **Bhowali** (5 per day 6:30am-1pm, 3hr., Rs30); **Ranikhet** (8, 10, 10:30am, and 3pm; 2½hr.; Rs20). **U.P. Roadways** is located down the steps: **Bhowali** (every 30min. 5-8am and 1:30-5pm, 2½hr., Rs29); **Delhi** (7am, 1, 3:30, and 5pm; 11hr.; Rs150); **Dehra Dun** (5am and 4pm, 12hr., Rs170); **Kausani** (7, 9, 9:30am, and noon; 2½hr.; Rs25); **Nainital** (8am, 3hr., Rs35); **Ranikhet** (6:30am, 1 and 2pm; 2hr.; Rs29).

Tourist Office: The **U.P. Tourist Office** (tel. 30180), 800m southwest of the bus stand on the road veering up from the Mall by the post office, carries information about Almora and Kumaon but keeps loose hours. Try M-Sa 10am-5pm. A better bet for information is one of the local **trekking companies,** including **Discover Himalaya** (tel. 31470; fax 31507; email joshi@n.d.e.vsnl.net.in), across from the post office, and **High Adventure** (tel. 31445), on the Mall a bit closer to town center. Mr. Shah at the Kailas Hotel is also very knowledgeable about the local sights.

Currency Exchange: State Bank of India (tel. 30048), on the Mall, near the town center. Changes AmEx checks in most currencies and grudgingly cashes Thomas Cook and Citibank checks (be persistent) but does not change foreign cash. Open M-F 10am-2pm, Sa 10am-12pm.

Bookstore: Shree Almora Book Depot (tel. 30148), next to High Adventure, carries paperbacks and regional guides. Open M-Sa 9:30am-8pm.

Pharmacy: The most fully-stocked pharmacy in town is the **Prakash Medical Store** located just as you enter the bazaar from the Mall. Open daily 7am-10:30pm.

Hospital: Civil Hospital (tel. 30025, emergency tel. 30064), up a short flight of stairs from the bazaar. Open daily 8am-2pm. Emergency open 24hr. **Base Hospital** (tel. 30012), 3km from town, is cleaner and less crowded. Open daily 8am-2pm.

Police: tel. 30323.

Post Office: (tel. 30019), on the downside of the Mall 600m southwest of the bus stand. *Poste Restante.* Open M-Sa 10am-6pm. **Postal Code:** 263601.

PHONE CODE	05962

ACCOMMODATIONS

Most of the hotels in town lie along the Mall, with dingier, cheaper places clustered around the town center. More relaxed accommodations dot the surrounding hills but are more difficult to reach (see **Near Almora,** p. 168).

Kailas Hotel (tel. 30624), across from the post office, 10m above the Mall. This place is the unrivaled sweet spot for foreign budget travelers in Almora. The Kailas is run by the incomparably charming 81-year-old Mr. Shah, who is a marvelous source for all sorts of tales and wisdom about the Almora district and Indian history. The rooms could be cleaner, but the place has a character that many find worth the price. Prices range from Rs65 for a single without bath to Rs365 for an in-season quint. Bargaining is futile.

KMVN Holiday House (tel. 30250), 1km southwest of the bus stand on the descending road. Typically pleasant and clean government accommodation, set apart from the rest of the noisy town, with its own garden and valley view. Combined seat/squat toilets for everyone. Dorms have bucket showers. Dorm beds Rs60; doubles Rs300; quads Rs600. Off-season: Rs50/225/450. Extra bed 20%. Extra person 10%.

Hotel Pawan (tel. 30252), across from Trishul, closer to town center. Don't be fooled by the "Enjoy Billiards" sign; it is only for local members of the Billiards Club (don't bother asking about membership, you don't qualify). Well-kept and sufficient, with bright rooms, large mirrors, and clean bathrooms with squat toilets. Room service available. Check-out noon. Singles Rs100; doubles Rs200; deluxe with TV Rs240.

Hotel Shikhar (tel. 30238), at the end of the Mall. Shikhar offers the most services of any of Almora's hotels with attached travel agency, general store, hair salon, restaurant, and STD/ISD. Rooms are spacious and very well lit. The balcony above the restaurant offers a dramatic view of the valley. Singles Rs150; doubles Rs245.

FOOD

Glory Restaurant, across from Mount View, up the road to the northeast. The 2nd floor's short ceilings and red lanterns lend this veg. restaurant an unusual amount of character. Cheese butter *masala* Rs40. Delicious *samosas* Rs8. Open daily 7am-10:30pm.

Hotel Himsagar Restaurant, has decent food at darn cheap prices. Great view, marble wash sinks, and all-veg. food (*dal makhani* Rs20). Open daily 8am-10:30pm.

Swagat Restaurant, on the side of the Hotel Shikhar, down the steps. An airy, homey place with a commanding view. No menus, only veg. *thalis* (Rs30) and some fried snacks (*pakora* platter Rs15). Open daily 7:30-9:30pm.

Mount View Restaurant, inside Hotel Shikhar, has dependable food. *Korma* curry Rs30; curry chicken Rs50. Open daily 6am-11:30pm. Off-season: 6am-10:30pm.

SIGHTS

Almora proper doesn't offer much in the way of sights, but the farther from town you go, the more interesting things get.

KASAR DEVI TEMPLE. The main attraction near Almora is the Kasar Devi Temple. The temple's spectacular setting emits an aura of mysticism. Views from a giant, sloping rock atop the mountain afford sweeping panoramas of the whole area, marred only slightly by the television antenna that shares the point, emitting an aura of its own. The temple is known as a center of spiritual energy—Swami Vivekananda came here to meditate, as have many soul-searching Americans and Europeans, some of whom still hang around the nearby tea stands today. Follow the trail past the temple through town for the best views of the distant Nanda Devi mountain range. *(Near the hamlet of Kasar Devi, 7km from Almora. Reachable by a long hike upwards past the Mall, forking left after the Hotel Shikhar. Taxi, Rs10 per person 1-way.)*

TRANQUILITY RETREAT. Wedged between two hills, and far from everything but its own splendor and jaw-dropping views, the Tranquility Retreat is a tiny utopia for the short- or long-term visitor. Now in its fourth year, Tranquility has grown to seven rooms, with an organic garden and an apiary (that's bees). Armelle and Kishan, French expatriate and Indian farmer, busily tend the garden, bake bread (7 loaves daily) and steaming scones served with homemade honey, and cook up a vegetarian storm—French and Continental mainstays with the occasional Indian touch—while exuding a warmth and compassion that keeps their contented guests from leaving the nest. And why would they, with fried vegetables (Rs35), garlic tomato pizza (Rs25), garden salad with vinaigrette (Rs10), and fresh bread (Rs15) for the taking? There are two paths leading from the road to Kasar Devi to Tranquillity Retreat. If you are walking towards Kasar Devi, look for a blue sign high in a tree on your left-hand side 10 minutes after passing the Research Institute for Yoga Therapy. If you are walking away from Kasar Devi, there will be a sign on your right-hand side 15 minutes down the mountain from the Kasar Devi Temple. For both paths, follow the blue blazes over the ridge. Write for reservations. *(Tranquillity Guesthouse c/o Kishan Joshi, 263601 Saria Pina Estate, Almora, VPM. Food is available 7am-10pm for casual visitors as well as guests. Doubles Rs1500 per month.)*

OTHER SIGHTS. Locals go to the locally important **Chitai Temple** to seek justice if they feel they've been wronged. Katermal (12.5km from Almora or 1.5km by foot) boasts an 800-year-old **Sun Temple.** Closer to town is the **Nanda Devi Temple,** which pays homage to the goddess of the distant mountain. The **Nanda Devi Fair** is held here in either the last week of August or first week in September. The **Brighton End**

Corner at the south end of town is a popular spot from which to watch the sunsets. A walk along the road above the Mall and bazaar offers stunning views and a serene atmosphere. The walk is punctuated by the **Bhairav** and **Patal Devi** temples. Both offer terrific views of the sunset amidst a holy setting. If you are looking to kill time while waiting for the bus to leave, walk across the street to the small, government-run **G.B. Pant Museum,** which features not trousers but tools and other artifacts from the Katyuri and Chanda dynasties *(open Tu-Su 10:30am-4:30pm, closed second Su; free)*. Aspiring musicians looking to hang around Almora for a while can seek tutelage at the **Bhadkande College of Music,** which has a branch in town. Wander through the **bazaar** (especially the lower region) and you'll note a lot of pots. Almora is the center of production of *tamta,* a silver-plated copper. **Anokhe Lal** sells these pots, though they'd be pretty heavy to carry in a backpack.

NEAR ALMORA

North and east of Almora lie many less-frequented treasures of the Kumaon region. Hundreds of temples and statues make up **Jageswar,** situated 38km from Almora in a valley surrounded by *deodar* trees. The temples were built by the rajas of the Chand dynasty and remain an excellent example of the regional architecture. There are many other less-touristed spots in the Almora and neighboring Pithoragarh districts. Of special note is the **Binsar Sanctuary,** 30km from Almora. Binsar was the summer getaway of the Chand rulers; now tourists come and lose themselves in the sanctuary's dense forests. There is a KMVN Tourist Rest House but few other hotels and services in the area (in-season doubles Rs300; 50% discount off-season; make reservations at the Almora tourist office).

For further immersion in Kumaon's natural beauty, consider going on a **trek** to one of the towering glaciers in the Indian Himalayas. **Discover Himalaya** offers trekking packages to all glaciers. Expect to pay Rs50-70 for their services on high-altitude treks. Make sure to inquire about the student discount. The most popular trek in Kumaon is the one to **Pindari Glacier** (90km). Rest houses line the trail at convenient distances, but the trek's popularity deters those seeking a true escape. Treks to **Milam Glacier** (200km), via stunning **Munsyari** in the Pithoragarh district, is prime for those hoping to avoid the slow-moving glacial crowds. The **Kafni Glacier** (90km) also provides fuel for high-altitude trekkers. Discover Himalaya also offers a short 4-day trek through the low Himalayas (200-2500m) to the **Barahi Devi Temple** at Devidhura, the site of a stunning ritual during the Rakshabandhan festival, around the third week of August. Two opponents, equipped with baskets as shields, throw rocks at each other. Blood from the ensuing wounds is collected and offered to the virgin goddess. (This and similar treks cost around Rs900 per person per day.)

KAUSANI कुसानी

At nearly 2000m above sea level, Kausani offers the most awe-inspiring views of the Himalayan peaks available in the U.P. Hills. Kausani's strategic location has helped inspire many notable Indians—Hindi poet laureate Sumitra Nandan Pant was born here, and, in 1929, Mohandas Gandhi spent time in the Anashakti Ashram. Kausani is basically a bus stop with a few restaurants and quite a few more hotels. It's a perfect spot for basking in the Himalayan splendor, just beyond earshot of the honking cars and busy daily life of the larger hill stations.

🔏 **ORIENTATION AND PRACTICAL INFORMATION.** **Buses** stop in Kausani's center, across from a colorful temple and marked by a three-way intersection between the main road and another road which begins to climb up the mountain. The **tourist office** (May-June: open daily 8am-8pm; off-season: M-Sa 10am-5pm) and **post office** are located on the main road before the center where the buses stop. The nearest **currency exchange** is in Almora or Bageswar. Buses leave frequently from the town center for Bageswar, Almora, Gwaldam, Ranikhet, Bhowali, and Haldwani. Inquire at the tourist office or ask locals (more than one!) about departure times. The **Sunil Medical store** is located on the walkway that climbs up the mountain (open daily 8am-8pm). The walkway continues, leading to the KMVN tourist rest house 2km away. Take a left instead at the Anashakti Ashram sign to get to many of the town's other hotels. Most hotels have **STD/ISDs,** and there is also a booth at the bus stop. **Telephone code:** 05962.

■■ **ACCOMMODATIONS AND FOOD.** Kausani plays host to a large number of pricey resort hotels advertising their magnificent view of the Himalayas. The good news is that these hotels do not have a monopoly on nature's beauty. The rooms at the **Hotel Uttarakhand** (tel. 45012), off the walkway, have unobstructed mountain views, and are far enough away from the town center to offer a modicum of peace and quiet (in-season doubles Rs200-300; off-season Rs50-150). The attached restaurant is one of the best in town with veg. fried rice for Rs25 (open daily 6am-11pm). Many of Kausani's nicer hotels in town are located on one strip of road above the town center. Your best choice here is the **Amer Holiday Home** (tel. 45015), which has modest-sized rooms, hot water, and a peaceful balcony (open May-July and Sept.-Dec.; in-season singles Rs150, doubles Rs300-500; off-season Rs100/200-350). On the same row of hotels is the **Anashakti Ashram** (sometimes called "the Gandhi ashram"). It is possible to stay in the ashram, though its large common hall has rope cots, and in the high season you may be awakened at daybreak by Indian tourists' children. But the ashram's immaculate grounds offer one of the most calming vista points on hotel row. Fees are paid on a donation basis, and the manager stresses that the ashram is only for those interested in spiritual living. **KMVN tourist rest houses** are always a safe bet in Kumaon, and the one in Kausani (tel. 45006), located 2km from town on a road that hugs the northern face of the mountain, is no exception. Book at least one month in advance during the high season, May to June and October. The attached restaurant is open 7am-10pm. (Dorm beds Rs60; doubles Rs300-800. 50% discount off-season.) Just past the KMVN is the **Hotel Sunrise** (tel. 45016). This new hotel has only six double rooms (Rs300) but maintains a five-person, full-time staff to meet all your needs. Good food is cooked as you like it (no menu, just tell them what you want); catch the sunrise and sunset from an unbeatable porch. Unfortunately, good cheap eats are much scarcer than cheap sleeps. Although you will probably end up just eating at your hotel, there are a few other options. The **Uttarkhand Restaurant** and the **Kitchen Restaurant,** next to the post office, offer reliable fare (the latter serves Rs35 *thalis*). The **Ashoka restaurant,** next to the Bhatt Clinic, serves up local dishes. The lentil-based *bara* dish (Rs35) accompanied by the local chutney is a tasty treat after weeks of *dal* and chow mein. Kumaoni dishes take a while to cook, so order early.

■ **SIGHTS.** As the man in the tourist office says with a smile, the main sights in Kausani are sunrise and sunset. These are also the best times to see the distant mountains when they are enveloped in clouds (summer and monsoon season, Apr.-Aug.). If gazing at the view and trekking around the area get tiring after a while, take a day trip to **Bajinath** (16km), the site of a group of ancient temples on the banks of the Gomti River (buses to Bajinath leave frequently from the town center, Rs8). Yogi's Uttarakhand Cycle Tours (tel. 45012), next to the Hotel Uttarakhand, rents **mountain bikes** and organizes tours through the surrounding area (from Rs375 per day).

THE U.P. PLAINS

AGRA आगरा

Over the last decade, the average tourist's stay in Agra has declined from 1.7 days to barely 12 hours. At the edges of all the roads and rail lines leading to Agra, the conventional wisdom has left behind a kind of verbal underbrush, and everyone seems to be mumbling the same thing: Agra is a dump. It is not difficult to see why visitors who arrive expecting some kind of exotic oriental Shangri-la—"the immortal city of undying love," according to the official literature—might leave Agra feeling more than just a little bit disappointed. The monuments are every bit as magnificent as they are hyped up to be; the problem is that most of the tourist literature omits mention of the parts of the city around and between its UNESCO-sanctioned sites. The main budget hotel center, Taj Ganj, is a powerful lesson of what happens when too many over-aggressive rickshaw-*wallahs* and rug vendors try to chase too many grungy backpackers down too few overcrowded streets. The city does have some nice areas, though. In the Cantonment area there are wide, clean streets, upscale stores, and a string of parks maintained by the local Sheraton, which has a multi-million dollar stake in seeing that Agra puts its best foot forward. But of course, Agra's real draw is the incomparably grand **Taj Mahal.**

Agra's monuments were all built under the Mughals, who swept into India from Central Asia early in the 16th century. At the Battle of Panipat in 1526, the Mughal warrior Babur crushed the ruling Lodi dynasty; as a direct result, the Mughals won a great South Asian empire, which included Agra, the Lodi capital. For the next 150 years, the site of the Mughal capital shifted repeatedly between Delhi and Agra, leaving each city with a host of beautiful landmarks. With the slow decline of Mughal power in North India, Agra fell on hard times; the British made Kolkata (and later Delhi) their capital, encouraging Allahabad to surpass Agra as the local political powerhouse.

WARNING. Agra, like all major tourist hubs in India, has a number of swindlers who'd love a chunk of that cash you're stashing. First, be aware that rickshaw charges are excessive; the commissions incentive means that *wallahs* will often try to take you to the hotel or restaurant of their (and not your) choice. Be firm, be insistent, and be prepared to walk away the moment a driver starts to tell you about his three brothers living in New York, London, and Sydney. Also beware of crafty salesmen who persuade tourists with "parties," tea, and sweet talk to buy rugs and jewels to resell back home. Numerous schemes (credit card fraud, false identities, etc.) can stem from this, so don't get lured in. (See also **Warning,** p. 21.) Walk away if the price you're quoted seems too high; there is no need to bother negotiating with those who make a living out of over-charging day-tripping tourists. See **Touts, Middlemen, and Scams,** p. 20.

Lately, Agra has worked hard to re-invent itself, funneling some of the hard currency it earns from tourists into smoggy industrial development. It sometimes requires great reserves of patience and magnanimity to rise above the temptation to scream and shout back at the persistent crowd that will follow your every step around Agra. But despite its irritations, Agra is well worth the effort it asks of you: the monuments remain serene and beautiful. Memories of the Taj at dawn will remain with you long after you have forgiven and forgotten the rickshaw driver who refused to take you anywhere but his uncle's diamond warehouse.

⎙ TRANSPORTATION

Airport: Agra's **Kheria Airport** is 9km southwest of the city (enquiry tel. 263982 or 301180, ext. 185). Flights to: **Delhi** (M and W 7:15pm, 40min., US$50); **Varanasi** (2hr., US$90) via **Khajuraho** (M and W 2:35pm, 45min., US$80). Book flights at the **Indian Airlines** office (tel. 360948 or 360190; open daily 10am-5:30pm), adjacent to Hotel Clarks-Shiraz, or from **Sita World Travel** (tel. 363013), on the north side of the main shopping bazaar, Sadar Bazaar.

Trains: Agra has several rail stations: **Agra Cantonment, Idgah, Agra Fort, Yamuna Bridge** (across the river), **Agra City** (north of town), and **Raja Ki Mandi** (northwest of Old Agra). Agra Cant. Railway Station (enquiry tel. 131 or 133), the main terminal, is southwest of the city at the west end of the Mall. A window at the computer reservation

Agra

ACCOMMODATIONS

A   Hotel Ritz
B   Pawan/Jalwal Hotel
C   Agra Hotel
D   Tourist Rest House
E   Hotel Akbar Inn
F   Hotel Safari

complex on the south side makes bookings for foreign tourists. Unless noted, fares listed are 2nd/1st class. To: **Bhopal** (*Shatabdi Exp.* 2002, 8:15am, 6hr., Rs640 A/C chair; *Punjab Mail* 1038, 8:30am, 8hr.; *Mangala Lakshadweep Exp.* 2618, 12:35pm, 8hr.; *Amritsar Dadar Exp.* 1058, 12:50am, 10½hr., Rs112/588); **Kolkata, Howrah Station** (*Udyan Abha Toofan Exp.* 3008, 12:40pm, 30hr., Rs201/1056); **Delhi** (*Shatabdi Exp.* 2001, 8:18pm, 2hr., Rs390 A/C chair; *Nizamuddin Intercity Exp.* 4003, 6am, 3½hr.; *Taj Exp.*, 6:45pm, 3hr., Rs53/279); **Gwalior** (*Kerala Exp.* 2626, 2:17pm, 1½hr.; *Punjab Mail* 2138, 8:30am; *Agra Kurla Lashkar Exp.* 1062, 8:50pm, 2hr., Rs36/189); **Lucknow** (*Ahmedabad-Gorakhpur Exp.* 5045, 6:50am, 6½hr.; *Marudhar Exp.* 4854 or 4864, 10:15pm, 6½hr., Rs79/415); **Mathura** (*G.T. Exp.* 2615, 7:30am, 1hr.; *Udyan Abha Toofan Exp.* 3007, 3:30pm, 1½hr., Rs23/173); **Mumbai** (*Punjab Mail* 1038, 8:30am, 23hr., Rs210/1103).

Buses: Most leave from **Idgah Bus Terminal,** just northeast of Agra Cant. Railway Station. To: **Ajmer** (9am, 5, 6, 9:30, and 10:30pm; 9hr.; Rs130); **Bikaner** (11am, 12hr., Rs198); **Delhi** (every 30min. 4am-10:30pm, 5hr., Rs74); **Fatehpur Sikri** (every 20min. 6am-6pm, 1½hr., Rs15); **Gwalior** (every hr. 6am-7:30pm, 3½hr., Rs43); **Jaipur** (every 30min. 6am-10:30pm, 7hr., Rs83) via **Bharatpur** (1½hr., Rs24); **Jhansi** (5am, 12:30, 3:30, and 8:30pm; 10hr.; Rs74); **Khajuraho** (5am, Rs100); **Mathura** (every hr. 6am-8:30pm, 1½hr., Rs80); **Udaipur** (6pm, 14hr., Rs224). Buses to **Varanasi** (5pm, 18hr., Rs220) leave from the **Agra Fort Bus Stand,** southwest of the fort. Deluxe buses leave frequently from other places—contact a Taj Ganj travel agent for details.

Local Transportation: Despite all the rip-offs, **cycle-rickshaws** are still a good way to get around. Pay no more than Rs15-20 for a cycle-rickshaw or **auto-rickshaw** going between railway or bus stations and Taj Ganj or Agra Fort. Auto-rickshaws can be hired for a day for Rs100-200, depending on your bargaining acumen. Agra is easy to zip around by **bicycle;** there are rental shops all around town. And if you have money to spare, hire a **car and driver** from one of the numerous places around the tourist centers: **R.R. Travels** (tel. 330055), Fatehabad Rd., in Taj Ganj, offers a 1-day tour (Rs650, Rs1100 with A/C) that includes Fatehpur Sikri. Open daily 10am-6pm.

✳ ORIENTATION

Agra is a large and diffuse city, most of which sprawls west from the banks of the **Yamuna River,** where the Taj Mahal and Agra Fort lie, separated by 1.5km and the **Shah Jahan Park. Yamuna Kinara Road** runs along the river's western banks from the Taj Mahal to **Belan Ganj,** a bustling neighborhood 1km north of **Agra Fort Railway Station,** where trains from eastern Rajasthan pull in. Tourist facilities cluster south of the Taj Mahal and Agra Fort. Bargain-basement backpacker dives crowd the streets of Taj Ganj, an unremittingly ugly and irritating rabbit-warren of hotels, restaurants, and souvenir shops that surrounds, chokes, and strangles the Taj Mahal. **Mahatma Gandhi (MG) Road, Gwalior Road,** and **General Cariappa Road** are three major thoroughfares that cross both the **Mall** and **Taj Road.** From the upscale **Sadar Bazaar,** which is nestled between MG and Gwalior Rd., it's 2km due west to **Agra Cantonment Railway Station** and its long-distance trains; 2km northwest along Fatehpur Sikri Rd. is the **Idgah Bus Stand.**

▟ PRACTICAL INFORMATION

Tourist Office: Government of India Tourist Office, 191 the Mall (tel. 363959 or 363377), across from the post office, is the most convenient and informative of Agra's 3 tourist offices. Open M-F 9am-5:30pm, Sa 9am-1pm. **U.P. Government Tourist Office,** 64 Taj Rd. (tel. 360517), near the Clarks-Shiraz. Friendlier but less well-stocked. Open M-Sa 10am-5pm. Their **branch office** (tel. 368598) is at Agra Cant. Railway Station, across from the enquiry booth. Open daily 8am-8pm. Arranges tours of Fatehpur Sikri, Sikandra, Agra Fort, and the Taj Mahal (Tu-Su 9:30am-6pm, Rs150).

Immigration Office: Foreigners Registration Office, 16 Old Idgah Colony (tel. 269563), near the bus stand, registers stays of over 3mo. Open M-Sa 10am-5pm, Su 10am-2pm.

Currency Exchange: State Bank of India, Fatehabad Rd. (tel. 330449), 1km from Taj Ganj; follow the blue "I" signs from the traffic circle at the Shah Jahan park entrance. Exchanges currency and traveler's checks up to US$200. Open M-F 10:30am-4pm, Sa 10am-1pm. **LKP Merchant Financing Ltd.,** Fatehabad Rd. (tel. 330480; fax 331191), in the tourist complex area next to Pizza Hut, changes traveler's checks and major currencies. Open M-Sa 9:15am-7pm. Outside these hours, the black-market opportunists in Taj Ganj will be more than happy to take your dollars from you. Many of the larger luxury hotels will also change money for a fee.

Luggage Storage: Agra Cant. Railway Station (Rs5 per 12hr.).

Market: Taj Ganj is a high-pressure, hassle-a-minute hustlers' hang-out where you are constantly urged to buy everything from toilet paper to miniature Taj Mahals in marble and plastic. **Old Agra** is one big bazaar for buying belts, shoes, car parts, and plastic buckets. **Kinari Bazaar,** extending northwest from the fort, is especially well stocked. Shop around, and always, always bargain hard (even if a sign claims fixed prices).

Bookstore: The Modern Book Depot (tel. 363133), in Sadar Bazaar, has an extensive selection of books, language dictionaries, and Hindi and English magazines. Open W-M 10:30am-9pm.

Pharmacy: Everywhere around the major tourist areas. **Shalya Medical Centre,** Fatehabad Rd. (tel. 331106), is well-marked and well-stocked. Open daily 8am-11:30pm.

Hospital: Sarojini Naidu Hospital (tel. 361318), west of Old Agra near Bageshwarnath Temple and Kali Masjid. **Shanti Manglik,** Fatehabad Rd. (tel. 332722 or 269474), provides 24hr. emergency assistance.

Emergency: Police, tel. 100 or 361120; Taj Ganj, tel. 331015. **Ambulance,** tel. 102.

Post Office: GPO, the Mall (tel. 361091). Opposite the tourist office. Massive, intimidating, and notoriously inefficient. Speed post and *Poste Restante* available M-Sa 10am-6pm. **Postal Code:** 282001.

Internet: Cyberlink, 3114 Thana Chowk, Taj Ganj (tel. 331275), just west of the hub at the first major crossing. The best of several places in and around Taj Ganj, Cyberlink has more computers than all its rivals put together and is run by a friendly, English-speaking staff. Rs30/hr. Fax, **free call-backs,** and collect calls (Rs10). Open daily 9am-9pm.

Telephone: Global Enterprises, Thana Chowk, Taj Ganj, allows international phone card calls for Rs3 per min. (open daily 8am-midnight).

PHONE CODE	0562

ACCOMMODATIONS

The area immediately to the south of the Taj Mahal testifies to how competition keeps prices in check. Rooms here are surprisingly cheap—except during peak times, there's absolutely no need to pay more than Rs100 for a decent double. This is where most budget travelers stay, and many cheap restaurants have sprung up to keep them watered and fed; however this area swarms with touts, con-men, and remarkably persistent rickshaw-*wallahs*. Most hotels boast rooftop views of the Taj—often little more than a blurred glimpse of a marble minaret through the brown haze and electrical wires. There are however several good budget options outside of Taj Ganj, often closer to the real center of the city, and only rarely more than a 10-minute rickshaw ride from the world's most talked-about tomb. Prices vary by season; around Christmas, the rates listed below may inflate to over 200%.

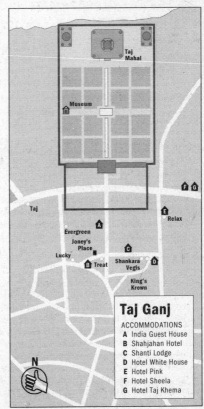

TAJ GANJ

The best way to orient yourself is to start with the central hub, the rickshaw-cluttered area in front of Joney's Place; Taj Ganj splits to the north (toward the Taj), east, and west. Roads also run along the sides of the Taj Mahal toward the gates.

Taj Ganj

ACCOMMODATIONS
A India Guest House
B Shahjahan Hotel
C Shanti Lodge
D Hotel White House
E Hotel Pink
F Hotel Sheela
G Hotel Taj Khema

Hotel Sheela, East Gate (tel. 33074). Just far enough away from the noise and the nastiness of the main hub, without being more than a couple of minutes' walk away from the you-know-what. Run by the V.P. of the Agra Hotel and Restaurant Association, this is strictly a no-commission, no-scams, no-rugs-or-knick-knacks zone. Pleasant rooms surround a garden patio restaurant. Check-out 10am. Doubles with fan Rs150, with bath Rs200, with air-cooling Rs300.

Shahjahan Hotel (tel. 331159). One of the oldest of the Taj Ganj budget places and still one of the most popular. The cushion-equipped rooftop chill-out area offers good views of the Taj. Two restaurants serve the standard fare; the manager is very eager to please. Singles Rs40-50; doubles Rs70-80, with attached bath Rs100-200.

India Guest House (tel. 330909). On the left side of the street between the hub and the Taj, within spitting distance of the gates. Run by a friendly family. Morning observances at the family shrine act as an effective wake-up call. Rooms with twin beds from Rs30.

Shanti Lodge (tel. 330900), on the left side as you walk east from the hub. The tallest hotel in Taj Ganj, Shanti has a rooftop restaurant with an unobstructed view of the Taj. Less grungy than many of the bargain-basement places nearby. Check-out 10am. Singles Rs100-120; doubles from Rs150; upstairs "rooms with a view" Rs200.

Hotel Taj Khema (tel. 330140), just east of East Gate, on the left; a short walk from the chaos of ground zero. The usual U.P. tourist bungalow set-up: clean but bland, over-priced but popular. Fully licensed bar and access to a grassy hillock with the best views of the Taj from any hotel in Agra. Singles from Rs275; doubles from Rs325.

CITY CENTER

■ **Tourists Rest House,** Kachahari Rd. (tel. 363961; fax 366910), next to Meher Cinema off Gwalior Rd., northeast of the GPO. Don't confuse it with impostors that go by similar names. Agra's best budget deal by far—spotlessly clean rooms (with soap, toilet paper, and clean towels) on a green garden courtyard. 24hr. STD/ISD, email facilities, and multilingual manager. Singles Rs65-120, with A/C Rs200; doubles Rs150/250.

Agra Hotel, FM Cariappa Rd. (tel. 363331; fax 265830), within walking distance of the fort. Good views of the Taj from garden deck-chairs. Being Agra's oldest hotel still in operation, it's beginning to show its age, but friendly management and mellow atmosphere keep it a good value. Attached restaurant. Singles Rs150; doubles Rs200-250.

Hotel Akbar Inn, 21 the Mall (tel. 363212), halfway between Taj Ganj and the railway station. A quiet place tucked away in the cool shade of the wide Cantonment streets, the Akbar feels a million miles away from the headaches and the hassles of the outside world. Some rooms a little small and stuffy. Singles Rs50-100; doubles Rs150-200.

Hotel Safari, Shaheed Nagar Shamsabad Rd. (tel. 360110), opposite Hotel Swagat and near the All India Radio station. Spotless rooms, 24hr. STD/ISD service, and free bicycles for those who want to cruise to the Taj (1.5km). Singles Rs150; doubles Rs200, with air-cooling Rs250.

Pawan Hotel, 3 Taj Rd., Sadar Bazaar (tel. 363716). The only hotel in the main Sadar strip, this huge, bright, sprawling, and slightly tatty hotel is well-placed for restaurants, bars, and auto-rickshaw tours of the world. All rooms have air-cooling. Singles Rs200-350, with A/C Rs600; doubles Rs250-450/700.

Hotel Ritz (tel. 269501), on the road running west from the Idgah Bus Stand. Best of the cheaper places for late-night or early-morning arrivals and departures. Otherwise unlikely to appeal much to the backpacking masses. Large, rather clean rooms with attached bath, air-cooling, and TV. Doubles Rs150-200; single occupancy Rs100-150.

◗ FOOD

Most of Agra's tourist-friendly restaurants are clustered around Taj Ganj, Sadar Bazaar, and other tourist centers south of the old heart of town. Most travelers tend to stick to places close to (or inside) their hotels. If you simply can't face the thought of another banana pancake or another plate of *chapati* and chow mein, then the best places to go for a really good meal are the extravagant restaurants in the five-star hotels to the south of Taj Ganj.

TAJ GANJ AREA

The restaurants near the Taj Mahal are disappointingly nondescript, offering bland Indian food and even blander Western dishes. The area is notorious for poor hygiene; most who stay more than a few days get the "Agra aches," akin to "Delhi

Belly." There have even been tales of restaurants deliberately poisoning guests and pocketing a percentage of the charges levied by the dodgy doctor conjured up to help the poor victim. For the most part, though, you are unlikely to catch anything worse than a mild case of boredom here. Most of the popular rooftop places are probably better for a sunset beer than a full-blown meal, unless you happen to have developed an addiction to greasy-finger fries.

Joney's Place, at the main hub of Taj Ganj. Hardly enough room to swing a kitten in this cozy little veteran of the Taj Ganj roadside racket. Friendly and reliable and, more or less, hassle-free. Renowned banana *lassis;* breakfasts (Rs15) are also good, but Indian dishes (Rs10-30) are somewhat variable. Open daily 6am-midnight.

Shankara Vegis and The Door's Cafe, just east of the hub. The most popular of the rooftop gathering points. Games like Connect 4 and a constant stream of Pink Floyd songs cover up any awkward evening silences. The food here won't win many prizes; still, you will eat far worse and survive. Happy hour daily 6-7pm and 9-10pm (beer Rs40).

Lucky Restaurant, west of the hub, but east of the road running along west Taj. A popular favorite with a stereo and air-cooler for a temperate, unassuming atmosphere. Delightful "Danish Farmoon" (Rs15), with coconut, chocolate, banana, and curd. Other species of *haute cuisine* lurk around the menu, disguised as spaghetti and vegetable sandwiches. Open daily 6am-midnight.

Treat Restaurant, at the Taj Ganj hub, south side, across from Joney's Place. Tiny little plastic-seated aerie with 4 different colors of light bulbs. Sit and shout abuse down to the rickshaw-*wallahs* below. Mini-breakfast (Rs15) is the best deal around. Also serves *thalis* (Rs25) and the usual grub. Open daily 6am-10pm.

CITY CENTER

The good news is that you are unlikely to starve in Agra, but if you eat all your meals in and around Taj Ganj then that's about where the good news ends. If you are interested in more than mere animal survival, then your first move should be to take a big step away from Taj Ganj. The places listed below all offer meals that spin around a different sun than the grotty omelettes and pancakes down the road.

Dasaprakash, 1 Gwalior Rd., next to Meher Cinema, opposite Tourists Rest House. With branches in Delhi, Madras, Mumbai, and Chicago, this is one of the best restaurants around. Excellent South Indian veg. dishes are well-worth the premium you pay for tasteful interior decor, unobtrusive and efficient service, and A/C. Delicious homemade pickles and excellent *thalis* (Rs100). Open daily 12:30-3pm and 6-11pm.

Zorba the Buddha, Gopi Chand Shivare Rd. (tel. 367767). In the shopping strip stretching north of the main part of Sadar Bazaar. Tiny, spick-n-span, A/C dining room decked with photos of meditation meister Osho. No smoking, no meat, no hassles. Very popular with the euro-tourist crowd. Most entrees Rs100-120. Open daily noon-3pm and 6-9pm; closed May 1 to July 5. Reservations necessary for large groups.

Priya Restaurant, behind Hotel Ratan Deep, off Fatehabad Rd. Cold and dark as a December cellar. Large menu of tasty Indian and Mughlai fare (Rs50-100) and a Shah Jahan *thali* (Rs225) that would feed a camel for a month. Open daily 7am-midnight.

Only Restaurant, 45 Taj Rd. Aptly named, since it is about the only place the rickshaw-*wallahs* will admit is still open and doing business. Bamboo ceilings, bamboo walls, and bamboo tables to drum on. Over-cooled and overpriced dude ranch attracts hordes of middle-aged, middle-class tourists. Live muzak nightly. *Navratan korma* Rs105, *rogan josh* Rs62. Open daily 11am-10pm.

■ SIGHTS

In Agra, more so than in other tourist hubs, sight-seers seem to have the same agenda. First is the Taj Mahal—preferably visited at dawn or dusk—followed by its next-door neighbor, the Agra Fort. Time permitting, tourists often squeeze in a trip to the Itimad-ud-Daulah and to the nearby city of Fatehpur Sikri (see p. 179).

UTTAR PRADESH

THE ULTIMATE KODAK MOMENT People come to the Taj Mahal to photograph it, or rather to be photographed in front of it, and the Taj does not disappoint. Friendly cameramen at the exit gate shoot tour-group after tour-group grinning in front of Shah Jahan's sublime expression of grief. They'll even work the perspective so it looks like you're lifting the tomb from its top, as if it were some oversized onion. "Gardeners" patrol the grounds, eager to show shutterbugs the right spot for that perfect angle in exchange for a little *baksheesh*. For the ultimate exposure, though, you'll have to go a little farther afield—to the other side of the Yamuna. Since there are no bridges near the tomb, this involves a lengthy auto-rickshaw journey (Rs30-40 round-trip) and a sizeable chunk of time. But if your camera craves that shot of the dome at dawn reflected in the river, it's worth the trek.

TAJ MAHAL

Open Tu-Su dawn-dusk. Rs15; Rs105 6-8am and 5-7pm. Free Fridays.

Even if they've never actually stood in front of its white marble domes, many people assume that their first visit to the Taj Mahal will provoke feelings of deja vu. Despite all the hype and hoopla, though, the sheer beauty of the place is so overwhelming that no amount of overexposure can diminish it. Especially at dawn and dusk, even the most jaded of globe-trotters often find themselves smiling in enraptured wonder as they behold it. Featured on the signs of a million and one restaurants, T-shirts, and biscuit tins the world round, this marble prima donna unofficially crowned by her ardent fans as "the most beautiful building in the world," remains undeniably India's ultimate must-see.

The tale of the Taj is a sad, sweet love story. When he became Mughal emperor in 1628, Shah Jahan brought to the throne a great many virtues, among them intellect, political acumen, and a passion for fine architecture. Three years after becoming emperor, Shah Jahan received news that broke his heart: after 18 years of marriage, his favorite wife, Arjumand Banu Begum, had died giving birth to their 14th child. In his grief, Shah Jahan decided that his beloved should be buried in a tomb of timeless beauty. As the Bengali poet Rabindranath Tagore said, the Taj Mahal was designed to be a "tear [that] would hang on the cheek of time."

Work on the Taj began in 1632, one year after the death of Arjumand Banu Begum. Marble was quarried in Makrana, Rajasthan, and precious stones were brought to Agra from Yemen, Russia, China, and Central Asia. Architects were brought in from Persia, and French and Italian master craftsmen had a hand in decorating the building; in all, nearly 20,000 people worked continuously on the construction of the Taj. By the time the Taj Mahal was completed in 1653, a great many things had changed—the Mughal capital had been moved from Agra to Delhi, the deceased Arjumand Banu Begum had become popularly known as "Mumtaz Mahal" ("Elect of the Palace"), and one of Shah Jahan's sons, Aurangzeb, had grown to manhood. In 1658, the severe, reclusive Aurangzeb staged a coup, violently surmounting the opposition of his three brothers and imprisoning his father in Agra Fort. Shah Jahan lived out his days under house arrest, staring out across the Yamuna River at the Taj Mahal. When the deposed emperor passed away in the winter of 1666, his body was buried next to his wife's.

The path to the Taj from the original entry arch (now the exit) is one of the most well designed architectural approaches in the world. The tomb itself rests on a large pedestal of white marble. Up close, the Taj is hardly white at all: delicately inlaid precious stones create meandering floral patterns framed by elegant Arabic script. While much of the tomb's interior is off-limits, visitors can enter the dim, reverberant chamber that contains the cenotaphs of Shah Jahan and Mumtaz Mahal, the latter's being inscribed with the 99 names of Allah. The tombs themselves lie directly below in a musty, unspectacular room. Outside, the **mosque** is to the west, and the **Jawab** ("Answer"), its architectural mirror, is to the east. North is the muddy Yamuna. A popular local myth says that Shah Jahan planned to construct a Taj replica of black marble across the river. A small **museum** on the west side of the gardens showcases paintings of Shah Jahan and Mumtaz Mahal and models of the complex, but few take the time to visit it *(open daily 10am-5pm)*.

If you don't mind ogling crowds, visit the Taj on a Friday, when admission is free. If you prefer a more serene, private audience, show up at dawn—you'll have the place practically to yourself, though you'll have to pay extra for the privilege. Also, keep in mind that changing light patterns affect the aesthetic experience of viewing the Taj. On a cloudless day, the Taj exudes a piercingly bright white light; in the early morning and toward twilight, the Taj has a softer glow.

AGRA FORT

Between Yamuna Kinara Rd. and Powerhouse Bus Stand, 1.5km upriver from the Taj Mahal. Open daily dawn-dusk. Rs15.

There aren't nearly as many restaurants named after Agra's fort, but it's a close second to the Taj on most visitors' check-list itineraries. Construction of the fort began under Emperor Akbar in 1565. Its fortifications were gradually strengthened over the years—the 2.5km bulky, red sandstone walls that enclose it were not completed until the time of Emperor Aurangzeb. Of the three outer gates that lead through the walls and into the fort, only the **Amar Singh Gate,** decorated with colorful glazed tiles, is accessible to the public. The gate is named for a Rajasthani maharaja who killed the royal treasurer before the emperor's eyes and then jumped from the walls here in 1644 to escape the guards.

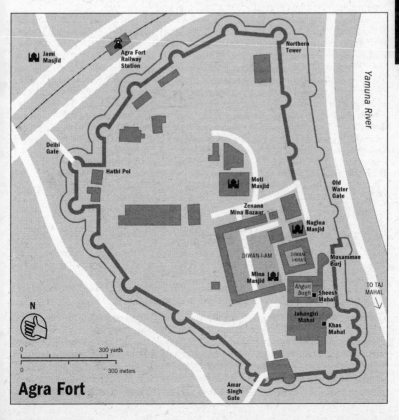

Agra Fort

Due north of the Amar Singh Gate is the breezy **Diwan-i-Am** (Hall of Public Audience), a low three-sided structure that served as Shah Jahan's court while Agra was the Mughal capital. In Agra's Mughal heyday, the Diwan-i-Am was filled with nobles, courtiers, and regal accoutrements. Shah Jahan had his throne here, on the graceful platform at the east side of the hall. The low marble platform in front of the throne was reserved for his chief minister. The tomb at the courtyard's center is that of a British officer who was slain here during the Mutiny of 1857.

The **royal chambers** are between the eastern ends of Diwan-i-Am and Agra Fort's ramparts; here the emperor's many needs were seen to in private. He also slept and prayed here from time to time. From Diwan-i-Am, the first chamber is the expansive **Macchi Bhavan** (Fish Palace), deriving its name from the stock that were dumped into its water channels so that the emperor could amuse himself with rod and reel. The chamber as it now stands is not as elegant as it once was—blocks of mosaic work and huge chunks of the royal bath have been pillaged over the centuries. In the northwest corner (left as you face away from Diwan-i-Am) of the Macchi Bhavan is the **Nagina Masjid** (Gem Mosque), built by Shah Jahan for the women of his *zenana* (harem).

Southeast of the Macchi Bhavan is the fabulous **Diwan-i-Khas** (Hall of Private Audience), completed in 1637, where the emperor would receive visitors. The **terrace** just east of Diwan-i-Khas offers classic views over the Yamuna to the Taj Mahal. Just south of the terrace is the sturdy, two-story **Musamman Burj** (Octagonal Tower), featuring delicate inlay work. Legend has it that Shah Jahan spent his final hours here, as a prisoner, gazing wistfully at his Taj Mahal, which is reflected in mirrors positioned at every angle in his cell. The emperor, meanwhile, is said to have enjoyed watching as men, tigers, and elephants were pitted against one another in the cramped area between the inner and outer walls.

Heading south from the tower, it's a hop, skip, and a jump to the **Sheesh Mahal** (Palace of Mirrors), where the women of the court bathed. South of Sheesh Mahal is a breezy enclosure that includes the 80 sq. m **Anguri Bagh** (Vine Garden). On the east side of the garden are three buildings. The **Khas Mahal** (Private Palace) is at the center, flanked by the **Golden Pavilions.** Rendered in cool marble, the Khas Mahal is supposedly where the emperor slept. The pavilions were women's bedrooms, with walls that were discreetly packed with jewelry. Note the pavilions' roofs, which were built to resemble roofs of Bengali thatched huts. The **Jahangiri Mahal,** the large sandstone palace to the south, was designed for the Hindu queen Jodhi Bai. The minute etchings and detail in the stone make it look as if it were made of timber. In front of the palace is a large tub, thought to have been where Queen Nur Jahan took her rose-scented baths.

OTHER SIGHTS

JAMA MASJID. The Jama Masjid (Friday Mosque), Agra's main mosque, is 100m west of Agra Fort Railway Station. Built in 1648 by Shah Jahan, out of sandstone spliced with ornamental marble, the mosque complex was damaged during the Mutiny of 1857, when British forces deemed its main gate a threat to the strategically important Red Fort; the gate was promptly leveled along with some of the front cloisters of the mosque. For a while during the uprising, the Jama Masjid was, in a sense, held hostage—the mosque was planted with explosives, and the British authorities loudly proclaimed that if the Mutiny gained a large enough following in Agra, the Jama Masjid would suffer the consequences. The building stayed standing, though it is in pretty bad shape today.

ITIMAD-UD-DAULAH. The so-called "Baby Taj," the **Himad-ud-Daulah,** is a small but exquisite marble tomb that is always less crowded than its cross-river rival. The tomb was built between 1622 and 1628 for Ghiyas Beg, a Persian diplomat who served as Emperor Jahangir's chief minister and was dubbed Itimad-ud-Daulah (Pillar of Government) for his loyal and exemplary service. Situated in an intimate garden designed by Ghiyas Beg himself, the tomb was built by his daughter Nur Jahan, whom the emperor married in 1611. The semi-precious stone inlay work on white marble enhances the tomb's dazzling beauty. Several of Nur Jahan's relatives were subsequently buried in the central tomb. *(Open sunrise-sunset. Rs12.)*

CHINI-KA-RAUZA AND RAM BAGH. One kilometer north of Itimad-ud-Daulah is the **Chini-ka-Rauza** (China Tomb), the decayed burial chamber of Shah Jahan's chief minister, Afzal Khan. Glazed tiles once covered the entire construction—the few that are left are severely weathered. As you continue north, it's 2km to **Ram Bagh,** a garden said to have been designed by Babur. The scruffy-looking garden is overgrown with weeds, but there is some talk of restoring it. Besides a few foreign visitors, only peacocks roam the ruins, giving the place an atmosphere of calm and peace rare in Agra. *(Both open sunrise-sunset. Women should not visit Ram Bagh alone.)*

NEAR AGRA: SIKANDRA सिकंद्र

A small town just outside Agra, Sikandra is famous as the home of **Akbar's Tomb.** Akbar, Mughal emperor from 1556 to 1605, was a great patron of the visual arts and a respectful admirer of Hinduism. The most impressive structure at the complex is the magnificent **Buland Darwaza** (Gateway of Magnificence), embellished with geometric patterns and Qur'anic inscriptions. The expansive tomb complex is divided into quadrants by wide pathways. The central mausoleum is sparsely adorned with colonnaded alcoves and marble domes. A narrow passageway to the south of the mausoleum leads down to the remarkably simple crypt itself, with its flickering candlelight and smoking sticks of incense. One of the many embroidered cloths that cover Akbar's grave was given by Indira Gandhi. Mornings and evening are less crowded, while on Fridays the joint jumps with the usual mix of hawkers, hustlers, and picnickers. The untended grassy area between the north wall of the mausoleum and the wall that encloses the entire complex is an entertaining place—monkeys, deer, and peacocks strutting around enhance the architectural grandeur of the tomb. Sikandra is quite accessible by **auto-rickshaw** (about Rs80 round-trip from Agra) or by one of the **buses** bound for Mathura, which board at the station and along Mathura Rd. (Open daily dawn-dusk. Rs12; free F.)

FATEHPUR SIKRI फ़तहपु सीकरी

Emperor Akbar, who ruled the Mughal empire from 1556 to 1605, was a man who had almost—but not quite—everything. Neither the absolute power he enjoyed throughout his vast territory, nor his three wives, nor any of his countless consorts and courtesans could satisfy his most powerful wish and give him what he wanted above all else: a male heir to succeed him. In time, Akbar's search became desperate, and he left Agra to wander across North India in search of help. His quest brought him to the village of Sikri, where Akbar came across a Sufi mystic named Shaykh Salim Chishti, who consoled the ruler and promised him no fewer than three sons. When, a year later, the first foretold son arrived, Akbar repaid the saint by naming his son Salim (he was later called Jehangir) and moving the entire court close to the saint's village of Sikri. To the surprise of the population of Agra, the palace of Fatehpur Sikri became the new capital of the Mughal empire.

Palaces, mosques, and battlements were hastily constructed, and Fatehpur Sikri served as the Mughal center for 15 years, before the court shifted back to Agra. Exactly what prompted the return to Agra remains uncertain. Some say that drought forced the Mughals out, while others claim that the death of Shaykh Salim prompted the move. In any case, the abrupt decision left an immaculate ghost-palace and abandoned city. Not much has changed here since, and an eerie air pervades the city's stone courtyards—it's as if the whole sleeping city might instantaneously awaken from its state of suspended animation. Fatehpur Sikri often casts a haunting spell on visitors, especially at dawn and dusk, when the sunlight and shadows whirl across the deserted palace courtyards.

UTTAR PRADESH

■ ORIENTATION AND PRACTICAL INFORMATION

Vehicles drive into Fatehpur Sikri from an access to the east of the palace complex. The deserted city looks down from a hilltop over the modern village of Sikri to the south. From the bus or train stations, it's a five-minute walk up the hill to the city. There is a bank near the bus station, but don't rely on it for currency exchange; ask around at the more upscale hotels. **Buses** head to: **Agra** (every 30min. 6am-7pm, 1hr., Rs12) and **Bharatpur** (5 per day, 1hr., Rs8). **Auto-rickshaws** also run to Bharatpur (30min., Rs50). **Trains** run daily to **Agra** (5:30, 11am, and 4:40pm; Rs8). **Telephone Code:** 05619.

■ ACCOMMODATIONS AND FOOD

Everything in Fatehpur Sikri is within walking distance of the palace. In peak season (Oct.-Mar.), hotels fill up and prices may rise by as much as 25%. Probably the best budget option in town is the recently opened **Ajay Palace Hotel,** just to the left as you come out of the bus station, offering four spotlessly clean rooms (doubles with bath Rs100-170). The cheapest place in town is the **Archaeological Survey Rest House** (tel. 882248), just east of Diwan-i-Am in the ruins. For only Rs9 per night, you're within sight of the palace and have access to an inexpensive, old-style dining hall. There are only three rooms available, though, and these must be booked ahead of time at the ASI office, 22 the Mall, Agra (tel. (0562) 363506). Down the path from the ruins to the bus stand, the **Shree Tourist Guest House** (tel. 882722) has a pleasant rooftop area and very basic rooms conveniently positioned in front of the "English Wine Shop" (singles Rs80; doubles Rs100). Down the road that heads back towards Agra, on the right-hand side just before the turn-off for the railway station, the **Hotel Goverdhan Tourist Complex** (tel. 882643) has large, neat and shiny rooms boasting such luxuries as running hot water and TVs (dorm beds Rs40; doubles Rs120, deluxe Rs200; triples Rs150). East of the Goverdhan, 1km from the monument, U.P. Tourism's **Gulistan Tourist Complex** (tel. 882490) has luxurious rooms at luxurious prices, as well as the standard swish-and-shiny restaurant around the standard dark-and-gloomy bar (doubles with air-cooling Rs575, with A/C Rs900; off-season discounts). For food, the restaurant in Hotel Ajay Palace is probably your best bet. Home-made cheese and mineral-water ice put this place in a different league from most roadside joints (Kashmiri *kofta* Rs40). The restaurant at the **Gulistan Tourist Complex** has large lunch and dinner buffets (Rs260). Of the several *thali* stalls up by the main gate to the old city compound, the best is probably the **Kallu Restaurant,** just in front of the gate (*thalis* Rs25).

■ SIGHTS

Wherever tourists and their buses congregate, so do **guides** eager to offer tours of the deserted palace. Many of these "guides" falsely claim to be licensed; others insist they are students whose "duty" it is to show you around, only afterwards whining for *baksheesh* or leading you into their handicraft shops. Ask to see proper ID. Official guides should charge around Rs40-50 for a tour of the monuments. All sights are open daily from dawn to dusk.

The base of the **Buland Darwaza** is 13m above street level, and its gate stands 40m above that, making it the tallest in Asia. The gate was added to the complex in 1595, following Akbar's triumph in Gujarat, and its style was copied in other Victory Gates around the country. As you pass through the gate, take off your shoes (either deposit them for Rs2 or tote them around). The head of the **Jama Masjid** is off to the left, facing Mecca. In the middle is the pure white **mausoleum** of Shaykh Salim Chishti, the sage who prophesied the birth of Akbar's sons. The core of the tomb is mother of pearl; visitors hoping for Shaykh Salim to intercede on *their* behalf hang threads from the marble latticework on the walls inside. The story of Shaykh Salim's "summoning" of Akbar's sons brings many heir-less women here to pray. Incense sticks burn inside the tomb, while musicians sit and play outside. It's

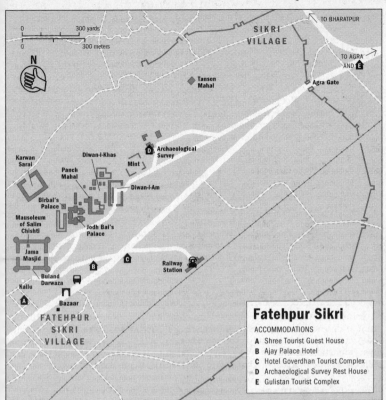

0   300 yards
0   300 meters

N

TO BHARATPUR

SIKRI VILLAGE

TO AGRA AND E

Tansen Mahal

Agra Gate

Karwan Saral

Diwan-i-Khas

D Archaeological Survey

Mint

Panch Mahal

Diwan-i-Am

Birbal's Palace

Mausoleum of Salim Chishti

Jodh Bai's Palace

Jama Masjid

Railway Station

C

B

Buland Darwaza

Kallu

A

Bazaar

FATEHPUR SIKRI VILLAGE

Fatehpur Sikri

ACCOMMODATIONS

A Shree Tourist Guest House
B Ajay Palace Hotel
C Hotel Goverdhan Tourist Complex
D Archaeological Survey Rest House
E Gulistan Tourist Complex

UTTAR PRADESH

customary to leave a small donation (Rs5-10) at the tomb itself. Coming out of the mosque, head left through the other main gate, **Badshani Darwaza,** and cross through the parking lot across the palace complex to the east.

Coming from the east, you'll pass the **Naubat Khana** (Drum House), which was used to signal the emperor's arrival, and the ticket office for the palace complex (Rs5, free on Fridays). A path leads around into the **Diwan-i-Am,** the court where, from a throne perched between two sandstone slates, the emperor would hear the pleas and petitions of common men. The stone ring in the grass to the northeast is thought to have held down either *shamiana* (huge canopies) or, as a more sinister version has it, the leash of the Elephant of Justice, who determined guilt or innocence by either trampling or sparing the accused men. To the west toward the throne is the main palace courtyard. To the right is the **Diwan-i-Khas** (Hall of Private Audience), where Akbar is thought to have spoken with VIPs and relatives. The hall is a massive chamber supported in the middle by one ornate column shaped like a budding flower. To the left is a meticulously carved gazebo, thought to be the sitting chamber of either the treasurer or royal astrologer.

The courtyard is dominated by the five-story **Panch Mahal** tower that looms up to the west of the Diwan-i-Khas. Steps to the west lead up through scores of intricately carved stone columns to the narrow fifth floor. Tourist access to the tower normally stops half way up, but even from here the breezes and the views can be breathtaking. On the south side of the courtyard is a grid tank called **Anup Talao,** the choice venue of legendary Mughal crooner Miyan Tansen (see also **Come On Baby Fight My Fire,** p. 392) More finely carved columns and walls decorate the nearby **Turkish Sultana's Palace.** To the north of Anup Talao stands what served as the royal **banquet hall.** The path from Panch Mahal leads west to **Birbal's Palace,** the residence of either the minister's daughters or one of Akbar's queens.

Before Panch Mahal, in the middle of the courtyard, is the small **Mariam's Palace,** once home to Akbar's Christian wife, where faded wall paintings are left over from the palace's glory days. From here, proceed south and cut right to the entrance of **Jodh Bai's Palace,** one of Fatehpur Sikri's largest and most atmospheric buildings. In the large courtyard, symmetrical patterns and sandstone flowers carved into the walls surround a central fountain. Most likely, this complex was used for the emperor's harem. Note the azure glazed tiles on the roof along the second story. To the rear of Jodh Bai's palace is the *haremsara*, which once housed the palace's many servants and attendants.

MATHURA मथुरा

The city of Mathura teems with thousands of temples, where devotees celebrate the birthplace of Krishna. Countless Vaishnava pilgrims come here every year for **Janmashtami,** the celebration of Krishna's birth, to pay homage to the blue-skinned hero of Hindu lore. They'll pass the butter pot on August 23, 2000 and August 12, 2001. Even outside the main festival season, Mathura hums with holiness. Thousands of pilgrims and priests throng the city, mingling saffron and incense with the dust and grime of the streets. Many tourists pass through Mathura on their way from Delhi to Agra.

🔢 ORIENTATION AND PRACTICAL INFORMATION

At the heart of Mathura is the bazaar, stretching north from **Holi Gate,** on the eastern part of town near the Yamuna River. The **old bus stand** is 500m south of Holi Gate, and the more frequently used **new bus stand** is 1km farther south. The town's most important landmark is the temple **Shri Krishna Janmasthan (Janmabhoomi),** built on the site of Krishna's birth, 2km northwest of the new bus stand.

Trains: The **railway station** is 1.5km south of the new bus stand. Fares listed are for 2nd/ 1st class. To: **Agra** (*Jodhpur-Varanasi Marudhar Exp.* 4864, 8:55pm, 1hr.; *Udyan Abha Toofan Exp.* 3008, 11am, 1½hr., Rs23/173); **Delhi** (*Punjab Mail* 1037, 5:39pm, 3hr.; *Kerala Exp.* 2625, 12:50pm, 2½hr.; *Dadar Amritsar Exp.* 1057, 1am, 4hr., Rs42/221); **Gwalior** (*Amritsar-Dadar Exp.* 1058, 11:44pm, 4hr.; *Nizamuddin Gwalior Taj Exp.* 2180, 9am, 3hr.; *Mangala Lakshadweep Exp.* 2618, 11:43am, 2½hr., Rs50/263); **Jhansi** (*Amritsar-Dadar Exp.* 1458, 11:44pm, 6hr.; *CST Punjab Mail* 2138, 7:40am, 3hr.; *Mangala Lakshadweep Exp.* 2618, 11:43am, 4hr., Rs67/352); **Kanpur** (*Jodhpur-Varanasi Marudhar Exp.* 4854 or 4864, 8:55pm, 6½hr., Rs78/410); **Mumbai** (*Paschim Exp.* 2926, 7:20pm, 20hr.; *Punjab Mail* 2138, 7:40am, 24hr., Rs200/1053).

Buses: From the **New Bus Stand** to: **Agra** (every 30min. 5am-10:30pm, 2hr., Rs20); **Bharatpur** (every 30min. 6:30am-10:30pm, 1hr., Rs15); **Delhi** (every 30min. 5am-10:30pm, 4hr., Rs53); **Jaipur** (every 30min. 7am-10:30pm, 6hr., Rs80). From the **Old Bus Stand,** U.P. Roadways buses run to: **Haridwar** (10pm; 8hr.; Rs125, "luxury" 155); **Varanasi** (6, 10am, and 2pm; 16hr.; Rs230); **Vrindaban** (4 per day, 30min., Rs5).

Local Transportation: Stretch **tempos** cruise to Vrindaban (Rs5) and around town, as do **cycle-** (temple to New Bus Stand Rs10) and **auto-rickshaws** (Rs15).

Tourist Office: U.P. Tourism (tel. 405351), at the north end of the old bus stand, 2nd fl. Campy brochures and no maps, but they know temples. Open M-Sa 10am-5pm.

Currency Exchange: Main Branch, **State Bank of India** (tel. 407647), 1km east of the new bus stand, near the railway, changes cash and traveler's checks.

Market: The **bazaar,** selling everything from chutneys to drums, extends just south and a long way north of Holi Gate. A **fruit market** is next to Jama Masjid.

Hospital: District Hospital (tel. 403006 or 406315), near the old bus stand. **Methodist Hospital,** Jaising Pura, Vrindaban Rd. (tel. 406032).

Post Office: A branch is in the complex next to the temple. **Postal Code:** 281001.

PHONE CODE	0565

ACCOMMODATIONS AND FOOD

The area near Holi Gate is the liveliest, noisiest part of town. Mathura has a few **ashrams,** including **Keshvjee Gaudig,** opposite the old bus stand (Rs50 per room). Across from the temple are several cheap *dhabas,* such as the **Prateek** and the **Madras Cafe,** that sell good South Indian food.

Hotel Brij Raj (tel. 406232), opposite Shri Krishna temple. Large rooms around a courtyard within chanting range of Krishna's birthplace. Doubles Rs200.

International Rest House (tel. 405888), in the complex just east of the entrance to the temple. Cheap, simple rooms for pilgrims, as well as a garden where they kick up their heels. Attached restaurant open 11am-3pm and 6:30-10:30pm for a "pious lunch and dinner." Singles Rs30; doubles Rs50, with bath Rs110.

Gaurav Guest House (tel. 406192). Walk 100m south of the Government Museum and turn left down a narrow alley; it's by the small pole and traffic circle. Large, clean, comfortable rooms in a quiet, peaceful neighborhood. Check-out noon. Singles with air-cooling Rs150; doubles Rs225, with bath Rs300, with TV Rs350.

Hotel Brij Raj Cafe, across from the temple, below and next to Hotel Brij Raj. Good *thalis* (Rs25), Gaylord's ice-cream treats, and fresh coffee. Open daily 7:30am-10:30pm.

Brijwasi, across from the temple, with another branch near Holi Gate. No real eats but tasty sweets. Open daily 7am-11pm.

Brij-Bhoj Restaurant, inside Hotel Mansarovar Palace. Cold enough to have numbed most of the waiters into a permanent state of frigid inactivity. *Pakora* as they're meant to be, *mutter paneer* (Rs55), and cucumber salad (Rs30). Non-veg. dishes from Rs135. Open daily 7am-11pm; snacks served 3-7pm, dinner 7-11pm.

SIGHTS

SHRI KRISHNA JANMASTHAN TEMPLE. Most of the sights in Mathura revolve around Krishna, whose birth here has given this otherwise unremarkable town its status as one of the holiest places in India. The most important site for pilgrims is the Shri Krishna Janmasthan temple, which marks the spot of Krishna's appearance—the original temple, Kesava Deo, was destroyed by Aurangzeb and replaced with a mosque. The similar histories of the temples here and at the birthplace of Rama in Ayodhya have made the authorities particularly cautious—visitors must check all belongings (bags, cameras, etc.) at the cloakroom off to the left (Rs1), pass through a metal detector, and undergo an overzealous frisking. Dotted amid all the souvenir shops inside are several small temples and shrines. The main shrine, at the back of the complex to the right as you come in, is a small, dimly lit room believed to mark the exact site of the birth. The room is designed to represent the prison cell where Krishna was born while the nefarious King Kamsa held his parents captive. Barbed wire and uniformed guards with guns stand at the rear of the shrine, between the temple and mosque. Nearby is **Potara Kund,** where baby Krishna's diapers were supposedly washed. *(Open daily 5-11am and 4-9pm.)*

JAMA MASJID. The Jama Masjid, Mathura's main mosque, was built by Abo-in Nabir Khan in 1661. The mosque is unusually colorful, its teal domes brightening up the already striking bazaar and fruit market. From its height above street level, visitors can observe the goings-on below. *(South from the bazaar.)*

GOVERNMENT MUSEUM. Founded in 1874, the Government Museum houses a large collection of ancient Indian sculpture. Its pieces shed light on Mathura's overall religious and cultural significance—for nearly 1200 years it was the artistic center for early Indian, Indo-Scythian, and visiting Hellenistic cultures. The museum contains several excellent examples of the mottled red sandstone sculpture for which the area is famous. The gems of the collection are two pristine Buddha statues from the 4th and 5th centuries. *(1km east of the new bus stand. Tel. 408191. Open Tu-Su 10:30am-4:30pm. Free; camera fee Rs20.)*

OTHER SIGHTS. Mathura's other attractions are on the east side of town. As you head north from the bazaar, the **Dwarkadheesh Temple** is on the left. Built in 1814 by local merchants, this temple is the main point of worship for local Hindus. Its interior colors are accentuated when the afternoon sun hits the wire-mesh roof. *(Open daily 5am-1pm and 4-9pm.)* A little south on the bazaar, the street forks off to the right toward the river and the sacred **Vishram Ghat,** where Krishna came to rest after slaying the menacing King Kamsa and where many priests, guides, and beggars now congregate. From the *ghats,* **boats** take visitors on an hour-long tour of the city's shore (Rs40-50), with a prime view of the dilapidated **Sati Bur,** built in 1570 and dedicated to the *sati* of Behari Mal. Sunset boat trips offer a front-row view of the nightly *aarti* ceremony, when priests bring fire to the sacred water amid the sound of gongs. You might be able to coax a few boat-*wallahs* into cruising you down the Yamuna all the way to Agra, a trip that involves an overnight stay (probably in a village barnyard). When negotiating a price, remember that you'll also have to buy food and whisky for the crew.

VRINDABAN ब्रिंबन

While Mathura draws its fair share of devotees, the main religious center of this area is actually the nearby town of Vrindaban, where Krishna is said to have performed the deeds which made him famous: lifting up **Mt. Govardhan,** jamming on his flute, and cavorting with all the *gopis* (milkmaids) he could find. Legend has it that in order to dance with several maidens at the same time, Krishna would simply multiply himself. Ever since the Bengali teacher Chaitanya discovered the site's importance, Vrindaban has been a huge draw for Vaishnava pilgrims, whose ashrams are maintained by wealthy devotees and ISKCON, the International Society for Krishna Consciousness (Hare Krishnas). As rustic as the town feels in places, there are a surprising number of con-men and would-be guides knocking about (pay no more than Rs30-50 for a tour). **Buses, trains,** and **tempos** from Mathura arrive south of the confusing tangle of narrow streets that makes up the heart of town. There are small restaurants, a few basic hotels, and tea stalls near the major temples for mid-worship munchies.

■ SIGHTS

KRISHNA BALRAM TEMPLE. None of the holy places in Vrindaban draws more foreigners than the Krishna Balram Temple, the dazzling marble house of worship of **ISKCON,** the International Society for Krishna Consciousness. The founder of the society, Srila Prabhupada, lived and worked here before embarking at the advanced age of 69 on a world tour to spread the word of "Krishna Consciousness." Next to three shrines and several murals of Krishna's exploits is a life-sized mannequin of Prabhupada over his burial site. The temple echoes with chants, drums, clicking beads, and donation requests. Still, the pervasive atmosphere of peace and serenity manages to rise above all the chaos and commotion. *(Temple open daily 4:30am-8:30pm.)* In the back is a **restaurant** serving good Indian breakfasts (Rs16) with ginger tea and *chiku* milkshakes (Rs8-12). There is also a **guest house** (tel. (0565) 442478) offering 45 clean doubles with attached baths (Rs200). Hare Krishnas, who come here from all over the world, are happy to talk to newcomers. The temple is likely to be full during August, September, and March. A **museum**

dedicated to Prabhupada displays the *swami's* rooms as he kept them, including books, clothes, jars of vaseline, and other bits of holy paraphrenalia he used while still contained within his mortal body *(museum open daily 9am-4:30pm; free).*

OTHER TEMPLES. The large, intricately carved **Govind Dev Temple** is one of the oldest in Vrindaban. It lacks the characteristic *gopuram* of most temples, and the top four stories were destroyed by Aurangzeb and never replaced. *(Open daily 5:30am-noon and 4-8pm.)* One hundred meters northeast of the Govind Dev is the **Rangnathji Temple,** India's longest. Seth Govind Das combined Rajput and South Indian designs when he built the temple in 1851. The 15m **Dhwaja Stambha,** the central column, is said to be plated in gold. Non-Hindus are not permitted inside, but you can catch a glimpse through either entrance. In two small galleries next to the entrance gate, electronic puppets dramatize episodes from Lord Krishna's life, including his mellow interaction with the ecstatic *gopis.* Among the other more notable temples in Vrindaban, the **Madan Mohan Temple,** on the banks of the Yamuna near Kali Ghat, has a small shrine in the base of its tall sandstone tower, which today boasts a good amount of vegetation. Other popular sights include the dilapidated **Radha Ballabh Temple,** dating from 1626; the more modern **glass temple,** east of the Rangnathji Temple; and **Bankey Bihari,** literally "crooked Krishna," named for Krishna's famously bent body. *(Open daily 9am-1pm and 6-10pm.)*

LUCKNOW लखनऊ

Despite the hissing, buzzing, helter-skelter hustle and bustle of the modern capital of U.P., Lucknow remains a city indelibly marked by its past. The city's skyline is dominated by crumbling monuments to the opulence of the nawab aristocracy of centuries past. Amidst the ruins stand the still-functioning battered souvenirs of the British Raj. Through it all one can always sense the busy hum of this modern city of over two million people. Lucknow's history stretches back into legend, but things didn't really start happening here until it became the capital of Avadh in 1775. The local nawab rulers, keen to assert the authority they had recently wrested from the Mughal rulers they had been sent to serve, embarked on ambitious building projects which soon thrust Lucknow forward to challenge Delhi and Kolkata for the title of India's most sparkling city. Before long, the British reduced the nawabs to mere puppet rulers, though under their patronage Lucknow flourished as a major center of Muslim poetry, music, and architecture. The British formally annexed Avadh in 1856, citing as their mandate the alleged "incompetence to rule" of the last nawab, Wajid Ali Shah, whom they subsequently sent into exile in Kolkata. The British take-over was one of the sparks that ignited the Indian Mutiny the following year, and the siege of the Lucknow Residency during the uprisings was to loom large in British legend until Independence.

Since Partition, when many of the city's Muslims fled to Pakistan, Lucknow is no longer the subcontinent's center for Indian Muslim culture, though many practices still survive. Local traditions such as *chikan* embroidery endure, however, and the Shi'a Muslim commemoration of Muharram (April 15, 2000; April 4, 2001)—a mourning for the martyrdom of Imam Husain (grandson of the Prophet) and his 72 companions—continues to be the most important event in Lucknow's religious calendar. Black-clad men and women march through the streets wailing laments as they carry replicas of Imam's tomb to the fire-walking ceremonies that take place in the *imambaras.*

⌷ TRANSPORTATION

Airport: Amousi Airport (tel. 436132 or 436327), 11km from Charbagh. Hire a tempo (Rs4) or auto-rickshaw (Rs100) in front of the main railway station. **Indian Airlines** (tel. 220927) flies daily to: **Kolkata** (2hr., US$140); **Delhi** (1hr., US$80); **Mumbai** (2hr., US$225); **Patna** (1hr., US$90).

NAWABS AND KEBABS Lucknow is popular today for the bygone nawabs as well as its tasty kebabs, which make for the city's interesting and assonant nickname, though each has nothing to do with the other. Even 150 years after the last of their numbers was dispatched into well-paid exile by the British in 1856, the nawabs still seem to be ubiquitous in Lucknow. The piscean pair that was their motif can still be found all over town, and many of Lucknow's hotels and restaurants are named after one or another of the men who ruled from here for 100 years. Particularly popular is the portrait of the last nawab, Wajid Ali Shah, whose left nipple peeks out from between his jewelled robes on walls all over Lucknow. Ali Shah's feckless lifestyle—he was rumored to be more interested in poetry and dance than in trade treaties or politics—so scandalized the British that they annexed Avadh in 1856 in order to "save" its people from the dissolute misrule of the playboy nawab. For the latter half of the city's nickname, however, try asking for a *kakori* or Avadhi kebab, minced lamb with herbs and spices wrapped on a skewer and cooked over charcoal.

Trains: Lucknow Station, Charbagh, 3km from Hazratganj. Tempos follow fixed routes between Station Rd. (100m in front of the station) and Chowk, Aminabad, Kaiserbagh, and Lalbagh/Hazratganj. A rickshaw from the station to Hazratganj should cost around Rs15. Fares listed are 2nd/1st class. To: **Allahabad** (*Saharanpur-Allahabad Nauchandi Exp.* 4512/4012, 6am, 5hr.; *Delhi Bareilly Exp.* 4556, 4:25pm, 5hr.; *Ganga Gomti Exp.* 4216, 6:20pm, 3½hr., Rs61/287); **Ayodhya** (*Farakka Exp.* 3484, Tu, Th, F, and Su 7:20am; *Saryu Yamuna Exp.* 4650, M, W, and Sa 6:10am, 3hr.; *Marudhar Exp.* 4854, M, Th, and Sa 4:40am, 3hr. Rs40/210); **Delhi** (*Avadh Assam Exp.* 5609, 5:30am, 10hr., Rs112/588; *Shatabdi Exp.* 2003, 3:20pm, 6½hr., A/C chair Rs640; *Lucknow Mail* 4229, 10pm, 9hr., Rs112/588); **Faizabad** (*Dehradun-Howrah Doon Exp.* 3010, 8:45am; *Ganga Sutlej Exp.* 3308, noon; *Jammu Tawi-Sealdah Exp.* 3152, 6:15pm, 3hr. Rs39/205); **Gorakhpur** (*Awadh Exp.* 5064, 8am, 6hr.; *Jammu-Tawi Gorakhpur Exp.* 5088, 3:55pm, 5½hr.; *Avadh Assam Exp.* 5610, 6:05pm, 6hr., Rs75/350); **Kanpur** (*Chhapra-Gwalior Exp.* 1144, 6:35 am, 2hr.; *Neeachal Exp.* 8475, 1pm, 2hr.; *Vaishali Exp.* 2553, 10:05pm, 1½hr., Rs28/173).

Buses: The **Charbagh bus station** is located on Station Rd. From the railway station, walk out the entrance 100m to the main road out front. Take a left; the station is 100m down on the right. Buses are cheap, but be prepared for frequent stops and overcrowding. To: **Agra** (every hr. 5:30am-10:30pm, Rs110); **Allahabad** (every hr., Rs90); **Ayodhya** (every hr., Rs50); **Gorakhpur** (every hr., Rs100); **Faizabad** (every hr., Rs44); **Varanasi** (every hr. 6:30am-10:30pm, Rs102). Another bus station, located in **Kaiserbagh** services **Delhi** (frequent, Rs183) and **Kathmandu.** Take a tempo from Station Rd.

Local Transportation: Unmetered **auto-rickshaws** and **tempos** wait outside Lucknow Station—be prepared to haggle. A rickshaw to Hazratganj costs Rs15. There are no official tempo stops, although they do follow a fixed route. Go to a main road, flag one down, and ask if the driver goes where you want to go. Repeat as necessary.

🛈 ORIENTATION AND PRACTICAL INFORMATION

Lucknow occupies the south bank of the **Gomti River** and extends far inland. **Hazratganj** is the center of the city—several bookstores, the post office, the police station, and many of the city's restaurants are here. The main road in this area is **Mahatma Gandhi (MG) Marg,** a wide street lined with shops, hotels, and restaurants. MG Marg runs through the city northwest to southeast before sweeping south and out of the city. To the northwest is **Husainabad.** Many of Lucknow's monuments are located on **Husainabad Trust Road.** The main railway station (and one of the bus stations) is at **Charbagh** in the south. The way from Charbagh to Hazratganj is a major route, going along **Motilal Nehru Marg** and then **Vidhan Sabha Marg** past the state legislature (Vidhan Sabha). **Subhash Road** goes almost directly from Char-

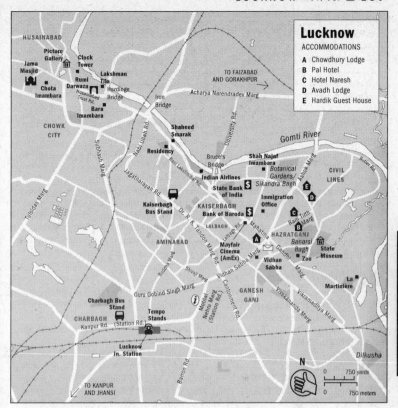

Lucknow

ACCOMMODATIONS

A Chowdhury Lodge
B Pal Hotel
C Hotel Naresh
D Avadh Lodge
E Hardik Guest House

bagh to Husainabad, completing the Hazratganj-Husainabad-Charbagh triangle. In the middle of the triangle is **Aminabad,** an old bazaar area.

Tourist Office: U.P. Government Tourist Reception Centre, Charbagh (tel. 452533). Inside the Lucknow Railway Station. Open daily 7am-8pm. **U.P. Tourist Office,** 3 Nawal Kishore Rd. (tel. 225165 or 228349), behind Hazratganj post office. There is another **tourist office** (tel. 226205) off Station Rd. **U.P. Tours** (tel. 212659) runs daily tours of the city starting from the Hotel Gomti (9:45am-2:15pm, Rs50).

Immigration Office: Jawaharlal Bhavan Marg (tel. 280635). Take a rickshaw from MG Rd. (Rs5). Open M-Sa 10am-5pm.

Currency Exchange: State Bank of India, Ashok Marg (tel. 226001), 300m up from MG Rd. on the right. Open M-F 10am-2:30pm and Sa 10:30am-12:30pm. Foreign exchange branch of the **Bank of Baroda,** MG Rd. (tel. 225267), opposite the turn-off onto Lalbagh road. Open M-F 10:30am-2:30pm, Sa 10:30am-12:30pm. **American Express,** MG Rd. (tel. 226534 or 212619; fax 212619), Mayfair Cinema Bldg., 2nd fl. Cash advances on AmEx. Cashes AmEx traveler's checks with no fee. Open M-Sa 9:30am-6:30pm, Su 10am-6pm.

Bookstore: Universal Bookseller, 82 MG Rd., Hazratganj (tel. 225894). Take a left onto MG Rd. from Vidhan Sabha Marg; Universal is on the right hand side. Good selection of imported and local English language books. Open M-Sa 10am-8pm.

Library: The **British Library** in Hazratganj, next to the Mayfair Cinema. Open Tu-Sa 10:30am-6:30pm.

Market: Main bazaars at **Aminabad** and **Chowk.** Tempos from Station Rd. go to both; those from Hazratganj go only to Chowk. Aminabad is a short rickshaw ride from Hazratganj. Open daily from dawn until late.

Hospital: The main civil hospital is **Balrampur** (tel. 220085), located on Gola Ganj, near Kaiserbagh (tel. 220085). The **New Modern Hospital and Heart Centre** (tel. 27158), at the end of Ran Tirth Marg, provides 24hr. emergency service. A smaller, private hospital is **Nishat,** 3 JC Bose Marg, Kaiserbagh.

Police: Hazratganj Police Station, MG Rd. (tel. 222555). Turn Left onto Hazratganj from Vidhan Sabha Marg. The police station is on the right-hand side, next to the Kashmir Government Arts Emporium.

Post Office: GPO, Vidhan Sabha Marg (tel. 222887). Take a right from MG Rd. to Vidhan Sabha. The GPO is the large yellow colonial building with the clock tower across the street. Open M-Sa 8am-7pm. **Postal Code:** 226001.

Internet: Internet Vision, G-28 Sriram Tower, Ashok Marg (tel. 282994), on the right hand side just before the State Bank of India. Rs3 per minute. **Fast Business Centre,** Faridi Building, 2nd fl., Hazratganj (tel. 2105923). From MG Rd. turn down Lalbagh. FBS is the first major building on the right. Private A/C browsing booths. Rs150 per hour.

Telephones: 24hr. STD/ISD, 39/55 Ram Tirth Marg (tel. 275910 or 275948), after the Hotel Naresh. Callbacks Rs5 per min. Collect calling at no charge through AT&T.

PHONE CODE	0522

ACCOMMODATIONS

Most of Lucknow's budget hotels are located in Hazratganj and in and around the Narhi Bazaar area along Ram Tirth Marg.

Avadh Lodge, 1 Ram Mohan Raj Marg (tel. 282861), a 10min. walk from MG Rd. Walk down Ashok Marg and turn right onto Ram Tirth Marg at the fruit market. At the end of the street turn left, then take your 2nd right; it's on the corner. This former residence of a Lucknow Raja features dusty old prints and animal heads hanging on the walls, along with a sorry-looking stuffed crocodile. *Fawlty Towers* with an Indian accent. Spacious, clean rooms with attached baths and fans. Common lounge with color TV. Check-out noon. Singles Rs200, with air-cooling Rs290; doubles Rs300/390.

Chowdhury Lodge, 3 Vidhan Sabha Marg (tel. 221911 or 273135), down an alley opposite the post office just before it intersects with MG Rd. Ideally situated in the heart of the city. Hot water Rs4 per bucket. Singles Rs80, with bath Rs125, with bath and air-cooling Rs200; doubles Rs170/230/245.

Hotel Naresh, Ram Tirth Marg (tel. 275160 or 285298), from MG Rd. towards the Allahabad Bank and onto Ashok Marg. Fork right onto Ram Tirth Marg at the fruit market. The hotel is 400m down on the left hand side, through the Narhi Bazaar. Check-out 24hr. Simple rooms with baths and air-cooling Rs130, with TV Rs150; doubles Rs190/210.

Pal Hotel, Ram Tirth Marg (tel. 229476), 50m down on the right. In the heart of Narhi Bazaar, this bare-bones, no-frills hotel offers reasonably clean, basic rooms. Hot water Rs4 per bucket. Room service Rs10-25. Check-out 24hr. Singles Rs100; doubles Rs120, with attached bath Rs170. Air cooler Rs25 extra.

Hardik Guest House, 16 Rana Pratap Marg (tel. 209497 or 209597). Turn left at the end of Ram Tirth Marg and then right at the traffic circle. Cool, quiet, clean, and friendly. Room service available. Check-out 24hr. Air-cooled singles/doubles with TV and attached bath from Rs400/500.

FOOD

Lucknow owes its reputation for a rich and refined cuisine to the nawabs. For the famous Avadhi kebabs you will either have to hit one of the big hotel restaurants or else sift through the small kiosks in the old city. Lucknow is also well known for its mangoes—the fruit market on Ram Tirth Marg is open every day.

Vyanjan Vegetarian Restaurant, on Ashok Ganj, by the State Bank of India on the right-hand side. Popular A/C restaurant serves a wide range of excellent veg. meals. Entrees Rs35-50. Open daily 9am-10:30pm.

Aahar Restaurant, Lalbagh. Turn left onto Lalbagh after the AmEx office on MG Rd., and walk to the traffic circle; it's on the left. Clean, cool place split over 2 levels serves excellent food (*paneer korma* Rs35) with a smile. Open daily 11am-11:30pm.

Moti Mahal, Hazratganj, on the left, opposite the police station. Look for the trademark golden arches. Air-conditioned restaurant upstairs serves Chinese food; neighboring Mini Mahal serves early breakfast and fast food and cakes until late at night.

Falaknuma Restaurant, Clark's Avadh Hotel, 9th fl. From MG Rd., take a 10min. rickshaw ride (Rs10). Overlooking the River Gomti on one side, the hushed and shiny A/C restaurant serves a full range of lamb and chicken kebabs (starting at Rs180). Though a good place to recuperate from the outdoor dust and grime, Falaknuma is a bit pricey (beer Rs150 a pop). Indian music starts at 8:30pm. Lunch noon-3pm, dinner 8-11pm.

Ranjana, MG Rd., past the police station. Something of a Hazratganj institution, this place has been around for years and is starting to show age. Tables and benches are set out on either side of a long, dark hall. Creaking ceiling fans keep the flies at bay. Good sized portions of cheap Indian and Chinese food. Open daily 10am-10:30pm.

🎵 ENTERTAINMENT AND SHOPPING

Lucknow isn't renowned for its nightlife, but if you need a drink to take the edge off a nerve-racking day, there are budget **bars** along Station Rd. and pricey drinks (Rs150-300) available in the **Falaknuma Restaurant** at Clark's Avadh Hotel, 9th floor. The only proper bar in Hazratganj is the pine-paneled **Tashna Bar** in the Hotel Gomti. Full of chain-smoking, hard-drinking local businessmen crowded around a small TV, this small and dark, A/C place serves booze (beer Rs100) and basic munchies. (Open daily 11am-10:30pm.) **Novelty Cinema,** on Lalbagh opposite Aahar's Restaurant, sometimes shows English-language movies. Lucknow is also home to one of the two major schools of **kathak Dance.** Check newspapers for information. **Aminabad,** to the south, is one of Lucknow's old bazaar areas and the best place to shop for Lucknawi crafts. Clothing with *chikan* embroidery comes in a wide variety with prices ranging from Rs50-5000 per piece. Also sold here are tiny bottles of *attar*, alcohol-free perfumes worn by Indian Muslims.

📷 SIGHTS

Most of what remains of old Lucknow's glittering mosques and flamboyant palaces is concentrated around the **Husainabad** area to the northwest of the city, far from the din of Hazratganj.

THE RESIDENCY

Off MG Rd., northwest of Hazratganj. Open daily from sunrise to sunset. Rs2, free on Fridays.

If the British Raj still governed India, the ruins of Lucknow's Residency would be one of its proudest monuments. One of the lengthiest struggles of the great uprising (the Indian "Mutiny" or "Revolt," depending on who's talking) took place when rebelling *sepoys* (Indians enlisted in the East India Company's army) besieged Lucknow's British community from June to November of 1857 (see also **Mutiny and Aftermath,** p. 74). The against-the-odds defense of the Residency was to leave a lasting impression on the colonial psyche. Once they had retaken the city, the British left the ruins as a monument to the stiff-lipped stubbornness and resilience of those trapped and killed inside. The battered remains of the Residency compound,

SNIFFING THE SUBCONTINENTAL SUBLIME

Mention India and odor in the same sentence and you're likely to get a less-than-positive reaction. Indeed, for many a traveler, India is The Land of Don't-Breathe-Too-Deeply. In Lucknow, though, olfactory observation is more likely to run along the lines of *eau de toilette* than *eau de* toilet: this is a center for production of *attar*, India's finest class of perfumes. For centuries *attar* has remained the aesthete's scent in both the secular and religious domains of Indian culture. The *attar* oil is extracted from pre-dawn flower buds and left in a large container of water. As the sun rises, the buds secrete an oily film which is then carefully preserved. There is an *attar* for every season and time of day: for summer, rose and Indian Jasmine; for winter, musk. The undisputed raja of Lucknow's perfume biz is the Azam Ali-Alam Ali Industry, renowned for authentic *attars* since Mughal days. Their products are sold all over India and have been worn by the likes of Empress Nuz Jahan and the late Princess Diana.

still visibly scarred by shots that pounded them 150 years ago, stand today within a shady green park near the center of the city.

The kind of heroic disaster so dear to English sensibilities, the siege began when news reached Lucknow of *sepoy* rebellions throughout the region. The Residency, a mansion for the East India Company's agent in Avadh, was turned into a fortress for the 3000 people who were trapped there. After three months Sir Henry Havelock arrived to relieve the Residency, only to wind up trapped with those he'd planned to liberate. It was another month and a half before new Commander-in-Chief Sir Colin Campbell was able to break the siege. The Residency was finally freed on November 17th, and the remaining survivors (less than a third of the original population) were evacuated to Allahabad. Meanwhile, the battle to take back the rest of the city raged on, and Lucknow was not completely back under British control until March of the following year.

As you enter the complex through the Ballie Gate there are several buildings on the right and left that were used during the siege as hospitals and armories. The Residency building itself is beyond a wide lawn containing a monument to Sir Henry Lawrence, who gathered the British together and organized the Residency's defenses, only to be killed after four days of the siege. One tall tower still stands on the Residency building. A British cemetery is located near the river. There is a tatty miniature version of the complex in the **Model Gallery,** along with several old weapons, prints, and a copy of the florid, jingoistic poem Tennyson knocked off to commemorate the event. Below the Model Gallery is the basement where many of the British women and children hid.

OTHER SIGHTS

BARA IMAMBARA. Marking the resting place of Asaf-ud-Daula and his wives, the Bara Imambara was constructed in 1784 as part of a a food-for-work program instituted in the wake of a great famine. An *imambara* is a replica of the tomb of an *imam*, a martyred descendant of the Prophet Mohammed revered by Shi'a Muslims. Dedicated to Hasan Ibn Ali, grandson of the Prophet, the Bara Imambara is the center of the Muharram festival in April which mourns his death. Domes and arches span the ceiling of the great blue hall, one of the largest vaulted spaces in the world at the time it was built. A staircase to the side of the main building leads up to the roof and toward the entrance to the **Bhulbhalaiya,** a multi-level labyrinth designed for the entertainment of the nawab's harem. A guide is not as necessary as the scouts downstairs suggest, although one might be helpful at places where dark, narrow passages turn suddenly and drop off into the sunlit courtyard 50m below. Straddling Husainabad Trust Rd. outside the Imambara is the **Rumi Darwaza,** another work of Asaf-ud-Daula's. This gate, intended as a copy of the Sublime Port in Istanbul, is covered by a spine of trumpets. *(Open daily sunrise to 7pm. Rs10, includes entry to the bauli, the Rumi Darwaza, and the Picture Gallery.)*

OTHER IMAMBARAS. Construction of the **Chota Imambara** was begun in 1837 by Nawab Mohammed Ali Shah. Two Taj-shaped buildings in the courtyard mask the tombs of the nawab's daughter and her husband. Ali Shah himself is buried below the main *imambara* structure. Inside are the nawab's silver-gilt throne and religious regalia used during Muharram, and dozens of dusty chandeliers. *(On Husainabad Trust Rd., past the 67m clock tower on the right. Open from sunrise to 5pm.)* North of the Hazratganj area is the **Shah Najaf Imambara.** The monument holds the tomb of Nawab Ghazi-ud-din Haidar (r. 1814-27) and was the base for the rebels of 1857. Its interior is dominated by one large dome whose inside is painted with leafy patterns and decked with chandeliers. Shi'a Muslims come here to express their devotion to Shah-i Najaf, the first Shi'a *imam*, and to the spiritual successor of the Prophet, Ali Ibn Abi Talib. On the fifth day of Muharram, fire-walking is conducted in the *imambara*'s complex. *(Open daily 6am-7pm.)*

LA MARTINIERE. The Martiniere school is one of Lucknow's most distinctive architectural survivals. Frenchman Claude Martin, money-lender and architectural advisor to the nawab as well as military man and colonial entrepreneur *par excellence*, designed this building as his own mausoleum after deciding toward the end of his life that he would live out his days in India. Martin built and owned dozens of houses throughout India, but his final creation is the only one to have survived intact, thanks to its conversion into a school shortly after his death. Described by one observer as a product of "the heterogeneous fancies of a diseased brain," La Martiniere is an eclectic mishmash of architectural styles and flavors. Startled-looking lions sling to colonnades, while a spritely collection of classical figurines congregates on the rooftop waving and pointing frantically at each other. A large turbaned turret completes the ensemble. Visitors are welcome, though you should first report to the principal's office if you come during school hours. *(Off MG Rd., southeast of Hazratganj. 10min. by rickshaw. Rs5-10.)*

MOSQUES. The **Jama Masjid,** another conspicuous sign of Ali Shah's legacy in Husainabad, is Lucknow's largest mosque. Though it is closed to non-Muslims, anyone can approach it and see its painted ceiling of leaf patterns and fruit bowls. *(Down Husainabad Trust Rd., around the corner, and down the road to the left after the Chota Imambara.)* To the right of the Bara Imambara is the beautiful **Asafi mosque,** built by Asaf-ud-Daula. This mosque is also closed to non-Muslims. Opposite the Asafi mosque is the **bauli,** once a spiralling series of water-cooled state apartments, now home to a viscous, green pool of algae and a colony of chattering bats (beware the strong fecal odor).

BOTANICAL GARDENS. Once the site of Nawab Wajid Ali Shah's pleasure garden, this is where the final battle for the relief of the Residency took place. Now the gardens, a big draw for early-morning walkers, contain the National Botanical Research Institute. *(Sikandra Bagh. Open Apr.-Oct. daily 5-8am; Nov.-Mar. 6-9am. Free.)*

PICTURE GALLERY AND ZOO. The **Picture Gallery,** located inside a summer house built by the nawab during the 19th century, has a collection of portraits of all the nawabs along with forlorn-looking busts of Dante and Aristotle *(in Husainabad, near the clock tower)*. Marked by a high-gated entrance, Lucknow's old and worn-looking **zoo** features an expanse of pleasant, green grounds and lots of animals housed in tiny cages with whatever the day's thoughtful visitors have seen fit to throw through the bars. *(Banarsi Bagh, southeast of Hazratganj; rickshaw from Hazratganj. Rs5. Open Tu-Su 8am-6pm.)* Within the same grounds is the **State Museum,** whose unremarkable collection includes an Egyptian mummy that was at least dead before it was put in its coffin *(open Tu-Su 10:30am-4:30pm)*.

FAIZABAD फैज़ाबाद

Once the capital of the kingdom of Avadh—until the nawab moved to Lucknow in 1775—Faizabad today serves travelers as a stop-off for day-trips to neighboring Ayodhya. Several monuments remain from the city's heyday, including the famous mausolea of Nawab Shuja-ud-Daula and his wife Bahu Begum (a rickshaw from the Chowk to see both tombs costs Rs15-20). Travelers headed for Ayodhya should take a train to Faizabad and then catch a tempo or bus, either at the bus station or in the Chowk area, to Ayodhya (10min., Rs3). There are a couple of cheap accommodation options in Ayodhya, but Faizabad has a greater number of "proper" hotels and restaurants.

⁊ ORIENTATION AND PRACTICAL INFORMATION. There are two main roads in Faizabad. **Station Road,** which starts at the railway station, becomes **Civil Lines** and eventually leads to the **Chowk** area, where hotels and sights are located. **National Highway (NH) 28** is the major bus route to Ayodhya and Gorakhpur. Rickshaw rides from the bus and train stations to the Chowk area average ten minutes. **Buses** head to: **Allahabad** (Rs60); **Delhi** (Rs190); **Gorakhpur** (Rs52); **Lucknow** (Rs46); and **Varanasi** (Rs65). There is no fixed timetable for the buses and no easy way to predict exactly when a particular bus is likely to scream through on its way down Highway 28. The helpful front-desk staff at the Tirupati Hotel just opposite the bus station speaks good English and may be able to help predict bus departures. **Tempos** to Ayodhya leave regularly from the Gurdi Bazaar, Chowk, and the bus station. **Trains** (fares listed are for 2nd/1st class) run to: **Delhi** (*Farakka Exp.* 3483, 4:55pm, 14hr.; *Saryu Yamuna Exp.* 4649, 10:08pm, 13hr., Rs131/688); **Lucknow** (4 per day, 3hr., Rs39/205); and **Varanasi** (6 per day, 5hr., Rs54/284). **The Regional Tourist Office** (tel. 813214) is located in an alley off Civil Lines. From the State Bank of India, turn left onto the main road and look for signs to the poorly marked office. The tourist officer speaks very little English but can be of help in deciphering bus and train schedules. (Open M-Sa 10am-5pm.) The **State Bank of India,** Civil Lines (tel. 20430 or 22210), changes AmEx traveler's checks. From the railway station, take Station Rd. to the traffic circle. Take the middle road at the traffic circle, and turn right at the end of the road. The bank is on the left. (Open M-F 10am-2pm, Sa 10am-noon.) The **police** (tel. 40236) are at Kotwali, Riedganj, and Chowk. Faizabad's **post office** (tel. 24227) is just off NH 28. With the bus stop behind you, turn left and walk towards the Chowk. Take the first major street to the left; the post office is on the right. (Open M-Sa 10am-5:30pm.) There are several **STD/ISD booths** in the area around the bus station. **Telephone Code:** 05278.

⁊⁊ ACCOMMODATIONS AND FOOD. There are several budget places in the Chowk area and a couple of cheap, clean hotels near the bus and train stations. Several of these have restaurants; otherwise, simple roadside *dhabas* are about the only place to eat. The well-appointed **Abha Hotel** (tel. 22550 or 22930), in an alley off Bajaja Rd. in Motibagh (5min. from the bus and tempo stops; the rickshaw drivers are familiar with it), is probably the best of the several small hotels in this area. All rooms have baths, and several have balconies (singles Rs120; air-cooled doubles Rs175). The A/C restaurant downstairs serves decent South Indian food (open daily 7am-10pm). The **Priya Hotel** (tel. 23783), down the same alley as the Abha, has tatty singles with baths and fans for Rs75 and doubles starting at Rs100. **Shane Avadh,** Civil Lines (tel. 23586 or 27075), has spacious, clean rooms with attached bath, cable TV, and same-day laundry service (singles Rs130; doubles Rs160). The restaurant downstairs has all the usual suspects out on parade (veg. chow mein strikes again!), along with noon-proof tinted windows and industrial strength A/C. The **Tirupati Hotel** (tel. 23231) next door has a very similar layout and offers the same amenities as its neighbor (singles with baths Rs120, with air-cooling Rs 195; doubles Rs150/245).

AYODHYA अयोध्या

All over India, the sacred and the profane jockey side by side competing chaotically for prominence. In Ayodhya, a small city dotted with dozens of temples and crowded by countless *sadhus* and other pilgrims, the sacred has definitely gotten the upper hand. Ayodhya has an ancient history as one of India's holiest cities. According to legend, the city was founded by the Hindu law-giver Manu. Lord Rama, hero of the Ramayana epic and the seventh incarnation of Vishnu, was born here into the ruling Surya dynasty. Many of Ayodhya's most important sites are sacred to him and to his faithful servant Hanuman, the monkey god.

A major pilgrimage destination for thousands of Hindus, Ayodhya sees few foreign visitors—a stay here offers a welcome break from the stresses and strains of some of India's more popular tourist destinations. Every street is home to at least one temple, and a peaceful air of quiet and calm pervades most everywhere. The dearth of Western tourists offers visitors a glimpse of the unspoiled (or at least unWesternized) heart of India.

Ayodhya made international news in 1992, when Hindu-Muslim unrest here sparked nationwide violence. The trouble began over the location of a mosque, the 16th-century Babri Masjid, which was built by the Mughal Emperor Babur on a site that many Hindus hold to be the birthplace of the god Rama. The mosque became a symbol for the resentment and prejudice many Hindus felt (and still feel) towards Indian Muslims. Hindu Nationalists such as the Vishwa Hindu Parishad (VHP) used the Babri Masjid as a rallying cry, and the mosque was eventually closed due to the controversy. On December 6, 1992, religious fervor turned to violence when 200,000 VHP-led militant Hindus (most of them from outside Ayodhya) descended on the town, smashing through police barricades to destroy the Babri Masjid and erect a makeshift temple in its place. Thousands were killed in the nationwide riots that followed, and Ayodhya has since remained a flash point for communal violence. Foreigners are unlikely to encounter any difficulties, but you should be sure to check the news before visiting, especially during the heady and unpredictable **Ramnaumi** festival celebration of Rama's birth (starts April 12, 2000).

⁊ ORIENTATION AND PRACTICAL INFORMATION. National Highway (NH) 28 cuts through Ayodhya on its way from Faizabad to Gorakhpur. The **railway station,** tourist bungalow, and several of the major sights (including Hanuman Gardhi and Kanak Bhavan) are located on either side of the highway, within walking distance of the bus station and tempo stop. Ayodhya is not a big city; it's not much more than a 15-minute walk from one side of town to the other along the main highway. The best way to see Ayodhya, though, is to escape as quickly as possible from the clamor of the built-up strip and walk north through the winding, climbing, temple-packed streets of the area between the highway and the river. The **tourist office** is inside the **U.P. Tourist Bungalow,** Pathik Niwas Saket. To get there, turn right with the bus station behind you, and walk down NH28 towards Faizabad. The bungalow is at the bottom of the lane, to the left before the railway station. The cheerful attendant will fish out a set of keys and unlock his secret stash of maps and pamphlets if prompted. (Open M-Sa 10am-5pm.) The **State Bank of India,** Shrinagar Hat (tel. 32053), has currency exchange (open M-F 10am-2pm, Sa 10am-noon). There is sporadic **train** service in Ayodhya (some stop for a minute or two on the way to or from Faizabad), but it's easier to catch trains from Faizabad. Regular **buses** to and from Gorakhpur stop briefly; catch them at the bus station on NH 28. **Sri Ram Hospital** (tel. 32026) is near the bus station. The **post office** (tel. 32025) is at Shrinagar Hat (open M-Sa 10am-5pm). **Telephone Code:** 05238.

⁊⁊ ACCOMMODATIONS AND FOOD. For lodgings, ashrams seem to be the most popular choice among the thousands of pilgrims who flock here every year. Better ashrams have single rooms (with attached bath and fan) and are concentrated near the bus station. Across from the bus station, the **Birla Dharamsala** is centrally located in a peaceful garden compound near the main road (singles with fan and attached bath Rs100, doubles Rs150; bring your own sheets and a mosquito coil). The small but beautiful **Birla Mandir** is just to the right of the ashram, in the same complex. Ayodhya's only "proper" hotel, the **Tourist Bungalow,** Pathik Niwas Saket (tel. 352435), houses the town's only "proper" restaurant. Unfortunately, neither is particularly inspiring. The somewhat drab and institutional hotel offers clean, large rooms (dorm beds Rs60; singles with bath Rs175; doubles Rs200, with air-cooling Rs260). The slow but steady restaurant is also nothing special but is just about the only place in town to get a decent meal. The vegetarian *thali* is a good deal at Rs30. (Open daily 7-10am, 12:30-3pm, and 7-10pm.)

⚅ SIGHTS. Ayodhya is a temple-lover's paradise. There really does seem to be at least one sacred site around every street corner. *Sadhus* and pilgrims are everywhere, and stalls selling cone-shaped piles of red and saffron *tilak* powder line the streets between temples. Many of the most important religious sites are within a few minutes' walk of the bus and train stations, but Ayodhya is not the kind of town that comes with a convenient checklist of must-see attractions. The whole of the town is really one huge stretching temple complex, marked by an atmosphere of holy hustle and bustle. The best way to drink in the atmosphere is to do as the *sadhus* do, and to let your footsteps lead you unhurriedly and at random from one temple to the next.

The **Babri Masjid** (known as Ram Janam Bhumi to Hindus) is the contested holy site that led to Hindu-Muslim clashes in 1992 and brought international attention to Ayodhya. It is primarily of interest to the history buff or the student of contemporary Indian politics. The mosque, built by the Mughal emperor Babur in the 16th century, was believed by some Hindus to occupy the birthplace of Lord Rama, or Ramjanambhoomi. On December 6, 1992, militants led by the Vishwa Hindu Parishad (VHP) razed the mosque to build a temple to Rama. The mosque is now a pile of rubble, and the makeshift Hindu temple erected in its place is nothing more than a tent. The compound is surrounded by high fences and hundreds of armed guards; visitors are often searched before they are admitted. No cameras are allowed. (Open daily 7-10am and 3-6pm.)

The **Hanuman Gardhi,** in a white fort to the left of the bus station, is one of Ayodhya's most important temples. It is abuzz with worshippers throughout the day and into the night. Supposed to mask the spot where Hanuman the monkey god sat guard in a cave overlooking Rama's birthplace, the main shrine is located at the top of a flight of 76 steps. Leave your shoes and socks at the bottom and look out for monkey droppings. To get to the **Jain Temple** on Hanuman Rd., take a right from the railway station, turn left at the end of the road, and the temple will be on the right after 600m or so. Other temples include the **Kanak Bhawan** (open daily 8:30am-12:15pm and 4:30-9pm), off the main road farther up from the **Hanuman Gardhi;** and the **Nageshwar Nath** temple, by the river **ghats** over on the east side of town (open daily 5-11am and 12-8pm).

GORAKHPUR गोरखपु

As the major transportation hub between India and Nepal, Gorakhpur is more often traveled through than to, and few people arrive here without definite plans to move on again as soon as possible. Buses leave regularly for the border, and the main railway station has trains to major cities in India (Gorakhpur is the headquarters of the North Eastern Railway), so getting out is easy enough—a good thing, as Gorakhpur offers little to the visitor. Founded around 1400 and named for the Hindu saint Gorakhnath, Gorakhpur still houses the temple of the patron saint of the Natha Yogis, located 4km from the railway station on Nepal Road. The Vishnu Temple on Medical College Rd. houses a 12th-century stone image of Vishnu that was carted off by Raj-era art collectors and taken to London, where it stayed until a court case ordered it returned to India. A major military center today, Gorakhpur became an army town under the Mughals and again under the British, who used it as a base for recruiting Gurkha soldiers from Nepal. Insect repellent is a must if you're going to be overnighting here; hungry mosquitos seem to penetrate even the most carefully netted hotel room windows.

🛈 ORIENTATION AND PRACTICAL INFORMATION

Most of Gorakhpur lies south of its **railway station.** Most of the budget hotels and restaurants are located on **Station Road,** directly across from the railway station. The road that runs straight down from the railway station's entrance leads to the **bus stand,** 400m south, before intersecting **Park Road,** which runs parallel to Station Rd. Park Rd. marks the beginning of the **Civil Lines** region.

Trains: Railway Station, Station Rd. Fares listed are 2nd/1st class. To: **Allahabad** (*Kashi Exp.* 1028, 5am, 11hr.; *Chauri-Chaura Exp.* 5004, 10:10pm, 10hr., Rs61/286); **Hajipur** (*Amritsar-Barauni Exp.* 5208, 5:25am, 5½hr.; *Shaheed Exp.* 4674, 11:35am, 6hr., Rs62/298); **Jhansi** (*Kushi Nagar Exp.* 1016, 7pm, 15hr.; *Chhapra-Gwalior Exp.* 1144, 12:10am, 14hr.; *Gorakhpur-Ahmadabad Exp.* 5046, 4am, 15hr., Rs122/641); **Kanpur** (*Vaishali Exp.* 2553, 4:40pm, 7hr.; *Avadh Exp.* 5063, 1:30pm, 7½hr.; *Chhapra-Gwalior Exp.* 1144, 12:10am, 8hr., Rs84/411); **Lucknow** (*Gorakhpur-Secunderabad Exp.* 5090, 5am, 5½hr.; *Vaishali Exp.* 2553, 4:40pm, 6hr.; *Chhapra-Gwalior Exp.* 1144, 12:10am, 6hr., Rs70/368); **Varanasi** (*Gorakhpur-Howrah Exp.* 5050, 3:15pm; *Gorakhpur-Varanasi Exp.* 5103, 5:10pm; *Krishak Exp.* 5001, 6:30am, 5½ hr., Rs62/326).

Buses: Gorakhpur Bus Station, across from the railway station. To: **Faizabad** (4hr., Rs51); **Kushinagar** (1½hr., Rs19); **Lucknow** (8hr., Rs98); **Sunauli** (frequent from 5am, Rs36). Ask for the next departing bus; just make sure you are getting on a government bus. There are many **private buses** to the border operating from the same area, but they tend to charge as much as Rs250 for tickets through to **Kathmandu** or **Pokhara.** The so-called "direct" service offered on these buses is, in fact, no faster than the government bus route. You will have to spend several hours at the border arranging your visa and switching buses in Nepal. For more information, see **Sunauli** (p. 773).

Tourist Office: 7 Park Rd. (tel. 335450), on Civil Lines, a short rickshaw ride from the railway station (Rs5-10). Not especially informative. Open M-Sa 10am-5pm. There is also a tourist information booth in the railway station, with city maps, information, and answers to train-related queries.

Currency Exchange: State Bank of India, Bank Rd. (tel.338497), Vijay Choraha. Cashes AmEx traveler's checks and U.S/U.K. currency. Open M-F 10am-2pm, Sa 10am-noon.

Post Office: There is a small sub-branch 100m left of the main exit from the railway station. Open daily 10am-5pm. **Postal Code:** 273001.

PHONE CODE	0551

🛏 ACCOMMODATIONS

There are several decent budget hotels directly opposite the railway station, along with several cheap restaurants and any number of young men competing to put you on a bus bound for Nepal. In the center of the city (Rs5-10 rickshaw ride from the station), there are a couple of mid-range options which are a bit quieter, if less conveniently located. Most places have 24-hour check-out. **Hotel Elora,** L-block, Station Rd. (tel. 200647), across from the railway station has simple, clean rooms with attached baths. Those at the back are away from most of the Station Rd. noise. (Singles Rs80; doubles Rs150; A/C rooms Rs350.) **Hotel Siddhartha,** Station Rd. (tel. 200976), past Hotel Elora is nothing to get excited about, but clean enough and enthusiastically run. Currency exchange available. (Singles Rs90, with air-cooling Rs140, with A/C Rs300; doubles Rs130/180/400; triples Rs180, with air-cooling Rs230.) **Hotel Marina,** Golghar (tel. 337630), is located in an alley off the main road in the center of town, with several other hotels and restaurants. More upscale than the rest, its large, clean singles and attached baths are popular with families. (Singles Rs165, with air-cooling Rs195; doubles Rs245/275.)

FOOD

Plenty of little places serving snacks and simple meals are located opposite the railway station and along the road leading down to the buses. For anything more elaborate, you'll have to make the hike into town. **Vardan Restaurant** is on Station Rd., between Hotel Standard and Hotel Elora. Small, dark, and cold, this is probably the best of the many places dotted around the station area. Food ranges from omelettes to *tandoori* dishes (Rs70-100); wine of any kind is "strictly forbidden." (Open daily 8am-11pm.) **Queen's Restaurant,** in the President's Hotel next door to the Marina Hotel, is a popular place serving excellent food (*nav ratan korma* Rs40, *rogan josh* Rs42) in a calm, quiet, and well-cooled setting (open daily 8am-11pm). **Hotel Ganges Deluxe Restaurant** is on Cinema Rd. in Golghar. If you've just missed your train out of town and need to drown your sorrows, or if you're looking for something to guarantee a good night's sleep on an overnight express, then this rough-and-tumble, spit-and-polish hotel bar's wide selection of beers and industrial-strength spirits could just do the trick. Basic food menu features cheap "Chinese" dishes and *tandoori* selections for Rs30-80. Open daily 10am-11pm.

KUSHINAGAR कुशीनगर

All things must pass. Decay is inherent in all things. With words to this effect, the Buddha preached his last sermon and breathed his last breath here in Kushinagar, where he was cremated and went on to attain the ultimate happily-never-after of *parinirvana.* For centuries after the Buddha's death, Kushinagar flourished as a major religious pilgrimage destination. Foremost among the rulers who patronized the place was Ashoka, whose conversion to Buddhism helped the religion prosper and spread throughout India.

With the decline of Buddhism in India during the 12th century, however, Kushinagar faded from prominence, and its many temples and monasteries soon fell into forgotten jungle decay. It was not until the mid-19th century, when a group of archaeologists working under the auspices of the East India Company started exploring the area with spades, that Kushinagar again rose to widespread attention. The *stupas* and images they unearthed and the inscriptions written on them were enough to establish beyond doubt Kushinagar's holy heritage, and the tiny town was soon back on the map as a major religious center.

A lot of money has made its way west into Kushinagar since then. Today, the streets are paved with shiny, new state-of-the-art tarmac and lined with temples, *stupas*, and study centers built in most of the architectural styles of Buddhist East Asia. Very much a beggar-free, truck-free, cow-free zone, Kushinagar is a small village remarkable for its pervasive air of peace and prosperity. Though it is small enough to be visited on a day-trip from Gorakhpur, it is worth an overnight stay to fully enjoy its atmosphere of untouristed calm and quiet. The main tourist season in Kushinagar runs from October to March; many hotels and restaurants close down completely out of season. Those listed below are open throughout the year.

⁊ ORIENTATION AND PRACTICAL INFORMATION. Fifty-one kilometers east of Gorakhpur, Kushinagar is located on **National Highway (NH) 28.** All the places of worship, tourist attractions, and accommodations are on Kushinagar's main road, **Buddh Marg,** which is entered through the **Buddha Dwar gate** off the highway. Regular buses go between Kushinagar and Gorakhpur, 1½ hours away. The **bus station** is in the neighboring town of **Kasia,** 3km from Kushinagar, but most buses from Gorakhpur will drop you right at the Buddha Dwar. The **Regional Tourist Office** is 100m down Buddha Marg on the right, in front of the Myanmar Temple and next to the Birla Buddhist temple. The tourist office has brochures, maps, and advice to dispense. (Open M-Sa 10am-5pm.) The **post office** (tel. 71029), which doubles as the **police station,** is a small white building opposite the Buddha Dwar on NH 28 (open daily 9am-5pm). **Postal Code:** 274403. **Telephone Code:** 05563.

▞▚ ACCOMMODATIONS AND FOOD. The cheapest accommodations in Kushinagar are at the **Linh-Son Chinese Temple** (tel. 71119) and the **Myanmar Buddhist Temple and Guest House** (tel. 71035). Both are on Buddh Marg, opposite the tourist office. Run by temple monks on a donation basis for pilgrims visiting Kushinagar's Buddhist sites, these places provide clean, basic accommodations in rooms adjoining the main temple buildings. (A donation of at least Rs50 is expected.) **Hotel Pathik Niwas,** Buddh Marg (tel. 05563 or 71038), 300m down from the tourist office on the right-hand side, offers a wide range of accommodations. A white-walled complex built around well-watered green gardens and lined with paintings depicting the life of the Buddha, the Pathik Niwas is run by a friendly and responsive staff. The rooms and bathrooms are clean, and sheets and towels are changed daily. (Singles with fan Rs300; doubles Rs400; A/C deluxe rooms Rs900/1000; small, kitchen-equipped "American huts" Rs700.) The restaurant offers everything from cheeseburgers (Rs30) to *paneer bhujia* (Rs35), as well as the obligatory chow mein-headed Chinese menu (open 6am-10pm). The **Yama Kwality Cafe,** next to the Myanmar Temple, is the only other restaurant open all year. Friendly and informative, the cafe serves up healthy-sized portions of noodles and fried rice and maintains a good selection of recent newspapers and magazines. It is a good place to sit and relax out of the mid-day sun.

◪ SIGHTS. Kushinagar's main attractions are the ancient *stupas* and images rediscovered here during the last century. These range along the kilometer or so of the main Buddh Marg stretch. Dotted between the historical remains are several modern temples and an expansive green **Meditation Park.** Next to the Myanmar Temple is Kushinagar's holiest site, the **Buddha Mahaparinirvana Temple,** said to mark the spot where the Buddha was liberated from the cycle of re-birth and attained the ideal state of *parinirvana.* Extensive traces remain of the original temple, and a 6m **reclining Buddha** survives inside the main temple building. Behind the reclining image is a large modern *stupa*, built to protect the age-weathered original beneath it. The original *stupa* is thought to contain a portion of the Buddha's cremated remains. Left out of the temple grounds and farther down Buddh Marg just as the road shifts left, the small **Matha Kunwar Temple** stands on the site of the Buddha's last sermon. One kilometer further down the road, past the Japanese, Korean, and Thai temples, is what remains of the **Ramambhar Stupa,** built on the sacred site of the Buddha's cremation. (*Stupas* open daily sunrise to sunset.)

VARANASI वाराणसी

For Hindus, Varanasi (also known as Benares or Banaras) is the holiest place on earth and the chosen residence of Shiva, who abides in the city's every nook and cranny. Hindus claim the whole city is a sacred zone with power so great that it permeates the city with its divine glow—hence the city's other name, **Kashi** (The Luminous). Those who die in Varanasi are guaranteed *moksha*, or liberation from the cycle of death and rebirth, and everyone here knows it. This otherworldly confidence (and a growing population of 1.2 million) has unfortunately shaped Varanasi into one of the world's grimiest and most tangled cities.

Shiva chose to settle in Kashi with his new bride Parvati, and he was so taken with the place that he vowed never to leave. Nowadays, Varanasi's glory takes time and timing to fully appreciate. At sunrise a quiet band of thousands descends to the riverside *ghats*, scorched by a godlike sun. The water oozes with disease; refuse and even human corpses can be seen bobbing by. But this has no apparent effect on Varanasi's popularity as a bathing spot, nor does it dissuade the drinking of its liberating waters. The Old City is a maze of tortuous lanes smeared with cow dung and congested with men and beasts. Small boys make fortunes guiding foreigners to the Golden Temple through little-used alleys. Dead bodies, sometimes stretched between two bicycles or tied to the roof of a jeep, are delivered to the pyre amid the traditional chant, *"Ram Nam Sata Hai"* (Ram is Truth). On the main street, buses honk madly and spew exhaust over strings of shaven-headed pilgrims, their baldness an expression of earthly loss and the small pigtail of hair a hook for the gods to grasp should they decide to snatch them up. The electricity fails almost every night; until the ugly fluorescent lights stutter back to life, the unprepared visitor must navigate the slippery lanes of the City of Light by the teasing flicker of a candle flame.

The physical condition of the city of Varanasi is due in part to five centuries (1200-1700) of Muslim levelings. No building in the city is more than 300 years old. But the attacks never really succeeded; they wiped out the city's temples and images but not the traditions that have kept Varanasi going from at least as far back as the 6th century BC. In the early days of Aryan settlement in India, Varanasi, one of the world's oldest continuously inhabited cities, sat at the great ford where traders traversing North India would cross the Ganga. It gained fame as a glorious bazaar town and also as a center for spiritual life. Teachers and ascetics came to mingle with the local deities in the ponds and rivers of the Anandavana, the Forest of Bliss, that grew here before the city. The Buddha came to Sarnath, on the outskirts of Kashi, to preach his first sermon. Varanasi's Hindu priests were active in developing their religion through the millennia, and the city itself soon became an object of worship: a holy place inhabited by holy beings and bounded by a holy river.

Neither a military nor a political powerhouse, Varanasi became a sanctuary for Indian culture, renowned for its silk brocades (Benares silk *saris* are still some of the best), its refined Sanskrit and Hindi, and its music. Today Varanasi, especially since the foundation of Benares Hindu University, continues to support a thriving arts culture. But piety and devotion are what bring the millions who come for brief glimpses of the city, and also for the many who come to settle and die in Varanasi. Here, the living can frolic knowing this life is their last.

▆ TRANSPORTATION

Airport: Babatpur Airport, 22km away. **Indian Airlines office,** Cantonment (tel. 343746 or 345959). To: **Agra** (Tu and Th 5pm, 2hr., US$95); **Delhi** (5pm, 2½hr., US$110); **Kathmandu** (Tu, Th, and Sa 12:50pm; 1hr.; US$71); **Khajuraho** (M and W 4:55pm, F 4pm; 1hr.; US$70); **Lucknow** (5pm, 45min., US$60); **Mumbai** (5pm, 4hr., US$210).

Trains: Varanasi Junction Railway Station, at the intersection of the Grand Trunk, Cantonment Station, and Vidyapith Rd. (Rs10 by cycle-rickshaw or Rs20 by auto-rickshaw from Godaulia Crossing). Fares listed are sleeper/2AC. To: **Allahabad** (*Mahanagri Exp.* 1094, 11:30am, 3hr.; *Kamayani Exp.* 1072, 3:50pm, 3hr.; *Poorva Exp.* 2381, 8pm, 2½hr., Rs124/418); **Ayodhya** (*Farakka Exp.* 3483, Tu, W, F, and Su 12:30pm, 4½hr.; *Marudhar Exp.* 4853, M, W, and Sa 4:20pm, 3hr., Rs104/451); **Delhi** (*Shramjeevi Exp.* 2401, 3:20pm, 14hr.; *Poorva Exp.* 2401, 8pm, 12hr., Rs114/275; *Rajdhani Exp.* 2309, 11pm, 11hr., Rs1130/1705); **Gorakhpur** (*Chauri Chaura Exp.* 5003, 12:15am, 6hr.; *Manduadih Gorakpur Exp.* 5104, 5:50am, 5hr.; *Howrah-Gorakhpur Exp.* 5049, 3:10pm, 6hr., Rs117/502); **Kanpur** (*Chauri Chaura Exp.* 5004, 4:50am, 6½hr.; *Farakka Exp.* 3483, 12:30pm, 10hr.; *Poorva Exp.* 2381, W, Th, and Su 8pm, 5½hr., Rs160/670); **Mumbai** (*Mahanagri Exp.* 1094, 11:30am, 28hr., Rs363/1020); **Patna** (*Shramjeevi Exp.* 2402, 2:45am, 4½hr.; *Bhiwani-Malda Town Farakka Exp.* 3414/3484, 3:20pm, 5½hr., Rs115/495); **Satna** (*Mahanagri Exp.* 1094, 11:30am; *Kamayani Exp.* 1072, 3:50pm, 6½hr., Rs151/642; a 4hr. bus ride takes you to **Khajuraho**).

Buses: Cantonment Bus Station, 200m to the left on Station Rd. as you come out of Varanasi Junction Station. To: **Agra** (5pm, 15hr., Rs220); **Allahabad** (every 30min. 4am-11pm, 3hr., Rs45); **Delhi** (7pm, 20hr., Rs273); **Gaya** (6am, 8hr., Rs70); **Gorakhpur** (10 per day 4:30am-11pm, 6hr., Rs82); **Kanpur** (9 per day 8am-11pm, Rs118); **Lucknow** (every hr. 5am-9pm, Rs104); **Sonauli** (8 per day 5am-8:30pm, Rs117). Buses to **Chunar** leave from a smaller station at Pilikothi, near the Varanasi City Railway Station east of the main Junction Station (every 30min. 6am-8pm, Rs10).

Local Transportation: Auto-rickshaws from Varanasi Junction Station to Godaulia or Cantonment area cost Rs20, shared Rs5. Cycle-rickshaws also run between all major points

Varanasi

ACCOMMODATIONS

A Hotel Relax
B Hotel Arya
C Hotel Arti
D Hotel Temple on
   the Ganges

UTTAR PRADESH

in the city. Don't take any nonsense from the drivers, who have grown accustomed to over-charging clueless tourists. **Tempos** run between less touristy spots, like Lanka and Ramnagar Fort (both Rs5), and the Civil Court and Sarnath.

⬟ ORIENTATION

Varanasi's city limits are marked by the **Varuna River** to the north and the **Assi River** to the south; hence the hybrid name of Varanasi. **Panch Koshi Road,** which circles around the city's 16km radius, marks the boundary of the sacred zone of Kashi. Old Varanasi is squeezed up against the western banks of the Ganga at a point where the river flows north, and there is virtually nothing on the east bank; it's believed that those who die there will return as donkeys. Uphill from the river rises a maze of narrow, winding streets lined with temples, shrines, budget hotels, and restaurants. Finding your way through this labyrinth can seem like a mission impossible at times, though many of the main backpackers' hang-outs are well marked and the *ghats* are clearly labeled in English. Be wary of accepting random offers of help in finding your way; lost-looking foreigners are easy targets for the hundreds of touts and commission-merchants that prowl the streets of the city.

Sticking to the river is the best way to navigate Varanasi, and most points of interest are along the waterfront. **Assi Ghat** marks the south end of the riverbank; **Raj Ghat** is farthest north. **Dasashwamedh Ghat,** the city's main *ghat*, is easily reached on **Dasashwamedh Road** from **Godaulia Crossing,** a central traffic circle. The surrounding area near the **Vishwanath Temple,** known as Godaulia, contains many of the budget hotels. Godaulia is connected to the northern parts of Varanasi by **Chowk Road,** one of the few roads near the *ghats* wide enough for cars. To enter Varanasi, trains from the east cross the **Malaviya Bridge,** next to Raj Ghat, and the railway stations are inland in the northern part of the city (20min. by rickshaw).

🔢 PRACTICAL INFORMATION

Tourist Office: The **U.P. Regional Tourist Office** (tel. 346370), in the main railway station, is small but helpful and well-run. Open M-Sa 8am-6pm. The **Tourist Bungalow,** Parade Kothi, Cantonment (tel. 343413), in the area directly in front of the railway station, distributes a similar selection of brochures, pamphlets, and advice. Has generally more detailed information on festivals and local events. Open M-Sa 10am-5pm.

Immigration Office: Siddh Giri Bagh (tel. 351968), a 10-15min. cycle-rickshaw ride from Godaulia Crossing. The office sends visa extension requests (granted under "special circumstances") to Delhi and may not get them back for weeks. Open M-Sa 10am-5pm.

Currency Exchange: State Bank of India, Cantonment (tel. 343410), between Hotel Saryu and Hotel Ideal Tops (20min. by cycle-rickshaw from the *ghats,* Rs20). Open M-F 10am-2pm, Sa 10am-noon. **Bank of Baroda,** Godaulia (tel. 321471), between Godaulia Crossing and Dasashwamedh Ghat, on the left. Conveniently located, but *only* gives advances on major credit cards (1% fee). Open M-F 11am-2pm, Sa noon-1pm.

Luggage Storage: Varanasi Junction Station (Rs5-7 per day). Open 24hr.

Market: Large fruit markets are located near the GPO at **Vishersarganj** and in **Chowk.** Hop in a rickshaw at Godaulia Crossing for the short ride north. Most of your mango and banana needs can also be met around **Dasashwamedh Ghat.**

Bookstore: Harmony: The Book Shop, B1/160, Assi Ghat, a few doors down from the Pizzeria Vaatika. Small and browser-friendly, they have an excellent selection from Indian and European literature to expensive coffee-table books. Open daily 10am-8pm. **Indica Books,** D40/18, Godaulia (tel. 321640). With your back to the river at Godaulia Crossing, turn left; Indica is 500m down on the right. It stocks an excellent range of India-related books, as well as the usual Western classics, paperbacks, and travel guides.

Pharmacy: Heritage Hospital Pharmacy, Lanka Crossing (tel. 366977-8). From Godaulia Crossing, take an auto-rickshaw (Rs20) toward Benares Hindu University. The hospital and its 24hr. pharmacy are on the left, right before Lanka Crossing. Just north of the Chowk down Kabir Rd. there are two 24hr. pharmacies: **Raksha Medical Store** (tel. 354219) and **Gangaly Medical Store** (tel. 354904), across from the emergency entrance of SSPG Hospital.

Hospital: The best private hospital in Varanasi is **Heritage Hospital** (see above) where you can usually see an English-speaking doctor right away. Also has an ambulance service. The hospital at **Benares Hindu University** (tel. 312542) is also reputable.

Police: Dasashwamedh Police Station (tel. 352650). **Emergency:** tel. 197.

Post Office: Kotwali (tel. 332090). A Rs10 rickshaw ride from Godaulia Crossing through Chowk. *Poste Restante.* Open M-Sa 10am-6pm. **Postal Code:** 221001.

Internet: Zee Services (tel. 391399), down a small lane to the right towards Dasashwamedh from Godaulia Crossing. Rs3 per min., Rs160 per hr. Open daily 6:30am-10:30pm. With more English, and more technical know-how, **Matronix,** Plot 101, Lane 2, Ravindrapuri (tel. 311721), is near the Bread of Life Bakery. With your back to the

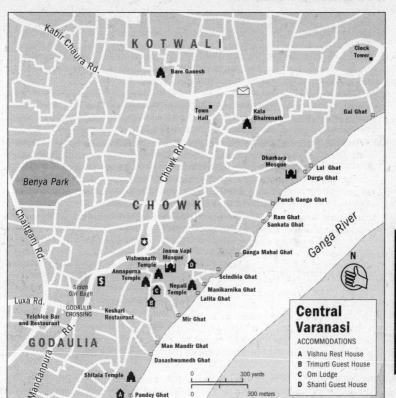

Central Varanasi

ACCOMMODATIONS

A Vishnu Rest House
B Trimurti Guest House
C Om Lodge
D Shanti Guest House

UTTAR PRADESH

bakery, turn into the lane on your right, take the first left, then the first left again; Matronix is 50m down on the left. Download email for Rs20. Open daily 9am-7:30pm.

Telephones: A 24hr. **STD/ISD** booth (no callbacks) is located on the left side of the railway station. Near the *ghats*, almost everybody with cabin space enough to squeeze a phone into seems to be offering STD services; most of these are open until 10pm.

| PHONE CODE | 0542 |

ACCOMMODATIONS

Dozens of budget hotels are packed into the winding maze of the Old City near Godaulia Crossing. Mid-range hotels can be found throughout the city, especially along Vidyapith Rd. and on the main streets in Godaulia. More expensive hotels tower above the Cantonment area north of the railway station.

Vishnu Rest House, D24/17, Pandey Ghat (tel. 329206). From Dasashwamedh Ghat facing the Ganga, walk right along the shore until you see "Pandey" written above the *ghats*. Not to be confused with the Vishnu Guest House or Old Vishnu Rest House. The Rest House pays no commissions, so rickshaw-*wallahs* often claim it's closed. The most popular budget hangout in town—this place fills up quickly. Cool terrace restaurant has superb views of the river. Restaurant open daily 7am-2pm and 6-9:30pm. Dorm beds Rs35; singles Rs60; doubles with bath Rs70.

Hotel Temple on Ganges, Assi Ghat (tel. 312340 or 315603), a 20min. walk (or boat ride) down from the "main *ghat*." A spotlessly clean place that offers facilities—

> **WARNING.** Rickshaw-*wallahs* in Varanasi often collect commissions from hoteliers for delivering guests. Beware of anyone who offers you a "ride anywhere" for "Rs5 only"; you will have very little control over your destination. Be firm about where you want to go, and don't believe your rickshaw-*wallah* if he tells you that the hotel you asked for is "full" or "closed."

including evening yoga lessons—way beyond most budget places around Dasashwamedh. Rooftop veg. restaurant has river views. All rooms have attached baths with hot water. ISD service. Dorm beds Rs50; singles Rs100-350; doubles Rs350-550.

Hotel Arya, Sonar Pura (tel. 313869), 1km from Godaulia Crossing on the main road to Assi Ghat. Just far enough from the action to allow you to catch your breath, but still only minutes from a plunge back into the thick of things. Hot water, international collect calling, and a very pleasant little rooftop restaurant. Bike rentals and extremely friendly, eager-to-please manager. Call ahead for a free pick-up from the railway station. Singles Rs125; doubles Rs175, deluxe with TV and air-cooling Rs250-300.

Shanti Guest House (tel. 322568), near Manikarnika Ghat. This huge place seems to stretch on forever in the narrow lanes that line the *ghats*. Rooms of all shapes and sizes are crowded around a steep staircase that leads up to a rooftop restaurant—which serves as Party Central for the Old City—with breath-taking views of the burning *ghats*. Clean sheets and soft mattresses. Changes many currencies and AmEx traveler's checks. Singles Rs30-60, with bath Rs80; doubles Rs50-80/125. Air-cooling Rs25.

Trimurti Guest House, CK35/12, Saraswati Phatak, Old City (tel. 323554). From Godaulia Crossing, follow Dasashwamedh Rd. toward Dasashwamedh Ghat. Take the last left before the *ghat* (there will be signs for Trimurti and for Kashi Vishwanath "Golden" Temple); the guest house is 200m down on the right. Simple but adequate rooms and views of the Golden Temple are as good as any you're likely to get if you're not a Hindu. Well-cooled with lots of plant life. Dorm beds Rs30; singles Rs50; doubles Rs80, with bath Rs120; triples Rs150.

Om Lodge, D12/26 Nichi Brahmapuri, Bansphatak area, Old City (tel. 392728). From Godaulia Crossing facing Dasashwamedh Ghat, turn left onto the road to Chowk. Take a right at the signs for Shanti and Om Lodge, and follow these down increasingly narrow and desolate alleys. Run by a friendly family headed by a welcoming, intelligent Santa-turned-*sadhu*. Extremely basic rooms, one with A/C. Yoga classes Rs30 per hr. Dorm beds Rs20-25; singles Rs40, with bath Rs60; doubles Rs60/100.

Golden Lodge, D8/35 Kalika Gali (tel. 323832), near the "Golden" Temple. Clean, simple, slightly shabby looking budget hotel offers "homely and comfortable staying" amidst "temple spires and holy zingling bells" (sic). Attached Fagin's Restaurant serves a good range of Indian and Western food and has A/C and satellite TV. Check-out 10:30am. Singles Rs50, with bath Rs80; doubles Rs80/100, with air-cooling Rs150.

Hotel Arti, Harischandra Ghat (tel. 313921), 200m back up the road from the second of Varanasi's burning *ghats*. A pleasant place with good views of the crowds on their way to the cremations. Clean, carpeted doubles have large bathrooms with hot water. Single occupancy Rs150; doubles Rs200-450.

Hotel Relax, Parade Kothi, Cantonment (tel. 343503), is a good late-night or early-morning train-dropping place. A short walk from the station. Decent rooms Rs100-200.

◘ FOOD

Keshari Restaurant, down a small alley on the right, off Dasashwamedh Rd. as you walk away from the river, almost directly opposite the La-Ra India Hotel. Cool, well-shaded, and normally packed full of prosperous-looking people, the Keshari serves good *thalis* and countless other Indian dishes (entrees Rs35-60). Open daily 10am-10:30pm.

Bread of Life Bakery and Western Restaurant, B3/322, Shivala (tel. 313912), on the main road between Assi Ghat and Godaulia. A world apart from most of Varanasi's restaurants, this place manages to (almost) capture the feel of a small European bistro.

The fried skillet breakfast (Rs125), pasta (Rs70), and chicken stroganoff (Rs125) are a welcome change. Good breads and pastries, and the closest thing to a decent cup of coffee you're likely to find in Asia. Open Tu-Su 8am-9pm.

Malika Restaurant, in Hotel Padmini. Classy and up-scale with arctic-standard A/C, wood paneling, mirrored walls, and a miniature railway for you to sit and play trains while you wait for your food to arrive. Western breakfasts and a good range of Indian meals. *Rogan josh* Rs85, chicken *korma* Rs95. Open daily 7am-10:30pm.

Yelchico Bar and Restaurant. A chain with two branches in downtown Varanasi. The first, near Godaulia Crossing, is just about the only place in the Old City where you can get your grubby hands on a glass of beer. As you approach the crossing from the river, it's down a flight of stairs one block up on the left. They have a decent range of Indian (Rs40-100) and international favorites (fish 'n' chips Rs40). The second branch, at Sigra Crossing, is much more of a civilized bar than a restaurant, though it does serve a range of meals. Open daily 12:30-10:30pm.

Shanti Guest House Rooftop Restaurant, near Manikarnika Ghat. With superb views over Manikarnika Ghat and the mighty Ganga, this is a very popular round-the-clock backpacker hang-out. Intrepid young curfew-breakers and other explorers congregate here to share tales of the day's events. The food itself is bland and unremarkable, and the service is slow. Things quiet down around 2am, when you can sit and enjoy the fine view of the Ganga. Guest house gate closes at midnight, but you can knock loudly for entry.

Pizzeria Vaatika, on Assi Ghat, in a hedged-off garden at the top of Assi Ghat. A good, mellow place to sit and munch on pizza (Rs45) or pasta (Rs30-40) to the sound of temple bells as the sun slips behind the city skyline. Open daily 7am-10pm.

Gazal Bar and Restaurant, inside Hotel Vaibhan, a short walk north of the main railway station, on the right-hand side. With its cold air, cold beer (Rs70), and free peanuts, this is a comfortable and spit-free alternative to the crowded railway waiting-rooms.

👁 SIGHTS

THE GHATS OF THE GANGA

A little religious imagination and some knowledge of what is going on at the city's countless sacred sites can help, but to truly experience the life and vibrancy of Varanasi—its crowded temples and is teeming *ghats*—all you really need are your five senses and an open mind ready to be bent gently out of shape.

The holy Ganga is what draws millions of pilgrims to Varanasi, and the series of **ghats** (steps) that line the river are at the heart of city life; thronged with crowds of people from before dawn until long after nightfall, the *ghats* are where the pounding pulse of the ancient city beats fastest. Thousands come at dawn to make offerings to the heavenly gods, but the *ghats* are not reserved purely for sacred activities. Teenagers dive bravely from the steps while others bathe and wash their clothes in the waters. The Ganga draws all sorts of life, and death as well; for in Varanasi, **cremations** are viewed as auspicious events (a reversal of traditional beliefs). They take place right on the *ghats*, rather than out of town on inauspicious soil. The bodies of those who can't afford cremation, as well as holy men and babies, are dumped straight into the river and can sometimes be seen floating by. It is largely for this reason that the waters are highly polluted, and **Let's Go strongly discourages bathing in the Ganga.**

The steps themselves are huge and usually number over 100 from top to bottom, though some are hidden when the water is high, and the name of each *ghat* is painted in large letters in both Devanagari and Roman scripts. Memorizing the location of at least some of the major *ghats* will make finding your way around the city a lot easier. A **boat ride** along the river is the highlight of any Varanasi itinerary. The best time to do this is at dawn, when the *ghats* are most crowded and the whole city shines like gold in the early-morning light. (A small boat seating 4-5 people should cost no more than Rs40 for an hour's trip from Dasashwamedh.) The *ghats* are presented here from south to north.

ASSI GHAT. The southern end of Varanasi's riverfront begins with Assi Ghat, a broad clay bank at the confluence of the Ganga and Assi Rivers. Assi Ghat is the southernmost edge of the sacred city and one of the busiest and most important of the bathing *ghats*. Its muddy banks are alive throughout the day with pilgrims crowding to pay their respects to the large Shiva *linga* that stands in the shade of a pipal tree just a few feet from the water's edge. Shops, drink-stalls, and restaurants make this a popular destination for non-religious travelers too. Assi Ghat is surrounded by temples, several of them among the most popular in the whole city (see **The Banks and Beyond,** below).

TULSI GHAT. Tulsi Ghat is the next significant *ghat* after Assi; the house where the great poet Tulsi Das once lived still stands at the top of the steps (see **The Banks and Beyond,** below). Back from the water above Tulsi Ghat is one of Varanasi's most ancient sacred spots, the **Lolarka Kund.** Sunk deep into the ground, this tank was at one time the site where early Hindus worshiped Surya, the sun god. Today it is a major point of pilgrimage only once a year (Aug. or Sept.) during the festival of Lolarka Shashthi, when thousands of couples come here to pray for sons.

HARISHCHANDRA GHAT. The next major *ghat* as you head north is Harishchandra Ghat, Varanasi's second most important cremation ground. It is distinguished by the spires of black smoke that rise throughout the day from the funeral pyres. The constant stream of mourners and attendants makes Harishchandra one of the busiest of all the *ghats*. Though widely believed to be the oldest cremation site in Varanasi, Harishchandra today is not accorded quite the same level of religious importance as Manikarnika farther north. **Photography is strictly prohibited at both cremation ghats.**

KEDAR GHAT AND CHOWKI GHAT. The *ghat* with the red-and-white circus stripes is **Kedar Ghat.** Kedar means "field," and this is the field in which liberation is said to grow; the Kedar Temple, one of Varanasi's oldest and most important Shiva temples, is so holy that just resolving to come here is enough to liberate a person from the accumulated sins of two whole lifetimes. The rough stone mound that marks Shiva's presence here is thought to be the oldest *linga* in the city. **Chowki Ghat** has a fierce collection of *nagas*, early aquatic snake-gods, around a central tree. From this point on, a long stretch of *ghats* used principally for laundry is marked by a collage formed of colorful *saris* and *lungis* stretched out to dry.

DASASHWAMEDH GHAT. The next major bathing spot and the most crowded *ghat* in Varanasi, Dasashwamedh Ghat is often referred to as the **"Main Ghat."** Every morning, busloads of pilgrims make their way past the fruit stalls and flower sellers that line the wide paved road leading to the *ghat*. Dasashwamedh is said to be the spot where the creator god Brahma performed 10 (*das*) royal horse-sacrifices (*ashwamedhas*) with the mythical King Divodasa. Bathing here is supposed to bestow on pilgrims all the benefits of ten horse sacrifices. On the *ghat* is **Brahmeshwar,** the *linga* that Brahma is supposed to have established here after performing his sacrifices. Just south of Dasashwamedh Ghat, the goddess of smallpox and other diseases, Shitala, is worshiped in the **Shitala Temple.** Adorned with colorful paint and tinsel, this square white temple is more popular than any of the *lingas* of Dasashwamedh.

MAN MANDIR GHAT TO LALITA GHAT. The next *ghat* from Dasashwamedh is **Man Mandir Ghat,** topped by one of the observatories built in the 18th century by Maharaja Jai Singh of Jaipur. Climb up on the right side of the building to see a collection of astronomical scales made of stone. Above **Mir Ghat** and **Lalita Ghat** are several important temples. The **Vishalakshi Temple** belongs to a "Wide-Eyed" local goddess, but it is also a *Shakti pitha*—the eye of the goddess Sati (or, by some accounts, her earring) is said to have landed here when she was chopped apart in the heavens (see **Divine Dismemberment,** p. 687). Nearby, a deep well, the **Dharma Kup,** marks the site where Yama, the god of death, paid homage to Shiva.

MANIKARNIKA GHAT. An axis of holiness runs between the **Vishwanath Temple** (see **The Banks and Beyond,** below) and the next *ghat*, Manikarnika Ghat. This is the most sacred of all the *ghats* and the final stop on the popular *panrahathirthi* pilgrimage, which leads pilgrims along the length of the city's riverside banks. Bathing here and worshiping at Vishwanath is a daily routine for many Benarsis and an essential part of any pilgrimage. Manikarnika Ghat takes its name from **Manikarnika Kund,** the small white tank just past the cremation grounds which Vishnu is said to have dug out at the beginning of time and filled with his sweat. This first pool of water so delighted Shiva that he dropped his bejeweled earring (*manikarnika*) in it. Vishnu's footprints are nearby, under a circular shelter.

The area just south of Manikarnika has become the city's **primary cremation ground.** Boats full of wood are moored here, and the pyres burn throughout the day and night, consuming the corpses of those lucky enough to have been liberated here. Bodies are carried on stretchers down the winding streets to the riverside, where they are dipped in the Ganga before being burned for three hours on fires lit from an eternal flame on the *ghat*. When the burning is complete, the eldest son of the deceased throws a pot of Ganga water onto the fire, and the ashes are sprinkled in the river. Above the *ghat* are hospices where the dying come to wait their turn. Visitors can watch the cremations from boats or buildings above the *ghat*, but you are likely to offend and upset mourners and workers if you linger too long or too conspicuously on the *ghat*. **Photographing the cremations is not permitted.**

SANKATA GHAT AND NORTHERN SIGHTS. Next in line is **Sankata Ghat,** above which is the baby-blue temple of **Sankata Devi,** a powerful mother-goddess. The next important bathing *ghat* is **Panchganga Ghat.** Five rivers are said to converge here: the Ganga, Yamuna, and Saraswati, which flow together from Allahabad upstream, and two old rivulets, the Dhutapapa and Kirana, which have now disappeared. Vishnu chose this place as the greatest spot in Kashi, and his creaky, painted **Bindu Madhava** temple sits above the *ghat*. During the month of Karthika (Oct.-Nov.) the temple and the *ghat* are decked with lamps at night. The rest of the year the most prominent feature of Panchganga Ghat is the tall **Dharhara Mosque** perched at the top. Emperor Aurangzeb built the mosque on the ruins of an earlier Bindu Madhava temple, and it now dominates a section of the riverbank skyline. It is closed to visitors because of threats from Hindu zealots to "take it back." A statue of a sacred cow at **Gai Ghat** watches over an array of Shiva *lingas*. Close to this is **Trilochan Ghat,** with the popular temple of the "Three-Eyed" Shiva. **Varanasi Devi,** the patron-goddess of Varanasi, also inhabits this temple.

North of this point, the *ghats* are spaced farther and farther apart and are less crowded than the more southern ones. This is the oldest part of the city, but as many Muslims settled in, several ancient Hindu sacred sites now lie forgotten. The next *ghat* of visible importance is **Raj Ghat,** the last before the Malaviya Bridge. This is the crossing-point where, since ancient times, traders have forded or ferried across the Ganga. The temple of **Adi Keshava** (Original Vishnu) sits on a high, lonely bank to the north of the bridge. Vishnu washed his feet here at the confluence of the Ganga and Varuna rivers, and the image inside the temple was shaped by Vishnu himself. The tall temple also marks the northern city limit of Varanasi.

THE BANKS AND BEYOND

THE VISHWANATH TEMPLE (GOLDEN TEMPLE). Up Dasashwamedh Rd. from the river and right through a temple-like archway, signs lead to the center of Varanasi's religious geography: the temple of Shiva as Vishwanath (Lord of All). Nicknamed the "Golden" Temple, it contains the Vishweshwar *linga*, the first one on earth and one of India's 12 *jyotirlingas*, which are said to have shot up from the ground as shafts of light. All of Varanasi is measured in circles around Vishwanath; it is the city's most important pilgrimage site. The temple is closed to non-Hindus, but shopkeepers across the road happily charge visitors for the view from their rooftops (Rs5). The temple's gilded spire soars high above the city, and bells chime at the many smaller temples that lead to it. There has been a Shiva temple on this site since ancient times, but the present building dates back only to 1777. Earlier temples here were repeatedly destroyed by wave after wave of Muslim invasions; the last of these took place in 1669, when the temple was torn down at the command of Emperor Aurangzeb.

JNANA VAPI MOSQUE. On top of the half-demolished ruins of an earlier Vishwanath Temple was constructed the Jnana Vapi Mosque, which still stands today surrounded by a cordon of barbed wire, iron fences, and soldiers. Hindu extremists have made repeated threats to destroy the mosque and "take back" the old holy site. In between the temple and the mosque is the **Jnana Vapi** itself, a "Well of Wisdom" said to have been in existence ever since the very beginning of the world. The waters that sprang up here when Shiva dug up the earth with his trident were the first pure waters anywhere on earth; the well's sacred waters of wisdom are ladled out daily under police supervision.

ANNAPURNA TEMPLE. The most important goddess temple in Varanasi is dedicated to Shakti, the divine embodiment of power or energy, and Shiva's consort, in the form of Annapurna. Armed with spoons and saucepans, Annapurna is a provider of food; a "Mountain of Food" festival occurs here in late October or early November. *(Across from Vishwanath, just down the lane. Closed to non-Hindus.)*

KALA BHAIRONATH. Once an angry and sinful form of Shiva, Kala Bhaironath (also known as Bhairava) chopped off the fifth head of the god Brahma after he failed to recognize Shiva, embodied in a shimmering *linga* of light, as supreme among all the gods. As punishment, the rotting head stuck to his hand, and for years Bhairava had to wander remorsefully around the whole of India, using the skull as a begging bowl for his food. It was not until he got to Varanasi that the head miraculously dropped from his hands. Shiva appointed Bhairava the "chief justice" of the sacred city. He keeps an eye on Varanasi's residents, devours their sins as they are washed away by the Ganga's holy waters, and metes out instant retribution for the accumulated misdeeds of previous lives to those who die here in order to pay their karmic debt. The temple is often crowded with supplicant sinners offering incense and garlands to the image of the holy police chief. *(Up Chowk Rd. from Godaulia, near the intersection with Kabir Chaura Rd. Open daily 6am-1pm and 3-9pm.)* Not too far away, on the other side of the Chowk-Kabir Chaura Rd. crossing, is the temple of **Bare Ganesh,** the central Ganesh shrine in Varanasi.

TULSI MANAS MANDIR. Built of white marble and flanked by palm trees, this modern Vishnu temple was erected in honor of Tulsi Das, the premier poet of the Hindi language who translated the Sanskrit epic, the *Ramayana*, into Hindi in the 16th century. The complete epic is inscribed on the inside walls in the poet's Hindi version, and painted depictions of scenes from the story also line the temple walls. Towards the back of the temple, behind glass, a collection of mechanical figures acts out the timeless tale to the delight of the pilgrims who flock here to watch. The great poet himself sits, book in hand, by the temple door. *(Up the road from the Assi Ghat, a short rickshaw ride from the river. Open daily 6am-noon and 4-10pm.)*

DURGA TEMPLE. The impressive red tower of this temple stretches up into the sky above the tank where the goddess is said to have rested after she had saved the world from an otherwise "unassailable" demon. Durga is regarded as the protectress of Southern Kashi to this day. The walls inside are inscribed with Tulsi Das's verses and adorned with paintings, the most notable of which is one depicting fraternal love: Bharat, Rama's step-brother, worships Rama's wooden sandals for the 14 years of Rama's exile (see p. 586). On the second floor at the back, there is a small collection of Hindu images. *(Next to the Tulsi Manas Mandir. Open 24hr.)*

It's a **big world.**

And **we've got** the **network** to cover it.

Use **AT&T Direct**® Service
when you're out exploring the world.

SANKAT MOCHAN TEMPLE. The Sankat Mochan Temple, inland from the river and south of the Assi Ghat, is dedicated to Hanuman, and is considered by locals to be one of the three most important temples in Varanasi; orange *sindur* smears attest to its popularity. *(Open daily 4am-noon and 4-10pm.)*

BENARES HINDU UNIVERSITY (BHU). Founded in 1916 by the reformer Madan Mohan Malaviya, the university was intended to merge modern ideas with tra-ditional Hindu learning. For those not planning to study Indian languages or philosophy, the campus has two places suited to shorter visits. The **Birla Vish-wanath Temple,** the largest temple in the city, has one large white spire modeled on the one knocked down by Aurangzeb in 1669. *(Open daily 4am-noon and 1-9pm.)* **Bharat Kala Bhawan,** the BHU museum, has an extensive collection of paintings, artifacts, and sculptures. The second floor boasts the sculptures and paintings of Alice Boner, the renowned Indophile who claimed to understand India on its own terms. There is plenty here from Varanasi, too, from 19th-century etchings of *ghats* to a great statue of Krishna lifting Mt. Govardhana. *(Across Panch Koshi Rd., at the south end of town. Museum open M-Sa 11am-4:30pm; May-June M-Sa 7:30am-12:30pm. Rs4.)*

RAMNAGAR FORT. The barren expanse of the Ganga's eastern shore does hold one point of interest: the Ramnagar Fort. This is the castle of Varanasi's maharaja, located in the village of Ramnagar opposite BHU at the south end of the city. The fort contains a **royal museum** with plenty of sedan chairs and swords from the royal family's past; most of the exhibits are quite dilapidated though. Ramnagar is prob-ably not worth the detour unless it's for the **Ramlila,** the festive *Ramayana* pag-eant *(Sept. 12-Oct. 12, 2000).* The river can be crossed on a pontoon bridge in winter or via ferry in summer.

BHARAT MATA TEMPLE. A spirit of urbane and modernized Hinduism can be seen in the Bharat Mata Temple, on the city's western outskirts south of the Can-tonment. Mahatma Gandhi inaugurated this temple, which has a swimming-pool-sized marble relief map of Mother India in place of a deity. The upper balconies offer great views of Varanasi.

🎵 MUSIC

Varanasi is well-known as a center for Indian classical music, and many Western-ers come to Varanasi to do a George Harrison and learn how to play the sitar or tabla. The best resource in this respect is the music school at **Benares Hindu Univer-sity** (tel. 310290, ext. 241), near Lanka Gate. Though the school itself only offers degree courses in Hindi and English, the faculty offers **private music lessons** and can also refer students to other teachers. Another good place to learn sitar or tabla is the **Triveni Music Centre** (tel. 328074), on Keval Gali in Godaulia, not far from Baba Restaurant. Instructor Nandu and his father come highly recommended; fees must be negotiated face-to-face. The **International Music Centre,** near Dasash-wamedh Ghat, offers private sitar and tabla lessons (Rs60 per hr.).

Buying musical instruments can be a tricky business. Sitar and tabla stores abound in the Old City. There is one sitar store recommended by the faculty at BHU; the proprietor, Mr. Nitai Chandra Nath, is a sage of string instruments and a true arti-san. From Godaulia Crossing, facing Dasashwamedh, turn right, go straight, and turn on the third lane on your left (1km from Godaulia Crossing); the Jangambali (Beagalitola) Post Office will be immediately on your left, and the unmarked sitar store is several doors down. (Sitars Rs2000-5000.) **Imtiyaz Ali,** Siddh Giri Bagh, is a tabla shop recommended by Mr. Nath. From Godaulia Crossing, with your back to Dasashwamedh Ghat, walk or take a rickshaw to the third big intersection (includ-ing Godaulia Crossing); turn right, and a kilometer down the small shop will be on the left. (Tablas Rs1500-2000.)

SHOPPING

Varanasi is famous for its silk, and the touts will never let your forget it. There are seven silk shops in Varanasi with fixed prices and government-enforced quality control. Three of these are located on Vishwanath Gali in the Old City, on the same road as the Golden Temple: **Mohan Silk Stores**, 5/54 Vishwanath Gali (tel. 392354), and **Bhagwan Stores**, D10/32 Vishwanath Gali (tel. 392365), both on the right-hand side shortly after the main gate leading off from Dasashwamedh towards the Golden Temple, and **J.R. Ivory Arts and Curios**, D20 Vishwanath Gali (tel. 321772), farther up the road on the left. Two others are at Sindhu Nagar, off Aurangabad Rd. near the intersection of Aurangabad and Vidyapith: **M/S Bhagwanlila Exports**, 41 Sindhu Nagar Colony, Sigra (tel. 221821), and **Mahalakshmi Saree House**, 10 Chandrika Nager, Sigra (tel. 221319). Also notable are **Chowdhary Brothers**, Thatheri Bazaar (tel. 320469), opposite the police station, and **Mehrotra Silk Factory**, SC21/22 Englishia Line, Cantonment (tel. 345289), off Cantonment Station Rd. just before it intersects with Vidyapith. Mehrotra also has a small branch in the Vishnu Rest House for everybody's "just-looking, just-looking" souvenir shopping convenience. It's a good idea to visit these shops to get a sense of the prices of top-quality silk before bargaining in the Chowk or Old City. (Shops open daily 10am-9pm.)

SARNATH सरनथ

In the wooded suburbs north of Varanasi lies Sarnath, a quiet and well-maintained site of ruins marking the site of Gautama Buddha's first sermon, the famous "Sermon in Deer Park." After the Buddha attained enlightenment in Bodh Gaya, he walked the 200km to Sarnath, with lotuses blooming where his feet touched the ground. Gathering his former companions here, among the deer and peacocks, he revealed the Noble Eightfold Path. In later years he occasionally returned to this quiet grove to meditate.

In the 3rd century BC, when the region was under the rule of the Mauryas, *stupas* were built to commemorate the Buddha's visits. This construction continued in force until the 4th century AD when the Hindu Guptas rose to power and Buddhist influence began to wane. Sarnath had achieved fame by this time with its sandstone images of the Buddha, many fine examples of which are displayed in the Sarnath's excellent archaeological museum. Sarnath's prestige as a center of Buddhism came to an abrupt end during the 12th century when it was demolished by Qutb-ud-din Aibak. Sarnath's Deer Park is dotted with the remains of numerous *stupas*, though only one monument, the Dhamekh Stupa, remains wholly intact.

Sarnath is a pleasant place for leisurely wandering. Even in the time-tired state they are in today, Sarnath's statues and monuments provide impressive evidence of the rich Buddhist culture that once flourished here and the importance the Buddha's philosophy once held throughout much of northern India. There has been little modern development in Sarnath since its monuments were excavated and explored by spade-*wallah* Sir Alexander Cunningham. With a bit of selective squinting, it is still possible to imagine Sarnath as it might have been when the Buddha himself walked through its woods more than two thousand years ago.

■ **ORIENTATION AND PRACTICAL INFORMATION. Ashok Marg**, which runs north from Varanasi, turns into **Dharmapal Road**. The **bus stand** is 500m away at a small intersection. Buses go to Lanka/BHU and the Varanasi Railway Station (frequent 7am-7:30pm, 15min., Rs5). **Tempos** go to the Civil Court, Cantonment, Varanasi (Rs20), and **auto-rickshaws** putter where you please (Rs50 to Varanasi). The **post office** (tel. 385013; open M-Sa 8:30am-4:30pm) and **Tourist Bungalow** are located opposite each other on a side road near the bus stand. From the bus stand as you face the sites, turn left onto a small road; they're 200m down on the left. There's a small information counter in the bungalow, which gives out maps of the sites (open M-Sa 10am-5pm). The **government hospital** is in a yellow building across from the Tourist Bungalow. **STD/ISD** booths are located nearby on Dharmapal Rd.

UTTAR PRADESH

ACCOMMODATIONS AND FOOD. Most tourists don't spend the night, but it's possible to stay in some of the monasteries for a small donation. The **Tourist Bungalow** (tel. 386965) is the standard U.P. government-issue, mid-range place: reliable, acceptable, clean, boring, and overpriced (dorm beds Rs70; singles from Rs250, with A/C Rs450; doubles from Rs300/550). The large **dining room** (open daily 7am-10pm) serves breakfast and all the usual Indian and Chinese dishes (Rs50-100). The only other restaurant worth mentioning is the **Rangoli Garden Restaurant,** 1km after the Tourist Bungalow on the left. The food here is not the best, nor is the service the quickest, but the place is clean, cool, and has a somewhat interesting menu (entrees from Rs50).

SIGHTS. Most of Sarnath's points of interest are piles of rubble only recently excavated: this is a place with more atmosphere and history than physical sights. The first stop on your way into the archaeological enclosure, however, is completely intact. The sandstone spires of the modern Buddhist temple **Mulgandha Kuti Vihar** beckon from the main gate. The peaceful interior is decorated with wall paintings inspired by the *Buddhacarita* (The Acts of the Buddha) by the Japanese artist Kosetsu Nosi. The pipal tree growing in the shrine is purportedly a close relative of the tree under which Buddha attained enlightenment. A small book stall inside the temple sells Buddhist-related literature. (From the bus stand, walk 100m along Dharmapal Rd., turn right under the arch, and walk 200m. Open daily 4-11:30am and 1:30-7pm.)

Looming above the temple as you exit is the **Dhamekh Stupa,** the only ancient structure left intact by Qutb-ud-din's armies. It commemorates the spot where the Buddha delivered his first sermon. Begun sometime in the 5th or 6th century, in the twilight of Buddhist predominance in North India, it remains unfinished. The bottom is made of elaborately decorated stone, with eight niches that once held images of the Buddha; the top is made up of little more than small clay bricks. Straight ahead lie the remains of the **Dharmarajika Stupa;** it must have been an impressive building in its day, but today only the foundations remain. It was built by the Mauryan emperor Ashoka in the 3rd century BC to house the relics of Buddha; Ashoka himself is thought to have come here to meditate in what was once a major monastic center. The structure was reduced to rubble in the 19th century by locals hunting for long-lost treasure.

Next to the *stupa* are the remains of the **Main Shrine,** built by Ashoka to mark a favorite meditation spot of the Buddha. At the end of the ruined structure, down a shallow well, is the bottom portion of **Ashoka's column.** The column is engraved with Buddhist edicts in Brahmi script that admonish Buddhist monks and nuns against creating rifts among the followers of the Buddha (the advice wasn't taken). The capital is one of the great masterpieces of early Indian art and is the centerpiece of the Archaeological Museum's collection. A high fence runs all around **Deer Park,** adjacent to the ancient ruins.

Opposite the main entrance to the Dharmarajika Stupa compound is the **Archaeological Museum.** The official entrance to the sites is 500m down on the left. On display directly in front of the museum entrance is the famous splendidly engraved capital from Ashoka's column, with its four roaring lions seated back to back. It was adopted as the emblem of the Indian republic and appears on all Indian currency. The museum's collection includes a number of excellent pieces, including at least one certifiable work of genius: a perfectly wrought teaching Buddha from the Gupta period. (Open Sa-Th 10am-5pm. Rs2.) One kilometer from the museum, on the road parallel to the Rangoli Garden Restaurant road, is a curious melange of Buddhist-Mughal architecture in the **Chowkhandi Stupa.** The rectangular Gupta-period foundation commemorating the site where the Buddha met his five disciples is topped by a crowning tower in the Mughal style. It was built by either Emperor Akbar or Raja Govandhan, the local ruler, to mark the site where Emperor Humayun once spent the night.

UTTAR PRADESH

ALLAHABAD इलाहाबाद

The holy city of Allahabad (ee-la-HA-bad) stands at the sacred *sangam*, or confluence, the meeting place of India's two most holy rivers, the Ganga and the Yamuna. Into these two rivers flows a third, the mystical Saraswati, river of wisdom. Lord Brahma called this spot Tirth Raj ("King of Pilgrimage Sites"), and all devout Hindus try to bathe in its waters at least once in their lives. For thousands of years, the city reaching back from the river bank was called Prayag (Confluence). While this name is sometimes used, more common is Allahabad, the Perso-Arabic name meaning "Place of God" given to the city by the Mughal emperors.

The British would later claim Allahabad as the capital of the United Provinces (Uttar Pradesh's precursor) after 1901. The Indian Independence movement was strongly rooted here due to the work of the Nehrus, the Allahabad family that forged a political dynasty after Independence. Now Allahabad is a rather quiet city of one million people. Few travelers bother to visit Allahabad, but it is well worth a couple of days. Quieter and calmer than most large Indian cities, Allahabad is mercifully free of predatory touts and rickshaw-*wallahs* and is a good place to recuperate if mainstream travel is starting to get you down. This atypical city, with its wide avenues and British buildings, becomes the focus of attention all around India every 12 years when it hosts the **Maha Kumbh Mela,** the most important Hindu festival. During this time, millions of pilgrims converge at the Sangam.

⌐ TRANSPORTATION

Trains: Allahabad Junction Railway Station, Leader Rd. Fares listed are 2nd/1st class. To: **Agra** (*Udyan Abha Toofan Exp.* 3007, 4:30am, 12½hr., Rs105/552); **Delhi** (*Howrah-New Delhi Poorva Exp.* 2381, 10:20pm, 10hr.; *Puri-New Delhi Purshottam Exp.* 2801, 7:05pm, 10hr.; *Allahabad-Ambala Unchchar Exp.* 4517, 3:25pm, 14½hr.; numerous other trains throughout the day, Rs142/649); **Gorakhpur** (*Chauri-Chaura Exp.* 5003, 9:15pm, 9hr.; *Kashi Exp.* 1027, 8:45am, 10½hr., Rs87/457); **Gwalior** (*Howrah-Gwalior Chambal Exp.* 1159, M, Tu, and Th; 1181, F 6:10am, 11½hr.; *Bundellchand Exp.* 1108, 6:35pm, 15hr., Rs106/557); **Kanpur** (*Poorva Exp.* 2381, 10:20pm, 2½hr.; *Muzaffarpur-Delhi Exp.* 5205, 6:25pm, 2½hr.; *Howrah Kalka Mail* 2311, 9am, 2hr., Rs54/285); **Lucknow** (*Triveni Exp.* 4269, 4:10am, 5hr.; *Mughalsarai Bareilly Exp.* 4307, 10:25pm, 7½hr.; *Allahabad-Lucknow Ganga Gomti Exp.* 4215, 6am, 3½hr., Rs59/310); **Satna** (*Varanasi-Chennai Ganga Kaveri* 6040, M and W 8:55pm, 3hr.; *Patna Karla Exp.* 3201, 8:30am, 3½hr.; *Gorakhpur Dadar Kashi Exp.* 1028, 4pm, 4hr., Rs52/273, then a 4hr. bus trip from Satna to **Khajuraho**).

Buses: Civil Lines Bus Stand, MG Rd., around the corner from the Tourist Bungalow, has buses to **Ayodhya, Gorakhpur, Lucknow,** and **Varanasi. Leader Rd. Bus Stand,** behind the main Allahabad Junction Railway Station, has buses to: **Agra** (3:30, 7am, and 7pm; Rs176); **Delhi** (6pm, 12-2am, Rs 227). **Zero Rd. Bus Stand** is north of Chowk.

Local Transportation: Cycle-rickshaws are Rs10 from the Allahabad Junction Railway Station to the Tourist Bungalow. **Tempos** wait at the bus or railway stations. To reach the Sangam, take a tempo to Daraganj Railway Station and walk south from the tracks.

⟁ ORIENTATION AND PRACTICAL INFORMATION

North of the railway tracks is the shady, British-built **Civil Lines** area, with all of its roads laid out in a grid; south is the congested and gritty **Chowk** area. The **Yamuna River** flows south of Allahabad until it reaches the sacred confluence point down at the southeastern extremity of the city. The Ganga flows down along the eastern edge of the city. In Civil Lines, **Mahatma Gandhi (MG) Road,** with its hotels, restaurants, and ice- cream stands, is the road to stick to for orientation; it is lined with tall and distinctive statues that make good landmarks. **Kamla Nehru Road** turns up from MG Rd. toward Allahabad University. **Leader Road** runs along the tracks on the Chowk side, while the **Grand Trunk Road** streaks through the heart of Chowk. Triveni Rd. leads from the Grand Trunk Rd. to the **Sangam.**

UTTAR PRADESH

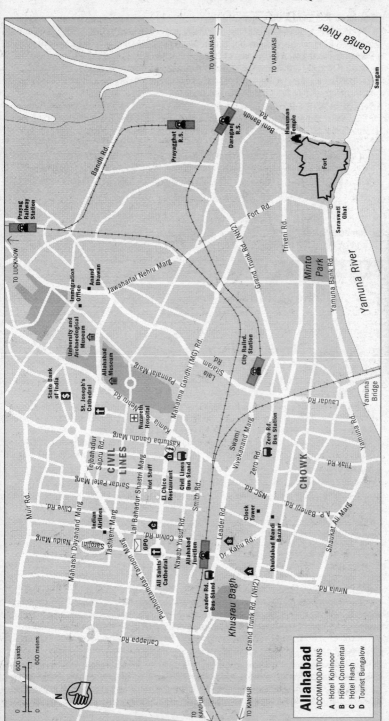

Allahabad

ACCOMMODATIONS
A - Hotel Kohinoor
B - Hotel Continental
C - Hotel Harsh
D - Tourist Bungalow

N

600 yards
600 meters

TO LUCKNOW
TO VARANASI
TO VARANASI

Ganga River
Sangam

Prayag Railway Station
Prayagghat R.S.
Daraganj R.S.
Hanuman Temple
Beni Bandh Rd.
Fort
Saraswati Ghat

Bandh Rd.

Immigration Office
Anand Bhawan
Jawaharlal Nehru Marg

University and Archaeological Museum
Allahabad Museum

Fort Rd.
Triveni Rd.

Minto Park
Yamuna Bank Rd.

Yamuna River

State Bank of India
St. Joseph's Cathedral
Nazareth Hospital

Pannalal Marg
Mahatma Gandhi (MG) Rd.
Lala Sitaram Rd.

City Railrd. Station

Nehru Rd.
Kamla
Kasturba Gandhi Marg

Mull Rd.
Clive Rd.
Maharshi Dayanand Marg
Naidu Marg
Sarojini
Indian Airlines
Tashkent Marg
Purushotamdas Tandon Marg

Tejbahadur Sapru Rd.
Sardar Patel Marg
Lal Bahadur Shastri Marg

CIVIL LINES

Hot Stuff
El Chico Restaurant
Civil Lines Bus Stand
Smith Rd.

Swami Vivekanand Marg
Zero Rd.
NSC Rd.
Zero Rd. Bus Station

Yamuna Rd.
Lauder Rd.
Yamuna Bridge

Colvin Rd.
GPO
All Saints' Cathedral
Allahabad Junction
Nawab Yusuf Rd.

Leader Rd.
Dr. Katju Rd.

Clock Tower
Khuldabad Mandi Bazaar

CHOWK

Tilak Rd.
A.P. Banerji Rd.
Shaukat Ali Marg

Leader Rd. Bus Stand

Khusrau Bagh

Grand Trunk Rd. (NH2)

Carlappa Rd.

TO KANPUR
TO KANPUR

Nirula Rd.

Grand Trunk Rd (NH2)

Tourist Office: Tourist Bungalow, MG Rd. (tel. 601440 or 611374). Just around the corner from the Civil Lines Bus Stand. Stern and serious-minded pamphlet custodians disperse maps and advice in return for patience and smiles. Open M-Sa 10am-5pm.

Currency Exchange: State Bank of India, 4 Kacheri Rd. (tel. 608224), near District Court. Open M-F 10am-2pm, Sa 10am-noon.

Market: There's a large fruit market at **Khuldabad Mandi Bazaar** near the clock tower, at the intersection of Dr. Katiu and Grand Trunk Rd.

Bookstore: M/S A.H. Wheeler Book Shop, 19 MG Rd. (tel. 624106). Facing away from the Tourist Bungalow, walk 5 blocks to the left. On the left side, to the right of the Palace Cinema. One of the best bookstores in U.P. Open M-Sa 10am-7pm.

Hospital: Nazareth Hospital, 13/A Kamla Nehru Rd. (tel. 600430). From the intersection of MG and Kamla Nehru Rd., it's 1km to the northeast, on the left side, marked by a red cross and a Hindi sign. The best private hospital in town, with a fully stocked **pharmacy.**

Police: (tel. 622592), on the main road that leads from All Saints' Cathedral to Allahabad junction railway station. **Emergency:** tel. 652000.

Post Office: GPO, Queen's Rd. Go left at the Tourist Bungalow until All Saints' Cathedral, then right for 1 block. *Poste Restante.* Open M-Sa 9am-5pm. **Postal Code:** 211001.

Internet: Pioneer PCO, MG Marg (tel. 624383), across from the Palace Cinema. Small and cramped but cool and well-run. E-mail Rs25 per 15min. Open daily 6am-11pm.

PHONE CODE	0532

■ ACCOMMODATIONS

Civil Lines lends luxury to the hotel scene. Quiet, mid-range hotels are along MG Rd. More cheapies are concentrated around Leader Rd., near the bus stand.

Hotel Harsh, MG Rd. (tel. 622197), on the right just before All Saints' Cathedral. A colonial-era hotel once open only to *pukka sahibs*, the Harsh is today a dusty, crumbling old ramshackle relic of times gone by. A team of friendly old men sits and waits patiently under creaking fans to welcome guests to huge, musty old rooms equipped with desks, chairs, beds, mirrors, and pink plastic buckets. Rooms with bath Rs200.

Hotel Kohinoor, 10 Noorulla Rd. (tel. 602031). From Allahabad Junction, take a right onto Leader Rd. and a left onto Noorulla; the hotel is 300m down on the left. Classy, well-kept place with tastefully decorated rooms overlooking a lawn and garden. A/C restaurant. Check-out 24hr. Singles Rs200, with air-cooling Rs300; doubles Rs250/400.

Tourist Bungalow, MG Rd. (tel. 601440), a short walk from Civil Lines Bus Stand. From the bus stand, walk left; it's on the left (rickshaw Rs10). Good, clean place with a pleasant garden. Downstairs restaurant open daily 6am-10pm. Bar serves liquor (Rs25-50) and beer (Rs60-100) daily noon-10pm. Check-out noon. Doubles from Rs300.

Hotel Continental, Dr. Katiu Rd. (tel. 652058). From Allahabad Junction Railway Station, walk to Leader Rd., make a right, and then a left onto Dr. Katiu Rd. An OK place to crash for the night for an early train out in the morning. Check-out 24hr. Singles with bath Rs140, with air-cooling Rs180, with A/C Rs400; doubles Rs180/240/450.

■ FOOD

Dining outside is the norm along MG Rd. Crowded benches surround fast food stalls serving Indian snacks, cold drinks, and imitation American junk food. More traditional Indian restaurants are located in Chowk, along Dr. Katiu and Nirula Rd.

El Chico Restaurant, MG Rd. Take a left from the Tourist Bungalow; it's on the right after the 4-way crossing. No enchiladas here; just a classy, unpretentious restaurant. Well-heeled crowd sits and sips at coffee and fruit juice, talking in hushed tones. Good Indian (*aloo dum kashmiri* Rs55) and Continental dishes, as well as the standard Chinese fried rice and noodles. Open daily 10am-10:30pm.

Bridges Restaurant, 22 Sardar Patel Marg. From the Tourist Bungalow, take a left and then a right at the four-way crossing; it's 500m down on the left in Hotel Vilas. Dimly lit and as cold as a Norwegian funeral parlor, this place claims to "bridge" the world by offering a choice of fine cuisines from around the world. Chow mein, omelettes, *thalis* Rs60, *shahi korma* Rs50, veg. noodles Rs50. Open daily 10am-10:30pm.

Hot Stuff, Sardar Patel Marg. From the Tourist Bungalow, take a left and a right at the four-way crossing; it's on the left after 300m. Allahabad's coolest fast food joint. The selection of ice cream, pizzas, and lamb-burgers draws crowds of hip, English-speaking college students. "Boyish Burger" Rs25.

Spicy Bite, left out of the Tourist Bungalow, is one of several good street-side open air stalls on MG Rd. Cheap, tasty Indian and Chinese dishes and a lively atmosphere.

👁 SIGHTS

TRIVENI SANGAM. Allahabad's chief attraction for millions of Hindu pilgrims is the Triveni Sangam, the confluence of the rivers Ganga, Yamuna, and Saraswati, and the site of the Kumbh Mela. The Yamuna skirts the south side of Allahabad, and the Ganga rushes along the east. The Saraswati, the mythical river of wisdom, is said to flow underground. For a negotiable fee (no more than Rs20) **boats** will take visitors by the fort to the meeting place of the rivers. The different colors of the Ganga and Yamuna's waters are also plainly visible from the shore. The water is warm and shallow in the summer; sometimes it's possible to walk to the Sangam over the floodplains that spread out from the city. Millions of pilgrims camp here during the **Kumbh Mela.** At other times, especially at dusk, the banks along the Sangam offer good views back towards the fort and the rest of the city background. Alongside the road approaching the Sangam is the **fort** built by Emperor Akbar in 1583. The Indian army still finds the confluence strategically important, so the fort is full of soldiers, and visitors are not allowed to enter.

HANUMAN TEMPLE. In the shadow of the fort's outer wall facing the Sangam side is the Hanuman Temple, dedicated to the monkey god. The temple itself is only a shed, but it's a very popular one (not to be confused with the multi-storied affair grinning out over the trees—that's the Shankar Viman Mandapam). A constant stream of chanting worshippers snakes around the tiny temple, showering offerings of flowers on the huge image of the god that lies smeared with vermilion just below ground level. The floodwaters are said to flow over Hanuman's feet each year before they recede. *(Open daily 6am-2pm and 5-10pm.)*

THE KUMBH MELA The Maha (Great) Kumbh Mela at Allahabad in 1989 set the record for the world's largest human gathering. An estimated 13 million people came to the city for this Hindu festival, the holiest time to bathe in the Sangam. Every 12 years, at one precisely calculated moment, all the pilgrims splash into the water in a ritual act believed to undo lifetimes of sin. Columns of charging *sadhus*, often naked and smeared with ash, are among the most zealous bathers.

The story behind the Kumbh Mela concerns a *kumbh* (pot) that is said to have contained an immortality-bestowing nectar. The demons battled the gods for this pot in a struggle that lasted 12 days, during which time four drops of the divine nectar were spilled. One landed at **Haridwar** (see p. 142), one at **Nasik** (see p. 418), one at **Ujjain** (see p. 374), and one at **Allahabad.** The mythical 12-day fight translates into 12 human years, the length of the festival's rotation between cities. Every three years a Kumbh Mela is held in one of the four cities in January or February. The Maha Kumbh Mela, held at Allahabad every 12th year, is the greatest of all. Smaller *melas*, known as Magh Melas, are held in Allahabad in off-years during the month of Magh (Jan.-Feb.). In the sixth year, midway between Maha Kumbh Melas, an Ardh ("Half") Kumbh Mela is held. The next Kumbh Mela is scheduled to occur in Allahabad in 2001.

ANAND BHAWAN. Once the mansion of the **Nehru family,** Anand Bhawan is now a museum devoted to their legacy. Independence leader Motilal Nehru, his son Prime Minister Jawaharlal Nehru, and Jawaharlal's daughter and future Prime Minister Indira Gandhi all lived and worked here, hosting meetings of the Independence movement. The Mahatma even had a room and working area here. The surprisingly modest Nehru showcase exhibits the family's passion for books—their bookshelves are stacked with everything from Roman Law to Tagore, and all the volumes can be peered at through glass panels. *(At the northeast corner of the city, close to the Civil Lines. Tel. 600476. Open Tu-Su 9:30am-5pm. Rs5.)* On the grounds, there's also a **bookstore** and a **planetarium** *(shows daily at 11am, noon, 2, 3, and 4pm; Rs10).* Next door is the **Swaraj Bhawan Museum,** the home of the patriarch Motilal Nehru. This mansion has an excellent sound and light show in Hindi which gives you a tour of the house while leading you through the events of the Independence movement. *(Open T-Su 9:30am-5pm. Show Rs5.)*

ALL SAINTS' CATHEDRAL. The boldest reminder of the British in Allahabad is All Saints' Cathedral, with its soaring Victorian gothic revival spires and its stained glass windows. It was designed by Sir William Emerson, the same architect who designed the Victoria Memorial in Kolkata. There are more weeds on the lawn than when the English last prayed from these pews for God, King, and Country, and more bats screeching and squealing up in the belfry, but it is not difficult to sense the ghosts of the empire click-clacking their heels through the reverberant hall and down the steps into the sunshine for tea and cakes with the rest of Allahabad's Sunday-best expatriate crowd. *(In Civil Lines, at the intersection of Mahatma Gandhi Rd. and Sarojini Naidu Marg.)*

KHUSRAU BAGH. If All Saints' is the most Raj-reminiscent relic in Allahabad, then Khusrau Bagh is the most impressive reminder of Mughal rule. These gardens hold the speckled tombs of Khusrau (a son of Emperor Jahangir) and his mother. Following Mughal royal family tradition, Khusrau plotted against his father and was subsequently murdered in 1615 by his brother, the future emperor Shah Jahan. The gardens, shaded by fruit trees and lined with paths, are a popular place for people to come and relax. In the evenings the place comes alive with games of cricket. *(In the Chowk area across the railway lines.)*

OTHER SIGHTS. Beyond the fort, on the bank of the Yamuna, is **Saraswati Ghat,** where boats dock and evening ceremony lamps are floated down to the confluence. Follow Yamuna Bank Rd. away from the fort to reach **Minto Park** on the right, where Lord Canning proclaimed in 1858 that India would be ruled by the Queen of England. Independent India has reclaimed the historic site by renaming the park for Madan Mohan Malaviya (an Independence figure and critic of the caste system) and erecting a part-Mauryan, part-Italian monument. Allahabad's teenagers have had the last word, however, with their graffiti. *(To reach the other side of the fort, take either a boat ride or detour through the fenced-off military installation behind the fort.)* The **Allahabad Museum,** Kamla Nehru Marg, has a large sculpture collection, including many terra-cotta figures from Kausambi, the ancient city and Buddhist center 60km from Allahabad. There is also a room with photographs and a few mementos of Jawaharlal Nehru. *(Tel. 600834. Open Tu-Su 10am-5pm. Rs2.)*

HIMACHAL PRADESH
हिमाचल प्रदेश

To travel through Himachal Pradesh ("Lap of Snow") is to experience complete detachment from the urban world, a rare feeling for most visitors to India. You'll walk through apple orchards and paddy fields and cross rivers swollen with glacial run-off, and mountain passes will leave you breathless with their soaring splendor. Different worlds coexist in Himachal: cross the Rohtang Pass and the rain-drenched forests of Manali suddenly give way to the rock, ice, and the harsh winds of the Lahaul Valley or the vast emptiness and harsh heat of Spiti; travel from Shimla to Kaza and Hindu temples gradually give way to Buddhist prayer flags and *gompas*. If you take the road from Manali to Leh, Kashmir, you'll experience an exhilaration that defies verbal definition.

Himachal is not all serene hillsides and remoteness, however. With the deteriorating political situation in Kashmir, Himachal has been "discovered" by tourists, and the three main towns in H.P. have become not only tourist-thronged getaways, but also gateways to the lands beyond. Dharamsala, which somehow manages to remain peaceful, has a strong Tibetan population and is the base for treks into the Dhauladars and the Pir Panjal. Manali and Shimla are favorite vacation spots with both Indian and foreign travelers. The less touristed rainshadow areas—Lahaul, Spiti, and Upper Kinnaur—can be reached from Manali via the Rohtang Pass or from Shimla via Kalpa and Kaza. Road maintenance is difficult in these places, and routes that are theoretically open from June to September may close down at any time. Although the tourist season in most of Himachal Pradesh runs from May to June and September to October, winter—when roads to Shimla, Manali, and Dharamsala and from Shimla to Chango remain open—is also an ideal time to visit. Prices are lower, and a blanket of snow softens the land's stark beauty.

HIGHLIGHTS OF HIMACHAL PRADESH

■ **The Kullu Valley's** towns **Manali** (p. 238), **Kullu** (p. 235), and **Naggar** (p. 236) are famous for green pastures, apple orchards, and great views of the Western Himalayas.
■ **Dharamsala** (p. 223) is where the mythic East meets and mixes with the equally mythic West, to the delight of hippies, addicts and pop stars.
■ From the green forests to the isolated, icy mountain-tops, H.P. offers some of the most beautiful **trekking** in India, particularly in **Kinnaur** and **Spiti** (p. 243).

SHIMLA सिमला

Stretching along a crescent-shaped ridge at an altitude of 2200m, Shimla casts a spell on the visitor with its cool air, magnificent views, and the lingering spirit of the Raj. A walk along the ridge can be strangely, though pleasantly, bewildering for the city's curious Western features—in the evening, a thick London fog rolls across a row of Scottish-style houses, while the monkeys Rudyard Kipling celebrated in his novels (Shimla was his base in India) scamper about.

Down the steps from the Mall runs a maze of alleys and crushed houses where, as Kipling once observed, you could stay hidden from the police for months at a time. In mid-winter, Shimla's 110,000 residents are immobilized under heavy

Himachal Pradesh

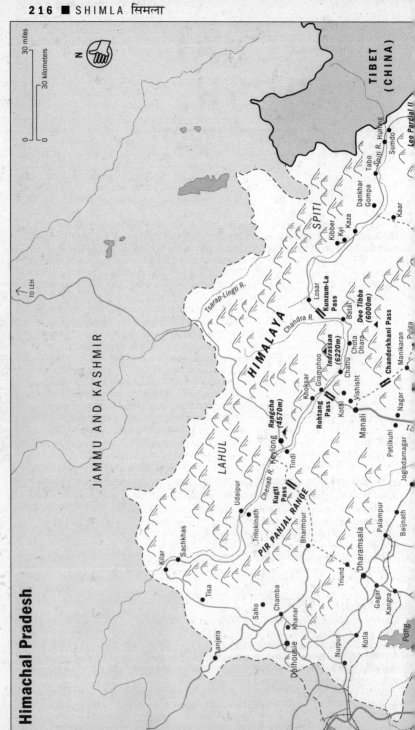

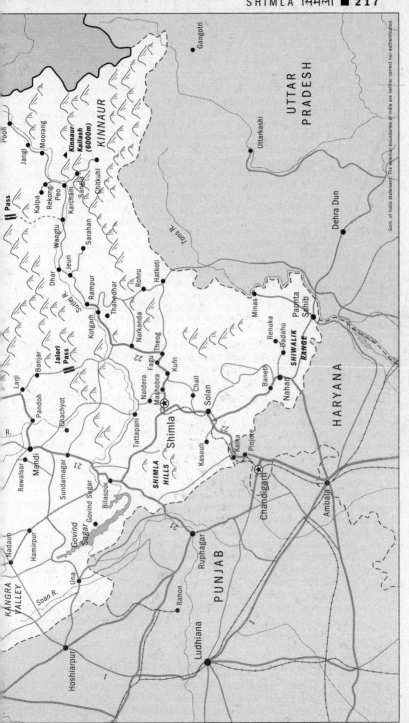

Govt. of India statement: The external boundaries of India are neither correct nor authenticated.

snows, to the extent that walking around town becomes difficult and even dangerous. There is actually little to do in Shimla except enjoy the views, so the city can
make a good stopover before you head to busier (or rougher) parts of the state. It
is connected by road to Kullu and Lahaul in the north, Kangra and Chamba in the
west, and Kinnaur and Spiti in the east.

The modern period of Shimla's history began in the 19th-century, when persistent Gorkha raiders ravaged the small village with stunning efficiency. Local rulers
appealed to the British for military aid; the British, seeing a chance to extend their
power into the Sutlej River area, obliged and defeated the Gorkhas in 1815. Over
the next half-century, British civil servants and injured soldiers flocked to Shimla
each summer seeking rest from the rigors of administration. In 1864, imperial
authorities made the summer haul to Shimla official, declaring that it would serve
as a seasonal capital for the Raj. Keep your eyes peeled in the Mall and you might
glimpse the aging, tweedy Brits who "stayed on" and still make their homes in
Shimla, 50 years later. In the summer Shimla is drenched by the monsoon, in the
winter it's buried in the snow, and during the months of May, June, September,
and October the whole area is flooded by crowds of heat-fleeing Indians who drive
up hotel prices and stir up such a ruckus that even the monkeys hide. When the
droves leave and the carless streets are once again blanketed by fog or snow,
Shimla attains a soothing serenity.

TRANSPORTATION

Airport: Jubbarhatti, 30km from town. Flights to **Delhi** (1 per day, 1hr., US$105) and
Kullu (1 per day, 30min., US$67). Book **Indian Airlines** flights and taxis to Jubbarhatti
at Ambassador Travels (see below).

Trains: Shimla is connected to **Kalka** via the narrow gauged train (10:20am from Town
Rail Station, 2:20, 5:30, and 5:45pm from Main Rail Station; 5hr.; 2nd class Rs32, 1st
class Rs173). From Kalka, connections can be made to: **Ambala** (7am, 6, and 9:20pm;
2hr.); **Amritsar** (4:20pm, 7hr., Rs120); **Delhi** (4:45 and 11:30pm, 7hr., Rs116).

Buses: There are 2 bus stands in Shimla. Most buses depart from the Main Bus Stand
next to Victory tunnel. To: **Chamba** (4:15am, 5, and 6pm; 14hr.; Rs205); **Chandigarh**
(every 15min. 6:30am-9pm, 10hr., Rs60); **Delhi** (10 per day 6am-10:30pm, 10hr.,
Rs160; deluxe 8:25am and 9pm, 9hr., Rs306); **Dharamsala** (8 per day 4:40am-
10:30pm, 8hr., Rs160); **Haridwar** via **Dehra Dun** (5:10am and 6:30pm, 10hr.,
Rs160); **Kazan** via **Peo** (8:15pm, 20hr., Rs220); **Manali** (8, 9:20am, 7, and 7:30pm;
10hr.; Rs170); **Pathankot** (5 daily 4:15am-5pm, 12hr., Rs185). From the Rivoli bus
stand, near the cinema, to: **Rampur** (every hr. 3:45am-7:30pm, 6hr., Rs65); **Rekong-
Peo** (4:30 and 6:45pm, 12hr., Rs120).

 WARNING. Foreigners planning to travel between Jangi and Sumdo in the
eastern regions of Kinnaur must obtain an all-inclusive **inner-line permit** from the
sub-divisional (or assistant) magistrate, as these areas are sensitive border
regions. In Shimla, see the **additional district magistrate,** on the second floor of
the left side of the green colonial building just north of the Mall beneath the telegraph office (open M-Sa 10am-5pm). Fill out an application and have a local
travel agent sign on as a sponsor. They should do it for free; in extreme cases, do
not pay more than Rs50. Bring two photos and lots of patience. There are also
offices in Rampur, Peo, Kaza, Chamba, and Kullen. In Peo you need 3 photos
and a photocopy of your passport, but no sponsor.

ORIENTATION AND PRACTICAL INFORMATION

Shimla stretches from west of Himachal Pradesh University across a ridge to the
area east of **Lakkar Bazaar,** where many of the town's 5000 Tibetan refugees live.
Major streets run from east to west, each at a different level of elevation. Trains

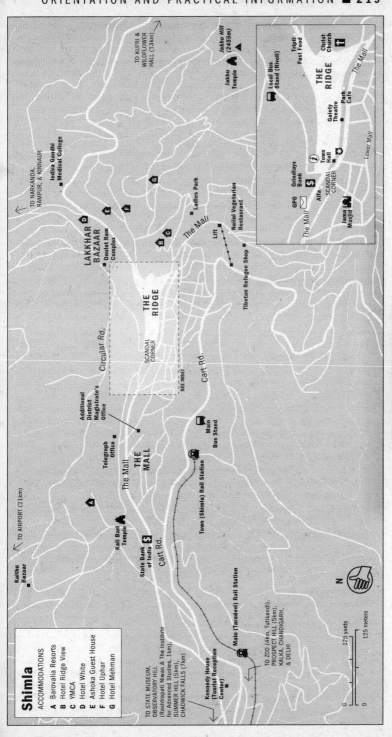

Shimla

ACCOMMODATIONS
A Barovalia Resorts
B Hotel Ridge View
C YMCA
D Hotel White
E Ashoka Guest House
F Hotel Uphar
G Hotel Mehman

TO STATE MUSEUM,
OBSERVATORY HILL
(Rashtrapati Niwas & The Institute
for Advanced Studies, 1km);
SUMMER HILL (5km),
CHADWICK FALLS (7km)

TO AIRPORT (21km)

TO NARKANDA,
RAMPUR, & KINNAUR

TO KUFRI &
WILDFLOWER
HALL (13km)

Jakhu Hill (2455m)
Jakhu Temple

Indira Gandhi
Medical College

Local Bus
Stand (Rivoli)

Tripti
Fast Food

Christ
Church

THE
RIDGE

The Mall

Galety
Theatre

Park
Cafe

Grindlays
Bank

Town
Hall

SCANDAL
CORNER

Alfa

Lower Mall

GPO

The Mall

Jama
Masjid

Ladies Park

LAKKHAR
BAZAAR

Daulat Ram
Complex

The Mall

Lift

Nalini Vegetarian
Restaurant

Tibetan Refugee Shop

THE
RIDGE

SCANDAL
CORNER

SEE INSET

Circular Rd.

Cart Rd.

Additional District
Magistrate's
Office

Telegraph
Office

THE
MALL

Main
Bus Stand

The Mall

Kaithu
Bazaar

Kali Bari
Temple

State Bank
of India

Cart Rd.

Town (Shimla) Rail Station

Main (Taradevi) Rail Station

Kennedy House
(Tourist Reception
Center)

TO ZOO (4km, Tutikandi),
PROSPECT HILL (5km),
KALKA, CHANDIGARH,
& DELHI

N

125 yards

125 meters

0

0

HIMACHAL PRADESH

and many buses arrive on **Cart Road.** Above Cart Rd. is the crowded jumble of the bazaar, and above the bazaar is Shimla's main drag, **the Mall,** which is off-limits to all motorized vehicles and contains hotels, restaurants, and banks. The easiest way to ascend and descend is to take the **tourist elevator** located on Cart Rd., where the street starts to bend right (open summer 6am-10pm, winter 7am-9pm). At **Scandal Corner** (so named for the elopement of a British soldier with an Indian princess), directly above the main bus stand, the Mall divides into a lower section and a wide upper section called **the Ridge,** which becomes Lakkar Bazaar as it curves left beyond the yellow **Christ Church.**

Tourist Office: Himachal Tourism Marketing Office (tel. 252561; fax 252557), next to Scandal Corner on the left. Offers brochures and guided tours of Shimla. 10 passenger min. Rs140 includes lunch, tea, and a guide. Open M-Sa 10am-6pm.

Budget Travel: There are travel offices on every corner of the Mall; all offer transport and trekking assistance. **Ambassador Travels** (tel 258014; fax 211139), below the mall near Gaiety Theatre, does airline booking and will sponsor your inner-line permit (see **Warning,** above). Open M-Sa 9am-6pm. **Transmount Adventures,** on the 2nd fl. of the Daulat Ram Complex in Lakkar Bazaar, specializes in adventure travel.

Currency Exchange: State Bank of India (open M-F 10am-2pm, Sa 10am-noon) and **ANZ Grindlays** (open M-F 9:30am-2:30pm, Sa 9:30am-12:30pm), both on the Mall, change cash and traveler's checks. Grindlays gives cash advances on MC, Visa for a Rs100 fee.

Library: Two colonial buildings shelter the **H.P. State Library.** The brown-and-white cottage next to Christ Church has a selection of scholarly books in English. The church-like structure above the telegraph office has a collection of books left behind by the British. Open W-M 11am-6pm. Closed last Sa.

Bookstore: Minerva Bookhouse on the Mall across from the Gaiety Theatre has books on Kinnaur and the Dalai Lama as well as computer manuals. Open M-Sa 10am-8pm. (Also see **Shopping,** p. 223.)

Pharmacy: Several along the lower Mall. **Vohra's** (tel. 205530). Open daily 9am-8pm. There is a pharmacy inside the **Indira Gandhi Medical College** complex, on Circular Rd. (tel. 203073). Open 24hr.

Hospital/Medical Services: Nehru Clinic, the Mall (tel. 201596), down a side alley. Consultation fee Rs40. Open M-Sa 10am-2pm and 4:30-6pm. **Shri Ram Medical Centre** (tel. 205300), just off the Mall. Open 9:30am-2pm and 3-7:30pm. For emergencies, call **Indira Gandhi Medical College** (tel. 203073). **Ambulance** (tel. 252102). **Tara Hospital** (tel. 203275) also has 24hr. service.

Police: Foreign tourists should contact the **Control Room** (tel. 212322), next to the town hall on the Mall. For inner-line permits, see the additional district magistrate's office, just north of the Mall below the telegraph office. Open M-Sa 10am-5pm.

Post Office: GPO, just above Scandal Corner. Speed post and *Poste Restante* available. Open M-Sa 10am-6pm. **Postal Code:** 171001.

Internet: Several stores along the Mall offer Internet access. The connection in the telegraph office is cheapest and most reliable (Rs37 per 30min.). Open M-Sa 10am-5pm. The tourist office has a connection, and the YMCA plans to open a cyber center in 2000.

Telephones: The telegraph office has 24hr. **STD/ISD.**

PHONE CODE	0177

▟ ACCOMMODATIONS

From May to June, September to October, and during Christmas season, vacancies become rare and pricey. For the rest of the year, Shimla's near-empty luxury hotels offer colonial comfort for a proletarian price. The really cheap places near Victory Tunnel and the bus station are congested dumps with common baths (Rs200-250 in-season). Nicer hotels are up the Mall. Expect discounts of up to 50% off season. Most hotels levy an additional 10% tax.

YMCA (tel. 204085 or 252375; fax 211016), up the stairs behind Christ Church. Not just for men, and quite possibly the last affordable, truly worthwhile place to stay in Shimla. Colonial grandeur blends seamlessly with kitsch. Rooms are standard but clean, and the rec. rooms have TV, billiards, and other diversions. Staff arranges treks and jeep safaris to Kinnaur, Spiti, Leh, and the Kullu Valley. Breakfast included. Hot water 7pm-9am. Prices are constant year-round. Doubles Rs250, with attached bath Rs430; single occupancy Rs125. Rs40 membership fee valid one week.

Hotel Mehman, Daisy Bank Estate (tel. 213692 or 204390). All rooms have plush wall-to-wall carpeting, color TVs, and attached baths with 24hr. hot water. Laundry service, doctor on call, and heat in the winter. Check-out noon. Doubles Rs550-1100. Off-season: Rs275-550. 10% tax. Credit cards accepted.

Hotel Ridge View, Ridge Rd. (tel. 255002), behind Christ Church; walk up the steps past Mayur Hotel. All rooms have carpeting, attached bath, and 24hr. hot water. Some have TV and Ridge views. Room service and doctor on call. Doubles Rs200-600. Off-season: Rs100-300. Extra bed Rs50.

Hotel Barovalia Resorts (tel. 252900) in Fingask Tourist Complex. Facing the State Bank of India, turn off the Mall to the left, and walk to the Palace Hotel; take the steps on the right, and then follow the narrow alley on your left 100m. Hidden from the bustle of the Mall but only a 5min. walk from it, Barovalia's offers sunset views of the Dhauladhars and personalized service. Rooms have TV, soft red carpeting, and white tiled bath with shower. Room service. Doubles Rs700-1200. Off-season: Rs350-600. 10% tax.

Hotel White (tel. 255276), Lahur Bazaar, 2min. from the ridge. All rooms have anti-quated but spotless toilets, TVs and, carpeting. Top floor rooms have balconies. Rooms Rs425-600. Off-season: 30% discount.

Hotel Uphar (tel. 257670). From the Ridge, walk up the path behind the clock and pass the Dreamland Hotel on your night. Unique rooms with baths of varying quality and size. Since Hanuman's temple is close by, all windows and balconies are barred to save you from the god's curious retinue. Doubles Rs250-450. Off-season: negotiable (haggling is the owner's sport, and even the duration of the "season" is fair game for bargaining).

Ashoka Guest House (tel 257280), right below Hotel Uphar. Good views, spacious rooms with baths and morning sun. Doubles Rs300-400. Off-season: 50% discount.

◐ FOOD

Though Himachali cuisine is as distinctive and varied as its regions, restaurants in Shimla seem to serve everything *but* regional specialties—from South Indian to Italian to Thai and Chinese. Snack stalls line the Ridge.

Nalini Vegetarian Restaurant, on the Mall, down past the lift. Crammed into two small rooms, Nalini is famed among locals for the best Indian cuisine in town. Steeper prices than in Lower Bazaar *dhabas*, but exquisite sauces and comfy chairs make a big difference. *Thali*s Rs70. Open daily 9am-10:30pm.

Park Cafe, on the slope between the Mall and the Ridge. Bamboo-decorated cafe keeps Western regulars enthralled with up-to-date pop music, English newspapers, and well-executed foreign standards. The wait can be long, but the pizza (Rs35) and the superb milkshakes (Rs20-30) are worth it. Open daily 8am-10pm.

Alfa, on the Mall near Scandal Corner. Soft brown chairs and benches, *masala chai* served in tin pots, and sweets brought in from the bakery shop in front prove that the Raj art of afternoon tea still survives. Full menu also available, but at a high price and with a long wait. Open daily 11am-10pm.

New Plaza Restaurant, on Lower Mall down the staircase from the Gaiety Theatre. A wide selection of Indian and Indianized Chinese meat and veg. dishes is served promptly by uniformed waiters. Chicken curry Rs50. Open daily 10am-11pm.

The Solitaire, on the Mall past the lift and Nalini's. Part lounge with plush sofas, part restaurant with delectable eats, The Solitaire makes for pleasant dining even if you're alone. Window seats offer splendid views of the valley below. *Malai* mushroom Rs80. Open daily noon-10pm.

HIMACHAL PRADESH

Tripti Fast Food, on the right between the Ridge and Lakkar Bazaar. A wide variety of South Indian *dosas* and *utthapams* prepared right before your eyes and served with special Tripti pickles. Meals Rs25. Open daily 10am-9:30pm.

ENTERTAINMENT

Most visitors are content to simply stroll along the Mall or the Ridge, enjoying the cool breezes and handsome architecture. A number of book shops and stores selling ice cream and other snacks line the Mall, also home to a dismal second-story billiard hall and numerous small video arcades. For sudsy diversions, there are a few pubs. **Himani's** serves drinks at inflated prices (beer Rs60-70) until 9 or 10pm. Other options are the bar at **Rendezvous,** just next to the statue of Lalalajpatrai (beer Rs40), and **The English Wine Shop,** which sells bottled spirits from a spot on just below Christ Church. For **movies,** head to **Rivoli** or **Ritz.** Rivoli, down the ramp nestled between ANZ Grindlays Bank and Rendezvous, usually shows its English-language flicks at 5pm (buy tickets by 4:30pm). Ritz, just east of Christ Church on the ramp leading up to the YMCA Guest House, usually screens sexy English-language films at 5:30 and 9pm. Just below Rivoli is an **ice-skating rink,** which rents skates and typically opens for the season in January.

SIGHTS

HIMACHAL PRADESH STATE MUSEUM. The long walk to the museum rewards the visitor with a widely varied collection accompanied by informative placards explaining the exhibits. The first floor houses remains of 2000 year-old sculptures and even older specimens of Indo-Greek coinage discovered by archaeological digs in H.P. On the second floor, there are a number of incredible Kangra Pahari miniature paintings and works by contemporary artists from the state. If you plan to hike up to the **Jakhu Temple** (see below), the precisely rendered "Hanuman Adoring Rama" is worth a special look. The collection of dolls and the Mahatma Gandhi exhibition complete the melange of Indian culture and history exhibitions. *(Walk west along the Mall until you reach a concrete ramp labeled "Museum," directly next to the Ambedkar Chowk sub-post office. Open Tu-Su 10am-1:30pm and 2-5pm. Free.)*

VICEREGAL LODGE (RASHTRAPATI NIVAS). The neo-Tudor style lodge, which houses the fellows of the Indian Institute of Advanced Study, was built between 1884 and 1888. This unabashedly grand building surrounded by well-manicured gardens was the summer headquarters of the Raj. The lodge was designed to impress—it was the first government building in British India equipped with electricity. In 1945, it was the site of important (but failed) negotiations between the would-be Indian and Pakistani leaders. *(Pass the entrance to the state museum and walk 10min. west along the Mall. Open daily 10am-1pm and 2-4:30pm. Rs10 admission includes a guide.)*

HIMALAYAN AVIARY. Opened in August 1994, this small, chain-link-enclosed aviary houses red jungle fowl, perky pheasants, and some magnificent peacocks. *(Opposite the entrance to the Viceregal Lodge. Open Tu-Su 10am-5pm. Rs5.)*

JAKHU TEMPLE. The red-and-yellow temple sits atop a 2455m hill, and the 20-minute walk to the top is a steep huffer and puffer, especially if you've been smoking too many *bidis.* The temple per se is architecturally uninspiring, but the views of the surrounding mountains more than make up for it. Inside the temple are what some believe to be the footprints of the monkey god Hanuman. Hordes of pesky monkeys revel in their heritage and in the snacks tourists feed them. The temple is surrounded by lush forests and has a canteen and a swing on its grounds. Two networks of paths lead back toward town. While both cut through magnificent, lush forests, the sinuous paths directly to the right of the temple afford better opportunities for enjoying the scenery and taking pleasant detours. Neither set of paths is marked, but they all eventually lead down. Allow 45 minutes to an hour to reach

town on the way down from Jakhu; expect to emerge from the ...
Bazaar, 15 minutes or so from Scandal Corner. *(At the east end of ...
beginning just left of Christ Church.)*

SHOPPING

Himachal's geographical isolation has allowed the evolution of a tradit... ...ut-of-the-ordinary handicrafts: fine woodwork, leather embroidery, engrave... metal-work, patterned carpets, and traditional woolen shawls. Check out any of the stores that crowd the Mall and Lakkar Bazaar. **Kashmir Craft Emporium,** 92 the Mall, has a particularly impressive collection of shawls (Rs100-5000) and silk *saris* (Rs250-4000). **Maria Brothers,** 78 the Mall, just below the church, specializes in bizarre and beautiful old books. Prices aren't cheap, but owner Rajiv Sud is equally friendly to browsers and buyers alike. (Open daily 10:30am-1pm and 3-8pm.)

DHARAMSALA धर्मशाला

After China's occupation of Tibet began in 1959, the 14th Dalai Lama and his Buddhist government were given asylum in Dharamsala, a former British hill station. Since then, a steady stream of Tibetan exiles has relocated here, some of them walking across the winter Himalayas to escape oppression and to be near the man they regard as their religious and political leader. Today, Upper Dharamsala, also called McLeod Ganj (named after David McLeod, a former governor of the Punjab), attracts students, tourists, and devotees of Buddhism to its monasteries, meditation centers, and Tibetan shops. The increasing popularity of the Tibetan cause over the past few years has begun to give this refugee community the feel of a crowded international crossroads.

Embraced by the craggy Dhauladar mountains covered with pine and deodar forests, Dharamsala offers fantastic views of Himalayan peaks and the Kangra Valley. Several easy hikes from McLeod Ganj lead to the slopes, while more serious treks head up and over the snowy passes. If your karma leads you to Dharamsala, in the summer, unfortunately, you'll face daily fog and rain. But no karma is wholly bad—in July and August the flowers blossom, infusing the mountain air with a sweet-smelling freshness that betrays Dharamsala's intrinsic charm.

TRANSPORTATION

Buses: Non-local **buses** usually arrive at and depart from the **New Bus Stand** in Lower Dharamsala. Booking Office (tel. 24903), open daily 8am-1pm and 2-7pm. To: **Amritsar** (5am, 6hr., Rs91); **Chamba** (5pm, 9hr., Rs130); **Chandigarh** (7:20 and 10:30am, 8hr., Rs170); **Dalhousie** (8am, 8hr., Rs80); **Delhi** (5 per day 5am-9:15pm, 13hr., Rs270; semi-deluxe 6 and 8pm, 12hr., Rs390); **Haridwar** (3pm, 12hr., Rs220); **Manali** (5 per day 4:15am-8:30pm, 9hr., Rs163); **Pathankot** (9 per day 7:40am-5pm, 3½hr., Rs51); **Shimla** (7 per day 5am-9:30pm, 8hr., Rs153; semi-deluxe noon, 5, and 7:45pm). From **Mcleod Ganj,** regular buses run to: **Delhi** (4am and 8:15pm, 14hr., Rs213); **Manali** (5pm, 10hr., Rs158); **Pathankot** (6 per day 10am-4pm, 3½hr., Rs52). Deluxe buses depart from McLeod Ganj to: **Dehra Dun** (8pm, 12hr., Rs220); **Delhi** (5, 6, 7, and 8pm; 12hr.; Rs405, semi-deluxe Rs350); **Manali** (9am and 9pm, 9½hr., Rs250). Book in any of the travel agencies. Buses to and from Manali and Chamba are sporadic during monsoon and snow seasons due to blocked roads and mudslides.

Local Transportation: Buses run between the New Bus Stand and McLeod Ganj (every 30min. 6:30am-8:30pm, Rs5). **Shared jeeps** that run between Kotwali Bazaar and McLeod Ganj (Rs5) are cramped but faster. Both bus and jeep are erratic, so if you're not carrying much, you can easily hike along Jogibara Rd. (1hr. up, 45min. down). Everything in McLeod Ganj is within walking distance. The **Taxi Union Stand** beside the bus circle has high fixed rates for most destinations—they're generally only worth it if you're heading up to Dharamkot or Bhagsu at night.

ORIENTATION

The town is split into two sections differing by 500m in altitude; the odd geography is the result of a massive 1905 earthquake which destroyed all of the buildings and killed 900 people in the Kangra Valley. Alarmed at the destruction, the British administration established **Lower Dharamsala,** which now houses mostly offices, banks, and the Indian population. The largely Tibetan enclave of **Upper Dharamsala (McLeod Ganj)** attracts the most tourist attention. Seven roads branch off the **main bus circle** in McLeod Ganj. The first is **Cantonment Road,** the route used by the bus to travel to and from Lower Dharamsala. As you go clockwise, the next road is **Taxi Stand Road,** which leads to the Tibetan Children's Village. Next is a steep road leading to **Dharamkot** (50min.). The fourth spoke off the bus circle is **TIPA Road,** which also leads to Dharamkot, passing the Tibetan Institute of Performing Arts (TIPA) on its way. Next, **Bhagsu Road** leads to **Bhagsu** (20min.) after passing many restaurants and hotels. The sixth road is **Jogibara Road,** chock full of restaurants and guest houses. Finally, **Temple Road** leads to the Dalai Lama's residence, Tsuglagkhang (Main Temple), and Namgyal Monastery. A steep 30-minute walk down either Jogibara or Temple Rd. lands you in Gangchen Kyishong, the Tibetan government-in-exile complex and home to the Library of Tibetan Works and Archives. From there, a 15-minute descent takes you to **Kotwali Bazaar** in the center of Lower Dharamsala.

🛈 PRACTICAL INFORMATION

Tourist Office: Himachal Tourism Marketing Office (tel./fax 24212), 50m below Kotwali Bazaar in Lower Dharamsala, distributes information on local sight-seeing, and books expensive Himachal Tourism-run hotels. Open daily 8am-8pm. The modern **McLeod Ganj Office** (tel. 21205), off Temple Rd. behind the State Bank of India, is less helpful. Open M-Sa 8am-5pm.

Budget Travel and Trekking: Most agencies in McLeod Ganj reserve bus and plane tickets; a few also organize treks. For computerized airline, train, and deluxe bus bookings, **Dhauladar Travel,** Temple Rd., accepts Visa, MC, and AmEx for charges above Rs500. Open daily 9am-1pm and 2-6pm. Farther up Temple Rd., **Ways Tours** (tel. 21910) and **Western Travels** (tel. 21926) are also helpful. Prem Sagar at **Occidental Travel** (tel. 21330), Taxi Stand Rd., a few meters from the bus circle, is the most knowledgeable *gaddi* (mountain nomad) in town. He can arrange treks for fully equipped individuals (US$10-20 per day). Trekking season in Dhauladhar runs from July to December; in the wet summer months you can see eight kinds of orchids and 130 kinds of herbs in bloom. **Yetti Trekking** (tel. 21032), 50m above the bus circle on the road to Dharamkot, and **Dhauladhar Adventures** (tel. 21017), next to the temple entrance in Bhagsu Nag, also organize treks. (For more information on **Trekking,** see p. 36.)

Currency Exchange: Bank of Punjab, Temple Rd., in McLeod Ganj, a few steps from the bus circle, changes currency and traveler's checks. Open M-F 10:30am-1:30pm, Sa 10:30-11:30am. **Western Union** money transfers are available at **Paul Merchants** (tel. 21418), in the **Surya Resorts Hotel,** a few houses after Bookworm bookshop. Open M-Sa 10am-7pm. **Bank of Baroda,** Lower Dharamsala, across from the Museum of Kangra Art, changes money and gives Visa and MC cash advances (Rs100 plus 1% service charge). Open M-F 10am-2pm, Sa 10am-noon. **State Bank of India,** Kotwali Bazaar, changes traveler's checks. Open M-F 10am-4pm, Sa 10am-1pm.

Bookstore: Bookworm, Temple Rd. At the fork, follow the sign to Hotel Bhagsu; it's 10m down on the right. Has the largest selection of Tibetan and Western classics. Open Tu-Su 9am-7pm; winter: 10am-5pm. For Buddhist literature, there are two options. **Little Lhasa Bookshop,** Temple Rd. Open Tu-Su 9:30am-7pm. **Namgyal Bookshop,** Namgyal Monastery, next to the Tsuglakhang. Open M-Sa 9am-5pm. **Charitable Trust Bookshop,** Jogibara Rd., near the prayer wheels, has books on yoga and Sanskrit and Tibetan language textbooks with tapes. Open Tu-Su 9am-7pm.

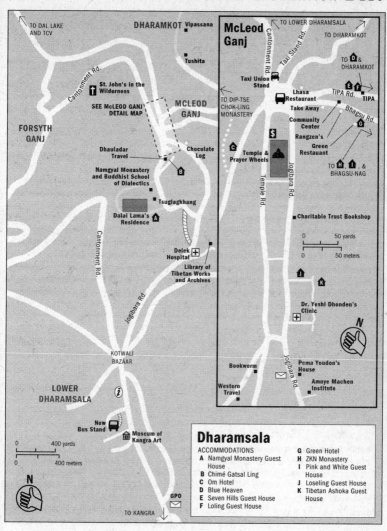

TO DAL LAKE AND TCV

DHARAMKOT — Vipassana

Tushita

St. John's in the Wilderness

SEE McLEOD GANJ DETAIL MAP

MCLEOD GANJ

FORSYTH GANJ

Dhauladar Travel

Chocolate Log

Namgyal Monastery and Buddhist School of Dialectics

Tsuglagkhang

Dalai Lama's Residence

Delek Hospital

Library of Tibetan Works and Archives

Cantonment Rd.

Cantonment Rd.

Jogibara Rd.

KOTWALI BAZAAR

LOWER DHARAMSALA

New Bus Stand

Museum of Kangra Art

0   400 yards
0   400 meters

N

GPO

TO KANGRA

McLeod Ganj

TO LOWER DHARAMSALA

TO DHARAMSALA

TO DHARAMKOT

TO DHARAMKOT

Taxi Stand Rd.

Cantonment Rd.

Taxi Union Stand

TIPA Rd.

TIPA

Lhasa Restaurant

Take Away

Bhagsu Rd.

Community Center

Rangzen's

Green Restauant

Temple & Prayer Wheels

TO DIP-TSE CHOK-LING MONASTERY

TO BHAGSU-NAG

Temple Rd.

Jogibara Rd.

Charitable Trust Bookshop

0   50 yards
0   50 meters

Dr. Yeshi Dhonden's Clinic

N

Jogibara Rd.

Bookworm

Western Travel

Pema Youdon's House

Amnye Machen Institute

Dharamsala

ACCOMMODATIONS
A Namgyal Monastery Guest House
B Chimé Gatsal Ling
C Om Hotel
D Blue Heaven
E Seven Hills Guest House
F Loling Guest House

G Green Hotel
H ZKN Monastery
I Pink and White Guest House
J Loseling Guest House
K Tibetan Ashoka Guest House

Laundry: McLeod Ganj abounds with launderers, and most places clean and dry within 24hr. Reliable **RK Laundry,** Bhagsu Rd., is the cheapest in town. Rs5 per pair of socks. Open daily 8am-8pm. Some hotels have their own laundry service.

Hospital: The Tibetan **Delek Hospital,** Jogibara Rd. (tel. 22053, 24hr. emergency tel. 23381), just before Gangchen Kyishong, has a good walk-in clinic. Open M-Sa 9am-1pm and 2-5pm. They have a branch in McLeod Ganj on Bhagsu Rd., just before the Green Cybercafe. **Dr. Yeshi Dhonden** (tel. 21461), off Jogibara Rd. in McLeod Ganj, practices Tibetan herbal medicine. The well-known doctor's 2-week herbal pill therapy makes you 90% immune to all stomach disorders (see below). Open Su-F 8am-1pm.

Police: The closest station (tel. 21483) is in Forsyth Ganj, west of McLeod Ganj. The **Superintendent of Police,** in Lower Dharmasala above the GPO, registers foreigners on non-tourist visas for long-term stays.

Post Office: GPO, Lower Dharamsala, 1km south of Kotwali Bazaar. **Post Office,** along Jogibara Rd., past the State Bank. Both have *Poste Restante* and EMS. Letters not addressed to McLeod Ganj end up at the GPO. Last mail leaves McLeod Ganj branch at 1:30pm, GPO at 2:30pm. Both open M-F 9am-2pm and 3-5pm. Airborne Express is available at **Western Travel,** Temple Rd. **Postal Code:** McLeod Ganj 176219. Lower Dharamsala (GPO) 176215.

Internet: Every hotel and shop in McLeod Ganj seems to be hooked up to the net. The connection is fast, and the standard price is Rs30 for the first 15min. and Rs1.50 for each minute thereafter. The largest labs (10 or more computers) are the **Green Cyberspace Cafe,** Bhagsu Rd., in Green Hotel (open daily 9am-10pm), and the cheaper **Emi Cafe,** Temple Rd. (Rs80 per hr.; open 24hr.).

Telephones: STD/ISD booths abound on Jogibara, Temple, and Bhagsu Rd.; some remain open until 1am. In many places you can use AT&T and MCI calling cards as well as receive callbacks. In both cases, the standard charge is Rs5 per min. **Western Travels,** Temple Rd., charges Rs3 per min. Open 24hr.

PHONE CODE	01892

■ ACCOMMODATIONS

Most tourists stay in McLeod Ganj, and guest houses continue to spring up along the already packed tourist sections of Jogibara, Temple, and Bhagsu Rd. A local joke advises against parking here—your car might be turned into a guest house while you're gone. If spiritual reasons are what draw you here, it might be best to stay in one of the monasteries. These fill up quickly, but if you put yourself on a waiting list when you arrive, you should get a room in a day or two. **Bhagsu** and **Dharamkot** are a 20-minute walk from McLeod Ganj and are generally much more peaceful. The areas are chock full of private houses that rent rooms (Rs50-90, Rs500-1000 per month). Dharamsala is usually packed in spring and autumn.

MCLEOD GANJ GUESTHOUSES

■ **Loling Guesthouse** (tel. 21072), 100m from the bus circle on TIPA Rd., has basic rooms that share the cleanest common bath you're likely to encounter in India. Hot shower Rs10. Singles Rs60; doubles Rs85. Winter: Rs10 discount. Obeying the same standards of hygiene, **Loseling Guesthouse** (tel. 21087), Jogibara Rd., 50m from the bus circle on the left, has spotless rooms, all with private bathrooms. Doubles with squat toilet Rs150, with seat toilet Rs190, with hot water Rs250.

Tibetan Ashoka Guest House (tel. 21763), off Jogibara Rd., on the left, 75m from the bus circle. With over 37 rooms, this place is likely to have a room for you during high-season. The common squat toilets are clean, and some rooms have valley-view balconies. Small, spare doubles Rs55 up to Rs330 with amenities like a view or a bathroom and water heater.

Seven Hills Guest House (tel. 21580), on the left side of TIPA Rd. 100m from the bus circle, is the only guest house in town with a garden and a beauty salon. The newly constructed restaurant and Internet lab make it entirely self-sufficient. All rooms have double beds, private baths, and great views. Doubles Rs150-250. Winter prices negotiable.

Om Hotel (tel. 21313), just down the paved path from the bus stand, to the right of Temple Rd. Travelers flock to the balcony restaurant to sip *chai* and enjoy a sunset view. The upscale rooms are large, and the attached bathrooms have seat toilets and hot water. In-house restaurant and laundry service. 2 rooms with common toilet each Rs80. Doubles Rs225-250, depending on the view. Off-season: Rs200.

Green Hotel, Bhagsu Rd. (tel. 21200), 150m from the bus circle, has more rooms than any of its neighbors, but still fills up for most of the year. Gates shut at midnight. Singles with bath and hot water Rs55-Rs80; doubles Rs250-350.

Tara Guest House (tel. 21181), next to the Chime Gatsal Ling monastery. Rooms are sparkling new, with hot showers and enormous built-in closets. The rooftop balcony has the best view of His Holiness' residence. The studios downstairs are an amazing deal if you are staying long term. Doubles Rs165-250. Studios Rs3000-3700 per month.

MONASTERIES

Dip Tse Chok Ling Monastery (tel. 21726), past Om Hotel and then a 10min. walk down the steps on the right, the isolated monastery seems far removed from the bustle on the ridge. Join in evening prayer with the *lamas*. All rooms have two single beds, writing tables, and a common, blue-tiled toilet. Rooms Rs120.

Zilnan Kagyeling Nyingmapa (ZKN) Monastery, 15min. up Bhagsu Rd. Turn left up the driveway just past Last Chance Tibetan Restaurant. Dimly lit, spare rooms with common bath line the sides of this new monastery. Step out of your room into the transcendental, temple-style courtyard. Singles Rs50; doubles Rs70.

Chime Gatsal Ling, Temple Rd. (tel. 21340), 10min. down, then left up the driveway across from the School of Dialectics—the big orange building is on the left after 75m. Part housing for Nyingmapa-sect monks, part hotel. Spotless, carpeted rooms are huge, and the roof is perfect for watching the sun set on the Dhauladars. Doubles Rs75, with bath (shower and seat toilet) Rs125.

Namgyal Monastery Guest House (tel. 21492) allows you to share a courtyard with His Holiness' residence and the Tsuglagkhang (Main Temple). The style of the cells matches the lavish surroundings. Doubles with bath Rs225.

BHAGSU AND DHARAMKOT

Pink and White Guest House, up the hill from the center of Bhagsu, a 25min. walk from McLeod. An array of faux-luxury rooms with private bath and 24hr. hot water. Room service 6am-11pm; entrees Rs20-35. Singles Rs200; doubles 350-500. Off-season: 40% discount.

Blue Heaven (tel. 21005), just below Dharamkot., a 20min. walk up steep TIPA Rd. Turn right on the forest path. This most tranquil of places has enormous doubles with or without cushy carpet and tiled bathroom. Doubles Rs150/200.

⚑ FOOD

The appearance of heavy, flat noodles and hunks of mutton reminds you that you're in Tibetan culinary territory. Yet the apple pie on the dessert menu leaves no doubt that Dharamsala is, at the same time, a tourist trap and a traveler's heaven—you can find just about any national cuisine represented here.

Amdo Cha-Chung Restaurant, Jogibara Rd., on the left past the post office. The owners toss up authentic *Amdo* cuisine from the northeastern region of Tibet. Try the *lanzhou* handpulled noodles (*thankthuk*) and szechuan hot sauce while you keep company with *Amdo* monks and other tourists. Chinese cable TV hums in the background.

Kunga Restaurant and Nick's Italian Kitchen, Bhagsu Rd., before the Green Hotel. A native New Yorker once taught his Bologna-acquired art to Tibetan chefs who have perfected the skill to the requisite *bodhisattva* level of perfection. The pasta is home-made, and the parmesan is flown in fresh from the Apennines. Open daily until 9:30pm.

Green Hotel and Restaurant, Bhagsu Rd. Carefully prepared Tibetan and Chinese dishes and a lip-smacking cappucino make it clear why this is a traveler's favorite. The banana chocolate wrap may not be the spiritual experience you came to Dharamsala for, but if nirvana took on a calorie-laden avatar, this is it. Open daily 7:30am-10pm.

Khama Nirvana, Temple Rd., above Western Travels. This most original of eateries serves comfortably cushioned guests pita sandwiches and *macho burritos* while drums and guitars flirt in the background. This happenin' joint features a "Sunday at Sunset" lecture series, Monday jam sessions, and an Interfaith Shabbat on Fridays. Inquire here for volunteer opportunities. Open daily 11am-9pm.

Rangzen's, Bhagsu Rd., just before Nick's Italian Kitchen, charms guests with its tininess and valley-views. The Tibetan brown bread sandwiches are good, but nothing surpasses the *tsampa* (barley porridge), a Tibetan staple cooked here according to a *Bonpo* shaman's magic formula (*Bonpo* is Tibet's ancient religion). Open daily 8am-10pm.

Om Restaurant, near the bus circle. The smiling Tibetan girls who serve food are supposedly as legendary as the famous veg. manchurians on the menu. The terrace makes a delightful spot to enjoy the sunset over a cup of tea. Open daily 8am-10pm.

Kailash Hotel and Restaurant, Temple Rd., near the bus circle. Owned by a warm Tibetan family, Kailash serves up spicy *momos* with a friendly spirit; wash 'em down with a cup of mild jasmine tea.

German Bakery and Restaurant, above the Pink and White Guest House, up the hill from central Bhagsu. This hungry hikers' haven has a tantalizing array of rye breads and apple pies to complement its assortment of homemade noodle soups. Open daily until 10pm.

🎵 ENTERTAINMENT

The market section of Jogibara Rd. is home to two hole-in-the-wall **movie houses** showing what seems like a random mix of recent American blockbusters and bizarre low-grade flicks. The wooden benches are only slightly more comfortable than the seats on a bus, but the big TV screens compensate with good reception. (Showings usually 5 and 9pm, Rs10.) **McLeo's** third-floor bar, on the bus circle, with its Hawaiian decor and endlessly looped Beatles cassettes, is a surreal place to swill (beer Rs75). Young, unemployed Tibetans gather here to mingle with and vent to the mobs of Westerners. Occasional **dance parties** start at 11pm and go until the 95% male dance floor clears. The **Tibetan Institute of Performing Arts (TIPA)** has cultural shows and performs a Tibetan opera for the New Year. Stop in for more details. (A 10min. walk up TIPA Rd. toward Dharamkot. Open M-Sa 9am-5:30pm, closed 2nd and 4th Sa. Tel. 21748. Call or stop by to check the schedule; if you want to see the theater, be persistent.)

👁 SIGHTS

GANGCHEN KYISHONG. The site of the administrative offices of the **Tibetan government-in-exile,** Gangchen Kyishong also houses several NGOs (Non-Governmental Organizations) including the **Tibetan Center for Human Rights and Democracy.** Stop by the Ministry of Information for an update on Tibet's political situation. The **Library of Tibetan Works and Archives,** at the far end of Gangchen Kyishong, has 10,000 volumes in English and other languages on Buddhism, Tibet, and related subjects. The books and many scholarly periodicals are available for general use in the reading room. If you have an institutional recommendation, you can obtain a borrowing privileges card. *(Library reading membership Rs15 per month, lending membership Rs150 per month.)* Language and philosophy courses taught by renowned *lamas* are offered as well. You can attend a session or two for free, although the Tibetan government would, no doubt, appreciate the registration fee. Common etiquette includes arriving on time for opening prayers and behaving respectfully during class hours: remove your shoes before entering the study hall, and, for philosophy sessions, don't stand up until the *lama* has left. *(9-month courses in Buddhist philosophy: M-Sa 9 and 11am, except 2nd and 4th Sa; Rs100 per month, plus Rs50 registration fee. Tibetan language courses: daily 10am spring, summer, and fall; Rs200 per month. Rooms available to students enrolled in 2 or more classes simultaneously, Rs500-2000 per month.)* The **museum** upstairs has beautiful *thankas*, Tibetan coins, and several rooms rescued from the pillage of the Chinese Red Guards *(Rs5)*. The **Nechung Monastery,** next to the library, is a peaceful spot for meditation. *(Halfway between McLeod Ganj and Lower Dharamsala on Jogibara Rd.; turn left through the archway. Tel. 22467. Open M-Sa 9am-1pm and 2-5pm, closed 2nd and 4th Sa and on Buddhist holidays. Free.)*

TSUGLAGKHANG TEMPLE. This temple (whose Tibetan name simply means "Main Temple") houses images of the Buddha, Padmasambhava, and Avalokiteshvara ("Chenresig" in Tibetan). This last image, representing the bodhisattva of whom the Dalai Lama is an incarnation, was rescued from the Tokhang Temple in Lhasa and brought here during the massive destruction wrought by the Chinese Cultural Revolution. Monks from the School of Dialectics come to

SO YOU THINK YOU'RE RICHARD GERE...

To schedule a private audience with His Holiness the Dalai Lama, send your request four months in advance and start praying. Private audiences are rare but not unheard of, particularly if your reason is truly specific to the Dalai Lama. Much more common are public audiences of 300 people or so, held once or twice a month for foreigners and recent arrivals from Tibet. At a public audience, the crowd files slowly past His Holiness, who takes time to speak and laugh with each person (despite his aides' attempts to speed things up). You need to bring your passport a few days ahead to be cleared for the audience. The best time to see and hear the Dalai Lama is during his public year 2000; teachings begin on February 17th and last for ten days. They are open to all. Occasionally, His Holiness gives public teachings during other times of the year, too. You can contact the Office of His Holiness the Dalai Lama by mail, phone, or email (Thekchen Choeling, McLeod Ganj, Dharamsala, H.P., 176219; tel./fax 21813; email ohhdl@cta.unv.ernet.in). Check with the security branch office near Hotel Tibet on Bhagsu Road to see when the Dalai Lama will next be in town.

debate—snapping, clapping, and shouting at each other—in the temple's courtyard in the afternoons. Each snap, clap, and stomp corresponds to a specific moment in the argument being advanced by the standing member of the debating pair. The debates proceed via an immensely complex system of logic, one of the defining features of the Gelugpa sect's teachings. *(Behind the Buddhist School of Dialectics; a 10min. walk from the bus circle in McLeod Ganj. Open daily sunrise to sunset.)*

THE BHAGSU-NAG TEMPLE. This serene temple rests beside several cool kunds (pools) where devout Hindus and monks bathe. According to legend, 9035 years ago, there was a drought in the kingdom of Ajmer, in present-day Rajasthan. In order to save his realm, King Bhagsu headed to a nearby peak 5400m high, where he discovered two lakes and trapped their waters in his bowl. But as the king lay down to sleep, Nag, the cobra who owned the lakes, challenged him to a fight. Mortally wounded in the ensuing struggle, he made a dying request that the people of Ajmer be rid of the drought. Impressed by Bhagsu's devotion to his people, Nag granted him his wish. The fruit of his efforts is today known as the Indira Gandhi Canal, which irrigates most of Rajasthan. The temple at Bhagsu-Nag marks the event and the snake-god's respect for the king. The **Bhagsu Waterfall** beyond the temple cascades for 30 spectacular feet during the monsoon season. There are small open-air cafes above and below the falls. The lower one has cold drinks, crackers, and a crowd of Indian bathers strutting around in their underwear (only in the summer). The upper one, Shiva Cafe, has hot meals, chessboards, and opium-inspired paintings. *(At the north end of Bhagsu; a 25min. walk from McLeod Ganj. The waterfall is 15min. beyond the temple; step through the chink in the wall to reach the path.)*

NORBU LINGKA. In order to see Tibetan art at its best, head to Norbu Lingka, a compound 10km from Dharamsala. Its bamboo groves enclose a rare display of Tibetan architecture designed to resemble the symmetries of a bodhisattva. The **Norbu Lingka Institute,** dedicated to preserving Tibetan culture in both its literary and artistic forms, is located here. It offers a unique opportunity to watch thanka masters, woodcarvers, metal-workers, and their pupils at work. The **Losel Doll Museum** exhibits costumes from every region of Tibet. *(Take the Palampur bus (Rs2) from Lower Dharamsala, and get off at Sacred Heart High School. From there it's a 20min. walk up the road to the left. Tel. 22664; www.norbulingka.org. Open M-Sa 9am-6pm; arrive before 4pm to see the workshops or catch a guided tour. Doll Museum Rs20.)*

THE TIBETAN CHILDREN'S HANDICRAFT AND VOCATIONAL CENTER. The vocational center instructs refugees in the arts of thanka painting, carpet weaving, and good old-fashioned capitalist marketing. The **Tibetan Children's Village School (TCV),** under the patronage of the Dalai Lama, has been housing, caring for, and educating more than 2400 orphaned Tibetan children since 1960. Foreigners are welcome to visit the school. A late afternoon soccer match with the kids is topped only by a weekend visit to help them practice English. You can volunteer here for a few months or sponsor a child (US$30 per month). Donations are welcome. *(The center is a 45min. walk up the hill from the McLeod Ganj taxi stand. The TCV is a 10min. walk farther uphill, past Dal Lake on the right. School open M-F 9am-4pm.)*

OTHER SIGHTS. The **Dip-Tse-Chok-Ling Monastery** is home to a small (and largely young) community of monks. The original monastery once lay south of Lhasa; in recent years, it has again become functional. Some of the monks alternate between the two locations. *(A 10min. walk from the bus circle down a stone path that begins just past Om Hotel. Open daily 7am-7pm.)* The church **St. John's in the Wilderness** is a functioning relic of the bygone British era. The kind pastor will happily converse with you about your country or his. Lord Elgin, an ex-Viceroy of India, is buried in the church cemetery, where dusk fog swirls around grave stones. *(Follow the narrow road from the Dip-Tse-Chok-Ling monastery guest house up to Cantonment Rd.; from there it's a 15min. walk downhill toward Lower Dharamsala. Open daily 9am-5pm. Sunday services in English 11:30am. Candle-light services on Christmas.)* The **Amnye Machen Institute** aims to bring Tibetan culture into the 21st century. The institute gathers contemporary writers and scholars, translates classical works into Tibetan, publishes journals on history and culture, and serves as the main cartographic center for Tibet. The Institute has film festivals, lectures, and other Tibet-related events; details are on their website. *(On Jogibara Rd. just past the post office. Tel. 21441; email ami@amnyemachen.org; www.amnyemachen.org.)* A pleasant day-hike from Dharamkot takes you to the rolling, grassy ridgetop of **Triund.** There's a small rest house here, as well as a comfortable cave 50m uphill. A second basic rest house is 5km up the trail at a spot where you can see the peaks in their massive entirety. Resist the urge to climb higher unless you've gotten good, detailed advice and have some mountaineering experience—it's an all-day endeavor even from here, and clouds rush up from the valley in the afternoon.

VOLUNTEER OPPORTUNITIES

In its struggle for freedom, the Tibetan community has deemed the ability to speak English a necessity; therefore, English teachers and simple conversationalists are welcomed and highly esteemed. The enthusiastic monks and Tibetan students, mostly McLeod Ganj regulars, often agree to exchange regular language lessons with foreigners. Any monastery in Dharamsala will be grateful for short- or long-term English teachers. Keep in mind that same-sex teachers are essential for reasons of modesty. The **Tibetan Children's Village** (tel. 21528) is always interested in committed, long-term English, math, and science teachers.

If you want to help, drop by the **Earthville Institute,** Temple Rd., at the Khana Nirvana Restaurant, an organization serving as a community center, non-profit educational society, and clearing house for information about volunteer opportunities in and around Dharamsala (tel. 21252; www.earthville.net; email mandala@del2.vsnl.net.in; or write to Mandala, Dalai Lama Temple Rd., McLeod Ganj, Dharamsala, H.P. 176219; open W-M 11am-9pm). The official **Community Center,** near Rangzen's on Bhagsu Rd., has postings on local events. The **Green Shop,** part of the center, employs a squad of dedicated workers who operate the recycling unit. Volunteers are also taught how to make paper or bind books. Contact Tsering Kyi (tel. 21059) at the Tibetan Welfare Office, Environmental Desk. If volunteering is not your cup of tea, the **Green Shop** offers many opportunities for small-scale environmentalism. Those interested in short-term or day projects should consider the **Yong Ling Creche** (tel. 21028), across from the nunnery on Jogibara Rd., where anyone can stop by for a conversation with the kids in the morning or with the adult students in the evening. Yong Ling also organizes a home-stay program (Rs200 per day including meals). With nearly every Tibetan organization wanting to be online, volunteers with graphic and web-designing skills are in high demand; try the **Amnye Machen Institute** (see p. 230). There may be opportunities at the

THE DALAI'S DAILY DUTIES Being a political leader, Nobel Peace Laureate, and world religious figure is a tall order for anyone. But the Dalai Lama's job description is even broader—it includes, for example, interviewing a man temporarily possessed by the Nechung oracle (which gives him the superhuman strength to leap around in an 50kg costume) in order to make political decisions. Other tools of statecraft include hiding fortune-cookie-type slips of paper in dough balls, rolling them in a bowl until one pops out, and reading the verdict. On a regular basis, His Holiness makes decisions regarding 1000-year-old politico-religious quarrels and also travels internationally, lecturing on Tibet's position in global politics. It's not exactly the easiest job in the world. Even divinity, it seems, has its downside.

Tibetan Centre for Human Rights and Democracy (Gangchen Kyishong, northern building; tel. 23363; email dsala@tchrd.org; www.tchrd.org); the **Tibetan Youth Congress** (Bhagsu Rd., opposite the Green Shop); the **Tibetan Women's Association** (tel. 21527 or 21198; fax 21528; email twa@del2.vsnl.net.in); and the **Tibetan Medical Institute** (tel. 22618, in the Delek Hospital). All have English publications and translations that need proofreading. You can contact any of the above institutions in writing: Name of the institution, P.O. McLeod Ganj, Dharamsala, H.P. 176219.

MEDITATION

Yoga and meditation courses abound in McLeod Ganj—check the postings at the Community Center or in most restaurants. The **Tushita Meditation Centre** (tel. 21866; email tushita@ndf.vsnl.net.in), 20 minutes from the bus circle in Dharamkot, offers 10-day or shorter residential courses that provide a good introduction to Tibetan Buddhism and analytical meditation. The classes (Mar.-June and Sept.-Nov.) are taught by a Tibetan *lama* and a Western monk. Register by phone or email two months in advance. (Open M-Sa 9:30-11:30am and 1-4:30pm; registration M-Sa 1:30-3:30pm.) The center also has a library with a good selection of books on Buddhism; anyone can borrow books after depositing a passport (Rs10 per book per week; open M-Sa 10am-4pm). For those whom the analytical approach does not suit, the **Vipassana Meditation Centre** (tel./fax 21309; www.dhamma.org), next door, runs residential courses in single point meditation. Vipassana has centers all over the world, so continuing elsewhere wouldn't be difficult. Register by mail by sending a brief resume. Registrations are not accepted over the phone. Both meditation centers operate on expected donations.

DALHOUSIE डलहौज़ी

Built around five ridges along the edge of the Dhauladar mountain range, Dalhousie was named after Lord James Ramsey, Marquis of Dalhousie, who became the Governor General of India in 1848. The hill station was founded in 1854, when the British rented the land from the largely autonomous Chamba raja in order to expand vacation options for their increasingly beleaguered colonial administrators. Today, Dalhousie is the prime destination for Indian honeymooners and Punjabi tourists escaping the sweltering heat. They come here for views of Pir Panjal and the nostalgic memory of the Raj, though the place also has its anti-British history. In the 1940s, Subhas Chandra Bose came here to secretly strategize for the Indian National Army, and today the nearby cantonment offers glimpses of Indian soldiers in all their finery.

⊠ ORIENTATION AND PRACTICAL INFORMATION. In Dalhousie, everything you need is within walking distance. The narrow road rising to the right from the **bus stand** leads to **Subhash Chowk** (a 10min. walk). The steps slightly to the left climb up to **Gandhi Chowk.** The chowks are connected by two horizontal roads, **Mall Road** on the northern side of the ridge and **Garam Path** to the south. Hotels and restaurants are located on these streets. Down from Subhash Chowk is **Sadar Bazaar,** where the locals live. **Buses** depart from the main bus stand to: **Chamba** via **Ranikhet** (5 daily 7am-4:30pm, 2hr., Rs30); **Dharamsala** (7am, 7hr., Rs75); **Pathankot** (10 daily 5am-4:30pm, 3hr., Rs40); and **Shimla** (12:45pm, 12hr., Rs185). For more buses to Dharamsala and for buses to **Amritsar** and **Jammu,** change in Pathankot (see p. 268). Two buses (9:30 and 10:10am) go to **Khajjiar, Chamba,** and back, stopping in each place for one-and-a-half hours (to Khajjiar only: 1hr., Rs15; roundtrip to Dalhousie: 8hr., Rs70). **Local buses** shuttle between the main bus stand and Gandhi Chowk (Rs4). The **Tourist Marketing Office** (tel. 42136), two houses down from the main bus stand, provides hotel information and booking (open daily 10am-5pm). **Treks 'n' Travels** (tel. 40277; fax 40476) books hotels in all of H.P, does ticket reservation, and organizes treks. **Punjab National Bank** (tel. 42190), next to Aroma 'n' Claire Hotel on the loop road off Subhash Chowk, changes traveler's checks (open M-F 10am-2pm, Sa 10am-noon). The **Civil Hospital,** near Aroma 'n' Claire, has bare-bones facilities. **St. Joseph's Clinic,** just up the road, is a little better (open daily 9am-4pm). The **police station** (tel. 42126) is across from Aroma 'n' Claire. The **Sub Post Office,** at Gandhi Chowk, has *Poste Restante* (open M-Sa 9am-5pm). **STD/ISD** booths cluster at the two chowks. **Postal Code:** 176304. **Telephone Code:** 01899.

⌖⌗ ACCOMMODATIONS AND FOOD. There are plenty of hotels in Dalhousie, and in the off season you can get a sizeable room with a view and private bath for Rs200. In season, prices can double. The season officially runs from April 15 to July 1 and from September 15 to November 15. In winter, there is usually a Rs100 per day charge for a space heater. Dalhousie has a water shortage problem, so during the season, running water is available for two hours in the morning and in the evening. As a consequence, some hotels charge heavy fines for washing clothes in the room. The serene and friendly **Hotel Crags,** Garam Sarak (tel. 42124), is a five-minute walk from Subhash Chowk. The view of the magnificent valley from the massive patio and from the rooms in front is unbeatable. Most rooms are equipped with wood-framed beds and mirrors, cable TV, and seat toilets. (In-season: Rs300-500. Off-season: Rs150-200. Curfew 10:30pm). Further along Garam Sarak is **Hotel Fain View** (tel. 42206), with large rooms and immaculate baths that, unlike in all the other hotels, have water all day (basic room with bath Rs175-350; with TV and hot water add Rs100). On Mall Rd. near Gandhi Chowk is **Mehar's Hotel** (tel. 42179), touted as the "Biggest Hotel in Dalhousie." The rooms have thick green carpets, wooden ceilings, cable TVs and clean bathrooms. The attached restaurant offers decent food and a clear day's view of the Pir Panjal range. (Doubles Rs350-500. 10% luxury tax.) If you are short on cash, take the road opposite State Bank of India up to the **Youth Hostel** (tel. 42189). The bathroom with squat toilets is not exactly spotless but is still bearable. Lights must be out at 10:30pm. No membership is necessary. (Dorm beds Rs30; floor mats Rs20.) The six-bed dorm in **Hotel Devdar** (tel. 36333) is an incredible deal for its spotless bed with luxurious private bath (Rs75). If the dorm is full, **Parne** (tel. 36344) has doubles for Rs300. At Subhash Chowk, **Punjabi Friends Dhaba** is well-known for food and dedicated service. At Gandhi Chowk, **Lovely Restaurant** serves the largest menu in town in a setting that matches its name. The Tibetans have monopolized **market** activities in town; aim for their stands at Gandhi Chowk and at the bus station if you need a watch or leather bag. For fruits and sweets, patronize the locals at **Sadar Bazaar.**

▨ SIGHTS. Most people who come to Dalhousie simply stroll between the *chowks* lined with oak, cedar, and pine trees looking for the views that present themselves in the occasional clearing. The **Garam Sarak walk** is especially nice because no cars are allowed on the road. Tibetan refugees have painted reliefs of Padmasambhava, Chenresig (of whom the Dalai Lama is an incarnation), and other Tibetan deities on the stone cliffs beside the road. There are also two old churches at the chowks, where you can take refuge from the world as well as from the multitudes of playful monkeys. Panch Pulla Rd., off Gandhi Chowk, leads to the dried **water spring,** notable because Ajit Singh, a supporter of Subhash Chandra Bose, died here on Independence Day. **Dainkunt Peak,** a beautiful 9km walk uphill from Gandhi Chowk, is the spot from where all the major rivers of the area—the Chenab, the Beas, and the Ravi—can be seen on a clear day. **Khajjiar,** a pristine meadow 22km from Dalhousie, is trumpeted by the local tourist industry as "the Switzerland of the East." The scenery is postcard-perfect, but be ready to share it with hundreds of Indian tourists arriving by the busload for the picnic and the perfect photo opportunity with the lake and the folk costume-clad villagers. Horse riding around the meadow is available for Rs50 per hour.

CHAMBA चम्बा

Locked in between four major mountain ranges (Shivalik, Dhauladhar, Pir Panjal, and Greater Himalayas), the region of Chamba is referred to as the lap of the Himalayas. At 990m, Chamba escapes the heat that scorches Punjab, yet it remains warmer and drier than Dalhousie or Dharamsala. The town itself sprawls in a medieval haze of porticoed homes and hidden temples on the slope above the Sal and Ravi Rivers. The town was founded in AD 940 as the new capital of an older princely state administered from Bharmour. Mountain ridges, isolation, attitude, and wily diplomacy have kept the Chamba Valley stubbornly independent ever since. The Mughals never managed to penetrate here; Chamba's temples were spared the fate of Hindu shrines in other parts of India. Even the British seem to have left little trace here: not much more than one hydro-electric plant. The result is a rich and relatively undisturbed local culture; Chamba and the surrounding area have developed trademark styles of cooking, politics, handicrafts, religious art, and even a regional literary dialect, Chambiali. Town spirit peaks in early August, when residents throw a riotous week-long harvest festival called Minjar.

🛈 ORIENTATION AND PRACTICAL INFORMATION. Most of the business in Chamba is concentrated around **Court Road,** which runs from the crowded **bus stand** area in the south of town along the eastern side of the **Chaugan,** Chamba's wide, grassy mall and cricket ground. Court Rd. becomes **Hospital Road** beyond Chaugan's shops and markets, then loops back through chicken shacks and liquor counters as **Museum Road.** Branching uphill off Court Rd., **Temple Road** leads to **Laxmi Narayan Temple** and into a maze of tight alleys which hide ancient shrines.

Buses leave for **Bharmour** (4 per day, 3½hr., Rs32); **Dalhousie** via Kajjiar or Banikhet (9 per day 6am-6pm, 2½hr., Rs28); **Dharamsala** (6am and 9:30am, 8hr., Rs110), via **Pathankot** (11:30am and 4pm, 10hr., Rs100) or via **Gaggal,** just 10km from Dharamsala (noon, 8hr., Rs80); **Manali** via **Kullu** (11:30am, 16hr., Rs242); and **Pathankot** (9 per day 4:30am-4pm, 5hr., Rs57). At the bus station there is a 24-hour cloak room (Rs5 per day). **Mami Mahesh Travels** (tel. 22507), next to the entrance to Laxmi Narayan Temple, helps with train reservations, treks, and information on temples. Farther down, on Hospital Rd., **Punjab National Bank** changes traveler's checks and foreign currency (open M-F 10am-2pm, Sa 10am-noon). **Pharmacies** line Hospital Rd., including **Shrikanth Chowfla and Sons** (tel. 22735), which proudly announces that it's also "Licensed to Deal Arms and Ammunition" (open M-Sa 9am-8pm). Medical facilities in Chamba are not first-rate, but there is a **District Hospital,** Hospital Rd. (tel. 22392), as well as a few private clinics nearby. The **police station** is on Hospital Rd. (tel. 22736). On the Chaugan, 20m past Hotel Inavati, is the antediluvian **post office,** which has *Poste Restante* (open M-F 9:30am-5:30pm). **Postal Code:** 176310. **STD/ISD** booths are scattered along Court and Hospital Rd. **Telephone Code:** 01899.

🛏🛏 ACCOMMODATIONS AND FOOD. Chamba's budget scene isn't spectacular. Most rooms are small, and hotels fill up fast in season (Apr. 15-July 1 and Sept. 15-Nov. 15). **Rishi Hotel and Restaurant** (tel. 24343), up Temple Rd. from Hospital Rd., crams guests into plain but clean rooms, all with attached bath. Get one of the four rooms overlooking the Laxmi Narayan Temple across the street. (Singles Rs110; doubles Rs165; "triple plus" Rs275.) The HPTDC runs **Hotel Champak** (tel. 22774), 50m behind the Tourist Development Office. The dimly lit, carpeted dorm room feels like a barracks. (Check-out noon. Dorm beds Rs75; doubles Rs220, with bath Rs275. 25% discount for single occupancy.) **Jimmy's Inn** (tel. 24748) is the first place you'll see after stepping off the bus. Standard rooms, all with bath, are poorly lit and somewhat polluted with bus station noise. (Check-out noon. Doubles Rs150-250.) ▓**Orchard Hut** (tel. 22507) is a wood and clay guest house and restaurant sitting atop the slope away from the Sal River, 5km from Chamba in the Panj-La Valley. Crisp *parathas* and homemade organic plum preserve will gratify your salivary glands' every desire. Enjoy your meal amidst the noise of a roaring river and a concerto of continual birdsong. Owner Prakash Dhami and his family can—and will—tell you everything you wanted to know about all things Chambiali. Call ahead or stop by the family-owned **Mami Mahesh Travels** (at the Laxmi Narayan Temple). To get to the Hut, take the Chamba-Sahoo bus from in front of the Brijeshwari Temple; get off at the Chaminu stop. Walk across the river and 20 minutes uphill; ask in the Chaminu store for directions. The Hut forms an ideal base for various treks. Accommodation ranges from simple tents to spacious doubles with homemade meals (Rs50-300). Cooking lessons are also available (Rs50).

Local cuisine can be hard to come by in Chamba. The **Olive Green Restaurant,** Temple Rd., tosses up the Chamba valley specialty *madhara*, a dish of kidney beans and curd cooked in *ghee* (Rs45). Chamba is equally well-known for its sweet-but-fiery chili sauce, *chukh*, which the bold palate can sample on gloriously deep-fried chicken available at shops on Museum Rd. Two floors above the shops, the **Park View Restaurant and Milk Bar** soothes twice-burnt tongues with the best sweets in town. Many fruit and vegetable vendors fill the steep alley between Temple and Hospital Rd.

▣ **SIGHTS.** For a synopsis of Chamba's royal and military past, head north on Museum Rd. and into the **Bhuri Singh Museum.** Named for Raja Bhuri Singh, ruler of the Chamba district from 1904-1919, the museum displays his collection of small weaponry, giant doors, musical instruments, *rumals* (a form of silk embroidery native to the valley), and other regal relics. Some of the carved stone slabs on display mark the sites of hidden springs in the hills. (Open Tu-Su 10am-5pm. Free.)

Chamba's charming collection of temples could exhaust even the most insatiable of temple appetites. The largest temple complex is that of the **Laxmi Narayan Temple,** up Temple Rd. across from the enormous Akhand Chandi Palace. The various shrines in the complex date from the 9th to the 10th centuries, when Chamba's founder commissioned the main temple and the statue of Laxmi Narayan (Vishnu) that it houses. Each temple's elaborate stone facade combines classical convention with Chamba's own highly developed local style. The copper statue of Gauri Shankar is a marvellous example of Chamba's renowned metal work. (Open daily 6am-9pm.)

A walk along the outskirts of town will take you past several other important holy sites. From the bus stand, a short climb south and east leads to the long staircase up to **Chamunda Devi Temple.** Chamunda Devi is the goddess Durga in a wrathful temper; the brass bells (meant to clear your head of worldly scheming) and stupendous view ensure that yours remains unruffled. At the northern edge of Chamba above the road to Sahoo sits the ancient and removed temple of **Vajreshwari** (Durga as the goddess of lightning). Tradition holds that this is Chamba's oldest temple, a thank-you note from Raja Sahil Varman to the family who donated the land for Chamba town. Although a number of stone carvings have been looted from the sides of the main shrine, finely crafted images of Durga, Undavi (the goddess of food), and other deities still grace its walls. Look for the Tibetan-style demonic faces on the rear of the main shrine—their presence here remains a mystery. The stone lions out front are the divine mode of transportation (not for hire).

When they weren't propitiating the gods at the temples, Chamba's 18th-century ruling elite retired to the Mughal-style corridors of the **Rang Mahal** ("Old Palace").

Dominating the upper center of Chamba, the palace currently houses the **Himachal Emporium,** a one-room shop selling *rumals*, hand-woven shawls, candleholders, and molded brass plates. Ask the shopkeeper to see the workshop upstairs, where some of these items are crafted.

NEAR CHAMBA: BHARMOUR भारमै

Bharmour, the capital of the Chamba valley kingdom from the 6th to the early 10th centuries, is a bus ride from Chamba town (3½hr.). Its temple square encloses 84 separate shrines, some of them 1100 years old. The most famous of these is the **Narsingha Temple** with its half-lion, half-man statue. Narsingha is the incarnation of Vishnu who transformed himself in order to destroy an evil spirit who could not be killed by either man or animal. Once Narsingha tasted blood, however, he kept on killing living creatures. Realizing the demonic powers within himself, he went up into the mountains where there was little to kill. The temple is supposedly built on the site where he secluded himself.

Bharmour is also the trailhead for **treks** over the Dhauladhar and Pir Panjal ranges. In the summer, you're likely to meet some of the rowdy *gaddis*, nomadic shepherds who make seasonal migrations up and down the valley. Bharmour is the launching point for the **Manimahesh Yatra,** a devotional procession that winds its way 34km up to the high-altitude lake at Manimahesh, where devotees worship and bathe in its icy waters. The procession takes place precisely 15 days after Jan-mashtami, Krishna's birthday, in September.

NEAR CHAMBA: SAHOO साह

The quiet farming village of Sahoo lies in the opposite direction, up the Sal River valley (1hr. bus ride from Chamba or a gorgeous 2hr. bike ride from the Orchard Hut). It boasts an 11th-century temple and breathtaking views of the Pir Panjal range. The **Chandra Shekhar** (moon-crowned Shiva) temple houses an ancient Shiva *linga*, said to be given to spurts of rapid and inexplicable growth—a hole had to be cut into the temple's stone ceiling to accommodate the *linga's* sky-high ambitions before a visiting priest was able to return it to a reasonable size. Today, devotees crawl through the (removed) holy ceiling-piece for luck and strength. Opposite the *linga* is a particularly fine stone sculpture of the ubiquitous heavenly vehicle, Nandi, with a ball hanging from his neck. In earlier times, when the temple bell was struck, the ball around the monolithic wonder's neck would resonate. Now, a thick layer of grease covers Shiva's carrier and muffles any sound.

KULLU कुल्लू

Kullu is tucked between two green mountains at the southern end of the Kullu Valley. At first glance, the city itself does not seem to have much to offer besides shawl shops and bus connections to bigger destinations. Given the in-season tourist glut in nearby Naggar and Manali, however, Kullu can be a pleasant stopover, offering a good look at small-town life in Himachal. Every year in early October, tourists and Indians crowd Kullu for **Dussehra,** a huge festival celebrating the 360 gods of the Himachal valley. An ideal daytrip from Kullu takes you up to the **Bijli Mahadev** ("God of Electricity") **Temple** where, legend has it, lightning strikes each year and breaks the massive *linga*, which then has to be painstakingly reassembled by a priest. Take a bus from town (Rs6) to the Chan Sari stop; from there, hike 3km uphill to the temple, which affords fantastic views and an opportunity to observe the pilgrimage rites.

🔁 ORIENTATION AND PRACTICAL INFORMATION. The main **bus station** is in the north end of town, next to the river. Across the footbridge and to the left extends the **market street,** leading to the **maidan,** Kullu's square and cricket ground. **Bhuntar Airport** is 10km to the south of town; local buses heading to and from Manali stop at the airport (Rs5), while taxis cost Rs100. **Ambassador Travel,** the only

HIMACHAL PRADESH

agent for Indian Airlines in town, has an office a short walk off the maidan on the road to Manali. **Flights** go to Delhi (M, W, and F 11:10am; US$130, under 30 US$105). **Buses** leave for: **Amritsar** (4 and 5:30pm, 14hr., Rs195); **Delhi** (5 per day 4am-5pm, 16hr., Rs225; semi-deluxe 6:15pm, 16hr., Rs280; deluxe 6:30pm, 13hr., Rs420); **Dharamsala** (5 per day 7am-8pm, Rs110-140); **Jammu** (6pm, 14hr., Rs190); **Leh** (7:30am, 48hr., Rs355); **Manali** (every 30min. 4am-7pm, 2hr., Rs20); **Manikaran** (7 per day 6:30am-3pm, 2½hr., Rs23); **Naggar** (every 30min. 4am-7pm, 1hr., Rs12); and **Shimla** (5 per day 4am-8:45pm, 9hr., Rs110-145). **Deluxe buses,** booked through **HARI Travel** in the maidan, go to: **Delhi** (6:15pm, 12hr., Rs325); **Dharamsala** (9pm, 8hr., Rs250); and **Shimla** (9pm, 8hr., Rs250). **Taxis** from the maidan can be hired to: **Delhi** (Rs5500); **Dharamsala** (Rs2500); **Haridwar** (Rs3500); and **Srinagar** (Rs7500). A **jeep** to **Leh** is Rs15,000 one-way. The **Tourist Office** (tel. 22349) is on the upper side of the maidan (open M-Sa 10am-5pm). The **State Bank of India,** 2km from the center of town, is the nearest place to exchange currency and traveler's checks (open M-F 10am-2pm, Sa 10am-noon). The **post office,** a few meters to the right off the maidan, has EMS and *Poste Restante* (open M-Sa 9:30am-5pm). **Hotel Rohtang,** at the far end of the maidan, lets you check email (Rs100 per hr.; open M-Sa 9am-7pm). **STD/ISD booths** cluster near the footbridge and in the maidan. **Postal Code:** 175101. **Telephone Code:** 01902.

■■■ **ACCOMMODATIONS AND FOOD.** Turn right at the top of the pedestrian market and walk 50m past the post office to reach **Baba Guest House** (tel. 22821), where an intelligent, friendly Baba rents tiny rooms with eagle's-nest views and access to a kitchen—budget backpacker paradise (Rs30-70). To the left of the bus station and over the footbridge is the immaculate **Aaditya Guest House** (tel. 23511), severed from the bus stand by a river, yet close enough that you can look out your window to make sure you don't miss the morning bus (doubles Rs100, with bath and carpet Rs200-400). The **Madhu Chandrika Guest House** (tel. 24395), next door, has spacious balconies that look out over the town and the surrounding mountains (dorm beds Rs40; doubles Rs150, with TV and bath Rs250; off season, 50% discount). **Hotel Bijleshwar** (tel. 22857), on the upper side of the maidan near the tourist office, lounges around a bird-and-flower-filled garden and patio restaurant (doubles with bath Rs250). Most of the food in Kullu takes the form of large, raw vegetables, or small, deep-fried ones. Kill your hankering for road-stall *samosas*, *pakoras*, and "sweets" at the pedestrian market street across the river from the bus stand. If you want to risk it, try the fried trout in the stall by the bridge. **Hotel Bijleshwar's** trout curry (Rs45) is a safer bet. In any case, be sure to stop for a beer (Rs90) and pizza (Rs40) at **Shobla Restaurant,** off the maidan; the view is astonishing, especially after a swig of potent Kingfisher (open 9am-10:30pm).

NAGGAR नाग्गर

Halfway between Kullu and Manali on the eastern side of the Beas River rests the hillside village of Naggar, blissfully blanketed by pine forests, apple orchards, and fields of cannabis. The regional capital until the mid-1600s, Naggar is now a serene little town with slate-shingled roofs, delicate temples, and perhaps the best art gallery in the Western Himalayas. Only a handful of hotels dot the village, making it an excellent place to get a sense of life in the Kullu Valley as it once was.

■ **ORIENTATION AND PRACTICAL INFORMATION.** Buses arrive and depart by the shops on the highway 1km below the **Castle.** To: **Manali** (every 45min., 1½hr., Rs12) and **Kullu** (every 45min., 1½hr., Rs15). Buses between Kullu and Manali on the other side of the river are more frequent and more reliable. Get off at Patilkahl, walk across the bridge, and then take the shortcut path along the creek in front of you; it's a 45-minute walk up to the Castle. There is a small **hospital** across from Hotel Alliance. The tiny **post office** on the narrow road below the Castle has *Poste Restante* (open M-Sa 9:30am-5pm). **Postal Code:** 175130. **Telephone Code:** 01902.

▮▮ ACCOMMODATIONS AND FOOD. Poonan Mountain Lodge (tel. 47747), 50m below the castle, blends with the traditional village architecture. The friendly owner will tell you about local traditions as you sit in the adjoining veg. restaurant. In addition to its regular rooms (doubles with tiled bath Rs200), Poonan rents a fully-equipped cottage, 1km above the village (Rs200). **Shertal Guest House** (tel. 47750), next to the castle, has rooms ranging from a dark double with common bath to a spacious room with shower and magnificent views from the balcony (singles with bath Rs500; doubles Rs125). Farther up the hill towards the Rerich gallery, **Hotel Alliance** (tel. 47763) has eagle's-nest rooms and an attached restaurant offering a melange of French and local cuisine (rooms Rs100-150, with bath Rs200-250). Also near the Castle, **Ragini Hotel** (tel. 47855) has large rooms, baths with tubs and 24-hour hot water, balconies, and a rooftop garden (rooms Rs450; off-season, Rs350). **La Purezza Hard Rock Cafe,** by the bus stop, loads you with much-needed Italian carbos before that climb up to the Castle (open daily 10am-10pm). **Chanchakhami Cafe,** on the road above the Tripuri temple, has such favorites as hummus and tofu. Before the entrance to the gallery, **Rag Cafe's** terrace serves tea while you drink in the surroundings.

▮ SIGHTS. Naggar's diminutive 504-year-old castle stands 1km up from the highway, housing a sacred slab of stone called **Jagti Patt.** Local legend says the valley's gods "transformed into honey bees endowed with great strength" to cut the hefty block and fly it up. Up the hill past the Castle Hotel, the **Tripuri Sundri Temple,** with its three-tiered pagoda roof, is the site of a local *mela* in mid-May. Further up the pine-lined road stands the **Nikolai Rerich Art Gallery.** Earlier in the century, the Russian artist N. Rerich settled here with his wife Yelema and their two sons. The house displays paintings of the mountains which uniquely capture the spirit of the Himalayas. Ask to be shown to the master's tombstone 100m below the house. The Rerich-founded **Urusvati Institute,** 200m farther, once had a faculty of leading scholars of Himalayan culture. *Urusvati* means "Light of the Morning Star," and the institute was supposed to "radiate" the sacred knowledge revealed by the mountains. Now it is the site of the **Himalayan Folk and Tribal Gallery,** which holds fine collections of traditional North Indian dress and metalwork. The gallery upstairs has some of Nikolai's earlier mystic paintings, a few works by his son Sviatoslav, and a number of contemporary paintings by local Kullu artists influenced by Rerich. (Both galleries open Tu-Sa 9am-1pm and 2-5pm. Rs10 ticket covers both.)

NEAR NAGGAR

Naggar is an ideal base for treks up the slopes of the Valley of Gods. **Himalayan Mountain Treks** (tel. 47748), at Poonam Lodge, is one of the most reliable trekking agencies in the valley (fully organized treks Rs1000 per person per day, treks with only a guide and a tent Rs500).

A hike (1-2 days) over the Chandrakhani Pass (3660m) takes you to **Malana,** a mountain village whose inhabitants claim to be descendants of Greek soldiers brought here by Alexander the Great. Malana has never come under the patronage of the Government of India Tourism Department, and visitors to Malana are not allowed to touch the villagers or the holy stones; the fine for violating this law is Rs1000. There is only one flea-plagued guest house with mattresses on the ground (Rs150), so you're better-off bringing your own tent. From here, you can continue farther, to the **Malana glacier** or to **Manikaran,** in the Parbatti Valley. The springs in Manikaran are said to cure rheumatism and soothe trekkers' strained muscles, but the town is less than charming. You're better off staying in the nearby village of **Kasol.** Raja Guest House has rooms (Rs50-100). Manikaran is the base for treks over the Pin-Parvati Pass (see **Treks around Kaza,** p. 248). Streams in both the Kullu and Parbatti Valleys are jumpin' with trout; many trekking agencies offer fishing trips (including instruction) and rent equipment. **Buses** run from Manikaran to Kullu (6 per day, 2½hr., Rs28).

HIMACHAL PRADESH

MANALI मनाली

Cradled between the mountains of the lesser Himalayas, Manali has long been the favorite hang-out of hashish-seeking hippies, Indian newlyweds, and travelers looking to rest before heading out on treks. Once serene and remote, Manali's apple orchards and pine forests are now peppered with wooden guest houses and concrete hotels as a result of the precarious situation in Kashmir which has sent tourists to Himachal Pradesh in search of a paradise lost. While the Mall and the adjoining Model Town are headquarters of the tourist invasion, the village life, friendly locals, and choice guest houses and restaurants of Old Manali are more inviting. The surrounding slopes offer superb hikes, and the nearby village of Vishisht, 3km away, is well worth a daytrip.

> **WARNING.** Manali, where cannabis grows wild, has been touted as the cool place to hang out and smoke hash, but stories of local use have been exaggerated. The drug is used by locals only under times of duress or in cold weather. Recently, harder drugs such as LSD and cocaine have hit Manali, and many predict that drug-related crimes and arrests will soon become a problem here. It may not seem so, but **hashish is illegal, even in Manali.** If you've got it, *don't* flaunt it.

TRANSPORTATION

Airport: The nearest airport is in **Bhuntar,** 52km from Manali (see **Kullu,** p. 235). **Matkon Travel** (tel. 52838), on the intersection of Old Manali Rd. and the Mall, is the agent for Indian Airlines. To **Delhi** (M, W, and F 11:10am; US$105). **Jagson Airlines** has flights to Delhi (1 per day, US$130). Open daily 9am-9pm.

Buses: The **bus stand** is smack dab in the center of the Mall. To: **Amritsar** (2pm, 14hr., Rs231); **Chamba** (2:55pm, 15hr., Rs240); **Dehra Dun** (5:15pm, Rs255); **Delhi** (5 per day 11:30am-5pm, 16hr., Rs240-265; deluxe 4:30 and 5pm, 14hr., Rs450); **Dharamsala** (5:30, 8:20am, and 6pm; 10hr.; Rs131); **Haridwar** (10am and 12:40pm, Rs235); **Keylong** (every 45 min. 4:30-9am and 2pm, 6hr., Rs60); **Kullu** (every 15min. 5am-6:30pm, 2hr., Rs20); **Leh** (10am, 2 days, Rs500); **Naggar** (every 30min. 5am-6:30pm, 1½hr., Rs10); **Shimla** (7am, 10hr., Rs135; semi-deluxe 6:30am, 6, and 7:15pm; 9hr.; Rs140); **Jammu** (4pm, 16hr., Rs215). Government deluxe buses can be booked at the **Himachal Tourism Marketing Office** (tel. 53531), on the Mall. The deluxe bus stand is at the southern end of town, a 300m walk down along the Mall. Be sure to confirm where your bus departs from. Private deluxe buses operated by **Matkon** or **Swagatam Travel** are usually cheaper and can be booked in any travel agency around town. To: **Delhi** (4:30 and 5pm, Rs400, 15hr.); **Dharamsala** (7:30pm, Rs250, 9hr.); **Leh** (6am, Rs800); **Shimla** (8:15am and 7:30pm, Rs250, 10hr.). For information on the **Manali-Leh Road,** see p. 251.

Local Transportation: Expensive **auto-rickshaws** throng Manali, Old Manali, and Vishisht. **Taxis** can be arranged at any tourist office or in front of Hotel Kunzam.

ORIENTATION AND PRACTICAL INFORMATION

Manali is structured roughly in the shape of a "Y." **The Mall** constitutes the trunk, where you'll find a **bus stand** and most services. Off either side are alleys lined with gift shops, *dhabas*, and provision stores that increase in concentration just behind and north of the bus stand. Following the left fork at the Nehru Statue leads you uphill 1km on the **Old Manali Road,** separating the **Model Town** on the left and the **Himalayan National Park** on the right, eventually making a sharp descent to the bridge over Manalsu River. Across the bridge, **Old Manali** spreads out along the uphill road to your left. Taking the right fork at the statue on top of the Mall lets you cross the **Beas River bridge.** Continuing 2km along the road upstream and turning right for a steep 1km ascent leads you to the village of **Vishisht.**

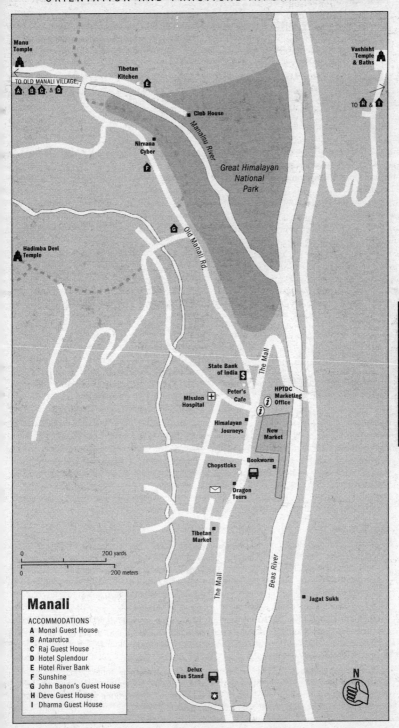

HIMACHAL PRADESH

Manu Temple

Vashisht Temple & Baths

TO OLD MANALI VILLAGE,
Ⓐ, Ⓑ Ⓒ, & Ⓓ

Tibetan Kitchen
Ⓔ

TO 🏠 & 🏠

Club House

Manalsu River

Nirvana Cyber
Ⓕ

Great Himalayan National Park

Hadimba Devi Temple

Ⓖ Old Manali Rd.

The Mall

State Bank of India
💲

Peter's Cafe

Mission Hospital ✚

HPTDC Marketing Office
ⓘ
ⓘ

Himalayan Journeys

New Market

Chopsticks

Bookworm 🚌

✉️

Dragon Tours

Tibetan Market

Beas River

0   200 yards
0   200 meters

The Mall

Jagat Sukh

Manali

ACCOMMODATIONS
A Monal Guest House
B Antarctica
C Raj Guest House
D Hotel Splendour
E Hotel River Bank
F Sunshine
G John Banon's Guest House
H Deve Guest House
I Dharma Guest House

Delux Bus Stand 🚌
✚

N

Tourist Office: Government of India Tourist Office (tel. 52175), on the Mall next to Hotel Kunzam. Open daily 10am-5pm. **HPTDC Marketing Office** (tel. 53531), on the Mall, in a large white building on your right as you face away from the bus stand, books HPTDC hotels and deluxe buses. Open M-Sa 9am-7pm, Su 10am-3pm.

Budget Travel: Plenty of Manali's travel agents offer treks (US$30 per person per day, all inclusive) and rafting trips (Rs850 and up per day). Two reliable companies are **Dragon Tours** (tel.52790; fax 52769), with offices opposite the bus stand and in Old Manali, and **Himalayan Journeys** (tel. 52365; fax 53065), just past the bus stand.

Currency Exchange: State Bank of India, Old Manali Rd., just past the Mall, abuses its monopoly with poor service and miserable rates. Accepts Thomas Cook, Barclay, Citicorp, and AmEx traveler's checks. Open M-F 10am-1:30pm, Sa 10-11:30am. The closest place to get credit card advances is in the Bank of Baroda.

Bookstore: Bookworm (tel. 52920), in the New Market behind the bus stand.

Hospital: Mission Hospital (tel. 52379), down the alley across from Hotel Kanzam. **Khana's Clinic,** Old Manali Rd. Open Sa 7:30am-1:30pm and 4-7:30pm, Su 10am-1:30pm. For holistic medicine, try **Kerala Ayurvedic Center** (tel. 54446), in Old Manali next to Tibetan Kitchen. Open M-Sa 9am-7pm.

Police: The **police station** (tel. 52326) is next to the deluxe bus stand.

Post Office: Sub Post Office, down the alley across from the bus stand and to the right of Monal Himalayan Travels. EMS available. They hold *Poste Restante* for up to a month. Open M-Sa 9am-5pm. **Postal Code:** 175131.

Internet: Valley of Gods, just off the road in Old Manali, 50m above Moondance. Plenty of computers; the carpet and pictures inside make surfing scenic. Open daily 9:30am-11pm. **Cyberia,** to the left of the bridge, is email central—the wait can be long. Rs100 per hr. Open daily 9am-10pm. **Nirvana Cybercafe,** on the road between Model Town and Old Manali, is almost as busy as Cyberia. Rs100 per hr. Open daily 10am-9pm.

Telephones: STD/ISD booths close by 11pm.

PHONE CODE	01902

ACCOMMODATIONS

Most travelers trek to Old Manali, where guest houses can't be told apart from village houses. The farther up the hill, the quieter the lodgings and the better the views. To avoid the crowds and enjoy a soak in some hot springs, head down to **Vishisht** (rickshaw from Manali Rs30 up, Rs15 down), where most guest houses are around the temple and hot baths. The area between the Old Manali Road and the Hadimba Temple, known as the **Model Town,** is an agglomeration of large hotels inundated by Indian tourists and honeymooners.

OLD MANALI

Hotel Splendour. Head up the hill in Old Manali and keep your eyes peeled for the signs on your right; 5min. down a side path takes you past other guest houses to Splendour, nested among apple orchards and cornfields. Each room has its own hot water heater and seat toilet. The friendly owners also run a restaurant and let you use the kitchen. Rooms Rs250. Off-season: singles Rs150; doubles Rs200. Pitch your own tent Rs75; 2-person tent rental Rs200.

Raj Guest House (tel. 53570), on the left of the path to Splendour. The older rooms share a bathroom and a porch with gorgeous views. The new rooms in the back all have tiled baths but lack the views. Attached garden restaurant. Older rooms Rs90; newer rooms Rs150. Off-season: Rs50/130.

Monal Guest House (tel. 53848). Perched on the top of the hill, Monal is the last house in the village. Large, wood-paneled rooms in front; rooms farther back with shared baths are perfect for long-term residents. Views are unbeatable, but bring a flashlight to find your way back at night. Front rooms Rs150; back Rs70.

Antarctica (tel. 53079), above the road to the left. All rooms have attached bath. The restaurant has a balcony. Rooms with hot showers Rs150; cold Rs100.

Hotel River Bank (tel. 53004 or 52968), to the right of the bridge in Old Manali. A typical concrete luxury complex. You'll feel like you're at a ski resort as you sip tea and recline in red velvet chairs on plush blue carpets. All rooms have attached seat toilets and hot water. Doubles Rs500, but bargain away. Off-season: Rs250.

VISHISHT

Dharma Guest House (tel. 52354), on a path 100m above the springs. The porch is ideal for meditative reading. Wooden doubles share a common toilet; the new concrete annex has rooms with extra facilities. Rs80; new rooms Rs200. Off-season: Rs50/150.

Kalp Taru Guest House (tel. 53443). A next-to-the-baths location gives you a chance to get steamed without being in the water. Doubles with bath Rs100. Off-season: Rs50.

MODEL TOWN

Sunshine (tel. 52320), halfway between the Mall and Old Manali. Each room has a private dressing room and bathroom, as well as a verandah overlooking the valley. Restaurant has an old-style dining room with a massive wooden table next to the fireplace. If you get cold, the staff supplies your fireplace with wood (Rs100 per day). Rooms Rs350. Closed Dec.-Mar.

John Banon's Guest House (tel. 52335 or 52388; fax 52392), a 5min. walk from the Mall up Old Manali Rd. One of the oldest hotels in Manali, it has its own private apple orchard prime for picking. Spacious rooms with huge windows and working fireplaces. Doubles Rs450-550. Reservations recommended one month in advance in season.

🔆 FOOD

There are a number of restaurants in Old Manali with inventive cooks—this place is heaven for a *thukpa*-tired stomach. Near the bus station, there's at least one *dhaba* down every alley. There are also many "German bakeries" which serve mean cream cheese sandwiches (Rs20) and apple strudels (Rs30).

📕 **Tibetan Kitchen,** 50m to the right of the bridge in Old Manali. This place, with tablecloths and well-decorated walls, wins the prize for cleanliness and style. Their Tibetan menu is the most exhaustive, while the Japanese and Chinese specialties are unrivaled. Hong Kong chicken Rs60. Open daily 8am-midnight.

Shiva Cafe, after the turn of the hill-road, has tasty Italian dishes and enormous servings of pudding. The covered verandah provides a happy hideout from the rain, and the garden allows you to bask in the sun. Lasagna Rs45. Open daily 8am-11:30pm.

Ristorante Italiano, across from Kunzam Hotel on the upper side of the Mall. Gabriele, the proprietor, makes Italian cheese, which he sprinkles on spaghetti bolognese for Rs90-100. *Secondi piatti* of meat (Rs80) accompanied by fresh bread and olive oil. Cap your lunch with a cappuccino (Rs15).

Chopsticks Restaurant, across the Mall from the bus stand, tries to serve authentic Tibetan/Chinese food, but since the local rice doesn't stick, chopsticks are useless, even for experts. Great Szechuan chicken Rs75. Open daily 8am-11pm.

Peter's Cafe, down a small, dingy lane in a small garden, near the State Bank. Psychedelic shack serves quiche (Rs20), pie (Rs25), and cheddar omelettes (Rs30) and garlic toast. Homemade preserves in reusable jars (Rs40). Pete has a razor-sharp wit and a collection of classical records, and he'll treat you to both. Open daily 8am-8pm.

Sher-e-Punjab, in the middle of the Mall. Authentic Punjabi food for those sick of Italian food and *momos*. Decently priced entrees (Rs30-55) and *makki-ki-roti* (Rs110) if you ask nicely. Open daily 9am-11pm.

Ranu Rooftop Cafe, in Vishisht, ensures that bathers do not run out of steam or fall behind the Manali crowd in terms of their gastronomic experience. Carbohydrates of both the pasta and *thukpa* variety. Open daily 8am-10pm.

♫ 🛍 ENTERTAINMENT AND SHOPPING

The Himachal Tourism-run **Club House** (tel. 52141), to the right of the bridge in Old Manali, offers sundry activities, not to mention a fully-stocked bar (beer Rs75.) Try your hand at billiards (Rs100 per hr.), *carom* (Rs40 per hr.), badminton (Rs60 per hr.), or just kick back in the plush lounge with one of the books from the library. (Open daily 10am-10pm.) In addition to the plethora of shawl shops on the Mall and on Old Manali Rd., the **Tibetan Market,** at the southern end of town, affords an opportunity for some hard bargaining. (Open daily 8am-10pm.)

👁 SIGHTS

HADIMBA DEVI TEMPLE. The four-tiered Hadimba Devi Temple, with a pagoda-shaped roof, is dedicated to the demoness-turned-goddess Hadimba, wife of Bhima. Valley residents claim that the king cut off the builder's hand to prevent the temple's duplication. Undaunted by the amputation, the builder trained his left hand and constructed a more elaborate temple at Tritoknath. That time, he lost his head. *(Walk 5min. along Old Manali Rd.; take a left, and follow the signs.)*

MANU TEMPLE. The Manu Temple, a pleasant 30-minute walk up the hill in Old Manali, is claimed to be the spot where Manu stepped onto the earth after a great flood. Manu, the first man to possess knowledge, and his wife Shatrupa had a series of thoughtful children who purportedly developed the world's religions. Vaulted ceilings, elaborate woodwork, and marble floors distinguish the temple, rebuilt in 1992. The townspeople appreciate foreigners who show respect by dressing appropriately and displaying reverence at the temple.

GREAT HIMALAYAN NATIONAL PARK. The Great Himalayan National Park shows visitors what the towering pine forests might have looked like before the modern architectural invasion. Moji, the manager, can arrange viewings of nature videos on Saturday afternoons. *(*Entrance at the Wildlife Information, Education, and Awareness Center, Old Manali Rd. *Open daily 10am-5pm. Rs2.)*

NEAR MANALI

The temple in Vishisht has free **hot baths,** separated for men and women (open daily 5am-9pm). Himachal Tourism runs a **Hot Bath Complex** in Vishisht, which has clean, private, tiled rooms with hot spring baths (Rs40 per person, Rs50 for 2). The **Mountaineering Institute** (tel. 52342 or 53789; fax 53509), 2km south of the bridge over the Beas River offers courses in mountaineering, skiing, and water sports throughout the year, with fees ranging from US$190 (skiing) to US$250 (a 4-week mountaineering course). Although some courses allow women, most are limited to men. The institute can also organize trips for larger groups. For more information, write to: Mountaineering Institute, H.P. 175131. Farther south is **Jagat Suk** and its glorious wood-and-stone Shiva temple. Alongside this 5000-year-old site, men play *carom* while women crush rocks to make gravel. The regular bus from Manali (every 15min. 5am-6:30pm, 30min., Rs3) will drop you in Jagat Suk, where you can check out the temple and drink *chai* with the locals. The **Rohtang Pass** (3998m), open erratically between June and September, is the only motorable way into the Lahaul-Spiti area from Manali (see **Kinnaur-Spiti Road,** below). Nowadays, it's best described as a polar dump; the place is a complete *mela* of tea tents, with debris scattered all around. But Rohtang can make for a decent trip if you're looking for high-altitude scenery without the exercise. Buses, as well as HPTDC tours (Rs150), will take you here, and you can rent fabulous fur coats on the way. Check out the creative HPPWD road advice on the way up, including slogans like "Divorce speed" and "Peep, peep, don't go to sleep."

KINNAUR-SPITI

One of the most incredible routes in the world, the road from Shimla cuts through mountains of solid rock and traverses Kinnaur, Spiti, and Lahaul, eventually crossing the Rohtang Pass and descending into Manali. The ride can be harrowing—at times the river churns violently hundreds of feet below the road, and you'll see the locals sitting next to you literally praying that the bus doesn't do the same. The reward for accepting the risks of transit here is an up-close and personal experience of some of the most awesome natural beauty in all of India. Each of the three regions incised by the road presents a distinct sublime landscape. The deep Sutlej Valley connects fertile valleys inhabited by the Kimmauri, round hut dwellers who all share the surname "Nogi", and a unique blend of religious traditions. The Spiti River cuts through mountain deserts dotted by green oases of barley fields and Tibetan enclaves. After crossing the Kunsum Pass, you enter the Lahaul Valley, a land of glaciers and moss-covered granite too rocky to sustain any life outside of fearless grass and herds of wild horses.

The road was opened to outsiders in 1992, and for some time Public Works Department (PWD) rest houses were the only accommodation options. Today, many lodges, hotels, and guest houses line the route. The road is technically open between June and October, but it is unlikely that you will make it through without encountering at least one road block or significant delay (mudslides, stone avalanches, etc.). The road conditions change in minutes, and bus drivers mostly rely on updates from passing vehicles. If you're traveling by bus, you can usually get off, cross the obstacle on foot, hike to the next town, and then catch another bus from there—but make sure you can reach the next town by nightfall. Also, hiking in the rain can be very dangerous on certain stretches of the road as rain-softened ground tends to loosen large boulders, which then come rolling down the slopes at speeds that make them difficult to dodge. Non-Indians traveling between Jangi and Sundo must obtain an **inner-line permit** (available from the sub-divisional magistrates in Shimla, Rampur, Peo, Kaza, Chamba, Kullu, Keylong, and the home office in Delhi; for more information, see **Warning,** p. 218). The **Kaza-Manali Road** is theoretically open from mid-June to mid-September, but weather makes it unreliable as well. **There are no facilities for currency exchange along the route.**

THE KINNAUR-SPITI ROAD

SUTLEJ VALLEY. From Shimla, the road climbs to **Narkanda** (60km, 2½hr. by bus) and then descends steeply to **Rampur** (120km, 3½hr. by bus). From **Jeuri** (or Jeori), 23km farther, you can reach the Kinnauri village of **Sarahan** (p. 244), site of the Bhima-Kali Temple. The green concrete building by the road in Jeuri has simple beds (Rs40)—an option if you get stranded there. Two hours up the road, a road cut into the rock takes you past a hydroelectric facility to **Wangtu**, the trailhead for treks over the **Bhaba Pass.** Another hour of prayers gets you to **Karcham,** where you can catch a bus heading up **Sangla** in the Lower Sangla Valley (see p. 244). You can get a bed in one of the shacks across the bridge over Baspa River (Rs50). From Karcham, it's one hour to **Rekong-Peo** (p. 245), the district headquarters of Kinnaur and gateway to **Kalpa** (p. 245), the winter residence of Shiva. From Peo onwards, the landscape becomes arid, and military bases multiply as you near the Tibetan border. You will need to show your permit and passport in **Jangi**—the bus will wait for you. At **Khab** (or Kabo), 70km (5hr. by bus) from Peo, the road turns left and starts climbing to the plateau above. In the middle of this brown plain is a splash of green: the village of **Kah.** Farther down, in **Yang Thang,** you can take a detour to see the Tibetan village of **Nako** (p. 246), cradled in a high altitude bowl with a green lake. The only guest houses around are in Nako, a 2km hike or 10km bus ride from Yang Thang. You can stay in **Chango**, 100km (3½hr.) from Peo, featuring a 13th-century temple supposedly hewn out of a single stone in one day.

SPITI VALLEY. The bus then goes through **Shalkar**, the checkpost at **Sumdo** (the Spiti boundary), and the truck-stop **Hurling** en route to the millennium-old *gompa* at **Tabo** (p. 246). After Sumdo, the responsibility for road maintenance passes from an army organization to the Public Works Department, and the transfer in authority shows—the ride becomes very bumpy. The 47km Tabo-Kaza stretch passes the villages of **Poh** and **Shichling**. A few hundred meters after Shichling, a road branches off up to **Dhankar Gompa**. Down the road 1km, a bridge leads off to the **Pim Valley**. Between Hurling and Tabo, and between Poh and Shichling, the road passes under mountains of mud—**do not attempt to walk this route in the rain.** From **Kaza** (see p. 247), the road takes another turn for the bumpier as it winds its way 50km up to the village of **Losar** (5hr.). Losar has two small guest houses and serves as the final launching point for the **Kanzam-La Pass** (4500m), 18km (1½hr.) away.

LAHAUL VALLEY. After the pass, the road drops steeply to the four tents that comprise **Batal**, in the Lahaul Valley (see p. 249); beds are available here. An 18km hike takes you to **Chandratal Lake**. After Batal, there is a *dhaba* in **Chota Dhara** (12km) and tented accommodations in **Chatru** (16km) before the route turns back onto a main road at **Gramphoo** (17km). From here it's a four-hour ride over the polar dump of Rohtang Pass to **Manali** (64km). The Lahaul Valley gets a lot of snow in winter, and the opening date of the segment between Losar and Gramphoo is entirely dependent on how long the snow takes to melt.

S A R A H A N सराहान

Nested 800m above the Sutlej River Valley, the Kinnauri village of Sarahan is notable for its impressive wooden **Bhima-Kali Temple** complex. The temple used to be the site of human sacrifice, until the practice was banned by the British. Inside the Durga shrine, the council of marble Buddhas, mountain deities, and Hindu gods is the most conspicuous evidence of the rich mingling of beliefs and traditions that characterizes the Kinnauri region. The views of the snowclad Shrimakand peak, endless fruit orchards, and groves of jacaranda pine provide a perfect setting for walks through the surrounding area. The Himalayan pheasant farm in the forest above the village is worth a visit. Buses from Jeuri go to Sarahan (4 per day 8:30am-5:30pm, 1hr., Rs11). The **Temple Rest House** (tel. 74248), in front of the temple, has brand new doubles with shining toilets (Rs200) and a grimy, cheap 12-bed dorm (beds Rs25). The huge **Shrimakand Hotel** (tel. 74234) is expensive, but the spacious eight-bed dormitory is a good deal, with pleasant views and large royal bathroom (beds Rs85). **Ajay Chinese Food,** next to the temple entrance, serves delicious noodles and Shanghai *momos*. **Telephone Code:** 01782.

LOWER SANGLA VALLEY सग्ंला

After a perilous 17km bus ride on a road carved out of the mountain face, with the Baspa River dashing hundreds of feet below, the deep canyon suddenly widens, and the fertile Sangla Valley unfolds in all its splendor. For centuries, the natural barriers of the wild river and the snow-capped peaks isolated the area from the surrounding region, and its distinct vegetative and cultural features developed free from outside influences. The area between **Sangla** and the last village of **Chitkuhl** is unforgettable. A day hike past charming villages allows you to witness amazing transformations of vegetation and landscape every few hundred meters. The valley was not open to outsiders (including Indians) until 1992, so **be very careful about where you wander.** If you happen upon a village festival, it's best to suppress your curiosity and head on—celebrations are often an extremely private affair.

From Sangla, a 2km road turning left past the police station leads to the village of **Kamru**, a former capital of the Baspa Kingdom. Perched atop a rock overlooking the entrance to the valley are a Buddhist temple with rich Tibetan wall-paintings and a Hindu shrine adorned with exquisite woodcarving. Looming above all of this is a temple dedicated to one of the mountain deities and guarded by a legion of lizards; ask permission before entering. From Chitkuhl it's another week farther up the valley and over a pass to the holy town of **Gangotri** (see p. 154) in U.P. You must be fully self-sufficient for this trek; there are no settlements of any type on the way. The **bus** from Karcham (8 and 10am, 1hr., Rs10) drops you off in **Sangla.**

Buses from Sangla go to **Peo** (7, 7:30am, and 3pm; 2hr.; Rs20) and **Rampur** (1pm). In the market in Sangla, there are a few eateries, guest houses, and a **National Travelers** branch (tel. 42358), which organizes treks. The wooden **Mount Kailash Guest House,** just off the road in Sangla, has a clean, four-bed dorm (beds Rs75) and several doubles (Rs300-400). On the first floor, there is a restaurant and an **STD/ISD** telephone. **Banjara Camps,** 6km up from Sangla, offers luxury tents with attached toilets (Rs1000, includes 3 meals and 2 snacks). Six kilometers along the route before you reach Rakchham village, **Fayal Guest House** has double rooms (Rs200-300), a dorm, and a restaurant serving local specialties. Down the path past Fayal is **Ganga Gardenview Guest House,** offering doubles (Rs250), local cuisine, and generous apple orchards. In Chitkul, **Chiranjan Guest House** has doubles (Rs100-250).

REKONG-PEO (PEO) पिओ

Halfway between Shimla and Tabo, Peo serves as the district headquarters of Kinnaur. Just off the main road, the town is a small collection of concrete military barracks, *dhabas*, and market stalls that do not merit longer than a few hours' visit. **Lavi Fair,** in the first week of November, however, is not to be missed. A variety of goods, including the prized Pashmina wool, dried fruits, and horses, are traded on the grounds near the District Commissioner's office. Peo is also famous for its nearby forests (10min. walk from the center of town). The site of a *kalachakra* ceremony performed by the Dalai Lama in 1992, a **gompa** with a massive statue of the Buddha is 20 minutes uphill from Peo, and the village of Kalpa (see below), is only 3km away. An overnight stay in Peo might be necessary if you need to catch an early morning bus. Although **buses** also stop in the market, it is better to catch them at the bus stand (a 10min. walk away) since the vehicles are usually packed by the time they reach the market. Buses run to: **Chandigarh** (5:30am, 15hr., Rs180); **Kalpa** (7:30, 9:15am, 1, 3:15, and 5:15pm; 30min.; Rs5); **Kaza** (7:30am, 13hr., Rs105); **Nako** (1pm, 5hr., Rs40); **Rampur** (11 per day, 2hr., Rs20); and **Sangla** (9:15am, 2hr., Rs20). The additional district magistrate that issues **inner-line permits** (see p. 218) for the road between Jangi and Sundo has an office on the first floor of the administrative complex near the market (open M-F 9am-5pm). The **police station** is in the same building. The **district hospital** is 2km above the town, on the road to Kalpa (open 24hr.). The **post office** is next to the bus stand (open M-Sa 9am-1pm and 2-5pm). **Postal Code:** 172107. **Telephone Code:** 017852.

The **Fairyland Hotel** (tel. 22477), above the market, has simple, clean rooms and an attached restaurant (doubles Rs220, with bath and 24hr. hot water Rs330). **Mayur Guest House** (tel. 22771), next door, is another option (dorm beds Rs40; rooms Rs125). The **Shivling View Guest House** (tel. 22421), near the bus stand, has carpeted rooms with hot showers, TVs, and a restaurant (doubles Rs300-400).

KALPA कल्पा

The village of Kalpa, or Chini-Gaon ("Chinese Village"), is noteworthy for its proximity to **Kimmer Kailash,** where, according to Hindu mythology, Shiva himself resides. It is believed that he moves to Kalpa's temple in the winter to escape the cold. Aside from its religious distinction, Kalpa offers a glimpse into traditional Kinnauri village life. Age-old festivals synthesizing traditions of Hinduism, Buddhism, and various mountain cults dominate the calendar; among these, **Fullaich,** the festival of flowers in September, is the most famous.

Kalpa's nucleus is a handful of wood and stone houses and Kinnauri shrines crammed onto an outcrop overlooking the valley. The rest of the village spreads up the ridge, and getting from one place to another can be a small trek in itself, but plentiful apricots, apples, plums, and blackberries along the way sweeten the climb. To reach Kalpa, walk from the bus stand along the road to the left until you reach Shivalik View Guest House. Behind the guest house begins the 3km path that takes you through chilgoza pine woods and past village houses (see below). Buses leave from the market and the **bus stand**. To: **Peo** (5 per day, Rs5) and **Shimla** (6am, 12hr., Rs120). From the market, the stone path leads to a paved road; turn right and walk 400m to reach **Aucktong Guest House** (tel. 26019), with bright flowers out front (doubles Rs200). The family prepares meals for their guests. The **Shivalik Guest House** (tel. 26158), just to the left of where the stone path reaches the road, offers rooms ranging in size and quality of view (singles Rs150; doubles Rs400). For luxury digs, head farther down to the left to **Kimmer Villa** (tel. 26079), offering luxurious rooms with a terrace (Rs900). Occasionally, it is also possible to stay in a village house—ask around the market. Food is available in the hotels and in the **Snow White Coffee House** in the market. Before leaving, check out the superb views from the soccer field by the school. The **sub-post office** is next to the temple (open M-Sa 9am-5pm). **Postal Code: 172108. Telephone Code: 017852.**

🚶 **TREKS AROUND KALPA.** The most popular trek within Kalpa itself is to **Chaka** (2hr. hike, one-way), a plateau above the village that makes an ideal camping or picnic spot. But Kalpa can also serve as a starting point for longer treks. The famed **Parikrama trek** begins at **Thangi** (60km from Kalpa, approachable by road) and ends 3-4 days later in Chitkul, with nights spent in a cave in the middle of the mountain. The descent to Chitkul is extremely steep, so walk in the opposite direction only if you wish to really challenge your knees. There are villages and shepherd huts on the way; tents and food supplies are therefore not necessary. Sleeping bags and good shoes, however, are a must as you reach altitudes of over 5000m. The climb can be done in August and September without any mountaineering equipment. **Timbuline Tent Camps** (tel. 26006), in Kimmer Villa, can arrange guides for Rs500 per day. The **National Travellers** office (tel. 22248), in Peo's market under the Fairyland Hotel, can also help. A seven-day trek takes you from **Wangtu** (3hr. by bus from Peo) over the Bhaba Pass to Pim Valley and Spiti. The most difficult route in this region—and one that should only be attempted by seasoned trekkers—is the trail leading up **Kinnaur Kailash** (6050m). The base of the mountain is in **Powari,** 20km from Kalpa. Expect the trek to take two days each way.

NAKO नाको

Fringing a small green lake in a high altitude bowl, this village of stone walls and mud-roof houses is one of the first fully Tibetan settlements along the way; the surrounding ridges are dotted by mud *gompas*, prayer flags, and piles of *mani* stones. The barren hills contrast sharply with the greenery of Kinnaur, and the vistas of the deep Spiti canyon and the distant white mountains complete the picture of this region's distinct landscape. A seven-hour hike takes you to an abandoned monastery near the Tibetan border where you can spend the night provided you bring a sleeping bag and food. A daily **bus** runs from to Nako from Peo (1pm, 5hr., Rs52) and returns the next morning at 6pm. You can also reach Nako by taking the Kaza- or Shalkar-bound bus and getting off at **Yang Thang**. From there it is a steep, 2km walk. To continue from Nako to Spiti, walk down and catch the Kaza bus that passes through Yang Thang (frequent after 11am). **Loulan Guest House,** next to the bus stand, has dorm beds (Rs50) and doubles with baths (Rs200-300). It also has the only *dhaba* in town, serving the local barley brew on request. Another guest house 100m up the path to the left has rooms (Rs200) and a porch where you can sleep (Rs25) if everything else is full.

TABO ताबो

The tiny hamlet of Tabo is home to some 350 intensely devout people, whose mud huts cluster around the Tabo *gompa* near the river. Tabo remained in virtual isolation until the Sino-Indian border disputes of the 1950s, when the geopolitical importance of this region brought it to center stage. Today the area is home to several Indian military outposts, and **foreigners must obtain a permit before visiting.**

Two **buses** pass through Tabo every day. The bus to Peo arrives any time after 10am (9hr., Rs120), and the bus to Kaza is due after 4pm (2hr., Rs30). Tabo's **Primary Health Center** (tel. 33325), at the edge of town, offers treatment and medicine and operates on donations (open M-Sa 9am-1pm and 3-5pm). The closest **police** assistance is in Sumdo or Kaza. The **post office** is located farther down the cow path in a barn (open M-Sa 10am-3pm). If the postmaster isn't there (most of the time he isn't), ask around for his whereabouts; you can usually find him having tea in one of the nearby *dhabas*. There is one **STD/ISD** booth at the back side of the Tenzin Restaurant behind the Temple Guest House. **Postal Code:** 172113. **Telephone Code:** 01906.

The wooden **Monastery Guest House** (tel. 33315) has a number of clean doubles (Rs150-250) and a spacious dorm (beds Rs50). Ask the receptionist to let you into the library, where you can read up on Buddhist thought or Tibetan *thankas* (open M-Sa 1-7pm). **Ajanta Guest House** (tel. 33312), also near the temple, has carpeted doubles with common baths (Rs200 second floor, Rs150 first floor). Food options are limited to the monastery restaurant and the Tenzin *dhaba* across the street, both with identical menus including round bread, *thukpas*, and *momos* (both open 5:30am-9:30pm). **Banjara Camps,** 4km outside Tabo in Kurith, a village of 22 (including sheep and goats) offers luxury tents with double beds and private baths (Rs1100, all meals included). In 2000, after performing the Kalachakra ceremony in Kyi, the Dalai Lama will offer four days of prayer in Tabo (Aug. 16-20).

🔳 **SIGHTS.** According to an ancient inscription, Tabo's founding has been dated to AD 996. The **Tabo Gompa** is the largest monastic complex in Spiti, as well as one of the largest in the Spiti valley, and one of the holiest sites in all of Trans-Himalayan Buddhist territory. Following the massive cultural purges of Tibet by the Chinese government, Tabo assumed the role of the treasury of Tibetan art. On the *gompa*'s 1000th birthday, the Dalai Lama came to perform the sacred **Kalachalena** ceremony, a rite of initiation, rejuvenation, and prayer offered once every four years. The monastery consists of what are believed to be five temples from the original settlement and four shrines that were added at a later date. At the core of the complex lies the Temple of the Enlightened Gods, otherwise known as the **Assembly Hall.** At the center, depicted turning the wheel of law, is a statue of the four-fold Vainocana, the divine being regarded by Vajnayana Buddhism as one of the spiritual sons of Adibuddha, the self-creative primordial Buddha. On brackets along the wall are stucco images of the other 33 deities of the pantheon. Hidden in darkness, the sanctum immediately behind Vainocana is richly adorned with wall paintings depicting the life of the Buddha. In the anteroom of the hall, ask the *lama* to show you the **Bom-khang,** the Temple of Wrathful gods. A *lama* shielded by protective meditation twice a day performs a secret ceremony to appease the fierce deities. Daily prayers are performed in the hall every morning at 6am. To the right of the Assembly Hall is the **Maitreya Temple,** with a 6m-high statue of the bodhisattva of the future. To the left is the **Mystic Mandala Temple,** where the initiation to monkhood takes place. Above the complex, on the sheer cliff-face overlooking the town, are a series of **caves** which once functioned as monastic dwellings. With a flashlight, you can see dim traces of the paintings that once adorned these walls. *(To visit the temples, ask at the reception of the monastery guest house for the temple keeper, and make sure to bring your own flashlight.)*

KAZA काज़ा

Strategically situated in the middle of the valley, Kaza has traditionally been the trading center of Spiti. Half an old village and half a government post, Kaza has become a base for travelers searching after the secrets of the long forbidden land. New hotels spring up every year, and the millennial **Kalachakra** ceremony in Kyi Gompa (Aug. 2-15, 2000) promises only to further the trend.

THE SPITI SPITE While tourists have been the invaders in recent years, the Spiti Valley has a history of periodical raiding by the Gorkhas and the Ladhakis. Unable to repel these intruders with force, the Spitians resorted to cunning. From posts on high cliffs (*dhankar*), watchmen could spot the invaders approaching and alert the people the people by lighting signal fires. The duly warned villagers would retreat to the safety of the high plateaus, descending only after the raiders left, empty-handed. Once, however, the Ladakhis managed to outsmart the Spitians by digging in for the winter in the valley. Unable to survive the cold months on the hills, the Spitians, pretending to accept defeat, returned to the valley and prepared a feast at Dhankar Gompa to honor their conquerors. The unsuspecting Ladakhis, jubilant in their victory, celebrated wildly. As the party progressed into the night with alcohol flowing freely, the Spitians brought the Ladakhis one by one to the cliffs and pushed them over the edge.

Both **Old Kaza** and **New Kaza** lie between the **main road** and the **river**—a small, often dry, **stream** separates the two. The **bazaar** and eateries are all in Old Kaza, while the **hospital, police station,** and government administrative buildings are in the new town. The **bus stand** is just off the main road in Old Kaza. Bus service to **Manali** (4am, 12hr., Rs100) begins in Spring in the Lahaul valley, sometime between early June and mid-August, and continues until October. Buses also go to: **Kibber** via **Kyi** (2pm, 1½hr., Rs12); **Lasar** (9am, 3½hr., Rs40); **Mikim,** in Pin Valley (9am, 2hr., Rs20); and **Peo** (7:30am, 12hr., Rs120) via **Tabo** (3hr., Rs35). Bus schedules depend on the whims of weather and drivers. The **hospital** (tel. 22218), in a big shed in New Kaza, runs an **ambulance** service. The **police** station and the sub-divisional magistrate office, which grants permits for the onward journey to Kinnaur, are both in New Kaza. The **post office** in Old Kaza, two minutes from the road, sells stamps (open M-F 9:30am-5:30pm). There's an **STD/ISD** booth near the market in Old Kaza (open daily 6am-10pm). **Postal Code: 172114. Telephone Code: 01906.**

Lodging in Kaza is available from April to November. In August 2000, due to the Kalachakra in Kyi, hotels are likely to fill up. **Mahabaudha** (tel. 22232), at the top end of the market road in Old Kaza, has the cleanest rooms in town (common bath with hot water) and a traditional Tibetan kitchen (doubles Rs150). **Snowlion** (tel. 22525), a few meters above, on the main road, offers rooms with baths and pleasant views from the porch (doubles Rs200). **Sakya's Abode** (tel. 22254), across the stream in New Kaza, is where tour groups stay (dorm beds Rs50; singles with bath Rs150; doubles with hot shower Rs350-500). **Milarepa** (tel. 22234), next door, has basic rooms (doubles Rs160-185). **Il Pomo d'Oro,** left of the market, is run by a globe-trotting Italian family who are a great resource for local wisdom. The veg. dishes (Rs50-80) display an artistic inventiveness, while the tender meats (Rs100) reveal the touch of a master chef. Try the rum-filled *tiramisu* (Rs50), and camp out in the garden if you cannot find your way back. A number of *dhabas* along the market serve *dal* and noodles; the one on the second floor near the bus station is frequented by bus drivers and serves as the best source for road information. The **bakery** next to Snowlion has whisperingly crisp *samosas* and tender round breads.

TREKS AROUND KAZA. The most popular trek takes you through the Pin Valley National Park and over the Pin-Parvati pass to **Manikaran** (6 days), where there are soothing hot springs and bus connections to Kullu and Manali. From Kaza, take a bus to **Mikim** (9am, 1hr., Rs15), where a *jula* will transport you on a rope across the river to the trailhead at Kaar village—ask for Chine Dorge, who can arrange guides for your trek. Instead of turning west over Pin-Parvati, you can continue south over Bhaba pass to **Wangtu** on the Shimla-Peo road (5 days).

NEAR KAZA

The largest fort monastery in Spiti, **Kyi** rests on the top of a cliff 12km from Kaza. Home to 1000 *lamas*, the monastery has an exquisite collection of *thankas*. The *gompa* has received a major face-lift in preparation for the **Kalachakra** ceremony: a road was cut through sand and stone to connect the brand new monastery guest house to the village, a large assembly hall was constructed on the hill, solar panels were installed, and repairs were made to the temples. The area will be incredibly busy from August 3rd to 15th, 2000. Large tents near the village will provide extra accommodations. To get to Kyi, put your faith in the erratic **bus** from Kaza (2pm), or just walk. If, on the way, a smiling young man in jeans whizzes past you in a Hyundai, you have just had the honor of a brush with His Holiness, the 19th incarnation of Kyi Gompa's head *lama*.

Perched on a hilltop in the shadow of the imposing Pasargla mountain, **Kibber** is a Tibetan village of white mud houses surrounded by pea and barley fields. At an altitude of 4250m, Kibber is reputed to be one of the world's highest villages reachable by motor vehicle. Kibber and the adjoining Kibber wildlife sanctuary offer many amazing day hikes and treks and a feeling of remoteness that has vanished from most other spots in the valley. A daily **bus** leaves Kaza (2pm, 1½hr., Rs12) and loops around at Kibber. If the bus driver is having a bad day, though, you might have to hike the 18km stretch or you can take a taxi (Rs250). The **Resang Hotel,** at the village entrance, has doubles with baths and a kitchen (Rs150). Farther down the road, **Pasargla Guest House** charges inflated prices for its rather bleak rooms (doubles Rs300, with bath Rs500). Many travelers report pleasant stays in village houses (Rs60-100 per night, including food)—ask around. In the village there is a huge prayer wheel and a *gompa* for curing spiritual afflictions and a "hospital" (a local healer) for bodily ones (open M-Sa 9am-1pm and 3-5pm).

Dhankar Gompa, named for its precarious location (*dhankar* means "cliff"), was one of the first fort monasteries incorporated into Spiti's defense system. It was also the site of a grisly feast (see **The Spiti Spite,** p. 248). The *gompa* is an 8km hike up from the road near Shichling. It is 20km from Kaza to Shichling, and you can either take the **Peo** bus (7:30am, 1hr., Rs15) or hitch a ride on one of the numerous trucks heading to a construction site nearby. The views and artwork here are amazing, and the *gompa* provides beds for Rs50.

LAHAUL VALLEY

With glaciers within a hand's reach, the canyon of the Chandra River takes you back to the end of the ice age. The valley below is watered by fresh water springs and melted snow, its grassy pastures grazed upon by wild horses. Above, framed by majestic peaks and massive glaciers, **Chandrathal Lake** is the jewel of the valley.

When road conditions permit, the Kullu-Kaza **bus** runs through the valley between **Gramphoo** and Batal. Many visitors, however, opt to hike the bumpy dirt road on foot. Situated on the Manali-Keylong road, Gramphoo's two *dhabas* have beds available (Rs50). Expect to be joined in bed by shepherds or family members at any time. It is 17km to **Chatru,** where food and tented accommodation (Rs30) are available; bring a sleeping bag unless you want to freeze to death. Chatru is the trailhead for a trek over the Hamta Pass to Manali. The hike takes two days on the way down and three days to return, and it can get incredibly wet during the monsoons. From Chatru, another 16km takes you to **Shkota Dhara,** where there is rice and *dal*, a campground, and accommodation in the PWD rest house for an outrageous Rs1000. Fortunately, it's only 12km to **Batal,** where there are cheap tents and bowls of *thukpa*. After the bridge in Batal, the road forks: the right branch scales the Kunzum-La Pass, while the left one stretches for 18km through the valley until it reaches **Chandrathal Lake.** There is an idyllic campground nearby Alternatively, you can descend to Chandrathal on a narrow path that starts at the *gompa* on the Kunzum-La Pass. From Chandrathal, it is another three days through high altitudes to **Baralacha-La Pass** on the Manali-Leh road. There are no accommodations between Batal and Baralacha-La, and the closest medical assistance is in Keylong.

HIMACHAL PRADESH

JAMMU जम्मु AND KASHMIR کشمیر

The northernmost state in India, Jammu and Kashmir rolls across 222,000 sq. km of mountains, valleys, and plateaus, only two-thirds of which are in fact controlled by India—the northwest and northeast portions of the state are ruled by Pakistan and China respectively. Kashmir is India's most volatile region, and travelers are advised not to visit the western part of the state, which is currently the site of an armed insurgency. So far, the violence has been confined to this area, which includes the predominately Muslim Kashmir Valley and the region of Jammu, populated by Dogra Hindus. The beautiful capital of Srinagar is overrun with army encampments and considered too risky to visit by most foreign state departments. The eastern part of the state, comprised of the Tibetan Buddhist regions of Ladakh and Zanskar, remains free from violence.

Kashmir's troubles began when India was partitioned along religious lines in 1947. Although the population of Kashmir was predominantly Muslim, the Hindu raja did not want to let his kingdom become part of Pakistan *or* India—and most Kashmiri Muslim leaders agreed with him. In late 1947, however, thousands of Pathan tribesmen, supplied with arms by Pakistan, crossed the border in an attempt to force Kashmir into Pakistan. Desperate, the maharaja turned his state over to India in exchange for military help. The Indian government accepted the offer, ensuring that a plebiscite would be held to determine whether the Kashmiri people, and not just the maharaja, wanted to join India. When the shooting stopped, however, Pakistan held a large chunk of Kashmir, and in 1962, China annexed the area of the state now known as Aksai Chin. India and Pakistan went to war over Kashmir again in 1965, but no territory changed hands. The 1948 cease-fire line remains the de facto India-Pakistan border, and the plebiscite promised by India has never been held. Kashmir is important to both India and Pakistan—as the only state with a Muslim majority, Kashmir is a vindication of India's tolerant secularism; and the desire to control the state is also a literal extension of Pakistan's founding theoretical precept (that all of South Asia's Muslims belong in a separate homeland). Within Kashmir, arguments have been made for the region's remaining part of India, joining Pakistan, and becoming an independent nation.

Since the 1947 conflict, both India and Pakistan have worked to integrate their slices of Kashmir into their respective nations. During the 1950s and 60s, the Indian portion of Kashmir remained somewhat autonomous, with a special status under India's constitution. But during the 1970s and 80s, the prominent Kashmiri leader Sheikh Abdullah, who had at times leaned toward independence, and his son Farooq Abdullah, who succeeded him, moved closer to Delhi. Kashmiri fears of absorption into India led to an outbreak of violence in 1989. Since that time, the western half of Indian-held Kashmir has been battered by the Jammu and Kashmir Liberation Front (JKLF), fighting for total independence; by various Islamic groups fighting for a merger with Pakistan; and by the Indian army which now occupies the state. While India accuses Pakistan of supplying arms to the rebels, human rights groups accuse the Indian army of torturing and summarily executing its opponents. In 1995, five foreign tourists were taken hostage in Kashmir; one of them was executed. Since then, Kashmir has shakily come under India's control, and elections were held in the state in May and September 1996, with decent voter turn-out. The large scale intrusion across the line of control in Kargil in early 1999 nearly escalated into another Indo-Pakistani war. With this increase in guerilla activity throughout the state Kashmir's future is once again uncertain.

AFGHANISTAN

CHINA

Disteghil Sar
7785m

Rakaposhi
7788m

UNDER
PAKISTANI
ADMINISTRATION

Gilgit

K2
8611m

Masherbrum
7821m

BALTISTAN

Nanga Parbat
8126m

KARAKORAM RANGE

UNDER
CHINESE
ADMINISTRATION

LINE OF ACTUAL CONTROL

Shyok River

Kargil

LADAKH

Sonamarg   Dras   Mulbekh

Baramula

Srinagar

Spituk   Leh

Lamayuru   Alchi   Tikse

Fulmarg

Khilanmarg   Pahalgam

Anantnag

Nun Kun
7135m

Hemis

LADAKH RANGE

TIBET
(CHINA)

Kishtwar

ZANSKAR

Padum

ZANSKAR RANGE

Indus River

PIRPANJAL RANGE

Batoti

Kud

Chenab River

Taglang
La Pass

RUPSHU

Jammu

Kathua

Chamba

Keylong

Manali

UNDER
CHINESE
ADMINISTRATION

OFFICIAL
INDO-PAKISTANI
BORDER

HIMACHAL
PRADESH

PAKISTAN

Jhelum River

VALE OF KASHMIR

N

Govt. of India statement:
The external boundaries of India are
neither correct nor authenticated.

PUNJAB

Jammu and Kashmir

HIGHLIGHTS OF JAMMU AND KASHMIR

■ The beautiful medieval town of **Leh** (p. 252), at 3500, is a base for treks through the surrounding mountain ranges and excursions to the *gompas* which dot the Indus valley.
■ Approached by the highest motorable pass in the world, the beautiful **Nubra Valley** (p. 259) features flower-filled villages, sand dunes, wild camels, and stunning views of the Karakoram.

THE MANALI-LEH ROAD

Two roads connect Leh to the rest of the world: the Manali-Leh Road and the Srinagar-Leh Road. Each is a two-day-plus haul involving crossing several passes well over 5000m. These roads are supposed to be open from mid-June to mid-September, but they can be washed out for days or even weeks by rains and mud-slides (if you're on a tight schedule and can get a seat, you might want to fly to Leh).

The **Manali-Leh Road** is perhaps one of the most beautiful overland journeys on the planet. The world's second-highest motorable road crosses the Rohtang Pass (3980m) to reach the rainshadow, and then the Baralacha-La (4892m) and Taglang-La (5325m) passes, before descending to Upshi and following the Indus River to Leh. **Bring warm clothes:** it can get below freezing at the high passes. The landscape changes constantly—the lush, green valleys of Manali give way to rugged gorges and barren plateau at first, and then to towering Himalayan peaks and sandstone cliffs. The trip ends when you enter green valleys speckled with herds of goats. Local and deluxe buses leave Manali (10 and 10:30am, Rs500/1000). It rarely rains along this road, but when it does, the muddy hills dissolve, taking the road with them. You may have to get off the bus and hike past the obstruction. Buses on the other side will usually take you on if you show them your ticket.

> **WARNING.** Following the large-scale Pakistani intrusion across the Line Of Control (LOC) in spring 1999, India has cemented its position in the Dras-Kargil area, leading to increased militant activity in northern and western Kashmir. Traveling on the **Srinagar-Leh Road** may be risky. If you do decide to travel, stay within the limits of the road, where a strong military presence reduces the risks.

The bus first descends into the Lahaul Valley, with an overnight stop in Keylong, Lahaul's administrative center; it leaves the next morning (4am). In Keylong, **Gyespa Hotel** (tel. (01900) 22207) has rooms with private toilets (Rs200) and hot showers (Rs250). At sunrise, the bus reaches **Darcha** (1hr.; *dhabas*, tents Rs35) the trailhead for treks into the **Zanskar Valley.** Over the next two to three hours, the bus climbs the main Himalayan ridge, crossing it at **Baralacha-La** (4892m). The three-day trail for **Chandratal Lake** begins (see p. 249). The first tea stop is in Bharatpur (tents Rs35), 3km below Baralacha-La. A gentle descent into a vast plain brings you to **Sarchu** (4hr.). After crossing the plain, the road makes 27 turns, climbing 1000m to cross the Zanskar range at **Lunga-lacha-La** (5059m). From here, it's "badlands" territory, with mounds of dried mud hanging precariously over the road. In **Pang** (8hr.; tents Rs30-50), the driver stops for lunch. After crossing an unimpressive, nameless pass, the road enters the plains of **Rupshu**. At the end of the plains below the glacier-lined **Taglang-La** (5325m) pass (12hr.) there are thousands of sheep, Pashmina-producing goats, and views of the Karakoram range and the Great Himalayas. The bus then descends into the Ladakhi village **Rumtse** (14hr.), dashing through more villages and *gompas* before it reaches **Upshi** (16hr.). From then on, it's smooth sailing down the main road to **Leh** (18hr.).

LEH

The capital of the former kingdom of Ladakh, Leh is remarkably distinct from cities farther south in Kashmir. In the middle of the Indus valley, halfway between Punjab and Yarkand on the "southern" silk route and halfway between the Tibetan plains and Kashmir, its location at the corner of a 3500m desert plateau has made it a vibrant meeting-place for Tibetan Buddhist culture from the east and Islamic influences from the west. Old Leh seems to remain in a time-warp, with a maze of deserted lanes dominated by the ruins of the Namgyal Palace above, while New Leh thrives on the steady stream of visitors that pours in during the summer. If the hawking of Kashmiri traders or the clicking of tourists' cameras become unbearable, you can seek refuge in one of the many beautiful *gompas* and deserted mountain trails in the vicinity. Some of these follow the same routes used for centuries by traders hauling goods from Western Tibet over the Chang-La (5547m) and Kardung-La (5602m) to Leh's bustling bazaar.

> **WARNING.** When you make the road journey, **carry your passport with you at all times.** The routes to Leh come close to areas under Pakistani and Chinese control. When arriving by plane, remember that Leh is 3505m above sea level. **Rest for at least one day** (that means not even walking around and definitely not consuming alcohol) before undertaking anything strenuous, and **watch for any signs of Acute Mountain Sickness (AMS).** The symptoms—headaches, breathlessness and nausea—normally develop during the first 36 hours (see **Trekking: Health and Safety,** p. 40). Leh has an emergency facility for dealing with AMS (24hr. tel. 52014 or 53629).

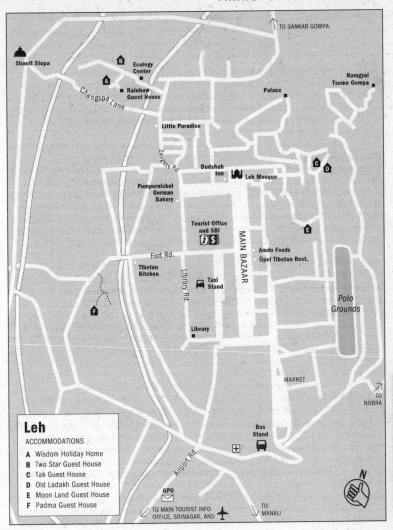

TO SANKAR GOMPA

Shanti Stupa

Ecology Center

Changspa Lane

Rainbow Guest House

Little Paradise

Zangsty Rd.

Budshah Inn

Leh Mosque

Pumpernickel German Bakery

Tourist Office and SBI

Fort Rd.

Tibetan Kitchen

Library Rd.

Taxi Stand

MAIN BAZAAR

Amdo Foods
Üpel Tibetan Rest.

Library

Palace

Namgyal Tsemo Gompa

Polo Grounds

MARKET

TO NOBRA

Bus Stand

Leh

ACCOMMODATIONS

A Wisdom Holiday Home
B Two Star Guest House
C Tak Guest House
D Old Ladakh Guest House
E Moon Land Guest House
F Padma Guest House

GPO

TO MAIN TOURIST INFO
OFFICE, SRINAGAR, AND

Airport Rd.

TO MANALI

N

◪ TRANSPORTATION

Airport: (tel. 52098), 4km from Leh down Fort Rd. (taxi Rs80). **Tushita Travel** (tel. 52076) is an authorized agent of Indian Airlines. Open M-Sa 10am-1pm and 2-5pm. During the summer, book several months in advance. If you have trouble getting a confirmed flight, talk to one of the more reputable tour agencies in town—they can work wonders and often convince Indian Airlines to send extra planes to clear out stranded tour groups. Flights are often delayed or cancelled due to bad weather. To: **Chandigarh** (Tu 7:30am, 1hr., US$70); **Delhi** (Tu, Th, Sa, and Su; 1½hr.; US$105); **Jammu** (Th and Su, 7:30am, 1hr., US$65); **Srinagar** (Sa 7:30am, 1hr., US$55). Batteries and lighters are not allowed in carry-on luggage flown out of Leh. Bags are checked at least twice.

Buses: The Tourist Information Office on Fort Rd. by the taxi stand has up-to-date schedules and prices. Fares listed are local/semi-deluxe. To: **Diskit** (Th and Sa 5:30am, 8hr., Rs50); **Hemis** (9:30am, 2hr., Rs20); **Kargil** via **Lamayuru** (5:30am, 12hr., Rs110/

143); **Matho** (2pm, 1hr., Rs15); **Manali** (4am, 48hr., Rs358/502); **Panamik** (Tu 5:30am, 8hr., Rs50); **Phyang** (8am and 4pm, 30min.); **Shey, Tikse,** and **Spituk** (every 30min. 7am-7pm); **Srinagar** (5:30am, 48hr., Rs220/286); **Stok** (8am, 2, and 4:30pm; 45min; Rs10). **Minibuses** go to **Alchi, Saspul, Likir,** and **Bagso** (all 4pm).

Local Transportation: The **taxi union** is in the center of town, near the top of Fort Rd. There are fixed rates for all destinations during the season (July-Aug.). Tourist season rates about Rs10 per km for a round-trip fare, Rs15 per km for one-way; bargain off sea-son. The best way around town is on foot, but **bikes** offer a convenient way of getting to the *gompas* in the Indus Valley. **Tomo-ri-ri Travels,** Fort Rd. (tel. 53622), rents mountain bikes (Rs200 per day with a US$100 deposit).

✴ ORIENTATION AND PRACTICAL INFORMATION

The **main bazaar** marks the western edge of the **Old City**. Running west from the center of the main bazaar is **Fort Road**, which has the highest density of restaurants, travel agents, and carpet shops. **Zangsty Road** begins at the north end of the main bazaar, con-nects to Fort Rd. via **Library Road,** and then runs north, where it sends two lanes, **Chang-spa** and **Karzoo,** to the left past several small guest houses. Buses arrive in the southern part of the town on **Airport Road,** a 10-minute walk from the bazaar.

Tourist Office: Tourist Information Centre (tel. 52297). Inconveniently located 2km from town on Airport Rd. The **Tourist Information Office,** in the State Bank of India com-pound on Fort Rd., has information on treks, local bus schedules, and festivals. Open M-Sa 8am-7pm. Off-season: 10am-4pm.

Trekking Agents: Although all agents are registered, not all are qualified to handle high-risk activities. Ask around to find out whom to trust. **RIMO Expeditions,** Zangsty Rd. (tel. 53348, in Delhi tel. 11 613 6568; www.atrav.com/rimo and **Snow Leopard Trails,** Fort Rd., P.O. Box 46 (tel. 52074; fax 52355), are reputable agencies that handle trek-king and rafting. Full expeditions with ponies and a cook US$20-25; only a guide US$8.

Currency Exchange: State Bank of India has an exchange counter in the same building as the tourist office, just off Fort Rd. Open M-F 10:30am-1:30pm, Sa 10:30am-noon. **Hotel Khangri,** farther down and just off the opposite side of the road, gives lower exchange rates but is less crowded. Open daily 6am-10pm.

Library: Jek State District Library, at the end of Library Rd., has two rooms filled with books in a variety of languages on a variety of subjects. Open M-Sa 10am-5pm.

Meditation Centers: Mahabodi Society, up Changspa Rd.; watch for signs on the right. Meditation meetings (M-F 5pm) are guided for 20-30min.; meditation goes on until 7pm. For longer meditation retreats, contact **Milarepa Meditation Centre** (tel. 44025), in Davachan, Choglamsar, on the road to Tikse.

Bookstore: Book Worm, Library Rd., next to Pumpernickel German Bakery, buys and sells backpackers' paperback favorites. Open daily 9am-8:30pm, Su noon-8:30pm. **Lehling Bookshop,** in the main bazaar, is well-stocked with books on Ladakhi and Buddhist art. Open daily 8am-8:30pm.

Laundry: All the runoff from laundry, done individually or by hotels, eventually finds its way into the river; it can be extremely polluting because of the use of non-biodegrad-able detergents. An eco-friendly women's organization runs **DZOMSA,** Zangsty Rd., which protects the river by using a desert pit away from Leh. The service is highly recom-mended (Rs8-10). Open M-Sa 8am-9pm, Su 8am-11am and 5-9pm.

Pharmacy: Himalaya Medical Store, opposite SNM Hospital. Open M-Sa and 2nd Su 9am-6pm.

Hospital: SNM Hospital (tel. 52014, 24hr. emergency tel. 53629), below the bus stand, is well maintained and has a special ward for tourists (most of them AMS-afflicted).

Police: (tel. 52018), halfway up Zangsty Rd. on the right.

Post Office: GPO, 2km from town on Airport Rd. *Poste Restante* held up to 1 month. Open M-F 10am-5pm. The itsy-bitsy branch in the middle of the Main Bazaar sells stamps. Open M-F 9:30am-4:30pm. **Postal Code:** 194101.

Internet: Gypsy's World, Fort Rd. (email matin.chunka@gems.vsnl.net.in), in the White House complex between town and the Indian Airlines office. Rs100 per page to send, Rs60 per page to receive. Open daily 9am-10pm.

PHONE CODE	01982

ACCOMMODATIONS

Most of the guest houses in Ladakh are run out of homes. Most of them are situated on the western outskirts of town in Karzoo and along Changspa Lane, where the vegetation is lush. The few guest houses in Old Town are off narrow lanes and in the shadow of the Namgyals Palace and within earshot of periodic prayer calls from the mosque. Prices are variable in June and from the end of August onward. Hot water usually costs Rs5 per bucket.

 Two Star Guest House (tel. 52250), in Karzoo, 20m past the path to Wisdom and Rainbow. You will be treated as family, as you sit in the windowed kitchen gazing at the snow-clad Stok Kangri. Ladakhi specialties take time, so tell "mother" a few hours ahead if you want *skiw* for dinner; ask for the unbeatable homemade pickles. Dorm beds Rs60; singles Rs80; doubles with huge windows and great views Rs150-300.

Old Ladakh Guest House (tel. 52951), Old Town. Facing the mosque, turn right into a narrow alley and continue for 150m through the labyrinth. Traditional Ladakhi rooms face a tiny courtyard shaded by hops—a perfect spot for postcard writing. The 2nd fl. doubles are well-lit, with private bath; the "triple" could easily house a rowing team. The eagle's-nest rooms on the roof get scorched by the sun but offer unbeatable views. Singles Rs80; doubles Rs150; triples Rs200.

Wisdom Holiday Home (tel. 52427), in Karzoo. Walk up Zangsty Rd., turn left after Mona Lisa Restaurant; continue along the road from the Ecology Centre, and follow the signs to either Wisdom or Rainbow. From its location in a wheat patch, this brand-new guest house offers views of a bleached-white *chorten* and the rugged cliffs behind it. Large doubles have picture windows and share a sparkling common bath with seat toilet. Doubles Rs150-200, with bath Rs300, with balcony Rs500.

Padma Guest House (tel. 52630). Walk 10min. down Fort Rd.; watch for a sign pointing to a path on the left. This 15-room complex with rooftop restaurant has sparkling new rooms that may seem expensive, but the hot shower is worth it. Older rooms have willow ceilings and clean common baths. Old rooms Rs250-300; new rooms Rs600-1000. Off-season: bargain mercilessly.

Tak Guest House (tel. 53643), across from the Old Ladakh Guest House, Old Town. Everything, from the rooms to the courtyard to the common toilets, is tiny but the friendliness of the Ladakhi family that runs it turns the small size into a plus. Singles Rs70; doubles with firm beds Rs150, with shower Rs250.

STRANGE MEDICINE Sniffly? Rheumatic? Plagued by vindictive demons? Ladakhi *lha-bas* can treat all of these afflictions by sucking the appropriate vile liquid directly through your skin! A *lha-ba* typically begins her therapeutic career by being possessed by spirits. Qualified *lamas* administer an initiation rite that enables her to control these spirits, channeling their influence into powers of healing. During a healing session, a *lha-ba* is first led into a trance by ritual drum-beating and singing. In that state she is able to locate the afflicting agent, in the form of internal fluids or objects, and draw them out with her mouth without breaking the patient's skin. Reports of these nasty substances (which the *lha-ba* repeatedly spits out during the process) cover everything from "red and lumpy" or "black and tarry" to "pebble" or "small, moving, salamander thing." *Lha-bas* still practice in Ladakh; ask around, but be warned—sessions can get violent to the point of necessitating slaps on the head with the flat of a sword. You should see a *lha-ba* only if you have a serious, long-term problem.

Moonland Guest House (tel. 52175), Old Town; continue 50m down the alley from Old Ladakh towards the polo ground and watch for signs on the right. Shiny-tiled bathrooms, thickly carpeted rooms, and the flower-filled patio stand out amid the dinginess of the Old Town. Here's your chance to experience medieval times while protected by modern comforts. Singles Rs100; doubles Rs200-250.

FOOD

With authentic Tibetan restaurants, not-so-authentic Italian ones, and Punjabi *samosa*/sweets/tea stalls in the bazaar, Leh is capable of satisfying any craving. Bottled mineral water is hauled over the passes on diesel-chugging Tata trucks; head to DZOMSA, on Zangsty Road, for pressure-boiled, eco-safe drinking water. Although there are more overpriced "German" bakeries in town than you can shake a strudel at, the tastiest bread is the Kashmiri *naan* sold in the bakeries behind the mosque. No restaurant serves Ladakhi food, but the family in your guest house will usually be happy to cook you *skiw* or *chutagi* if you give them enough notice.

- **Upel Tibetan Restaurant,** in the middle of the Main Bazaar, 3rd fl. The Darjeeling cooks seem to have mastered the culinary arts of Tibet and China. Eggplant with hot garlic sauce (Rs30) captures the unique taste of Szechuan. Open daily 7:30am-9:30pm.

- **Budshah Inn Restaurant,** at the end of the Main Bazaar, just to the left of the mosque. The only place in Leh (outside of the kebab vendors of the evening bazaar) to get Kashmiri cuisine. *Rista* (Rs70) and various *tandoori* meats are accompanied by enough rice to feed an army. Open daily 8am-10pm.

- **Amdo Foods Restaurant,** in the middle of the Main Bazaar, 2nd fl., serves Tibetan cuisine to the accompaniment of Amdo singers. *Nakin* noodles Rs35. Open daily 8am-10pm.

- **Tibetan Kitchen,** 5min. down Fort Rd., just before the White House. Clean tablecloths and artistic decor add another dimension to unique Tibetan specialties like *shaba-gleb* (meat bread Rs40) and Amdo bean stew (Rs45). The menu is topped off with Indian and Continental items. Wash it all down with a pot of mint tea in a funny looking *lama* hat teapot. Open daily 8am-3pm and 6-11pm.

- **Pumpernickel German Bakery,** between Fort Rd. and Zangsty Rd. As much an expat community center as an eatery. Bulletin board posts notices about taxis to Manali and ads for more trekking partners. Desserts (Rs30-45), an excellent yak-cheese and tomato sandwich (Rs30), and huge breakfasts (Rs50). Open daily 7:30am-9pm.

- **Little Paradise,** Zangsty Rd., next to the Mona Lisa Restaurant. This candle-lit bistro (and its fanatically enthusiastic *maître d'*) serve up homemade tagliatelle, roast chicken, and full breakfasts. Topped with garlands of garlic, fresh tomatoes, and a neon-red sauce, the *napoletano* (Rs40) is deliciously authentic. Try the great coffee (Rs7) but avoid the thin apple pie. Open daily 7am-9:30pm.

SIGHTS

SENGGE NAMGYAL PALACE. The nine-story palace which towers above the Old Town was built in the 1630's to emphasize Leh's ascendancy over Shey as the Ladakhi capital. It is said to have inspired the Potala Palace in Lhasa. The opening of the East Gate here used to be ceremoniously marked by the roar of a caged lion; now the gate serves as the entrance to the only well-maintained room of the palace, which houses old *thankas* and swords. Badly damaged in a war, the rest of the palace is in ruins. *(Open daily 7am-5pm. Rs20).*

SHANTI STUPA. Referred to by locals as the **Japan Stupa,** the Shanti Stupa in Changspa village is at the top of 560 steps. When you've stopped panting and puffing, feast your eyes on the legacy of Fujii Guraji, a Japanese Buddhist who moved to India in 1931. One of many Japanese-built stupas, this Peace Pagoda built in

THE LION KING The mysterious circumstances surrounding King Sengge Namgyal's birth provide a fairy-tale accompaniment to his castle's splendor. In the early 1600s, Ladakhi king Vamyang Namgyal's army was thoroughly defeated by the Balti king Ali Min. Ladakh was looted, its king imprisoned, and impending doom was nigh. Then, inexplicably the Balti forces withdrew. Vamyang was subsequently restored to power, and he married one of Ali Min's daughters. A few months later, she bore a son. Legend tells of a romance between the imprisoned king and the beautiful Balti princess, resulting in an illicit pregnancy. Balti sources record a dream of king Ali Min's in which he saw a lion jump out of the river and enter his daughter; at that instant, she conceived a baby, Sengge. The greatest of Ladakhi kings, Sengge Namgyal ("Lion Victorious") left the region with a legacy of grand castles and monasteries.

1983 features gilt panels depicting episodes from the life of the Buddha. (3km west of the bazaar; walk to Changspa and follow a direct line to the stupa. Open 24hr.)

NAMGYAL TSEMO GOMPA. Nestled high above the palace, the red Namgyal Tsemo Gompa is distinguished by its *gon-khang*, which features sculptures of wrathful deities and wall-paintings of benign *bodhisattvas*. *(Open briefly in the morning and evening when a lama climbs up from Samkar to light the butter lamps. The inside is dark— bring a flashlight.)*

OTHER SIGHTS. The imposing **masjid** at the end of the main bazaar was built in 1666 by the Ladakhi King Deldan Namgyal as a vassal's offering to the Mughal Emperor. The mosque displays a style more Ladakhi than Islamic, and the *namaaz* prayer calls can be heard five times a day in every corner of Leh. The **polo grounds** above the Old Town is site of annual tournaments and of occasional games between locals and soldiers, who chase the ball on sturdy ponies amid clouds of dust, parked trucks, and barking dogs. If you see a man with a bat, riding through town on horseback, hurry to the polo grounds to witness the spectacle. The **Sankar Gompa**, the official local residence of the reformist Gelug-pa ("Yellow Hat") sect, houses the image of a fearsome deity—the hundred-headed, thousand-armed Avalokitesvara *(walk along the footpath across the fields from the Ecological Centre; open daily 7-10am and 5-7pm; Rs15).*

 SHOPPING

There are plenty of opportunities to shop (and get swindled) in Leh. Masks, carpets, jewelry, shawls, and so-called "antiques" abound in the shops along Fort Rd., but prices are often significantly higher than those in Delhi, Shimla, or Dharamsala. Most of the traders are Kashmiris who come to Leh only during the tourist season. The **Tibetan Children's Village Handicrafts Centre,** on the road towards Choglamsar, sells crafts made at the Tibetan Children's Village (open M-Sa 9:30am-5pm). The **Tibetan Handicraft Emporium,** in the main market, is approved by the Dalai Lama (open M-Sa 9am-1pm and 2-7pm). Stop by the **Ecology Centre's** handicraft store for local Ladakhi goods (open M-Sa 10:30am-4:30pm). The **Co-operative store,** in the Galdan Hotel complex just off Fort Rd., sells similar items. These places support the local community and have fixed prices. **Cashmere Ladakh Arts,** on Zangsty Rd., is a private shop that prides itself on and fixed prices and no-hassle salesmanship. Shopping elsewhere is much like a sophisticated mugging.

VOLUNTEER OPPORTUNITIES

Travelers who would like to volunteer either with the Leh Women's Alliance or the Ecology Centre, or those wishing to arrange homestays at a Ladakhi farm (1 month min.) should contact **The International Society for Ecology and Culture (ISEC),** Apple Barn, Week, Dartington, Devon TQ9 6JP, U.K. (tel. (44 1803) 868650; fax 868651; email isecuk@gov.ape.org; www.isec.org.uk), preferably a year ahead.

The organization's aim is to re-establish the relationship between the community and its land. ISEC runs the **Ecological Development Centre,** left from Zangsty St. in Leh, which examines conventional notions of development and rethinks policy prescriptions for Ladakh. The center has ongoing projects which need volunteers from time to time and can also refer would-be volunteers to other local organizations. (Open M-Sa 10:30am-4:30pm.) For short-notice volunteering, the **Student Educational and Cultural Movement of Ladakh** (SECMOL), at the Ridzong Labrang Complex in Old Leh (tel. 52421; fax 53012), between the bazaar and the polo grounds, has volunteer positions at its camp for Ladakhi youth in Choglamsar.

 ## TREKKING AROUND LEH

> **WARNING.** In case of accidents, the only available rescue is the military heli-copter that operates at a cost of Rs40,000 per hour, flying out only if there is a guarantee that the cost will be met. Before setting out on a trek, whether you're alone or with an organized group, be sure to leave the following with your guest house owner in Leh: detailed itinerary; photocopies of your passport, visa, and insurance policy; three filled-out forms guaranteeing payment; acceptance certif-icate; and indemnity bond—all available from any travel agent in town.

Set between the world's two highest mountain ranges, which protect it from rain, Ladakh is a favorite destination of trekkers who come both for the scenery and relatively reliable weather. During the trekking season (June-Oct.), the days are scorchingly hot and nights bitterly cold. Depending on your experience, you may or may not want to hire a porter or a guide, but you should not attempt treks deep in the mountains with less than three people. Consult one of the many **trekking agents** in town (see p. 254). You can rent and occasionally buy equipment (tent Rs100 per day, stove Rs15 per day) in the **White House,** Fort Rd. (tel. 53048).

The **Likir-Khalse** trek (2-4 days) also known as the "Baby Trek," leads over moderate passes to more villages and *gompas.* One of the routes best suited to solo trekking is the one through the **Markha Valley** (7-9 days), which starts either in Stok or Spitak and ends in **Hemis.** There are supplies along the route and no difficult river crossings, though passing the Stok-La (4900m) on the second day is a challenge. The demanding **Lamayuru-Padum-Darcha** trek (19 days), which crosses both the Samskar range and the Himalayas, is probably the best known and most traveled trek in the Western Himalayas. Provisions are sold in tents along the way.

The **Karzok-Kibber trek,** also very demanding, is one of the best in the area. The route starts at **Tso-Morari Lake,** one day from Leh by car (you need a **permit** to reach Tso-Morari; see p. 260), and takes you through **Rupshu,** inhabited by the nomadic Changpas. On day four, you'll cross the Ohirsta Phu River, which usually flows from Tibet to Tso-Morari, but reverses flow seasonally. The difficult crossing requires proper equipment. From there, the trek climbs to the **Parang Pass,** from where it descends to the beautiful village of **Kibber** in Spiti (see **Near Kaza,** p. 249).

NEAR LEH

Fifteen kilometers up the main road from Leh lies the ancient Ladakhi capital of **Shey.** The surrounding hillsides are home to the famed giant twin images of Sakyamuni. The one of gilt copper is a part of a palace temple; the other, supposedly made in the 17th century by Nepalese craftsmen, is in a large temple 300m from the palace, past a group of *chortens* (open daily 6am-8pm; Rs15). Four kilometers farther up the road, perched on a craggy bluff, is Ladakh's most photographed *gompa* of **Tikse.** A few kilometers above Tikse, you can get off the bus and cross the Indus to reach the **Stakma Gompa,** rising dramatically from the flat Indus Valley on a 60m-high rock. The three temples of the *gompa* are small but well-maintained, and the views from the temple windows are gorgeous. (Admission Rs20.)

From Stakma, you can make out the **Matho Gompa** to the southwest, set on a hill at the foot of the glacier-carved mountain. Separated from the Stakma *gompa* by 7km of meadows and barley fields, Matho is the only monastery in Ladakh belonging to the Saskya-pa sect and is famous for the oracles delivered here. Every three years, *lamas* are chosen by a traditional procedure and then spend several months following a strict regime of fasting and prayer regimen until they are able to perform miraculous feats and deliver prophecies. The tiny *gon-khang* at the top of the *gompa* containing fierce images of deities armed with shining sabres, is likely to terrify you. Unlike in most other *gon-khangs*, the ferocious faces here are not covered; women are therefore not allowed to enter.

From Matho, descend to the left and follow the path at the foot of the ridge 12km until you reach **Stok.** The palace in Stok is the current residence of the Namgyal dynasty. The queen has converted four rooms into a museum that displays *thankas* and precious family heirlooms. The turquoise-inlaid crown once belonged to a Chinese princess of the Tang dynasty who married a Tibetan king; curiously enough, this is China's oldest claim to Tibet. (Museum open daily 7am-7pm. Rs25). The last bus back to Leh departs at 4:30pm.

Four kilometers from **Saspol** (up the Indus Valley from Leh) and across the river is Ladakh's oldest and most precious *gompa*, **Alchi,** a village founded in the 11th century. Volumes have been written about the wall paintings inside the two low buildings, praised for the individualistic touches they exhibit, features noticeably absent in later Tibetan art. Make sure you read up about the area before you come, and bring a strong flashlight; the *gompa* is dark inside. **Lotsava Guest House,** 50m to the left from where the taxis stop, has a secluded garden and immaculate bathrooms (singles Rs80; doubles Rs150).

THE NUBRA VALLEY

For centuries, caravans have traversed Khardung-La on their way between Punjab and Yarkand. The Nubra Valley, literally "Green Valley," used to be the fuelling stop before or after the scorching trials of the Karakoram. Surrounded by the mighty mountains of Ladakh, the Nubra Valley has a highly varied landscape, covering areas of barren desert and lush greenery. Recent conflicts have reduced the passage of caravans, and only a segment of the valley (between Panamik and Hunder) is now open to the latest sources of foreign exchange: tourists. A new road has made Khardung-La the highest motorable pass in the world, plied daily by military and tourist convoys and the occasional wild camel.

 WARNING: Four newly opened areas in Ladakh—the Drok-pa area, Nubra Valley, Pangong Lake, and Tso-Morari Lake—require a special permit issued by the Deputy Commissioner, 1st fl. of the government building just above the polo grounds, Leh. The 7-day permit, issued to groups of 4 or more, can be obtained only through a travel agent; bring a photocopy of your passport and visa. Expect to pay Rs100 each. The permit takes a day to arrange. You will be asked to leave a copy of your permit at every check-post; bring at least 5 photocopies with you.

DISKIT

Diskit is the administrative headquarters of the Nubra Valley. The western part of the village is an unimpressive collection of ugly concrete buildings, while the eastern part is a jumble of village houses and barley fields. The *chortens* have paths on both sides, but you should not tread the ones on the left. Similarly, the prayer-wheels should be turned only in a clockwise direction. From the prayer wheel on the main road, it is a 30-minute climb, along the path to the left over a hill covered by *chortens*, to the *gompa*. The windows of the large, new *du-khang* (assembly hall) afford great views, and you can visit the protective deities in the *gon-khang*—the deities' fierce faces are unmasked on only one day of the year; their veils, however, make it possible for women to enter (Rs20).

Guest houses line the *mani* wall. Coming from the *gompa* and the main road, **Sunrise Guest House** (tel. 20011) is on your right. The common baths are brand new, and food is served in the kitchen or in the garden. (Doubles Rs150; triples Rs200.) **D. Khangsar Guest House** (tel. 20014), farther down a path to the right, is probably the best place to experience village life—you'll be shacking up with the cows. Despite your bovine suitemates, rooms are clean, carpeted, and dirt cheap. (Rooms Rs50; breakfast Rs15, dinner Rs25.) Follow the road for 10 minutes to New Diskit, near the bus stand, where the only restaurant in town serves rice and *dal* (Rs25). **Buses** from Leh go to Diskit (Th and Sa 5:30am, 8hr., Rs50).

HUNDER

At the end of New Diskit, a dirt road turns off to the right into barley fields, continuing along spectacular pastures, creeks, and sand dunes for 7km until it reaches Hunder. This easy walk is one the valley's most picturesque; along the way you are likely to spot a family of wild Bactrian camels against the background of the glaciered mountains. On the main road that skirts Hunder, there is a *gompa* by the bridge, but this is as far as your permit allows you to go. The most interesting sites lie outside of the *gompa* itself. The paintings inside the biggest *chorten* are 50m below it, and the temples are on the ridge above.

Once in Hunder, walk with the military barracks on your left until you see a sign for the **Snow Leopard Guest House** on the right (singles Rs50; deluxe doubles with bath Rs150). The enormous dinner (Rs40) lets you sample the bounty of the vegetable fields and the cows that surround the house; unfortunately, it is served in the impersonal, office-like dining room instead of the kitchen. **Moon Land (Nerchungpa) Guest House,** deeper inside the village, is somewhat hard to find, but rooms are spacious (Rs75) and meals (Rs40) can be taken in the flower-filled garden.

SUMUR

A large village well worth exploring, Sumur is lined by *chortens* and a *mani* wall. Keeping these always on your right, walk up to **Sampan Ling Gompa.** Almost as big as Diskit Gompa, it has a less spectacular setting but equally spectacular views. It contains a school for young monks whom you can watch turn into little devils in the glacier stream during breaks from lessons. There are a number of guest houses along the way; **Stakrey Guest House,** farther to the right and somewhat hard to find, is the best—ask locals for directions. Doubles with semi-private, clean bathrooms are Rs200, including breakfast and dinner. **Tashis Khahgsar Guest House,** 30m off the main road next to the school, has new rooms with common baths (doubles Rs150) and a spacious, shaded garden. Sumur can be reached by crossing the Shayuk River from the bridge near Khalsar.

SRINAGAR سرینگر

> ⚠ **WARNING.** Tensions in Kashmir have eased significantly since 1996, but travel to the western half of Jammu and Kashmir (including the Kashmir Valley) is still risky. **Foreign tourists have been the targets of acts of extreme violence as recently as 1995.** Border skirmishes between India and Pakistan erupted into a crisis in Kargil in June 1999, and militant activity remains widespread in rural areas. Travelers are strongly advised to stay within the limits of Srinagar city, where the strong presence of the Indian Army somewhat mitigates the risk.

From Goa to Delhi to Leh, you are bound to meet at least one zealously friendly Kashmiri who's convinced that his houseboat in Srinagar is the place for you. For about seven years (between 1989-1996), this was an invitation to probable disaster—kidnappings, bomb blasts, and random gunfire in the streets made the once-idyllic Vale of Kashmir off-limits to Western tourists. Recently, however, such vacation plans have been upgraded from impossible to dangerous-but-doable. While *Let's Go* is neither smarter nor better connected than your embassy (which will most likely advise against traveling anywhere in Western Kashmir), we offer a few suggestions if you do decide to go.

Srinagar is situated on the Dal Lake and the Jhelum River. Despite the decreased political tensions in Srinagar proper, it's better to fly in and out rather than to take the **bus** ride through the still-hazardous outlying areas. It's also easier to get a seat on a Srinagar-Leh flight than on a Delhi-Leh flight. Srinagar's **airport** is currently operating out of a military air base, so the baggage claim is a free-for-all coming in, but security is extremely tight going out. All your worst suspicions about military police will be confirmed, but at least you'll feel safe in the knowledge that your socks have been checked for hidden explosives. Indian Airlines flies to Srinagar from Delhi (1 per day, US$115).

After nine years of relative stagnation, though, even mainland life is beginning to attract tourist interest. Incredible Kashmiri dishes can be sniffed out in parts of the city. **Adhoo's,** Residency Rd., serves superb Srinagar standards (Rs50-100); and **Mughal Darbar,** two blocks from Adhoo's on Residency Rd., offers good food at slightly higher prices and has a well-deserved local following.

Many of Srinagar's world-renowned Mughal Gardens have been closed, largely because the military government refuses to fund their maintenance. **Shalimar Garden** is open, but parts of its central fountains are under repair. The awe-inspiring **Nishat Garden,** however, is in full working order. (Both gardens open in the summer sunrise-7pm, until 6pm in the winter.)

No one escapes Srinagar without some exposure to high-intensity Kashmiri salesmanship—whether it's carpets, papier-mache, silver, or shawls, you'll be tempted to drop some serious rupees. Prices for Kashmiri **handicrafts** are generally better here than anywhere else, and there's also less hassle; most salesmen aren't working for a commission. Family-owned or collective outfits are the most reliable sources for quality products. **Honey** is one of the least expensive and most enjoyable specialties available here. **The Oriental Apiary,** between Dal and Nagin Lakes, has been producing a wide variety for 45 years.

HOUSEBOAT STAYS. A trip to Srinagar would be incomplete if you didn't stay in one of Dal Lake's **houseboats,** especially since the hotels on land are pricier and often remain occupied by the boys of the Indian Army. Pre-booking your trip in Delhi or Goa saves you a lot of hassle, provided the travel agent doesn't charge a steep commission. Any tourist office will be able to recommend a reliable travel agent who books accommodations in Srinagar (most agents book for only one houseboat or group of houseboats); ask to see pictures of the houseboat on which you'll be staying. Houseboats come in five classes with government-set rates (deluxe Rs1500, A Rs1000, B Rs700, C Rs600, and D Rs200 per double room). The decimated tourist trade in Kashmir allows you to demand up to 50% off these rates. The more expensive boats are definitely worth the extra money.

An alternative to pre-booking is to hire a *shikhara* (canvas-roofed canoe) at Dal Lake and shop around. **Swan Houseboats,** just off Dal Lake, comprises a luxurious, well-maintained group of boats run by an honest, exuberant family and their staff (deluxe Rs750, A Rs650, B Rs525, C Rs480; Rs50 discount for *Let's Go* users). Reservations can be made at **Merrygo Travels,** Connaught Pl. (tel. 3347364; fax 3347365; email travels.merrygo@axcess.net.in), in Delhi; or directly (tel. (0091) 194 475038). Be aware that other agencies have spent much of 1999 forging Merrygo signs and business cards; make sure you have the right place.

A stay on the houseboat often includes a meal-and-tour package. It can be extremely expensive (up to US$300 for 4-5 days), but it's not a bad idea to have someone to accompany you around the city, especially since wandering about on your own is dangerous. A guide can partially protect you from would-be abductors. The treks outside Srinagar are spectacular, but a recent increase in military operations in outlying areas of the Kashmir Valley makes trekking foolhardy.

PUNJAB ਪੰਜਾਬ AND HARYANA ਹਰਿਆਣਾ

When the 1947 Partition divided the northwestern state of Punjab between India and Pakistan, only two of the five rivers to which the Persian *punj aab* refers were still contained within India's borders. Nineteen years later, what was left of the Indian state was divided again, this time along the linguistic lines of Punjabi and Hindi, forming the states of Punjab and Haryana. Despite linguistic differences, Haryana and Punjab share a capital (Chandigarh), a fertile geography, and the pride of overcoming a long and turbulent history to become one of India's most prosperous regions. Together, the two states produce more than half of India's wheat and rice supply.

Punjab has long been the foyer through which aggressive guests have entered the subcontinent—and stayed. The Aryans' arrival here in 1500 BC led to the writing of the *Vedas* and the *Mahabharata*. With the 1526 Battle of Panipat came the Mughals, though the advent of the British viceroyalty in 1739 and 1761 precipitated the decline of its once-influential Muslim rulers. Punjab has had a strong cultural impact on India, largely through its Sikh religion, founded in the 15th century by Guru Nanak. Although Nanak's religion spread throughout India, the majority of Sikhs—and their holy city of Amritsar—are in Punjab (see **Sikhism,** p. 88).

But prosperity and peace have not gone hand in hand, and there has long been friction in Punjab between moderates and Sikh militants of the Shiromani Akali Dal party who demanded the formation of an independent Sikh nation, Khalistan ("Land of the Pure"). Things came to a head in 1983-84, with Sikh-militant massacres of Hindus and a subsequent army raid on the militants' headquarters in Amritsar's Golden Temple. The siege of the holy site led to Sikh army desertions, mutinies, and, eventually, the murder of Indira Gandhi by two of her Sikh bodyguards. Subsequent Hindu rioting, in which thousands of Sikhs were slaughtered, meant an increase in support for the Khalistan movement that has only recently begun to wane. Although separatist groups continue to demand independence, they lack popular support and pose no threat to travelers.

HIGHLIGHTS OF PUNJAB AND HARYANA

■ Amritsar's **Golden Temple** (p. 272), the most sacred site of the Sikh religion, welcomes visitors with its beauty, holiness, and hospitality.

■ Modern **Chandigarh's** pre-planned sectors and structures offer a history of Indian futurism, set in pre-poured concrete (below).

CHANDIGARH ਚੰਡੀਗੜ੍ਹ चंडीगढ़

Chandigarh was born of the starry-eyed optimism of India's newly independent government. The Punjab (including present-day Haryana) had been partitioned, and its original capital, Lahore, lay across the border in Pakistan. A new capital was needed, and Nehru's government decided on the present site of Chandigarh because of its scenic views and fertile land. Nehru employed a team of crack Western architects, transplanting their ideas for a functional, well-organized European habitat into an Indian setting. The most prominent of the architects, Le Corbusier (the artist formerly known as M. Charles Jeanneret), seized this opportunity to mobilize his plans for a revolution in urban landscape; the result was a huge grid of broad, park-filled avenues and clean-cut "sectors." Today, Le Corbusier's California dream of "sun, space, and silence" has become crowded and polluted, but it still has some tranquil and refreshing spots that provide a welcome contrast to traditional India, and a brief vacation from the furious swirl of other Indian cities.

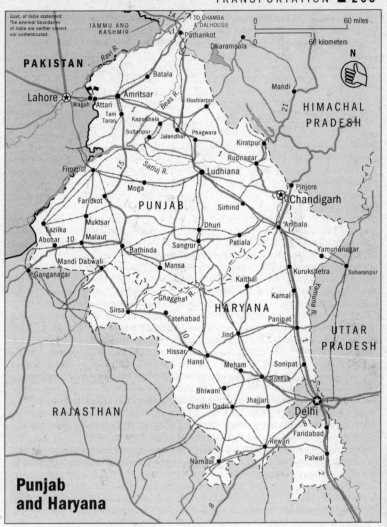

Govt. of India statement:
The external boundaries
of India are neither correct
nor authenticated.

Punjab and Haryana

▐ TRANSPORTATION

Airport: 11km out of town, a Rs80-120 auto-rickshaw ride. **Indian Airlines** (tel. 704539) accepts credit cards to book flights. To: **Delhi** (W and F 3:20pm, 40min., US$65); **Leh** (W 9:20am, 1hr., US$70). Book 2 months early to guarantee a ticket to Leh.

Trains: Chandigarh's **railway station** is 8km to the southeast of town. Local bus #37 connects the railway station with the bus stand (20min., Rs5). Auto-rickshaws will go the distance for Rs20-30. On the 3rd fl. of the bus stand, the **Railway Reservation Office** (tel. 708573). Open M-Sa 8am-8pm, Su 8am-2pm. To: **Delhi** (*Shatabdi Exp.* 2006, 6:50am; *Shatabdi Exp.* 2012, 12:20pm, 3½hr., A/C chair Rs435). For **Jammu, Amritsar,** and **Rishikesh**, go to **Ambala** (several daily, 1hr., Rs45) and get your connection there. Tickets for trains from Ambala can be obtained in Chandigarh if booked a day in advance. For **Shimla,** it is necessary to change in **Kalka** (several daily, 30min., Rs24) for the narrow-gauged rail. Tickets sold only in Kalka.

Buses: Inter-State Bus Terminal, on the southwest side of Sector 17, across from the hotels in Sector 22. Buses depart for **Amritsar** (every 20min. 4am-11pm, 5hr., Rs90); **Dehra Dun** (every 10min. 4:30am-11pm, 5½hr., Rs100; deluxe every hr. 4:30am-11pm, Rs200); **Delhi** (frequent 4am-midnight, 5½hr., Rs91; deluxe Rs182); **Dharamsala** (9 daily 4:40am-1am, 8hr., Rs107; deluxe 2:30am and 11:15pm, Rs220); **Jaipur** (6 daily 6:10am-7pm, 12hr., Rs183; deluxe 4 and 5:30pm, Rs372); **Jammu** (7, 10am, and 7pm; 8hr.; Rs120); **Manali** (7 daily 5:10am-3:30pm, 12hr., Rs155); **Rishikesh** (10:30am and 8:30pm, 8hr., Rs108); **Shimla** (frequent 5am-7pm, 4½hr., Rs59; deluxe 9:30, 11:30am, and 12:45pm). **Dalhousie** or **Chamba** can be reached by a bus to **Pathankot** (5hr., Rs90). Pathankot to **Dalhousie** (10 per day 6:40am-5pm, 3½hr., Rs40).

Local Transportation: Cycle-rickshaws charge Rs10 for a 2-sector trip. The blue **auto-rickshaws** charge twice as much. All local **buses** originate at the main bus station, Sector 17. Bus #13 goes to the Rock Garden (15min., Rs5) and Bus #37 to the train station (20min., Rs5).

✴ ORIENTATION

No one can say that Chandigarh is illogical—the whole city is a massive grid that makes disorientation unlikely, except that its avenues all appear nearly identical. The streets run northwest to southeast and northeast to southwest, dividing the town into 50 sectors. Each sector is a self-sufficient unit with its own market places and shopping centers. **Sector 1** is to the north, where the main government buildings, **Sukhna Lake,** and the **Rock Garden,** are situated. The rest are numbered from west to east, then east to west, in rows proceeding to the south. **Sector 17** is the heart of the city where most services, including the **bus station,** are located. The adjacent **Sector 9** affords a look into Chandigarh's affluent homes and suburban tranquility. **Sector 22** has its share of cheap restaurants and hotels, and its several temples proffer spiritual nourishment.

▨ PRACTICAL INFORMATION

Tourist Office: The Chandigarh Industrial and Tourism Development Corp. (CITCO), (tel. 704614, railway station tel. 658005) has offices upstairs in the bus stand (open M-Sa 9am-5pm) and at the railway station (open during train arrivals). Both offices give sight-seeing information and book rooms in expensive government hotels. If you can't find the right bus or cheap accommodation, ask in the bus stand's central cafeteria for **Narinder Singh.** This elderly Sikh in a blue turban has made it his full-time hobby to help out-of-town visitors; chances are he will find you before you find him. His services and city tour are the best in town. At the bus stand, there are also **Punjab** (tel. 711878), **U.P.** (tel. 707649), and **H.P.** (tel. 708569) **Tourist Information Centres.** Open M-F 9am-5pm. All offer brochures and arrange hotel reservations.

Budget Travel: Indian Airlines, Sector 17C (tel. 704539), opposite the library, accepts credit cards to book flights all over India. Open M-Sa 10am-5pm.

Immigration Office: Foreigners Registration Office (tel. 702810), in SSP, Police Headquarters, across from Sector 9, registers foreigners with non-tourist visas. Open M-Sa 10am-6pm.

Currency Exchange: Banks cluster around the "Bank Square" in Sector 17B. **Bank of Baroda** (tel. 709692) changes traveler's checks and gives cash advances on Visa and MC for Rs100 plus a 1% fee. Open M-F 10am-2pm, Sa 10am-noon. **State Bank of India** (tel. 708359), in the 3rd fl. office, changes cash and AmEx and Thomas Cook traveler's checks. Open M-F 10am-2pm, Sa 10am-noon.

Luggage Storage: The cloak room at the bus terminal charges Rs2-3 per day. Open daily 9am-5pm.

Market: Although each sector has its own market, Sector 22 is the place where most locals come for their vegetables. The south end of Sector 17 offers a more high-brow experience.

Chandigarh

ACCOMMODATIONS

A Sector 22 Gurudwara
B Shivalik Lodge
C Julundur Hotel
D Hotel Divyadeep
E Panchayat Bhawan
F Sector 19 Gurudwara

N

0   600 yards
0   600 meters

Sukhna Lake

Sukhna Choa

Boat Rental

CAPITAL COMPLEX
■ Open Hand Monument
■ High Court
■ Rock Garden
■ Legislative Assembly
■ Secretariat

Rajindra Park

Patiali Rao

Uttar Marg

Saelvari Path

TO RAILWAY STATION AND SHIMLA

SECTOR 1
SECTOR 2
SECTOR 3
SECTOR 4
SECTOR 5
SECTOR 6
SECTOR 7
SECTOR 8
SECTOR 9
SECTOR 10
SECTOR 11
SECTOR 12
SECTOR 14
SECTOR 15
SECTOR 16
SECTOR 17
SECTOR 18
SECTOR 19
SECTOR 20
SECTOR 21
SECTOR 22
SECTOR 23
SECTOR 24
SECTOR 25
SECTOR 35
SECTOR 36
SECTOR 37
SECTOR 38
SECTOR 40
SECTOR 41
SECTOR 42

Post Graduate Institute

Museum and Art Gallery 🏛
Indian Airlines
State Bank of India $
KC's Mezbaan
Central State Library 🏛
Shangri-La
Indian Coffee House
Inter-State Bus Terminal
CITCO
Local Buses
Pub 22
Hot Millions
Rose Garden

Madhya Marg
Himalaya Marg
Jan Marg
Dakshin Marg
Udyan Path
Vidya Path
Paschim Marg

Tagore Theatre 🎭

Leisure Valley
Fitness Trails
Atawa Club

TO DELHI

PUNJAB & HARYANA

Library: Central State Library, Sector 17B (tel. 702565), has an excellent selection of Indian and world books, dictionaries, and Indian periodicals. File a membership application on the 2nd fl. and attach a Rs100 refundable deposit. Open M-F 10am-5:30pm, Sa 10am-1:30pm; closed the last Sa of every month.

Bookstore: The English Bookshop, south of Sector 17C, supplies dictionaries, travel books, and scholarly works on subjects ranging from Sikh hair to the female body. **Capital Book Depot,** farther west along the row past the cinema, has an almost complete collection of the Penguin Classics. Both open M-Sa 10am-8pm.

Pharmacy: Chemists abound around the medical center in Sector 17. In Sector 22-C are several late-night pharmacies, such as **Anil and Co.,** Bayshop #42 (tel. 777565). Open daily 8am-9:30pm. Both hospital pharmacies require membership.

Hospital/Medical Services: Post Graduate Institute (PGI), Sector 12 (tel. 746018). The best hospital in Chandigarh and one of the most reputable in India. 24hr. emergency services. **Government Medical College and Hospital,** Sector 32, Dakshin Marg (tel. 665545-49, emergency ext. 1200), has an ambulance service.

Emergency: tel. 100 to report a bomb and other emergencies.

Post Office: GPO, Sector 17A, has *Poste Restante* and EMS. Open M-Sa 10am-5pm. There are also DHL and other express couriers in Sector 17. **Postal Code:** 160017.

Internet: Cyber Club, Sector 17B (tel. 712209), across from the KC Theater. The connection is more reliable in the evenings. Rs75 per hr. Open M-Sa 9am-8pm.

Telephones: Many **STD/ISD** booths at the station and in every sector.

PHONE CODE	0172

ACCOMMODATIONS

Accommodations in Chandigarh are relatively easy on the wallet and can be an experience in themselves. Treat yourself to simplicity in that bastion of Sikh hospitality, the **gurudwara,** where stubborn persistence in the face of glowering, spear-wielding guardians will be rewarded. *Gurudwaras* are Sikh temples open to the public, and each one has a large room with floor mats open to everyone, usually for free. Unless you plan to stay in one in Amritsar, don't pass up this chance to see Sikhism from the inside. No cigarettes, alcohol, or other intoxicants are allowed inside the compound. If this isn't quite your cup of tea, you can always trot across the street from the bus station into the hotel jungle of Sector 22, or you could try the government *bhawan,* which fills up quickly.

Gurudwaras. The Sikh owners of Sector 19's Gurudwara are extremely friendly and eager to instruct you about their faith, once you persuade them to let you stay. Rooms with double bed, fan, and private tiled bath Rs60, plus Rs100 refundable deposit. Sector 22 and Sector 9 Gurudwaras have large rooms with communal squat toilets (free).

Hotel Divyadeep, 1090-91, Sector 22B (tel. 705191), on the southwest side of Sector 22, 250m from the bus station. Immaculate, spacious, old-style, wood-paneled rooms with seat toilets. Room service (veg. only) 6am-10pm. Doctor on call. Check-out 24hr. Singles Rs250, with A/C Rs450; doubles Rs300/500. **Bhol Restaurant** downstairs has a rich *thali* for Rs60.

Panchayat Bhawan, Sector 18 (tel. 780701), on the northeast side. Enormous, well-appointed rooms around an unspoiled courtyard. Doubles with bath Rs80; with A/C, TV, and huge closets Rs400. Fills up quickly; reservations recommended.

Shivalik Lodge, Sector 22B (tel. 774540), just behind the restaurant/hotel opposite the bus station. Clean bathrooms with squat toilets and hot water. Check-out noon. Doubles with air-cooling and TV Rs300.

Jullundur Hotel, Sector 22 (tel. 706777 or 701121), opposite the bus station, next to Sunbeam. The best bet for spare-your-wallet rooms. Courteous staff, hot water, and attached restaurant. Check-out noon. Singles with A/C Rs550; doubles with TV and A/C Rs750.

FOOD

There's no dearth of restaurants in wealthy Chandigarh. Sector 17 offers a combination of somewhat pricey restaurants and indigenous variations of American style fast-food joints. If you are searching just for some plain, wholesome food, head to any market outside of Sector 17. To escape the glitz and sample the local *thalis*, *samosas*, and "sweets," simply wander through the markets of any Sector besides 17 or 22.

KC's Mezbaam, Sector 17, on the north side, behind the KC Cinema. KC's presents the mosaic of styles that are the result of Muslim influence—feast on Nawab of Avadh's favorite *gushtaba* (Kashmiri meatballs in a yogurt sauce, Rs125) or on Nizam of Hyderabad's beloved *mung malai tikka* (Rs125) amidst flowers, fountains, and arches. Open daily 11am-11:30pm.

Shangri-La, SCO 96, Sector 17C. At first, Shangri-La's red paneling, dragon paintings, and silk lanterns promise an authentic Chinese experience, but the picture of the Dalai Lama reveals a hint of Tibet. In fact, both the chef and staff are Nepalese. Szechuan-style sliced lamb Rs90, jasmine tea Rs12. Open daily 11:30am-11:30pm. Delivery noon-11pm.

Indian Coffee House, on Sector 17's main square, has the town's largest selection of *dosas* (Rs20-30), served by waiters in cute little hats. There is only one kind of coffee, but the *lassi* selection more than matches the diversity of the *dosas*.

Hot Millions, Sector 17. So popular that, soon, Sector 17 might be renamed Sector Millions because of the restaurant's 4 branches. 3 of them serve quick-n'-greasy Indian, Chinese, and Continental food. Chicken burger Rs38, pizza Rs45-80. The fourth is a classy restaurant on the 2nd fl. with an amazing, stomach-safe salad bar (9-salad combination platter Rs110). Open daily 11am-11pm.

City Heart Restaurant, Sector 22, directly across from the bus station, is the place to refuel between exhausting bus rides. Helpings of veg. fried rice (Rs22) and *matar paneer* (Rs20) are huge, but prices still leave you enough for that ticket to Dharamsala.

Nanak's Sweets Shop, Sector 19D, next to the 19D *gurudwara*. Brave palates will be rewarded with a chalky, dough-based taste-sensation. The shop is run by three friendly Sikh brothers. Beware the strength of their whiskey-and-beer aperitif. Chocolate, coconut, and pineapple *barfis* Rs80.

NIGHTLIFE AND ENTERTAINMENT

The basement of **KC's Mezbaam** (see **Food,** open until 11:30pm) caters to the beer-deprived with Thunderbolt on tap (Rs25). If you need longer hours to thunder, **Pub 22,** Sector 22, directly across from the bus station, is open later (beer Rs25; open until 1am). Both pubs, however, serve nothing but beer, so if you need snacks in between the strong brew (8% alcohol content), **Ambrozia Restaurant and Pub,** Sector 17C across from the library, is an option. Small plates of *tandoori* and Chinese specialties cost Rs35-80, and the Riviera wine is Rs65. (Open until 11:30pm.) For some discotheque action, head to **Las Vegas Den,** SCO 915, Kulka Highway (tel. 554487), where you can dance to a curious blend of Indian and Western beats (couples Rs150, single women Rs50, single men often not allowed). For a more refined experience, head to the **Tagore Theatre,** Sector 18 (tel. 774278), which stages Shakespeare in Punjabi and features dancing troupes in costumes. Movies play at Sector 17's five cinemas (tickets Rs15 and Rs25).

SIGHTS

ROCK GARDEN. The birth of the city of Chandigarh as a government-supervised golden child gave rise to heaps of concrete waste and piles of debris. In 1985, however, a road construction supervisor Nek Chand used one of the many government dumps as a playground for his imagination, turning it into a garden well beyond the ken of the government and most other earthlings. Visit Nek Chand's Rock Garden, and you'll never look at Indian concrete the same way again. The former road-construction worker has brought this humble material, and even some road trash, into a state of grace, assembling an escapist wonderland that now meanders through 40 surreal acres. Highlights include stone duck armies, waterfalls, dancers, and a forthcoming glass-and-plastic fantasy. *(Sector 1, near the Capital Complex. Open daily Apr.-Sep. 9am-1pm and 3-7pm; Oct.-Mar. daily 9am-1pm and 2-6pm. Rs5. Appointments with Nek Chand, the garden's creator, occasionally available; inquire at the ticket window.)*

OTHER SIGHTS. Sector 1 plays host to other notable attractions. The **Capital Complex,** with its monumental concrete buildings, was Le Corbusier's way of staging the functions of government in symbolic and geometric relation to one another and to the rest of the city (as "head" to "body"—the parks were to be the "lungs"). The **High Court** and **Open Hand Monument** are more accessible than the **Legislative Assembly** and heavily-guarded **Secretariat.** Also in the north is **Sukhna Lake,** a small reservoir-turned-tourist trap with cafeteria, pub, mini-amusement park, and paddle boats. Come at sunset, hop in one of the **swan boats** and float over to the mangrove **alcoves** across the lake. *(2-seater Rs25 per 30 min., 4-seater Rs50 per 30 min.)* **Leisure Valley** is the term Le Corbusier used for the long parkland stretching through the heart of Chandigarh. It is meant to provide "care for the body and spirit." The highlight of this public park is the Dr. Zakir Hussain **Rose Garden,** off Jan Marg in Sector 16, which features fountains and 4000 species of roses. In February, the garden hosts the giant Rose Festival. Also worth visiting is the **Chhatbir Zoological Park,** 15km from Chandigarh, where you can meet (hopefully not face-to-face) the Royal Bengal Tigers or take a lion safari.

AMRITSAR ਅਮ੍ਰਿਤਸਰ

Named for the sacred tank or "pool of immortal nectar" at its heart, the holy city of Amritsar (pop. 800,000) is the largest city in partitioned Punjab and the focal point of Sikhism. An awe-inspiring monument to the Sikh faith, Amritsar's Golden Temple is a must-see for all visitors. Guru Ram Das initiated the construction of the temple in 1579, but the city did not begin to form around it until the fifth Guru, Arjun, enshrined the Sikh holy book, the Granth Sahib, here. Centuries of Mughal invasions started a cycle of destruction and reconstruction of the Golden Temple, and this streak of calamity continued up to the 1980s. Early in the 20th century, Amritsar played an important role in the formation of the Indian nationalist movement. In 1919 British Brigadier General REH Dyer massacred 400 unarmed Indians in the closed compound of Jallianwala Bagh, sparking a wave of protest all over India. Tanks bulldozed through the gates as the government put down an uprising of Sikh extremists in 1984. In spite of its blighted past, Amritsar today is a thriving industrial center beyond the 20 gates that form the ramparts of the old city. The city's proximity to the Pakistan border is itself an attraction; each evening an elaborate military ceremony accompanies the closing of the border gates.

▣ TRANSPORTATION

Airport: Raja Sanhsi Airport, 12km northwest of town, has a small tourist office and other basic services. To: **Delhi** (M and F 9am, W and F 2:20pm; 2hr.; US$90). Book from the **Indian Airlines** office, Court Rd. (tel. 213392), halfway between Albert and Mall Rd. Open M-Sa 10am-5pm.

Trains: The **computer reservation** complex (tel.562811 or 562812) is on the south end of the railway station; walk on the bridge over the platforms. Open M-Sa 8am-1:30pm and 2-8pm, Su 8am-2pm. Fares listed are for 2nd/sleeper class. To: **Agra** (*Amritsar-Nanded Exp.* 2716, 5:45am, 11hr., Rs300/800); **Delhi** (*Shatabdi Exp.* 2014, 5:25am and 5:10pm, 5½hr., Rs645; *Flying Mail Exp.* 4648, 6:20, 11:50am, and 2:40pm; 8hr.; Rs150/365); **Haridwar** (3:30am and 9pm, 12hr., Rs187/650); **Jaipur** (3:30pm,

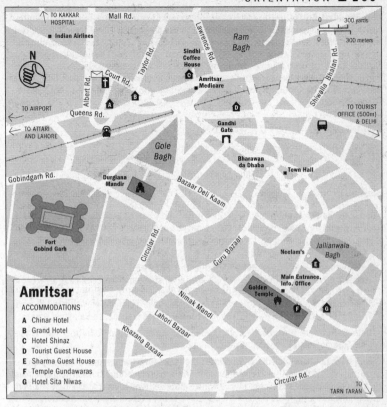

Amritsar

ACCOMMODATIONS

A Chinar Hotel
B Grand Hotel
C Hotel Shinaz
D Tourist Guest House
E Sharma Guest House
F Temple Gundawaras
G Hotel Sita Niwas

19hr., Rs280/1200); **Lahore, Pakistan** (*Lahore Exp.* 4607, M and Th 9:30am, 4hr., Rs50; no reservations—purchase ticket at the platform at 9am); **Lucknow** (*Amritsar-Howrah Exp.*, 5:45 and 6:30pm, 18hr., Rs265/736); **Mumbai** (*Paschim Exp.* 2926, 8am, 31hr., sleeper Rs430; *Golden Temple Mail* 2904, 9:30pm, 33hr., Rs105/193); **Patna** (*Amritsar-Howrah Exp.*, 5:45 and 6:30pm, 34hr., Rs350/936).

Buses: Enquiry office (tel. 551734). Times and prices tend to change frequently. To: **Attari,** near the Pakistan border (every 15min. 7am-6pm, 1hr., Rs11); **Chandigarh** (every 20min. 4:40am-5pm, 5hr., Rs90; deluxe 9am, noon, and 3pm, Rs150); **Dehra Dun** (5:40 and 7:30pm, 9hr., Rs155); **Delhi** (several daily 5:40am-10:30pm, 9hr., Rs166; deluxe 9pm, 8hr., Rs300); **Dalhousie** (6am, 6hr., Rs70); **Dharamsala** (6am, 7hr., Rs82); **Jammu** (every 30min. 6am-3:30pm, 6hr., Rs90); **Shimla** (7:20am, 10hr., Rs150; or go to Chandigarh and change there). For connections at friendlier hours, go to **Pathankot** (every 15min. 5am-8pm, 3hr., Rs40). From Pathankot to **Chamba** (11 per day 5:30am-5:30pm, 5hr., Rs58); **Dalhousie** (10 per day 6:40am-5pm, 3hr., Rs40); **Dharamsala** (9 per day 4:45am-9:30pm, 3½hr., Rs47).

Local Transportation: Bicycle rental available at **Raja Cycles,** across the street north of the bus stand, next to Janta Stores signs. Rs25 per day plus a Rs1000 deposit. Open M-Sa 9am-8pm. **Cycle-rickshaws** will take you anywhere in town for Rs10-15. In the "new sections," **auto-rickshaws** can speed things up; in the old parts they have to follow the snail's pace of the cycle-rickshaw-dominated narrow streets.

✦ ORIENTATION

Amritsar's **railroad tracks** divide the city into northern and southern sections. The older, livelier section of the city is beyond the gates to the south of the railway.

The **Bhandari Bridge** is the major vehicle conduit connecting north and south. North of the bridge is the **Ram Bagh** park and the modern parts of the city. The old town is farther south, enclosed by **Circular Road** which runs where the wall once stood. The Golden Temple marks the center of the circle. Though most visitors venture only into the temple compound and the area immediately north of it, the maze of alleys and bazaars south and west of the temple capture the feel of old Amritsar. The **bus stand** is northeast of the center, on the road from Delhi to the **railway station.**

🚹 PRACTICAL INFORMATION

Tourist Office: Punjab Government Tourist Office, Grand Trunk Rd. (tel. 231452), 1km east of the bus stand; ask a rickshaw to follow the road to Delhi. The office is on the left just before the Shell gas station on the right. Although in a decrepit state, its friendly staff knows a lot about Sikh Gurus and nearby towns. Open M-Sa 9am-5pm. There is also a helpful **Information Centre** at the Golden Temple (see p. 272).

Foreigner Registration Office: (tel. 228786), in the office of the Senior Superintendent of Police at the Court government compound just past the intersection of Court and Mall Rd. Visitors with non-tourist visas must register for long term stays. Tourist visas can only be extended in Delhi. Open M-Sa 10am-5:30pm.

Currency Exchange: State Bank of India (tel. 556763), next to the town hall, will exchange traveler's checks. Cash exchange against a purchase certificate. Open M-F 10am-2pm, Sa 10am-noon. **Grindlays Bank** (tel. 224626), at the intersection of Lawrence and Mall Rd., accepts traveler's checks. Cash advances on Visa and MC for a flat Rs100 fee. The railway area also has several offices that change **Pakistani rupees.**

Luggage Storage: The cloakroom at the railway station charges Rs5-6 per day. Open 24hr. Some hotels also offer this service upon request.

Market: The **bazaar** immediately in front of the main entrance to the Golden Temple carries a wide selection of merchandise, from Rajasthani shoes to Sikh daggers and swords. The steel bracelets *(kara)* worn by all Sikhs, symbolizing strength of will and determination, are available here. Be discriminating—*kara* that are not made of stainless steel will certainly erode after a few months of wear. Each narrow lane south and west of the shrine specializes in a particular product or craft.

Library: Sri Guru Ram Das Library, in the basement of Hargobind Niwas next to the Golden Temple, has a good collection of English-language books about Sikhism and the temple, as well as daily periodicals. Open M-Sa 9:30am-5pm.

Bookstore: Booklover's Retreat (tel. 545666), on Hall Bazaar, south of Gandhi Gate. Teetering stacks of new and used books include everything from *Sex, Scotch, and Scholarship* to Shakespeare. Open M-Sa 9am-8pm.

Pharmacy: Although chemists can be found all over town, several are clustered on Cooper Rd., around the corner from Crystal Restaurant, several blocks northeast of the railway station. Among these, **Sham Medicine** (tel. 228905) carries tampons and is otherwise well-stocked. Open daily 8:30am-10pm.

Hospital: Kakkar Hospital, Green Ave. (tel. 506015 or 506075), near the intersection of Mall and Albert Rd., is the most reputable in town; enough people know the name to point the way. **24hr. Emergency Room** on Mahna Singh Rd., in the Golden Temple area.

Post Office: Court Rd. (tel. 566032), northwest of the railway station. *Poste Restante* (c/o Post Marshall) and EMS speed post. Open M-Sa 9am-5pm. The **Golden Temple Post Office** sells stamps. Open M-Sa 9am-6pm. **Postal Code:** 143001 for main GPO, 143006 for Golden Temple area.

Internet Access: Infonet Services (tel. 210706), at the intersection of Queens and Lawrence Rd., across the street from Hotel Astoria. Has a state-of-the-art lab on the 2nd fl. Rs50 per hr. Open daily 9am-11pm. **Tourist Guest House** also has one computer hooked to the World Wide Web.

Telephones: STD/ISD booths near Golden Temple, railway station, bus stand, and one block east of Tourist Guest House.

PHONE CODE	0183

ACCOMMODATIONS

Amritsar's hotels are found in three parts of the city: the bus stand, railway station, and Golden Temple areas. Though undoubtedly the cheapest are near the bus stand, these are neither sanitary nor safe—over the years the area has become a red-light district where rooms are rented out by the hour. A number of decent, reasonably-priced hotels near the railway station await travelers anxious to keep distance from the heart of the city. Hotels near the temple are more scarce, but this is the most vibrant part of the city. The best place to stay, of course, is in the temple compound itself, although the strict rules become taxing after a few days.

INSIDE THE GOLDEN TEMPLE

Sri Guru Ram Das Niwas Gurudwara, outside the east gate of the temple past the community kitchen. All guests can use the washing spouts, showers, and toilets. Foreign guests sleep on floor mats in an open-ceilinged bunker. No smoking and drinking allowed, and prayers broadcasted periodically through the courtyard add to the mellow feel. Foreign compound is guarded 24hr., but lock all your valuables in the in-house closets. Donations at the charity box up front are appreciated.

Sri Guru Hargobind Niwas (temple manager tel. 553953, Hargobind Niwas ext. 323), 100m south of Ram Das Niwas Gurudwara. If the free digs are a bit too free for your taste, pay a token tariff for a sparkling new, marble-covered double with attached bath. As a rule, the place is always full, but if you are persistent, or if you keep coming back, you'll be rewarded. No drinking or smoking. Doubles with bath Rs50.

GOLDEN TEMPLE AREA

Sharma Guest House, Mahna Singh Rd. (tel. 551757), on the street between the main and the eastern entrances to the temple. Owned by two brothers, Sharma's prides itself on its family atmosphere and excellent room service. Clean, air-cooled doubles have seat toilets, cable TV, and phones. A few rooms look into Jallianwalla Bagh. Check-out 24hr. Doubles Rs200-300; deluxe Rs300-350. Reservations recommended.

Hotel Sita Niwas (tel. 543092), near the eastern temple entrance. Signs aplenty—you can't miss it. Among the 85 rooms that open into a big indoor courtyard you are sure to find the one that suits you. Singles are a little cramped; doubles with TV, tub, and seat-toilet have great temple views. STD/ISD. Doctor on call 24hr. A lift is being for access to 3rd fl. views. Check-out 24hr. Singles Rs150; doubles Rs550.

Shri Gujrati Lodge and Guest House (tel. 557870), a block in front of the main temple entrance, next to the infamous passage to Jallianwala Bagh. The 8-bed dormitory overlooks the memorial park, while the cramped doubles with tiny bathrooms open into Amritsar's central market. The huge 3rd fl. balcony is ideal for a game of cricket. TV and food in the lobby. Doubles equipped with phone and seat toilet. Dorm beds Rs60; doubles Rs200. No reservations accepted.

RAILWAY AREA

Tourist Guest House, GT Rd. (tel. 553830), near Nandan Cinema on the road from the bus stand to the railway station. Fifty years ago, a British colonel turned his mansion into this guest house; since then, tourists have flocked here for a taste of the Raj lifestyle. Rooms feature high ceilings, some with TVs. The colonel's 90-year old widow will keep you company for a chat over a beer. Internet connection in the living room Rs 2 per min. Dorm beds Rs85; doubles with fans and bath Rs125-250.

Grand Hotel (tel. 562424), directly opposite the railway station. Well-kept rooms surround a pleasant courtyard with a garden and lawn chairs. All rooms have attached baths with seat toilets, running hot water, and color TV. Room service 7am-10pm. Check-out noon. Singles Rs395, with A/C Rs600; doubles Rs500/700. 10% surcharge.

Hotel Shinaz (tel. 565157). Follow Queen's Rd. from the train station; look for the sign on the left just before Ram Bagh. Large clean rooms have TVs and seat toilets. No hot water. Room service 7am-11pm. Check-out noon. Singles Rs300; doubles Rs400; triples with air-cooling Rs500; add Rs100 for A/C. 10% surcharge.

Chinar Hotel, Railway Links Rd. (tel. 54655). A half-block up from the railway station. Moderately clean, with huge front-side rooms. Room service 6am-midnight. Check-out noon. Doubles Rs150, with bath Rs350, with A/C Rs550. 10% surcharge.

◖ FOOD

Eat at least one meal in the Golden Temple itself—the *dal* may surprise you and bring you back for more. There are also plenty of cheap and clean restaurants that serve the standard Indian-Chinese fare. Amritsar pales in comparison with Chandigarh's royal feasts; it is much more suited to the middle class palate and wallet.

▩ **Neelam's,** a few doors down from the entrance to Jallianwala Bagh. Cushy booths and A/C makes it the most comfortable *dhaba* in the temple neighborhood. The enormous portions ensure satisfaction. Noodles Rs25. Don't miss the *masala dosa* (Rs15). Open daily 10am-10pm.

Sharma Vaishno Dhaba, downstairs in the Hotel Sharma, has Amritsar's largest selection of *paneer* and inexhaustible supplies of cheap curd. *Shahi Paneer* Rs32.

Bubby Dhaba, directly in front of the main temple entrance, provides a standard menu. Relax in the hidden A/C room in the back if the heat is unbearable, or stay up front to chat with the cooks. Open daily 4:30am-1:30am.

Bharawanda Dhaba, across from Town Hall and next door to Punjab National Bank. Well-known, well-stocked, well-lit cafeteria with superb *thalis* (Rs30). Speedy service and foreigner friendly. Open daily 8:30am-11:30pm.

Subhash Juice Bar, one block southwest of Gandhi Gate. Sit in black, mirrored booths, and enjoy the colorful selection of juices and shakes. Mango shake with *pista badam* Rs15. Open daily 6am-11:30pm.

Sindhi Coffee House, Lawrence Rd., across from Ram Bagh Gardens. Dim lights, comfy chairs, brown carpet, and waiters dressed in brown. Here is where an Indian takes a date or sister for ice-cream. They also serve the standard menu and palatable coffee (Rs20). "Cock rolls" (spring rolls) Rs30-50. Open daily 9am-10pm.

◉ SIGHTS

THE GOLDEN TEMPLE

No matter what you choose to call it—the Golden Temple, Hari Mandir, or Darbar Sahib (as it's known in Punjabi)—Amritsar's focal monument is inspiringly beautiful and hauntingly serene, oblivious to the grind and grime only a few feet outside its walls. The Golden Temple's tranquility is especially impressive given the tumultuous history of the Sikhs and that of the temple itself. The nearly 400 years of the temple's existence have been marked by incessant destruction and desecration from outsiders. All Sikhs (and quite a few members of other religions) try to make a pilgrimage here at least once in their lifetime. The best time to visit is at night—gone is the blinding sunlight reflected in the temple's gold and white dome, and the lights sparkling in the blackened tank and the lanterns illuminating the causeway impart a soft, ethereal glow to the place of worship.

VISITOR'S INFORMATION. Golden Temple Information Centre (tel. 553954; open daily 8am-8pm, Sept.-Mar. 8am-7pm) is on the northeast side of the complex (open

HEADLESS HEROISM In 1761, the Mughal Ahmad Shah Abdali blew up the Golden Temple and filled the sacred tank with refuse. As a result, Baba Deep Singh, an understandably miffed Sikh leader, began a defense of the desecrated temple from 10km outside Amritsar. Baba Deep had sworn to reach the temple, but halfway there, he had his head cut off by a Muslim soldier. Disembodied head in hand, the Sikh leader trudged on, eventually crossing the temple's gates and plopping it in the water before finally expiring. On the site where he discarded his head is a shrine. Another memorial is on the road to Tarn Taran on the spot where Baba Deep Singh is thought to have started his zealous scuffle. All passing vehicles slow down here to offer a token of their appreciation for the man's spectacular exploits.

daily 24hr., free). No tobacco, alcohol, or narcotics of any kind are allowed in the temple complex. Visitors must deposit cigarettes a block away from the temple's entrance. Shoes, socks, and umbrellas must be left at free depositories at each of the main entrances or at the Tourist Information Center. Visitors must rinse their feet in the tanks in front of the entrances. Photography is allowed inside the temple complex but not inside the temple itself. Head-coverings are required at all times inside the temple. They are available for free at the Information Centre and for sale (Rs10) outside the temple, but any scarf, hat, or towel will suffice.

HISTORY. Although Guru Nanak, the founder of Sikhism, once lived near the site of the modern tank, it was **Guru Ram Das** who sparked the growth of a religious center when he began building the pool in 1574. That task was completed under Guru Arjun 15 years later, when the area was named Amritsar. Guru Arjun built the **Hari Mandir** in the tank's center and placed the Guru Granth Sahib, the Sikh holy book, inside it. A series of destructive Mughal invasions followed the 1601 completion of the temple. It fell alternatively under Mughal and Sikh control until Ahmad Shah Abdali took the temple and, taking no chances, blew it to smithereens. Finally, under the leadership of Punjab ruler Maharaja Ranjit Singh, the Sikhs reclaimed the site. The one-eyed maharaja rebuilt the complex, beautified parts with marble and copper, and coated the newly built Hari Mandir with gold leaf. In the 19th century, the British assumed less-than-reverent management of the temple. It wasn't until the 1920s that the practice of pure Sikhism was restored within the temple's walls.

Sadly, the temple has continued to be a site of frequent violence, even into recent times. The 1980's saw the rise of a vocal Sikh militant group, that called (and, in small factions, continues to call) for the creation of an independent Sikh nation. Tensions began to peak in 1983, when the movement's leader, Sant Bhindranwale, sequestered himself in the Golden Temple and incited acts of violence against Hindus. With over 350 Hindus killed by the summer of 1984, Indira Gandhi ordered the national army to storm the temple, in a plan dubbed **Operation Bluestar**. But what was intended as a commando raid became a three-day siege. When the smoke had cleared, more the 750 people were dead, including Bhindranwale and 83 soldiers. Tour guides and brochures are hush-hush about this latter-day violence, emphasizing instead historically distant bloodbaths and the site's current state of peace.

PARIKRAMA. The main entrance to the Golden Temple is on the north side, beneath the **clock tower.** Here also is the main shoe depository and the **Tourist Information Centre,** which provides informative brochures about the temples and Sikhism and also conducts hourly tours in English. The clock tower leads to the Parikrama, the 12m wide marble promenade encircling the tank. The four entrances to the temple and the complex symbolize an openness to friendly visitors from all sides—both geographically and metaphorically in terms of caste and creed. Guru Arjun once exclaimed, "My faith is for people of all castes and all creeds from whichever direction they come and to whichever direction they bow." Traffic moves clockwise around the Parikrama. Here, the **68 Holy Places** represent the 68 holiest Hindu sites in India—to merely walk along this northern edge, Guru Arjun declared, is to attain the holiness a Hindu takes a lifetime to acquire. Some of these have been converted into the **Central Sikh Museum,** or Gallery of Martyrs, housed in the northern part of the temple complex; the entrance is to the right of the main gate. There are portraits of renowned Sikhs, including Baba Deep Singh and Sevapanthi Bhai Mansha Singh, who swam across the tank amid gunfire to keep the temple lit. The display of heavy duty arms includes everything from spears to blunderbusses. Paintings of martyred bodies that were boiled or sawed at Chandni Chowk in Old Delhi and photographs of slain Sikh martyrs with pop-eyed, bloody faces spare no detail and are not for the faint of heart. *(Open daily 7am-7pm. Free.)* The small tree at the northeast corner of the tank is said to have been the site of a miracle healing of a cripple; today the healthy, wealthy, crippled, and destitute alike seek the benefits of the tank's curative powers at the adjoining **bathing ghats.** Just next to the *ghats* along the tank is one of four booths in which priests read from the Guru Granth Sahib. **Ongoing readings** are meant to ensure the continuation of Sikh beliefs; with each priest reciting for three hours, a complete reading takes 50 hours. The eerie tranquility of the temple is enhanced by other speakers perpetually piping *kirtans* (devotional songs) from inside the Hari Mandir.

On the east side of the Parikrama are the **Ramgarhia Minars,** two brick towers that were damaged when tanks plowed through this entrance in 1984. This access leads to the Guru-ka-Langar, the communal kitchen, and the *gurudwaras,* the housing for temple pilgrims. The south side of the tank has a shrine to **Baba Deep Singh,** whose headless exploits made him a Sikh hero (see **Headless Heroism,** p. 273). The west end of the tank has several notable structures. The first window is where devotees collect *prasad,* the sweet lumps of cornmeal used as an offering inside the Hari Mandir. Farther on (clockwise), across from the entrance to the Hari Mandir, is the **Akal Takhat,** the second-holiest place here. Guru Hargobind, the sixth Sikh guru, built the Akal Takhat in 1609 as a decision-making center. Many weapons, fine pieces of jewelry, and other Sikh artifacts are stored here. The two towering flagstaffs next to the Akal Takhat represent the religious and political facets of Sikhism; the two are joined by the **double swords of Hargobind,** demonstrating how intertwined these aspects of Sikhism are. Illuminated at the very top, the poles are intended as beacons for pilgrims heading into Amritsar. Near the flag-staffs is the shrine to the last and most militant guru, Gobind Singh. The last noteworthy spot along the Parikrama, other than the Hari Mandir itself, is the 450-year old **jujube** tree under which the Baba Buddhaja, the temple's first priest, is thought to have spent time. The tree is thought to bring fertility for those who touch it.

HARI MANDIR. Seeming to float in the middle of the tank, the Hari Mandir is the holiest part of the complex. Photography is not allowed past the gate to the temple walkway. The architecture of the Golden Temple fuses Hindu and Muslim styles—this is most noticeable in the synthesis of the Hindu temple's rectangular form with the domes and minarets of the Muslim mosque. The three stories of the Hari Mandir, capped by an inverted-lotus dome, are made of marble, copper, and about 100 kilograms of pure gold leaf. Inside the temple on the ground floor, the chief priest and his musicians perform the *gurbani* (hymns) from the Guru Granth Sahib. Devotees sit around the center and toss flowers and money toward the jewel-studded canopy, where the silk-enshrouded Guru Granth Sahib lies.

The **Guru Granth Sahib** (considered by the Sikhs as a living teacher, more than just a book) is brought to the temple from the Akal Takhat each day and returned at night. The morning ceremony takes place at around 3:30am, the procession at 10pm. Arrive about an hour early to observe the ceremony on the second floor of the Hari Mandir. Hymns echo through the building before the book is finally revealed and the priest takes over the prayers; he chants, folds the book in gold leaf and more silk, and finally places it on the golden palanquin. Head downstairs at this point, and you may end up in the line of devotees pushing each other for the privilege of bearing the holy burden. Finally, a blaring serpentine horn and communal drum beating signal a final prayer that puts the book to bed, near the flag-staff. The entire ceremony lasts about an hour and a half.

GATAKA: 400 YEARS OF COOL WEAPONS

The Sikhs' success in resisting centuries of oppression is in part due to their skill as warriors. Through countless battles, the group developed a martial art known as *gataka*. Today, young would-be warriors practice *gataka* on the roof of the Guru-ka-Langar (daily 8:30-11pm). They enjoy having visitors watch as they deftly wield the *neja* (spears), swords, bamboo sticks, and other ancient weapons and practice *talwar baji* (fencing), or as it's more bluntly known, *kirpan* (the art of stabbing). The most impressive weapon is the *chakkar*, a wooden ring with stone spheres dangling off it by 4-foot strings. The warrior stands in the middle and spins the ring, the whirling balls forming a barrier around him, then tosses it up into the air (still spinning) for someone nearby to catch. Watching the nightly spectacle is exciting, but participating is even better—the warriors will often let you try the weapons out. To really indulge in *gataka*, they recommend heading out to Raia, 50km outside of Amritsar, where Baba Bakala, the training center for the most hard-core students, is located on GT Rd.

AROUND THE TEMPLE. Step outside to the left (north) side, onto the *pradakhina*, the marble path leading around the temple. On this north side is a stairwell leading to the second floor, where flowers, animals, and hymns ornament the walls and where you can catch a good look at the procession and Adi Granth below. On the east side of this floor is a small *shish mahal* (hall of mirrors). Once occupied by the gurus, the halls now reverberate with the voices of modern-day priests engaged in the *akhand path*, the ongoing reading of the holy book. The **Har-ki-Pari** (Steps of God), on the ground floor on the temple's east (back) side, allows visitors easy access to the most sacred section of the tank's waters.

No visit to the Golden Temple is complete without a meal at the **Guru-ka-Langar,** the enormous community kitchen characteristic of all Sikh temples. Sikh founder Guru Nanak instituted the custom of *pangat* (dining together) to reinforce the idea of equality. *Pangat* continues in the dining hall, where basic meals are dished out daily to the rows of hungry thousands who sit together, regardless of wealth or caste. As one row eats, the next gathers in an ongoing cycle. The meal consists of basically all-you-can-eat *dal-chapatis;* simply hold out cupped hands as the *chapati* chap walks by and he'll toss you more. Afterwards, kindly leave a donation in one of the charity boxes, since this ongoing charity is largely funded by such contributions. A glimpse of the kitchen reveals the heaps of *chapatis* that are flipped nimbly on flaming woodstoves and a gigantic cauldron of simmering *dal*.

Just beyond the more modern Hargobind *gurudwara* to the south is the nine-story **Tower of Baba Atal Rai.** According to legend, the tower is named after the son of Guru Hargobind, who perturbed his father with his precociousness, performing a miracle at age nine. In shame, the young *baba* came to this spot and died. On the first floor are some detailed miniatures depicting episodes from Guru Nanak's life and a *nagarah* (drum) for your beating pleasure. The other floors are empty, but you can climb past them to the top for an unsurpassed view of Amritsar, the Golden Temple, and the tank of Kamalsar to the south.

OTHER SIGHTS

JALLIANWALA BAGH. Although the Golden Temple taps most of Amritsar's touristic energies, the city does have other interesting sights. About two blocks north of the temple's main entrance is Jallianwala Bagh, the site of one of the most horrific moments in colonial—and world—history. On April 13, 1919, crowds filled Jallianwala Bagh to peacefully protest a law allowing the British to imprison Indians without trial. British Brigadier-General Reginald EH Dyer was brought in to quell the disturbance. Dyer stood behind 150 troops in front of the main alley, the only entrance and exit to the compound, and ordered his men to open fire without warning on the 10,000 men, women, and children who had gathered there. The shooting continued for an estimated 6 to 15 minutes. People were shot as they perched to jump over walls; others drowned after diving into wells. Dyer's troops had fired 1650 rounds, and nearly all of them found their mark. In all, about 400 people died, while 1500 were left wounded. The massacre sparked a rallying cry for Indian insurgence. The Bengali poet Rabindranath Tagore, who had been knighted after winning the Nobel Prize for Literature in 1913, returned his knighthood after the massacre. Dyer was reprimanded and relieved of his duties but never charged with any crime. In 1997, Queen Elizabeth II visited Jallianwala Bagh. Although no official apology was made during her controversial visit, the British Monarch remarked on the regrettability of the massacre, and laid a wreath at the memorial to the victims. Today, Jallianwala Bagh is a calm garden, frequented by college kids and picknicking families. The stone well is a monument to the drowned Indians who jumped in attempting to flee, and the **Martyr's Gallery** features portraits of heroes involved in the event. (Open summer daily 9am-5pm, winter daily 10am-1pm and 3-7pm.)

RAM BAGH. In the northern part of Amritsar, Ram Bagh is a park between Mall and Queens Rd., northeast of the railway station. At the park's south edge, the impressive **Darshani Deorhi** gate testifies that the park was originally encircled by solid ramparts and a moat. On the northwest corner of the park stands a menacing statue of Maharaja Ranjit Singh, the Sikh responsible for the early 19th-century restoration of the Golden Temple and, along with Napoleon, supposedly the greatest man of his time. Ram Bagh served as his summer residence between 1818 and 1837, and the central building now houses the **Ranijit Singh Museum,** containing oil paintings, weapons, manuscripts, and miniatures from the maharaja's era. The tourist office's pamphlet, *Amritsar: Spiritual Centre of Punjab*, is a good guide to the museum. *(Museum open Tu-Su 10am-4:45pm; Rs5.)*

DURGIANA MANDIR. The high profile of the Golden Temple overshadows the existence of the tiny Hindu shrines tucked into alleyways in the immediate vicinity, as well as the more impressive Durgiana Mandir. This temple, set back from the busy street four blocks northwest of the Golden Temple, honors the goddess Durga. The exterior, set on a platform in a medium-sized tank, is surprisingly evocative of the Hari Mandir.

INDIAN ACADEMY OF FINE ARTS. Across the street from Ram Bagh on Lawrence Rd., east of the Sindhi Coffee House, the Indian Academy of Fine Arts puts on periodic exhibitions of modern Indian art *(open daily 9am-7pm; free, but* baksheesh *to the guard who opens the gallery just for you would be appropriate).*

NEAR AMRITSAR: TARN TARAN ਟਰਣ ਟਰਨ

Once the Hari Mandir has whetted your appetite for shiny, golden Sikh temples, head 22km south to the town of Tarn Taran. Buses leave every half-hour from the main stand (1hr., Rs9). From the Tarn Taran bus stand, it's a 15-minute walk along the main road and then through the narrow alley of the bazaar up to the local *gurudwara*. Its founder, Guru Arjun Dev, built the temple in 1768 to commemorate Guru Ram Das, who, in an act of selfless concern, slept side-by-side with a

BORDER BALLET A few people go to Wagah to *cross* the border, but a crowd always shows up to *watch* the border. A half-hour before sunset, an elaborate nightly ritual accompanies the Indo-Pakistani border's closing and the lowering of the neighboring nations' flags. Tourists crowd around the spiked gate on either side and jostle for the best views. Right on schedule, with a near-farcical dose of solemnity, the ceremony unfolds. As one officer barks an order and another follows with furious stomping and wild high-stepping, the audiences on both sides break into raucous applause. After some machismo-packed face-offs and lengthy siren-like yells, the respective flags are lowered, the lights go bright, the bugles blare, and the visitors mob the gate for a glimpse of the faces on the other side—or for a chance to toe one of the world's most famous white lines.

leper. Though local clinicians don't provide any evidence for the common belief that the water here cures leprosy, they do attest to its curative effects on several minor skin conditions. The architectural style here resembles that of the Amritsar complex, and the *parikrama* encircling the still waters is actually larger than its counterpart in the Golden Temple. The *gurudwara* provides decent rooms (free) in the large yellow building just outsides the west (not the main) entrance.

 ## PAKISTAN BORDER

> **WARNING.** If you want to cross into Pakistan, **make sure you have your Pakistani visa and that your Indian visa allows multiple entries.** Crossing the line isn't easy. For more information, please see **Surrounding Countries**, p. 13.

Amritsar is the first or last stop in India for travelers heading to or from Pakistan; the *only* border crossing between the two countries is at **Wagah,** 28km from Amritsar. Take a **bus** to **Attari** (every 15min. 7am-6pm, 1hr., Rs11), and on the right look for the impressive Khalsa College. From Attari it is a 2km rickshaw ride to the border (Rs10). The border opens daily from 10am to 4pm. If you only wish to visit the border, wait until after 4pm, or better still, for the 7pm ceremony (see below). The last bus to **Amritsar** leaves Attari at 6pm so if you are here for the 7pm flag ceremony, you can take a cab back (Rs50). If you are crossing over, pass through the customs on the left and then walk the remaining 200m to the actual line. To enter Pakistan, take the **train** from Amritsar to **Lahore** (M and Th 9am). For the trains, all checking is done in Attari. There is also a direct **bus** between Delhi and Lahore (Tu, W, F, and Sa).

At Wagah, **Punjab Tourism,** just behind the check-post at the entrance, supplies the standard, outdated brochures and maps (open M-Sa 10am-4pm). Next door, the **State Bank of India** changes traveler's checks but not Pakistani rupees (open 11am-4pm). The money-changers, however, will. There is also a **post office** for last minute send-offs. If you are stranded overnight, **Neem Chameli** (tel. 382646) provides both spacious (Rs400) and cramped (Rs200) rooms. However, some sinks are missing and the bedsheets are unmilitarily disordered.

RAJASTHAN
राजस्थान

Unflinching valor, dauntless courage, and steadfast honor are values sown deep into this "Land of Kings," a region whose soil has been soaked by massive blood-baths raining from the hearty Rajput people's unyielding defense of their territory. In the cliff-top fortresses of the Thar Desert, Rajput women and children followed their fallen warriors in honorable death, choosing mass immolation (*jauhar*) over surrender. Perhaps it was the stark desert and merciless heat that bred the raw intensity of the legendary warrior clans who ruled these parts for a millennium; the stubborn loyalty and pride of Rajasthan's people prevails to this day.

Rajasthan's fiercely independent maharajas made the region a mess of uncooperative kingdoms that was easily conquered by the powerful, united Mughal Empire. The Mughals quickly realized, however, that granting the Rajputs some power in their ruling hierarchy was more effective than engaging in punishing battles with unwavering foes. When the British overthrew the Mughals, the maharajas collaborated with the Raj; in return, they were given license to live in utter decadence, depleting the state's resources and arresting its social and economic development. Through it all, though, the common people remained loyal to their ruling elites. To this day, the people's unequivocal pride, expressed so poignantly in the traditional folk verse of the region, complements—rather than counters—the enduring culture of privilege so apparent in the lavish palaces, *havelis*, temples, and pavilions throughout the state. The close relationship between maharaja and subject, often one of *noblesse oblige*, persists in the politics of today, where Rajasthani royals running for office are enthusiastically elected by their loyal citizens.

Rajasthan can be divided into three geographical regions. The flat lands of the east feature rich national parks and cosmopolitan centers like Jaipur, the state's capital and the western corner of India's "Golden Triangle" of tourism. In the western "Marwar" region, the plains gradually yield to the arid lands of the Thar Desert and its imposing forts. In the south, the majestic Aravalli Mountains of the "Mewar" region decorate the landscape with lush valleys and mountain lakes.

HIGHLIGHTS OF RAJASTHAN

- **Jaipur** is Rajasthan's most popular destination. Its **City Palace** (p. 289), **Hawa Mahal** (p. 290), and **Amber Fort** (p. 290) are worth all the hype.
- The **lake palaces** of **Udaipur** (p. 310) have long been a draw for honeymooners and secret agents alike—one glimpse of the sunrise city and you'll see why.
- **Jaisalmer's** illuminated fort sates most tourists' cravings for a taste of life in the middle ages—the rest journey into the desert on the hump of a camel.
- Peaceful **Pushkar** (p. 297) is a quiet oasis, soothing weary pilgrims and travelers 361 days a year. The four-day **Pushkar Fair** (p. 300) is another story entirely.

Today, Rajasthan's colorful history and relics of the *richesse* (in various states of preservation) that lured Mughal invaders have inspired a tourist siege, making Rajasthan the most visited state of India. Palaces have been converted into "heritage hostels," and camera-toting tourists now walk the halls of former residences of maharajas. The tourist boom has made the state wealthier and has created a well developed infrastructure, but it has also had deleterious effects—a fiercely competitive clamor for dollars, pounds, and yen, and an over-abundance of tourist traffic obscure the local culture in many cities. Nevertheless, while some Rajputs have traded their swords for cell-phones, you will still be able to catch occasional glimpses—in the colored *bandhani* cloth of Jaipur's markets, the fortress at Chittaugarh, the pastoral lifestyle of the hill country, the camels in Pushkar, and the opulent palaces of Udaipur—of the state's rich heritage.

JAIPUR जयपु

Rajasthan's most popular tourist destination, Jaipur forms the southwest corner of India's "Golden Triangle," together with Delhi and Agra. Although many tourists only stay long enough to have their pictures snapped in front of all the major attractions, you may want to dig in for a longer stay to more fully experience the culture; its easy-going, cosmopolitan spirit and elegant architecture give an unmistakably regal air to the Rajasthani capital.

The city was conceived out of the vision and prudent urban planning of the remarkable 18th-century Rajput leader Maharaja Sawai Jai Singh II, ruler of the region from 1699 to 1744. By all accounts, he possessed a rare erudition and a ferocious curiosity for the sciences. During the early years of his reign his kingdom was threatened by both the Marathas and the Mughals. But fortune favored the maharaja; his intelligence won him the respect and alliance of Mughal emperor Aurangzeb, and his military savvy led the Rajput forces to crushing victories against the Marathas. By the mid-1720s, having established political stability in his territories, Jai Singh decided to move the capital from its hillside fort in Amber to a new city of his own design. With help from the renowned Bengali architect Vidyadhar Chakravarti, the maharaja built the magnificent walled city of Jaipur.

While carefully laying out Jaipur according to a mathematical grid model of the ancient Hindu map of the universe, Jai Singh and Chakravarti made the city both beautiful and functional. High walls were constructed for the city's defense, and the entrances to stores and homes were placed on side streets so that the Maharaja's massive royal processions could pass without disturbing the daily life of Jaipur's residents. Wide sidewalks and streets were designed to facilitate the easy flow of pedestrian traffic. A complex system of underground aqueducts brought ample drinking water into the fortified city.

The British imperial presence in the 19th century brought about a drastic cosmetic transformation that has persisted to this day. To celebrate a visit in 1856 by Prince Albert, the city painted itself pink. Newsman Stanley Reed dubbed Jaipur the "Pink City," and the name stuck. Modern Jaipur, with its population of 1.8 million, has long since outgrown the walls of Reed's Pink City, but this old world enclave remains Jaipur's cultural and commercial center, replete with extraordinary museums, forts, temples, and palaces, as well as the crowded markets and congested streets that characterize India at its hectic best and worst.

▗ TRANSPORTATION

Airport: Sanganer Airport (enquiry: Indian Airlines tel. 721333 or 721519; Jet Airways tel. 551729 or 551733), 15km south of the city. Buses (Rs4-5) leave Ajmeri Gate for the airport every 30min. Taxis cost Rs200-300. To: **Ahmedabad** (3 per week, 1hr., US$95); **Kolkata** (3 per week, 2½hr., US$200); **Delhi** (2-3 per day, 40min., US$55); **Jodhpur** (2 per day, 1hr., US$70); **Mumbai** (2-3 per day, 1½-3½hr., US$140); **Udaipur** (1 per day, 45min., US$70); **Jaisalmer** (3 per week, 1hr., US$110). **Air India,** Ganpati Plaza, MI Rd. (tel. 368569 or 368742; fax 360756). Open M-Sa 9:30am-1pm and 2-5:30pm, Sa 9:30am-2pm. **Indian Airlines,** Nehru Place, Tonk Rd. (tel. 514407 or 515324; fax 510344). Open daily 10am-1pm and 2-5pm. The more centrally located **Satyam Travels and Tours,** Jaipur Towers ground floor (tel. 378794; fax 375426), is an authorized agent for Indian Airlines. Books, changes, and delivers tickets at no extra fee. Open M-Sa 9:30am-7:30pm. **Jet Air Limited,** Jaipur Towers first floor, MI Rd. (tel. 375430 or 367409; fax 374242), is an agent for Gulf Air, Royal Jordanian, Bangladesh Biman, TWA, and Air Canada. **Jet Airways,** (tel. 360763 or 370594; fax 374242) is in the same office as Jet Air Limited. **Air France,** Jaipur Towers 2nd fl. (tel. 377051 or 370509). Open M-Sa 9:30am-5:30pm. **KLM,** Jaipur Towers 2nd fl., MI Rd. (tel./fax 360053). Open M-Sa 9:30am-6pm. **British Airways,** Usha Plaza, MI Rd. (tel. 370374). Open M-F 9:30am-6pm, Sa 9:30am-2pm. **Lufthansa,** Saraogi Mansion, MI Rd. (tel. 562822; fax 562944), near New Gate. Open M-F 9:30am-6pm, Sa 9:30am-2pm.

RAJASTHAN

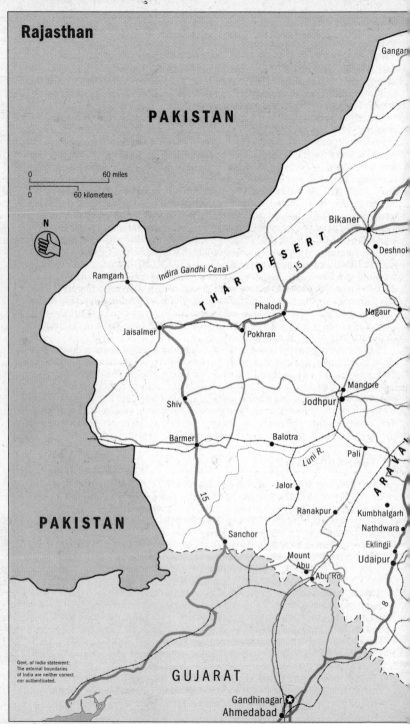

Rajasthan

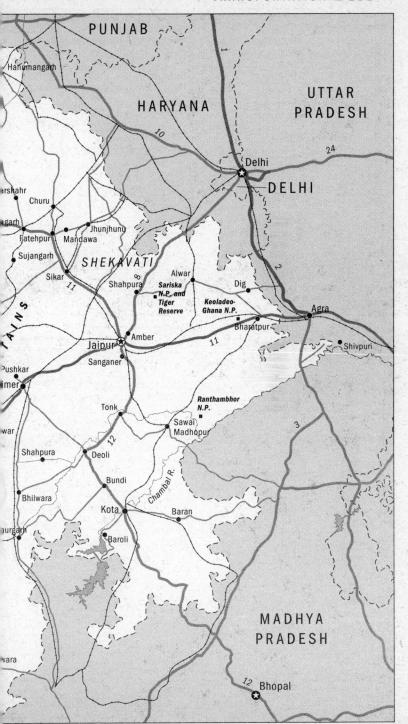

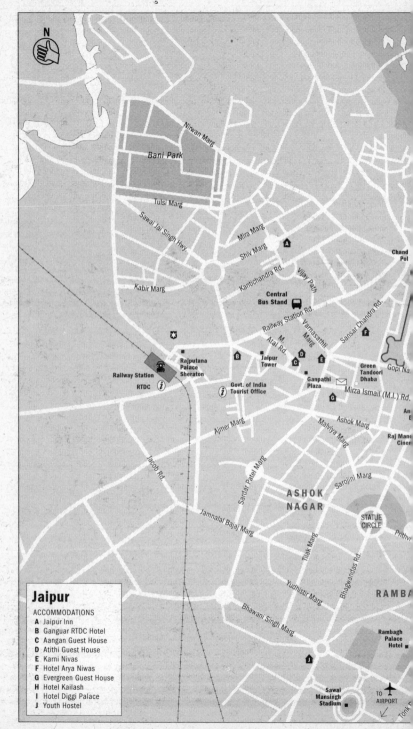

N

Nirwan Marg

Bani Park

Tulsi Marg

Sawai Jai Singh Hwy.

Mira Marg

Shiv Marg

A

Chand
Pol

Kantichandra Rd.

Vijay Path

Kabir Marg

**Central
Bus Stand**

Railway Station Rd.

Varnasathi Marg

Sansar Chandra Rd.

F

Atal Rd.

M.

Railway Station

**Rajputana
Palace
Sheraton**

B

**Jaipur
Tower**

D

E

**Green
Tandoori
Dhaba**

Gopi Na.

RTDC

ⓘ

**Govt. of India
Tourist Office**

ⓘ

**Ganpathi
Plaza**

✉

Mirza Ismail (M.I.) Rd.

G

Ashok Marg

An
E

Ajmer Marg

Malviya Marg

**Raj Mand
Ciner**

Jacob Rd.

Sardar Patel Marg

Sarojini Marg

**ASHOK
NAGAR**

Jamnalal Bajaj Marg

Tilak Marg

Bhagwandas Rd.

**STATUE
CIRCLE**

Prithvi

RAMBA

Yudhistir Marg

Bhawani Singh Marg

J

**Rambagh
Palace
Hotel**

Jaipur

ACCOMMODATIONS
A Jaipur Inn
B Ganguar RTDC Hotel
C Aangan Guest House
D Atithi Guest House
E Karni Nivas
F Hotel Arya Niwas
G Evergreen Guest House
H Hotel Kailash
I Hotel Diggi Palace
J Youth Hostel

**Sawai
Mansingh
Stadium**

TO
AIRPORT

Tonk

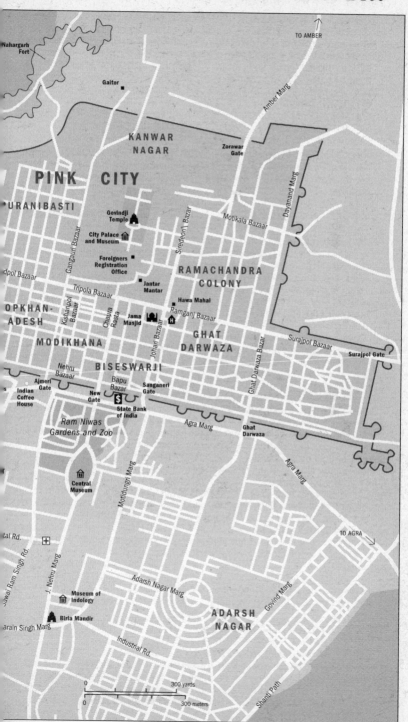

TO AMBER

Nahargarh
Fort

Gaitor ■

KANWAR
NAGAR

Amber Marg

Zorawar
Gate

PINK   CITY

URANIBASTI

Govindji
Temple

City Palace
and Museum

Gangaur Bazaar

Siredeoh Bazaar

Motikala Bazaar

Dayanand Marg

Foreigners
Registration
Office

dpol Bazaar

Tripola Bazaar

Kishanpol Bazaar

Chaura Rasta

Jantar
Mantar

RAMACHANDRA
COLONY

OPKHAN-
ADESH

MODIKHANA

Jama
Masjid

Johari Bazaar

Hawa Mahal

H

Ramganj Bazaar

GHAT
DARWAZA

Surajpol Bazaar

Surajpol Gate

Ghat Darwaza Bazaar

BISESWARJI

Nehru
Bazaar

Ajmeri
Gate

Indian
Coffee
House

New
Gate

Bapu
Bazaar

Sanganeri
Gate

State Bank
of India

Agra Marg

Ghat
Darwaza

Ram Niwas
Gardens and Zoo

Motidungri Marg

Agra Marg

Central
Museum

TO AGRA

tal Rd.

Jawai Ram Singh Rd.

J. Nehru Marg

Adarsh Nagar Marg

Govind Marg

Museum of
Indology

Birla Mandir

arain Singh Marg

Industrial Rd.

ADARSH
NAGAR

Shanti Path

0   300 yards

0   300 meters

Trains: Jaipur Railway Station (tel. 131). **Advance Reservation Office** (tel. 135), to the left of the station. English-speaking staff. Open M-Sa 8am-8pm, Su 8am-2pm. Fares listed are 2nd/1st class. To: **Agra** (*Marudhar Exp.* 4864, 7hr., Rs77/564); **Ahmedabad** (*Delhi Mail* 9106, 4:30am, Rs187); **Ajmer** (*Shatabdi Exp.* 2015, M-Sa 10:40am, 2hr., Rs290); **Bikaner** (*Intercity Exp.* 2468, 3:20pm, 7hr., Rs89/643; *Bikaner Exp.* 4737, 9pm, 10hr., Rs127/643); **Chennai** (9767, Tu, F and Su 4:15pm, Rs410); **Delhi** (*Intercity Superfast* 9760, 6am, 5½hr., Rs77/236; *Jammu Tawi Exp.* 2414, 4:30pm, 5½hr., Rs110/564; *Shekhavati Exp.* 9734, 5:45pm, 5½hr., Rs110/564); **Jodhpur** (*Marudhar Exp.* 4863, 12:25pm; *Superfast Exp.* 2307, 4:05pm; *Intercity Exp.* 2465, 5:30pm, 5hr., Rs79/573); **Mumbai** (*Superfast Exp.* 2956, 1:40pm, 18hr.; *Exp.* 9707, 7am, 24hr., Rs277/1357); **Udaipur** (*Chetak Exp.* 9615, 9:50pm, 13½hr., Rs141/700).

Buses: Sindhi Camp Central Bus Stand, Station Rd. (tel. 205790 or 205621). To: **Agra** (13 per day 5:30am-midnight, 5hr., Rs110); **Chittaurgarh** (9:15, 10am, noon, 11pm, and midnight, 8hr., Rs140); **Delhi** (every 15min. 5:30am-12:30am, 5½hr., Rs190); **Jaisalmer** (10:45 and 11:30pm, 13hr., Rs290); **Jodhpur** (5 per day 5am-8pm, 7hr., Rs160); **Mt. Abu** (7:30am, 12hr., Rs246); **Udaipur** (6 per day 9:15am-9:30pm, 9hr., Rs200). **Private buses** depart from the same stand. Private bus companies line Station Rd. and Motilal Atal Rd., off MI Rd.; most hotels can make reservations too.

Local Transportation: Unmetered **auto-rickshaws** and **cycle-rickshaws** are the best way to get around the city; prepare for heavy haggling (Rs15-30 by auto-rickshaw between places in the old city). **Local buses** depart from the Central Bus Stand, from all the sights, and at most major intersections every 5min. within the old city and every 10-15min. in other areas (Rs4-10). Ambassador **taxis** can be picked up at the railway station (Rs10-13 per km). **Cars** (with driver) can be hired from the RTDC at the Tourist Hotel on MI Rd. (Rs140 per hr., Rs715 per day) and from some private companies as well. **Bicycles** are convenient for exploration, and many budget hotels will arrange rentals. Near Ajmeri Gate in **Kishanpol Bazaar**, you can rent bicycles for Rs35-50 per day. Open daily 8am-10pm. **Mohan Cycle Works,** MI Rd. (tel. 372335), across from the Indian Coffee House, charges Rs25 per day (10 day min.). Open M-Sa 10:30am-8pm.

✦ ORIENTATION

Though Jaipur is a good-sized city, getting around is made easy because of its wide, straight streets, provided you can keep track of street name changes. The walled **Pink City**, encompassing most of the sights, is in the northeast; the **new city** sprawls south and west. The most important roads in the new city are **Mizra Ismail (MI) Road, Railway Station Road,** and **Sansar Chandra Road,** which intersect one another in the vicinity of the **railway station,** the **Central Bus Station,** the GPO, and most budget hotels and restaurants. MI Rd., which is Jaipur's main east-west thoroughfare, becomes **Agra Marg** after it skirts the three gates that lead into the heart of the Pink City: **Ajmeri Gate, New Gate,** and **Sanganeri Gate.** From Ajmeri Gate, **Kishanpol Bazaar** (which becomes **Gangauri Bazaar**) leads north into the Pink City and **Sawai Ram Singh Road** leads south to the new city. From Sanganeri Gate, **Johari Bazaar** (which becomes **Hawa Mahal Bazaar**) runs nearly 2km north. Just south of New Gate and beyond the **Ram Niwas Gardens, Jawaharlal Nehru Marg** runs south for nearly 2km before changing names and continues past the Birla Mandir, east of the Ram Bagh Palace and the station. The Pink City's western gate is **Chand Pol.** The road that runs under it is called **Nirwan Marg** outside the Pink City, but it changes names four times before leaving the city at its eastern gate, **Suraj Pol.**

✦ PRACTICAL INFORMATION

TOURIST AND FINANCIAL SERVICES

Tourist Office: RTDC Tourist Information Bureau (tel. 375466), platform 1 of the railway station. Provides useful maps and brochures. Accommodating, English-speaking staff. Open daily 7am-6pm. A second branch (tel. 370180) is in the Tourist Hotel, off MI Rd., near the GPO. Open M-Sa 10am-5pm. **Government of India Tourist Office,** in Hotel

Khasi Kothi (tel./fax 372200), near MI Rd. and Station Rd. intersection. Open M-F 9am-6pm, Sa 9am-4:30pm. The monthly publication *Jaipur Vision,* available at most bookstores for Rs20, has lots of useful tourist information as well.

Tours: RTDC offers full-day and evening **city tours,** which jam the Pink City into a compact, unimaginative, and uncomfortable drive-by (half-day Rs75; full-day Rs115; does not include entrance fees). Arrange all tours through the Tourist Information Bureau at the railway station. Both the RTDC and the Government of India Tourist Office can arrange government-approved private **guides** (half-day Rs230 for up to 4 people). For more information about private guides, contact the **Guide Room** at Rambagh Palace Hotel (tel. 381919). If you want to avoid paying inflated prices at the appointed RTDC lunch spot, pack your own lunch.

Budget Travel: Rajasthan Tours, Rambagh Palace Hotel (tel. 381668; fax 381784). Open daily 7:30am-6pm. **Tourist Guide Service,** MI Rd., near Panch Batti (tel. 367735; fax 376251). Open daily 9am-6pm. **Priti Travels and Tours,** 180 Guru Nanak Pura (tel. 566806; fax 561492), in Raja Park outside Hotel Meru Palace. Open daily 8:30am-9pm.

Immigration Office: Foreigners Registration Office (tel. 669391), behind Rajasthan Police Headquarters near Jantar Mantar. Contact at least 1 week before visa expiration date. Open M-Sa 10am-5pm. Closed 2nd Sa. of each month.

Currency Exchange: State Bank of India (tel. 561163; fax 564597), off MI Rd. near Sanganeri Gate. Currency exchange and traveler's checks. Open M-F 10am-2pm and 3-5pm, Sa 10am-noon and 12:30-2pm. **Andhra Bank,** MI Rd. (tel. 374529; fax 365094), near Panch Batti. Cash advances on Visa, MC. 1% Service charge per transaction. Open M-F 10am-2pm, Sa 10am-noon. **Thomas Cook,** Jaipur Tower, 1st fl. (tel. 360940; fax 360974), near the intersection of Station and MI Rd. Currency exchange, traveler's checks, and money wiring. Open M-Sa 9:30am-6pm. **American Express,** MI Rd. (tel. 367735; fax 376251), in the Tourist Guide Service. Open daily 9am-6pm.

LOCAL SERVICES

Luggage Storage: Jaipur Railway Station, Rs5-7 per item per day. Open 24hr.

Market: Food and vegetable stalls abound in the old city—most near Chand Pol and along MI Rd. Most bazaars open dawn-dusk, closed Su; Bapu Bazaar is open Su, closed M.

Library: Radhakrishnan Public Library, Jawaharlal Nehru Marg (tel. 516694). Tourists aren't allowed to check out books, but they may browse. Open W-M 7am-7pm.

Bookstore: Books Corner, MI Rd. (tel. 366323; fax 366313), near Niro's Restaurant. Good collection of English books and international periodicals. Open daily 10am-11pm. **The Book Shop** (tel. 381430), in Rambagh Palace Hotel, off Bhawani Singh Marg, has an expansive, expensive selection of books about India. Open daily 7am-11pm. Bookstores line Chaura Rasta near Tripola Bazaar. Most open daily 10am-8pm.

EMERGENCY AND COMMUNICATIONS

Pharmacy: Pharmacies cluster around hospitals. There is also one in Shiv Marg, across from Jaipur Inn. Most open daily 8am-10pm. There pharmacy in front of Santokba Durlabhji Memorial Hospital (tel. 571301) is open 24hr.

Hospital/Medical Services: Sawai Mansingh Hospital, Sawai Ram Singh Rd. (tel. 560291). Government-run, large, efficient, organized, and English-speaking. Among the many **private hospitals,** the best (English-speaking, clean, 24hr.) are **Santokba Durlabhji Memorial Hospital,** Bhawani Singh Marg (tel. 566251 or 566258), and **Soni Hospital,** Kahota Bagh (tel. 571122 or 571123; fax 564392), off Jawaharlal Nehru Marg.

Police: Main Police Station (tel. 565555), in King Edward Memorial Bldg., near Ajmeri Gate. Branches are abundant—look for the red-and-blue diagonal pattern.

Post Office: GPO, MI Rd. (tel. 368740). Contains a museum filled with old stamps and weapons carried by mail runners of yore. Open for *Poste Restante,* counter 5, M-Sa 10am-6pm. Stamps sold M-Sa 8am-7pm, Su 10am-6pm. **Branch offices** are in Tripolia Bazaar, Bapu Bazaar, Jawahar Nagar, and Shastri Nagar. **Postal Code:** 302001.

RAJASTHAN

Internet: Communicator, G-4/5 Jaipur Tower ground floor (tel. 368061 or 204100; fax 374413; email pravin@jp1.dot.net.in). Internet use Rs4 per min. Also offers email, ISD/STD, and fax. Open M-Sa 9:30am-8pm. **Universal Courier and Communications,** M.I. Road (tel. 36790 or 367903; fax 375970), across from Indian Coffee House. Internet use Rs4 per min. Open daily 8:30-8:30pm. Atithi Guest House, Aangan Guest House, and Evergreen Guest House offer Internet access at Rs4 per min. to guests and non-guests. Hotel Arya Niwas charges Rs75 per 30min.

PHONE CODE	0141

▚ ACCOMMODATIONS

The budget hotel situation is frustratingly competitive. Upon exiting the bus or railway station you will be mobbed by rickshaw drivers prodding or pushing you to a particular hotel. It's a win-win-win situation for them: if you choose their hotel, they get a 50% commission, which will show up on your hotel bill; if you insist on another budget hotel, they simply charge you triple fare (or refuse to take you); and if you opt for a higher-end hotel, they quadruple their fare since you're "rich." Your cheapest bet is to shell out the triple fare and go where you want. Or just walk down a block (or three) and find less ruthless local transportation.

Hotels cluster around the bus and railway stations, and a fair number occupy MI Rd. and vicinity. Unfortunately, few hotels can claim the Pink City proper as turf. It may be worth looking into home-stay accommodations, arranged through the tourist office at the railway station (Rs150-800 per night).

■ **Jaipur Inn,** Shiv Marg (tel./fax 201121). From Sawai Jai Singh Highway, go right onto Shiv Marg 5min. down the circle, and into the large, inoffensively pink building. Clean, well-lit, plant-filled corridors, teem with loitering backpackers. Incredible roof-top restaurant. Facilities include ping-pong table, laundry service, and store. More expensive rooms offer attached baths, air-cooling, and great views. Lockers. Check-out 10am. Camping in the front garden Rs50 per person; dorm beds Rs70; singles Rs150-400; doubles Rs200-500. Reservations recommended.

■ **Atithi Guest House,** 1 Park House Scheme (tel. 378679; fax 379496), MI Rd. Owners Vijay and Poorva welcome guests to this home-away-from-home with bright, airy, and refreshingly immaculate rooms all with attached baths and telephones. Garden with waterfall in front and plant-filled rooftop terrace provide peaceful getaway from bustling locale. Great veg. food and attentive service. Hot water 8am-12:30pm and 7-10:30pm or on request. STD/ISD, fax, email, and Internet. Check-out noon. Air-cooled singles begin at Rs300, with A/C Rs600; doubles Rs350/650.

Hotel Diggi Palace, Sawai Ram Singh Marg (tel. 373091; fax 370359), about 1km south of Ajmeri Gate. A spacious, 200 year-old converted palace in a mellow location. All food in the terrace restaurant is organically grown by the owner, and the cooking fuel is produced from the manure of his cows and polo horses. Surrounded by a beautiful garden, all the rooms look in on courtyards with outdoor sitting areas. Unreliable but friendly service. Check-out noon. Singles Rs100, with bath Rs250; doubles Rs100/250-950.

Aangan Guest House, 4 Park House Scheme (tel. 373449; fax 364596; email aangan25@hotmail.com), off M.I. Rd., near All India Radio. A homey, friendly place with aging rooms and relaxing garden. STD/ISD, fax, telephones, Internet, and car hire. All rooms with attached bath (hot water!) and air-cooling. Check-out noon. Singles Rs175-400, with A/C Rs500; doubles Rs250-500/600. Extra beds Rs50. TVs Rs50.

Hotel Arya Niwas, Sansar Chandra Rd. (tel. 372456; fax 364376; www.indobase.com/aryaniwas; email aryahotel@jp1.dot.net.in). A large, simple, well-run hotel built in a renovated *haveli*. Lots of natural light and cross-ventilation keep the place bright and cool. STD/ISD, email, Internet, currency exchange, and small shop. All rooms have attached bath and air-cooling. Check-out noon. Singles Rs300-500, with A/C 400-600; doubles Rs400-600. Extra bed Rs100; extra person Rs50. Reservations essential Oct.-Mar.

Evergreen Guest House (tel. 363446 or 362415; fax 204234; email evergreen34@hotmail.com), off MI Rd. Head past the GPO on the left, and take the next right. Mingle with other tourists all day and night. Rooms (all with attached bath) are rather bare. Swimming pool, STD/ISD service, email, Internet, and luggage storage. Buckets of hot water on request; 24hr. hot water for pricier rooms. Check-out 10am. Singles Rs100, with air-cooling Rs200, with A/C Rs450; doubles Rs120/250/490. Reservations recommended Oct.-Mar.

Shahpura House, D-257 Devi Marg (tel. 203069; fax 201494), Bani Park, 1km from the railway station. Old-style *haveli* with elegantly painted walls run by royal family of Shahpura. Pricier rooms are spacious with ornately carved furniture and great baths. Smaller, less expensive rooms are not as indulgent. Garden sitting area, small collection of English books and magazines, laundry service. Check-out noon. Rooms Rs500-750.

Karni Niwas, Moti Lal Atal Rd. (tel. 365433 or 216947; fax 375034; email karniniwas@hotmail.com), behind Hotel Neelam. Simple rooms adorned with Mughal paintings in a homey atmosphere. Restaurant, laundry service, complimentary pick-up at train or bus station. Check-out noon. Singles 225-400; doubles Rs275-450.

Hotel Kailash, Johari Bazaar (tel. 565372). Look for the narrow door between stores. One of the few located in the heart of the Pink City. Sure, it's noisy, but it's where the action is. Adequate rooms, with central air-cooling, telephones, black-and-white TV, and hot water until 10am (free buckets after 10am). Check-out 24hr. Singles Rs130-160, with bath Rs190-325; doubles Rs150-200/220-370. Reservations recommended.

Youth Hostel (HI/AYH), Bhagwandas Rd. (tel. 518330), near the intersection of Bhawani Singh Rd. Clean common baths and inexpensive lodging at the expense of a little freedom. Curfew 10pm, lights out 11pm, liquor and drugs prohibited, 5-day max. stay. Guests not allowed in rooms 11am-4pm for cleaning. Linen charge Rs10 per week. Check-in 7-11am and 4-9pm. Check-out 10am. Dorm beds Rs20, nonmembers Rs40; singles Rs100/150; doubles Rs 100/150.

🍴 FOOD

Jaipur doesn't have its own renowned specialties, but you'll find a range of Rajasthani classics. For cheap quickies, the *bhojnalyas* (diners) on Station Rd. in the old city are where the locals go. For those with a sweet tooth, the *mishri, mawas,* and *ghevars* of Jaipur are the best in the state.

Shri Shanker Bhojnalya, Station Rd., outside Chand Pol. Perhaps the most popular *bhojnalya* in town. Cheap, quality food: excellent *thalis* (Rs30) and tandoori that never fails to draw a local crowd. Open daily 9am-11:30pm.

Surya Mahal, MI Rd. (tel. 369840), next to Niro's and Books Corner. Popular among local businessmen, families, coquettish teens, and tourists alike. Specializes in South Indian, Chinese, and pizza. A/C sweet shop in the back. Most entrees under Rs65. Open daily 8am-11pm.

LMB, Johari Bazaar. Incredible veg. food in a quirky A/C environment. Dishes a range of Subcontinental specialties (Rs30-60). Try not to fill up first at the sweet shop in front. Open daily 8am-11:30pm.

Niro's, MI Rd., near Panch Batti. Their card justly claims "quiet grandeur, warm hearted courtesy, personalized service." Add A/C to get the best non-veg. dining experience in town in spite of the touristy crowd. The melange of Indian, Chinese, and Continental dishes comes at a steep-but-worth-it Rs100-150. Open daily 10am-11pm.

Green Tandoori Dhaba (tel. 362791), off MI Rd. near Indian Panch Batti. Locals come here for quality non-veg. food at great prices. Tandoori oven heats up the street along with delicious *rotis* and kebabs (Rs50-70). Those with adventurous tastebuds can munch on *magaj* (goat brain) for a mere Rs30. Open daily 11am-11pm.

Fun and Food Garden Restaurant, Meel Bhawan (tel. 331034), opposite Jyoti petrol pump, 8km from town. The garden atmosphere, complete with live geese, provides the "fun" (not the "food") in this all-veg. restaurant. Generous and tasty entrees make the hike worth your while. Entrees Rs30-55. Open daily 9am-11pm.

Hanuman Dhaba, Road 1, Raja Park (tel. 620582), near where Govind Marg turns into Industrial Rd. Locals go here for quality veg. food at cheap prices (Rs20-45). Street-side seating with views of the busy kitchen. Open daily 9:30am-11pm.

Milky Way, off Bhagwandas Marg. Midway between MI Rd. and Statue Circle, on a side street to the left. Best ice cream in town, thick shakes (Rs25), fountain sodas (Rs10), and sundaes (Rs30). Unique "Herbonic Shake" Rs30. Open daily 9am-midnight.

Indian Coffee House, MI Road (tel. 369008), next to the "Arrow" sign. The notorious chain that serves filling dosas (Rs10-20) and tasty coffee (Rs5). Open daily 8am-9pm.

📺🎵 NIGHTLIFE AND ENTERTAINMENT

BARS AND NIGHTCLUBS. Due to a strange prohibition law that's been in effect for years, only hotels can legally serve alcohol stronger than beer. For air-conditioned, high-class boozing, try the popular **Polo Bar** (tel. 381919) in Rambagh Palace, off Bhawani Singh Rd. (open daily 11am-11:30pm). **Rana Sanga Roof Top Bar** (tel. 378771, ext. 2677), in Mansingh Palace off Sansar Chandra Road, has a 24-hour coffee shop on the ground floor (open daily noon-3pm and 6:30-11pm). The **Sheesh Mahal** (tel. 360011, ext. 1713), in the Welcomgroup Rajputana Palace Sheraton near the railway station, is open daily 11am to 11pm. Getting sloshed at cheaper prices with locals and budget tourists is better accomplished at the **Talab Bar** (tel. 200595), in Swagatam Tourist Bungalow (open noon-3pm and 6-11pm). Other cheap bars include **Amrapali Bar** (tel. 206300), in Chandragupt Hotel across from Sindhi Camp Bus Stand (open daily 7am-11pm), and **Dubki Bar,** Moti Lal Alal Rd., in Hotel Sangam near the Ganpati Complex (open daily 10am-11:30pm).

FESTIVALS. Although discovering Jaipur is a treat year-round, its festivals are especially exciting times to see the city. The **Gangaur Fair,** dedicated to the goddess Gauri, celebrates women and lasts for 18 days after Holi (beginning Apr. 7-8, 2000; Mar. 28-29, 2001). The festival is accompanied by singing, dancing, and parades with incredible costumes and decorations. The **Elephant Festival** features elephant polo and a tug-of-war pitting man against beast (March 19, 2000; March 9, 2001). The **Teej Fair** (Festival of Swings) celebrates the monsoon (Aug. 2-3, 2000; July 23-24, 2001). Decorated swings are hung from trees, and the city goes wild.

THE ARTS. For authentic, traditional Rajasthani dance and music, the **Panghat Theater** (tel. 381919), in Rambagh Palace off Bhawani Singh Rd., offers in-season nightly performances in high-class surroundings for Rs300 per person. Shows are generally 7-9pm. Be sure to call in advance. **Ravindra Manch** (tel. 669061), in Ram Nivas Gardens, offers evening performances of Rajasthani dance, music, and plays, usually for Rs20 or less. Occasional films and fashion shows can be more expensive. The Modern Art Gallery upstairs (tel. 668531) is open daily 10am to 5pm and is free. **Jawahar Kala Kendra,** Jawaharlal Nehru Marg (tel. 510501), offers regular in-season performances of Rajasthani dance and music as well as plays in Hindi and Rajasthani. Performances in the indoor theater are Rs5, and those in the open-air theater are free. There is also an arts library and modern art gallery.

OTHER DIVERSIONS. Jaipur's 16 **cinemas** are packed with people at every show-ing. Regardless of your interest in or comprehension of Hindi films, the plush, lux-urious, world-renowned Raj Mandir Cinema (tel. 374694), off MI Rd., is an experience in itself. The four daily showings are *always* sold out; arrive *at least* 1 hour in advance to get tickets. Look for the tourist/student queue. ("Diamond box seats" Rs46, "Emerald" Rs34, "Ruby" Rs30, or "Pearl" Rs15.) **Swimming pools** abound in the hotels and stadiums of Jaipur. The Evergreen Guest House (tel. 363446), off MI Rd., lets outsiders use their pool (Rs75). Monsingh Palace (tel. 378771; fax 377582), off Sansar Chandra Rd., charges Rs200 for the use of their pool (daily 7am-8pm). For a glimpse of "authentic" **village life,** Chowki Dhani, 20km south of the city, promises a night of wild entertainment. Camel and ox rides, parrot astrology, palmistry, snake charming, *mehendi* hand-art, puppet shows, acrobatics, and music, all in traditional style, are available in this exhibition of village living. The highlight of the evening is the over-spiced dinner, served on leaf plates in a large mud hut. (Open daily 6-11pm. Auto-rickshaw Rs250 round-trip.)

SIGHTS

THE CITY PALACE

In the center of the Pink City, flanked by Gangauri Bazaar to the west and Siredeori Bazaar to the east. Open daily 9:30am-4:45pm. Rs110, children Rs75; video fee Rs100. No photography inside the galleries. Government-authorized guides Rs150.

Built between 1729 and 1732 by Jai Singh as a home for himself and his successors, the City Palace encompasses nearly 15% of the Pink City's total area. As the home of the current maharaja, Sawai Bhawani Singh, much of the palace is off-limits, but what you can see is delightful. The palace's architecture has changed little since it was built, but its character and the culture it has accommodated have changed substantially. Until the decline of the Rajputs during middle and late 19th century, the maharaja of Jaipur was the most important ruler in what is now eastern Rajasthan. Early maharajas filled the palace with scientific and artistic treasures. Others concentrated on public affairs. Those more interested in pleasure than in business cultivated a lively palace harem, which, reputedly held over 1000 women into the 20th century. In recent decades, the palace has taken on a new public role in the life of the city: it opened to tourists in the 1950s, and over 400 films—including *North by Northwest* and the Errol Flynn version of Rudyard Kipling's *Kim*—have had scenes shot within its walls.

Upon entering you'll find yourself in a large courtyard enclosed by red-and-yellow mortar walls with decaying arches and balconies, at the center of which is an attractive, albeit nondescript, building adorned with carved patterns, marble pillars, and arched balconies. This once served as a secretariat, containing the offices used by the maharaja for state business. Today, the ground floor is occupied by the offices of the director of the palace, a museum complex, and a library that is accessible only with the permission of the director. The library holds nearly 90,000 items, including centuries-old manuscripts collected by the maharajas, photo albums, and recent periodicals. The second floor of the building houses a **Textile Museum,** with collections of cloth and costumes, including the massive robes of the notorious "Fat Maharaja," Sawai Madho Singh I, who was 2.15m tall and reportedly weighed over 250kg. Also noteworthy are the harem mock-up and the exhibit of 19th-century prints from nearby Sanganer. The prints were made by a traditional wood-block process still used by the village artisans.

Up the stairs in the northwest corner of the courtyard is the **Arms and Weapons Museum.** Just to the right of the entrance is one of the best displays, the exhibit of daggers with elaborately crafted hilts concealing secret chambers and gunpowder holders made of seashells. For those less martially inclined, the museum offers some attractions not designed to inflict bodily harm. The ceilings are expertly decorated with mirrors, paintings, and dense floral patterns. The museum also offers hokey pleasures—keep your eyes peeled as you enter and exit for a somewhat disturbing "WELCOME" and "GOODBY" spelled out in daggers and pistols.

Exiting the courtyard, you'll pass through an elaborate gate with massive brass doors flanked by two marble elephants and several red-turbaned soldiers. Centering the next courtyard is the **Hall of Private Audience,** where two *gangajalis,* silver urns built to contain incredible quantities of Ganga River water, are on display. A sign notes that each urn holds 9000 liters of water and weighs 345kg, giving them the Guiness-certified distinction of being the largest pieces of silver in the world. In the corner of the courtyard is the **Hall of Public Audience,** housing the **Art Museum,** which displays a hodge-podge of terrific objects collected by the mahara-

MEETING THE MAHARAJA The current maharaja of Jaipur, Sawai Bhawani Singh, is a man of refinement and verve. Paying him a visit is about the coolest thing you can do in Jaipur. An old military man, the maharaja is an avid polo player who enjoys driving fancy cars and talks with excitement about computers and ham radio. The maharaja typically grants **private audiences** to visitors on weekdays. Appointments are necessary. To make an appointment, ask at the main entrance of the City Palace for the ADC (Aide de Camp) Office. Be persistent in confirming the date and time of the appointment. There you can speak with the PPS (Principal Private Secretary), who organizes the maharaja's schedule. It's best to give the PPS a couple of days' advance notice. Throughout the process, modest, respectful clothing and behavior are expected.

jas over the centuries. The walls are lined with massive Persian-style carpets. A large collection of manuscripts demonstrates the maharajas' traditional patronage of learning, and the collection of works on astronomy includes a 16th-century translated edition of Aristotle's scientific writings. One of the museum's highlights is its outstanding collection of miniature paintings. Particularly interesting is the **Well of Mercury,** a painting of a beautiful woman in front of flowing water. The work has caused some controversy among scholars because, while traditionally it has been understood strictly as an illustration of a Hindu myth, some argue that it is a coded visual explanation of how to extract mercury from the earth. Exit the courtyard, and you'll find yourself in a smaller one, surrounded by four gates, each representing a different season. Lording over the courtyard is the **Chandra Mahal,** the maharaja's residence. Parts of the first floor are open to the public.

ALSO IN THE PINK CITY

HAWA MAHAL (PALACE OF WINDS). Jaipur's most recognizable landmark, the Hawa Mahal's five-story pink sandstone edifice was built in 1799. Maharaja Sawai Pratap Singh built the palace as a comfortable retreat where he could go to compose his devotional songs to Krishna. Some of his songs are still sung in the nearby Govindji Temple. Designed to catch the breeze, the Hawa Mahal was named for the many brass wind vanes that adorned it until the 1960s. Spacious underground tunnels connected the palace to the harem. Some claim the edifice was constructed in order to enable the ladies of the harem to watch the street below. Behind the Hawa Mahal sits the ornately sculpted **Govindji Temple,** perhaps the most popular Hindu temple in town, dedicated to Krishna. *(On the east wall of the City Palace, facing Siredeori Bazaar. Open daily 9am-4:30pm. Rs2; camera fee Rs30; video Rs70.)*

JANTAR MANTAR. The largest stone observatory in the world, Jantar Mantar is one of the Maharaja Jai Singh's most conspicuous contributions to the Jaipur cityscape. Before building, Jai Singh sent emissaries to the East and West; they returned with cutting-edge technical manuals, including a copy of La Hire's "Tables," which the maharaja had coveted. Ironically, after building the Jantar Mantar, Jai Singh found that it produced readings 20 seconds more accurate than those reported by La Hire. The observatory features 18 large instruments, including a 30m sundial—impressive, but incomprehensible without a guide or a solid knowledge of astronomy. *(Next to the City Palace entrance. Open Sa-Th 9am-4:30pm. Rs4, free M; camera fee Rs50; video Rs100. Guides, Rs80.)*

NORTH OF THE PINK CITY

AMBER FORT. Standing sentinel over the Pink City below, the three Garland Forts dominate the northern horizon. Foremost among these is Amber Fort. Amber today is a reflection of the legendary Kachhwaha dynasty, a Rajput clan that dominated the area from the 12th to 18th centuries. Constructed in 1592 by Raja Man Singh, Amber is a blend of Hindu and Islamic architecture. Defense was clearly the top priority in Amber's design—hence its hilltop location, winding roads, and solidly fortified gates—but decorative artwork and many creature comforts are smoothly integrated into the fort's martial features.

Half the fun is getting up to the fort from the main road. A 15-minute walk up the steep, curvy road affords beautiful views of the surrounding valleys. Other means of access include jeep (Rs100) or elephant rides (a whopping Rs400 for up to 4 people); rates include round-trip fare and an hour-long wait at the fort. To the side of this courtyard is the **Shri Sila Devi Temple,** dedicated to the goddess of strength. Entry through the majestic silver doors leads to a black marble idol of the deity. *(Closed daily noon-4pm.)* From the main courtyard, a flight of stairs leads to **Diwan-i-Am** (Hall of Public Audience), a pillared, latticed meeting gallery. Opposite is the magnificently frescoed, mosaic-tiled **Ganesh Pol,** marking the entrance to the maharaja's former apartments, with their labyrinthine corridors, balconies, terraces, and rooms. Parts are in poor repair but some, like the famous **Jai Mandir** (Hall of Victory), are in better condition, exhibiting blinding mirror work and beautiful, well-preserved coloring. Other attractions include the **Sheesh Mahal,** the original private chambers of the maharaja, whose walls and ceilings are completely covered with colored glass and mirrors, and the **Sukh Mahal** (Pleasure Palace). The lake below the fort offers **paddle-boat** rental. *(11km north of Jaipur. Bus leaves from the front of the Hawa Mahal every 15min., Rs5. Open daily 9am-4:30pm. Rs4, children under 7 free; camera fee Rs50; video fee Rs100. Boats Rs40 per 30min., up to 4 people.)*

JAIGARH FORT. From the Amber Fort balconies, you can see this stocky fort, the second in the Garland trio, perched on a nearby hilltop. Its chambers and courtyards are hardly as elaborate as Amber's, but it does possess the gigantic **Jaivana,** the largest wheeled cannon in the world. It once was capable of firing a shot 35km. The main courtyard contains three enormous underground water tanks: one originally used by prisoners for bathing; one that held the gold and jewels that financed Jaipur's founding; and one, the largest, that was found to contain nothing at all when the Indian government ransacked it in 1976 in a futile attempt to locate legendary treasure. Jaigarh's museum contains a rather bland selection of relics. The view of Amber Fort and Jaipur from the ramparts is breathtaking. *(500m southwest of Amber. The fort can be reached by jeep or via a 20min. climb from Amber. Open daily 9am-4:30pm. Rs15, free with City Palace ticket stub; camera fee Rs50; video Rs100.)*

NAHARGARH FORT. The third Garland Fort, the Nahargarh, is also known as the Tiger Fort. Painted floral patterns brighten the walls of this fort's many chambers strung together in a labyrinthine floorplan to add to the solitary romantic atmosphere. The fort's view of the nearby valleys is stunning. A shaded, open cafeteria next door offers overpriced food and drink. *(A shadeless 20min. walk uphill from the road leading from Amber to Jaigarh. Open daily 10am-5pm. Rs4, guides Rs100; camera fee Rs30; video Rs100. Jeep to all three forts Rs300 for up to 4 people.)*

SOUTH OF THE PINK CITY

LAKSHMI NARAYAN MANDIR. The Lakshmi Narayan Mandir is rapidly becoming one of Jaipur's most beloved sights. Commonly called the **Birla Mandir,** the white marble temple was built by the wealthy Birla family, a dynasty of Indian industrialists. True to the family's multi-denominational approach to religion, the temple has three domes, each styled according to a different type of religious architecture. The theme of pluralism is further evident in the artwork of the *parikarima*—done by a Muslim—and the pillars flanking the temple, which include carvings of Hindu deities as well as depictions of Moses, Christ, Zarathustra, Socrates, and many others. *(Nehru Marg, where it intersects with Narain Sing Marg. Open daily 6am-noon and 2-9pm. Free guide available 8-11am and 4-7pm.)*

CENTRAL MUSEUM. Ram Niwas Gardens shelters Jaipur's Central Museum, often called **Albert Hall.** The museum complex is a mixture of pillars, arches, and courtyards adorned with murals. The ground floor of the museum showcases various facets of Rajasthani culture and history, including miniature paintings and ivory carvings, shields depicting scenes from Hindu epics, costumed mannequins, and stone sculptures. *(In the Ram Niwas Gardens, south of the old city. Open Sa-Th 10am-5pm. Rs30, M free. Photography prohibited.)*

MUSEUM OF INDOLOGY. The eccentric, encyclopedic, privately funded Museum of Indology features the troves of Vyakul (poet, painter, and super-nice guy who has been collecting stuff since he was 13 and can't bear to part with any of it): knick-knacks, curio pieces, and some real treasures. The museum holds a collection of textiles, designs, architectural drawings, and 20,000 buttons. In one room, the marriage contract of the last Mughal emperor vies for attention with a grain of rice on which a full-color map of India has been drawn. The volume, rarity, and oddity of Vyakul's collection make it worth a look. *(About 500m south of the Central Museum, just off Nehru Marg. Open daily 10am-5pm. Admission with guide, Rs40.)*

OTHER SIGHTS. On the hill overlooking the Birla Mandir are the crumbling remains of **Motidungri Fort,** owned but not maintained by the maharaja. The fort complex encloses a **Shiva temple** and is open to the public only once a year, on Shivaratri in the first week of March. Off Agra Rd. is the pilgrimage destination of **Galta (Monkey Temple).** A series of temples and pavilions hidden in a gorge surround a sacred spring. Hundreds of monkeys scamper around the washing wells as devotees engage in ceremonial cleansing. The best time to visit is before noon, when the tide of worshippers is at its fullest. Follow the road up behind Galta for a steep ten-minute climb to the **Sun Temple,** which offers a great view of the city and a popular picnic spot. Keep in mind that flowers and food may elicit unwelcome attention from the monkeys. *(Buses go to Galta from Badi chopar for Rs4-5. A round-trip auto-rickshaw ride for Rs100-200 provides a more scenic route through the mountains.)*

 SHOPPING

Jaipur is essentially a series of interconnected bazaars. Shopping here means heavy bargaining and constant harassment—it can be draining, but the effort is well worth it. You'll find a huge assortment of handicrafts, clothing, textiles, jewelry, and perfumes. Unique local specialties include *meenakari* (enamel work on silver and gold) and blue pottery. The jewelry and gem work of Jaipur are world-famous and remarkably inexpensive, but be on the lookout for scams. Remember, you are under no obligation to buy anything, no matter how kindly you are treated. In the Pink City, **Johari Bazaar** and two lanes off it—**Gopalj ka Rasta** and **Haldiyon ka Rasta**—are the prime spots for jewelry and gem stores and gold and silver smiths. Parts of the bazaar are closed on Sunday. Connecting the Ajmeri, New, and Sanganeri Gates are **Nehru Bazaar** and **Bapu Bazaar.** These specialize in textiles, unique perfumes, camel-skin shoes, and *mojiris* (a type of sandal). These bazaars are closed on Sundays and Mondays respectively. **Tripolia Bazaar** and **Charra Rasta,** closed Sundays, have a variety of stores selling lace work, ironwork, miscellaneous wooden and ivory relics, and local trinkets. Watch master carpet-makers at work in **Siredeori Bazaar,** and find exquisite marble sculpture and carvings in **Chandpol Bazaar.** (Most stores open 10am-8pm.)

◢ SARISKA TIGER RESERVE AND NATIONAL PARK

The dry, temple-studded Aravalli Mountains, 108km northeast of Jaipur and 200km west of Delhi, is home to the 866 sq. km Sariska Tiger Reserve and National Park (tel. (0144) 41333), featuring a rich population of wildlife: *nilgai* (blue bulls), *sambar* (large deer), spotted deer, wild boar, common langur, rhesus monkeys, leopards, hyenas, wild dogs, and peafowl. Unfortunately, this former hunting ground of the royal family of Alwar is seriously threatened by poaching, and Sariska is now a protected reserve under the Indian government's "Project Tiger."

Three-hour tours of the reserve are given upon request by both hotels and the Tourist Reception Centre (jeep for up to 5 persons Rs500-700). Animal activity is at its peak around 7am and 3pm. Most tours visit **Hanuman Mandir** and the **Pandu Pole Temple,** where pilgrims go to wash away their sins in the jungle pools and streams (open daily Oct.-Mar. 7am-4pm; Apr.-Sept. 6am-4:30pm; gates close at dusk; Rs100 per person, Rs125 per jeep; Rs200 video camera fee). Tickets can be bought from the booking office across from Hotel Sariska Palace. While most jeep drivers know the English names of the animals in the reserve, guides can be hired from the booking office (Rs150, 3hr.). **Buses** head to Sariska from Alwar (every 30min. dawn-midnight, 1hr., Rs9-14) and from Jaipur (regular until 7pm, 2½hr., Rs48). Buses from Sariska to Alwar (every ½hr. 6am-10pm, Rs9-14) and Jaipur (every hr. 6am-10pm, Rs48) leave from the booking office. You can also rent a **jeep** that seats up to five people (Rs600). Accommodations include the popular **Hotel Tiger Den** (tel. 41342), next to the park entrance, which offers clean, spacious, though over-priced rooms. (Check-out noon. Singles Rs550, with A/C Rs700; doubles Rs600/825. 20% discount for multi-night stays Apr.-Sept.) The Sariska Palace Hotel changes currency at times, but it's best to come with all the cash you'll need.

BHARATPUR भरतपर

A convenient stop on the popular tourist route between Agra (56km) and Jaipur (172km), Bharatpur's spectacular Keoladeo-Ghana National Park, one of the premier bird sanctuaries in the world, merits attention in its own right. Founded by Badan Singh in 1733 as a princely state, Bharatpur soon became known for the fierce armies of Suraj Mal, who plundered Delhi in 1753 and occupied Agra from 1761 to 1774. The state of Bharatpur was recognized as autonomous by the Mughals, and it successfully resisted two attacks by the British before being captured by Lord Combermere in 1826; after Independence, it became a part of Rajasthan. But history isn't what draws thousands of migrating birds and foreign travelers each winter—it's the rich ecosystem of the impeccably maintained park.

7 ORIENTATION AND PRACTICAL INFORMATION. Both the bird sanctuary and the adjacent hotels are a few km southeast of the center of town. **Buses** coming from Jaipur drop passengers off on the west side. **Rickshaws** (Rs15-20) make the journey to the hotel areas. At the core of town lie the ruins of the old fort. The area between **Jama Masjid** and the **Old Laxman Temple** functions as a sort of downtown, and it is here that you'll find the densest population of services. Nearer to the sanctuary, **Hotel Saras,** right at the intersection of the road to Fatehpur Sikri, serves as a good starting point to look for rooms.

Trains leave from the station (tel. 131), north of town. Fares listed are 2nd/1st class. To: **Mathura** (*Golden Temple Mail* 2903, 3:30pm; *Mumbai-Dehra Dun Exp.* 9029, 1am; *Mumbai-Firozpur Janata Exp.* 9023, 8am, ½hr., Rs30/300) en route to **Delhi** (3½hr., Rs62/475). **Buses** leave from the main bus stand (tel. 23434) on the southwest side of town, but most, particularly those heading toward Agra, can be waved down near the Hotel Saras. Buses go to: **Agra** (every 30min. 5am-8:30pm, 1hr., Rs22; deluxe 9am, 1hr., Rs27); **Delhi** (every hr. 5:30am-10:30pm, 5hr., Rs67); **Fatehpur Sikri** (9 per day 7:30-4pm, 1hr., Rs8); **Mathura** (every 30min. 5:30am-8:30pm, 1hr., Rs16); **Ajmer** (11 per day 7:45am-11:30pm, 7hr., Rs124); **Bikaner** (12:45pm, 12hr., Rs200); and **Udaipur** (7:45am, 2:15 and 7:45pm; 14hr.; Rs235). The bus stand also has government or private transport to **Jaipur** (every 30min. 5am-12:30am, 4hr., Rs45/71) and **Udaipur.** You can rent **bicycles** at several hotels near the sanctuary (Rs30-50 per day). The **RTDC Tourist Reception Centre,** adjacent to the Hotel Saras, has basic booklets about the area and Keoladeo and city maps for Rs2 (tel. 22542, open M-F 10am-5pm). The **State Bank,** near Binarayan Gate, northwest of Birdland, exchanges currencies and traveler's checks, but has a US$100 limit (tel. 22441, open M-F 10am-5pm, Sa 10am-2pm). **Luggage storage** on platform #1 of the train station is open 24 hours (Rs5-7 per day). **Pharmacies** are common throughout the city, except near the bird sanctuary. **Lokesh Medicos** (tel. 26879), near the **General Hospital,** Station Rd. (tel. 23633, emergencies 22451), 3km from the railway station, is open 24 hours. The **post office** is across from Jama Masjid to the east (tel. 23586, open M-Sa 6am-6pm). Collect calling and callbacks are available at **Shree Prabhu** (tel. 25446), between Hotel Pratap Palace and Hotel Sunbird, on the road leading to the sanctuary (open 24 hours). **Emergency:** tel. 22451. **Police:** tel. 22526. **Postal Code:** 321001. **Telephone Code:** 05644.

📷🛏 ACCOMMODATIONS AND FOOD. Unless noted, all hotels and restaurants listed below are a short jaunt from the park. Many hotels rent bicycles, binoculars, and birding books. Room prices soar in the high season (Oct.-Mar.), particularly around Christmas; prices listed here are high season. Prices are much higher inside the park. If you're looking to go low-end, try the popular **Tourist Lodge**, Gol Bagh Rd. (tel. 23742), near Mathura Gate 2km from the train station, about 1½km from the park. Simple, aging rooms in a less touristed area, with 24-hour hot water. (Check-out noon. Singles Rs50, with bath Rs75, with air-cooling Rs125; doubles Rs80/125/150). The **Saras Tourist Bungalow** (tel. 23700) is a well-run but uninspiring RTDC hotel. Still, it has a great garden and restaurant, plus clean rooms with chairs, sinks, and mirrors. Free bucket hot water. (Check-out noon. Dorm beds Rs50; singles Rs300, with air-cooling Rs450, with A/C and TV Rs600; doubles Rs350/550/700; extra bed Rs75-125.) Up the road toward the park, **Hotel Sunbird** (tel. 25701; fax 28344) has clean, spacious rooms with attached baths, air-cooling, and 24-hour hot water. (Check-out noon. Singles Rs200, deluxe Rs500-600; doubles Rs250/550-650. 50% discount off-season.) Closer to the sanctuary, **Hotel Pelican** (tel. 24221) is efficiently run, and the owner (also owner of the Tourist Lodge in town) is a chatty naturalist (singles Rs50; doubles Rs80, with bath and hot water, Rs150-300). **Hotel Pratap Palace** (tel. 24245; fax 25093), also on the road to the sanctuary, offers clean, simply decorated rooms. 24-hour hot water. (Check-out noon. Singles Rs200, deluxe Rs600; doubles Rs300/700.)

Most of the hotels have attached restaurants, some with rooftops for sunsets and binocular-aided birding. The **Spoonbill** has Mughlai, South Indian, Chinese, and Continental dishes freshly prepared for courtyard dining. Veg. and non-veg. entrees run Rs20-60. (Open daily 6am-10pm.) The **Krishna Restaurant,** in Pratap Palace, has pricier veg. and non-veg. dishes (Rs30-80). **Annexy Restaurant,** in Hotel Pelican, offers ultra-rich *lassis* (Rs20) and many delicious dishes, and they'll pack you a lunch (Rs30-60, with tea or coffee in a thermos) to take to the park.

📷 SIGHTS. The main reason foreigners flock to Bharatpur is to go cuckoo for the hordes of birds at Keoladeo Ghana National Park (see below). Still, if you're in town and are sick of binoculars, check out the town's 18th-century **Lohagarh Fort**, near Nehru Park, north of the center of town. The fort was built by Maharaja Suraj Mal and has been notoriously resistant to attack; heavy British armaments are said to have bounced off the walls. The **museum** here features three large galleries of ancient Jain sculpture and fort artifacts (open Sa-Th 10am-4:30pm; Rs3).

🏞 KEOLADEO GHANA NATIONAL PARK. Bharatpur's 29sq. km of pride and joy, the Keoladeo Ghana National Park annually plays host to one of the world's most impressive assemblages of feathered friends, a whopping 375 species in all. The marshes, woodlands, and grassy pastures draw hundreds of bird species each year, including VIBs (Very Important Birds) such as the rare Siberian crane, the painted stork, shoveller, widgeon, and grey, purple, and night herons. Together with the birds, there are pythons, spotted deer, jackals, and other mammals and reptiles. Ironically, the local maharaja originally set aside the land as an elaborate hunting ground, and the bloodsport didn't end until 1972. Now the grounds are suprisingly serene and well-maintained—ideal for a relaxing stroll and, of course, bird watching. Early morning and dusk are particularly beautiful and bountiful.

Visitors must rent a **bicycle** or **cycle-rickshaw** to explore the grounds because motor vehicles are not allowed past Keoladeo's only entrance. The **main office** at the gate rents bicycles for Rs20 (deposit your passport or Rs1000), and many local hotels do the same for Rs30-50. Only rickshaws that wear a special "yellow plate" have paid their dues and are certified to enter. Inside the office, a small visitors center features nests, eggs, and stuffed specimens, as well as a color map of the park. Tongas (Rs60 per hr.) and cycle-rickshaws (Rs30 per hr.) depart from the gate. Some rickshaw drivers know enough to serve as guides, but while your wallet is open, it might be better to hire one of the certified naturalist **guides** from the office (Rs35 per hr.)—they have keen eyes for spotting and identifying birds. Inside the park you can hire a **boat** in season for up to four people (1hr., Rs80), or inquire in the office in front of the park about one of the suggested **walking tours**. A reference book with all the English and scientific names of the various species is available for Rs50. To preserve the tranquility of the park, there are strict rules against smoking, noise-making, and other polluting activities. *(Tel. 22777. Open daily sunrise to sunset in-season, 6am-6pm during the monsoon. Rs100 for non-Indians; with cycle additional Rs3; with video camera additional Rs200.)*

AJMER अजमेर

The bustling town of Ajmer, 132km west of Jaipur in the heart of the Aravalli Mountains, is hailed by tourists more for its proximity to Pushkar than for its own sights. Nevertheless, Ajmer is remembered as the final resting place of Khwaja Muin-ud-din Chishti, founder of India's premier Sufi order. As a result, thousands upon thousands of Muslims and Hindus make a pilgrimage to Ajmer during the annual Urs Ajmer Sharif (Sept. 9-14, 2000). During this time, the town bursts at its seams with people and festivities. The annual Pushkar Camel Fair attracts even wilder crowds. The rest of the year, Ajmer's winding bazaars and less touristed streets make for interesting people watching and good bargaining.

⛐ ORIENTATION AND PRACTICAL INFORMATION. Ajmer is a small town, only about 3km long, and if you wander around for a bit, its geography becomes clear. If wandering is not your thing, all of the standard modes of transport apply. For Rs10-25, cycle- and auto-**rickshaws** will get you anywhere. Crowded **tempos** charge Rs2. Popular in Ajmer are motorized **tongas,** which charge Rs5-10 to get around town. **Station Road** runs north-south in front of the **railway station,** whose reservation office is on the second floor above the main entrance (enquiries tel. 131, reservations tel. 431965; open M-Sa 8am-8pm, Su 8am-2pm). Fares listed are 2nd/1st class. Trains head for **Delhi** (*Shatabdi Exp.* 2016, M-Sa 3:30pm, 7hr., A/C chair Rs580; *Ahmedabad-Delhi Mail* 9105, 8:30pm, 9hr., Rs163/700); **Jaipur** (*Shatabdi Exp.* 2016, 3:30pm, 2hr., A/C chair Rs290; *Ahmedabad-Delhi Mail* 9105, 8:30pm, 3hr., Rs72/365); and **Udaipur** (*Chetak Exp.* 9615, 1:40am, 8hr., Rs130/350). The main **tourist office** (tel. 52426) is on the west side of town, next to the Hotel Khadim (open M-Sa 10am-1:30pm and 2-5pm). From the railway station, points of interest are straight ahead in **Diggi Bazaar,** the main commercial area, and to the right toward the **GPO,** which has *Poste Restante* services (tel. 432145, open daily 10am-6pm). **Postal Code:** 305001. **Telephone Code:** 0145.

From the intersection near the GPO, **Kutchery Road** darts southeast, joining **Jaipur Road,** before passing the **Main Bus Stand** (tel. 429398), which is 2km southeast of the railway station. To: **Ahmedabad** (5 per day 12:30am-8:45pm, 13½ hr., Rs190); **Abu Road** (5:45am, 3:30 and 8:15pm, 9hr., Rs137); **Mt. Abu** deluxe (10:45pm, 9hr., Rs165); **Bikaner** (11 per day 6:15am-11:45pm, 7hr., Rs108); **Chittaurgarh** (every hr. 5-1am, 5½ hr., Rs72); **Jaipur** (every 15min., 3hr., Rs52; deluxe 9 per day 7:45am-10:30pm, 3hr., Rs62); **Jaisalmer** (8am, 12hr., Rs190); **Jodhpur** (every 30min. 6am-11pm, 5hr., Rs81); and **Udaipur** (12 per day, 7hr., Rs112; deluxe 4:15pm, 7hr., Rs135). The **Pushkar Bus Stand,** near the Station-Kutchery Rd. junction, sends buses to (surprise!) Pushkar every 15 minutes (5am-midnight, 30min., Rs5). **Private bus** companies line Kutchery Rd. and have deluxe buses to most destinations. Most will pick up in Pushkar if needed; check in advance.

Bicycles can be rented through the Tourist Information Bureau, near the Main Bus Stand, for Rs1 per hour. The **Bank of Baroda,** Station Rd. (tel. 432124), near the GPO, changes foreign currency, traveler's checks, and cash advances on Visa, MC, AMEX (open M-F 10am-2pm, Sa 10am-noon). Dr. Yadava's **Pratap Memorial Hospital,** Kutchery Rd. (tel. 426406), the best private hospital, has a 24-hour **pharmacy** in front. The **Main Police Office** (tel. 425080 and 431251) is opposite the railway station. **STD/ISDs** abound near the railway station (most open 7am-11pm).

▌▛▐▛ ACCOMMODATIONS AND FOOD. Ajmer has a disappointing selection of hotels. Most tourists head to Pushkar for a wider range of accommodations, and visit Ajmer on a daytrip. Across from the railway station is a noisy bunch of no-frills, dirt-cheap hotels. Prithviraj Marg and Kutchery Rd. host similar congregations of hotels. Hotels are booked heavily, so call in advance. Prices skyrocket during the Urs Ajmer Sharif and the Pushkar Camel Fair. The **City View Paying Guest House,** Nalla Bazaar (tel. 431243), a five-minute walk from the railway station, is a tiny, family-run hotel on a narrow, winding street in the old city. The rooms are very basic but spacious, and the rooftop offers spectacular views. (Singles Rs50-75, with bath 100-150; doubles Rs100-200.) The best of the cheapies is **Bhola Hotel,** Agra Gate (tel. 432844), with simple, well-decorated rooms (singles Rs125; doubles Rs200; extra bed Rs50; air-cooling Rs50). The **Hotel Nagpal,** Station Rd. (tel. 429503), features clean rooms with phones and attached baths. (Check-out 24hr. Singles Rs175, with TV and air-cooling Rs300, with A/C Rs650; doubles Rs300/400/1000; extra person Rs150.) **Hotel Moti Mahal,** JLN Hospital Rd. (tel. 622446 or 622440) in front of Anasagar Lake, offers clean rooms decorated in royal red, with 24-hour hot water and STD/ISD telephones in all the rooms. Laundry service is available. (Check-out 24-hr. Singles Rs300, with A/C and color television Rs450; doubles 350/550.)

There aren't many **restaurants** in Ajmer, but the few you'll find are decent. For a quick bite, jet over to the snack, juice, and egg stalls around Delhi Gate. For non-veg. Persian food and great street views, the **Madeena Hotel,** Station Rd., opposite the railway station, is cheap (Rs45 or less) and friendly (open daily 7am-11pm). **Rasna,** Prithviraj Marg, has pure veg. food (entrees Rs24-45) served in underground A/C bliss (open daily 8am-11pm). For the best of both worlds, the **Honeydew Restaurant,** Station Rd. (tel. 622498), offers Continental, Chinese, and Indian cuisines in a clean and calm environment (most entrees Rs28-50; open daily 8am-11pm).

◙ SIGHTS. When thousands of devotees flock to Ajmer during the Urs Ajmer Sharif, **Dargah** is their destination. On the north side of town in the old city, the tomb of the Sufi saint **Khwaja Muin-ud-din Chishti** looms above the surrounding bazaars at the foot of a hill on the left side of Dargah Bazaar. Originally a simple brick cenotaph, Dargah has expanded to an elaborate marble complex as rich rulers have paid tribute. A tall, elaborate gateway leads to the first courtyard, where two massive cauldrons called *degs* are filled with rice that is then sold to devotees as *tabarukh,* a sanctified food. Akbar's mosque is to the right, and Shah Jahan's grand mosque is farther inside. The tomb of the saint himself is in a central marble mosque, encircled by silver railings. The sight draws huge crowds, making it difficult to see the tomb for extended periods of time. Keep a close eye on your personal belongings when you enter. Respectful behavior and a small donation are expected at Dargah—at the very least buy flowers (Rs11) for the grave site.

Continuing on the road past Dargah about 500m brings you to the **Adhai-din-Ka-jhonpra** (Mosque of Two-and-a-Half Days) named for the time the legendary Muhammad of Ghur took to build it in 1193. Giant pillars loom behind the facade, whose seven arches are decorated with elaborate Persian calligraphy. The magnificent red of the **Nasiyan Temple** in the bazaars near Agra Gate houses a museum where the Jain conception of the universe is illustrated with golden models. A wealthy local Jain family used over 1000kg of gold to construct the exhibit in 1865, and the project took 20 artisans 40 years to complete. The colored glass that decorates the walls and columns is said to conceal enormous diamonds. (Open daily 8:30am-5:30pm. Rs3. Photography prohibited.)

On the northeast side of town, the 11th-century artificial lake **Anasagar** offers a nice spot for a stroll or picnic. The **Dault Bagh** gardens along its bank boast marble pavilions built by Shah Jahan. Boats can be rented from the newly built Luvkush Gardens (pedal boats Rs30 per ½hr.; motor boats Rs15 per person per 5min.)

RAJASTHAN

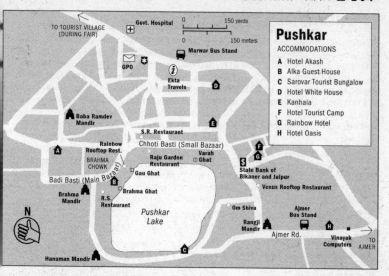

PUSHKAR पुष्कर

Legend has it that at the beginning of time Lord Brahma dropped a *pushkara*, or lotus flower, into the desert. Where the flower fell, a holy lake sprang up and became a place where pilgrims could be cleansed of all their sins. The lake is now the central attraction of the calm town of Pushkar, the site of the only Brahma temple in all of India. Some Hindu pilgrims consider Pushkar their final stop, and a dip in the waters completes the circuit of redemption. Besides spiritual enlightenment, Pushkar offers respite from the hassles of bigger cities. The noisy autorickshaws that plague other cities are delightfully absent in Pushkar; a stroll around the 1km long city is peaceful and relaxing. This serenity is transformed into a beehive of activity in November for the annual Pushkar Fair (Nov. 9-11, 2000; Nov. 27-30, 2001), but otherwise a mellow mood prevails. While the abundance of tourists has obvious drawbacks, Pushkar's popularity has given rise to a wealth of inviting hotels and restaurants.

> **WARNING.** Given its religious and cultural roots, Pushkar is a purely vegetarian town, with strict prohibition of alcohol and drug use (the drug and alcohol scene in this quasi-hippie town is entirely underground). Although Pushkar's policies may clash with many Western conceptions of a good time, being respectful of the heritage and traditions of the town is probably wise.

TRANSPORTATION

Buses: Ajmer Bus Stand, Ajmer Rd. To: **Ajmer** (every 15min. 5:30am-8:30pm, 30min., Rs5). All other destinations can be reached through the **Main Bus Stand** (tel. 429398) in Ajmer. Daily buses going directly to **Jaisalmer, Jodhpur, Udaipur, Mumbai,** and **Delhi** leave from the Marwar Bus Stand. **Private bus** companies line Chhoti Basti and the area around Marwar Bus Stand. For most destinations, they provide free jeep transportation to Ajmer, where their main offices are located and from where most of their buses depart. **Ekta Travels** (see below) is the only government-recognized agency in Pushkar. Most hotels make private and government bus and train arrangements for guests.

Local Transportation: Most visitors travel everywhere on foot. **Bicycles** can be rented from several shops near the Ajmer Bus Stand (Rs3 per hr., Rs20 per day).

ORIENTATION AND PRACTICAL INFORMATION

Pushkar runs less than 1km in each direction, so getting lost is hardly an issue. Most travelers arrive from Ajmer at the **Ajmer Bus Stand,** on **Ajmer Road** in the southeast side of town. In town, Ajmer Rd. becomes **Chhoti Basti (Small Bazaar),** the main thoroughfare, which follows the north shore of **Pushkar Lake.** Chhoti Basti becomes **Badi Basti (Main Bazaar),** winding south and ending on the west side of town, near **Brahma Mandir.** A right turn on one of the meandering side streets off Chhoti Basti leads to the road that marks the northern boundary of the town and hosts the GPO, the **Marwar Bus Stand,** and the government hospital.

Tourist Office: Ajmer's Tourist Information Bureau (tel. 52426) has information about Pushkar. Open M-Sa 10am-1:30pm and 2-5pm. During the Pushkar Fair, the RTDC-run **Tourist Village** (tel. 72074) provides a wealth of information. **Ekta Travels** (tel. 72131; fax 72921), near the Marwar Bus Stand, is an authorized agent for Indian Airlines and Indian Railways and provides brochures and maps. Open daily 7am-10pm.

Currency Exchange: State Bank of Bikaner and Jaipur, Chhoti Basti (tel. 72006), opposite Varah Ghat, exchanges foreign currency and traveler's checks. No service charges. Open M-F 10am-2pm, Sa 10am-noon.

Bookstore: Lalchand Ranchand Company, Chhoti Basti (tel. 72599), has a decent new and used collection of French, German, Italian, Spanish, Hebrew, and English paperbacks. **British Book World,** next door, has a good selection of (yes) British books. Both open daily 8am-11pm.

Pharmacy: Most pharmacies line the northern side of town near the hospitals and Marwar Bus Stand, but several dot Chhoti Basti as well. Most open daily 8am-8pm.

Hospital: Government Community Hospital (tel. 72029), near Marwar Bus Stand. English-speaking staff, reputable, and open 24hr. for emergencies. Open for consultations daily 9am-3pm.

Police: Main Police Station (tel. 72046), across from the Government Hospital. Tourist-friendly and English-speaking. Open 24hr.

Post Office: GPO (tel. 720222), on the north side of town next to the police station. *Poste Restante.* A branch office is on Chhoti Basti. Both open M-Sa 9am-5pm, 9am-2pm for parcel post and registered mail. **Postal Code:** 305022.

Internet: Vinayak Computers (tel. 72760), next to the Hotel Oasis and near the Ajmer Bus Stand, charges Rs4 per min. for Internet use. Open daily 9am-10pm. **Kamal and Co.,** Chhoti Basti (tel. 72041; fax 72244; email krishnamantri@hotmail.com) also near the bus stand, has the same rates. Open daily 11am-9:30pm.

Telephones: Mahesh Pal Communication, Ghumar Niwas (tel. 72486 or 72596), across from the Government Hospital has free callbacks. Open 24hr.

PHONE CODE	0145

ACCOMMODATIONS

Most of Pushkar's plentiful budget digs are converted houses with clean cots and common baths. Hotels have different policies regarding drinking, smoking, and curfews—check in advance if you have preferences. Also remember that Pushkar is so small that you can safely check out all the hotels one by one with baggage in arms. During the Pushkar Fair, when prices can be more than 10 times as high, it is cheapest to stay in Ajmer and commute to Pushkar.

Alka Guest House, Badi Basti (tel. 72738), near Rainbow Restaurant. Spacious, clean rooms overlooking the lake run by a friendly family establishment. Excellent common baths. The rooftop commands beautiful views of the lake and the desert. The terrace restaurant offers a huge selection of food and Indian music. Luggage storage. Check-out noon. Singles Rs70; doubles Rs100; deluxe room with view of lake Rs150.

Kanhaia (tel. 72146), between Chhoti Basti and Marwar Bus Stand, near Old Rangnath Temple. A new and already very popular hotel run by a very friendly family. Clean, spacious rooms with bright sheets, soothing blue walls, *mehendi* upon request, travel service, and 24hr. room service. Check-out noon. Dorm beds Rs30-40; singles Rs50-80, with bath and air-cooling Rs100-250; doubles Rs150-250.

Rainbow Hotel (tel. 72167 or 72044), off Chhoti Basti, near the State Bank of Bikaner and Jaipur. Rooms are small but bright and clean in this fledgling hotel. 24hr. room service, laundry service, rooftop restaurant. Check-out noon. Singles Rs60, with bath Rs150; doubles Rs100/200-250.

Hotel White House (tel. 72147), between Chhoti Basti and Marwar Bus Stand. Spacious, spotless rooms around an airy, open courtyard. Surrounding gardens. Rooftop restaurant with sweet views and even sweeter complimentary mango tea upon arrival. 24hr. room service. Check-out 10am. Dorm beds Rs20; singles Rs100-150, with bath and air-cooling Rs200-350, with A/C Rs450; doubles Rs100-150/200-350/600.

Hotel Akash (tel. 72498), near Brahma Mandir. A small hotel run by a gracious family. The rooms are clean but very basic and surround a central garden. Travel services, laundry, room service, roof top restaurant. Check-out noon. Singles Rs30, with bath Rs80-100, with air-cooling Rs120; doubles Rs70/80-100/120.

Hotel Oasis, Ajmer Bus Stand (tel. 72100). Large, simple rooms, all with attached baths, some with balconies. 24hr. room service, swimming pool. Check-out noon. Singles Rs100-150, with air-cooling Rs200, with A/C Rs500; doubles Rs200-250/300/800.

Sarovar Tourist Bungalow, Ajmer Rd. (tel. 72040), 100m west of the Ajmer Bus Stand. A government building with character. RTDC-run establishment has nice, cool rooms and a pool with a mountain view. Check-out noon. Dorm beds Rs50; singles Rs125, with bath Rs250, deluxe Rs300, with lake view Rs375; doubles Rs200/300/350/500.

Hotel Tourist Camp (tel. 72920), off of Chhoti Basti beyond Rainbow Hotel. Aged, dimly lit rooms, but at a great price. Check-out noon. Singles Rs40, with attached bath Rs50; doubles Rs70/100.

⌂ FOOD

While Pushkar has its share of good Indian cuisine, most travelers indulge in the local interpretations of Western food. For quick snacks and sweets, a stroll down Chhoti Basti should satiate most cravings.

S.R. Restaurant, Badi Basti near Gau Ghat. This open-air restaurant whips up delicious food in enormous helpings at great prices. Entrees Rs15-45. Massive special *thali* Rs45. Open daily 9am-10:30pm.

Rainbow Rooftop Restaurant, near Brahma Temple. Delightful, well-prepared Indian and Western dishes and a menu as stunning as the rooftop view. Homemade peanut butter (Rs15), *falafel* (Rs40-90), banana fritters (Rs30), real cappuccino (Rs15), homemade pasta (Rs55-70), mouth-watering chocolate truffles (Rs10), and the best lemon soda (Rs15) in town. Open 8am-11pm.

KNEAD IT, FLIP IT, TASTE IT Just as any meal is incomplete without *chapati*, a visit to Rajasthan is incomplete without learning the art of *chapati*-making. For eight tasty *chapatis*, add a dash of salt to 300g of wheat flour. Slowly add water and knead the mixture until it becomes doughy (too much water will make the mixture sticky). Divide the dough into eight little balls and roll them in extra flour until lightly coated. Grab your *belan* (*chapati* roller) and roll away to make eight, flat, circular pieces. Warm up your *tawa* (flat metal plate used for cooking) at a low heat and lather it with *ghee* (clarified butter). Cook them one at a time, continuously twisting it around to ensure even cooking. Once browned (about one minute), flip the *chapati* over. When the top starts to puff up, remove from heat. Don't be dismayed if your first batch of *chapatis* is sub-par: practice makes perfect.

R.S., opposite Brahma Temple. Great Indian dishes (Rs20-28), as well as spaghetti and macaroni (Rs30-40). Popular among locals with garden and terrace seating. STD/ISD service with free callbacks. Fresh juice (Rs10-15). Open daily 7am-10:30pm.

Raju Garden Restaurant, Badi Basti. Refreshingly small selection of international cuisine. Tasty Indian entrees (Rs20-50). Lakeside view. Open daily 8am-10pm.

Venus Rooftop Restaurant, Chhoti Basti. Another multi-cuisine restaurant, but with particularly tasty Indian dishes (Rs15-40), fresh juice (Rs10-12), and a rooftop view of the lake and the bustling street below. Limited *thalis* Rs25. Open daily 7am-10:30pm.

ENTERTAINMENT

The annual **Pushkar Fair** is an event of colossal numbers, crowding 200,000 people from all over the world into one square kilometer. Thousands of pilgrims bathe in the lake's holy waters seeking redemption for their sins. Concurrently, an enormous camel fair brings in over 50,000 camels, who excite the masses in races, auctions, contests, parades, and safaris. Stalls selling handicrafts from all over India fill the streets, punctuated by performers at every corner. And it wouldn't be a fair without food—specialty cuisines abound as well. At night, the air is filled with the sounds of bells and songs and with scented smoke from campfires at the edge of town. The dates vary each year with the lunar calendar (Nov. 9-11, 2000; Nov 27-30, 2001). Make hotel reservations well in advance. Prices will skyrocket.

If you come during one of the other 361 days of the year, though, Pushkar is simply a wonderful place to relax. Most visitors enjoy meandering along the tiny streets, visiting the temples and *ghats*, and perhaps hiking up a nearby hill for the views. Camel safaris into the desert are becoming increasingly popular in Pushkar, along with camel treks across the desert to Jaisalmer, Jodhpur, or Bikaner. Most hotels and travel agents can make these arrangements for you; expect to pay around Rs350 per day for a good camel safari. If you don't have enough time for a safari or trek but want to befriend a hump-back, go for a camel ride—loops around the city cost Rs40-50 per hour.

SIGHTS

Most of Pushkar's 540 **temples** were rebuilt after assorted raids and pillages by the Mughal emperor Aurangzeb in the 17th century. A few of the temples are open only to Hindus. The most frequented temple is the **Brahma Mandir,** the only temple in India dedicated to Brahma, the Hindu creator-god. Expect to be mobbed by eager guides, though their services are hardly necessary to view the temple.

Two major hillside temples in Pushkar offer superb vistas of the town and valley, especially at sunset and sunrise. Named for two of Brahma's wives, **Savithri Mandir** and **Gayatri Mandir** crown hills on the east and west side of town (each a 1½hr. climb). Other temples of interest include **Rangji Mandir,** with its white stone facade, the **Hanuman Mandir,** a colorful tower depicting Hanuman's exploits, and the turquoise-green **Baba Ramdev Mandir.** Encircling Pushkar Lake are broad **ghats** connecting the temples and the holy waters. Of Pushkar's 52 *ghats*, the most important are the **Gau Ghat,** where an assortment of politicians, ministers, and VIPs have paid their respects, **Brahma Ghat,** which Brahma himself is said to have used, and the central **Varah Ghat,** where Vishnu is said to have cameoed in the form of a boar. Signs in hotels instruct visitors to remove their shoes and to refrain from smoking and taking photographs. Pilgrims and tourists at the *ghats* request local priests to perform a Pushkar *puja*, a ceremony of scripture-reading and flower-scattering, for a donation. Do not feel pressured into donating the exorbitant amounts that the priests insist are "standard." After the *puja*, your patronage is officially recognized with a red wrist-band—the "Pushkar Passport"—giving you the freedom to visit *ghats* and stroll around town without priestly harassment.

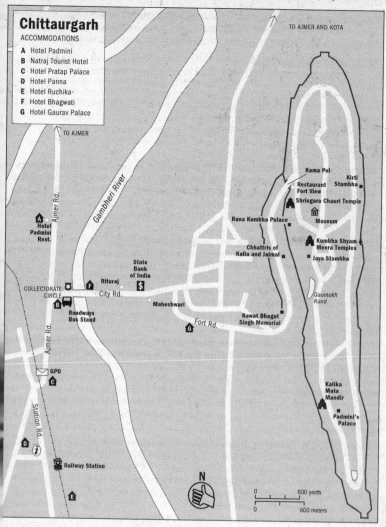

Chittaurgarh

ACCOMMODATIONS

A Hotel Padmini
B Natraj Tourist Hotel
C Hotel Pratap Palace
D Hotel Panna
E Hotel Ruchika
F Hotel Bhagwati
G Hotel Gaurav Palace

CHITTAURGARH चित्तौड़गढ़

Rajasthan has many wind-swept cities with impressive forts, but few loom with Chittaurgarh's tragic nostalgia. Enjoying a prime location on a rocky plateau 115km northeast of Udaipur, the Chittaurgarh Fort has a past shadowed with misfortune. In 1303, the Delhi Sultan Ala-ud-din Khilji besieged the fort in an attempt to capture the beautiful Padmini, wife of Maharaja Ratan Singh. When Padmini fell into the maharaja's hands, Rajput women were outraged by the loss of their queen. In an act of bitter sacrifice, 13,000 of them declared *jauhar* (self-immolation) and jumped onto a burning funeral pyre, infuriating the Sultan and prompting him to ravage the city. Barely two centuries later in 1535, the Sultan Bahadur Shah attacked by surprise, annihilating another generation of Rajput warriors even as their wives immolated themselves. In 1568, the Mughal emperor Akbar laid siege to the city, killing over 30,000 inhabitants; again, the women committed *jauhar*. The fort today is a 5km stretch of ruins of former palaces and temples, the only vestiges of the city's past glory. Though proud of its turbulent history, Chittaurgarh has simmered down significantly; the only invaders these days are a handful of tourists pursuing their photographic plunder at the city's attractions.

▣ TRANSPORTATION

Trains: Railway Station, Station Rd. (tel. 40131). Reservation office open daily 10am-5pm. Fares listed are 2nd/1st class. To: **Ahmedabad** (*Ajmer-Ahmedabad Mail* 9943, 1:50pm, 15hr., Rs155/707); **Ajmer** (*Meenakshi Exp.* 9770, 5:15am, 4½hr.; *Poorna-Ajmer Passenger* 582, 3pm, 7hr., Rs96/451; *Chetak Exp.* 9616, 9:40pm, 4hr., Rs48/388); **Jaipur** (*Meenakshi Exp.* 9770, 5:15am; *Chetak Exp.* 9616, 10:15pm, 7½hr., Rs133/605); **Udaipur** (*Chetak Exp.* 9615, 6:30am, 3hr., Rs36/348; *Ajmer-Ahmeda-bad Mail* 9943, 1:50pm, 3½hr., Rs35/348).

Buses: Roadways Bus Stand (tel. 41177). Fares listed are regular/deluxe. To: **Ahmedabad** (8am and 5:30pm, 10hr., Rs135); **Abu Road** (7am, 10hr., Rs124); **Bundi** (10:30 and 11:15am, 5½hr., Rs67); **Jaipur** (13 per day 5am-8:45pm, 8hr., Rs112/136) via **Ajmer** (5hr., Rs73/89); **Jodhpur** (4 per day 10:30am-9:30pm, 8hr., Rs124/141); **Kota** (7 per day 6:30am-4:30pm, 5½hr., Rs51-82/93); **Udaipur** (frequent 7:30am-2am, 2½hr., Rs44/53). **Private bus** companies on Station Rd. service most destinations.

Local Transportation: Unmetered **auto-rickshaws** and horse-drawn **tongas** are the most common modes of transport. An auto-rickshaw ride within town costs Rs3-5, to the fort Rs15-20 (tongas won't make the climb); a round-trip up to the fort and all the sights should cost Rs100, Rs70 off season. **Bicycles** can be rented (Rs25 per day) from shops near the railway station. You'll have to walk the bike up to the fort, but the cruise down is thrilling. **Taxis** in front of the bus stand charge Rs3 per km.

▣ ORIENTATION AND PRACTICAL INFORMATION

Chittaurgarh (or "Chittore") is too spread out to navigate on foot. The **railway station** is on the west side of town. **Station Road** becomes Ajmer Road, which continues north to Ajmer after intersecting with **City Road.** The GPO and General Hospital are near this junction, called **Collectorate Circle.** City Rd. passes the **Roadways Bus Stand** before crossing the **Gambheri River** and proceeding to the base of the Fort, where it turns into **Fort Road.** The main commercial area and the **new city** are here. Fort Rd. zig-zags steeply up to the **Fort,** which sprawls 5km across the plateau. One main road loops inside the Fort and leads to Chittaurgarh's major sights.

Tourist Office: The **Tourist Reception Centre,** Station Rd. (tel. 41089). Friendly and helpful English-speaking staff provides maps and travel information. Open M-Sa 10am-1:30pm and 2-5pm.

Budget Travel: Keerti Tour and Travels (tel. 43245; fax 41042), in the fort near the main entrance. Knowledgeable staff leads pricey but extensive tours and arranges jeep and camel safaris. Open daily 7am-9pm.

Currency Exchange: State Bank of Bikaner and Jaipur, Collectorate Circle (tel. 40933), cashes traveler's checks. Open M-F 10am-2pm, Sa 10am-noon.

Market: Food, provisions, and crafts market around Fort Rd., across the river from Roadways Bus Stand. Most stalls open daily 9am-8pm.

Pharmacy: Chittaurgarh Cooperative (tel. 41276), on the General Hospital compound, is the only 24hr. pharmacy. Other pharmacies cluster near the hospital.

Hospital: General Hospital, Station Rd. (tel. 41102). English-speaking, large, and efficient. Open 24hr. Private hospitals abound with comparable facilities.

Police: Main Police Station (tel. 41060), opposite the bus stand. Open 24hr.

Emergency: Fire, tel. 41101. **Ambulance,** tel. 41102.

Post Office: GPO, Station Rd. (tel. 41159), near the railroad crossing. *Poste Restante.* Open M-Sa 7-10:30am and 2:30-6pm. **Postal Code:** 312001.

Telephones: STD/ISD booths dot Station and City Rd.

PHONE CODE	01472

RAJASTHAN

ACCOMMODATIONS

Hotels are concentrated near the railway station along City Rd. and also on Fort Rd. as it passes the bus stand and crosses the river into the old city. Be aware that rickshaw-*wallahs* operate on commission. Budget hotels in Chittaurgarh tend to be very basic and not very well maintained.

Hotel Ruchika (tel. 40419), near the railway station; follow signs to Hotel Meera. A delightful, family-run hotel with friendly staff. Basic, clean rooms. 24hr. room service. Free buckets of hot water; attached baths have 24hr. hot water. Singles Rs40, with bath Rs100, with air-cooling and TV Rs125; doubles Rs60/150/175. Extra bed Rs35.

Hotel Gaurav Palace (tel. 47207), off Fort Rd. on the first big side street to the right as you move away from the City Rd. intersection. All rooms in this modern hotel have attached baths with hot water. Check-out noon. Singles Rs300, with balcony and TV Rs400, with A/C 600; doubles Rs400/500/700. Extra person Rs125.

Hotel Bhagwati, Fort Rd. (tel. 46226 or 42275), across the bridge from the Roadways Bus Stand, near the old city. Large, dimly lit rooms with attached baths encircle a tiled courtyard. 24hr. room service and a *bhojnalya* downstairs serving Rs25 *thalis*. Check-out 24hr. Singles Rs80, with air-cooling and hot water Rs120; doubles Rs125/200. TV Rs25 per person. Extra bed Rs30.

Natraj Tourist Hotel (tel. 41009), near Roadways Bus Stand., has simple rooms, 24hr. room service, STD/ISD facilities. Hot water buckets Rs3. Singles Rs40, with bath Rs60 with air-cooling, phone, TV, and hot water Rs125; doubles Rs60/100/175.

Hotel Panna, Udaipur Rd. (tel. 41238), in front of the railway station. Standard RTDC tourist bungalow accommodations—well-maintained, spare rooms with faded red carpet, phones, and attached baths. Dining hall, bar, room service. Check-out noon. Dorm beds Rs50; singles Rs175, with air-cooling and hot water Rs275, with TV and A/C Rs475; doubles Rs225/350/575. Extra bed Rs75/100/125.

Hotel Pratap Palace, Station Rd. (tel./fax 40099), midway between the bus stand and rail station. English-speaking staff. Beautiful lobby and clean, well-furnished rooms with phones and TVs. 24hr. hot water, laundry service. Singles Rs250, air cooled Rs375, with A/C Rs500, deluxe Rs550; doubles Rs300/425/580/625. Extra bed Rs250.

Hotel Padmini, Chanderiya Rd. (tel. 41718 or 41997). Huge rooms with clean baths and phones. Relaxing outdoor garden. 24hr. hot water. Check-out noon. Singles Rs400, with A/C Rs800; doubles Rs500/1000.

FOOD

For cheap eats in Chittaurgarh, your best bet is to head towards the Roadways Bus Stand, where *bhojnalyas* lining the road serve steaming *thalis* (Rs25-30).

Maheshwari Restaurant, off Fort Rd. on the second big street to the right after the river crossing, behind Kazi Chal Phir Shah Mosque. Decidedly local restaurant doesn't have menus or cold drinks, but they do have boiled drinking water and substantial veg. *thalis* (with a mango) for Rs25. Open daily 10am-3pm and 6:30-10:30pm.

Rituraj Restaurant, City Rd., near the State Bank of India. A small but popular shop specializing in snacks, *tandoori,* and South Indian dishes, all under Rs45. Delicious *lassis* (Rs10) and fresh juices (Rs10). Open daily 7am-11pm.

Shakti Restaurant, Hotel Pratap Palace. Quiet, comfortable garden dining with a range of cuisines. Most dishes Rs25-50; excellent Continental breakfast (Rs80), full *tandoori* chicken (Rs120), and lip-smacking buffet dinner (Rs240). Open daily 7am-10:30pm.

Hotel Padmini Restaurant, Chanderiya Rd., about 3km from the Station and City Rd. intersection. Garden dining in a beautiful resort, far removed from the noise and pollution of the city. Air-cooled dining hall is also available. Indian and Continental dishes Rs20-45. Open daily 7am-11:30pm.

Restaurant Fort View, in the fort, near Rama Pol. The only restaurant in the fort itself dishes out *thalis* (Rs60) in a garden area with a spectacular view. Open daily 7am-9pm.

RAJASTHAN

🔍 SIGHTS

THE FORT. Jutting abruptly from the flat plateau below, the Chittaurgarh Fort is perhaps the single most impressive structure in all of Rajasthan. **Padan Pol** is the first *pol* (gate) in a series of seven that meanders a kilometer from the east side of town to the fort entrance. The climb to the top is gruelling; even auto-rickshaws struggle. Near the second *pol* are the *chhattris* (cenotaphs) of heroic martyrs Kalla and Jaimal, who died in the third sacking of Chittaurgarh in 1568. The final gate, **Rama Pol,** serves as the entrance to the fort proper. All the sights of interest in Chittaurgarh are inside the fort, and the view from the ramparts on all sides is spectacular. Although rickshaw drivers will offer rides around the fort, it's worth taking the time to walk the narrow tree-studded streets from sight to sight. *(Rs50, ticket valid for 2 days; video fee Rs25.)*

THE SHINGARA CHAURI MANDIR. The 15th-century Shingara Chauri Mandir is a Jain temple whose elaborate decoration betrays its Hindu influences. The inner statue was plundered during one of the Mughal sieges. The stone wall that extends to the right and left of Shingara Chauri Mandir was hastily constructed by Banvir Singh, cousin of Udai Singh. Legend has it that even when the young Udai Singh's father died in battle and his mother immolated herself, Banvir Singh devised a plan to kill the prince and take over the throne. The prince's nurse, Pannadhai, discovered Banvir Singh's plan and sacrificed her own son, switching him with the prince, whom she whisked away to safety. When Banvir Singh learned of the young prince's survival, he began partitioning the fort in the hopes of sharing power with Udai Singh. He conveniently constructed the wall so that his section of the fort included the treasury and the residential area (along with its tax-paying inhabitants). But Banvir Singh was dethroned by his cousin before his scheming could be completed. *(From the main road, the temple is just inside the fort to the left.)*

THE JAYA STAMBHA. The Jaya Stambha (Tower of Victory) is the monument on the cover of every brochure and postcard of Chittaurgarh. The sandstone tower boasts Chittaurgarh's story and glory from an imposing 37m. Elaborate multi-denominational sculptures grace the exterior. The tower's construction began in 1458 to commemorate an important victory in 1440, and it took 10 years to complete. You can climb eight of its nine stories; the view at the top is breathtaking. The ramparts around the tower are a popular hang-out. The **Sammidheshwar Mandir** is nearby on the hill. Thousands of *sati* handprints of women who immolated themselves on the funeral pyres of their husbands mark the solemn site of the **Mahasati** nearby. *(Follow the shady Fort Rd. south. Rs3, free on Friday; video fee Rs25.)*

THE RANA KUMBHA PALACE. The quasi-ruined Rana Kumbha Palace is believed to be where Chittaurgarh's third *jauhar* took place in an underground tunnel leading to Gaumukh Kund. After the siege of the city, only stables (including a stable said to house Genda Hathi, a militarily adept, sword-wielding elephant) and a Shiva temple remained. Toward the back is the nurse's palace, where Pannadhai's son was reputedly slain in the place of the young prince. Also nearby are the elegant **Meera Mandir,** which honors the Jodhpuri mystic poetess Mirabai (see **Mirabai,** p. 310) and the towered **Kumbha Shyam Mandir.** *(To the right off the main road.)*

OTHER SIGHTS. The **Gaumukh Kund** (Cow's Mouth Tank), off the main road, features a carved cow who fills the tank with water. Farther down is **Padmini's Palace,** a dainty but run-down palace set in a shallow pool. According to legend, Ala-ud-din-Khilji saw beautiful Padmini's reflection in a palace mirror and, setting his sight on her (and his army on Chittaurgarh), he staged the first siege of Chittaurgarh. The **Kalika Mata Mandir,** directly opposite, was originally dedicated to the sun god Surya in the 8th century but now pays tribute to the goddess Kali. The road loops past the often-empty **Deer Park,** quiet **Bhimlat Tank,** and a small crack in the fort's wall where traitors and political prisoners were thrown to their deaths. The road then turns north again past **Suraj Pol,** the eastern gate of the fort, and the **Kirti Stambha** (Tower of Fame). Built by a wealthy Jain merchant, the tower features decorative images of the Jain pantheon, particularly that of Adinath, the first *tirthankara,* to whom the tower is dedicated.

NEAR CHITTAURGARH

Forty kilometers south of Chittaurgarh is **Bijaipur,** a less-than-spectacular village with a spectacular 200-year-old palace which has been converted into the **Hotel Castle Bijaipur** (tel. 76222). This palace hotel offers fancy rooms, excellent dinners (Rs300), and blissful solitude, along with jungle trekking and safaris of the horse-and-village variety. (Check-out noon. Singles Rs910; doubles Rs1015; extra bed Rs250.) Reserve ahead at Hotel Pratap Palace (tel. 01472-40099) in Chittaurgarh. Buses run from Chittaurgarh to Bijaipur (5 per day, 1½hr., Rs10). **Bassi,** a small town 25km east of Chittaurgarh, is renowned for its wooden crafts. The town bursts with activity during the annual **Teejaji Fair** in late August and early September. Buses en route to Bundi or Kota from Chittaurgarh stop in Bassi.

UDAIPUR उदयपुर

Udaipur, City of Sunrise, epitomizes Rajasthan's romantic allure; countless visitors who plan three-day tours end up staying for weeks in this veritable oasis in the Thar desert. The old city overlooks the green Lake Pichhola, whose postcard perfection is removed from the industrialization farther out. Rooftop restaurants boast spectacular views and offer lazy-day releases from the bonanza of craft and jewelry stores below. Belittling the domain of cobblestone streets, modernization has reaped grim benefits—logging barons have left the once luscious valleys barren; crowds and chaos fill the new urban center outside the old city walls. Still, Udaipur's architectural offerings are surpassed only by Jaipur's, while its lakeside languor is surpassed by none.

Maharaja Udai Singh II founded Udaipur when he fled after Chittaurgarh's final siege in 1568. Four years later, Udai Singh's son and his troops successfully defended Udaipur against invasion by Akbar's fierce forces. The next 150 years were peaceful for the thriving city; miniature painting became a specialty, and architects beautifed the town with majestic palaces. In 1736 the city was crippled by the mighty Marathas, but it bounced back with British aid, somehow remaining firmly independent. Since then, the city's arts have continued to flourish, James Bond films notwithstanding (yes, *Octopussy* was filmed here). The **Mewar Festival** (April 7-8, 2000; March 28-29, 2001) brings in colorful dances, music, fireworks, and a scintillating lake parade.

▗ TRANSPORTATION

Airport: Dabok Airport (tel. 655453), 25km east of Udaipur (taxi Rs200). **Indian Airlines,** Delhi Gate (tel. 410999). Open daily 10am-1:15pm and 2-5pm. **U.P. Air,** Blue Circle, 1-C Madhu 1 (tel./fax 528666), near the GPO. Open daily 10am-6pm. To: **Aurangabad** (daily, 40min., US$105); **Delhi** (1-3 per day, 2hr., US$95); **Jaipur** (daily, 40min., US$70); **Mumbai** (1-3 per day, 2hr., US$110).

Trains: Udaipur City Railway Station (tel. 131). Reservation office open M-Sa 8am-8pm. Fares listed are 2nd/1st class. To: **Ahmedabad** (*Mewar Fast Passenger* 931, 9:10am, 12hr., Rs39/315); **Ajmer** (*Chetak Exp.* 9616, 6:20pm, 8hr., Rs130/564; *Mewar Fast Passenger* 932, 7:05pm, 12hr., Rs130/370); **Chittaurgarh** (*Ahmedabad-Delhi Mail* 9944, 8:30am, 4hr.; *Mewar Fast Passenger* 932, 7:05pm, 5hr., Rs22/348); **Delhi** (*Chetak Exp.* 9616, 6:20pm, 21hr., Rs223/1039); **Jaipur** (*Chetak Exp.* 9616, 6:20pm, 12hr., Rs161/725).

Buses: Main Bus Stand (tel. 484191). Fares listed are regular/deluxe. To: **Ahmedabad** (12 per day 5am-11pm, 7hr., Rs88; deluxe 6hr., Rs114); **Bikaner** (4:30pm, 15hr., Rs214); **Chittaurgarh** (6am-10pm, 3hr., Rs48/60); **Delhi** (5 per day, 15hr., Rs261/388); **Jaipur** (frequent 5am-10:30pm, 10hr., Rs165/200) via **Ajmer** (7hr., Rs114/145); **Jodhpur** (10 per day 5:30am-10:30pm, 7hr., Rs114/130); **Mt. Abu** (5 per day, 6hr., Rs76) via **Ranakpur** (2½ hr., Rs 35/40). Many companies have **private buses** to major cities (see **Budget Travel,** below).

Local Transportation: The best way to get around is by **bicycle**. **Vijay Cycles,** BC (tel. 411274), next to Raj Palace Hotel, rents bikes for Rs20 per day. Scooters Rs150 or Rs25 per hr. **Heera Cycle Store,** Gangaur Marg (tel. 523525), across from the road to Lal Ghat, rents bikes for Rs25 per day. Scooters Rs100-200 per day, motorcycles Rs250 per day. Open daily 7:30am-9pm. **Auto-rickshaws** are unmetered but not exorbitant. **Taxis** can be hired from through travel agents (Rs3-5 per km).

✴ ORIENTATION

One hundred thirteen kilometers southwest of Chittaurgarh and 270km south of Ajmer, Udaipur rests in the shadows of the Aravalli mountains. The **Old City** straddles the northeast bank of Lake Pichhola; the **New City** expands to the north, east, and south. The **Udaipur City Railway Station** sits to the southeast of town along **City Station Road.** The **bus stand** is 2km north of the station, opposite **Udai Pol,** one of the four main entrances to the Old City. The main road leads to **Suraj Pol,** another city entrance which also opens onto the two main shopping streets, **Bapu Bazaar** and **Bara Bazaar.** Bapu Bazaar runs parallel to **Town Hall Road,** home to many banks, and leads north to **Delhi Gate.** From Delhi Gate, the road left leads west down Ashwani Rd. and **Hathi Pol,** on the north end of the Old City. Going right at the gate leads to **Shastri Circle,** which includes the Tourist Bungalow, the GPO, and the General Hospital. **Chetak Circle** is about 1km down Hospital Rd. to the left. Hathi Pol affords the easiest access to the **City Palace** and **Jagdish Mandir** by way of the **clock tower.** From the clock tower, the right fork uphill leads southwest toward the Mandir, and the left leads east down Bara Bazaar to Suraj Pol. The road to **Gangaur Ghat** extends to the north from Jagdish Mandir. **Lal Ghat** extends behind the temple to the lake. From Jagdish Mandir, **Bhatiyani Chohotta (BC)** leads south, becoming **Lake Palace Road** before dead-ending in Bapu Bazaar. Heading north on BC takes you past the palaces and the *ghats* to the **Chand Pol** and west and north over bridges to the beautiful but less regal **Fateh Sagar Lake.**

❷ PRACTICAL INFORMATION

Tourist Office: Tourist Reception Centre, Suraj Pol (tel. 411535), has current maps and brochures and arranges home stays (see **Accommodations,** below). Open M-Sa 10am-5pm. Closed 2nd Sa. **Tourist Information Bureau,** at the railway station, has less information. Open M-Sa 8-11am and 4-7pm. Closed 2nd Sa. A small **information counter** at Dabok Airport (tel. 655433) is open when flights arrive and depart.

Budget Travel: Agents line City Station Rd. and the Jagdish Mandir area, with more around Delhi Gate and Chetak Circle. Most hotels double as travel agencies, which can book train, bus, and plane tickets; city tours by car (Rs350-450); airport taxis (Rs200); camel, horse, and elephant safaris (from Rs400 per day); and bus tours. Competition keeps prices virtually equal. **Shrinath Travels,** Udai Pol (tel. 422201; fax 422206), near the bus stand. Open daily 8:30am-11pm. **Rajasthan Tours,** Lake Palace Rd. (tel. 525777; fax 414283), near Gulab Bagh. Open daily 7am-7pm. **Gangaur Tour 'n' Travels,** 28 Gangaur Ghat (tel. 411476 or 415247; fax 561121), sells Indian Airlines tickets and reconfirms international flights. Open daily 9am-9pm.

Currency Exchange: Andhra Bank, Shakti Nagar Rd. (tel. 410699), advances cash on Visa and MC (Rs50 for up to Rs5000 advance) and exchanges foreign currency and traveler's checks. **State Bank of India,** Hospital Rd. (tel. 528857), exchanges foreign currency. Both open M-F 10am-2pm, Sa 10am-noon.

Market: In addition to Bara Bazaar and Bapu Bazaar, market areas, food stores, and food stalls are located around Jagdish Mandir, the clock tower, Chetak Circle, and all of the gates. Most open daily 8am-10pm.

Bookstore: Mayur Book Paradise, 60 BC (tel. 410316; fax 412160), opposite Hotel Shakti Palace. Wide multilingual paperback selection and some international 'zines. Open daily 10:30am-8pm. **English Book Shop,** Lal Ghat (tel. 418924), sells and

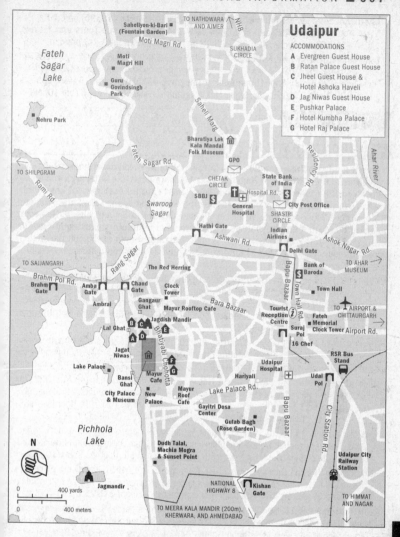

Udaipur

ACCOMMODATIONS

A Evergreen Guest House
B Ratan Palace Guest House
C Jheel Guest House &
    Hotel Ashoka Haveli
D Jag Niwas Guest House
E Pushkar Palace
F Hotel Kumbha Palace
G Hotel Raj Palace

exchanges books. Open daily 10am-10pm. The **book stall** at the railway station has an unusually good collection of English novels. Open daily 7-10am and 4-8pm.

Pharmacy: Hospital Rd. and Udai Pol have several pharmacies. Most open daily 7am-9:30pm. **Udaipur Hospital** (tel. 421900) has a well-stocked 24hr. pharmacy.

Hospital: RNT General Hospital, Hospital Rd. (tel. 528811 to 528817). Government-run. **Udaipur Hospital,** Gulab Bagh Rd. (tel. 420322), near Udai Pol, has excellent facilities and a pharmacy. Both English-speaking and open 24hr.

Police: A major police station is at every gate. The biggest are at **Delhi Gate** and **Udai Pol.** There are also stations near the bus and railway stations. Police superintendent (tel. 413949). Police control room (tel. 23000).

Post Office: GPO, Chetak Circle (tel. 528622). Open M-F 10am-6pm, Sa 10am-1pm. **Shastri Circle** (tel. 413905) has *Poste Restante.* Open M-Sa 10am-6pm. **Postal Code:** 313001.

Internet Access: Mewar Internet & Email, BC (tel. 410364; fax 410395), in the Raj Palace Hotel, charges Rs5 per min. Open daily 9am-10pm. **Titanic Tours and Travels,** Lake Palace Rd. (tel. 527895), outside Hotel Jhala Maan, charges Rs3 per min.

Telephones: Mewar International, 3 Lal Ghat (tel. 522992 or 521140; fax 520023) allows credit card/calling card calls (Rs4 per min.), collect calls, and callbacks (Rs2 per min). Open daily 7am-10pm. **Central Telegraph Office** (tel. 520275; fax 529922), in the GPO, has STD/ISD, fax, telex, and telegraph services. Open daily 7am-10pm.

PHONE CODE	0294

ACCOMMODATIONS

Though many of Udaipur's 200-plus hotels pay auto-rickshaw drivers to deposit wayfarers at their doorstep, you can ask to be dropped at one hotel area and easily check out the others nearby. The hotels on the beautiful **east bank** of Lake Pichhola are far better than any others in the city, with those along **Lake Palace Rd.** and **BC** coming a close second. Hotels in the **new city** are noisy and cheap. **Homestay** accommodation is an alternative, with more than 80 families participating. The Tourist Reception Centre (see above) makes arrangements (Rs50-500 per night). Most hotels listed below have laundry, travel, and 24-hour room service.

Hotel Raj Palace, BC (tel. 410364; fax 410395), between Jagdish Mandir and the City Palace. Great location, service, and food. The rooms have stained-glass windows, alcoves, fancy mirrors, spotless bathrooms, and garden views. 24hr. hot water. Check-out 10am. Dorm beds Rs75; standard rooms Rs150-350; deluxe singles Rs400, super-deluxe Rs590; doubles Rs500/690.

Hotel Ashoka Haveli, Gangaur Ghat (tel. 422303; fax 561121), has big, well-decorated rooms, an excellent rooftop restaurant, and a jovial atmosphere. Nightly puppet show on roof. 24hr. hot water. Doubles Rs80-100, with bath Rs150-400.

Jheel Guest House and **Paying Guest House,** 56/52 Gangaur Ghat (tel. 421352; fax 520008), on the edge of the lake. Spacious, well-kept, breezy rooms. All baths have hot water. Check-out 10am. Singles Rs50-80, with bath Rs100-200; doubles Rs80-100/150-350. Deluxe rooms with balconies overlooking the lake Rs600-700.

Pushkar Palace, 93 BC (tel. 417685), near Asha Pala Temple. Family-run "palace" offers huge, well-kept rooms around beautiful courtyards. Great common baths, funky bedspreads. Check-out 10am. Singles Rs50, with bath Rs60-80; doubles Rs80/100-120.

Ratan Palace Paying Guest House, 21 Lal Ghat (tel./fax 561153). Family-run place with clean, well-decorated rooms. Vibrant courtyard and terrace overlooking the lake. Check-out 10am. Singles Rs250, with 24hr. hot water Rs300; doubles Rs250/350-400.

Hotel Kumbha Palace, 104 BC (tel. 422702). The central garden borders the city walls. Distinctive rooms have colorful stained-glass windows and decorations from the Jaisalmeri desert, as well as attached baths and air-coolers. Check-out 10am. Singles Rs100-150; doubles Rs150-200. Discount Apr.-June.

Evergreen Guest House, 32 Lal Ghat (tel. 421585), set in an area frequented by Westerners. Cool, basic, aging rooms enhanced by good views. Art shop below offers free lessons. Luggage storage and free 24hr. hot water. Check-out 10am. Singles Rs100, with bath Rs200; doubles Rs150/250. Extra bed Rs50.

Jag Niwas Guest House, 21 Gangaur Marg (tel. 410303), near Jagdish Mandir. No longer owned by the Maharaja, but it still has style. Well-maintained rooms with attached baths and air-cooling. Check-out noon. Singles Rs120; doubles Rs200-300.

FOOD

Udaipur has a fairly good range of restaurants to choose from, many of which offer (you guessed it) non-stop screenings of *Octopussy.* Most are hotel rooftop eateries, but less-touristed finds are growing in number.

Mayur Cafe, Jagdish Mandir. Quality food, quick service and an A/C dining hall make the Mayur a popular local haunt. Leafy garden dining in back for those willing to forgo A/C pleasure. Especially popular are the Indian dishes (Rs25-50) and the easternized Western entrees, including Rajasthani pizza (Rs35). Open daily 8am-10pm.

Ambrai, Panch Devri Marg, in Amet-ki Haveli outside Chand Pol., clinches the romantic dining cliche with its underneath-the-mango-tree lakeside setting. You couldn't get any closer to the Lake Palace without getting wet. Wonderfully prepared veg. and non-veg. Indian dishes (Rs35-100). Open daily 9am-11pm.

The 16 Chef Restaurant, 16 Gyah Marg, near Suraj Pol. A huge red sign showing a bear hugging the number 16 invites you into a spectacular garden restaurant inaugurated by the Maharana of Mewar himself. Indian, Continental, and Chinese food galore, all (even *tandoori!*) for under Rs40. Open daily 9am-10:30pm.

The Red Herring Restaurant, Chand Pol. The chef's fingers are golden at this lakeside garden restaurant run by a gracious family. Indian (Rs25-30) and Swiss (Rs20-30) dishes. The view is fabulous and the garden lovely. Open Aug. to mid-Feb. daily 7am-11pm, mid-Feb. to July daily 8am-4pm.

Gayitri Dosa Centre, Lake Palace Rd. Bond with locals as you queue up for scrumptious *dosas* (Rs12-15) at this quasi-stall eatery. Open daily 7am-11pm.

Mayur Roof Cafe, Shakti Palace Hotel, 76 BC. The best of the rooftop restaurants, with views to kill for. Groove to the Hindi film music that plays in the background. Good Indian selection, some Continental and Chinese dishes (veg. generally less than Rs35, non-veg. Rs35-60). Open daily 7am-11pm.

Hariyali Restaurant, RMV Rd., off Lake Palace Rd. Specialty veg. South Indian cuisine; Continental and Chinese also available. Secluded atmosphere saves the lush garden for your eyes only. Most entrees Rs35-50. Open daily 9am-11pm.

Jagat Niwas Palace Hotel, Lal Ghat. Affordable, lake-view dining luxury at this renovated palace. The rooms here are expensive, but dinner is not (veg. entrees Rs35-50; non-veg. Rs45-70; beer Rs70). Have a romantic meal for two in the center alcove on the balcony. Attentive service. Open daily 7:30am-10:30pm.

🎵🛍 ENTERTAINMENT AND SHOPPING

Udaipur's charm isn't confined merely to lakeside palaces and museums. Traditional **Rajasthani folk dances** and music performances, involving a dazzling blend of tribal trances and circus-like balancing feats, take place at **Meera Kala Mandir** (tel. 583176), near the Pars Theater in Sector 11, a Rs25-30 rickshaw ride from the old city. (Shows held M-Sa 7-8pm. Tickets Rs60. Book at Heera Cycle Store, Gangaur Marg, across the road leading to Lal Ghat. Tel. 523525. Open daily 7:30am-9pm. Tel. 523525). For information about **puppet shows** at the Bharatiya Lok Kala Folk Museum and **folk dances,** see Shilpigram, p. 311.

 Shopping here can be addictive. Countless clothing, jewelry, textile, and handi-crafts shops pepper the areas around Jagdish Mandir, Lake Palace Rd., and Bara and Bapu Bazaars. They carry wares from all over Rajasthan at inflated but nego-tiable prices. **Miniature painting** is an Udaipuri specialty, and Lake Palace Rd. has shops where skilled artists can be observed without your feeling any obligation (despite coercion) to buy. In general, it's best to explore the areas on your own..

📷 SIGHTS

Udaipur's skyline may be dominated by the elegant palaces rising from the deep green of Lake Pichhola, but the historical focal points are the **City Palace** and **Jagdish Mandir,** to the west of the old city. A good way to take in the sights in a quick daytrip is with the RTDC city tour (8am-1pm, 5hr., Rs53), departing from Hotel Kajri. Reserve ahead at Kajri Tourist Bungalow (tel. 410501).

MIRABAI Visitors from far and wide come to Chittaurgarh to visit Meera Mandir, a tribute to the mystic poetess Mirabai, whose *bhajans* (devotional songs) grace the airwaves nationwide. Born in the 15th century to a Rajput family in the village of Kurki, outside of Jodhpur, Mirabai displayed an early affection for the Lord Krishna—she claimed him as her husband at a tender age. When she was matched with a mortal spouse, Raltan Singh of Chittaurgarh, Mirabai persisted in her devotion. She defied her new family (staunch Shiva devotees) and Rajput customs by leaving the fort to worship Krishna. The final straw for the royal family was her refusal to commit *sati* upon her husband's death. She claimed her true spouse was Krishna, citing his immortality as a reason for not mourning. Members of the enraged royal family plotted to take her life, first by sending her poison to drink and then by releasing a black cobra to kill her. Mira consumed the poison as if it were a *lassi*, and the cobra became a garland of flowers around her neck. After the attempts on her life, Mirabai took her statue of Krishna and fled to Dwarka in Gujarat. When Udai Singh came to power, he attempted to redress his family's transgressions and invited Mirabai back to Chittaurgarh. Legend has it that, after a visit to the Krishna temple that housed her statue, she was never seen again—she disappeared into the statue. Mirabai's cherished Krishna icon is now the personal property of the royal family of Udaipur. The songs Mirabai composed out of her devotional love (*bhakti*) remain a popular means of Krishna worship.

CITY PALACE. The toast of Udaipur is its grand palace, begun in 1559 by **Udai Singh,** the proud Mewar migrant who founded the city. An amalgamation of the architectural efforts of more than 20 kings, the City Palace is currently part museum, part royal residence, and part luxury hotel. Before entering the museum, note the two large paved stone indentions—they were once elephant beds. The museum opens into the **Raja Angan Chowk,** surrounded by rooms of Udaipuri miniature paintings, one of which appears in three dimensions when viewed at a distance. This vast courtyard was once a Holi playground. The palace is filled with tributes to Rana Pratap, Udai Singh's legendary son; among them are an eerie, larger-than-life marble bust and 400-year-old armor worn by his equally brave Arabian steed, Chetak (see **A Helluva Horse,** p. 312). The palace is best known for the **Mor Chowk,** with its blue and green inlaid glass peacocks and convex mirrors. **Krishna Vilas,** a small room with walls completely covered by miniature paintings, is dedicated to Krishna Kumari, a 16-year-old princess who was betrothed to two princes and chose to commit suicide to avoid the war for her hand. The **Zenana Mahal,** the women's quarters, is disappointingly ill-maintained and houses little more than Maharaja Bhopal Singh's 1922 Rolls-Royce. *(West of the city. Open daily 9:30am-4:30pm. Rs25; camera fee Rs50; video fee Rs300. Tours Rs95 per hr.)*

JAGDISH MANDIR. A 17th-century temple built by Maharaja Jagat Singh and dedicated to Vishnu's avatar Jagannath, whose black marble image resides in the sanctum, the Jagdish Mandirl lies in the heart of the old city. Legend has it that Jagat Singh received the inspiration for the temple in a dream. The outer structure rises in a pyramid-like shikhara of worn stone decorated with rows of elephants and apsaras, along with figures from Mewari mythology. The entrance is guarded by a large bronze Garuda, Vishnu's mount. The cornerstone at the left base of the stairs bestows good luck on anyone who rubs it seven times. The central dome teems with mythological figures, and a huge silver bed meant for the gods rests in front of the sanctuary entrance. (Down the steep hill from the City Palace. *Open daily 5am-2pm and 4-10:30pm. Winter: open 5:30am-2pm and 4-10pm.)*

JAG NIWAS (LAKE PALACE). Once the royal summer palace, the Jag Niwas seems to float gently on the waters of Lake Pichhola. The Lake Palace, now a luxury hotel, is worth the buffet dinner that comes with short boat rides from **Bansi Ghat.** The palace grounds and open-air courtyard cafes, with marble inlay and corner towers and turrets, are stunning. Jag Mandir can be visited on non-dinner cruises as well—jaunts around the lake leave from Bansi Ghat. *(Dinner buffet Rs600, a la carte Rs110-190. Reserve ahead; tel. 527961. Cruises daily 10am-5pm; Rs75 per 30min.)*

BHARATIYA LOK KALA MANDAL FOLK MUSEUM. A large complex intended as a center for the preservation and diffusion of tribal folk arts, the museum has several rooms off one main hall, each containing a variety of items ranging from colorfully painted masks to clay figure dioramas of local festivals to a rather dusty collection of life-sized models of local tribals. The museum's highlight is the collection of traditional Rajasthani **puppets** called *kathpurli*—wide-eyed wooden string puppets dressed in bright, traditional costumes. A **minimalist puppet show** is put on every 20 to 25 minutes in the puppet theater—music accompanies the shimmying hips of wooden dancing girls. The puppets are expertly (and a trifle obscenely) manipulated. The Lok Mandal also puts on dance performances. *(Saheli Marg, just past Chetak Circle. Tel. 529296. Museum open daily 9am-6pm. Rs10; camera fee Rs10, video fee Rs50. Dance performances daily noon-1pm and 6-7pm. Rs30.)*

SHILPIGRAM. A self-dubbed "rural arts and crafts complex," Shilpigram has wide paths leading to model homes from specific rural and tribal communities of Rajasthan, Gujarat, Maharashtra, and Goa. Styles range from the circular, white stone, clay-roofed homes of the Meghwal Bahni to the thatched-roofed, square home of a Kohlapuri shoe maker. The village supports itself with tents selling the work of potters and cloth makers. and lively performances by musicians and dancers from various rural communities who inhabit the village for short periods of time. (West of Udaipur, off Lake Fateh Sagar. Rickshaws around Rs70-100 round trip. Tel. 431304. Open daily noon-8pm in summer. Winter: open daily 11am-7pm. Rs10.)

GARDENS. Udaipur's famous gardens are extremely well-maintained but also quite tourist-trampled. **Nehru Park,** built in part as a public works project to create jobs during a famine, sits pretty in Fateh Sagar. It is spread over fairly open and fountain-sprinkled grounds, with beige-domed cupolas, swaying palm trees, and bright bushes of bougainvillea. Small, crowded boats leave the banks of Fateh Sagar every 20 minutes for the island park. They offer a quaint, if slightly harrowing, adventure. It is also possible to take a 30-minute tour around the lake. *(Open daily 8am-7pm in summer. Winter: open daily 8am-6pm. Rs5. Boats Rs40 for up to 4 people.)* The 18th-century **Saheliyon-ki-Bari** (Garden of the Maids of Honor), built by Maharana Sangram Singh for the maharani and her corps of friends and servants, lies 2km to the north of town. The verdant garden, with its palm-lined walks and lotus pool, is more of a tourist sight than the refuge it was meant to be. During the monsoon rains, the pool is spectacular. *(Open daily 9am-6pm. Rs2.)* **Sajjan Niwas,** on Lake Palace Rd., and the nearby **Gulab Bagh** (Rose Garden) are sprawling, thickly vegetated dream gardens. The former's wide paths are lined with local flora, including giant umbrella neem trees. *(Open daily 5am-8pm. Free.)*

OTHER SIGHTS. Not far from the Lake Palace, on another island, is the **Jag Mandir,** a domed pavilion famous for the safety it provided to the exiled Shah Jahan, a prince who led a revolt against his father Jahangir, and later to English women and children during the Mutiny of 1857.For a mind-blowing view of the city and valley, head to **Sajjangarh (Monsoon) Palace.** If you're biking it there, good luck—even auto-rickshaws barely sputter their way up. *(On a steep hill 5km west of Udaipur. Auto-rickshaws Rs100-150 round-trip. Palace closed to visitors.)* **The Dudh Talal and Sunset Point** offers more solitary, serene lake views (off Lake Palace Rd.).

NEAR UDAIPUR: EKLINGI इकलिंगी

Twenty-two kilometers north of Udaipur, in the heart of marble-producing territory, is the inspiring village of **Eklingi,** home to a magnificent temple of Shiva. The temple itself is vanilla-colored marble and encloses a four-faced solid black image of Shiva. Silver doors, silver lamps, silver parcels, and a solid silver bull adorn the interior, and the exterior and surrounding shrines are decorated with impressive stonework. The complex, erected in AD 734, houses a total of 108 temples. (Open daily 4:30-6:30am, 10:30am-1:30pm, and 5:30-6:45pm. Photography is not permitted.) Many tours stop at Eklingi, which is also accessible by **bus** from Udaipur (every 30min. 5am-9:30pm, 45min., Rs10).

RAJASTHAN

A HELLUVA HORSE The cow might be an object of worship for Hindus, but the Rajputs of Rajasthan have a special place in their hearts for a certain white stallion named Chetak. Indeed, his name lives on in Udaipur's main circle and graces the main express train in Rajasthan. Chetak, whose statues abound in Udaipur, was the loyal battle companion of Rana Pratap. At the famous bloodbath of Haldighati in 1532, Chetak's leg was cut by an enemy elephant wielding a machete in its trunk; Pratap was also wounded. Though hobbled, Chetak bravely carried his master from the battlefield through a narrow passage, leaping over a 3m crevice before finally coming to rest under a tree 6km away. Having saved his master's life, poor Chetak breathed his last. Many tours of the area surrounding Udaipur stop at Haldighati to pay respects at Chetak's tomb and hear the tale of his valiant death.

NEAR UDAIPUR: NATHDWARA नाथद्वारा

Forty-eight kilometers north of Udaipur is the important Vaishnava pilgrimage site of **Nathdwara,** built entirely around its incredible **Nathji Mandir,** a temple dedicated to Krishna's avatar as Sri Nathji. Legend maintains that, in the 17th century, a chariot en route from Mathura to Udaipur bearing Krishna's image inexplicably became trapped in the mud; the bearers interpreted the situation as a divine signal and built a temple on the spot. The image of Sri Nathji, with blazing diamond-studded eyes and Mughal dress, is found on decorative items in households all over India. The stalls outside the temple have commercialized the image—the assortment of Krishna paraphernalia is vast, and prices are high. Although the temple's architecture is a visual feast, far more interesting are the evening (5pm) ceremonies following a ritual schedule of feeding, bathing, and resting the image. For each *darshan*, a different backdrop is displayed behind the statue in order to depict a different scene of Krishna's life. Viewing the image is only possible at certain times of the day, and after 3pm, the temple re-opens at 4:45 for only 15 minutes of viewing. The mad rush that ensues is enough to make even the most crowd-loving person claustrophobic. It also serves pick-pockets well, so guard your belongings. Photography is strictly prohibited in the temple.

Nathdwara is a stop on many buses and is accessible by **bus** from Udaipur (every 30min. 5am-9:30pm, 1hr., Rs21). RTDC runs a bus (M-F 2pm; returns 7pm; Rs85) to Haldighati, Eklingi, and Nathdwara that leaves from the Kajri Tourist Bungalow (tel. 410501) in Chowk Circle. Make reservations in advance at Kajri.

NEAR UDAIPUR: RANAKPUR रनकपु

Eighty kilometers northwest of Udaipur, roads zig-zag through the verdant Aravalli range's valleys to Ranakpur's superb Jain temples, a complex rivaling Mt. Abu's Dilwara. The main, white marble **Chaumukha Temple,** built in 1439, is dedicated to Adinath, the first *tirthankara* (Jain teacher). The three-tiered entry facade is delicately crenulated and punctuated by squashed spires along both sides. Inside, each of the 29 halls, 80 domes, and 1444 pillars (no two of them alike) is intricately carved and sculpted—every last bead on a dancer's earring is rendered meticulously in stone. The temple's most intricate carvings surround a four-faced image of Adinath in the innermost sanctum. Within the complex are smaller shrines to Parshvanath and Neminath and a Hindu temple to Surya. Its sculpture and latticework are striking, although a bit weathered. (A rickshaw to the temple should cost about Rs35. Temple open to non-Jains daily noon-5pm. Camera fee Rs25. Menstruating women not permitted to enter.)

Most **buses** from Udaipur to Jodhpur stop at Ranakpur (3hr.; Rs35-40; see **Udaipur,** p.305). Be sure the driver knows that you want to be dropped off in Ranakpur. Private bus companies in Udaipur and Mt. Abu arrange frequent departures and tours to Ranakpur as well. Private buses bound for Jodhpur, Jaipur, and Udaipur leave Ranalpur from in front of the *chai* stand on the main road (approx. every 2hr.). There is a **post office** in Shilpi Tourist Bungalow (open M-Sa noon-5pm). **Telephone Code:** 02934.

There are only two accommodation options in Ranakpur proper. The **dharam-shala** (tel. 85019) offers simple lodgings (Rs5 per bed, donations appreciated) and basic but plentiful veg. lunches and dinners (Rs13). Alcohol and smoking are prohibited, and lights-out is at 10pm. The **Shilpi Tourist Bungalow** (tel. 85074), just up the road from the temples, has spacious, clean rooms and an expensive restaurant. All rooms have attached baths. (Dorm beds Rs50; singles Rs200, with air-cooling Rs250; doubles Rs250/350/500.) The **Roopam Restaurant** (tel. 85321), 2km past the Tourist Bungalow, is an open-air establishment set among several forest villages (most entrees Rs35-55; open daily 7am-11pm).

MOUNT ABU आबू

Situated 1220m above sea level on a temperate plateau with lush vegetation and bearable temperatures year round, Mt. Abu, Rajasthan's only hill station, is a popular destination for Indian (mainly Gujarati) families and honeymooners. Some are drawn by the ecological richness of the area—the most impressive natural sights are the winding rivers flanked by palm trees and shadowed by mammoth rock outcroppings. Others come to Mt. Abu with a more divinely inspired mission. Once part of the kingdom of the Chauhan Rajputs, the hill station is now an important Hindu pilgrimage site. Thought to be the home of Vashishta, the sage whose sacrificial fire gave rise to the five Rajput clans, Mt. Abu also boasts the holy waters of Nakki Lake, held to be as purifying as those of the Ganga. Jains also make spiritual journeys here, to worship at the architecturally breathtaking Dilwara temples. Despite the strongly religious atmosphere, though, sacred Mt. Abu

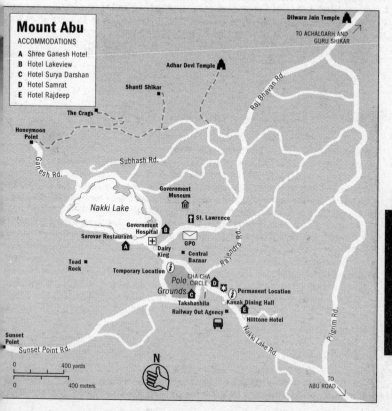

Mount Abu

ACCOMMODATIONS
A Shree Ganesh Hotel
B Hotel Lakeview
C Hotel Surya Darshan
D Hotel Samrat
E Hotel Rajdeep

Dilwara Jain Temple

TO ACHALGARH AND
GURU SHIKAR

Adhar Devi Temple

Rai Bhavan Rd.

Shanti Shikar

The Crags

Honeymoon
Point

Ganesh Rd.

Subhash Rd.

Government
Museum

Nakki Lake

St. Lawrence

Government
Hospital

Sarovar Restaurant

Dairy
King

GPO

Central
Bazaar

Rajendra Rd.

Toad
Rock

Temporary Location

Polo
Grounds

CHA CHA
CIRCLE

Takshashila

Railway Out Agency

Permanent Location

Kanak Dining Hall

Hilltone Hotel

Nakki Lake Rd.

Pilgrim Rd.

Sunset
Point

Sunset Point Rd.

N

0   400 yards
0   400 meters

TO
ABU ROAD

does not inhibit frolicking honeymooners in their more worldly enjoyments. Bangle stores, milkshake shops, and galloping ponies cater to the throngs of Gujarati tourists who come to Mt. Abu to enjoy a liquor-filled weekend of leisure. During the annual Summer Festival (June 1-3), tourists from nearby areas head here to cavort amid tribal dances and folk music. With its palm trees and grand sunsets over the ridged lake, Mt. Abu offers a pleasant and festive desert oasis retreat.

TRANSPORTATION

Trains: Trains depart from **Abu Road Railway Station** (tel. 22222), 27km from town (see **Local Transportation,** below). **Railway Out Agency,** Nakki Lake Rd. (tel. 38697), next to the bus stand, handles reservations. Open M-Sa 9am-1pm and 2-4pm, Su 9am-noon. Fares listed are 2nd/1st class. To: **Ahmedabad** (*Ahmedabad Mail* 9106, 1:10pm, 5hr., Rs96); **Delhi** (*Ahmedabad Mail* 9105, 2:40pm, 14hr.; *Superfast* 2915, 9pm, 13hr., Rs250/1080); **Jaipur** (*Ahmedabad Mail* 9105, 2:40pm, 7½hr., Rs161/755).

Buses: Main Bus Stand (tel. 43434). To: **Ahmedabad** (10 per day 6am-9pm, 6hr., Rs70); **Jaipur** (9:45am, 12hr., Rs201; deluxe, 6:30pm, 12hr., Rs244); **Jaisalmer** (6:15 and 7am, 11hr., Rs178); **Jodhpur** (6:30am, 7½hr., Rs118); **Udaipur** (8:45 and 9:30am, 6hr., Rs76; deluxe 1:30 and 4pm, 6hr., Rs137). **Private bus companies** lining the main road service Rajasthan and Gujarat. Recommended agencies are **Shobha Travels** (tel. 38302; open daily 7am-10:30pm), near Hotel Samrat; **Baba Travels** (tel. 38747; open daily 7am-11pm), near the taxi stand; and **Natraj Travels** (tel. 38083; open daily 8:30am-10:30pm), across from the Telecom office. Private buses depart from the taxi stand and along the main road. All bus transportation arranged in Mt. Abu departs from Mt. Abu proper, but arrangements made in other cities for service to Mt. Abu may only come as far as Abu Road, 1hr. away—be sure to check in advance.

Local Transportation: Buses to Abu Rd. frequently depart from the Main Bus Stand (every 30min. 6am-9pm, 1hr., Rs15). Jeeps and vans serving as local **taxis** depart from the taxi stand. A shared jeep to Abu Rd. Rs15 per person; a private taxi Rs200 one-way. To the Dilwara Temples, private taxis Rs50-60 one-way and shared jeeps, leaving from Cha Cha Cir., Rs3 per person.

ORIENTATION AND PRACTICAL INFORMATION

The railhead at **Abu Road,** 27km downhill, serves Mt. Abu. The small town can be traversed in 25 minutes, and buses will drop you off within walking distance of several hotels, but too far from the lake. The main drag, **Nakki Lake Road,** leads into town from Abu Rd., passing the Railway Out Agency, Tourist Reception Centre, Main Bus Stand, police station, and **Cha Cha Circle.** A left after the police station takes you past the taxi stand; the road curves around the **Polo Grounds** and, continuing along the right fork, reunites with Nakki Lake Rd., which then continues on to the **Central Bazaar.** A right at the Central Bazaar takes you past the hospital, the **GPO, St. Lawrence Church,** and, much farther on, the **Dilwara Temples.** Veering left from the Central Bazaar takes you to **Nakki Lake.**

Tourist Office: Tourist Reception Centre (tel. 43151), in the RTDC youth hostel located off Nakki Lake Rd., at the end of the Polo Grounds closest to the lake. Provides good maps, brochures, travel information for all of Rajasthan, and city tours (8:30am and 1:30pm, 5hr., Rs35-40). Open M-Sa 10am-1:30pm and 2-5pm.

Currency Exchange: State Bank of India (tel. 43136; fax 38882), near General Hospital, exchanges currency and wires money. **State Bank of Bikaner and Jaipur** (tel. 3224), behind the GPO, changes traveler's checks and currency. **Bank of Baroda** (tel. 43166), near the taxi stand, gives cash advances on Visa, MC, and AmEx (service charge Rs100). All open M-F 10am-2pm, Sa 10am-noon.

Market: The **Central Bazaar** is Mt. Abu's main market. Open daily 9am-10pm.

Hospital: J. Watumull Global Hospital and Research Centre (tel. 38347 or 38348), 1km out of town on the road to the Dilwara Temples, is an ultra-clean, ultra-modern private facility. Open M-Sa 9am-1pm and 3-5pm. Open for emergencies 24hr.

Police: Main Police Station (tel. 43333), near the Main Bus Stand. English-speaking and tourist-friendly. Open 24hr.

Post Office: GPO (tel. 43170). *Poste Restante* M-Sa 10am-5pm. Registered mail and parcel service M-F 10am-3pm, Sa 10am-2pm. **Postal Code:** 307501.

Telephones: The **Telecom Centre** (tel. 43107; fax 38900), near the taxi stand, offers STD/ISD, fax, and telegraph services. Open M-Sa 8am-8pm.

PHONE CODE	02974

ACCOMMODATIONS

Most of the hotels in Mt. Abu cater to honeymooners, so doubles are the norm. Visitors arrive here in droves from April to June and September to December, and especially around **Diwali** (Oct. 26, 2000). Prices of accommodations at least triple during these peak times, and reservations are essential. In the low season (Mar.-Apr. and July-Sept.), room rates are negotiable. As in most tourist locales, touts will accost you at the bus and taxi stands. The dozens of "youth hostels" around town are intended principally for students attending Mt. Abu private schools. Most hotels have travel, laundry, room service, and 9am check-out.

Shree Ganesh Hotel (tel. 43591), near Nakki Lake on the road up to the Maharaja of Jaipur's summer palace. Popular because of its value and isolation from the main clusters of hotels. Sparse rooms have attached baths. Garrulous owner. Low season: doubles Rs100, with TV and 24hr. hot water Rs150; triples and quads Rs150-210. Extra bed Rs25. Kitchen facilities Rs75 per day. High season: singles Rs250; doubles Rs300.

Hotel Surya Darshan (tel. 43165; fax 38900). The best value of the western Polo Grounds group. Rooms are slightly stuffy but big and clean, with attached baths. Low season: singles Rs100, with color TV and views of the Polo Grounds Rs200-300; doubles Rs150/250-300. High season: singles Rs250-500; doubles Rs300-600.

Hotel Lakeview, Nakki Lake (tel. 38659). An odd, off-white building with a garden in front. Big, well-lit rooms with tie-dyed bed spreads and attached baths. Lakeside balconies have swings and excellent views. Hot water 7-11am. Rooftop restaurant, STD/ISD. Singles Rs100-200; doubles Rs300-400; luxurious lakeside rooms Rs500-700.

Hotel Rajdeep (tel. 43525), opposite the bus stand, in an arched building that has seen better days. Still, the rooms here are large and the lawn is a nice place to relax. Attached baths and hot water in buckets Rs5. Low season: doubles Rs150-250; 20% discount for single occupancy. High season: doubles Rs250-350.

Hotel Samrat International (tel. 43173 or 43153), on the main road opposite the Polo Field. Ordinary rooms are simple, clean, and comfortable. The honeymoon and VIP suites have arched wooden bed frames, swings, and baths with romantic touches—mild erotica on the tiles and mirrored ceilings. Singles Rs70, with bath and TV Rs130; doubles Rs200; honeymoon suites Rs450; VIP suites Rs450, with A/C Rs700.

FOOD

Restaurants in Mt. Abu serve both Gujarati and Rajasthani cuisines, and many offer Punjabi and Chinese dishes as well. Between the Central Bazaar and the main bus stand, *dhabas* offer quick service and roadside seating.

Hilltone Hotel, near the Main Bus Stand. There are two excellent restaurants and a bar in this large, luxurious hotel. The veg. **Handi Restaurant** offers indoor or garden seating. The food is superb and most entrees are Rs45-75. Open daily 7-11pm. The **Kalali Bar** has domestic and imported drinks (Rs80-120). Open daily 11am-3pm and 7-11pm.

Kanak Dining Hall, near the Main Bus Stand. Come around lunchtime to see stainless steel fly in this spacious, undecorated dining hall. Crowds swarm around the excellent all-you-can-eat Gujarati *thalis* (Rs45). Open daily 7am-10pm.

Takshashila Restaurant, in Hotel Samrat. The best veg. food in town, according to the locals. The restaurant is elegantly decorated with covered wooden chairs, marble floors, and red and white tablecloths. Indian, Chinese, and Continental entrees (Rs40-60) and Aquaguard water! Open daily 7am-11pm.

Veena Fast Food Corner, Nakki Rd., opposite the Bank of Baroda. Good, fast meal and snack joint specializing in South Indian food. Not as fast as King's Food, but more sanitary. Twist your hips to Hindi pop as you munch on a *dosa* (Rs20-40) or dare to try a veg. cheeseburger (Rs30). Open daily 7am-midnight.

Sarovar Restaurant, Nakki Lake. The RTDC finally gets creative—a fake plaster boat jutting into Nakki Lake houses this little snack-bar. The view is beautiful, with the lake up front and gardens to the rear. Occasionally, fishermen try their luck on the deck as well. Snacks Rs8-20, *chai* Rs5. Open daily 8am-10pm.

👁 SIGHTS

DILWARA JAIN TEMPLES. The marble Jain temples house within their simple, worn stone exteriors some of the country's most amazing marble sculpture. Sarnavasaian workers toiled on this colossal sculptural achievement for 14 years. The artisans were paid in amounts corresponding to the weight of marble they removed and were thereby given incentive to create the finest, most intricate carvings. The main temple, constructed in the 11th century by Vimal Shah, Chief Minister to the Solanki King, is dedicated to the first *tirthankara* ("crossing-maker"), Adinath. Devotees of art and Adinath alike flock to Dilwara to see the exquisitely carved pillars of dancers and spiralling lotus domes that adorn the halls. Fifty-seven *tirthankara* statues line these halls under a ceiling depicting different myths. One playfully illustrates Krishna with his *gopis;* others depict various goddesses soaring overhead, rendering them in minutest detail, right down to the fingernails. The central dome is alive with more dancing and a triumphant marble elephant who turns up his trunk in homage to Adinath. The balconies to either side of the main sanctuary, built by two brothers, are identically decorated save for the last figure on the left, who is bent in due respect to the work of the elder.

The dome and walls of the outer sanctuary, on the other hand, were purposefully left undecorated to avoid distracting meditators. The statue of Adinath is modeled on a 3500-year-old granite statue housed in the back corner of the temple. According to legend, Vimal Shah discovered the statue on this very spot under a sweet-smelling *champa* tree revealed to him in one of his dreams.

Even more intricate than the decoration on the main temple are the curling arches of the second largest temple, dedicated to Neminath, the 22nd tirthankara and a cousin of Krishna. Its tiered lotus dome was carved from a single block of marble. Both temples enclose marble memorials to their patrons, depicted sitting atop models of the elephants who transported the building materials to the site.

There are three other temples in the complex, including a 16th-century shrine to Mahavira and another commemorating Adinath Rishabdeo. The third is a memorial to the skilled workers who contributed to the complex; it is constructed of many types of stone and dedicated to tirthankara Parshvanath. Unofficial guides give tours and appreciate a tip or a donation to the temple. *(A peaceful 45min., 3km walk northeast of town. Jeeps from Cha Cha Circle head to the temples every 15min. for Rs3. Open to non-Jains noon-6pm. Free. Photography and leather items prohibited. Menstruating women not permitted entrance.)*

NAKKI LAKE. Visiting Nakki Lake, where most of Mt. Abu's activity is focused, is a bit like attending a carnival—crowding the short street to the lake are small shops alongside popcorn sellers, fast-food restaurants, photo stalls, and brightly decorated **ponies** *(rides Rs40 per 30min.).* Mobs constantly clamor for the paddle

boats or rowboats available at the dock *(Rs25 per 30min.)*. The festive atmosphere tends to obscure the religious significance of the lake, thought to contain holy waters because it was dug out by the *nakh* ("nails") of a god. To experience the lake's serenity, take a scenic walk along the left bank, past the small **Ragunath Temple,** and to the quiet bank opposite lined with huge estates and stately homes.

VIEWPOINTS. Sunset Point lies along the left fork from the main road past the taxi stand. Although it does offer a beautiful view of the setting sun, the constant rabble of tourists has made it much more of a people-watching spot. A similar fate has befallen **Honeymoon Point,** off the road leading northwest behind Nakki Lake. Though the view from here is also superlative, it is the name that has drawn newlyweds by the dozen.

ADHAR DEVI TEMPLE. A left off the northeast road to Dilwara leads to the base of a good 30-minute heart-pumping trek up 360 steps to the mountain-top Adhar Devi Temple. Dedicated to the patron goddess of Mt. Abu, the "temple" is actually a natural cleft in the rock that can be entered only by crawling on all fours. It offers a spectacular view of the green valleys below.

GOVERNMENT MUSEUM. Back in town across from the GPO is the bizarre **Government Museum,** with its huge collection of stone chunks and slabs from various archaeological hunts. Most of the artifacts come from Jain temples built between the 8th and 12th centuries. *(Open Sa-Th 10am-4:30pm. Rs3, students Rs1, free on M.)*

NEAR MOUNT ABU

Eight kilometers past Dilwara is **Achalgarh,** where a small 9th-century temple to Achaleshwar Mahadev, an incarnation of Shiva, stands amid the heavy, sweet scent of the plentiful *champa* trees. The temple marks a small, supposedly bottomless crater that was created by the impact of Shiva's big toe. The temple also contains a Nandi statue made of 4320kg of silver, brass, gold, copper, and tin. Outside the temple is a tank which, according to legend, was once filled with *ghee.* Lard-loving demons, dressed as buffalo, attempted to lap up the grease, but the king, ever-vigilant when it came to clarified butter, killed them. The three stone buffalo flanking the tank are the beasts' remains. Another five minutes up this same road is **Guru Shikar** (1721m), the highest point in Rajasthan, marked by a small Vishnu temple. **Buses** head to Achalgarh from the main bus stand (10am and 4pm, 30min., Rs5; return buses 10:30am and 5pm). The RTDC leads tours that stop at Dilwara, Achalgarh, and Guru Shikar (8:30am and 1:30pm; 5½hr.; Rs20, deluxe Rs35). Tour buses depart from the main bus stand.

JODHPUR जोधपर

Once the capital of the state of Marwar ("Land of Death") and home to the warrior clans of Rathore, Jodhpur (pop. 1,000,000) has a past rife with tales of royalty and valor. In the 18th century the city was overrun by the Mughals, and Maharaja Ajit Singh was exiled to Afghanistan and then murdered. The Mughals tried to legitimize their rule by claiming that there was no one left to take the throne of Jodhpur. Thirty years later, Maharaja Ajit Singh II—kidnapped as an infant and brought up secretly in a tiny Himalayan village—rode through the city gates at the head of an enormous army and drove out the Mughals, who never returned.

Modern Jodhpur is still haunted with legends from its past. As the sun rises on the eastern edge of the Thar Desert, daylight first gilds the elaborate towers of Jodhpur's ancient buildings, reminiscent of a vivid history of maharajas and princesses, of caravans crossing sand dunes, of city walls protecting from the beasts and bandits of the desert night. As daylight penetrates into the streets below, Rajasthan's second largest city comes to life, and the fairy tales mix with the realities of industry, grime, and poverty. Jodhpur, however, remains vibrant and its people resilient. The aptly named "Sun City" is awash with color, from the deep reds and blues of *bandhani* cloth to the fuchsia of bougainvillea, from the brilliant yellow of the scorching desert sun to the sea-blue walls of the old city houses.

TRANSPORTATION

Airport: Jodhpur Airport (tel. 142 or 630617), 6km from the city center, down Airport Rd. 15min. from town by auto-rickshaw (Rs60-80) or taxi (Rs90-100). To: **Delhi** (3 per week, 2hr., US$95); **Mumbai** (6 per week, US$135); **Udaipur** (3 per week, 45min., US$55). **Indian Airlines,** Airport Rd. (tel. 636757 or 636758). Open daily 10am-1:15pm and 2-4:30pm.

Trains: Jodhpur Railway Station, Railway Station Rd. (tel. 131 or 132). Prices are 2nd/A/C class. To: **Ahmedabad** (*Marwar Exp.;* Tu, Th, and Su 3:15 and 6:30pm; 8hr.; Rs166/730); **Bikaner** (*Jammu Exp.* 4806, 8pm, 6hr., 2nd class Rs122); **Delhi** (*Mandore Exp.* 2462, 7:30pm, 12hr., Rs227/976); **Jaipur** (*Intercity Exp.* 2466, 5:45am, 5hr., Rs104/292); **Jaisalmer** (*Jaisalmer Exp.* 4810, 11:30pm, 7hr., Rs124/568). Reserve at the **Advance Reservation Office,** Station Rd. (tel. 636407), located to the right of the GPO. Although a separate tourist quota line is available, plan to be there at least an hour. Reservations for long trips should be made several days in advance. Open M-Sa 8am-1:45pm and 2-8pm, Su 8am-1:45pm.

Buses: Main Bus Station, High Court Rd. (tel. 544686 or 544989). Features a retiring room and a disorganized ticket-purchasing system. To: **Ahmedabad** (5 per day 6:30am-7:30pm, 12hr., Rs159; deluxe at 6, 9, and 10pm, 10hr., Rs189); **Agra** (7am, 4:15 and 8:45pm; 12hr.; Rs220); **Bikaner** (12 per day 5am-10:30pm, 6hr., Rs101); **Delhi** (5 per day 9am-8:15pm, 14hr., Rs232; deluxe at 4pm, 11hr., Rs347); **Jaipur** (every hr. 5:15am-10:15pm, 8hr., Rs129; 5 deluxe per day 11am-11:30pm, 7hr., Rs158); **Jaisalmer** (1:30pm, 7hr., Rs89; deluxe at 5:30am, 6hr., Rs133); **Osian** (every 30min., 5:30am-9pm, 2hr., Rs25); **Udaipur** (6 per day 7am-10pm, 8hr., Rs105; deluxe 5:30am, noon, 3, and 10:30pm, 7hr., Rs129). **Private bus companies** number in the dozens; most are located along High Court Rd. Their fares are generally lower than the government bus fares, but their departure times are even less rigid. Tickets can be booked in one of the many travel agencies that line High Court Rd. near the main railway station. **Solanki Tours,** Station Rd. (tel. 620332), located opposite the railway station, rents buses to tourists for Rs6 per km, minimum 300km per day.

Local Transportation: Small, convenient local **buses** run by the railway stations, the bus stand, and along all major roads every 2-10min. for Rs2-7. A/C **taxis** at all the major sights and in front of the tourist bungalow are at least Rs3 per km., minimum Rs60. Smaller side streets are inaccessible by taxi, particularly in the old city. **Car hire** from the Tourist Reception Centre and private travel agencies cost Rs3-6 per km, minimum 100km. **Auto-rickshaws,** the best way to maneuver through the small streets of the old city, congregate around all the major sights and stations. Rates are unmetered and negotiable, but should take you anywhere in the city center for Rs10-30. **Tempos,** though less common than auto-rickshaws, can be found all over the city for Rs1-5. **Bicycles** are a fun way to explore the city. **Prem Cycle Store,** a few doors down from Kalinga Restaurant opposite the railway station, charges Rs2 per hr., Rs10 per day.

ORIENTATION

Winding streets dotted with traffic circles and the absence of street signs make Jodhpur difficult to navigate. Jodhpur's **sher,** or old city, is enclosed by a stone wall with eight entrance gates, of which **Jalori Gate** and **Sojati Gate,** on the south side of town, are the most important—the busiest commercial centers surround them. The **new city** expands to the south and east of the *sher.* **Jodhpur Railway Station** lies to the southwest of Sojati Gate along **Station Road.** Outside the station, three main roads fan out from a statue of a horseman. **Olympic Cinema Road,** to the far left, leads to the **telegraph office.** The road directly in front of the statue leads to Jalori Gate, which is the best way into the old city. Station Rd., leading off to the right toward Sojati Gate, is lined with cheap hotels and restaurants. **High Court**

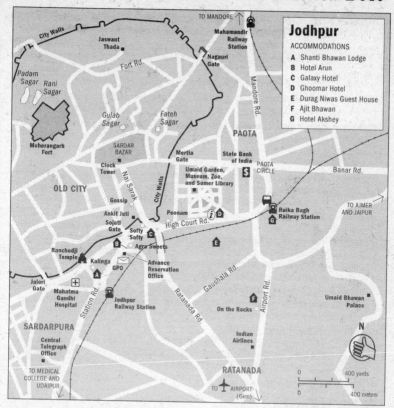

Jodhpur

ACCOMMODATIONS

A Shanti Bhawan Lodge
B Hotel Arun
C Galaxy Hotel
D Ghoomar Hotel
E Durag Niwas Guest House
F Ajit Bhawan
G Hotel Akshey

Road is the main east-west avenue, running from Sojati Gate past the **Umaid Gardens** and the **Tourist Reception Centre** to the distant **Raika Bagh Railway Station**, just opposite the **bus stand**, where it bends north toward **Paota Circle**.

Nai Sarak, or New Road, leads through Sojati Gate to the old city's biggest shopping thoroughfare and then to the market area, **Sardar Bazaar**, at the base of the **clock tower** that marks the center of Jodhpur. The magnificent **Meherangarh Fort** (above the city) and **Jaswant Thada** can be seen from almost everywhere. Both can be reached by a short auto-rickshaw ride up a winding mountain road or a steep five-minute walk through the *sher*. The **Umaid Bhawan Palace** sits alone in the distance to the southwest of the **clock tower**. The **airport** is a 15-minute drive south.

ℹ️ PRACTICAL INFORMATION

Tourist Office: Government of Rajasthan Tourist Reception Centre, High Court Rd. (tel. 545083). Up Station Rd. past Sojati Gate to High Court Rd., on the left beyond the Umaid Gardens. Helpful, English-speaking staff provides maps (Rs2), train and bus schedules, and reservations. **Sight-seeing tours** operate daily 9am-1pm and 2-6pm for Rs63 per person (min. 4 people) plus Rs100 in entry fees. Open daily 8am-7pm.

Currency Exchange: State Bank of India (tel. 544247), near Paota Circle on campus of Rajasthan High Court. Changes currency and traveler's checks with no service charge. Also offers money-wiring and telex services. **Bank of Baroda,** Sojati Gate (tel. 636539), just below Hotel Arun. Traveler's checks and cash advance with major credit cards. Both open M-F 10am-2pm, Sa 10am-noon. Many banks and hotels also exchange currency but don't cash traveler's checks.

Luggage Storage: Jodhpur Railway Station, in the cloakroom. Rs5 for first day, Rs6 for the second, and Rs7 per additional day. Store at your own risk.

Market: High Court Rd., Nai Sarak, and Sardar Bazaar are the main shopping areas. Fresh fruit and vegetable stalls and stores are found in Sardar Bazaar and along Station Rd. Most stores open daily 10am-9pm, closed one weekday near the end of each month. Stores near Sojati Gate market occasionally close on Su and M.

Library: Sumer Public Library, High Court Rd., in Umaid Gardens, has a small collection of English books and newspapers. No check-out fee. Open daily 8am-7pm.

Bookstore: Rathi's Media Centre, Ratanada Rd. (tel. 634580), on the bridge over the railroad tracks. Has a large collection of assorted paperbacks, children's books, reference works, and current best-sellers, plus newspapers and international magazines (including *Time, The Economist,* and *Vogue*). Open daily 8am-9pm.

Pharmacy: Chemists abound near hospitals, around Sojati and Jalori Gates and along Nai Sarak. Most open M-Sa 8am-10pm. **Manoj Chhajer Medical Provision Store,** Nai Sarak, on the right in front of the Sardar Bazaar. Open M-Sa 8am-10pm, Su 8am-3pm.

Hospital: Mahatma Gandhi Hospital, Mahatma Gandhi Hospital Rd. (tel. 636437), between Sojati and Jalori Gates, also accessible from the Station Rd. side. English-speaking staff. Open 24hr. **Private hospitals** abound. **Goyal Hospital,** Residency Rd. (tel. 432144), near the Medical College is one of the best. Open 24hr. Some English spoken. **Sun City Hospital,** Mandore Rd. (tel. 545455), just past Paota Circle away from town. Open 24hrs. Some English spoken.

Police: Ratanada Rd. (tel 633700). English-speaking, particularly helpful to tourists. **Police Control Room** (tel. 547180), at the intersection of Nai Sarak and High Court Rd. is also helpful in an emergency.

Post Office: Jodhpur Head Post Office, Station Rd. (enquiries tel. 636695, postmaster tel. 636746). Large building on Railway Station Rd., near the main railway station toward Sojati Gate. Entrance on the left side, closest to the station. *Poste Restante.* Open M-Sa 10am-6pm, Su 10am-4pm. **Postal Code:** 342001.

Telephones: Directory assistance tel. 197.

PHONE CODE	0291

■ ACCOMMODATIONS

Budget hotels abound near the Jodhpur Railway Station and along Nai Sarak. Travelers staying in these central locations will feel the heart of the city pulsing around them. Hotels on Airport Rd. and near Raika Bagh Railway Station offer rest from the clamor of the city but not from the honking of incoming trains. The Tourist Reception Center will set up tourists with local families for Rs1000 per night.

Hotel Akshey (tel. 612481 or 437327), behind Raika Bagh Railway Station. Though away from the bustle of the city, Akshey's immaculate rooms resonate with the sound of passing trains. Travel services, currency exchange, room service, TVs and phones, STD/ISD at reception, running hot water. Check-out 24hr. Dorm beds Rs50; singles Rs175, with air-cooling Rs250, with A/C Rs400; doubles Rs225/325/550. Extra beds Rs50.

Durag Niwas Guest House, 1st Old Public Park (tel. 639092), south of the tourist office, near K.M. Hall Girls' College. One of the best of the paying guest houses, it provides a homey atmosphere at good prices. Owner "Mr. Desert" and family are very knowledgeable about the Jodhpur area. Air-cooled rooms with 24hr. hot water for Rs150-500. Not to be confused with the neighboring **Durag Villas** (tel. 621300), which offers similar amenities and more ornate rooms for Rs150-750.

Shanti Bhawan Lodge, Station Rd. (tel. 621689; fax 639211), opposite the railway station. Former residence of Jodhpur's prime minister. Small, clean, basic rooms overlook a noisy main road and open courtyards. Friendly staff, STD/ISD, and travel agency which offers reconfirmation for international tickets. Midtown Restaurant is right underneath. Deluxe rooms have 24hr. hot water; others get bucketfuls. Check-out 24hr. Singles Rs70-100, with bath Rs175-200; doubles Rs180/250; deluxe Rs300-700.

Hotel Arun, Sojati Gate (tel. 620238 or 621824; fax 634228), opposite Sojati Gate. Moderately sized rooms give great views of the crazy streets below. Quiet and clean, despite its location. 24hr. room service, dining hall (open 6am-10:30pm), travel agency, laundry, STD/ISD, fax, massage. Dorm beds Rs80; singles Rs120-170; doubles Rs180-250; triples Rs350; quads Rs400. Extra person Rs50. Air-cooling Rs50 extra. Reservations recommended and accepted 8am-6pm.

Galaxy Hotel, Sojati Gate (tel. 620796), at the intersection of High Court and Ratanada Rd. A complicated maze of hallways leads to sparse rooms that surround flowery courtyards and offer intimate views of the heart of the city. 24hr. room service, laundry, and 24hr. hot water. Singles Rs80, with bath Rs150, with air-cooling Rs195; doubles Rs240-650; triples Rs300-750. Extra person Rs100. Kitchens Rs500.

Ajit Bhawan, Airport Rd. (tel. 437410; fax 637774), before the Indian Airlines office. Peacefully located away from the commotion of the city, this hotel features walkways shrouded by latticed vines, footpaths that coil through lush gardens, and individually decorated cottages. Fantastic restaurant. Not cheap, but you won't want to leave. Half-day village safaris Rs450. Singles Rs1550; doubles Rs1800. Extra bed Rs500. Off-season (Apr.-Sept.): singles Rs1400; doubles Rs1650.

Ghoomar Hotel, High Court Rd. (tel. 544010 or 548010), abuts the tourist office. Large, simply decorated rooms have phones and hot water. Crafts shop, restaurant, travel agency, laundry, and fax. Doctor and folk music on call. 3-day max. stay, unless you get manager's permission. Check-out noon. Dorm beds Rs50; singles Rs300, with air-cooling Rs500, with A/C Rs650; doubles Rs375/600/750. Discounts in May and August.

🍴 FOOD

Jodhpuri dishes such as *kabuli* (rice preparation) and *chakki-ka sagh* (spongy wheat dish) are definitely worth a try, preferably over a refreshing *mousmi* (orange drink) or a cold glass of saffron-flavored *makhania lassi*. Along Nai Sarak and near Sojati and Jalori Gates you'll find a medley of small **fast-food restaurants** and **stalls** selling drinks, fresh fruits and vegetables, and snack foods.

Midtown Restaurant, in the Shanti Bhawan Lodge. A great introduction to Rajasthani cuisine, this veg. restaurant features a host of local specialties, including *kabuli* (Rs50) and *chakki-ka sagh* (Rs55), as well as the ubiquitous Continental and Chinese food. The *Rajasthani maharaja thali* (Rs80) samples many Jodhpuri specialties. Rooftop seating affords a spectacular view of the fort and palace. Open daily 7am-11pm.

On the Rocks, Ajit Bhawan (tel. 611410), adjacent to Ajit Bhawan Hotel, on Airport Rd. Excellent Indian, Chinese, and Continental food (entrees Rs40-170). Free live Indian classical music Sa and Su. Well-stocked bar and beautifully illuminated courtyard in the evenings. Open daily 11am-11pm.

Poonam Restaurant, High Court Rd., near the intersection with Nai Sarak. Choose from over 200 dishes as you sit under fans in dark wood-panelled and mirrored rooms. All-Jain food (pure veg. and nothing that grows underground). Almost everything is Rs10-40. Open daily 11am-4pm and 6-11pm.

Kalinga Restaurant, Station Rd. (tel. 627338), in the Adarsh Niwas Hotel. Indian, Continental, Chinese, Italian—a veritable, if typical, potpourri in an elegant setting. The *paneer khas-e-kalinga* (Rs65) and Kalinga special of vanilla, chocolate, and strawberry ice cream with fresh fruit (Rs4) will surely satisfy. Open daily 11am-3pm and 6-10pm.

Gossip Restaurant, 32 Nai Sarak, in the City Palace Hotel. A much less shameful indulgence than its name would suggest. Excellent North and South Indian, Chinese, Continental, and Rajasthani veg. food. The dark, cool, **Classic Bar** downstairs takes music requests. Entrees Rs38-50. Open daily 7am-10:30pm.

Ajit Bhawan Palace Hotel Restaurant (tel. 37410), off Airport Rd., before the Indian Airlines office. Buffet dinner has superb food and live Rajasthani folk music and dance, all for Rs300. Buffet breakfast Rs185, lunch Rs240. Explore the majestic grounds while you're here. Open daily 7am-11pm. Reservations recommended 2hr. in advance.

Agra Sweets, Sojati Gate (tel. 615260), directly opposite Sojati Gate. The oldest shop in Jodhpur, where mobs descend on the best *makhania lassi* in town at Rs10 a hit (*Gourmet Magazine* once wanted the recipe). Try *mava kachori* (Rs9) over a warm cup of *espresso* (Rs6), the shop's specialty. A wide range of sweets and Rajhasthani snacks are also available. Open daily 8am-10:30pm.

🎵 ENTERTAINMENT

What little nightlife Jodhpur has is geared to foreign tourists. **On the Rocks** and **City Palace Hotel** both have popular bars. There are **Hindi cinemas** everywhere; one of the most popular is Girdhar Mandir Cinema (tel. 547371), on Nai Sarak. Showings at noon, 3, 6, and 9pm; tickets Rs6/10/21/27. The annual **Marwar Festival** (Oct. 12-13, 2000; Oct. 31-Nov. 2, 2001) showcases local culture, history, dance, art, and most of all, food. All restaurants load their menus with high-priced regional specialties.

👁 SIGHTS

MEHERANGARH FORT. Rising magnificently above Jodhpur, Meherangarh dominates the city's landscape. The fort is a blend of well-designed defense systems and amazing artistry. Eight *pols* (gates) mark the various entrances to the fort. The formidable **Jayapol** is the main entrance commemorating Maharaja Man Singh's military achievements. The impressive **Fatehpol** (Victory Gate), created by Maharaja Ajit Singh after his return from exile, marks the original entrance into the fort. The **Lohapol** (Iron Gate), where 15 handprints mark the *sati* sacrifice of Maharaja Man Singh's widows, is particularly dramatic. Despite modern anti-*sati* sentiment, Jodhpuris pay tribute at this gate daily. The final gigantic **Surajpol** leads to the tiny **Fort Museum,** located in the sculpted red sandstone palace. Filling its halls are extravagant *howdahs* (elephant mounts), exquisite wood and ivory artifacts, a weapons room, the royal dumbbells of the maharani, a beautiful 250-year-old tent canopy, 150 types of cannon, fancy baby cradles, musical instruments, and a 300-piece turban collection. Of particular interest is the **Phool Mahal** (Flower Palace), an elaborately mirrored hall. The **Moti Mahal** (Pearl Palace), a conference room with a glass and gold ceiling, is opulent yet serene. (*Open daily 9am-5pm. Rs50. Camera fee Rs50, video fee Rs100. Government guided tours for Rs100 available at ticket counter.*)

UMAID BHAWAN PALACE. The Umaid Bhawan Palace is a majestic marble and sandstone palace, the eminent edifice of the eastern part of the city. The palace offers well-kept, picnic-perfect gardens. A grandiose hotel and restaurant consume half the palace, while an eccentric but boring museum containing traditional art, weapons, trophies, and miscellaneous relics—all belonging to the maharaja—occupies the rest. (*Open daily 9am-5pm. Rs40, including tour. Cameras strictly prohibited.*)

OTHER SIGHTS. The **Chamunda Temple,** near the fort, offers a good view of the blue city-scape. Don't bother taking the lift; the view is better if you walk. As you exit, noisy "traditional" musicians will surround you, demanding *baksheesh.* The **Jaswant Thada,** a pillared marble memorial to the beloved Maharaja Jaswant Singh II, was erected by his wife after his death. Locals liken it to a miniature Taj Mahal, and the structures are quite similar, as are the legends explaining their constructions. (*10min. from the fort, down a windy road. Open daily 9am-1pm, 2-5pm. Rs10. Photography not allowed inside.*) Back in the center of the city, the **Clock Tower** marks the center of the *sher* and the splenetic Sardar Bazaar. Along High Court Rd. are Jalori Gate and Sojati Gate—large, simply carved structures interesting for their adjoining commercial centers. The **Umaid Gardens,** near the Tourist Bungalow, make for pleasant strolling. (*Gardens open Sa-Th 10am-4:30pm, Rs3. Zoo open daily 10am-6pm, Rs1.*)

SHOPPING

The **Sojati Gate** and **Nai Sarak** areas, especially **Sardar bazaar** by the Clock Tower, are constellations of stalls, markets, emporia, and department stores. Everything can be found here, from craft works to stereo equipment. Haggling is expected nearly everywhere, and the best deals await those willing to brave the cacophonous bazaar scene. For jewelry, utensils, and decorations, try **Satyam Shivam Sundaram Jewelers,** next to Sojati Gate (tel. 622526; open Tu-Su noon-9pm).

Handicraft is one of Jodhpur's largest industries, and art shops such as **Rajasthan Arts and Crafts** (tel. 639220; open M-Sa 9am-7:30pm) and **Ajay Art Emporium** (tel. 624636; open daily 9am-8pm), both near Circuit House on Umaid Bhawan Palace Road, offer excellent selections of items in wood, brass, marble, iron, clay, *papier mâché*, and textiles—all hand-made in Rajasthan. **Bhandari Exports,** near Hotel Akshey on Bank Colony Rd. offers everything ranging from small keepsakes to massive furniture (tel. 636821, fax 437674; open daily 9am-7pm). For reasonable prices and a more intimate atmosphere, try the **Emporium Marusthaly,** High Court Road, between Nai Sarak and the tourist office (tel. 547684; open M-Sa 10am-8pm). Also available are the beautiful and fabulously colorful cloths and *saris* of Rajasthan, including the traditional *bhandani saris,* which are tie-dyed. On Nai Sarak, the **National Handloom Corporation,** Rajasthan's largest department store, sells *saris,* carpets, and cotton cloth, with prices starting at Rs95 (tel. 623096; open daily 10am-9pm). **Lovely Silk Palace,** Railway Station Rd. (tel. 621590; open M-Sa 9:30am-9pm), and **Lucky Silk Stores,** Sojati Gate (tel. 622221; open daily 10:30am-9pm), both sell cloth and hand-made *saris* from all over India.

VILLAGE SAFARIS

Guided tours of the villages in the desert around Jodhpur allow visitors to witness and participate in carpet-making, weaving, spinning, foraging, indigenous medicine, and cooking. In particular, the villages of the **Bishnoi** leave visitors feeling enlightened and environmentally conscious because their religion, which originated in the 15th century, is devoted to environmental protection and conservation. Maharaj Swaroop Singh (not the maharaja himself but a member of his family) sometimes personally leads tours, arranged through the Ajit Bhawan Hotel (tel. 437410; 5hr., 8:30am-2pm in winter, 8am-1:30pm in summer, including lunch; Rs450 per person). Mr. Parbat Singh (tel. 543805) arranges tours and cross-desert camel safaris as far as Jaisalmer and Bikaner for Rs500-900 per person per day.

NEAR JODHPUR

Once the capital of Marwar, the town of **Mandore,** 9km north of Jodhpur, still houses the cenotaphs (tombs) of the Rathore maharajas, including that of Ajit Singh. Near the tidy garden where the cenotaphs stand is the **Hall of Heroes,** a series of 15 colorful, life-size statues of Hindu gods and Rajput warriors carved out of one large rock wall. Also nearby is the **Shrine of the 330 Million Gods,** a site of polytheistic celebration and triumph. The vibrant gardens and peaceful atmosphere make it a welcome escape from the hum of the city. Mandore is accessible from Jodhpur by local buses (Rs2-4). Flag down a small 18-seater bus on High Court Rd. in front of the tourist reception center. Most small buses end their routes at the gardens, but you should enquire before boarding. Return buses leave frequently from the gate in front of the garden.

Osian, an ancient town surrounded by sand dunes, is home to 16 sculpted Jain and Hindu temples from the 8th-11th centuries 65km north of Jodhpur. Osian is accessible by regular buses from Jodhpur (see **Transportation,** p. 318).

For prime picnic spots, visit **Kailana Lake,** about 11km from town on Jaisalmer Rd., or **Balsamand Lake and Palace,** about 7km from town (Rs75-100 by autorickshaw). Both are man-made tanks. Balsamand Lake is encircled by 12th-century mango, guava, papaya, and date groves.

JAISALMER जैसलमेर

In the heart of the Thar Desert, 285km west of Jodhpur and 100km from the Pakistan border, lies the "Golden City" of Jaisalmer (pop. 40,000). Once a Rajput stronghold and dusty medieval city, Jaisalmer was built originally as a strategic fort. After being twice sacked and conquered by Muslim invaders, the city became a prosperous trade center for camel caravans in the 17th century. Maritime trade under the British eclipsed the desert trade routes, and the Partition of 1947 cut them off altogether, thus diminishing Jaisalmer's wealth and importance. With the Indo-Pakistan tensions of the 1960s, however, Jaisalmer once again became a military outpost. The heavy army presence is a source of income second only to the booming tourism industry. Now Jaisalmer offers camel safaris to Jain temples, desert craftwork and cuisine, and peerless *havelis* (royal mansions) that retain sandstorm-sculpted memories of the city's golden years.

Though at times the city seems trapped within the confines of its old ramparts, walking the streets of Jaisalmer is like strolling into a fairy tale. Its inhabitants' warmth and hospitality provide a peaceful escape from the madding crowd of winter tourists that flock to this enigmatic and charming Rajput city.

▐ TRANSPORTATION

Airport: Jaisalmer Airport (tel. 51952), 5km from the city center down Sam Rd. 15min. by auto-rickshaw (Rs50-60). To: **Delhi** (3per week, 2hr., US$140); **Jaipur** (55min., US$110); **Mumbai** (3 per week, 2½hr., US$175) via **Jodhpur** (30min., US$60). **Crown Tours Limited,** Sam Rd. (tel./fax 51912), in the Moomal Tourist Bungalow, books tickets. Open daily 9:30am-8:30pm.

Trains: Jaisalmer Railway Station (tel. 52354; enquiry 51301), 10min. out of Gadi Sagar Pol, on the left. Reservation counter open M-Sa 8am-1:45pm, 2-8pm; Su 8am-2pm. Platforms are open to passengers 1hr. before the departure of each train. Passenger trains leave for **Jodhpur** (*1JPJ,* 7am; *Exp.* 4809, 10:30pm, 8hr., Rs124/323).

Buses: Main Bus Stand (tel. 51541), near the Railway Station. Open daily 5am-11pm. To: **Ahmedabad** (6pm, 11hr., Rs180); **Bikaner** (6:30 and 9am, noon, and 1:30pm, 9hr., Rs84; deluxe 5, 8:30, and 10pm, 7hr., Rs133); **Jaipur** (7am, 15hr., Rs199; deluxe 5:30pm, 12hr., Rs288); **Jodhpur** (7am, 6hr., Rs69; deluxe 5:30pm, 5hr., Rs131); **Mt. Abu** (6am, 11hr., Rs177). Advance booking for deluxe buses and ticket purchase for express buses available at the **private bus stand** on Station Rd., behind Hotel Neeraj. Tickets for all classes are available at the Main Bus Stand. **Private buses** leave frequently, but departure times are less strict. All hotels and all travel agents can arrange both government and private bus reservations.

Local Transportation: On foot, it takes 15-20min. to cross the city. Auto-rickshaws are unmetered and ubiquitous except in the fort during peak tourist hours (8am-noon and 4-7pm), when they are not permitted to enter. Most charge Rs10-15. Bicycles are a convenient means of touring Jaisalmer, except for the hills. Try shops inside Amar Sagar Pol and near the fort gate (Rs2-3 per hr., Rs10-15 per day). Jeeps available at Hanuman Cir. are needed to get to places outside of the city. Expect to pay at least Rs5 per km. Travel agents and hotels can rent out their own jeeps at cheaper rates for fixed tours.

✳ ORIENTATION AND PRACTICAL INFORMATION

Hanuman Circle is just outside **Amar Sagar Pol,** the main entrance to the old city, and adjacent to a market. Littered with jeeps, buses, and taxis for hire, Hanuman Circle is easily identified by a strangely stationed jet fighter, a relic from a war with Pakistan. **Sam Road** heads east from the circle into the city. Just inside Amar Sagar Pol is **Gandhi Chowk,** the main market area. The entrance to **Badal Mahal,** the old royal palace, is just inside the gate area on the right. This same road leads narrowly through the market to the **fort.** The road continues to the north of the fort to the **Gopa Chowk** market before winding its way to **Gadi Sagar Pol,** the east gate of

Jaisalmer

ACCOMMODATIONS

A Hotel Anurag
B Hotel Pleasure
C Hotel Swastika
D Hotel Renuka
E Hotel Nachana Haveli
F Hotel Simla
G Deepak Rest House
H Hotel Paradise
I Hotel Jaisal Castle

N

0   200 yards
0   200 meters

TO BIKANER
AND JODHPUR

TO BARMER

Main Bus Stand

Railway Station

Barmer Rd.

Gadi Sagar
(Lake Gadisan)

Kishanghat Pol

City Walls

Gadi Sagar Rd.

Tilon-ki-Pol
and Jaisalmer
Folklore Museum

Gadi Sagar Pol

Govt. of
Rajasthan

Jama Masjid

Malka Pol

Salam Singh-
ki-Haveli

Natraj

Midtown

Patwon-
ki-Haveli

Kanchan
Shree

GOPA
CHAUK

Monica

Charanpura St.

Nathmalji-
ki-Haveli

Sahara
Travels

Station Rd.

Kalpana

Man
Bhavan

FORT
Palace

H

C

B

A

GANDHI
CHAUK

D

E

Trio

F

G

Jain
Temples

I

Amar
Sagar Pol

Badal Mahal/
Mandir Palace

Chandani
Shrree

HANUMAN
CIRCLE

GPO

City Walls

Private
Bus Stand

Sam Rd.

Bara
Bagh

Ramgarh Rd.

Moomal Tourist
Bungalow

Government
Museum

Jawahar
Niwas
Palace

TO AIRPORT,
AMAR SAGAR, & SAM

RAJASTHAN

the city. From here the road becomes **Gadi Sagar Road** and ends at Lake Gadisan, or Gadi Sagar. A left turn just outside of Gadi Sagar Pol leads to the remote **Main Bus Stand** and **Railway Station.**

Tourist Office: Government of Rajasthan Tourist Reception Centre (tel. 52406). Exit Gadi Sagar Pol and turn right at the first intersection. The tourist bureau is on your right after a 3min. walk. Helpful, English-speaking staff provide bus, train, plane, and camel safari information, maps of Jaisalmer (Rs2), and hotel reservations. Offers tours to Sam to see the sunset (3:30-4pm, Rs100). Open M-Sa 10am-5pm. The **Moomal Tourist Bungalow** (tel. 52392; fax 52545), on the other side of town, off of Sam Rd., provides basic information.

Budget Travel: Safari Tours, (tel. 51058; fax 51158), near Amar Sagar Pol. An excellent source of information on everything in and around Jaisalmer. Open daily 8:30am-7pm. For more information, see **Camel Safaris,** p. 330.

Currency Exchange: Bank of Baroda, Amar Sagar (tel. 52402), just inside Amar Sagar Pol on the right. Currency exchange, traveler's checks, and cash advances on credit cards. Open M-F 10am-2pm, Sa 10-11am.

Market: Gandhi Chowk is the main commercial center. **Hanuman Circle** and the **Fort Gate area (Gopa Chowk)** are also shopping districts. Fresh fruit and vegetables are sold from stalls mainly in Gopa Chowk. Most stores open daily 8am-9pm.

Bookstore: Bhatia News Agency, Gandhi Chowk (tel. 52671), on the right past Nachana Haveli, coming from Amar Sagar Pol. A generally attractive selection of multi-lingual books, magazines, and newspapers, new and used. Open daily 8am-8pm.

Pharmacy: The **Government Pharmacy** outside Shri Jawahar Hospital is open 24hr.

Hospital: Sri Maheswari Hospital (tel. 50024; direct to doctors 52721), on the right of Sam Rd. after the government hospital past Hanuman Circle. Private, extremely modern, and clean, with helpful, English-speaking staff. **Sri Jawahar Government Hospital** (tel. 52343), in the large pillared building on the right of Sam Rd. past Hanuman Circle, away from the Old City. Not particularly clean.

Police: Main Police Office (tel. 52322, emergency 100), south of Hanuman Circle on the right. On the road that extends to the left out of Hanuman Circle as you walk away from Amar Sagar Pol. English-speaking and very helpful to tourists.

Post Office: GPO (tel. 52407 or 51377), south of the police station, 5min. from Amar Sagar Pol. Offices around the city. All open M-Sa 9am-5pm. **Postal Code:** 345001.

Internet: Kuri Travel and Tours (tel. 51582), down the road to your right as you exit the fort. Rs7 per min. for less than 30min., Rs5 per min. over 1hr. Open daily 9am-10pm.

Telephones: Bantu's STD/ISD (tel. 51539), in the fort is open 24hr. Follow the signs in front of the city palace (after midnight, ring doorbell for service).

PHONE CODE	02992

▶ ACCOMMODATIONS

Jaisalmer bristles with budget hotels. New ones pop up by the month as tourism takes over more and more of the city. Large clusters of hotels are found in the fort area and outside the city walls along Sam Rd. All hotels without exception offer **camel safaris** (see p. 330 for more information on the insanely competitive safari market) as well as other travel services. Expect rates to at least double during the Desert Festival. (Feb. 17-19, 2000. See **Entertainment,** p. 328.)

Hotel Pleasure, Gandhi Chowk (tel. 52323), in Amar Sagar Pol to the left. The Holy Grail of the budget traveler with simple, tiled rooms of moderate size. The owners (two brothers) speak excellent English. Breakfast room service, free luggage storage while on camel safari (even a competitor's safari), free callbacks, refrigerator/freezer, and free washing machine (soap not included). Rooms have air-cooling. Check-out noon. Singles Rs50, with bath Rs60; doubles Rs70/90. Camel safaris Rs350 per day.

Deepak Rest House (tel. 52665 or 52070; fax 52070; www.offthebeatentrack.net), in the Fort near the Jain temple. The best budget hotel in the fort with fantastic desert views from clean, modest rooms in the fort wall, some of which occupy large, windowed bastions. Run by a friendly family fluent in English. Good rooftop veg. restaurant. Check-out 9am. Dorm beds Rs20; singles Rs40-50, with attached bath Rs60-80; doubles Rs80-150/100-450. Excellent camel safaris Rs250-750 per day.

Hotel Simla (tel. 53061 or 53113), in the fort. This renovated *haveli* has a little something for everyone, from lavishly decorated rooms with comfortable beds draped in silks to budget rooftop accommodations. Doors close at 10:30pm. Rs25 to sleep on roof, Rs50 with tent. Singles Rs100-350; doubles Rs150-550.

Hotel Paradise (tel. 52674), in the fort to the left. Once a part of the Diwanon-ki-Haveli. Friendly, family-run with carpeted rooms around a central garden. Rooftop restaurant offers glorious sunset panoramas and traditional music and dance at sunset; tips expected. 24hr. room service. Check-out 9am. Hot water 7am-noon, 5-10pm, and on request. Singles Rs80, with bath Rs350-850; doubles Rs120-250/Rs400-850. Rooms with balcony Rs400/850. Award-winning camel safaris Rs250-350 per day.

Hotel Anurag, Gandhi Chowk (tel. 50276). A small family hotel with rough-and-ready accommodations for very low rates. Rooms are clean and the atmosphere is informal and welcoming. Complimentary *chai* in the morning and upon arrival. Rooftop snack shop in season. STD/ISD. Check-out 9am. Singles Rs50, with bath Rs80-125; doubles with bath Rs100/150. Camel safaris Rs350 per day.

Hotel Renuka, Chainpura St. (tel. 52757; fax 51414). Enter Amar Sagar Pol, left on Chainpura, 5min. down on the left. Familial and clean, basic rooms. 24hr. room service from rooftop veg. restaurant. For Rs500, the owners can arrange to have 3-5hr. dance and music performances on the rooftop. Doors close at 11pm. Check-out 9am. Hot water 8am-noon, 6-9pm. Singles Rs40-60, with bath Rs80-120; doubles Rs100/150-200. Reservations recommended. Rs250/750 per day for 2½-day jeep/camel safari.

Hotel Swastika, Chainpura St. (tel. 52483). Similar to Hotel Renuka. Well-run, decently sized rooms gird a sunlit courtyard. No restaurant, but they make a mean bread, jam, and tea breakfast. Laundry service. Free callbacks. Check-out 9am. Singles Rs80, with attached bath Rs200; doubles Rs200/250. 50% discount May-Jun. Reservations recommended. Camel safaris Rs300 per day.

Hotel Nachana Haveli, Gandhi Chowk (tel. 52110; fax 52778), inside Amar Sagar Pol to the right. Imperial relatives provide royal treatment that doesn't cost a king's ransom. A renovated *haveli* with traditional room decor that includes bear skins and spears. Large, spotless rooms with air-cooling and attached bathrooms; deluxe rooms have bathtubs. Extremely competent staff. Check-out noon. Singles Rs550, deluxe Rs950; doubles Rs750/1150. 50% discount May-Jun.

Hotel Jaisal Castle (tel. 52362; fax 52101), in the fort. Every room has windows and a balcony in this former Maharaja's palace, and the bathrooms are absolutely spotless. Gracious staff, huge, hand-carved beds, a beautifully tended courtyard, and a rooftop from which to see the most splendiferous sunset in town. Singles Rs650; doubles Rs850; triples Rs1050. Extra bed Rs200. Reservations recommended.

FOOD

The main reason to eat here is the rooftop view, but Jaisalmer also has an earthy desert cuisine not found elsewhere. While every restaurant features Continental and Chinese food, local specialties are basic and savory. Be sure to experience *ker sangri*, a mix of desert capers and beans (it looks like a bundle of gravied twigs); *gatte*, a *garam* flour preparation; and *kadi pakoras*, a yogurt-based appetizer.

Trio Restaurant, Amar Sagar Pol (tel. 52733), next to the Badal Mahal, in Gandhi Chowk. Considered by many to be the best restaurant in Jaisalmer, Trio (tr-EYE-oh) features first-class service, well-prepared specialties (like the delectable Royal Safari soup Rs40), and traditional Rajasthani music at a very reasonable price. The view is great, and a backup generator keeps things humming during power outages. Entrees Rs25-80. Open daily 7am-10:30pm. Reservations recommended in season.

Man Bhavan (tel. 50408), at the base of the fort, slightly hidden. Serves delicious South Indian, Bengali, Gujarati, and Rajasthani food for under Rs32. Open 7am-11pm.

Midtown Restaurant, Gopa Chowk (tel. 50242). Dim red lamps give it an atmosphere as intimate as the view of the Fort. Popular with western tourists. The menu contains the usual items, in addition to some unusual desserts. The homemade Dutch apple pie (Rs50) is delicious. Rajasthani *thalis* Rs50. Open daily 7am-11pm.

Monica Restaurant, Gopa Chowk (tel. 51586), left of the fort gate. A local favorite with a range of cuisines. Every night, local musicians perform just a betel-spit from the fort. Beer Rs70-75. Entrees Rs30-75. Open daily 8am-2pm and 6:30-10:30pm.

Kalpana Restaurant, Gandhi Chowk (tel. 52469). Located in the heart of Gandhi Chowk, Kalpana offers a rooftop view, specialty *tandoor* cuisine, and one of the best bars in the city. Popular with tourists and locals alike. Entrees Rs30-35. Open daily 7am-11pm.

Natraj Restaurant, Asni Rd. (tel. 52667), near the Salam Singh-ki-Haveli. Good food for slightly higher prices. Decorated with surrealist paintings and a striking rooftop view of the Salam Singh-ki-Haveli. The only A/C dining room in the city. Standard range of dishes, all well-prepared. Entrees Rs35-60. Open daily 8am-11pm.

Chandan Shree Restaurant, Amar Sagar Pol. Exit the old city and join locals as you enjoy cheap, filling *thalis* (Rs20-25) served by friendly youths. Open daily 8am-11pm.

🎵 ENTERTAINMENT

Jaisalmer has little nightlife, but plenty to keep you occupied. For the wildest time in Jaisalmer, come to the annual **Desert Festival** (Feb. 17-19, 2000; see **Mr. Desert,** p. 329). Prices double (at least), and tourists mob the place, but you'll still be able to enjoy traditional music and folk dance, camel races, camel polo, camel dances, puppeteers, moustache contests, and more. RTDC sets up a special tourist tent-village for accommodations.

Other diversions include **swimming** in Lake Gadi Sagar (free) or at Narayan Niwas Palace's indoor pool (near Patwon-ki-Haveli, Rs100). Film fans can indulge at Hindi **cinemas,** including **Ramesh Talkies** (tel. 52242), near Patwon-ki-Haveli.

👁 SIGHTS

The city's many tourist attractions form a unique "Jaisalmer experience" that is more than just the sum of its tourist spots. Camel safaris, rolling dunes, and the sand-dusted fort of the old city are all part of Jaisalmer's mysterious medieval charm. Intricate carvings, centuries-old abodes, and architectural wonders grace every alley of the old city.

JAISALMER FORT. Jaisalmer's fort, founded in 1156 by Maharaja Jaisal, a king of the Bhatti clan of Rajputs, overlooks the city from the south. Its 99 circular bastions surround a labyrinthine world of small homes and shops along narrow gullies that wind around the old palace. Enter from Gopa Chowk, the commercial square outside the fort's main gate. The **City Palace,** just inside the fort, is open to visitors. It is composed of five smaller palaces, one of which has a dancing hall decorated with blue Chinese tiles and green screens from the Netherlands. The old stone rooms are half-preserved; some even remain closed by their original locks, while others store decaying elephant howdahs (saddles). A climb to the windy ramparts affords a great view of the fort and the old city. It is said that the fort does not have a single cemented joint in its foundation but was constructed stone upon stone from the ground up. (Open summer daily 8am-1pm, 2:30-5pm; winter 9am-1pm, 2:30-5pm. Rs10. Camera fee Rs20; video fee Rs50.)

MR. DESERT Moustaches twisted to follicular perfection, camels dripping in shells, mirrors, and buttons, and turban-tying professionals await those willing to brave the onslaught of tourists at the annual Desert Festival of Jaisalmer (Feb. 17-19, 2000). The event kicks off with a procession of "ships of the desert" and local bands followed by an odd assortment of competitions: tug-of-war, turban tying, a battle of the moustaches, camel racing, camel decoration, and, arguably the high point of the festival, the "crowning of Mr. Desert." The prestigious and lucrative title is bestowed upon the man who best epitomizes Rajasthan—he who exudes masculinity in his traditional dress, bushy beard, and gravity-defying moustache. Past winners include Mr. Shri Laxmi Narain Bissa, proud owner of Sahara Travels near the fort. After capturing the crown for four consecutive years, Shri Laxmi Narain Bissa hung up his turban and was bestowed with the title "Mr. Desert Emeritus." His face can now be seen staring out of *haveli* windows on posters promoting Rajasthani tourism and gracing advertisements for Jaisalmer Cigarettes, a stint that earned him the title "The Indian Marlboro man."

JAIN TEMPLES. A cluster of seven interconnected Jain Temples (two of which are open for touring) lies within the fort. Built on a raised platform, the temples' low archways and tiny halls display amazing sculpture, the intricate work covering every visible inch. A winding staircase leads to a circular balcony with an open view of the sanctuary and the temple domes below. (A short walk from the entrance to the palace along the 2nd road to the right. Open daily 7am-noon. Free. Camera fee Rs50, video fee Rs100. Menstruating women prohibited.)

OLD CITY HAVELIS. Any walk through the old city will inevitably bring you to one of the three large *havelis*, or mansions. **Patwon-ki-Haveli,** the most impressive of the three, is composed of five joint *havelis* built in the early 1900s by a family of wealthy merchants. The single golden facade rises four dramatic stories, each fitted with stone balconies topped by arched stone umbrellas and exquisite lattice-work windows. While parts of the *haveli* are now occupied by shops selling jewelry and embroidered cloth, two doors still open to reveal stairs up to the building's towering rooftop view of the surrounding sand-brick street. (*Open daily 10am-5pm. Rs2.*) **Nathmalji-ki-Haveli** is another architectural monument built by two rather stubborn Muslim brothers, Lalu and Hat, who each took one half of the building's face. The divergent, intricate carvings on the left and right sides of the main door belie this sibling rivalry. Inside, stairs lead up from a central courtyard to the elaborately carved dancing room. (*Open daily 8am-1:30pm, 3-8pm. Donations requested for maintenance.*) **Salam Singh-ki-Haveli,** with peacock buttresses adorning its exterior, was built by the infamous prime minister Salam Singh Mohta around 1800. Considered a tyrant for his crippling taxes, he is said to have attempted to construct two additional levels on his own *haveli* in order to make his home taller than the maharaja's, but the maharaja had the levels torn down. Ultimately, Salam Singh's audacity drove the maharaja to have him assassinated. Salam Singh's descendants have graciously opened their doors to the public. (*Open daily 8am-6pm. Rs15.*)

LAKE GADI SAGAR. An artificial reservoir constructed in 1367, Lake Gadi Sagar was once Jaisalmer's only source of water. Today, it is frequented by bathers, *dhobis*, and visitors who come to view the **Folklore Museum,** which contains quirky paintings, carvings and relics of Rajasthani art and culture (*open daily Aug.-Mar. 8am-6:30pm, Apr.-Jul. 4:30-7:30pm. Rs10*). Gadi Sagar's other attraction is a yellow sandstone gateway, the **Tilon-ki-Pol.** With its grand arched windows, this portal once held beautifully carved windowed rooms in which the royal family stayed during the monsoon. Said to have been built by the king's chief courtesan, the gate was once a source of great controversy for the town's citizens, who refused to allow their womenfolk to walk beneath the "tainted" creation. As a compromise, a smaller entrance to the lake was built to the right side. The lake is now decorated with a few royal stone *chhattris* (cenotaphs). **The Desert Culture Centre and Museum** holds a collection of 19th-century Ravi Varma paintings, petrified wood fossils, old coins, and regional musical instruments. (*Gadi Sagar Pol, next to the tourist office. Open daily Aug.-Mar. 10am-6:30pm, Apr.-July 9am-noon, 3-6pm. Free with stub from folklore museum.*)

RAJASTHAN

🛍 SHOPPING

Jaisalmer is a haven for **crafts,** including embroidery, patchwork, leather goods, and mirror work, as well as stone carving, silver, and pottery. Bargain hard, and don't attempt to shop during the Desert Festival. **Gandhi Chowk** and the main road past the fort to Gadi Sagar Pol are the main commercial areas. Among fixed-priced shops, government shops tend to be cheaper than private ones, the drawback being that you must arrange shipping yourself. The **Rajasthali Government Emporium,** just outside Amar Sagar Pol, south of Sam Rd., offers a vast selection of Rajasthani desert handicrafts in brass, silver, wood, and textiles, as well as carpets and paintings (tel. 52461; prices start at Rs50; open daily 10am-8pm). For a basic explanation of art, culture, and architecture in Jaisalmer, L.N. Khatri's *Jaisalmer: Folklore, History, and Architecture* (Rs75) can be purchased at the author's craft store, **Desert Handicraft Emporium,** (tel. 50062) Gandhi Chowk, on the right as you walk away from Amer Sagar Pol. (open daily 9:30am-11:30pm). Manak Lal Soni, owner of **Parmar Jewelers Emporium,** in the fort opposite the palace runs a wholesale and custom made jewelry business out of his home (tel. 51373).

CAMEL SAFARIS

A wonderful way to experience the Thar Desert, camel safaris are the heart and soul of Jaisalmer's tourist trade. The camel safari business has become ruthlessly competitive. Every hotel offers camel safaris, as do several independent agencies. But few hotels actually have their own camels; most safaris operate through independent agencies. Hotels pay the agencies about Rs100 per day just for the camels, with food and equipment costs added. For the hotels to make a profit, they must charge at least Rs200 per day. **Indeed, the tourist office recommends spending at least Rs350 per day on safaris.** Deluxe safaris with tents, quality food, portable bars, dancing, music, and other goodies can cost over Rs2000 per day.

If you take the train or bus to Jaisalmer from Jodhpur, expect to be hassled by hotel agents en route. You will be offered incredible deals such as Rs10 hotel rooms, provided you go on that hotel's safari. When you arrive in Jaisalmer, you will be mobbed by touts offering similar deals. All will offer free transportation to the hotel in question. They will often then give you a story about that hotel being closed or full, and try to take you to their hotel. Some hotels do provide free transportation without hassle. Look for hotel banners, not business cards. Also, lookout for hotel scams. At some hotels, if you go on another hotel's or agency's safari, you will be kicked out. Hotel agents will follow you around town making sure you don't visit other places. If you go on your own hotel's safari, you may be kicked out the next day as more tourists arrive. Be very selective about whom you trust and always get at least one other opinion. If you have been taken advantage of—overcharged, not given the proper amenities, kicked out of your hotel—don't be afraid to go to the police. Sometimes just threatening to involve the police will suffice.

Once you've chosen a safari, still be wary. Cheap safaris often have **hidden costs** (e.g., Rs50 or more for bottles of mineral water). They also often skimp on basic amenities such as blankets (it gets very cold in the desert at night) and English-speaking guides. Furthermore, several scams exist to steal your possessions on the return trip. **Never accept offers to watch your luggage** while you explore a sight.

Of course, not all hotels run scams. Many hotels have honest, decent, and inexpensive safaris. The most reliable camel safaris are booked through independent agents. **Safari Tours,** just inside Amar Sagar Pol, is excellent for general tourist information and safari specialties (tel. 51508, fax 51158; open daily 8:30am-7pm). Basic safaris cost Rs500 per day, and deluxe safaris start at Rs1500 per day. Safari Tours is one of the few that genuinely tries to keep the desert clean. **Royal Safari** (tel. 52538), in Nachana Haveli, offers basic for Rs450 per day and deluxe for Rs1050-2000 per day. **Sahara Travels,** near the Fort Gate, charges basic Rs350 per day and deluxe Rs500 per day (tel. 52609, open daily 7am-10:30pm). **Ask safari agents to specify all food and equipment; "deluxe" and "basic" can mean many things.**

Camel safaris often head to the spectacular Sam sand dunes, stopping at villages along the way. A round-trip takes 4½ days. All hotels and agents offer shorter jeep/camel combos for assorted prices, but you might not get the chance to sleep under the stars in the Thar Desert. Longer cross-desert safaris to Bikaner, Pushkar, or Jodhpur are also available from all of the safari companies listed above.

NEAR JAISALMER

The areas surrounding Jaisalmer are as interesting as the city proper. Camel and hybrid camel/jeep safaris stop at many of these locales on their way to the sand dunes and are the best means of introduction to them. They are, however, accessible by bus, jeep, and even bicycle. The area 45km west of Jaisalmer is restricted because of border disputes, and special permission (never granted for reasons of tourism) is required from the **District Magistrate Office,** near the police station.

About 5km north of Jaisalmer is **Bada Bagh,** where 500-year-old sculpted sandstone cenotaphs stand next to the 300-year-old mango trees of the royal garden. The most recent tomb is to the far left, constructed in 1991 for the grandfather of the current maharaja. The plush gardens, which used to supply food to all of Jaisalmer, are a popular picnic spot. (Open daily 8am-8pm. Admission Rs10.) Another well-known tiffin spot is **Amar Sagar,** 5km northwest of Jaisalmer, where a beautifully carved Jain temple, constructed under the orders of Majaraja Amar Singh, guards a lake and fertile gardens. (Open daily 6am-9pm. Admission free. Camera fee Rs50, video fee Rs100. No menstruating women permitted inside.) The **Mool Sagar Garden Palace,** located 7km to the north of Jaisalmer was once the decadent picnic palace of the former Maharaja. (Open daily 8am-8pm. Admission Rs10.)

Once the capital of the region, **Lodurva** now lies in ruins 15km north of Jaisalmer. Rebuilt Jain temples are the only remnant of the town's former splendor. An amazing 1000yr. old archway from the original temple still stands in the courtyard. A cobra occasionally emerges from a small hole in the temple; glimpsing the snake is deemed auspicious. (Open 24hr. Free. Camera fee Rs50, video fee Rs100.)

One way or another, most camel safaris end up in **Sam,** an expanse of rippling, desert 42km west of Jaisalmer. The dunes are beautiful at any time, but especially at sunrise and sunset. Most safaris spend the night on the dunes, sleeping under the stars or in a tent. The RTDC-run Hotel Sam Dhani is also available. Camel rides are available (Rs55 per hour). There are two daily buses from Jaisalmer, one in the late morning or early afternoon and one in the early evening.

BIKANER बीकानेर

The fourth largest city of Rajasthan, Bikaner (pop. 500,000) has been trying to draw in tourists, but its remote location and competition from its higher profile neighbors (Jaisalmer to the west and Jodhpur to the south) have been obstacles for the RTDC in this desert city. While maddening traffic circles and long stretches of road best traversed by rickshaw keep some visitors at bay, those who trek here are rewarded with Jain temples, an enchanting fort, scores of havelis, and (this is, after all, Rajasthan) lots of camels. Moreover, for those weary of the tourists that descend upon the rest of the state, Bikaner is an undiscovered oasis. The fact that modern Bikaner doesn't depend on your money is a welcome change, but it also means that the minimal tourist infrastructure makes guest services sparse.

Founded in 1488 by Rao Bika, Bikaner originally was a stop on the Silk Route as well as an important center for camel breeding. In the 16th century, its maharaja, Rei Singh, became one of the most successful generals in Emperor Akbar's nearly invincible army. By the 18th century, Bikaner had become a power to be reckoned with, a mortal enemy of Jodhpur, and the home of the legendary Bikaner Camel Corps. Since Independence, the city has been almost exclusively concerned with its own economic advancement, and thus has become increasingly industrialized and well integrated with the rest of India. Only recently has Bikaner looked to tourism as another possible avenue for economic development. The city's new interest in generating a tourist industry is apparent in the grand show it puts on for the annual Camel Festival (Jan. 20-21, 2000; Jan 8-9, 2001), a celebration of food, music, and all things camel: races, contests, parades, trading, and safaris aplenty. Prices of everything double (at least) as Bikaner fills with tourists.

▐ TRANSPORTATION

Trains: Bikaner Railway Station (tel. 131 or 132), a Rs20-30 auto-rickshaw ride from anywhere in the city. Fares listed are 2nd/1st class. To: **Delhi** (*Bikaner Exp.* 4790, 8:40am, 10½hr., Rs104/535; *Bikaner-Delhi Link Exp.* 4710, 5:50pm, 11hr., Rs166/535; *Bikaner Mail* 4792, 7:45pm, 8½hr., Rs166/535); **Jaipur** (*Intercity Exp.* 2467, 5am, 7hr., Rs99; *Bikaner Exp.* 4738, 8:30pm, 10½hr., Rs88/663); **Jodhpur** (6am, 6½hr., Rs45; 8:40am, 6hr., Rs70). **Advance Reservation Office** (tel. 523132), next to the railway station. Open M-Sa 8am-8pm, Su 8am-2pm.

Buses: Central Bus Stand (tel. 523800), 3km north of the city, across from Lalgarh Palace. To: **Ahmedabad** (1:30pm, 10hr., Rs249); **Ajmer** (13 per day 6am-11:30pm, 7½hr., Rs106); **Delhi** (6 per day 5:15am-7:30pm, 11hr., Rs175); **Jaipur** (8 per day 5am-10pm, 7hr., Rs137; deluxe 7:45am, 6½ hr., Rs166); **Jaisalmer** (5 per day 6am-9pm, 7½hr., Rs84; deluxe 5am and 10:30pm, 7hr., Rs133); **Jodhpur** (13 per day 12:45am-4:30pm, 5½hr., Rs101); **Udaipur** (6:30pm, 12hr., Rs213). **Private buses** can be arranged through hotels, excursion agents, and the bus agencies that congregate around Goga Gate, south of Kote Gate, and behind the fort. Private buses leave frequently for all major cities from the Central Bus Stand.

Local Transportation: Auto-rickshaws are unmetered and will take you anywhere around the city for Rs15-30. **Bicycles** can be rented from cycle stores opposite the police station on Station Rd. **GNP Cycle Store** and **Baba Cycle Store** both charge Rs2 per hr, Rs15 per day. Both open daily 8am-9pm. **Jeeps** can be found near the railway station and across from the Fort's front entrance. They can be rented for Rs3-5 per km.

▐ ORIENTATION AND PRACTICAL INFORMATION

Bikaner lies in the center of the hot Thar Desert, 240km northeast of Jodhpur. The layout is pretty straightforward outside the old city. Noisy **Station Road** is the hotel strip and runs parallel to the tracks in front of the **railway station.** To the right of the station, Station Rd. intersects the main commercial thoroughfare, **KEM Road,** and then continues to the **Junagarh Fort** and the GPO. A left turn on KEM Rd. leads to **Kote Gate,** the main entrance to the walled **old city;** a right leads to the front side of the fort, where you'll find the **State Bank of Bikaner and Jaipur** and the **Central Telegraph Office.** Back at the railway station, a left on Station Rd. leads past the **Clock Tower** through two intersections. A left at the second intersection will lead you to Ambedkar Circle. From the circle, the right road leads to the **PBM Road,** home of the aptly named **PBM Hospital.** PBM Rd. ends in **Major Puran Singh Circle,** close to the **Golden Jubilee Museum.** Going left at the circle takes you back to KEM Rd. Because of the large distances between locales, the city is best traversed by rickshaw.

Tourist Office: Tourist Reception Centre, Hotel Dhola Maru Complex (tel. 544125). From PBM Rd., turn right at Major Puran Singh Circle. Dhola Maru is on your left. Helpful English-speaking staff. Open M-Sa 10am-5pm.

Budget Travel: Desert Tours (tel. 521967; fax 525150), behind the GPO, provides tourist information. Mr. Kamal Saxena organizes horsecart tours of the city and environs: Rs95 for ½day, Rs175 for full day. Camel tour Rs350-550. Open daily 8am-8pm.

Currency Exchange: Bank of Baroda (tel. 545053), opposite the railway station, changes currency and traveler's checks. Open M-F 10am-2pm, Sa 10am-noon.

Luggage Storage: Railway Station Cloak Room, Rs5-7 per item per day.

Market: Most of Bikaner's stores and bazaars are open daily 8am-9pm.

Bookstore: Nauyug Giranth Kuteer (tel. 520836), inside Kote Gate, on the right. Books, international magazines, and newspapers. Open daily 9am-9pm.

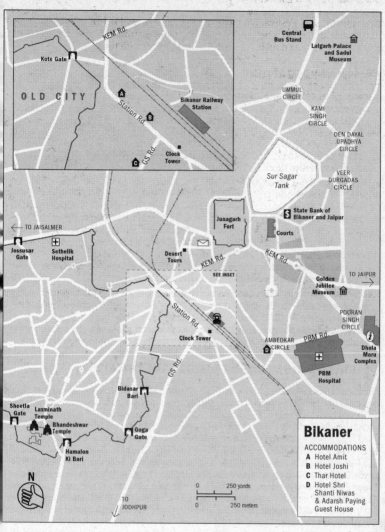

Pharmacy: PBM Hospital and MN Hospital (tel. 544423) both operate 24hr. pharmacies. Others pepper the areas around the hospitals and Kote gate.

Hospital: MN Hospital (tel. 544122), near Kerni Singh Stadium and **Sethelik Hospital** (tel. 528811), inside Jessusar Gate, are clean and modern with English-speaking staff.

Police: Main office (tel. 200840), next to the railway station. Open 24hr. The Superinten-dent of Police (tel. 545173) speaks English. Open M-F 9am-5pm.

Post Office: GPO (tel. 524185), behind Junagarh Fort. *Poste Restante.* Open M-Sa 10am-6pm. **Branches** near PBM Hospital, inside Kote Gate, and near State Bank of Bikaner and Jaipur. **Postal Code:** 334001.

Telephones: Central Telegraph Office (tel. 523144), near State Bank of Bikaner and Jaipur. Open M-Sa 8am-8pm, Su 8am-3:30pm.

RAJASTHAN

PHONE CODE 0151

ACCOMMODATIONS

Most of Bikaner's budget options are clustered on noisy Station Rd., and all are pretty much the same. Hotels are being established near Junagarh Fort and in other areas, though, so choices should rapidly increase. Homestays with local families can be arranged through the tourist office (Rs80-750 per night). A lethargic tourist industry keeps hotel prices steady year round, but expect drastic jumps in fares during the annual camel festival (Jan. 20-21, 2000; Jan 8-9, 2001).

Hotel Shri Shanti Niwas, GS Rd. (tel. 521925; fax 524231), perpendicular to the railway station. Simple, clean rooms in a central location. No alcohol or non veg. food allowed on premises. Check-out 24hr. Singles Rs60, with bath Rs75, deluxe Rs175; doubles Rs100/ 125/250. Extra bed Rs25.

Hotel Joshi, Station Rd. (tel. 527700; fax 52123), about 1½ blocks from the railway station. Modern and centrally located, the Joshi offers a pleasant escape from the heat, dust, and noise of Bikaner. Good veg. restaurant, elevator, STD/ISD, currency exchange, and laundry services. All rooms have attached bath. Check-out 24hr. Singles with air-cooling Rs300, with A/C & TV Rs575; doubles Rs375/675. Enormous A/C deluxe double Rs875. Reservations recommended in season.

Hotel Amit, Station Rd. (tel. 544451), on a side street near the Evergreen Hotel. Basic but clean, cramped rooms, all with attached baths. Hot water buckets Rs5 each. Check-out 24hr. Singles Rs100, with air-cooling Rs150; doubles Rs125/200. Extra bed Rs25. Black and white TV Rs25.

Thar Hotel, PBM Hospital Rd. (tel. 543050; fax 52150), next to Ambedkar Circle. Good-sized, quiet rooms. Room service, puppet show, folk music, TVs, telephones, excellent restaurant. Camel safaris Rs600-900 per day. All rooms have attached bath. Singles with air-cooling Rs450, with A/C Rs700; doubles Rs650/800. Extra bed Rs100. Off-season: 20% discount.

Harasar House (tel. 527318 or 209891; fax 525150), near Karni Singh Stadium. Enjoy enormous, intricately carved wooden beds and sparkling bathrooms at plebeian prices. Rooftop terrace with view of fort and city palace. Good veg. restaurant. Singles 300, with A/C 600; doubles 300/800. Reservations recommended.

Adarsh Paying Guest House, GS Rd. (tel. 523965), perpendicular to the railway station. Basic rooms in a family environment. Singles Rs50, with bath Rs80-100; doubles Rs75/ 100-150. Reservations accepted.

Bhairon Vilas (tel. 544751), next to the fort, opposite the GPO, a few minutes from the bus stand. Splurge to stay in the same suite that Lord Mountbatten did for less than Rs1000 off season in this posh *haveli*-hotel. Lofty ceilings, silk-covered furniture, and luxurious baths with tubs to melt away heat exhaustion. Delicious (if pricey) meals served in attached restaurant. Save up for this one. Singles Rs1100; doubles Rs1600. Low-season: 25% discount.

FOOD

Bikaner's restaurants are spread throughout the city. Station Rd. is a haven for inexpensive sweet shops and street stands frying up loads of *samosas* (Rs 7-12).

Tripti Restaurant, opposite Thar Hotel. Affordable entrees (Rs30-50) and inexpensive *thalis* (Rs38) under a red ceiling and romantic red lanterns. Open daily 10am-10pm.

Moomal Restaurant, Panch Sebi Circle. Worth the 20min. walk. A large, dark, air-cooled veg. restaurant presenting standard Chinese, Continental, and Indian cuisine. Fast service. Rs60-100 for a hearty dinner. Open daily 11am-3pm and 6-10pm.

Metro Bar and Restaurant, at the front of the fort near Sadul Singh Circle. Air-cooled restaurant with plush booths on 3 levels and standard entrees (Rs30-70). Beer Rs45-60. Open daily 8am-10:30pm.

Restaurant Amber, Station Rd., across from the Hotel Joshi. An A/C escape from noisy Station Rd. Red cushioned booths and dim lighting make you savor your *dosas* (Rs18-34) all the more. Entrees Rs30-45. Open daily 7am-10:30pm.

Hotel Sagar, Lalgarh Palace, across from the bus station. Less palatial than its stately neighbor, it features a wide range of entrees, most for under Rs50. Some unusual items are deep pan pizza (Rs25-40) and apple onion soup (Rs45). Open daily 6am-10:30pm.

🎵 ENTERTAINMENT

Although nowhere near Jaisalmeric proportions, **camel safaris** have recently become quite popular in Bikaner. Most of these begin with a tour of the city and nearby sights. A trek through the desert often follows, with frequent stops at rarely touristed traditional villages where you can witness local handicrafts and desert lifestyles. Also common are **intercity safaris** to Jaisalmer and Jodhpur. As in Jaisalmer, the safaris can often involve combinations of jeep, horse, and camel travel. Few hotels offer safaris, and those that do operate exclusively through independent agencies. Vino Desert Safari (tel. 204445, fax 525150), near Gopeshwar Temple, organizes camel safaris for two to thirteen days at Rs400-600 per day. The agency is run by a group of musicians, teachers, and social workers who use the revenue to fund classes in basic literacy, English, math, history, geography, and crafts in the slums of Bikaner. The knowledgeable and friendly Vinod Bhojak is an excellent source for information on Bikaner and the surrounding areas. (Open daily 8am-5pm.) Desert Tours (tel. 521967), located behind the Fort near the GPO, offers a wide range of safaris for Rs350-1000 per day. Rajasthani Safaris & Treks (tel. 543718; fax 520321), in BASSAI House near Junagarh Fort, organizes camel and jeep safaris for Rs1200-1600 per day (open M-Sa 10am-5pm).

🐾 SIGHTS

Essential to any visit to Bikaner is a stroll through the old city, where narrow streets lined by *havelis* snake through metal, spice, sweets, bangle, and vegetable markets. The wealth brought by camel caravans is reflected in over 200 towering *havelis*. Particularly interesting are those of the Ramapuria estate, fashioned out of Bikaner's red sandstone.

JUNAGARH FORT. Bikaner's grandest attraction, Junagarh Fort was built in 1589 by Rai Singh and is distinguished as one of the few in the country that has never been conquered. The fort is a solid, densely packed ground-level structure whose 986m-long wall is capped with 37 bastions and surrounded by a 9m-wide moat. Pretty damn impregnable. The fort entrance is on the east side through a succession of gates. Near the second, **Daulat Pol,** are 24 dramatic hand marks of women who performed a *sati* self-sacrifice after their husbands had perished in a successful attempt to prevent a siege. The fort's main entrance is the **Suraj Pol** (Sun Gate), a large iron-spiked door flanked by two stone elephants.

The fort is an intricate complex of palaces, courtyards, pavilions, and temples (37 in all) added to the original structure by successive rulers. Each new addition was built to connect harmoniously to the previous structures, so that there appears to be one elaborate but continuous palace. The **Karan Mahal,** constructed after an important victory over the Mughal army of Emperor Aurangzeb, features gold-leaf paintings and the silver throne of Lord Karan Singh. The **Chandra Mahal** (Moon Palace) is a beautifully painted *puja* room adorned with Hindu gods and goddesses. To the side is the **Sheesh Mahal** (Mirror Palace), a room studded with mirrors that provide a magnificent glitter—light a match or shine a flashlight and enjoy the dazzle. **Shardaw Miwas** was the music room of the fort; it features old instruments and an ancient system of air-cooling. **Hanuman Temple** is filled with arrays of swords, saws, spears, and nails, which are danced upon by *fakirs* from neighboring villages every January. The **Ganga Singh Hall,** the last portion of the fort, houses a **museum** whose collection of weapons and various relics includes a World War I biplane. *(Open daily 10am-4:30pm. Rs50, includes group guide; camera fee Rs30; video fee Rs100. Authorized government guides Rs80-100, non-English Rs150.)*

RAJASTHAN

RODENT REVERENCE At the Karni Mata Temple in Deshnok, 30km from Bikaner, thousands of holy rats called *kabas* run rampant at the feet of thronging worshippers, who bask in the auspiciousness of the fleeting footsteps of the *kabas*. Those lucky enough to see a white rat can consider themselves blessed. These rodent rapscallions consume massive quantities of grain and milk and play all day to work it off. According to regional legend, the Bikaner patron deity Karni Mata was once asked to resurrect her favorite nephew, who died drowning. She called up Yama, the god of death, who told her the boy had already been reborn as a rat, and that all her male descendants would first be born as rats in her temple at Deshnok. The *kabas* are fed *prasad* every morning—what's left is given to worshippers, who eat it without compunction, as the *prasad* anointed with the animals' spit is also considered auspicious. The best time to visit is during the Navratri festival in March, when the temple is swamped with devotees. The temple is not for the faint of heart, but it is worth visiting for reasons other than its burgeoning rodent population—namely the magnificent solid silver gate donated by Maharaja Ganga Singh, and ornate stone carvings. The temple is accessible by taxi (about Rs200 round-trip) and by bus from Bikaner (every 15min. 5:15am-12:45am, 40min., Rs9-14), and is a stop on the city tours. Capture the scene of a lifetime for a Rs20 camera fee or Rs50 video fee. (Open daily 4am-10pm.)

LALGARH PALACE. The large, multi-tiered palace, made of red sandstone was designed for Maharaja Ganga Singh in 1902, in an attempt to fuse European opulence, "Oriental" majesty, and Rajasthani tradition—unfortunately, it falls short of all of those ideals. The royal family of Bikaner lives in part of it, a luxury hotel takes up some more space, and the **Sri Sadul Museum** occupies the rest. The museum houses every remaining personal item of Maharaja Ganga Singh and his son, Maharaja Karni Singh. Its seemingly endless corridors and halls are filled with everything from a picture of Ganga Singh signing the Treaty of Versailles to his son's personal effects, including his electric toothbrush, Ray Ban sunglasses, and a rifle from the 1960 Olympics, where he was a silver medalist in diving. *(Three kilometers north of the city, across from the Main Bus Stand. Tel. 540201. Museum open Th-Tu 10am-5pm. Rs55. Guided tours Rs40-50.)*

JAIN TEMPLES. Following the main road through Kote Gate will eventually lead you to the base of the old city, where two extraordinary Jain temples, built by merchant brothers in the 16th century, can be found. The **Bhandeshwar Temple,** one of the most spectacular in India, is adorned with gilded floral motifs painted by Persian artists from Emperor Akbar's court. Fifty years, 500 laborers, and 40,000kg of *ghee* went into its construction (the *ghee* was used in place of water to make the temple's cement foundation). On hot days, the temple's base is said to ooze the clarified butter. The **Sandeshwar Temple** also features intricate gold-leaf painting and sculpted marble rows of popular saints. **Laxminath Temple,** next door, is a masterfully carved stone temple with superb views of the desert and city. *(Bhandeshwar open daily 6am-7pm in season; Sandeshwar and Laxminath open daily 6am-1pm. Free; camera fee Rs10 at Bhandeshwar. All temples require the removal of shoes. Sandeshwar and Laxminath do not allow socks, shorts, umbrellas, watches, cameras, or leather goods.)*

SHOPPING

Bikaner is a prime location to shop for desert **handicrafts.** The main commercial areas are **KEM Road** and almost all of the **old city.** Just inside Kote Gate on the left are cloth and textile stores and a fruit market. Leather and other craft stores cluster near the Jain temples. The government-approved **Abhivyakti** (tel. 522139), located just inside the Fort, sells high-quality wares from 115 villages around the city. Shop hassle-free, and rest assured that proceeds go to artisans and projects that promote health care, literacy, and women's rights. (Open daily 9am-6:30pm.)

NEAR BIKANER

Devikund Sagar contains the marble and red sandstone royal *chhattris* (cenotaphs) of Bikaner rulers and their wives and mistresses, whose handprints commemorate their self-sacrifice. There is a *sati* temple where the spirits of the women who immolated themselves here are worshipped. It all surrounds a tranquil lake inhabited by pigeons and peacocks. (8km west of Bikaner.)

The nearby **Camel Breeding Farm** is the largest in Asia, producing 50% of India's bred camels. In the early evening hundreds of camels of all ages return here from the desert. During World War II, the British Imperial Army's Camel Corps was drawn from the stock of this farm. Of course, during the Camel Festival (Jan.), this place goes ballistic. (10km south of the city. Round-trip auto-rickshaw Rs60-80. Open M-Sa 3-5pm. Free. Government authorized guides Rs100 per person. Photography permitted outside only.)

Gajner Wildlife Sanctuary was once the location of the royal hunting grounds. It then became a resort for important visiting dignitaries and now stands as a sanctuary for antelopes, black bucks, gazelles, and assorted birds. Famous Siberian imperial sand grouse migrate here every winter. The elegant palace on the lake has been converted into the upscale Gajner Palace Hotel. (32km west of Bikaner. Buses depart the Central Bus Stand: 7 per day 7:15am-6:30pm, 40min., Rs9-14. Entrance Rs500 per jeep; Rs1100 for guided jeep tour.)

RAJASTHAN

GUJARAT ગુજરાત

One of India's richest industrial regions, Gujarat has much to offer, in part because it sees fewer travelers than its neighbors Rajasthan and Maharashtra. Gujarat is also one of the safest places to travel because of alcoholic prohibition and the lack of mass tourism. The former makes it safer for women to travel alone, even at night, and the latter keeps tourists from being taken advantage of by local touts.

Originally settled as part of the Indus Valley civilization in 2500 BC, Gujarat prospered under several empires, including the Solanki dynasty in the 11th and 12th centuries, which imbued the region with a culture influenced by a blend of Jainism and Hinduism. In 1299 the area was conquered by Muslims, who formed the Sultanate of Gujarat. The Portuguese stormed onto the scene in the 16th century, capturing the ports of Diu and Daman. During India's struggle for Independence, Gujarat gained visibility as the birthplace and operational base of Mahatma Gandhi and as the home to Muhammad Ali Jinnah, architect of Pakistan.

Gujarat can be divided geographically into three vastly different regions. The eastern region, containing the capital Gandhinagar, the metropolis Ahmedabad, and the commercial cities of the mainland strip, is characterized by its modern industrialization. The northwestern quasi-island of Kutch is a dry and isolated area renowned for its many traditional villages. The Kathiawar Peninsula (also known as Saurashtra), features lush land, breathtaking beaches, rich temples, forts, palaces, and all things Gandhi.

HIGHLIGHTS OF GUJARAT

■ Gandhi and gingham combine in **Ahmedabad** (below), at the Mahatma's **Sabarmati Ashram** (p. 344) and the **Calico Museum of Textiles** (p. 345).
■ India sets its western compass point at **Dwarka** (p. 355), where pilgrims congregate and antique lighthouses afford sublime sunset vistas.
■ One of India's most isolated regions, beautiful **Kutch** (p. 356) is home to unique tribal cultures and the labyrinthine port of **Mandvi** (p. 359).

AHMEDABAD અમદાબાદ

Ahmedabad (AHM-da-vad), the largest city in Gujarat (4.4 million people), ranks among the most eccentric and fascinating cities in all of Asia as well as one of the most congested. In the old part of the city, booming industries and businesses envelop spectacular mosques, temples, and museums. Across the river lies the new city, with its expansive web of shopping arcades and cinemas interrupted only by the occasional old-world oxcart or camel.

Founded in 1411 by Sultan Ahmed Shah, the city rapidly expanded as traders, craftsmen, and artisans flocked in. The construction of countless mosques in the Indo-Saracenic style imbued the city with the decidedly Muslim character it retains today. Through the centuries Ahmedabad's prosperity see-sawed as devastating famines periodically checked its growth, but the city's fortes have always been textiles and handicrafts—especially since the establishment here of the ashram that became the center of Gandhi's *swadeshi* movement. Today, Ahmedabad merits recognition as home to the second largest textile industry in the country. While meandering through the old city streets, don't be surprised to see craftsmen adding the finishing touches to *batiks* drying in the morning sun.

▐ TRANSPORTATION

Airport: Ahmedabad International Airport, 10km northeast of the city center (tel. 642 5633). Taxis into the city cost Rs200, auto-rickshaws Rs75-85, and buses run to Lal

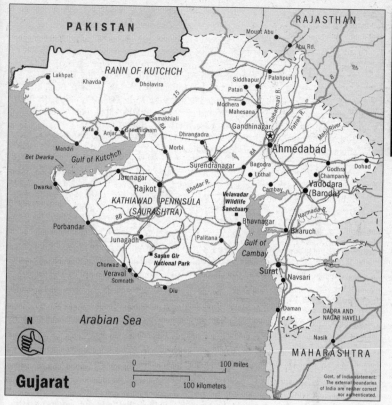

Gujarat

PAKISTAN
RAJASTHAN

Mount Abu
Abu Rd.

RANN OF KUTCHCH
Lakhpat
Khavda
Dholavira
Siddhapur
Palanpuri
Patan
Modhera
Mahesana
Gandhinagar
Samakhiali
Kera
Anjar
Gandhidham
Dhrangadra
AHMEDABAD
Mandvi
Morbi
Godhra
Champaner
Dohad
Bet Dwarka
Gulf of Kutch
Surendranagar
Bagodra
Vadodara
(Baroda)
Jamnagar
Lothal
Dwarka
Rajkot
Bhadar R.
Cambay
KATHIAWAD PENINSULA
(SAURASHTRA)
Velavadar
Wildlife
Sanctuary
Bharuch
Porbandar
Junagadh
Palitana
Bhavnagar
Gulf of
Cambay
Sasan Gir
National Park
Surat
Navsari
Chorwad
Veraval
Somnath
Diu
Daman
DADRA AND
NAGAR HAVELI
N
Arabian Sea
Nasik
MAHARASHTRA

0   100 miles
0   100 kilometers

Govt. of India statement:
The external boundaries
of India are neither correct
nor authenticated.

Darwaja Bus Stand (every 30min., Rs4). Bus #102 heads to the airport from Lal Darwaja, and bus #18 heads to the airport from the railway station, both during flight times. **Air India** (tel. 658 5633 or 658 5644; fax 658 5900), behind the High Court off Ashram Rd., west of the Gandhi statue. Open M-F 10am-1:15pm and 2-5:15pm, Sa 10am-1:30pm. **Indian Airlines,** Lal Darwaja (tel. 550 3061; fax 550 5599), near the east end of Nehru Bridge. Open daily 10am-1pm and 2-5:15pm. **Jet Airways,** Ashram Rd. (tel. 754 3366), 1km north of Gujarat Tourism. Open M-F 10am-7pm, Sa-Su 10am-5:30pm. The *Times of India* Ahmedabad edition has updated flight and train information on the second page. To: **Bangalore** (3 per week, 1½hr., US$200); **Kolkata** (1 per day, 2½hr., US$205); **Chennai** (1 per day, 2½hr., US$220); **Delhi** (2-3 per day, 1½hr., US$120); **Hyderabad** (4 per week, 1½hr., US$150); **Jaipur** (3 per week, 1hr., US$95); **Mumbai** (2-3 per day, 1hr., US$75).

Trains: Ahmedabad Railway Station (tel. 131 or 1331), on the east side of town. The **Reservation Office** (tel. 135) is in the station. Open M-Sa 8am-8pm, Su 8am-2pm. Fares listed are 2nd class/2nd class A/C. To: **Abu Road** (*Delhi Mail 9105,* 10am, 4½hr., Rs76/451); **Bhopal** (*Rajkot-Bhopal Exp.* 1269, 7pm, 14hr., Rs207/950); **Kolkata** (*Howrah Exp.* 8033, 9:20am, 43hr., Rs389/1920); **Chennai** (*Navajivan Exp.* 6045, 6:35am, 22½hr., Rs378/1828); **Delhi** (*Delhi Mail* 9105, 10am, 8hr., Rs259/1146; *Sarvodaya Express,* Tu, W, and Sa noon, 17hr., Rs287/1328); **Dwarka** (*Saurashtra Mail 9005,* 6:15am, 10hr., Rs168/737); **Jaipur** (*Delhi Mail 9105,* 10am, 14hr., Rs207/946); **Junagadh** (*Girnar Exp.* 9946, 9pm, 9hr., Rs146/663; *Sommath Mail* 9924, 11pm, 10hr., Rs146/663); **Mumbai** (*Gujarat Exp.* 9012, 7am, 9hr., Rs172/759; *Shatabdi Exp.* 2010, 2:45pm, 9hr., Rs570 A/C only); **Rajkot** (*Saurashtra Exp.* 9215, 8pm, 5hr., Rs112/502); **Udaipur** (*Udaipur Exp.* 9944, 11pm, 9hr., Rs132/

548); **Varanasi** (*Sabarmati Exp.* 9165, 8pm, 42hr., Rs352); **Veraval** (*Girnar Exp.* 9946, 9pm, 11hr; *Sommath Mail* 9924, 11pm, 12hr., Rs161/725).

Buses: The **S.T. Bus Stand** (tel. 214 764) is for intercity buses. To: **Abu Road** (every 30min. 5am-11:30pm, 6hr., Rs85; deluxe 2:30 and 11:30pm, 5hr., Rs100); **Bhuj** (12 per day 5:30am-11pm, 8hr., Rs90; deluxe 8, 11am, and noon, Rs120); **Bikaner** (5:30pm, 15hr., Rs256); **Chittaurgarh** (9am and 10pm, 9hr., Rs135); **Diu** (8am, 10hr., Rs89); **Dwarka** (8:30, 10am, 4, and 7pm, 11hr., Rs100; deluxe 6, 8am, 10:30, and 11:30pm, Rs120); **Jaipur** (4:30 and 9:30pm, 15hr., Rs245; deluxe 6pm, Rs303); **Jaisalmer** (7pm, 12hr., Rs180); **Mt. Abu** (7 per day 6:30am-3pm, 6hr., Rs70); **Mumbai** (2, 3:30, 4:15, and 9:45pm; 12hr.; Rs150); **Rajkot** (express every 30 min. 4:30am-1am, 5hr., Rs53; deluxe 7:45 and 10:30am, Rs71); **Ranakpur** (6:30, 7:15am, and 7:45pm; 8hr.; Rs130); **Udaipur** (16 per day 4am-11:30pm, 6hr., Rs88; deluxe 11:30am and 10:30pm, Rs112); **Una** (6am, 7, and 8pm; 10hr.; Rs87); **Veraval** (6, 7, 10am, 7, 8, and 8:45pm, 12hr., Rs73; deluxe 8am, Rs90). Opposite the S.T. Bus Stand are dozens of **private bus** company stalls, but most are ticket agents only; most private buses depart from the main company office. The best companies are **Punjab Travels,** Embassy Market (tel. 658 9200), off Ashram Rd., north of the tourist office (open daily 6am-10:30pm); and **Shrinath Travels,** Shahi Bagh (tel. 562 5351; fax 562 5599), near the police commissioner's office (open daily 6am-midnight).

Local Transportation: Auto-rickshaws are the most convenient mode of local transport. Insist on the meter, and ask to see the fare card. **Local buses** are extensive and inexpensive. The **Lal Darwaja Bus Stand** (tel. 550 7739) is the local bus stand. #82 and 84 cross the river and run north up Ashram Rd.; #32 runs to the S.T. Bus Stand and southeast to Kankaria Lake; #34 and 112 run past the Civil Hospital; and #131 and 133-135 run to the railway station. Fares are less than Rs6. Besides lining Lal Darwaja (Rs200 to cross the city), A/C Ambassador **taxis** can also be found at the two bus stands, the airport, the railway station, and V.S. Hospital.

ORIENTATION

Ahmedabad is separated into two parts by the **Sabarmati River,** which cuts a north-south path—the river bed is usually dry and filled with grazing water buffalo—between old and new sections of the city. The **Lal Darwaja (Red Gate)** opens into the old city on the river's east side, and the newer industrial and urban centers lie westward. The two parts of the city are connected by a series of five bridges. The most frequently used are **Ellis** and **Nehru,** the safer and preferred bridge connecting the centers of the old and new cities.

East of the old city, the **Ahmedabad Railway Station** is connected to Lal Darwaja by **Relief Road** (officially known as **Tilak Road**) and **Gandhi Road,** both running through the heart of the old city. The **local bus stand** is located in Lal Darwaja near the end of Gandhi Rd. The **Central Bus Stand** is south of town near the end of **Sardar Patel Road,** which leads southeast from Ellis Bridge to **Astodia Darwaja. Vivekanand Road** leads from Astodia Darwaja to the railway station. **Ashram (RC) Road** is a major commercial strip conveniently lined with banks and big stores. **Gujarat College** and the **Law Gardens** are off Ashram Rd. just north of Ellis Bridge.

Most of Ahmedabad's modern facilities are found in the ever-expanding **new city,** to the west of Sabarmati. Ashram Rd., **Panchwati Circle,** and **CG Road** are bustling areas full of helpful services, but they are far away from the traditional old city, the area of primary interest to tourists.

PRACTICAL INFORMATION

Tourist Office: Tourist Information Bureau (Gujarat Tourism), HK House (tel. 1364 or 658 9683), off Ashram Rd. and down a side-street opposite the South Indian Bank, between Gandhi and Nehru Bridges. Helpful English-speaking staff offers an assortment of brochures. City maps Rs4, Gujarat maps Rs20. Open M-Sa 10:30am-1:30pm and 2-6pm. Closed 2nd and 4th Sa. The **tourist counter** at the airport has limited information.

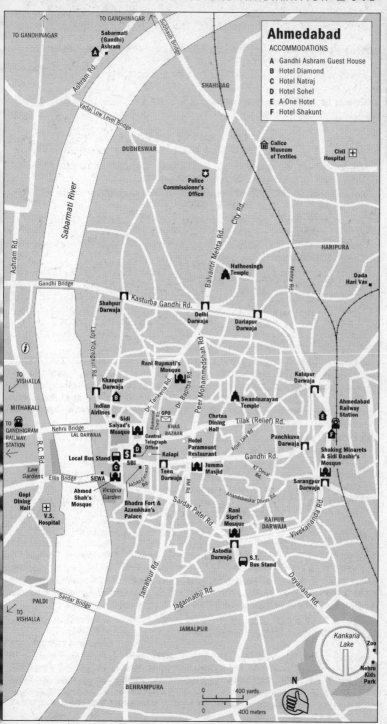

Ahmedabad

ACCOMMODATIONS

A Gandhi Ashram Guest House
B Hotel Diamond
C Hotel Natraj
D Hotel Sohel
E A-One Hotel
F Hotel Shakunt

City tours depart from the tourist window at the Lal Darwaja Bus Stand (9:30am and 3pm; 4hr.; Rs40, A/C Rs60).

Immigration Office: Foreigners Regional Registration Office (FRRO), Commissioner of Police, Dr. Tankeria Rd., 3rd fl. (tel. 562 0990; fax 562 4526), in Shahi Bagh 3km north of Lal Darwaja. Contact at least 15 days prior to visa expiration. Open M-Sa 10:30am-2pm and 3:30-6pm, closed 2nd and 4th Sa.

Currency Exchange: State Bank of India, Lal Darwaja (tel. 550 6116), near Lal Darwaja bus stand. **Bank of Baroda,** Ashram Rd. (tel. 658 0362; fax 658 5175), south of the Gandhi statue, gives cash advances on Visa, MC. 1% service charge. Open M-F 11am-2pm, Sa 11am-noon. **Dena Bank,** Ashram Rd. (tel. 568 4292; fax 658 8613), north of Nehru Bridge. Open M-F 10am-2:30pm. All exchange currency and traveler's checks.

Luggage Storage: The railway station offers luggage storage (Rs5 per item for the 1st 24hr., Rs11 for the 2nd, and Rs18 per additional 24hr.).

Market: Relief, Gandhi, Sardar Patel, Ashram Rd., and **Khas Bazaar** are the main commercial areas. Most stores open daily 9am-9:30pm.

Library: British Library, Bhaikaka Bhawan (tel. 646 4693; fax 644 9493), near the Law Garden. Non-members are allowed to browse but cannot check out books. Open Tu-Sa 10:30am-7:15pm. **M.J. Public Library** (tel. 657 8513) at Ellis Bridge and Ashram Rd. Decent English collection. Open daily 7:30am-7pm.

Cultural Centers: See *Times of India* for notices. **British Library,** Bhaikaka Bhawan (tel. 646 4693; fax 644 9493), near the Law Garden. Organizes lectures and video shows. **Alliance Francaise** (tel. 656 0271), opposite Gujarat College. Small library with French books and newspapers. Organizes cultural activities and exhibitions. Open M-F 10:30am-6:30pm, Sa 11am-5pm. **The Indian Cultural Centre,** Spandan G-11 Balaji Ave., Judge's Bungalow Rd. (tel. 675 7880), hosts traditional folk dance training rehearsals. Call in advance to watch rehearsals.

Bookstore: Crossword, Sri Krishna Shopping Centre, Mithakali (tel. 402238), west of Ashram Rd. and south of Nehru Bridge. Books of all types, magazines, newspapers, stationery, computer games, and a cafe. Open daily 10:30am-8:30pm. **Sastu Kitab Dhar,** Relief Rd. (tel. 535 1785), near Relief Cinema. Gracious staff and good selection of paperbacks. Open M-Sa 9:30am-6:45pm. Lots of **book stalls** with smaller collections line the west end of Relief Rd.

Pharmacy: Pharmacies are especially numerous around the 3 main hospitals (see below). Most open daily 9am-7pm, but some are open 24hr.

Hospital: Good government hospitals are **New Civil Hospital,** Shahi Bagh (tel. 212 3721), 3km north of the railway station off Khandubhai Desai Rd.; and **Sheth Vadilal Sarabhai Hospital,** also called **V.S. Hospital** (tel. 657 7621), south of the intersection of Ashram Rd. and Ellis Bridge. The best private hospital is **Chaturbhuj Lajpatrai Hospital,** also known as **Rajasthan Hospital,** Dr. Tankeria Rd. (tel. 286 6311), south of the police commissioner's office. English-speaking, modern, efficient. Well-stocked 24hr. pharmacy. All hospitals open 24hr.

Police: Major police stations are **Karanj,** in Teen Darwaja; **Shaherkotada,** opposite the railway station; and **Ellis Bridge,** at the intersection with Ashram Rd.

Post Office: GPO, Mirzapar Rd. (tel. 550 0977), near Lal Darwaja. *Poste Restante.* Open M-Sa 8am-7:30pm, Su 10:30am-1:30pm. Branches at the airport, Gandhi Ashram, and opposite the railway station. Open M-Sa 10am-5pm. **Postal Code:** 380001.

Internet: Random Access, Panchwati Circle, Agarwal Arcade, Ambavadi Rd. (tel. 656 6337). The city's first real cyber-cafe, featuring great coffee and super-fast connections (Rs50 for 30min., Rs90 for 1hr.). Open daily 10am-midnight. **Interactive Technologies,** CG Rd., Mardia Plaza (tel. 656 6111 or 656 2307), above Tomatoes Restaurant. Rs30 for 15min., Rs100 for 1hr., Rs150 for 1½hr. Open daily 9am-9pm. **Apple Telecom,** Lehanpur Chakla (tel. 550 4053), near Hotel Diamond charges Rs2.50 per min. Open 24hr. **Suroor Telecommunications,** Relief Rd. (tel. 535 1221; fax 535 0291), opposite Relief Cinema. Open daily 9am-midnight.

Telephones: **Central Telegraph Office,** Lal Darwaja (tel. 550 2139; fax 550 0066), offers telex and telegraph services. Open 24hr.

PHONE CODE	079

ACCOMMODATIONS

The best budget hotels are conveniently scattered around the west half of the city center. Luxury hotels cluster around Khanpur Darwaja, between the Gandhi and Nehru Bridges on the east side of the river. All hotels add 10-15% luxury tax.

Hotel Sohel, Lal Darwaja (tel. 550 5465 or 550 5466), on a side street off Advance Cinema Rd. Spotless rooms in a great location await you in this fresh, new hotel. 24hr. hot water, TVs, phones, and 24hr. room service. Check-out 24hr. Singles Rs190-200, with A/C and balcony Rs300; doubles Rs350-360/400. Rates include tax.

Hotel Natraj (tel. 550 6048), next to Ahmed Shah's Mosque south of the local bus stand. Rooms with balconies overlooking the gardens of the mosque next door offer the best view in the city proper. Rooms are large but boring. All have attached baths. Check-out 24hr. Singles Rs120; doubles Rs200; triples Rs270. Extra bed Rs40.

Gandhi Ashram Guest House (tel. 755 9342), opposite Gandhi Ashram. Located away from the city, this guest house catches some of the peaceful vibes from the ashram across the street. Room decor is enhanced by abstract art and Grecian busts, phones, and TVs. Run by Gujarat Tourism—the staff is well-informed about the city. Good veg. restaurant. Check-out 9am. Singles Rs325, with A/C Rs525; doubles Rs500/750. Room rate includes breakfast.

Hotel Diamond, Khanpur (tel. 550 3699; fax 550 5330), near Gujarat Samachar Press. A good deal for the facilities. Well-kept rooms with baths, TVs, telephones, spotty red carpet, and bland beige bedspreads. Check-out 24hr. Singles Rs175, with A/C Rs260; doubles Rs225/325; triples Rs270/350. Extra bed Rs75.

Hotel Shakunt (tel. 214 4615), opposite the railway station. A modern hotel with a pleasant terrace garden and friendly staff. Rooms are stuffy but have TVs, phones, and baths. Check-out 24hr. Singles Rs210, deluxe Rs345, with A/C Rs400; doubles Rs360/400/500; triples Rs300. Extra bed Rs125.

A-One Hotel (tel. 214 9823), opposite the railway station. The undecorated, unfurnished, nondescript, and slightly grungy rooms are barely larger than the beds, but the price can't be beat for the locale. Check-out 24hr. Dorm beds (men only) Rs60; singles Rs90, with TV and bath Rs175; doubles Rs140/250; triples 190/325.

FOOD

Gujarati *thalis* blend several local specialties in a delightful, often sweet, mix. For quick and spicy stall food, **Khas Bazaar** can't be beat.

Gopi Dining Hall, off Ashram Rd. near V.S. Hospital on the west side of river; look for the sign above the building. Excellent, enormous Gujarati *thalis* (Rs45) served on fine stainless steel in a packed den. Come early, or be prepared to wait. Unbeatable service and the price is right. Open daily 10:30am-3pm and 6-11pm.

Colours of Spice, Piyuraj Chambers, Swastik Cross Roads, Navrangpura (tel. 644 2324), in the heart of the new city. The finest dining in Ahmedabad. Indonesian, Thai, Chinese, and Indian entrees are all delicious down to the last bite. A full meal will run about Rs150. Goodies from the attached sweets shop are divine. Open daily 11am-11pm.

Kalapi Restaurant, near Advance Cinema, Lal Darwaja. One of the best bargains in town, evidenced by the steady stream of locals entering through the tinted glass door. Dim lighting, A/C, and no smoking. All veg. fare is excellent, well-presented, and cheap. Madrasi specialties Rs12-22. Open daily 9am-11pm.

Hotel Paramount, near Khas Bazaar. Bland, vinyl-booth atmosphere, but dim lights and A/C make it comfortable. Good seafood dishes for under Rs45, veg. entrees under Rs40. Open daily 9:30am-11:15pm.

Sunrise Restaurant, Reid Rd., across from the railway stations near Hotel Shakunt. A busy diner where the *dosas* are cheap (Rs13-22) and the cold coffee ice cream floats (Rs25) are to die for. Open daily 6am-12:30am.

Chetna Dining Hall, Relief Rd., almost directly north of the Jama Masjid. Your standard *thali* house, with stainless steel everywhere and waiters rushing from table to packed table with pots of steaming vegetables. South Indian dishes (*dosas* Rs20-22) downstairs, substantial *thalis* (Rs55) upstairs. Open daily 10:30am-3pm and 6:30-10pm.

Tomatoes Restaurant, CG Rd., in the new city. If you miss Western food, this '50s diner is your chance to splurge and satisfy your cravings as you (and many Indian teens) pay tribute to Elvis. Entrees Rs75-200. Open daily noon-11pm.

👁 SIGHTS

SABARMATI (GANDHI) ASHRAM. Each year thousands of admirers and followers of Mahatma Gandhi descend upon Ahmedabad to visit the ashram from which much of Gandhi's spiritual and political influence emanated. The original ashram, in the middle of the city, was founded in 1915, upon Gandhi's return from South Africa. A city-wide plague in 1917 caused Gandhi to relocate it to a plot of donated land on the banks of the Sabarmati River. Gandhi resided here until 1930, along with his wife, Kasturba, and 600 other residents. His simple living quarters are on display, as is an impressive exhibition on his achievements, philosophy, paintings, photographs, quotes, political cartoons, and stamps. The focus is on Gandhi's role in the revitalization of the Ahmedabad textile industry.

The museum library, accessible to residents and visitors, holds a mammoth collection of over 36,000 of Gandhi's letters. Also of interest is **Pasana Mandir,** a small plot of land overlooking the river where Gandhi and his fellow ashram inhabitants recited daily prayers. Evening prayer sessions are still held in the same spot by current inhabitants of the ashram *(6:30pm).* Beyond **Vinoba/Mira Kutir,** the modest abode of two particularly fervent devotees, lies a large building referred to as the "hostel." The hostel was the first building erected in the ashram. The room on the riverside was Gandhi's original dwelling and work room for three months. The building is now home to 2000 orphans and children from impoverished families living in nearby slums. Those interested in spending time at the ashram should contact the management directly by phone. For shorter stays, of one to two weeks, contact Jayesh Patel (tel. 755 8052 or 755 7702; email: safai@ad1.vsnl.net.in), next door to the ashram. The Department of Gandhian Studies (tel. 754 0746) of Gujarat Vidyapith offers classes structured after Gandhian principles. *(Ashram Rd., north of the Gandhi Bridge; take local bus #81, 82, 83, 84, 86, 87, 200, or 300. Tel. 755 7277. Open daily 8:30am-6:30pm. Free. Sound and light show Su, W, and F 8:30pm. Rs3.)*

> **LET'S GO: FLY A KITE** For three nights in January, the skies of Ahmedabad are speckled with kites of all styles, colors, and sizes. Enthusiasts from all over the world descend upon the city for the **International Kite Festival,** the largest kite-related happening in the world. For the weeks leading up to the event, local shops and stalls sell an enormous variety of kites and kite-flying equipment, and experts roam the streets offering lessons on the finer points of the craft. In the festival itself there are competitions for kite size, originality, and beauty. At night the skies light up with kites' illuminated tails. Dancing, singing, shows, parades, and general merriment round out the festival's lighter side. The festival ends with a highly competitive contest in which kite strings are coated with adhesive and ground glass, turning them into razor-sharp lines. Kites are then sent flying into one another to slash at each other's lines until one kite emerges victorious. In 2000, the festival runs January 13-15.

CALICO MUSEUM OF TEXTILES. Creatively housed in the *haveli* of the city's richest family, India's premier textile museum is split into two sections surrounded by peacock- and fountain-filled gardens. The first half displays non-religious textiles and features an enormous collection of textile items made from every possible fabric, in every possible style, for every possible purpose, and from every part of India. The white-on-white translucent shadowwork is remarkable, as are the lavish silk embroideries. Other highlights include beautiful *saris* (valued at Rs80,000 and up) made according to a highly complex method—one tiny mistake in the sewing ruins the entire piece—and clothes so heavily laden with gold lace that their weight exceeds 9kg. The second half of the museum displays textiles for religious use and features an exquisite, 8m-long pictorial scroll, many old tapestries, and a series of rooms explaining the methods in minute detail—every knot, stitch, thread type, dye, bead, and mirror technique imaginable is explained. *(Shahi Bagh, 3km north of Delhi Gate; take local bus #101, 102, or 106. Tel. 786 8172. Open Th-Tu. Guided tours of Foundation galleries, 10:30am; of textile collection, 2:45pm; both 2hr. Unguided visitation 10:30am-12:30pm. Free. Photography permitted only in the gardens.)*

JAMA MASJID. Built in 1424 by Sultan Ahmed Shah I, the Jama Masjid ("Friday Mosque") opens onto a large marble courtyard centered on a small reflecting pool often surrounded by devotees. The structure's 15 domes are supported by 256 pillars with detailed carvings, most of which are Hindu-themed. The curious black slab by the main massive archway is said to be an inverted Jain image. Through the left gate of the courtyard are the **Tomb of Ahmed Shah** and the **Rani-ka-hazira,** the tomb of his queens. The cenotaphs, in vast pillared chambers, are covered with fancy gold-laced cloths. A guard can lift one for you to reveal some fine stonework. *(Gandhi Rd. Women are prohibited from entering the chambers which hold tombs of male members of the family.)*

SIDI SAIYAD'S MOSQUE. Constructed in 1573 by one of Ahmed Shah's slaves, Sidi Saiyad's Mosque, in Lal Darwaja, is the image that graces at least half of Gujarat Tourism's literature. The interior of the mosque is quite impressive, with elaborately carved ceilings and domes, but the real highlight is the delicate latticework on the screens lining the upper walls. Most are floral or arboreal in nature, with windy threads of marble meandering through one another. *(Women are not allowed to enter, but they can view the screens from the gardens.)*

OTHER MOSQUES. **Rani Sipri's Mosque** is near the railway station, on Sardar Patel Rd. Also known as **Masjid-e-Nagira** (the "Jewel of a Mosque"), it was built in 1519. The central grave holds Rani Sipri, who ordered the mosque built after her son was executed for a petty crime. The mosque is known for its exquisite latticework. The tomb itself is surrounded by 12 pillars under a single stylish dome. Near Sarangpur Darwaja are the famous **Shaking Minarets** and **Sidi Bashir's Mosque.** A huge arch supporting two 21m-high minarets explains half the name. These are balanced such that if one shakes, the other will move to counteract the tremor, allowing the mosque to survive jostles by earthquakes and colonialist bombardments alike. Shaking the minarets is now prohibited.

TEMPLES. The **Swaminarayan Temple,** on the north side of the city, is a temple dedicated to Vishnu and Lakshmi. Built in 1850, this barrage of rainbow and metallic colors contrasts dramatically with Ahmedabad's stonework. The temple's fine woodwork and bright, detailed painting rival the mosques' stonework in intricacy. *(Open daily 6am-8pm; cameras prohibited.)* The **Hatheesing Temple,** north of Delhi Lake, is one of a few Jain temples in the city. Built in 1848 and dedicated to the 15th *tirthankara,* Dharamarath, this white marble temple has a design that is typically Jain, with detailed carvings of dancers and floral patterns. *(Buses headed to the airport pass by both Swaminarayan and Hatheesing Temple; be sure to let the driver know where you are going. Hatheesing Temple open to non-Jains daily 10am-noon and 4-7:30pm.)*

MUSEUMS. The **Mehta Museum of Miniatures** has a large collection of miniature paintings, most of them modern, from throughout India *(west of the city, near the uni-*

versity; tel. 646 3324; open Tu-Su 10:am-5:30pm; free). Next door, the **L.D. Institute of Indology** offers more miniatures, manuscripts, and carvings (bus #52 from Lal Darwaja and bus #56 from the railway station serve both museums; tel. 644 2463; open M-Sa 10am-5:30pm; free). The **Shreyas Folk Museum,** west of the city, displays folk work—costumes, handicrafts, and textiles—from all over Gujarat (bus #41 from Lal Darwaja; tel. 660 1338; open Tu-Su 10:30am-1:30pm and 2:30-5:30pm; Rs40). The **Tribal Research and Training Museum** showcases similar crafts from regional tribal peoples and explains their customs (north of Ashram Rd., on the campus of Gujarat Vidyapith; tel. 754 1148; open M-Sa noon-6pm; free).

NEAR AHMEDABAD

ADALAJ VAV. Nineteen kilometers north off the road to Gandhinagar, the step-well Adalaj Vav ranks among the most impressive in the state. Built in 1499 by Rani Rudabai as a summer retreat, it now serves mainly as a popular relaxation spot for locals. The gardens around it are pleasant enough, but the carvings on the well are the main attraction. Intricate lattices and detailed carvings of mythological scenes adorn the walls, pillars, and platforms of the five-story well. The best time to visit is just before noon, when sunlight illuminates the stonework all the way to the bottom. Buses going to Mehsama Kalol from the S.T. Bus Stand pass Adlaj Vav (every 30min. 6am-10pm, 30min., Rs6).

SARKHEJ. Eight kilometers southwest of Ahmedabad is Sarkhej, the erstwhile summer retreat of Gujarati sultans and a present-day suburb, a town whose pacific atmosphere makes it seem much more removed from the city than it really is. Set on one side of an artificial lake is the tomb of Sheikh Ahmed Khattu Ganj Buksh, the spiritual mentor and unofficial advisor of Ahmed Shah. The largest **mausoleum** in the state, it has a huge central dome supported by pillars and decorated with exquisite marble, brass, and wood ornamentation. Sultan Muhammed Beghada's mausoleum and that of his wife Rajabai are interesting as well. It was Sultan Beghada who transformed the solemn Sarkhej complex in the 1500s by adding palaces, gardens, fountains, and courtyards. It has declined over the years, but it is still an attractive place for peaceful wandering. **Bus** #31 from Lal Darwaja and #150 from the railway station make the trip here.

LOTHAL. The site of Lothal, "place of the dead" in Gujarati, 90km southwest of Ahmedabad, shook the archaeological community when it was discovered in 1945. Lothal is what remains of a city of the ancient Indus Valley Civilization dating from 2400 to 1900 BC. Lying in ruin are old roads, a bathhouse, a sewer, houses, and shops; the discovery of a dock and a cargo warehouse has led to the conclusion that Lothal was a major port city. A **museum** showcases the findings of years of excavation. (Open Sa-Th 10am-5pm.) To reach Lothal, take the **bus** to Bhavnagar (every 30min. 7am-1am, 2hr., Rs33), get off at Dholka, and take one of the frequent buses from there. Alternatively, catch a bus to Bagodra (every hr. 6am-7pm, 1hr., Rs21), and take a rickshaw from there to the site (Rs150 round-trip).

MODHERA. The unassuming town of Modhera, 100km northwest of Ahmedabad, is home to an extraordinary, Jain-influenced **Sun Temple** built in 1026 by the Solanki King Bhimdev I. Following Sun Temple norms, the temple was constructed and positioned so that, at the time of the equinoxes, sunlight falls directly on the image of Surya, the sun god, in the sanctuary—many worshippers come to see this sacred event. The main pillared entry hall is adorned on the sides with 12 *adityas* representing the sun's phases through the year. Guides (working for tips) will eagerly point out the multitude of Kama Sutra-esque carvings that adorn the inner sancta and outer walls. The step-well in front of the temple holds over 100 smaller temples. (Open daily sunrise to sunset. Rs2; video fee Rs25.) Stop for replenishing *chai* (Rs5) and *thalis* (Rs38) at the GTDC-run **Torah Garden Restaurant** (tel. 02734-84334), at the front of the temple (open daily 9am-6pm). **Buses** run frequently to Modhera from the S.T. Bus Stand (ever 30min. 9:30am-4pm, 3hr., Rs42) and from Mehsana, which is connected to Ahmedabad by rail.

GANDHINAGAR. Thirty-two kilometers northeast of Ahmedabad is Gandhinagar, the capital of Gujarat and the second state capital in India planned and constructed after Independence. Designed by Le Corbusier, the French architect who planned Chandigarh (see p. 262), the city might strike some as boring for its symmetry and numbered sectors. **Buses** run to Gandhinagar from the S.T. Bus Stand (every 30min. 4am-midnight, 1hr., Rs7).

VISHALLA. The Gujarati village mock-up of Vishalla, 4km south of Ahmedabad, offers a night of earthy village dining and rustic entertainment. Eat plentiful, spicy food from leaf plates and drink from clay cups while musicians play and attendants dressed in traditional village garb fan insect-repelling, scented smoke in your face. The buffet dinner is an expensive Rs175-250, but snacks are also available (open daily 7-11pm). Bus #31 from Lal Darwaja and #150 from the railway station run past the Octori check post—specify where you want to be let off. From the checkpoint, Vishalla is a seven-minute walk or a short rickshaw ride (Rs5-10).

RAJKOT રાજકોટ

Rajkot is a clean, relaxed, typical Gujarati town, primarily of interest to travelers as a gateway to the Kathiawar Peninsula. Founded in the 16th century, it was the capital of the state of Saurashtra and an important administrative center for the Raj. It most recently attained fame for its connection to Mahatma Gandhi, who spent his youth here. It was in Rajkot that Gandhi went to school, married, and received permission from his mother to go to England—the rest is history.

TRANSPORTATION

Airport: Rajkot Airport (tel. 454533), 4km northwest of town. **Indian Airlines,** Dhebar Rd. (tel. 234122; fax 233329), near the circle. Open daily 10am-1pm and 2-5:30pm. Purchase tickets before 4:30pm. **Jet Airways,** 78 Bilkha Plaza, Kasturba Rd. (tel. 479623 or 479624; fax 479624), opposite Lord's Banquet Restaurant. Open M-Sa 9:30am-7pm, Su 9:30am-6:30pm. Flights to: **Mumbai** (4 per week, 50min., US$75).

Trains: Rajkot Railway Station (tel. 131). Reservation office (tel. 135). Open M-Sa 8am-8pm, Su 8am-2pm. Fares listed are 2nd/1st class. To: **Ahmedabad** (*Intercity Exp.* 9154, 6:40am; *Bhopal Exp.* 1269, 2:35pm; *Saurashtra Mail* 9006, 5:30pm, 5hr., Rs62/489); **Dwarka** (*Saurashtra Mail* 9005, 10:40am, 6hr., Rs62/489); **Junagadh** (*Passenger,* 8:15am and 6:15pm; *Veraval mail* 9838, 11:15am, 3-4hr., Rs22-33); **Veraval** (*Veraval Mail* 9838, 11:15am, 6hr., Rs52).

Buses: Main Bus Stand (tel. 235025). To: **Ahmedabad** (every 15min., 4hr., Rs54/62); **Bhuj** (12 per day 4:45am-11:15pm, 6hr., Rs60); **Diu** (1 and 2:30pm, 6hr., Rs56); **Dwarka** (12 per day 5:30am-9:30pm, 5½hr., Rs51); **Junagadh** (every 30min. 4am-midnight, 2hr., Rs60); **Somnath** and **Veraval** (14 per day 6am-11pm, 4½hr., Rs36/40). **Private bus companies** opposite the bus stand serve many cities in Gujarat and Rajasthan. **Eagle Travel Agency,** Moti Tonki (tel. 450300), is 5min. from the Playing Fields. Take the road leading west off the northwest corner of the Playing Fields; at the traffic circle, take the road to the upper right. Open daily 6am-midnight.

Local Transportation: Unmetered **auto-rickshaws** buzz to the airport (Rs25). **Local buses** can take you anywhere in the city (Rs5 or less)—ask locals to help you find the right bus. **Chakka-rickshaws** (tempo-motorcycle hybrids) go to most points in the city (Rs5-10).

ORIENTATION AND PRACTICAL INFORMATION

Everything of interest in Rajkot is sandwiched between the **railway station** to the north and the **bus stand** to the south. The bus stand is on **Dhebar Road,** which darts north to **Trikonbaug,** a major circle that marks the city center. East of the circle is **Lakhajiraj Road;** west is an intersection at the eastern edge of the **Playing Fields.** Toward the left, **Dr. Yagnik Road** heads south and circles the fields, and to the right, **Jawahar Road** runs north past Jubilee Gardens to the Civil Hospital and **Junction Road.** A right at Junction Rd. and a left onto **Station Road** takes you to the railway station. From the Civil Hospital, **Kasturba Road** leads southwest to the **race course** west of the Playing Fields.

Tourist Office: Tourist Information Bureau (tel. 234507), behind State Bank of Saurashtra at the south end of Jawahar Rd.; 2nd fl. of the yellow brick building. Maps of Gujarat (Rs20) but none of Rajkot. Open M-Sa 10:30am-6pm, closed 2nd and 4th Sa.

Currency Exchange: State Bank of India, Jawahar Rd. (tel. 226416-7), north of Jubilee Gardens. Changes cash and traveler's checks. Open M-F 11am-3pm, Sa 11am-1pm.

Market: The main commercial areas are in the old city, on Lakhajiraj Rd., and along Dhebar-Jawahar Rd. Most stores open M-Sa 9am-1pm and 3-10pm.

Hospital: Civil Hospital (tel. 440298; fax 445868), at the intersection of Kasturba and Jawahar Rd. 24hr. pharmacy. Clean facilities and English-speaking staff.

Police: Police Commissioner's Office (tel. 444288), opposite the race-course next to Galaxy Cinema. The **control room** (tel. 457777) is open 24hr.

Post Office: GPO (tel. 228611), west of Jawahar Rd., opposite Jubilee Gardens. Open M-Sa 8am-7pm. **Postal Code:** 360001.

Internet: Wesphil C.C. (tel. 237290), 2nd fl. of the Galaxy Building, just below the hotel. Surf the web for Rs100 per hr. Open daily 8am-midnight.

Telephones: Telegraph Office, Jawahar Rd. (tel. 227592; fax 221452), opposite Jubilee Gardens. **STD/ISD,** fax, and telegraph services. Open 24hr.

PHONE CODE	0281

■ ACCOMMODATIONS

Budget hotels dot the railway station area and Lakhajiraj Rd. Business hotels surround the Playing Fields. There are plenty of both types behind the bus stand.

Vishram Guest House, Lakhajiraj Rd. (tel. 32183), the blue-and-white building opposite Rainbow Restaurant. By far the best deal in town, Vishram has spotless rooms with attached baths and TVs to help while away the time. Check-out 24hr. Singles Rs140-175, with air-cooling Rs190-200; doubles Rs250-300/300-350. Extra bed Rs60.

Hotel Moon Guest House (tel. 225522), behind the bus stand. Don't be deterred by the betel-stained walls on the way up. Clean, sparsely decorated rooms with clean bathrooms and great city views from the terrace. 24hr. room service. Check-out noon. Singles and doubles Rs125, with bath Rs175.

Galaxy (tel. 222904), in the Galaxy Building overlooking the Playing Fields. Rajkot's "premier hotel" has the largest singles in town. Room service, laundry, phones, TVs, currency exchange, nice bathrooms, and 24hr. hot water. Check-out noon. Singles Rs400-500, with A/C Rs600-900; doubles Rs600-760/900-1350. 15% tax. AmEx, Visa, MC.

■ FOOD

Rajkot's eateries have their share of modern Indian cuisine, but *thali*-lovers will surely be appeased as well; many of Rajkot's restaurants specialize in ice cream.

Havmor Restaurant, Jawahar Rd., south of Jubilee Garden. Delight in Punjabi, Chinese, and Continental entrees in the A/C, mirrored, and marbled dining room. Havmor's food is renowned locally, but service lags when they're busy. Veg. dishes Rs35-60, non-veg. Rs60-75. Open daily 9am-11pm.

Lord's Banquet Restaurant, Kasturba Rd. Gaudy chandeliers, A/C, cushy booths, and an enormous selection of Chinese, Continental, and Indian veg. specialties (Rs27-68). Open daily 11am-3pm and 7:30-11:30pm.

Rainbow Restaurant, Lakhajiraj Rd., under the Himalaya Guest House. Cheap South Indian veg. snacks (Rs15-30), Punjabi and Chinese dishes, and over 40 novelty ice cream confections. Dodge the flies and head upstairs (A/C). Open daily 10am-11pm.

SIGHTS

Flanked by stone lions, the **Watson Museum** is curiously dedicated to Col. John Watson, a 19th-century British political agent. The museum houses artifacts from the Indus Valley Civilization, exquisite miniature paintings, and Rajasthani brass- and silver-work. (In the Jubilee Gardens. Open M-Sa 9am-1pm and 2-6pm. Closed 2nd and 4th Sa. Rs0.50.) The **Kabo Gandhi no Delo** was the Gandhi family's residence when they moved here in 1881. It now features a small collection of photographs and memorabilia. (Ghitaka Rd. Open M-Sa 9am-noon and 3-6pm. Small donations appreciated.) The **Playing Fields** (or **maidan**) host a few concerts a week—check the *Times of India* Ahmedabad edition, *Gujarat Samachal*, or *Phul Chab* for local listings.

DIU દીવ

Life on the small island of Diu ("DEE-ooh" to islanders, "Doo" to mainlanders), off the southern coast of Gujarat, revolves around the pursuit of fish and alcohol. A Portuguese colony until 1961, when India reclaimed it, Diu is now considered part of a Union Territory rather than part of Gujarat. As a result, Gujarat's alcoholic prohibition laws don't apply here, making it prime party ground for the thousands of Gujaratis who descend upon the island every weekend. Diu's marvelous beaches and relaxed pace cheer up even the most hung-over of revelers, but tourists are also drawn to the island's colorful buildings and impressive fort.

TRANSPORTATION

Airport: Diu Airport, 5km west of Diu Town, north of Nagoa Beach (auto-rickshaw Rs50). **Gujarat Airways** (tel. 52180; fax 52372), off Bunder Rd. next to the GPO. Open M-Sa 9am-1pm and 3-6:30pm, Su 9am-1pm and 3-6pm. Flights to: **Mumbai** (50min., US$95). Departures often delayed or cancelled.

Trains: Delwada Railway Station (tel. 22226), between Una and Goghla, 8km from Diu Town (auto-rickshaw Rs100). To: **Junagadh** (Rail Bus 1, 1:30pm, 7hr., Rs27) via **Sasan Gir** (5hr., Rs16); **Veraval** (*Veraval Local*, 6:30am, 4½hr., Rs16).

Buses: S.T. Bus Stand, just outside the city's northern gate. Most buses depart 6-8am or noon-3pm. Buses depart from the Main Sq. before 7am. To: **Ahmedabad** (7am, 8½hr., Rs75); **Rajkot** (7 per day 4:45am-5:25pm, 6½hr., Rs60); **Una** (every 30min. 7am-9:30pm, 40min., Rs5); **Veraval** (4am and 2:15pm, 2½hr., Rs30). The **Una Bus Stand** (tel. 31600) services: **Ahmedabad** (10 per day 6am-8pm, 8hr., Rs87); **Junagadh** (6 per day 3am-3pm, 5hr., Rs42) via **Veraval** (2hr., Rs25); **Rajkot** (5 per day 5:30am-7:45pm, 6hr., Rs55). **Private bus companies** surround the Main Sq. **Gayatri Travels** (tel. 52346; fax 53019), next to the Bank of Saurashtra. Open daily 9am-noon and 3-8pm. Avoid Sunday night buses out of Diu; they're inevitably filled with drunken Gujaratis.

Local Transportation: Auto-rickshaws travel within Diu Town (Rs5-10) and go to Nagoa Beach (Rs30) and Una (Rs100). A 3hr. tour will run you Rs150. Night travel out of Diu Town extra Rs20. The **local bus stand,** west of Main Sq., services Nagoa Beach (departs 7, 11am, and 4pm; returns 1:30 and 6pm; Rs5) and Delwada (every 30min. 6:30am-7pm, Rs5). Buses from S.T. Bus Stand to Una (see above) stop at Delwada (Rs5-10). **Kismat Cycle Store** (tel. 52971), behind Main Sq. near the high school, rents **bikes** (Rs15 per day) and **mopeds** (Rs100 per day). Open M-Sa 9am-8pm, Su 9am-1pm.

🛈 ORIENTATION AND PRACTICAL INFORMATION

Diu Island spreads 12km from east to west at a width of 3km. One enters Diu via the port town of **Una** in Saurashtra, past the **railway station** in the town of **Delwada** and through the little island of **Goghla,** off the northeastern tip of Diu Island. **Diu Town** occupies the eastern tip of the island. From there, roads head west through the southern half of the island past **Chakratirth Beach, Sunset Point,** the village of **Fudam, Diu Airport,** and the famous **Nagoa Beach** before ending in **Vanakbara,** at the western tip of the island. Diu Town itself is set apart by a north-south wall stretching across the eastern tip. **Bunder Road** leads past the **S.T. Bus Stand** into town through the northern gate, then runs along the coast to the **local bus stand** and the **Public Gardens** before dead-ending at **Diu Fort,** which marks the extreme eastern tip of the town and island. **Jampa Gate,** in the middle of the wall, leads to the old city's disorienting cobweb of tiny lanes. The road entering town to the south runs along **Jallandhar Beach,** bending past the hospital and St. Thomas' Church to Bunder Rd.

Tourist Office: Tourist Information Bureau, Bunder Rd. (tel. 52653), near Main Sq., has maps and information. Open M-F 9:30am-1:30pm and 2:15-6pm, Sa 9:30am-1:30pm.

Currency Exchange: State Bank of Saurashtra (tel. 52135 or 52492), around the corner from the tourist office, behind the GPO. Open M-F 10am-2pm, Sa 10am-noon.

Market: Most markets and stores open daily 8am-7pm; many are closed 1-3pm and on Su. The **fish market** is behind Main Sq., and the **vegetable market** is farther down Bunder Rd., 200m past Main Sq. Vegetable market open daily 8am-noon.

Pharmacy: Shops in Main Sq. sell basic meds and toiletries. Most open daily 10am-6pm.

Hospital: Government Hospital (staff tel. 102), in St. Francis of Assisi Church, 200m north of Jallandhar Beach. English-speaking. Pharmacy for patients. Open 24hr. for emergencies. Open 9am-1pm and 2:30-5pm for consultations.

Police: Bunder Rd. (tel. 52133), past the Public Gardens on the left. Open 24hr.

Post Office: GPO, Bunder Rd. (tel. 52122), in Main Sq. *Poste Restante.* Open M-Sa 8am-noon and 2-4pm. **Postal Code:** 362520.

Telephones: STD/ISD booths line Bunder Rd. Most open daily 8am-10pm.

PHONE CODE	02875

♙♙ ACCOMMODATIONS AND FOOD

Considering that most visitors to Diu are only looking for a place to black out after a night of drinking, hotels have no real incentive to impress. Off-season (roughly Apr.-Nov.) discounts can be substantial, but you'll need to bargain. Camping is no longer permitted on Diu's beaches. Free-standing bars are prohibited, so they parade as restaurants, providing only the minimum amount of food required by law; hotels are the best bet for decent food.

▧ **Jay Shankar's Guest House** (tel. 52424), Jallandhar Beach. This guest house, diner and bar caters to backpackers. Small, clean, sea-blue rooms are homey. Restaurant serves Indian and Western dishes of all sorts—french toast served all day—but it's the seafood that makes it stellar. Check-out noon. Dorm beds Rs40; singles Rs100-125; doubles with balcony Rs200. Off-season: Rs30/60-80/125-150.

▧ **Ganga Sagar Rest House** (tel. 52249), Nagoa Beach. The relaxing outer courtyard sits right on the shore. Small, bare, clean rooms. Decent restaurant and bar offer limited room service. Check-out 8am. Singles Rs150, with bath Rs300; doubles Rs300/400. Off-season: singles Rs100/150; doubles Rs150-300/300.

Hotel Mozambique, Burden Rd. (tel. 52223), in a distinctly Portuguese building in the heart of the vegetable market. Big, not-especially-clean rooms draw in a nice breeze through balconies with seaside or market views. Good restaurant serves cheap seafood.

Check-out noon. Singles Rs175, with bath Rs225; doubles with bath Rs250-325. Off-season: Rs100/125/200-250.

Hotel Prince, (tel. 52265), northwest of the Main Sq. What this hotel lacks in character it makes up for in cleanliness. Large rooms have mirrors and phones. Check-out noon. Singles Rs200, with TV Rs250, with A/C Rs500; doubles Rs400/500/1000. Off-season: singles Rs125/175/300; doubles Rs250/350/600.

Rio Restaurant (tel. 52209), in Fudam. A little out of the way, Diu's only luxury hotel, **Kohinoor,** has a good restaurant serving Indian and Chinese delicacies (Rs35-100) and beer (Rs35-50). Open daily 11:30am-3pm and 7-11:30pm.

👁 ◗ SIGHTS AND BEACHES

The massive **Diu Fort,** built in 1591, is guarded by a tidal moat which once made it virtually impenetrable. There is little to do here except wander among the cannons and cannonballs and catch the beautiful sunset views of the sea and town. The fort doubles as the island jail. (At the end of Bunder Rd. Open daily 7am-6pm.) Wandering the labyrinthine streets is the best way to see the sights of the Portuguese-influenced old city. **Nagar Seth's Haveli** is considered the most impressive and distinctively Portuguese building in Diu Town (ask for directions once you're in the old city). **St. Paul's Church** is badly weathered but still has grand ceilings and arches, excellent paintings, and a beautiful organ. Mass is still held here each Sunday. (Open daily 8am-9pm.) Nearby, **St. Thomas' Church** houses the **Diu Museum,** with its Catholic paintings and statues (open daily 8am-9pm).

Travelers sick of (or from) drinking might enjoy one of Diu's excellent beaches. The island's longest, most famous, and filthiest beach is **Nagoa Beach,** 7km west of town. On the south side of Diu Town, **Jallandhar Beach** is rocky but great for wading. **Chakratirth Beach,** to the west of Diu Town, is better for swimming, and the nearby **Sunset Point** is a favorite local hangout. Across the bridge from Diu Town, **Goghla's** long beach is great for swimming, with fewer tourists, but also fewer palms, than Nagoa Beach. **Auto-rickshaws** shuttle from the bazaar to Jallandhar Beach and Chakratirth (Rs15), Goghla Beach (Rs20), and Nagoa Beach (Rs30).

VERAVAL વેરાવળ AND SOMNATH સોમનાથ

The busy city of Veraval is Saurashtra's most important port, home to over 1000 boats and a thriving *dhow* (an hand-built Arab boat) industry. While the docks may provide for an intriguing, if smelly, stroll, Veraval is more important as a stepping stone to nearby Somnath, 5km away. Known for its once-magnificent temple, Somnath is a popular vacation spot for many Gujaratis. Old city streets, refreshingly free from the stench pervading Veraval's port, laze in the shadow of the towering *mandir* while peaceful ocean waves lap the shore.

🔢 ORIENTATION AND PRACTICAL INFORMATION. Veraval's main thoroughfare runs roughly northwest-southeast past the **bus stand** (tel. 21666), through the center of town marked by the **clock tower,** dead-ending at the port. At the Clock Tower, the left road heads northeast, past the GPO down the first street on the left, and forks just past the State Bank of India (no foreign exchange facilities). The fork's left branch leads to the **Veraval Railway Station** (tel. 20444 or 131; reservation office open M-Sa 8am-8pm, Su 8am-2pm). Fares listed are 2nd/1st class. To: **Ahmedabad** (*Girnar Exp.* 9945, 7:30pm, 10hr., Rs166/730); **Junagadh** (*Rajkot Exp.* 9837, 11:30am; *Somnath Mail* 9923, 5pm; *Girnar Exp.* 9945, 7:30pm, 2hr., Rs96/334); and **Rajkot** (*Rajkot Exp.* 9837, 11:30am, 5hr., Rs62/280). From the station, the road leads to another that bends around Veraval Harbor, past the Temple of Somnath to Somnath's **bus stand.** Buses go to: **Ahmedabad** (8, 11am, and 7:30pm; 10hr.; Rs89; deluxe 10pm, Rs107; **Diu** (7:30, 9:30am, and 4:30pm; 3hr.; Rs26); **Dwarka** (6:30am, noon, 2:30, and 3pm; 6hr.; Rs50); **Junagadh** (every hr. 5:30am-10:30pm, 2hr., Rs28); and **Rajkot** (every hr. 7:30am-10:30pm, 4hr., Rs49). From the clock tower, **local**

buses run from Veraval to Somnath and back (every 30min. 6am-11pm, Rs3-5). **Auto-rickshaws** make the same trip for Rs25. The **State Bank of Saurashtra**, Shubash Rd. (tel. 21266), past the clock tower and towards the port, changes US$, UK£, and traveler's checks (open M-F 11am-3pm, Sa 11am-1pm). The **police station** (tel. 20003) is to the right of the tower (open 24hr.). The **GPO** (tel. 21255) is open M-Sa 10am-6pm. **STD/ISD** booths are concentrated in the center of town (most open daily 10am-9pm). **Postal Code:** 362265. **Telephone Code:** 02876.

ACCOMMODATIONS AND FOOD. Hotels line the route between the bus stand and the railway station. Although staying in Veraval is convenient, the two hotels in Somnath are cheaper and far more peaceful, if slightly spartan. Most restaurants in Veraval lie between the bus stand and the clock tower, and *dhabas* dot the city. Somnath has many food stalls but no real restaurants. Though Veraval is a fishing town, pious Gujarati culture keeps seafood confined to a handful of hotels and Muslim restaurants—don't even *think* about meat in Somnath. **Hotel Kaveri,** Akar complex, 2nd fl. (tel. 20842 or 43842), is on the first side street to the left after you exit the bus station. The cleanest rooms in the city have TVs, phones, and 24-hour hot water. The hotel also has laundry service and 24-hour room service. (Check-out 11am. Singles Rs150, with balcony Rs225, with A/C Rs425; doubles Rs180/270/480; suites with swings Rs800-850. Extra person Rs50.) The **Mayuram Hotel** (tel. 20286), near the bus stand in Somnath, has large, spotless rooms. The bed covers grow on you, and mosquitoes are noticeably absent. Attached baths and noon check-out round out the pretty picture. Awaken to the sound of softly chanted hymns coming from the nearby temple. (Singles and doubles Rs200; triples Rs300; quads Rs400.) **Hotel Ajanta** (tel. 23202 or 23203), on the right as you exit the Veraval bus stand, has quiet, moderately clean rooms in a central location with laundry and 24-hour room service (check-out 11am; singles Rs100-150, with A/C Rs300; doubles Rs150-200/350; triples Rs200; quads Rs250; extra bed Rs50). **Jill Restaurant** (tel. 20713), halfway between the bus stand and the clock tower, has an A/C dining hall with tall, cushioned booths and a chef that's liberal with the *ghee* (veg. Punjabi, South Indian, Chinese, and Continental dishes Rs20-50; open daily 8am-11pm).

SIGHTS. Somnath is renowned throughout Gujarat for the **Temple of Somnath**, also known as **Prabhas Pratan Mandir**, one of India's 12 *jyotirlingas*. According to popular myth, the temple site was dedicated to *soma*, the plant of hallucinogenic properties which appears often in the *Vedas*, written between the 12th and 2nd centuries BC (see **Vedic Literature**, p. 82). The temple was built first of pure gold by Samraj the moon god, then of silver by Ravana the sun god, then of wood by Krishna, and finally of stone by the Pandava brother Bhima (of *Mahabharata* fame). Historians counter that the temple was built in the early 10th century AD and that it has always been made of stone. Staffed by hundreds of dancers and musicians, the temple was once so rich that its coffers were stuffed with gold and jewelry. The notorious Mahmud of Ghazni raided and destroyed the temple in the early 11th century, effectively starting a cycle of sacking and rebuilding that persisted until Aurangzeb's final plundering and restoration in 1706. Sardar Patel, the philanthropist who funded the temple's reconstruction in 1950, is commemorated with a statue outside the temple. The history of the temple is more interesting than the building itself; very little of the original structure remains. The stonework is quite elaborate in places, but the sea winds have worn down the carving on the ocean-side walls. (Open daily 6am-9:30pm; *puja* 7am, noon, and 7pm. No cameras allowed inside.) The **Prabhas Pratan Museum** holds the eclectic remains of the temple's past glories, including paintings, latticework, stone sculptures, and pottery (near the temple; open M-Sa 9am-noon and 3-6pm, closed 2nd and 4th Sa; Rs0.50).

JUNAGADH જૂનાગઢ

Less than 100km north of Diu, the lively town of Junagadh, also known as Junagarh, is refreshingly free of Western influence. From the 4th century BC until Emperor Ashoka's death, Junagadh was the capital of Gujarat under the Mauryas. Control of the town then passed through several hands before falling under Muslim rule, where it remained until Independence. Although its rulers wanted to unite Junagadh with Pakistan, the town's Hindu majority insisted on joining India. Situated at the base of Mount Girnar, Junagadh's wealth of temples, *havelis*, mosques, and vibrant bazaars makes it a fascinating place to visit at any time. The town hosts a wild, nine-day party during the **Shivaratri Festival** (Feb.-Mar.).

⊅ ORIENTATION AND PRACTICAL INFORMATION. Junagadh is a rather difficult city to navigate, but it's too small to really get lost in. Dhal Rd. runs east from the bus stand across the railroad tracks on its way to **Chittakhana Chowk,** the central bazaar, and eventually to Uperkot Fort.The **S.T. Bus Stand** (tel. 630303), on the west side of town, is just off **Dhal Road,** the main, roughly east-west thoroughfare. Buses go to: **Ahmedabad** (23 per day 5:30am-1am, 7hr., Rs74; deluxe 5 per day 4:30am-5:45pm, Rs1101); **Bhuj** (8 per day 5:45am-10pm, 6hr., Rs81); **Diu** (2:30, 2:45, and 3:30pm; 6hr.; Rs48); **Dwarka** (5:45, 7, 10am, and 4pm; 5hr.; Rs54); **Rajkot** (every 30min. 6:30am-1am, 2hr., Rs30/35); and **Veraval** (every hr. 4:30am-11:30pm, 2hr., Rs27). **Private bus companies** along Dhal Rd. run comfortable minibuses and buses to Mumbai and towns in Gujarat. **Station Road,** which intersects Dhal Rd. east of the bus stand, takes you north to **Junagadh Railway Station** (tel. 131). Fares listed are 2nd/1st class. Trains run to: **Ahmedabad** (*Somnath Mail* 9923, 7pm; *Girnar Exp.* 9925, 9:13pm, 9hr., Rs146/663); **Rajkot** (*Fast Passenger* 341, 6:15am; *Fast Passenger* 347, 9:45am, 3hr., Rs22; *Saurashtra Mail* 9837, 1:30pm, 2½hr., Rs33); and **Veraval** (*Fast Passenger* 342, 5am, 2½hr., Rs15; *Somnath Mail,* 9am; *Saurashtra Mail,* 2:20pm, 2hr., Rs30). **Auto-rickshaws** can get you around town (Rs20) or to Mt. Girnar (Rs35). **Local buses** run to Mt. Girnar (every hr. 6am-5pm, Rs3) from the local bus stand on MG Rd.; early morning buses are the most reliable. **Bikes** (Rs3 per hr., Rs25 per day) can be rented from several locations around Chittakhana Chowk.

At Chittakhana Chowk, **Mahatma Gandhi (MG) Road** branches south passing the **Government Hospital** (tel. 620652; open 24hr.), the **local bus stand,** the **GPO** (tel. 623701; open M-Sa 9:30am-5pm), the main **police station** (tel. 627001, emergency tel. 100), and the **Bank of Baroda** (tel. 654684; open M-F 11am-3pm) on its way to Kalwa Chowk, another market area. Roughly halfway between Chittakhana Chowk and Uperkot Fork, **Jhalorapa Road** branches south off Dhal Rd. through Diwan Chowk, near the **State Bank of India** (tel. 621094; open M-F 11am-3pm), which exchanges US$ and UK£. **Pharmacies** can be found in Kalwa and Chittakhana Chowk near the General Hospital. **Shree Medical Stores,** Dhal Rd. (tel. 631820), is just west of the railway crossing (open 24hr.). Many **STD/ISD** booths are sprinkled throughout the town (most open daily 8am-10pm). **Postal Code:** 362001. **Telephone Code:** 0285.

⌖⌕ ACCOMMODATIONS AND FOOD. Most hotels are in Kalwa Chowk and along Dhal Rd., west of Chittakhana Chowk, but a few reside near the S.T. Bus Stand and the railway station. Reserve well in advance during Shivaratri. The gracious and incredibly helpful staff at ⌖ **Hotel Relief,** Chittakhana Chowk (tel. 620280), has unofficially assumed the role of the town's tourist information center. Average-sized rooms are tastefully decorated and have attached baths. The hotel has 24-hour room service, travel services, and a decent restaurant. (Check-out 10am; extensions granted. Singles Rs100; doubles Rs200; either with A/C Rs500.) **Hotel Anand,** Dhal Rd. (tel. 630657), between the S.T. Bus Stand and Chittakhana Chowk, has dimly lit, well-kept rooms with attached baths and TVs in a somewhat noisy area (check-out 9am; singles Rs150, with A/C Rs500; doubles Rs250/600). **Hotel Somnath** (tel. 624645), near the railway station, is far from town but near the sights. It offers clean, well-furnished rooms with clean attached baths. (Check-out noon. Singles Rs100, with TV Rs200, with A/C Rs545; doubles Rs150/200/545. Extra bed Rs60, in A/C room Rs80.)

Although there are a number of food stalls and *dhabas* in Chittakhana and Kalwa Chowks, you'll find better food at the hotel restaurants in town. **Sagar Restaurant,** Riddhi Siddhi Complex, 1st fl. (tel. 623661), near Kalwa Chowk, serves the best food in town in its dimly lit A/C dining room (entrees Rs20-40; open daily 9am-3pm and 5-10:45pm). **Swati Restaurant,** Jayshree Rd., Kotecha Complex, 1st fl. (tel. 625296), is near Jayshree Cinema. Hindi pop reverb fills the air as friendly waiters serve spicy entrees (Rs20-50) in this ever-crowded veg. restaurant. (Open daily 9am-3pm and 5-10pm.) **Santoor Restaurant,** MG Rd. (tel. 625090), near Kalwa Chowk, is a popular A/C eatery. Its somewhat shabby exterior is redeemed by the colorful glass chandeliers inside. Indian veg. dishes (Rs12-45) are artfully presented. (Open daily 9:45am-3pm and 5-11pm.)

⚅ **SIGHTS.** The impressive **Uperkot Fort,** sitting stoutly atop a mini-plateau in the middle of the town, ranks among the best in the state. Built in 319 BC, it was ignored for 1300 years until its rediscovery in AD 976. Over the next 800 years, it was besieged a whopping 16 times; one unsuccessful siege lasted 12 years. A high stone *tripolia* gate marks the entrance to the fort and the start of the twisty cobblestone path that meanders to the **Jama Masjid,** built on top of a Hindu temple. Once an impressive edifice with 140 pillars supporting its high ceiling, the mosque has suffered from years of neglect. The fort also holds two *vavs* (step-wells): the **Adi Chadi Vav** has 170 steps descending into the dimness below, and the extraordinary **Navghan Kuva** has a unique 11th-century circular staircase that winds more than 50m down the well. (Fort open daily 7am-6:30pm. Rs1.) Near Diwan Chowk outside the fort is the standard **Durbar Hall Museum** (open Th-Tu 9am-12:30pm and 3:30-5:30pm; Rs3). The **Babupyana Caves,** south of the fort, and the **Khapra Kodia Caves,** north of the fort, are popular for spelunking.

On the road to Mt. Girnar is the **Baha-ud-din-Bhar Muqbara,** with its spiraling minarets, curved grand arches, and numerous domes. The mausoleum's complex design and opulent interior, including carved silver doors, make it unlike any other in Gujarat. Also on the way to Mt. Girnar is the granite boulder inscribed with **Ashokan edicts.** Dating from the 3rd century BC, these edicts teach moral lessons of *dharma*, tolerance, equality, love, harmony, and peace. The Sanskrit inscriptions, which refer to flooding in nearby areas, were added by later rulers.

Mount Girnar, 4km east of Junagadh, is an 1100m extinct volcano that has been sacred to several religions since 300 BC. Nearly 5000 steps wind through forests and sun-scorched stone outcroppings leading to the summit. Approximately halfway up the mountain, you'll come upon a cluster of intricately decorated Jain temples. The marble **Neminath Temple** is dedicated to the 22nd *tirthankara* who, according to legend, died on Mount Girnar. A black marble image of the ascetic sits amid finely carved pillars, domes, and arches. Another 2000 steps take you to the mountain's peak, where the small **Amba Mata Temple** and several other shrines offer a breathtaking view. Since a visit to the temple is said to guarantee a happy marriage, the summit sees many newlyweds. (Begin your hike before 7am to avoid the heat. Drink stalls line the ascent.)

NEAR JUNAGADH: SASAN GIR NATIONAL PARK સાસાણ ગીર

Sasan Gir, 65km from Junagadh, is the last stronghold of the **Asiatic lion.** The Indian variety, nearly 3m in length, can be distinguished from its African cousin by its bigger tail tassel, bushy elbow tufts, larger belly folds, and smaller mane. These big cats once roamed forests and grasslands stretching from Greece to Bengal, but by the turn of the 20th century, there were only 239 left on the planet. In 1900, the Nawab of Junagadh invited Lord Curzon, then Viceroy of India, to a lion hunt on his land, the only place outside of the African continent in which wild lions could still be found. The two met a barrage of criticism for further endangering the threatened species, and Lord Curzon cancelled the hunt, advising the Nawab to protect the lions. The forest became a wildlife sanctuary in 1969, and it now covers over 250 sq. km. The lion population, which today exceeds 300, is gradually increasing at a healthy rate. The park's forests and grasslands are also a sanctuary for peacocks, hyenas, panthers, and several varieties of deer.

The park is accessible by **train** (*Delwara Local* 352, 6:10am, 3hr., Rs15) and **bus** (every hr. 7am-1pm, 2hr., Rs32) from Junagadh. **Shared jeeps** are required to tour the park (Rs400 for up to 6 people; departs 7am and 3pm). Sasan Gir is open from September 16 until the monsoon hits. Jeep and entry fees total about Rs80, and the camera fee is Rs40. An average trip through the park takes about 45 minutes, and at least one lion sighting is probable, though you shouldn't be disappointed if all the beasts do is stare at you and lick their chops.

DWARKA દ્વારકા

Most Hindu legends are in agreement on the subject of Dwarka's holiness. Designated in the *Puranas* as one of the seven holy cities in which pilgrims can attain *moksha*, Dwarka is also associated with Vishnu in a number of legends. Krishna set up his capital here, on the westernmost point of the Kathiawar peninsula, after being forced to flee Mathura in Uttar Pradesh; Vishnu descended to Dwarka in the form of a fish to battle local demons; and the 9th-century saint Shankara established a monastery here, marking it as India's western *dham*. The few tourists who come here remark on the sense of peace inspired by the town's active temple, sea breezes, and mystical remoteness.

◪ ORIENTATION AND PRACTICAL INFORMATION. Dwarka is small enough to wander through on foot, but **auto-rickshaws** are plentiful (Rs10 to the railway station). The main road into the city bends right as it joins the road between the main gate into the **old city** and the **railway station** (tel. 34044 or 131; reservations office open daily 9am-noon and 3-5pm). Fares listed are 2nd/1st class. Trains run to: **Ahmedabad** (*Saurashtra Mail* 9006, noon, 10hr., Rs105); **Mumbai** (*Saurashtra Mail* 9006, noon, 20hr., Rs172/1163); and **Rajkot** (3 per day, 5-7hr., Rs61/470). Just before reaching the **main gate**, the road turns right, skirting a huge empty field, then bends left. After the bend is a set of three arches—the second gate into the old city—on the right. Going straight leads to a road that runs along the coast, and the main road bends left, passing the **main bus stand** (tel. 34204) and a small building that serves as the **GPO** (tel. 34529; open M-F 7:30am-12:30pm and 4-6pm, Sa 7:30am-12:30pm), and the **Telegraph Office** (tel. 34037; open M-Sa 8-11am and 2-6pm) on its way to Okha, the port for Bet Dwarka. **Intercity buses** run to: **Ahmedabad** (6 per day 6:15am-6:45pm, 10hr., Rs112; deluxe 8:45pm, Rs125); **Bhuj** (7pm, 9hr., Rs73); **Junagadh** (9:30, 11am, 1:30, and 2:15pm; 7hr.; Rs55); **Mandvi** (7:30am, 10½hr., Rs97); and **Rajkot** (14 per day 5am-9pm, 5hr., Rs64; deluxe 12:45am, Rs81); **Veraval** (6 per day 5:45am-6:45pm, 6hr., Rs58). **Local buses** shuttle to **Okha** (every 15min. 6:45am-10pm, 45min., Rs9). The old city is a maze of tiny streets centered around the Dwarkadish Temple, with the main **police station** (tel. 34523) next door. Dwarka Lighthouse sits on the western outskirts of the old city. The best hospital in town, **Navajyot Hospital** (tel. 34419), 400m toward the coast from the main gate, has a 24-hour **pharmacy** (open daily 9am-1pm and 4:30-8:30pm for consultations, 24hr. for emergencies). **STD/ISD** booths abound in the old city (most open daily 9am-1pm and 4-9pm). **Postal Code: 361335. Telephone Code: 02892.**

▣▢ ACCOMMODATIONS AND FOOD. Most lodgings are clean and well-maintained with attached baths. ▨ **Hotel Rajdhani,** Hospital Rd. (tel. 34178), is on the first road to the right off the main road from the bus stand to the temple. Plush rooms feature marble bed frames, color TVs, phones, and room service. (Check-out 3pm. Doubles Rs200, with A/C Rs450; triples Rs300/600. Extra bed Rs50.) **Hotel Meera** (tel. 34031), near the main gate into the old city, boasts spotless white-washed rooms and a familial staff (singles Rs80-150, with A/C Rs350; doubles Rs120-200/575). The **Meera Dining Hall** serves delicious bottomless *thalis* for Rs25 (open daily 11am-3pm and 7-11pm). **Radhika** (tel. 34754), a stone's throw from the bus stand, has rooms as nice as Meera's, adorned with pictures of local sights (check-out 24hr.; doubles Rs200, with A/C Rs450; triples Rs300/600). The **Toran Tourist Guest House** (tel. 34013), near the coast, offers a peaceful seaside location.

Run by Gujarat Tourism, it features big, well-kept rooms and a knowledgeable staff. Mosquito nets are provided. (Check-out 9am. Dorm beds Rs50; singles Rs200; doubles Rs300; triples Rs350. Aug.-Sept.: 50% discount.) **Guruprerna** (tel. 34512), on the way to the temple from the bus station, features an A/C garden restaurant as well as an outdoor fast-food joint offering cheap, tasty Punjabi and Chinese dishes (Rs15-40) and *lassis* (Rs6; open daily 7:30am-3pm and 5:30-11pm).

🧭 **SIGHTS.** Dwarka's principal attraction is the staggering **Dwarkadish Temple,** marking the center of town with its six-story, 50m-high main spire. While the spiky exterior stonework is a bit weathered, elaborate carvings of various incarnations of Vishnu are visible on the temple's inner walls. Sixty columns support the main structure, which houses a black marble Krishna image in a silver-plated chamber. Smaller shrines decorate the edges of the complex. (Temple open daily 7am-1pm and 5-9:30pm. Non-Hindus must sign a release form to enter.) The **Dwarka Lighthouse** offers spectacular views of the sunset over the Arabian Sea (open daily 4:30pm-sunset; Rs1). The long, clean **beach** nearby, which is rarely crowded (except Su), is great for wading and wandering past the small beach temples.

No pilgrimage to Dwarka is complete without a visit to the tiny island where Vishnu slayed the demon Shankasura. **Bet Dwarka,** at the tip of the peninsula, has a number of architecturally uninspired Krishna temples, where devotees come for *prasad* and *puja.* The main temple, which marks the spot of Krishna's death, has a central well that is said to bring up sweet-tasting water, although it apparently draws from the surrounding ocean. Dwarka's real appeal, however, is its eery quietude, broken only by the howling of dogs and the chanting of old women. The island is accessible by the port at **Okha,** an hour north of Dwarka. Rickety, overloaded, pastel-colored boats make the crossing (every 20min., 30min., Rs2).

KUTCH કચ્છ

One of the most isolated regions in India, Kutch (also spelled Kachch, Kuchch, or Kachchha) is bordered on the west and north by the Gulf of Kutch and the Arabian Sea and on the east by the Rann of Kutch, a marsh in the Thar desert which is home to pink flamingoes and the rare wild ass. The Sultans who ruled Gujarat made repeated attempts to cross into Kutch, but it remained independent, developing its own customs, laws, and a thriving maritime trade with Muscat, Malabar, and the African coast. Kutch was absorbed into the Indian Union in 1948. During the monsoon season, floods in the Rann of Kutch cut the region off from its neighbors Saurashtra (Gujarat) and Sindh (Pakistan), causing varying degrees of damage, but the Rann is scenic during the rest of the year. The dry northern part of Kutch is not arable, but the southern district of Banni used to be one of India's most fertile regions. Though drier today, Banni still produces cotton, castor-oil plants, sunflowers, and wheat. When climatic changes caused Kutchis to abandon agriculture, they turned to handicrafts—the villages of the region are famed for their mirrorwork, beaded embroidery, gold and silver jewelry, leather work (mostly in the villages of Dhordo, Khavda, and Hodko), woodcarving (in Dhordo), silver engraving (in Bhuj), and *bandhani* cloth (mainly in Mandvi and Anjar).

BHUJ ભુજ

Located in the center of the region of Kutch, Bhuj is used by most tourists as a base for exploring outlying villages, but the city offers far more than just a place to leave your pack—labyrinthine old-city bazaars, interesting museums, and eclectic architecture, including a decadent palace and an array of interesting temples. Bhuj was founded in the 16th century as the capital of Kutch by Rao Khengarji, a Jadeja Rajput, and it remained the region's center of economic activity until the establishment of the city of Gandhidam and the port of Kandla to the east. Today, as the limits of the new city expand, the old city preserves the peaceful way of life that keeps those willing to brave the bus ride coming back, time and time again.

TRANSPORTATION

Airport: Bhuj Airport (auto-rickshaw Rs40-50, taxi Rs150). **Indian Airlines,** Station Rd. (tel. 50204 or 21433). Open daily 10am-5:30pm. **Jet Airways,** Station Rd. (tel. 53671 or 53674). Open M-Sa 8am-7pm, Su 8am-4pm. **Gujarat Airways,** ST Rd. (tel. 52286). Open daily 9-11:30am and 3-7:30pm. Flights to: **Mumbai** (1 per day, 1½hr., US$100-125).

Trains: **Bhuj Railway Station** (tel. 20950), 1km north of town (auto-rickshaw Rs20). Reservations office (tel. 131 or 132). Open M-Sa 8am-8pm, Su 8am-2pm. To: **Gandhidam** (4 per day, 2hr., Rs11) for trains to Ahmedabad and Rajkot.

Buses: S.T. Bus Stand, ST Rd. (tel. 20002). To: **Ahmedabad** (15 per day 5am-11pm, 8hr., Rs96; deluxe 11am, 5:45, and 8:30pm, Rs144); **Barmer** (noon, 11hr., Rs146); **Dwarka** (6 and 10:45am, 11hr., Rs100); **Junagadh** (5 per day 5am-9:30pm, 9hr., Rs91); **Mandvi** (every 30min. 4:30am-10:30pm, 1½hr., Rs12/19); **Rajkot** (every 30min. 5am-9:30pm, 6hr., Rs65). **Private bus companies** line ST Rd. **Shree Shajanand Travels** (tel. 22437), west of the bus stand. Open daily 6am-9:30pm.

Local Transportation: Auto-rickshaws are unmetered (in town Rs5-10). **Taxis,** found opposite the bus stand, take you to villages around Bhuj (Rs3 per km).

ORIENTATION AND PRACTICAL INFORMATION

Bhuj's main **bus stand** is on **ST Road,** which runs roughly east-west along the southern edge of the old city. From **Mahadev Gate** at the west end of ST Rd., **Uplipar Road** runs north along the eastern edge of Hamirsar Tank past the Swaminarayan Temple and the walled complex that contains the Prag and Aina Mahals. **College Road** leads south from the complex past the Kutch Museum, the **police station,** and the Folk Art Museum. **Museum Road** wanders along the southern edge of the tank, bending north at **Sharad Bagh.** At the eastern end of ST Rd., **Waniawad Road** leads north to old city's **Shroff Bazaar.** From the northern edge of the old city, roads lead to the **railway station** and the **airport,** 6km north. **Station Road** runs north along the eastern side of the old city, and **Hospital Road** runs south from Station Rd.

Tourist Office: Tourist Information Office (tel. 20004), in Aina Mahal. Maps of Bhuj (Rs5) and Gujarat (Rs2), and books about Kutch. Open Su-F 9am-noon and 3-6pm.

Currency Exchange: Dena Bank, Hospital Rd. (tel. 20339), exchanges foreign currency and traveler's checks. Open M-F 11am-2:30pm. **State Bank of India,** Hospital Rd. (tel. 56100) does the same. Open M-F 10am-2pm.

Market: ST Rd. and **Shroff Bazaar** are the main market areas.

Library: Maharao Shree Vijay Rajji Public Library, south of Hamirsar Tank, allows tourists to check out books. Open Tu-Su 8am-noon and 4-8pm.

Pharmacy: Many on Hospital and Station Rd. Most open daily 8am-1pm and 2-9pm.

Hospital: Seth Gophandas Khetsey Hospital (tel. 22850), on the road to Gandhidam, is clean and modern with English-speaking doctors. Also has a 24hr. **pharmacy.**

Police: The main **police station** (tel. 53050), on the east side of College Rd., has English-speaking officers. To get permits for the sensitive border area north of Bhuj, go to the **District Superintendent of Police** (tel. 53593, ext. 132), east of College Rd.'s south end, down the road across from the Collector's Office. Bring 2 copies of your passport and visa. Open M-Sa 10:30am-2pm and 3-6:15pm, closed 2nd and 4th Sa. The office will give you forms to take to the Collector's office, College Rd (tel. 52347). Open M-Sa 10:30am-2pm and 2:30-6:10pm, closed 2nd and 4th Sa.

Post Office: GPO (tel. 22952), off Station Rd. south of ST Rd. Open M-Sa 10am-5:45pm. Small branch on Langa Rd., opposite the City Guest House (tel. 22650). Open M-Sa 9am-5pm. **Postal Code:** 370001.

Telephones: Central Telegraph Office, Station Rd., Krishna Chambers, 2nd fl. (tel. 20250), has **STD/ISD,** fax, and telex services. Open M-Sa 7am-10pm, Su 8am-4pm.

PHONE CODE	02832

ACCOMMODATIONS

City Guest House, Langa St. (tel. 21067), in the main market. Favored among back-packers, it features small, spotless rooms livened up by bright linens. Indoor courtyard and 24hr. *chai* service promote a social atmosphere. Check-out 24hr. Singles Rs60, with bath Rs130-170; doubles Rs130/130-170.

Hotel Annapurna, Bhid Pol (tel. 20831). Simple rooms with balconies allow you to observe the city's commotion from a distance. Check-out 24hr. Singles Rs30, with bath Rs90; doubles Rs70/150. Extra bed Rs30.

Hotel Jantaghar, ST Rd. (tel. 54456; fax 51428). Austere rooms are quite clean. A/C dining hall serves Gujarati *thalis* (Rs40). Check-out 5pm. Dorm beds Rs30; singles Rs50, with bath Rs75; doubles Rs75/125; triples Rs100/175; quads Rs125/225.

Hotel Lake View (tel. 53422), south of Hamirsar Tank. This luxury hotel far from the noisy ST Rd. has rooms with TVs, spotless baths, and cushioned wooden furniture. Slightly murky swimming pool is open to non-guests (Rs10 for 45min., guests free). Check-out noon. Singles Rs350, deluxe Rs600, with A/C Rs750; doubles Rs400/700/850.

FOOD

Annapurna Restaurant, Bhid Pol, in Hotel Annapurna. Popular *thali* house serves spicy, mouth-watering dishes on a pay-for-what-you-eat basis. Veg. dishes (Rs5), sweets (Rs6), rice (Rs5), and *chapatis* (Rs1) are skillfully prepared. Open M-Sa 10:30am-3:30pm and 7-11:30pm, Su 10:30am-3:30pm.

Hotel Noorani Restaurant, near the vegetable market as you walk through the main bazaar from Aina Mahal. Indulge in cheap, fresh non-veg. dishes. Chicken *tandoori* (half-order Rs60), mutton *biryani* (Rs24). Open daily 9am-3:30pm and 6:30-10pm.

Hotel Anam Dining Hall, ST Rd., near the intersection with Station Rd. A very popular *thali* joint with black-and-white wildlife pictures all over the walls. Gujarati *thalis* Rs50. Open daily 11am-3pm and 7-10pm.

Resoi Restaurant, ST Rd., in Hotel Abha. A/C dining with Punjabi, Chinese, or Continental (Rs35-55), or a bottomless *thali* (Rs60). Open daily 11am-3pm and 7-10pm.

SIGHTS

AINA MAHAL (OLD PALACE). The decadent palace of Maharao Lakhad, also known as Lakhpatji, renowned for his celebration of the arts which now distinguishes the region of Kutch, is a small, fortified structure in the old city. One room displays a raised platform surrounded by a pool of water and spurting fountains on which the maharao would sit as musicians entertained him. The maharao's *chakri* (slippers) sit on the platform; they were designed to produce an olfactory warning of his proximity—with each step a flower at the toe of the slippers opens to release scented powder. The maharao's bedroom, inside the hall of mirrors, has gone virtually untouched since his death. Inside the Aina Mahal, the beautifully designed **Maharao Madansinji Museum** is filled with artifacts and memorabilia from his reign. *(Open Su-F 9am-noon and 3-6pm. Rs5. Photography prohibited.)*

PRAG MAHAL (NEW PALACE). This beautiful red sandstone palace built in 1816 is now filled with hunting trophies. Marble stairs ascend to the main hall beneath curving arches and sandstone columns. The main hall is a macabre monument to death and a is taxidermist's nightmare—the floor is covered with decaying heads of lions, tigers, leopards, sambar, deer, and wild cows. A spiral staircase leads to the top of the bell tower, where fantastic views await. *(Open M-Sa 9-11:45am and 3-5:45pm. Rs5; camera fee Rs15, video fee Rs50.)*

SHARAD BAGH MUSEUM. This beautifully kept museum at the southwestern corner of Hamirsar Tank was the residence of the last Maharao of Kutch until his death in 1991. Near the entrance, a small greenhouse guarded by two stone lions sits beside a small bamboo forest. The museum is much as the maharao left it, with his TV and VCR set among his hunting trophies and Chinese vases. *(Tel. 20878. Open Sa-Th 9am-noon and 3-6pm. Rs5; camera fee Rs10, video fee Rs50.)*

OTHER MUSEUMS. Bhuj's museums are an excellent place to learn about Kutch culture before heading out to the villages. The **Kutch Museum,** the oldest in the state, has excellent anthropological and archaeological exhibits on the region *(College Rd.; tel. 20541; open Th-Tu 9am-noon and 2:45-5:45pm, closed 2nd and 4th Sa; Rs0.50, camera fee Rs2 per shot).* The **Bharatiya Sanskriti Darshan** boasts a small collection of local textiles, embroideries, paintings, and bead work, supplemented by a library of related sources. The highlight of the museum is its reproduction of Rabari *bhungas* (huts) with their delicately decorated inner walls. *(Mandvi Rd., at the south end of College Rd. Tel. 21518. Open M-Sa 9am-noon and 3-6pm. Rs5; camera fee Rs30.)*

OTHER SIGHTS. On the way to Harmisar Tank from the Darbargadh Complex lies the **Swaminarayan Temple.** This technicolor, early 19th-century temple actually consists of two single-sex temples and a third for men and women. *(Open daily 7-11am and 4-8pm.)* South of Hamirsar Tank, in the midst of a sandy, deserted plain, the eerie **Memorial Chattris** commemorate some of the previous maharaos of Kutch and their wives who committed *sati.* The red sandstone memorial to Maharao Shri Lalehpatjo (1710-1761) and his 15 wives is the largest of the bunch.

VILLAGE TOURS

Many tourists use Bhuj primarily as a base from which to explore the nearby villages. While these tours offer a glimpse of village life and plentiful opportunities for the purchase of local handicrafts, the experience has been soured a bit; many villages have responded to the tourist trade with aggressive merchandising and exorbitant prices. Tours can be made by **taxi** (Rs750-800 for up to 4 people for a full day tour to several villages) or, more slowly, by **bus** from Bhuj. Contact the tourist office for more information on arranging village tours.

The village of **Sumrasar,** just outside of Bhuj, is home to **Kala Raksha** (tel. 77238), a research institute and women artists' cooperative focused on the "preservation of traditional arts." Founded in 1993, the center has a large collection of embroidered textiles from around Kutch. A small store sells local work that has been adapted to a Western aesthetic. Profits go directly to the artisans. For information on research opportunities and accommodations at Kala Raksha, contact Judy Frater, Project Coordinator (tel. 53697; fax 55500; email judyf@ad1.vsnl.net.in). From Bhuj, take a rickshaw (Rs100) or a bus (to nearby Hajipar, Rs6).

Kera, 22km south of Bhuj, is home to a Shiva temple thought to have been built in the 10th century (buses every hr. 6am-9pm, 45min., Rs5). Farther south is the Rabari village of **Tundawadh** (best reached by car), famed for its exquisite embroideries. **Anjar,** 40km southeast of Bhuj, is a mecca for handicrafts enthusiasts, with weapons, nut-crackers, jewelry, and textiles (buses every 30min. 5am-11pm, 2hr., Rs16-19). For block printing aplenty, head to **Dhamandka,** east of Bhuj (buses every hr. 6am-10pm, 1½hr., Rs11). The village of **Khavda** specializes in pottery (bus 9am, 2hr., Rs15), and **Bhirendiara** is a known for its embroidery, weaving, and leather work (buses 9am, noon, and 3pm; 1hr.; Rs10). **Zura,** home of the copper bell, and **Nirona,** specializing in lacquer work, are accessible by the same bus (8am, Rs8-10).

Those who've had their fill of handicrafts can head 60km northwest of Bhuj to the remote **Than Monastery** (buses 8am and 5pm, 2hr., Rs15). The ruins of **Dholavira,** one of the largest sites uncovered in the Indus Valley, dates to around 2500 BC. The vast site is assessable from Rapar (buses from Bhuj 6 and 8am, 4½hr., Rs25).

MANDVI માંડવી

Once an important port city, Mandvi was the center of trade between the Middle East and India. The Arab and European traders who settled here in the 18th century left behind grand mansions in the winding lanes of the old city and a dwindling boat-building industry. Pushcarts and auto-rickshaws seem to be propelled by the breeze, and hand-built wooden *dhows* lean lazily against the docks, beached by the tide. Shop-owners rest quietly on the steps of medieval buildings while blacksmiths and welders send dust and sparks into the salty evening air.

▨ ORIENTATION AND PRACTICAL INFORMATION. The unnamed **bridge** over the salt flats leads directly to **New Station Road**, which runs north-south along the western edge of the estuary. A right turn from **Mandvi Gate** at the end of the bridge takes you along the northern city wall to the **GPO**, 1km away (tel. 20266; open M-F 10am-6pm, Sa 10am-1pm). Straight ahead is the **Shree Gokul Hospital** (tel. 20361), a very clean, modern facility with an English-speaking staff (open M-F 9am-1:30pm and 4-6:30pm for consultations, 24hr. for emergencies). There are many **pharmacies** near the hospital (open M-Sa 9am-9pm). A left takes you down New Station Rd. past the main **police station** (tel. 20008; open 24hr.), opposite **Sadaya Gate**, which opens onto the salt flat and the **S.T. Bus Stand** (tel. 20004). Buses travel to: **Ahmedabad** (6:45, 8:45am, 5, and 7:15pm; 12hr.; Rs98); **Bhuj** (every 30min. 6:15am-8:45pm, 1½hr., Rs19); **Dwarka** (9:30am, 11hr., Rs100); **Junagadh** (7:15am, 11hr., Rs85); and **Rajkot** (6:15, 8am, 2, and 8:45pm; 7hr.; Rs75). The road then curves west, joining **Bandar Road,** which leads past the **State Bank of India** (tel. 20031; foreign exchange open M-F 11am-3pm, Sa 11am-1pm) to the port at the southern end of the city. All roads to the right lead into the **old city.** Bandar Rd. runs north behind the petrol station, past several sawmills, to the southern end of **Bhid Chowk,** the central market area. **Postal Code:** 370465. **Telephone Code:** 02834.

▨▨ ACCOMMODATIONS AND FOOD. ▨ **Vijay Vilas Palace** (tel. 20043), 9km west of town, but reserve ahead. And—it's not exactly budget. Bare but regal rooms pale in comparison to those of the nearby palace, but they offer some solitude. (Singles Rs500-600; doubles Rs700-800.) The sweet proprietor serves a delicious veg. *thali* for dinner (order in advance; Rs70). He can also make arrangements for **camping** on the maharaja's private beach (Rs200 per person). **Sahara Guest House,** Bhid Chowk (tel. 20272), south of the market, is isolated from the noise of hawkers and sawmills. The beds are soft, the rooms are bright, and the attached baths are spotless. (Check-out noon. Singles Rs125; doubles Rs200.) More expensive lodgings are available at the maharaja's guest house. Hundreds of stalls in Bhid Chowk and along New Station Rd. serve snacks that defy the imagination. **Zorba the Buddha,** in the market, dishes out unlimited *thalis* (lunch Rs40, dinner Rs20) to a constant stream of locals (open daily 11:30am-2:30pm and 7:30-9:30pm). **Hotel Krishna,** Bhid Chowk, has excellent veg. food served by a friendly staff (entrees Rs25-40, *thalis* Rs35-45; open daily 11:30am-4pm and 5-10:30pm).

▨ SIGHTS. Mandvi is blessed with many beautiful haunts—the old city walls, the port with its wooden ships perched on the salt flats, the canyon-like streets with stone mansions, and the temples and mosques that crowd the eastern side of the salt flats. But the **Vijay Vilas Palace,** 9km west of town, is Mandvi's biggest draw. A domed, latticed mansion set on 692 acres, the palace was built in 1927 as a summer home for the maharao of Kutch. Spotless marble floors, walls delicately inlaid with floral patterns, and decadently gorgeous carved rosewood and teak furniture decorate the inside. From the third floor, a rusting spiral staircase leads to a domed terrace with a view of the Arabian Sea and the coconut trees and windmills of the flat, green Kutch. Perhaps the highlight of the palace, though, is its private **beach,** 1km away. The nearly 2km stretch of sand is litter-free and blissfully unpopulated. Nearby are the royal **cenotaphs** and **sunset pavilion.** (Past the GPO. Open daily 9am-1pm and 2-6pm. Rs5; camera fee Rs30, video fee Rs200. Vehicle charges: bike Rs2, scooter Rs4, others Rs6-10.)

MADHYA PRADESH
मध्य प्रदेश

True to its name, Madhya Pradesh ("Middle State") stretches across the belly of the country. Although covering a larger area than any other state, Madhya Pradesh, due to an arid and inhospitable climate, has a population of fewer than 80 million (less than 10% of the country's total population). Besides the heavily-populated and very arable Narmada River Valley, scrubby hills and ravines dominate the topography of the densely forested state, providing a home for *dacoits* (bandits), tigers, and Gond and Bhil tribals alike. For years, this terrain has sheltered natural and historical treasures that might otherwise have disappeared. The forests conceal the ruined cities of Mandu and Orchha and the erotic carvings of the infamous temples at Khajuraho.

Historical remains in Madhya Pradesh date back to the 3rd century BC, when the Emperor Ashoka founded Sanchi as a religious center. A succession of Buddhist and Hindu dynasties gave way to Muslim marauders from the north, each reinventing the land. The Mughal emperors eventually lost control of the region to the Marathas, whose leading families ruled until Independence. Today, although 93% of the state's population is Hindu and its politics are dominated by the BJP, the landscape of Madhya Pradesh—from commercial centers to Buddhist pilgrimage sites to national parks—preserves the many aspects of its rich past.

HIGHLIGHTS OF MADHYA PRADESH

■ Madhya Pradesh has India's largest tiger population, and **Kanha National Park** (p. 377), of *Jungle Book* fame, is the best place to see them.
■ The northern village of **Khajuraho** (p. 379) is famous for its exquisite (and highly explicit) erotic sculpture.
■ The ruins of the town of **Mandu** (p. 372) open a window onto the Muslim Malwa culture of the 14th century.
■ The fort in **Gwalior** (p. 392) is one of the most impressive in all of India.

BHOPAL भोपाल

With 1.2 million inhabitants, a thriving arts community, and a lively Muslim bazaar quarter, the state capital of Bhopal serves up a rich slice of North Indian culture. In the first half of the 18th century, Dost Mohammed founded modern Bhopal, laying its foundations on the site of an 11th-century city established by Raja Bhoja. A sequence of women rulers who embarked on a program of civic improvements during the 19th century has left the city interspersed not only with lakes and parks but also punctuated with the minarets of massive mosques. Bhopal, a good staging point for visits to the nearby Buddhist ruins at Sanchi and other sights in the state, is also a pleasant city in its own right. Mention Bhopal today, though, and many pale, remembering the city as the site of the worst industrial accident in history. In the middle of the night on December 2, 1984, a cloud of lethal methylisocyanate gas leaked from the Union Carbide fertilizer factory in the north of the city. Two thousand people died, and thousands more were crippled for life. The plant has long since closed, and though the effects of the tragedy continue to be felt, Bhopal moves forward, justly proud of its beautiful sights and cool lakeside breezes.

TRANSPORTATION

Airport: Agra Rd. (tel. 521789), 12km from city center (taxis Rs100-150, rickshaws Rs80-100). **Indian Airlines** (tel. 770480), next door to the Gangotri Building in TT Nagar, 100m on the left past the Rang Mahal cinema. Open M-Sa 10am-1pm and 2-5pm. To: **Delhi** (M, Tu, Th, and Sa 12:55pm, 1-2hr., US$105) via **Gwalior** (45min., US$70); **Mumbai** (6:20pm, 2hr., US$115) via **Indore** (30min., US$50).

Trains: The **railway station** (tel. 540170), down the street that leads off the bend in Hamidia Rd., 1km east of the bus station. Reservation office outside platform #1, on the far right as you face the station. Open M-Sa 8am-8pm, Su 8am-2pm. Fares listed are for 2nd/1st class. To: **Agra** (*Shatabdi Exp.* 2001, 2:30pm, 6hr., Rs640/1325; *Goa Exp.* 2779, 7:15pm, 9hr., Rs120); **Delhi** (*Shatabdi Exp.* 2001, 2:30pm, 7½hr., Rs850/Rs1800); **Gwalior** (*Shatabdi Exp.* 2001, 2:30pm, 4½hr., Rs700/Rs1300); **Hyderabad** (*Dakshin Exp.* 7022, 9am, 24hr., Rs300; *Andhra Exp.* 2723, 3:40pm, 20hr., Rs300); **Indore** (*Narmada Exp.* 8234, 5:40am, 6hr., Rs90/305); **Jabalpur** (*Narmada Exp.* 8233, 10:40pm, 7hr., Rs79/388); **Jalgaon** (*Pushpak Exp.* 2134, 5:40am, 3½hr., R95); **Jhansi** (*Shatabdi Exp.* 2001, 10:40pm, 3hr., Rs67); **Mumbai** (*Pushpak Exp.* 2134, 5:40am, 15½hr., Rs223/669).

Buses: The **Nadra Bus Stand,** Hamidia Rd. (tel. 540841), west of the train station, 1km down on the right. Frequent departures for **Indore** (every 10min. 6am-6:30pm, 5hr., Rs58); **Sanchi** (every hr. 6am-6pm, 1½hr., Rs14); and other cities around the state. For longer distances, private operators nearby offer more luxurious vehicles.

Local Transportation: Metered **auto-rickshaws** will take you anywhere, including the airport (Rs80-100), but **minibuses** will whisk you almost as far for much less (Rs2 a pop). Minibus #9 goes from the railway station to TT Nagar; #7 and 11 go by Sultania Rd.

ORIENTATION AND PRACTICAL INFORMATION

The huge **Upper Lake** and smaller **Lower Lake** separate Old Bhopal in the northwest from the **New Town** in the southeast. **Hamidia Road** runs near the Taj-ul-Masjid (the city's largest mosque) on the western fringes of the old town, past the bus stand to the railway station in the east. There, amid many cheap hotels and restaurants, it turns right and runs south toward the new town and government center. The MPTDC, Indian Airlines office, and the State Bank with foreign exchange facilities (a rarity) reside in **TT Nagar,** one of the many neighborhoods in the sprawling area.

Tourist Office: MPTDC main office, 4th fl., Gangotri Building, TT Nagar, New Town (tel. 774340), just past the Rang Mahal cinema. Staff can reserve rooms at all MPTDC hotels in the state. Open M-Sa 10am-5pm. Other branches are located in the airport and the railway station. Open M-Su 7am-8pm.

Currency Exchange: State Bank of India, Main Branch, Parcharad Building, New Market Rd., TT Nagar (tel. 551804 or 556299). Foreign exchange upstairs. Open M-F 10:30am-2:30pm, Su 10:30am-noon.

Luggage Storage: In the railway station. Open 24hr. Rs5 per piece.

Market: The wholesale **fruit and vegetable market** stretches to the left off Hamidia Rd. and into the bazaars as you go from the railway to the bus stations. Open 4am-late. **New Market,** directly behind it, is a lively market area with clothes and just about anything else you can imagine.

Bookstore: Books World, 33 Bhadbhada Rd., TT Nagar (tel. 554061), stands out for its quirky selection and jumbled shelving system. Open daily 10:30am-9pm. Numerous other bookstores with more organized shelving systems are located on the same street.

Hospital: Hamidia Hospital, Sultania Rd. (tel. 540222), near Taj-ul-Masjid, also houses a **24hr. pharmacy.**

Police: Sultania Rd., Jehangirabad (tel. 555911). **Emergency:** tel. 100.

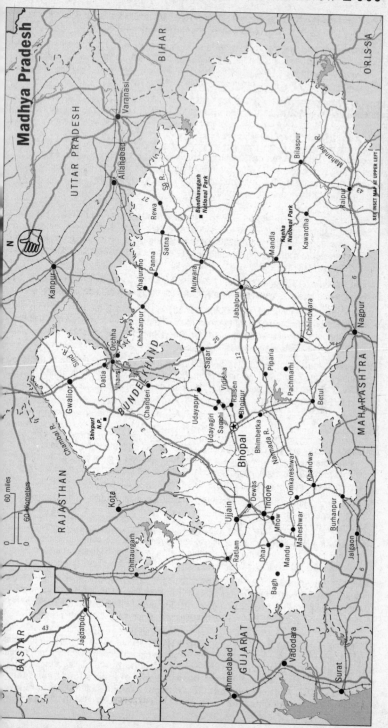

Madhya Pradesh

Post Office: GPO, Sultania Rd., near Taj-ul-Masjid. For unreliable *Poste Restante* ask at enquiry counter #3. Open M-Sa 10am-7pm. **Postal Code:** 462001.

Internet Access: Compquest Consultants, 36 Bhadbhada Rd., 1st fl., New Market, TT Nagan (tel. 234440). Look for the Thunderball pool sign and go up the stairs to this pool parlor/cybercafe. Given the uncertainty of their modem connections, calling ahead is probably a good idea. Rs60 per hr. Open daily 10am-11pm.

PHONE CODE	0755

ACCOMMODATIONS

Hotels in Bhopal cater mainly to a largely male clientele of business travelers, thus leaving few real cheapies. To add insult to injury, they all levy taxes and service charges of up to 20%. This does mean, though, that luxuries like TVs, telephones, and attached bathrooms are pretty standard.

Hotel Taj, 52 Hamidia Rd. (tel. 536261), across from the Hotel Ranjit, toward the bus station. Though rates run up to Rs1200, even guests in the cheap rooms enjoy good service and the attention of the bellboys, bearers, and cleaners. The atrium design insulates guests from the Hamidia hullabaloo. Check-out 24hr. Singles Rs200; doubles Rs350. Visa, MC, AmEx, DC.

Hotel Gulshan, 3 Hamidia Rd. (tel. 73506), in the alleyway next to Hotel Ranjit. It's cheap but it lacks the usual perks (telephone, TV). Singles Rs55, with bath Rs110.

Hotel Ranjit, 3 Hamidia Rd. (tel. 533511 or 535211), between the bus and train stations, on the right 200m before the road turns. The diminutive rooms share a building with Bhopal's busiest restaurant and bar. Check-out 24hr. Singles Rs150; doubles Rs200. Reservations are a necessity.

Hotel Meghdoot, Hamidia Rd. (tel. 534093), on the leg of the street south of the train station, on the right 200m before the turn. One of the cheapest deals in Bhopal, it has all the standard facilities but in a noisy, betel-stained atmosphere. Check-out 24hr. Singles Rs100 (without phone, TV); doubles Rs140.

FOOD

Manohar Dairy and Restaurant, 6 Hamidia Rd., across from the Hotel Taj. Good, cheap South Indian fare. Lively evening scene, fast turnover, and a great menu. Choose from *shami dosa* (Rs24), *dami challa samosa* (Rs12), fresh juices (Rs12-20), pizza (Rs30-40), shakes, and a wide variety of desserts (Rs4-30). Open daily 6am-midnight.

Hotel Gaurav, Hamidia Rd., near Meghdoot. The all-veg. menu features many *paneer* specialties in a pleasant decor complete with French doors and Indian miniature paintings. Try the *palak paneer* (Rs28). Open daily 7am-11pm.

Indian Coffee House, Hamidia Rd., across from Hotel Ranjit. The unruffled waiters in ruffled headgear serve delightful South Indian snacks to delighted guests. Special *dosa* or *utthapam* (Rs16). Delicious sugarless coffee (Rs5). Open daily 7am-10pm.

Ranjit, 3 Hamidia Rd., inside Hotel Ranjit. Bhopal's most popular dinner joint features many dimly lit levels of bar and restaurant. Large portions of Indian chicken or mutton (Rs60), veg. fare (Rs14-70), *kaju* curry (Rs55), and Chinese dishes (Rs30-50). Also serves alcohol (beer Rs63-72). Take-out available. Open daily 11:30am-11pm.

ENTERTAINMENT AND SIGHTS

BHARAT BHAVAN. A cultural center producing exhibitions of theater, music, poetry, and the fine arts, the Bharat Bhavan is one of India's finest museums. Architect Charles Correa crafted it into a charming public space with multi-layered courtyards overlooking the scenic Upper Lake. The three oddly shaped and

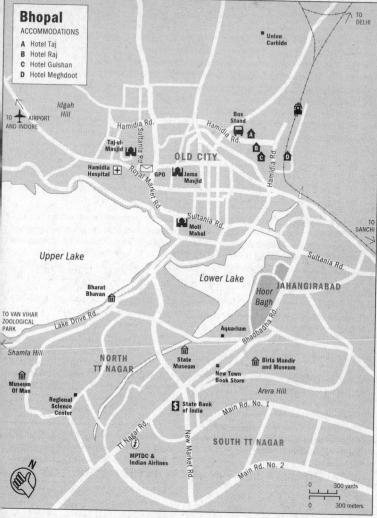

more oddly decorated protuberances are skylights that illuminate subterranean galleries featuring modern tribal and non-tribal art. A repertory company performs throughout the year. Past seasons have featured works by Jean-Paul Sartre and Samuel Beckett (*Gouda la Dekhat Han*, a Chattisgarhi version of *Waiting for Godot*, premiered in 1997). The Bhavan also hosts classical music concerts and poetry readings; check at the ticket office for schedules. A library and cafe (featuring "French Tries") complete this culture vulture's oasis. (*Upper Lake Rd., in the new town. Auto-rickshaw from downtown Rs40. Open daily 1-7pm; Feb. 1-Oct. 31 Tu-Su 2-8pm. Rs2.*)

OLD TOWN. Bhopal's status as an independent, Muslim-ruled princely state until 1952 endowed the city with a strong Muslim character and a wealth of mosques. The old Muslim bazaar quarter, or **Chowk,** wedged in the crook of a turn in Hamidia Rd., has the strongest Islamic flavor. Most of the area's old buildings have disappeared, but skull-capped men returning from pilgrimages to Mecca and women in *chadors* continue Bhopal's Muslim traditions.

The **Taj-ul-Masjid,** Bhopal's biggest mosque, is a spectacular illustration of Bhopal's Islamic tradition. The plans of the original builder, Victorian Nawab Shajehar Begum, were so grandiose that they have not been completed to this day. The 18-story minarets, the vast courtyard, the three huge domes over the prayer hall filled with Qur'anic students, and the river nearby combine together to create a grand impression. Don't be fooled by the huge staircase on Sultania Rd.—the mosque can only be approached from Royal Market Rd. *(Open dawn-dusk. Free.)*

The **Jama Masjid,** built by Kudsia Begum in 1837, displays impressive gold-spiked minarets. The **Moti Mahal,** constructed in 1860 by Kudsia Begum's daughter Sikander Jehan continues the Mughal tradition of small-scale, elegant, more "personal" mosques. Although less opulent than its big city counterparts, this mosque imitates many features (including striped domes) of the Jama Masjid in Delhi.

TRIBAL HABITAT (MUSEUM OF MAN). The Tribal Habitat reconstructs the dwellings of various indigenous Indian tribes, attempting to provide a glimpse of actual tribal life. The open-air exhibition matches the natural surroundings of the tribal villages. Boats can be rented along Lake Drive Rd. *(Shamla Hills, close to Bharat Bhavan. 1km auto-rickshaw ride to exhibition area. Open Tu-Su 10am-6pm. Free.)*

OTHER MUSEUMS. The **Regional Science Center** is a science museum boasting nearly 300 participatory exhibits in the "Invention" and "Fun in Science" galleries and Planetarium *(Shamla Hill; open Tu-Su 10:30am-6:30pm; Rs2)*. The **government archaeological museum** has a small collection including several noteworthy sculptures collected from various parts of Madhya Pradesh, tribal art, and paintings from the Bagh Caves near Mandu *(Banganga Rd.; open Tu-Su 10am-5pm.; free)*. The **Birla Museum** features a collection of 9th- and 10th-century sculptures from the Raisen, Sehore, Mond Saur, and Shahdol districts of M.P. *(Arera Hill; open Tu-Su 10am-5pm; Rs3.)* Next door, the **Birla Temple** boasts another scenic view of the city, especially at night *(open dawn to dusk; free).*

SANCHI सांची

In the 3rd century BC, the emperor Ashoka founded the Buddhist retreat at Sanchi as a haven for meditation, and 22 centuries have still not undermined his purpose. Sanchi only re-entered the limelight when a British officer, roaming India in search of a civilizing mission, stumbled across its ruins in 1818. The huge, white *stupas*, with later additions of exquisite sculpture, were named a UNESCO World Heritage site in 1989. Despite increased visibility, Sanchi remains a tiny village, rewarding visitors with a near complete compendium of Buddhist architectural history.

🛈 ORIENTATION AND PRACTICAL INFORMATION

One road leads from the **railway station,** past the few budget hotels and the **police station,** and up a hill to the **main gate** of the ruins. The road to Bhopal crosses this street at a right angle, continuing on to Vidisha, 10km to the northeast. The **small market** and **bus stand** occupy the quadrant on the station side of the main road and the Bhopal side of the cross road. **Buses** leave for Bhopal (at least every hr. 6am-6pm, 1½hr., Rs14), but some take the slow route through Raisen. Although Sanchi sits on the main line from Bhopal to Delhi, express **trains** only stop here for 1st class or A/C passengers who have traveled at least 161km or 2nd class passengers in groups of 10 who have racked up 400km. The Bhopal station masters seem more officious in this matter than those at Sanchi, so although you may have trouble getting here by train (from Bhopal: *Punjab Mail* 1038, 4:30pm; 1457, 2:25pm, 1hr.), you should be able to snag a seat on the way back (*Dadar Exp.* 1457, 3:15pm, Rs16). If you're coming from Agra (Rs104), Delhi (Rs135), Gwalior (Rs82), Itarsi (Rs41), or Mumbai (Rs161), then you can invoke the 161km clause if you have the extra cash to pay for 1st class. Alternatively, you can get on or off the train at Vidisha (*Punjab Mail* 2138, 3:40pm, 1hr., Rs16) and take the bus to Sanchi (every 10 min. 6am-10pm). There's an **STD/ISD** booth at the bus stand. **Telephone Code:** 07482.

ACCOMMODATIONS AND FOOD

Though many visitors see the sights in a couple of hours, accommodations are plentiful—most convenient are the **railway retiring rooms,** complete with dressing room, shower-less bathroom, and mosquito nets (doubles Rs100-150). The **Sri Lanka Mahabodhi Society Guest House** (tel. 62739), on the left just outside the station, has a range of rooms, though the Sri Lankan pilgrims for whom the guest house was built have first priority. The **Tourist Cafeteria** (tel. 62743), just before the museum, has bright, airy, spotless rooms (singles Rs200; doubles Rs290; Rs50 for use of cooler). The cafeteria serves the standard MPTDC fare (entrees Rs12-90, *channa masala* Rs25, *chicken murgh masala* Rs45; open daily 7am-10pm). Near the railway station, the **Pathak** and **Rohit** restaurants serve basic Indian fare.

SIGHTS

THE GREAT STUPA

Even though the Enlightened One never visited Sanchi (as far as is known), the complex of temples and monasteries here chronicles the entire ancient history of Indian Buddhism. Mauryan Emperor Ashoka himself erected a pillar at the Great Stupa, and sculptures dating from the end of the Buddhist period resemble deities from the Hindu pantheon. Surprisingly, even though Sanchi was an active Buddhist site for over 1000 years, only a few scattered references to Sanchi have been identified in the vast corpus of Buddhist literature. Thus, archaeology provides the only hints about the history behind the hilltop ruins here. When the ruins were first unearthed, archaeologists were less than delicate in their rush to unlock the site's secrets; they nearly destroyed the Great Stupa in their search for valuable artifacts before discovering that there was no treasure inside—the *stupa* was solid throughout. It was later restored, and today, along with its amazingly well-preserved gateways, the Great Stupa reigns over the rest of the crumbling edifices surrounding it on the hill. The Great Stupa is open daily from dawn to dusk.

In the first century BC, the Satavahanas tacked on Sanchi's richest addition: the four monumental gateways facing the cardinal directions. Archaeologists attribute the intricate sculpture to ivory carvers accustomed to making maximum use of minimum surface; the theory is borne out by a Pali inscription on the south gate. Since all the sculpture, except the four **seated Buddhas** inside each gate, dates from the Theravada period, no direct depictions of the Buddha appear on the gates. He is referred to only obliquely, with symbols such as the lotus flowers (for his birth), the pipal tree (for his enlightenment), and the wheel (for his sermons). Figures commonly depicted include six *manushis*—Buddha's predecessors who appear as *stupas* or trees, each of a different species. *Jatakas* (tales from the Buddha's previous lives) such as the **Chhadanta Jataka,** in which the Buddha, as an elephant, helps a hunter saw off his tusks, and stories from the subsequent history of Buddhism, particularly those detailing the distribution of the Buddha's relics, are also illustrated on the pillars of the temples.

SOUTH GATEWAY. The south gate was once the main entrance, as evidenced by the stump of a pillar erected by Ashoka, a local *zamindar* ("landlord") who broke off the rest to use in a sugarcane press, and the staircases leading to the raised balcony. The middle rung of the south gateway shows one of the latter: Ashoka's army has arrived (on the right) at the last of the eight original *stupas* containing the Buddha's relics at Ramagrama. But he is prevented from carting off the loot (as he had in the other seven) by the army of snake people to the left. On the inside, the middle rung depicts the Chhadanta Jataka, with the Buddha as the six-tusked elephant; above this scene are the trees and *stupas* of the *manushi* buddhas. The bottom rung shows the siege of Kushinagar (see p. 196), a historical nod to Buddhist non-violence wherein eight armies' imminent clash over those sought-after relics was averted by equitable distribution.

WEST GATEWAY. The front face of the west gateway features (from top to bottom) more *manushis*, the Buddha's first sermon (note the wheel), and more scenes of Chhadanta. Inside, the top two rungs show more wrangling over relics, and the bottom reveals the Buddha attaining enlightenment despite the distracting demons sent by Mara. On the south pillar of this gate, the **Mahakapi Jataka** shows the Buddha as a monkey turning himself into a bridge so that his brethren can escape to safety over a river.

NORTH GATEWAY. The north gateway, less scarred by the ravages of time than its counterparts, shows the **Vessarkara Jataka,** around both sides of the bottom rung, in which the Buddha gives up successively a magic elephant, his horse and chariot, and his wife and children before being reinstated to his princedom.

EAST GATEWAY. While the upper registers of the east gateway repeat earlier scenes, the south pillar depicts the Buddha walking on water (on the outside) and facing a fearsome cobra (on the inside). Below this scene is a depiction of villagers trying to make a sacrificial fire which won't light without the Buddha's permission.

MUSEUM. A small museum holds a modest collection of statues unearthed at Sanchi, including some impressive lion-headed Ashokan pillar capitals (just past the Tourist Cafeteria; closed F). A kiosk in front sells tickets good for entry both to the exhibit inside and to the hilltop ruins. A road winds circuitously up the hill, but, if you're on foot, the steep staircase leading off to the right is the more direct route to the ruins. (Rs5. Free F.)

INDORE इोर

With a population of 1.2 million, Indore is the Mammon of Madhya Pradesh. More people pack its cityscape, more businesses clutter its buildings, more industries sear its escarpments, and more money flows through its coffers than any other city in the state. Only the cows sitting placidly in the back allies seem untouched by the urban bustle. The old-town market will reward travelers who wander its warrens long enough, but most hurry to jump the next bus to Mandu or Ujjain.

⌐ TRANSPORTATION

Airport: 10km west of town center along MG Rd. (taxi Rs150, auto-rickshaw Rs40). To: **Bhopal** (11:45am, US$50); **Delhi** via Bhopal (US$120); **Gwalior** (M, Tu, Th, and Sa; 11:45am; US$95); **Mumbai** (7:15pm, US$80). The **Indian Airlines** office (tel. 431595 or 431596) is on Dr. RS Bhadari Marg, 1 block north of MG Rd., 2 blocks east of RN Tagore Rd. in Khelprashal Stadium. Open daily 10:05am-1:15pm and 2:15-5pm.

Trains: The **railway station** is on Station Rd. Despite being a commercial hub, Indore sits astride one of the Western Railway's most antiquated and inefficient lines, which demands time-consuming changes and recouplings when joining the main routes. Prices given are for sleeper class. To: **Delhi** (*Intercity Exp.*, 1pm and 4pm, 13-14hr., Rs262); **Mumbai** (3:45pm, 16hr., Rs284); **Udaipur** (4:20pm, 16hr., Rs155/529).

Buses: Sarawate Bus Station, at the intersection of MY Hospital and Station Rd. To: **Bhopal** (every 10min. 4:30am-2:30am, 4½hr., Rs58/88); **Maheshwar** (8:15am and 6:45pm, 3hr., Rs28); **Omkareshwar** (frequent morning departures, 3hr., Rs25); **Sanchi** (6:15am and 4:45pm, 8hr., Rs100); **Ujjain** (every 15min. 5am-11pm, 2hr., Rs18). **Gangawal Bus Stand** serves **Mandu** via **Dhar** (every 30min. 6am-6pm, 3-4hr., Rs32).

Local Transportation: English street signs are rare, and the old part of town is a labyrinth. Take advantage of the ubiquitous, metered **auto-rickshaws.** Base fare Rs5; most destinations in town Rs10-20. Pre-paid auto-rickshaw stand in Sarawate Bus Station next to the Inquiry Office.

▐ ORIENTATION AND INFORMATION

Indore is bisected by **Station Road,** which leads south from the railway station to the **Sarawate Bus Stand** 500m away. In the market to the west, narrow streets lined with stalls predominate; to the east, workshops and businessmen's hotels occupy new and unremarkable concrete row houses. **Mahatma Gandhi (MG) Road** is the main east-west artery, and **Maharuja Yeshwant Hospital Road** leads southeast from the station area to the GPO and the bank.

MADHYA PRADESH

Tourist Office: MPTDC, RN Tagore Rd. (tel. 528653 or 521818), behind Ravindra Natya Graha Hall, a half block south of MG Rd. Lethargic staff offers free brochures of Mandu, Maheshwar and Omkareshwar. Open daily 10am-5pm.

Currency Exchange: State Bank of India, Main Office, Agra-Bombay Rd., south of MY Hospital Rd. on the left. Foreign exchange on the 1st fl. Open M-F 10:30am-2:30pm, Sa 10:30am-12:30pm. **Trade-Wings Ltd.,** Exchange Bureau, 6/2 South Takoganj, 308 Man Heritage, 3rd fl. (tel. 510600, residence tel. 553273) near High Court.

Bookstore: Shri Indore Book Depot, 504 MG Rd. (tel. 432479), 2 blocks before the Indian Coffee House and across the street, has lots of used books. Exit railway station, turn left, and walk for a block—numerous stalls sell English books.

Pharmacy: Medico Corner (tel. 467691), one block to the right when exiting Sarawate bus station. Open M-Sa 8am-10pm, Su 2-8pm.

Hospital: Choithrom Hospital, Monik Barg Rd. (tel. 362491).

Police: (tel. 464488), in the blue booth in Sarawate Bus Station, under the staircase in front of the booking office.

Post Office: GPO, Agra-Bombay Rd., (tel. 700244), between the State Bank of India and the museum, on the left just south of MY Hospital Rd. Open M-Sa 8am-7:30pm, Su and holidays 10:30am-3:30pm. **Postal Code:** 452001.

Internet: The Web People, B-17 (L6), Chetak Centre (tel. 528794; www.indorecity.com/thewebpeople), in the basement of the tall white commercial building across from the Hotel President. Rs60 per hr., Rs1.50 per min. Open daily 9am-10:30pm.

PHONE CODE	0731

▐ ACCOMMODATIONS

Hotels in Indore fill up quickly with itinerant businessmen, especially at the beginning of the month. The cheaper places behind the Sarawate Bus Station cater to the middle class Indian entrepreneur, usually offering 24-hour check-out, TVs, and phones. Generally, rooms with grandiose titles like "VIP" and "deluxe" yield only a few extra knick-knacks and thin carpeting. Prices quoted do not include state taxes of 10%. The predominantly male clientele means that females may not feel comfortable walking around alone at night.

Hotel Sant Plaza, 9/1 Kibe Compund, Chhoti Gwaltoli Chouraha (tel. 463166 or 283203), on Station Rd. Clean standard businessman's hotel with good service. Singles Rs145, with air-cooling Rs195, with A/C Rs450; doubles Rs195/245/550.

Hotel Dayal (tel. 462865 or 462866), next to Sant Plaza. This cheapie fills up quickly so reserve in advance. Singles Rs80, with air-cooling Rs100; doubles Rs110/130.

Hotel Ashoka, 14 Nasia Rd. (tel. 465991 or 475496), opposite Sarawate Bus Station, 100m to the right as you exit. Rooms feature TV, phone, and bathroom with hot water. Indulge and get a quieter room in the back, away from bus stand noise. Singles Rs140, with air-cooling Rs200, with A/C Rs300; doubles Rs190/250/350.

Hotel Uday Palace, 7 Kibe Compund (tel. 762688 or 762703), next to Madhumilan Cinema off Station Rd. Pricier and nicer rooms. Check-out noon. Singles Rs195, with air-cooling Rs250, with A/C Rs425; doubles Rs275/350/525. MC, Visa.

Hotel Payal, 38 Chhoti Gwaltoli (tel. 463202 or 478460), in the row of hotels hidden behind the Patel flyover, just around the corner from Sarawate. The real penny pincher might want to consider the subterranean rows of dorm beds before succumbing to the TV'd, toilet-ed rooms above ground. Dorm beds Rs20; singles Rs120; doubles Rs165.

🍴 FOOD

Indian Coffee House, MG Rd., on the left inside a courtyard (look for the "Deadend Jeans" sign on the archway); from the city center, 100m past the Central Hotel. Part of an India-wide chain, trusty old ICH serves tasty *masala dosas* (Rs16) and *sada dosas* (Rs13). The real highlight is, as always, the waiters attired with their elaborately pleated headpieces. A second location, opposite the MY Hospital, features outdoor tables in a small park. Open daily 7:30am-10pm.

Woodlands Restaurant, Hotel President, 163 RN Tagore Rd., next to the Nehru statue. A respite from the frenzy of Indore, Woodlands features pricey set breakfasts (Rs65-85), a great all-you-can-eat lunch buffet (Rs82), typical dinner fare (Rs38-68), and all-day snacks (Rs24-48). Open daily 7am-11pm; meals 7-11am, noon-3pm and 7-11pm.

Siddharth Restaurant, opposite Sarawate Bus Station on the left. This dark and somewhat eerie bar has a tree growing through the middle of the dining room. The veg. menu is better for bar snacks than meals, with tasty yellow *dal* fry (Rs15) and butter *paneer masala* (Rs30). Cold beer (Rs55-65). Open daily 6am-11pm.

👁 SIGHTS

For most pilgrims, Indore is little more than a waystation. After pausing to hop on a connecting bus, they are off to the next *yatra*. If stuck with time to kill in Indore, however, you can spend a pleasant day checking out the following sights.

LAL BAGH PALACE. Although travelers generally stop in for a look at the Lal Bagh Palace, a British manor house built by the Holkar Maharajas in the 1870s, there is little to see here. Fortunately, it is conveniently located on the road that runs from the bus and railway stations to the Gangawal Bus Stand. Although the building could be gone over with the proverbial fine-toothed comb in under an hour, the roped-off rooms prevent such an examination. Along with the usual grotesque stuffed wildcats, the house features an underground tunnel connecting the main house with the kitchens on the opposite side of the river and several intricately carved rooms. Don't jump out of your *chappals* when a statue of a stern Queen Victoria greets you at the exit. If nothing else, the grounds provide the widest expanse of green that you'll find in Indore's urban sprawl. *(Agra-Bombay Rd., beyond the GPO. Open Tu-Su 10am-5pm. Rs2. English/Hindi guidebooks Rs3.)*

CENTRAL MUSEUM. Indore's Central Museum presents religious sculptures from Madhya Pradesh and exhibits on the area's pre-history. Although some of the museum's works are quite beautiful, poor presentation does little to illuminate cultural context. Unlike in Western museums, however, touching the sculptures is acceptable, and the pieces scattered outside in the grass make the art accessible. Appreciate the pieces for their aesthetic merits alone, or kindly ask one of the many museum attendants for a tour. *(Open Tu-Su 9am-5pm. Free.)*

OTHER SIGHTS. The **Rajwada Jata Chock** is an interesting building surrounded by a lively market area (open daily 6am-8pm). The nearby **Kach Mandir,** a Jain temple made entirely of mirrored tiles, forms part of a neighborhood containing several more buildings of architectural interest. Finally, the **Gonndhihall,** a Municipal Corporation building built during the Raj, located in the park just over Shastri Bridge in the town center, forms a cheery backdrop to the park.

NEAR INDORE: MAHESHWAR महेश्वर

Both the *Ramayana* and the *Mahabharata* mention **Maheshvari,** once a glorious city and the capital of King Arjuna Kartavirya's domain around 200 BC. The city lapsed into oblivion for about two millennia, until the late 18th century, when the Holkar Queen Ahalya Bai made it her capital, building a fortified palace and a pair of richly decorated temples along the Narmada River. Known today as Maheshwar, it remains a small and somewhat out-of-the-loop town whose name is famous throughout India because of the fine, handloomed *saris* made here.

To reach the sights, clustered inside the **fort,** head due south through the village. The left of the fork in the village road ascends to the fort. Its bulbous battlements dwarf the houses in the village below; past the main gate, a smaller gate leads into the palace grounds, where a two-room museum contains a jumble of broken statuary and Holkar dynasty paraphernalia. The gate to the left of the museum leads to steps down to the **sari workshop** and the temples and *ghats* below. The workshop at the top of the stairs, run by the Rehwa Society (established in 1978 to preserve Maheshwar's silk-cotton *sari*-weaving tradition), is set up for the benefit of tourists. In a dark, low, historic building lit by fluorescent tubes, workers, most of them women, spin and weave material in a stunning array of colors and designs. The manager, who sits just inside the door, will call someone to show you around. Though *saris* are most vehemently *not* sold on the premises, they are available in town for Rs400-2500. (Open W-M 10am-5pm. Free.) Past the *sari* workshop, at the bottom of the stairs, Maheshwar's **temples** are pressed into small courtyards that make them seem larger than they really are. They tower over the *ghats* below, the *sati* stones sunk in the quay, and the pilgrims bathing in the sacred Narmada.

A three-hour bus ride from either Indore (Rs38) or Mandu (Rs20) will deposit you at the **bus stand. Buses** return to Indore every hour and leave for Mandu and Omkareshwar in the early morning and afternoon. On your way to the sights, you'll pass several **STD/ISD** telephone booths. **Ajanta Lodge** (tel. 07283 or 73226), 100m west of the bus stand on the main road, provides clean rooms (singles Rs40, with bath Rs50; doubles Rs55/70). As for food, **VIP Cottage,** 400m east of the bus stand on the main road, just over the bridge, has veg. (Rs14-35) and non-veg. (Rs15-130) items and snacks (Rs2-120).

NEAR INDORE: OMKARESHWAR ओमकेश्वर

For many years, Omkareshwar, an island shaped like the holiest of all Hindu symbols, the "Om" (ॐ), has drawn pilgrims to its temples and *ghats*. With sounds of chanting day and night, repeated intonations of *"Hare Om,"* and the incessant buzz of flies, Omkareshwar, with its scores of fervent believers, resembles a miniature Varanasi. Still, Omkareshwar's landscape of temples rises steeply out of the jagged cliffs, and *ghats* emerge serenely from the Narmada and Kaveri rivers.

To reach the temples, just continue to walk through the village until you reach the newly constructed bridge spanning above the deep gully that divides the island. The view from the bridge reveals the city's two major temples: the exceptionally detailed **Shri Omkar Mandhata,** home to one of only 12 *jyotirlingas* (manifestations of Shiva as brilliant columns of light) in India, and **Siddhnath Temple,** an early medieval Brahmanic temple.

A **bus** from Indore (11 per day, 3hr., Rs25) or Ujjain (1 per day, 5hr., Rs37) directly connects Omkareshwar. There are frequent departures to Indore (every 30min. from 9am, 3hr., Rs25); Ujjain (noon, 5hr., Rs37); and Maheshwar (1pm, 3hr., Rs20). Trains from Indore stop at the Khandhwa/Omkareshwar Rd. **railroad station,** 12km from Omkareshwar's bus station. The **police station** (tel. 344015; open daily 9am-5pm) and the **post office** (tel. 71222; open M-Sa 9am-5pm) are near the bus station. There is no place in town to change currency. From the bus station, a three-minute walk through the village leads you past the **Government Hospital** on the right (open daily 8am-noon and 5-6pm) and the **pharmacy** on the left (open daily 7:30am-9:30pm). The only **STD/ISD** booth lies just beyond the pharmacy at Jyoti General Store. **Telephone Code:** 07280. The **Yatrika Guest House** (tel. 71308) is behind the bus station (singles Rs100, with bath and air-cooler Rs150). For nicer rooms and scenic views try **Hotel Aishwarya** (tel. 71325 or 71326), where prices are negotiable (singles Rs250, with air-cooling Rs400; doubles Rs300/450; 10% luxury tax). Restaurants abound in the village.

MANDU मंडु

Mandu, aptly named the "City of Joy," is the India that you've seen advertised in glossy tourist brochures. Goats gambol in the lush green vegetation surrounding the ruins while women with pots on their head sashay by and children run over to say "hello." If the past is a country we can never visit, Mandu probably allows us a glimpse over the fence, for life continues here largely untouched by modernization. Stretched out atop a narrow plateau in the Vindhya range, the city was fortified as long ago as the 6th century. Mandu's golden age lasted from 1401 to 1526, when the Muslim rulers of the kingdom of Malwa called it their home, building mosques, palaces, and pleasure domes in stone and marble across the length of the plateau. Five centuries later, their monuments still stand in a tranquil, under-populated mountain region set against a backdrop of great natural beauty.

ORIENTATION AND PRACTICAL INFORMATION

After passing through a series of narrow gates, the bus ascends to the plateau. The **main road** runs south through the village, past the **market square** and **Jama Masjid**, ending at the **Rewa Kund** ruins at the far end of town. All the hotels, as well as the **post office** (tel. 63222; open M-Sa 9am-5pm), **police station** (tel. 63223), and restaurants, are on the main road. The **pharmacy** (open daily 9am-7pm) and several doctors' offices are located on the main road, but Indore hosts the closest hospital facilities. The sights around town are well-marked, and signs in English and Hindi direct visitors to the ruins. There is no tourist office in Mandu, but the **MPTDC** in Indore can help with hotel reservations (recommended in winter). **Buses** depart from the market square heading to: **Dhar** (14 per day, 1½hr., Rs15); **Indore** (5-6 per day, 3hr., Rs25); and **Maheshwar** (7:15am, 3hr., Rs20). Bus service is less frequent during monsoon season. The easiest and most pleasant means of getting around Mandu is by bicycle. You can rent **bicycles** from Ajoy's Bicycle Shop on the main road, just south of the square (Rs2 per hr., Rs25 per day). Alternatively, Nitin Traders will provide **auto-rickshaws** (Rs150-200 for 3-4hr.) and expensive private **taxis** to Indore (Rs725, notify 1½hr. before departure). They're located just south of the square across from the Jain temple; look for the sign. (Open daily 8am-8pm.) **STD/ISD** calls can be placed from a market square stall (open daily 8:30am-9pm) or from the Rupmati Hotel. Power outages are frequent, and phone lines are often down during the monsoon. **Postal Code:** 454010. **Telephone Code:** 07292.

ACCOMMODATIONS AND FOOD

SADA's tourist rest house (tel. 63234), at the corner of the main square across the side street from the Jama Masjid, has rooms in dank cement bunkers with squat toilets (doubles Rs125). **MPTDC** has two excellent but pricey hotels in Mandu. The **Travelers' Lodge** (tel. 63221), 1km north of the square on the main road, has scenic views over the eastern ravine from its comfortable, seat toilet-equipped double rooms (singles Rs290; doubles Rs375). The **MPTDC Tourist Cottages** (tel. 63235), on the main road 2km south of the square, has better rooms in small cottages with lake views (singles Rs350, deluxe with TV Rs550, with A/C Rs750; doubles Rs450/650/850; extra person Rs75-125). Both lodgings charge 10% luxury tax but offer 25% discounts in May and June; reservations can be made in any MPTDC office. Both have **restaurants** (cottages outdoor, lodge indoor) with the standard MPTDC menu of snacks (veg. sandwiches Rs16, fish fingers Rs40), continental dishes (fish and chips Rs60), and veg. (*paneer shahi korma* Rs30) and non-veg. (mutton curry Rs40) options. (MPTDC restaurants open daily 8-10am, noon-3pm, and 7-11pm; snacks available between meal times. The **Rupmati Hotel** (tel. 63270, in Indore tel. 702055), the nicest in town, offers lovely views of the ravine, excellent service, and large, clean rooms (singles Rs300; doubles Rs375, with A/C Rs750; 10% luxury tax). The Rupmati restaurant is more affordable than the rooms. The open-air pavilion overlooking a landscaped lawn, complete with swings and slides, serves veg. (Rs20-50) and non-veg. (Rs40-210) dishes. The restaurant also holds the only liquor license in town. (Beer Rs60. Open daily 7am-11pm.) The **Relax Point Restaurant,** in the main square, offers huge, excellent helpings of veg. *thalis* for only Rs25 (open daily 8am-10:30pm).

👁 SIGHTS

Ruins punctuate Mandu's entire landscape, from the arched gateways you pass on the way into town to the mosque and tomb in the market square, from the crumbling houses along the sides of the main street to the palace at the very tip of the plateau. The big attractions fall into three main areas: the **Royal Enclave** in the north, the **central group,** and the **Rewa Kund complex** in the south.

THE CENTRAL GROUP. In the middle of both the plateau and the village, the central group includes Mandu's beautiful **Jama Masjid,** one of India's largest mosques. Like the other monuments here, it typifies the austere style of architecture imported from Afghanistan by Hoshang Shah. Reputedly designed after the mosque in Damascus and completed in 1454, the Jama Masjid is remarkable for its sheer scale and simplicity. Hoshang Shah's son built a white marble **mausoleum** behind the Jama Masjid for his father. The structure so inspired Shah Jahan that he sent his architects to study it before they began work on the Taj Mahal. Opposite the Jama Masjid, the over-ambitious and underachieving **Ashrafi Mahal** proves, by contrast, that less patience and skill went into Mandu's other monuments. In the 15th century Mahud Shah Khilji tried to slap together a huge tomb and seven-story victory tower so carelessly that most of it has since collapsed, leaving only the remains of a *madrasa* (theological college) complete with students' cells.

THE ROYAL ENCLAVE. The Jahaz Mahal Rd., next to Hoshang Shah's tomb, continues to the Royal Enclave. The sybaritic Sultan Ghiyas Shah constructed the huge Jahaz Mahal, just inside the gateway, to house his equally large harem. The long, narrow design (120m by 10m) and the two artificial lakes on either side earn the building its nickname of "Ship Palace," especially during the rainy season when water runs through the complex system of pools and conduits. With its cool breezes and views, it evokes images of the Love Boat it once was. Behind stands the Hindola Mahal, an audience hall nicknamed the "Swinging Palace" because its sloping buttresses look like they're swinging out at an angle. Ghiyas Shah had a ramp built so that he could ride to the upper floor without going through the hassle of dismounting from his elephant. Numerous other ruins, including **Dilwar Khan's mosque** and **Gada Shah's Shop,** are also in this enclave. *(Open dawn-dusk. Rs2.)*

NIL KANTH TEMPLE. At the southern end of the village, a fork leads right (west) from the main road to the Nil Kanth Temple, 3km away. Originally a Mughal pleasure pavilion complete with water flowing over ribbed stones in front of candles to create visual effects, the temple today has been taken over by the Shaivites. From this inspirational spot perched just below the clifftop on the valley slopes, they worship an incarnation of Shiva whose throat turned blue when he drank poison.

REWA KUND. The main road ends 5km from the square, at the **Rewa Kund** complex, named after the tank that used to supply water to the nearby palaces. Baz Bahadur, the last independent ruler of Mandu, built his eponymous **palace** in the 16th century as a quiet retreat with views of the surrounding greenery. But even this tranquil spot would not satisfy the stunning Roopmati, the sultan's favorite dancer. Life on the plateau made this plains-dweller homesick. As legend has it, Roopmati demanded that Baz Bahadur build her a pavilion on the crest of a hill, from which she could see her former village in the Narmada Valley far below. No sooner had the dutiful sultan completed **Rupmati's Pavilion** than the jealous Akbar marched on Mandu in order to seize the renowned dancer. Baz Bahadur fled, Roopmati swallowed poison, and Akbar, after a brief stay, let his testosterone guide him to the next desirable dancing girl (see **Orchha,** p. 386), leaving Mandu desolate. The unparalleled view over the plains from the palace is sobering—villages, trees, and fields recede in a patchwork haze to where the silver smudge of the Narmada River swerves into the horizon.

UJJAIN उज्जैन

Ujjain's long, eclectic history began in the 3rd century BC, when the city was the imperial seat of Ashoka, Buddhism's first patron. Later, Ujjain served as the capital of two other empires as well as a development center for Indian astronomy. Long before the prime meridian, Hindu stargazers made Ujjain India's Greenwich. An 18th-century observatory on the southwestern side of town is still in use today. Ujjain is also among the holiest of holy Hindu cities; every twelve years during the festival of **Kumbh Mela** (see p. 213) Ujjain attracts devotees by the millions with the promise of a hard-earned space along the city *ghats* for a dip in the sacred River Shipra. Because Ujjain's temples can be less than inspiring, the time to come—if you can handle the crush of millions of pilgrims—is during the Mela.

ℹ ORIENTATION AND PRACTICAL INFORMATION

Hemmed in by the **River Shipra** to the west and the **railroad tracks** to the south, Ujjain's **old city** charms visitors with many small shops and narrow lanes that frustrate even the most state-of-the-art navigation tools. There are no street signs, few landmarks, and countless non-linear byways. The temples and *ghats* are within walking distance, but other destinations require a rickshaw ride. Thankfully, the railway station, bus stand, GPO, and most hotels cluster around one intersection.

Trains: The **railway station** is on Subash Rd., 100m west of the bus station. Fares listed are for 2nd/1st class. To: **Bhopal** (*Intercity Exp.* 7:25am; *Malwa Exp.* 2:30pm; both 3hr., Rs52/573); **Delhi** (*Malwa Exp.* 4667, 2:45pm, 17hr., Rs160/846; *Indore-Nizamuddin Exp.* 4005, 5:55pm, 12hr., Rs128/641); **Gwalior** (*Malwa Exp.* 4667, 2:45pm, 2nd class Rs148); **Mumbai** (*Indore-Bandra Avantika Exp.* 2692, 5:30pm, 10hr., 2nd class Rs160). To reach **Orchha,** change trains in Ahmedabad.

Buses: Mahakal Bus Stand, on the corner east of the train station. To: **Bhopal** (8 per day; 5hr.; Rs58, night bus Rs67); **Indore** (every 10min. 4:30am-9:30pm, 2hr., Rs18).

Local Transportation: Sights are spread out, and most **auto-rickshaw** drivers refuse to use meters. Bargain them down; the longest ride should cost no more than Rs25-30.

Tourist Office: MPTDC Hotel Shipra, Vishva Vidhyalaya Rd. (tel. 551495 or 551496). Exit the railway station through the stairway overpass. Cross the road and turn right; the hotel is 200m on the right. Although there is no tourist office per se, the helpful staff at the reception desk will give you a free map of Ujjain. Raju Bawar, the only government-licensed guide of Ujjain, can also provide reasonably priced tours of the city.

Currency Exchange: The closest place to exchange currency is in Indore.

Pharmacy: Radhaswami Vijayraj Medical Store, behind the Civil Hospital, near the maternity home. Open 24hr.

Hospital: Civil Hospital, Ager Rd.; from the train station, 100m beyond Mahakal bus stand on the opposite side of street. Open daily 8am-1pm and 5-6pm. For private medical assistance, contact Dr. Bishi or Dr. Rita Shinde anytime (tel. 555067).

Police: tel. 552140.

Post Office: GPO (tel. 551024), behind the bus stand at the 2nd gate on the left. Open M-Sa 7am-8pm, Su 10am-4pm. **Postal Code:** 456001.

PHONE CODE	0734

🏠 ACCOMMODATIONS

Most budget hotels are located near the railway station. Prices listed do not include state taxes of 5% on rooms Rs60-149 and 10% on rooms Rs150 and above.

✦ **Hotel Shipra,** Vishva Vidhyalaya Rd. (tel. 551495 or 551496). See **MPTDC** directions above. Ujjain's lap of luxury run by the MPTDC, this is the place to splurge. Clean rooms have big windows, high ceilings, and desks. Helpful staff provide impeccable service. Check-out noon. Singles Rs350-690; doubles Rs390-790. MC, Visa, AmEx.

Hotel Rama Krishna (tel. 557012), across from the train station to the left. The staff is friendly, and as long as you're not a big fan of flesh, it's a good choice—no meat is allowed on the premises. Avoid the stuffy interior rooms. All rooms have air-cooling and attached bathrooms. Check-out 24hr. Singles Rs130-200, with A/C Rs450; doubles Rs170-250/550. 5% service charge.

Hotel Chandragupta (tel. 561600), next to the Rama Krishna. The reception is up a flight of stairs. Slightly cheaper and less clean than its neighbor. Hot water available in buckets. Attached bathrooms have squat toilets and wall faucets. The ground floor has a decent veg. restaurant. Check-out 24hr. Singles Rs100-165; doubles Rs150-170.

Hotel Ajay, 12 Dewas Gate (tel. 550856 or 551354), on the street opposite the bus station. Small but clean rooms are a good deal. Singles Rs66, with bath Rs88, with air-cooling Rs165; doubles Rs100/110/240.

◉ FOOD

Sudama Restaurant, across from the railway station, next to Hotel Ramakrishna. Contemplate the fascinating cut-mirror decor while chowing down on *paneer korma* (Rs28) and other veg. fare (Rs16-40). Dinner only after 7pm, but snacks (Rs25-40) and good veg. fried rice (Rs28) all day. Open daily 9am-11pm.

Navratna Restaurant, inside Hotel Shipra. The standard M.P. Tourism menu, including scrambled eggs and toast (Rs28), decent coffee (Rs15), and a range of both veg. and non-veg. Indian dishes (Rs126-150). Beer (Rs90) must be consumed in the separate bar. Open daily 7am-3pm and 7-10:30pm.

Chanakya Restaurant, on the ground floor of Hotel Chandragupta. The whole extended family can fit into one of the giant booths. Large selection of beer and spirits. Don't miss the pseudo-erotic sculpture or the amusingly kitschy Indian imitations of Western alcohol ads on the wall. Veg.-only dishes Rs12-63. Open daily 8am-11pm.

◉ SIGHTS

Even if you picked up a map, start praying now—it's hard to find anything without faith. The largest temples and *ghats*, though, aren't far from the railway station.

THE TEMPLES. The **Gopal Mandir** (Ganesh Temple) sits behind a high, onion-domed, whitewashed fortification in the midst of a busy market square where vendors display the season's most sought-after devotional paraphernalia. Inside, pilgrims lounge under the arched platforms that circle the complex's perimeter, while in the sumptuous main hall, a figure of Ganesh sits obediently between figures of his parents, Shiva and Parvati. *(In the center of town.)*

Slightly farther away, the rosy-spired main building at **Mahakaleshwar Mandir** caps a series of long, narrow tunnels that eventually lead to an underground room containing the **Shivalinga**, one of twelve *jyotirlingas*. Moving on, the passage leads into a spacious, well-swept courtyard where several smaller shrines and temples await. *(Walk 10min. down the narrow street in front of the bus station; the temple is down one of the biggest side streets to the left.)*

The **Harsiddhi Mandir,** the large temple complex behind high white walls just to the right, forms the focal point of Devi worship. It marks the spot where Parvati's arm was severed when Shiva pulled her from her *sati* pyre (see **Divine Dismemberment**, p. 687). A famous image of the goddess Annapurna is housed in the temple shrine. *(Take the road that passes by the side of the temple complex into and over the marsh beyond; when you hit dry land again, you've reached the Harsiddhi temple complex.)*

THE VEDHA SHALA. The instruments of the Vedha Shala (Veda School) sit in a compound behind a gate with a sign reading "Shree Jiwagi Observatory." The mathematically-inclined will wonder at the precision of doo-dads like the parallel sundials on either end of a meter-high cylinder. Each side tells the time for exactly half the year. Acrest a hill with a view of the river and fields beyond, the observatory would be a pleasant vista if it weren't for the non-stop truck traffic just outside the gate—the world of machines and modernity is never far away. *(On a road leading southwest from the back of the railway station, atop a hill.)*

OTHER SIGHTS. Seeing the other sights requires booster shots of patience and fortitude (not to mention energy). The **Ram Ghat** is the largest, although not always busiest, of the long row of ghats on both sides of the river. Near the north end of the row, the **Bhartirihari Caves** are home to the hoop-earringed Kanphata yogis. (The streets and paths beyond the Harsiddhi Mandir all lead to the ghats.)

JABALPUR जबलपु

The Madhya Pradesh tourism office tries to promote protracted sojourns in this dusty town of just over one million people (it seems more like 100,000) on the basis of some scenic white cliffs nearby. Basically, though, there is very little to see in Jabalpur; as far as most tourists are concerned, the city is merely a staging point for Kanha and Bandhavgarh National Parks.

ℹ ORIENTATION AND PRACTICAL INFORMATION

Collectorate Road curves north from the east end of the **railway station** past the hospital and Gothic High Court to the **clock tower,** marking the beginning of the **bazaar area. Station Road,** in front (south) of the station, leads east to **Residency Road** and west toward the center of town. Two hundred meters before Empire Cinema, the street to the right passes under the railroad tracks and leads to **Russel Chowk,** the center of the city. A fork to the right just beyond the underpass runs by the State Bank of India on its way to Collectorate Rd. From Russel Chowk, the main drag heads north to the bazaars over the **Navdra Bridge,** and another leads west past the museum, the **tempo stand** for the Marble Rocks, and a bridge to the **bus station.**

Trains: The **railway station** (tel. 1311132), a Rs15 rickshaw ride to the east of Russel Chowk. Reservation office open M-Sa 8am-8pm, Su 8am-2pm. Window #3 serves tourists. Fares listed are 2nd/1st class. To: **Bhopal** (*Narmada Exp.* 8234, 10:15pm, 7½hr., Rs81/398); **Kolkata** (*Mumbai-Howrah Mail* 3004, 2:10pm, 23hr., Rs194/980); **Delhi** (*Gondwana Exp.* 2411, 3:40pm, 23hr., Rs167/805); **Jalgaon,** for Ajanta Caves (*Ajanta Exp.* 3201, 3pm; *Mahangawi Exp.* 1094, 7:15am, 11hr., Rs122/604); **Patna** (*Janta Exp.* 3202, 3:45pm, 16hr., Rs185/883); **Satna** (*Howrah Mail* 3004, 2:10pm, 3hr., Rs53/258); **Varanasi** (*Mehanagri Exp.* 1093, 4:35pm, 10hr., Rs182/546); **Umaria,** for Bandhavgarh National Park (*Narmada Exp.* 8233, 6:20am, 1hr., Rs31).

Buses: The chaotic **bus stand** has both public (MPSRTC) and private sections. For all but the short regional trips, shop around for the comfiest private service; or better yet, take the train. For **Kanha National Park,** go to **Kisli** (7am, 6hr.; 11am, 7hr., Rs50). Alternatively, the MPTDC runs a bus from the train station (8am, 4hr.; Rs100). To reach **Mukki,** take a bus to Malajhund (9am, 10hr., Rs65) and ask to be let off at Mukki. For **Bandhavgarh,** take the train to **Umaria** and switch to the Bandhavgarh bus there (4 per day, 1hr., Rs10). To: **Khajuraho** (9am, 10hr., Rs100).

Local Transportation: Auto-rickshaws and **cycle-rickshaws** are unmetered. **Tempos** run from the museum to the White Rocks for Rs8.

Tourist Office: MPTDC (tel. 322111), inside the railway station, makes reservations for MPTDC facilities at Kanha and Bardavgarh. In-season (Dec.-Mar.) bookings for accommodations in parks should be made at least 72hr. in advance from this or any other MPTDC office; 100% payment required. Open daily 6am-10pm.

Currency Exchange: State Bank of India (tel. 322259), opposite Hotel Rishi Regency, near the railway underpass. The international banking division is upstairs, past a pair of botanically lush murals. Open M-F 10:30am-2:30pm.

Hospital: Medical College, Nagpur Rd. (tel. 322117), 8km south of the bus stand, also has a 24hr. **pharmacy.**

Police: Collectorate Rd., Civil Lines (tel. 320352), in front of the clock tower.

Post Office: GPO, Residency Rd. Out of the station, turn left on Station Rd. and then right on the next main road. The GPO is 500m down on the left. *Poste Restante* at counter #6. Open M-Sa 10am-6pm. **Postal Code:** 482002.

Telephones: 24hr. **STD/ISD** booth at the railway station.

PHONE CODE	0761

ACCOMMODATIONS AND FOOD

Most hotels slap on a 15-20% tax and have 24-hour check-out. Reserve in advance.

Hotel Natraj (tel. 310931), near Karamchand Chowk. Heading north (away from Russel Chowk), take the right fork after crossing the Navdra bridge, and take the first major right when you see the JFK quote ("Ask not what your country can do for you..."); it's on the left, opposite the Indian Coffee House. Rooms with attached baths have TV, air-cooling, and hand-held showers. Singles Rs20; doubles Rs120, with TV Rs130.

Hotel Utsav, Surya Commercial Complex, Russel Chowk (tel. 26038 or 23538), where the roads meet. Economy rooms have all the amenities, including A/C. Singles Rs250; doubles Rs325.

Hotel Swayam (tel. 325377), opposite Jyoti Talkies, at Navdra Bridge. In a noisy part of town. Rooms have attached baths and TVs. Singles Rs50; doubles Rs90.

Indian Coffee House, Malaviya Marg, near Karamchand Chowk, opposite Hotel Natraj. The mother ship of the ICH chain. Sky-high ceilings, rock-solid tables, wicker chairs, and vintage advertisements make this a classic. The usual *dosas* and *utthapams* (Rs13) as well as other snacks and great, unsweetened coffee (Rs4). Open daily 7am-9:30pm.

Hotel Republic Bar, just over Navdra Bridge, on the right. Rows of tall, straight-backed chairs and the no-nonsense Sikh owner behind the bar give the Republic a wild west feel. Butter chicken (Rs70) is their speciality, and they also offer veg. dishes (from Rs15) and a full range of booze. Open daily 10am-11:30pm.

Hotel Kalchuri, across from the GPO. Comfort and reassurance await at this MP Tourism hotel, which features the standard MPT menu, prepared by an above-average MPT chef. Open daily 7:30am-10:30pm.

SIGHTS

On the road from Russel Chowk to the bus stand is a local **museum,** which houses temple sculpture from the region (open Tu-Su 10am-5pm; free). About 20km from the city, the Narmada River passes through the white-cliffed gorge featured in the MPTDC brochures. For Rs10 per person, you can view the rocks from a rowboat. The **Marble Rocks** are fully illuminated at night to maximize tourist viewing hours. On the way, tempos (Rs8) pass the old grand fortress of **Madan Mahal.**

KANHA NATIONAL PARK

Gorgeous Kanha has a conflicted history. The same Brits who cantered across the continent with their rifles, driving game to the brink of extinction, also set aside Kanha as a hunting preserve. This doubtlessly saved it from the encroachment of the local population until Kanha became a wildlife reserve in 1933 (although hunting continued until 1955). The result of these preservation efforts is nearly 2000 sq. km of bona fide *Jungle Book* jungle—Rudyard Kipling set many of his stories here. Sightings of tigers are frequent; there are currently 114 tigers in the park, and the number is increasing (though not too quickly, as the males display a predilection to eat their own children). Once a tiger is spotted, it is held at bay by elephants

PROJECT TIGER Faced with a shocking drop in the tiger population due to hunting and India's industrialization, Indira Gandhi inaugurated a drastic initiative to save tigers in 1973. **Project Tiger** set aside nine areas of tiger territory as national parks and hired a staff of armed guards to patrol the areas and thwart poachers. The plan was initially successful, and the tiger population grew from several hundred to several thousand. Ten more national parks were eventually set aside. Lately, however, poaching has increased as the forces protecting the sanctuaries have become less formidable than they were initially. Tiger products—some believed to have healing and aphrodisiacal properties—fetch incredibly high prices on domestic and international markets. The tiger remains an endangered species, and some fear it could face extinction soon. The best places in India to try to catch a glimpse of the beasts are **Corbett** (see p. 156) and **Kanha National Parks** (see below).

until everyone in the area gets a look. Besides the well-fed cats, one may view their friends and food: leopards, deer, sambar, wild boar, bears, pythons, porcupines, and over 300 species of birds. Your chances of safely seeing one here are better than anywhere in India—the Sundarbans in West Bengal have more, but some of them seem to have developed a taste for human blood.

The park is open from November 1 through June 30, and it closes completely during the monsoon months. Peak season is March to April. There is a one-time permit fee of Rs100 (Rs10 for Indians), plus a camera fee (Rs10 for still 35mm).

GETTING TO THE PARK. The park has two main gates, one at **Kisli,** in the northwest, and another at **Mukki,** in the center on the west side. **Buses** depart from Jabalpur to **Kisli** (7 and 11am, 6-7hr., Rs50; MPTDC bus, 8am, 4hr., Rs100), stopping on the way at Khatia gate near the **Visitors Center,** where most non-MPTDC accommodations and food can be found. A daily bus also runs from Jabalpur to **Mukki** (9am, 10hr., Rs65). Buses return to Jabalpur (8am, 7hr., Rs50; noon, 6hr., Rs50; 1pm, 3½ hr., Rs100). For more information, see **Jabalpur: Practical Information,** p. 376. Both Kilsi and Mukki have visitor centers run with the assistance of the U.S. National Park Service, as does Kanha, in the middle of the park's core area. These centers have informative displays and sell brochures and supplies; they also show nature films in Hindi (open daily 9am-noon and 6:30-8pm). All transport beyond Khatra gate is conducted via private or gypsy **jeeps** (Rs9 per km). To get between Khatra and Kisli after the bus drops you off, wait for a full jeep to pass and ask for a ride; the last jeeps cruise by around 8pm. **Walking the 4km is prohibited.**

LODGES AND FOOD. Except for the MPTDC hotels, all accommodation is outside the park, concentrated at **Khatia,** 4km from Kisli. The MPTDC requires prepayment in full for their accommodations, leaving last-minute visitors at a loss. Risk-takers will delight in the small range of budget accommodation at Khatra, most of which double as restaurants and jeep pickup points. **Van Vihar,** on the right as you walk away from the gate, has comfy doubles 200m from the road with private baths and bucket showers (Rs50 per person) and a restaurant ("jungle" *thali* Rs30); it also arranges jeep trips. Next door is **Motel Chandan** (tel. 77220 or 77233), with passable doubles (Rs300, with bath Rs400, with hot water Rs500) and one unwholesome "economy" room (Rs200); prices go down drastically off season and whenever demand is low. Chandan also arranges jeep trips, and its restaurant's food is edible. The **MPTDC** operates **Baghira Log Huts** (posh singles Rs590; doubles with private bath Rs690), a **Tourist Hostel** near Kisli (dorm beds Rs250, bland snacks in a depressing canteen included), and the **Kanha Safari Lodge,** near Mukki (singles Rs390; doubles Rs490). These prices do not include the 10% state tax. For information or reservations, contact one of the MPTDC offices in major Madhya Pradesh cities or in Mumbai, Kolkata, and Delhi. The head office is in Bhopal (tel. (0755) 764397). It's a good idea to book MPTDC hotel rooms in advance during high season. Baghira has the only restaurant in Kisli, with a few bland choices, but it's better than the canteen (Rs50-100). At Khatra, the food doesn't get much better, but at least there are options—try your luck at the various lodges (*thalis* Rs25-30).

ACTIVITIES. Although you might catch one of the nightly nature films or take the somewhat disorienting 1.5km **jungle walk** at Khatra gate, you're really here to see the law of the jungle at work. Jeep trips, the only way to go, run Rs400-600 plus sundry nominal fees (Rs50-100 per trip), and can be split between a maximum of six passengers. Consult the manager of your hotel for a berth. Trips run in the morning (6am, 4-5hr.) and afternoon (around 3pm, 2-3hr.). Morning is usually a better time for sightings; if there are tigers about, your jeep will take you to an **elephant** (Rs50) for closer, more silent viewing. Bring warm clothing and a blanket in winter, as the mornings are very cold and the evening chill sets in quickly. Morning trips make a breakfast stop (fritters and *chai* Rs9) and stop again at the Kanha visitors center. Walking in the jungle is prohibited.

KHAJURAHO खजुराहो

The once-forgotten village of Khajuraho, stuck in the middle of nowhere in northern Madhya Pradesh, has recently become one of the most visited places in India, thanks to the remarkable erotic sculpture adorning the walls of its temples. This dusty litle hamlet might not look like the kind of place that would inspire such uninhibited passionate expression, but nowhere else in India are so many couples shown so prominently copulating in every position and direction imaginable. Each explicit detail is meticulously rendered in the sandstone facades, leaving nothing to the imagination but the question of what might have inspired it all in the first place. Many visitors to Khajuraho come as much to study the art as to gasp and giggle. The unavoidable souvenir stands are full of pocket paperback editions of the *Kama Sutra* translated into all of the world's major languages, and late-night conversation in the town's restaurants and cafes seems to focus predominantly on the advisability—or even the possibility—of some of the things depicted here.

But there is a lot more to Khajuraho's temples than a few exquisitely executed sex scenes. The erotic sculptures themselves are far from being pornographic; they are imbued with a sincere and tender exuberance for life and a luxuriant sensuality that transcend the physical acts they depict. For all the attention they are given, though, these scenes represent only a part of the wealth of fascinating cultural insight offered by these holy sites. From war to love and from joy to sorrow, the carvings range the breadth of the human experience.

Construction of the temples, which took place between AD 900 and 1100, was sponsored by the reigning Chandela dynasty, a Rajput clan claiming to be descended from the moon god. When Chandela power waned, the temples were forgotten and lay hidden deep in the jungle for 700 years before the outside world (in the form of the British officer T.S. Burt) stumbled across them in 1838. (See **Sex in Khajuraho**, p. 383). Of an original 85 temples, only 25 still stand today.

The morning is the coolest and quietest time to make a tour of Khajuraho's temples. Since almost all of the temples face east, the early light reveals sculptures and relief detail hard to see later on. Khajuraho's temples are conventionally divided into three groups; the Western Group contains the most famous and impressive of the temples, although all of them are stunning. For the biggest event in Khajuraho, the annual **Festival of Dance** in March, the government flies in India's best classical dancers to perform in front of the temples (March 2-8, 2000).

▐▀ TRANSPORTATION

Airport: Khajuraho Civil Aerodrome, 6km south of the Western Group. **Indian Airlines,** Main Rd. (tel. 44035; airport office tel. 44036), next door to the Clarks Bundela Hotel. Open daily 10am-1:15pm and 2-5pm. To: **Agra** (M and W, 45min.; US$70); **Delhi** (M, W, and F; 1½hr.; US$90); **Varanasi** (M, W, and F; 45min.; US$70). Advance reservations are essential year-round.

Buses: Buses are the only ground transport to Khajuraho. The clean station posts English schedules and has frequent departures for the nearest railheads at Satna, Mahoba, and

Jhansi. To: **Agra** (9am, 12hr., Rs132); **Bhopal** (8am and 7pm, 10hr., Rs141); **Gwalior** (9 and 11:15am, 6hr., Rs95); **Jabalpur** (7:30am, 12hr., Rs100); **Jhansi** (9am, 4hr., Rs60), continuing to Gwalior and Agra; **Mahoba,** for trains to **Varanasi** (10:15am, 2:30, and 6:30pm; 3hr.; Rs30); **Satna,** for trains to **Varanasi** (7 per day, 3½hr., Rs41). There is one direct bus to **Varanasi** (4pm, Rs144). **MPTC** runs a "luxury" coach that coordinates with the *Shatabdi Exp.*, leaving Khajuraho at 4pm and continuing to Gwalior (Rs95). The last buses to Khajuraho leave Satna at 3:30pm, Jhansi at 1:15pm, and Mahoba at 5pm.

Local Transportation: Bicycles, the most practical mode of transport, can be rented at hotels or stands in the square for Rs20 per day. The few **auto-rickshaws** are overpriced. A **cycle-rickshaw** trip should cost between Rs5-10. It is a 20-25 minute walk from the Western to the Eastern Group.

🛈 ORIENTATION AND PRACTICAL INFORMATION

You would have to try very hard to get lost in Khajuraho. There is only one main road, which leads up from the airport in the south to the main temple complex **(Western Group)** and the mess of hotels, restaurants, and postcard shops which comprise the "new village." **Jain Temple Road** leads east from here to the second main group of temples **(Eastern Group)** and then to the old village. The bus stand is on **Link Road Number Two,** South of Jain Temple Road, a 10-minute walk from the main group of temples.

Tourist Office: Main Rd. (tel. 42347), opposite the Western Group. Distributes maps and brochures and helps arrange sight-seeing with one of its 50 licensed guides (Rs230 half-day, Rs345 full day for up to 4 people). Also recommends various jeep excursions to nearby waterfalls and wildlife parks. Open M-F 9am-5:30pm. **MP Tourist Information Center** (tel. 44163), at the bus stand. Open M-Sa 9am-6pm.

Currency Exchange: State Bank of India, Main Rd. (tel. 42373), opposite the Western Group, cashes traveler's checks and changes over 20 currencies. Open M-F 10:45am-2:45pm and 4-6pm, Sa 10:45am-12:45pm and 3:30-4:30pm.

Hospital: 500m down the road in front of the Western Group, on the left side, are 2 small clinics and a **pharmacy**. Open daily 8am-noon and 5-9pm. Dr. R.K. Khare (tel. 44177, residence tel. 42273) is recommended by local luxury hotels. His **clinic** is located in the strip mall beside the bus station. Open M-Sa 9am-1pm and 6-9:30pm. Medical facilities are limited; serious cases are sent to Jhansi or Satna.

Police: (tel. 44032), in the booth opposite the Western Group and by the bus stand.

Post Office: Opposite the bus stand. Open M-Sa 10am-6pm. **Postal Code:** 471606.

PHONE CODE	07686

🛏 ACCOMMODATIONS

Prices are highly variable between seasons. There is a mini-boom during July and August, but rates drop off between April and June. The high season runs from November to March, when most hotel owners drastically inflate their prices; it is common for a Rs50 room to go for Rs200, leaving budget travelers with no option but to fork out the money. Book in advance at peak times.

Yogi Lodge, Main Sq. (tel. 44158), down an alley by the Terazza Restaurant, on the left side of the square as you face away from the Western Group. Simple, clean rooms have baths with hot water. Air-cooling available. The owner, an established yoga instructor, offers services free of charge. Singles from Rs60; doubles Rs100; triples Rs120.

Hotel Surya, Jain Temple Rd. (tel. 42341), on the right 200m from the main road, opposite Ristorante Mediterraneo. Spacious, spotless rooms, some with balconies overlooking the green lawn. Singles Rs175; doubles 250, "deluxe" with air-cooling Rs360.

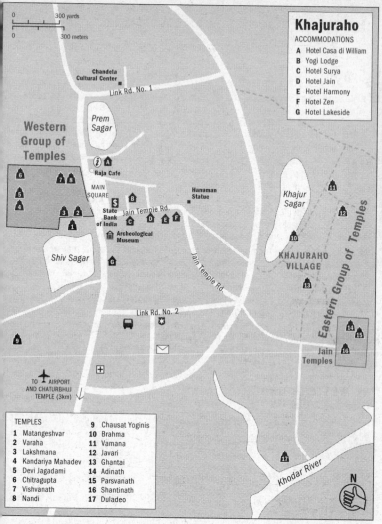

Khajuraho

ACCOMMODATIONS

A Hotel Casa di William
B Yogi Lodge
C Hotel Surya
D Hotel Jain
E Hotel Harmony
F Hotel Zen
G Hotel Lakeside

Western Group of Temples

Prem Sagar

Chandela Cultural Center

Link Rd. No. 1

Raja Cafe

MAIN SQUARE

State Bank of India

Jain Temple Rd.

Hanuman Statue

Archeological Museum

Shiv Sagar

Khajur Sagar

KHAJURAHO VILLAGE

Eastern Group of Temples

Jain Temple Rd.

Link Rd. No. 2

TO AIRPORT AND CHATURBHUJ TEMPLE (3km)

Jain Temples

Khodar River

N

TEMPLES

1 Matangeshvar
2 Varaha
3 Lakshmana
4 Kandariya Mahadev
5 Devi Jagadami
6 Chitragupta
7 Vishvanath
8 Nandi

9   Chausat Yoginis
10 Brahma
11 Vamana
12 Javari
13 Ghantai
14 Adinath
15 Parsvanath
16 Shantinath
17 Duladeo

Hotel Zen, Jain Temple (tel. 44228), farther down the road on the right-hand side from the Hotel Surya. A classy new place with well-furnished rooms, slippery pitter-pat marble floors, and a "zen" garden. Most rooms have a garden view. Off-season: doubles Rs100-200. In season, expect to pay at least double.

Hotel Harmony, Jain Temples Rd. (tel. 44135). Air-cooled rooms with wooden furnishings and attached baths. 2nd fl. rooms have garden views. Off-season: doubles Rs200, with A/C Rs250; single occupancy Rs150. In-season: from Rs350.

Hotel Lakeside, Main Rd. (tel. 44120), opposite Shiv Sagar Lake, next door to the museum. Popular budget place with good rooftop views over the lake towards the temples. Off-season: dorm beds Rs30; singles Rs100; doubles Rs150-250. In season, prices jump 20-100%.

Hotel Jain, Jain Temple Rd. (tel. 42352), next to Hotel Surya. Cheap, clean, friendly— what more do you want? Rooms with attached baths around central courtyard. Singles from Rs80; doubles from Rs125.

Hotel Casa Di William, Prem Sagar Lake Rd. (tel. 44244), on the 1st road that turns right after the Western Group. As clean and homey as your grandmother's kitchen. Rooms have baths with hot water and air-cooling. Rooftop terrace restaurant offers great temple views. Doubles Rs250, with A/C Rs600; single occupancy Rs100/500.

🕐 FOOD

🔪 **Ristorante Mediterraneo,** Jain Temple Rd., 200m from Main Rd., on the left opposite Hotel Surya. 1000km from the nearest source of mozzarella, the Mediterraneo beats the odds. An Italian chef serves up pizza and pasta, with wine-sized bottles of well-chilled beer, to a European crowd that chatters the night away on the rooftop terrace. Pasta siciliane Rs85, pizzas Rs120-145, crepes Rs30-70. Open daily 7:30am-10pm.

Raja Cafe Swiss Restaurant, Main Rd., in a shaded courtyard directly opposite the Western Group. Popular place to sit eating pancakes and fighting off flies. Simple fare includes veg. curry (Rs20) and a large, set breakfast (Rs70). Open daily 8am-10pm.

La Terrazza Restaurant, just opposite the Western Group, on the left of the square at the corner that turns off towards Yogi Lodge. Another good rooftop place with views to the temples and terraces beyond. Menu includes usual breakfast items, *thalis* (Rs40), mutton *masala* (Rs60), and a selection of Chinese dishes (Rs50). Open daily 10am-10pm.

Safari Restaurant, Jain Temple Rd., 20m from the intersection with the main road on the left. Street-level, open-air place offering no-nonsense breakfasts (omelettes Rs20) and standard Indian (Rs40-80), Chinese (Rs40-80), Italian (Rs80), and Continental (Rs40-80) fare. Open daily 6am-10pm.

Madras Coffee House, directly opposite the Western Group, next to the main compound containing the State Bank of India. Popular with Indian tourists. The usual range of Indian and "Chinese" dishes, as well as some thoroughly unremarkable coffee, served at a long, narrow, and slightly cramped row of tables.

👁 SIGHTS

THE WESTERN GROUP
Open sunrise-sunset. Rs5.

The Western Group of temples, in a grassy, fenced-in compound administered by the Archaeological Survey of India, contains many of the best examples of Khajuraho's magnificent architecture. The custom of *pradakshina* dictates that you walk around the whole group clockwise and circle each temple the same way.

LAKSHMI AND VARAHA TEMPLES. The first stop on your *pradakshina* is the least impressive: the **Lakshmi Temple,** a small shrine that 19th-century repairs left with a jagged cement roof. Next door, the open-air, 10th-century **Varaha Mandap,** built for Vishnu's avatar as a boar, offers a more promising beginning. The huge sandstone boar is so well polished that it shines like glazed porcelain, and it is covered with hundreds of tiny gods and goddesses, including those of the sacred rivers Ganga, Yamuna, and Saraswati.

LAKSHMANA TEMPLE. The magnificent Lakshmana Temple, across from the Lakshmi and Varaha temples, is one of the largest in Khajuraho and contains some of the most famous sculpted images. It is also one of the oldest of the Western Group temples, dating from around AD 941. A frieze depicting a military procession winds around the base of the temple; elephants, horses, and soldiers march together in riotous disorder. Here and there the carving is of scenes more reminiscent of an orgy than a goose-stepping drum-banging parade. The temple itself has four halls leading up to its *shikhara* and secondary shrines at the four corners of its platform. A band of hulking elephants in the stonework supports the temple; higher up are several of the erotic scenes that put Khajuraho on the map and which continue to elicit giggles and blushes from visitors. High up on the west side, one figure arches her back away from the viewer, her clothes dripping wet as

SEX IN KHAJURAHO

> The sculptor had at times allowed his subject to grow rather warmer than there was any absolute necessity for his doing; indeed, some of the sculptures here were extremely indecent and offensive.
> —T. S. Burt, describing Khajuraho, 1838

Ever since it was discovered by an itinerant Victorian officer, art historians and religious scholars have wracked their brains trying to figure out why so much sex has been carved onto the walls of Khajuraho's temples. Some have suggested that the sculptures were used for sex education, while others maintain that they were offerings to voyeuristic gods, especially Indra, the lord of lightning, who had to be entertained lest he destroy the temples. A more plausible theory lends the sculptures deeper significance, explaining that Tantric cults, conceiving of sexual intercourse as symbolic of the male and female elements in the universe uniting to make the world turn, used the temples for ritualized sex. More mainstream Hindus hold that much of the sculpture in Khajuraho can be read as part of the wedding myth of Shiva and Parvati. The posing women, who have been caught unaware looking in the mirror, have stopped whatever they were doing in order to watch the wedding procession. All the other gods are here as guests. And, of course, finally, the wedding is consummated—in a great lovemaking session that lasts 1000 god-years. Not all the sculptures fit into the wedding story, and some of the more bizarre scenes may be due to the private jokes of the craftsmen.

she leaves her bath. Two-thirds of the way around (clockwise), another female figure picks a thorn from her foot, illustrating a common Khajuraho theme. The interior of the temple has columns—as if it were an audience hall for the presiding Vishnu—and numerous sculptures of gods and *apsaras* paying him homage.

KANDARIYA MAHADEV TEMPLE. Straight ahead at the far end of the park, three temples stand together on the same platform. Built between 1025 and 1050 and dedicated to Shiva, the Kandariya Mahadev Temple, on the left, is the tallest temple in Khajuraho and is also outstanding for the quality and variety of its sculpture. A waterfall of cascading rock pours down from the temple roof and over the perforated honeycomb stone to the lower walls, which are endlessly indented, projected, articulated, refracted, and retracted to create an intricate 3-D effect. A sex scene on the southern walls delights gaggles of gawkers, but the famous erotic scenes are really just one part of a wide variety of superlative sculpture here. The Kandariya Temple's beauty and the intricacy of its adornments are enhanced because it hasn't blackened with age as many of the other temples have. Over the doorway hangs a stone garland of flowers; inside the sanctum is a *linga*.

MAHADEV SHRINE AND DEVI JAGADAMI TEMPLE. Next to the Kandariya Temple on the same platform is the **Mahadev Shrine,** which contains sculpture showing a human figure grappling with a lion. It has no religious significance; the scene is thought to be a Chandela symbol. The same pair of figures can be found all over Khajuraho. On the other side of the Mahadev Shrine is the **Devi Jagadami Temple.** Though smaller than the Lakshmana and Kandariya temples, it has some superb sculpture, most notably its directional guardians, who are stationed between boldly flirting women and delicate sensual scenes. The image inside is of Kali, but images of Vishnu cover its inside and outside walls.

CHITRAGUPTA TEMPLE. The overall shape of the Chitragupta Temple, Khajuraho's only temple to Surya (the sun god), is identical to that of Jagadami. Small processions run around the lower portion of the temple wall, and higher up are many amorous couples. The damaged wall and roof were repaired with concrete, and most of the statues inside the temple have been decapitated, but the main image of Surya, driving his chariot across the sky, is missing only the arms.

VISHVANATH TEMPLE. Continuing around the circuit, you next come to the small and damaged **Parvati Temple,** but it is overshadowed by the more spectacular Vishvanath Temple next to it, a large Shiva temple dated to 1002 from an inscription inside. Notice the elephant guardians as you approach the stairs to the temple: the *mahout* on the right side seems to have fallen asleep. The bawdy sculptures on the Vishvanath Temple are some of the best: depicted are whole dramatic scenes in which the couples' attendants also get caught up in the action. There are some fascinating sculptures of posing women here—look for the one on the south side twisting her hair to dry and the one on the ceiling inside holding a tiny baby. Some of the figures are sculpted in astonishing detail, down to the cuticles. The Vishvanath Temple originally had a shrine at each corner of its foundation, like the Lakshmana Temple does, but only two remain. In front of the temple is the **Nandi Mandap,** an open shrine where Shiva's bull, Nandi, sits gazing into the temple.

MATANGESHVAR TEMPLE. The two members of the Western group that stray outside the fence are older and noticeably different from the others. Just over the fence from the Lakshmana Temple is the Matangeshvar Temple. Built around AD 900, it is the only temple in the compound that's still in use—more people come here to worship than to view the architecture. It is a relatively plain temple with only thin stripes of carving. Inside, a *linga* sits on top of a huge stone platform. The temple's upper-level terrace has good views of the Lakshmana Temple.

CHAUSAT YOGINIS. Along the south side of the **Shiv Sagar tank,** a small lake bordered by the main road, a narrow, tree-lined path leads off to the right and out to the temple of Chausat Yoginis ("Sixty-Four Goddesses"). The high building is made of crudely cut blocks of granite piled together like sandbags. Around the top is a gallery of empty shrines—there were once 64 of these little windows. but only 35 remain. The Chandelas used this temple for worship early in their reign; it is the oldest temple in Khajuraho, dating from the 9th century.

ARCHAEOLOGICAL MUSEUM. Across the street from the Western Group enclosure, the Archaeological Museum houses sculptures separated from their temples. A wonderful dancing Ganesh stands in the entrance hall. In the center of the Miscellaneous Gallery on the right, a stout king and queen sit together making an offering; this is possibly a portrait of the sculptor's Chandela patrons. Also note the unfinished amorous couple whose small noses have been left stuck together with a gooey thread. In truth, there are few pieces here to compare with the best sculpture still on the temples. The museum is worth a visit, though, if only for the opportunity it offers to get good close-up views of some of the sculptures. *(Open Sa-Th 10am-5pm. Free with Western Group ticket.)*

EASTERN AND SOUTHERN GROUPS

Open sunrise-sunset.

Scattered in and about Khajurajo village, the temples of the Eastern Group are not as stunning as those in the Western Group. But since they are visited by fewer people, they have an atmosphere of relative quiet and seclusion lacking around the temples of the main group. The so-called "Southern Group" is comprised of two temples farther apart from one another than from either of the other two groups.

EASTERN GROUP. Along Jain Temple Rd. is a **Hanuman Shrine** containing one of the oldest sculptures in Khajuraho, a large *sindur*-smeared Hanuman image that dates from the 9th century. Crossing the bypass road and entering Khajuraho village, the path veers to the left along the side of a seasonal pond called the **Khajur Sagar.** Not far along it on the left is the small **Brahma Temple,** misnamed by 19th-century art historians. A four-faced Shiva *linga* sits in the sanctuary, and Vishnu is carved on the lintel above the door. The **Vamana Temple,** at the end of this lakeside path, is as large as some of the temples in the Western Group, simpler in design, and boasts slightly less impressive sculpture and decoration.

Down a path just south of the Vamana temple is the **Javari Temple,** which features a number of interesting pieces despite its small size and relatively simple design. The women that dance around the temple walls manage to look remarkably life-like and spritely even though most of them had their heads knocked off centuries ago. A section of the Eastern Group consists of several Jain temples walled into a Jain monastery complex on the far side of Khajuraho village. The old temples here are interspersed with the new ones. This mixture is embodied in the **Shantinath Temple,** which was built recently but has heavy pillars and doorways taken from older temples. Inside the temple is a collection of photographs, posters of Jain pilgrimage sites and plenty of sculptures of naked Jain monks.

To the left of the Shantinath Temple is the best of the Jain temples, the **Parsvanath Temple.** It is noted for its simple design—there are no balconies—and the small shrine at the back. In addition to Jain *tirthankaras* (saints), the sculptures on the outside depict just about every major Hindu deity; it is thought that this was once a Hindu temple. Some of the most famous sculptures in Khajuraho are here, including one of a woman putting on ankle-bells and another of a woman applying her make-up. On the other side of a big mango tree, **Adinath Temple,** whose porch has been reconstructed in concrete, features supple women climbing up the walls. Shiny black *tirthankara* images sit inside both temples.

SOUTHERN GROUP. A paved road off to the right of Jain Temple Rd. (marked "Dhulade") leads to the **Duladeo Temple.** This temple dates from around 1100, by which time standards had started to slip in Khajuraho—the sculpture here is generally held to be inferior to that of the other temples. There are still plenty of interesting little scenes, though: numerous dragon-like mythical beasts and people depicted going about their daily lives. At the southern end of the temple is a pair of dioramas showing first a man and then a woman unsuccessfully imitating one of the other sex-in-stone scenes so prevalent in Khajuraho. The *linga* inside the temple is overlaid with dozens of tiny replicas of itself, giving it a curiously scaly appearance. The *mahamandapam*, a hall with a great rotunda ceiling, has an elaborate star shape. By the time this temple was built, sculptors were getting so carried away with the embelishing ornaments and jewelry on their human figures that the quality of the sculptures themselves began to decline.

Chaturbhuj Temple is 3km south of Khajuraho down the main road. It's a trip best made in the late afternoon; Chaturbhuj is the only big temple in Khajuraho that faces west. The evening light shines warmly on its 2.7m *dakshinamurti* statue: one stone, three deities. This huge image is thought to be a combination of Shiva, Vishnu, and Krishna. The sculptures around the outside feature another interesting hybrid: on the south side, an image of Ardhanarishvara (half-Shiva, half-Parvati) is split down the middle illustrating the motif of male and female union that was so significant to those who produced the marvelous sculptures at Khajuraho.

JHANSI झाँसी

Jhansi is one of those places you only come to in order to get to somewhere else. There are worse places than this in India, to be sure, but apart from those with a particular interest in dusty urban ugliness, most travelers would be well advised to take a good long look at the timetables before coming to Jhansi: this is not the kind of town you want to get stranded in for long. Jhansi draws tourists due to its proximity to Orchha and its function as a railhead for Khajuraho. Schedules may conspire to detain you here, in which case you can while away the hours in rapt contemplation of Maharani Lakshmi Bai's last stand at the city's otherwise uninspiring fort. A celebrated revolutionary, she joined the anti-British *sepoys* in the Mutiny of 1857. As the British recaptured the region, Jhansi was one of the last rebel holdouts. Dressed as a man, her guns blazing, the *maharani* rode out into battle to meet her final demise 180km from Jhansi.

MADHYA PRADESH

⁊ ORIENTATION AND PRACTICAL INFORMATION. Downtown Jhansi covers a 5km span from the **railway station** in the west to the **bus stand** in the east. About 1km north of the station, **Shivpuri Road** runs straight-ish all the way across town. The **U.P. Tourism Main Office** (tel. 441267) is in the Hotel Veerangana on **Sipri Road.** To get there, take a left on **Station Road,** go straight to Sipri Crossing, and take a right; the hotel is on the left. (Open M-Sa 10am-5pm.) There is an **MPTDC** booth on platform #1 of the railway station (tel. 442622; open daily 6am-11pm). **Buses** for Khajuraho leave from the railway station (6 and 7am) and from the bus stand (11:45am and 1:15pm, Rs60). The superfast A/C *Shatabdi Exp.* 2001 departs to: **Delhi** (5:45pm, 4hr., Rs525) via **Agra** (2hr., Rs295) and **Gwalior** (1hr., Rs200). Trains also run to **Bhopal** (*Shatabdi Exp.* 2002, 10:45am, 3hr., Rs450) and **Jabalpur** (*Mahakoshal Exp.* 1450, 10:45pm, 12hr., Rs119/625). **Tempos** for Orchha (Rs6) leave directly from the bus stand. The **State Bank of India** (tel. 330298), Jhokar Bagh Rd., at the center of town near Elite Crossing, changes AmEx traveler's checks (open M-F 10am-2pm, Sa 10am-noon). The **telegraph office**, Gwalior Rd., is opposite Hotel Pujan (open M-Sa 10am-5pm). The government **hospital** (tel. 440521) is on Mani Chowk, the market at the base of the fort. The **police station** is located on the Main Rd. (tel. 440538). There's a 24-hour **STD/ISD** booth on platform #6 at the railway station. **Postal Code:** 284001. **Telephone Code:** 0517.

⌂⌦ ACCOMMODATIONS AND FOOD. ⬚ **Hotel Prakash** (tel. 448822), in Civil Lines not far from the railway station, is stretched out around a pleasant lawn of grass and weeds. It offers good-sized rooms with attached baths. (Singles from Rs200, with A/C Rs350; doubles from Rs250/450.) **The Prakash Regency Guest House,** Sardarilal Lal Market, Civil Lines (tel. 330133 or 330226), just south of the fort, offers pleasant mid-range lodgings. The air-cooled rooms feature wall-to-wall carpeting, air-cooling, and twin beds (Rs250, with A/C Rs550). **Hotel Veerangana** (tel. 442402), run by U.P. Tourism, has clean dorms (beds Rs60) and large, clean rooms (singles Rs200, with air-cooling Rs300; doubles Rs275/375). The downstairs restaurant has a small, dark, A/C bar. The restaurant in the ⬚ **Hotel Sita,** Shivpuri Rd., serves absolutely first-rate food in a civilized and climate-controlled environment (open daily 6:30am-10pm). The Prakash Regency Guest House also has a decent restaurant and bar called **Sagar,** where brave souls can sample *paneer pasendida,* "stuffed with sultans," (Rs35; open daily 6:30am-11pm). For a place with character as well as flavor, the restaurant in the colonial-era **Jhansi Hotel** is well worth a try. Stuffed animal heads hang from the walls, and the bar is open most of the day to see to the G&T needs of the dress-for-dinner crowd.

☗ SIGHTS. The **Jhansi Fort** has nothing much to recommend it apart from the views from its ramparts. Most of the fort itself is an empty and decrepit-looking home to bands of monkeys and bats. Outside the fort, along the southern wall as you approach the main entrance, there's a bizarre life-size model depicting a battle between heroic Indian freedom-fighters and their dastardly red-coat oppressors during the Mutiny of 1857. Local mailmen joined in the resistance by converting old letterboxes into weapons. These ailbox cannons appear to have inflicted mortal wounds on several Brits, much to the satisfaction of Indian onlookers. This stirring scene may quicken the pulse—"Who cannot remain unimpressed by this life-like picturisation?" asks a sign next to the diorama—but the nearby **museum** is sure to induce catatonia. (Open 10am-5pm. Rs0.25.)

ORCHHA ओरछा

A feeling of wistfulness is inspired by the ruins speckling the small town of Orchha, located on a loop in the Betwa river 16km from Jhansi. An abandoned 17th-century city rises out of the hills and trees, its crumbling towers still clinging to the rocky rubble. During its heyday in the 16th and 17th centuries, Orchha was the capital of a small Bundela kingdom. It was abandoned in 1783 when the continual onslaught of Mughal and Maratha attacks became too much for the city to withstand. Raja Rudra Pratap Bundela chose Orchha as his capital in 1531, and the Bundelas' fortunes grew as they kept the Mughal Empire at bay. Raja Bir Singh Deo (r. 1605-27), the greatest Bundela king, befriended the emperor Jahangir and even had him visit here in 1606. Under Bir Singh Deo, the Bundelas expanded to control the whole region of Bundelk-hand, which still bears their name. Later Bundela rulers were less successful at appeasing the Mughals, and once the emperor Shah Jahan attacked Orchha, the kingdom's long, slow decline became inevitable.

The Bundelas left a landscape filled with palaces and temples, and nothing but the forces of nature disturbed them for two centuries. Orchha, meaning "hidden," lives up to its name—when human rulers gave up the attempt to con-ceal the city from invaders, nature took up the challenge. The ruins are over-grown with trees and weeds, cracked walls are shrouded with vines, and empty palace courtyards echo with lonely birdcalls.

ORIENTATION AND PRACTICAL INFORMATION

Tempos sputter to Orchha from Jhansi (Rs6) and from the intersection of **Orchha Road** with the highway running from Jhansi to Khajuraho, spitting out their passengers just south of the village's only **crossroads.** South past the bus and tempo stand lies the pricey MPTDC Betwa Cottages complex, as well as some royal cenotaphs and the new five-star Orchha Resort on the banks of the **Betwa River.** The right-hand (eastern) crossroad, heading up from the bus sta-tion, leads to the bridge connecting the main palace complex to the village. You'll first pass the **Post Office.** Towering over the village are Orchha's best-preserved sights; the enormous Jehangir Mahal and the decorated Raj Mahal. From the crossroads, the MPTDC's second property, the Mansarovar Hotel, the Chaturbhuj and Ram Raja temples, and the Palki Mahal Hotel, lie on the way to the Lakshminarayan Temple at the western edge. **Police:** tel. 52622. Most guest services are in Jhansi.

ACCOMMODATIONS AND FOOD

The MPTDC has converted an 18th-century palace in the middle of Orchha's ruins into the moderately priced **Sheesh Mahal Hotel** (tel. 52624), where the suites are really only moderately palatial. Wherever you end up, though, you get to gaze out over the deserted turrets to the woods and fields beyond. The best rooms are stuffed with rugs and carpets and have nooks and alcoves full of hookahs, tin drums, and TVs. Be prepared to shell out Rs2990 for the maha-raja treatment. (Singles with bath Rs490; doubles Rs590; suites with air-cooling Rs1990. Off-season: 25% discount.) The hotel's **restaurant,** open to guests and non-guests, features standard entrees, as well as breakfast and snacks (open daily 7am-10pm). Try to book at an MPTDC office up to a month in advance during busy times. The local SADA runs three budget lodges, none of which is really anything special. **Palki Mahal,** inside the Phool Bagh Palace (next door to the Ram Raja Temple), combines dorm beds (Rs25) with history, while the **Mansarovar** (tel. 52633), by the crossroads, mixes threadbare sheets with tatty modernity (doubles Rs75). The final SADA offering is the **Pryatak Guest House,** with cement cottages complemented by a cement courtyard (rooms with bath Rs75). There are plenty of *dhabas* in the market, but for any-thing more than a simple snack, you'll have to head down towards the river to the **Orchha Resort.** There, a shiny, A/C, all-veg. restaurant serves excellent meals for Rs70. (Open daily 8am-10pm.)

◉ SIGHTS

THE RUINS

All locations open 8am-5pm. Rs30 for a ticket that covers all the main sights. Walkman tour 2hr.; Rs50, Rs500 deposit.

The ruins of Orchha are scattered all over this bend in the Betwa and they spill across from the main "island" to the modern town and beyond. Nothing much has happened in Orchha over the past 200 years to clear them away, and nothing of any consequence has been built here since the Bhundelas closed shop and left the place to the winds. The old buildings still enjoy uncontested hegemony over the landscape and skyline, and the shells of abandoned palaces and temples stand alone and undisturbed amidst the encroaching grasses and trees. Slumping towers and overgrown archways are everywhere, most of them unnamed and unmarked. Hotel Sheesh Mahal offers a **walkman tour** that covers the three main palaces. This is well worth taking for the historical background, though you'll probably find your finger twitching over the fast-forward button from time to time as the breathless narrator launches into yet another dramatic "picture-the-scene" sequence.

PALACES. The **Raj Mahal,** on the left side as you face the hotel, was the king's residence, with a room for his private audiences and several chambers for his harem. One of the oldest buildings in Orchha, the palace lacks any notable ornamental features. The building itself is somewhat blocky and relatively unimpressive, though the walls and ceilings of many of the rooms are painted with intricate botanical patterns and murals depicting religious and mythical scenes. The top windows offer a good view of the town. The steps to the right of the Raj Mahal lead down to the **public audience hall,** after which the path veers down and to the right again through numerous unmarked ruins.

The next complete palace is the **Rai Praveen Mahal,** built and named for Raja Indramani's favorite dancing concubine. This palace was intended to be level with the treetops in the Anand Mahal gardens behind it. These can still be seen from the second floor, and, though neither the palace nor its gardens have exactly improved with age, it is still possible to imagine (as your audio-guide will constantly remind-ing you) that this must once have been quite a nice place to kick back and relax after a long hard day spent wielding supreme executive power.

If you walk through the arch and head up the hill to the right (you'll pass the camel stables), you should be able to enter through the main door of the stunning **Jahangir Mahal** palace. Built for Emperor Jahangir when he visited Orchha in 1606, this palace surpasses anything else the Bundela ever built in Orchha. Two ele-phants nod in welcome on either side of the entrance. Inside, the Jahangir Mahal is filled with balconies, walkways, and railings. Traces of Islamic style are visible in the stone screens and decorated domes. The views to the east from the third-floor balconies are some of Orchha's best: the Betwa river curls through the country-side and into the village, winding its way past the palaces. Throughout the palace are numerous fine carvings of peacocks, parrots, snakes, and other animals.

TEMPLES. The north end of Orchha's island is reached by turning left after pass-ing through the **Royal Gate,** then passing through another archway in a wall. This is a good place to fight back the thornbushes and explore—it's dotted with **old tem-ples** that have been neglected and are now surrounded by small wheat farms. Peo-ple still dip into the ancient wells for their drinking water here, and, in some cases, the temples have become makeshift toolsheds and kitchens.

Back on the other side of the river, beyond the intersection with the main road, are several more minor palaces, as well as a number of important Bundela tem-ples, the two most prominent of which share an interconnected history. The devout Raja Madhukar Shah had a dream in which Lord Rama appeared and instructed him to bring an image of the Lord to Orchha from his holy hometown of Ayodhya. The king did as he was told but arrived back in Orchha before his work-men had completed the temple designed to house the image, so he decided to keep the holy image in his own palace until the temple could be completed. When the time came to relocate him, though, Lord Rama refused to budge. The palace had to be given up, and it became the **Ram Raja Temple,** where Rama has been worshipped in his role as a king ever since. Painted pink and yellow and overlooking a cobbled square, Ram Raja is now a popular temple. (Temple open daily 8am-1pm and 8-10pm.) The **Chhaturbhuj Temple,** however, is defunct, left only with a great arching assembly hall and several large spires. Spiral staircases at each corner of the cross-shaped floorplan lead to high lookout points.

At the crest of a hill 1km west of town is the **Lakshminarayan Temple**. Its location seems fit for a fort, and the temple is built like one, with four high walls, turrets at the corners, and two mighty stone lions standing guard at the entrance. Inside the temple are the best paintings to be found anywhere in Orchha. Some of them date from as late as the 19th century, including one fabulous post-Mutiny scene of British soldiers swarming around an Indian fort. The lookout above the entrance offers a pleasant view of the temples and palaces. (Open daily 10am-5pm.)

Clustered along the peaceful, tree-lined banks of the Betwa river, just south of town, is a series of box-like royal **chhattris** (cenotaphs). The Bundelas, being a Hindu people, cremated their dead. This custom did not, however, stop them from borrowing the Mughal custom of mausoleum-building.

MADHYA PRADESH

GWALIOR ग्वालियर

India is covered in ruins of one kind or another; but there are few anywhere that can rival those in Gwalior, the largest city in northern Madhya Pradesh (pop. 800,000). For centuries, Gwalior has been legendary for the massive fort that looks down upon the city from high above. Emperor Babur called the fort "the pearl amongst the fortresses of Hind," and generations of conquerors have gazed down on the world from here, from the Rajputs and Marathas to the Mughals and the British, to the Scindia family, who dominate local politics today. During the Raj, the Maharaja of Gwalior earned one of only five 21-gun salutes accorded Indian potentates by the British, in recognition of his loyalty during the Mutiny. This royal treatment stands in stark contrast to the fate of Maharani Lakshmi Bai, who resisted the British in nearby Jhansi (see p. 385). The Scindia royal family is still the focus of Gwalior's civic pride: their palace, a 19th-century shrine to conspicuous consumption, offers a glimpse into a fairy-tale world of kitschy chaos and conforms to every stereotypical preconception of what a maharaja's house should be.

▐ TRANSPORTATION

Airport: Bhind Rd. (tel. 310348), 10km northeast of the city. **Indian Airlines,** MLB Rd. (tel. 326872), opposite Shelter Hotel. Open M-Sa 10am-5pm. Flights to: **Bhopal** (M, W, F, and Su 5:10pm; 1hr.; US$70); **Bombay** (5:30pm, 3hr., US$108); **Delhi** (M, Tu, Th, and Sa 2:05pm; 45min.; US$60); **Mumbai** (M, W, F, and Su 5:10pm; 3hr.; US$145); **Indore** (5:30pm, 2hr., US$95).

Trains: Railway Station, MLB Rd., Morar (tel. 341344). *Shatabdi Exp.* fares are for A/C chair-car; others are listed 2nd/1st class. To: **Agra** (*Shatabdi Exp.* 2001, 7pm, 1hr., Rs225; *Mangala Lakshadweep Exp.* 2617, 10:40am, 1½hr.; *Punjab Mail* 2137, 3pm, 1½hr., Rs36/189); **Bhopal** (*Shatabdi Exp.* 2002, 9:15am, 4½hr., Rs505; *Mangala Lakshadweep Exp.* 2618, 2:15pm, 6hr.; *Nizamuddin Habibganj Exp.* 2156, 3am, 6hr., Rs106/557); **Delhi** (*Shatabdi Exp.* 2001, 7pm, 3½hr., Rs465; *Punjab Mail* 2137, 3pm, 6hr.; *Dadar Amritsar Exp.* 1057, 9:55pm, 7hr., Rs77/405); **Jhansi** (*Shatabdi Exp.* 2002, 9:15am, 1hr., Rs200; *Chhathisgarh Exp.* 8238, 11am, 2hr.; *Maha Koshal Exp.* 1450, 9:10pm, 2hr., Rs31/173); **Kanpur** (*Ahmedabad-Gorakhpur Exp.* 5045, Tu 4:15am, 7½hr., Rs49/246; *Gwalior Baranni Mail* 5224, 11:15am, 7hr., Rs50/263); **Lucknow** (*Ahmedabad-Gorakhpur Exp.* 5045, 4:15am, 9hr.; *Gwalior Baurani Mail* 5224, 11:15am, 9hr., Rs531/279); **Mathura** (*Mangala Lakshadweep Exp.* 2617, 10:40am, 2½hr.; *Punjab Mail* 2137, 3pm, 2½hr.; *Dadar Amritsar Exp.* 1057, 9:55pm, 3hr., Rs50/263); **Mumbai** (*Punjab Mail* 2138, 10:25am, 21hr., Rs200/1050).

Buses: State bus stand (tel. 340192), near the railway station off MLB Rd. To: **Agra** (14 per day 5am-9:30pm, 3hr., Rs45); **Bhopal** (7:30 and 11am, 16hr., Rs142); **Delhi** (7 per day 5am-9:30pm, 8hr., Rs120); **Jhansi** (every 30min., 3hr., Rs38); **Khajuraho** (8am, 8hr., Rs95). The **private bus stand** is in Lashkar, not too far from Bada Chowk.

Local Transportation: Tempos cruise down MLB Rd. from one side of town to the other. Fares are typically Rs2. **Auto-rickshaws,** the best way of getting around, are everywhere; their meters are purely decorative.

ORIENTATION AND PRACTICAL INFORMATION

Gwalior is quite spread out, wrapped in an irregular "U" shape around the **fort.** The **Old Town,** containing the **railway station** and the state **bus stand,** lies to the east of the fort; the **Morar** area, dominated by the gaudy **palace,** is to the southeast; and the **Lashkar** area is in the southwest. Lashkar is the heart of modern Gwalior, with a bazaar area and **Bada (Jiyaji) Chowk,** where the GPO and State Bank of India are located. **Maharani Lakshmi Bai (MLB) Road** runs across town from northeast, near the station, to Lashkar. Gwalior's **business holiday** is Tuesday.

Tourist Office: MPTDC (tel. 345379), platform #1 of the railway station. Friendly officer distributes maps and pamphlets about M.P., arranges city tours (9:30am-2pm, Rs40), and provides bus transportation (6:30pm, Rs25) for the fort's sound and light show (Indians Rs20, foreigners Rs50). Open M-Sa 8am-7pm. The **main regional tourist office,** Gandhi Rd. (tel. 340370), is inside the Hotel Tansen.

Currency Exchange: State Bank of India, Bada Chowk (tel. 422968). The foreign exchange desk, on the 1st fl. of the main building next to the GPO, changes traveler's checks and foreign currency. Open M-F 10:30am-2:30pm, Sa 10:30am-12:30pm.

Hospital: Royal Hospital, Kampoo (tel. 332711), near Roxy Cinema. Recommended private hospital with doctors available 24hr. and ambulance service. **Kasturba Medical Stores,** 6 Kasturba Market (tel. 310953), 1km away, is open 24hr.

Police: Jayendra Ganj (tel. 326037).

Post Office: GPO, Bada Chowk, has *Poste Restante.* Open M-Sa 8am-8pm, Su 10am-6pm. **Postal Code:** 474001.

Internet: Bhargava Computers, opposite the Miss Hill School, Lakshmi Bai Colony (tel. 428946). Web access Rs75 per hr. Open daily 9:30am-9:30pm.

PHONE CODE	0751

ACCOMMODATIONS

In addition to the listings below, there are several acceptable budget hotels lining the market in front of the railway station. Most of these have 24-hour check-out.

Hotel Mayur, Paday (tel. 325559). Turn right out of the railway station and fly over the flyover; turn back down the small service road and look for the signs on the left. Spotless rooms. Check-out 24hr. Dorms Rs55; doubles Rs120, with bath Rs150.

Hotel Fort View, MLB Rd. (tel. 423409). One of a string of places along the main road in the shadow of the fort. Attached bar and restaurant. Good views of the fort from one side. Check-out noon. Doubles with bath Rs225, deluxe from Rs400.

Hotel Midway, MLB Rd. (tel. 424392), 2.5km from the rail station, opposite the *gurudwara.* A sterile complex with clean sheets and towels, satellite TVs, phones that work, hot water, and generator-powered email facilities. Clean, air-cooled rooms. Check-out noon. Doubles Rs300, single occupancy double Rs250; deluxe with A/C Rs500.

Regal Hotel, Shinde Ki Chhawanii, MLB Rd. (tel. 334469). Another decent place facing the main road, the Regal has rooms for kings and queens of all shapes and sizes. Breezy garden terrace upstairs and airless beer bar downstairs. Check-out noon. Singles with air-cooling Rs200; doubles with bath Rs250, deluxe with A/C Rs400.

Hotel Meghdoot, Padav (tel. 326148), next to the Indian Airlines office just after the flyover leading back to the railway station. Standard budget hotel, good location for rail access. Singles with bath Rs140; doubles Rs200; A/C suite Rs525.

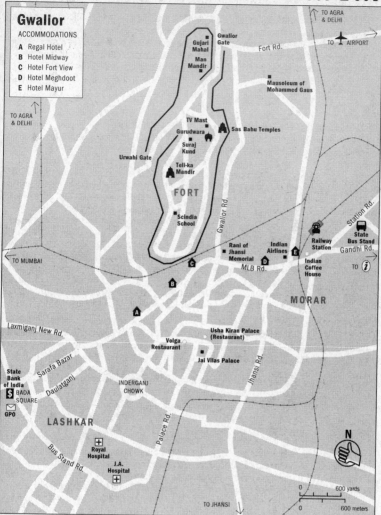

Gwalior

ACCOMMODATIONS

A Regal Hotel
B Hotel Midway
C Hotel Fort View
D Hotel Meghdoot
E Hotel Mayur

FOOD

Volga Restaurant, Tayendra Ganj, inside Hotel Surya. The *malai-de-la-malai* of Gwalior society frequent this chandeliered, A/C bastion of the *bourzhaozya*. Gentle lighting, lsoft music, and efficient service with a smile. All this and good food too. Entrees around Rs50. Open daily 11:30am-4:30pm and 7-11pm.

Indian Coffee House, Station Rd. From the station, turn right, then head left at the traffic circle. Same old reliable veg. snacks as always, served up by friendly waiters in white with feathers in their caps. Just out of the fumy haze of Station Rd., and a good place for a revitalizing cup of decent coffee. Open daily 7am-8pm.

Kwality Restaurant, Deendayal Market, MLB Rd. Chalk up another one for the dim, non-descript, A/C chain with a spelling problem. Standard range of north Indian veg. (Rs18-50), chicken (Rs45), and mutton (Rs40) dishes. Open daily 11:30am-11pm.

Usha Kiran Palace, Jayendraganj, Lashkar. This tasteful cold-as-Greenland restaurant inside Gwalior's most beautiful hotel is the place to come if the luxury at nearby Jain Vilas palace has whetted your appetite for the finer things in life. Lots of plants to talk to as you wait for your meal to arrive. *Haute cuisine* from around the world, and everything from fish 'n' chips (Rs200) to a pageful of "peony's favorites" (Rs110-225).

🔍 SIGHTS

GWALIOR FORT

Fort open daily 8am-6:30pm. Free.

Gwalior's amazing fort, almost 3km long and at points 1km wide, dominates the city from 90m above, behind hulking 10m-high walls. It has been the center of the region's power for all of recorded history. According to legend, it was built in the first century AD by a king named Suraj, who was cured of leprosy here by a holy hermit named Gwalipa. Out of gratitude to his healer, Suraj named the fort Gwalior. Since then, the fort has come to be ruled by all of the region's succeeding dynasties: Rajputs, Delhi Sultans, Mughals, Marathas, and eventually the British. Since 1886, the fort has belonged to the Scindias, Gwalior's present royal family. Through the ages, the fort has accumulated palaces and temples within and, most recently, a prestigious boys' school, a TV relay station, and two post offices.

There are two entrances to the fort: **Gwalior Gate** on the northeast side, adjacent to the Old Town; and **Urwahi Gate** on the southwest, which is approached through a long gorge. Both have long, steep ramps which must be climbed on foot, although cars and taxis (but not auto-rickshaws) can enter through Urwahi Gate. It's worth entering at Gwalior Gate for the view of the Man Mandir Palace's picture-postcard towers above.

THE PALACES. At the base of the hill just inside Gwalior Gate is the **Gujari Mahal Palace,** built by Man Singh Tomar for his favorite queen. Inside the palace courtyard is an **archaeological museum** with a melange of sculptures and paintings from the region. The curator keeps a Salabhanjika miniature sculpture of the tree-goddess Gyraspur—a priceless piece of art history—under lock and key, but he might be coaxed into showing it. *(Museum open Tu-Su 10am-5pm. Rs2.)*

The northeastern ramp continues up through a series of archways past Jain and Hindu shrines. Looming overhead are the blue-splotched towers of the **Man Mandir Palace.** As you pass through the Elephant Gate (there was once a big stone elephant here) into the fort itself, Raja Man Singh Tomar's creation on your right becomes livelier, with blue, green, and yellow tiles forming pictures of plants and ducks. Inside the palace are many small rooms split by lattices carved in the shape of animals and dancers. These elaborate, perforated screens with a *dandia-ras* motif bear witness to the *purdah,* or veiling system, that is customary among certain groups of Hindus and Muslims. Noble women would be expected to spend much of their time sitting behind these screens, peering through them at the world outside. A flashlight will help lead the way down to the bat-infested dungeon complex where, in the 17th century, the Mughal emperor Aurangzeb had his brother Murad chained up and slowly killed through starvation and intoxication, feeding him nothing but boiled and mashed-up poppies. Near the Man Mandir Palace is a **museum,** run by the Archaeological Survey of India. It's not as impressive as the

---

COME ON BABY, FIGHT MY FIRE Legend has it that Akbar's greatest court singer, Miyan Tansen, learned the powerful *raga dipak* after having seen a twig spontaneously catch fire in a songbird's beak. The *raga*, when performed with the full intensity, supposedly turns the practitioner's vocal chords into ashes. When Tansen's jealous rivals challenged him to sing *dipak* for the emperor, he welcomed the opportunity. Little did the baddies know that the savvy musician had trained his wife in the rain-inducing *raga mahar* to counter *dipak*'s fiery impact. When the crooner began to ignite, his wife was called in, and the subsequent duet of fire and water so impressed Akbar that he aided Tansen's ascendancy in the imperial court.

one at the bottom of the hill, but it's free and the staff sells cold drinks. *(Open Sa-Th 10am-5pm.)* On the other side of the Elephant Gate from the Man Mandir Palace are seats for the nightly **sound and light show** *(8:30pm, Rs50).*

To reach the north end of the fort, pass through the gate on your right as you exit the Man Mandir Palace. This area is a barren landscape where ruined palaces and dried-up tanks cling to the edge of the hill. There are four palaces here, two built by the Tomar Rajputs and two by the Mughals. The huge **Jauhar Tank** next to them is remembered for the *jauhar* (mass suicide) of Rajput queens here in 1232, when Sultan Iltutmish of Delhi was on the verge of capturing the fort.

THE TEMPLES. About midway along the eastern edge of the hilltop are the **Sas Bahu** temples, built in 1093. One temple's spire has fallen, but its assembly hall, still standing, has a beautiful stack of skewed false stories. The edge of the fort here offers a drab view of the city, but at least the big brown dome of Muhammad Gaus's tomb is visible. The west side of the fort affords better views of the sprawling city and its craggy landscape. The nearby **Bandi Chhor Gurudwara** is a Sikh pilgrimage site that marks the spot where the sixth Sikh Guru, Hargobind, was imprisoned for two years by Emperor Jahangir. Ritual cleansing is required for entry, and cloths are provided for you to cover your head before entering the *gurudwara.* Inside, men sit and chant Sikh scriptures above a sunken silver chamber marking the guru's jail.

The **Teli-ka Mandir** ("Oilman's Temple") is a tall building, though not tall enough to rival the nearby TV mast. The Mandir dates from the 9th century. It was once a Vishnu temple, but when the British occupied the fort in the 19th century, they turned it into a soda-water factory. The southwestern entrance passes through the long Urwahi Gorge, a natural rift in the hillside. Its walls are adorned with rows of **Jain sculptures** dating from between the 7th and 15th centuries. These figures of *tirthankaras* still stand impassively above the road, despite the efforts of Mughal conqueror Babur, who damaged many of the statues by smashing in their faces and genitals. One statue, an image of Adhinath, is 19m tall. More of these carvings are on the southeast side of the fort, including one still used as a Jain shrine.

OUTSIDE THE FORT

JAI VILAS PALACE. Maharaja Jiyaji Rao Scindia commissioned a British architect to erect this great white whale of a complex to impress the Prince of Wales (later Edward VII) on his state visit in 1875. Generations of Scindias since then have filled it with the most outrageous *objets d'art* and kitsch; now part of it is open as a **museum** (the rest is still the maharaja's residence). Furniture from Versailles, crystal and marble staircases, and a set of shimmering crystal furniture are just a few of the palace's notable features. Tatty stuffed tigers fill up the "Natural History Gallery." From the gilded ceiling of Durbar Hall hang two enormous Belgian chandeliers, each weighing 3.5 tons, and below them is the largest handmade carpet in Asia. Downstairs, the dining table has tracks for a silver toy train that once wheeled around after-dinner brandy and cigars. *(Open daily Th-Tu 10am-6pm. Rs175 for foreigners. Keep your ticket stub for entry to both wings.)*

OTHER SIGHTS. To the east of the fort in the Old Town is the **Mausoleum of Sheik Muhammad Ghaus.** The sheik was a Muslim saint who helped the Mughal emperor Babur capture Gwalior Fort. The walls of this fine early Mughal monument are made up of a series of cut-stone screens carved into beautiful geometric patterns. *(Open daily sunrise-sunset.)* The **Tomb of Tansen,** in the same graveyard, evokes a different kind of rhythm: the 16th-century *raga*-singer was one of the greatest musicians in Indian history. (See **Come on Baby Fight my Fire,** above.) A prestigious classical music festival takes place here in November or December. Chewing the leaves of the tamarind tree near the tomb is supposed to make your voice as sweet as Tansen's. In the Lashkar area, **Bada Square** is one of the most scenic parts of Gwalior. Palm trees, benches, frilly arches, and a clock tower are ringed around a statue of Maharaja Jiyaji Rao Scindia. Gwalior's newest big thing is its **Sun Temple,** in the Morar area. A scaled-down knock-off of the Sun Temple in **Konark** (see p. 619), it was built by the philanthropic Birla family. *(Open daily 6am-noon and 2-7pm.)*

MAHARASHTRA
महाराष्ट्र

Maharashtra, the "Great Country," straddles the Indian Peninsula, from the tropical coast to the arid Deccan Plateau, from the fringes of the hot and hectic Gangetic Plain to the palmier, balmier, more easy-going south, and from isolated villages to metropolitan Mumbai. From the Hindu devotees immersing themselves en masse in the sacred Godavari at Nasik to the giddy, red-robed, Birkenstock-clad acolytes of the Osho Commune to the businessmen and billboards of Mumbai, the state encompasses both the sacred and the profane. Over half of India's foreign trade and nearly 40% of its tax revenue flows from the state, yet almost two-thirds of Maharashtra's population still survives on subsistence-level agriculture. Most Maharashtrians proudly embrace the bold martial tradition and a fierce regional autonomy of their forbears, the Marathas, hardy fighters bred in the rocky hinterland. This heritage is singularly embodied by the warrior-king and folk-hero Shivaji (1627-80) and is currently exploited by the ruling Shiv Sena (literally, "Shivaji's Army") Party, a Hindu nationalist ally of the BJP. Perhaps all Indian states can be fairly described as *mirch masala* amalgams; what distinguishes Maharashtra is its hard-working and strident citizenry.

HIGHLIGHTS OF MAHARASHTRA

■ The intricately carved **cave temples** at **Ajanta** (p. 434) and **Ellora** (p. 432), both UNESCO World Heritage Sites, are architectural wonders par excellence.
■ Bombay by any other name smells as sweet—well, maybe not, but **Mumbai** (below) impresses with its sights, sounds, nightlife, and ceaseless energy.
■ The ruins of the village and impregnable fort at **Daulatabad** (p. 432) offer a peek at the genius, and lack thereof, of some of India's great ancient despots.

MUMBAI (BOMBAY) मुंबई

India's largest city, in attitude as well as population, Mumbai unites all of the country's languages, religions, ethnicities, castes, and classes in one heaving, seething sizzler of a metropolis. Mumbai blends myriad traditions and innovations from each region, city, and village in India and beyond, offering everything from *bhel puri* to bell-bottoms. Trade through the city accounts for 50% of India's imports and exports and its densest concentration of industry, as well as the nation's largest stock exchange. Rupee and dollar billionaires, film stars, models, and politicians flock to frolic at the many opulent hotels, expensive discos, and ritzy restaurants. But Mumbai also harbors more of the desperate poor than any other Indian city; the endless shantytown at Dharavi has expanded into Asia's (and perhaps the world's) largest slum. As many as half of Mumbai's 16 million residents live in shacks or on the street. Still, an estimated 10,000 flood into Mumbai daily, most from the countryside, to make their homes and seek their fortunes.

The huge population, combined with arcane rent control provisions that prohibit the conversion of industrial to residential property, has driven real estate prices beyond those of Manhattan or Tokyo—in a country in which the yearly per capita income is just US$350. Right-wing and sectarian politicians stoked this pressure-cooker of economic disappointment, inconceivable crowding, wretched sanitation, choking pollution, and religious tension until it exploded into riots and bomb blasts in 1992-93. The city often serves as the arena for India's social strug-

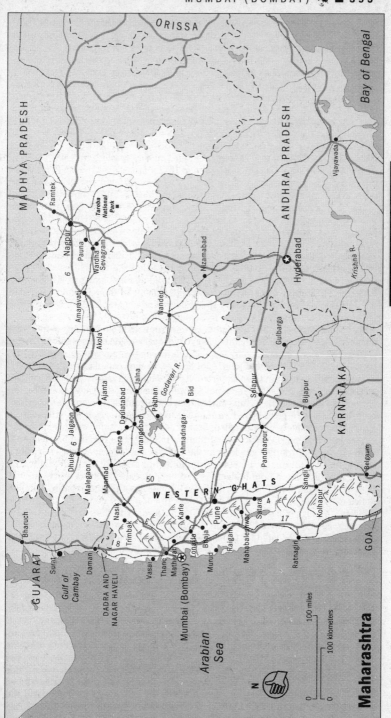

MAHARASHTRA

Maharashtra

gles (witness a 1999 scheme by the Shiv Sena to deport all of the bazaar district's Bengali-speaking Muslims to Bangladesh) and as the lair of the nation's only urban crime syndicate. The recent upheavals don't seem to be slowing down the metropolis. The decade-long bull run on Dalal Street brings the Bombay Stock Exchange and its millions of minions to face the new millennium from uncharted heights.

This urban extravaganza began modestly. Artifacts found in the suburb of Kandivli prove that the original seven islands which make up the city have been inhabited since the Stone Age. Successive dynasties ignored Mumbai's potential as a port, but when the Portuguese acquired the islands in 1534, they called them Bom Bahia ("Good Port"). The British made good on the name after the dowry of Catherine of Braganza brought the islands to Charles II of England. The fourth East India Company Governor of Bombay, Gerald Aungier, set his grandiose dreams in motion by ordering a construction spree in 1672. Zoroastrians fleeing Persia built their first fire temple in 1675, initiating a flow of affluent refugees. Bombay became the capital of the Company's regional holdings in 1687—the rest is history.

The shortage of cotton in Britain due to the American Civil War prompted a boom in Bombay, resulting in an impressive array of late Victorian public works, including the consolidation of the seven islands into one through the initial reclaiming of land from the Arabian Sea. Around the same time, a fledgling organization called the Indian National Congress held its 1885 inaugural meeting in Bombay. It was at another Bombay session in 1942 that the group first voiced its demand for full independence. After India realized that ambition in 1947, disputes between the Marathi- and Gujarati-speaking segments of the population ended in the partition of Bombay State into Maharashtra and Gujarat in 1960. Even during the conflict, the economy boomed, as it continues to do today. In 1995, the flick of a Shiv Sena-backed politician's pen gave the new and ancient city a new and ancient name—Mumbai, from Mumbadevi, the local version of the goddess Durga.

Despite such changes, the city formerly known as Bombay remains wholly irrepressible. Slum-dwellers find jobs if not houses, so they can blast the latest Bollywood blockbusters from their imported VCRs—Mumbai makes more movies than any other place in India, and India makes far more movies than any other place on earth. Cat-callers whistle at miniskirted teens, while lunch delivery men overload their bicycles with pickles and *papads* for businessmen. Even the architecture expresses a uniquely urban schizophrenia: Victorian-Gothic vestiges share the streets with high rises, Art Deco apartments, Hindu shrines, and bamboo lean-to's.

The throngs of tourists gawking at the city's insane extremes causes hardly a ripple. As an addition to the standard, guidebook-friendly array of sights, the manic mix of London double-deckers and bullock carts, *sadhus* and stockbrokers, and the perpetual motion of it all will floor any first-time visitor. Mumbai defies expectations of an India filled only with pot-bellied cows and ramshackle temples, although it has plenty of both. The city forces travelers to confront a hitherto unimagined fusion of development and despair. But whether it delights or disgusts, it cannot be denied that this unexpected, ebullient, eclectic city leads the vanguard of emerging modern India. *Salaam* Bombay, indeed.

▄ GETTING THERE AND AWAY

INTERNATIONAL FLIGHTS

Sahar International Airport, Vile Parle (tel. 836 6700; Air India flight information tel. 836 6767; all other airlines tel. 836 6200), 20km north of downtown Mumbai. This chaotic, mosquito-ridden complex prepares arriving travelers for the continent beyond. Though it's slightly overpriced, the easiest way to get between the airport and downtown Mumbai is by **pre-paid taxi** (Rs250 to Colaba as opposed to Rs200 by meter, 1½hr.). The non-pre-paid drivers at the airport are not to be trusted, but from Mumbai to the airport, any cab in which the driver sets the meter will do. Allow two hours during rush hour (to the city 8-11am, from the city 5-8pm).

NOTE. There is a Rs500 **departure tax** which all travelers must pay before going through customs and leaving India (Rs250 if you're headed to another South Asian country). Most airlines do not include this tax in their ticket prices. Set aside enough cash for the tax before exchanging your last rupees. For more information on **Customs,** see p. 14.

INTERNATIONAL AIRLINES. Air India, Air India Building, Marine Drive, Nariman Point (tel. 202 4142). Open M-Th 9:15am-6:30pm, F 9:15am-6:15pm, Sa-Su 9:15am-5:15pm. **Air Lanka,** Mittal Tower, "C" Wing, Nariman Point (tel. 282 3288 or 284 4156). Open M-F 9:30am-5:30pm, Sa 9am-4pm. **Bangladesh Biman,** Airline Hotel Building, 199 J. Tata Rd., #32, Churchgate (tel. 282 4580). Open M-F 9am-5:30pm, Sa 9am-3pm. **British Airways,** 202-B Vulcan Insurance Building, Veer Nariman Rd., Churchgate (tel. 282 0888). Open M-F 9:45am-6pm, Sa 9:30am-5:30pm. **Cathay Pacific,** Taj Mahal Hotel, Apollo Bunder, Colaba (tel. 202 9113). Open M-Sa 9:30am-1pm and 1:45-5:30pm. **Delta,** Taj Mahal Hotel, Apollo Bunder, Colaba (tel. 288 3274 or 288 5652). Open M-Sa 9am-1pm and 1:30-5:30pm. **Emirates,** Mittal Chambers, 288 Nariman Point (tel. 287 1649 or 287 1650). Open M-Sa 9am-5:30pm. **Lufthansa,** Express Towers, Nariman Point (tel. 202 3430 or 287 5264). Open M-F 9am-1pm and 1:45-5:45pm, Sa 9am-1pm. **Pakistan International Airlines,** Mittal Towers, Nariman Point (tel. 202 1598). Open M-Sa 9am-1pm and 2-5:30pm. **Royal Jordanian,** Jollymaker Chamber #2, Nariman Point, 4th fl. (tel. 202 2779). Open M-F 9am-1pm and 2-5:30pm, Sa 9am-3pm. **Royal Nepal,** 222 Maker Chamber V, Nariman Point (tel. 283 6197 or 283 5489). Open M-F 10am-6pm, Sa 10am-2pm. **Singapore Airlines,** Taj Mahal Hotel, Apollo Bunder, Colaba (tel. 202 3316 or 202 2747). Open M-Sa 9:15am-5:30pm. **Thai Air,** World Trade Center, Shop 15, Ground Floor, Cuffe Parade (tel. 218 5426). Open M-F 9:30am-5:30pm.

DOMESTIC FLIGHTS

Santa Cruz Airport, 20km northeast of downtown, 3km from Sahar International Airport. The new Terminal 1A is for Indian Airlines and 1B is for all private carriers; **free shuttle buses** connect the two (every 15min. 4am-midnight). Free shuttle buses also depart from both terminals to the international airport (every hr.). Take a metered auto-rickshaw (about Rs180) from the airport to the Andheri East Railway Station, buy a ticket for any **city-bound train** (45min., 2nd class Rs2), and get off at Churchgate Station, or vice versa. There are no **pre-paid taxis** from the airport, but the ones at the stand outside should follow the meter one-way (Rs200 to downtown; under Rs75 to Sahar International Airport).

DOMESTIC AIRLINES. Indian Airlines, Air India Building, Marine Drive, Nariman Point (enquiry tel. 140 or 141 for 24hr. service, reservations tel. 289 6161). Open M-Sa 8:30am-7:30pm, Su 10am-1pm and 1:45-5:30pm; ticketing office at domestic airport open 24hr. **Jet Airways,** Amarchand Mansion, Madam Cama Rd. (tel. 287 5086 or 287 5087). Open M-Sa 10am-5:30pm. **Modi Luft,** Bhulabari Desai Rd., Breach Candy (tel. 367 8871 or 363 1921). Open M-Sa 9am-7pm. **Sahara India Airlines,** Maker Chamber V, Nariman Point (tel. 283 2369 or 283 1790). Open M-Sa 10am-6pm. **Skyline NEPC,** Lyka Labs Building, 77 Nehru Rd., Vile Parle East (tel. 610 7356). Open M-Sa 10am-6pm. Indian Airlines flies to: **Ahmedabad** (2 per day, 1hr., US$75); **Aurangabad** (1 per day, 1hr., US$65); **Bangalore** (3 per day, 1½hr., US$125); **Bhopal** (1 per day, 2hr., US$115); **Bunbaneshwar** (4 per week, 3hr., US$225); **Kolkata (Calcutta)** (2 per day, 2½hr., US$205); **Calicut** (1 per day, 1½hr., US$140); **Chennai (Madras)** (3 per day, 2hr., US$115); **Cochin** (1 per day, 2hr., US$150); **Coimbatore** (1 per day, 2hr., US$135); **Delhi** (8 per day, 2hr., US$155); **Goa** (1 per day, 1hr., US$75); **Hyderabad** (3 per day, 1½hr., US$105); **Indore** (1 per day, 1hr., US$80); **Jaipur** (1 per day, 3½hr., US$140); **Mangalore** (1 per day, 1½hr., US$115); **Trivandrum** (1 per day, 2hr., US$175); **Udaipur** (1 per day, 2½hr., US$110); and **Varanasi** (1 per day, 5hr., US$120). Flights booked from abroad must be reconfirmed 72hr. before departure. Passengers under 30 eligible for a 25% reduced Indian Airlines "Youth Fare."

MAHARASHTRA

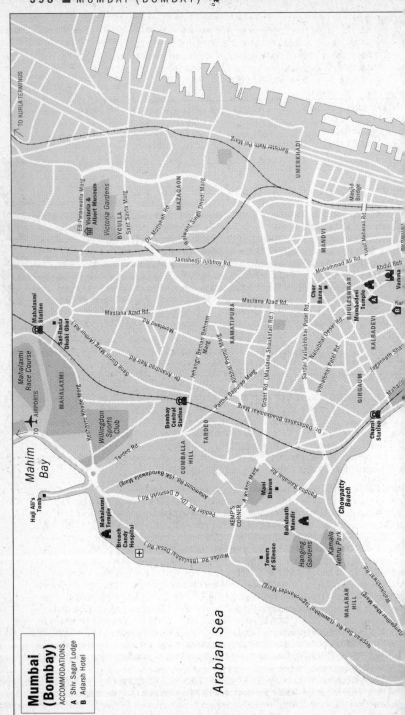

Mumbai (Bombay)

ACCOMMODATIONS

A Shiv Sagar Lodge

B Adarsh Hotel

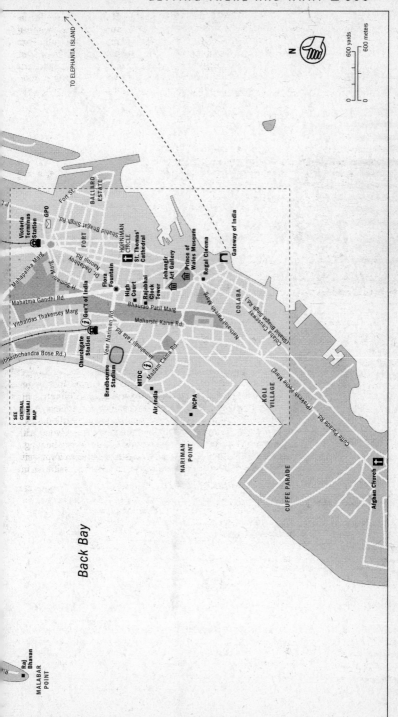

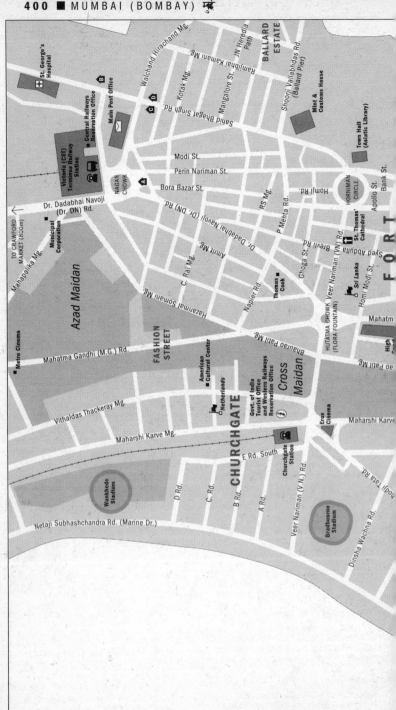

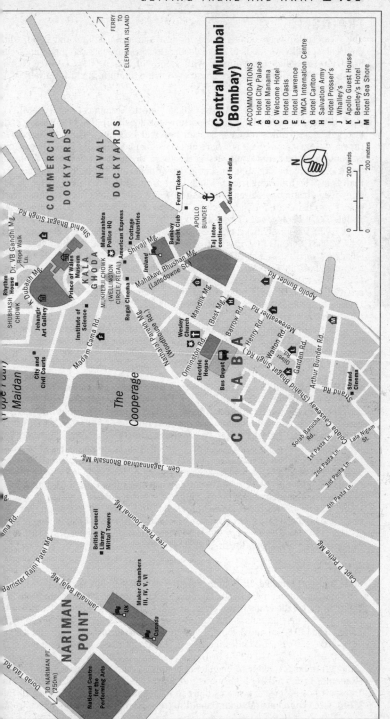

Central Mumbai (Bombay)

ACCOMMODATIONS
A Hotel City Palace
B Hotel Manama
C Welcome Hotel
D Hotel Oasis
E Hotel Lawrence
F YMCA Internation Centre
G Hotel Carlton
H Salvation Army
I Hotel Prosser's
J Whalley's
K Apollo Guest House
L Bentley's Hotel
M Hotel Sea Shore

TRAINS

The Western Railways connects the city to Gujarat, Rajasthan, and Delhi, while the Central Railways tends to serve destinations to the east, also including Dehli. For train **schedules** arm yourself with a copy of *Trains at a Glance* (Rs25). Depending on which railways service your destination, head to either VT or Churchgate Station.

CENTRAL RAILWAYS. Reservation Office, Victoria Terminus (enquiry tel. 135 or 269 5959; automated arrivals and departures tel. 265 6565). Head for **Window 7,** the Foreign Tourist Guide (open M-Sa 9am-1pm and 1:30-4pm). They sell tickets for rupees or for US$ or UK£ if you have an encashment certificate. They release tourist quota seats on a first-come, first-served basis on the day *prior* to departure for trains departing before 2pm, or on the day *of* departure for trains departing later than 2pm. The following trains, which leave from **Victoria Terminus (VT),** officially known as **Chhatrapati Shivaji Terminus (CST),** are only a select few of those available. Fares listed are for 2nd/1st class. To: **Agra** (*Punjab Mail* 2137, 7:10pm, 22hr., Rs200/1050); **Aurangabad** (*Tapovan Exp.* 7617, 6:10am, 7½hr.; *Nanded-Devgiri Exp.* 1003, 9:20pm, 7hr., Rs88/462); **Bangalore** (*Udyan Exp.* 6529, 8am, 24hr. Rs201/1056); **Bhopal** (*Firozpur-Punjab Mail* 2137, 7:10pm, 14hr., Rs158/830); **Earnakulam** (*Netravathi Exp.* 6635, from Kurla Terminus, 15km northeast of downtown, 4:40pm, 28hr., Rs207/1087); **Kolkata (Calcutta)** (*Gitanjali Exp.* 2859, 6am 35hr.; *Howrah Mail* 8001, 8:15pm, 35hr., Rs253/1418); **Chennai (Madras)** (*Mumbai-Chennai Exp.* 6011, 2pm, 27hr.; *Dadar Chennai Exp.* 1063, 7:50pm from Dadar, accessible by either Churchgate or VT, 24hr., Rs203/1066); **Hyderaba** (*Mumbai-Hyderabad Exp.* 7031, 12:35pm, 19hr.; *Hussainsagar Exp.* 7001 9:55pm, 15½hr., Rs151/793); **Madgaon** (*Mumbai-Madgaon Konkan Kanya Exp* 0111, 11:30pm, 11hr., Rs124/651); **Pune** (*Mumbai-Bangalore Udyan Exp.* 6529 8am, 4hr.; *Mumbai-Pune Pragati Exp.* 1025, 4:20pm, 3½hr., Rs53/279); **Trivandrum** (*Mumbai-Kanyakumari Exp.* 1081, 3:40pm, 42hr., Rs256/1465).

WESTERN RAILWAYS. Western Railways, Churchgate Reservation Office, Maharishi Karve Rd., Churchgate (enquiry tel. 131, booking information tel. 209 5959 arrivals from Delhi tel. 132, from Gujarat tel. 133). Across the street from Churchgate Station, in the same building as the Government of India Tourist Office. T get to the **Foreign Tourist Counter,** ignore the first reservation office and walk pas the tourist office; it's the next door on your left. Tourist quota tickets are as at V (see above), but here an agent is specially assigned to help you. Open M-F 9:30a 1:30pm and 2-4:30pm, Sa 9:30am-2:30pm. The following trains leave from **Mumb** **Central,** which can be reached from downtown Mumbai (see **Getting Aroun** below). To: **Ahmedabad** (*Mumbai-Ahmedabad Karnavati Exp.* 2933, 1:40pm 8½hr., Rs107/562; *Mumbai-Ahmedabad Shatabdi Exp.* 2009, 6:25am, 7hr., A/ chair Rs630); **Delhi** (*Mumbai-Amritsar Golden Temple Mail* 2903, 9:30pm, 22h Rs212/1113; *Rajdhani Exp.* 2951, 16½hr., A/C 3-tier sleeper Rs1485); **Jaipu** (*Jaipur Exp.* 2955, 7pm, 18½hr., Rs184/966).

BUSES

State Transport Terminal, JB Behran Marg (tel. 307 4272 or 307 6622), opposite Cer tral Railway Station, next to the Maratha Mandir Cinema. **Maharashtra State Roa Transport Corporation** runs relatively quiet, comfortable, and expensive buses to th major tourist destinations in the state; services are cut back during monsoon. T **Aurangabad** (10:30am and 3:30pm, 10hr., Rs168); **Mahabaleshwar** (7am and 8:30p 7hr., Rs120/130). For other destinations in Maharashtra, travelers must book at th ASIAD office (tel. 413 6835) in Dadar, or at an MTDC luxury service offic although trains are likely to be quicker and more convenient. **Goa State Transpo** (Kadamba) runs a daily luxury bus to **Panjim** (5pm, 15hr., Rs240). **Gujarat Sta Transport** has at least 2 services daily to **Ahmedabad** (3 and 7pm, 12hr., Rs168 **MTDC,** CDO Hutments, Madam Cama Rd. (tel. 202 6713), also runs buses to **Ga**

patipule (8:30pm, 8-10hr., Rs200); **Mahabaleshwar** (in-season 7am, 7hr., Rs200); and **Shirdi** (2pm, 7hr., Rs225). Their services change frequently, so check with them for current route information.

⊑ GETTING AROUND

The hurly-burly of Bombay wouldn't be what it is were it not for the towering red double-decker buses spinning around the chowks; the endless passenger trains that chug up and down from Churchgate and VT, bulging with passengers at each doorway; or the city's black-and-yellow taxis, graceful and clumsy like a school of fish. Become a part of the scene, and exploit the reasonable fares.

LOCAL BUSES

Buses are slightly easier to deal with than trains and, for most tourists, more useful. Try to learn the Marathi numerals so you can recognize the bus as it approaches (the Roman numeral and English destination are written only down on the side—often visible too late to secure footing before the bus roars off again). Red numbers indicate "limited" services, which supposedly stop less frequently and cost marginally less, but no fare within the city should exceed Rs3, limited or otherwise. Climb in the rear door only (the front is for exiting, except in double-deckers, where the rear does double duty), be ready to name a destination for the conductor, buy a ticket on the bus as the conductor approaches, and don't lose it.

Bus #	Marathi	Route and Destination
1 ltd.	१	Colaba-Regal-Flora-VT-Crawford Market-Mahim
3	३	Afghan Church-Colaba-Regal-Flora-VT
6	६	Colaba-Regal-VT-Crawford-Byculla
62	६२	Flora-Metro-Marine Lines-Mumbai Central-Dadar Station
61	६१	Regal-Metro-Opera House-Mumbai Central-Dadar Station
81 ltd.	८१	VT-Kemp's Corner-Breach Candy and Haji Ali-Nehru Planetarium
91	९१	Mumbai Central-Dardar-Kurla
106	१०६	Afghan Church-Colaba-Regal-Chowpatty-Kamala Nehru Park
108	१०८	VT-Regal-Chowpatty-Kamala Nehru Park
125	१२५	Colaba-Crawford Market-Haji Ali-Worli Village
132	१३२	Regal-Churchgate-Breach Candy and Haji Ali
188 ltd.	१८८	Borivli (E)-Sanjay Gandhi NP-Kanheri Caves
231	२३१	Santa Cruz (W)-Juhu Beach
321 ltd.	३२१	Airport-Vile Parle (E)
343	३४३	Goregaon (E)-Film City

LOCAL TRAINS

Mumbai's commuter rail system is complicated. **Western Railways** runs one line, from **Churchgate** through Mumbai Central, Mahalaxmi, Dadar, Bandra, Santa Cruz (for Juhu), Andheri (for the airports), plus a dozen other stations before Borivli (Sanjay Gandhi NP) and beyond. The **Central Railways** runs to and from **VT**, sometimes in parallel with one another (check the final destination: be sure you're on the right line), and tend to be of less use to the tourist. However, most trains out of VT stop at Dadar, where you can cross the platform and change onto a Western train. One-way tickets (Rs2-8 2nd class, Rs8-32 1st class) are sold at windows in each station. When boarding a train, check the illuminated display—the first letter code is the first letter of the final destination, the second code is the time, and the

MAHARASHTRA

A BOMBAY BY ANY OTHER NAME... Most tour-

ists spin or stroll down Netaji Subhas Chandra Bose Rd. in Mumbai several times without even realizing it. They, like all the city's residents, know this street by its colonial
name, Marine Dr. No matter how civic-minded or patriotic the new designations
selected by the municipal corporation, latter-day Bombayites rebel against today's
authorities by refusing to relinquish the monikers of past oppressors. Nepean Sea Rd.
is never Laxmibhai Jagmohandas Marg; even the bus conductors say Ridge Rd. for Bal
Gangadhar Kher Marg; Shahid Bhagat Singh Marg evinces blank stares from taxi
drivers—but everyone recognizes Colaba Causeway. On the rare occasions when Bombay's citizens accept the new names, they inevitably abbreviate them beyond recognition: Sir Pherozeshah Mehta Rd. becomes PM Rd.; and Doctor Dadabhoy Naoroji
barely escapes as Dr. DN.

Bombay's name game developed from small-scale civil disobedience to big-time politics, as the Hindu nationalist Shiv Sena party, senior partners in the state's coalition
government, decided that streets by any other name would smell more sweet. In 1995
the Sena dropped their biggest bomb—literally. They renamed the whole city Mumbai,
in line with its perceived "traditional" Marathi name (Madras followed suit in 1996,
switching its name to the hardly homophonic Chennai). But the struggle continues as
urbanites now wryly refer to the city as "Slumbai."

"F" or "S" indicates whether the train is fast or slow. Fast trains skip the stations
whose names are illuminated on the board below. That's right, the names that are
lit up brightly by the train are the **places it does not go.** There are special, less
crowded cars exclusively for women on all trains. Keep hold of your ticket, and be
on the lookout for your stop since the platform side varies.

TAXIS

Taxis rule Mumbai since auto-rickshaws aren't allowed in the downtown area and
public transport is so crowded. Set the meter and go—this shouldn't be too much
of a struggle unless it's very late or the weather's very bad. You pay roughly 11
times what the meter shows—for the precise figure, consult the chart that the
driver should carry. He may deny it at first, but an imperious "chart *de* do" usually
works. **Auto-rickshaws** only roam the suburbs; you pay about seven times the meter.

▓ ORIENTATION

The urban heart of Mumbai is shaped like a vast lobster claw making a back-
handed grab at the Arabian Sea. The long pincer, **Colaba**, where you'll find most of
the budget hotels, faces the shorter, residential neighborhood of **Malabar Hill**,
across the choppy waters of **Back Bay.** North of these two are piled successively
the business and financial district, the bazaar district, the old mill areas, and the
endless suburbs, which stretch all the way to the end of Bombay Island, 50km
north of the city center. Most tourists only catch a fleeting, jet-lagged glimpse of
the suburbs of **Vile Parle** and **Santa Cruz**, 20km from downtown, on their way to or
from the international and domestic airports. Instead, the Colaba district, centering on **Colaba Causeway (Shahid Bhagat Singh Marg),** claims most of their time. The
Causeway ends at **Wellington Circle,** universally known as **"Regal"** because of the
movie theater that presides over it. From Regal, **Madam Cama Road** runs west (left)
to **Nariman Point,** Mumbai's most prestigious corporate address, which houses the
offices of many international banks, airlines, and even a few consulates. North of
Regal, **Mahatma Gandhi Marg (MG Rd.)** runs past the Prince of Wales Museum, the
High Court, and Bombay University to **Flora Fountain (Hutatma Chowk).** From here,
Veer Nariman (VN) Road leads left to **Churchgate Station** and **Marine Drive;** or to the
right, it heads to the heart of **Fort,** Mumbai's oldest neighborhood. **Dr. Dadabhoy
Naoroji (Dr. DN) Road** proceeds north from Flora to **Victoria Terminus (VT),** officially
called **Chhatrapati Shivaji Terminus (CST),** the colonial colossus from which many of

Mumbai's short- and long-distance trains depart. Beyond VT, Dr. DN Rd. comes to a halt at **Crawford Market,** the beginning of the **bazaar district.** Meanwhile, Marine Drive follows Back Bay from Nariman Point all the way up to **Chowpatty Beach,** at the crotch of the lobster's claw. A 10-minute ride to the north lies **Mumbai Central,** another major railway station and the terminus for state-run buses.

⁊ PRACTICAL INFORMATION

TOURIST AND FINANCIAL SERVICES

Tourist Office: Government of India Tourist Office, 123 Maharishi Karve Rd. (tel. 203 3144 or 203 3145), 100m along the road running down the right of Churchgate Station as you face it. The place looks like a travel agency, but those printers are churning out computerized tourist information for all of India. Friendly staff has a few non-electronic brochures and can answer questions about Mumbai. Open M-F 8:30am-6pm, Sa 8:30am-2pm. Also at **Sahar International Airport** (tel. 832 5331, open 24hr.) and at Santa Cruz Domestic Airport (tel. 614 9200, open during flight arrival times). **Maharashtra Tourism Development Corporation (MTDC),** CDO Hutments, Madam Cama Rd. (tel. 202 6713). From the Air India building, walk away from Marine Dr. on Madam Cama Rd.; it's is on the left, after the giant Nehru statue. The staff sells maps, but they are little more than glorified booking agents for MTDC tours and hotels. Open M-Sa 9am-7pm, Sa 9:30am-2pm. Other offices at Santa Cruz airport, Sahar International Airport, Churchgate Station, and the Gateway of India.

Help Line: Ask Me (tel. 261 6666). The helpful staff will answer questions about Mumbai, from the esoteric to the inane.

Diplomatic Missions: Australia, Maker Towers, 16th fl. (tel. 218 1071), Cuffe Parade. Open M-F 9am-5pm. **Canada,** 41/42 Maker Chambers VI (tel. 287 6027), Nariman Point. Open M-Th 9am-5pm, F 9am-3pm. **Ireland,** Royal Mumbai Yacht Club, Apollo Bunder (tel. 202 4607), Colaba. Open M-F 9am-5pm. **Netherlands,** The International Bldg., 3rd fl., Marine Lines Cross Rd. #1 (tel. 201 6750), Churchgate. Open M-F 9am-4pm. **South Africa,** Gandhi Mansion, Altamount Rd. (tel. 389 3725), near Kemp's Corner. Open M-F 9am-5pm. **Sri Lanka,** Jehangir Wadhwa, 1st fl., 34 Homi Modi St. (tel. 204 5861 or 204 8303), Fort. Most visas obtainable on arrival in Sri Lanka. Open for visas M-F 9:30-11:30am. **Thailand,** Malabar View Bldg. (tel. 363 1404), near Purandevi Hospital, Chowpatty Beach. Visa Rs400, 2 months. Many nationalities can enter for under 2 months. without a visa. Open for visas M-F 9am-noon. (For more information, see **Surrounding Countries,** p. 13.) **U.K.,** Maker Chambers IV, 1st and 2nd fl., 222 J. Bajaj Rd. (tel. 283 3602 or 283 0517), Nariman Point. Open M-F 8am-4pm. **U.S.,** Lincoln House, 78 Bhulabhai Desai Rd. (tel. 363 3611 or 363 3617), Breach Candy. Registers citizens, issues travel advisories, and lists doctors and dentists. Open M-F 8am-5pm.

Currency Exchange: Hong Kong Bank, 52160 MG Rd. (tel. 267 4921), Flora Fountain. Cash advances on Visa and MC. On-site **ATM** is connected to the Plus network. Open M-F 10:30am-3:30pm, Sa 10:30am-1pm. **Standard Chartered,** Ismail Bldg., Dr. DN Rd. (tel. 204 5056), near Flora. On the right-hand side as you walk from Flora to VT. **24hr. ATM** connects to the Plus and Cirrus systems. Office open 9am-6pm. **Thomas Cook,** Thomas Cook Bldg., Dr. DN Rd. (tel. 204 8556), Fort. On the left-hand side 2 blocks up as you walk from Flora to VT, with the bright red sign. Cashes Thomas Cook traveler's checks for free; Rs20 per transaction for other brands. Open M-Sa 9:30am-6pm. **American Express,** Regal Cinema Bldg., Shivaji Marg (tel. 204 6361), on Wellington Circle.

LOCAL SERVICES

Luggage Storage: Cloak Room at VT (Rs5-7 per day, 31 day max.), inside the station building, near platform 13. Similar facilities available at all big stations. Bags must be locked closed (including the unlockable portion of backpacks). Don't lose the receipt. Limited space. Open daily 12:30-7:30am, 8am-3:30pm, and 4pm-midnight.

Market: M Phule Market, north end of Dr. DN Rd. Universally known as **Crawford Market,** despite the best efforts of several governments. A huge warren of fruit, vegetable, meat, and dry goods. Open M-Sa 6am-6pm.

Library and Cultural Center: The Asiatic Society Library, Town Hall, SBS Marg (tel. 266 5139), Horniman Circle. A beautiful old cavern of a reading room in the old town hall, and a great place to read and browse. **American Center (USIS) Library,** 4 New Marine Lines (tel. 262 4590), Churchgate. The barricaded building on the right-hand side as you walk from Churchgate. For Rs15 per day, non-members may lounge in the A/C calm and read dated U.S. papers or indulge in the library's reasonable American fiction collection. Open M-Tu and Th-Sa 10am-6pm. **British Council,** A Wing, Mittal Towers, 1st fl. (tel. 282 3560), Nariman Point. Although short-term visitors cannot join the library, they are allowed to glance through its papers. Open Tu-F 10am-5:45pm, Sa 9am-4:45pm.

Bookstore: The Strand Book Stall, Sir PM Rd. (tel. 266 1994), just above Horniman Cir., Fort. Favorite of the Bombay intelligentsia, the Strand's crowded collection is hand-picked. Search carefully for discounts. **Crossword Bookstore,** Mahalaxmi Chambers, 1st fl., 22 Bhulabhai Desai Rd. (tel. 492 4882), Breach Candy. Look up for the yellow sign in the window. Inside, Mumbai's best browse through the English language selections. Indian and foreign magazines, music, and games. Open daily 10am-6pm.

EMERGENCY AND COMMUNICATIONS

Pharmacy: New Marine Lines is lined with late night chemists, such as **Mumbai Chemists** (tel. 200 1173), opposite Liberty Cinema, Churchgate, next to Bombay Hospital. Open daily 7am-11pm. **Wordell Chemist,** 5B Stadium House (tel. 282 1644), Churchgate, a stone's throw from the platforms. Open 24hr.

Hospital: Breach Candy Hospital, 60 Warden Rd. (tel. 363 3651), Breach Candy, just past the American Consulate and the Breach Candy Swimming Club. Not near Colaba, but one of the most modern hospitals in Mumbai and accustomed to dealing with for-eigners. Open 24hr. **Bombay Hospital,** 12 New Marine Lines (tel. 206 7676). Modern, established, and centrally located. Open 24hr.

Emergency: Police, tel. 100. **Fire,** tel. 101. **Ambulance,** tel. 102.

Police: Police Commissioner's Office, Dr. DN Rd. (tel. 100), Crawford Market. Opposite the market building behind an iron fence. You can report thefts at this head office; expect an endless bureaucratic nightmare, but miracles have been known to happen.

Post Office: GPO, W. Hirachand Marg (tel. 262 0956). The huge stone building next door to VT, off Nagar Chowk. *Poste Restante* at counter 2 or 3 (not counter 93, as posted), on the left as you enter the main hall. Open M-Sa 9am-8pm. Counters 87-89 sell stamps M-Sa 9am-8pm, Su 10am-5pm. To mail letters abroad, head to counter 3. **EMS Speed Post** resides at counters 13-14, in the apse on the left of the main hall. Open M-Sa 9am-7pm, Su 10am-4:30pm. The whole building is open M-Sa 9am-8pm, Su 10am-5pm. **Postal Code:** 400001.

Internet: L.S.M. PCO Service, Abubakar Mansion, Lansdowne St. (tel. 202 2452; fax 283 6417), Colaba. To your left, 20m down a drippy burrow on the southwest side. Web access (Rs100 per hr.) with a discount payment plan (Rs800 for 10hr., etc.). Open daily 9am-11pm. **Internet Cyber Cafe,** 74 Nagindas Master Rd., Modi and Modi Bldg. (tel. 267 1331 or 267 1525; fax 261 0095), Fort. From Flora walk south on the road immediately to the left and parallel to MG Rd.; it's 200m down on the right. Web access Rs80 per hr. Open M-Sa 10am-8pm. **Arvind Copy Centre,** Bharucha Marg (tel./fax 266 9018), between Colaba and Fort, half a block in from MG Rd., before POW Museum. One terminal, plus printing facilities (Rs80 per hr.). Open M-Sa 9am-9pm.

Telephones: The **Government Telephone Office,** MG Rd., Videsh Sanchar Bhavan; the huge building, covered with antennae, just north of Flora. Telegrams and telexes. Open daily 8am-8pm. **Directory Assistance:** tel. 197 or 1952.

| PHONE CODE | 022 |

▚ ACCOMMODATIONS

Budget hotels can be found in different parts of the city, but foreign tourists gravitate toward the peaceful, remodeled mansions of Colaba despite its proximity to Gateway of India touts and the (decidedly non-budget) Taj Mahal Hotel. Note that Mumbai real estate being what it is, "budget" means something entirely different in this city than it does elsewhere in India; even bottom-of-the-barrel digs charge tariffs that would mortify any self-respecting concierge in a smaller Indian city. Reservations are a good idea at any time, especially in high season (Nov.-Feb.).

COLABA

Hotel Lawrence, 3rd fl., ITTS House, 33 Sri Sai Baba Marg (Rope Walk Ln.; tel. 284 3618), off K Dubash Marg. The entrance is a few steps up from the Prince of Wales Museum, to your right. Nine decent sized rooms with clean bathrooms, a friendly Goan staff, and a few potted palms make it the best budget hotel in Mumbai. Singles Rs300; doubles Rs400; triples Rs600. Breakfast included. Reserve 2 weeks in advance.

YWCA International Centre, 18 Madam Cama Rd. (tel. 202 5053 or 202 9161; fax 202 0445), 5min. from Regal on the left. Although more expensive than most budget hotels, you get your money's worth at the Y—rates include all-you-can-eat buffet breakfast and dinner, TV lounge, daily room cleaning, telephones, and towels in spotless, airy rooms with breezy balconies. All have attached bathrooms. Check-out noon. Dorm beds Rs529; singles Rs626; doubles Rs1157; triples Rs1626. Additional Rs60 membership fee (good for 90 days). Reserve 15 days in advance.

Whalley's, Jaiji Mansion, 41 Mereweather Rd., Apollo Bunder (tel. 282 1802 or 283 4206). A renovated, big, breezy villa surrounded by greenery, where the birds make more noise than the traffic. Breakfast included. Check-out noon. Singles Rs550, with bath and TV Rs650, with A/C Rs800; doubles Rs650/950/1200.

Salvation Army, 30 Mereweather Rd. (tel. 284 1824), behind the Taj Mahal Hotel. High ceilings, dim lighting, and pistachio-green walls lend the big complex an institutional feel. Passable dorms and large, nondescript doubles. Dorm guests must rent lockers (Rs3 per day, Rs50 deposit). Check-in 10am, check-out 9am. Dorm beds Rs100, with full board Rs140; doubles with bath and full board Rs400, with A/C Rs500.

Hotel Carlton, Florence House, 12 Mereweather Rd. (tel. 202 0642 or 202 0259), 1 block north of the Salvation Army, behind the Taj. The veranda, equipped with tiny tables and red plastic chairs, allows residents to escape their cramped but clean quarters for an interesting glimpse of cathouse life across the street. All rooms have TVs. No luggage storage. Check-out noon. Singles Rs350; doubles Rs450, with bath and A/C Rs950; triples Rs700/1250.

Hotel Sea Shore, 1-49 Kamal Mansion, 4th fl., Arthur Bunder Rd. (tel. 287 4237 or 287 4238). From Regal, follow the Causeway to Arthur Bunder, 9 blocks down on the left. The entrance to Kamal Mansion is on the right down an alley before Arthur Bunder hits the ocean. The rooms range from tiny, but clean cubicles to large, airy, ocean-view suites. Common bath. Check-out noon. Singles Rs300; doubles with TV Rs400-500.

Bentley's Hotel, 17 Oliver Rd. (tel. 284 1474 or 284 1733; fax 287 1846). A real treat—vintage rooms with hardwood floors, whitewashed balconies, and mosaic tiling. Individual baths, TVs, and breakfast included in price. Rooms of varying size Rs700-1000. A/C Rs200 extra. Visa, MC.

Hotel Prosser's, Curzon House, 2-4 Henry Rd., Apollo Bunder Rd., (tel. 284 1715 or 283 4937). Where Henry Rd. (the 6th left off the Causeway south of Regal) meets the sea. High ceilings make the spacious rooms look like corridors temporarily filled with metal beds and dusty mattresses. Common bath. Check-out noon. Singles Rs400; doubles Rs600. Off-season: Rs350/500.

Apollo Guest House, Dhun Mahal, ground fl., Garden St. (tel. 204 1302). Turn left on Garden St., 8 blocks down Colaba Causeway, from Regal; it's on the left. Beyond the plush lobby are tiny rooms off a cramped, noisy warren with a less-than-immaculate common bathroom. Singles with bath Rs350; doubles Rs400, with bath Rs600, with TV and A/C Rs800-1000.

BEYOND COLABA

Hotel Manama, 221/225 P D'Mello Rd. (tel. 261 3412; fax 261 3860). With your back to the GPO, head left on Hirachand Marg, then take a left on D'Mello; Manama is on the right. This crowded, middle-class Indian hotel is a good value. Bellhops in the lobby and TVs in all the rooms. Doubles Rs400, with bath and shower Rs550, with A/C Rs700.

Hotel Oasis, 276 Shahid Bhagat Singh Rd. (tel. 269 7886; fax 262 6498). With your back to the GPO, head left on Hirachand Marg, then right onto Sahid Bhagat Singh; it's on the right. Pleasant, immaculate rooms with phones and TVs. Singles (no TVs) Rs410; doubles Rs600, with A/C Rs750; super deluxe Rs875. No advance booking for singles.

Shiv Sagar Lodge, 144/146 Kalbadevi Rd. (tel. 240 4753 or 240 3938), 1km north of Metro Cinema, opposite the Cotton Exchange. Nestled in the densely packed garment district of Bhuleshwar, the Shiv Sagar offers clean, well-appointed rooms with TVs, phones, and attached baths. A good location in the city's less touristy side. Check-out 8am. Singles Rs450, with A/C Rs650; doubles Rs550/750. Extra person Rs150.

Adarsh Hotel, Kalbadevi Rd. (tel. 208 4989 or 208 4960), at PH Purohit Marg, 250m south of Shiv Sagar Lodge. Opulent marble hallway leads to smallish, well-kept rooms with phones and room service; some have TV, A/C, and attached bath. Check-out 8am. Singles Rs275-500; doubles Rs750-1000; triples Rs700-950. 4% tax.

Welcome Hotel, 257 Shahid Bhagat Singh Rd. (tel. 261 2196 or 261 7474), near Hotel Oasis, across the street. Glamorous and clean, with TVs and phones. Breakfast and morning and evening tea included. Check-out noon. Singles Rs550, with A/C Rs800; doubles Rs800/1100; rooms with bath Rs850-2000.

Hotel City Palace, 121 City Terrace, W. Hirachand Marg (tel. 261 5515 or 261 4759; fax 267 6890), opposite VT. Most rooms cost more than they're worth, but the ground-floor A/C cubicles with common bath are cheap. Check-out noon. Prices include morning tea. Singles Rs450, with bath Rs700, with A/C and bath Rs1050; doubles with bath Rs650, with A/C and bath RS1200; triples Rs1050/1350. Tax not included.

🍴 FOOD

Eating in Mumbai can result in anything from gastronomical delight to gastrointestinal distress. The distinctive street food is a constant temptation, while the city's restaurants beckon with the best foreign fare in India as well as every conceivable type of Indian cuisine, including a few (Parsi, Malvani) not to be found anywhere else in the world. There is no better place to splurge while dining out. Serious eaters should refer to the *Mid-Day Good Food Guide* (Rs50).

COLABA

🍴 **Trishna,** 7 Sri Sai Baba Marg (tel. 267 2176 or 265 9644). Follow Dr. VB Gandhi Marg past Rhythm House, turn left at the first intersection, and walk 2 blocks; it's on the right. Trishna started out as a food stall and, by word of mouth, became Mumbai's trendiest seafood restaurant. Serves freakishly sized shellfish at dirt-cheap prices. Medium prawns (large ones are 15cm long, so these are still pretty big) with butter, pepper, and garlic are worth every paise of the Rs160. Pomfret (enough for two) Rs270, crisp calamari Rs130. Reservations essential for dinner. Open M-Sa noon-4pm and 6pm-midnight, Su noon-4pm and 7pm-midnight.

🍴 **Sahakari Bhandar,** to the right as you stand facing the Regal Cinema. Fast, friendly, Sindhi-snacks-oriented. A convenient and safe place to cut your teeth on *bhel puri: sev puri* (Rs12) and *pao bhaji* (Rs22), etc. Duck the fruit garlands on your way in, and don't miss the Chicu Milkshake (Rs24). Great, cheap South Indian tiffins (*dosas* Rs15). Open M-Sa 9am-9:30pm.

🍴 **Ling's Pavilion,** 19/21 KC College Hostel Bldg., Landsdowne Rd., (tel. 285 0023). Up the Causeway, turn right on the lane before Metro House; it's on the right. Ultra-swank Ling's serves Chinese fare free of mutation *a la masala*. Cantonese dishes include *dim* *sum* for two (Rs100) and a variety of tasty meat, seafood, and veg. options (entrees Rs100-200). Check out the iridescent fish frolicking in the purple pond. Open M noon-3pm and 6-11:30pm, Tu-Su noon-11:30pm.

Olympia Restaurant and Coffee House, Rahim Mansion, opposite Mondegar's, SBS Marg, Colaba. Time stands still in this 2-tiered, turn of the century *Irani* cafe. Today's owners are Bengali Muslim, but they've preserved the ancient carved chairs, marble-topped tables, and affordable Iranian cuisine that characterize one of Bombay's most distinctive genres of food. Brain *masala* fry (Rs27) is their most famous dish, but not-so-trippy eaters will also be satisfied. Mutton *biryani* (Rs14). Open daily 11am-11pm.

Madras Lunch and Coffee House, 56 Dr. VB Gandhi Marg, to the left as you face the Rhythm House. Clean breakfast, lunch, and South Indian snack joint. *Dosas* (Rs12-25); *upma, utthapams, idlis,* and *vadais* (Rs10-18). Open M-Sa 8:15am-7:30pm.

Delhi Darbar, Holland House, Colaba Causeway. On the right side, 100m from Regal. Upscale A/C joint offers good North Indian cuisine to faint cheesy 80s music. Not a hint of alcohol, but the zealous use of *ghee* provides debauchery enough. Try the Parsi specialty *dhansak* (Rs85). Entrees Rs70-95. Open daily 11:30am-12:30am.

Majestic, Colaba Causeway, opposite Mondegar's, up a few stairs. Simple entrees (Rs18-40) and basic *thalis* (Rs20) served in a huge hall of low tables under whirring fans. And you thought there was no budget in Mumbai. Open daily 7am-11pm.

Mondegar's Cafe, Metro House, Colaba Causeway. The first corner on the left after Regal. Cartoon murals provide distraction while you eat your breakfast (Rs50-65) or Continental meal (Rs45-80). The same thing as better-known Leopold's, with better rates and fare. Beer (Rs90 per bottle). CD jukebox helps pack 'em in. Open daily 8am-11pm.

Khyber Restaurant, 145 MG Rd. (tel. 267 3227). Where MG Rd. meets the Prince of Wales Museum. Lavish antiques-and-mirrors decoration; M.F. Hussain murals; intimate, multi-storied nooks and crannies; and, above all, the finest Mughlai cuisine in all the city conspire to make this expensive hotspot Mumbai's most popular restaurant. Chicken *makhanwala* (Rs200) swims in thick, tangy tomato sauce, and chicken *badami* (Rs200) sends a thrill through taste buds. Open daily 12:30-3:45pm and 7:30-11:45pm. Reservations essential.

STREET EATS IN MUMBAI—HOW BRAVE ARE YOU?

Life in the streets of Mumbai is tough—it takes guts of steel just to eat there. But a streetwise stomach unlocks some of the city's greatest culinary pleasures. At every major intersection food stalls, Mumbai's truest "budget" food source vie for the attention of passersby. One common sidewalk staple, **pao bhaji,** consists of batter-fried balls of potato and chilies served on white bread. Vendors also sell roasted peanuts, chickpeas, and **Bombay Mix** in small servings. The veggie sandwiches, spread with butter and green chutney, are stuffed with potatoes, cucumber, tomato, onion, and an optional slice of beetroot. But the most popular pavement peddling is the **bhel puri.** *Puri,* innocent-looking fried pastry shells, appears in both flat, disc-like and hollow, spherical avatars. The disc form serves to scoop up a sticky mixture of green chutney, tamarind sauce, chili paste, fried vermicelli, puffed rice, potato, tomato, onion, green mango, and coriander to create the full-blooded *bhel.* The *chaat* at Chowpatty Beach is said to be the world's best. In **sev puri,** a species of the genus, the crunchy frisbees act as platters for the same vegetable mix, minus the starch and plus *sev:* red, crunchy, and MSG-packed. *Chaat-wallahs,* as the snack merchants are known, fill the spherical version with a thin sauce or a spiced curd to create **pani puri** and **dahi puri,** respectively. Round off a full meal with fresh fruit or slab of *kulfi,* and to wash it all down, **coconut water, nimbu pani** (lemonade), or (if you're into typhoid roulette) **sugarcane juice.** At Rs6 each, they'll leave you with money enough for medicine, should the unfortunate occur.

BEYOND COLABA

🔖 **Bharat Lunch Home (the Excellensea),** 317 Mint Rd., Fort (tel. 261 8991), just north of Horniman Circle, where SBS Marg forks. Two restaurants in one. Bharat, the budget option, sits on the ground floor in non-A/C splendor, replete with tubfuls of live crabs, an artificial waterfall, and uniformed, barefoot busboys by the brigade. Prawn *gassi* with *idlis* (Rs60), and draft beer (Rs35), fried squid *koliwada* (Rs80). The A/C Excellensea beckons with longer menus, bigger bills, giant lobsters, and Italian decor. Open daily 11:30am-3:30pm and 5:30-11:30pm.

🔖 **Cafe Naaz,** BG Kher Rd. (Ridge Rd.), Malabar Hill (tel. 367 2969), opposite the Hanging Gardens (or Sir PM Gardens), just beyond Kamala Nehru Park. Perched on the tip of posh Malabar Hill, this open-air cafe commands unparalleled views of all of Mumbai, from Chowpatty to Nariman Point and Colaba. The Irani meals (Rs35-80) are tasty, but most come here for beer (Rs60-75), ice cream, juices, shakes, and sundaes (Rs20-50) after a stroll in the nearby parks. Open M-Sa noon-10pm.

Rajdhani, Sheikh Memon St. (tel. 342 6919), opposite Mangaldas Market, near Crawford Market. From Crawford, look down the crowded lanes opposite Dr. DN Rd.; Rajdhani is on the right of the lane with the turreted white building at the far end. Mumbai's best, richest Gujarati lunchtime *thali* (Rs85); Maharashtrian, Kathiawadi, and Rajasthani *thalis* served for dinner. Open daily 11:30am-3:30pm and 7-11pm.

Jimmy Boy Cafe, 11 Bank St., Fort (tel. 270 0880), one block south of Horniman Cir., at Green St. A sleek Anglo-U.S. fast-food conceit hides very Parsi roots. Preserve the illusion with burgers and sandwiches (Rs40-60), but even better are the veg. or non-veg meal (Rs80-100), the *sassan-i-machli* (a spicy fish curry), and the *khir ghosh*, each served in a donut-shaped bed of saffron rice. Open M-Sa 11am-11pm.

Under the Over, 36 Altamount Rd., Kemp's Corner (tel. 386 1393), just beyond (and "under") the flyover at Kemp's Corner. This place imitates American food better than any other in Mumbai. Barbecued chicken with fries and cornbread (Rs185) and chicken chimichangas (Rs175) all taste like the real thing. Brownies (Rs85) or cheesecake (Rs110) wind it up. Open daily 12:30-3:30pm and 7:30-11:30pm.

Samrat, Prem Court, J Tata Rd., Churchgate. From Churchgate, on the left side of the road that leads to the right of Eros. Fancy, pure-veg. restaurant specializes in the slightly sweet Gujarati *thalis* (Rs100-120). You can wash down the all-you-can-eat *chapati, dal,* and vegetables with a bottle of beer (Rs80). Open daily noon-10:30pm.

The Pizzeria, 143 Marine Drive, Churchgate (tel. 285 6115). Where VN Rd. meets Marine Drive. The cool bay breeze and the straw blinds that help keep it out lend the joint a Mediterranean feel. The pizza itself is as authentic as Mumbai can muster. Choices include margherita (8in. Rs90, 12in. Rs150) and the stuffed-crust mixed seafood Fisherman's Wharf (Rs165). Pasta dishes (Rs135-190). Open daily noon-11:30pm.

Gaylord's, VN Rd., Churchgate (tel. 282 1259), on the left as you walk from Churchgate to Marine Drive. The sidewalk cafe, barricaded by potted plants, offers a pleasant compromise between indoors and out. Pastries Rs50, grilled sandwiches Rs70-85. Open daily 10am-11:30pm.

THE THIRD SEX India has an entire subculture of **hijras,** which translates very roughly as "those between" or "shifters." Some *hijras* are hermaphrodites, others castrated or emasculated, while the rest have functioning male sex organs. They live with other *hijras* in modern-day *zenanas*. Their ambiguous sexual orientation and their dabbling in prostitution earn *hijras* little status in Indian society, and most Indians are reluctant or unable to explain exactly what they are. However, when a baby is born, a group of *sari*-clad *hijras* will show up at the hospital, where the proud parents welcome their bawdy blessing (which involves singing, dancing and, often, throwing the baby in the air) with *baksheesh*, for it is considered quite auspicious.

⊠ NIGHTLIFE

Unlike most cities in India, Mumbai has nightlife. Barbaric backpackers will be pleased to discover nary a hint of culture at the city's many pubs and discos, but beware the pervasive (if sporadically enforced) "couples only" policies on busy nights and the occasional refusal of t-shirted or sandaled sybarites.

⊠ **The Ghetto,** 30 Bhulabhai Desai Rd., Breach Candy (tel. 492 1556), in an alley on the seaward side of the road, just before Mahalaxmi. Mumbai's most happening bar fills with yuppie kids every night. Beers Rs50, spirits Rs50 and up. Open Su-W 7pm-2am, Th-Sa 7pm-4am.

⊠ **Three Flights Up,** Shivaji Marg, Colaba (tel. 282 9934), next to the Cottage Industries. Probably the least 'regional' club in the city. Follow the neon trail down the mirrored black hallway, and up to the longest bar (40m) in the city. Rs100 cover goes toward beer (Rs75, pitcher Rs200) and cocktails. Semi-enforced 'couples-only' on the dance-floor. Open daily 7:30pm-1:15am; busiest W, F, and Sa.

Gokul's Permit Room, Tullock Rd., parallel to the Taj, one street behind Colaba. Adjoining Gokul's Communication Centre, Wine Shop, etc., this ever-expanding working man's beer-and-scotch joint is as authentic an Indian watering hole can be. Escape glitz and have a bottle of beer (Rs50) and a plate of fried Bombay duck (Rs45).

The Other Room at Sundance Cafe, (tel. 202 3583), Eros Building, opposite Churchgate Station. The entrance to The Other Room (not to be confused with the main Sundance Cafe) lies in an alley down the left-hand side of the building. A cool, secluded spot for a quiet daytime drink. Draft beers Rs40-45; snacks Rs40-105. Open daily 11am-11pm.

Leopold Cafe, Colaba Causeway, Colaba (tel. 202 0131), 3 blocks down from Regal, on the left side. A landmark stop for burnt-out escapees from both the West and the East. The dimly lit A/C upstairs hosts the serious drinkers. Beers Rs58, pitchers Rs200. Open daily 1pm-1am. Downstairs open daily 8am-midnight.

Voodoo, Arthur Bunder Rd., Colaba, 4 doors up on the left from the sea front. Mumbai's—and one of India's—only above-ground gay bar attracts fashion designers and filmmakers, especially on Sa. India's most famous gay rights activist, Ashok Rao Kavi, is a regular. Cover charge Rs110. Beers Rs55. Open daily 7pm-12:30am.

The Pub at Rasna, J Tata Rd., Churchgate (tel. 282 0995), on the left on the road that leads to the right of Eros from Churchgate, just after the small circle. Futuristic—if the future hinges on tall metal chairs, neon lights, streamlined decor, and a confusing floor plan. The children of Mumbai's jet-set jam up against the aerodynamic bar, leaving breathing space only on the small dance floor. Beer Rs60. Open daily 7pm-1am.

The 'Q' Room, Strand Rd., Colaba, opposite the old Strand Theatre. A small, bright, and serious pool room. Bring a beer and wait at the outside cafe for a table to open up. Rub shoulders with the African, Arab, and Russian tourists who hang around here, but watch out for sharks. Rs30 per rack. Open daily 11am-11:30pm.

♫ ENTERTAINMENT

Check the *This Fortnight,* or *Bombay Times* in the *Times of India* for the weekly bulletin of the latest concerts and plays at the **Tata Theatre,** the **Nehru Centre,** and a host of smaller venues.

Nehru Centre, Dr. Annie Besant Rd., Worli (tel. 492 8192 or 492 6042). In the same complex as the Nehru Planetarium, on the right side just past Mahalaxmi race course. Indian and Western classical music performances as well as some theater.

Tata Theatre, Marine Drive, Nariman Pt. (tel. 282 4567), at the very tip of Nariman Pt., just beyond the Oberoi. The compound houses a main theater, an experimental theater, and a third venue scheduled to open soon. More European and American offerings than at the Nehru, but good Indian music and theater, too.

Prithvi Theatre, Janki-Kutir, Juhu-Church Rd. (tel. 614 9546), along a lane that juts off the main road leading to the Juhu bus station. The theater hall here is appropriately among Mumbai's most popular, with performances in many languages. Tickets Rs60. English-language shows Sa-Su 6 and 9pm.

◉ SIGHTS

The Raj may have ended over half a century ago, but the most British-influenced area continues to dominate the sight-seeing scene in modern Mumbai, for better or for worse.

COLABA

THE GATEWAY OF INDIA. A good starting point from which to lose yourself in the endless metropolis is the Gateway of India. Built to commemorate the visit of King George V and Queen Mary in 1911, this Indianized triumphal arch stands guard over the harbor next to the Taj Mahal Hotel. With a cosmopolitan nonchalance typical of Mumbai, the gateway combines carved brackets derived from Gujarati temple architecture with Islamic motifs such as the minaret-like finials in a purely European building type. Especially in the evening, the gateway plays host to strolling couples, camera-happy tourists, peanut vendors, snake charmers, and touts pushing do-it-yourself embroidery kits with which to make your very own velour rendition of the celebrated archway. In the small nearby park stands an imposing equestrian statue of the great 17th-century Maratha leader **Shivaji Bhonsle** (see p. 425). The reputation of this historical king and legendary hero has been hijacked by the right-wing Maharashtrian party, Shiv Sena, which decks out the unwitting image in marigold garlands and saffron flags.

TAJ MAHAL HOTEL. The modern tower of the Taj Mahal Hotel dwarfs Shivaji, and the building's older wing is a real eye-catcher. Jamshedji Tata, one of India's first industrialists, built this luxurious Mumbai landmark in 1899 in retaliation against the Europeans-only policies of Raj-era hotels. Like all the other Tata enterprises, which dominate today's Indian economy, the Taj soared to success, monopolizing both the hotel industry and the city's early skyline. A self-assured expression wins even grubby backpackers access to the reverberant A/C corridors.

AFGHAN CHURCH. Down at the southernmost end of the Causeway stands the 19th-century Afghan Church, built to commemorate the first soldiers who died to keep the Khyber Pass British, as well as an old colonial cemetery, and the now-defunct Colaba **lighthouse.**

KALA GHODA

PRINCE OF WALES MUSEUM. Opposite the Regal Cinema stands the Prince of Wales Museum. The intervening gardens provide a buffer between the newly restored domed gallery and the breakneck traffic outside. By far the most impressive exhibit, more than enough reason alone to visit the museum, is the collection of miniature paintings from the 16th to 18th centuries. These painstakingly detailed works showcase the various Rajasthani, Deccani, and Mughal schools in scenes of palace life, Hindu mythology, and animals. Other areas of the museum feature cluttered displays of everything from exquisite Mughal miniatures to stuffed animals and fourth-rate oil paintings. The first hall houses an amazing trove of archaeological treasures dating back to the Indus Valley civilization. They include exquisitely preserved stone tools and home burial urns from both Harappa and Mohenjo-Daro. Another highlight is the collection of 16th- to 18th-century metal deities, including a depiction of Shiva as Natraj, the king of dancers. *(Open Tu-Su 10:15am-6pm. Tel. 284 4484. Adults Rs5, college students Rs3, children Rs1.)*

The **Jehangir Art Gallery,** just behind the Prince of Wales Museum, hosts temporary art exhibits. The displays focus on contemporary Indian painting, providing a fascinating counterpoint to the miniatures next door. The quality of the art here is mixed, but it's free and A/C. *(Tel. 284 3989. Open daily 11am-7pm.)*

THE GRRLS OF MUMBAI The Koli fisherwomen of Mumbai swear, spit, scream, and will seek retribution if you dare turn up your nose at them, let alone hold it as you walk by. In Marathi, Koli means "contentious woman." If you want icons of women's liberation, skip the bourgeois short-skirted babes of Breach Candy and extol these authentic anti-chicks instead. Utterly unrefined (every conversation starts with a profanity and sounds like a cat fight) and completely self-sufficient, Koli women will douse with reeking fish water those passersby who note, under their breath, the Kolis' putrid stench. They rise at dawn, head to the wharf to purchase the day's catch, return home after the entire load is sold, only to be greeted by a slew of domestic duties. Indeed, amid the cosmopolitan chaos of Mumbai, these "traditional" types perform, with superior agility, the working woman's balancing act. Then again, most of Mumbai's *Femina*-flaunting females are too busy holding their noses to notice.

NEAR MUMBAI UNIVERSITY. The buildings of Mumbai University and the **High Court** line the left side of MG Rd. from the Prince of Wales Museum to Flora Fountain—their finest facades face the Oval Maidan, one block to the west. These Victorian-Gothic extravaganzas, centering on the 85m **Rajabai Clock Tower,** used to occupy the sea front until the Art Deco neighborhood opposite was built on reclaimed land in the 20s and 30s *(open daily 11am-5pm).*

THE FORT AREA

Another area of sights stretches north from **Flora Fountain,** now renamed **Hutatma Chowk (Martyrs' Square)** in honor of the protesters who died agitating for a separate Marathi-speaking state in 1959-1960. Flora is lined by still more detailed Raj-era Gothic buildings now inhabited by foreign banks.

HORNIMAN CIRCLE. Horniman Circle strikes a calm, dignified note in the midst of the surrounding commercial hubbub. The elegant Neoclassical colonnade faces the early-19th-century **Asiatic Society Library** (originally the Town Hall) over a small park complete with fountain. The neighboring **Mint and Customs House** also dates from the early 1800s. But Mumbai's oldest English building is **St. Thomas' Cathedral,** on the southwest corner of the Circle. Although begun by East India Company Governor Gerald Aungier in 1672, when Surat was still the capital of the Bombay Presidency, St. Thomas' remained incomplete until 1718. The interior reveals a fascinating slice of colonial life with its *punkahs* (hand-operated cloth fans) and endless marble memorials to English colonials. *(Open daily 6:30am-6pm.)*

NORTH FORT. At the northern edge of the fort area stand the grand colonial edifices of the GPO and **Victoria Terminus.** Opposite VT, the **Bombay Municipal Corporation Building** comes as close to scraping the sky as any Victorian building could. The 76m dome can be viewed from the interior during office hours. **Crawford Market** sends a lesser, if equally architecturally improbable spire into the sky. Lockwood Kipling, Rudyard's father, designed the rather condescending sculptures on the exterior during his tenure at the nearby art school. *(MJ Phule Market, a quick stroll up Dr. DN Rd. from VT, past the huge Times of India building and the Mumbai School of Art.)*

CHURCHGATE AND BACK BAY COAST

NEAR CHURCHGATE STATION. The pink-and-white wedding cake of **Eros Cinema** in the middle of this period-piece area exemplifies Mumbai's unparalleled wealth of interwar architecture. Some of the surrounding buildings, on the same square as Churchgate Station, have been restored to their original waxy, zig-zag glory, but most have suffered from damp, salty air and landlords constrained by rent control. Visitors strolling down the side of the maidan from Churchgate will find it hard to believe that these dilapidated apartments fetch millions of dollars on the rare occasions when they come up for sale.

KOLI VILLAGE. From the maidan, Maharishi Karve Rd. merges with Cuffe Parade Rd., where an abrupt gap in the land reclamation schemes has left a small bay between the towers of Nariman Point and the Cuffe Parade Extension. A fishing village, still populated by the original inhabitants of Mumbai, the Kolis, lines the shore here (see **The Grrls of Mumbai,** below). The incongruous juxtaposition of the carved wooden boats and shanties without power or running water with the high-rises of the multinationals next door strikes even the most hardened tourist.

MARINE DRIVE. In the opposite direction from Churchgate, Marine Drive stretches all the way from Nariman Point around Back Bay to Chowpatty Beach at the foot of Malabar Hill. Up to the beach, the Drive is lined with over-flow from the supply of massive, grey "tetropods" that prop up downtown Bombay from the waves below. At sunset, Mumbaiites love to stroll, power-walk, and jog along the seaface, chatting, buying snacks, and treating their children to rides on toy cars and makeshift merry-go-rounds. During the monsoons, tremendous waves crash down on the street, but its roasted-corn hawkers, buses, and cars seem unperturbed. At night, neon ads and streetlights transform the seaside strip into what was once known as the **Queen's Necklace.**

MALABAR HILL

Beyond the beach rises Malabar Hill, home to Mumbai's wealthiest jet-setters.

BANGANGA TANK. The Walukeshwar Temple hides in one of the many old back streets lined with bright flower stalls and renegade chickens that wind through Malabar. In local legend, the area hosted the banished hero of the *Ramayana,* Rama, and his brother Lakshmana, as they traveled south to free Rama's wife from captivity in Ravana's kingdom. In order for Rama to perform his daily worship, Lakshmana had to bring a *linga* from far off Varanasi. He was late one day, prompting Rama to make one from the only material he had, sand (*waluk*), thus creating a *walukeshwar* ("sand god"). The temple's massive gray *shikhara* sits at the head of Banganga Tank, a huge rectangular pool of greenish water surrounded by jagged lines of rundown settlements and as full of legend as it is of bathers and *dhobis.* The thirsty Rama created the tank by shooting his arrow into the ground, at which point water began to gush forth to relieve the parched deity. What was once a celestial drinking fountain is now a glorified sink. Just behind the temple, the maze of *dhobi ghats* along the shore is crowded with row upon row of half-dressed washermen crouched low on the rocks, beating the washables of every-one else in the city. The city boasts even more impressive *dhobi ghats* near the Mahalaxmi race course, but these are less accessible to most tourists.

THE HANGING GARDENS. The city's two most famous gardens are also located at the top of Malabar Hill. Sir Pherozeshah Mehta Garden, locally known as the Hang-ing Garden, sits right at the terminus of buses #106 and 108 *(open daily 5am-9pm; Free).* Along with the **Kamala Nehru Children's Park** across the street, it entices visi-tors with topiary, penguin-shaped trash cans, a life-sized reproduction of the shoe in which the old lady lived, and stunning views of the city *(open daily 5am-8pm).*

Crowning Malabar Hill are the seven massive **Parsi Towers of Silence,** upon which Zoroastrians set out their dead for vultures to eat. The whole complex is screened from sight by artful landscaping, but the funeral customs of the Parsis nonetheless caused a stir a few years ago when the vultures threatened to contaminate the city's water supply by dropping leftover morsels in the nearby reservoirs.

BABULNATH MANDIR. The entrance to **Babulnath Mandir** on Babulnath Mandir Rd. is an unassuming set of three connected small stone arches, seemingly held up by the throngs of flower sellers, holy men, and worshippers around their base. The gates open up to a world far removed from the jams of Marutis below, where a concert of blaring bells and voices reciting *aarti* blankets the path up the stone stepped hill. The temple itself, with its small shrine, is loudly alive during worship times. As you head back down, your ears still ringing, don't be surprised to find

nes of women squatting beside baskets of coiled cobras asking for money to feed
ilk to their serpents—feeding them on certain days of the week is considered an
spicious tribute to Shiva.

ANI BHAVAN. As the site of the first meeting of the Indian National Congress,
umbai fittingly pays tribute to the Father of the Nation and one-time citizen of
e city, Mahatma Gandhi. The Mahatma stayed at Mani Bhavan during his fre-
ent political visits to Mumbai. The building now houses a **museum** to the great
an, with a huge research library on Indian history, Gandhi, and Independence.
long with a film archive, the museum includes a small collection of old photos
d a "look-and-see" diorama version of the great moments in Gandhi's life and the
ruggle for Independence. *(19 Laburnum Rd., on a quiet, leafy lane in the streets behind the
mple. Open Tu-Su 9:30am-6pm. Admission Rs5.)*

AHALAXMI AREA

AHALAXMI TEMPLE. The Mahalaxmi Temple's patron goddess (like Mumbai)
evotes herself to wealth and beauty, making this *mandir* the city's most popular.
addition to a depiction of Lakshmi riding a tiger (normally Durga's vehicle), the
mple contains images of Kali and Saraswati, two other major goddesses of the
indu pantheon. *(North past the flyover-ed shopping hub of Kemp's Corner, near the sea on
arden Rd., also called Bhulabhai Desai Rd.)*

OMB OF HAJI ALI. Just beyond Mahalaxmi, on an island in the middle of the
rabian Sea, the shrine of the Sufi saint Haji Ali battles the waves daily. The bright
hite building stands out against the pacific blue or stormy gray of the ocean like
beacon to all camera owners. The narrow causeway to the island disappears at
gh tide and during the monsoon storms, but at other times even non-Muslims
n stride past the expectant rows of beggars as far as the outer chambers. It's bet-
r seen from a distance. On dry ground next to Haji Ali, the **Mahalaxmi Racecourse**
its a green gash through the gray cityscape. The races (and betting) run on week-
ds from December to May.

EAR WORLI. Farther north still, on the edges of the upscale neighborhood of
orli, the **Nehru Centre** showcases Indian history, culture, and scientific achieve-
ent. The theater offers both Indian and Western performing arts (see **Entertain-
ent,** p. 411). The **Nehru Science Museum** (tel. 494676), whose park is dotted with
imal rides and old train cars, is mostly geared to children but also offers an
hibit on Indian contributions to science, from ancient ayurvedic medicine and
e dawn of mathematics to current genetic discoveries by H.G. Khorana. *(Open
ily 11am-5pm.)*

ENTRAL AND NORTHERN MUMBAI

est of Crawford stretches an endless string of bazaars: first **Zaveri (Silversmiths)
azaar,** then **Bhuleshwar Market**—offering produce and housewares—near the
umbadevi Temple, and finally **Chor (Thieves) Bazaar,** northward by Johar Chowk.
rolling and shopping here provides a more traditionally Indian commercial foil
the faxes and stock-options of Nariman Point.

YCULLA. North again from Johar Chowk along Sir JJ Rd., in the neighborhood of
yculla, the **Victoria and Albert Museum** (now Veermata Jijabhai) receives relatively
w foreign tourists. The exhibits on Mumbai's history include the carved stone
ephant that gave Elephanta Island its name. *(Open Th-Tu 9:30am-5pm. Admission
2.)* For the real thing, head next door to **Mumbai's Zoo,** where mangy animals
bsist in depressing surroundings. The adjacent **Botanical Gardens** provide a more
lubrious setting for a stroll *(open Th-Tu 10:30am-4:30pm; admission Rs2).*

ANJAY GANDHI NATIONAL PARK. The Sanjay Gandhi National Park features
er 100 rock-cut caves, although few of them amount to more than holes in the
all. Nonetheless, those planning to hit Ajanta, Ellora, or Karla and Bhaja can

come here for a quick prep course, while others can visit for consolation. Cave 3, a *chaitya* hall guarded by two huge standing Buddhas, makes for the most interesting exploration. *(In the northern suburb of Borivli. Take the train to the Borvili stop. Open daily 9am-5:30pm. Admission Rs2.)*

ESSELWORLD. A visit to the 35-ride Esselworld, the larger of Mumbai's two amusement parks, can serve sociological as well as recreational purposes. Esselworld exhibits middle-class urbanite life at its most packaged and plastic for ruin-weary travelers. *(From the Borvili railway stop, head to Govai Creek (Borivli-W), where free ferries depart for Corao Island. Tel. 492 0891 or 807 7321. Open daily 11am-7pm; ferries 10:30am-7:30pm. Admission Rs150; children Rs128.)* Your ticket also grants admission to the neighboring **Water Sports Complex.**

SHOPPING

Like some enormous, quasi-tropical Mall of India, Mumbai can fulfill every material need and wanton consumer desire in every price range. A two-minute walk north from Flora Fountain leads to a part of MG Rd. known as **Fashion Street,** an endless chain of street stalls selling cheap, disorientingly similar merchandise. The hawk-eyed hawkers of hackneyed, Western designer cast-offs can spot naive tourists from miles away, so bargain without shame. (Open daily, roughly 10am-8pm.) For those who need a hiatus from haggling, **Cottage Industries Emporium** Shivaji Marg, offers a government **fixed-price** alternative. Though it's unabashedly geared toward tourists and, compared to the chaos of the streets outside, rather sterile, you're guaranteed good quality and reasonably fair prices. The emporium is also a pathetically convenient one-stop souvenir shop, proffering such wares as batik fabrics, handmade silk Nehru jackets and scarves, and all things sandal-wood. (Open M-Sa 11am-7pm. Accepts major credit cards and exchanges money.)

The more upscale **Mumbai Store** (tel. 288 5048; fax 287 3478) burrows along Si PM Rd. in Fort. Formerly known as the Mumbai Swadeshi Store, the A/C store's gleaming glass cases and polished hardwood shelves bear little resemblance to the *swadeshi* movement's spinning wheels and simple, homemade cloth. Like a department store specializing in "ethnic" merchandise, this is sterile, spoon-fed shopping, but the quality and selection is commendable. (Open M-Sa 10:30am-8:30pm, Su 11am-7pm. Major credit cards accepted.) Finally, travelers with particularly fat wallets should head over to **Warden Rd.** (Bhulabhai Desai Rd.), near Kemp's Corner. The line of stores is the place to go to match, thread for thread, the clothing donned by Mumbai's hipsters.

NEAR MUMBAI: ELEPHANTA ISLAND

About 10km northeast of the Gateway of India, the island of Elephanta, in Bombay Harbor, offers travelers a fleeting glimpse of a quaint Indian fishing village in its heyday. Then it delivers a full-barreled assault—Elephanta is what happens to the quaint village when more tourists than gilled wildlife are dragged in from the water. Elephanta's 8th-century cave temples have lured in thousands of visitors, and locals haven't hesitated to capitalize. Point your Nikon at picturesque fisher-women draped in emerald, magenta, and lime *saris*, and risk the repercussions—they will chase you, squawking demands for *baksheesh* (without upsetting the silver *mutkas* balanced on their heads). Also be prepared for free-roaming monkeys who readily strip tourists of chips, Frootis, and bananas.

In spite of its hassles (the ferry ride itself is an adventure), Elephanta remains justly renowned for its truly extraordinary **cave temples.** At the end of a 125-step climb up the mountainside, the cave itself covers over 5000 sq. m, much of which is filled with moss and bats. The main chamber has a cross-like arrangement of massive pillars with no functional purpose. The image of Shiva as the cosmic dancer Nataraja is carved in detail near the entrance; the damage is due to the Portuguese who reportedly used it for target practice when they occupied the island in the 1800s. A weathered and beaten-up panel of Lakulisha, a saint considered to be an incarnation of Shiva, stands opposite. The main **Linga Shrine** in the center of the cave is accessed by entrances on all four sides, each flanked by a pair of *lwarapalas*, guardians who are at least as vicious as the fisherwomen. The other attractions in the cave are the elaborate **wall panels** depicting assorted scenes from Shiva mythology in remarkable detail. On the north side is a lively panel depicting Shiva as Bhairava killing the demon Andhaka, who was attempting to steal a divine tree. The three panels on the south side of the temple are the caves' central attraction. The 6m-tall bust of Shiva as the three-faced Trimurti, Lord of the Universe, is also of note. To the sides, the Descent of the Ganga and Shiva as Ardhanarishvara (half male, half female) are shown, while near another entrance there is a detailed panel showing Ravana's attempt to uproot Mount Kailasa.

Elephanta is accessible by a one-hour **ferry ride** from the Gateway of India. It is not unheard of for the slow-moving ferries to ram into each other. Only luxury boats run in the monsoon months (roughly June-Sept.), and then only when waters are navigable. (Enquiry tel. 202 6364. Depart every 30min. 9am-2:30pm, return 11am-6:30pm. Round-trip Rs50, children Rs30; luxury Rs70/Rs45, includes the fee for a government-approved guide's tour through the caves).

MATHERAN मथेरान

Formerly an exclusive retreat for Raj-era White Men, the station of Matheran (95km east of Mumbai) today swarms every weekend from September to June, shutting down when the monsoon rains arrive. For frazzled Bombayites and urban-weary travelers alike, the posh full-board resorts, absence of motor vehicles, networks of foliage-canopied red clay paths, troops of wandering monkeys, and magnificent vistas are just the ticket for a few days of relaxation.

⚑ ORIENTATION AND PRACTICAL INFORMATION. The access point for Matheran is the small town of **Neral**, which lies at the base of the hill station. From Mumbai VT Station, local trains to **Karjat** stop at Neral Junction, as do some on the Mumbai-Pune route (every hr. 6am-11pm, 3hr., Rs14). Express trains (*Deccan Exp.*, 6:40am; *Koyana Exp.*, 8:45am; 2½hr., Rs30) run the same route. From Neral, Matheran is 6.5km up the hill. It's a toss-up as to which option for this ascent is more nerve-wracking—a **taxi** hired at the station (Rs45 per person shared) or the **miniature train** (8:40, 11am, and 5pm; return 5:45am, 1:10, and 2:35pm; 2½hr.; Rs21/140). If you opt for the former, be forewarned that the taxi cannot take you all the way into town. The taxi stand/drop-off is 2.5km north of the railway station, and to complete the trip you're left with a 40min. hike, a rocky but fun horse ride (Rs80), or a hand-pulled rickshaw (Rs120). During monsoon season, mini-train service is sporadic and may be cancelled entirely around June 20. Matheran levies an entry tax on all visitors (adults Rs10, children Rs5).

The miniature train pulls into the **Matheran Railway Station**, located on the main road, **Mahatma Gandhi Marg (MG Marg)**, marking the center of town. The **tourist office** is opposite the railway station and has town maps (open M-Sa 9:30am-5:30pm; closed during the off-season). Moving south down MG Marg—right if you're facing the railway—the **GPO** is on the left. Past the GPO, a fork to the right passes the **police station** before continuing on to **Charlotte Lake**. **Currency exchange** is available only in the top hotels, usually for guests only. **Telephone Code:** 02148.

☎☗ ACCOMMODATIONS AND FOOD. Matheran is intended to be a resort town, thus prices can be high, especially in season when reservations are required. In the off-season, many hotels close down or offer substantial discounts. Midweek in Matheran, rates are generally negotiable but single rates are rare, and many family resorts will turn away solo travelers. Check-out times are drastically early (7am is standard), and hotels will gladly bill you for another half-day if you sleep in. **Hope Hall Hotel**, MG Rd. (tel. 30193 or 30253), south of the railway station, is a family-run budget place offering clean rooms with attached baths and hard beds (in-season doubles Rs390; off-season Rs200). The **Hotel Prasanna** (tel. 30258), with all-Hindi signs, is across from the train station; it's a step up with tidier-than-usual bathrooms and warm showers (in-season doubles Rs600; off-season Rs300). For a more resorty option with 24-hour room service, a pool, and a playground, there's also the **Gujarat Bhavan Hotel,** Maulana Azad Rd. (tel. 30278, in Mumbai (022) 203 0876). Walk south on MG Rd. and then follow the signs. The five types of rooms range from Rs500 to Rs1500 in season, but all are 40% less in the off-season. Many hotels offer full- or half-board, and there are several simple restaurants on MG Rd. south of the railway station. There's slim pickins in the off-season, though, when snack shops are the only non-hotel options. Local specialties include *chikki*—a sweet, sticky, crunchy peanut brittle—and mango fudge, which tastes much better than it sounds (or looks, for that matter).

⊡ SIGHTS. Matheran is known for the numerous viewpoints marking the borders of the hill station. All offer views of the surrounding valleys from sheer cliff outcrops. Those on the western side, including **Porcupine and Louisa Points,** have views of Neral in the distance. **Panorama Point,** to the far north, has breathtaking views. Also popular are **Monkey Point** to the north, which includes Porcupine and Louisa Points, and **Alexandra Point** to the south. The viewpoints are very romantic at sunset and sunrise, as the mobs of embracing honeymooners can attest. Women are advised not to explore the more remote viewpoints alone at night.

NASIK नाशिक

Blackened bursts of diesel fumes, swirls of red and orange *kum kum* powder, and clouds of dust kicked up by thousands of bare feet all mingle in Nasik, along the banks of the sacred Godavari River. Nasik is believed to be the site where Ravana abducted Rama's wife Sita in the *Ramayana*, igniting one of the greatest metaphysical match-ups in Hindu religious lore (see **The Ramayana,** p. 586). Today, Nasik's purity as a religious haven seems to be threatened by the metastasizing growth of industrial plants along the riverbanks. The jingle of temple bells and the humming of the meditative syllable *om* combine discordantly with the chug and spit of smokestacks and exhaust pipes. Nevertheless, every year thousands of devotees head to Nasik to trek the same pathways that their gods and goddesses once did. Nasik reaches the height of its fame as it plays host to the **Kumbh Mela** festival (see p. 213) every 12 years. During the Mela, one of the most auspicious moments in the Hindu calendar, millions of Hindus flock to Nasik to take a purifying dip in the waters of the Godavari.

▐ ORIENTATION AND PRACTICAL INFORMATION

Nasik's spiritual life is centered along the banks of the **Godavari River,** 565m above sea level. Its commercial heart lies a couple of kilometers from the river, however, near the **Central Bus Stand (CBS)** at the intersection of **Sharanpur** and **Old Agra Roads.** Running parallel and to the north of Sharanpur Rd. is **Gangapur Road.** To the south is **Trimbak Road. MG Road,** from which one can access the river area in the city's northwest corner, is off Old Agra Rd. to the north. The **Nasik Road Railway Station** is 8km southeast of the CBS and is preceded by chaotic **Dwarka Circle.**

Trains: The **railway station** (tel. 561274) is 8km from the city center. As you leave the platforms, the booking office is on the left. Fares listed are 2nd/1st class. To: **Mumbai** (10 per day 7am-12:10am, 4hr., Rs53/304); **Nagpur** (12:20, 2:30am, 7:10, and 11:45pm; 12hr.; Rs225/718).

Buses: Central Bus Stand, Sharanpur Rd. (tel. 572854). To: **Ahmedabad** (7 per day noon-1am, 12hr., Rs121); **Aurangabad** (7 per day 6:45am-7:30pm, 4½hr., Rs85); **Mumbai** (every hr., 5hr., Rs75); **Nagpur** (10pm, 15hr., Rs295); **Pune** (every 30min. 5hr., Rs92). Buses from Mumbai go to **Mahamarga Bus Stand,** 7km away.

Local Transportation: Auto-rickshaws rule the road and are grudgingly subject to meters.

Tourist Office: MTDC, T-1, Golf Club, Old Agra Rd. (tel. 570059). From the CBS, head down Old Agra, past the State Bank. Turn right at the 2nd major intersection; the MTDC is 5min. down on the right. Mediocre Nasik maps, train and bus schedules, and a few pamphlets about nearby destinations. Sight-seeing tours 8:30am-5:30pm, Rs60. Open M-F and 1st and 3rd Sa 10am-5:30pm.

Currency Exchange: State Bank of India, Old Agra Rd. Go right from the CBS; it's 200m after the intersection on the left. Open M-F 11am-5pm, Sa 11am-2pm, but no foreign exchange on Sa. **Trade-wings,** 1st fl. Manoram Arcade, Vakil Wada, off MG Rd., by Pancharati Hotel. Open M-Sa 9:30am-5:30pm.

Hospital: Lifeline, Wadala Rd. (tel. 591634 or 597904, mobile ambulance 982300 6666), near Dwarka Circle. Nasik's best. **Ambulance,** tel. 576106 or 591634.

Police: Police Commissioner's Office (tel. 570183), off Sharanpur Rd.

Post Office: GPO, Trimbak Rd. (tel. 502141). Go down Old Agra Rd. from the CBS, and turn left at the first major intersection. The GPO is on the right, beyond the next intersection. *Poste Restante* should be addressed to the Postmaster. Open M-Sa 10am-6pm, Su 10am-2pm. **Postal Code:** 42001.

Internet: Cyber Space, Vakil Wadi Rd. (tel. 575881), on the right off MG Rd., next to Trade-wings. Rs 60 per hr. with free printing.

PHONE CODE	0253

ACCOMMODATIONS AND FOOD

Budget hotels cluster near the CBS on Shivaji and Old Agra Rd. and along Dwarka Circle. Most have noon check-out. Good luck finding a room during the Mela. Excellent *thalis* are to be had at the three **Panchavati** hotels on MG Rd. in Vakil Wadi and the one at the intersection of Thimbak and Boys Town Rd.

Hotel Basera, Shivaji Rd. (tel. 575616 or 575618). Cross the intersection from the CBS and then head down the small alley on the left. Reception is to the right, 1st fl. Simple rooms all have TVs and telephones. Corridors encircle an open space, revealing the building's bowels and restaurant fumes. Singles Rs210, with A/C Rs350; doubles Rs325/475, unattached double Rs200; triples Rs400; quads Rs500.

Raj Mahal Lodge, Sharanpur Rd. (tel. 580501; fax 571096), across from the CBS. Basic rooms, unbeatable location, and relatively cheap rates conspire to fill the Raj's rooms early, so act fast. 24hr. STD/ISD in the lobby, TVs and telephones in all the rooms. Singles Rs170; doubles Rs230, with half-bath Rs340, deluxe with bath Rs425, with A/C Rs500; triples with bath Rs400; quads with bath Rs425.

Hotel Siddharth, Nasik-Pune Rd. (tel. 553376 or 552618; fax 554288), near the Nasardi Bridge, 2km past Dwarka Circle on the right. Dark halls lead to sunny rooms with sparkling white walls, attached baths, TVs, and telephones. An expansive, well-maintained lawn in the back is ideal for evening lounging. Singles Rs350, with A/C Rs500; doubles Rs500/700.

Samrat Restaurant, Hotel Samrat, Old Agra Rd. Across from the State Bank. Pure veg., Gujarati *thalis* (Rs63), a diner's dream, are popular with locals. Canteen-like ambience is in step with the bus stand hullabaloo nearby. Open daily 11am-3pm and 7-10:30pm.

Nandinee Woodlands Restaurant, Nasik-Pune Rd., in the plaza across from Hotel Siddharth. Sleek decor and Western clientele belie the taste explosion provided by its South Indian dishes (Rs14-40). Also serves Western snacks (pizza Rs72, french fries Rs33). Open daily 9am-11pm. Meals 11am-3pm and 7-11pm.

SIGHTS

GODAVAR RIVER. The widely worshipped Godavari River is most easily accessed via the narrow, meandering alleys that shoot down from MG Rd. The downsloping pathways quickly swap thick traffic fumes for the clatter of candy, *kurta,* and

MAHARASHTRA

cloth vendors. They end at a Nasik strikingly dissimilar to the industrial center just a few blocks back. Just beyond the Old Quarter, shallow squares of murky water are visible next to the **Santar Gardhi Mahara Bridge.** Most mornings they are merely a gathering place for hundreds of *dhobi-wallahs* percussively scrubbing clothes on the Godavari's stone steps while huge groups of *baksheesh* babies tenaciously follow more upper-class visitors. Every 12 years, however, these *ghats* experience the onslaught of thousands of Hindu devotees who flood Nasik during the **Kumbh Mela.** Nasik's next Mela is scheduled for the year 2003, but it's not impossible to imagine the frenzied cacophony that ensues at this time—one glance at the sprawling **market** directly behind the *ghats* will give you an idea. Rickety wooden stalls provide row upon cluttered row of religious paraphernalia, as well as a gleaming glut of fruits, vegetables, nuts, lentils, and less perishable steel jewelry, carved statuettes, and bronze vessels.

OTHER SIGHTS. Interspersed among the market stalls and around the *ghats* are many sites steeped in mythology. Nasik's religious focal point, several meters to the left of the **Ram Sita footbridge,** is the **Ram Kund.** Thousands of Hindus immerse themselves here in order to purify themselves of sin. The tank's waters are also said to possess the unusual power to dissolve bones; the remains of several celebrities and top politicians (from members of the Nehru-Gandhi dynasty to Rama's father, King Dasharatha) are rumored to languish here in the **Astivilaya Tirth** ("Bone Immersion Tank"). Up the hill from Ram Kund is the **Kala Ram Mandir,** a temple at the site where, according to the *Ramayana*, Rama's brother Laxman sliced off the nose (in Sanskrit, *nasika)* of Ravana's monstrous sister, Shurparnakha. The *mandir*, which may not be open to Western visitors, boasts slick ebony images of the myth's main protagonists. Sita's cave, or **Gumpha,** is the site where the Hindu goddess was abducted by the lascivious demon Ravana.

PUNE पु

As Mumbai becomes increasingly congested and cosmopolitan, the drip-drip of daily commuters between Mumbai and Pune (POO-nuh) has deluged into a mini exodus to the cooler, more relaxed Pune, a four-hour climb up the Deccan Plateau. Birthplace of the Maratha hero Shivaji, capital of his successors, and an almost purely Marathi-speaking city, Pune lays a much more credible claim to son-of-the-soil status than its upstart cousin on the coast. Some of Mumbai's urban sophistication has migrated to Pune, due to its many internationally respected colleges and strategic position on road and rail routes. The biggest dose of internationalism, though, springs from Pune's infamous ashram, the Osho Commune International of the late export guru Rajneesh. Drawn from all parts of the world, the Birkenstock-clad clientele in maroon robes (called Sannyasins) converge on Pune to undergo Osho's various meditation therapies.

Despite its vast reserves of intellect, discipline, and religiosity, Pune's biggest selling point is its citizens' gregarious demeanor. Punenites offer warm smiles, advice, and stories while chomping *chaat* under the cooling shade of a large palm frond or sweltering in interminable queues for train tickets. Although Pune's attractions may not be as renowned as its ashram, there are enough friendly people and engaging things to do to here to make any length of stay worthwhile.

▐ TRANSPORTATION

Airport: Pune Nagar Rd. (tel. 668 5261), 10km from the city center. An Ex-Servicemen' bus leaves every hour from outside the GPO (Rs25). **Indian Airlines,** Ambedkar Rd. (tel. 632140 or 632141), near the Sangam Bridge, in Camp. **Jet Airways** (tel. 668591 or 668592). **NEPC,** 17 MC Rd. (tel. 633128), in Camp. **Span Aviation,** Vishnu Darshan 113213, Fergusson College Rd. (tel. 685614), in Deccan Gymkhana. To: **Bangalore** (Indian Airlines, Tu, Th, Sa, and Su; Jet Airways, daily; 1½hr.; US$130); **Mumbai** (Jet Airways, 2 per day, 35min., US$75); **Delhi** (Indian Airlines and Jet Airways, 1 per day,

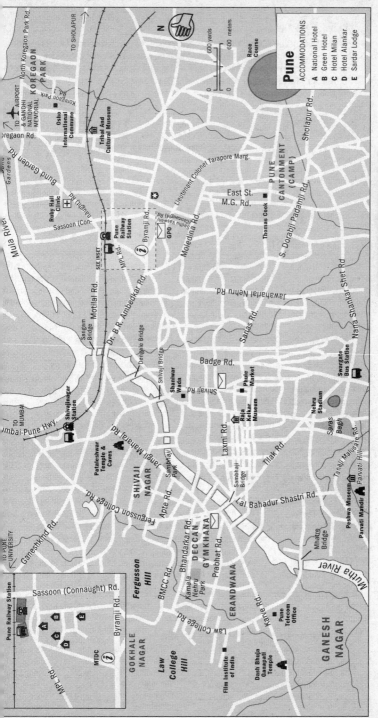

Pune

ACCOMMODATIONS
A National Hotel
B Green Hotel
C Hotel Milan
D Hotel Alankar
E Sardar Lodge

N

600 yards
600 meters

Race Course

TO SHOLAPUR

TO SHOLAPUR

North Koregaon Park Rd.
KOREGAON PARK
Koregaon Park Rd.

TO AIRPORT & GANDHI NATIONAL MEMORIAL
Koregaon Rd.

Osho International Commune

Tribal And Cultural Museum

Bund Garden Rd.

Bund Garden Rd.

Mula River

Reby Hall Clinic

Sassoon (Con-

Pune Railway Station

Byramji Rd.

GPO

Sadhu Vaswani (Connaught) Rd.

Moledina Rd.

Lieutenant Colonel Tarapore Marg.

East St.
M.G. Rd.

PUNE CANTONMENT (CAMP)

Thomas Cook

S. Dorabji Padamji Rd.

Sholapur Rd.

MPL Rd.

Motilal Rd.

Dr. B. R. Ambedkar Rd.

Sangam Bridge

Dengle Bridge

Shivaji Bridge

Jawaharlal Nehru Rd.

Sarjas Rd.

Nana Shankar Shet Rd.

Shivajinagar Station

TO MUMBAI

Mumbai-Pune Hwy.

Pataleshwar Temple & Caves

Jangli Maharaj Rd.

SHIVAJI NAGAR

Shaniwar Wada

Shivaji Rd.

Badge Rd.

Phule Market

Raja Kelkar Museum

Laxmi Rd.

Tilak Rd.

Swargate Bus Station

Nehru Stadium

Saras Bagh

TO PUNE UNIVERSITY

Ganeshkind Rd.

Ferguson Hill

Fergusson College Rd.

Apte Rd.

Sambhaji Park

Sambhaji Rd.

DECCAN GYMKHANA

Bhandarkar Rd.

Prabhat Rd.

BMCC Rd.

Kamala Nehru Park

Sambhaji Bridge

Lal Bahadur Shastri Rd.

Tanaji Malusare Rd.

Peshwa Museum

Parvati Mahdir

Parvati Hill

Mhatre Bridge

Mutha River

GOKHALE NAGAR

Law College Hill

ERANDWANA

Law College Rd.

Kanve Rd.

Pune Telecom Office

GANESH NAGAR

Film Institute of India

Dash Bhuja Ganapati Temple

INSET:

Pune Railway Station

Sassoon (Connaught) Rd.

Byramji Rd.

A B E
C
D

MTDC

GOKHALE NAGAR

MPL Rd.

2hr., US$185); **Goa** (Gujrati Ways, in-season: daily; off-season: M, W, and F, 1hr., US$90); **Madras** (Indian Airlines, Tu, Th, and Sa; Jet Airways, daily; 3hr.; US$155).

Trains: Railway Station, MPL Rd. The booking office, on your left as you face the station, has separate sections for local tickets, reservations, and Mumbai trains. Fares listed are 2nd/1st class. To: **Bangalore** (2:35am and noon, 20hr., Rs304/986); **Hyderabad** (5pm, 13hr., Rs214/925); **Miraj** for Goa, (1:30 and 10:15pm, 6½hr., Rs85/393); **Mumbai** (5 per day, 4hr., Rs78/196).

Buses: Pune has 3 main state stations and many private carriers. The most convenient station for tourists is right next to the railway station. To: **Mumbai** (every hr. 5am-10pm 4½hr., Rs58/90); **Mahabaleshwar** (6 per day, 4hr., Rs55/72); **Panjim** (4 per day, 12hr., Rs195). For **Aurangabad,** head to **Shivajinagar Station** in Deccan Gymkhana (every 30min. 5am-6pm, 6hr., Rs50/100).

Local Transportation: Auto-rickshaws are the best means of getting around in Pune. The conversion rate for auto-rickshaws is roughly 4-5 times the meter reading; ask to see a chart. Local **bus** #4 goes to Deccan Gymkhana, while #5, 6, and 31 go south towards Swargate bus station and the old town.

ORIENTATION

Although Pune seems quiet by comparison to Mumbai, it is a large city supporting a population of three million which sprawls over two vaguely defined sections: the **Camp** and **Old Town.** The railway station and a major bus stand rub shoulders in Camp between **Sassoon Road** (formerly part of Connaught Rd.) to the east and MPL **Road** to the south. A 10-minute rickshaw ride west of here is the Old Town, where traditional *wadas* (extended family houses) surround the **Swargate Bus Terminal Raja Kelkar Museum, Phule Market,** and the ruined **Shaniwar Wada Palace.** Farther west across the Mutha River, the middle class neighborhood of Deccan Gymkhana stretches to Fergusson College Rd., where Pune's students hobnob in a string of restaurants and cafes. The Koregaon Park suburb to the northeast of Camp, home to the indefatigable **Osho Commune,** can be identified as a third segment of town occupying its own distinctive physical (and psychological) space.

Street names can be confusing in Pune. The old Connaught Rd. is now called Sassoon Rd. north of its intersection with Byramji, and it is called Sahu Vaswani to the south even though it is essentially one street. Sassoon Rd. and Bund Garden Rd. flow into each other in a similar fashion, as do Ambedkar and Moledina Rd.

PRACTICAL INFORMATION

Tourist Office: MTDC, I block of Central Building Complex on Byramji Rd. (tel. 626867 o 628169; fax 628189). From the bus station, head south (or right) on Sassoon Rd. Turn right at the first roundabout onto Byramji Rd.—the Central Building complex is about a 5min. walk down on the right. Enter through the main gate, and follow the road straight back. The MTDC is the first building on the left after the road curves. Bland brochures and MTDC hotel reservations. Open M-F 10:30am-4pm. The **Bus Station Branch Office** (tel. 625342) offers fifteen-point sightseeing tours of Pune (9am, 7½hr., Rs70).

Budget Travel: Apple Travels, Amir Hotel, Connaught Rd. (tel. 628185 or 632325; fa 625421), in Camp, at the junction of Sassoon and MPL Rd. Arranges domestic and international air travel. Open M-Sa 9:30am-6pm.

Currency Exchange: AXE Central Bank of India, MG Rd. (tel. 631413 or 631415), in Camp, 5min. south of Moledina Rd. Up to US$500 cash advance on Visa or MC. Open M-F 11am-1:30pm. **Thomas Cook,** ground floor, 13 Thacker House, 2418 General Thim imaya Rd. (tel. 646171 or 643026), in Camp. A 10min. walk down MG Rd. from Mole dina Rd. Turn left down the sidewalk next to the villa labeled M. Nusserwanji. They cash their own checks for free and others for Rs30 per transaction. Open M-Sa 10am-5pm.

Bookstore: Manney's Bookstore, 7 Moledina Rd., Clover Centre (tel. 631683), in Camp. English books galore, travel guides, and maps of major Indian cities (Rs30). The best source for Pune maps. Open M-Sa 9:30am-1:30pm and 4-8pm.

Pharmacy/Hospital: Pune Medical Foundation, Ruby Hall Clinic, 40 Sassoon Rd. (tel. 623391), in Camp. From MPL, turn left on Sassoon Rd., cross the railroad tracks, and follow the road to the right. The clinic is on the left, immediately past Domino's Pizza. Pharmacy open 24hr.

Police: Bund Garden Station, Byramji Rd. (tel. 62202 or 100). From MPL Rd., head south (or right) along Sassoon Rd. and make your first left on to Byramji. The station is the small house on the right immediately after the first intersection. Open 24hr.

Post Office: Sadhu Vaswani Rd. A Victorian-domed stone building on the right, 5min. south of the intersection of Sassoon Rd. and MPL Rd. *Poste Restante* at the Enquiries counter. Open M-Sa 10am-4pm. Stamps sold M-Sa 10am-6pm. **Postal Code:** 411001.

Internet: Institute of Computer Education, 113 Ashoka Mall, Bund Garden Rd. (tel. 636611), opposite the Holiday Inn. Surf the web for Rs30 per hr. in the office or the new cafe. Open Tu-Su 8am-6pm. **Internet Vision,** 7 Moledina Rd., Clover Centre Basement 42 (tel. 633099). Web browsing Rs30 per hr. Open daily 10am-7pm.

PHONE CODE	020

ACCOMMODATIONS

Almost all budget hotels in Pune cluster within the square-shaped **Wilson Garden** area. Though most of these buildings were once opulent personal *wadas* (mansions), they now stand in dilapidated decadence. To reach the area, take the small lane to the left of the National Hotel and turn right at the corner.

National Hotel (tel. 625054), opposite the railway station. Vast verandahs seem to sprout from the well-tended gardens in this 150-year old palace-turned-hotel. All rooms except singles have attached bath. Check-out noon. Singles Rs150; doubles Rs300-350; triples 350-400; quads 400-450.

Sardar Lodge, Wilson Garden (tel. 625662), across the park from the main road. Friendly staff and well-maintained rooms make Sardar's a perfectly palatable palette. Check-out 24hr. Singles Rs110; doubles Rs160, with bath Rs235, with bath and TV Rs310.

Green Hotel, 16 Wilson Garden (tel. 625229). The sensational decor—replete with stained glass, wood finish, wrought iron, and old furniture—makes the Green the most unique budget dive in Pune. Check-out 5pm. Singles Rs175; doubles Rs250, with bath Rs275; triples Rs300; quads Rs400.

Hotel Alankar, 14 Wilson Circle (tel. 620484). A decorative frieze featuring female musicians enlivens the otherwise simple rooms (some with balconies) lined along long, quiet corridors. Check-out 24hr. Singles Rs200; doubles Rs235; triples Rs375.

Hotel Milan, 19 Wilson Garden (tel. 622024). One of the cheaper places with TVs and telephones, although the rooms themselves aren't extraordinary. Check-out 5pm. Singles Rs225, with bath Rs325-375, with TV and bath Rs410-450; doubles Rs260/425/525; triples Rs340/525/575. Four, five, and six-bed rooms are also available.

FOOD

Lieutenant Colonel Tarapore Marg, which crosses Sadhu Vaswani Rd. a block before Moledina Rd., functions as a huge open-air cafe in the afternoons and evenings. Countless drink and *chaat* stalls lure revelers into street side seats (or squats) to gossip and people-watch (closed on Sundays). The area between the bus stand and the railway booking office is full of fruit carts, providing perfect provisions for a peelable early-morning breakfast.

The Place: Touché the Sizzler, 7 Moledina Rd., Camp. A trendy, 2-tier, A/C hotspot. The dimmed lights and Tudor interior pack in Pune's carnivorous yuppies for "sizzlers"—iron skillets filled with mixed vegetables, fries, and a choice of entree (veg. Rs90, non-veg. Rs110-175). Traditional *tandoori* dishes also available (Rs70-125). Open daily 11:30am-3:30pm and 7-11pm.

Woodlands Restaurant, Woodland Hotel, Byramji Rd., Camp. Go south along Sassoon Rd. and turn right at the first intersection. The comforting canopy of the Woodland and sumptuous entrees make it a welcome refuge from sun or rain. Punjabi, Mughali, and Chinese dishes Rs50-75. South Indian fare, like the magnificent Mysore *dosa* (Rs33), tickles the taste buds. Open daily 7-11am, 12:30-3pm, and 7-11pm.

Coffee House, 2 Moledina Rd., Camp. This A/C hang-out's simple name belies the scope of its culinary offerings: an array of Chinese and Indian dishes are available (Rs30-55) alongside caffeinated quaffs. Tables are jammed with locals at peak hours; don't be surprised to be seated at a table already occupied by other diners. Open daily for snacks 8am-11:30pm; meals 11am-3pm and 7pm-11:30pm.

Shabree, Hotel Parichay, Fergusson College Rd., at the corner of Shola Rd. opposite Deendayal Hospital. One option—the ultimate, unlimited *thali* (Rs60)—is served up by a line of majestically uniformed waiters. Earthen walls, mirrorwork-adorned arches, and patchwork ceilings recreate a genuine *ghara* (Maharashtrian home). Open daily 11:30am-3:30pm and 7:30-11:30pm.

The German Bakery, North Koregaon Park Rd. From the Osho ashram, take a right at the gate, walk to the end of the road, and turn left; it's on the right. Homesick Sannyasins spill crumbs from feta rolls (Rs20) and apple strudel (Rs22) on their maroon robes. More upbeat devotees can chat over cappuccino (Rs20) or "sterilized" pineapple juice, all the while pondering the merits of the acupuncture, *tai chi,* and Tao healing lessons advertised colorfully around them. Open daily 7am-midnight.

Domino's Pizza, Graficon Arcade, at the corner of Sassoon Rd. and Dhole Patil Rd. (tel. 633022 or 657585), across from Ruby Hall clinic. An undeniable symbol of Pune's increasing worldliness, Domino's will serve up the same well-manufactured pie you get at home (reg. Rs85, med. Rs100, lg. Rs170, toppings Rs15-45). And yes, they deliver within 30min. (within the 3km delivery area), or it's Rs30 off. Open daily 11am-11pm.

🎵 ENTERTAINMENT

One of the few discos around to cater to Mumbai wanna-bes is the **Black Cadillac,** Grafikon Arcade, Sassoon Rd. (tel. 622864), in Camp opposite the Ruby Hall Clinic and behind Domino's Pizza. The flat beer on tap (Rs55) contrasts with the bubbling scene as the student-dominated crowd, long repressed in single-sex secondary schools, grind away to the glory of their newfound unchaperoned liberty. (Open daily noon-3pm and 7pm-midnight.) **Alankar Cinema,** Sassoon Rd., and **West End Cinema,** next to Touché the Sizzler on Moledina Rd., are among the many theaters that show Bollywood flicks to huge crowds, afternoon and night. **The Film Institute of India,** Law College Rd., offers more substantive movies, but (at least in theory) you have to be a member to get in. **Nehru Memorial Hall,** Moledina Rd., and **Bal Gandharva Theater,** Jangli Maharaj Rd., stage performances of Indian drama, music, and dance. For more detailed listings and schedules, see the "Pune Plus" section in the *Times of India.*

👁 SIGHTS

OSHO COMMUNE INTERNATIONAL. Upwardly mobile meditators worldwide flock to Pune's infamous ashram. Here, followers of the late guru Osho (also known as Bhagwan Shree Rajneesh) gather to practice his New Age meditation techniques among the lush tropical plants and simple marble structures of the park. There is a wide range of facilities, including an open-air meditation hall, swimming pool, library, bookstore, vegetarian canteen, jacuzzi, and "*zen*nis courts." However these are only vaguely visible from the tour; to be a real part of the Osho Commune requires an HIV test (Rs125), two passport photographs, three robes, and Rs100 per day. Apart from six daily meditations—which encourage you to "become an empty vessel" or engage in the cathartic explosion of "shouting wildly the mantra 'Hoo!'"—all courses, food, and other services cost extra. *(17 Koregaon Park, in the northwest part of Camp. Tel. 628561; www.osho.org. Visitors' Center open daily 9:30am-1pm and 2-4pm. Daily guided tours 10:30am and 2:30pm, 1hr., Rs10. One day advance ticket purchase recommended.)*

SHANIWAR WADA. Amid the narrow winding streets of Old Town, the remains of the massive Shaniwar Wada palace (built in 1736) harken back to an age when fortifications were a necessary part of opulence. At the height of its glory, the walls enclosed the multi-story home of the Peshwa rulers. Unfortunately, the inner structures burned down in 1828, leaving only their foundations and the palace's outer walls and gates for tourists to climb and explore. After wandering the Wada, visit the Raja Kelkar Museum and the Peshwa Museum on Parvati Hill to find artifacts and information that can help dust off some of the stone fortress' cobwebbed past. *(Shivaji Rd. Open daily 8am-6pm. Rs2.)*

RAJA KELKAR MUSEUM. The pack rat passion of the late Dr. D.G. Kelkar, the museum's founder, has resulted in a vast collection that is both eclectic and exceptional. Enthusiastic guides lead groups through three floors of galleries highlighting unique exhibits and their peculiarities: an elephant-shaped foot scrubber; eight images of Lord Ganesh carved on a bean; a brass scorpion which, if you pull the tail, reveals a secret lock. More than a melange of bric-a-brac, the exhibits delightfully articulate the diversity of India's cultures in a spunky, subtle voice that is often missing in displays of more esoteric *objets d'art*. *(Baji Rao Rd., Deccan Gymkhana. Open M-Sa 8:30am-6pm, entrance closes at 5:30. Rs30, children Rs15.)*

TRIBAL AND CULTURAL MUSEUM. It is estimated that India has over 600 tribal communities, involving 67.7 million people—9% of the nation's population. This obscure gem of a museum celebrates those cultures and their craftwork with over 2,000 artifacts primarily from the 47 Maharashtran groups. The museum is spare on informative English placards, but the staff of published anthropologists more than compensates, offering unparalleled explanations of the "tribals'" cultural practices and survival concerns. *(Koregaon Park Rd., just south of the railroad tracks. Open M-F 10am-5pm. Free.)*

SHIVAJI Pune is justly proud to be the birthplace of one of India's great national heroes, Shivaji Bhonsle. By the time of his birth in 1630, Muslims had dominated the subcontinent for 400 years with widespread persecution of their Hindu subjects. Against this backdrop of oppression, the 16-year-old nobleman from the landholding Hindu Bhonsle family of the Maratha region of the Bijapur Sultanate declared his divine mission: the violent restoration of religious tolerance.

Shivaji's cunning and courage always kept him one step ahead of his main nemesis, the ardently Muslim Mughal emperor Aurangzeb. In 1659, he lured the Bijapur Sultan's Muslim general, Afzal Khan, into a discussion, then embraced him closely and ripped out his innards with his *wagh nakh,* or metal "tiger claws." Meanwhile, his troops ambushed and destroyed the Bijapuri army.

In 1666, Shivaji gave himself up at Agra, only to smuggle himself out of house arrest in a basket of candy. On another occasion, he captured the sheer-walled fort of Simhagad (near Pune) by training lizards to carry ropes up the cliff face.

Shivaji ruled his Maratha Confederacy with religious impartiality, recruiting officers from among both the Hindu and Muslim faiths. Even after he died in 1680, the Confederacy prospered, until the British came. In the 1950s, Balasaheb (Bal) Thackeray, a journalist-turned-cartoonist, revived Shivaji's status as a folk hero and founded a political party in Maharashtra named Shiv Sena in his honor. The party, however, does not share Shivaji's tolerance, opting instead for a doctrine of rigid Hindu nationalism and hostility towards Muslims.

MAHARASHTRA

PATALESHWAR TEMPLE CAVES. Almost overshadowed by the modern temple next door, the Pataleshwar Caves exude humble elegance and spirituality. A circular stone gazebo (a Nandi *mapandapam*) stands by the entrance to the small underground temple, adding to the peace and simple beauty of the site and making it a marvelous respite from the Pune bustle. *(On Jangali Maharaj Rd., near the intersection with Shivaji Rd.)*

OTHER SIGHTS. The **Ghandi National Memorial** is unfortunately neglected. The elegant architecture of the Aga Khan Palace, where Gandhi was imprisoned at one time, fades behind the crumbling paint and stained floors you see as you approach. A time line of Gandhi's life, in similar condition, leads you through a few rooms and, outside, to the *samadhis* containing the ashes of Gandhi's wife. *(Aga Khan Palace, Pune-Nagar Rd., on the way to the airport. Open daily 9am-5:45pm. Requested donation Rs5, children Rs2.)* **Parvati Hill,** at the far southwest corner of Pune, offers a pleasant view of the city and its environs. A sloping staircase leads from a side street off Tanaji Malusane Road up to two temples, several outlooks, and the **Peshwa Museum** *(open 7:30am-8pm, Rs3).*

NEAR PUNE: LONAVLA लोनावला

Lonavla, 60km west of Pune, is a popular destination for both foreign and Indian tourists due to its proximity to the **Buddhist caves** at Karla and Bhaja. Lonavla is easily accessible by train and bus on the Mumbai-Pune routes. From the **train station,** the center of town is up the stairs and to the right on the **pedestrian bridge,** down the last set of stairs and right, around the field, to **Mahatma Gandhi Road.** Lonavla's **bus station** is at the intersection of **Shivaji Road** and **National Highway (NH) 4** (reservations M-Sa 8am-2pm and 2:30-8pm, Su 8am-2pm). Leaving the train station, turn right on MG Rd. and follow it over the bridge to the intersection with NH4; turn right, and then take the first right on Shivaji Rd. The bus station is on the left. **Buses** head to Pune (every 15min., 2hr., Rs36) and Mumbai (every 15min., 3hr., Rs52), and to the Karla and Bhaja caves (see below). **Trains** to Mumbai (3½hr., Rs39/196) and Pune (2hr., Rs26/129) depart frequently. Shivaji Rd., MG Rd., and NH4 have more **STD/ISD booths** than you'll ever need. **Telephone Code:** 02114.

Most of the tourists in Lonavla are families from Mumbai and Pune looking to splurge on resort-style, hill station living. For this reason, budget travelers have few accommodation options, especially during the high season, from April until June. About 100m to the left of the bus station on Shivaji Rd., the **Hotel Chandralok** (tel. 72294 or 72921), with its clean bathrooms and friendly staff, is probably the best bet (Rs325). A less tidy budget option is the **Adarsh Hotel** (tel. 72353), across Shivaji Rd. from the Chandralok (economy double Rs300). The area around the bus station has the best selection of restaurants (the railway station neighborhood is dominated by shops and the produce market). Eat your fill at the **Mehfill,** on the corner of Shivaji and NH4. The **Kumar Resort** restaurant, at the intersection of NH4 and MG Rd., also has a large menu of tasty stuff (entrees Rs80-100). Snack stands all around the bus station offer quicker and cheaper options.

Most foreign tourists to Lonavla distract themselves with the exquisite first-century B.C. Buddhist cave architecture at nearby **Karla** and **Bhaja.** Several buses per day shuttle the 12km from Lonavla's bus station to Karla (Rs5). At Karla, a steep staircase leads up from the small bazaar to the outcropping high above the plain where the main cave is located. A Hindu shrine and pillar capped by four lions obscure the entrance to the *chaitya* hall. The pipal-tree-shaped window, which signifies learning, illuminates the Buddhist *stupa.* (Karla caves open daily 8am-6pm. Rs2.) It's a 5km walk or rickshaw ride from the base of the Karla steps to those of Bhaja. To walk, go back along the Karla road, cross over the main road, and keep going straight. Turn right immediately after you cross the Malouvil Station tracks, and follow the road to the Bhaja steps. This staircase leads up to 18 caves that date from the second century BC. The *chaitya*s and *vihara*s feature some lovely sculpture, including a celebrated relief of a war elephant tearing up trees in its path. (Bhaja caves open dawn-dusk. Free.) If you have time after the caves, check out the Maratha-era **Lohagad** and **Visapur Forts**.

About 5km south of town is Lonavla's most popular attraction during the monsoons, the **Bhushi Dam.** The dam has rock steps along part of its face, and at the peak of the rainy season the dam overflows, allowing foamy water to spill down these stairs, where tourists and locals delight in the bubbles.

MAHABALESHWAR महाबलेश्वर

Mahabaleshwar is Indian hill station vacationing at its finest. Thirty viewpoints, several waterfalls, a lake, and historic architecture beckon those eager to escape the hustle of Pune or Mumbai. In the dry season, a clear day reveals the ocean from **Arthur's Seat,** and the surrounding countryside provides a pleasant panorama from other outlooks such as **Bombay** and **Kate's Ports. Venna Lake** in the north offers boating and fishing, and nearby **Old Mahabaleshwar** enchants with its endless historic cobblestone streets and two ancient temples—**Panchaganga Mandir,** which is purported to contain the springs of five rivers, and the **Mahabaleshwar Mandir,** which encloses a natural rock *linga*. The historic **Pratapghad** and **Kamalghad Forts** are also nearby. During its particularly rainy monsoon season (mid-June to mid-Sept.), however, thick fogs greatly reduce visibility. Visitors are charged an entry tax of Rs10.

The main part of the town is south of Old Mahabaleshwar. **Dr. Sabane Road (Main Street)** runs east-west and contains the bazaar at the heart of Mahabaleshwar. The **bus station** is at the far west end of Main St. **Masjid Road** runs parallel to Main St. to the north, and **Murray Peth Road** is parallel to the south. **Buses** run to: Pune (11 per day 6:30am-6:15pm, 4hr., Rs53/70); Satara (for train connections; 11 per day 5:30am-3pm, 2hr., Rs22/80); and Mumbai (4 per day 9:15am-9pm, 7hr., Rs20/120). **Exchange currency** at the State Bank of India, Bank of Maharashtra, on the left of the second floor, a five-minute walk east down Main St. from the bus stand (open M-F 10:30am-2:30pm, Sa 10:30am-12:30pm). The **police station** (tel. 60333) is on the right a bit farther east (open 24hr.). The **GPO/Telephone Office,** FG Rd., is just north of the bus station. **Postal Code:** 6061. **Morarji Gokuldas Rural Hospital,** Shivaji Circle (tel. 60247), with a 24-hour pharmacy, is farther north. **Bicycles** can be rented cheaply at the east end of the bazaar. **Taxis** can be found at the stand (tel. 60931) across from the bus station; they offer tours (2½hr.; Rs280) of Mahabaleshwar and nearby Panchgari. The **Tourist Office** (tel. 60318), 2km south of the bus stand at the MTDC Holiday Resort, also arranges tours (in season Rs70). **Telephone code:** 02168.

During the wet season, reasonably nice hotels go for a song. In season, however, rates can more than triple. The closest thing to a true budget option, especially in season, is the **MTDC Holiday Resort,** which has dorm rooms (in-season Rs100; off-season Rs50), as well as clean doubles with 24-hour hot water (in-season Rs350; off-season Rs200). **Hotel Aman,** Masjid Rd. (tel. 61087 or 60417), has clean rooms with 24-hour hot water (in season), phones, and TVs (in-season doubles Rs800; off-season Rs200). Food options are plentiful year-round. **Rick's Restaurant,** east of the bus station on Main St., is a friendly spot for tasty meals (even breakfast). Mahabaleshwar is famous for its berries and berry-products, which can be found in season at stalls and restaurants all over the hill station.

AURANGABAD (SAMBHAJINAGAR) औरांगाबाद

Cradled within the crags of the desiccated Deccan Plateau and named after the orthodox Mughal ruler Aurangzeb, Aurangabad (pop. 1,000,000) breathes a distinctively Persian air. Founded in 1610 by Abyssinian minister of the Ahmadnagar Sultanate Malik Ambar, the city became an important center for Muslim culture; poetry and silk shawls were its claim to fame. Square stone homes line the street in some sections of town, and 52 ancient gates tower over seemingly insignificant roadways. Thousands of travelers visit Aurangabad in transit to its more famous neighbors Ajanta and Ellora, and stop to enjoy the city itself for its peaceful atmosphere and almost un-Indian cleanliness. As a result of this constant influx, the tourist infrastructure is somewhat better developed in this city than in most throughout the state. Right-wing Shiv Sena city councilors, meeting in the shadow of Mughal monuments, recently voted to rename Aurangzeb's capital in honor of Sambhaji, Shivaji's son and a Maratha Hindu hero in his own right. Few use the new name, Sambhajinagar, and the city's Muslim flavor endures amid the tourist boom and economic development typical of Mumbai's hinterland.

▐ TRANSPORTATION

Airport: Located at Chikalthana, Jalna Rd., 8km from city center. Buses run to and from the railway station (Rs5). **Indian Airlines,** Jalna Rd. (tel. 485421 or 483392), 150m west of Rama International Hotel. Open daily 10am-1pm and 2-5pm. To: **Delhi** (1 per day, 3½hr., US$150); **Jaipur** (1 per day, 2½hr., US$125); **Mumbai** (*Alliance Air,* 1 per day, 50min., US$65); **Udaipur** (1 per day, 1hr., US$105).

Trains: Railway station, Station Rd. (tel. 331015). Fares listed are 2nd/1st class. To: **Bhopal** (12:25pm, 13hr., Rs251/667); **Agra** (12:25pm, 20hr., Rs344/937); **Dehli** (12:25pm, 24hr., Rs380/1090); **Mumbai** (2:45 and 9:35pm, 10hr., Rs157/487).

Buses: Bus station, Dr. Ambedkar Rd. (tel. 331217), 2km north of the railway station along the continuation of Station Rd. W. To: **Ahmedabad** (9pm, 9hr., Rs180); **Hyderabad** (3pm, 12hr., Rs200); **Jalgaon** (10 per day 6am-9pm, 3hr., Rs50); **Mumbai** (8, 8:30am, 8:50, 10pm; 10hr.; Rs165); **Pune** (every hr., 6hr., Rs100). Frequent local buses head to **Ajanta** (Rs40); **Daulatabad** (Rs6); **Ellora** (Rs12).

Local Transportation: Auto-rickshaws are easy to catch and convenient to take, but insist that *wallahs* use the meters. **Bicycles** for rent at the Railway Station. Rs2 per hr., Rs15 per day.

▐ ORIENTATION AND PRACTICAL INFORMATION

Tourist facilities can be found along **Station Road,** which has two branches: the western half runs north from the railway station to the bus stand, and the eastern branch runs northeast past several hotels and restaurants to **Kranti Chowk,** an important business area. From Kranti Chowk, **Jalna Road** runs east to airline offices and the airport, while **Dr. Rajendra Prasad Marg** cuts back west to intersect Station Rd. North of this intersection, Station Rd. becomes **Dr. Ambedkar Marg** near the bus stand. Its terminus on the north end of town lies near the Bibi-Ka-Maqbara and the Aurangabad Caves.

Tourist Office: Government of India Tourist Office, Krishna Vilas, Station Rd. (tel. 331217), on the right-hand side of the main (western) branch of Station Rd., about 250m from the station. City and regional maps, brochures, and general information, as well as guides for both MTDC and MSRTC tours (given in Hindi or English, no tours M). Open M-F 8:30am-6pm, Sa 8:30am-1pm. **MTDC,** MTDC Holiday Resort, Station Rd. E. (tel. 331198). Daily tours of Ajanta (Tu-Su 8am-6pm, Rs150); Ellora, Daulatabad, Aurangabad (Tu-Su 9:30am-6pm, Rs115); and Paithan (M 3:30-9:30pm, Rs115). Open daily 7am-8pm. **MSRTC** (tel. 331647) also offers tours to Ellora, Daulatabad, Aurangabad (Tu-Su 8am-6pm, Rs57); and Ajanta (Tu-Su 8am-6pm, Rs137, not including entrance tickets). The MSRTC tours are arranged through the booking office at the Central Bus Stand. Both tour agencies are overly ambitious; they do not allow much time at any of the sites, and tour takers will miss some of Ellora's best caves.

Budget Travel: Classic Travel, MTDC Holiday Resort, Station Rd. (tel. 335598 or 337788; fax 338556; email ravindra@bom4.vsnl.net.in), inside the lobby to the right. Can arrange bus, train, and air travel. Open daily 7am-9p.■. MC, AmEx, Visa. Also located in Hotel Ajanta Ambassador, Airport Rd. (tel. 486399 or 485211; fax 484367).

Currency Exchange: State Bank of India, Dr. Rajendra Prasad Marg, Kranti Chowk, on the NW corner. Foreign exchange upstairs to the right. Open M-F 10:30am-2:30pm, Sa 10:30am-12:30pm. **Trade-wings,** Dr. Ambedkar Marg (tel. 332952), across from Hotel Printravel. Open M-Sa 8:30am-2:30pm, on call Su.

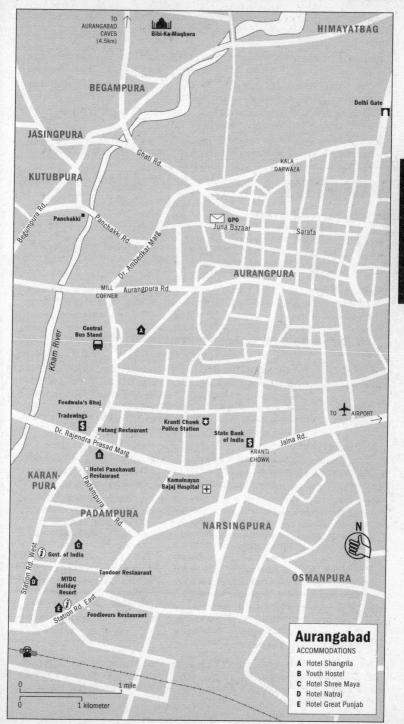

TO
AURANGABAD
CAVES
(4.5km)

Bibi-Ka-Maqbara

HIMAYATBAG

BEGAMPURA

Delhi Gate

JASINGPURA

Ghati Rd.

KALA
DARWAZA

KUTUBPURA

Begampura Rd.

Panchakki

Panchakki Rd.

Dr. Ambedkar Marg

GPO
Juna Bazaar

Sarafa

AURANGPURA

MILL
CORNER

Aurangpura Rd.

Central
Bus Stand

Kham River

Foodwala's Bhoj

Tradewings

Patang Restaurant

Dr. Rajendra Prasad Marg

Kranti Chowk
Police Station

State Bank
of India

TO ✈ AIRPORT

Jalna Rd.

KRANTI
CHOWK

Padampura Rd.

Hotel Panchavati
Restaurant

KARAN-
PURA

Kamalnayan
Bajaj Hospital

PADAMPURA

NARSINGPURA

N

Station Rd. West

Govt. of India

Tandoor Restaurant

OSMANPURA

MTDC
Holiday
Resort

Station Rd. East

Foodlovers Restaurant

MAHARASHTRA

0   1 mile
0   1 kilometer

Aurangabad
ACCOMMODATIONS

A   Hotel Shangrila
B   Youth Hostel
C   Hotel Shree Maya
D   Hotel Natraj
E   Hotel Great Punjab

Market: The Aurangpura neighborhood is a giant market, selling everything from *himroo* to chandeliers to pomegranates at local prices—a much better shopping spot than the tourist bazaars near the caves.

Hospital: Kamalnayan Bajaj Hospital (tel. 321329, 321352, or 334447), down a lane 100m west of Kranti Chowk, on the right if coming from town center. **24hr. pharmacy.**

Police: Kranti Chowk Police Station (tel. 331773), 150m west of Kranti Chowk on a parallel street. Turn north at the water tower and then left; the station is on the left

Post Office: GPO, Juna Bazaar Chowk, Bazaar District. *Poste Restante* at Counter 1. Open M-F 10am-4pm, Sa 10am-1pm. **Postal Code: 431005.**

Internet: Cyber Mall, Dr. Ambedkar Rd. (tel. 350007), north of the intersection with Dr. Rajendra Prasad Marg, and right at the next major intersection. Cyber Mall is a 5min. walk on the right. Rs100 per hr. Open daily 8am-11pm.

PHONE CODE	0240

ACCOMMODATIONS

Hotels cluster in the areas immediately surrounding the three major transportation hubs: budget hotels tend to be found around the railway station and bus stand, while luxury accommodations are near the airport.

Youth Hostel (HI), Station Rd. W. (tel. 334892), 1km from the station, just before the intersection with Dr. Rajendra Prasad Marg, on the right. Well-run and spotless. Gender-segregated student hostel with cheap, mosquito-netted dorm beds, warm water bathrooms, and cafeteria (breakfast Rs12, lunch and dinner Rs22). Check-in 7-11am and 4-8pm. Curfew 10pm. Check-out 9am. Dorm beds Rs20, nonmembers Rs40; doubles Rs100. Extra bed Rs50. One-time linen charge Rs5.

Hotel Shree Maya, Bharuka Complex (tel. 333093 or 333094; fax 331043). Walking north on Station Rd. from the Government Tourist Office, take the first two right turns; it's 100m on the right. Shree Maya beckons with marble halls and attractive rooms with telephones, TVs, spacious attached squat-toilet baths, and 24hr. hot water. Internet services 8-9:30pm, Rs120 (guests 30% off). Check-out 24hr. Singles Rs145-195, with A/C Rs350; doubles Rs195-245/350. Extra bed Rs45, in A/C room Rs75.

Hotel Great Punjab, Station Rd. E. (tel. 336482 or 338735), on the left, 100m from the station gates. Stained walls and mosquitoes but helpful staff. Rooms include satellite TV, balconies, squat toilets, morning bucket baths, soap, towels, and a daily paper. Check-out 24hr. Singles Rs195; doubles Rs275, with A/C Rs375.

Hotel Natraj, Station Rd. W. (tel. 324260), 100m north of the station on the right. This quiet, lime-green single-story hotel has been run by two Gujarati brothers since 1938, and management has only recently been handed down to an equally kind younger generation. Clean rooms with attached baths (squat toilets, morning bucket baths). Singles Rs70; doubles Rs100; triples Rs150.

Hotel Shangrila (tel. 336481 or 329917), across from the Central Bus Stand, down the lane by the taxi stand. Lobby decorations with posters of the white Goan sands are the closest it gets to its namesake, but still a comfortable haven with clean bathrooms, and 24hr. hot water, although the beds could be softer. Check-out 24hr. Singles Rs100; doubles Rs175, with bath Rs250, with A/C Rs350.

FOOD

A company called Foodwala's has a lock on the non-hotel restaurants in Aurangabad. To escape their monopoly, try one of the ever-popular garden restaurants or check out the small restaurants, snack shops, and street vendors near the railway station along Station Rd. E.

Foodwala's Bhoj, Dr. Ambedkar Rd., in a big building 200m south of the bus stand on the right, 1 floor up. Classy touches like painted fan blades and a small rock fountain centerpiece mark this pure veg. joint as a hideaway for Aurangabad's elite. *Thalis* Rs45, *dosas,* and *utthapams* Rs12-18. Open daily noon-3pm and 7-11pm.

Tandoor Restaurant, Shyam Chambers, Barsilal Nagar, Station Rd. E. Egyptian kitsch decor does not detract from the quality of classic Mughlai (Rs80), Chinese (Rs40-70) and Butter chicken (Rs105) either. Yet another subject of the Foodwala Empire. Open daily noon-4pm and 6:30-11:30pm.

Foodlovers Restaurant, Station Rd. E., on the right, 250m from the station. This dirt-floored, open-air thatched hall stands as proof of Aurangabad's garden-restaurant fetish. Mammoth menu (353 items) helps diners select chicken (Rs80-100), Chinese (Rs42-65), and veg. dishes (Rs28-48). If you spend Rs100 or more you get a future discount. Beer comes in a teapot. Open daily 1pm-midnight.

Patang Restaurant, Hotel Printravel, Station Rd. W., on the right just after the intersection with Dr. Rajendra Prasad Rd., 1km north of the railway station. The expensive circular doorway, pink-highlighted alcoves, and avant-garde chairs justify the slightly higher prices. *Dosas* Rs10-30, *utthapams* Rs18-20, *thalis* Rs50. Beer Rs65. Open daily 7am-11pm; meals served 7am-3pm and 7-11pm.

Hotel Panchavati Restaurant, Hotel Panchavati, Station Rd. W. This cheapie doubles as a watering hole, with canteen-like benches and bare walls. *Utthapams* Rs10, veg. and non-veg. dishes Rs15-58. Open daily 6am-midnight.

SIGHTS

AURANGABAD CAVES. Aurangabad's cave temples often get eclipsed by the glamour surrounding their counterparts at Ellora and Ajanta, but they remain a wonderful introduction to the breathtaking sculpture to be found all along the Maharashtrian cave trail. Split into western and eastern sections, these important examples of Buddhist art and architecture were excavated by two great dynasties during the 6th, 7th, and 8th centuries. The western caves, numbers 1 through 5, are off the dirt road atop a treacherous climb up winding stone steps. The third and most beautiful cave, supported and guarded by several wide and ornately carved pillars, was a vihara (residence hall), for the wandering Buddhist bikshus (monks) of the time who gathered in monastic communities' caves like these around the state. Some fragments of the original paintings depict stories from the Jataka about the Buddha's previous incarnations upon earth. The fourth cave is a chaitya hall, used for congregation and prayer. Even ordinary speech echoes enough to fill the space with a rhythmic chant-like sound. The eastern caves, numbers 6 through 9, lie at the end of the right fork and afford an incredible view of the surrounding landscape and the silhouette of Bibi-Ka-Maqbara against the city in the distance. The seventh cave greets visitors with lotus-framed apsaras (celestial dancing nymphs) at the entrance to the crypt. The shadowed Buddha sits peacefully within the sanctuary surrounded by the frozen faces of intent listeners at his feet. Visit the caves early in the morning when few tourists are there. Beware of the colony of slumbering bats who find the caves as wonderfully isolated and peaceful as tourists do but don't appreciate the flashlight's illumination quite as much. (In the hills behind the Bibi-Ka-Maqbara, up the dirt road that leads past the tomb; 10min. by auto-rickshaw. Open dawn-dusk. Free. Bring a flashlight—the caves are not artificially lit.)

BIBI-KA-MAQBARA. Aurangzeb's milk-white monument to his wife Begum Rabi'a Durani suffers much ridicule as an inferior Taj Mahal knock-off. The Bibi-Ka-Maqbara does deserve recognition as an important addition to the tradition of Mughal mausolea, but the relatively small tomb could never have challenged the Taj even if cash shortages had not forced ungainly corner-cutting, such as the abandonment of marble for plaster one meter up the wall. Nevertheless, the building and grounds remain an ingenious compression and simplification of the Taj's plan, complete with elegant floral reliefs and ornate jali screens. *(Open daily dawn-10pm. Rs2, under 15 free.)*

PANCHAKKI. The Mughal water mill at Panchakki is a good stopover on the return trip from the caves or Bibi-Ka-Maqbara. Located 11km from the actual grindstone, the mill was constructed in 1624 in honour of Muslim saint Baba Shah Musafir to help feed the hundreds of orphans, paupers, and fakirs who were his devotees. The water gushes through earthen pipes, is raised by a siphon, and then dropped with intense force upon the blades of the water wheel. The output, in the Panchakki's heyday, was almost four tons of finely ground grain. Today, Panchakki has been reduced to a breeding ground for hawkers and crafts shops selling the city's special himroo fabric, polished-stone necklaces, wood-carved boxes, and bidri jewelry. (Panchakki Rd. Open daily 7am-8:30pm. Rs2.)

NEAR AURANGABAD:
DAULATABAD दौलताबाद AND KHULDABAD खुन्दबाद

There are several important sights on the road between Aurangabad and Ellora. The most impressive of these is the **Daulatabad fortress,** crowning a tall hill 13km from Aurangabad. A series of despots have endowed this formidable complex with a colorful history. In the 14th century, Muhammad Tughlaq, the Sultan of Delhi decided it was just the spot for a capital. Rather than leave the development of a thriving city to chance, the not-so-savvy sultan decided to march the entire population of Delhi 1000km across India to people his new metropolis. Needless to say, the small proportion of the deportees who did not die on the way greeted life in the Deccan with a sullen resentment not conducive to prosperity. The Sultan abandoned his brainchild after only eight years and marched the few survivors back home. Nevertheless, Daulatabad did grow to be an important city, and the fort itself is considered India's second most impregnable after Rajasthan's Amber Fort. Now, the ruins of town and fort are peopled only by langur monkeys, lizards, chipmunks, and tourists.

Through the first gates, spiked as usual to prevent elephant attacks, a huge ruined city awaits the visitor. The **Chand Minar** victory tower, built in 1435, rises over a mosque cobbled together with columns pillaged from temples and a water tank from Daulatabad's advanced hydraulic system. Beyond, a series of steps leads up the hill past ruined palaces to the **Chini Mahal,** with its trace blue tiles, where the last king of Golconda met his end. On top of the small tower next door a recreation of a cannon called Qila Shikan (Fort Breaker) points menacingly at the horizon. From here, the defenses begin in earnest; one must cross a moat to enter the sheer-walled citadel. Inside the fort's walls is a completely dark passage designed as an ambush path for intruders. A guide will take you through it with a kerosene lamp, in anticipation, of course, of a little *baksheesh.* Endless stairs lead ever upwards, reemerging into daylight and a further series of palaces coating the slope to its summit. From the top, magnificent views reveal Aurangabad and the surrounding country through the Deccan dust. (Open daily 6am-6pm. Rs2.)

Back toward Aurangabad lies **Khuldabad,** or Rauza, a small, strongly Muslim town where the Emperor Aurangzeb finally found rest from the struggle to subjugate Maharashtra. In a departure from the grandiose mausolea of his Mughal forebearers, not to mention his wife, Aurangzeb asked for a modest grave funded by the proceeds from his own transcription of the Qur'an. The nearby shrines to various Sufi saints far outshadow it.

ELLORA इलोरा

Ellora's Buddhist, Hindu, and Jain **"caves"** comprise, along with similar structures at Ajanta, Maharashtra's most celebrated tourist attraction. Generations of India's most skilled artisans chiseled a series of temples and residence halls from the solid rock of the hills. Though still referred to as caves, they are actually man-made architectural and sculptural wonders. Ellora also boasts the **Ghrashneshwar Temple,** one of India's *jyotirlingas* where Shiva is said to have burst from the earth, making it a pilgrimage site as well as a lovely temple in its own right. The same square also houses three ancient temple-like structures said to be the tombs of Shivaji's father and grandfathers—locals maintain that this village, not Pune, is Shivaji's birthplace.

A mere 29km from Aurangabad, Ellora usually gets relegated to daytrip status. The main road runs west from the bus stand by the site entrance, currently concealing one budget hotel amid trinket and cold drink stands. (Frequent **buses** via Daulatabad 6am-6pm, 45min., Rs12; shared taxis from the taxi stand across from Aurangabad's Central Bus Station, Rs15.) The MTDC's **Kailas Hotel** (tel. 44543 or 41067) is clean and well run, with a variety of rooming options (dorm beds Rs100; singles with hot water Rs500; doubles Rs200, with hot water Rs700, with A/C Rs1000.) Food options in Ellora include sodas and unsanitary *pakoras* and a few minimalist restaurants. The **Kailas Hotel Restaurant** serves *thalis* for Rs50, breakfast for Rs80, and dinner entrees for Rs40-70 (open daily 7am-9:30pm; off-season: breakfast 7-9:30am, lunch noon-3:30pm, snacks 4:30-7pm, and dinner 7-9:30pm). Ellora's best restaurant, **Hotel Milan,** offers pure veg. entrees for Rs15-40 and a good *thali* for Rs30 (open for breakfast 8-11am, lunch 11am-5pm, and dinner 8-11pm). **Telephone Code:** 02437.

 SIGHTS

THE CAVES

Caves open Tu-Su. Cave 16 open Tu-Su 6am-6pm. Rs5, children under 15 free; video fee Rs25, exterior only. All other caves free.

Of the 34 caves, numbers 1 through 16 give the clearest impression of Ellora's development over the centuries, culminating in the masterpiece of the Kailasa Temple (number 16). Starting at the southernmost cave (right as you face the caves, number 1 according to the Architectural Survey of India) allows for a roughly chronological sequence.

CAVES 1-12. The first set of caves date from Buddhist India's twilight in the 6th to 8th centuries (see **Trade and the Growth of Buddhism,** p. 70). The caves in this group grow increasingly elaborate even as Buddhism fades due to the popular revival of Hinduism evidenced by the neighboring Shiva temples whose construction began in the 7th century. Of the first nine *viharas* (monastery caves), individual cells with statues of the Buddha and *bodhisattvas,* **Cave 5** stands out. The flat, low ridges in the floor probably served as benches to make a community dining hall. The stern Vajrapani (the *bodhisattva* who holds a thunderbolt) and the more forgiving Padmapani (flower-power in the form of a lotus-totin' *bodhisattva*) preside over the meals from the sides of the central shrine.

Cave 10, Ellora's only *chaitya* hall, echoes earlier structures at **Ajanta** (p. 434), **Karla** (p. 426), and elsewhere in the state. Octagonal pillars flank the walls and create an ambulatory around the *stupa*, while a window and balcony above provide illumination and a great vantage point. The carved beams in the ceiling imitate wooden rafters from Karla and presumably earlier free-standing halls. The last Buddhist gasp at Ellora, **Cave 12** contains some beautiful sculpture on the third level. *Bodhisattvas* line the side walls, while the seven previous incarnations of the Buddha flank the main shrine. A different type of tree shades each Buddha, exhibiting a symbology developed at Sanchi in Madhya Pradesh and other early Buddhist monuments. Traces of paint in the sanctum and chamber hint at the once bright decoration of the caves.

CAVES 13-29. Dating from Ellora's Hindu era, which lasted late into the 9th century, these more elaborate, densely sculptured temples share many motifs: Shiva appears most often on Mount Kailasa playing dice with wife Parvati while a demon tries frantically to dislodge him, but in vain; at other times he dances with both legs bent as Nataraja, whose gyrations shook the world into being and will one day destroy it. Vishnu crops up as Narasimha (the man-lion), Varaha (the boar), and most commonly, asleep in the coils of a serpent floating on the cosmic sea. From his navel grows a lotus, out of which Brahma emerges to create the world. The image of the Seven Mothers, buxom god-desses with children, flanked by Kala and Kali, also appears regularly. All of these sculptures appear in **Caves 14** and **15.** The latter also houses a depiction of Shiva emerging from a *linga*, while Brahma and Vishnu kneel before him—testimony to Shiva-worship among Ellora's patrons.

Ellora's Hindu epoch and Maharashtrian rock-cut temples in general reach their climax in **Cave 16,** the **Kailasa Temple.** This massive 8th- and 9th-century building was excavated from the top down by several generations of impecca-bly skilled craftsmen. The sheer scale of this replica of Shiva's home in the Himalayas begs belief even before you consider the technical challenge of slic-ing it from just one solid rock. Traces of plaster and paint bear witness to fur-ther decorative complexity on top of the elaborate sculpture and architecture. The paved road in front of Cave 16 (to the left if you're facing it) leads to the remaining caves—don't let the stairs on the right fool you. **Cave 21** repeats Cave 14's iconographic scheme.

Cave 29, with its view of a rainy season waterfall, contains perhaps the only mooner protected under UNESCO world heritage provisions: in another panel of Shiva ignoring Ravana's ruckus, you'll notice a dwarf baring his ass. Ellora's second-largest cave, it is also among the most structurally impressive, with three lion-guarded entrances protecting it. Cave 29 sees almost no tourists since the Aurangabad-arranged tours skip all the higher-numbered caves.

CAVES 30-34. Caves 30-34 date from Ellora's third and final phase of construc-tion under Jain patrons during the 9th and 10th centuries. **Cave 32** depicts the *tirthankara* Gomatesvara so deep in meditation that he has not noticed the vines growing on his limbs or the animals surrounding him.

AJANTA अजन्ता

Ajanta remains almost as remote today as it was in the 2nd century BC, when it was a Buddhist retreat. Its architects chose a sheer cliff-face above a horseshoe shaped canyon of the Waghora River to render their contemplative spiritual visions in painting and sculpture. During the 7th century AD, the monks aban-doned their 29 *chaityas* and *viharas* (and the astonishingly life-like art with which they had filled them) to an even greater obscurity. Only the local tribespeo-ple knew of the masterpieces, prowled by tigers and overrun with creepers, until one of those red-coated hunting parties that infested the forests of imperial India spied Cave 10 from the opposite ridge in 1819.

Would-be visitors no longer have to beat back the brush, but they do have to suf-fer through a long, hot, jolting **bus** ride to get here. Many buses stop at Ajanta between Jalgaon (58km north) and Aurangabad (108km south), starting early in the morning and ending at 5:30pm in Aurangabad and 6:30pm in Jalgaon. You can come from one town, leave your well-locked bags to be guarded in the cloak room at the base of the caves (theoretically free) while sightseeing, and proceed to the next in the evening. **Telephone Code:** 02438.

The MTDC, naturally, runs the **hotel** and **restaurant** (tel. 4226) at the caves them-selves. Their rooms are clean but spare, with balconies and common bathrooms. (Singles Rs150; doubles Rs250. Attached restaurant: entrees Rs22-50; open daily 9am-5:30pm.) For reservations, call the regional MTDC manager in Aurangabad (tel. 331198). A far-preferable housing option is the **Forest Guest House,** 500m back down the road. It has two air-cooled doubles with hot water, a cook, mosquito nets, and a wicker-furnished and flowery veranda for those who book in advance at the Divisional Forest Officer, Opp. Government, Engineering College, Osman-pura, Aurangabad (tel. 334701; Rs100 per person).

 **THE SIGHTS**

THE CAVES

Open Tu-Su 9am-5:30pm. Rs5; additional Rs5 "light" fee for caves 1, 2, 16, and 17; video fee Rs25, exterior only; guide Rs100.

The caves are located up the steps behind the drink stands and over the rise. The guided tours, although interesting, rely primarily on gimmicks: "See the expression of the Buddha change when I move the light" and "see the very first Bermuda shorts in history." They do guarantee decent lighting while you visit, but your own flashlight will do just as well.

CAVES 1-2. Cave 1, which dates from the 5th century AD, contains some of Ajanta's most naturalistic paintings. As with all of Ajanta's art, the life-like jewelry, clothing, and domestic objects matter more than the stories behind them. On the left-hand wall, a king, newly converted to Buddhism, abandons earthly pleasures for a life of meditation. Just to the left of the rear shrine, a painting depicts the elegant Padmapani (the lotus-holding *bodhisattva*), while Vajrapani stands sentry to his right with his thunderbolt. Four deer sharing a single head gaze out contentedly at the tourists from several capitals on the right-hand side of the hall. In **Cave 2,** paintings to the left show the dream of a six-tusked elephant which foretold the Buddha's conception, and his miraculous birth directly into the arms of his mother. In the right-hand rear corner, a sculptural frieze of a classroom depicts an ill-behaved student pulling the hair of the girl in front. Above to the right, the demon Hariti dances furiously while, on the left, his teachings have lulled a princess into a peaceful repose.

CAVES 9-26. The *chaitya* hall in **Cave 9** dates from the Theravada era, during which the Buddha was not directly depicted. In the stead of traditional images are oblique references to the Enlightened One, including the pipal-tree-shaped window in the facade, signifying learning, and the huge *stupa* in the apse, symbolizing (somewhat more literally) the relics of the Buddha. The same goes for **Cave 10,** which dates from the 2nd century BC, although here millennia of sunlight and the scratchings of graffiti artists have obscured most of the paintings. In **Cave 16,** the most celebrated fresco shows yet another princess swooning in distress as her husband throws in the worldly towel. *Jataka* stories about the Buddha's earlier incarnations fill the walls of **Cave 17.** In the *vishavantara*, on the left-hand wall, a well-intentioned prince gives away his father's magic elephant, his cart and possessions, and even his wife and children, renouncing all earthly ties before entering into the final life-phase of hermitage. On the opposite wall, confusing tales of seductive beauties and bloodthirsty demons are depicted in surprisingly accurate anatomical detail. The tour guides love to create a 3-D effect by shining their flashlights on the princess' pearls in the upper-right-hand corner of the right wall.

The elaborate interior and exterior sculpture of **Cave 19** indicates the Buddhist response to the Hindu renaissance of the 6th century AD. A columned *chaitya* hall, Cave 19 dates from the Mahayana period, during which depictions of the Buddha were permitted. The most splendid example of this freedom reclines along the left-hand wall of **Cave 26:** Buddha on the verge of attaining nirvana, surrounded by disciples. The path behind Cave 26 leads down the hill to a bridge. From here, intrepid visitors can climb to a **viewpoint** to relive the astonishment of the British in 1819. A second path along the river will guide the less historically minded to a rainy-season waterfall and washing pool for villagers.

NAGPUR नागपुर

Located smack dab in the center of India, Nagpur is the hub for virtually every major road and rail route. But it certainly doesn't *feel* like the entire subcontinent rotates around this city of two million. Here, the streets are filled with tattered *tongas* and auto-rickshaws rather than taxis and aggressive Tata two-tonners. The seat of the state legislature alternates between Nagpur and Mumbai, but Nagpur lacks the skyscrapers and concrete that characterize other cities of its size. In fact, with its numerous parks and playgrounds, Nagpur is the second greenest cosmopolitan area in India. Most of its visitors are corporate types who come to attend conferences (or convert to Buddhism, as a few hundred thousand of Dr. B. R. Ambedkar's Untouchable followers did here in 1956). For tourists who find themselves at the center of things, however, Nagpur is subtle and sweet and makes a good starting point for excursions into the national parks nearby.

🚩 **ORIENTATION AND PRACTICAL INFORMATION.** Nagpur's pulse originates at the **railway station** (tel. 131 or 1331), on **Central Avenue Road;** the tracks split the city into eastern and western halves. Central Avenue Rd. becomes **Kingsway Road** after the railway station. Running parallel to and south of Kingsway Rd. is **Palm Road.** Farther south is the tourist center, **Sitabuldi,** with shining shops and a smattering of cheap hotels. North and west of Sitabuldi lies the **Civil Lines** area. **Wardha Road (NH7)** runs parallel to the train tracks and leads to the **airport** (tel. 260348 or 260433), 8km from the city center. The **Indian Airlines office** (tel. 523069; open M-Su 10am-1pm and 2-5pm) is on Palm Rd. Flights are available from Nagpur to: **Delhi** (9:25pm, 1½hr., US$135); **Hyderabad** (Tu, Th, and Sa 8pm; 1hr.; US$95); **Kolkata** (Tu, Th, and Sa 7:30am; 1½hr.; US$150); and **Mumbai** (7:30am and 9pm, 1½hr., US$115). **Trains** (fares listed are 2nd/1st class) go almost anywhere, including: **Chennai** (*Tamil Nadu Exp.* 2622, 2:35pm, 19hr., Rs315/1007); **Delhi** (*Tamil Nadu Exp.* 2621, 2pm, 14hr., Rs310/1047); **Hyderabad** (*Andhra Pradesh Exp.* 2724, 10:25am, 10hr.; *Hyderabad Exp.* 7022, 6pm, 11hr., Rs213/676); **Kolkata** (*Howrah Mail* 8001, 11:30am, 17hr.; *Gitanjali Exp.* 2859, 8:15pm, 17hr., Rs317/1028); and **Mumbai** (*Gitanjali Exp.* 2860, 7:45am, 14hr.; Rs285/875). The **State Bus Stand,** 1.5km south of the railway station, has buses to: **Hyderabad** (3 and 5pm, 12hr., Rs237), **Indore** (5:30am, 16hr., Rs187); **Jabalpur** (11am, 1, 9, and 11pm; Rs88, 109, 96, and 118 respectively); and **Pune** (1 and 4:45 pm, 14hr., Rs315).

The **MTOC tourist office,** Dr. Munje Rd. (tel. 533325), off Buty Rd., can provide information on area parks and lakes (open M-F and 1st, 3rd, and 5th Sa 10am-5pm). The **State Bank of India,** Kingsway Rd. (tel. 521196/7, ext. 416; open M-F 10:30am-2pm), near the railway station exchanges currency and cashes traveler's checks at the **foreign exchange office** in the center of the left-hand building. The **GPO** (open M-Sa 10am-5pm) is on Palm Rd. **Mayo Hospital** (tel. 72126 or 728623) is near the railway station. **Postal Code:** 440001. **Telephone Code:** 0712.

📞🛏️🍴 **ACCOMMODATIONS, FOOD, AND ENTERTAINMENT.** The steady traffic of business travelers through Nagpur sustains an abundance of accommodations. A service charge of 10% and a luxury tax of 4% are often added to basic room rates. The thickest tangle of budget (and disorientingly similar) hotels is on **Central Avenue Rd.** and its arteries. **Hotel Blue Diamond,** 113 Central Ave., Dosar Chowk (tel. 727461/69), is a good bet if you think you can handle its huge psychedelic honeycomb for a cheap room with a common bath (singles Rs55-130; doubles Rs120-200; TV add Rs40). Nearby, **Hotel Midland** (tel. 726131) has tidy rooms, disinfected marble bathrooms, and funky-smellin' hallways (singles Rs275-300; doubles Rs400-550; A/C rooms from Rs650). The cluster of cheapies in **Sitabuldi,** in the heart of Nagpur's market district, are less consistent in terms of quality but are well-suited to those inclined to explore. Head east on Mahatma Gandhi Rd., away from his statue, and take the third left to reach **Hotel Amrta,** Modi No. 3 (tel. 543762; fax 553123). Even the "regular rooms" in this aqua oasis put other dwellings to shame. (Check-out 24hr. Singles Rs350-475; doubles Rs400-550. Visa, MC, AmEx.) **Hotel Agrawal** (tel. 552021 or 536447), across the street, offers a wide variety of rooms. (Check-out 24hr. Dorm rooms Rs60-70; singles Rs115, with bath Rs195; doubles Rs195/250; reserve in advance).

Fine food is the dear domain of the five-star luxury hotels, but a few other establishments challenge their authority. **Nanking,** Mount Rd., Sardar, is the best-known best-value establishment for a Chinese feast (chicken Rs70-95, seafood Rs75-120, veg. fare Rs45-90; open Tu-Su noon-3pm and 6-11pm).

The Zodiac, 24 Central Bazaar Rd., in the Hotel Centre Point (tel. 520910), a popular spot among locals, is the most happening pub-cum-discotheque in town (open for "jam sessions" W 1-5pm; Rs150 per couple). For those seeking to see rather than to be seen, **Liberty Cinema,** Residency Rd., in Sardar, shows fairly recent English-language films (daily 10:30pm, Sa-M 11am). **Ambajhari Lake and Garden,** on the western outskirts of Nagpur, is ideal for early morning or evening strolls (open daily 9am-sunset).

NEAR NAGPUR: SEVAGRAM

Sevagram, literally the "Village of Service," is where Mahatma Gandhi founded an ashram after he left his Sabarmati retreat in Ahmedabad, Gujarat (see p. 344) in 1936. From Sevagram, Gandhi directed the independence movement, leading India to victory against the British in 1947 with his policy of non-violence. The community continues to thrive, with simple living and self-sufficiency the paradigm. The town is also the site of the **Nai Talimi Sangh,** the university founded by Gandhi to ensure that the town could meet its own aesthetic, spiritual, and intellectual needs. Far from the bustle of the rest of urban India, Sevagram is a breath of fresh air: clean, serene, and spiritual. Even people with little interest in Gandhi will find Sevagram a delightful place to relax for a few days.

Sevagram Ashram has kept all of its original buildings and Gandhi's personal belongings intact, complete with explanatory English signposts. Ashramites will also gladly answer questions and provide free English pamplets. (Open sunrise to sunset.) A shop near the entrance sells Gandhi's books and *khadi*, the hand-spun cloth that played an important role in the freedom movement, signifying *swaraj* (self-sufficiency) and a rejection of the reliance upon imported textiles. The *chakra* (wheel) that Gandhi used to spin the cloth now figures as the central motif on India's flag. Across from the ashram, the **Gandhi Picture Exhibition** displays a photographic timeline of Gandhi's life (open Sa-Th 10am-6pm; free). In the neighboring town of Wardha, the **Magan Nadi,** the home of Gandhi's nephew, provides a history of *khadi*.

The Center of Science for Villagers, 4km away, devotes itself to explaining Gandhi's philosophy of village-based economics (open daily 9am-1pm and 2pm-5pm; free). Adjoining the center is the **Leprosy Home,** where lepers engage in a variety of tasks including agriculture, shoe-making, weaving, and spinning.

The women who run **Vinobaji's Ashram** in Gopuri, 3km away, provide a living testament to the self-sufficient community that Gandhi envisioned. A fervent disciple of Gandhi, Vinoba Bhave was a social activist reformer who advocated land reform and the eradication of caste hierarchy. **Vinobaji's Museum** has exhibitions explaining Gandhi's and his efforts to get landlords to give land to the destitute (open daily 9am-1pm and 2pm-5pm; free).

Trains from Nagpur to Mumbai will stop at **Wardha,** 8km away from Sevagram (express 1hr., Rs30). Frequent MSRTC **buses** also run from Nagpur to Sevagram and Wardha (2½hr., Rs26). From Sevagram, an auto-rickshaw ride to the ashram is Rs25; from Wardha, it is Rs40. Buses also run from Wardha to the ashram (every 10min. 7:30am-8pm, 15min., Rs2). Although the **MTDC** offers basic accommodations for Rs150-220, **Sevagram Ashram** is cheaper and nicer (rooms Rs30; meals Rs10-13). **Yatri Nivas,** across from the ashram, offers rooms and meals for the same price. **Vinobaji's Ashram** (tel. 43518), in Paunar (3km away), prefers to house only women and requires advance notification by mail (Vinobaji's Ashram, Paunar, District Wardha, Maharashtra, 442111) or by telephone. **Telephone Code:** 07152.

GOA गोवा

Renowned for its sun-bathed white beaches, the charm of its lingering Portuguese colonial presence, and its easy-going, free spirit, Goa has long been a prime destination for all kinds of travelers. Unfortunately, though, the Goan idyll has recently begun falling beach by beach to the vanguard of invading tourist culture. As battalions of red Coca-Cola umbrellas crawl up the shores, regiments of middle-class Brits are marshalled off of charter flights and into resort complexes, while pan-European techno junkies groove en masse to the pedestrian reveille of rave after identical rave. The past twenty years have witnessed the fossilization of many of Goa's legendary attractions: the flea-market mayhem, bacchic revelry, Edenic splendor, and unconventional spirituality have been supplanted by an invasion of conventional tourist culture. The legends, spread worldwide, have returned to usurp the very things they touted, thereby giving today's travelers exactly what they expect. Homes have been converted into guest houses; restaurants, whose chefs have mastered the art of banana pancakes, have surfaced from the sand; and five-star resorts have invaded pristine beaches with their capitalist megaplexes. These sit amid moss-covered Baroque churches, leafy coconut groves, and soft-sanded shorelines strewn with fishing nets: relics of an older way of life that lives on overshadowed by the platoons of Kashmiri rug sellers and sun-loving surfers.

The West has been encroaching on Goa since 1498, when the Portuguese explorer Vasco da Gama landed on the Keralan coast in search of spices. Portugal was seeking a foothold on India's west coast, and in 1510 Goa ended up becoming a Portuguese colony. In the 16th century, Goa became a prosperous trading city where Portuguese soldiers and adventurers mixed with the locals, many of whom converted to Catholicism and married Europeans. Through the guidance of the Jesuits and the terror of the Inquisition, Goa also developed into a stronghold of Christianity in India. Portugal prevented Goa's absorption into the British Raj and held on until 1961, when Indian troops annexed the region. Thus, Goa holds the distinction of being both the first piece of subcontinental soil clutched by European colonizers and the last to be liberated. Goa first became a Union Territory and eventually, in 1987, an official state.

Some would say that the invasion of hippies and wealthy tourists in search of paradise has made Goa a colony once again. But indulging in its pleasures need not be an exploitative venture. After five centuries of Portuguese rule, Goa is unique among Indian states: you are as likely to meet a Portuguese-speaking Roman Catholic dressed in jeans and a muscle shirt as you are to encounter a *lungi*-clad fisherman shouldering his day's catch. About 30% of Goa's inhabitants are Christian, and the state has literacy and income levels among the highest in India. Goa is small enough to explore thoroughly on a moderate stay, and the locals are usually eager to share their vanishing paradise with visitors.

WHEN TO GO

Goa's northern beaches are hopping from early November to late March, when near perfect weather (sunny, hot, and cloudless) draws sun-lovers in droves. Beach fever is intense in the weeks before and after Goa's psychedelic Christmas; the months of December and January are considered peak season. Practically everything closes down during the monsoon (June-Sept.), and guest house prices bottom out as Westerners move out and head to Manali. The monsoon cools Goa and fills its wells, but the showers often cease for long sunny stretches. Other holidays well worth the trip are the Carnival, Panjim's pre-Lent revelry (Mar. 5-7 2000), and the more solemn festivities in honor of Goa's favorite Saint, Francis Xavier, held in Old Goa on December 3 every year.

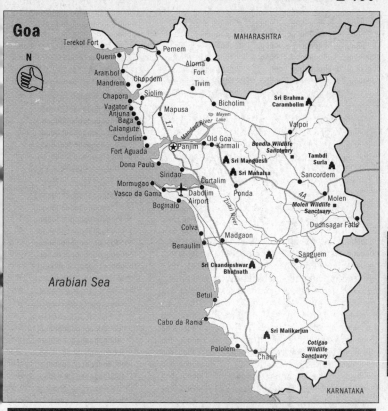

Goa

MAHARASHTRA

N

Terekol Fort
Querim
Pernem
Arambol
Mandrem
Chopdem
Aloma
Fort
Tivim
Chapora
Siolim
Vagator
Mapusa
Bicholim
Sri Brahma
Carambolim
Anjuna
Baga
Mayem
Lake
Valpoi
Calangute
Mandovi River
17
Candolim
Old Goa
Karmali
Bondla Wildlife
Sanctuary
Fort Aguada
Panjim
Sri Manguesh
Tambdi
Surla
Dona Paula
Sri Mahalsa
Siridao
Cortalim
Sancordem
Mormugao
Ponda
Vasco da Gama
Dabolim
Airport
Molen
Bogmalo
4A
Molen Wildlife
Sanctuary
Juari River
Dudhsagar Falls
Colva
Madgaon
Benaulim
Sanguem
Arabian Sea
Sri Chandreshwar
Bhutnath
Betul
Cabo da Rama
Sri Malikarjun
Cotigao
Wildlife
Sanctuary
Palolem
Chauri
KARNATAKA

GOA

HIGHLIGHTS OF GOA

■ India's most legendary (and decadent) nightlife raves away at the northern beaches of **Anjuna** (p. 452) and **Calangute** (p. 449) all winter.
■ Time stands still in **Old Goa** (p. 446), home to Portuguese monuments, cathedrals, and the interred remains of **St. Francis Xavier** (p. 446).
■ **South Goa** (p. 459), particularly the beach towns of **Benaulim** (p. 462) and **Palolem** (p. 463), offers sandy respite from the northern tourist frenzy.

HOW TO GO

Most travelers reach Goa from Mumbai, 600km to the north.

DOMESTIC FLIGHTS. Dabolim Airport (info tel. (0854) 512644), 29km south of Panjim, is primarily a domestic hub. Indian Airlines and Jet Airways both offer flights to and from: **Bangalore,** via Mumbai (M, 1hr., US$100); **Delhi** (1 per day, 2½hr., US$200); and **Mumbai** (1 per day, 1hr., US$50). There is a Rs750 airport tax for all flights. During peak season, seats on the Mumbai-Goa flight can be difficult to procure. Reserving months ahead for Christmas week is common practice.

Dabolim's prepaid **taxi** counter, outside the airport's main entrance, will ferry visitors to most anywhere in Goa. A board to the left of the ticket counter lists fares (to Panjim Rs300). Off season (May-Sept.), when the resorts are empty, touts clutter the main exit, threatening to whisk you off to a plush hotel you've never heard of. **Local buses** run to nearby Vasco da Gama (8am-8pm, Rs5), with connections for Panjim and Madgaon.

> **DON'T MESS WITH GOA** Goa's tourist boom has speckled its coast with huge resorts and small guest houses, all of which consume a hefty share of resources. The flood of thirsty (and dirty) travelers depletes Goa's freshwater resources so much that village wells run dry or are contaminated by salty seawater. Hotels drilling private wells and filling Olympic-sized swimming pools deserve most of the blame for water waste. But backpackers too can have an effect. There are simple ways to conserve water—taking bucket baths, turning off the shower while soaping, and giving clothes to a *dhobi* instead of washing them in your room. Beaches once trodden only by fishermen are now littered with Bisleri bottles, plastic bags, and light bulbs. Fishermen still fish here, and people (including you) still eat the fish they catch. But now, in addition to fish, the ocean is violently belching up tourist trash—take the hint and don't litter. If you are considering a long stay, volunteering for one of Goa's Non-Governmental Organizations (NGOs) allow you to help on a local level. ECOFORUM in Mapusa publishes a book, *Fish Curry & Rice* (Rs200), which has a listing of Goa's activist groups. For more information, see **Environmentally Responsible Tourism,** p. 59.

TRAINS. After years of waiting and wondering, you'll be pleased to know that the **Konkan Railway** is finally complete. Now, travel to the south from Mumbai is speedier and more comfortable; as the tracks wind through lush tropical forests and over more than one hundred bridges, the passing scenery is even more beautiful. The only drawback is that the tracks were laid 15 to 20km outside city stations, so the railway only skirts major towns. *Mumbai-Madgaon Express* trains from **Mumbai** (#0111, 1 per day) stop at three stations in Goa: **Tivim,** in the north, 20km due east of Vagator beach (arrives 9:15am, 11hr.); the centrally located **Karmali,** 12km due east of Panjim (arrives 9:45am, 11½hr.); and **Madgaon,** in the south, 5km outside the city (arrives 10:15am, 12hr.). All Mumbai fares are Rs231 for non-A/C sleeper and Rs597 for 3-tier A/C with blanket and pillow. Other trains continue down, eventually connecting Mumbai with Mangalore, Bangalore, and the tip of the sub-continent, Kanyakumari. Trains for **Delhi** leave daily from the coastal town of **Vasco da Gama,** near the airport (*Goa Exp.* 2779, 12:15pm, 41hr., Rs425/1750).

Note: Expect delays of one to five hours, especially in the monsoon season. Even the mighty Konkan must yield to Mother Nature.

CATAMARANS. Frank Shipping (tel. 374 3737), in Colaba, runs a catamaran service between Panjim and Mumbai (open M-F 9am-5pm, Su 10am-6pm). The service operates between late September and May. From Mumbai to **Panjim** (W 10am, F-Su 10:30pm; 8hr.; Rs1600/1800 or Rs9000 per 5-person cabin). In late December, reserve a seat several weeks in advance; at other times, 3-5 days is sufficient. The catamaran leaves Mumbai from the "Ferry Wharf" dock along P D'Mello Rd., 3km north of Victoria Terminus. From Panjim to **Mumbai** (Tu, Th, and F-Su 10am). Frank's Panjim office (tel. (0832) 228 711), opposite the Hotel Mandovi on the Mandovi River, is open late September to May). Going either direction, it's best to book through their central office in Mumbai, opposite the Oberoi Hotel, Nariman Point (tel. 285 2272 or 285 2274; open year-round M-F 9am-5pm, Su 10am-6pm).

BUSES. Buses are the cheapest way to reach Goa from: **Bangalore** (16hr.; see p. 466); **Mangalore** (12hr.; see p. 489); **Miraj** (7hr.); **Mumbai** (15hr., see p. 394); **Mysore** (16hr.; see p. 477); and **Pune** (12hr.; see p. 420). In most cities, you can buy the tickets on the bus. Alternatively, intrastate buses go between the **Kadamba Bus Terminals** in the transport hubs of Panjim, Mapusa, and Madgaon. **Private carriers** offer more extensive services, and their coaches are generally more comfortable (except for the infamous "video coaches"). Book private coaches through a travel agency or one of the shacks near the bus terminals in Goa. For details on interstate bus travel, see listings for **Panjim** (p. 442), **Mapusa** (p. 447), and **Madgaon** (p. 459).

HOW TO GET AROUND

Traveling by bus along Goa's narrow roads is not as stomach-wrenching as in other parts of the country; the popular routes are generally packed, but they are mercifully short. Local **buses** run extensively, frequently, and cheaply. **Express buses,** available only for certain routes, are the fastest; others stop in every village and paddy as locals hop on and off. There are few real bus stops in the state, and most locals simply flag down non-express buses as they pass by.

Tourist vehicles (expensive minivans) and **taxis** are available for short jaunts or longer-term rentals (Rs250-300 for 40km). **Auto-rickshaws** disclined to set their meters zip between beaches or herd passengers in at rickshaw stands in town. Their fares tend to be a little more than half of what taxis charge. During the off-season and when heading to more remote areas, all require return fares. The distinctly Goan **motorcycle-rickshaws** or **pilot taxis** are the cheapest options.

The simplest, riskiest, and sexiest transportation method employed by many visitors is an automatic Enfield, Honda Kinetic, or Yamaha **motorcycle,** which can be rented by the day or month through most hotels and guest houses in virtually every town and beach. You must obtain an Indian or international driver's license in order to drive one (see **Driving Permits and Car Insurance,** p. 49). Goan police have been known to relish busting unlicensed bikers in the cities, but license enforcement on the beaches is notoriously lax (except in Anjuna during Wednesday's flea market). If you are pulled over by a police officer and you do not have a valid license, keep your cool and remember that a little *baksheesh* might go a long way. **Helmets** can be hard to come by, but, with a little prodding, some official bike rental places might be able to find you one. An alternative is to pick up a helmet (with a visor to block dust) in Panjim or Mumbai and keep it as a souvenir.

Short distances, lack of direct bus service, and an overabundance of motorcycles make hitchhiking an attractive proposition, although riding with a stranger is inherently dangerous and *Let's Go* does not recommend it. **Bicycles** (Rs3-5 per hr., Rs30-50 per day) are a non-polluting alternative and can be rented through hotels and guest houses. You can pedal along the entirety of Colva Beach when the tide is out. Plan to get wet, and bring plastic bags for cameras and valuables. Cycling any long distance is tough; rental bikes have one gear, and there are many, many hills.

NORTH GOA

PANJIM (PANAJI) पणजी

Small and mellow for a state capital, the city of Panjim (pop. 100,000) covers the south bank of the Mandovi River. Its Portuguese past is most obvious in the porticoed, red-tiled mansions that crowd the narrow streets of the Fontainhas area, fulfilling the romantic, colonialist dream of a miniature Europe transplanted into the East. Shop signs in Portuguese and whitewashed churches speckling the countryside complete the picture. In 1759, the viceroy shifted his residence from Old Goa to Yusuf Adil Shah's old palace in Panjim (today's Secretariat), and from that point the city really began to grow, eventually becoming the capital in 1843. Relative to the rest of the state, Panjim bustles with activity, but there's a politeness in the "taxi, friend?" of the rickshaw-*wallah* that's rare in urban India.

▐ TRANSPORTATION

Airlines: Air India, 18th June Rd. (tel. 231101 or 231104), next to Hotel Fidalgo. Open M-F 9:30am-1pm and 2-5pm, Sa 9:30am-1pm. **Skyline NEPC,** BG Rd. (tel. 229234), behind the Hotel Delman. Open daily 9am-6pm. **Indian Airlines,** DB Marg (tel. 223826). Open M-F 10am-1pm and 2-5pm. **Jet Airways, Air France, TWA, Gulf Air, Air Canada,** 102 Rizvi Chambers (tel. 226154). Open M-F 9am-1pm and 2-5:30pm, Sa

9:30am-1pm. **British Airways,** MG Rd. (tel. 224336). Open M-F 9am-5:30pm, Sa 9:30am-1:30pm. **Thakkers Travel Service,** 2nd Mahalaxmi Chambers (tel. 226678), is an agent for KLM. Open M-F 9:30am-1pm and 2-5:30pm.

Buses: Kadamba Bus Terminal, Patto. Dual prices are for regular/deluxe service. **Interstate buses** to: **Bangalore** (3:30 and 7pm, 13hr., Rs223); **Bijapur** (8am, 10hr., Rs107); **Mangalore** (6:15am, 7, 8:30, and 11:15pm; 12hr.; Rs132/145); **Miraj** (10:30am, 7hr., Rs96); **Mumbai** (4 and 5pm, 15hr., Rs307); **Pune** (6:15am and 7pm, 12hr., Rs150/250). Advance reservations are recommended and can be made at the booking office. Most counters open 9am-6pm, but try to show up before 4pm, as some close early. **Private buses** departing for the same destinations can also be booked at many hotels and travel agents, or just show up at the bus stand (north of Kadamba under the overpass) along the river, and look for the sign with your destination. **Intrastate buses** zip to destinations throughout Goa 6am-8pm. To: **Calangute** (every 15min., 45min., Rs5); **Mapusa** (every 15min.; express 20min., regular 40min.; Rs4); **Madgaon** (every 30min., 1hr., Rs12). Reservation office for **Konkan Railway** and **Mumbai Terminal Lines** is upstairs. Open daily 9am-6pm.

Local Transportation: Taxis hover in front of the Hotel Mandovi. **Auto-rickshaws** line up near the market and the Municipal Gardens. When the weather's fair, budding capitalists hawk **motorbikes** across the street from the GPO. It's inadvisable to rent in Panjim without an international driver's license. Heavy, one-speed **bikes** are available at Daud M. Aga (tel. 222670), across from the Cinema National entrance for Rs2 per hr. Open M-Sa 9am-1pm and 2-7pm, Su 9am-1pm.

ℹ ORIENTATION AND PRACTICAL INFORMATION

Situated on the south bank of the **Mandovi River,** Panjim is easily navigated on foot. The **Ourem River** joins the Mandovi at Panjim; on the east bank of the Ourem is the **Patto** area, enclosing the chaotic **bus terminal. Emidio Gracia Road** leads west uphill from the Ourem to **Church Square,** dominated by the white facade of the **Immaculate Conception Church.** Here, the **Municipal Gardens** stretch northward almost all the way to the Mandovi River and the **Secretariat.** Past the Secretariat runs **Dayanand Bandodkar (DB) Marg (Avenida Dom Joao Castro),** which follows the bank of the Mandovi River. **18th June Road,** featuring many hotels, restaurants, and shops, leads southwest from Church Square.

Tourist Office: Government of India Tourist Office, Communidade Building, Church Sq. (tel. 223412). Disappointing brochure selection, but plenty of booklets including comprehensive railway schedules. Open M-F 9:30am-1pm and 2-6pm, Sa 9:30am-1pm. **Goa Tourism,** Patto Tourist Home, Dr. Alvares Cross Rd. (tel. 225715; fax 223926), between the traffic bridge and the footbridge on the bank of the Ourem River. Arranges tours and sunset kitsch cruises on the river. Open 24hr.

Currency Exchange: State Bank of India, DB Marg (tel. 226091), across from the Hotel Mandovi. Open for exchange only M-F 10am-2pm and 3-4pm, Sa 10am-noon. **Thomas Cook,** DB Marg (tel. 221312), exchanges cash and all traveler's checks at better-than-bank rates. Open Oct.-Mar. M-Sa 9:30am-6pm, Su 10am-5pm.

Bookstore: Hotel Mandovi has a decent bookstore with travel guides, novels, language books, and decade-old back issues of *Mad* magazine. Open daily 9am-9pm.

Pharmacy: Hindu Pharmacy, Cunha Rivara Rd. (tel. 223176), to the left of the Hotel Aroma and next to the Municipal Gardens. Open daily 9am-1pm and 3-8pm.

Hospital: Dr. Bhandare Hospital, Fontainhas (tel. 224966). Go south on 31st January Rd., passing the Panjim Inn; bear left where the road forks and continue to the gates of the hospital. Walk-ins admitted. **Ambulance** (tel. 224096).

Police: Police Headquarters (tel. 223124), 2 streets to the left of the Hotel Mandovi. Visa extensions are available in emergencies, but they take a while.

Post Office: From the traffic bridge at the Ourem River, continue along the road into Panjim. The **GPO** is on the left behind a garden. The desk to the left as you enter handles

GOA

Panjim

ACCOMMODATIONS

A Youth Hostel H1
B Tourist Hotel
C Mandovi Pearl Guest House
D Park Lane Lodge
E Panjim Inn
F Patto Tourist Home

Mandovi River

Mandovi Bridge

TO MAPUSA

Ribandar Causeway

TO OLD GOA AND PONDA

TO MERCES

Fishing Jetty

PATTO

Kadamba Bus Terminal

GTDC

Patto Bridge

Footbridge

Ourem River

Ourem Rd.

Frank Shipping Ferry Terminal

State Bank of India

Customs House

Secretariat

Abbé de Faria Statue

Dom João Castro

Avenida

GPO

Quem Rd.

Hotel Vihar Restaurant

Hotel Venite Restaurant

G.P. Rd.

31st January Rd.

C.A. Rd.

Emídio Gracia Rd.

School

Chapel of St. Sebastian

FOUNTAIN-HAS

Armada Portugesa Rd.

TO AIRPORT & MARGAO

Karnataka Tourist Office

Church of the Immaculate Conception

CHURCH SQ.

Dr. R.S. Rd.

Govt. of India Tourist Office

Municipal Gardens

Cunha Rivara Rd.

Hotel Mandovi

Sher-e-Punjab Classic

Cine National

Phone Office

Central Telegraph Office

Ormuz Rd.

Dr. Pisurleka Rd.

Sher-e-Punjab

Avenida

Pe. Agnelo

Dr. Dada Vaidya Rd.

Goenchin

Mahalaxmi Temple

Azad Maidan

Mahatma Gandhi Rd.

Malaca Rd.

Central Library

Ferry Ramp

Dayanand Bandodkar Marg

Swami Vivekananda Rd.

Shiu Sagar

Hotel Fidalgo

Dr. P. Shirgaonkar Rd.

National Parks Office

Ashok and Samrat Cinemas

Gen. Costa Alvares Rd.

Heliodoro Salgado Rd.

Indian Airlines

Municipal Market

Gen. Bernardo Guedes Rd.

Don Bosco School

18th June Rd.

Dr. Amaleam Botkaro Rd.

Dr. Gama Pinto Rd.

TO TALEIGAO

Children's Park

TO DONA PAULA, MORMUGAO, MIRAMAR, & A

Dayanand Bandodkar Marg

Dr. Brazanga Pereira Rd.

N

200 yards

200 meters

Poste Restante (M-Sa 9am-5pm), and the counters in the right wing sell stamps (8am-noon and 1-6pm). **Postal Code:** 403001.

Internet: Connections are slow; the nearest server is in Mumbai. **NetMagic,** 7 Shanta Bldg., 18th June Rd. (tel. 224106), behind Don Bosco High School, past the petrol station; go right onto 18th June. NetMagic is 5 shops down on the left. Web access. RS2 per min., Rs100 per hr. Open M-Sa 9am-1pm and 3:30-6pm.

Telephones: Panjim has recently switched from 5- to 6-digit phone numbers. Replace the leading 4 with 22 or 42 in any 5-digit numbers you may stumble across.

PHONE CODE	0832

◤ ACCOMMODATIONS

Guest houses and swanky hotels do a brisk business, but since most folks only stay a night or two before heading beachward, same-day accommodations can be easily arranged. Standards (and, sadly, prices) are high for the region, and tariffs often double around Christmas.

Panjim Inn, 31st January Rd., Fontainhas (tel. 226523; fax 228136; email Panjimin @bom2.vsnl.net.in), on the left, south from Emidio Gracia Rd. 17th-century mansion with a vine-covered veranda and antique furniture. Internet service. Hot showers in all attached baths. Check-out 9am. In-season: singles Rs495; doubles Rs630; suites Rs720. A/C Rs225 extra. Peak-season (Dec. 21-Jan. 10) add Rs100-150. Off-season: Rs360/585/140. Rooms at the equally beautiful adjacent annex, **Pousada,** 10% cheaper, but call in advance for a reservation. Check-out 9am. Both accept MC, Visa.

Park Lane Lodge, Fontainhas (tel. 227154 or 220238), near St. Sebastian Chapel. Head north along 31st January Rd.; the lodge is visible from the main road. Cozy common TV room/study and terrace. Rooms with common bath are more spacious than those with attached bath. Lockers. Check-out 8am. In-season: doubles Rs240-300. Peak-season: Rs400-450. Off-season: Rs160/200.

Patto Tourist Home (tel. 225715), between the bus terminal and the Ourem, is a great option for penny-pinchers. Packed to the rafters Dec.-Jan. Must be in group for dorm beds. In season: Rs50. Off-season: Rs40.

Tourist Hotel, Dr. Alvares Costa Rd. (tel. 227103), a few blocks northwest after crossing Patto Bridge. GTDC institutionalism breeds cleanliness, but also sterility—even the welcome mats in the rooms are government-issued. Rooms have attached baths, fans, phones, clean sheets and towels; some have TVs. Check-out noon. In-season: doubles Rs500, with A/C Rs605-770. Peak-season: 10% increase. Off-season: Rs250/550.

Youth Hostel H1 (tel. 22533), in suburban Miramar, a 30min. walk from the town center along DB Marg. Less-crowded, dirt-cheap dormitory choice requires some chores. Meals Rs20-30. Check-out 8am. Dorm beds Rs40, H1 members Rs20.

Mandovi Pearl Guest House, (tel. 223928), just scamper up the hill behind the Tourist Hotel. Large rooms with an eccentric blend of carpet and furnishings, but well-kept. All have attached baths, some with seat toilets. Hot water Rs5 per bucket. Check-out 9am. In-season: singles Rs350; doubles Rs450. Off-season: Rs150/175.

◪ FOOD

Panjim's myriad top-drawer eateries may be the best reason to stay in the city longer than it takes to hail a beach-bound taxi. Visitors pick from chow mein, lasagna, South Indian snacks, Gujarati *thalis*, Punjabi *dal*, and Goan fish curry.

Shiu Sagar, MG Rd., in Shiu Sagar Hotel. The best veg. fare in Panjim. Crowded with middle-class families and the occasional business deal. North Indian veg. dishes Rs35-50 and non-veg. under Rs50. Open daily noon-3pm and 7-11pm.

Sher-e-Punjab Classic, on the 1st fl. of Hotel Aroma, on the west edge of the Municipal Gardens. The delicacies that emerge from the restaurant's well-known *tandoor* (entrees Rs50-90) will remind you why you eat meat in the first place. A well-deserved A/C respite from the heat. Open daily noon-3:30pm and 7pm-midnight.

Sher-e-Punjab, 18th June Rd., on the right as you walk away from the river. A huge local favorite swarming with satisfied customers. Lively bar scene at night. Entrees under Rs60. Open daily noon-11pm.

Hotel Vihar, around the corner north of Hotel Venite. Enormously popular, this stainless steel and formica joint serves up meal-sized *dosas* and *samosas* (Rs12) masquerading as snacks. Veg. *thali* Rs19. Open daily 7am-10pm.

Goenchin, Dr. Dada Vaidya Rd. on the left as you come from Church Sq. The delicious Chinese food is only slightly Indianesque (you can even request chopsticks), and the ambience is lush. Most entrees go for Rs80-90, with veg. choices going for Rs60-70. Open daily 12:30-3pm and 7:30-11pm.

Hotel Venite, on 31st January Rd. near the river. A sign will direct you up a narrow stair-case. Macaroni and cheese (Rs65) for the homesick, but Venite's crowd-pleasers are its fish curry (Rs80) and nightly specials (Rs60-100). Have a beer or a *feni* (coconut or cashew Rs20), or try the artery-clogging *bebinca.* Open M-Sa 8am-3pm and 7-10pm.

NIGHTLIFE AND ENTERTAINMENT

Panjim provides generously for the timeless recreation of consuming alcohol. Local brews are sold in small shops, and tiny bars dot the city, especially in Fontainhas. Try **Kwality Bar & Restaurant,** Church Sq., a place where Chinese flavor, wicker lanterns, Stevie Wonder tunes, and Goan hipsters all come together.

Government and private companies still organize **evening cruises** on the Mandovi River. The cruises feature traditional dancing—*denki, fijddi,* Portuguese, and *corredmino* dances—and, depending on the time, a stunning view of the sunset at sea. Book at any GTDC office, or just show up at the pier and look for the boat. Check an English-language newspaper to find what's showing at Panjim's three **cinemas:** the **Samrat** and the **Ashok** (which shows the dregs of English and American cinema) are in the same building on 18th June Rd., and the **Cine National** is behind the Hotel Aroma on Ormuz Rd.

SIGHTS

Not even the tourist offices pretend that there are any honest-to-goodness sights in Panjim. Still, it's a pleasant place for idle meandering, particularly in the Fontainhas area on the west bank of the Ourem.

The bright white **Chapel of St. Sebastian,** dating from the 1880s, stands at the end of a short street opening off 31st January Rd. The life-sized crucified Jesus statue that used to hang in the Palace of the Inquisition in Old Goa hangs here now, head unbowed. (Open daily 6:30-8am.) In Church Sq. stands the **Mary Immaculate Conception Church (Igreja Maria Immaculada Conceicao),** the top tier of a stack of white and blue criss-crossing staircases. The original chapel, consecrated in 1541, was the first stop for Portuguese sailors thanking God for a safe voyage. The chapel was renovated in the 17th century. This is the main place of worship for local Christians, and its musty, dark interior is heavy with silence and prayer. (Open Su and holy days 10:30am-1pm and 6:15-7pm, other days 9am-1pm and 3:30-6pm.)

The **Secretariat** sits on the banks of the River Mandovi. The grand white building was constructed in the 16th century as a palace and fortress for Yusuf Adil Shah of Bijapur. The Portuguese rebuilt it in 1615, and in 1759 it became the palace of the Portuguese viceroy. A bit farther downstream lies Panjim's most auspicious monument—a dark statue of a man hypnotizing a buxom lady. The man is Abbé José de Faria, an expatriate Goan priest who gained fame (and eventually infamy) as a hypnotist in 19th-century Paris. Faria was ruined by rumors that he took undue liberties with his female groupies, rumors that the monument does little to dispel. The **Mahalaxmi Temple,** with a large open sacred space, can be reached by following Dr. Dada Vaidya Rd. southwest from Church Sq.

OLD GOA ओल्ड गोवा

Tourists who don't venture inland from the beaches might think European fascination with Goa began in 1970s Calangute. Old Goa, 9km east of Panjim along the Mandovi River, proves them wrong, evoking the 16th-century glory days of Portuguese rule, when the city of 200,000 was hailed as the "Rome of the Orient," and the Inquisition was in full swing. The euphoria began in 1510, when Alfonso de Albuquerque, the original Portuguese man-o'-war, trounced the Bijapur Sultan and seized the capital on the Mandovi, then known as Ela. Regional control gave the Portuguese a valuable monopoly, allowing the city to attract wealth, sailors, and the epic debauchery such elements helped to touch off. Galvanized by tales of sin, the Jesuits arrived shortly thereafter, proselytizing to hedonists and heathens with the same zeal that built Old Goa's staggeringly ornate cathedrals. The city's demise, concurrent with Portuguese India's decline, was hastened by malaria epidemics and silting in the Mandovi; by the 17th century the party had ended for good, and the seat of government moved to Panjim. Today's viceroys are not aristocratic *hidalgos* but rather the Archaeological Survey of India, plastering the churches to keep them from crumbling in the monsoon.

Auto-rickshaws (Rs50), **motorcycles,** and **bicycles** easily make the scenic 9km trip along the Mandovi riverbank from Panjim to Old Goa. **Buses** also shuttle from Panjim's bus terminal (every 15min. 7am-7pm, 20min., Rs3). Unofficial guides, frequenting the churches for earthly reasons, are chock full of history and legends, and they expect to be tipped. For eats, *dhabas* serve snacks (Rs10-20) and "tourist restaurants" serve bland *thalis* (Rs20-50), but the best deal is a coconut split open, full of water you can trust (Rs10).

■ SIGHTS

CATHEDRAL OF ST. CATHERINE DA SE. At the center of Old Goa, along the main road from Panjim, the yellow Cathedral of St. Catherine da Sé looms to the left from an expanse of the green-trimmed lawn. Erected by the viceroy in 1564, the vast, three-naved cathedral took 80 years to build. One of the cathedral's twin towers was destroyed by lightning in 1775, and the other houses the mellow-toned **Sino du Ouro (Golden Bell),** said to be the largest bell in Asia. Scenes from the life of St. Catherine are carved into the grand golden altar; and fourteen smaller ones are set within the cavernous church. Large pillars and somber silences may inspire, but try not to vocalize your reactions too loudly; this is still an active place of worship. Also in the Cathedral complex is the former **Convent and Church of St. Francis of Assisi.** Tread softly upon the church floor—it's paved with coats of arms marking family graves from as early as the 16th century. Gold ornamentation and oil paintings adorn the walls, holding fast against the advancing orange water stains. Mary and Jesus are depicted with dark hair and complexions, similar to the dark-skinned cherubs in the Sé Cathedral. The attached convent is now the **Archaeological Museum,** exhibiting portraits of the viceroys, currency from "India Portuguesa," Christian icons, and sculpture from Goan Hindu temples. *(Open Sa-Th 10am-5pm.)*

BASILICA DE BOM JESUS. The Basilica de Bom Jesus, (Cathedral of the Good Jesus), with its dark orange stone walls, may be Old Goa's most legendary site. The Basilica was built between 1594 and 1605 to house the remains of St. Francis Xavier. Its interior is an explosion of gold, attesting to the former wealth of the Goans in India. At the far end of the nave, above the altar, is a painting of St. Francis Xavier embracing Christ on the cross. The saint's mausoleum is set off to the right of the altar behind a curtain of stars. Inside the windowed silver casket, a lightbulb shines on St. Francis' shriveled body, which was "donated" by Cosimo III de Medici in exchange for a pillow on which the saint's head rested. A doorway to the left of the mausoleum leads to a small room with historical "tidbits" and photographs of the relic at different stages. Stairs lead to an **art gallery** with modern religious works, scenes from the life of Goa's favorite do-gooder, and an aerial view of the casket. *(Opposite the Sé Cathedral. Open M-Sa 9am-6:30pm, Su 10:30am-6:30pm. Gallery open Sa-Th 9:30am-12:30pm and 2-5:30pm, Su 10:30am-12:30pm and 2-5:30pm.)*

STUDENT TRAVEL

Planning Trips for Generations X, Y and Z.

STA TRAVEL

(800) 777-0112

We've Been There.

BOSTON   NEW YORK   SEATTLE   CAMBRIDGE   WASHINGTON   MIAMI   AUSTIN
CHICAGO   LOS ANGELES   ORLANDO   BERKELEY   MINNEAPOLIS   ANN ARBOR
SAN FRANCISCO   SAN DIEGO   PHILADELPHIA   TEMPE   PALO ALTO   GAINSVILLE
TUCSON   CHAMPAIGN   CHARLOTTESVILLE   TAMPA   BATON ROUGE   MADISON

www.statravel.com

OTHER SIGHTS. To the west of the Sé Cathedral, the **Church of St. Cajetan** was, according to local lore, built atop an ancient Hindu temple by Italian friars of the Order of Theatines in the 17th century. Today it's known for its unique dome (modeled after St. Peter's in Rome) and the elaborate woodwork of the interior. Here, the ruined gate to Yusuf Adil Shah's collapsed palace rises in a forlorn tribute to pre-Portuguese Goa. Up the road toward the Mandovi River, the **Viceroy's Arch** patiently waits to receive another incoming Portuguese viceroy, who would be handed the keys to the capital as he ceremoniously passed under the arch. There is an inscription on the arch left by Governor Francisco da Gama (r. 1597-1600) in memory of his great-grandfather Vasco. Up the hill to the west of the Basilica de Bom Jesus are the ruins of the **Church of St. Augustine.** The 46m tower has stood since 1602. Gravestones line the floor, and the knobby alcoves hint at carvings. Across the street, at the **Church and Convent of St. Monica Christon,** the "miracle cross" probably won't open its eyes, bleed from its wounds, and try to speak, as it did for patrons in 1636, but catching a glimpse can't hurt. *(Churches open daily 8am-5:30pm but may close for a 12:30-3pm siesta.)*

NEAR OLD GOA

A handful of Hindu temples lurk deceptively near the Portugese ruins of Old Goa, on NH4 and between Panjim and Ponda. Although far from India's finest, they provide day-trippers with an interesting glimpse of the Hindu majority behind coastal Goa's Portuguese facade.

Six temples hide near NH4, conveniently becoming less interesting the closer one gets to drab **Ponda.** Thus, for visitors who tire of the temples, it's a simple matter of hopping a bus back to **Panjim** (every 15-20min. 6am-5:40pm, 1hr., Rs8). Buses from Panjim are often full—be sure to stand near a door so you can fight your way out, and tell the conductor where you want to get off. The first temple is at **Mangeshi** (also called Priol) village, where a colorful arch on the left highlights the walkway to the **Sri Manguesh** temple. Like most of the temples in this area, it was built in the 18th century to house deities smuggled inland in the 16th century from the Inquisition-ravaged coast. Just a 15-minute walk south leads to the more sedately decorated **Sri Mahalsa,** acclaimed for the wood carvings on the facades of its *mandapam* (sloping roof). Veering right off NH4, 10 minutes farther south, the paved road winds west to **Vingua** village. As the town square with its cement shine looms into view, a gate and steps lead south to the **Sri Laxmi Narcenha.** The interior is closed to non-believers, but heathens can gawk at the temple's lovely water tank. From here, it's best to hop a bus the 4km stretch to the Farmagudi junction, where an equestrian statue of Shivaji points down a narrow back road through **Nageshi** village to the **Sri Naguesh** temple. Colorful woodcarvings in the entrance hall depict scenes from the **Ramayana** (see p. 586), though it's difficult to piece together the narrative. Lumbering down the road another 20 minutes (keep right), hordes of buses indicate you've arrived at **Sri Shantadurga,** notable for its size, Western influences, and tourist multitudes.

MAPUSA म्हापूसा

Mapusa (MAP-sa) is on a hillside 30km north of Panjim and 10km inland from the topping beaches at Anjuna, Calangute, and Baga. This major area of North Goa is mostly of interest to travelers for its bus terminal. Beach-cravers from Mumbai or Bangalore jump off the bus at Mapusa and head straight for the sand.

Mapusa is not paradise, but at least it's easy to leave; throngs of buses shuttle frequently from the **Kadamba Bus Terminal** to the North Goa beaches, Panjim, and Madgaon. Most buses run from 6am to 8:20pm and travel to: **Anjuna** (every 30min., 45min., Rs5); **Arambol** (11am, 1hr., Rs10); **Baga and Calangute** (every 20min., 30min., Rs4); **Madgaon** (every hr. 6am-8:20pm, 1½hr., Rs17); **Panjim** (every 15min.; express 20min., local 40min.; Rs5); and **Siolim** (every 15min.,

DIVINE DISMEMBERMENT, PART TWO When

he was 36, Spanish saint Francis Xavier was dispatched to Goa by the king of Portugal, who was worried by reports of hedonism practiced by his Portugese subjects there. Although Xavier engaged in social work among Euro sybarites for a few months, he found his forte among Subcontinentals: Xavier won converts by the thousands in India, and whole villages would embrace Christianity mere days after his arrival. Undoubtedly, part of his appeal lay in his aptitude for curing the dying, raising the dead, and performing miracles. God and duty called Xavier on missions to the rest of Asia, until his death in 1552 at the age of 46. He was buried on the Malaysian coast.

But this was only the beginning for Francis Xavier, known as *Goench Sahib* (Lord of Goa), who performed some of his greatest miracles as a corpse. When, after five months, his body was disinterred to bring the bones back to Goa, it was found to be "fresh as on the day it was buried." Jesuit priests in Goa plunged their fingers into a hole in Xavier's chest and examined the blood for preservatives, but the blood was "smelt and found to be absolutely untainted." Soon everyone wanted a piece of the soon-to-be-canonized Xavier. When the saint's body was installed in the Basilica of Bom Jesus, the Pope got his right arm and parts of his intestines were dispatched to southeast Asia, while Japan cashed in on Xavier's hand. An enshrined fingernail still sits in the Braganza-Perriera mansion in Chandor. Most infamously, during an exposition of the body in 1634, an ecstatic devotee bit off St. Francis' big toe, which gushed blood from her mouth all the way home. Since the canonization in 1622, St. Francis Xavier's relics (minus a few) have been housed in the Basilica de Bom Jesus, where a marble pedestal and a fence restrain the overzealous from swarming the corpse. An exposition is held every ten years (the next is in 2004), during which the wilted body is placed on view in the Sé Cathedral.

Rs5). **Motorcycle rentals** are hard to come by, due to Mapusa's police crackdown on foreigners without papers; would-be easy-riders rent in the resort villages. If you're heading to Mumbai, Bangalore, or Pune, there's no reason to go to Panjim to catch a bus—the area around Kadamba teems with private coach operators, and state-run buses also make the haul (long distance booking office, opposite bus stall 8; open daily 6am-1pm and 2-8pm). Buses go to: **Hubli** (11am, 5hr., Rs57); **Miraj** (10:45am, 5hr., Rs96); **Mumbai** (4, 4:30, and 7pm; 17hr., Rs307); and **Pune** (regular 6:30am, deluxe 7:30pm; 14hr.; Rs203/250). For currency exchange, the **State Bank of India** is north of the bus terminal at the Gandhi-less roundabout (open M-F 10am-2pm, Sa 10am-noon). Two blocks west are the **police station** (tel. 262231) and the **GPO.** Though the post office is open for *Poste Restante* (M-Sa 9am-11am and 3-5pm), the offices in tourist-saturated Anjuna and Calangute are more efficient. **Postal Code:** 403507.

Finding lodging in Mapusa presents a catch-22: if you've planned ahead there shouldn't be any need to stay here; if you haven't, you're unlikely to find any vacancies. In an emergency, taking a taxi to Calangute or Panjim might be more expedient than trying to find a good place on short notice in Mapusa. If it is necessary to stay overnight, however, the **Tourist Hostel** (tel. 262694), at the Gandhi-statued roundabout south of the bus terminal, will make you feel like the just-off-the-bus tourist that you are (check-out noon; doubles Rs280, quads Rs350; off-season: Rs240/300). To the left of the Tourist Hostel at the next roundabout stands the **Hotel Satya Heera** (tel. 262849), with spacious rooms, spectacular views (on the upper floors), and even an antiquated TV (check-out 9am; doubles Rs300, with A/C Rs600; triples Rs400/700; MC,Visa). **Ruchira**, the hotel's rooftop restaurant, serves Goan, Chinese, and pan-Indian dishes (Rs10-60; open daily 7-11am and 11:30am-10:45pm). Food stalls around the bus terminal serve delicious, greasy fare, but Mapusa's **market**, southeast of the bus terminal, is an adventure: a more authentic version of the Anjuna flea market (every F early morning-late afternoon).

CALANGUTE कालांगुद AND BAGA बागा

Once winter hangouts of the backpacker set, Calangute and Baga have largely sold out to the security of package tourism. Calangute is now densely commercialized; guest houses, restaurants, and Kashmiri rug shops abound. Wizened locals, expats, and travel guides tantalize newcomers with tales of Calangute in its late-70s hedonistic heyday, full of free drugs, free love, and—for the voyeuristic Indian gawkers who came in droves—a free peep show. Today, it's difficult to see what all the fuss was about. Certainly, the *laissez-faire* attitude is gone. Police strictly enforce the beaches' "no nudity" ordinance and frequently shut down the rickety shacks fronting the beach on the slightest suspicion of drug-peddling. Rampant development has narrowed what was never an expansive beach with resorts and seafood shacks that stretch all the way to Baga village, 2.5km north. Today, while the sunsets are rarely enhanced with anything stronger than an ice-cold Kingfisher, Calangute and Baga still provide a brief, sunny escape to lots of travelers.

🛈 ORIENTATION AND PRACTICAL INFORMATION

Most buses plod into **Calangute market** at the base of the main road heading west to the **beach.** Proceed straight along this road for about 1km and make a right at the **roundabout** (before the beach) and onto the **Calangute-Baga strip,** where most budget accommodations are found. There are two main roads in Calangute and Baga: an east-west road leading from the **market** west to the **beach,** where the hotels and restaurants of Calangute proper are concentrated, and a north-south road which intersects it at the roundabout before heading 2km north to Baga.

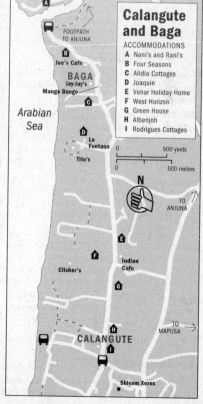

Calangute and Baga
ACCOMMODATIONS
A Nani's and Rani's
B Four Seasons
C Alidia Cottages
D Joaquin
E Venar Holiday Home
F West Horizon
G Green House
H Albenjoh
I Rodrigues Cottages

Buses: Buses stop at the stand at **Calangute market** before proceeding some 800m to the beach. Buses from Mapusa turn at the main roundabout and head north to **Baga,** then return on their way back to **Mapusa** (Rs3 to Baga, Rs9 to Mapusa). Buses to and from **Panjim** (Rs5) stop at the market, the roundabout, and just before the beach.

Local Transportation: Tourist taxis go between Calangute and Baga for Rs40-50. **Rickshaws** and **motorbikes** do the route for about Rs30-40 (to Panjim Rs70-150, to Anjuna Rs50-100). All three types of vehicles hover near the Calangute bus stand. **Motorcycle** rental is common in season—look for signs. Otherwise, ask taxi drivers or enquire near the gas station west of the market. For **bicycle** rental, look for signs or try Jay-Jay's, on the road between Baga and Calangute (Rs40-55). Open daily 8am-7pm.

Budget Travel: MGM Travels (tel. 276073), on the Calangute roundabout, sells plane and catamaran tickets and has **STD/ISD** telephone services. In-season: open daily 9am-7pm. Off-season: open M-Sa 9:30am-6pm.

Currency Exchange: State Bank of India, at Calangute market. Open M-F 10am-2pm, Sa 10am-noon. **Prince Santosh** (tel. 276417), on the inland side of the Calangute-Baga Rd., exchanges all major traveler's checks and currencies. Open daily 9am-10pm.

Bookstore: Rama Books & Jewelry, at the roundabout right before the Tourist Hostel, swaps English, German, and French books. Open daily 9am-7pm.

Pharmacy: Calangute Medical Stores, Shop #B-11 of the beachfront "Tourist Complex," stocks its shelves with over-the-counter goodies. Open M-Sa 9am-9pm, Su 9am-7pm.

Post Office: In a cute pink building south of the market. Open 9am-2pm and 2:30-5pm.

Internet: The Computer Spot, (tel. 276290), has web access for Rs120 per hr. Open M-Sa 9am-1:30pm and 2:30-6:30pm.

PHONE CODE	0832

▲ ACCOMMODATIONS

Most cheap accommodations are around the main villages and the road between them. In general, the ones close to Baga offer more pleasant surroundings, though most places between the villages are far from the beach. Haggling can be fruitful until around mid-December, when prices may as much as double until mid-January. Try to visit before then or call ahead to reserve rooms at better rates. Flats and houses for longer stays, the best ones being just north of Baga, are usually still available in early December. Look for signs and ask around.

Venar Holiday Home (tel. 276867), halfway between Calangute and Baga on the inland side of the road. The world's nicest family rents several rooms in a large house and several more in separate cottages. All have fans and 24hr. running water; hot water is available by the bucket. Check-out noon. Sometimes closed off season. In-season: singles Rs150, doubles Rs250.

Albenjoh (tel. 276422), just north of Calangute on the inland side. Resort-style white-wash, terraces, and lovely gardens at guest house prices. In-season: Rs600-800. Off-season: Rs250.

Alidia Cottages (tel./fax 27901; emergency tel. 276835), farther along the road to Baga behind a white church on the left. Another friendly, family-run establishment. Wander through the back gate, past the tiny fishing village, and right onto the blissful beach. In-house restaurants for guests. Check-out 11am. In September, rates begin to increase, reaching Rs800 by winter. Off-season: doubles Rs150. Discounts for long-term singles.

Joaquin (tel. 279696—the home of the proprietress' sister), just off the east-west road that leads to Tito's. From the main north-south road, head east between the Sunshine Beach and Miranda Resorts and look for signs on your right. Beautiful rooms with sparkling attached baths. Guests savor the thatched roof patio. Check-out 10am. In-season: Rs400-500. Off-season: Rs150-300.

Four Seasons (formerly Lucky Bar & Restaurant), along the main road in Baga. Rents rooms in a building near the beach or in brightly painted cottages with attached bath and 24hr. running water. In-season: doubles Rs300, with hot water Rs400; triples Rs400/450; cottage doubles Rs250. Off-season: rooms Rs100-150.

Nani's and Rani's, (tel. 277014), north of Baga, across the river. The cream of the northern crop. Splendid doubles (all attached) cluster around the house's popular restaurant. Singles with common bath Rs150; doubles with fan Rs250. One A/C room Rs450.

Rodrigues Cottages (tel. 276458), across from the Calangute Association building. Basic rooms strung around a courtyard, all with attached bath. Proprietress is amenable to further discounts for "poor" travelers. Rooms Rs100-150.

West Horizon (tel. 276489), seaward from the main north-south road at the sign for Hotel Cary's; follow the road to the Beach Queen Guest House. Turn due left; it's 100m away through the pines. A ramshackle hut with brightly painted concrete rooms added on for guests. Bathroom fixtures are relatively new and clean, and the place gets bonus points for beach proximity. In-season: doubles Rs200. Off-season: doubles Rs150.

Green House (tel. 277434), inland on the main north-south road. The smallest single may be the cheapest in town. Clean enough, especially considering what you're paying. Common baths. Rooms Rs100-150.

FOOD

You can't please all the people all the time, but that doesn't stop the throngs of touristy seafood shacks here from trying. Copycat menus proffer mediocre renditions of regional delights and favorites from home, whether that's Beijing, Boston, or Bologna. Still, the seafood is good, and if you're just craving a good spot to meet fellow travelers over a cold beer and a sunset, try the popular and serviceable **Britto's** or **St. Anthony's,** side by side on the Baga beachfront, or the reasonably cheap **Inspiration,** on the beach between Baga and Calangute.

Indian Cafe, midway between Calangute and Baga; look for the sign on the main north-south road. Excellent lunchtime retreat serves delicious *masala dosa* (Rs20). Open daily 8am-6pm. Closed Jun. 1-Sept. 31.

La Fontana, next to Joachim, across the street from Tito's. Superb seafood, pasta, and veggies in a friendly atmosphere allow you to transcend your belly troubles and contemplate higher things. Fresh pasta Rs35-60, fish Rs70-100, crepes Rs20-40. Open daily 8:30am-midnight.

Infanteria Pastry Shop, to the right from the roundabout, by the church. Pastries galore, donuts (plain Rs8, chocolate Rs12), pizzas, and fresh soups. Open daily 8am-9pm. Table service stops 30min. before closing.

Clisher's, just west of the West Horizon Guest House. Follow the large, fish-shaped sign from the Calangute tourist complex along the beach. Excellent, moderately priced seafood in surroundings so tranquil you can hear the waves lapping on the shore. Indian dishes Rs20-50, seafood Rs60-300. Closed Jun. 1-Aug. 31.

Joe's Cafe, on the southern outskirts of Baga, serves cheap, tasty breakfasts and fresh juice on tables cunningly constructed on curvy brick pillars. Omelettes Rs20. For health nuts and those needing to dry out, a variety of fresh juice combos are available, with or without spirulina. Open daily 8am-6pm.

NIGHTLIFE

Despite a raucous past, nightlife in today's Calangute and Baga tends to wind down early and errs on the side of resort-area hokeyness. The more upscale hotels pack their bar-restaurants with the sort of live "musicians" who'd be confined to street-performing back home, though there are worse places to begin or end a night of drunken revelry. Aside from surf-splashing and beer-swilling, there's little to do here—but isn't that why you came in the first place?

For nightlife without the schmaltz, the reggae-themed **Mango Bongo** bar—a beach shack transplanted onto the main Baga road—plays tunes and serves until as late as 1am in season. But even their bartenders acknowledge that there's only one after-hours game in town: **Tito's,** a bar-restaurant on the Baga beach with a dance floor and boomin' hi-fi, serves expensive drinks often until the break of dawn. Outside the village proper, the **West End,** a somewhat tame party venue on the road between Calangute and Panjim, hosts parties regularly in December and January. Watch for their flyers, or ask area bartenders and taxi-*wallahs* eager to take you there (Rs50-150). Calangute isn't well-connected to the norther party scene, but closer to Baga you'll catch word of happenings in Anjuna or Vagator.

GOA

GOA TRANCE At least one aspect of Goa's party scene has transcended international borders. **Goa trance music,** also known as "psychedelic" or "psyche" trance (because of its supposed psychoactive effects), has emerged as one of the most popular forms of techno music. Relying on multi-layered, harmonic synthesizer patterns rather than thick, pounding bass pulses, Goa trance is said by fans to represent the merging of technology with spiritualism. Don't be fooled—there's nothing Indian about this music, except for the occasional Sanskrit chant or catch-phrase ("Bom Shankar!" or "Om Shiva!") sampled over the sound. Rather, Goa trance emerged from the backpacking subculture of India, making it possible for partiers from the rest of the world to taste the Goa freak scene without ever leaving home.

BEACHES

 WARNING. The water on some beaches is off-limits during the monsoon season because of rough waves and dangerous undertow. Ask before taking a dip, and watch for boulders and steep drop-outs.

The strip between Calangute and Baga is good, if not great, as Goan beaches go. Despite the development, the sands are very quiet in the morning, and the water is incredibly calm. Towards noon, however, crowds of daytrippers and package tourists begin to trickle in from the village. The beach widens as it bleeds into Baga, the crowds grow thinner, and the bodies get younger as backpackers strive to work up a credible tan before heading north. South of Baga, a strip of beach has been designated for water sports. **Goan Bananas** (tel. 276362) has a fleet of boats for the gamut of tourist water-sports (water-skiing Rs550 for 15min.; parasailing Rs900 for 15min.; being dragged behind the boat on a giant inflatable banana Rs200 for 15min.; ubiquitous Goan puns free). Next door, **Atlantis** rents sailboards (Rs250 per hr.). **Fishing boats,** chartered by numerous companies in season, make the wet 'n wild journey to the Anjuna flea market every Wednesday and offer dolphin-, crocodile-, and hippie-spotting tours for Rs200-500 per day.

NEAR CALANGUTE: FORT AGUADA AND CANDOLIM

Mocked and scorned by scenesters farther north, the resort-packed village of **Candolim** is largely the preserve of well-off, older package tourists. But the hillside south of the Taj hides the impressive 17th-century **Aguada Fort,** which guards the mouth of the Mandovi. Follow the Candolim road south past the Taj, and keep right as it winds 3km uphill. If you're on foot, take a left at the end of Candolim's north-south road (there's a bus stop), then a right at the chapel; a series of dirt paths winds to the top of the hill. The citadel commands an excellent view of the Mandovi and the southern coast but, if you can find someone to let you in the oddly shaped lighthouse, the view is even better.

Between the citadel and the river lurks the **Central Aguada Jail,** filled with native and imported drug offenders. From the citadel, follow the road east as it curves downhill and southwest. Charitable folks eager to perform good works (or those just hungry for juicy conversation) can show up to chat with inmates who don't already have another monthly visit scheduled (Tu and F 9am-noon and 3-5pm).

ANJUNA अंजुना

Seaside restaurants and low, red-roofed cottages run along Anjuna's shore to the hill in the distance. For many a budget hedonist, the Goan ideal—idyllic beachside days, wild, raving nights, and liberal doses of cheap drugs to smooth the transition between the two—can only be realized here. October through March, Anjuna buzzes with beach raves, full-moon parties, jungle boogies, and all the accompanying psychedelic mayhem. The village's charms (or vices, for in Anjuna, they're one

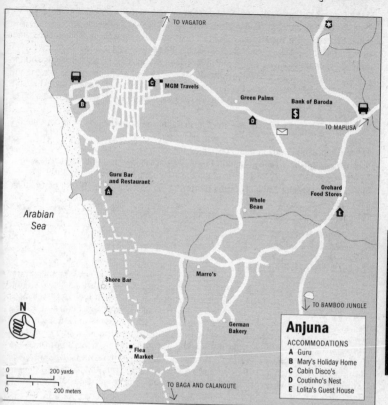

Anjuna

ACCOMMODATIONS
A Guru
B Mary's Holiday Home
C Cabin Disco's
D Coutinho's Nest
E Lolita's Guest House

and the same) have been more resistant to police crackdowns than those of its southern neighbors, but Anjuna continues to pass the time with festivity—a beautiful sunset tags each day, each week brings free-market mayhem in the form of Anjuna's famous flea market (closed off-season), and the world-renowned full-moon raves mark the months. As Christmas approaches, the parties escalate in intensity and frequency. Despite attempts to tame its wild side, Anjuna still plays host to a crazy cast of characters from freaks to fishermen, package tourists to smacksters, Euro-yuppies to Kashmiri handicraft hawkers—which are you?

> **! WARNING. Theft occurs frequently in Anjuna,** particularly on party nights. Carry important documents and valuables with you or lock them somewhere safe.

🛈 ORIENTATION AND PRACTICAL INFORMATION

From Anjuna's main intersection (crowned by the Starro Restaurant), roads lead west to the beachfront and bus stand, east to Mapusa and most banking facilities, south to the flea market grounds and restaurants, and north to Vagator and some of the main party venues.

Buses: Buses stop at the end of the road above the beach and at several places along the road away from the beach. To: **Calangute** and **Baga** (20min., Rs5); **Mapusa** (20min., Rs9); **Panjim** (30min., Rs10); **Vagator** (10min., Rs3). If your bus doesn't appear, hop on one to Mapusa and make your connection there.

Local Transportation: Taxis and **auto-rickshaws** wait near the bus stand. **Motorcycles and bicycles** can be rented along the main road at standard rates.

Budget Travel: MGM Travels (tel. 274317) deals with plane tickets, reconfirmations, and car rentals. In-season: open M-Sa 9am-6pm. Off-season: open 9:30am-6pm.

Currency Exchange: The exchange at **Orchard Food Stores.** Open daily 8am-9pm, shorter hours in the off season. **Bank of Baroda** (tel. 273228), on the main east-west road, gives cash advances on Visa, but their hours are short and wildly variant. Open M-W and F 9:30am-1:30pm, Sa 9:30-11:30am. Many guest houses and restaurants also change money.

Bookstore: Johnson's Library and **The South Anjuna Information** are both on Anjuna's main drag.

Police: On the road away from the beach, on the left.

Post Office: Sub-post office, 2km up the road from the beach on the right. *Poste Restante.* Open M-Sa 9:30am-12:30pm and 2:30-4:30pm. **Postal Code:** 403509.

Internet: St. Anthony Communication Center, at the post office. Rs150 per hr. Open M-Sa 8am-11pm, Su 9am-11pm.

Telephones: Nehal Communications, across from the bus stand, has 24hr. **STD/ISD.**

PHONE CODE	0832

ACCOMMODATIONS

Anjuna has acquired a somewhat undeserved reputation as a difficult place to find a bed, particularly during the peak season. A lack of phones in most guest houses rules out reservations, but those who show up are generally rewarded with a room. Additionally, because of the large number of long-termers in Anjuna, houses here aren't as prone to the insane Christmas price fluctuations of their southern counterparts. Guest houses hug the beachfront and Mapusa Road. South of the flea market grounds lies a veritable tourist colony for long-termers, a good place to look for bare-bones house- or room-lodgings for stays ranging from a week to a few months. Prices listed are in-season; bargain away at other times of the year.

Mary's Holiday Home (tel. 273216), behind the Sea Rock Restaurant. Though close to the beachfront action, the attached rooms face inland, providing quiet, communal tranquility. Satisfied customers sing the praises of the showers. Doubles Rs200-250.

Coutinho's Nest (tel. 274386), a 15min. walk down the main road. An excellent, affable place to tuck your head under your wing after a hard day of beachcombing. Doubles with shared (but shiny and convenient) bathroom Rs150-250.

Cabin Disco's, on the south side of the road, about 1km from the sea. Cool clientele boogie-oogie-oogie their way into comfy rooms after a mellow evening in the groovy bar-restaurant. Doubles Rs300-400.

Guru Bar-Restaurant and Guest House. Bare rooms are airy and serviceable, but outdoor common shower is a bit muddy. For better or worse, the bar is a hub of the beachfront dope scene. Singles Rs100; doubles Rs150. Off-season: some rooms go for Rs75.

Lolita's Guest House, just north of the Orchard Store, a 30min. walk from the beach. The homey, freshly painted bungalows are an excellent place for a rendez-vous with the nymphet of your dreams. Immaculate doubles, each stocked with a fridge and a sound system, may prove to be the light of your life. In-season: Rs500. Off-season: Rs250.

FOOD

Anjuna seaside fare is fast, cheap, greasy, and plentiful. Those not blessed with stomachs of steel will be better off at the restaurants lining the road that curves away from the **Shore Bar**—they pack more variety and flavor than their seaside brethren. On Wednesday, an abundance of food stalls materializes out of the ether to make the **flea market** Anjuna's premier spot for lunch or early dinner—the atmosphere is unbeatable. These places, and those listed below, are closed off-season.

German Bakery, on the road inland from the Shore Bar; watch carefully for the sign. Not to be confused with the German Bakery at the Paradise Restaurant on the main road. Batik-printed hippie boys and angst-ridden babes lounge and sip cappuccinos. The laid-back atmosphere comes complete with savory baked goods in the morning (Rs15-30), veg. North Indian chow at night (Rs35-60). Open daily 7am-midnight.

Marro's, near the German Bakery on the way back to town. Marro's specialty, believe it or not, is Thai (though pizza is thrown in for good measure). Jumps at night with refugees from the Bakery as well as irreverent revelers on their way to Bamboo's. Entrees Rs50-90. Open daily 8am-11pm.

Green Palms, on the Mapusa road about 1.5km inland. Enjoy the delicious falafel sandwich (Rs40), a banana milkshake (Rs25), and bittersweet Israeli pop music (free). Open M-Sa 9:30am-9:30pm.

Whole Bean, along the road east of the Shore Bar. For every vegan who's stared enviously while a fellow patron slurped down a delicious banana *lassi*, this small tofu shop pours out soy milkshakes in a variety of flavors (Rs30-45). Homemade tofu and tempeh sandwiches (Rs60). Open M-Sa 9am-5:30pm.

◤ NIGHTLIFE

THE RAVES. Anjuna's sloping hills have gained international renown as a rave venue. The monthly coming of the full moon summons the werewolf lurking within many of Goa's tourists, transforming them from placid beach-chillers into wild, snarling party-beasts, especially during Goa's peak season. New Year's Eve and Christmas Eve are the biggest nights, but things slow only somewhat during the interval between. Roads are rife with people cycling from party to party, and huge fields are deluged with ravers. Domestic and European DJs of varying quality broadcast the rave's techno sound track to a core of gyrating dancers, themselves surrounded by crowds of people resting and chilling, even as the Goan minions serve them tea, omelettes, chocolate, and smack. Understandably, many locals bemoan these monthly debauches, and participants should be considerate, responsible, and, of course, careful.

OTHER NIGHTLIFE. If there isn't any scheduled action, most of the crowd heads to the **Shore Bar,** right in the middle of the beach. The terraced steps leading down to the beach throng with beer-guzzling sunbathers or stargazers, depending on the hour. Upstairs, the requisite black lights flicker and imported DJs of varying acumen pilot the gargantuan sound system, while techno ravers go for broke on the small, sandy dance floor. Hours vary wildly by season. The **Sea Rock Restaurant,** just south of the bus stand, is another popular hangout, especially for Westerners. Don't worry if you're not hungry—only a few of the packed restaurant's occupants are dining at any one time; the rest are having coffee, tea, or juice, scoping each other out, or sneaking a joint. Farther south, the **Guru Bar,** with a much laxer drug policy, serves tall cold ones late into the night. Its southerly neighbor, **Francis Bar and Restaurant,** occasionally catches the Saturday night fever, stacks up the tables and chairs, and hires a DJ and sound system for a night of techno and dancing.

◤ BEACHES

Perhaps the most stereotypically Goan of the state's beaches, Anjuna's postcard-pretty shores draw understandably large crowds and tanned, toned ravers in various states of inebriation who crash all along the strip. Perhaps the sloth of the average Anjuna beachgoer accounts for the variety of the beach's annoyingly convenient hawkers. It's quite easy to slurp down cold drinks and tropical fruit all day, while having a bogus ear-cleaning and full-body massage—practically the only things the hawkers aren't se.lling are tranquility and solitude. Thronged with tourists, particularly on Wednesdays, this is the beach to sea and be scene, but for peace and quiet, look elsewhere.

GOA

VAGATOR वागातोर

Of all the northern beach towns in Goa, Vagator strikes the superlative balance between hotspot and hideaway. Popular but not over-populated, scenic but not seedy, Vagator suns all day and raves all night without losing its cheerful, down-home vibe. A shortage of guest houses makes the town home to mostly longtime dwellers, but the regulars here seem less jaundiced than their southern counterparts, probably because the rigors of the tourism boom have yet to sap Vagator's easy, jubilant grace.

⚑ ORIENTATION AND PRACTICAL INFORMATION. Most resources for the budget traveler in Vagator line the east-west street running inland from Big Vagator Beach. The **Primrose Bar and Restaurant** (heading inland, it's the first right past the See Green Restaurant), besides being a nighttime hot-spot, does **currency exchange** into the wee hours of the morning. **Su Jata Travels** (tel. 273308), just inland from the big beach, handles bookings and reconfirmations (open M-Sa 9am-6pm). **Buses** stop at the crossroads about 1km inland. They shuttle between **Mapusa** and **Chapora** (every 30min. 6am-6pm to Mapusa, 6am-7pm to Chapora; Rs4). Buses also shuttle between **Anjuna**, Chapora, and Vagator every hour (Rs3).

Prakash Motors, on the main road, rents and repairs **motorcycles** at good rates (Rs150-250 per day or Rs3000-5000 per month, depending on bike model; open daily 8am-8:30pm, but emergency help from adjoining **tailor shop** until midnight). **Touts** along the road from Ozran Beach also rent motor bikes at similar rates. This area is also a good place to ask about **bicycle rental. Taxis** cluster behind Big Vagator Beach. Rates are almost identical. During peak season, this is a good place to get a taxi to the north (Rs150, to Mapusa Rs50, to Anjuna Rs50, between Vagator and Chapora Rs40). Plunk away on the **Internet** at Lalita Communications (tel. 274481), just inland on the main road (Rs150 per hr.; open daily 8am-midnight). The nearest **post office** is in Anjuna.

▰▱ ACCOMMODATIONS AND FOOD. Vagator housing still caters primarily to folks here for the long haul. Follow the yellow signs north of Big Vagator road to **Dolrina** (tel. 273382), a large and popular guest house run by a friendly family (doubles Rs200, with bath Rs250; off-season Rs150-200; book in advance in season). **Balbina's** (tel. 27303) has its own set of signs north of the road. The ballyhooed "fort view" is a bit overrated, but the lush valley this small guest house overlooks is easy on the eyes. (Doubles with toilet and common shower Rs200.) As the paved Big Vagator road curves in front of the beach and narrows to a dirt path, **Yellow House** is on the right, with airy, sparsely furnished rooms and clean common toilets and showers (in-season doubles Rs150). The **Blue Bird Cafe,** near the seashore along the Ozran Beach road, is particularly mellow and cozy, even by Vagator standards. Patrons play backgammon under the thatched roof and over delicious, reasonably priced veg. and non-veg. Indian and French cuisine. (Entrees Rs50-80; open 8:30am until the last diner leaves.) The attached guest house has homey rooms at decent rates (in-season attached doubles Rs150-250). **Abu John's,** Big Vagator road, with its open kitchen and a jovial, well-dressed crowd, is a popular dinner spot for *tandoori* and barbecue dishes (Rs30-50; open daily 8am-noon and 6pm-midnight; closed during monsoon season). Next door, the **Garden Villa** offers slightly better prices and food and nightly bootlegged American movies on the TV (entrees Rs25-40; open daily 8am-11pm; movies 7:30pm).

▟ NIGHTLIFE. Vagator's bars remain lively all night in December and January—proprietors will serve beer until no one's standing upright to drink it. The **Primrose Restaurant and Bar** is the local answer to Anjuna's Shore Bar, with late nights, black lights, and techno DJs of varying skill levels. The Primrose is also a good source for information about upcoming full moon parties, raves, and other debauches. (Entrees around Rs60, mixed drinks Rs40.) A new rival, the **Loot Discotheque** at the Alcove Restaurant overlooking Ozran Beach (signs are everywhere), has recently sprung up, but the beats there aren't as thumpin', and the crowd is rarely as hyped as at the Primrose. Parties often break out between Vagator and Anjuna, with partiers commuting back and forth in search of the hippest scene.

SIGHTS AND BEACHES. Ozran Beach reigns as Vagator's mellowest, most picturesque strip of sand—something like Anjuna in miniature, minus the vendors and the daytrippers. Farther north, Vagator's distinctive grassy, gently shelving hills lead, like giant steps, to the shore at **Little Vagator Beach,** a rocky bit of nothing remarkable only for the large, grassy field separating it from the hills—the best place in the north for a seaside picnic. **Big Vagator,** just north past the hills, is the longest expanse of fine white grains around; it is occasionally cramped by the big crowds it draws from **Sterling Vagator Resort** and the nearby bus stand. Towering over the whole scene to the northeast are the ruins of the 17th-century **Portuguese Fort** which separates Chapora from Vagator. Today the ruins only shelter the occasional errant cow or enterprising cold drinks salesman, but the quick clamber up to the fort rewards with a smashing panoramic sampling of the whole scene—beach blanket bingo to the south, fishermen hauling in their nets to the east, and lush, unspoiled territory looming across the Chapora River to the north.

NEAR VAGATOR: CHAPORA चापोरा

Separated from Vagator by a ruined fort and a few hundred meters, Chapora isn't graced with anything resembling Vagator's beachside charm, or even anything resembling a beach, but that's the secret of its entropic appeal. The abundance of bars and restaurants crowding its main drag fill daily with folks anxious to eat, drink, and unwind away from the beachside bustle. The languor affects even the usually industrious **taxi drivers,** who huddle under the banyan tree playing cards on Chapora's main street instead of hustling for fares to Panjim (Rs200), Mapusa (Rs50), Anjuna (Rs50), and Vagator (Rs40). **Buses,** unperturbed, turn around and head back to Mapusa, via Vagator (every 20min.). Chapora's short-term accommodations are limited to a few overpriced, under-impressive guest houses along the main road. Commuting from Anjuna, Baga, or Calangute until something long-term pops up would be a better move, but if you're bent on staying here, **private rooms** (inquire at the restaurants) are a good alternative; two can sleep well for under Rs100 per night. In the eats department, **Preyanka,** off the main Chapora road, exudes atmosphere, with tablecloths, colored lamp shades, and sweet '70s rock. The food's good, too—cheap, no-nonsense Indian, Continental, and Chinese victuals and a Rs35 veg. *thali.* (Open daily 6am-11pm.)

ARAMBOL (HARMAL) आरामबोल

In the Beatles-esque nomenclature used by backpackers to categorize North Goan beaches, Arambol is "the remote one." Though a bridge over the Chapora river is slowly (*very* slowly) nearing completion, the city is currently accessible only by ferry. Thus, Arambol's proximity to pristine beaches, a freshwater lake, and scenic vistas just outside the clutches of the long arms of the law and the package tour trade continue to appeal to rugged souls looking to get away from it all. Remote, however, is relative. During peak season, the many seaside cafes and bars swarm with daytrippers and fortnighters seeking solitude and driving the die-hard sociopaths south to Mandrem, north to Querim Beach, or into the trees. North of the main beach, along a rocky path negotiable only by foot, lies the smaller, more secluded **Paradise Beach** with a lovely aquamarine **freshwater lagoon.** Farther inland from the lake (a 15min. walk into the forest), the wafting odors of *cheeba* and the plaintive thum-thum of flea-market congas signal a peaceful enclave of peace-seekers holding court under the sheltering branches of a great banyan tree.

7 ORIENTATION AND PRACTICAL INFORMATION. Buses arrive in **Arambol Junction** from Chopdem in the south. From the junction, backtrack south and take the first right, where the narrow road winds about 400m to the beach. The road heads north to the region's only **petrol station.** Gas up here before heading north to Querim or Terekol; there may be folks in the Querim village willing to sell you water bottles full of petrol, but don't bet on it. To reach Arambol from south of the Chapora River, journey to Siolem—there are **buses** from Mapusa (every 30min.), and it's a quick 8km along the riverside from Chapora by bike—and take the **river ferry** to Chopdem (every 15min. 6am-10pm; 10min; Rs3, with bike Rs5). From the ferry dock, buses shuttle at least every hour between Arambol and Chopdem (15min., Rs5). If you're self-propelled, just veer right from the dock and take a left at the first intersection (following the signs to Harmal). Buses run directly from Mapusa to Arambol (daily 8, 10am, and 1pm; 1hr.; Rs10). **Boats** from Baga make the popular daytrip to Arambol every morning (Rs200 round-trip) and the **Welcome Restaurant** near the beach sends boats to Anjuna every Wednesday morning (Rs150 round-trip). **Taxis** in Vagator, Chapora, Mapusa, and Siolem carry you to Arambol, though outside of December and January you'll have to pay for a round-trip (at most Rs400) even if you're only going one-way. **Tara Travels** (tel. 297751), just north of the junction, handles transport bookings and reconfirmations and does **currency exchange** (open daily 8am-8pm). Just south of the beach road, the tiny **post office** has *Poste Restante* (open M-Sa 10am-1pm and 2-5:30pm).

7 ▄ **ACCOMMODATIONS AND FOOD.** Most visitors here return year after year and rent houses for several months. A few new guest houses are available for short-term stays, and even during peak season, accommodations can be arranged with a little legwork. During the monsoon, most lodges and restaurants are simply closed. **Houses** may be rented for Rs100-150 per night or Rs2000-5000 per month. Sizes and facilities vary as widely as the prices: many houses have no toilets or running water, only access to nearby bushes and wells (respectively). **The Ganesh Bar** (tel. 238522) has rooms ideally situated on the cliffs midway between the two beaches (doubles Rs200). **Tara Travels** books a few rooms a bit farther from the surf; they fill up more slowly. Even in season you can usually bargain a double with bath down to Rs125. Where the road intersects the beach, the **Sea Horse Restaurant** serves up Goan, Continental, and Chinese cuisine to a packed house (Rs20-90; open daily 9am-11pm). Just south of Paradise Beach, **Lake Paradise** has fresh *hummus* (Rs50), milkshakes (Rs15), a paperback exchange, and, in season, puppies (open daily 7am-10pm). The **Ganesh Bar** and the rasta-themed **Jah Kingdom,** on the southern end of the main beach, offer food and drink (seafood Rs55-70, Indian Rs40-50; open daily 9am-1am), and the dozen-or-so bars along the main road pour fizzies to fuzz your mind. All of these restaurants are closed off season.

NEAR ARAMBOL: MANDREM मांद्रे

Over-endowed (even by Goan standards) with palm trees and white sand and overlooked by backpackers on their northward push to Arambol, Mandrem is a paradise waiting to be lost to the yet-dormant devils of tourist culture. The lucky vacationer who makes it here tends to stay—many come for ongoing yoga classes. Although the town's innocence and unparalleled solitude will be lost someday, for now there are already plenty of destinations nearby with varying degrees of backpacker culture to keep tourists away from this hidden gem.

"Beach" is a bit of a misnomer for Mandrem's seaside landscape. It's more like "desert." Vast expanses of sand stretch over 100 unspoiled meters inland at their widest, and it's rare to see more than a dozen beachcombers sauntering about, even on the busiest days. Mandrem village lies on a short stretch of road branching off of the main thoroughfare between Arambol and Chopdem. Travel amenities are scarce. For currency exchange, buses, or even rickshaws, denizens must schlep 5km or so up the road to Arambol. Accommodations, both short and long-term, are more plentiful there, but restaurant-affiliated "guest houses" are excuses for eager villagers to whisk you around until you find something to your liking.

More of a retreat than a guest house, the **Villa River Cat** (tel. 297346) bathes its residents in aesthetic grace and careful hospitality. From the beach, it's north of the river, between the tragically hip **Groovy Train** and sedate **La Brasserie** beach shacks. If you're self-propelled, head west from the main (not beach) Arambol-Chopdem road at Junuswaddo, and be prepared to ask around. (Doubles Rs350-650, 25% off during the monsoon; reserve well in advance). The **Miau** restaurant is the Villa River Cat's back porch, but non-guests are welcome to partake in the fantastic family-style meals. (Breakfast 7-11am; Rs125 dinner served around 8pm; call first). **Groovy Train,** near River Cat on the beach, serves yummy shakes (Rs25) to sophisticated slackers, while small clusters of shacks a few hundred meters north and south of the Villa serve standard shack fare (meals Rs40-60).

NEAR ARAMBOL: QUERIM खेरीम (TEREKOL तेरेखोल) BEACH

North of Arambol junction, virtually all traces of backpacker culture vanish. Beyond the pale of hippie settlement, though, a couple of spots stand out. The first is Querim Beach, a fir-backed strip of the white stuff where you can vegetate from Noel to New Year's and see nary a Kodak or dreadlock. Querim (Keri) Beach is a two-hour walk north from Paradise Beach in Arambol, or you can head north from the Arambol junction, following the signs to Keri (about 10km). Faint white writing on the road will point you to the beach, also known as Terekol Beach. Nowadays, **Terekol Fort,** as if tired of living a lie, has given up trying to be an impressive 400-year-old fort, and is now a spruced-up, overpriced hotel and restaurant. **Buses** make the long trip from Panjim and Chopdem/Arambol, but getting there is all the fun. The journey north to Terekol has some spectacular scenery and the fort is in excellent, whitewashed repair, but it isn't worth the trip if you don't have your own bike. Buses from Chopdem and Arambol slog to Querim every hour or so (Rs5), stopping at the Terekol ferry. **Ferries** cross the Terekol from Querim (every 30min. daily 6am-10pm; 5min.; Rs1, with bike Rs3). From there it's just a few kilometers west—a 15-minute hike or Rs20 taxi ride—to the fort.

SOUTH GOA

MADGAON (MARGAO) मारगंव

Capped with a shaking arterial highway, bounded by the glinting rails of the Konkan, and fed from the dusty maw of the gigantic KTC bus terminal, Madgaon is very much a transport hub. Most travelers spend enough time in the capital of agriculturally-rich Salcete Province only to catch their next connection. Tourist-hungry accommodations lie less than 30 minutes away in Colva and Benaulim, though it's not unbearable to stay the night in the city; Magdaon doesn't exactly teem with attractions, but a few hours here can be very well spent.

🚩 **ORIENTATION AND PRACTICAL INFORMATION.** Madgaon is centered on the rectangular **Municipal Gardens,** which are brushed on their west side by **National Highway 17.** South of the Municipal Gardens along Station Rd. is a bustling market district. **Trains** leave from Madgaon Railway Station, 4km southeast of the municipal gardens and 2km south of the old railway station on Station Rd. The Konkan Railway's major station has trains to: **Mangalore** (*Madgaon Mangalore Passenger* KR1, 2:10pm, 7hr., Rs52); and **Mumbai** (*Mumbai-Madgaon Exp.* KRO112; 7:25pm; 11hr.; Rs231 non-A/C sleeper, Rs597 3-tier A/C with pillow and blanket). **Buses** leave from the **KTC Bus Stand,** 2km north along the road to Panjim, bound for: **Hubli** (7 per day 6am-1:45pm, 6hr., Rs50); **Mangalore** (6am and 6:30pm, 10hr., Rs135); **Mumbai** (2:30pm, 16hr., Rs390); and **Pune** (5pm, 14hr., Rs265). Travel agents around the tourist hostels book frequent private buses to the same destinations. **Intrastate buses** depart for: **Colva** via **Benaulim** (every 30min. 7am-8pm, 30min., Rs4); **Chaudi** (every hr. 8am-8pm, 1hr, Rs10); and **Panjim** (frequent 6am-

9:15pm; Rs12). Buses to and from Colva and Benaulim also stop on the side of the Municipal Gardens, while those heading to other intrastate destinations stop on the western side.

West of the Municipal Gardens is the **State Bank of India** (open M-F 10am-2pm, Sa10am-noon), and to the north is the **police station** (tel. 722175) and the **GPO** (open M-Sa 7am-6:30pm). *Poste Restante* can be received at an office nearby: from the GPO hang a right, then take the third left (open M-Sa 8-10:30am and 3-4:30pm). **Postal Code:** 403601. A dependable pharmacy is **Raikar Medical Stores,** along Station Rd. (tel. 732924; open M-Sa 8am-8pm). For high-tech communication, head 50m directly up the road from the Tourist Hotel to the Rangavi Complex shopping center on the left. Internet access is available in shop #9 on the ground floor at **Cyberlink** (tel. 712079; Rs170 per hr.; open M-Sa 8am-6:45pm). **Telephone Code:** 0834.

[icon] ACCOMMODATIONS AND FOOD. Most foreigners stay one night at most in Magdaon; the steady influx from the trains and buses ensures that most hotels along Station Rd. (between the market and the old railway station) fill up quickly each day. Both **Rikresh** (tel. 721709) and **Milan** (tel. 722715) are located along Station Rd., marked by signs on the northwest side of the street. Reserve in advance for their clean and airy rooms. (Singles around Rs100; doubles around Rs180.) The **Tourist Hotel** (tel. 721966), just south of the Municipal Gardens, is overpriced but dependably institutional and a good bet if you haven't reserved ahead. All rooms have attached baths. (In-season: singles Rs200; doubles Rs280, with A/C Rs350. Off-season: Rs150/240/300.) Excellent, cheap vegetarian fare can be enjoyed in air-conditioned comfort at **Kamat,** in the Milan hotel (*samosas* Rs10, *thalis* Rs22; open daily 6:30am-9:30pm), and **Cafe Tato,** one block east of the Municipal Gardens on the north-south Valaulikar Rd. in the Apna Bazaar Complex (excellent *thali* Rs24; open M-Sa 7am-9:45pm). **Longuinhos** (tel. 721038), across the street from the Tourist Hotel, dishes up cheap Goan delights and copious cocktails (open daily 8am-10:45pm). The god-fearing **Crislene Cafe,** west of the GPO, serves yummy victuals in a sweltering box (open 7:30am-8pm).

[icon] SIGHTS. Free of the weight of cultural or aesthetic significance, Magdaon's sights don't range far beyond the pleasant and can be seen at leisure within an hour. The **Municipal Gardens** are a well-maintained, colorful public park, festooned with flowers and shrubs of all ilk and bronze busts of Portuguese dignitaries: a respite for the eyes, if not for the ears, as traffic screams outside the topiary. As the sun ascends, folks clear out of the walls into the scant shady places, leaving the majority of the park eerily deserted. Almost 1km north of the Gardens, at Largo de Igreja, stands the **Church of the Holy Spirit,** a classic Goan cathedral with nifty carvings of the apostles and a history of religious conflict—it was built on the ruins of a Hindu temple sacked by Muslims and rebuilt by persistent Catholics (open daily 6-9am). To the west is a road leading up Monte Hill to **Our Lady of the Mount Chapel,** a 15-minute hike or quick drive leading to excellent views of Madgaon's hills. From here, it looks like the quintessential sleepy subtropical city.

The most interesting things to see in Madgaon are actually not in Madgaon at all, but in smaller towns to the east, accessible by bus. In **Rachol** (7km from Madgaon, buses every 30min., 25min., Rs4), the **Museum of Christian Art,** at the Rachol Seminary, provides an elegant overview of Goan Christianity. The treasures include an 18th-century palanquin used to carry around ecclesiastical high rollers, a portable altar for mobile missionaries, and an enormous, kingfisher-shaped silver and wood monstrance looted from the Sé Cathedral in Old Goa. (Open daily 9am-1pm and 2-5pm. Rs5.) On the kitschier side, **Ancestral Goa,** in Loutilim (10km east of Madgaon; buses every hr., 30min., Rs4), provides an eclectic presentation of Goan village life as it was in ye olde days, the Limca World Record Book's longest laterite sculpture, a garden full of edible foliage, and a tour to tie these wildly disparate elements together (open daily 9am-6pm; Rs20). To get from Rachol to Loutilim without going back to Madgaon, take the first right past the arch leading out of the seminary and then the first left; walk to a market where you can pick up a motorcycle taxi to Loutilim (Rs25). Several stately old **Portuguese villas** also grace Loutilim, but to see these, you've got to make an appointment through the GTDC.

One kilometer east of the KTC bus terminal looms the largest football arena in Goa, with a capacity of 40,000. If you're a fan, consult **Goa Today** or ask around for upcoming games, but be prepared to fight your way to the ticket windows.

COLVA कोल्वा

If first impressions told the whole story, any self-respecting backpacker would tuck tail and run after being dumped at Colva's beachfront. An unsightly mass of concrete pavement, garish resorts, and skeletal construction sights, Colva's beachfront is a prime example of the overdeveloped resort scene in Goa. As you move away from the beachfront, however, the concrete jungle recedes and rich Mumbaiites and extortionist scarf sellers are less of a presence. Though far and away the south's most touristed beach, Colva has far less traffic than you'll find in the north, and the mellow, young crowd here suns and funs much less frantically.

⁊ ORIENTATION AND PRACTICAL INFORMATION. Colva's main strip, **Madgaon Road** winds westward. The road then passes through **Colva Village,** a crossroads leading south to Benaulim and north to Vasco da Gama, and peters out 1km away at a beachfront **roundabout. Buses** from Madgaon stop at the crossroads and at the roundabout, going to Benaulim from the crossroads (every 30min., Rs3). For other destinations in Goa it is necessary to travel first to Madgaon. **Auto-rickshaws** from the beach roundabout and the main road go to Benaulim (Rs35) and Palolem (Rs175). **Taxis** charge twice as much. **Bicycles** and **motorbikes** can be rented at many shops and resorts, including **Maria Joanna Cycle Shop,** east of the roundabout. West of the church in the village, the **Bank of Baroda** gives cash advances on Visa (open M-Tu and Th-F 9am-1pm, Sa 9am-11am). Any resort with an ounce of pretension will also **exchange currency,** but their rates are less than ideal. Trashy paperbacks in many tongues can be bought or swapped at **Damodar's Books,** north of the roundabout (open daily 9:30am-9:30pm). Just east of Damodar's is the **tourist police** station and its crack detective squad (open 24hr.). *Poste Restante* is available at the **sub post office,** just southeast of the church (open 9:30am-noon and 2:30-4pm). **Postal Code:** 403708. Internet services are available at **WorldLinkers** (tel. 732004), east of the roundabout on the main road (Rs240 per hr.; open daily 8am-midnight). **STD/ISD** booths are scattered along the main road.

⌐⌐ ACCOMMODATIONS AND FOOD. Transients holing up in Colva after a tour of duty in the north will be pleasantly surprised by the area's digs. Facilities vary widely, but prices are little more than half what you'd pay for comparable rooms north of Panjim. Additionally, outside of Christmas week, only the hyperpopular lodges fill up, and bargaining may pay off, particularly for loners and longtermers. A thicket of budget guest houses nestles in the **4th ward** area, due northwest of the crossroads; from there, head west, bearing left at the fork, and then north when you reach a cluster of signs. **Rennie's Cottages** (tel. 721926) is the best bargain. Six well-kept concrete blocks with attached baths sit in a remote, relaxed neighborhood, about 500m off the road down a winding sandy path. (Doubles Rs100-150.) **Jinson's Cottages** (tel.736481), near Rennie's, is a bit more pleasant and comes with an attached Goan restaurant (Rs25-30; doubles Rs200-300).

The small road leading north from the beachfront roundabout heads towards the **Hotel Colmar** (tel. 721253), a happening place providing resorty perks. The relatively posh rooms on a lush garden are cool and airy. (Doubles Rs500. Off-season: Rs250.) The pasta dishes (Rs50-75) at the attached **Pasta Hut** supersede standard Indo-Italian fare, and the restaurant's bar is a popular watering hole (open daily 8:30am-11pm). North of the Colmar is **The Fisherman's Cottages** (tel. 734323), distinguished by a freshly whitewashed facade in view of the rolling surf and 24-hour

GOA

running water. True to its name, the place is operated by local fishermen; they occasionally leave their nets in the hall. (Doubles Rs200. Off-season: Rs100.) **Lucky Star** (tel. 730069), just north of Fisherman's, isn't as well-kept as its competitor but is cheaper. Six attached rooms are on the second floor above the eponymous bar and restaurant. (Doubles Rs200. Off-season: Rs100.) Backpackers flock to the **Tourist Nest Hotel** (tel 723944), north of the crossroad; take a left at "La Touche." This 200-year-old Portuguese mansion in a tangled grove operates as a guest house in the old Goan tradition—light on price and amenities, heavy on hospitality. Out back are two cottages with attached baths; one has a kitchen. (Doubles Rs80, with bath Rs85. Cottages Rs300 per night, Rs5000 per month.) **The Sea Pearl,** north on the first road east of the roundabout, draws a huge crowd for seafood specials (Rs50-175) so fresh they ought to be slapped (open daily 8:30am-2pm and 6-11pm; no kitchen orders past 10pm).

🎵🏖 NIGHTLIFE AND BEACHES. Nocturnal Colva never slams, and outside Christmas week, it rarely works up more than a dull thudding. The beach bars south of the roundabout host most of the action. The homogeneity of the beach bar scene has barmen wracking their brains to come up with amusements, from star-gazing to volleyball. **Splash's** touted "fire party" rarely amounts to more than a few baby boomers busting the White Man's Overbite on the dance floor, but they pull in a lively crowd. Nearby **Ziggy's** is also popular, albeit nondescript.

As far as globe-trotting budgeteers are concerned, the southern beaches begin at **Colva beach,** but the village actually lies midway along the states' longest beach. Decked out in 26km of sparkling white and emerald blue, the strip is long enough to make bicycles the preferred mode of waterfront locomotion. At high tide, it's possible to wheel on wet, packed sand along the beach's entirety. Although the sand may seem crowded around Colva, solitude awaits those willing to venture 1km north or south. Between Colva and Benaulim, the relatively quiet water makes for pleasant swimming surf. Balmy breezes and mildly rippin' tubes make **boogie boarding** and **windsurfing** popular here. Shacks south of Colva beach lease equipment (boogie board Rs30 per hr.; sailboard 200 per hr.).

BENAULIM बेनावलीम

Just a 20-minute walk south of Colva, Benaulim (been-AH-li) is marked by a rapidly disappearing buffer zone of small-scale agriculture between the beach and the guest houses. The sobering presence of non-tourist business keeps the action relatively low-key, but developers are still trying to buy up the remaining land (sometimes seizing it illegally) to erect resort complexes, forcibly bending Benaulim towards the appearance of its northern neighbors. For now, though, the rooms are cheap and plentiful, the food is more than decent, the nightlife is hip, and the long walk to the beach still affords the visitor a pleasant encounter with local life.

🛈 ORIENTATION AND PRACTICAL INFORMATION. Two parallel north-south roads—comprising the heart of Benaulim Village—intersect the east-west Madgaon Road's march towards the beach. **Buses** stop at the eastern (Marin Hall) crossroads. Benaulim is on both the Madgaon-Mobor and Madgaon-Colva lines (every 30min. 8am-8pm), with departures to: **Colva** (10min., Rs3); **Madgaon** (25min., Rs4); and **Varca** (10min., Rs3). **Taxis** wait at the drop spot to whisk you off to the shimmering sands 2km away (Rs20), or to Madgaon (Rs70) or Colva (Rs60). **Autorickshaws** go to all corners of Goa as well and cost only marginally less. Benaulim is a 50-minute taxi ride from Dabolim **airport** (Rs300). At the western crossroads, the north-south road fronts the majority of the village's numerous guest houses and is cluttered with signs and entrepreneurs touting **motorcycle** (Rs125-200) and **bicycle** rentals (Rs50). The **Bank of Baroda,** located at the Marin Hall crossroads in town, only does cash advances on Visa cards (open M-Tu and Th-F 9am-1pm, Sa 9-11am). **Currency exchange** is left to the travel agents with offices lining the western crossroads (some open 24hr.). The **Benaulim Medical Store** (tel. 71214), situated right beside the Bank of Baroda, has medications, toiletries and cheap film developing (open M-Sa 9am-1pm and 4-9pm, Su 9am-1pm). Benaulim's **post office** and telegraph, south of Marin Hall and west just past the Holy Trinity Church (in Trinity Hall), sell stamps (open M-Sa 9am-noon and 2-4pm).

⌐⌐ ACCOMMODATIONS AND FOOD. For those averse to squatting in the half-finished beachside resort complexes, cheap comfortable guest houses line the Madgaon road and the two north-south streets. To reach those listed below, head south from the western crossroads and watch for signs. **Diogo Con** (tel. 733749), 100m east of the Meridian Restaurant on a dirt road, is one of Benaulim's best kept secrets, offering freshly painted, petite rooms with shiny, tiled attached baths (singles Rs100; doubles Rs200). **Lacy Rose** (tel. 721813), on the main east-west road between the two crossroads, is an airy, brightly painted house boasting spacious singles (Rs80) and doubles (Rs150) with shared baths and balconies. The in-house restaurant serves excellent, cheap food (entrees Rs30-40). **Casa De Caji Cottages** (tel. 722937), in an idyllic spot west of the western north-south road (watch for the sign), has a location, proprietress, and rooms that all radiate a charm unique in Benaulim. Calling them "common" does the spotless toilets and bath a disservice. (Doubles Rs125, with balcony Rs150. Off-season: Rs50-60.) For an entirely different experience, stay at **Ravi Kurj** (tel. 734503), on the eastern crossroads; follow the road as it hooks east, then north. It's run by the local pharmacist, who is happy to supplement his posh accommodations—amenities include bath, mosquito netting, and power bidet—with late-night medical assistance. (Doubles Rs150-200.)

On the beachfront, **Johney's Restaurant** distinguishes itself with late hours and good deals. The prawns *amotik* (Rs60), prepared with fiery chilies and whole cloves of garlic, is unsubtle and undeniably tasty. (Open daily 8am-midnight; closed intermittently during monsoon season.) **Pedro's**, right next door, excels with its breakfast offerings (authentic French toast Rs20) as well as Chinese and *tandoori* dishes (Rs35-70; open daily 9am-midnight). Farther inland, **Lacy Rose** (see above) is a treat, and **Amal-M**, on the western north-south road just past the Meridian Restaurant, dishes out tasty *tandoori* (Rs50-60) with Elvis and Kenny Rogers in the background (open daily 8am-midnight). After dark, a few beach shacks south of the road play host to slacking and mellowing. The drinking, smoking, and debauchery continue until the wee hours, but the partying seems somewhat sporadic; however, Colva is always just a 20-minute walk north on the beach.

PALOLEM पाल्लैनेम

When overworked desk jockeys daydream of telling the boss to shove it, quitting the rat race, and starting life anew in a tropical paradise, Palolem is what they envision. Strolling along its kilometer-long crescent of sand, you may find it hard to shake the feeling that you've unwittingly walked into a dream. The tiny cove flanked by forested hillocks and black rocks gives the impression that this is the only place on earth, while the bathing beauties strolling the sand raise hopes that sweet-but-fleeting tropical romance is only a couple of fruity cocktails away. Hammocks strung between densely packed palm trees shelter guitar-strumming hippies, and the tide recedes to connect the northern end of the beach with an island inhabited by black-faced monkeys. The only tropical beach virtue Palolem doesn't exemplify is quiescence, but the crowds, under the beach's spell, are mellower, happier, and more content than most: Palolem has plenty of paradise to go around.

The road from Chaudi (33km south of Madgaon) zigzags 4km northwest to Palolem, running parallel to the surf midway along and intersecting the 100m beach road at the northern end of the sand. During peak season, **buses** run regularly to Madgaon (every 30-90min. 6:45am to 4:30pm), but service is less frequent at other times. Fortunately, most guest house owners double as accurate bus timetables. If you miss the direct services, the bus from Chaudi to Madgaon (every hr. until 8:30pm, 1½hr., Rs10) is a viable option. You can also take a **rickshaw** (Rs30) or **taxi**

(Rs50), or you can take a hike (4km). Signs on the Chaudi road also tout **bike** (Rs3 per hr.) and **motorcycle rental.** Some restaurants (including the Sun'n'Moon) will **exchange currency,** but their rates will have you wishing you'd brought enough cash. The nearest **post office** is in Chaudi.

Compared to Colva and Benaulim, Palolem's accommodations are overpriced and underkept—expect to pay Rs200 in season for the privilege of crashing in a cramped, charmless double and using an outhouse. A stay in one of the straw hut colonies on the beachfront provides a more photogenic alternative. Midway down the beach, on the low end of the scale, the **Deena Bar and Restaurant** (tel. 643449) rents simple huts with one light bulb, one bed, and one chair; the common toilet is squat, the shower is bucket, and there's a safe for valuables (Rs150). Just south of Deena, **Island View Cottages** (contact via the adjoining **Cressida** restaurant, tel. 634258) offers the same minimal accommodations (Rs150, off-season Rs120). **Cocohuts** offers weirder digs—huts raised up off the ground on stilts—along with lockers, electric fans, and a more sophisticated common toilet. Those who like to make a wild ruckus behind closed doors should bear in mind that the thin layer of dried vegetation offers very little privacy. (Doubles Rs350.)

The sole bright blip on Palolem's otherwise dreary restaurant radar is the **Sun'n'Moon,** which serves delicious sizzlers (Rs45-80) to a lively young crowd (open daily 8am-10:30pm). When it closes, folks can be found blowin' in the wind at **Dylan's** on the beach. Late at night, the rest of the town is Desolation Row.

NEAR PALOLEM: AGONDA

Those who tire of paradise populated with like-minded folk should wend their way northwest 15 minutes to the as yet uncontaminated **Agonda Beach.** A cove almost as picturesque as Palolem's (although it doesn't match it palm-for-palm), Agonda lacks everything but surf and sand—wide-eyed refugees from Palolem stop their bikes, get agoraphobic, and leave. Supplies (petrol, cold snacks) are available from the garage-like complex of stores on the left as you head towards the beach (most close at 7pm).

NEAR PALOLEM: CABO DE RAMA

Farther northwest (30min. by scooter), the immense ruins of a Portuguese fort wait for the invasion that never happened in **Cabo de Rama,** a town consisting only of a name, a fort, and a few bars scattered along the main and only road. The ruins overlook an endless sea front and exude a quality of quiet grandeur that fits right in with a picnic. Neither the fort nor Agonda, however, are really worth the trip without a motorbike—taxis are expensive (Rs250-300 from Palolem), and the two daily buses to Cabo de Rama from Madgaon (1 and 5:30pm) take two hours to complete the journey to a destination only worth a half-hour visit.

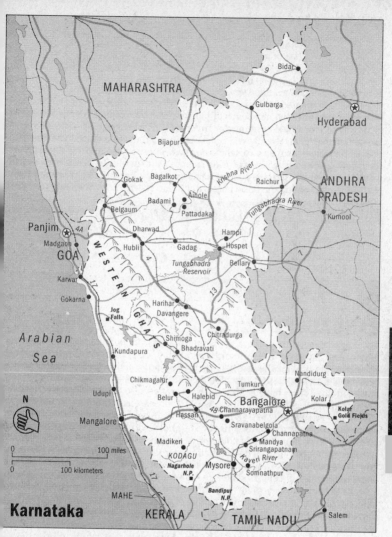

KARNATAKA

ಕರ್ಾಟಕ

Karnataka, home of exquisite beaches, ancient ruins, and fabulous palaces, captures the romantic stereotype of South India; it is still much less touristed than its sister states in the south. Though its residents are as mild as the temperate climate, the attitude here is neither overly traditional nor alarmingly cosmopolitan, and Karnataka is one of India's most progressive states. With years of Muslim rule first under the Muslim Sultanate, then under Haider Ali and his son Tipu Sultan (after a brief snatch of power by the Wadiyar Rajas), Karnataka grew in eminence, with the city of Mysore catapulting into political and architectural fame. The British had direct control of Mysore State for a little while, and the native maharajas who ruled until 1947 gave it a cohesive vision to propel it into a future with independent India. In 1956, Kannada-speaking regions in the north were added to the Mysore State, creating a Kannada-speaking state, renamed Karnataka in 1973. The coastline is dominated by the jagged Western Ghats, which shield the Deccan Plateau from the torrential monsoons of the coast. On the plateau, orange-red earth gives way to green fields and narrow waterways. The area upland of the *ghats* is forested with teak and sandalwood, and the rivers produce so much hydroelectric power that Karnataka used to sell its surplus energy to neighboring states. The rocky terrain around the *ghats* provided material for some of India's ancient architectural masterpieces: in the north, Chalukyan temples and the Vijayanagar ruins at Hampi; in the south, the florid temples at Belur, Halebid, and Somnathpur.

HIGHLIGHTS OF KARNATAKA

■ India's technology capital, **Bangalore** beckons with pubs, gardens, unbelievable shopping, and all things cyber (p. 466).
■ The **Maharaja's Palace** (p. 481) is a fairy-tale vision set amidst the laid-back, sweet-smelling chaos of **Mysore** (p. 477).
■ Hippie-tested and UNESCO-certified, **Hampi's** extensive and intricate **ruins** (p. 493) are nice enough to make you glad to be in the middle of nowhere.

BANGALORE ಬೆಂಗಳೂರು

The city of Bangalore is where the West makes its cameo in the Deccan, clad in Indian garb—a city where American and Indian execs down *dosas* streetside, where families open cyber-cafes in their backyards, and where auto-rickshaws beckon with web addresses posted in their rear windows. A city of direct satellite links and three-*lassi* lunches, Bangalore is ground zero for India's technological revolution. A sizeable chunk of the world's software is written here, and in the conference rooms along MG and Residency Roads, India's wired elite drafts marketing strategies to sell the trappings of technology to the world's largest middle class—hundreds of millions of potential customers.

When Kempegowda, a petty chieftain under the Vijayanagar Empire, founded Bangalore in 1537, his son built four watchtowers marking the boundaries of the city. Four and a half centuries later, the towers still stand, but modern Bangalore spreads far beyond these limits. The growth of India's fifth largest city (pop. 4.5 million) has been accelerated by the influx of rural Karnatakans, as well as Tamils, Keralites, and North Indians lured by mild climes and metropolitan madness; all are drawn by the urban utopia that Bangalore promises. Though residents continue to bemoan the congestion caused by this growth, Bangalore still rightfully deserves its sobriquet as the "Garden City." The numerous lakes, parks, gardens, and broad, tree-lined avenues make Bangalore one of India's most pleasant cities.

▐▛ TRANSPORTATION

BY AIR

The Airport is 8km southeast of the city from the MG Rd. area (Rs45-50 auto-rickshaw ride). It has a 24-hour pre-paid taxi booth. Unless otherwise noted, airline offices are open M-F 9:30am-1pm and 2-5pm, Sa 9:30am-1pm.

Domestic Airlines: Indian Airlines, Cauvery Bhavan, Kempegowda Rd. (tel. 526 6233), offers the most flights; check with other airlines for better fares. Open M-Su 6am-5:30pm. Airport office (tel. 526 6898 or 526 1926). Open daily 8:30am-8:30pm. **Jet Airways,** 22 Ulsoor Rd., Unity Building (tel. 227 6617 or 227 6620), behind the Taj Residency. Open M-F 8:30am-7pm, Sa 9am-5pm. **Sahara,** Sahara Nirvana Building,

Richmond Circle (tel. 224 6435 or 224 6439). Open M-F 8am-8pm, Sa 10am-5pm. Airport branch (tel. 526 2531 or 527 0626). **Indian Airlines** has flights to: **Ahmedabad** (M, W, and F 3:30pm; 2hr.; US$200); **Kolkata** (6am, 2½hr., US$240); **Chennai** (M-Sa 3pm, Su 8:50pm; 40min.; US$65); **Cochin** (11:20am, 50min., US$70); **Delhi** (6:50am, 4:30, and 7:50pm; 2½hr.; US$230); **Goa** (M, W, and F 11:30am; 55min.; US$95); **Hyderabad** (10:05am and 5:45pm, 1hr., US$95); **Mangalore** (Tu, Th, and Sa; 45min.; US$70); **Mumbai** (8:35am, 1:20, and 8pm; 1½hr.; US$125); **Pune** (Tu, Th, and Sa 3:50pm; 1½hr.; US$130); **Trivandrum** (Tu, Th, Sa, and Su 11:25am; 1hr.; US$105).

International Airlines: Air India, JC Rd., Unity Bldg. (tel. 227 7747; fax 227 3300), 1 block from Corporation Bldg. **Air Canada** (tel. 558 5394; fax 558 6098), **Air France** (tel. 558 9397), **Kuwait Airways** (tel. 558 9021; fax 558 6098), and **Gulf Air** (tel. 558 4702), are in Sunrise Chambers, 22 Ulsoor Rd., 1 block north of MG Rd. behind the Taj Residency. **British Airways,** St. Marks Rd. (tel. 227 1205; fax 224 1503). **KLM,** West End Hotel (tel. 226 8703). **Lufthansa,** 42-2 Dickenson Rd. (tel. 558 8791), near Munipal Center. Open M-F 9am-5:30pm, Sa 9am-1pm. **Swissair,** 51 Richmond Rd. (tel. 221 1983), opposite BPL Plaza. Open M-F 9:30am-5:30pm, Sa 9:30am-1:30pm. **Qantas,** 13 Westminster Cunningham Rd. (tel. 225 6611), near Wockhardt Hospital. Open M-F 9:15am-1pm and 2-5:30pm, Sa 9:30am-12:30pm. **Singapore Airlines,** Richmond Rd. (tel. 221 3833). **Thai Airways,** Imperial Court, Cunningham Rd. (tel. 226 7613). **United Airlines,** 12 Richmond Rd. (tel. 224 4620).

BY LAND

Trains: City Railway Station (24hr. arrival and departure information tel. 131 or 133), at the end of Race Course and Bhashyam Rd. The **reservations counter** (tel. 132) with special counters for women and foreigners, is in the building on your left as you face the station. Open M-Sa 8am-8pm, Su 8am-2pm. The **enquiries** counter (tel. 1361-3) is in the main building. Open daily 7am-10:30pm. Go to the foreigner counter (#14) for regular booking. Trains are often booked weeks in advance—if there is no space available, you may get on the emergency quota. Fares listed are 2nd/1st class. To: **Kolkata** (*Howrah Exp.* 6512, F 11:50pm, 38hr., Rs417); **Chennai** (*Lalbagh Exp.* 2608, 6:30am, 5hr.; *Shatabdi Exp.,* 4:20pm, 4½hr.; *Mysore Exp.,* 9:15pm, 7hr., Rs152/482); **Coimbatore** (*Intercity Exp.,* 6am, 15½hr.; *Kurla Exp.,* 13hr., Rs89/282); **Delhi** (*Karnataka Exp.* 2627, 6:25pm, 42hr., Rs399/1687; *Rajdhani Exp.* 2429, W and F 6:45pm, 34hr., Rs422/1796); **Hospet** (*Saptagiri Exp.* 6057, 9:55pm, 10hr., Rs135/464); **Mangalore** (*Bangalore Tiruchi Exp.* 6532, 10:10pm, 26hr., Rs116/400); **Mumbai** (*Mumbai Exp.,* 6am, 26hr.; *Udyan Exp.* 6530, 8:30pm, 24hr., Rs330/1075); **Mysore** (*Mysore Exp.* 6222, 7:15am, 3hr.; *Chamundi Exp.* 6216, 6:15pm, 3hr., Rs41/138).

Buses: KSRTC Bus Stand, Bhashyam Rd. (tel 287 3377 or 287 1261), has a reservation counter open 7am-11pm. To: **Badami** (5:30 and 9pm, 9hr., Rs134); **Bijapur** (8 per day 4:30-10:15pm, 11hr., Rs154/183); **Chennai** (9 per day 9:30am-10:30pm, 7hr., Rs75/112); **Cochin** (4 per day 4-7:30pm, 12hr., Rs162/220); **Hassan** (every hr. 6am-11:40pm, 4hr., Rs48/65); **Hospet** (10 per day 4:30-10:30pm, 8hr., Rs90/119); **Hyderabad** (5 per day 4:30-10:30pm, 12hr., Rs174/219); **Kodaikanal** (9:15pm, 10hr., Rs133); **Mangalore** (frequent 8am-11:20pm, 8hr., Rs93/122); **Mumbai** (2 and 4pm, 24hr., Rs292/343); **Mysore** (frequent 5:45pm-midnight, 3hr., Rs48/63); **Panjim** (4:45pm, 11hr., Rs203); **Ooty** (8:30, 10am, and 10pm; 8hr.; Rs103); **Trivandrum** (4pm, 16hr., Rs270). **Private buses** to Mumbai, Ooty, Mysore, and other destinations leave from the KSRTC bus stand area. Their agencies line the streets near the bus stand.

Local Transportation: Don't be shy about insisting that **auto-rickshaws** use their meters—it's the law and common practice (Rs7 for the 1st km, Rs3.40 each additional km). The auto-rickshaw stand in the northeast corner of the railway station parking lot has a policeman there to ensure meter use. From 10pm-6am, expect to pay double the meter charge. Two kinds of **local buses** leave from the city bus stand: ordinary buses and the more expensive Pushpak buses. Buses to MG Rd. leave from platforms 17/18 (frequent 6:30am-10pm, Rs2-5). Route#7 serves the Corporation Building and MG Rd. (every 20min., Rs4). For Whitefield, take the #333E or 334 bus (1hr., Rs8). **U-Rent Services,**

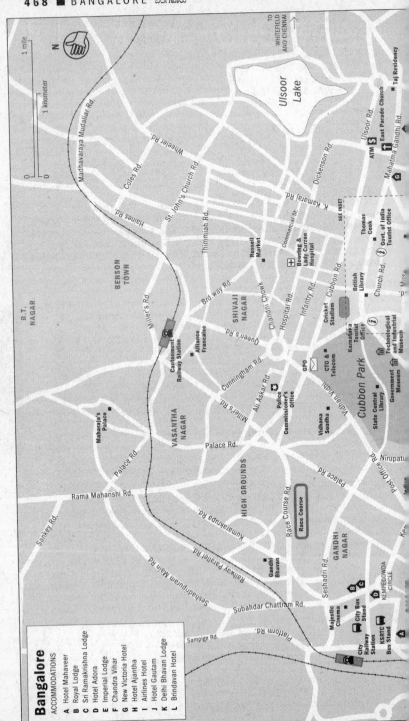

Bangalore

ACCOMMODATIONS

A Hotel Mahaveer
B Royal Lodge
C Sri Ramakrishna Lodge
D Hotel Adora
E Imperial Lodge
F Chandra Vihar
G New Victoria Hotel
H Hotel Ajantha
I Airlines Hotel
J Hotel Gautam
K Delhi Bhavan Lodge
L Brindavan Hotel

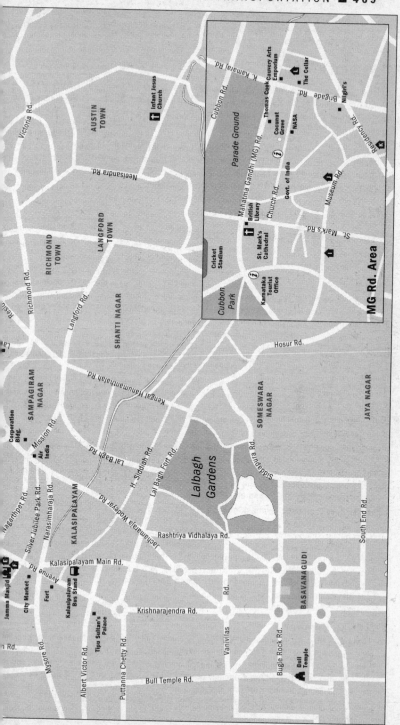

MG Rd. Area

Parade Ground

K. Kamaraj Rd.

Cubbon Rd.

Thomas Cook

Cauvery Arts Emporium

The Cellar

Brigade Rd.

Nilgiri's

Coconut Grove

NASA

Mahatma Gandhi (MG Rd.)

Residency Rd.

Church Rd.

Govt. of India

Museum Rd.

British Library

St. Mark's Rd.

St. Mark's Cathedral

Cricket Stadium

Cubbon Park

Karnataka Tourist Office

Infant Jesus Church

Victoria Rd.

AUSTIN TOWN

Neelasandra Rd.

RICHMOND TOWN

LANGFORD TOWN

Richmond Rd.

Langford Rd.

Re...

La...

SHANTI NAGAR

Hosur Rd.

Kengal Hanumanthaiah Rd.

SAMPAGIRAM NAGAR

SOMESWARA NAGAR

JAYA NAGAR

Corporation Bldg.

Air India

Mission Rd.

Lal Bagh Rd.

H. Siddiah Rd.

Lal Bagh Fort Rd.

Jachamaraja Wodeyar Rd.

Lalbagh Gardens

Siddapura Rd.

Nagarthpet Rd.

Silver Jubilee Park Rd.

Narasimharaja Rd.

KALASIPALAYAM

Rashtriya Vidhalaya Rd.

Jamma Masjid

City Market

Avenue Rd.

Fort

Kalasipalayam Bus Stand

Kalasipalayam Main Rd.

Tipu Sultan's Palace

Krishnarajendra Rd.

South End Rd.

BASAVANAGUDI

Mysore Rd.

Albert Victor Rd.

Puttanna Chetty Rd.

Vanivilas Rd.

Bugle Rock Rd.

Bull Temple

Bull Temple Rd.

n Rd.

19 RBDGT Bldg., rents **mopeds;** as you head out of the railway station, turn right and scan the sidewalk for their wooden sign (24hr. rental Rs200, Rs0.20 per km oil charge; open daily 9am-6pm).

✴ ORIENTATION

The hub of modern, international Bangalore is at the intersection of **Mahatma Gandhi (MG)** and **Brigade Roads.** South of MG Rd. are **Church Street** and **Residency Road,** home of hi-tech pubs, high-class hotels, and high-price shops. North of MG Rd., the aptly named **Commercial Street** leads west towards **Shivajinagar,** a bustling market district that is Bangalore's downtown. Most of the museums are in **Cubbon Park,** which stretches along **Kasturba (Gandhi) Road** from **Ambedkar Road** to MG Rd. The **Majestic** area, near the **City Railway Station** and **bus stand,** is fertile ground for budget hotels. South of the Majestic lies the frenetic **City Market** area, with its unpaved narrow roads, bullock carts, temples, and mosques.

✴ PRACTICAL INFORMATION

TOURIST AND FINANCIAL SERVICES

Tourist Offices: Government of India Tourist Office, 48 Church St. (tel. 558 5417). From Brigade Rd., turn right; the office is on the right inside the KFC building. Ask for a copy of *Bangalore This Fortnight,* an excellent guide to the city. Open M-F 9:30am-6pm, Sa 9am-1pm. **KSTDC,** 104/1 Kasturba Rd. (tel. 221 2901), near the junction with MG Rd., opposite the Queen Victoria statue in Cubbon Park, 2 flights up in a big, off-white building. Operates daily Bangalore bus tours (Rs80) and tours of Belur and Halebid. They will also book a night in one of KSTDC's myriad Mayura hotels. Open M-Sa 10am-5:30pm. Closed 2nd Sa. Another KSTDC branch in Badomi House, opposite the City Corporation Office, N.R. Square (tel. 221 5869). **Tourist Information Centers** in the Railway Station (tel. 287 0068) and the airport (tel. 526 8012). The **Department of Tourism,** KG Rd., Cauvery Bhavan, F block, 1st fl. (tel. 221 5498).

Budget Travel: Scores of travel agencies line the streets near the railway and bus stands; they offer sight-seeing tours and run coaches to Mumbai, Mysore, Ooty, and other locales. For car rental, bus, rail, air, and tour reservations, go to **Trade Wings,** 48 Lavelle Rd. (tel. 221 4595), across from the Airlines Hotel. Open M-F 9:30am-1pm and 2-5:30pm, Sa 9:30am-1pm.

Immigration Office: Foreigners Registration Office is at the **Office of the Commissioner of Police,** 1 Infantry Rd. (tel. 225 6242, ext. 251). Walk north along Cubbon Park past the GPO onto Queen's Rd., then left 1 block later onto Infantry. Open M-Sa 10am-5:30pm. For visa extensions, head to Rm. 224 in Vidhana Soudha, the office of L. Shanmukha, Undersecretary to Government, Home and Transport Dept. Open M-F 3:30-5:30pm.

Currency Exchange: Thomas Cook, 55 MG Rd. (tel. 558 1340), just before the intersection with Brigade Rd., is the fastest place to change foreign currency or traveler's checks. Open M-Sa 9:30am-6pm. A 24hr. **ATM,** Municipal Center, 47 Dickenson Rd., outside the Hong Kong Bank, accepts cards with Plus or Global Access logos. Walk east on MG Rd., 1 block past the parade grounds. The Prestige Meridien Building, 2 MG Rd. has a 24hr. **Citibank ATM** which accepts Visa, MC, Citibank, and all Cirrus/Plus logo cards. Turn left on Dickenson Rd. at the East Parade Church. **Bank of Baroda,** Bluemoon Complex, 66 MG Rd. (tel. 559 6981-2), gives cash advances on Visa and MC. 1% commission. Open M-F 10:30am-2:30pm, Sa 10:30am-12:30pm.

LOCAL SERVICES

Market: Nilgiri's, Brigade Rd., has luscious fruit in outside stalls. Open M-F 9:30am-2pm and 4-8:30pm, Sa 10:30am-1:30pm. **Russell Market,** 2km north of MG Rd. off Cunningham St., Shivajinagar, is an indoor market selling fruit, flowers, veggies, meat, antiques, and bric-a-brac. Generally open M-Sa 9:30am-1:30pm and 4-8pm. **City Market,** 1.5km southwest of City Railway Station, near Jamma Masjid, is a wholesale bazaar selling silk fabric, in addition to food and flowers. Open dawn-dusk.

Library: State Central Library, Cubbon Park (tel. 221 2128). Approach Cubbon Park from Kasturba Rd. and follow Lavelle Rd. into the park; the library is in a red building with green sills. Open Tu-Su 9am-7pm. **British Library,** 29 St. Mark's Rd. (tel. 221 3485), off MG Rd. near Koshy's. They supposedly don't allow non-members, but you can sneak in. Membership Rs300 plus Rs20 per book. Open Tu-Sa 10:30am-6:30pm.

Cultural Center: Bharatiya Vidya Bhavan (tel. 226 7421), opposite the race course on Race Course Rd. The Bangalore branch of this national organization sponsors cultural and literary activities. Library open M-F 10:30am-5:30pm, Sa 10:30am-1:30pm.

Bookstore: Gangaram's Book Bureau, 72 MG Rd. (tel. 558 6189). Three immense floors are filled with books on fiction and social science, stationery, postcards, and travel guides for India and elsewhere. Open daily 10am-8pm. Closed 2nd Su. **Nationwide Books,** 39 MG Rd. (tel. 558 2080), offers a 10% discount on a wide range of books. Open M-Sa 10am-8pm, Su 10am-2pm. **Premier Bookshop,** 46/1 Church St. (tel. 558 8570), around the corner from Berry's Hotel. Stuffed with paperbacks. Open M-Sa 10am-1:30pm and 3-7:30pm. Sidewalk vendors are the cheapest option for books; there are a few near the Cauvery Arts Emporium.

EMERGENCY AND COMMUNICATIONS

Pharmacy: Al-Siddique Pharmaceutical Centre (tel. 605491), near City Market. **Hosmat,** 45 Maganath Rd. (tel. 559 3796 or 559 3797), off Richmond Rd. Open 24hr.

Hospitals: The most respected government hospital is **Bowring and Lady Curzon Hospital** (tel. 559 1362, ext. 244 for emergencies), off Hospital Rd. 2km north of MG Rd. **Mallya Hospital,** 2 Vittal Mallya Rd. (tel. 227 7991); **Manipal Hospital,** 98 Rustumbagh Airport Rd. (tel. 528 7749 or 528 7751); and **St. John's Medical College and Hospital,** Sarjapur Rd. (tel. 553 0724 or 553 0734) offer excellent private care.

Police: Commissioner's Office, 1 Infantry Rd. (tel. 225 4501). From the intersection of MG and Kasturba Rd., walk northwest with Cubbon Park on your left; follow Queen's Rd. to Infantry Rd. and take a left. **Headquarters,** Nirupatunga Rd. (tel. 221 1803), next to the YMCA. Cubbon Park branch, Kasturba Rd. (tel. 556 6242), next to the aquarium.

Post Office: The **GPO** is a stone colossus on the corner of Raj Bhavan and Ambedkar Rd. in Cubbon Park. Also a branch on Brigade Rd., halfway between KFC and Wimpy's, across the street. Branch on Museum Rd., at the junction with St. Mark's Rd., is a computerized post and telegraph office. All open M-Sa 10am-6pm. **Postal Code:** 560001.

Internet: Bangalore has the best Internet access in all of India. **Cyber Club,** 31 Brigade Rd., 1st fl. (tel. 558 2028), in the alley opposite the post office. Open daily 9am-noon. Branch at Curzon Complex, Brigade Rd. Open daily 7.30am-9pm.

Telephones: The 24hr. **Central Telegraph Office** (tel. 286472) and **Public Telecom** (tel. 286 4019) are behind the GPO on Raj Bhavan Rd.

PHONE CODE	080

ACCOMMODATIONS

It might be difficult to find a decently priced room in the hip, hi-tech, and happening **MG Road** area. Book at least a week in advance. The area around the bus stand and railway stations has plenty of cheap places to stay, but they are a good 5km away from MG Rd.'s services. The lodges in **City Market** are cheap but close to the traffic and noise. Prices do not include 5-10% taxes.

MG ROAD AREA

Hotel Ajantha, 22-A MG Rd. (tel. 558 4321; fax 558 4780), 10min. from Brigade Rd. Clean, reasonably-priced rooms, helpful staff, and great location. Color TV and 24hr. hot water. Check-out 24hr. Singles Rs175; doubles Rs300, with A/C Rs550. Reserve up to 3 weeks in advance.

Brindavan Hotel, 108 MG Rd. (tel. 558 4000), has pretty inexpensive rooms considering its great MG Rd. location. Check-out 24hr. Singles Rs190-260, with A/C Rs550; doubles Rs310-425/950; quads Rs400. Extra person Rs60/100. Reserve ahead.

Hotel Imperial Lodge, 93-94 Residency Rd. (tel. 558 8391 or 558 5473) has plain, functional rooms with large windows and a cheery atmosphere. Squat toilets, hot water in the morning. Attached restaurant. Upcoming renovations might up prices a bit. Check-out 24hr. Singles Rs170; doubles Rs300. Extra person Rs120.

Airlines Hotel, 4 Madras Bank Rd. (tel. 227 3783 or 227 3786), off Lavelle Rd., 10min. from MG Rd. Rooms aren't sparkling, but they're well-furnished: towels, seat toilets, and hot water until 10am. Check-out 24hr. Singles Rs275; doubles Rs385. Extra bed Rs120, extra person Rs75. Visa, AmEx.

New Victoria Hotel, 47-48 Residency Rd. (tel. 558 4076 or 558 5028). Lost in trees and wildflowers, the New Victoria's bungalows were a British military canteen and library until about 1935. Attached baths have 24hr. hot water and seat toilets. Rooms are average but most have Star TV. Check-out 24hr. Singles Rs400; doubles Rs1050. Service charge 10%. Credit card and traveler's checks.

Hotel Gautam, 17 Museum Rd. (tel. 558 8475 or 558 8137), 5min. from Brigade Rd. Spacious, serene rooms have 24hr. hot water, Star TV, and balconies. Travel agency and attached veg. restaurant. Singles Rs400; doubles Rs450.

RAILWAY STATION AND BUS STAND AREA

⬚ **Sri Ramakrishna Lodge,** SC Rd. (tel. 226 3041), next to Kapali Theater. Rooms have extra-cushiony beds and immaculate bathrooms with squat toilets. Each floor has a pleasant verandah. 24hr. hot water., laundry, room service, TVs, and phones. Two attached restaurants (*thalis* Rs19), travel counter, and pharmacy. Check-out 24hr. Singles Rs150; doubles RS250.

Royal Lodge, 251 SC Rd. (tel. 226 6951). Basic rooms in a calm and welcoming atmosphere, with attached bath and hot water 6:30-9am. Check-out 24hr. Singles Rs100; doubles Rs253.

Hotel Mahaveer, 8-1 Tankbund Rd. (tel. 287 3670), on the corner of Chickpet Rd. on the right outside the rail station exit. Over sixty modern, boxy-but-clean rooms have TV, phone, and attached bath with seat toilet. Friendly management provides running hot water 6-9am, same-day laundry service, foreign exchange. Check-out 24hr. Singles Rs225; doubles Rs450, with A/C Rs850; triples Rs625. Visa, MC.

Hotel Adora, 47 SC Rd. (tel 220 0324). Very clean rooms have phones but the barest of furnishings. Room service from the attached veg. restaurant, laundry, and travel services. Check-out 24hr. Singles Rs150; doubles Rs253.

CITY MARKET

Chandra Vihar, MRR Ln. (tel. 222 4146), opposite City Market Bldg., 1 block from Jamma Masjid. Phones and TVs in all 50 rooms. Check-out 24hr. Singles Rs210; doubles Rs303. Extra bed Rs75.

Delhi Bhavan Lodge, Avenue Rd. (tel. 287 5045). Standard, clean rooms. Hot water 6-9am. Check-out 24hr. Singles Rs125; doubles Rs205. Extra bed Rs30.

◖ FOOD

Bangalore, inundated with Western food chains, boasts some of the best restaurants in India. Whether you're into *tandoori* or KFC, burgers or *bhel puris*, lasagna or *lassis*, Bangalore has enough variety to delight the pickiest palate.

⬚ **Cafe Schorlemmer,** Max Mueller Bhavan, 3 Lavelle Rd. Operated by a German expat, this rooftop cafe serves up probably the best apple strudel (Rs30) in all of South Asia and great homemade delights, such as cheesecake (Rs30), chocolate cake (Rs15), and kugel (Rs20). Rotating art exhibits add a classy touch. Full German lunch of the day (veg. Rs70, non-veg. Rs110), sandwiches (Rs30-40), loaves of freshly baked brown bread (Rs60), and baguettes (Rs30). Open M-Sa 9am-8pm.

Java City, 24/1 Lavelle Rd. Popular coffee house serves espresso (Rs15) and cappuccino (Rs20). Italian sodas of many flavors (Rs50) and an array of fresh desserts and pastries. Delicious chocolate mousse (Rs35) and chocolate fondue (Rs135-260). Open daily M-Su 11am-11pm.

Sunny's, 35/2 Kasturba Cross, off Lavelle Rd. near Trade Wings travel agency. A tiny Mediterranean bistro with a vivid orange-and-blue color scheme. Delicious *gazpacho* (Rs75), pasta (Rs150-200), and freshly made desserts from the bakery below (chocolate ganache tart Rs58). Timely servers bring you delicious bread and garlic butter with every order. Rs200 min. per head, plus 10% service charge. Open Tu-Th 1-3pm and 6-9:30pm, Sa-Su open until 10:30pm.

Casa Picolla, Devatha Plaza, 131 Residency Rd. (tel. 221 2907), 10min. from the Brigade Rd. area. Relatively inexpensive food tastes surprisingly good in a pleasantly airy setting complete with seaside murals. Lasagne *verde* (Rs69) and steak (Rs85) are filling, but save room for those delicious crepes (Rs53), profiteroles (Rs39), and a cappuccino (Rs12). Open daily 11:30am-10:30pm. Delivery 10% charge within 2km.

The Only Place, 158 Nota Royal Arcade, Brigade Rd. This restaurant has been serving hamburgers (Rs39-69), pizza (Rs49-76), pasta (Rs69-76), apple pie (Rs40), pancakes (Rs35), and lasagna (Rs75) for years. Though no longer the only place serving them, it's a Bangalore institution. Open daily 11am-3:30pm and 7-11pm. MC, Visa, AmEx.

Indian Coffee House, 78 MG Rd. The cheapest and smartest sit-down place on MG Rd. to grab a cuppa joe (Rs5) and smoke a cigarette. The brew is served by festooned waiters. Peruse a newspaper over scrambled eggs with toast (Rs12) or a *masala dosa* (Rs9). Open daily 8:30am-8:30pm.

Kamat, Unity Bldg., JC Rd. One of Bangalore's best-value Indian restaurants. Huge *thalis* available noon-3pm (Rs40, Rs55 in the A/C section). Sweets counter, too. Open M-Sa 8am-11pm, Su 10am-3pm (snacks only) and 7-11pm.

Nilgiri's Cafe, 171 Brigade Rd., attracts a clientele so well-scrubbed that they look fresh from the dairy farm Nilgiri's founded in 1905. Huge grilled sandwiches (Rs38-60) and doughy cheese pizzas (Rs65-90). Hazelnut milkshakes (Rs30) and fried ice cream (Rs40) delight customers. Open daily 9am-11pm.

Karavalli, 66 Residency Rd., in the Gateway Hotel. Bangalore's most elegant coastal Keralan cuisine. *Appam,* with fish or veg. stew, is the specialty, but you shouldn't miss the coconut curries. Lunchtime *thalis* (Rs215-250). French wine (Rs90 per glass). Count on Rs300 per person. Open daily 12:30-3:30pm and 7:30pm-midnight.

The Coconut Grove, 86 Church St. Reasonable prices and subtle tropical decor helps you discover the culinary gems of Kerala, Karnataka, and Tamil Nadu. Try the *kaikari kootu* (Rs45), a dish of lentils and grated coconut, or feast on an unbeatable *thali* (Rs55 veg., Rs75 non-veg.) for lunch. Seafood specialties (Rs105-115). Pineapple-based *kaidachakka halwa* makes for a heavenly dessert. Open daily 12:30-4pm and 7-11pm.

■♫ NIGHTLIFE AND ENTERTAINMENT

PUBS AND BARS

Though plagued by water shortages, Bangalore is never dry. Its burgeoning pub culture has earned the city the title "Bar Galore." Most pubs are clustered around Brigade Rd., and the regulars who frequent them greet the pubs' godfather-esque owners with hearty hugs and know the bartenders by name. Pubs may serve alcohol only from 11am to 2:30pm and from 5:30 to 11pm. The police come by around midnight, suggesting that "good people sleep early" as stragglers exit quietly through the back door. Sometimes pubs may refuse admission to unaccompanied women. Most accept major credit cards.

The Cellar, 7 Brigade Rd., Curzon Ct., opposite the intersection with Church St. Wooden decor and cushy booths. The mellow afternoon may have been invented here. Proportionate representation of the sexes. Chinese, Continental, and *tandoori* cuisine (Rs60). Pitchers Rs150, mugs Rs35. Open daily 11am-12:30pm and 5:30-11pm.

The New Night Watchman, 46/1 Church St., near Berry's Hotel. Catering to a largely North Indian crowd, it's one of the few pubs that plays *bhangra*. Shaped like a mini-stadium, with the bar in the center, the pub is one big "happy" family—happy hour (11am-2:30pm) offers discounted drinks (pitchers Rs125, mugs Rs25; other times Rs140/28). Full lunch and dinner menus available.

Peco's Pub, 34 Rest House Rd., one street south of Church St. off Brigade Rd. Hendrix, Marley, Joplin, and Zeppelin grace the walls. 3 floors packed with college-aged guzzlers imbibing mugfuls (Rs30). Rooftop has relaxing chairs. Open daily 10:30am-2:30pm and 5:30-10:30pm.

The Pub World, 65 Residency St., opposite Galaxy Theatre. Marginally more chi-chi than its neighbors, with oak banisters, lace curtains, and tapestried footstools. Well-lit, too, so you won't feel like a reprobate for drinking in the middle of the afternoon. Bartenders have honors degrees in chivalry. Pitchers (Rs150), mugs (Rs30).

The Black Cadillac, Mohan Towers, 50 Residency Rd., a few blocks west of Brigade Rd.; look out for the red neon sign (you can see only a giant cursive "C"). Called "BC" by regulars, this is where the city's fashionable elite go to see and be seen (model want-ads grace the walls). Sublime in the sublime garden area. Pitchers (Rs175), mugs (Rs35).

NASA, 1/4 Church St. The walls are decorated with pictures of spaceships, astronauts, and...Michael Jackson? The interior is correspondingly out of *Captain Eo*. Beer is pricey (pitcher Rs150, mugs Rs30), but atmosphere (laser shows et al) comes at a price.

The Underground, 61/1 MG Rd., Bluemoon Complex, derives its inspiration from the London underground. "Oxford Circus" resembles a hopping pub in London. "Kensington" is more a country-style pub catering to families and children. Mugs Rs30, pints Rs60, pitchers Rs150. Veg. lunch (Rs35), non-veg. (Rs45), and snacks (Rs30-60).

DISCOS

Another much-loved city ordinance, the one against the late operation of discos, prevents a full-fledged club scene from taking root. Still, a few clubs have managed to stay open. By far the most popular club is **The Club Inferno,** Mysore Rd. (tel. 860 0665), outside of town. (Rs200-400 for a one-way rickshaw ride). Unfortunately, lack of neighboring competition has meant that the club can play nonstop, overpoweringly loud techno music and be less than friendly to its patrons who don't seem to groove much to the music. (Open M, W, and F-Sa 9pm-5am; Rs300 per couple). Two other clubs in town draw significantly smaller crowds and thus have more space for personal creative expression: **Orion,** on Residency Rd. (tel. 227 3546), above the Black Cadillac (open W and F-Sa 9:30pm-2am) and **JJ's,** Airport Rd. (tel. 526 1929), just before the airport (open M, Th, and Su 10:30pm-2am, Rs150; W and F-Sa 1-5am, Rs100). However, the party doesn't get started until past midnight. Don't miss Sunday **jazz night,** where patrons relax to groovy old rock and jazz. **Time and Again,** Brigade Rd. (tel. 558 5845) is a more centrally located, if pricey, club (open daily from 7pm; Rs250 per couple; beer Rs60). Farther out, **The Rocks,** Allasandra Bellamy Rd. (tel. 846 2776) is fun for weekend clubbing (open F-Sa from 9:30pm; Rs150 per couple; beer Rs80).

OTHER DIVERSIONS

Several cinemas in the MG Rd. area show English-language flicks. **The Plaza,** 74 MG Rd. (tel. 558 7682), **The Rex,** Brigade Rd. (tel 571350), and **The Symphony,** 51 MG Rd. (tel. 558 5988) all show not-too-old American movies (Rs15-45). Try to buy tickets at least an hour in advance. The **Windsor Manor Sheraton,** 25 Sankey Rd. (tel. 226 9898), near the High Grounds, will let you use their outdoor swimming pool for Rs390 (open daily 7am-7pm). If you don't mind a much less luxurious atmosphere, go for a dip in the public **Kensington Swimming Pool** (tel. 536413), opposite Ulsoor Lake (membership fee Rs100, plus Rs3 per hr.; open daily 6am-5pm).

⬤ SIGHTS

CUBBON PARK AND MUSEUMS. Set aside in 1864 and named for the former Viceroy of India, Lord Cubbon, the park consists of 300 acres of lush greenery in the center of the city. The park extends from the corner of MG Rd. to the Corporation Building, providing much needed shade and refuge from the city traffic surrounding it. The park is also home to several museums. The **K. Venkatappa Art Gallery** exhibits watercolor landscapes by K. Venkatappa, the Mysore court artist who painted much of the Maharaja's Palace in Mysore. The second floor displays rotating exhibitions of contemporary Karnatakan artists. The 112-year-old **Government Museum,** one of India's oldest, is a fine example of monumental neoclassical architecture. The first floor houses some interesting archaelogical artifacts and stone Hoysalan sculptures. *(Museum and gallery open Tu-Su 10am-5pm. Rs4.)* Next door, the **Visveswaraya Industrial and Technological Museum** celebrates Bangalore's industrial progress from 1905, when City Market lit India's first light bulb, to Bangalore's current boom in information technology. Use your mind and muscle power to learn about the inner workings of the pulley, the computer, and the nuclear bomb. The park also has an aquarium and a children's park, **Bhal Bhavan,** complete with boat, pony, and toy train rides, a doll museum, and a children's theater which stages plays and screens films *(open daily 10am-5:30pm; Rs10).* Across the park lies the red **Attara Kachari,** which housed the 18 departments of the secretariat until 1956 (*attara* means "eighteen" in Hindi).

VIDHANA SOUDHA. One of Bangalore's most recognizable landmarks, the Vidhana Soudha houses the Secretariat. In the early 1950s, a visiting Russian delegation pointed out the abundance of European architecture in Bangalore. Spurred to action by the Russians' remarks, the chief minister of Mysore state decided to construct this spectacular neo-Dravidian temple-style structure. The Vidhana Soudha became not only an affirmation of Indian sovereignty but also an assertion of Bangalore's new legislative power. It was built out of pure granite by craftsmen from Andhra Pradesh (one of Bangalore's largest slums was formed by the displaced masons' families). Atop the main entrance sits Emperor Ashoka's four-headed lion (the symbol of the Indian nation and the watermark on all rupee notes). Statues of Jawaharlal Nehru and B.R. Ambedkar stand in the front lawn, gesticulating at each other beneath the self-congratulatory inscription, "Government Work is God's Work." The building is closed to the public but lit up every Sunday night. *(Across the street from Cubbon Park to the northwest.)*

BANGALORE FORT. Built in mud and brick by Chikkadevaraga Wadiyar in the late 1600s as an extension of another of Kempegowda's forts, the Bangalore Fort was later refurbished by Haider Ali and Tipu Sultan in the 18th century. It originally encompassed the area between the Corporation Offices and City Market. Though most of it was destroyed in the Anglo-Mysore War, the remains are beautifully preserved, with ornately carved Islamic-style arches and turrets and an exquisite **Ganpati Temple** inside. *(Krishnarajendra Rd., opposite Vanivilas Hospital.)*

TIPU SULTAN'S SUMMER PALACE. Tipu liked to call his Summer Palace Lask-e-Jannat, "The Envy of Heaven," but the palace is really just a low-budget replica of Daria Daulat in Srirangapatnam. It took 10 years to complete because Haider Ali was killed during its construction and Tipu was busy avenging his death. Most of the original wall paintings have been obscured by shiny brown paint. *(500m south of the fort. Open daily 9am-5pm.)*

BULL TEMPLE. The Bull Temple's massive black Nandi, over 500 years old, draws devotees from all around India. Legend has it that a raging bull used to torment local farmers by ravaging their fields at night. The frustrated farmers finally hired a night watchman to kill the bull with a crowbar. The next morning, they discovered that the carcass had transformed into a solid granite bull. Look closely, and you'll see the crowbar embedded in the poor beast's back. *(Bull Temple Rd., south of the Summer Palace. Open daily 8am-8pm.)*

THE BOY WONDER With his expansive coiffure, saffron robes, and beatific smile, photographs of **Satya Sai Baba** decorate and bless restaurants, hotels, homes, and autos throughout India. Millions of faithful devotees worldwide believe that he is an avatar of God and a reincarnation of an earlier saint, Shirdi Sai Baba. Born in the tiny village of Puttaparthi, the young Satya first displayed his spiritual leanings at the young age of 13. Some say he was stung by a scorpion, and subsequently fell into a trance from which he awoke chanting Sanskrit passages. His parents thought him possessed and called in an exorcist who tried to beat the devil out of him, but Satya responded by materializing sweets out of thin air. Finally his father cried, "Who are you?" to which his son answered, "I am Sai Baba."

Since then, Satya Sai Baba has achieved renown by performing feats such as raising the dead, healing the sick, and producing diamonds out of thin air. However, he considers the miracles secondary to his main task of promoting the values of truth, peace, non-violence, love, and righteousness. Thousands upon thousands of Indians and foreigners flock to Sai Baba's ashrams in Andhra Pradesh and Karnataka, hoping to observe, learn, and bask in the peaceful aura that radiates from the master.

LALBAGH GARDENS. Haider Ali laid out Lalbagh Gardens in 1760, and his son Tipu Sultan later expanded the 16-hectare gardens to 96 hectares and added the mango grove. After Tipu's demise in 1799, the British took over Lalbagh, and Prince Albert Victor of Wales built the Glass House to resemble London's Crystal Palace in the late 1800s. The gardens are home to 150 different varieties of roses and 1000 kinds of tropical and subtropical flora and fauna, a giant floral clock, a lotus pond, a deer park, and innumerable walkers, joggers, cyclists, and monkeys. One of Kempegowda's four watchtowers marking Bangalore's city limits in 1537 can still be seen here. *(2km south of Cubbon Park. Open daily dawn-dusk. Rs2.)*

ULSOOR LAKE. The Ulsoor Lake spreads over northeastern Bangalore, its 1.5 sq. km of water speckled with tiny, picturesque islands. Enjoy a boat ride or swim in the Kensington pool nearby (see **Other Diversions**, p. 474). During the annual Ganesha Festival (Aug.-Sept.), devotees dunk a statue of Lord Ganesha, decked out in ceremonial regalia, in the lake. Local Bengalis follow a similar ritual during the Dussehra Festival in October when they submerge a statue of the goddess Durga. *(2 blocks north of MG Rd. on Gangadhana Chetty and Kensington Rd, near the Taj Hotel and Cottage Emporium. Open daily dawn-dusk.)*

OTHER SIGHTS. The eight-year-old **Jawaharlal Nehru Planetarium** was built to commemorate the 100th birthday of the freedom fighter and prime minister who called Bangalore "India's city of the future" *(T Chowdiak Rd., across from Raj Bhavan; tel. 220 3234; open Tu-Su, closed 2nd Tu; English shows at 4:30pm; Rs15).* The **Gandhi Picture Gallery**, on the second floor of **Gandhi Bhavan**, affords a well-organized journey through the Mahatma's life, with grainy blown-up photographs, quotations full of Gandhian wisdom, and artifacts such as Gandhi's wooden *chappals*, drinking bowls, and letters to Franklin Roosevelt, Tolstoy, Gokhale, and Nehru. Few visit this jewel; there's no permanent staff, and you'll need to ask to have the door unlocked. The library downstairs sells cheap copies of Gandhi's writings. *(From Windsor Hotel, across the Golf Course High Grounds, down Kumara Krupa Rd. Tel. 226 1967. Open M-Sa 10:30am-1:30pm and 3-5pm. Free.)*

 SHOPPING

Even if you've spent all your money in Bangalore's bars, you should still check out the city's arts and crafts emporia, which sell tables that are handpainted or inlaid with precious gems, *saris* fit for a rani, and life-size sandalwood Krishnas. The government-run **Cauvery Arts Emporium,** 45 MG Rd. (tel. 558 1118), near Brigade Rd., has fair prices and a decent selection, but the salespeople are practically comatose (open M-Su 10am-1:30pm and 3-7:30pm). Check out **Nateson's Antiquaries,** 76 MG

Rd. (tel. 558344; open M-Sa 10am-8pm). **Himalayan Dowry,** 72 MG Rd. (tel. 536 9567), an "anti-dowry store" sells Kashmiri and Tibetan handicrafts and donates a portion of its proceeds to anti-dowry campaigns (open M-Sa 10am-9pm). In general, the MG Rd. area is the emporiophile's paradise, with arts and handicrafts shops selling stuff from all over India, at prices to match the superlative quality. Luckily, most accept credit cards, so you can rue the purchase of that antique jade Buddha later. On **Commercial St.,** you'll find *salwar kameez* and *saris* in unimaginable permutations of style, color, and price.

NEAR BANGALORE

Satya Sai Baba's Karnataka ashram (Brindavan) is in the town of **Whitefield,** 16km from Bangalore. Although he spends most of the year at his main ashram in Puttaparthi, Andhra Pradesh, Sai Baba often spends the summer months here in **Brindavan.** Sai Baba has established free hospitals, schools, and countless public aid projects, including "The Water Project" which brought running water to several neighboring villages. Sai Baba, affectionately referred to as "Swami," customarily gives morning and afternoon *darshan*, at which he meanders among the crowds of devotees who have assembled here from countries all over the world. Devotees and interested travelers can stay there for a nominal charge. For information call the ashram office (tel. 845 2233). City **buses** #333E and 334 ply to Whitefield (1hr., Rs7). **Trains** also service the town (*Marikuppan* 256/254, 6:45am and 6:10pm; *Chennai Passenger* 96, 10:30am, 1hr., 2nd/1st class Rs10/65).

Nrityagram Dance Village (tel. 846 6313; fax 846 6312; www.allindia.com/nritya), in Hessaraghatta, 35km from the city on the Bangalore-Pune Highway, is run by Protima Gauri, possibly the best *odissi* dancer in the country. Dancers from all over India come to train here, and Gauri also conducts classes for children from neighboring villages. Tours of the architecturally award-winning village include an hour-long lecture-demonstration of *odissi* and *kathak* dance, a lecture on Indian philosophy and culture, and an organically grown lunch. (Casual tours Rs20 per person.) In the first week of February, the dance village conducts an all-night dance and music festival. The festival is free of charge, featuring performances by Gauri and her students, as well as musical faves Zakir Hussain and Amjad Ali Khan, in front of an audience of more than 25,000. Get there by 5:30pm if you want a seat. (Dance performance Rs1100, min. 10 people; advance booking required. Village open Sept.-May Tu-Su 10am-5pm.) **Buses** run regularly from Bangalore (#253, 253A, 253D, and 253E from City Market) to Nrityagram, but the village is 5km from the bus stand, and there aren't many auto-rickshaws around. It's easier to arrange a private **taxi** (about Rs500 round-trip) or book through either Cosmopole Travels (tel. 228 1591) or Cox and Kings Travel (tel. 223 9258).

MYSORE ಮೈಸುರು

Sandalwood capital of Karnataka and home to the breathtaking Mysore Maharaja's Palace, the city of Mysore rewards visitors with one of the few places in India that surpasses the tourist brochures. The Wadiyar dynasty ruled Mysore from the 15th century until Independence in 1947. As capital of a princely state until 1956, when Bangalore claimed the title, grand old palaces and other maharaja ex-haunts, as well as monuments, temples, gardens, and parks, fill the city. Mysore is home to a thriving incense industry, churning out hundreds of thousands of trinkets, key-chains, incense sticks, and beauty products every year. The city explodes during the annual Dussehra festival, a ten-day celebration in October.

▛ TRANSPORTATION

Trains: The **railway station** is at the intersection of Irwin and Jhansi Laxmi Bai Rd. The enquiry and reservations desks (tel. 131 or 520103) are open M-Sa 8am-8pm, Su 8am-2pm. Fares listed are 2nd/1st class. To: **Bangalore** (5 per day 6am-10:30pm,

3hr., Rs25/41); **Chennai** (*Shatabdi Exp.* 2008, 2:10pm, 7hr., Rs630; *Chennai Exp.* 6221, 6:05pm, 10½hr., 2nd class Rs186).

Buses: Long-distance buses leave from the **Central Bus Stand** (tel. 520853), on B-N Rd., near Wesley Cathedral. Reservations desk open daily 7:30am-9pm. To: **Bangalore** (every 15min. 5:45am-9:30pm, 3hr., Rs36/48); **Belur** (7am and 1pm, 5hr., Rs41); **Bijapur** (1pm, 18hr., Rs183); **Chennai** (7pm, 12hr., Rs115); **Coimbatore** (11 per day 6am-11:30pm, 6hr., Rs49); **Hassan** (every 30min. 4:30am-10:30pm, 3hr., Rs31); **Mangalore** (frequent 4:45am-11:30pm, 7hr., Rs68/89); **Ooty** (8 per day 7am-3pm, 5hr., Rs43). The bus to **Somnathpur** (11:45am, Rs13) leaves from the street in front of Wesley Cathedral, but you can also take a bus to **Bannur** (every hr., Rs10), 7km from Somnathpur, and then catch a bus from there (every 30min., Rs3). Near the cathedral, **private bus** companies vie for space and customers. Most are open late into the night.

Local Transportation: Local buses leave from the **City Bus Stand** (tel. 425819), off K-R Cir. Fares are Rs3-6. To: **Brindavan Gardens** (#301 and 304-6, every 30min., 30min.); **Chamundi Hill** (#201, every 20min., 40min.); **Srirangapatnam** (Platform 6 #313, 316; every 20min.; 45min.). **Taxis** cluster in Gandhi Sq.; fares are subject to negotiation. **Auto-rickshaws** *should* be metered (Rs7 for the 1st km, Rs6 per subsequent km).

✦ ORIENTATION

Although Mysore is dotted with rotaries and streaked with unforgiving twisty-turny roads, the city itself is actually quite compact. The summit of **Chamundi Hill** looms southeast of the city. Running north-south, **Sayajit Rao Road** bisects Mysore proper into roughly equal halves, cutting through **K-R Circle**, the true center of the city. The **City Bus Stand** is off the southeast quarter of K-R Cir. If you head east from K-R Cir., you'll walk along the outskirts of the gigantic **Maharaja's Palace.** About 300m north of K-R Cir., Sayajit Rao Rd. meets the east-west **Old Bank Road (Sardar Patel Road).** Old Bank Rd. leads east to a granite obelisk, a smaller rendition of Delhi's **Gandhi Memorial**; this is **Gandhi Square,** where you'll find a number of tourist accommodations. About 75m southeast is a tall **clock tower;** south of that, the road intersects Sri Harsha Road, which leads east to a north-south thoroughfare, **Bangalore-Nilgiri (B-N) Road.** North on B-N Rd., across from Wesley Cathedral, is the **Central Bus Stand,** and farther north is **Irwin Road,** which leads west past the GPO, the State Bank of Mysore, and the tourist office. One block farther west, set back from the road, is the domed **railway station.**

🔢 PRACTICAL INFORMATION

Tourist Office: Karnataka Tourist Office, Old Exhibition Bldg. (tel. 442096), at the corner of Irwin and Diwan's Rd., 1 block east of the railway station. Helpful staff. Open M-Sa 10am-5:30pm. Closed 2nd Sa. The **KSTDC** (tel. 423652), on Jhansi Laxmi Bai Rd., adjacent to the Hotel Mayura, will book you on day tours of Mysore. The cheap, low-stress tour includes Somnathpur, Srirangapatnam, Chamundi Hill, Maharaja's Palace, and Brindavan Gardens (7:30am-8:30pm; Rs110, not including admission fees). Tours of Belur, Halebid, and Sravanabelagola (Tu-W, F, and Su 7:30am-9pm; Rs160) and Ooty (M, Th, and Sa 7am-9pm; Rs200). Open 24hr.

Budget Travel: Many travel agencies are located in the vicinity of Gandhi Sq. **Dasprakash Travel Agency** (tel. 529949), in the eponymous hotel complex off Gandhi Sq., books tours and air and rail tickets. Open daily 6:30am-10pm. **Indian Airlines,** Hotel Mayura Complex, Jhansi Laxmi Bai Rd. (tel. 421846 or 426317). 250m south of the railway station. Open M-Sa 10am-1:30pm and 2:15-5pm.

Foreigners Registration Office: Police Commissioner's Office, Lalitha Mahal Rd. (tel. 226203), 3km from the city center. May grant free 3-month visa extensions, which take 1 week to process, but a trek out to Bangalore may be necessary.

Currency Exchange: The **State Bank of Mysore** (tel. 443866) has a foreign exchange branch at the junction of Sayajit Rao and Old Bank Rd. The **State Bank of India,** K-R Cir. (tel. 437650) changes US$, UK£, and traveler's checks. Both open M-F 10:30am-2:30pm, Sa 10:30am-12:30pm.

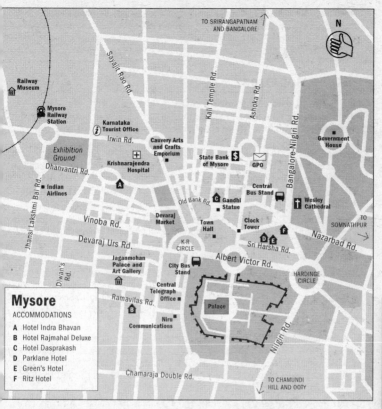

TO SRIRANGAPATNAM AND BANGALORE

N

Railway Museum

Mysore Railway Station

Exhibition Ground

Karnataka Tourist Office

Irwin Rd.

Cauvery Arts and Crafts Emporium

Sayajit Rao Rd.

Kali Temple Rd.

Ashoka Rd.

Bangalore-Nilgiri Rd.

Government House

State Bank of Mysore

GPO

Krishnarajendra Hospital

Dhanvantri Rd.

Indian Airlines

Jhansi Lakshmi Bai Rd.

Central Bus Stand

Wesley Cathedral

Old Bank Rd.

Gandhi Statue

TO SOMNATHPUR

Vinoba Rd.

Devaraj Market

Town Hall

Clock Tower

Nazarbad Rd.

Devaraj Urs Rd.

K-R CIRCLE

Sri Harsha Rd.

Diwan's Rd.

Jaganmohan Palace and Art Gallery

City Bus Stand

Albert Victor Rd.

HARDINGE CIRCLE

Central Telegraph Office

Ramavilas Rd.

Niru Communications

Palace

Mysore

ACCOMMODATIONS

A Hotel Indra Bhavan
B Hotel Rajmahal Deluxe
C Hotel Dasprakash
D Parklane Hotel
E Green's Hotel
F Ritz Hotel

Chamaraja Double Rd.

Nilgiri Rd.

TO CHAMUNDI HILL AND OOTY

KARNATAKA

Luggage Storage: Railway Station. Rs5-7. Open daily 6am-11:30pm.

Market: Devaraja Market, tucked behind the glitzy *sari* shops on Sayajit Rao Rd. and the sandalwood shops on Dhanvantri Rd. Sells fresh vegetables and fruit, color film, and *kum-kum,* the brightly colored powder used for *bindis.* Open daily dawn-dusk. **Pick 'n' Pack Mini Supermarket,** Hotel Luciya complex, Old Bank Rd. (tel. 425445), between Gandhi Sq. and Sayajit Rao Rd. Open M-Sa 9am-9pm, Su 9am-2pm.

Library: Mysore City Central Library, at the intersection of Irwin and Sayajit Rao Rd. Full of musty books, but as airy as a library should be. Periodicals room is packed. Open Tu-Su 8:30am-8pm. Closed 2nd Sa.

Bookstore: Ashok Book Centre (tel. 435553), on Dhanvantri Rd., near Sayajit Rao Rd. A post-colonial paradise, rife with the latest Rushdie, Mehta, and Ishigaro. Open M-Sa 9:30am-2pm and 3:30-8:30pm.

Pharmacy: Many are clustered near the hospital grounds, on Sayajit Rao and Dhanvantri Rd. **Ismail Optical Co.** (tel. 422786) quickly fills medical and optical prescriptions and has contact lens supplies. Open M-Sa 9:30am-9:30pm, Su 9:30am-3pm.

Hospital: K-R Hospital (tel. 443 3000), at the corner of Sayajit Rao and Irwin Rd., opposite Cauvery Emporium, is the main government hospital. The private **Holdsworth Memorial (Mission) Hospital,** Sawday Rd. (tel. 521650), is nicer and cleaner.

Police: Branch offices across from the GPO and at the Central Bus Stand (tel. 522 2222).

Post Office: GPO (tel. 22165), intersection of Ashoka and Irwin Rd., 750m east of the tourist office. Open M-Sa 10am-6pm. **Postal Code:** 570001.

Internet: Coca-Cola Cyber Space, #2 Madvesha Complex, Nazarbad (tel. 565574 or 522740) charges Rs60 per hr. or Rs1 per min.; confirm before you start browsing. Open M-Sa 10am-10:30pm, Su 10am-8pm.

Telephones: 24hr. **STD/ISD** booths near Gandhi Sq. and at the **Central Telegraph Office,** south of K-R Cir., before Ramavilas Rd. Callbacks Rs1 per min.

PHONE CODE	0821

ACCOMMODATIONS

Mysore is full of reasonably priced, centrally located hotels. Many have built devoted followings, so advance reservations (a week ahead in season, a few days otherwise) are a good idea. There are state taxes of 5-10% on expensive rooms.

Parklane Hotel, 2720 Sri Harsha Rd. (tel. 434400 or 437370). Small but clean rooms. Popular restaurant on the terrace. Hot water 6-10am; squat toilet on the ground floor, seat toilet on the first floor. Check-out 24hr. Singles Rs100 (ground-floor), Rs125 (1st floor, away from the busy restaurant bustle); doubles Rs149; triples Rs200; quads Rs240. Extra person Rs40.

Green's Hotel, 2722/2 Sri Harsha Rd. (tel. 422415), next to Parklane Hotel. Dusty dark corridors lead into surprisingly nice and inexpensive rooms. Mostly Indian clientele. Bucket hot water. Check-out 24hr. Attached restaurant and bar open 10:30am-2:30pm and 5:30-11pm. Singles Rs60; doubles Rs90.

Hotel Dasprakash (tel. 442444 or 444455), on the corner of Gandhi Sq. and Old Bank Rd. Spacious and airy. Palm-fringed courtyard houses an ice cream parlor, astropalmist, and a travel agency. Hot water 4am-11am; towels and soap provided. Seat or squat toilets. Veg. restaurant. Check-out 24hr. Singles Rs135-310; doubles Rs275-435, with A/C Rs575. Major credit cards.

The Hotel Rajmahal Deluxe, Lakshmivilas Rd. (tel. 421196), to the right as you walk out of Jaganmohan Palace. Large, spotless rooms have huge windows, baths (seat toilets), and hot water 6:30-8:30am. Some have TVs. 24hr. room service, friendly staff, laundry service, and travel counter. Check-out 24hr. Singles Rs140, with TV Rs175; doubles Rs200/225; triples with TV Rs285.

The Ritz Hotel, 5 B-N Rd. (tel. 422668), 100m south of the Central Bus Stand, on your right as you exit. High quality, batik-decorated rooms are usually booked solid. Attached baths have seat toilets and 24hr. hot water. Terrific restaurant/bar. Check-out noon. Doubles Rs300. Visa, MC.

Hotel Indra Bhavan, Dhanvantri Rd. (tel. 423933), on the SRRD side. Manned by cordial and sweet old men who are inflexible about 3 rules: no alcohol, no meat, and no dirt. Rooms are well-lit and ugly in a cheerful sort of way. Attached baths and telephones. Good attached restaurant. Local tour info, newspapers, 24hr. STD/ISD service, and laundry. Check-out 24hr. Singles Rs140; doubles Rs150-240; quads Rs270.

FOOD

Mysore's cheapest, tastiest, and most authentic food can be had at one of the myriad "meals" or "tiffins" cafes, where dingy, painted signs proclaim "Meals Ready!" in Kannada and English. *Idlis* (Rs5) or *thalis* (Rs15) are ready in minutes.

Parklane Hotel, Sri Harsha Rd., near New Statue Circle. The menu solemnly notes that "disposable vomit bags are available on request in case of need, and out of consideration for fellow diners." Secluded booths are ideal for twilight wining and dining. Good daily specials. Great *kadai paneer* (Rs50), *tandoori* items (60-150), and veg. *pulao* (Rs36). Beer Rs32-55. Open daily 10am-11:15pm.

Akshaya Vegetarian Restaurant, in the Hotel Dasprakash, serves brimming *thalis* (Rs25-40) to hordes of locals and travelers. Open daily noon-3pm and 7:45-10pm. Tiffin 6-10:30am and 4-10pm.

Samrat, Dhanvantri Rd., inside Hotel Indra Bhavan. The North Indian veg. menu will satisfy your penchant for *paneer.* (16 varieties may well be a Mysore record!) North Indian *thali* Rs55. Open daily noon-3pm and 7-10:15pm.

The Ritz Hotel, 5 B-N Rd. Standard fare attentively spiced and delicately crafted. Candlelit dining and garden patio. Kebab platter Rs70, veg. dishes Rs35-55, meals with drinks from Rs100. Open daily 7am-11pm. Bar open daily 11am-11pm.

Jewel Rock Restaurant, 2716 Sri Harsha Rd., at Hotel Maurya Palace. Serves delectable *tandoori, tikkas,* and *ghee*-laden *biryanis* (Rs38-60). Gingham-checked tablecloths, dim lighting, and jazz muzak. Try the Jewel Special: a sampling of chicken, mutton, and fish kebabs (Rs75). Open daily 11am-3:30pm and 6:30-11pm.

Mylari Hotel, Door #738, Nazarbad Main Rd., past Shree Krishna Continental Hotel. Popular tiffin room is constantly packed with locals enjoying the 2 items on the menu: *dosas* (Rs10) and *idlis* (3 for Rs10). Open 7-11am and 4-7pm.

🎵🛍 ENTERTAINMENT AND SHOPPING

Sterling Cinema in Vidyaranyapuram, near the government silk and oil factories, screens English-language films (Rs30). Take the bus (#3, 8, 11, 13, 14, or 44; every 10min.; 15min) to Vidyaranyapuram. **Bure's Concert Pub,** Sivarampet Rd., Balajee Complex, next to the Rajkumar Theatre, offers a selection of spirits that attracts foreigners and locals alike (open 11am-midnight).

Mysore produces half of India's **sandal oil** as well as massive quantities of **silks, sandalwood,** and **jewelry.** The state government's **Cauvery Emporium,** Satyajit Rao Rd. (tel. 521258), is a giant warehouse of such exotica. They accept AmEx, Visa, MC, and traveler's checks and will arrange packing and export for an extra charge. (Open daily 10-11:30am and 3-7:30pm.) Cauvery has an open-air annex near the Palace (open M-Sa 10am-1:30pm and 3-7:30pm). Cheaper mini-emporia with better prices crowd Dhanvantri Rd. near its intersection with Sayajit Rao Rd. Farther down Sayajit Rao Rd., near K-R Cir., silk stores sell enough *saris* to drape the earth. Many stores' tailors alter dresses or shirts in an afternoon. The **Government Silk Weaving Factory** (tel. 481803), in Vidyaranyapuram, allows tours with prior permission. Here you can watch your silk being woven and buy it later at mill prices. (Open M-Sa 9:30am-4:30pm.) Next door is the **Government Sandal Oil Factory** (tel. 481803), where, with permission, you can schedule a tour (open M-Sa 8am-5pm).

👁 SIGHTS

THE MAHARAJA'S PALACE. The home of the current maharaja and the jewel of the dusty Mysore plateau, the Maharaja's Palace (Amber Vilas) is impressive for its girth (it covers more than 3.5 sq. km) and worth (construction cost Rs4.2 million, not a small sum 100 years ago). Built in the Indo-Saracenic style, the palace is visited daily by slow-moving streams of tourists. In 1897, during the reign of Krishnaraja Wadiyar IV, who had been reinstated as ruler by the British 16 years earlier, the original wooden palace burned to the ground. Immediately afterward, a certain Henry Irwin was commissioned to rebuild it. The task took him and his team of Indian artisans 15 years. Durbar Hall is plastered with murals depicting scenes from the Dussehra festival, complete with scores of cavalry in various stages of uniform. The museum is a must-see for those with an itch for kitsch: gold chariots, slightly androgynous Wadiyar family portraits, a weapon room with scintillating scythes, Ganesh stained-glass windows, and a wax effigy of the maharaja. The **Maharaja's Residential Palace,** visible from the exit of the Palace, with its tarnished cutlery and shabby school uniforms, is rather disappointing. But you don't have to go in to take a camel or elephant ride around the compound. On Sunday nights and government holidays, the palace is illuminated with 80,000 delightfully ostentatious light bulbs. *(Purandara Dasa Rd. Open 10am-5:30pm. Rs10; Residential Palace Rs10. Camel rides Rs10; elephant rides Rs25; horse carriage ride Rs25.)*

CHAMUNDI HILL. Even if you're not religious, Chamundi Hill can be a spiritual experience. The ride affords a divine view of the Deccan plain, with its squares of saffron and green, and other angles present terrific views of Mysore City—even at a distance, you can see the Maharaja's Palace in all its splendor. At the top of the hill, 16m-high Mahishasura, the buffalo demon who plagued Mysore (and from whom the city takes its name) greets you in all his gaudiness. The **Sri Chamundeswari Temple,** with its 40m *gopuram*, derives its name from Chamundi, an incarnation of the goddess Durga who smote Mahishasura. The area is a bit of a madhouse (mind your shoes!), but the rest of the hill is quite peaceful. *(Chamundeswari Temple open 7:30am-2pm and 4-8pm.)* The tiny **Godly Museum,** near the Mahishasura statue, is filled with dioramas depicting various stages of spiritual life. One exhibit delineates "Today's Problematic World," in which troubles all seem to stem from overpopulation. Note the picture of a family of seven on one bicycle and the prophetic sketch of the crowded bus you'll take down the hill. This is also your source for holographic Om stickers. *(Open daily 10:30am-7pm. Free.)* Pilgrims ascend or descend Chamundi Hill's 1000 steps, a journey that takes at least two hours and will have you exclaiming "My-sore feet!" at the end of it all. If you opt to hike it, however, don't miss the **Shiva Temple** one-third of the way up. A granite statue of a corpulent Nandi, Shiva's bull, guards the temple. Nandi has been protecting the temple for 300 years, and it's whispered that each year he, like all of his stone brethren, grows an itsy-bitsy bit. It is expected that in 300 more years, Nandi will grow so large that he'll sit atop Mysore—but that may just be a lot of bull. *(Southeast of town. City bus #201 and special buses, Rs5. Taxis Rs125-175 round-trip. Shiva Temple open 7:30am-2pm and 3:30-9pm.)*

OTHER SIGHTS. The **Jaganmohan Palace,** containing the **Jayachamarajendra Art Gallery,** holds a jumble of ill-exhibited *objets d'art*. A few gems are on display: Rabindranath Tagore watercolors and Raja Ravi Varma oils; a collection of tablas, sitars, and veenas; a series of Buddhas carved on an elephant tusk; and ancient silk game boards. *(2 blocks west of the Maharaja's Palace. Open daily 8am-5pm. Rs10.)* Indian tourists flock to the **Brindavan Gardens** and **Krishnarajendra Dam** on the weekends. The dam was built across the Kaveri River at the turn of the century by Maharaja Krishnaraja Wadiyar Bahadur. The gardens lack flowers, but the fountains are let loose at night, with a much hyped light show accompanied by Hindi and Kannada music. *(City bus #201. Open M-F 7am-8:30pm, Sa-Su 7am-9:30pm. Rs5; camera fee Rs25. Light show M-F 7-7:55pm, Sa-Su 7-8:55pm.)* As Indian zoos go, the **Mysore Zoo,** which spreads over 250 green acres, is rather pleasant. Plenty of tigers (including the endangered white) prowl about their lush, enclosed grounds. Pure white peacocks, languid emurs, ponderous pachyderms, and elegant emus eke out an existence here amidst expertly groomed topiary and gazing *Homo sapiens*. Efforts to house animals in their most natural habitats led to the 1994 escape of two vagrant crocodiles into rural Karnataka. *(Open W-M 8am-5pm. Rs8.)*

NEAR MYSORE: SOMNATHPUR ಸೋಮನತಪುರ

A tiny village 38km east of Mysore, Somnathpur is the site of the famous and beautiful **Keshava Temple,** built in 1268. The village was established and the temple commissioned by Soma, a high officer under the Hoysala King Narasimha II—hence the name Somnathpur. Legend has it that when the temple was completed, the gods deemed it too beautiful and grand (despite its height of only 10m) for this earth and wanted to transport it to heaven. The temple quaked and began to levitate, and the chief sculptor, in his horror, mutilated some of the images on the outside wall to avert such a catastrophe. The slightly disfigured temple came crashing back down to earth. These events explain why the *garudagamba* (stone pillar depicting the divine mount, the eagle Garuda) is not exactly opposite the entrance, as is traditional, but slightly skewed to the northeast. The Keshava Temple contains six strata of carved friezes—elephants, scrolls, geese, and scenes from the *Bhagavad Gita*, *Mahabharata*, and the

Puranas border the exterior, and scores of deity images fill the interior. Though it's dark inside, you can tell that Indra and company were justified in their covetousness—it *is* too beautiful for this earth. To get to Somnathpur, take a private bus from near Wesley Church, or hire a taxi. See **Buses,** p. 478. (Open daily 9am-5:30pm. Rs2; video fee Rs25.)

NEAR MYSORE: SRIRANGAPATNAM ಶ್ರೀರಂಗಪಟ್ಟಣ

Sixteen kilometers from Mysore, Srirangapatnam was the site of Tipu Sultan's island fort and the seat of his vast kingdom until the fourth Anglo-Mysore war in 1799. Tipu and his forces raised quite a fight against the British in South India. Tipu's father, Haider Ali, defeated Mysore's Hindu raja in 1761. In 1782, Tipu inherited the throne and his father's rivalries with the Marathas, the French, and the British. He proved especially fearsome to the East India Company, to whom he dealt two sound defeats before the colonialists turned the tide against him. Tipu met his final defeat here in 1799, ending his subcontinental conquest and opening up the path for the East India Company's expansion in South India. Today, Srirangapatnam is a history buff's heaven—this is, after all, where the roguish ruler and warrior met his demise in an series of legendary events. Barraged by redcoat bullets, Tipu toppled off his horse into a pile of the dead and dying. A British soldier, catching a glimpse of Tipu's ostentatious gold belt buckle, tried to snatch it for booty. But the barely-breathing Tipu lanced the soldier with his ever-ready sword. Alas, the soldier was merely injured and was still sharp enough to lodge a bullet in Tipu's temple. It is rumored that, in the depths of the Karnatakan night, the ghost of Tipu wanders around his former digs in search of his stolen belt buckle. This legend, along with the utter lack of hotels and restaurants in Srirangapatnam, explains why the town is relegated to daytrip status.

Turn left from the bus stand to reach the **Jama Masjid,** the mosque Tipu built on the grounds of an old Hindu temple. Remnants of walls put up to keep the British out encircle the area. According to the Archaeological Survey of India, they are "protected and ancient monuments," but local woman use them to dry cow-dung patties. **Daria Daulat,** Tipu's summer palace, is about 1km from the village (rickshaw Rs20; to walk, make two rights from the bus stand and turn left at the sign). Tipu's main palace was destroyed in 1807 by a Brit, Colonel Wellesley, and its timbers went to build the maharaja's palace in Mysore and St. Stephen's Church in Ooty. The manicured lawns and splendid palace recall a bygone era of pomp and luxury; today, you'll share Tipu's old stomping grounds with busloads of tourists and vagrant Architectural Survey of India guides looking for work. The palace, built in 1784 in an Indo-Islamic style, is now a **museum** housing some marvelous murals of Tipu's battles and portraits of the entire Tipu Sultan clan, including a portrait of Tipu wearing his signature tiger stripes which gave him the title "Tiger of Mysore" (open Sa-Th 9am-5pm). The hospital that housed Colonel Wellesley and company is also on the premises, as is an obelisk commemorating British lives lost in the siege, and the dungeons where Tipu held British soldiers (open Sa-Th 9am-5pm; Rs2). Beyond Daria Daulat, another 1km down the road, lies **Gumbaz,** the mausoleum where Tipu and his father Haider Ali lie (at least during the day). The **Sri Ranganatha Temple,** the town's namesake, dates from the Hoysala age (open daily 8am-1pm and 4-8pm). To reach Srirangapatnam, take a **bus** from Mysore (every 30min. 6am-8pm, Rs7; last return to Mysore 9pm).

HASSAN ಹಸನ

The busy industrial city of Hassan has little tourist appeal and no sights of its own, but its location 40km from the temple villages of Halebid and Belur has ensured its place along South India's tourist trail. Hassan's railway station, bus stands, hotels, and modern conveniences make it a practical place to spend your nights while visiting these nearby areas.

🔼 ORIENTATION AND PRACTICAL INFORMATION

Most hotels and lodges are within 500m of the **bus stand,** which is at the intersection of **Bus Stand Road** (north-south) and **Church Road** (east-west). Running parallel to Bus Stand Rd. 200m to the east is **Race Course Road.** It intersects the second east-west thoroughfare, **Bangalore-Mangalore (B-M) Road,** 300m to the south. The **railway station,** on B-M Rd., is 1km to the east. The city center hugs the bus stand and the intersection of Race Course and B-M Rd.

Trains: The **railway station** serves **Mysore** (#86, 6am; #861, 6:30pm, 3hr., Rs23) and **Arsikere** (#862, 11am, 1½hr., Rs10). Both connect to Bangalore, but Mysore is faster.

Buses: The **bus stand** (tel. 68418) is across from Maharaja's Park. To: **Belur** (every 30min. 6am-8:30pm, 1½hr., Rs10); **Bangalore** (every 15min. 5:30am-7:45pm and midnight, 4hr., Rs50/60); **Halebid** (every 30min. 7:30am--7pm, 1hr., Rs8); **Mangalore** (20 per day 6am-6:30pm, 3½hr., Rs50). To get to **Sravanabelagola,** first go to **Channarayapatna** (every 15min. 5:15am-7:45pm, 1hr., Rs13), from where buses depart (every 20min., 15min., Rs4). For **Hospet/Hampi,** head to **Shimoga** (15 per day 5:30am-8:15pm, 4hr., Rs45) and transfer. Hordes of **private bus** companies go to Bangalore (Rs50). **Tempos** also frequently service Belur and Halebid; from the bus stand, make a left onto Church St., take the first right, and proceed for a few blocks.

Tourist Office: Regional Tourist Office, Vartha Bhavan, B-M Rd. (tel. 68862). From the bus stand, walk 1 block south, turn left onto B-M Rd., walk a few blocks; it's on the left. Friendly and helpful. Open M-Sa 10am-1:30pm and 2-5:30pm.

Immigration Office: Foreigners Registration Office, B-M Rd. (tel. 68000), at the Police Station in the women's grievances office. Open M-F 10am-5:30pm.

Currency Exchange: State Bank of Mysore (tel. 68407), on the corner of Bus Stand and B-M Rd. Changes US$, UK£, and traveler's checks in U.S., Canadian, British, German, and French currencies. Open M-F 10:30am-2:30pm, Sa 10:30am-12:30pm.

Market: The market to the west of the bus stand has pyramids of tangerines, grapes, apples, and mangoes alongside *chaat* carts, *chai* stalls, and omelette fryers.

Pharmacy: Gopal Medicines (tel. 68678), opposite Karnataka Bank. Open 9am-9:30pm.

Hospital: CSI Redfern Memorial Hospital, Race Course Rd. (tel. 67653), 1 block north of the intersection with Church Rd. **Mangala Nursing Home** (tel. 67236).

Post Office: Bus Stand Rd. Open M-Sa 10am-6pm, Su 10am-1pm. **Postal Code:** 573201.

PHONE CODE	08172

◤ ACCOMMODATIONS

Vaishnavi Lodging, Harsha Mahal Rd. (tel. 67413). Exit from the northeast corner of the bus stand, walk east on Church Rd., and turn left. Big rooms with heavy-duty fans, clean sheets, fluffy pillows, phones, and attached baths (squat, baby, squat). Hot water 6-9am. Check-out 24hr. Singles Rs100; doubles Rs140.

Hotel New Abiruchi, B-M Rd. (tel. 67852). From the bus stand, walk 2 blocks south on Bus Stand Rd. and take a right after the police station. Clean rooms and spotless bathrooms with seat toilets. Attached restaurant. Hot water 6-9am. Check-out 24hr. Singles Rs80, with TV Rs145; doubles Rs140/200.

Hotel Suvarna Regency, B-M Rd. (tel. 64006). From Bus Stand Rd., turn right after the police station and follow B-M Rd. to where it turns south; look for the Suvarna Regency's towers. Star TV, phones, seat or squat toilets, travel services, and fluffy towels. Check-out 24hr. Singles Rs280; doubles Rs392, with A/C Rs560; family Rs840.

⬛🅽 FOOD AND NIGHTLIFE

Hotel Sanman, M-O Rd. From the bus stand, head south on Bus Stand Rd. and take the last road before B-M Rd. The fresh and steam-filled *puris* are piled mile-high. Open daily 6am-9:45pm. *Thalis* (Rs15) served 11:30am-4pm and 7-9:45pm.

Suvarna Sagar, B-M Rd., attached to Hotel Survarna. Dishes out adequate if costly South Indian (Rs18-36) and North Indian (Rs35-55) *thalis* and tiffins in a tapestried hall. They've scooped the competition when it comes to ice cream (Rs9-35). 10% surcharge to sit in the A/C section. Open daily 7am-10:30pm.

Hotel GRR, Bus Stand Rd., opposite the bus stand. This Andhran eatery focuses its culinary energy on banana-leaf *thalis* (Rs15). Ornate wooden chairs and stone kitchen enhance the dining experience. Open daily 11:30am-4:30pm and 7:30-11pm.

Golden Gate, behind Suvarna Sagar. For those who can't handle another *thali,* this pricey restaurant offers Continental food such as spaghetti "nepolitine" (Rs50). Indian (Rs30-140) and Chinese (Rs30-70) fare also available. This nightspot for Hassan's well-to-do serves alcohol (Rs30-120) and cocktails (Rs80). Open noon-3pm and 7-11pm.

Malanika Restaurant, Race Course and Hospital Rd., atop the Hotel Amblee. Malanika's is lit with dim, colored light bulbs. Hallucinogenically tinted windows help intensify the buzz (beer: mild Rs44, *super* strong Rs48). Watch out for the mosquitoes in the rooftop garden. Open daily noon-3pm and 7-11pm.

NEAR HASSAN: SRAVANABELAGOLA ಶ್ರವಣಬೆಳಗೊಲ

Sravanabeagola's 17m-high statue of the Jain saint Bahubali is said to be the world's tallest monolithic statue. The beatific smile of the naked holy man, also called Gomateshvara, blesses the tiny town with serenity. The streets are clean and empty, the air is suffused with calm, and the touts are less aggressive than their postcard-pushing brethren in most temple towns. While the main attraction is, of course, the towering statue, Sravanabelagola is also the site of some important and even longer-standing Jain *bastis* (temples).

The **bus stand** is on **Bangalore (CR Patna) Road,** across from the Chandragiri hilltop Jain *bastis.* Buses leave for **Bangalore** (6:45, 8, 10am, and 3pm; 3hr.; Rs38); **Chanayapatna** (every 15min. 6am-8:30pm, 15min., Rs3); **Hassan** (6, 7:45, 8:30am, and 1:45pm; 45min.; Rs10); and **Mysore** (7:15am, 2½hr., Rs31). Make a right from the station onto Bangalore Rd., and your first right will be **Kalyani Road,** which fronts many small stores and cold-drink shops and leads to **Temple Road.** The hill upon which Bahubali and many of the *bastis* stand looms to the right, with the KSTDC **tourist office** (tel. 57254) at its base. The staff speaks little English, but their tours (Rs100) are helpful. (Open M-Sa 10am-5:30pm.) **Telephone Code:** 08176.

Most visitors make Sravanabelagola a daytrip, but the town has plenty of accommodations, in part because of the Mahamastakabhisheka ceremony, which attracts thousands of Jain pilgrims here every 12 years. Visitors should respect the Jain prohibitions of meat and alcohol. The Jain **lodging houses,** which must be reserved through the central **Accommodations Office** (tel. 57258), have quiet, clean doubles with attached baths (seat toilet) for Rs50. Turn left from the bus stand; they're on the left. Farther down the street, **Yatri Nivas** has bigger, marginally more luxurious rooms also reserved through the Accommodations Office (singles Rs60; doubles Rs80-160; triples Rs210).

Built around AD 980, the **Bahubali statue,** sitting atop Indragiri Hill, is a relatively recent fixture in Sravanabelagola. Son of the first Jain *tirthankara,* and a saint in his own right, Bahubali wears an enlightened smile and not much else. Vines creep up his legs, snakes coil around his feet, and anthills fester at his ankles, all symbolizing the renunciant's detachment from the world of sense. The 620 steps leading to the statue require about 15 to 20 minutes of dedicated climbing. Wear a pair of thick socks if your soles are not ascetically hardened to the touch of burning granite. A group of tired-looking old men can carry you up in a chair for Rs80. (The temple housing the statue is open daily sunrise-sunset. *Puja* 8am and 8pm. Visit in the morning to avoid the crowds and the heat.)

ROAD WRITING The backsides of Indian motor vehicles make for interesting recreational reading. Even the most fume-filled of city drives can be brightened by a simple game of "guess-the-rickshaw-driver's-religion-from-his-bumper-stickers." Similarly, road trips offer the eye-candy of those humorously ominous warnings painted on the backs of lumbering Tatas and Ashok-Leylands. The most pervasive genre of this lorry literature is the proper-horn-use statement: "Soundhorn," "No Horn!," and the ubiquitously inane "Horn OK Please." The latter phrase finds its origins in the days when many Indian goods carriers had a centered, cyclopic brake light. The "Horn Please" directed drivers to signal if they wished to pass the larger, slower vehicle. If the truck driver saw fit to allow such a maneuver, he would tap his brake, and the center light, labeled "OK," would flash. Eventually the one taillight became two, but by then word order stayed. "Horn OK Please" was fixed in the mind and tailgate of Indian automotive consciousness.

Every 12 years the Jain mega-festival **Mahamastakabhisheka** is held here. On the eve of the ceremony, scaffolding is erected behind the monument, and 1008 pots of sacred and colored water are placed in front of the statue. Priests and wealthy devotees chant *mantras* as they anoint Bahubali with water, milk, dates, bananas, jaggery, curds, *ghee*, sugar, almonds, and gold and silver flowers. Thousands of awe-struck pilgrims attend the sticky ceremony in pin-drop silence. The next Mahamastakabhisheka is scheduled for 2005.

Tall, naked ascetics tend to get all the attention, and Bahubali is certainly no exception. However, the hills surrounding him have been a Jain pilgrimage site long before the statue was carved. The Jain *bastis* scattered throughout the town were built over several centuries, forming an architectural history of the hills. The Mauryan emperor Chandragupta alighted upon Sravanabelagola in 300BC, when he abdicated his throne to retire here as an ascetic. His guru Bhadrabahu reached enlightenment here and passed away in a cave on Chandragiri Hill. Chandragupta, after whom the hill is named, faithfully spent days inside the cave worshipping the footprints of his deceased teacher until he, too, died of starvation. The site still attracts pilgrims who believe that viewing the prints cures all illness.

HALEBID ಹಳೇಬೀಡು

Visitors may find it difficult to imagine Halebid in its heyday in the 12th and 13th centuries, when it was "Dwarasamudram," the capital of the magnificent Hoysala Empire famed for its wealth and culture. Halebid's current name means "Destroyed City," a fitting description; the village today is home to more cows and goats than kings and sculptors. But the aged grandeur of Halebid's temple seems oddly fitting for this serene village of 6000. With the Western Ghats rising in the distance, small children playing games in the road, and old men gossiping over *chai* in mud cottages, Halebid indulges all romantic stereotypes of India's long-lost simplicity. That is, until one of the sweet children morphs into a vehement postcard tout, lurching you back to reality.

Halebid has more 12th-century shrines than banks, police stations, hospitals, and telephones combined. The **Hoysalesvara Temple,** the only star-shaped soapstone edifice in town, is hard to miss. Across from it lies the **bus stand.** Buses go to: **Arsikere** (10 per day, 3hr., Rs18); **Belur** (every 30min. 7am-6:30pm, 45min., Rs3); and **Hassan** (15 per day 6:30am-7pm, 1hr., Rs8). Private **maxicabs** going to Hassan and Belur aggressively bid for potential customers in front of the temple. To the right of the bus stand, the Department of Tourism runs the village's only lodging, the **Hotel Mayura.** An enormously energetic, safari-suited employee will supply you with information on every subject from their **Tourist Help Desk** (open M-Sa 10am-5:30pm). The **Jain Mandir (Bagadi Hall)** is 500m down, after you turn left at the fork in the road. The **post office** is located on the street to the left of the bus stand (open M-F 9:30am-5:30pm, Sa 10am-1pm). **Postal Code:** 573121. **Telephone Code:** 08177.

Halebid's **Hotel Mayura** (tel. 73224) is the only lodging in town. All rooms have attached baths and 24-hour hot water. (Singles Rs100; doubles Rs150/200; quads Rs250.) The attached **restaurant** serves a standard tourist menu with Indian and Chinese food (*thalis* Rs20; open 7am-11pm). The bus stand also has a **restaurant**, with *thalis* (Rs14) and good *dosas* (Rs9; open 5:30am-8:30pm).

👁 SIGHTS

HOYSALESVARA TEMPLE. The largest of the Hoysalan temples, **Hoysalesvara Temple** overlooks the vast Dwarasamudra Lake and is surrounded by immaculately tended gardens. Construction began in 1121, but before it could be completed, the armies of the Delhi Sultanate sacked the temple and town. By the time of India's Independence, only 14 of the original 84 large statues remained, and only one of the "bracket figures" (the mini-statues for which Belur's temple is famed) was left. Those that were not destroyed or vandalized were stolen—British museums display quite a few of them. The Archaeological Survey of India took over the temple in 1952 to protect it from the elements and graffiti-writing vandals; today the detail, humor, and accuracy of the temple's engravings are awe-inspiring.

The temple is actually composed of two Shiva temples situated on a single, star-shaped platform. The larger of the two was commissioned by the Hoysala king Vishnuvardhana, and the smaller one by his senior wife, the famed dancer Shantaladevi. Like all Hoysalan temples, the deities face east towards the sunrise, though the absence of a *gopuram* indicates that it's no longer a place of worship. Over 20,000 elaborate figures remain in and around the temple, and the unusually funny and well-informed ASI-sanctioned **guides** will point out the best and the brightest (*guides Rs30 for up to 5 people*).

Six strata of **frieze work** border the base of the temple: elephants, lions, geese, horsemen, scrolls, stories from the *Puranas* and epics. Larger, gorier engravings of gods and goddesses line the upper exterior walls: Shiva killing an elephant demon by severing his trunk and then dancing in the pachyderm's stomach in celebration; Vishnu peeling off the face of a demon as you would peel a banana; and Bhima tossing elephants over his shoulders like grenades. The carvings have provided scholars with anthropological and historical information. One scene, for example, depicts a monarch peering through a surprisingly modern-looking telescope. The temple also houses two *lingas* and a platform once used for devotional dances. Leave your shoes at the entrance (Rs1).

OTHER SIGHTS. The **Archaeological Museum,** a stone's throw from the temple, houses deity statues from the town's temples and nearby ruins. Half of it is outdoors, and some of the statues—fortunately, they're labeled—sit in a pretty garden with a fountain. (*Open Sa-Th 10am-5pm. Free.*) The 12th-century **Jain Bastis,** built by King Vishnu Vardhevna before he converted to Hinduism, are styled much like the town's Hindu temples, though the images etched in soapstone tell stories of a different faith. The most prominent of these is the **Parswanathasamy Temple,** held up by 12 columns. Their simple design—so smooth you can see your own reflection—is meant to convey the serenity of meditation and worship. (*500m south of the temple. Open 10am-5pm. Puja 9am.*)

BELUR ಬೇಲೂರು

Belur, a little town on the right bank of the Yagachi River, was the capital of the Hoysalan empire before Halebid usurped this honor in the 12th century. Seven hundred years and several dynasties later, Belur has become a blink-and-you'll-miss-it town. Its two roads are lined with dank eateries, tea stalls, and a few meager stores which betray none of the town's gilded history. Only the Chennakeshava Temple, set apart from the town by its tall *gopuram*, reminds visitors of its glorious past. Although Belur has more hotels and restaurants than Halebid, most tourists prefer Halebid's peaceful village feel to Belur's rough small-town vibe.

KARNATAKA

◪ ORIENTATION AND PRACTICAL INFORMATION. There are two roads in Belur. **Main Road** is roughly perpendicular to **Temple Road,** which runs from the **bus stand** to the Chennakeshava Temple. Buses to: **Arsikere** (every 30-60min. 6am-7pm, 1½hr., Rs13); **Halebid** (every 30-60min. 6am-8pm, 45min., Rs4-5); **Hassan** (every hr. 5:30am-11:30pm, 1hr., Rs10); **Mangalore** (every hr. 5:30am-11:30pm, 5hr., Rs58-68); and **Mysore** (every hr. 5:30am-6:45pm, 4hr., Rs35). **Auto-rickshaws** head to the temple (Rs5), but you can walk there in under 10 minutes. From the bus stand, turn left onto Main Rd.; the **post office** is a few blocks down on the left. On the way, you'll pass the **Karnataka Tourist Office,** inside the Mayura Velapuri Hotel Complex (tel. 22209; open M-Sa 10:30am-5:30pm); if no one's there, check inside the hotel or restaurant. The unmarked **Government Hospital** (tel. 22333) is just past the hotel complex, and the **State Bank of Mysore,** farther down, changes currency (open M-F 10:30am-2:30pm, Sa 10:30am-12:30pm). **Postal Code:** 573115. **Telephone Code:** 08177.

◪◪ ACCOMMODATIONS AND FOOD. The limited lodging options in Belur run the gamut from cheap and functional to cheaper and less functional—no A/C or TVs here. Dining is best done in one of the hotels. You won't see roaches scuffle across the clean floor of **Hotel Mayura Velapuri** (tel. 22209), the priciest hotel in town. Utilitarian, though dark, rooms and a gregarious proprietor let you know you're livin' large. (Singles Rs135-160; doubles Rs200.) The **restaurant** at Hotel Mauryan dishes up *thalis* (Rs25) and Continental snacks (open daily 6:30am-10:30pm). **Swagath Tourist Home** (tel. 22159), a few minutes' walk down Temple Rd., is cheaper, cheerier, and more intimate than its neighbors. Owned by the family who runs the market below, the Swagath has pretty pink balconies overlooking a tiny courtyard. (Check-out 24hr. Doubles Rs60.) **Hotel Annapoorna** serves a good *thali* (Rs15; open daily 6am-10pm) and has decent doubles with bath (Rs150).

◙ SIGHTS. Perhaps Vishnu's fearsome eagle-mount Garuda, who guards the famous **Chennakeshava Temple,** saved it from the brutal ransacking Halebid suffered. Along with those at Somnathpur and Halebid, this temple is considered one of the best examples of Hoysala architecture. The Hoysala king Vishnuvardhana commissioned the temple to commemorate his conversion from Jainism to Hinduism, and even though three generations of sculptors devoted their lives to its construction, the Chennakeshava Temple was never finished.

Like the temples at Halebid and Somnathpur, Chennakeshava has a base covered with astoundingly detailed horizontal friezes. To bear the weight of the temple, 644 stone elephants, each one unique, stand at the bottom. Nine statues of Vishnu surround the exterior. The emblem of the Hoysalan empire—its first emperor smiting a half-lion, half-tiger beast—also stands outside. When he was a boy, the emperor Sala and his guru were sitting under a tree when this ferocious animal appeared. Sala stared the beast down as his guru shouted **"Hoy, Sala"** ("Kill, Sala"). The courageous boy founded the great Hoysalan Empire, which ruled over Karnataka and parts of Tamil Nadu from the 10th to 14th centuries.

The temple is renowned for the 42 mini-statues, or **bracket figures,** which line the interior ceilings and exterior walls. The detail of these sculptures is incredible. Voluptuous women with jingling bangles and head pendants are carved out of a single stone. Another wears an expression of longing as she holds a letter to her far-away lover while a lusty monkey tugs at the edge of her *sari*. The famed **Thribhanghi Nritya,** a classical dancer, contorts her body in such a way that a drop of water from her right hand grazes the tip of her nose, then her left breast, and then hits the thumb of her left hand before it lands at the arch of her right foot.

Inside the temple is a platform once used by the *devadasis* (temple dancers), a waiting area for the audience, and several four-ton columns which were so heavy that they had to be turned by elephants while sculptors detailed them. The **Narasimha Pillar** at the center of the temple contains miniature replicas of all of the temple's other carvings. One square is left empty to indicate that, despite the efforts of the earthly artists, God can never be truly depicted.

Two images of Vishnu sit inside the **sanctum**—a large, silver-plated image to which pilgrims still pray daily and a smaller wooden sculpture used in temple processions. Carved on the wall in front of the image is a strange creature with a peacock's tail, a boar's body, a lion's feet, a crocodile's mouth, a monkey's eyes, an elephant's trunk, and a cow's ears. The animal possesses the best part of each of the animals, making it more perfect than any single animal and, thus, fit to guard Vishnu himself. (Non-Hindus may view the images. *Puja* 9am and 7pm.)

The Vijayanagar Dynasty constructed the temple's original **gopuram,** which has since been rebuilt due to a fire. On the bottom right-hand corner, as you exit the temple, are some particularly erotic engravings, and if you hire one of the authorized ASI **guides** (Rs30 for a very well-done 1hr. tour), he'll be sure to point them out to you. Leave your shoes and inhibitions at the door. (Temple open daily 8am-8:30pm. Inner sanctum closed 1-3pm. Free; Rs1 for shoe storage.)

MANGALORE ಮಂಗಳೂರು

An important trading port for centuries and a major shipbuilding center during the 18th century, the city of Mangalore retains its mercantile feel but little of its erstwhile glory. Nowadays, Mangalore has distinguished itself as India's major cashew and coffee processor and *bidi*-production center—it's little wonder that Mangalore isn't exactly a tourist magnet. Nevertheless, it's a modern, bustling city with plenty of budget hotels and cheap restaurants. As a transport node between Goa and Kerala, Mangalore makes a fine stopover and, with the recent completion of the Konkan Railway, its importance to travelers will only increase.

▐ TRANSPORTATION

Airport: Bajpe Airport, 22km from town, can be reached by local buses #47A and 47B or by taxi (Rs250). **Indian Airlines** (tel. 455259), on Hat Hill (rickshaw Rs12 from Rao Rd.). Open daily 9:30am-1pm and 1:45-4pm. To: **Bangalore** (3 per week, 1hr., US$70); **Chennai** (3 per week, 2hr., US$95); **Mumbai** (1 per day, 1hr., US$115). **Jet Airways,** KS Rao Rd. (tel. 440694 or 752709), has flights for the same prices to Bangalore (daily) and Mumbai (12 per week).

Trains: The **railway station,** 300m south of the Rao and Lighthouse Rd. intersection. Reservations open M-Sa 8am-8pm, Su 8am-2pm. Fares listed are 2nd/1st class. To: **Calicut** (6 per day, 5hr., Rs61/319); **Chennai** (*Mangalore-Chennai Mail* 6602, 11:45am, 18hr.; *West Coast Exp.* 6628, 6:55pm, 18hr., Rs253/825); **Ernakulam** (*Parsuram Exp.* 6350, 3:23am, 10hr.; *Malabar Exp.* 6030, 4:30pm, 10hr., Rs155/496); **Madgaon** (*Kurla Superfast* 2620, 9pm, 5hr., Rs124/450); **Mumbai** (*Kurla Superfast* 2620, 9pm, 15hr., Rs320/830); **Trivandrum** (*Malabar Exp.* 6030, 4:30pm, 15hr., Rs220/678).

Bus: Private buses run from the new bus stand located near the intersection of Maidan and W. Maidan Rd. Many companies have offices at the old bus stand, in the alleyway near the intersection of Lighthouse Hill and KS Rao Rd. **Ganesh Travels** (tel. 441277) sends buses to: **Bangalore** (9 per day, 8hr., Rs165/180); **Cochin** (8:10pm, 10hr., Rs210); **Mumbai** (4 per day, 22hr., Rs350/400); **Mysore** (5:30am and 10:30pm, 7hr., Rs135); **Panjim** (9:30pm, 9hr., Rs150). There are also several small travel operators in and around Hampankatta who can get you to most places. **KSRTC Bus Stand** is located 3km from the center of town in Bijai, a Rs15 auto-rickshaw trip from Hampankatta. Its buses go to: **Bangalore** (14 per day, 8hr., Rs135); **Hassan** (every 30min., 4hr., Rs65); **Mysore** (15 per day, 7hr., Rs135); **Panjim** (2 per day, 10hr., Rs122).

Local Transportation: Most **local buses** stop on Dr. UP Maliya Rd., near Town Hall. **Auto-rickshaws** are the easiest way to get around. Except for those around the bus and railway stations, most will use the meter with a Rs7 flag-fall.

▐ ORIENTATION AND PRACTICAL INFORMATION

Mangalore's mangled street plan can make navigation tricky. In the heart of the city, **Hampankatta** consists of a chaotic traffic circle from which six major thoroughfares radiate. Down the hill, about 300m to the south, is the **railway station;** on the other side of the hill, heading north, is **KS Rao Road,** home of most budget hotels and restaurants; heading west toward the ocean is **Maidan Road,** which runs past the **Town Hall;** and heading east, sharply uphill, is **Lighthouse Hill Road.**

Tourist Office: Department of Tourism Information Office, in Hotel Indraprastha, Lighthouse Hill Rd. (tel. 442926). No maps, but the friendly staff answers questions and gives directions. Open M-Sa 10:30am-1:30pm and 2:30-5:30pm.

Currency Exchange: State Bank of India, KS Rao Rd., exchanges cash and traveler's checks. Open M-F 10am-2pm and 2:30-3:30pm, Sa 10am-12:30pm.

Bookstore: Higginbothams, Lighthouse Hill Rd. (tel. 427585), near the intersection with KS Rao Rd., has a small section of fiction and textbooks. Open M-Sa 9:30am-1:30pm and 3:30-7:30pm. **Athree Book Centre,** 4 Sharavathi Bldg., Balmatta Rd. (tel. 425161), close to the intersection with Lighthouse Hill Rd., has a better selection but is far from the city center. Open M-Sa 8:30am-1pm and 2:30-8pm.

Pharmacy: City Drug House (tel. 217357), next to City Hospital. Open 24hr.

Hospital: Government-run **Wenlick Hospital** (tel. 425038), in Hampankatta. **City Hospital** (tel. 217424), in Kadri, 3km from Hampankatta (take a rickshaw).

Police: (tel. 426426), close to the central post office just beyond Shetty Circle.

Post Office: Dr. UP Mallya Rd., southwest from Town Hall past Shetty Circle. *Poste Restante:* c/o Postmaster, Central PO, Mangalore. Open M-F 10am-6pm.

Internet: I-net 107 Cyber Cafe, KS Rao Rd. (tel. 441042; email inet107@hotmail.com), in the Classique Arcade, has 10 terminals, each with full web access (Rs65 per hr.), plus cold drinks and techno music. Save money at **Kohinoor Computer Zone,** Lighthouse Hill Rd., close to Hotel Indraprastha (Rs50 per hr.). No techno.

Telephones: 24hr. **STD/ISD** booths abound on KS Rao Rd., and a few allow callbacks. The main **Telegraph Office,** Dr. UP Maliya Rd., next to the GPO, allows collect calls.

PHONE CODE	0824

▲ ACCOMMODATIONS

Weary travelers need look no farther than KS Rao Rd., where the hotels are uniformly cheap, clean, and pleasant. Most own back-up generators, so you can lounge in well-fanned, Star TV'd bliss all day long.

Hotel Naufal (tel. 428085). With the Town Hall on your left, follow Maidan Rd. to Mission St.; it's on your right. A so-so hotel at so-cheap prices. Smiling staff guides you to spartan rooms (no top sheets—just like in Sparta) and bathrooms with seat toilets; hot water 6-9am. The waterfront is only a short walk away. Jasmine Restaurant downstairs serves basic fare. Singles Rs100; doubles Rs150; triples Rs200.

Hotel Shaan Plaza, KS Rao Rd. (tel. 440312). This large well-kept hotel distinguishes itself by its staff who, unsolicited, brings extra towels, enquires after your meals, and generally anticipates your every unspoken need. Huge rooms have heavy-duty fans. Room service, telephones, seat toilets, and Star movies, too. Singles Rs270; doubles Rs350, with A/C Rs600. Extra person Rs70, in A/C room Rs100.

Hotel Mangalore International, KS Rao Rd. (tel. 444860). Though it's a bit pricier, the staff takes personal pride in the hotel and is keen to point out its virtues, of which cleanliness and modernity are prominent. Complimentary breakfast brought to your room. Check-out 24hr. Singles Rs450, with A/C 650; doubles Rs550/750.

Hotel Roopa, Balmatta Rd. (tel. 421271), Hampankatta. A good alternative for those wishing to avoid "hotel central" on KS Rao Rd. Uninspired decor but functional and comfortable. Check-out noon. Singles Rs125; doubles Rs175, with A/C Rs450.

FOOD

Janatha Restaurant, in the Hotel Shaan Plaza. This busy restaurant serves up North and South Indian dishes along with ice cream treats (Rs10-24). The mushroom *masala* is yummy and affordable at Rs28. Open daily 7am-10:30pm.

Pai Cafe, in Hotel Navaratna. An excellent veg. restaurant, with delectable *puri thalis* (Rs16), *chaat*, South Indian breakfasts, and Bengali sweets. Open daily 6am-10pm.

Tai Chien, in Hotel Moti Mahal, Fahir Rd., just beyond Milagres Church. An impeccable spread of silverware, porcelain, linens, sauces, and pickles is only vaguely discernible in the dim light of Chinese lanterns, but the food is so good you won't need to see it. Szechuan pork ribs Rs75. Beer and liquor available. Open daily 7-10:30pm.

The Galley, in Manjuran Hotel (tel. 420420). Don your last clean t-shirt and take a rickshaw (Rs10 from KS Rao Rd.) to Mangalore's fanciest address. Pricey, but the food and atmosphere are scrumptious. The menu offers Indian and Continental dishes, but the kitchen takes requests. Enjoy the delicate fish almondine (Rs120) as you sway to the sounds of Urdu love songs, performed live Sa-Su evenings. Frequent special *prix fixe* meals (Rs150). Open daily 12:30-3pm and 7:30-11pm.

SIGHTS

LIGHTHOUSE HILL. The **Lighthouse** by itself, orange racing stripe and all, is not worth the walk up the hill, but situated in Tagore Park, it is surrounded by lovely gardens with fine views of the city—a fair reward for a bit of sweat. Just beyond the lighthouse to the left is the Jesuit **St. Aloysius College Chapel,** whose painted ceilings date from 1899. *(Chapel open daily 8:30-10am, noon-2pm, and 3:30-6pm. English mass M-Sa 6:30 and 7am, Su 6:30 and 8am; ceiling ogling not welcome during Sa-Su services.)*

MANJUNATH TEMPLE. Once a center for the Shaiva and Tantric Natha-Pantha cult, the temple is noted for its bronze figures, including a 10th-century seated Lokeshvara, considered among India's finest. The gabled, towered temple complex is surrounded by nine tanks. A path opposite the temple leads to several shrines, then to the **Shri Yogishwar Math,** whose Tantric *sadhus* are depicted contemplating Kala Bhairawa (a terrifying aspect of Shiva), Agni (the god of fire), and Durga. *(5km north of the city center at the bottom of Kadri Hill. Various city buses go there; rickshaws Rs25 round-trip.)*

SULTAN'S BATTERY. Sultan's Battery, on the headlands of the old port, is a fort constructed by Tipu Sultan. There's not a great amount to see here, but it's a peaceful river scene. Check out the hundreds of scurrying fiddler crabs—the ones with those big asymmetric front claws—down by the river. *(5km north of the city center; take the #16 bus or a rickshaw for about Rs45 round-trip.)*

HOSPET ಹೋಸಪೇಟ್

The famed Vijayanagar king Krishnadevaraya built Hospet between 1509 and 1520 and it quickly became one of his favorite haunts. Today, all traces of the Vijayanagar Empire have been effaced and Hospet embodies humdrum Karnataka, treading the line between heavy industrialization—blaring, barreling trucks transporting the products of a burgeoning steel industry—and village life—pigs, roosters, and dogs sifting through the streetside trash. The only visible reminders of the Vijayanagar heyday are the regular buses to Hampi, where most of the ruins remain. Although food and lodging can also be found in Hampi, Hospet offers easy access to transportation and a modicum of luxury unavailable in Hampi.

TRANSPORTATION

Trains: Hospet Junction Station (tel. 131), 750m from the bus stand at the end of Station Rd. Enquiry counter open 24hr. Reservation counter open daily 8am–8pm. To: **Ban-**

KARNATAKA

galere (*Hampi Exp.*, 6:30am and 8:10pm, 11hr., Rs577/183); **Gadag** for connections to **Bijapur** (*Hampi Exp.* 6592, 7:30am; *Amaravati Exp.* 7225, 10:30am, 2½hr., Rs30); **Guntakal,** for **Delhi** and **Mumbai** (*Hampi Exp.*, 8:10 and 11pm, Rs30); **Hyderabad** (*Hampi Exp.* 7316, 11pm, 12hr., Rs645/202).

Buses: The **bus station,** Station Rd. (tel. 28802), across from Hotel Vishwa. Enquiry counter open 24hr. Reservation counters open 8am-noon and 3-6pm. To: **Badami** (6:45, 9:30am, and 1pm; Rs51); **Bangalore** (15 per day 5:30am-2:45am, 9hr., Rs92/119); **Bijapur** (7 per day 5:30am-1pm, Rs62); **Hassan** (10am and 11:30pm, 10hr., Rs90); **Hyderabad** (6 per day 9:30am-1am, 11hr., Rs113); **Mangalore** (7:30 and 8:30pm, 13hr., Rs137); **Mysore** (7 per day 5am-10:30pm, Rs115/135).

Local Transportation: Auto-rickshaws (Rs60-80 to Hampi) are unmetered, and **cycle-rickshaws** abound (Rs8 to the railway station). **Local buses** go to **Hampi** from platform 10 (every 30min. 6am-7:30pm, Rs3-4). **Khizer Cycle Market,** Station Rd., Thaluk Office Complex, rents **bikes** (Rs3 per hr., Rs30 per day). Open daily 7am-6pm.

🔢 ORIENTATION AND PRACTICAL INFORMATION

Life in Hospet revolves around **Station Road** (occasionally called MG Road), which runs roughly north to south from the **railway station** past the **bus station,** turning into **Main Bazaar Road** in Hospet's commercial area. It bridges two canals in the process, as well as the northeast-running **Hampi Road** and the **Tungabhadra Dam Road,** which runs west and skirts the market area.

Tourist Office: Karnataka Dept. of Tourism and **KSTDC,** whose commercial wing organizes tours, share an office (tel. 28537) at the corner of College and Old Bus Stand Rd. Make a left onto Station Rd. from the bus station; take your first left onto College, then your first left onto Old Bus Stand Rd. **Tours** of Hampi and the Tungabhadra Dam Rs60. Decent maps of Hampi and information about Karnataka's other hotspots. Dept. of Tourism open M-Sa 10am-5:30pm. Closed 2nd Sa. KSTDC open daily 7:30am-10pm.

Budget Travel: Monika Travels, Station Rd. (tel. 27446), left from the bus station, on the left. Books air, rail, and bus tickets, and rent cars. Open daily 9:30am-9pm.

Currency Exchange: State Bank of India, Station Rd. (tel. 25478), a few steps north of Hotel Priyadarshini. Changes US$ and UK£ only. **State Bank of Mysore,** Station Rd., Thaluk Office Compound (tel.24918), changes traveler's checks and US$ and UK£. Both open M-F 10:30am-2:30pm.

Pharmacy: Several cluster around Hotel Priyadarshini.

Hospital: Government General Hospital (tel. 28444, emergency tel. 28199), west on College Rd. and left immediately after the college. Cross a canal and continue; the hospital is on the right. Refurbished and very clean. **Medinowa** is a new private hospital.

Police: (tel. 24833), 200m south of the tourist office.

Post Office, Station Rd. (tel. 28210), south of the bus stand. Open M-Sa 8am-12:30pm and 2-5:30pm. **Postal Code:** 583201.

| **PHONE CODE** | 08394 |

📷 ACCOMMODATIONS

📷 **Malligi Tourist Home,** 6/143 JN Rd. (tel. 2810106), 250m south of the bus stand; turn left before the 2nd intersection. Regular rooms are a good value, but luxury digs are spectacular. New pool open Tu-Su 7am-7pm (Rs25 per hr. non-deluxe room guests). Check-out 24hr. Singles Rs140-170; doubles Rs140-170; deluxe Rs550-1600.

Hotel Priyadarshini, V/45 Station Rd. (tel. 28838), 500m south of the railway station. 82 spacious rooms with phones, heavy-duty fans, room service, and same-day laundry. Each has a balcony, some with nice views. Hot water 6:30-10am. Two good attached restaurants. Check-out 24hr. Singles Rs175; doubles Rs250. A/C rooms Rs675.

Hotel Shalini, Station Rd. (tel. 28910), 300m south of the railway station. With flowering trees in front of its tiny pink facade, the place makes up for in character what it lacks in convenience or cleanliness. Squat toilets and bucket hot water 7-9am. Bring your own sheets. Check-out 24hr. Singles Rs50; doubles Rs80; triples Rs90; quads Rs150.

FOOD

Waves Restaurant, in Malligi. This ultra-slick restaurant overlooking the swimming pool could just as easily be Bangalore's hippest hot-spot. Expect to pay Rs100 for a meal. Kashmiri *pulao* Rs50, chicken *tikka* Rs55, delicious pancakes with honey Rs30. Open daily 6:30am-11:30pm.

Manasa, in Hotel Priyadarshini, fulfills your cravings for Continental cuisine with shepherd's pie (Rs55), farmer's bake (Rs45) and fruit trifle (Rs20), but it also offers Indian and Chinese dishes (non-veg. Rs45, veg. Rs25-30), beer (Rs50-60), and spirits (Rs17-60). Open daily noon-3pm and 7-11pm.

Naivedyam Restaurant, also in Hotel Priyadarshini, dishes out fresh, huge portions. North and South Indian *thalis* (Rs18-35) with your choice of *chapati* or *puri*. *Alu* and *palak* prepared a million different ways (Rs16-24). Open daily 7am-10:30pm, for *thalis* noon-3:15pm and 7-10:30pm.

HAMPI ಹಂಪೆ

It is said that gold once rained down on Hampi, figuratively, if not literally. The city was awash in rubies and diamonds, and wealth dripped from its corniced rooftops, flowing into its gutters and filling its sacred tanks. The Vijayanagar king would regularly distribute his weight in precious metals to the area's needy. But riches eventually begat ruin. Five dynasties ruled the resplendent kingdom and its capital from 1336, building all manner of temples, pavilions, aqueducts, and palaces, but a confederacy of Muslim sultans from the north annihilated the empire in 1565 and sopped up Vijayanagar's wealth, leaving the once thriving capital dry and desolate.

Despite ongoing attempts by UNESCO and the Archaeological Survey of India to restore the Vijayanagar ruins to their 15th-century splendor, Hampi may never dispense with the pervading aura of decay embodied by its desolate landscape, languid pace of life, and utterly decadent tourist culture. Hampi has become one of India's hottest hippie hang-outs. After the Christmas raves in Goa, the crew packs up and heads to the banks of the Tungabhadra River, bringing their acid parties with them, much to the frustration of the town's residents. Hampi's season runs from September to March, peaking between December and February, but more than a few expats have turned a week's stay into years, using the ruins for drug dens or eloping with Hampiites and settling down on the other side of the Tungabhadra River to avoid the police. Isolated from time and urbanity, Hampi is an alluring permanent oasis for any traveler seeking to slow down; the chance you take by going to Hampi is that you might decide never to leave.

ORIENTATION AND PRACTICAL INFORMATION

The ruins of Vijayanagar spread 26 sq. km, and the bulk of them start at **Kamalapuram,** a village 4km southeast of **Hampi Bazaar.** The paved road from Kamalapuram skirts the **Palace Area,** the **Zenana Enclosure,** the **Krishna Temple,** and many other shrines, boulder formations, coconut groves, and sugarcane fields before reaching the Hampi Bazaar. The bazaar is actually a clump of guest houses, restaurants, and bauble shops that cluster around the **Virupaksha Temple** and its 53m *gopuram.* About 2km to the northeast of the bazaar lies the other major area of ruins, including the **Vittala Temple.**

> **WARNING.** Muggings and rapes have been reported in past years in the area near Vittala Temple. **Foreigners are asked to register with the police at Hampi** when they first arrive in town.

Local Transportation: Buses to **Hospet** depart from the intersection of Hampi Bazaar and the road to Hospet (every 30min. 7am-8pm, 45min., Rs3-4). **Auto-rickshaws** shuttle between Hampi Bazaar and **Kamalapuram** (Rs5) and **Hospet** (Rs50). Prices double at night. The best way to get around town is to rent a **bike** at Guru's Bicycle Shop, right behind the tourist office (Rs25-30 per day; Rs3-5 per hr.). Open daily7:30am-6pm.

Tourist Office (tel. 41339), 100m towards the Virupaksha Temple from the bus stop. Get a detailed map of the ruins, and hire an approved **guide** (in season Rs100-500, off season Rs100). Government of India guides charge Rs400 because they are approved to provide information on places outside Hampi. Open M-Sa 10am-5pm. Closed 2nd Sa.

Currency Exchange: Canara Bank (tel. 41243) exchanges only AmEx and Thomas Cook traveler's checks in U.S., British, and French currencies. Open M-F 11am-2pm. In season, various travel agencies exchange currency—try **Modi,** next to the tourist office.

Hospital: The nearest medical services are in Hospet.

Police: (tel. 41241), inside the Virupaksha Temple, immediately to your right. Registering here when you get in town takes 2min. Open 24hr. (closed for breaks). There's also a branch in Kanakpuram (tel. 41240), east of the bus stand.

Post Office: (tel. 41242), just outside the temple, beside the *gopuram. Poste Restante.* Open M-Sa 8:30am-1:30pm and 2-4:30pm. **Postal Code:** 583239.

Telephones: The bazaar's **STD/ISD** booths are open 24hr. in season.

PHONE CODE	08394

ACCOMMODATIONS

To 15th-century traveler Domingo Paes, the Hampi Bazaar was "a broad and beautiful street, full of rows of fine houses and mantapas…[where] you will find all sorts of rubies, and diamonds, and emeralds, and pearls and seed pearls, and every other sort of thing there is on earth that you wish to buy." To the 20th-century tourist, Hampi Bazaar is important not for its magnificent architecture, glimmering jewels, or vivid silks, but rather for its cheap rooms, pancakes and spaghetti, and stone(r)s of a different variety. Staying in the guest houses of the bazaar, most of which are portions of homes, usually requires a lack of concern for cleanliness, a fondness for squat toilets, and a tolerance for buggies, doggies, and froggies.

Shanthi Guest House (tel. 41568). From the bus stand, walk toward the Virupaksha Temple, turn right and walk around the Sree Rama Lodge. Enclosed garden, cheerful exterior, and clean common baths (cold showers) make it a wellspring of tourist camaraderie. Check-out 10:30am. Singles Rs100; doubles Rs150. Mar.-Dec.: Rs60/80.

Gopi Rest House (tel. 41695). Clean rooms have flowered sheets, large windows, and pink mosquito nets. Friendly proprietor creates a pleasant atmosphere. Rooftop restaurant with nice views. Rooms Rs50, with bath Rs80. Off-season: Rs30.

Vicky Guest House (tel. 41694), 200m behind the tourist office. Huge beds, fans, and attached baths. The rooms downstairs, super-modern by Hampi's standards, are a great bargain. Attached in-season restaurant. Check-out 11am. Doubles Rs80. Mar.-Nov.: Rs125.

Lakshmi Guest House (tel. 41287), behind the tourist office. The mattresses are hard but the sheets are clean. Common trough baths. Bring your own padlock. Check-out noon. Doubles Rs150. Off-season: Rs80. Try bargaining for better prices.

Sree Rama Tourist House (tel. 41219). A safe bet for clean doubles, but look elsewhere for singles. Fickle lighting. Attached musty bathrooms with squat toilets and showers. Check-out 24hr. Singles Rs50; doubles Rs100.

FOOD

The open-air cafes that line the main bazaar are probably the only places in Karnataka that serve hummus and "fal-fel." Sub-standard pseudo-Western food, including fruit *parathas*, chocolate *lassis*, and *masala* macaroni, may leave you craving a *thali*, though you'll be hard-pressed to find one here.

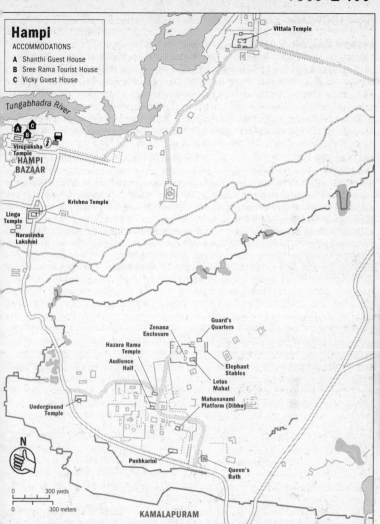

Hampi

ACCOMMODATIONS

A Shanthi Guest House
B Sree Rama Tourist House
C Vicky Guest House

Tungabhadra River

Virupaksha Temple

HAMPI BAZAAR

Krishna Temple

Linga Temple

Narasimha Lakshmi

Vittala Temple

Zenana Enclosure

Guard's Quarters

Hazara Rama Temple

Audience Hall

Elephant Stables

Lotus Mahal

Underground Temple

Mahanavami Platform (Dibba)

N

0   300 yards

0   300 meters

Pushkarini

Queen's Bath

KAMALAPURAM

KARNATAKA

Raju Rooftop Restaurant, near Shanthi Guest House. Gnocci (Rs30) and tomato pasta (Rs30) combined with the spiked punch of a sangria (Rs30), capture the delightful oddity of Hampi's restaurant menus. Raja even has its very own cat named Sheila, a friendly gray creature. Open daily 7am-10pm.

Bom Shankar Restaurant. Facing the Vittala Temple, turn right on the street before Hampi Bazaar. Incredible river views and freshly caught fish (small Rs25, large Rs150). Menu also offers pasta (Rs25-30), 12 kinds of pancakes (Rs15-25), and *kheer* (Rs25). Open daily 7am-10pm.

Welcome Restaurant, Hampi Bazaar. Popular for its pasta (Rs30-40) and pancakes, hummus, and falafel. Also offers the rare Indian *thali* (Rs25), rice pudding (Rs20), and espresso (Rs30). Open daily 7am-9:30pm. Off-season: 7:30am-9pm.

Hotel Mayura Bhuvaneswari, Kamalapuram. The only enclosed restaurant in the whole area, it has *thalis* on Su (Rs22-35), and veg. (Rs12-30) and chicken (Rs40-45) curries all the time. Beer Rs50-55. Open daily 6:30am-10pm.

👁 **SIGHTS**

VIJAYANAGAR RUINS

Though it won't enable you to see *all* the 26 sq. km of ruins, you can soak up most of the major sights in one foot-killing, back-aching, thigh-throbbing day. Renting a bike in Hospet, Kamalapuram, or Hampi Bazaar will help you see everything except the Vittala Temple area to the northeast, where the path is too rocky to ride; you can lock your bike and leave it with the tourist office or approach Vittala from the southeast, along the tour bus route. Mind your belongings and carry only a small quantity of cash. **Avoid walking along the river or behind the Vittala Temple alone,** though the path to the temple is considered safe.

THE SACRED CENTER. At the east end of Hampi Bazaar is the imposing **Virupaksha Temple,** once the king's personal temple. Inside is a marriage hall and an assembly hall, and towards the rear you can enter a small room an upside-down image of the *gopuram* is projected on the wall. Walk back toward the *gopuram* and take a right before exiting. Hike up the stony hill past the **Jain Temples** on your right, from which a beautiful view of Hampi can be had. Veer left, and you'll approach some boulder-caves where armies used to chill in the shade. The road down below eventually leads to Kamalapuram and the ruins of the Royal Center, but before you see these, you will pass the **Krishna Temple** on your right. Make a right on the dirt path to reach the **Narasimha Lakshmi statue.** When Muslim sultans sacked the city, they sliced open Narasimha's belly to see if the 7m-high monolith had eaten any gems. They found nothing, and Narasimha remains disfigured, although he is considered one of Hampi's most striking figures. Around the back you can see the hand of his consort Lakshmi, who was probably depicted resting on Narasimha's thigh. The ASI is trying to restore Narasimha to his original wholeness, although this would mean sacrificing his monolithic nature to mortar. Beside the statue is the **Linga Temple,** which contains the second-largest *linga* in India.

THE ROYAL CENTER. Back on the main road, continue on to the Royal Center until you see a sign for the Lotus Mahal. On your right will be the **Underground Temple,** which fills up with rainwater and fish during the monsoon season due to a collapsed roof. Follow the signs to the Lotus Mahal at the end of the road. Make a left, walking away from the **Hazara Rama Temple** past the pink Archaeological Camp House. Here you'll see the **Zenana Enclosure,** a stone wall within which the ladies of the court used to stay, protected from male ogling *(open daily 8am-6pm; Rs5).* To the right is the pink stucco **Lotus Mahal,** a sweet little example of Indo-Saracenic architecture. The nearby **watchtower** was used either to survey the terrain for enemies or, according to some accounts, to provide a vantage point for the king's wives to watch the goings-on without being spotted. Across from the Lotus Mahal are the **Guard's Quarters,** with high arches and polished floors.

To the east and through the stone walls are the 11 domed **Elephant Stables,** where more than 15,000 of the royal beasts slept, rested, and ate a whole lot of elephant food in the 15th century. Backtrack to the sign pointing to the Mahanavami Dibba, and take that road south; on your right will be the **Hazara Rama Temple.** The enclosure walls are carved with scenes from the *Ramayana* on the inside and with a parade of horses, elephants, dancing girls, and soldiers on the outside. Two rare images of Vishnu incarnated as the Buddha are inside the sanctum.

Continue on the road, and just as the path veers east (to your left), you will see a large platform, which was once the **Audience Hall.** The **Mahanavami Platform,** also on your right, is crossed by ancient aqueducts and now-dry stone canals. This platform, where the gala Dussehra Festival was held, is one of the tallest and most ornate around, and the throne stored inside is covered with gold and gems. Because it was carved out of granite like most other Vijayanagar monuments, the frieze is not very detailed, but what it lacks in embellishment it makes up for in stature. South of the platform is the recently excavated **Pushkarini,** a deep sacred water tank with unbelievably regular steps. Just before the dirt road joins with the main paved road to Kamalapuram, you will see on the left the **Queen's Bath,** a giant stone enclosure surrounded by a moat. The inside has a huge pool where the queen used to kick back after a hard day. *(Open daily 8am-6pm. Rs5.)*

VITTALA TEMPLE. Kamalapuram lies another 600m down the road. You can continue this way and ride on the paved road 5km north to the Vittala Temple, or you can backtrack to the Hampi Bazaar and walk 2km along the river to the temple. Though Vittala seems small and unimpressive from the outside, you'll know you're there when you see the cold-drink dealers and tourist buses. Construction of the temple, which was never finished or consecrated, was begun around 1513 by the Vijayanagar king Krishnadevaraya, and the work was probably halted when the city was destroyed in 1565. A competing bit of lore has it that Vittala, the incarnation of Vishnu to whom the temple is dedicated, came to look at the temple, found it too grand for him, and hightailed it back to his humbler home in Maharashtra. Indeed, the carvings here are certainly the most ornate of any around the ruins. Each of the 56 musical pillars inside the temple sounds a different note when tapped, but the security guards glare sternly at tourists who try to play a tune. Outside the temple is the massive stone chariot of Vishnu's mythical bird Garuda.

ANEGUNDI

The ancient cave temples at Anegundi are seldom visited by tourists. The Archaeological Survey of India isn't in charge here, and getting to the caves is an adventure in itself. Because there are no signs, it may be best to solicit the assistance of a certified **guide** at Hampi's tourist office (Rs100-500 in season, Rs100 off season).

From the Vittala Temple, continue on the main paved road along the Tungabhadra River. Eventually the road deteriorates into a path leading to the river bank, where two grass-basket boats shuttle people, bicycles, and (more perilously) motorcycles to and from Anegundi. Once you reach the other side, walk straight up a small slope and you'll see the village. If you don't, just ask your boat-*wallah* ("Anegundi?"), and he'll point you in the right direction. A left turn at the first opportunity and then a left at the next fork in the road will lead you past the Andhra Bank and under a small gate. After the gate, turn left onto the paved road that cuts through the rice paddies. A dirt path veers off to the left; take it and you'll be at the base a rocky hill. Midway up the hill is a **Durga Temple,** thought to be the site at which Rama killed the monkey king Vali. The active temple is especially favored by soldiers who perform *pujas* to gain strength. A *bidi*-smoking *swami* offering *chai* and other treats will point you past his shrine and up the hill to the **Laxmi Temple.** Here, Sita prayed for Rama's forgiveness after she had been banished, demonstrating her devotion to her doubting husband, as well as the purity of her mind, body, and soul. The nearby **Pampasarovara Pond** is believed to be the site where Parvati quite successfully prayed for a husband—the reward for her efforts was Shiva himself. A small 7th-century temple marks **Hanuman Hill,** the monkey-god's birthplace. His simian descendants still scampering about are irreverent enough to snatch cameras and lunches.

BADAMI ಬಾದಮಿ

This jumping little town in the middle of nowhere was the capital of the mighty Chalukyan Empire from AD 543 to 757. The town's ancient cave temples and edifices are situated high in the mountains surrounding an ancient Chalukyan tank, around which echo the thwacking and thumping of women doing the family laundry; the brilliant green hue of the tank's water is actually due to overabundant algae which thrives on detergent. Badami is also the town closest to Pattadakal, 20km away, where Chalukyan kings were crowned, and Aihole, 47km away on the Malaprabha River, the first Chalukyan capital. Together, these three towns are a fascinating study in the development of Indian temple architecture. Aihole is considered the birthplace of the now-dominant style—its structures were built up rather than carved out, as older cave temples were. The cave temples of Badami and the later temples at Pattadakal illustrate the evolution of an increasingly sophisticated style. Though less aesthetically impressive than what you'll find in

Belur, Halebid, and Somnathpur, the Chalukyan temples served as a template for styles which later emerged throughout the country.

⚡ ORIENTATION AND PRACTICAL INFORMATION. Badami's main road, **Station Road,** is probably the only straight path in the entire village. From the **railway station** in the north, it runs 5km south to the **bus stand** and eventually to the routes to Pattadakal and Aihole in the south. Buses run to: **Aihole** (5:30 and 8:15am, 6hr.; Rs8); **Bangalore** (5:30am, 5:30, and 8:30pm; 8hr.; Rs135); **Bagal Pot** (every 1½hr.; Rs10—transfer to Bijapur permitted); **Bijapur** (6:45, 8:15, 9am, and 6:30pm; 4hr.; Rs46); **Hospet** (5:30, 7:15, 9:15am, and 1:30pm; 5hr.; Rs60); and **Pattadakal** (5:30 and 8:15am, 1hr., Rs6). The only **private bus** service in town goes to Bangalore (9:30pm, 9hr., Rs150); book through Hotel Mookambika Deluxe (tel. 65067). Private **maxicabs** are another way to reach Pattadakal. **Trains** run only to **Bijapur** and **Gadag** for connections to Hospet and Bangalore. **College (Ramdurg) Road** runs east from Station Rd., south of the bus stand, and winds around to the KSTDC hotel and **Tourist Information Center** (tel. 65414; open M-Sa 10am-5:30pm; closed second Sa), 1km later. The Bhutanatha Temples are north of **Agastyatirtha Tank.** The **police station** (tel. 65133) is opposite the bus stand. The **GPO** (open M-Sa 7-11am and 2-5pm) is supposedly open 24hr. **Telegraph Office** (tel. 65030) are just north of the bus stand. **Postal Code:** 587201. **Telephone Code:** 08357.

🍴🛏 ACCOMMODATIONS AND FOOD. Compared to Aihole and Pattadakal's sparse offerings, Badami's possesses an abundance of accommodations, most of which are located near the bus stand. **Hotel Mookambika Deluxe** (tel. 65067) is the cheeriest and cleanest in that area. Screened windows look out upon the Chalukyan hills, and an in-house travel agency will help get you there. Be sure to bargain off season. (Singles Rs150, deluxe with TV Rs300, with A/C Rs600; doubles Rs200/350/650.) The attached restaurant serves food made-to-order. Cheaper options include **Hotel Anand** (tel. 65074), across from Hotel Mookambika (singles Rs50, with bath Rs70; doubles Rs120/150), and across the street, the somewhat brighter **Hotel Satka** (tel. 65417; singles with bath Rs70; doubles Rs100-150, with A/C Rs350). If proximity and *paise*-pinching are not your top priorities, consider the **Hotel Mayura Chalukya,** College Rd. (tel. 65046). Turn right from the bus stand, walk 500m, and turn right on the first paved road; the hotel is 1km down on the right. This is monkey territory, but the huge rooms are relatively clean and look out on overgrown gardens. Seat and squat toilets are available, and hot water flows night and day. The attached restaurant serves mediocre cuisine. (Check-out noon. Singles Rs168; doubles Rs200; triples Rs250.) For cheaper food, try the stand-up, no-nonsense **Geeta Darshini,** just north of the bus stand, where nothing on the menu costs more than Rs7 (open M-Sa 6:30am-9pm). Next door, the **Hotel Parimal** serves *masala dosas* (Rs7) and tomato omelettes (Rs8; open M-Sa 6:30am-9pm).

📷 SIGHTS. The **South Fort cave temples,** carved out of the red sandstone cliff and connected by steps, are some of the most important cave temples in India. The first three temples are Hindu, though Jain and Buddhist influences are apparent. **Cave 1,** the oldest of the bunch, is dedicated to Shiva in his different guises. On the right front wall is an 18-armed dancing Shiva, and there is a *linga* protected by granite cobras in the back of the cave. **Cave 2** is dedicated to Vishnu, as is **Cave 3,** the largest and best-sculpted of the group, dating from AD 578. The 21m-long facade of Cave 3 is carved with figures of humans, gods, and dwarves, as are the pillars and the steps leading to the foundation. In one scene, Vishnu reclines on a serpent's lap, and though the asp's mouth looms over him, the god remains sedate. Though the caves were once painted, the only traces of color which remain are on the ceiling of Cave 3. The path up to Cave 3 leads past a natural cave once used as a Buddhist temple; the Buddha image has since been defaced. **Cave 4,** probably the only cave here ever used as a Jain temple, overlooks the lake. The pillars appear to be held up by an assortment of creatures, including one which bears a startling resemblance to Yoda from *Star Wars.* (From the bus stand, head right on Station Rd. past College Rd.; from the perspective of the Dr. Ambedkar statue, turn left and follow that road to the end. Temples open daily 6am-6pm. Rs2. Guides Rs175 for a 2-3hr. tour or Rs350 for a full day.)

Across the lake from the cave temples lie a number of other temples. The **Upper Shivalaya Temple** is one of the oldest of the group at Badami, and its carvings depict scenes from the life of Krishna. The most spectacular of the temples is the **Malegetti Shivalaya,** with its pillared hallway flanked by Shiva on one side and Vishnu on the other. The temple is perched precariously on top of the hill, offering spectacular views of the village and the fields below. Located in town by the 6th century **Agastyatirtha Tank,** the **Jambulinga Temple** was built in AD 699 by the Vijay-anagars. The peaceful **Bhutanatha Temples** are on the opposite side of the tank. To reach the temples and the **Archaeological Museum** (open Sa-Th 10am-5pm; free), head right from the bus stand and follow a sign which will lead you through a tiny neighborhood on narrow stone paths.

NEAR BADAMI: AIHOLE ಐಹೊಳ

Forty-four kilometers northeast of Badami on the banks of the Malaprabha River, Aihole offers spectacular opportunities for temple viewing. The litter of beautiful, half-finished temples was once the playground of a civilization hell-bent on build-ing the greatest architecture in the region. Aihole's 100 temples combine elements of both Dravidian and Northern Nagar styles—note that there are *gopurams* of both styles. The temples' square pillars and flat roofs, which gently slope down-wards on the periphery, reflect a distinctly Chalukyan element.

The most impressive temple within the main compound is the **Durgigudi Temple,** dedicated to Vishnu but so named because it sits next to a fort, or *durga*. The tem-ple's Islamic-style perforated windows have a round shape evocative of Buddhist *chaitya* halls. (Open daily 6am-6pm. Rs2.) The Jain **Meguti Temple** has a stone inscription in Old Kannada script that has been dated to AD 634, making it one of the oldest dated temples in India. A relatively unadorned Buddhist temple is just below. Farther south in the main compound, the **Ladh Khan Temple** is named after a 19th-century Muslim who set up house in the sanctuary. Because of its similarity to megalithic caves, this temple was once thought to date from the 5th century; now it is believed to have been built in the early 8th century. The structure com-bines elements of Dravidian style with hints of typical Chalukyan architecture. The compound also has an **archaeological museum** (open Sa-Th 10am-5pm). Out-side the compound and off the main road, but still within walking distance, is **Ravan Phadi,** a precursor to the more sophisticated cave temples of Badami.

Buses go to Badami (1 and 4pm, 2hr., Rs8). The **Tourist Home Aihole** (tel. 68041) is the only place for non-locals to lay their weary heads. The manager is gracious, the food is cooked to order (*thalis* Rs20-25), and there are no postcard touts hanging around. Standard, clean rooms cost half of what they would in Badami. (Singles Rs35; doubles Rs60; triples Rs75.)

NEAR BADAMI: PATTADAKAL ಪಟ್ಟದಕಲ್

Twenty kilometers between Badami and Aihole, **Pattadakal** was the Chalukyan capital during the 7th and 8th centuries, and its temples are the most stylistically advanced in the region. The ancient structures are clustered at the base of a pink sandstone hill. Pattadakal's only active temple, the **Virupaksha (Lokeshvara) Temple,** has a three-story spire with a chlorite stone Nandi sitting in front of it. Passages lead around the shrine past carvings which depict episodes from the *Ramayana* and *Mahabharata*, as well as scenes of Chalukyan martial triumphs. The other prominent temples in the compound are the **Mallikarjuna Temple** and the **Papanatha Temple.** About 1km south of the compound, the **Jain Temple** has an upper-story sanctuary accessible by a staircase and guarded by a crocodile-carved gate. Your climb to the top will be rewarded with a lovely view. (Temple compound open daily 6am-6pm. Rs5. Guides Rs50, or bargain for a shorter tour.)

Since there are no accommodations, travelers must daytrip here from Badami or Aihole. **Buses** (every 45min. 6am-7pm, Rs5-7) and private **maxicabs** make the 45-minute trek to Badami. Buses also go to Aihole (7, 8, 9, 10am, and 4pm; Rs6).

KERALA കേരളം

Kerala's A-to-Z representation of religious minorities stems from a complex history. As early as the 3rd century BC, Egyptians, Phoenicians, Chinese, and Babylonians had established trade relations with this center of maritime commerce. In AD 52, St. Thomas the Apostle purportedly arrived here, establishing strong Christian roots in India, and in AD 70, Jews fleeing Roman persecution in Palestine landed on Kerala's palm-lined shores. Beginning in the 8th century, Arabs dominated Keralan trade, spreading Islam throughout the region, until the Portuguese landed at Calicut in 1498 and muscled their way to exclusive trading rights. Meanwhile, rivalry between the port cities of Cochin and Calicut weakened both, and the Dutch and British ejected the Portuguese from their forts early in the 17th century. Kerala came under the rule of the British Raj during the 18th century.

After Independence, the princely states of Cochin and Travancore were joined to form the state of Kerala, and in 1956 Kerala's boundaries were redrawn along linguistic (Malayalam) lines. One year later, Kerala's electorate became the first in the world to freely choose a Communist government. The state's leftist tradition has brought many advantages to its citizens: despite a low per capita income, reforms have given Kerala the most equitable land distribution in India, and Kerala's literacy rate—around 90%, twice the national average—is the country's highest. Also in contrast with much of India, Kerala's low rates of female infanticide and high standards for health care has populated the state with more women than men. Vestiges of ancient matrilineal, polyandrous systems, such as those still practiced by the Nayar caste, have lent a somewhat higher status to women in Kerala, and the U.N. has commended the state for its exemplary women's rights record.

The state's famed beaches and palm-tree-lined backwaters have made it a genuinely laid-back corner of the subcontinent. Forty lazy rivers run from the Western Ghats to the sea, channeled through canals and rice paddies, past islands of palm groves. This picture-postcard scenery has made Kerala particularly amenable to tourism, and it has become second only to Goa in hosting droves of certified sun-worshippers and bona fide beach bums.

HIGHLIGHTS OF KERALA

- The cool **backwaters** of **Cochin** (p. 516) and **Alleppey** (p. 524), shrouded in greenery and plied by fishing boats, offer a look at Keralan village life at its most idyllic.
- **Periyar Tiger Reserve** (p. 513), in Kerala's eastern hills, is home to laughing thrushes, flying squirrels, and a few very big, very shy cats.
- Kerala has produced one of the world's more extraordinary dance forms, **kathakali**. The best place to see performances is **Cochin** (p. 518).
- Sun-seekers find solace, if not solitude, in sandy **Kovalam** (p. 506) and **Varkala** (p. 511).

TRIVANDRUM (THIRUVANATHAPURAM)
തിരുവനന്തപുരം

While most foreign tourists consider it a piddling stop-off on the way to the balmy beaches of Kovalam and the beckoning backwaters of Alleppey, Kerala's state capital of Trivandrum deserves a closer look. Speckled with parks, palaces, monuments, and museums, it provides plenty of opportunities for checking out Kerala's cultural offerings. Though it became the capital of Kerala when the state was formed in 1956, Trivandrum had been the capital of Travancore for two centuries, and it still retains its trademark red-tiled, pagoda-roofed houses, winding streets, tiny cafes, and beautiful gardens. The city's Malayalam name refers to Anantha, the serpent who holds the reclining Lord Vishnu (Lord Padmanabha) in the Shree

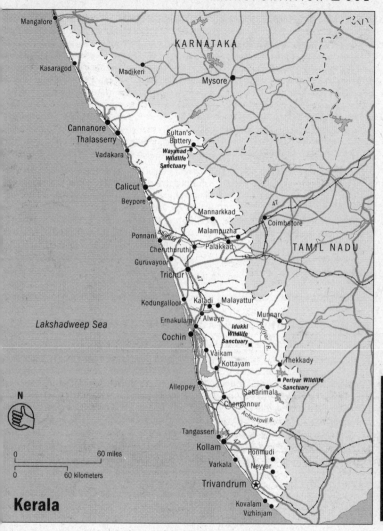

Kerala

Padmanabha Swami Temple. Though the inner temple is open only to *dhoti*-clad Hindus, the zoo and museums, set in the town's lovely public gardens, require no specific religious allegiance. An inviting respite from beach-hopping, Trivandrum makes a fitting beginning or end to any trip through South India.

▐ TRANSPORTATION

Airport: Trivandrum's **international airport** is 6km outside town. Buses for the airport leave from the city bus stand at East Fort (every 30min., Rs3). Auto-rickshaws cost Rs50. Flights to and from **Male** in the Maldives (Indian Airlines Tu, Th, Sa, and Su; 1hr.; Rs3000) and **Colombo,** Sri Lanka (Air Lanka M-Sa; Indian Airlines M, W, and F, 1hr., Rs2410). **Indian Airlines,** Museum Rd. (tel. 501537), 1 block left from the intersection with MG Rd. (open M-Sa 10am-1pm and 1:35-5:35pm). **Jet Airways** (tel. 500860) also has flights. To: **Bangalore** (Tu, Th, and Sa; 1hr.; US$105); **Chennai** (M, W, F, and Su;

1hr.; US$105); **Delhi** (1 per day, 5hr., US$325); **Mumbai** (2 per day, 2hr., US$175). Up-to-date schedules of trains and planes are published every Monday in *The Hindu.*

Trains: The **railway station,** Station Rd., a few min. east of MG Rd. Reservations counter open M-Sa 8am-8pm, Su 8am-2pm. Fares listed for 2nd/1st class. To: **Alleppey** (*Intercity Exp.* 6342, 4:30pm, 3½hr., Rs43/220); **Bangalore** (*Island Exp.* 6525, 9:20am, 20hr., Rs156/766); **Chennai** (*Chennai Mail* 6230, 1:30pm, 20hr., Rs168/814); **Cochin** (several per day 5am-9:40pm, 5hr., Rs61/294); **Delhi** (*Kerala Exp.* 2625, 11am, 55hr., Rs326/2040); **Kanyakumari** (12:20 and 3:20pm, 2hr., Rs30/161); **Kollam** (several per day 5am-9:40pm, 1½hr., Rs26/129); **Madurai** (*Madurai Passenger* 0728, 8:30pm, 10hr., Rs80/342); **Mangalore** (*Parasuram Exp.* 6349, 6am; *Malabar Exp.* 6329, 5:40pm, 16hr., Rs132/650); **Mumbai** (*Kanyakumari Exp.* 1082, 7:10am, 46hr., Rs256/1445); **Varkala** (several per day 5am-9:45pm, 1hr., Rs21/112).

Buses: The **long-distance KSRTC bus station,** Station Rd., opposite the railway station. To: **Alleppey** (every 15min., 3½hr., Rs55); **Cochin** (every 30min., 6hr., Rs65); **Kanyakumari** (10 per day, 2½hr., Rs20); **Kollam** (frequent, 1½hr., Rs25); **Varkala** (12 per day 7:50am-9:30pm, 1½hr., Rs16); **Thekkady** for Periyar (4 and 8:45am, 8hr., Rs80). The **Tamil Nadu Transport Office** (tel. 327756), at the far east end of the KSRTC bus station, runs buses to cities in Tamil Nadu. Open daily 7am-9pm. To: **Chennai** (9 per day 11:30am-8pm, 17hr., Rs201); **Madurai** (6 per day 10:30am-10:30pm, 7hr., Rs88); **Pondicherry** (4pm, 16hr., Rs173). The **local bus station,** MG Rd., is a few min. south of the train tracks at East Fort. Buses to **Kovalam** (every 20min. 5:50am-8:30pm, Rs5) depart from the bus stand on Overbridge Rd., 100m south of the local stand.

Local Transportation: Auto-rickshaws should use meters; base Rs6. Rs50 to Kovalam.

⏐ ORIENTATION AND PRACTICAL INFORMATION

The streets tangle over 74 sq. km of coastal hills, but navigation is easy if you stick to the few main drags. The north-south **MG Road** dumps all its traffic onto **Museum Road,** at the north end of town. To the south, MG Rd. cruises down a hill to a hectic intersection with the city's other main drag, **(Central) Station Road.** One hundred meters left on Station Rd. from MG Rd., **Manjalikulam Road** leads north to the budget hotel district. Farther down Station Rd., the **long-distance bus stand** is on the left, opposite the **railway station.** MG Rd. becomes **Overbridge Road** when it heads south over the railway tracks to the **East Fort** area. A great white gate marks the entrance to **Shree Padmanabha Swamy Temple,** opposite the **local bus stand.** Behind the stand, **Chalai Bazaar Road** leads east through the bazaar.

Tourist Office: Tourist Facilitation Centre, Museum Rd. (tel. 321132), opposite the museum compound. Open M-Sa 9am-5:50pm. **KTDC Reception Centre,** Station Rd (tel. 330031), in front of Chaitram Hotel, next to the bus stand. This office promotes KTDC tours. Open M-Sa 6:30am-9:30pm. Smaller tourist offices at the **KSRTC Bus Stand** (tel. 327224) and the **train station** (tel. 334470). Both open M-Sa 10am-5pm

Budget Travel: Travel Destinations, Chaitram Hotel lobby, Station Rd. (tel. 330702) between the intersection with MG Rd. and the long-distance bus stand. Confirms airline tickets (Rs50) and books flights, trains, and private buses. Open M-Sa 9am-9:30pm.

Immigration Office: Foreigners Registration Office, Residency Rd. (tel. 3213909); ask for the "foreigners section." Rickshaw ride Rs10. Extensions for student and entry visa "with proper documents." The process should take 2 weeks, but "urgent" applications might be processed in 4 days; bring a copy of your passport. Open M-Sa 10:15am 1:15pm and 2-5:15pm. Closed 2nd Sa.

Currency Exchange: Central Bank of India (tel. 330359), in the Chaitram Hotel lobby Exchanges foreign currency and major traveler's checks. Open M-F 10am-2pm, Sa 10am-noon. The **Canara Bank,** MG Rd. (tel. 331536), at Spencer Junction just north of the Secretariat, gives cash advances on Visa. Open M-F 10am-2pm, Sa 10am-noon.

Market: Chalai Bazaar Road, which intersects MG Rd. at the local bus station.

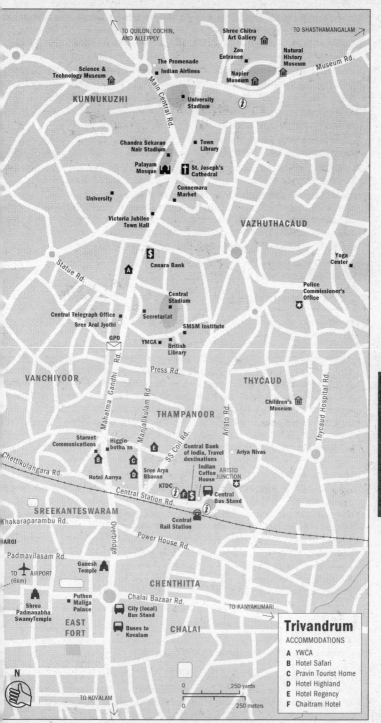

TO QUILON, COCHIN, AND ALLEPPEY

TO SHASTHAMANGALAM

Shree Chitra Art Gallery

Zoo Entrance

Natural History Museum

Museum Rd.

The Promenade
Indian Airlines

Napier Museum

Science & Technology Museum

KUNNUKUZHI

University Stadium

Main Central Rd.

Chandra Sekaran Nair Stadium

Town Library

Palayam Mosque

St. Joseph's Cathedral

University

Connemara Market

Victoria Jubilee Town Hall

VAZHUTHACAUD

Statue Rd.

Yoga Center

Canara Bank

Central Stadium

Police Commissioner's Office

Central Telegraph Office
Sree Aral Jyothi

Secretariat

SMSM Institute

GPO

YMCA

British Library

Mahatma Gandhi Rd.

Press Rd.

VANCHIYOOR

Manjalikulam Rd.

THYCAUD

Thycaud Hospital Rd.

Children's Museum

THAMPANOOR

Aristo Rd.

Starnet Communications

Higgin-bothans

SS Coil Rd.

Central Bank of India, Travel destinations

Ariya Nivas

Chettikulangara Rd.

B

C

Indian Coffee House

ARISTO JUNCTION

Hotel Aarrya

D

Sree Arya Bhavan

KTDC

Central Station Rd.

F

Central Bus Stand

SREEKANTESWARAM

Central Rail Station

Thakaraparambu Rd.

Overbridge

Power House Rd.

ARGI

Padmavilasam Rd.

Ganesh Temple

TO AIRPORT (6km)

Puthen Maliga Palace

CHENTHITTA

Shree Padmanabha SwamyTemple

EAST FORT

Chalai Bazaar Rd.

City (local) Bus Stand

TO KANYAKUMARI

Buses to Kovalam

CHALAI

N

TO KOVALAM

0   250 yards

0   250 meters

KERALA

Trivandrum

ACCOMMODATIONS

A YWCA
B Hotel Safari
C Pravin Tourist Home
D Hotel Highland
E Hotel Regency
F Chaitram Hotel

Library: British Library, off Manjalikulam Rd. where it swerves left, is officially open only to card-carrying members, but they may let you browse. Open Tu-Sa 11am-7pm. The **town library,** still marked "Victoria Diamond Jubilee Library," is housed in a colonial building on MG Rd., south of Museum Rd. Open daily 8am-8pm.

Bookstore: Higginbothams, MG Rd., north of Station Rd. Open M-Sa 9:30am-7:30pm.

Pharmacy: Vishnu Medicals (tel. 449447), across from Cosmopolitan Hospital, has a particularly friendly and efficient staff. Open daily 8:30am-9:30pm.

Hospital: Cosmopolitan Hospital (tel. 448182), in the northwest area of town (Rs20 rickshaw from Station Rd.), is considered the best private hospital in the city.

Police: Thampanoor Police Station, Station Rd. (tel. 326543), near the long-distance bus station, near Aristo Junction. Outpost inside the museum compound (tel. 315096).

Post Office: GPO, MG Rd., south of the Secretariat. Open M-Sa 8am-8pm, Su 10am-4pm. Poste Restante sent here sometimes ends up in Kovalam. **Postal Code:** 695001.

Internet: Starnet Communications, Old Sreekanteswaram Rd. (tel. 464550), south of Ayurveda College Junction, offers the best deal on Internet access (Rs75 per hr.). Open M-Sa 9am-9pm. The **Central Telegraph Office,** opposite the Secretariat, has 2 terminals (Rs80 per hr.) available daily 7am-10pm.

Telephones: The **Central Telegraph Office** allows collect calls. Open 24hr.

PHONE CODE	0471

ACCOMMODATIONS

While MG and Station Rd. offer plenty of large hotels, Manjalikulam Rd. is the real budget hotel district.

Hotel Regency (tel. 330377). Follow Manjalikulam Rd. to the first cross-street, then turn right. Fancier than usual, with big clean rooms and satellite TVs. A choice of restaurants (including one on the roof), obliging room service, and framed Rajasthani miniatures on the walls make this a luxurious option. Seat toilets and hot water. Currency exchange. Singles Rs275, with A/C Rs550; doubles Rs450/650. MC, Visa.

Pravin Tourist Home, Manjalikulam Rd. (tel. 330443), a 2min. walk north from Hotel Regency, on the left. Super-friendly proprietor. Fairly moderately sized rooms have big windows and attached bathrooms (seat and squat toilets). TV in the lobby. Singles Rs98; doubles Rs172; triples Rs226; quads Rs279. Prices include tax.

Hotel Highland, Manjalikulam Rd. (tel. 333200 or 333421), near Central Station Rd., on the left. Large, popular hotel has big rooms. A/C rooms have TV. Seat toilets. Singles Rs200, with A/C Rs460; doubles Rs260/540.

YWCA (tel. 477308), 4th fl., Indian Overseas Bank Building opposite the Secretariat. Lovely, Lysol-christened rooms with attached baths are refreshingly clean. No unmarried couples allowed. Singles Rs150; doubles Rs200, with A/C Rs350; family room Rs300.

Hotel Safari, MG Rd. (tel. 477202), a few min. north of Central Station Rd. Standard accommodation, but the A/C rooms are cushy—bathtubs, hot water, and lots of space. Pleasant restaurant has city views. Lone women may want to steer clear of the hotel bar. Singles Rs185, with A/C Rs400; doubles Rs230/450; triples Rs280/550.

FOOD

It's difficult to find authentic Keralan food in Trivandrum, as most South Indian restaurants dish out a more Tamil-influenced menu.

Sree Arya Bharan, on the corner of SS Coil and Station Rd., 100m west of Hotel Chairam. This hole-in-the-wall serves terrific North Indian veg. fare. The *chapatis* may not emerge from the kitchen quite as fast as you'd like in this popular place, but it is a gem nonetheless. Chalkboard menu changes daily. *Aloo simlamirch* (Rs17) will keep you coming back for more. Open daily 8:30am-3pm and 7-11pm.

Hotel Aarrya, Central Station Rd., between Hotel Chaitram and the intersection with MG Rd. Offers simple but smashing South Indian fare. Good *masala dosas* (Rs10) and Keralan meals (Rs18). Open daily 7am-10pm.

Maveli Cafe (Indian Coffee House), facing the bus station; it's the red, spiraling building on the left. The coolest structure in Trivandrum, its Tower-of-Pisa grandeur must be seen to be believed. Standard *dosas* (Rs8) and coffee. Open daily 7:30am-10pm.

Ariya Nivaas, around the corner from the station, towards Aristo Junction. Popular up-market veg. restaurant caters to middle-class families. Fancy *thali* served on a banana leaf (Rs45 in the A/C upstairs) is especially recommended. Open daily 7am-10pm.

Sree Aral Jyothi, MG Rd., opposite the Secretariat. Enjoy authentic Keralan "raw rice meals" (Rs19) and *masala dosas* (Rs15) in this crowded restaurant. Pass up the gloomy, windowless A/C space in the back in favor of the heart-o'-town street-life views in front. Meals served daily 3-10pm.

ENTERTAINMENT

FESTIVALS

The Shree Padmanabha Swamy Temple holds the **Festival of Attakul Pongala** on the day of Holi in early March, though the festival itself is not connected to the holiday. Tens of thousands of women converge on Trivandrum during this time, each one setting up a miniature kitchen on the streets in the center of town. The women offer Pongala by cooking a meal in an earthenware pot over sanctified fire from the temple. Trivandrum's center is closed to traffic and takes on an uncharacteristically peaceful air as the smoke from thousands upon thousands of cooling fires drifts heavenwards. The **Swati Music Festival** (late Jan.-early Feb.) presents evenings of classical music on the lawn of the Puthen Maliga Palace. The annual **Nishagandhi Dance Festival,** with outdoor classical performances, takes place during the last week of February. Contact the KTDC for a complete festival schedule.

DANCE AND THEATER

MARGI (tel. 478806), a school at West Fort, occasionally performs **kathakali dance drama** and **kutiyattum theater** (Keralan martial art) in the evenings. Follow MG Rd. south over the train tracks, turn right at the corner temple, walk 10 minutes into West Fort until the street comes to a final "T," and turn right. MARGI is behind Fort High School on your left—look for a big banyan tree. The sign on the door is in Malayalam, but the image of a dancer gives it away. Performances are not regularly scheduled and often take place in local temples; call for details. Trivandrum has 18 **movie theaters.** Sree Kumar and Sree Visakh (both near the Chaitram Hotel), and New Theatre (walk east on Central Station Rd., turn left in front of the railway station) screen English-language films.

SIGHTS

MUSEUM COMPOUND. A big red gate marks the entrance to the lovely, 20-hectare public gardens dotted with moon-eyed couples, two museums, two galleries, and the town's zoo. The **Natural History Museum** features dioramas of natural history, a model of a traditional upper-class house in Travancore (mid-pageant it seems, with *kathakali* dancers—check out the skin color of the *brahmin* denizens), and a life-sized, ivory model of a human skeleton made for Marthandavarma Maharaja in 1853. To the right of the Natural History Museum is the **K.C.S. Paniker Gallery,** which features paintings by the eponymous 20th-century Indian artist. Sadly, the musty gallery does not do justice to the artist's beautiful work. Better maintained is the **Shree Chitra Art Gallery,** across from the Napier Museum, decked with Western-style portraits by the famed Raja Ravi Varma (1848-1906), Tibetan

thankas, Japanese, Chinese, and Balinese paintings, 400-year-old Rajasthani min
iatures, and modern Indian works. Dedicated to the last Maharaja of Travancore
the gallery also boasts an authentic royal carriage.

Set in front of these three galleries is the **Napier Museum,** which looks suspi
ciously like a Walt Disney spin-off—florid gables and red, black, and pink brick
and tiles decorate the outside, while the inside is striped in yellow, pink, red, and
turquoise. In reality, the building is an Indo-Saracenic experiment by Robert Fel
lowes Chisholm, who attempted to marry traditional Keralan and colonial archi
tectural styles. The museum's forte is, surprisingly, Southeast Asian and Balines
art. A fine wooden temple car is one of the museum's more indigenous pieces
Some of the kitsch on display, including an engraved plate to mark Kuwait Air
lines' inaugural flight to Trivandrum, were gifts from foreign rulers to erstwhil
first ministers of Kerala. *(Museum Rd. Galleries open Tu and Th-Su 10am-5pm, W 1-5pm
Rs5 for all four museums. Purchase tickets at the Natural History Museum from 10am-4pm.)*

The compound also contains a **zoo.** Though the animals probably live better tha
their colleagues elsewhere in India, some are kept in frighteningly small cages. I
might be worth a visit, however, to see its impressive roost of wild fruit bats. *(Ope
Tu-Sa 9am-6:30pm. Rs5; camera fee Rs10, video Rs1500. Tickets sold until 5pm.)*

PUTHEN MALIGA PALACE (HORSE PALACE). Every inch of the palace of Princ
Swati Tirunal, also a famed musician and court composer, is exquisitely adorned
Its beautiful carvings were completed in four years, and the surly Swati Tiruna
subsequently occupied it for only one year, leaving in a huff. The Puthen Malig
Palace or "Horse Palace," so-named for the 122 galloping horse sculptures beneath
its eaves, provides some fascinating insight on how the other half once lived. Th
palace also functions as a museum (i.e. repository of old stuff), featuring life-siz
kathakali figures in full regalia, paintings of the rajas and ranis of Travancore
weapons, and thrones in ivory and Bohemian crystal. *(Open Tu-Su 8:30am-12:30pr
and 3-5:30pm. Rs20; camera fee Rs15, photography prohibited inside. Official museum guide
who expect* baksheesh, *are required to accompany you.)*

SHREE PADMANABHA SWAMY TEMPLE. Marked by a large white gate, the Shre
Padmanabha Swamy Temple features a 6m-high statue of the reclining Vishnu
The whole of the god's body is made visible by the opening of three doors—one a
the sacred head, one at the divine midsection, and one at the holy feet. The presen
gopuram was built in 1566 and subsequently acquired two extra stories, but th
current structure was not completed until 1733. Although the temple itself is ope
only to Hindus wearing *dhotis* or *saris*, non-Hindus may climb the steps and se
the less sacred images. The lane leading up to the temple, through a thicket o
handicraft hawkers, houses a large green **tank** used by bathing pilgrims.

KOVALAM കോവളം

The pounding of hammers and pouring of concrete have forever altered the caln
landscape of Kovalam's black sands and turquoise waters. Since the arrival of hip
pie sun- and soul-searchers in the 60s, Kovalam has fast become Kerala's mos
popular beach resort and one of the most popular in India. Restaurant sound sys
tems play Jimi Hendrix and Pink Floyd as Kovalam struggles to remind itself of it
hippie past and aspires, Goa-like, to a psychedelic present. The busy beachfron
has been consumed by hotels, downcast but persistent touts, and thieves in th
guise of tailors and handicraft sellers. Enjoy the carnivalesque atmosphere—i
was created just for you. Beyond the tourist enclave, local fishing boats still p
the bays, and life continues as it always has amid thatched huts and rice paddies.

🛈 ORIENTATION AND PRACTICAL INFORMATION

Kovalam Beach is composed of three coves divided by rocky promontories. A
lighthouse both marks and names the southernmost **Lighthouse Beach.** From here
Lighthouse Road, crawling with seafood restaurants, leads down to the water an

the budget hotels favored by Western tourists. **Eve's Beach** lies north of a rocky promontory. The headland is home to the chi-chi **Ashok Hotel** (Kovalam Hotel), north of which is **Samudra Beach,** delightful but largely ignored by the crowds who flock to Lighthouse and Eve Beaches. A road leads up from Eve's Beach past several travel offices, handicraft shops, and tailors to the **bus stand** at the entrance to the Kovalam Hotel. The road to Trivandrum leads first to **Kovalam Junction,** 2km away, where a left turn at the fork brings you to the **post office.** Between Lighthouse Rd. and the road to the bus stand, paths twist through the palm trees, connecting the beach to some of the quieter restaurants and hotels.

 WARNING. The undertow and rip currents here can be very strong, so follow the warnings of the signs, flags, and whistle-toting lifeguards. Also, public displays of female flesh are frowned upon, and women in swimsuits inevitably attract negative attention. Consider swimming in light pants and a t-shirt instead.

Buses: The **bus stand** is at the top of the path from the north end of Eve's Beach. There is no ticket office, but the Tourist Facilitation Centre (see below) can give bus schedules. Tickets are purchased on the bus. To: **Cochin** (7am, 6hr., Rs65) via **Kollam** (2hr.) and **Alleppey** (4hr.); **Kanyakumari** via **Nagercoil** (4 per day 9am-6:20pm, Rs23); **Trivandrum** (every 15min. 5am-9:30pm, 20min., Rs5).

Local Transportation: **Rickshaws** and **taxis** hover at the bottom of Lighthouse Rd., the bus stand, and Kovalam Junction. A ride to Trivandrum should cost under Rs100.

Tourist Office: **Tourist Facilitation Centre** (tel. 480085), near the bus stand. Run by the Kerala Department of Tourism, the office has information about Kerala, books hotels all over India, and arranges tickets for the Kollam-Alleppey backwater cruises (Rs150) and commission-free local backwater trips (Rs300). Open in season M-Sa 10am-5pm.

Budget Travel: **Western Travels** (tel. 481307), next to the bus stand. Energetic and helpful staff confirms plane reservations for the price of the phone call. Also makes plane, bus, hotel, and train bookings (Rs50 service charge). They organize **sightseeing tours** in season, which include the Quilon-Alleppey backwater trip (run 7:30am-6:30pm, 6hr., Rs550). Currency exchange and cash advances on credit cards. Taxis for hire. Open daily 6:30am-12:30am. Off-season: 7am-9pm. MC, Visa, AmEx.

Currency Exchange: Some shops on the beach exchange currency. The reception desks at **Wilson's Tourist Home,** behind Hotel Neelakanta (open daily 9am-6:30pm), and **Hotel Neptune,** on the southern edge of Lighthouse Beach (open 24hr.), both offer bank rates. The **Central Bank of India** has a branch in the Kovalam Hotel shopping complex. Open M-F 10:30am-1:30pm, Sa 10:30am-noon.

Library: **Jungle Book Library** (on the way to Lonely Planet Restaurant from Hotel Neptune) lends (Rs5 per day) and sells books in English, French, German, and Dutch. Deposit required. Open daily 10am-4pm.

Bookstore: Many shops on the beach sell musty used books. **Anjana Emporium,** in the Ashok Hotel, has more expensive English-language books, magazines, and postcards. Open M-Sa 10am-8:30pm, Su 10:30am-5pm.

Hospital: Upasana Hospital (tel. 480632), off the road to Kovalam Junction, a 10min. walk from the bus stand. **Pharmacy** is open M-Sa 9:30am-1pm and 4:30-8:30pm, Su 9:30am-1pm. In an emergency, you can call Dr. Chandrasenan at home (tel. 457357).

Police: (tel. 480255), left off the road to Kovalam Junction, 10min. from the bus station on the left. In season, the **Tourist Aid Post** is on the beach. Open daily 9am-7pm.

Post Office: The **GPO** can be reached by taking a left at Kovalam Junction. *Poste Restante.* Open M-Sa 9am-1pm and 1:30-5pm. *Poste Restante* sent here sometimes ends up at in Trivandrum. **Postal Code:** 695527.

Internet: **Alpha Internet Services** (tel. 481951), right on Lighthouse Beach, close to the southern end, has 2 terminals (Rs180 per hr.). Open daily 8am-9:30pm.

KERALA

| PHONE CODE | 0471 |

ACCOMMODATIONS

Prices peak December to January. Off season and during the monsoon, bargain hard—don't let persistent touts determine where you will stay. All accommodations listed are located on Lighthouse Beach and come with attached bathrooms.

- **Wilson's Tourist Home** (tel. 480051), behind the beachfront restaurants, close to Hotel Neelakanta. Rooms arranged around a large courtyard, each with massive bed and balcony. Friendly female staff is a draw for women traveling alone. Doubles Rs350, with A/C Rs1000. Off-season: Rs250/700. Visa.
- **Green Valley Cottages** (tel. 480636). From the beach, walk straight past Hotel Neptune and follow signs back to the paddies. Forsaking the beachfront has its advantages—lower prices and tranquility, for instance. Each immaculate room has a private balcony and chairs to loll around in. Doubles Rs550-700. Off-season: Rs150. In season, reserve at least one month in advance.
- **Jeevan House** (tel. 480662), set slightly back from the beach, midway down the cove. Pleasant, airy rooms have balconies. Doubles Rs200-300, with A/C Rs800-1200.
- **Sumangali Tourist Home** (tel. 481729), behind the Achutna Restaurant on the beach. Clean and simple, but with hot water. Doubles Rs200, with balcony Rs300.

FOOD

The restaurants spread in an almost uninterrupted sweep all the way along the beaches. What little Indian food there is has been de-spiced to appease Western palates. Alcohol is served at many beachfront establishments (beer Rs70).

- **Red Star Restaurant,** though little more than a bamboo hut at the south end of the beach, is the best place in Kovalam to get a feel for the old days. Its one table means you have to hang out and chat with the owner, Mani, who's serious about his restaurant's name—the only decor is a poster of Jyoti Basu, West Bengal's Communist chief minister. *Masala dosa* Rs15, Keralan meal Rs20. Open daily 6am-10pm.
- **German Bakery,** towards the south end of Lighthouse beach. You're a long way from home, but you wouldn't know it taking a bite of that cinnamon-apple strudel (Rs25). Service lacks Teutonic efficiency, though. Open daily 7am-11pm.
- **Santana.** Makes great *masala* and *tandoori* seafood (market price Rs150 for a decent-sized fish) and chocolate banana pancakes (Rs30). Open daily 7am-10pm.
- **Lonely Planet Restaurant.** Follow directions for Green Valley cottages (above) and take a left at the fork; it's on your right, marked by a sign. Veg., mainly Indian fare. *Masala* fried potato Rs25, *thali* Rs40. No liquor allowed. Open daily 7:30am-10pm.

BILE BALANCE The predominant medical tradition in Hindu culture is associated with *ayurveda,* which translates literally as the "knowledge of long life." Practitioners of this wisdom are called *vaidyas.* Ayurvedic medicine takes a holistic approach to diagnosis (a broken heart is as much an ailment as a broken leg) and to treatment (a combination of herbal potions and life notions). The earliest known herbal prescriptions date back to the *Atharva Veda* (c. 1000 BC), when *vaidyas* were performing surgery on external wounds long before their Western counterparts. Ayurvedic medicine, however, is primarily associated with maintaining a balance between the three bodily essences or *doshas: vatta* (wind), *pitta* (bile), and *kapha* (phlegm). *Vatta,* associated with the nervous system and movement, represents kinetic energy. *Kapha,* which opposes *vatta,* is potential energy and is associated with lymph and mucus. Finally, *pitta* mediates between these two forces, governing digestive and metabolic processes. Balance between the three *doshas* is essential to good health, but decadent *doshas* develop distortions.

KERALA

Garzia, on the northern end of the beach. Fresh pasta is a treat, although their version of mac 'n cheese (Rs40) ain't so Kraft-y. Fresh seafood Rs100; cheese, tomato, and garlic pasta Rs55. Open daily 7am-10pm.

👁 🎵 SIGHTS AND ENTERTAINMENT

Tired of the waves? Wave good-bye to your aches and pains with an **ayurvedic massage.** Kerala is currently touted as an ayurvedic haven, and numerous establishments in Kovalam hawk these treatments. Wilson's Tourist Home (tel. 480051) has a masseur for gents and a masseuse for ladies (Rs200 per blissful hr., Rs300 to have your head seen to as well; open M-Sa 9am-5pm). The tourist office promotes "rejuvenation" vacations during the ayurvedic-friendly monsoon months. Peak season also means **yoga** season at many hotels and private institutions. Hotel Neptune offers classes (1hr. session Rs150; 2 per day for a week Rs1200).

During peak season, "cultural nights" featuring **kathakali dance** (see p. 522) take place at the Hotel Ashok (tel. 480101; Tu-F, Rs150) and Hotel Neptune (tel. 480222; M, W, and Sa, Rs100). Make-up starts at 5pm; the dance program begins at 6:45pm. Pirated **movies,** complete with laughter from the original audience, show nightly at several restaurants, including Hotel Flamingo (tel. 480421) and Hawah Beach Restaurant (tel. 48431). The Tourist Facilitation Centre arranges commission-free **backwater cruises** that circle an island 5km from Kovalam. The Rs300 fee covers transportation to the boat, two hours of cruising time, and the return trip to Kovalam. Unlike in the Alleppey-Kollam tour, the boat used in season is a traditional, non-motorized vessel with a rat-tan shade; off season, an uncovered boat is used. If, after spending too much time in Kovalam, you've forgotten that you're in India, take the 20-minute stroll along the coastal road to the ramshackle village of **Vizhinjam** (VEER-in-yam). Only ruins of some small shrines remain in this former capital of the Ay Kings. Brightly painted fishing boats fill the harbor, which is crowned at the north end by a dizzying pink-and-yellow **mosque.**

KOLLAM (QUILON) കൊല്ലം

The appellation "Quilon" is slowly giving way to the town's ancient name "Kollam" (Koy-LAM). Called "Kaulam" Mall by ancient Arabs, and "Coilum" by Marco Polo in the 13th century, the port was the center of the "heroic rebellion" against British rule led by Veluthambi Dalava. Little of this former glory, however, is visible in Kollam today. It is still an active industrial town and exporter of coconuts, but a shopping mall and modern storefronts have obliterated ancient palaces and most of the ancient streets, leaving very little of interest to tourists.

🚌 TRANSPORTATION

Trains: Fares listed are 2nd/1st class. To: **Alleppey** (*Intercity Exp.* 6342, 5:50pm, 1½hr., Rs30/159); **Bangalore** (*Island Exp.* 6525, 10:50am, Rs147/726); **Chennai** (*Chennai Mail,* 2:55pm, 16hr., Rs158/767); **Delhi** (*Kerala Exp.* 2625, 12:10pm, 53hr., Rs319/1983); **Ernakulam** (*Intercity Exp.,* 5:50pm, 3hr., Rs42/213); **Kanyakumari** (10:30am and 1:30pm, 4hr., Rs46/223); **Mangalore** (*Parasuram Exp.* 6349, 7:20am; *Malabar Exp.* 6329, 7:15pm, 14hr., Rs120/598); **Mumbai** (*Jayanthi Janatha* 1082, 8:40am, 46hr., Rs256/1444); **Trivandrum** (several per day 6:35am-8:30pm, 1½hr., Rs26/129); **Varkala** (several per day 6:35am-8:30pm, 30min., Rs18/100).

Buses: **KRSTC bus station,** Jetty Rd., north toward the river and the boat jetty. To: **Alleppey** (every 30min.; 2hr.; Rs26 regular, Rs30 express); **Ernakulam** (every 30min., 3½hr., Rs53); **Trivandrum** (every 10-30min.; 2hr.; Rs22 regular, Rs25 express); **Varkala** (11 per day 6:30am-8pm, 1½hr., Rs11).

KERALA

☀ ORIENTATION

Kollam's streets follow the bends of the canals, turning at confusing angles. The main drag, **National Highway (NH) 47** runs southeast to northwest through town. Beginning in the southeast end of town, NH47 passes the **railway station** before crossing the tracks to the congested center of town, marked by the **clock tower,** where it intersects with **Main Road.** From the intersection of NH47 with **Tourist Bungalow Road,** it twists in a northwest direction past the **post office,** the sprawling Bishop Jerome Nagar Shopping Centre, and the wild Shrine of Our Lady of Velankanni. The next junction is with **Jetty Road,** which leads to the right to the **KSRTC bus station** and the **ferry jetty,** 100m away. A 10-minute walk to the left leads to the sprawling fruit and vegetable **market,** housed in small stores with red-tiled roofs.

Tourist Office: District Tourism Promotion Council (DTPC) has outposts at the railway station (open M-Sa 9am-5:30pm) and near the Tourist Bungalow (tel. 742558; open M-Sa 10am-5pm), but the bus station branch (tel. 745625), staffed by the super-competent Usha, is especially helpful (open M-Sa 6am-6pm). Backwater-tour booking, hotel reservations, and, at the bus station, foreign exchange. Expect heavy promotion of *their* backwater tour (over the ATDC's version) and *their* hotel, Yatri Nivas.

Currency Exchange: State Bank of India, NH47, 100m south of the railway station. Open M-F 10am-2pm, Sa 10am-noon. Gives advances on MC, Visa, and AmEx. The tourist information office at the bus station also changes currency. Open M-Sa 10am-5pm.

Market: A fruit and vegetable market occupies a few blocks of the road that leads from the boat jetty into town (15min. walk from the boat jetty). Another market in front of the flyover in the center of town offers mangoes and international editions of *Newsweek.*

Bookstore: Chani Bookseller, NH47 (tel. 743973), in the Bishop Jerome Nagar Shopping Center. Open M-Sa 9am-8pm.

Pharmacy: Kochappally Medicals, Tourist Bungalow Rd. (tel. 749286), just southwest of the main intersection with NH47 and Main Rd. Open daily 8am-9pm.

Hospital: Nair's Hospital (tel. 742413), 1.5km northeast of the jetty.

Police Station: (tel. 742072), right from the railway station, next the large temple.

Post Office: Head Post Office, NH47, northeast of the intersection with Tourist Bungalow Rd. on the left. *Poste Restante.* Open M-Sa 7am-7:30pm. **Postal Code:** 691001.

Internet: Net4you (tel. 741266), 2nd fl. in the Bishop Jerome Nagar Shopping Centre. Several terminals in shiny and new A/C luxury. Rs90 per hr. Open daily 9am-9pm.

PHONE CODE	0474

⚑ ACCOMMODATIONS AND FOOD

■ **The Tourist Bungalow (Government Guest House),** Tourist Bungalow Rd. (tel. 743620), a few km outside of town (take a rickshaw). This beautiful old British mansion with a huge, echoing ballroom hung with quietly mildewing prints has rooms with 3m-high ceilings and sparse antique furniture. Recently refurbished, it's more gorgeous than ever. Wonderfully romantic and almost always full—come for a look around even if you can't get a room. Attached bathrooms (seat toilets) with tubs and dressing rooms. Singles Rs50; doubles Rs100. Student discounts. Reservations highly recommended.

Yatri Nivas (tel. 745538), opposite the lake from the boat jetty—phone from there for a pickup in their speedboat (Rs10); otherwise, hire a rickshaw (Rs10). Clean rooms have attached baths. Singles Rs110-165; doubles Rs165-220, with A/C Rs385. Extra person Rs50. Reservations recommended.

Hotel Shah International, Tourist Bungalow Rd. (tel. 742362), 100m from NH47. A large place with grand aspirations it doesn't quite live up to. A good value and quiet and conveniently located. All rooms have balconies and attached baths with seat toilets, towels, and soap. Singles Rs180, with A/C Rs380; doubles Rs230/450.

Jala Subhiksha, next to the boat jetty, is a floating restaurant in a lovely traditional *kettuvallam* (boat). Delicious Chinese and Indian dishes: *saiwoo* chicken Rs55, Manchurian tofu Rs45. Open daily 6pm-10pm.

Indian Coffee House, Main Rd., near Iswarya Lodge. From the post office, turn right on NH47, then take the second right. Once a franchise, always a franchise. Masala *dosa* Rs8, banana fry Rs3. Separate rooms for women and families. Open daily 8am-9pm.

Supreme Bakers, from the post office, turn right onto NH47, then take an immediate right; it's on the left. This spic-n-span bakery serves fresh cakes and breads: plain croissant Rs4, pastries Rs4-12. Cold drinks, spicy snacks, and A/C offer relief from the sugar overload. Open M-Sa 9am-8pm.

👁 🎵 SIGHTS AND ENTERTAINMENT

BACKWATER CRUISES. The main attractions in Kollam are the backwater cruises to Alleppey. The boat can take both you and your luggage, making this a convenient and beautiful mode of transport north up the Keralan coast. Many of the cruises make several stops along the way, including one at the Mata Amrithananda Mayi Mission (see below). Cruises are run by the District Tourism Promotion Council (DTPC). For more information, see p. 513. *(Tours depart 10:30am from the DTPC office near the KSRTC bus stand and the boat jetty and arrive in Alleppey 6:30pm. Report to the office by 10am. Rs150, Rs100 for ISIC holders.)* The KDTC office at the bus station organizes additional backwater tours, including a popular **village tour** *(daily 9am departures from KDTC; Rs300, 15% discount if purchased directly from KDTC).*

SHRINE OF OUR LADY OF VELANKANNI. This towering shrine rises above everything in its wake. Festooned with bright plastic flowers and tinsel, the shrine occupies a central place in Kollam's religious life. Although a mere 13 years old, the adolescent shrine has already gained a reputation for healing and performing miracles. On Wednesdays, crowds line up inside, fingering rosaries and praying for hours. *(NH47, near Jetty Rd. Mass W 8am and noon; 5pm mass usually in Malayalam.)*

MATA AMRITHANANDA MAYI MISSION. Backwater cruises frequently stop to pick up and drop off passengers at the ashram of one of India's few female gurus, Mata Amrithananda Mayi Devi. Particularly popular with Westerners, this place boasts its own accommodation block (Rs150 per day, including food). The backwater-cruise boats honor partially used tickets—a single ticket will take you from Kollam to the ashram and, a few days later, on to Alleppey (or vice versa).

NEAR KOLLAM: VARKALA

The town of Varkala, with its quiet beach and towering cliffs, just might rescue South India's growing reputation for over-commercialized beaches. Though Varkala, 25km from Kollam, is slowly developing an affinity for tourist dollars, for the time being it retains some of the beauty and tranquility for which Kovalam was once famed. The town's only real beach sits at the base of a 32m cliff which shoulders the burden of most of Varkala's tourist infrastructure. Beach Road takes you past the Devaswom Building, beside the temple pond, where you can see **kathakali dance** performances staged by the Varkala Cultural Club (tel. 603612; M, W, and F 6:45pm, Rs100). On the cliff-top north of the beach, various operations, including the **Scientific School of Yoga and Massage** (1½hr. massage Rs300), promise a combination of spiritual and physical rejuvenation.

Buses stop at the temple junction, a short walk from the beach. To: Trivandum (6 per day 6am-5pm, 1½hr., Rs15) and Kollam (8:30am and 8:45pm, 1-2hr., Rs11). The **railway station** is a couple of kilometers from the temple junction (Rs15 autorickshaw ride). To: Trivandum (several per day 7am-9pm, 1hr.) and Kollam (several per day 6am-10:40pm, 40min., Rs18/100). Presiding over the temple junction is the **Bureau de Change,** which lives up to its name providing STD/ISD, fax, Internet services (Rs150 per hr.), and tourist information, including bus and train schedules.

KERALA

The cliff-top overlooking the beach is crowded with hotels, including the **Seaview Cliff House** (doubles with bath Rs250-500) and **Hill View** (doubles Rs250). Views cost money in Varkala, so wander inland if your budget is tight. Varkala's restaurants, which open early and close late, invariably have lengthy menus featuring everything from hash browns to *pad thai*. The **Clafouti Bakery** has excellent croissants (Rs10) and brownies (Rs18; open Sa-Th 8:30am-6pm).

ALLEPPEY (ALAPPUZHA) ആലപ്പുഴ

The two canals that carve out the center of Alleppey were once the major arteries of a great shipping center, but now tangles of water lilies fill the waterways. Today, most of the town's activity is derived from the prodigious amount of *coir* (woven coconut fiber) products shipped through here on small boats propelled by pole. Partly because of the town's falling economic star, Alleppey provides a prime example of a traditional Keralan town, replete with steeply pitched red-tiled roofs. But the town's several snake-boat races, especially the annual Nehru Trophy Boat Race (2nd Sa in Aug.), also attract the attention of international tourists.

■ **ORIENTATION AND PRACTICAL INFORMATION.** The town is sandwiched between two east-west canals: the **North Canal** and the **South Canal,** about a 10-minute walk apart. The streets between the two canals are laid out in a simple grid. The **railway station** is near the beach 4km southwest of the town center. Trains go to: **Ernakulam** (8 per day 6am-7:20pm, 1½hr., Rs11/25); **Kollam** (*Trivandrum Exp.* 6324, 7:15pm; *Nagercoil Exp.* 6305, 12:55am, 2hr., Rs40/131); **Mumbai** (*Mumbai Exp.* 6332, F 7:20am, 44hr., Rs355/1385); and **Trivandrum** (*Guruvayur-Nagercoil Exp.* 6305, 12:55am; *Ernakulam-Trivandrum Exp.* 6341, 7:15am, 3hr., Rs40/220). The **KSRTC bus station** is at the east end of **Boat Jetty Road,** which runs along the south bank of North Canal. An auto-rickshaw to the boat jetty or bus station will cost you Rs35. Buses go to: **Cochin** (every 20min., 2hr., Rs17); **Kollam** (every 20min., 2hr., Rs26); **Kottayam,** for buses to Periyar (every hr. 5:50am-9pm, 1½hr., Rs15); and **Trivandrum** (every 20min., 4hr., Rs47). The **District Tourism Promotion Council (DTPC),** Boat Jetty Rd. (tel. 253308 or 251796), west of the bus station, distributes maps and sells tickets for boat rides and the Nehru Trophy Boat Race (open M-Sa 9am-6pm). Public and private boats depart from the jetties nearby.

Mullakal Road, the large cross-street that bridges the North Canal, leads to the fruit and vegetable **market** north of town. Immediately after crossing the canal, take a right and then a left to reach the new branch of the **ATDC Tourist Office** (tel. 243462; open daily 8am-8pm). South from the North Canal, on Mullakal Rd., the **Indian Bank** is past the intersection with Cullen Rd., on the left (open M-F 10am-2pm, Sa 10am-noon). **Medical College Hospital** (tel. 251611), 1.5km south of the intersection of Boat Jetty and Mullakal Rd., houses a 24-hour **pharmacy.** Continue south until Mullakal Rd. ends at the South Canal, then turn right to reach a small branch of the **post office** (open M-Sa 9am-5pm). The **Head Post Office,** 500m to the west and then right on Exchange Rd., has *Poste Restante* (M-Sa 9:30am-2:30pm) and sells stamps (M-Sa 9:30am-5:30pm). **Postal Code:** 688001. Stone Bridge, which takes Church Rd. over the South Canal, leads south to **Atlanta Computers** (Internet access Rs90 per hr.; open M-Sa 9:30am-7:30pm, Su 2-5pm). **Telephone Code:** 0477.

■ **ACCOMMODATIONS AND FOOD.** Most hotels are just north of North Canal, 10 minutes from the bus stand, but the **Arcadia Hotel,** next to the bus station, is more conveniently located. Partially renovated, the hotel has comfortable rooms that have been freshly painted in a cheerful pink. (Singles Rs125; doubles Rs200-300, with A/C Rs750.) The **Komala Hotel,** Mullakal Rd. (tel. 243631), is north over the North Canal traffic bridge. Turn right, then left; the hotel is set back on the right. Attached baths (some seat and some squat toilets) have gleaming white tiles. (Singles Rs118, with A/C Rs495; doubles Rs172/605; triples Rs195.) **Karthika Tourist Home** (tel. 245524), 50m north over the North Canal traffic bridge, is painted a pleasant blue. This well-run establishment has great prices, but the rooms could be cleaner. Attached baths have seat or squat toilets. (Singles Rs60; doubles Rs100; groovy circular room Rs150.) **Mutteal Holiday Inn,** Nehru Trophy Rd. (tel. 242955), east of the footbridge, has double rooms for Rs300. Farther afield (Rs20 by auto-rickshaw, Rs1 by bus), the brand-new **Yatri Nivas Hotel** (tel. 244460) offers big, comfortable rooms (singles Rs100-200; doubles Rs150-300). The standard ruffle-clad waiters at the **Indian Coffee House,** Mullakal Rd., a few blocks south of the North Canal, serve *masala dosas* (Rs8) and meals (Rs13; open daily 8am-9pm). **Hotel Annapoorna,** Boat Jetty Rd., near the bus station, serves standard South Indian veg. fare in a sterile environment (meals Rs14-18; open daily 7am-9pm). **Cafe Venice,** so-named for its location overlooking a fetid canal, is a KTDC-run, A/C restaurant serving Keralan meals (Rs20-25) and chicken *masala* (Rs50). It also serves as a convenient breakfast stop for departing backwater trippers. (Open daily 8am-10pm.) Most of Alleppey's hotels also have restaurants.

SIGHTS AND ENTERTAINMENT. Though the main reason people come to Alleppey is in order to leave it via some means of backwater transport, the palm-lined town is pleasantly attractive and laid-back. Much of the traditional architecture has yet to be converted into concrete block constructions, and wandering along the South Canal takes you by many of Alleppey's traditional red-tile-roofed houses, with their deep, shady eaves and decorated gables.

The highlight of Alleppy's tourist calendar is the annual **Nehru Trophy Boat Race,** held on the second Saturday of August in the lake east of town. Hundreds of oarsmen are required to crew each of the 65m-long snake-boats, traditional Keralan battle vessels. The first race was held in honor of Prime Minister Jawaharlal Nehru during his visit here in 1952. Nehru was so flattered and fascinated by the race that he awarded the race's winners with a trophy; henceforth, the event developed into an Alleppey institution. Tickets are available from the DTPC and may be purchased up to one month in advance (Rs10-250). Other snake-boat races are held throughout the year, among them the **Moolam Boat Race** at Champakulam in July. The ATDC arranges backwater boat rides to the race (Rs100 round-trip).

For most of the year, daily **backwater cruises** run the 80km of green canals that separate Alleppey from Kollam. Trips often include visits to an 11th-century statue of the Buddha, a temple, a *coir*-producing village, a swimming hole, and an ashram (see p. 511). A traditional Keralan meal is served on a banana leaf for lunch. The ATDC and DTPC both operate cruises (10:30am departure, 6:30pm arrival; tours operate in both directions). Make reservations at either office before 10am at least one day in advance. During the off season (June-Aug.), trips with less than 10 people will be cancelled. Both the ATDC and DTPC charge Rs150 for the trip, but the DTPC gives a Rs50 discount to ISIC cardholders and children under 12. The ATDC and other private agencies along Boat Jetty Rd., including Penguin Tourist Service (tel. 261522; open daily 8am-6pm), arrange shorter trips on boats of varying size and means of propulsion. Private agencies also arrange stays on traditional "rice" boats—converted **houseboats** with tiny bedrooms, bathrooms, dining areas, and two men to pole the boat around (one night's stay for 2 including food, Rs4300). The ATDC can also arrange **village stays** for Rs300-500. The public **ferry ride** to and from Kottayam is a shorter, cheaper, but still pleasant option (7 per day 7am-6:30pm, 2½hr., Rs8).

PERIYAR TIGER RESERVE പെരിയാർ

Situated in 777 sq. km of lofty woodlands interspersed with grasslands on the border of Tamil Nadu, Periyar Tiger Reserve surrounds the artificial Periyar Lake. The woods around the lake were set aside as Reserved Forests in 1899, becoming the Nellikkampatty Sanctuary in 1934. Renamed and merged with the forest department in 1966, Periyar was incorporated into **Project Tiger** in 1979 (see p. 378).

KERALA

⚡ ORIENTATION AND PRACTICAL INFORMATION

Periyar encompasses the reserve and a small collection of hotels at the town of **Thekkady**. Most park activities, boat rides in particular, are based here. Most tourists, however, stay in **Kumily**, north of the park. There are plenty of cheap hotels and other amenities along **Thekkady Road**, which runs from the Kumily bus station, on the border of Tamil Nadu, all the way to the boat jetty at the end of Thekkady. The entrance to the reserve is about 1.5 km from the bus stand; it's another 3km to the boat jetty. Walking through the park is permitted, as long as you stay on the road, but you may not enter the forest without a guide. With few exceptions, most tourist needs are met in Kumily rather than Thekkady. Unless otherwise noted, the following listings are for Kumily.

Buses: Both private and KSRTC buses operate out of **Kumily Bus Stand** on the Tamil Nadu border, but you've got to walk across the border for Tamil Nadu buses. From Kumily to: **Allepey** (11:45am, 5hr., Rs35); **Ernakulam** (every hr. 5:30am-10:30pm, 6hr., Rs55); **Kottayam** (every 30min. 2am-11pm, 4hr., Rs28); **Madurai** (every 30min., 4hr., Rs30); **Munnar** (4 per day 6am-1:30pm, 5hr., Rs39). From Thekkady (buses stop in Kumily approximately 15min. later) to: **Ernakulam** (6:45am and 2:45pm); **Trivandrum** (8:15am and 3:15pm, 8hr., Rs71).

Local Transportation: Taxis, jeeps, and **auto-rickshaws** to the boat jetty in Thekkady are readily available from the Kumily bus stand (Rs40). There's a lot to be said for walking through the reserve; even in the middle of the day, the road is pleasantly shaded, and you stand a good chance of seeing (and hearing) some of the wildlife.

Tourist Office: The **Government of Kerala Tourist Office** (tel. 322620), 5min. from the bus station towards the reserve; it's on the left, away from the road up the stairs in a yellow building. Arranges private tours of local spice plantations (Rs600 per jeep; 3hr.). Open M-Sa 10am-5pm. For information on activities in Periyar, see the **Wildlife Information Centre** (tel. 322028), at the boat jetty in Thekkady. Open daily 6:30am-5pm.

Currency Exchange: The State Bank of Travancore, behind the bus station, exchanges foreign currency and AmEx and Thomas Cook traveler's checks. Open M-F 10am-2pm, Sa 10am-noon. Some hotels also exchange currency and traveler's checks.

Bookstore: DC Books, next to the tourist office, has a large selection of books on India and plenty of fiction. Open daily 9:30am-9:30pm.

Pharmacy: High Range Drug House (tel. 322043). Open M-Sa 8:30am-8:30pm.

Hospital: St. Augustine Hospital, Spring Valley (tel. 322042), 3km from the town center.

Police: (tel. 322049), beyond the bus station toward the Tamil Nadu border. **Tourist Police Office,** Thekkady Rd., before the Ambadi Hotel. Open daily 8am-8pm.

Emergency: Police, tel. 100. **Fire,** tel. 101. **Ambulance,** tel. 102.

Post Office: Near the bus stand on the main road. Open M-Sa 9am-5pm (packages accepted until 3pm). *Post Restante.* There is also a branch at the park entrance. Open M-F 9am-5pm, Sa 9am-1pm. **Postal Code:** 685509.

Internet: Rissas Communication (tel. 322103), opposite the Lake Queen Tourist Home, has the only terminal in town. And is it *slow!* Rs125 per hr. Open daily 6am-midnight.

PHONE CODE	0486

◤ ACCOMMODATIONS

There are only three hotels inside the reserve, and all are run by the KTDC. So be prepared to spend more to stay there; otherwise, plan to shack up in Kumily.

🏨 **Lake Queen Tourist Home** (tel. 322084), 200m down the main road. Run by a charitable foundation and managed by a retired military man, this place exudes a kind of regimented warmth. "Special" doubles feature mosquito nets, towels, and soap. All rooms have attached baths with seat toilets. Singles Rs107-215; doubles Rs161-268.

Hotel Ambadi (tel. 322193), 1km from the bus stand. Slightly dark cottages are a great deal. Nice rugs and furniture and large attached baths with seat toilets, towels, and toilet paper. Check-out 10am. Cottages (for 2) Rs425; rooms Rs690-990. Visa, MC.

Periyar House (tel. 322026), 2km inside the reserve, is the cheapest of the KTDC hotels in the park. Attached baths with seat toilets. Breakfast and dinner included. Singles Rs500-1300; doubles Rs700-1500. Off-season: Rs300-750/500-950. Visa, MC.

Hotel Regent Tower (tel. 322570), 50m from the bus stand on the main road. Big, functional rooms with access to balconies overlooking the...bus station. Attached baths with seat toilets. Doubles Rs250-350.

Coffee Inn, 200m beyond Hotel Ambadi. 8 basic rooms, including a couple of rustic bamboo shacks (with mosquito nets). A fun alternative. Singles Rs100; doubles Rs150, with bath Rs250.

🍴 FOOD

Hotel Ambadi Restaurant, one of the town's best, offers the standard Indian, Chinese, and Continental fare. The "Kerala meal" (Rs20) is delicious, and mashed potatoes (Rs40) and French onion soup (Rs30) are good, too. Open daily 6:30am-10:30pm.

Coffee Inn, 500m before the park entrance. This popular tourist joint features porridge (Rs25), pizza, and potatoes (mashed, Rs30). The shady garden is a nice place to while away the hours before your food arrives. That's right, *hours*. Open early-late.

Snack Shop, near the Thekkady jetty, is the only non-hotel restaurant in the reserve. Sodas and pre-packaged cookies help get you through the day. Open daily 8am-6pm.

Sabala Restaurant, Karthika Tourist Home. Though Sabala is recommended for good, cheap South Indian food, the clientele seem to prefer curious liquids—it may not be an ideal hang-out for single women. Beer Rs80, *thalis* Rs16-25. Open daily 7am-10pm.

⚠ THE RESERVE

Open daily 6am-6pm. Rs50 for 3 days (foreigners). **Boat Tours** *(7, 9:30, 11:30am, 2, and 4pm; Rs50 top deck, Rs25 lower deck). In season, purchase tickets a day ahead at the Wildlife Information Centre (Rs25) or the KTDC ticket booth at the boat jetty. If a particular boat cruise is sold out, enquire at the reception desk of the Aranya Nivas Hotel, up the steps behind the jetty; the hotel allocates a number of spots for its guests, many of which don't show up.* **Jungle walks** *(7:30am, 3hr., Rs10);* **elephant rides** *(30min., Rs30).*

KERALA

The reserve is home to a variety of animals, including wild boar, monkeys, the Nilgiri langur, Malabar giant squirrels, barking deer, and gaur. Most people, however, come to Periyar to see its main attractions: wild elephants and the extremely elusive tiger. Unfortunately the golden cats, hunted to the brink of extinction, are a rare sight; Periyar currently claims to be home to 49 of the world's 3700 remaining wild tigers. At a cool 900 meters, Periyar is a good place to relax, start short treks, or take an elephant ride. November and May are the best months to visit, and April and May brings many animals down to the lake to drink.

> **⚠ WARNING.** So-called "official" guides often approach tourists with offers of jungle walks and jeep tours—contracting them is illegal, and you may be fined.

The two main modes of exploring the Reserve are by boat tour and trekking. Early morning and evening are the best times to see the animals. Jungle-walking groups are small during the monsoon, when you should come prepared to encounter leeches. At other times of the year, the group may have as many as ten people, so it might be wise to hire a private guide from the information center. Elephant rides are purely for entertainment, so you probably won't see much. One of the best ways to see the wildlife is to spend a night in an **observation tower.** The Wildlife Information Centre handles the necessary reservations. The tower houses a maximum of two people, who must provide their own food, water, and bedding. The center will arrange transportation by boat (Rs100 per person, boat fee Rs15).

COCHIN (KOCHI) കൊച്ചി

In 1341, torrential floods from the Western Ghats hollowed out Lake Vembanad
giving Cochin a perfect harbor. Over the next few centuries, the quiet fishing vil
lage spread over a cluster of islands and narrow peninsulas transformed itself into
a wealthy, cosmopolitan port. Arab, Jewish, and Syrian Christian settlers from the
Middle East started the long trend much before Portuguese and Dutch sailors
scrambled for access to the Malabar Coast and the lucrative spice trade centuries
later. The Portuguese, Cochin's first colonial rulers, were followed by the Dutch
and then the British, who briefly ruled the Madras Presidency from here.

Cochin's cultural grafts have thrived; "Fort Cochin" is renowned for its tangle of
different traditions, heritages, and architectures. Chinese fishing nets line the har
bor's mouth, Dutch-style houses cram narrow streets, and Jew Town is a five
minute stroll from the raja's palace (known locally as "The Dutch Palace"), built
by the Portuguese, filled with murals depicting scenes from the Hindu epics. Con
trasting with the archaic, vaguely European feel that Fort Cochin has managed to
preserve, Ernakulam plays the part of its modern alter-ego. Frantic, brash, and pol
luted, Ernakulam is as bustling as Ft. Cochin is bucolic and provides tourists to
Fort Cochin with every imaginable amenity.

█ TRANSPORTATION

Current plane, train, and bus schedules can be found in *Hello, Cochin* (free) or
Jaico Timetable (Rs5), available from most tourist offices.

Airport: At the south end of Willingdon Island. **Indian Airlines,** DH Rd., Ernakulam (tel
370242), near the Foreshore Rd. intersection. Open daily 10am-1pm and 1:45-5pm
To: **Bangalore** (1 per day, 1hr., US$70); **Chennai** (4 per week, 1hr., US$105); **Delhi** (
per day, 4hr., US$300); **Mumbai** (1 per day, 2hr., US$150); **Goa** (1 per day, 1hr
US$110). **Jet Airways** (tel. 369423) also has 2-3 daily flights to Mumbai and 4 flight
per week to Chennai.

Trains: Cochin has 3 stations. **Ernakulam Junction Railway Station,** 2 blocks east of Jo
Junction, gets the most use. **Ernakulam Town Railway Station,** 4km farther north alon
Banerji Rd., is far from MG Rd. **Cochin Harbour Railway Station,** on Willingdon Island
is serviced by few trains. Fares listed are 2nd/1st class. From **Ernakulam Junction** to
Alleppey (7 per day 6:15am-11:50pm, 1½hr., Rs23/125); **Mumbai (Kurla)** via Madg
aon (Netravati Exp. 6636, 4:45am, 26hr., Rs337/1255); **Trivandrum** (6 per day 4am
5:15pm, 4½hr., Rs61/294). From **Ernakulam Town** to: **Bangalore** (*Bangalore Exp
6525*, 2:35pm, 13hr., Rs124/611); **Calicut** (*Parsuram Exp. 6349*, 11am; *Malaba
Exp. 6329*, 11pm, 4½hr., Rs53/254).

Buses: The **KSRTC Bus Stand,** 2 blocks east of Senoy Junction, central Ernakulam. To
Alleppey (every 30min., 1½hr., Rs25); **Bangalore** (8 per day 6am-9:15pm, 14hr.
Rs220) via **Mysore** (10hr., Rs120); **Calicut** (every hr., 5hr., Rs75); **Coimbatore** (fre
quent, 4½hr., Rs54); **Munnar** (6:30am, 5hr., Rs46); **Trivandrum** (very frequent, 4½hr
Rs80). Tamil Nadu State Transportation services: **Chennai** (3:30pm, 15hr., Rs199) an
Madurai (8:15am and 8:30pm, 10hr., Rs89). **Private bus companies** also run long
distance buses from several termini in Cochin: Ernakulam South, opposite the Ernak
lam Junction Railway Station, and High Court Junction, at the end of Shanmugham R
Several agencies, such as **Indira Travels** (tel. 360693), have offices around Jos Jun
tion, Ernakulam. Deluxe coaches depart from **Jos Junction** to: **Bangalore** (9 per da
12hr., Rs240); **Chennai** (4, 4:30, and 5:30pm; 15hr.; Rs300); **Coimbatore** (9 per da
4hr., Rs120); **Munnar** (7am from Ernakulam South; 6:30am and 12:30pm from Hig
Court Junction, 5hr., Rs39).

Ferries: The best way to move from one island to another, frequent commutes cost les
than Rs2 and run at least 6am-9pm (no services from Ernakulam's Main Jetty to Fo
Cochin noon-1pm, and vice versa 1:20-2:55pm). From **Ernakulam: Main Jetty,** mid
town, to Willingdon Island and Fort Cochin (buy tickets at the SWTD counter to avoi

KERALA

Elamkulam Rd.

KP Vallon Rd.

TO TRIVANDRUM

Azad Rd.

Warriom Rd.

KSRTC Bus Stand

Charara Cultural Center

Ernakulam Junction Railway Station

See India Foundation

Kerala Ayurveda Pharmacy

Cochin Cultural Center

Parambhihara Rd.

Ernakulam Town Railway Station

ERNAKULAM

Veekshanam Rd.

Inman Kovil Rd.

Chittoor Rd.

Ernakulam South Bus Stand

Mannam Rd.

Andhra Bank

Banerji Rd.

Jews St.

Mahatma Gandhi Rd.

Indian Coffee House D

JOS.

Medical Trust Hospital

TD Rd.

Gopalaprabhu Rd.

Convent Rd.

Coco Cabana

Bimbi's/ Khyber

Bimbi's/ Khyber

Hot Breads

Chinese Garden

Delhi Durbar

Thomas Cook

Mathai Manjooran Rd.

Market Rd.

Princess Room/ Suvarna

Press Club Rd.

GPO

Indian Coffee House

Park Ave

Hospital Rd.

Church Landing Rd.

Dinbur Hall Rd.

Indian Airlines

Foreshore Rd.

Police Commissioner's Office

High Court Junction Bus Station

Broadway

Shanmugham Rd.

Current Books

Marine Dr. Walkway

KTDC Tourist Reception Center

State Bank of India

Main Jetty

Tourist Desk

Sealord Jetty

GCDA Shopping Centre

High Court Jetties

Bolghatty Island

Vembanad Lake

Willingdon Island

TO AIRPORT

KERALA

Arabian Sea

Embarkation Jetty

FTDC

Malabar Hotel

Milne Rd.

Milne Jetty

Terminus Jetty

Cochin Harbour Railway Station

Bristow Rd.

Indira Gandhi Rd.

Customs Jetty

Mattancherry Jetty

Dutch Palace

Synagogue

Moutran Azad Rd.

MATTANCHERRY

Hotel Seagull Rest.

Bazaar Rd.

Padinara Mosque

Jain Temple

Nehru Memorial Town Hall

Santo Gopalan Rd.

Gundu Island

N

Vypeen Island Jetty

Vypeen Island

Calvathy Rd.

Palace Rd.

FORT COCHIN

Bastian St.

Beach Rd.

300 yards

300 meters

0

0

SEE FORT COCHIN MAP

Napier St.

Cochin
ACCOMMODATIONS
A Basoto Lodge
B Hotel Aiswarya
C Hotel Sangeetha
D Woodlands Hotel
E Hotel Luciya

being double-charged); **High Court Jetty** to Vypeen Island and to and from Bolghatty Island. From **Fort Cochin: Customs Jetty** to Willingdon Island's Terminus and Malabar Hotel Jetties (M-Sa), then on to Ernakulam's Main Jetty (last ferry 6:30pm); **Vypeen Island Jetty** (across from the bus stand) to Vypeen Island. From **Mattancherry** (the jetty is across from the Dutch Palace) to Willingdon Island. From **Willingdon Island: Embarkation Jetty** (northeast side) to Vypeen Island and Ernakulam; **Terminus Jetty** (southwest side) to Ft. Cochin and Mattancherry. From **Vypeen Island:** to Ft. Cochin, Willingdon Island's Embarkation Jetty, and Ernakulam's High Court Jetty.

Other Local Transportation: Local buses are cheap (under Rs4) and orderly. In Ernakulam local buses depart frequently from the KRSTC bus station and can also be nabbed as they pass through town. Buses to Ft. Cochin depart from the east side of MG Rd., south of Jos Junction. In Ft. Cochin, local buses run from the bus stand (across from the Vypeen Island jetty) over the bridge onto Willingdon Island, past the airport, across the bridge to Ernakulam, and up MG Rd. In Ernakulam, **taxis** and **auto-rickshaws** are plentiful during the day but scarce at night. In Ft. Cochin, buses and taxis do not operate, but cycle- and auto-rickshaws can be found near the jetties. Auto-rickshaw-*wallahs* may refuse to use the meters, but most in-town fares should be less than Rs15. The peninsula is navigable by foot, and **bike** rentals are available from the Vasco Hospitality Center (Rs5 per hr., Rs35 per day) and the Tharavadu Tourist Home (Rs40 per day).

✴ ORIENTATION

Cochin is spread around **Lake Vembanad** and consists of **Ernakulam** on the shore of the mainland, **Fort Cochin** and **Mattancherry** on the peninsula, Vypeen Island, and the smaller Willingdon, Vallarpadam, Gundy, and Bolghatty Islands. The central railway and bus stations and most of the hotels are along the eastern shore of Lake Vembanad, but tourists generally devote their waking hours to the other side of the lake and the sight-filled peninsula.

Ernakulam's three main streets, **Shanmugham, Mahatma Gandhi (MG),** and **Chitoor Roads,** run north-south, parallel to the shore. MG Road is intersected by three major cross-streets which lead to the lake shore: **Convent Road** intersects at **Shenoys Junction** a couple of blocks west of the **central bus station;** three blocks south of Shenoys Junction, **Hospital Road** runs between MG Rd. and the lake-front; farther south, **Jos Junction** marks the intersection with **Durbar Hall (DH) Road.**

Princess Street, at the northern tip of the peninsula, is Fort Cochin's main drag. It extends to **Calvathy Road,** which skirts the shore. **Jew Town** and Mattancherry, home of the Dutch Palace, are on the eastern side of the peninsula. In the early 20th century, a mammoth dredging project created **Willingdon Island,** sandwiched between Ernakulam and the peninsula. Willingdon is home to the **airport** and, 2km south, the **Cochin Harbour Railway Station.** With a 270° view of the harbor, the Taj Malabar Hotel sits at the northern tip of the island.

🛈 PRACTICAL INFORMATION

Tourist Office: There is a privately run **Tourist Desk,** Ernakulam (tel. 371761), at the dock-side ticket office at the Main Jetty. In season the friendly and helpful staff posts cultural events on the board outside. Open daily 9am-6pm. (For information on their **Backwater Cruises,** see p. 524.) **KTDC Tourist Reception Centre,** Shanmugham Rd., Ernakulam (tel. 353234), next to the State Bank of India, offers backwater and city tours. Open daily 8am-7pm. The **tourist police booth** in Ernakulam Junction Railway Station is surprisingly helpful and may even have a map. Open daily 9am-5:30pm. There are a number of privately run tourist offices in and around Princess St., Ft. Cochin, including the **Vasco Information Centre** (tel. 229877), which distributes the informative map and brochure *Walking Through Ft. Cochin.* Open daily 9:30am-11pm.

Immigration Office: Police Commissioner's Office, Banerji Rd., Ernakulam. East of High Court Jetty, on the corner of Shanmugham Rd. on the left. **Visa extensions** (student and entry visas only) take up to 10 days, and you may need to leave your passport for the duration. Open M-Sa 10:15am-1:15pm and 2-5:30pm. Closed holidays and 2nd Sa.

Currency Exchange: Thomas Cook, MG Rd., Ernakulam (tel. 373829), near the Air India building. Open M-Sa 9:30am-6pm. **South Indian Bank,** Ft. Cochin (tel. 226824), opposite the Santa Cruz Basilica, exchanges all traveler's checks. Open M-F 10am-2pm. **Andhra Bank,** MG Rd. (tel. 363920), 2 blocks south of Jos Junction, gives cash advances on credit cards. Open M-F 10am-2pm, Sa 10am-noon.

Market: In Ft. Cochin, beach shacks sell fresh fish. In Ernakulam, there are shops of every stripe at Jos Junction and a lot of shopping action on and around Broadway. The area near the jetty features roadside hawkers, used-book kiosks, and fruit stands.

Bookstore: Idiom, Mattancherry, across from the Pardesi Synagogue. Crusty classics and Indian fiction. Open daily 10am-6pm. They've opened a new branch on Bastion St., in the center of Ft. Cochin. Open daily noon-9pm. **Current Books,** Press Club Rd., Ernakulam, is open M-Sa 9:30am-7:30pm.

Hospital: Medical Trust Hospital, MG Rd., Ernakulam (tel. 371852), 3 blocks south of Jos Junction, is currently being renovated and installed with new U.S. equipment. The **pharmacy** inside is open 24hr. **Gautham Hospital,** Ft. Cochin (tel. 223055), is difficult to find; it's best to take a rickshaw or call an ambulance.

Police: Police Commissioner, Banerji Rd., Ernakulam. East of the High Court Jetty, on the corner of Shanmugham Rd. on the left. The **police station** (tel. 394500) is north of the commissioner's office, on the left around the curve to the right. **Fort Cochin Police** is behind the bus station opposite the Vypeen Island Jetty.

Post Office: Kochi Head Post Office, Ft. Cochin, has *Poste Restante*. Open M-Sa 9am-5pm. Telegrams and stamps sold M-Sa 9am-5pm. Parcels accepted M-F 9am-3pm, Sa 9am-2pm. Ernakulam's **GPO,** Hospital Rd., between Foreshore and MG Rd. Open M-F 8am-8pm, Sa 9:30am-2:30pm and 4-8pm, Su 10am-4pm. **Postal Code:** 682001.

Internet: Raiyaan Communications, MG Rd., Ernakulam (tel. 351387), at Padma Junction, offers web access (Rs60 per hr.). Open M-Sa 8am-8pm, Su 9am-1pm. Fort Cochin's internet services seldom cost under Rs100 per hr. **Call'n'Fax,** Princess St. (tel. 223438; email callnfax@md3.vsnl.net.in), next to Elite Hotel (Rs120 per hr.). You can receive email at their address. Open daily 8am-11pm.

PHONE CODE	0484

 ## ACCOMMODATIONS

ERNAKULAM

Narakathara Road, south of Shenoys Circle, heading west off MG Rd., is home to several cheap hotels with basic rooms in the Rs100-200 range.

Hotel Luciya (tel. 381177), behind the KRSTC bus station, is well-run and of good value. Its enormous size almost ensures room availability. Singles (squat toilet) Rs110, with A/C Rs250; doubles (seat toilet and balcony) Rs220/375.

Basoto Lodge, Press Club Rd. (tel. 352140), close to Market Rd. Comfortable, high-ceilinged house with basic facilities is very popular with foreigners. Check-out 24hr. Singles Rs60; doubles with bath (squat toilets) Rs120; triples with bath Rs160.

Hotel Sangeetha (tel. 368487), east from Jos Junction towards the railway station. Take the first left; Sangeetha is on the left. Smiling staff escorts you to clean rooms with Star TV and soft beds. Breakfast at attached restaurant included. Check-out 24hr. Singles Rs330, with A/C Rs550; doubles Rs470/660. Extra person Rs125. Visa, MC.

Hotel Aiswarya, Warrion Rd. (tel. 364454), near Jos Junction where Warrion meets DH Rd. Cool marble floors, decent furnishings, and funky bedspreads that are whisked away once you check in. All rooms have TV and bath with hot water and seat toilets. Check-out 24hr. Singles Rs300, with A/C Rs450; doubles Rs400/500. Visa, MC.

Woodlands Hotel, MG Rd. (tel. 382051), 1 block north of Jos Junction. Popular with Indian businessmen and foreigners, Woodlands is in the commercial heart of Ernakulam. Color TVs and carved furniture grace the rooms. Marble bathrooms have hot water. Lobby travel desk is helpful. Check-out 24hr. Singles Rs350, with A/C Rs525; doubles Rs475/700. Extra person Rs75/100. Visa, MC, AmEx, traveler's checks.

FORT COCHIN

Flee the bustle of Ernakulam for the Olde Worlde tranquility of Ft. Cochin. High season (Dec.-Jan.) accommodation in Ft. Cochin, however, may be limited.

🖼 **Spencer's Tourist Home,** Parade St. (tel. 225049). Turn right off of Rose St.; Spencer's is the handsome, rambling old house on the left. Run by 3 friendly brothers. Dorm beds in a big room with cable TV, couch, and reading materials. Large, clean rooms; attached baths have seat toilets. Dorm beds Rs40; singles Rs60; doubles with bath Rs250-300.

🖼 **Delight Tourist Resort,** Rose St. (tel. 228658), south from St. Francis Church; on the left before the end of the field. This family run hotel hardly qualifies as a resort, but it's certainly a delightful place to stay. Large rooms with attached baths, set in a lovely house with a large library. Doubles Rs250-700. Off-season (Apr.-Nov.): 50% discount.

Chiramel Residency, Lilly St. (tel. 227310), close to the intersection with Parade St. A small, family run guest house. Mosquito nets supplied by the staff in this comfortable place with great home-cooking. Doubles Rs350, with bath Rs500, with A/C Rs1000.

Tharavadu Tourist Home, Quiros St. (tel. 226897). From the south end of Princess St. turn right, and then left. Well-maintained, 400-year-old house has dimly lit stairs leading to 8 fairly clean rooms, some with common bath (seat toilet and shower). Rooms Rs135-205, based on size and availability of the "Goofy" bedspread.

Hotel Park Avenue (tel. 222671), at the intersection of Princess and Bastion St. A marble-faced monstrosity, this is nevertheless a great place to stay. Modest-sized rooms have attached baths, and everything works. Check-out noon. Singles Rs200, with A/C Rs500; doubles Rs300/850. Off-season (Apr.-Sept.): knock off 30%.

Vasco Hospitality Centre (tel. 229877), on the corner of Bastion and Rose St., offers 7 basic rooms in a tired old house. Local legend has it that Vasco da Gama expired here on Christmas Eve, 1524. But don't be put off; it's since come under new management. The obliging owner provides tourist information, bike rentals (Rs5 per hr., Rs35 per day), and Internet access (Rs120 per hr.). Singles Rs75; doubles with bath Rs100-150.

🗋 FOOD

ERNAKULAM

Influenced by the heavy maritime traffic, Ernakulam's eateries present a mishmash of international cuisines. But be sure to sample local foods like *appam*, a thick *dosa* served with fish stew and coconut dishes.

🖼 **Delhi Durbar,** MG Rd., a few blocks south of Jos Junction. Here you'll find Ernakulam's best slice of North Indian cuisine: succulent chicken *tikka masala* (Rs60) in A/C comfort. Open daily noon-3:30pm and 6pm-midnight.

Bimbi's, Jos Junction. The chaotic ambience of this local landmark is mesmerizing, its food good and cheap. Pay at the register, claim your chow at the appropriate counter, then sit down and watch the world go by. Excellent *masala dosa* Rs10. Huge selection of Indian and Western sweets at the front. Open daily 8am-9:30pm.

Coco Cabana, Convent Rd., near the intersection with MG Rd. Ernakulam's most chic shake and juice joint. Select the fruit for your Rs15 beverage. Open daily 10am-10pm.

Khyber Restaurant, Jos Junction, upstairs from Bimbi's. Dimly lit, marble-floored, and more expensive than its downstairs neighbor, the mildly A/C-ed Khyber offers Chinese and Indian fare. Luscious *kadai* (ginger) *paneer* (Rs38), incredible garlic *naan* (Rs16) and smooth, creamy *lassis* (Rs12). Open daily 11am-11pm.

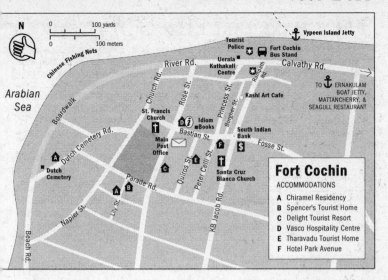

Hot Breads, Warriom Rd. Follow MG Rd. south from Jos Junction and turn right; it's on the right. Ernakulam's best spot for warm treats has fresh pastries and cakes, including apricot croissants (Rs10) and chocolate brownies (Rs13). Pizza, burgers, and sandwiches, too. Open daily 9am-9pm.

Chinese Garden, Warriom Rd., west of the intersection with MG Rd. This dimly lit Chinese restaurant offers seafood specialties and other fare as well: fried rice (Rs55) and beer (Rs80) to wash it down. Classy but inadequate A/C makes the dark space rather claustrophobic. Open daily 11am-11pm.

The Princess Room and **Sayanna,** in the Sealord Hotel. The A/C Princess Room, 2nd fl., has lush decor and fawning service at a price: Keralan dishes Rs65-95. Open daily 7am-11pm. The rooftop Sayanna offers a nice view of the harbor below, and its **Golden Jug Bar** can bring the view to life: beer (Rs90), spirits, and champagne. Sayanna open daily 6-11pm. Golden Jug open daily 11am-11pm.

Indian Coffee Houses, one across from Main Boat Jetty, the other in Jos Junction, opposite Bimbi's. Beloved by locals and tourists, ICH is convenient and fast. Veg. *biryani* (Rs15), banana fry (Rs3), and *dosas* (Rs8). Open daily 7:30am-8:30pm.

FORT COCHIN

Fort Cochin has few restaurants, but there are shacks on the sea-front that grill fish to order. Bakeries and vegetable stores can be found at the intersection of Bastian St. and the main road, and fruit is sold near the bus stand.

Hotel Seagull Restaurant, Calvathy Rd. Go upstairs for the real view of the harbor (follow the stairs on the left, disregarding the "Families Only" sign). Though it's primarily a watering hole these days, you can still enjoy seafood (fried, *tandoori,* or *masala*) while you watch boats and dolphins cruise by below. Ginger fish Rs80; crab fry Rs60; mixed vegetable curry Rs30. Beer (Rs60) to wash it all down. Open daily 7am-10:30pm.

Kashi Art Café, Burgher St., one block from Princess St. A tad pretentious perhaps—all that art on the walls—but you can reacquaint yourself with *real* coffee (Rs30). Light Western meals, including breakfast. Open M-Sa 8:30am-6:30pm, Su 8:30am-2:30pm.

Elite Hotel Restaurant, Princess St., on the ground floor of the hotel. Catch up on the latest news from Goa, and try the seafood of the day with finger chips (Rs40). *Dosas* (Rs15) served after 6pm. Open daily 8am until the crowd trickles out (10 or 11pm).

DON'T MAKE THAT FACE OR IT'LL STICK
THAT WAY **Kathakali,** which means "story play," is one of India's four major schools of classical dance. Transformed into gods and demons by the application of wildly colored make-up, massive golden headdresses, and skirts bright and full enough to put any ballerina to shame, the performers are traditionally men who have studied scripture, Kalaripayatu, ayurvedic massage, and music for eight years beginning at age 10 or 12. They are then trained in dance for four years. Emphasis is given to proper lifestyle and the deep understanding of archetypes portrayed in the *Vedas.* The dancers communicate through the use of 24 *mudras,* hand gestures augmented by convulsive movements of the eyes and facial muscles and the pounding dancing of belled feet. By using combinations of these 24 *mudras* (signifying "love," "courage," "bee drinking from a lotus flower," etc.), they tell stories from the *Ramayana* and *Mahabharata.* Piercing drums and classical vocals narrate the story. Although traditional *kathakali* was—and still is on special holy days—performed as part of a temple ritual, the modern art of *kathakali* has been truncated neo-colonial style: now most shows last only one hour and are given in theaters filled with tourists who come to "watch the Gods dance."

🎵 ENTERTAINMENT

For those with an itch to disco, **Ice's,** Ravipuram, near MG Rd., spins Western and Hindi hits, as well as Pepsi and ice cream (but no booze). It has an outdoor patio and an ancient dance floor. If that isn't your style, the resident band in the Princess Room at the **Sealord Hotel** cranks out a good "Mustang Sally," with ice cream *and* alcohol available (band plays 8-11pm, club closes at 1 or 2am). The **Sridar** movie theater, across from the GCDA Shopping Centre, screens English-language films in Dolby stereo and A/C comfort.

The **Cochin Cultural Centre** (tel. 380366) teaches dance, yoga, music, costume making, and more (for directions, see below). The traditional Keralan martial art of Kalaripayatu, dating from medieval times, is taught at the **ENS Kalari Centre** (tel. 809810), 9km from the city center; call for directions.

The **Kerala Ayurveda Pharmacy,** Warriom Rd. (tel. 361202), just east of MG Rd., is one of many places in Cochin offering **ayurvedic massage** (Rs350, with steam wash Rs450; open daily 9am-5pm). **PNVM Santhigiri Ayurvedic Hospital,** Azad Rd. (tel. 348757) offers massage (Rs250) and consultations (Rs50). To get there, take one of the frequent buses running from Jos Junction to Palarvattom Junction (not far from Ernakulam Town Railway Station), and then walk ten minutes down Azad Rd. to the clinic. (Open daily 11am-6pm.) As it's an important component of *kathakali,* several dance centers also offer ayurvedic massage by appointment: Cochin Cultural Centre (380366), Chavara Cultural Centre (tel. 368443), and Kerala Kathakali Kendra (tel. 740030). For more on **Ayurvedic Medicine,** see p. 508.

DANCE PERFORMANCES
Cochin offers spectacular nightly performances of **kathakali dance** (see p. 522). Geared toward tourists, these performances are usually prefaced by elaborate make-up demonstrations, an explanation of the music and hand-symbols, and a synopsis of the tale to be enacted. Performances last from one hour to 90 minutes.

Cochin Cultural Centre (tel. 380366). From Jos Junction, south on MG Rd., left on South Overbridge Rd., right on Chittoor Rd., and then left onto Manikath Rd. A green *kathakali* visage is painted on the wall. Make-up 5:30pm, performance 6:30pm; Rs100.

See India Foundation (tel. 369471). From MG Rd., head east on Warriom Rd. for 2 blocks; the Foundation is on the right under the huge painted face of a *kathakali* dancer. Director Devan has been performing here for 26 years. 6pm, 6:45pm; Rs100.

Kerala Kathakali Centre, in the Cochin Aquatic Club near the Fort Cochin bus stand, features a young troupe of artists. 5pm, 6:30pm; Rs70.

Kerala Kathakali Kendra, Bolghatty Island (theater tel. 355003; office tel. 740030), in the Bolghatty Palace Hotel near the jetty. A good pretext for visiting this erstwhile palace built by the Dutch in 1744. 4pm prayer, then dance at 6pm; Rs100.

☀ SIGHTS

FORT COCHIN

The romantic image of ancient churches kissed by the orange glow of the setting sun as it slips into the Arabian sea behind Chinese fishing nets, Fort Cochin makes the typical fantasy of South India a reality.

ST. FRANCIS CHURCH. The first European church in India, St. Francis Church (locally called the Vasco da Gama Church), was built by Portuguese Franciscan friars in 1503. The stone version, constructed a few years later, still stands among the houses built by British traders and Dutch farmers. When Vasco da Gama died in Cochin in 1524, his remains were buried under the church floor. Fourteen years later, the remains of the remains were transferred to Lisbon, but his tombstone remains here. Cochin fell to the Dutch in 1663, and the church was Protestantized in 1779. Although the British occupied Cochin in 1795, the church remained a Dutch stronghold—the walls are still lined with Dutch memorials. It became Anglican in 1864, and the Church of South India, which has since dedicated it to St. Francis, now carries the ecclesiastical baton. *(Open M-F 9:30am-1pm and 2:30-5:30pm. English services Su 8am.)*

SANTA CRUZ BASILICA. A church was first built on this site in 1505, but it was replaced by a cathedral in 1558. The current cathedral, consecrated in 1902, is new by Ft. Cochin standards, but its bizarre interior merits a quick look around nevertheless. *(Bastian St.; follow Princess St. south and turn left. English mass Su 4:30pm.)*

OTHER SIGHTS. Crumbling tombs disintegrate beside the beach at the **Dutch Cemetery** *(turn left from the gates of St. Francis Church, then right onto Dutch Cemetery Rd.).* A driveway next to PWD Guest House leads to the **beach,** where the crowd consists of fishermen, fish sellers, fish buyers, and fish. The nearby skeletal **Chinese fishing nets** were brought to Kerala by Chinese traders in the 13th century. As massive cargo ships pull into the harbor, fishermen return from the sea in long canoe-like boats with the day's catch. High tide is the time to see them in action.

MATTANCHERRY

It's a 45-minute stroll from Ft. Cochin to the heart of Mattancherry. Follow Calvathy Road to the Customs Jetty, and keep going as it turns into Bazaar Rd.—it's a pleasant walk past rows of export warehouses, where rich smells of tea, pepper, and spices waft out of every alley. The olfactory kaleidoscope can also be sampled, along with a few exhaust fumes, in an auto-rickshaw (Rs10 from Ft. Cochin).

THE DUTCH PALACE. The **Mattancherry Palace** (a.k.a. the Dutch Palace) was built by the Portuguese in 1557 for Raja Virakerala Varma; its construction was a "goodwill gesture," probably in exchange for trading rights. During their occupation in 1665, the Dutch renovated and renamed the palace. Two **temples,** one dedicated to Krishna and the other to Shiva, were built on the palace grounds by the Portuguese, but today only Hindus may enter. Detailed **murals** depicting scenes from the *Ramayana* and the *Puranas* in distinct Keralite style cover nearly 300 square meters of the palace walls. Downstairs in the queen's bedchamber, a number of less detailed paintings show divinely sexual scenes set in a beautiful forest. In one, Krishna uses six hands and two feet to pleasure a group of admiring *gopis* (milkmaids) and two more hands to play the flute. An attached **museum** houses oil portraits of Cochin rajas with their palanquins, robes, weapons, and umbrellas *(museum open Sa-Th 10am-5pm; no photography permitted).*

JEW TOWN It is believed that the first Jews came to Kerala in the 10th century BC as traders from King Solomon's Israel. The destruction of the Second Temple in Jerusalem by the Romans in AD 70 led to the dispersion of the Jewish people, some of whom landed in Shingly (30km north of Cochin, now known as Cranganore) a few years later. Around AD 500, another large group of Jews immigrated here from Iraq and Iran. With the onset of Portuguese persecution in the 16th century, the Jews were expelled from Shingly. Legend has it that Joseph Azar, the last surviving Jewish prince, swam to Cochin with his wife on his shoulders. The Jewish Keralans placed themselves under the protection of the Raja of Cochin, who gave them a parcel of land next to his palace for a synagogue (see above).

Emigration to Mumbai and Israel has pared Cochin's Jewish population down to a geriatric 17, but you'll still see menorahs in some of the windows. There has been no rabbi here for several years, so the elders of the synagogue conduct ceremonies and make decisions regarding Jewish law. Happy to discuss their future with visitors, the remaining Jews seem unconcerned about the survival of their community. Eighty or so Jews remain in Kerala, along with some four to five thousand in all of India as a whole, most of them residing in Mumbai.

PARDESI SYNAGOGUE. Originally built in 1568 (though the current structure dates from 1664), the synagogue is lit by 19th-century oil-burning chandeliers suspended over a floor of blue-and-white Cantonese tiles. The synagogue's Torah is written on sheepskin scrolls and stored in ornate metal canisters, one of them a gift from the Raja of Cochin. The true antiquity of the Jewish community in Kerala can be witnessed in a Helnas-inscribed stone set into an outside wall of the synagogue: it comes from a now-defunct synagogue built in 1344 in Kochangadi. You can still visit the synagogue, located in **Jew Town,** tucked in an alleyway parallel to Bazaar Rd. The area is teeming with stores selling curios and antiques—bargain hard. *(5min. from the Dutch Palace. Walk away from Ft. Cochin until the road makes a right turn; the synagogue is at the end of the street to the right. Open Su-F 10am-noon and 3-5pm. Rs2.)*

VYPEEN ISLAND

Miles of ignored **beaches** roll along the Arabian Sea on Vypeen Island, passing a **Lighthouse** at Ochanthuruth (open daily 3-5pm) and the early 16th-century **Palliport Fort** (open Th 10am-5pm). The beaches are empty, except for herds of sunbathing cows and a few fishing boats, until high season, when all the foreigners arrive. Men come from the nearby villages to see the show—women are advised to swim in a t-shirt and shorts or pants. **Cherai Beach** (4km, Rs20 by auto-rickshaw) is more frequented by foreigners and is probably safer for women than the others. Coconut quaffs can be sipped at a **toddy bar** on the right side of the main road, a five-minute walk from the jetty (closes around 9pm). **Ferries** run between Vypeen Island and Ernakulam's High Court Jetty (every 20min. 6:30am-9pm). The same is true of ferries to Ft. Cochin, which depart from the launch opposite the bus stand.

BACKWATER CRUISES

Beyond the city lie magical green fields, towering palms, and lazy backwaters—some of India's most remarkably verdant and beautiful landscapes. Kerala's tourist industry has capitalized on the greenery by offering backwater tours on non-motorized boats through the maze of lagoons, lakes, canals, and streams. A guide paddles the vessel (which can hold no more than 6 people) for several enchanting hours, stopping for a fresh coconut break and a stroll through paddy fields. The whole natural scene is enthralling, especially for bird-watchers. The tours also offer a unique opportunity to see Keralan village life up close. **Moonlight cruises** on full moon nights are offered in season. The **Tourist Desk,** Main Jetty (tel. 371761), charters daily tours. In season, reserve at least one day in advance; off season, show up 30 minutes before departure. (Tours 9am-1:30pm and 2-6:30pm, Rs275.

Save Rs50 by booking directly at the Tourist Office.) Backwater tours (9am and 2pm; Rs300) are also offered by **Tourist Land,** Market Rd. (tel. 365163), close to the Main Jetty. For a more idiosyncratic backwater experience, and one that can last up to 12 hours, contact Sabu, the caretaker at the **PWD Rest House,** Ft. Cochin (Rs500; 5 person min., 10 person max.). The **KTDC** also provides backwater tours on country boats (8:30am and 2:30pm; Rs300). They also offer a sunset tour (daily 5:30-7pm; Rs30) and a tour of Periyar Tiger Reserve (departs Sa 7:30am, returns Su 8pm; accommodation not included).

MUNNAR വുന്നാർ

At an elevation of 1500m, Munnar provides an invigorating antidote to the steamy heat of the plains, and it has scenery superlative enough to match Anaimudi (2700m), the highest peak in India south of the Himalayas. The area was the fiefdom of generations of Scottish tea-planters; it was a Scot, J.D. Munro, who initiated the town's development in the 1870s. Today the Scots have long since departed, leaving their rolling ocean of exquisitely maintained tea estates in the hands of Tata Tea Ltd., an offshoot of the same Parsi-owned mega-company that built the bus that brought you here. Still a tea town in many ways, Munnar is rapidly reinventing itself as a hill station, and its attractive mix of climate, wildlife, and scenery will not go unnoticed for long.

▨ ORIENTATION AND PRACTICAL INFORMATION. In Tamil, Munnar literally means "Three Rivers," and the heart of the town is centered on their confluence. The road from Cochin enters the relatively flat valley alongside the main river 3km south of Munnar's town center. Several budget hotels, restaurants, banks, the post office, and the bus stand are spread out on either side of the river. Munnar proper, however, begins with the **Tata Tea Regional Headquarters,** beyond the bazaar. From here, several roads wind up each of the river valleys: the one heading north past the mosque goes to **Ernakulam National Park** and Coimbatore, while another heads east across the river behind towards Madurai. **Buses** depart from the KSRTC bus station, 2km south of town. To: **Cochin** (6:30 and 11:40am, 5hr., Rs40); **Kottayam** (4 per day 6:30am-5:30pm, Rs40); and **Trivandrum** (4 per day 10:30am-5:30pm, 8hr., Rs110). The private bus stand in town services: **Cochin** via **Alwaye** (12 per day 5:20am-6:30pm, 5hr., Rs40) and **Coimbatore** (6:30am and 3:45pm, 6hr., Rs48). **Jeeps** and **rickshaws** (Rs10 for the length of the town) are the most common forms of local transport. **Matha Cycle Shop,** in the middle of the bazaar, rents "mountain bikes" (Rs3 per hr.; open daily 9am-6pm). Joseph Iype, in his tiny **tourist information shop** close to the western end of the footbridge, is keen to share the delights of the region (open daily 9am-noon and 3-7pm). The **State Bank of Travancore** is opposite the Tata Tea Headquarters (open M-F 10am-2pm, Sa 10am-noon). There are several **pharmacies** scattered throughout the bazaar. The **post office,** across the river from Tata Tea, has *Poste Restante* (open M-Sa 9am-5:30pm.) **Postal Code:** 685612. **Telephone Code:** 0486.

▨☖ ACCOMMODATIONS AND FOOD. Most affordable food and accommodations options can be found along the bazaar. **Hilltop Lodge** (tel. 530616) is probably the best of Munnar's basic lodges. Clean, compact rooms come with attached squat toilets. (Singles Rs110; doubles Rs160.) **Government Guest House** (tel. 530385), just above town, is a great place to stay if you can get in. A handful of large double rooms with roomy bathrooms in old colonial stone bungalows go for Rs550. Meals are served in a handsome dining room (lunch Rs35). **Hotel Hajrath,** in the produce market, is justly popular (veg. entrees Rs12; open daily 6:30am-9:30pm). **Aiswarya Restaurant,** under the Hilltop Lodge, offers great views in addition to great food in an airy ambience (veg. entrees Rs12; open daily 7am-9pm). **Brothers Restaurant,** 100m from Aiswarya, is little more than a dark shed, but they grill great fish for Rs25 (open daily 6am-9pm).

KERALA

■ ♙ **SIGHTS AND HIKING.** Munnar is all about strolls through undulating tea gardens and splashing around in waterfalls, but there are also more energetic alternatives. **Ernakulam National Park,** 15 km away, encompasses much of the bulk of Anaimudi and most of the world's population of the endangered Nilgiri tahr, a species of mountain goat. It's a 2km walk up the switchbacks to Rajmalai Gap (1975m) on the shoulder of the mountain. A narrow road heads off along the ridge to the right, ultimately reaching the most accessible of Anaimudi's summits. Visitors are not permitted to stray from the road in February and March, when the tahr are breeding. (Rickshaw Rs80, round-trip including waiting time Rs125. Park admission Rs50 per person.)

Lockhart Mountain offers another superb mountain ridge hike. Take a bus (Rs3) or a rickshaw (Rs120) to Lockhart Gap. The round-trip hike will take about three hours, and you'll be rewarded with spectacular mountain views. A more sedate way to take in the scenery is to bus it to **Top Station.** The first bus of the day (7:15am, 1½hr.) should get you there before the clouds come down and the haze comes up. You can also make a three-day trek to **Kodaikanal** from Top Station; two villages en route provide basic accommodations.

Munnar doesn't boast a great nightlife, but a visit to the **High Range Club,** at the end of a footbridge across the river from the SN Tourist Home, is an excellent substitute. The club is formally open only to members and high-paying guests, but proper dress (a collar and long sleeves are required of men in the evening) and a polite word with the Club Secretary might give you access to the planters' social world. The walls of the "Men Only" bar (women admitted occasionally) sag under the weight of hunting trophies and a collection of ancient headgear (beer Rs50).

With all that tea around, it's understandable to be curious about how those cute, tubby little green bushes get converted into a Twinings tea bag. While Tata Tea isn't too keen on conducting **tours** of its factories, a little polite persistence and a healthy dose of patience might prove fruitful.

TRICHUR (THRISSUR) തൻശൂർ

With its high concentration of universities, museums, and temples, Trichur bills itself as the "cultural capital of Kerala," but most foreign visitors only come for the annual **Puram Festival** held in April and May. During Puram, deity-bearing revelers from neighboring villages, heralded by musicians and brightly bedecked elephants, descend on the town. Although Trichur usually isn't worth a detour, its extensive temple and park make it a perfectly pleasant stopover.

⚅ ORIENTATION AND INFORMATION

Trichur is laid out like a wheel. The hubcap is the vast, green **Swaraj Round,** on which stands **Vadakkunathan Temple,** and the major roads are the spokes: moving clockwise from the western edge, these are **Mahatma Gandhi (MG), Shornur, Palace, College, High, Municipal Office, Kurrappam,** and **Marar Roads.** Most hotels and restaurants are clustered on these roads, near the Round. The KSRTC **bus stand** and **railway station** are both 500m south of the Round; head down Kurrappam Rd. until you pick up Railway Station Rd.

Trains: The **railway station** is on Railway Station Rd. (tel. 423150). Fares listed are 2nd/ 1st class. To: **Bangalore** (*Bangalore Exp.* 6525, 12hr., 4:30pm, Rs113/556); **Calicut** (6 per day 4am-6pm, 3hr., Rs36/180); **Chennai** (6 and 7:45pm, 12hr., Rs131/632); **Delhi** (*Kerala Exp.* 2625, 5:20pm, 43hr., Rs308/1879); **Mangalore** (*Malabar Exp.* 6329, 12:25am; *Parasuram Exp.* 6349, 12:30pm, 10hr., Rs81/398); **Mumbai** (*Netravati Exp.* 6636, 6:15am, 24hr., Rs241/1309); **Madgaon** (*Parasuram Exp.* 6349, 12:30pm, 8hr., Rs151/752); **Trivandrum** (8 per day, 6hr., Rs73/361).

Buses: The **KSRTC bus stand,** Masjid Rd. (tel. 421150), close to the railway station. Frequent buses to: **Alleppey** (3½hr., Rs70); Calicut (3hr., Rs45); **Ernakulam** (2hr., Rs30)

Kottayam (3hr., Rs50); **Mangalore** (9pm, 12hr., Rs147); **Trivandrum** (7hr., Rs105). **Sakthan Thampuran Bus Stand,** TB Rd., 1.5km south of the Round, has frequent private buses to Calicut, Guruvayur, Cochin, and Trivandrum.

Local Transportation: Most of Trichur's sights and accommodations are within walking distance. **Auto-rickshaws** are plentiful, however, and meters are the norm. Rs5 first km, Rs3 per km thereafter.

Tourist Office: KTDC (tel. 332333), Yatri Nivas Hotel, is helpful but cartographically challenged. Open 24hr. **DTPC,** on the corner of Palace and Museum Rd., sometimes has decent maps and brochures, but the staff's English is lacking. Open M-Sa 9am-5:30pm.

Currency Exchange: State Bank of India, on the Round near Palace Rd., changes foreign currency and traveler's checks (US$ and UK£). Open M-F 10am-2pm, Sa 10am-noon.

Library: Public library in the Town Hall, Palace Rd. Open M-Sa 8am-8pm, Su 8am-noon.

Bookstore: Current Books, MG Rd., on the Round. Large selection of highbrow reads (Camus, Naipaul) and juicy trashies. Open M-Sa 9am-8pm. **Kairali Pusthakasala,** Sakthan Thampuran Bus Stand, has a decent selection. Open M-Sa 4:30am-7:30pm.

Hospital: West Fort Hospital, W. Fort-Punkunnam Rd. (tel. 382130), off MG Rd.

Police: Market Rd. (tel. 421400), off Round South.

Emergency: Police, tel. 100; **Fire,** tel. 101; **Ambulance,** tel. 102.

Post Office: GPO, near the Sakthan Thampuran Bus Stand. *Poste Restante* at the enquiry counter. Open M-Sa 8am-6pm. More convenient is the **Trichur City Post Office,** Korappatu Lane, 200m north of the Round. Open M-Sa 9am-5pm. **Postal Code:** 680001.

Internet: Bhavana Systems and Communications, MO Rd. (tel. 442429), 3rd fl. of the building opposite the Municipal Office. Rs70 per hr. Open M-Sa 8:30am-7pm.

PHONE CODE	0487

ACCOMMODATIONS AND FOOD

During Puram, the room rates listed below triple or quadruple. Visitors choose between cheap South Indian coffee-house fare and overpriced hotel meals.

Hotel Elite International (tel. 421033), on the Round, between Kurrappam and Municipal Office Rd. Comfortable place boasting huge beds, 24hr. hot water, phones, seat toilets, and city-view balconies. Attached restaurant. Check-out 24hr. Singles Rs210, with A/C and TV Rs410; doubles Rs260/480; quads Rs400.

Alukkas Tourist Home (tel. 426067), in an alley off Railway Station Rd. near the station. The dribbling, artificial waterfall outside makes for an irresistible welcome to this busy hotel. Basic, reasonably sized rooms have seat toilets. Singles Rs61; doubles Rs215.

Ming Palace, across from the Elite Hotel, on the 2nd fl. of the Pathans building. Chinese dishes (Rs25-50) served by a courteous staff. Alcohol-free, but the red lanterns and chintzy furniture make for an intriguingly seedy air. Open daily 11am-10pm. Visa, MC.

Hotel Bharath Restaurant has cheap South (*thali* Rs17) and North Indian veg. fare (*aloo gobi* Rs17). Frenetic at mealtimes and justly popular. Open daily 6:30am-10:30pm.

SIGHTS AND ENTERTAINMENT

Most tourists know Trichur only by its association with the annual **Puram Festival** in April and May. Featuring a multitude of elephants, masses of onlookers, and noisy bands, the festival is Indian pageantry at its very best. Hotels fill up fast and charge extravagant rates during the festival, so plan well in advance. It is held on the grounds of the **Vadakkunathan Temple,** the oldest and largest temple complex in the state. Dedicated to Shiva, the temple sits on the site where Nandi, Shiva's bull, is said to have rested. The temple is closed to non-Hindus. There is a local **zoo,** in the northeast corner of Trichur, 2km away from the Round (open Tu-Su 9am-5:15pm; Rs5). The "multipurpose" **art museum** on the same grounds

KERALA

contains plenty of dusty *kathakali* dance costumes, some decent sculpture and carving, and lifesize stuffed zoo animals are presumably the stuffed remains of erstwhile zoo occupants (open Tu-Su 10am-5pm; free, camera fee Rs3). You'll find more carvings at the **Archaeological Museum,** 100m farther along Museum Rd. (open Tu-Su 9:30am-5pm; free). The **market area** behind Municipal Office Rd. is worth exploring.

CALICUT (KOZHIKODE) കോഴിക്കോട്

Calicut was once among India's most celebrated seaports. As early as the 7th century it was the harbor of choice for Chinese and Middle Eastern spice traders. In 1498, Malabar-man Vasco da Gama tread his first subcontinental steps just north of here, inadvertently initiating three centuries of mercantile mayhem that culminated in Tipu Sultan's trashing of the region in 1789. The British took over three years later and managed to immortalize Calicut by coining the word "calico" for the locally produced fabric. Present-day Calicut, however, bears little imprint of its colorful past. Those who imagine a city filled with ruined forts, wharfside temples, and cartloads of black pepper have probably been reading too much Rushdie (part of his *The Moor's Last Sigh* is set here) and will be disappointed to find a dearth of potential Kodak moments in this small, bustling city which serves mostly as a stopover between Cochin and Mysore.

▐▛ TRANSPORTATION

Airport: The airport is in Karippur, 23km from Calicut; take a taxi. **Air India** and **Indian Airlines,** Eroh Centre, Bank Rd. (tel. 766243 or 755343). To: **Chennai** (3 per week, 2hr., US$80); **Coimbatore** (10 per week, 30min., US$35); **Mumbai** (2 per day, 1½hr., US$140). **Jet Airways,** Mavoor Rd. (tel. 356518), also has daily flights to Mumbai.

Trains: The **railway station** (tel. 703822), 1km south of the park; follow Town Hall Rd. Fares listed are 2nd/1st class. To: **Delhi** (*Mangala Exp.* 2617, 5:30pm, 40hr., Rs315/ 1933); **Ernakulam** (5 per day, 4½hr., Rs53/259); **Mangalore** (8 per day, 5hr., Rs61/ 294); **Mumbai** (*Netravati Exp.* 6636A, 9:45am, 20hr., Rs251/1408).

Buses: **KSRTC Bus Stand** (tel. 723796), near the intersection with Bank Rd. Slightly dirty, but at this point in your travels, so are you. To: **Bangalore** (9 per day, 8½hr., Rs122); **Cochin** (30 per day, 5½hr., Rs75); **Mangalore** (4 per day, 7hr., Rs92); **Mysore** (19 per day 12:30am-8pm, 5½hr., Rs60); **Trivandrum** (15 per day, 10hr., Rs150). Cleaner, cheaper **private buses** run from the bus stand farther down Mavoor Rd. To: **Cochin** (16 per day, Rs56); **Devala,** near Ooty (2:15pm, 10hr., Rs40); **Mangalore** (5:45am, 9:30, and 10:30pm; 6hr.; Rs58); **Mysore** (6 and 8:30am, 6hr., Rs56).

Local Transportation: **Auto-rickshaws** are your best bet (Rs3 per km). **Taxis** are unmetered and readily available. **Local buses** run around town and to the beach.

▐ ORIENTATION AND PRACTICAL INFORMATION

At the center of town is **Ansari Park,** flanked by **Town Hall Road** on the left and **Bank Road,** which turns into **GH Road** as it heads south, on the right. **Mavoor Road (Indira Gandhi Road)** veers right off Bank Rd. in the north, leading to the KSRTC and private **bus stations.** To the south, GH Rd. intersects with **MM Ali Road,** which leads east to an older part of the city. The **railway station** is on Town Hall Rd., southwest of the park. The **beach,** 2km west of town center, is reputedly unsafe at night.

Tourist Office: The **KTDC** office (tel. 721394 or 721395), at the reception desk of the Malabar Mansion on the south side of the park. Staffed 9am-5pm, but the hotel will help out with information 24hr. Good luck getting a map. The **information booth** at the railway station can also be very helpful. No maps, no telephone, but plenty of information and smiles. Open M-Sa 10am-1pm and 2-5pm.

Budget Travel: PL Worldways, 3rd fl., Lakhotia Computer Centre (tel. 722564), at the intersection of Mavoor and Bank Rd. Books airline reservations and obtains foreign visas. Open M-F 9:30am-1pm and 2-5:30pm, Sa 9:30am-1:30pm.

Currency Exchange: State Bank of India, Bank Rd. (tel. 721321), changes foreign currency and traveler's checks. Open M-F 10am-2pm, Sa 10am-noon. **PL Worldways** (see above) also cashes traveler's checks.

Market: There is an extensive fruit and vegetable market around the old bus station on the left side of MM Ali Rd., as you head away from GH Rd.

Library: Kozhikode Public Library, on the right of Malabar Mansion, has a decent selection and an original painting by Keralan homeboy M.F. Hussain. Open Tu-Su 2-8pm.

Hospital: National Hospital, Mavoor Rd. (tel. 723061 or 723062), near its intersection with Bank Rd., is the best in town. Its **pharmacy** is open 24hr.

Police Station: (tel. 703499), near the railway station.

Post Office: (tel. 722663), on the west edge of the park. The shiny marble-and-granite post office sells stamps M-Sa 10am-7:45pm, Su 2-4:45pm and mails parcels M-Sa 4-7:30pm, Su 2-4:30pm. *Poste Restante* c/o Postmaster. **Postal Code:** 673001.

Internet: W3 Internet Access, AB Rd. (tel. 365219), in the KM Building; it's immediately across the railway tracks from the Crown Cinema on Town Hall Rd. at the corner of the park. Calicut's best service with several terminals. Rs75 per hr. Open M-Sa 8:45am-9:30pm, Su 1-9:30pm. More conveniently located, **SR Enterprises** (tel. 722851), in the Lakhotia Computer Bldg., at the intersection of Mavoor and Bank Rd., has one terminal available (Rs80 per hr.). Open M-Sa 8:30am-8:30pm.

PHONE CODE	0495

🛏 ACCOMMODATIONS

Sasthapuri Tourist Home (tel. 723281), a ways down MM Ali Rd. on the left. Not the most efficient of institutions, but a good value in a lively part of town. Attached squat toilets. Check-out 24hr. Singles Rs75, with bath Rs100, with A/C Rs350; doubles Rs100/150/400.

Malabar Mansion (tel. 722391), on the south side of the park. KTDC-run, with a tourist reception desk, A/C restaurant, and beer parlor. All rooms have TV, phone, and attached bath. A/C rooms are huge and well-outfitted. Singles Rs175, with A/C Rs360; doubles Rs225/400; quads Rs350. Extra person Rs60, in A/C rooms Rs120.

Metro Tourist Home (tel. 766029), at the junction of Mavoor and Bank Rd. With a great location in the whizzing, grinding heart of town, it's grimy but still good. Deluxe rooms have breathing room and seat toilets; non-deluxe rooms are tiny, and you'll have to squat. Singles Rs130; doubles Rs185, with A/C Rs425; deluxe Rs225.

Kalpaka Tourist Home (tel. 720222), Town Hall Rd., just south of the park. Run by a cadre of efficient women. Big beds, big rooms. Hot water 24hr. Singles Rs180, with A/C Rs450; doubles Rs225/550. MC, Visa.

🍽 FOOD

Woodlands Restaurant, in the Hotel Whitelines on GH Rd. not far from the intersection with MM Ali Rd. Set in a groovy circular, maroon dining room, this restaurant feels more like a diner than a *dhaba,* but its excellent all-veg. food is the real thing. *Thalis* Rs25-40. Open daily 8am-10pm.

Kalpaka Restaurant, Kalpaka Tourist Home. A variety of veg. Indian, Chinese, and pseudo-Continental dishes (Rs15-35). Capsicum pizza Rs30. Open daily 7am-10pm.

Cochin Bakery, across from the State Bank of India. Spicy snacks, cold drinks, and scrumptious pastries from Rs2. Open daily 9:30am-9pm.

Dakshin-The Veg, Mavoor Rd., close to the intersection with Bank Rd. Strange name, but pretty generic restaurant consisting of a self-service area downstairs and A/C and non-A/C restaurants upstairs. North Indian veg. dishes Rs35, South Indian *thali* Rs25.

HOW THE WEST WAS WORN

While many Indians currently seek to adopt ever more Western forms of dress, a number of supposedly Western fashion concepts came from the subcontinent in the first place. What goes around comes around—call it clothing karma.

calico [Western corruption of "Calicut," see p. 528]: Cotton cloth with prints (in the U.S.) or without (in the UK). Also an epithet for splotchy cats.

cashmere [from Kashmir, see p. 250]: See "shawl," below.

dungarees [from Hindi *dungri*]: Pants made of coarse calico.

jodhpurs [from Jodhpur in Rajasthan, see p. 317]: Pants for horseback riding, tight at the ankles.

khaki [from Urdu for "dusty"]: Everyone's favorite junglewear.

pajamas [from Urdu *pay jamah,* or "leg garment"]: Europeans in India and thereabouts copied the silk pants worn all around them, but only nocturnally.

seersucker [Indian corruption of Persian *shir o shakkar,* or "milk and honey"]: A striped and puckered fabric, and the most evocative word in this box.

shawl [from Persian *shal*]: Originally made in Kashmir from the wool of the highland shawl-goat *(Capra lanigera)*.

KERALA

  ## SIGHTS AND ENTERTAINMENT

! WARNING. The beachfront is reputed to be home to a dangerous drug culture. Heed local cautions and avoid the beach after dark.

Calicut's long, sandy **beach,** just 2km from the city center, warrants a visit. The areas close to town can be profitably overlooked, but farther to the north, fishermen and their colorful boats take over the scene. The **Pazhassiraja Museum** is one of those Indian general-purpose museums featuring everything anyone ever thought of putting in a museum. Most of it is junk, but downstairs there are a number of well displayed stone carvings. (East Hill, 5km from Calicut; rickshaw Rs35.) Next door, the **Krishna Menon Museum** houses the personal belongings of the late Indian president (b. Calicut 1896, d. Delhi 1974), and the **Art Gallery** has a collection of paintings by Raja Ravi Varma. (Museums and gallery open Th-Su 10am-5pm, W 1-5pm.) Movie buffs should check out the handsome art deco **Crown Theatre,** Town Hall Rd., at the corner of the park, which screens Western movies. Every evening at the park, a little guy in a box madly flips switches to manipulate a **Music Fountain** choreographed to Hindi pop (show at 6:30pm, 2hr.; Rs3).

Ten kilometers—and 100 years—away from Calicut is the ship-building town of **Beypore** (auto-rickshaw Rs80 round-trip). Under thatched roofs, but otherwise exposed to the elements, master woodworkers carve, scrape, and pound huge beams into 200 ft. barges. Everything is done by hand—even the vast trees destined to become the boats' beams are shifted using only a few crowbars. These boats are ocean-going monsters destined for a life of trading between India's west coast and the Arabian peninsula—an extraordinary glimpse of living nautical history. (Inquire in Calicut as to whether construction is currently underway.)

 ## SHOPPING

Calicut has always been a trading city, and doing a bit of it yourself can provide plenty of entertainment. Fancy clothing stores line "Sweet Meat Street" (SM St.) and Mavoor Rd., and jewelers pack into tiny shops on Palayam Rd., near the fruit and vegetable market behind the KSRTC bus stand. A journey over the railway tracks and down towards the ocean along Big Bazaar Rd. offers a view of the wholesale side of the spice trade. The **Comtrust Store,** south of the park and just off Town Hall Rd., is the outlet store for the impressive Raj-era factory next door that produces hand-loomed fabrics (open M-F 10am-1pm and 2:30-7pm).

Tamil Nadu

TAMIL NADU
தமிழ் நாடு

The southernmost state in mainland India, Tamil Nadu (literally, "land of the Tamils") is the heartland of Dravidian culture and the stronghold of conservative Hinduism. Over three millennia, Tamil Nadu has cultivated a spirit and heritage of its own. Some of the finest temples in India can be found here; *gopurams* (gateway towers) can be seen towering over huge temple-city complexes with dusty streets spiraling around a central shrine. The state is also home to the sounds of Carnatic music and *bharat natyam*, India's most popular classical dance form.

Tamil Nadu is peopled by Dravidians, the oldest known inhabitants of the subcontinent, though little is known about their immigration into India. The Dravidian family of languages is older than the Indo-European languages, and some historians believe that the peoples of the Indus Valley Civilization, who were displaced by the Aryan invasion of 1500 BC into other parts of the subcontinent, spoke a Dravidian language—traces of Dravidian are also found in tribal dialects of Bihar and some spoken dialects of southern Pakistan. Since the first century, the state has nurtured South India's oldest literary tradition in its mother tongue, Tamil. The refusal to welcome Hindi, India's national language, into its schools and administration, has tinged the state's history with separatism and linguistic pride.

During the last few centuries BC, Tamil Nadu was ruled by three rival dynasties: the Cholas, the Pandyas, and the Cheras. By the 4th century AD the Pallava kingdom had risen to power, only to be stopped in the 9th century by the unconquerable Cholas, who grew to rule all of South India. Not until the 14th-century growth of the Vijayanagar Empire was the present-day area of Tamil Nadu ruled by a kingdom based outside its borders. Under the British, Tamil Nadu was part of the Chennai Presidency, which included parts of present-day Andhra Pradesh, Kerala, and Karnataka; this entity was split into four separate states in the 1950s.

The state's geography features the eastern plains along the Coromandel Coast, and the northern and western hills which culminate in the Nilgiris, where the Eastern and Western Ghats meet. Its only perennial river, the Kaveri, flows into the state from Karnataka; it has been dammed heavily and is now a mere trickle in places. From the paddy-fields and red, tilled earth of the coastal plains to the spice plantations of the Cardamom Hills; from the sun-drenched beaches of Pondicherry to the peninsula's tip at Kanyakumari, kissed by the waves of the Arabian Sea, the Bay of Bengal, and the Indian Ocean; Tamil Nadu is a veritable country in itself.

HIGHLIGHTS OF TAMIL NADU

■ A fascinating cultural mix distinguishes **Pondicherry** (p. 557), the former capital of French India, now home to the famously surreal **Aurobindo Ashram** (p. 561).

■ Thousands flock to the **Meenakshi Amman Temple** in **Madurai** (p. 577), where some 30 million sculptures provide an artistic counterpoint to a lively city.

■ **Kodaikanal** (p. 589), in the Western Ghats, features the standard hill station amusements set against some of India's finest film-grade scenery.

CHENNAI (MADRAS) சென்னை

Dubbed the "Gateway to the South" by its champions, Chennai is India's fourth largest city and the first stop for most sojourners in Tamil Nadu. The capital of the state, this metropolis on the Coromandel Coast is a bastion of South Indian culture, with its dance and music festivals attracting more crowds than the few sights sprinkled within the city limits. As if to relieve the weary visitor, Chennai's cityscape is punctuated with large expanses of green which complement its lazy stretches of sand by the Bay of Bengal.

From its humble origins as a tiny fishing village, Chennai started expanding in 1639, when a British official of the East India Company, Francis Day, founded a trading outpost here. Soon, a fort and a church were built, and an Indian weaver's colony called Chennaipatnam sprung up north of the fort; to accommodate the new arrivals, the Company agents purchased great swaths of land. Unfortunately, for the British, French forces stormed, seized, and sacked the city in 1746. While Madras (as it was called until 1996) ceased to be a place where crucial political decisions were made, it became a thriving economic center, and its sprawling factories spun out thousands of bales of export-grade cotton clothing throughout the late 19th and early 20th centuries. Like other big cities, Chennai proffers the downside of the urban dream: congested streets, aggressive auto-rickshaw-*wallahs* and the incessant blare of traffic horns. But, as if undaunted by all the mayhem around them, Madrasis remain relaxed and friendly, never losing their cool.

Recently, Chennai has been swept up in India's wave of politically motivated name changes. Many of the town's major thoroughfares have been stripped of their colonial titles and renamed in honor of Tamil leaders. In 1996, the city's former name, "Madras," was officially replaced by "Chennai," a Tamil name that invokes the original Indian settlement of Chennaipatnam.

▛ GETTING THERE AND AWAY

FLIGHTS

Chennai Meenambakkam is not as heavily used as Mumbai's or Delhi's airports, making Chennai a relatively peaceful port of entry and exit. There are a number of transport options to the city center, 16km north of the airport. **Local buses** (#21G, PP21, 52B, and 60E; Rs13) are too crowded to be useful; luggage is a hassle even if you only have a small bag. A **minibus service** runs between the airport and the major hotels (Rs100). This is a slow but sure and comfortable way of making it into the city. Book your tickets at the counter in the International Terminal. The **pre-paid taxi booth** inside the International Terminal operates at fixed rates; a ride downtown should cost about Rs200. Regular **taxis** charge upwards of Rs250, while **auto-rickshaws** cost Rs150 with some fierce haggling. A final option is the urban **train** system; it runs from Tirusulam station (a short walk from the terminals) to Egmore and other downtown destinations. It costs Rs40 for the 40-minute ride to Egmore Station, the drop-off point for a number of cheap hotels. You may get a few unkind stares if you squeeze onto a crowded train car with a bulging pack.

INTERNATIONAL AIRLINES. American Airlines, Air Canada, and **TWA** share an office at 43-44 "Thaper House," Montieth Rd. (tel. 859 2915 or 859 2564); **Air France,** 47 White's Rd. (tel. 855 4894); **Air India,** 19 Marshalls Rd. (tel. 827 4477); **Air Lanka,** 76 Cathedral Rd. (tel. 826 1536 or 826 1537); **British Airways,** Alsa Mall Khaleeli Centre, Montieth Rd. (tel. 855 4752 or 855 4726); **Delta Airlines,** 47 White's Rd. (tel. 852 5655 or 852 5647); **Gulf Air,** 52 Montieth Rd. (tel. 855 4417 or 855 3101); **Lufthansa,** 167 Anna Salai (tel. 852 3272); **Malaysia Airlines,** 498 Anna Salai (tel. 434 9651); **Singapore Airlines,** 108 Dr. Radhakrishnan Salai (tel. 852 2871 or 855 2883); **Swiss Air,** 47 White's Rd. (tel. 857 4783 or 852 2541). **Thai Airways, United Airlines, SAS, Air New Zealand,** and **Varig Airlines** share an office at the Malavikas Centre, 144 Kodambakkam Rd. (tel. 822 6149 or 822 6150). All are open M-F 9:30am-6pm and Sa 9:30am-7pm, with the exception of British Airways, open M-Sa 9:30am-6pm. Air Lanka and Air India both fly to Colombo, Sri Lanka (4-5 per day, 1½hr., US$90).

DOMESTIC AIRLINES. Jet Airways India, Thaper House, 43-44 Montieth Rd. in Egmore (tel. 855 5353; fax 858-8493; open daily 10am-5pm), has daily flights between Chennai and **Bangalore** (US$67); **Coimbatore** (US$62); **Delhi** (US$235); **Mumbai** (US$154); and **Trivandrum** (US$105). **Indian Airlines,** 19 Marshalls Rd. (tel. 855 3039; fax 855 5208) gives 20% discounts for all travelers under 30 and other special deals. To: **Ahmedabad** (3 per week, 3½hr., US$220); **Bangalore** (3-4 per day, 1hr., US$65); **Bhubaneswar** (3 per week, 1½hr., US$180); **Kolkata** (1-2 per day, 2hr., US$200); **Calicut** (4 per week, 1hr., US$80); **Cochin** (4 per week, 1hr., US$105); **Coimbatore** (3 per week, 1hr., US$80); **Delhi** (2 per day, 2½hr., US$235); **Goa** (4 per week, 2½hr., US$125); **Hyderabad** (2-3 per day, 1hr., US$95); **Madurai** (1 per day, 1hr., US$80); **Mangalore** (4 per week, 2hr., US$95); **Mumbai** (3 per day, 2hr., US$145); **Port Blair** (3 per week, 2hr., US$195); **Pune** (5 per week, 3hr., US$155); **Tiruchirappalli** (3 per week, 1hr., US$70); and **Trivandrum** (1 per day, 2hr, US$105).

TRAINS

Chennai has two principal train stations, one for intra-state and the other for inter-state travel, both located in the northern part of town near Periyar EVR Rd. (Poonamallee High Rd.). For **arrival and departure information,** call 131 and dial the train number after the beep.

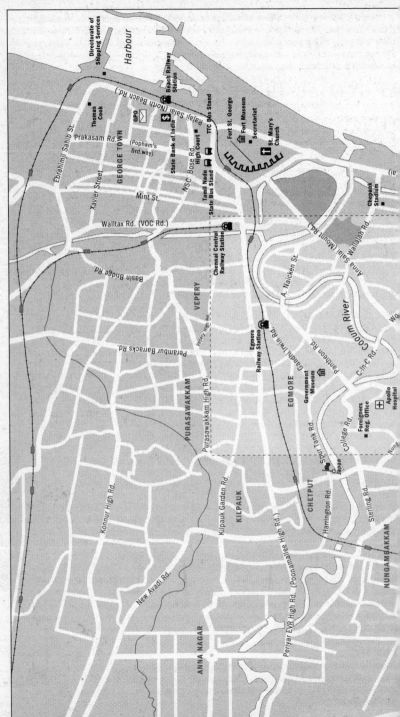

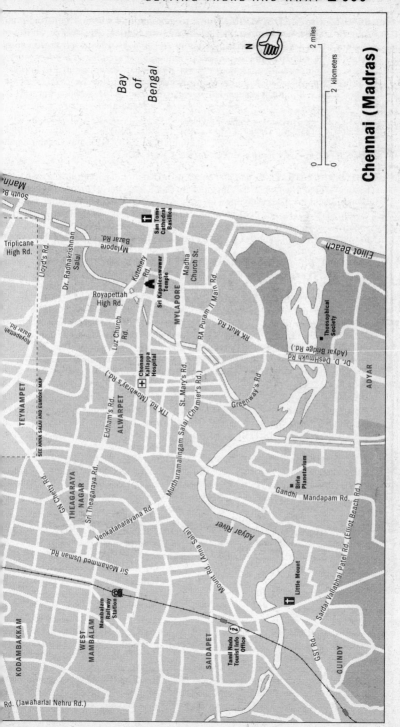

Chennai (Madras)

Bay
of
Bengal

N

2 miles

2 kilometers

Triplicane
High Rd.

Lloyd's Rd.

Dr. Radhakrishnan
Salai

Mylapore
Bazar Rd.

San Tome
Cathedral
Basilica

Kutchery
Rd.

Royapettah
High Rd.

Sri Kapaleeswarar
Temple

MYLAPORE

Madha
Church St.

RA Puram II Main Rd.

RK Mutt Rd.

Royapettah
Bazar Rd.

SEE ANNA SALAI AND EGMORE MAP

Luz Church
Rd.

Chennai
Kaliappa
Hospital

TTK Rd. (Mowbray's Rd.)

St. Mary's Rd.

Eldham's Rd.

ALWARPET

Murthuramalingam Salai (Chamiers Rd.)

Greenway's Rd.

Dr. D. Deshmukh Rd.
(Adyar Bridge Rd.)

Theosophical
Society

ADYAR

Elliot Beach

South Be... Marin...

TEYNAMPET

CN Chetty Rd.

THEAGARAYA
NAGAR

Sri Theagaraya Rd.

Venkatanarayana Rd.

Sir Mohammed Usman Rd.

Mount Rd. (Anna Salai)

Adyar River

Birla
Planetarium

Gandhi Mandapam Rd.

Little Mount

Sardar Vallabhai Patel Rd. (Elliot Beach Rd.)

KODAMBAKKAM

WEST
MAMBALAM

Mambalam
Railway
Station

SAIDAPET

Tamil Nadu
Tourist Info
Office

GST Rd.

GUINDY

Rd. (Jawaharlal Nehru Rd.)

EGMORE RAILWAY STATION. Trains to destinations within Tamil Nadu and Andhra Pradesh depart from the Egmore Railway Station. The station is north of Gandhi Irwin Rd. The reservation counter (tel. 135) is to your left as you enter (open M-Sa 8am-2pm and 2:15-6pm, Su 8am-2pm). Fares listed are for 2nd/1st class. To: **Chidambaram** (*Rameswaram Exp.* 6101, 8:25pm, 6hr., Rs117/351; *Cholan Exp.* 6153, 8am, 6hr., Rs77/232); **Kodaikanal** (*Pandian Exp.* 6717, 7:15pm, 12hr., Rs186/587); **Kumbakonam** (*Rameswaram Exp.* 6101, 8:25pm, 6hr. Rs143/440; *Cholan Exp.* 6153, 8am, 8hr., Rs94/262); **Madurai** (*Pandian Exp.* 6717, 7:15pm, 13hr., Rs186/587); **Rameswaram** (*Rameswaram Exp.* 6101, 8:35pm, 18hr., Rs230/734); **Thanjavur (Tanjore)** (*Rameswaram Exp.* 6101, 8:35pm, 9hr., Rs91/389; *Thanjavur Fast Passenger* 628, 10:20pm, 6hr., Rs76/343); and **Tiruchirappalli** (*Rockfort Exp.* 6877, 6am and 9:45pm, 6½hr., Rs146/451).

CHENNAI CENTRAL. Long-distance trains arrive and depart from Chennai Central, in George Town near the Buckingham Canal, also fairly close to the hotels of Gandhi Irwin Rd. The reservation counter is located upstairs in the administrative building—the 10-story, yellow concrete structure to the left of the huge red station (open M-Sa 8am-8pm, Su 8am-2pm). Here on the first floor, a special desk attends to tourists. General inquiries tel. 132. Fares listed are for 2nd/1st class. To: **Ahmedabad** (*Navjivan Exp.* 6046, 9:30am, 35hr., Rs406/1819); **Bangalore** (*Brindavan Exp.* 2639, 7:15am, 6hr.; *Bangalore Exp.* 6023, 1pm, 7hr.; *Chennai-Bangalore Mail* 6007, 10pm, 7hr., Rs155/482); **Kolkata** (*Coromandel Exp.* 2842, 9am, 28hr., Rs406/1755; *Howrah Mail* 6004, 10:30pm, 32hr., Rs386/1480); **Coimbatore** (4 per day, 7hr., Rs186/587); **Delhi** (*Tamil Nadu Exp.* 2621, 10pm, 34hr.; *Grand Trunk Exp.* 2615, 11pm, 37½hr., Rs450/1994); **Hyderabad** (*Charminar Exp.* 2759, 6:10pm, 276/1150; *Hyderabad Exp.* 7053, 4pm, 15hr., Rs242/1055); **Mangalore** (*Mangalore Mail* 6601, 7pm, 18hr., Rs260/871); **Mumbai** (*Chennai-Mumbai Mail* 6012, 11:45am, 28hr., Rs335/1091); **Tirupati** (*Tirupati Exp.* 6053, 1:50pm, 3hr., Rs61/176); **Trivandrum** (*Trivandrum Mail* 6319, 6:55pm, 18hr., Rs225/830); and **Varanasi** (*Ganga Kaveri Exp.* 6039, M and Sa 5pm, 39hr., Rs427/1543).

BUSES

Most buses to tourist destinations leave from the **State Express Transport Corporation Bus Stand,** on the south side of George Town (in an area officially known as Park Town; tel. 534 1835; open daily 7am-9pm). To take any inter-city bus, you need a reservation form (Rs0.25) from the reservations counter upstairs. TTC runs to: **Bangalore** via **Kanchipuram** or **Vellore** (#831, 21 per day, 9hr., Rs84); **Chidambaram** (#304, 300, and 326; 12 per day; 5hr.; Rs42); **Coimbatore** (#460 and 883, 9 per day, 12hr., Rs90); **Kanyakumari** (#282, 8 per day, 18hr., Rs115); **Kodaikanal** (#461, 5:45pm, 14hr., Rs87); **Kumbakonam** (#303, 33 per day, 7hr., Rs64); **Madurai** (#137, every hr., 10hr., Rs76); **Mysore** (#863; 5, 6, and 8pm; 11hr.; Rs137); **Ooty** (#468S, 7pm; #860, 6pm, 14hr., Rs94-120); **Pondicherry** (#803, every 30min., 4hr., Rs30); **Rameswaram** (#166, 5:45pm, 14hr., Rs93); **Thanjavur (Tanjore)** (#323, 9hr., Rs57); **Tiruchirappalli** (#123 and 124, 6hr., Rs70); and **Tirupati** (#902 and 911, every hr., 4hr., Rs46). **Broadway Terminal,** across the street from State Express stand, is somewhat nightmarish, and necessary only for travelers headed to **Kanchipuram** (#76, 79, and 130; every 30min.; 3hr.; Rs12) or **Mahabalipuram** (#19C, 119, 188, and 189; every 30min.; Rs10).

BOATS

Adventurous travelers might consider the long (56hr.) boat ride to the **Andaman Islands.** Fares are Rs1200 for a bunk, Rs2400 for a 2nd class cabin (with common bath), Rs3600 for first class (with attached bath), and Rs4800 for a deluxe cabin. Meals are available at the on-board restaurant. To purchase tickets, foreigners need four passport photos (get them at one of the shops on Anna Salai). For more information, contact the Deputy Director of Shipping Services, Andaman & Nicobar Administration, NSC Bose Rd. (tel. 532 1401; open daily 8am-5pm).

TAMIL NADU

▐ GETTING AROUND

AUTO-RICKSHAWS

Like those of most Indian cities, the streets of Chennai are infested with buzzing swarms of auto-rickshaws, probably the best way to navigate the city. Though the minimum charge is Rs1 per km (Rs7 min.), many drivers tamper with the meters or ask for more money. This is technically illegal, except at night. Be prepared to be "taken for a ride" if you hop in without any sense of direction. If possible, figure out the route before you step in, and bark at the driver if he, in hopes of upping his profits, strays from it. Rs25 is a typical fare between two downtown destinations. From the airport and railway station, take pre-paid rickshaws. Most rickshaw-*wallahs* will happily agree to meet you at your hotel in the morning or will take you around town for the day—simply discuss your plans beforehand and agree on a lump sum. Always insist that your driver use the meter; if he claims that it's "broken," find another driver. If you have serious trouble with a driver, threaten to take down his number (located on the back of the vehicle or on a black pin worn on his shirt) and report him to the police.

TAXIS

Taxis are much less common and about twice as expensive as auto-rickshaws. One advantage, however, is that taxis will allow you to cram in up to five passengers. While most have meters, it's best to fix a price beforehand. Expect to pay at least Rs100 from the railway stations to Anna Salai or to Triplicane.

LOCAL BUSES

The mere idea of boarding an Indian bus deters many, but the bus system in Chennai is efficient, frequent, and (marginally) less crowded than those of Mumbai, Delhi, and Kolkata. Many public buses are green and have their final destination printed on the side. Bus stands are located every few blocks throughout the city—if there's no awning, seek out the throngs of locals. Try to avoid rush hour (7:30-10:30am and 5:30-7pm).

Buses are boarded from the rear. Inform the conductor of your destination and pay up (usually Rs2-3). Note that many buses are unofficially segregated by gender—women on one side, men on the other. Married couples are an exception to this rule. Nevertheless, out of respect for custom (and women's safety—women are frequently sexually harassed on buses), it's best to follow the locals' lead.

Bus #	Route
22, 27, 27B, 29A	Egmore-Triplicane
PP23C	Egmore-Anna Salai-Adyar Depot
22, 23, 17, 17E, 9, 10	Egmore-Central
17D, 17K, 9, 9A, 10	Broadway-Egmore
21G, PP21, 60E	Broadway-Guindy National Park-Airport
9, 10	Parry's Corner-Central-Egmore
9A, 17D	Parry's Corner-Nungambakkan
60A, 18A, A18, 52B, 60	Parry's Corner-Anna Salai-Airport
21G	High Court-Adyar-Guindy National Park-Airport
4, 23C, PP23C	Anna Salai-Besant Nagar (Adyar)
21, 1A, 19M, 3A, 5	Anna Salai-Mylapore
17A, 17G, 25E, 25B	Anna Salai-Nungambakkan
40, 27A, 25B	Anna Salai-Triplicane-Egmore
23A, 23B, 23C, PP23C	Adyar Bus Depot-Anna Salai-Egmore

MOPEDS

You need an international license to rent a moped (Rs75 per day). If you're craving your own pair of wheels, check out **U-Rent Services Ltd.,** 36 II Main Rd. (tel. 491 0838), in the Gandhi Nagar district in the southern part of town, past the Adyar river (open daily 8:30am-8pm).

✴ ORIENTATION

Chennai is a massive, sprawling city, extending more than 15km along the western shores of the **Bay of Bengal.** While the city feels like an agglomeration of several small neighborhoods, it can be divided into three distinct sections. The northern-most is **George Town,** an area of long, straight streets which run south to **Fort Saint George** and the **Central Railway Station.** George Town's major east-west artery is **NSC Bose Road,** which ends at its intersection with **Rajaji Road (North Beach Road)** and runs north-south close to the shore and parallel to **Prakasam Road (Broadway). Parry's Corner,** at the intersection of NSC Bose and Rajaji Rd., is the wheeling, deal-ing locus of the market area, the city's **bus terminals,** and many rickshaws.

The southernmost of Chennai's three sections is 10km south of George Town and stretches from **Mylapore** in the north to the residential areas south of the **Adyar River.** This section is pleasant, but it has little of tourist interest besides the **Guindy National Park,** south of Adyar in the city's nether regions.

Wedged between George Town and Mylapore is Chennai's lively center, which includes **Egmore** and **Anna Salai (Mount Rd.),** Chennai's longest, busiest street. Anna Salai runs northeast to southeast and houses many tourist services. North of Anna Salai lies the congested Egmore area, full of cheap, convenient hotels. Egmore's northern boundary is **Egmore Railway Station,** just off hotel-saturated **Gandhi Irwin Road. Pantheon Road** runs parallel to and south of Gandhi Irwin Rd., while **Periyar EVR Road (Poonamallee High Rd.)** is to its north. Perpendicular to both are **Com-mander-in-Chief Road (C-in-C Rd.)** and, farther southwest, **Nungambakkam High Road (NH Rd.),** two busy streets where many of Chennai's businesses are located. Just 2km south of Egmore Railway Station is the **Cooum River,** which skirts just north of Anna Salai. **Triplicane** is a fun neighborhood just south of Anna Salai near the coast.

🛈 PRACTICAL INFORMATION

For the most current information, tourists should pick up a copy of **Hallo! Madras,** which details everything from practical information to sights and shopping.

TOURIST AND FINANCIAL SERVICES

Tourist Office: Government of India Tourist Office, 154 Anna Salai (tel. 852 4295 or 852 4785; fax 852 2139), at the corner of Clubhouse Rd. The best place to start col-lecting information on Chennai, Tamil Nadu, or the country. Helpful, English-speaking staff. Open M-F 9:15am-5:45pm, Sa 9am-1pm. There's also a **GOI information counter** in the domestic airport (tel. 234 0569). Open daily 6am-9:30pm. **Tamil Tourism Devel-opment Corporation (TTDC) Office** (tel. 535 3351), near Chennai Central RW Station, offers an assortment of brochures, reserves hotels, and books TTDC tours. Open daily 7am-7pm. **Kerala Government Tourist Information Office,** 28 C-in-C Rd. (tel. 827 9862). Open M-Sa 10am-5pm (closed second Sa).

Budget Travel: TTDC (see above) has affordable excursions to nearby cities. Daytrips to Pondicherry and Mahabalipuram from Rs 200; trips to Tirupati Rs350. Government-approved **Sita Travel,** 26 C-in-C Rd. (tel. 826 8861; email sitamaa@sita.sprint-rpg.ems.vsnl.net.in), just past Hotel Connemara, north of Anna Salai Airline office, has ticketing and currency exchange. Open M-F 9:30am-6pm, Sa 9:30am-1:30pm.

Diplomatic Missions: Australia, 114 NH Rd. (tel. 827 6036). Open M-F 9:30am-4pm. **France,** 202 Prestige Point Bldg., 40 College Rd. (tel. 826 6561). Open M-F 10am-3pm. **Germany,** 22 Ethiraj Salai (tel. 827 1747). Open M-F 9am-noon. **Indonesia,** 5 North Leith Castle Rd., Santhome (tel. 234 1095). Open M-F 10:30am-12:30pm.

Japan, 60 Spur Tank Rd. (tel. 827 5594). **Malaysia,** Asst. High Commissioner, 6 Sri Ram Nagar, North St. (tel. 434 4048). Open M-F 9-11:30am. **Netherlands,** Catholic Center, 64 Armenian St. (tel. 584894). Open M-F 10am-4pm. **Philippines,** 86 Radhakrishnan Salai (tel. 235 1016 or 235 0427). Open M-F 10am-4pm. **Sri Lanka,** 9D Nawab Habibullah Ave. (tel. 827 0831). Open M-F 9am-5:15pm. **U.K.,** 27 Anderson Rd. (tel. 827 3136). Open M-F 8:30am-4pm. **U.S.,** 220 Anna Salai (tel. 827 3040), at Cathedral Rd. Open M-F 9:30am-6pm.

Immigration Office: Foreigners Registration Office, Sastri Bhavan Annex, 26 Haddows Rd. (tel. 827 5424), off NH Rd. Three-month visa extensions take about 2 working days and cost Rs900; be sure to take along 3 passport-size photographs. The office also issues special permits for restricted areas. Open M-F 9:30am-6pm.

Currency Exchange: Bank of America, 748 Anna Salai (tel. 855 2121), 2 blocks west of the tourist office and across the street. Open daily 10am-7pm. **CitiBank,** 768 Anna Salai (tel. 852 2484), diagonally to the left of the government tourist office, has 24hr. ATM machines which accept international cards. Open M-F 10am-2pm, Sa 10am-noon. **State Bank of India,** 46 Cathedral Rd. (tel. 827 8091). Open M-F 10am-2pm, Sa 10am-12pm. **Thomas Cook,** Eldorado Building, 112 NH Rd. (tel. 827 2610). Extra charge for non-Thomas Cook traveler's checks. The private **Forexpress,** 1 Prestige Point, 16 Haddows Rd. (tel. 827 6597), guarantees 5min. exchange. Open daily 9am-7pm. **American Express** (tel. 852 3628), Anna Salai, 1st fl. of Spencer Plaza Mall, across from the government tourist office on Anna Salai. Open M-Sa 9:30am-6:30pm.

LOCAL SERVICES

Markets: Parry's Corner, NSC Bose Rd., in George Town northeast of the city center, is an unofficial market where you can find anything, from carnations to computers. The nearby **Burma Bazaar** carries imported goods. **Foodworld,** 769 Anna Salai, in Spencer Plaza Mall, provides a more bourgeois shopping experience. Open M-Sa 9am-6pm.

Libraries: Connemara Public Library, Pantheon Rd. (tel. 826 1151). No membership required. Open M-F 9am-7:30pm, Sa-Su 9:30am-6pm. **American Library,** U.S. consulate building (see **Diplomatic Missions,** above). Day membership Rs30. Open M-Sa 9:30am-6pm. **British Council,** 737 Anna Salai (tel. 852 5002). 1-month membership Rs550. Open Tu-Sa 8:30am-7pm.

Cultural Centers: Max Mueller Bhavan, 13 KN Khan Rd. (tel. 826 1314), screens German movies and has a collection of German books. Open M-F 9am-6:45pm, Sa 11am-6:30pm. **Alliance Francaise,** 40 College Rd., Nungambakkam (tel. 827 2650), brings that neo-imperialist *je ne sais quoi* to Chennai. **Soviet Culture Center,** 27 Kasturi Ranga Rd. (tel. 499 0050).

Bookstore: Landmark, Apex Plaza, 3 NH Rd., is a huge bookstore. **Higginbothams,** 814 Anna Salai (tel. 852 2440). Open M-Sa 9am-7pm. **Odyssey,** 6 First Main Rd., Adyar, Gandhi Nagar (tel. 442 0393). Open daily 10am-8:30pm. **Fountainhead,** Laxmi Towers, 27 Dr. Radhakrishnan Salai (tel. 828 0867). Open Tu-Su 9:30am-8:30pm.

EMERGENCY AND COMMUNICATIONS

Pharmacy: Emsons Medicals, 105 Poonamallee Rd. (tel. 825 5232). Open daily 8am-10pm. **Spencer & Co.,** Spencer Plaza, Anna Salai (tel. 826 3611). Open M-Sa 8am-7pm. **Anbu Pharmacy,** 684 EVR Periyar High Rd. (tel. 613 867). Open daily 8am-10pm.

Hospital: Apollo Hospital, 21 Greams Rd. (tel. 827 6566), with attached 24hr. pharmacy. **K.J. Hospital,** 496 Periyar EVR Rd. (tel. 825 5331). **Malar Hospital,** 52 1st Main Rd. (tel. 491 4023), near Adyar Bridge, Gandhi Nagar. Attached pharmacy. Open 24hr.

Police: Stations in **Adyar** (tel. 491 3552), **Anna Salai** (tel. 852 1720), **Egmore** (tel. 825 0952), **Guindy** (tel. 234 1539), **Kodambakkam** (tel. 483 8902), and **Mylapore** (tel. 498 0100).

Emergency: Police, tel. 100. **Fire,** tel. 101. **Ambulance,** tel. 102. English understood, but speak calmly and slowly.

TAMIL NADU

Post Office: GPO, Rajaji Salai (tel. 524 4338, enquiries tel. 514289). **Mount Rd. Head Post Office,** Kennet Ln. (tel. 852 1947), Egmore. Convenient *Poste Restante:* Anna Salai Head Post Office, Madras 600002. Open M-Sa 10am-4pm. **Postal Code:** 600001-600099.

Internet: netcafé@india.com (tel. 826 3779, 822 5427), just off Cathedral Rd. next to the Music Academy. You can't miss the neon-yellow signboard. Web-browsing and email (Rs50-60 per 30min.), as well as snacks and coffee (Rs20-65). Open daily 7am-11pm. **World Link,** Apex Plaza (tel. 822 7388), above Landmark Books. Cheaper (Rs75 per hr.), but connections are less reliable. In Egmore, check out **Web Surf,** #6 Gandhi Irwin Rd., Hotel Imperial Complex (tel. 825 4908 or 825 5965). Open daily 10am-10pm (Rs75 per hr.).

Telephones: Callbacks sometimes allowed at **STD/ISD** booths; fees at the proprietor's discretion, but expect to pay around Rs5 per min. **Directory Assistance:** tel. 197.

PHONE CODE	044

▐ ACCOMMODATIONS

Hotels in Chennai cater to virtually every budget, but this is a big city, and travelers scraping the dregs of the barrel may find Chennai pricey. Budget hotels are concentrated on or around Gandhi Irwin Rd., but most of the cheaper ones follow a strict "no foreigners policy." Still, good deals can be found almost anywhere. If you're looking for a piece of the action, consider staying in Triplicane. The chi-chi restaurants, highbrow shops, and most tourist services are but a stone's throw away. Reserve in advance. Most hotels have 24-hour check-out.

Dayal-De Lodge, 486 Pantheon Rd. (tel. 822 7328), just west of the intersection with Kennet Ln. Driveway leads to an elegant villa removed from the hectic Pantheon Rd. High-ceilinged, pastel rooms have French-style windows and phones. Aging bathrooms have either squat or seat toilets. Check-out 24hr. Singles Rs160; doubles Rs264.

Hotel Regal, 15 Kennet Ln. (tel. 823 1766), behind Hotel Masa. Get your daily fix of Doordarshan TV from the comfy beds. Squat toilets, but would you have it any other way? Attached restaurant. Check-out 24hr. Singles Rs258; doubles Rs330, with A/C Rs480. MC, Visa, AmEx.

Hotel Pandian, 9 Kennet Ln. (tel. 825 2901; fax 825 8459). More upscale, but it won't bust your bank account. Eager staff shows off the "luxuries" that come with the plain rooms: soap, TV, towel, phone, and seat toilet. Lovely attached restaurant and bar (open 11am-11pm). Check-out 24hr. Singles Rs400-500, with A/C Rs750; doubles Rs600/850.

Hotel Dasaprakash, 100 EVR Periyar Salai (tel. 825 5111), parallel to Gandhi Rd., north of Egmore Railway Station. An old Indian favorite, the charming, brightly-colored hotel occupies a location favored for its proximity to the train station. Polished wood rooms are classy, complete with daily newspaper, change of towels, seat toilets, and balcony views. Attached restaurant and ice cream parlor. Check-out 24hr. Singles Rs250-340, with A/C Rs400-480; doubles Rs480/600. 20% luxury tax.

YWCA International Guest House, 1086 EVR Periyar Salai (tel. 532 4234; fax 532 4263). Removed from the noisy streets by a tree-filled courtyard, the YWCA has bright white rooms and spotless bathrooms and an attached restaurant. If you're not a member, you can purchase a month's YMCA membership (Rs20). Check-out 24hr. Singles Rs450, with A/C Rs630; doubles Rs580/630.

Broadlands, 16 Vallabha Agraharam (tel. 854 8131), Triplicane, opposite Star Theaters. Steeped in backpacker lore, the labyrinthine villa has been around for nearly 50 years. All that mileage has lent the place loads of character, allowing one to overlook the slightly decomposing state of the rooms. Passport required for room rental. 10pm curfew. Check-out 24hr. All non-A/C singles Rs120-175; doubles Rs150-390.

Hotel Comfort, 22 Vallabha Agraharam (tel. 858 7661; fax 854 9671), Triplicane High Rd., down the street from Broadlands. Your typical medium-grade Indian "luxury" hotel, with TVs and phones in every tidy room. Check-out 24hr. Singles Rs250, with A/C Rs350; doubles Rs325-350/485. Extra person Rs140. 20% luxury tax.

FOOD

Dining in Chennai constitutes many travelers' first exposure to South Indian food and its rice-based dishes, but here one can also find Tamil Nadu's finest gourmet cuisine. Take advantage of Chennai's pastry and fruit juice shops during your stay; you probably won't see anything like it in more rustic towns.

EGMORE

For the most part, budget dining in Egmore is a strictly proletarian experience. So roll up those sleeves, wash your hands, and plunge your fingers into that *thali*.

Vasanta Bhavan, at the corner of Gandhi Irwin Rd. and Kennet Ln. The South Indian restaurant with which you will soon (or already have) become familiar, replete with *thalis* (Rs20) and the requisite *dosas*. A tempting array of calorie-laden Indian sweets are sold up front, including *badam* (Rs5) and *laddu* (Rs10). Open daily 8am-midnight.

Ceylon Restaurant, 15 Kennet Ln., in front of Hotel Mass. A hybrid of the whirring *thali*-joint and the hotel restaurant, Ceylon is calmer than its brethren across from the railway station. Fresh food is popular with Indians and foreigners. Try some fruit salad (Rs12) or *biryani* (Rs32). Open daily 7am-11:30pm.

Raj, 9 Kennet Ln., attached to Hotel Pandian. A typical hotel restaurant with the A/C humming away and virtually no decor (any splash of color would spoil the perfectly institutional atmosphere). *Tandoori* and Chinese dishes supplement the usual Indian fare. Entrees Rs30-75. Open daily 6am-11pm.

Jewel Box Restaurant, 934 EVR Periyar Salai, next to Hotel Blue Diamond. A more sophisticated dining option. Continental breakfasts (Rs45) and savory garlic chicken (Rs70) are served to you Italian style, on red and white checkered table cloths by candlelight. Open daily 7:30am-11pm.

ANNA SALAI AND TRIPLICANE

Some of the city's classiest restaurants sit along its main thoroughfare. With prime location and extra pampering, however, come prices more inflated than a politician's ego. Still, bargains can be found.

House of Dasaprakash, 806 Anna Salai, in a white cottage somewhat set back from the street. Although best known for its ice creams (Rs50-175), Dasa also serves up soups and salads (Rs125), gourmet spaghetti burmese (Rs90), and ravioli (Rs90) that will send your salivary glands into overdrive. Open daily 12:30-3pm and 7-11pm.

Buhari's, 83 Anna Salai, across from the Tarapore Towers, near where Anna Salai veers slightly to the right. Their specialty is decadent *tandoori* cooking (9pm-midnight). Locals wolf down chicken *biryani* (Rs28) in the cool, crowded dining hall. At night, take in the cityscape from the terrace. Open daily 8am-11pm.

Hotel Maharaja, Triplicane High Rd., at the Wallajah end. Enjoy your *thali* (Rs15) with a smattering of backpackers who stayed at the infamous Broadlands hotel. Veg. *tandoori* fare Rs15-30. Open daily 7am-11pm.

Southern Chinese Restaurant, 683 Anna Salai (tel. 852 2515). Small and romantic, with red decor and tables for two. Delicious food and attentive service. Non-veg. options include beef dishes (Rs55-70). Open daily 11:30am-3pm and 6-10:30pm.

Annalakshmi, 804 Anna Salai, next to the House of Dasaprakash Restaurant. Unquestionably one of the most cushy settings in all of Tamil Nadu—eating here is like being in a palace, and it shows on your bill. Exorbitant prices (Rs300-500) for slightly better-than-average South Indian set menus. Minimum Rs150 charge. Open daily noon-3pm and 7-9pm.

TAMIL NADU

Aavin, on Anna Salai, between the GOI and Tamil Nadu tourist offices. Get to know the name of this ice-cream/flavored-milk bar; you'll be seeing its blue-and-white stalls all across the city. Rich dairy goodies like mango ice cream (Rs12) and "African delight" (Rs75). Open daily 6am-8pm.

Cakes 'N' Bakes, 22 NH Rd. (tel. 827 7075), off Anna Salai's southern end. Try a slice of black forest cake (Rs15) or some mango pudding (Rs20). Tasty milkshakes (Rs30) wash down the heavy desserts. Open daily 10am-10pm.

Fruit Shop on Greams Road, 11 Greams Rd., north of Anna Salai. A cool, colorful oasis from the blistering heat. Unique fruit cocktails made before your eyes with mineral water. Sit upstairs and try the "Sheikh shake" (Rs65) or the "Jughead Special" (Rs50). Open Su-F 11am-midnight, Sa 11am-1:30am.

MYLAPORE AND ALWARPET

The eateries that dot the Mylapore/Alwarpet area are hidden gems—less crowded, they often boast a menu and ambience that even the more upscale competition on Anna Salai can't match.

Kabul, 35 TKK Rd. The restaurant receives rave reviews from all the locals, with good reason: waiters move to your assistance at the drop of a napkin, serving you succulent kebabs (Rs120) so soft that you can cut them with a spoon and savory *biryani* (Rs90-120). Open daily noon-3pm and 7pm-midnight.

Hotel Saravana Bhavan, 57 Dr. Radhakrishnan Salai. *Idli* (Rs10) and *thalis* (Rs20) served in a sparkling clean environment. Watch them squeeze that pulp out of fresh mangoes to make your juice (Rs8-21) at the juice counter up front. Open daily 5am-midnight.

Woodlands, 72/75 Dr. Radhakrishnan Salai, attached to the New Woodlands Hotel. Efficient service in cool surroundings. South Indian *thali* (Rs45), *idli* (Rs10), *vadai* (Rs15), and *dosa* (Rs18-50) served promptly. Open daily 7am-10pm.

Snofield, Amaravati Complex, 1 Cathedral Rd., just off Anna Salai. Opposite Music Academy. Your source for vaguely erotic sundaes—"One Exciting Night," "Sweet Dreams," "Playmate," and yes, "Stimulator" (sundaes Rs48-60). Open daily 10am-1am. Indulge in sweets like "cashew cutley" (Rs8) at **Nala's,** next door. Open daily 9am-11pm.

Coastline, Kaaraikudi, The Dhaba, and **Shogun,** at the Kaaraikudi Complex, 84 Dr. Radhakrishna Salai, where seafood, kebabs, Chinese food, and South Indian food are served respectively. Gives one the opportunity to sample the spectrum of Near and Far Eastern cuisine, with entrees Rs60-Rs120. Open daily 11:30am-3:30pm.

Gem Restaurant, at the corner of Peter's Rd. and Anna Salai. Candlelight, gilded swans, and exquisite cuisine make this place a true gem. Succulent Reshmi kebab (Rs70), non-veg. selections (Rs70-100), and fruit drinks (Rs40). Open 11am-midnight.

◩ NIGHTLIFE

Tamil Nadu only recently repealed its prohibition laws, and a controversy created by a recent bar-related murder in Delhi has ensured that Chennai remain a pretty dry town—alcohol consumption is still stigmatized. Most bars have heavily tinted windows and doors, as if to obscure the shameful goings-on inside. Nearly every three-to-five-star hotel has its own permit room. But don't expect to find your quaff of choice, since most permit rooms are stocked with just about any IMFL the owners can get their hands on. Near Egmore, decent bars are attached to the Hotel Imperial (**Sherry's,** 6 Gandhi Irwin Rd.; tel. 825 0376) and the Hotel Chandra Towers (**Bon Sante;** tel. 823 3334), where suspicious brands of beer (Rs100-160) flow freely. (Both open 11am-11pm.) For the serious action, posh hotels are the venues to look into, as young, designer-jean-clad Chennaiites are apt to know. Only the trendiest frequent **Socko,** Ambassador Pallava, 53 Montieth Rd., Egmore (tel. 855 4476), a popular disco that churns out techno rhythms for gyrating collegiate types (Rs300 per couple; open W 8pm-11pm).

Anna Salai and Egmore

ACCOMMODATIONS

A Hotel Dasprakash

B YWCA International
  Guest House

C Hotel Masa
  and Hotel Regal

D Dayal-De Lodge

E Hotel Pandian

F Comfort Hotel

🎵 ENTERTAINMENT

Chennai is home to India's second-largest film industry, so if you have time, take in a Tamil talkie, too. Language barriers won't prevent you from understanding the show—and you'll leave the theater with a new insight into the culture. Cinemas surprise you on every corner; many screen English-language movies. **Sathyam,** 8 Thurni Vika Rd., off Peters Rd., near New College; **Woodlands,** Royapettah High Rd. (tel. 852 7355); and **Devi,** Anna Salai (tel. 855 5660), all show four films per day. You might want to prop your feet up on the seat in front of you—rats enjoy the theater's darkness. Unfortunately, so do some of the male movie-goers looking to cop a feel; women should beware. Sound is also an on-again/off-again phenomenon. *The Hindu* has listings of films, special screenings, cultural events, etc.

There are music performances and dance dramas at the city's various music and dance academies. The **Carnatic Music and Dance Festival** takes place annually, from December 2 to January 15. Scout newspapers, like *The Hindu,* to find out what's going on. **The Music Academy,** 115 E. Mowbray's Rd. (tel. 827 5619), often gives away free tickets for shows.

🔘 SIGHTS

For a city of six million, Chennai has a surprisingly slim menu of sightseeing picks. If you're in town for a day, avoid overdosing on unimpressive monuments—either head for Marina Beach and the city's sumptuous shores or wander in the greenery of the Theosophical Society gardens.

FORT ST. GEORGE. Foremost among the city's traditional attractions, Fort St. George is a massive structure, once an enclave of British power, where the British Regiment and East India Company were housed in 1640. Many of the original buildings were damaged or destroyed during mid-18th century French attacks, though some remain. These days, the fort complex is home to Tamil Nadu's state government. The government's occupation of the complex has diminished its appeal as a tourist attraction. *(500m south of Parry's corner; 3km east of Egmore. Tell your rickshaw driver to take you to the Secretariat (SECK-reh-tree). Open daily 9am-5pm. Rs2.)*

Amid the everyday workings of the Tamil Nadu Legislative Assembly and Council, the ghost of the fort's colonial past lingers. To get a sense of what Fort St. George used to be like, head for the **Fort Museum,** housed in the fort complex's Exchange Building. Established in 1944, the museum displays an eclectic assortment of items from British Madras, including old uniforms, coins, and weapons from the Raj. On the upper floors, you can browse through a superb collection of lithographs from colonial times—the images subtly betray the British view of things. Also on display are original writings by Robert Clive, an adventurer of that era who laid the foundation for British rule. *(Museum open Sa-Th 10am-5pm.)*

South of the museum, on the opposite side of the gray and white Fort House, sits the modest and rather schizophrenic **St. Mary's Church,** the oldest Anglican church east of the Suez. Consecrated in 1679, the church was built with a vaulted, bombproof ceiling to withstand the frequent attacks on the fort. The interior of the church is cluttered with assorted memorabilia and plaques commemorating British colonists and their descendants. The altar is tastefully simple, graced by a solemn painting of *The Last Supper*. *(St. Mary's open daily 9am-5pm. Services Su 9am.)* Finally, the fort complex houses the wholly unimpressive homes of Robert Clive and Elihu Yale, the founder of Yale University and governor of Madras.

MARINA BEACH. Extending south from Fort St. George all the way down to Mahabalipuram, this 12km stretch of sand is the second longest in the world. The beach is spectacular at dusk; the setting sun casts an iridescent glow, and peddlers hawk everything from roasted peanuts to balloons to ice cream, and hundreds of Chennai residents amble away their worries along the shore. On isolated patches of sand, fortune tellers and palm readers lure customers, soothsaying with the aid of seashells and tarot cards. Despite the heat, few locals use the beach for all-out swimming, in part because of the dangerously strong tides, and in part because of the social current—wearing a swimsuit in public is seriously frowned upon. Instead, residents are content to wade along the shore, or simply sit on the beach and drink in the atmosphere. Near the beach are **Anna Park** and the antenna-like **MGR Samadhi,** memorials to former Tamil Nadu Chief Ministers C.N. Annadurai and M.G. Ramachandran. There is also a slimy aquarium and several decrepit swimming pools which are best avoided. Tourists should stick to the more crowded areas, especially at night. Deserted areas of the beach are often unsafe.

GOVERNMENT MUSEUM. An archipelago of six buildings in varying states of dilapidation, the Government Museum was established in 1857 by British imperial authorities. Its collection boldly seeks to cover everything from archaeology to modern art. The highlight of the museum is the free-standing **bronze gallery,** west of the ethnology galleries. This unparalleled collection of Chola bronzes includes a complete set of characters from the *Ramayana* and a succession of excellent

I'M NOT A POLITICIAN, BUT I PLAY ONE IN REAL LIFE

Residents of Tamil Nadu have cultivated their penchant for electing members of the immensely popular local film industry to positions of power. In 1977, the film star M.G. Ramachandran ("MGR") won a landslide victory on behalf of the All-India Anna Dravida Munnetra Kazhagam (AIADMK), a breakaway faction of the ruling DMK. That was only the beginning. In 1990, the most (in)famous of AIADMK's leaders, Jayalalitha Jayaram, came to power. The former actress and dancer quickly became embroiled in a veritable mini-series of corruption and scandal. She was forced to make a hasty exit in 1995 as her unfolding political drama was too much for her fans (or was it voters?) to handle. Her successor, the DMK-backed N. Karunanidhi, is the bald, grinning man sporting dark glasses, whose unflattering mug is immortalized in statues and billboards in every town in the state. A former screenwriter for Tamil films, Karunanidhi is often depicted alongside Rajnikant, a feather-haired, mustached actor who is deeply concerned, naturally, for a variety of social causes. For now, Karunanidhi runs a fairly clean ship (of state), but locals jokingly wonder what sort of high-stakes *filmi* scandal this writer will dream up.

11th-century renderings of Shiva in the guise of Nataraja (King of Dance). West of the bronze gallery is the less-than-thrilling **Children's Museum**, graced with a much-photographed pair of dinosaurs out front. Next door is the **National Art Gallery**, housed in a splendid Indo-Saracenic edifice, built in 1906. Framed by such an elaborate exterior, the collection inside is somewhat anticlimactic. Finally, the **Museum of Contemporary Art** contains, well, a collection of contemporary art, that varies greatly in quality. *(Pantheon Rd., south of Egmore Station. Open Sa-Th 8am-5pm; ticket booth closes at 4:30pm. Rs3; camera fee Rs10. Free tours at 10am, noon, 2, and 4pm.)*

SRI PARTHASARATHY TEMPLE. Originally raised by the Pallavas in the 8th century, then renovated by the Cholas and the Vijayanagar kings, the temple is dedicated to Krishna, who served as the chariot driver (Sarathy) to Arjuna (Partha) in the Mahabharata. The distinguishing feature of this temple is that it contains the images of four avatars of Vishnu: Varaha (boar incarnation), Narasimha (lion incarnation), Rama, and Lord Venkatakrishna. The principal image of Lord Venkatakrishna is made of black granite. *(Triplicane, west of South Beach Rd. Open daily 7am-noon and 4-8pm. Admission to inner sanctum Rs3.)*

SRI KAPALEESWARAR TEMPLE. After an earlier temple on the same site was destroyed by the Portuguese, the Vijayanagar Kings rebuilt the present structure in the 16th century, including the majestic 37m *gopuram* (gateway) at its entrance. The great saint Ugnanasambandar is said to have sung a hymn to Lord Kapaleeswarar in order to bring a girl who died of a snake bite back to life; in front of the temple, a shrine and statue commemorate this sacred event. The temple's name is derived from a story involving Brahma and Shiva. At a meeting on Mount Kailas, Brahma did not proffer the due respects and courtesies to Shiva. An angry Shiva plucked off one of Brahma's *kapalams* (heads), and in an act of regretful penance, Brahma came to Mylapore and installed the *linga* himself. Non-Hindus are allowed only in the outer courtyard, which houses a shrine to Parvati in peacock form. *(Mylapore, off Kutchery Rd. Open daily 5:30am-noon and 4-9:30pm. Puja every hr.)*

SANTHOME CATHEDRAL BASILICA. The basilica is an important pilgrimage site built over the tomb of the apostle St. Thomas. It is believed that Thomas arrived in India from Palestine in AD 52 and was killed 26 years later. A millennium passed, and Thomas's remains were moved inland and a new church was built, likely by Madras' Persian Christian community. In 1606, the church was refurbished and made into a cathedral, and in 1896 it was rebuilt as a basilica. Santhome is more interesting for its history than for its aesthetic appeal, although the church sanctuary is pleasant and peaceful and bears a large stained glass window depicting the apostle's life. A **museum** on the premises contains a 16th-century map of South Asia. *(Eastern Mylapore, 6km south of Egmore. Open daily 6am-6pm. Museum open M-F 9:30am-12:30pm and 2-5:30pm.)*

LITTLE MOUNT AND ST. THOMAS MOUNT. Just south of the Adyar River is **Little Mount,** a complex of mildly interesting caves where St. Thomas the Apostle led the life of an ascetic, occasionally offering prayers and sermons from his rocky pulpit. The cave once inhabited by St. Thomas now bears only a small cross. According to local legend, the impressions in the caves are St. Thomas's handprints. Little Mount has two churches, both of which attract plenty of pilgrims. The older church was built in 1551 by the Portuguese, while the newer, Our Lady of Health, was constructed in 1971. About 5km southwest of Little Mount, 160 steep steps lead pilgrims to the 95m-high **Saint Thomas Mount (Great Mount),** where Thomas is said to have been killed after fleeing his home at Little Mount. The Portuguese church atop the Mount was raised in 1523 on the site of a church that had been constructed nearly 1000 years earlier by Armenian traders. It is said that the current church's altar is built on the very spot where Thomas died, and that the paintings over the altar were done by St. Luke. The altar cross is named "the bleeding cross." Legend has it that the red stains on the carving are patches of blood that reappear annually on the 18th of December. The somewhat taxing climb is actually worth the toil—the gorgeous view makes you realize just how much green relief there really is in Chennai. *(Little Mount is 10km south of the city center. St. Thomas Mount is 5km farther. Auto-rickshaws from downtown Rs30-40.)*

OTHER SIGHTS. Guindy National Park is a peaceful, though increasingly scruffy, expanse. Popular with families, its zoo is home to some deer and the occasional jackal, mongoose, and monkey. *(1km south of Little Mount. Open daily 8:30am-5:30pm. Rs3.)* Also on the premises is the popular **Snake Park,** with the usual representation of reptiles—king cobras, adders, pythons, vipers, and crocodiles *(open daily 9am-5:30pm; demonstrations every hr. 10am-5pm; Rs2).* Eastern Adyar harbors the headquarters of the **Theosophical Society** (tel. 491 7198), a spiritual movement founded by a pair of Americans in 1875. The mansion is surrounded by elaborate gardens, home to "The Great Banyan Tree," one of the largest of its kind in the world; over 100 years old, its branches span over 40,000 square feet. *(Open M-F 8-11am and 2-5pm, Sa 8-11am.)* On the southern edge of George Town, not far from Fort St. George, rise the minarets of the **High Court** and the **Law College,** constructed in an Indo-Saracenic style in the mid-19th century. Both buildings are still in use today, and men in black judicial robes traverse the busy streets surrounding the edifices.

🛍 SHOPPING

Before you bust your wallet, take a moment to reflect on your itinerary. Many crafts and silks can be had for considerably less in smaller towns, where you can purchase goods directly from the artisans. Still, **street shopping** can be rewarding since hawkers are common and often offer good deals. Dozens of makeshift shops also line the streets in **Luz** (directly south of city center in **Alwarpet**). **Radha Silk House (RASI),** 1 Sannadhi St., Mylapore (tel. 494 1906), next to the Kapaleeswarar Temple, is a hot favorite among foreigners, with silk *saris,* and silk fabric of all kinds in a profusion of colors. The basement boasts an excellent selection of gift items, wooden carved boxes inlaid with ivory, brassware, and paintings. (Open daily 9am-9pm. Accepts all major credit cards.) Also of interest are more glitzy shopping plazas, such as **Alsa Mall,** 149 Montieth Rd., Egmore, where (after some serious bargaining) beautiful *salwaar kameezes* can be purchased. **Victoria Technical Institute (VTI),** 765 Anna Salai (tel. 852 3141), is somewhat overpriced, but its hassle-free environment lets you select paintings, woodwork, exquisite sculpture, brassware, and pottery at leisure. The proceeds of this state-run shop go to charity. (Open M-F 9:30am-6pm, Sa 9:30am-1:30pm.)

Kanchipuram

ACCOMMODATIONS
A Hotel Baboo Surya
B Hotel Abirami & Lodge
C Rajam Lodge
D Hotel Jaybala Int'l

KANCHIPURAM காஞ்சீரம்

From the dusty streets to the towering *gopurams*, Kanchi is a city of temples, "the Varanasi of the South." Counted among Hinduism's seven most sacred cities, Kanchi derives its name from the words *Ka* (another name for Brahma, the creator) and *anchi* ("worship"). Brahma is said to have worshiped Vishnu and the goddess Kamakshi here, and the magnificent temples constructed by the Pallava kings (4th-8th centuries AD) in their capital city reinforce the story. Kanchi was also the episcopal seat of the guru Shankara, also known as Sankaracharya (AD 780-820), and has been a center of philosophy and learning ever since. Officially, Kanchi is divided into two parts: Little Kanchi houses the important Vishnu temples, and Big Kanchi has over a thousand temples dedicated to Shiva. Modern Kanchipuram is a place where the smell of *chakra pongal*, the sound of temple bells, and the sight of dazzling silks in every storefront conspire to launch a sensory assault. When in town, look out for the elegant threads worn by Tamil women—Kanchipuram silk *saris* are famous all over India.

ORIENTATION AND PRACTICAL INFORMATION

The **bus stand** has one main entrance on **Kamarajar Street** (formerly known as Kossa St.), which runs north-south through the center of town, where many shops and eating places are located. You can also find food and lodging on **Nellukkara Street,** which runs perpendicular to Kamarajar St. at its northern end. **Gandhi Road** runs parallel to Nellukkara St., about 500m down from the bus stand, turning onto **Nambi Koil Street.** These roads house the bulk of Kanchi's most famous silk emporiums. One block east of the Nellukkara-Kamarajar intersection, **East Raja Veethi** shoots northward, leading out of town.

Trains: The **railway station** (tel. 23149), on Station Rd., is east of the Vaikuntha Perumal Temple. Take E. Raja Veethi north and follow the signs. 2nd class only to: **Chennai** via **Chengalpattu** (7, 8:40am, noon, and 6:10pm; Rs7).

Buses: The chaotic **bus stand,** hidden behind storefronts at the intersection of Kamarajar and Nellukkara St., can be accessed from either thoroughfare. To: **Chennai** (#76B and 76C, every 30min., 2½hr., Rs15) or Point-to-Point (PP) bus (every 30min, 1½hr., Rs17); **Mahabalipuram** (every 15min., 2hr., Rs12); **Vellore** (every 30min., 2½hr., Rs12); **Chengalpattu** (#212H and 212B, every hr., 1½hr., Rs8). Frequent buses to **Pondicherry** depart from Chengalpattu.

Local Transportation: Auto rickshaws can be flagged down on Kamarajar St. or Gandhi Rd. or picked up next to the bus stand. A ride from the bus stand to the outskirts of town should cost no more than Rs25. For those willing to combat the usual chaos of Indian traffic, **bike rental** is available at the shop outside Perumal Temple and at the stall near the railway station (Rs15 per day).

Tourist Office: While there is no official tourist office, some basic information and maps can be obtained from the TTDC-sponsored **Hotel Tamil Nadu,** Railway Station Rd. (tel. 22553 or 22554). Follow E. Raja Veethi north from the bus station. Turn right at the sign, and follow this street to its end at Railway Station Rd. Turn right again; the main entrance is just ahead.

Currency Exchange: The nearest place to change foreign currency is in Chennai.

Market: Rajaji Market, at the intersection of Railway and Gandhi Rd., sells all the fruits, vegetables, and mutton you could want. Open daily 7am-7pm.

Pharmacy: Tamil Nadu Medicals, 25 Nellukkara St. (tel. 22285), west of the intersection with Kamarajar St. Open M-Sa 8am-11:30pm.

Hospital: Government Hospital, Railway Rd. (tel. 22307). Open 24hr.

Police: Police Control Room, Kamarajar St. (tel. 22000).

Post Office: GPO, Railway Rd. Open M-F 9am-5pm. **Postal Code:** 631502.

PHONE CODE	04112

 ACCOMMODATIONS

Kanchipuram's budget hotels are usually rather dank and windowless, and many tend to fill up quickly. They cluster near the bus station, close to the intersection of Kamarajar and Nellukkara St.

Hotel Jaybala International, 504 Gandhi Rd. (tel. 24348). Rooms have all the amenities, including towel, soap, satellite TV, elevator access, phone, safe deposit box, room service, and a doctor on call. Seat and squat toilets. Check-in 24hr. Singles Rs120; doubles Rs275, with A/C Rs475; triples Rs400. 20% luxury tax.

Rajam Lodge, 9 Kamarajar St. (tel. 22519), near the bus stand entrance. Vertigo-inducing M.C. Escher-type tiles on the floor add character. Ask for a double on the 2nd floor—in return you'll get windows (a scarce commodity in this town). Squat toilets attach to moderately clean rooms. Singles Rs70; doubles Rs110; triples Rs145.

Hotel Abirami & Lodge, 109B Kamarajar St. (tel. 20797). Rub-a-dub-dub: being in here is like living in a bathtub (walls & floors are covered in brown and white tile). Phones in the rooms, but no windows or sheets. Seat and squat toilets. Padlocks. Singles Rs70; doubles Rs110; deluxe Rs145.

Hotel Baboo Surya, 85 E. Raja Veethi (tel. 22555 or 22556), near the Perumal Temple, about a 5min. walk from the bus stand. The poshest place around, Baboo Surya flaunts a glass-windowed elevator and circular driveway. You get what you pay for: immaculate rooms, seat toilets, and the morning paper. All rooms have Star TV. Singles Rs270, with A/C Rs375; doubles Rs320/450. MC, AmEx. 20% luxury tax.

FOOD

Hotel Saravana Bhavan, 504 Gandhi Rd., next to Hotel Jaibala International. Suited officials bring order to the masses by way of an intricate token system and assigned seating. Undoubtedly the most popular spot in town—for good reason. Splendid "rice meals" from 10am-4pm (Rs28) and sweet *badam halwa* (Rs10) make a sticky mess. Open daily 9am-6pm.

Hotel Shakti Ganappatti, on E. Raja Veethi St., about 2min. north from the bus stand. A bigger, newer South Indian diner that serves your old favorites. *Masala dosa* (Rs12) and steaming hot *idli* (Rs3 per piece). Open daily 5:30am-8:30pm.

Kanchi Woodlands, inside Hotel Baboo Surya, allows for an undisturbed veg. meal in its silent, slightly chilly atmosphere. Pick from a wide variety of *dosas* (Rs10-16), *paneer* (Rs33), and rices (Rs20-40). Open daily 6am-10:30pm.

Abirami, 109B Kamaraj St., underneath the hotel of the same name. Despite its somewhat run-down appearance, the *thali* (Rs15) receives good reviews from locals. Cheap *dosas* (Rs3) and *idli* (Rs8). Open daily 6am-10pm.

SIGHTS

Far more than historical relics, these constructions rank among India's most sacred locales for contemporary Hindus. Since the temples are fairly spread out, a walking tour may not be the best option. Auto-rickshaw drivers will ask for Rs150-200 for a tour, including "waiting charges"—bargain them down if you can. An alternative is to rent a bicycle for the day. Below, the temples are arranged in a roughly clockwise order.

SRI KAILASANATHA TEMPLE. Built by Rajasimba Pallava in the first quarter of the 8th century, the temple is the oldest construction in Kanchipuram. Its relatively modest size and the use of the soft amber sandstone are characteristic of Pallava temples; the famous shore temple at Mahabalipuram was erected by the Pallavas at roughly the same time. The temple is a quiet and largely untrafficked site; most visitors opt for either the Kamakshi Amman or Sri Ekambaranathar temples in the center of town. The interior of the wall surrounding the shrine is marked by a row of 58 uncomfortably small meditation chambers, where *sadhus* reflect in quiet solitude. In some of the small cubbyholes, traces of the temple's frescoes are still visible. Unfortunately, most of the wall paintings were destroyed by the British in their attempt to "preserve" the monument by encasing it in plaster and stripping it of its fragile artwork. On the sanctum's rear wall are carvings of Shiva performing the Urdhwa Tandava dance of destruction. The inner sanctum (closed to non-Hindus) houses a *linga* to which it is believed Vishnu prayed for help in defeating the demon Tripurantaka. To walk around the image, worshippers must first crawl on all fours through a hollow. *(1.5km out of town. Follow Nellukkara St. westward until it becomes Putteri St. Sri Kailasanatha is on the right past a small lake. Open daily 8:30am-noon and 4-6pm. Free. If you want to see much, plan to visit before sunset.)*

SRI EKAMBARANATHAR TEMPLE. The magnificent white *gopuram* of the Sri Ekambaranathar Temple dominates the skyline in the northern part of town, dwarfing all neighboring structures and mesmerizing visitors. The origins of the temple are recorded in the *sthalapurana*, which recounts an incident when Parvati jokingly covered the eyes of her consort, upsetting the process of creation and destruction. So angered was Shiva that he ordered Parvati to earth to expiate her wrongdoings. On earth, Parvati came to a mango tree on the banks of the river Kampa in Kanchipuram and fashioned a *linga* out of sand. To test her devotion, Shiva placed before her all sorts of obstacles, which Parvati overcame. Finally, Shiva let flow the Ganga from his hair, hoping to inundate Kanchi and wash away the *linga*. Yet Parvati's devotion was such that she held tight, protecting the *linga* through the torrent. Shiva was pleased and took her once again as his consort.

Shiva & Parvati were married under this same mango tree by which Parvati knelt. The tree itself is housed within the temple. Each of its four branches—they represent the four books of the Vedas and are supposedly 3500 years old—is said to produce a different type of leaf, as well as fruit of a different taste. Locals believe that eating the fruit cures women of infertility. The temple derives its name from this tree, the root "Eka" meaning "mango tree."

Also within the inner sanctum of the temple is the *linga* that Parvati fashioned, one of five in Tamil Nadu devoted to the elements. A cavernous hallway surrounding the sanctum houses many *lingas* and statues of the 63 Alvar poet-saints. These colorful works are displayed during the temple's car festivals in April and July. *(Puthupalayam St. leads directly north to the temple. Open daily 6am-12:30pm and 4-8pm. Free; camera fee Rs3. Puja 6, 7am, noon, 4, 5, and 9pm.)*

KAMAKSHI AMMAN TEMPLE. *Gopurams* cast in soft shades of yellow, green, and pink and capped with tiny wooden spires adorn this temple dedicated to Kamakshi, the town's resident deity. A local incarnation of the goddess Devi, Kamakshi is said to have Lakshmi, Parvati, and Saraswati as her eyes. The temple is one of the three sacred *shakti peeths* of India, sites devoted to the worship of the female element in creation. The inner sanctum (inaccessible to non-Hindus) is a squarish chamber with inscriptions on all sides. The image of Kamakshi faces southeast; *darshan* is possible only during prescribed *aarti* times. Outside, the *mandapam* is graced by a golden *vimana* which glows with a blinding brilliance under the South Indian sun. It is believed that the grounds were once filed with *champaka* trees, whose reddish blossoms exude a sweet scent. The sacred tank in the back is also steeped in legend—Vishnu sent two servants-turned-demons to bathe here to cleanse them of their evil ways. The temple also houses a shrine to **Sri Sankaracharya,** the first in a famous line of Hindu saints known as *acharyas*. A small gallery next to the *mandapam* bears the images of more recent holy men in this line. It is said that Sankaracharya appeased the goddess Kamakshi with prayer when she was causing trouble in town in the form of Kali. Kamakshi promised Sankaracharya that she would not go into town without his permission. Even today, when her image leaves the temple for the annual **Silver Car Festival** (June), a ceremonial stop is made before Sri Sankaracharya's shrine to symbolically request his permission to go. *(From W. Raja St., turn right onto Amman Koli St. Open daily 5am-12:30pm and 4-8:30pm. Free. Photography not permitted.)*

VAIKUNTA PERUMAL TEMPLE. This temple, dedicated to Vishnu, is deserted, and its sculptures have been repaired with plaster by the Archaeological Survey of India. Legend holds that a Pallava king performed an elaborate *puja* at the Sri Kailasanatha Temple on the holiday of *Maha Shivratri*. Ancient texts proclaim that those who worship devotedly on *Maha Shivratri* will have sons who will be devotees of Vishnu. The courtyard surrounding the inner sanctum is lined with granite pillars and carvings that depict the Pallava kings, battle scenes, and musicians. The left corner at the back has a panel showing Hsuan Tsang, the Chinese Buddhist pilgrim who traveled all over India in the 7th century.

The inner sanctum (with its images of Vishnu) is usually locked, but generous *baksheesh* to the key-wielding guard can work wonders. The central spire houses three images of Vishnu, one on top of the other. On the ground floor he is seen sitting; on the second floor, reclining on the serpent *ananta*; on the top, standing in an ascetic pose. A small walkway around the *vimana* is filled with well-preserved panels of Vishnu and his consort Lakshmi. *(From E. Raja St., turn right; the temple is several hundred meters ahead. Open daily 8am-noon and 4-8pm. Free.)*

 SHOPPING

The biggest and most reputed of Kanchi's silk *sari* shops is **Nalli Silks,** 54 Nellukkara St. (open M-Sa 9am-11pm). You can also try **Srinivasan Silk House,** 17A TK Nambi St. (open daily 8:30am-11pm). Most owners will gladly take you to the back of the stores to show you silk yarn and demonstrate the process of making *zari*

pure gold thread) designs onto *saris*. Turn right onto the road perpendicular to Sannadhi St. (outside Varadaraja Perumal Temple), and take a left at **Ammangar Street,** which teems with silk weavers who will willingly demonstrate their craft. Weavers' cooperatives tend to cluster near temple entrances, so you'll probably be accosted by salesmen wielding business cards. Each *sari* is handwoven and takes fifteen days to a month to complete. Kanchipuram silks start at around Rs1000 and skyrocket into the tens of thousands for elaborate wedding *saris*. Expect to pay at least Rs3000 for a good quality *sari* with a fair amount of *zari* and an intricately woven *pallu* (the part that drapes over the shoulder). Store owners should give you at least a Rs1200 "discount" off the first price named.

VELLORE வெல்லூர்

Vellore, 145km southwest of Chennai, is not for the claustrophobic. Vendors cram into every inch of the excruciatingly narrow streets, while masses of pedestrians push to gain right of way in their frantic attempt to reach the city hospital. The Vellore hospital dominates the center of town and is famed throughout India, drawing hundreds waiting to be healed, on a daily basis. For travelers without physical ailments, however, Vellore's well-preserved historical relics provide insights into Vellore's past as a medieval city of the Vijayanagar kingdom.

Everything of use to visitors can be found in the immediate vicinity of the **CMC Hospital** (tel. 222102; open 24hr.), which marks the center of town. Most restaurants can be found on **Ida Scudder Road,** which runs directly parallel to the hospital. **Babu Rao Street,** which runs parallel and south of Ida Scudder Rd., and **KVS Chetty Street,** south of Babu Rao St., front most of Vellore's hotels and lodges. The **Main Bazaar** lies two streets south and parallel to KVS St., and leads straight to the fort and temple entrances. The temple's major cross street is **PTC Road;** turning right onto it will bring you to the **bus stand.** To: **Chennai** (every 10 min., 3½hr., Rs28); and **Trichy** (5 per morning, 5hr., Rs60). PATC goes to: **Bangalore** (every 30min., 6hr., Rs48); **Tirupathi** (every hr., 3hr., Rs15); **Kanchipuram** (every 30min., 2hr., Rs13); and **Chennai** (every 15min., 4hr., Rs26). The nearest place to **exchange currency** is in Chennai. The **pharmacy** (tel. 222121) attached to the hospital is open 24 hours. **North Vellore Police Station** (tel. 200021), on the corner of PTC Rd. by the bus station, is open 24 hours. The **post office** is on Katpadi Rd. (open M-F 10am-5pm, Sa 10am-4pm). **Postal Code:** 632004. **Telephone Code:** 0416.

Hotel vacancies increase the farther one gets from the hospital. **VDM Lodge** (tel. 224008), on the corner of Beri Baukali St., has small but clean, pastel rooms. Only doubles have decently clean attached baths. (Check-out 24hr. Singles Rs50; doubles Rs90.) **Srinivasa Lodge** (tel. 226389), opposite VDM Lodge, has well-lit rooms that are slightly bigger than VDM's, all with attached bath and free hot water from 6am to 8am (singles Rs70; doubles Rs110). At Vellore's grimy diners, even the toughest tummies might encounter some grief. **Hotel Susil Classic,** 64 Arcott Rd., past the hospital, has dimly lit A/C or non-A/C dining. Vegetable clear soup (Rs13) or South Indian staples such as *dosa* (Rs18) and *idli* (Rs8) are among the picks. Open daily 7:30am-10:30pm.) **Chinatown,** on Arcott Rd. above Hotel Susil Classic, has bow-tied waiters serving fried rice (Rs35), wonton soup (Rs30), and *naan* (Rs18) in the small, cool dining room (open daily noon-3pm and 6-11pm).

◼ SIGHTS. Legend has it that the **Vellore Fort** was created in an attempt to lift a curse on the temple that had been built earlier on its site. Erected in the 13th century under the rule of the Vijayanagar kings, this sprawling granite fortress surrounded by a beautiful moat became the nucleus around which the town of Vellore grew. For a few turbulent centuries, beginning in the 1600s when the Bhamini Sultans occupied it, control of the fort kept changing hands. The Sultans were ousted by the Marathas, who, in turn, were booted by the Mughals. War between the Mughals and Marathas continued for some time; Vellore shuttled back and forth between the two powers, but eventually the Mughals' rule became solid. In the 18th century, the British replaced the Mughals as the fort's controllers. The fort was also the scene of the short-lived **Vellore Mutiny,** in which the South Indian troops employed by the British protested changes in headgear and traditional uniform by unsuccessfully storming the fort. About 130 British officers were killed before the mutiny was put down in a few hours by Colonel Robert Gillespie. Today, there are several government offices, schools, and private businesses inside, as well as a **museum** containing some interesting stone carvings. (Located on PTC Rd. Fort open daily 6am-8pm; free. Museum open Sa-Th 9:30am-5pm; free.) The beautiful limestone **Jalakanteshwara Temple** was built a couple of years before Vellore's fort, and despite constant invasion by non-Shavaite worshipping, the white statues and carvings have remained in superb condition. On top of the *gopuram* above the main entrance, amidst smaller carvings of deities, is a small carving of the fort's builder and his wife. To the left of the entrance, a series of spectacularly carved outer pillars support a great hall—all of these pillars are carved from one stone. (Temple located inside the fort. Leave shoes for Rs5.)

NEAR VELLORE: TIRUVANNAMALAI திருவண்ணாமலை

Though the major attraction of Tiruvannamalai is its **Siva-Parvati Temple of Arunachaleswar** (open daily 6am-8pm), a truly awe-inspiring monument, the town's tranquility is a welcome relief from the bustle of other South Indian towns. A truly blissful morning can be had watching the sun rise over the ivory-colored *gopurams* and then exploring the five gigantic courtyards. **Buses** go to and from **Vellore** (every 15min., 2hr., Rs15) and **Villapuram** for connecting buses (every 15min., 3hr., Rs15). Across from the eastern temple wall (the first wall you see when coming from the bus stand), **Sri Kalaimagal Lodge,** N. Othavadai St. (tel. 24215), has large rooms with floors so clean you could eat off them (singles Rs100; doubles Rs150). Down the street, near the entrance of the temple is **Hotel Dibum,** one of the town's few non-grimy, open-air restaurants. Basic *dosa* (Rs9) and *idli* (Rs29) are all these restaurants tend to offer. (Open daily 6:30am-10:30pm.)

MAHABALIPURAM மஹாபலிபுரம்

Officially known as Mamallapuram, the village of Mahabalipuram rests comfortably on the shores of the Bay of Bengal, disturbed only by the pungent odors of its fishermen's bounty and the suspiciously "herbal" stench left in the wake of the many tourists who drift up and down Mahab's sandy beaches. The town's foreign appeal is so great that there is even a festival devoted to its visitors: the **Tourist Dance Festival** (Jan. 15-Feb. 15). During the festival, just about every door on E. Raja St. seems to belong to a hotel, restaurant, or overzealous tour operator, and the air is filled with the monotonous hammer and clang of artists carving stone. The craft of stonework has long been a tradition in Mahabalipuram, beginning with the reign of the Pallavas during the 4th-8th centuries.

◪ ORIENTATION AND PRACTICAL INFORMATION

Finding your way around in Mahabalipuram is a cinch. From the **inter-city bus stand,** it's a five-minute walk due north (turn left when exiting the bus stand) along **East Raja Street** to the **tourist office,** which is next to the **post office.** On the way you'll cross two east-west streets. The first is the unmarked **Othavadai Road,** which leads east to a number of lodges and restaurants. A bit further north, **TKM Road** cuts across E. Raja St. on its left-hand side, leading to the **bank** and **pharmacy.** At the tourist office, E. Raja St. becomes **Kovalam Road,** a long, solitary thoroughfare which stretches out of town, passing a bunch of fancy beach bungalows as it goes **West Raja Street** runs parallel to E. Raja St. The **beach** is a few hundred meters from the village; walk east from E. Raja St. To get to the **Shore Temple,** take a right from the bus stand onto E. Raja St. and then a left onto **Shore Temple Road.** If you want to see the **mandapams** and surrounding caves, take a left on the same road (in the opposite direction from the temple).

Mahabalipuram (Mamallapuram)

ACCOMMODATIONS
A Ramakrishna Lodge
B Lakshmi Lodge
C Mamalla Bhavan Annexe
D Hotel Tamil Nadu II:
 Camping

WARNING. The Bay of Bengal can be very dangerous, and every year many people drown. Before venturing into the water, ask at the tourist office and at your hotel about the advisability of swimming. Even if you are an experienced swimmer, don't underestimate the force of the undertow. If you have been drinking alcohol, don't even *look* at the water.

Bus: The **bus stand** is on E. Raja St. To: **Chengalpattu** (#212H and 108B, frequent, 45min., Rs6); **Chennai** (#118, every 15min., 2hr., Rs12); **Kovalam** (#118 and 188V, every 30min., 30min., Rs4); **Thirupporur** (#119, every 40min., 2½hr., Rs12); **Kanchipuram** (#157M and 212H, every 10min., 2½hr., Rs13); **Pondicherry** (every 30min., 2½hr., Rs19).

Local Transportation: Auto-rickshaws and **tourist taxis** wait outside the bus stand, but you won't need them in this small town unless you stay at one of the beach resorts outside Mahabalipuram proper. Many cycle shops rent 2-wheeled wonders. **Nathan Cycle Works,** opposite TTDC, rents bicycles (Rs15 per day) and mopeds (Rs175 per day).

Tourist Office: TTDC, E. Raja St. (tel. 42232), in a house at the end of the street, on the right-hand side near Kovalam Rd. Will load you down with maps from all over Tamil Nadu. Bus schedules posted on the wall. Open daily 10am-6pm.

Budget Travel: Stores along E. Raja St. charge somewhat exorbitant prices for tourist taxis and trips to sites. None are government-approved since TTDC has its own tours to pitch. **JRS** (tel. 42285) can arrange trips for all over India starting at Rs950 per day. Many other travel agencies rub elbows on E. Raja St.

Currency Exchange: Indian Overseas Bank, 130 TKM Rd. (tel. 42222). Go north on E. Raja St. and turn left onto TKM. Changes AmEx, Thomas Cook, and Visa traveler's checks. Open M-F 10am-2pm, Sa 10am-noon.

Pharmacy: Revathy Medicals, about 10 doors up from the bank, near E. Raja St. Open daily 9am-9pm.

Hospital: Government Primary-Care Facility, adjacent to the Township Office, on E. Raja St. south of the tourist office. Has less than a dozen beds and is not a good option. In an emergency, the tourist office recommends the private **Suradeep Hospital,** Thirukula St., (tel. 42389 or 42448). Doctors available 7am-10pm and 24hr. nurse service. Your best bet is to go to Chennai.

Police: Vandavasi Police Station, Kovalam Rd. (tel. 42221), just north of town. 24hr.

Post Office: E. Raja St. (tel. 42230), near the tourist office. Open M-Sa 9am-4pm. Telegraph services attached. **Postal Code:** 603104.

Internet Access: Several places along E. Raja St. allow email and web browsing. **VAT Telecom Center** (tel. 42711) is in the middle of the road. Rs2 per min. online, Rs20 per page offline typing, and Rs15 per page printout. Open daily 7:30am-10:30pm.

Telephones: STD/ISD booths are on E. Raja and Othavadai St. Booth at the intersection of Othavadai St. and E. Raja St. is open 24hr.

PHONE CODE	04114

▚ ACCOMMODATIONS

Plenty of inexpensive lodgings have sprung up to cater to the droves of tourists who descend on Mahabalipuram during high season. The cheapest accommodations can be found on or near E. Raja or Othavadai St. For those with some extra cash, a number of resorts line Kovalam Rd., offering private beaches, extravagant buffet feasts, and oodles of services. During low season, some of these resorts are a superb bargain. If you do decide to stay out along Kovalam Rd., the town and its attractions are but a short, invigorating bike ride away.

Ramakrishna Lodge, 8 Othavadai St. (tel. 42331 or 42431), in a pink and red painted building. Wide rooms house big beds, clotheslines, and mosquito screens. Seat toilets and hot water. Inner garden adds artistic flair. Singles Rs75; doubles Rs125.

Lakshmi Lodge, 29/A2 Othavadai Street (tel. 42463), down the dirt road on the right at Tina Blue View Restaurant. This sea-side lodge is crammed full of foreigners. Standard rooms vary in price according to view (patio or beach). Most bathrooms have seat toilets. Staff will arrange practically anything for guests, including massage and astrology readings. Attached rooftop restaurant. Singles Rs100-150; doubles Rs150-200.

Hotel Tamil Nadu II: Camping Site (tel. 42287), on the road that veers south in the middle of Shore Temple Rd. You can't miss the billboard. This government-run hotel is a tad pricey, but its rolling gardens are immaculate and the site is serene (pitch a tent outside if you want). Rooms have modern wooden furnishings. Hot water in all bathrooms. Dorm beds Rs50; cluster cottages Rs300; sea-view cottages Rs350, with A/C Rs450.

Hotel Sea Breeze (tel. 43035), the first side street off Othavadai St., on the right side. Fuchsia mosquito netting, shiny marble floors, polished wood furniture and breezy balconies create a classy environment. Singles Rs250; doubles Rs400-550, with A/C Rs750. Off-season: Rs250/350-400/650. 15% discount for cash.

Mamalla Bhavan Annexe, 104 E. Raja St. (tel. 42060). By far the most luxurious hotel in town, with an eager team of blue-uniformed employees. Spacious rooms have marble tiled floors with luxurious double beds, phones, and cable TVs. Two deluxe rooms have full-sized baths attached. Attached restaurant. Doubles Rs300, with A/C Rs525; deluxe Rs650. 20% luxury tax.

FOOD

Mahabalipuram overflows with restaurants proffering European "health food" and seafood (only during the high season). You'll have a surprisingly difficult time finding unembellished Indian food.

Pallais Croisette, Othavadai St., on top of the Ramakrishna Hotel. Everything seems to taste good in this airy rooftop restaurant. The rice pudding (Rs20) is mouth-watering; golden, hearty pancakes (Rs15-25) will make you ask for seconds. Acclaimed German bakery re-opens December 1999. Open daily 7:30am-10:30pm.

Curiosity Restaurant, Othavadai St., near Hotel Sea Breeze. Don't worry, there is nothing "curious" about the food; it's actually quite tasty. Excellent vegetable *biryani* (Rs25) and banana shakes (Rs15) are palate-pleasing. Open daily 7am-10pm.

Mamalla Bhavan, E. Raja St., opposite the bus stand. A typical Indian eatery, with a battalion of fans whirring above and tons of locals below. Try *thalis* (Rs12) and spicy, non-pricey *masala dosas.* Open daily 8am-10pm.

Moonrakers, Othavadai St. next door to the Ramakrishna Hotel. European breakfasts popular with tourists (muesli and yogurt Rs40), but travelers linger here throughout the day. Lemon tea (Rs15), fish and chips with salad (Rs60), chicken in lime-mint sauce (Rs60), and honey "pancakes" (crepes Rs25). Open daily 7am-1am.

Golden Palate Restaurant, 104 E. Raja Street, inside Mamalla Bhavan Annex. Fresh pink flowers on the tables mark this as a more upscale place to enjoy Indian fare. Enormous, elaborate *thalis* (Rs50) and ice cream sundaes (Rs45-70). Open daily 7am-10:30pm.

SIGHTS

While most of Mahabalipuram's magnificent rock carvings have been weathered by the sun, sand, and surf, the town boasts an incredible concentration of well preserved sculpture. Each stone breathes with life and sings the glory of the Pallavas. Little is known about life in the area when local sculptors produced the work they did, but scholars agree that most of these masterpieces were produced under the patronage of the 7th-century Pallava leader Narasimhavarman I, who went by the fearsome name Mamalla ("Great Wrestler")—hence the town's name. All of the sights are conveniently clustered near the southern part of town.

SHORE TEMPLE. Dedicated to Shiva and Vishnu, the temple was built at the turn of the 8th century and is thought to have been the first South Indian temple built entirely of stone. The Pallavas' maritime activities diffused Pallava culture—echoes of the Shore Temple's lion carvings and stocky spires can be seen in South Asian temple architecture of the period. The interior of the temple houses a flower-strewn image of Vishnu reclining on the serpent Ananta and a broken, fluted granite Shiva *linga.* Outside the temple, carved panels depict historical scenes of its Pallava creators. Though the area around the temple boasts a profusion of sacred *Nandi* (bull) images, there has been speculation that the Shore Temple once served as a lighthouse, due to its oddly elongated and narrow *vimana.* (On Shore Temple Rd., 1km to the right of the bus stand, jutting into the Bay of Bengal. Open daily 8am-6pm. Rs5 includes admission to the 5 Rathas, free on Fridays.)

ARJUNA'S PENANCE. This is reportedly the world's largest *bas*-relief sculpture, measuring 9m x 27m. Particularly impressive is the elegant, witty depiction of animals and birds—look for the delightfully out-sized renderings of an elephant family and the wry depiction of an ascetic, meditating cat surrounded by jolly dancing rats. While it is easy enough to admire the visual spectacle, scholars have had a hard time figuring out exactly what all the sculpture represents. According to the widely accepted "Arjuna's Penance" theory, it depicts a well-loved story from the *Mahabharata*—the scrawny man standing on one leg is the archer Arjuna, who is gazing through a prism doing penance and imploring Shiva for the *pashupatashastra*, a powerful magic arrow. Other historians believe that the images

TAMIL NADU

represent Rama's ancestor, Bhagiratha, begging the gods to give the Ganga river to the people of the world (see **Flashing Eyes, Floating Hair, Holy Dreds,** p. 146). The gods have agreed to comply with Bhagiratha's request, and the whole of creation—including the elephants—has turned out to watch the miracle of Ganga gushing down from the Himalayas. *(In town, just behind W. Raja St.)*

MANDAPAMS AND SURROUNDING MONUMENTS. The area to the west, from Koneri Rd. in the north to Dharmaraja Mandapam in the south, has an eerie, ashen ambience. The hilly area is strewn with massive boulders and ten small **mandapams** (cave temples), which depict tales from Hindu mythology. Finding your way from one *mandapam* to the next can be difficult, and making a systematic tour is tough. Still, getting a bit lost and stumbling upon *mandapams* can be lots of fun. Just around the corner to the northwest from the bas-relief is the **Ganesha Ratha,** a massive, free-standing monolith dedicated to the elephant-headed son of Shiva and Parvati. Two elaborate pillars mark the front, and a number of intricate columnar forms have been hewn from the stone. North of the *ratha* and off to the left is **Krishna's Butterball,** a massive boulder precariously balanced on the side of a hill. The name comes from popular stories of Krishna's youth, which recount an incident when the baby Krishna was caught stealing solidified *ghee* from an urn. North of the Butterball, the **Trimurti Cave,** next to a Pallavan water tank, boasts shrines to Shiva, Vishnu, and Brahma; all are depicted with their right hands in the *abhya* pose, which indicates a blessing. Each divine image is surrounded by kneeling devotees and flying dwarf *ganas*. The **Kotikal Mandapam,** which dates from the turn of the 7th century and is regarded as the area's oldest *mandapam*, is down the hill to the left. A small cell in the back is guarded by stone carvings of female attendants.

Heading south back toward the *bas*-relief, you first pass the 7th-century **Varaha Mandapam,** displaying four panels that represent the goddess Varaha raising the earth from the ocean. Most impressive is the one on the left depicting Vishnu in the form of a boar with the goddess Bhumidevi (Earth) seated in his lap. Another panel depicts the goddess of wealth, Lakshmi, accompanied by elephants. The trough in front of the *mandapam* was used by worshippers to wash their feet before entering the temple. From the Varaha Mandapam, walk 150m southeast to the exquisite **Krishna Mandapam,** a large mid-7th-century *bas*-relief which depicts Krishna raising up Mount Govardhana to protect his relatives from the god Indra. Other panels depict scenes from Krishna's life, including his play *(lila)* with the *gopis*, or milkmaids. A covered *mandapam* was added several centuries ago. The *mandapam* is also easily accessible from W. Raja St., south of Arjuna's Penance.

Directly west of the Krishna Mandapam and up the steep hill rests the decaying **Rayala Gopuram.** This uncompleted construction bears slender vertical panels that portray the ten incarnations of Vishnu. From the Krishna Mandapam, it's a short walk south to the **Ramanuja Mandapam,** built in the mid-7th century and almost completely ruined by vandals of later times who chiseled away at and destroyed many of the temple's elaborate panels. From there, the 100-year-old **New Lighthouse** is in view. Next to the New Lighthouse is the **Old Lighthouse,** a Shiva temple perched at an especially high elevation that was used as a lighthouse with a bonfire on top until the turn of the century.

FIVE RATHAS. A collection of stunning monoliths were carved during the reign of Narasimhavarman I Pallava; they are known as the **Pancha Pandava Rathas,** full-size models of temples known to the Dravidian builders of the 7th century. The complex includes life-size depictions of animals as well as five temples influenced by Buddhist temple architecture and named for the five Pandava brothers, the heroes of the *Mahabharata*. The largest of the temples, the **Dharmaraja Ratha,** is adorned with various carvings of demi-gods and Narasimhavarman. *(About 1.5km south of town along E. Raja St. Rs5, including admission to the Shore Temple.)*

GOVERNMENT COLLEGE OF SCULPTURE AND ARCHITECTURE. Hundreds of artisans learn their craft at this sprawling seaside complex. Though there are sculptors busying themselves with hammer and chisel throughout Mahabalipuram, the ever-lively Government College can be a fun place; ask at the tourist office or contact the college directly to make an appointment to have a look around. *(About 3km north of central Mahabalipuram along Kovalam Rd. Tel. 42261.)*

CROCODILE PARK. Indians from far and wide come to Vodanammali (a small town north of Mahabalipuran) to see this privately owned "collection" of over 3,500 specimens of crocs and alligators from around the world. The thousands of seemingly lethargic reptiles, separated by their "nationality" or breed, snap at one another in various water holes throughout the park. Due to unfortunate occurrences a few years back, signs have been plastered everywhere to warn visitors who think it might be okay to pet the ferocious scaly beasts. Next door to the croc farm is the government-run **Snake Venom Extraction** facility. Poisonous invertebrates slither here and there (in a controlled pit, of course) and from time to time are grabbed by attendants who provoke snakes into striking position and then squeeze the poison into containers as a public demonstration. Do not come here if the sound of hissing irks you. Hisssss... *(15km north of Mahabalipuram. Crocodile Park open daily 8am-5:45pm. Rs15, kids under 10 Rs5. Snake facility open W-M 9:30am-5pm; Rs5.)*

PONDICHERRY பாண்டிச் சேரி

Many visitors to Pondicherry expect the one-time capital of French India to be a wholly unadulterated enclave of European culture, but this coastal town's claim to fame is a little tinged with hyperbole: Pondicherry isn't Paris. It's a decidedly divided town, split geographically and culturally by a narrow canal. To the west, Pondicherry is Pondy, your basic, bustling mid-sized South Indian city. To the east of the canal, Pondicherry is *Pondichéri*. The streets here are well-kept, the cops sport red *képis*, restaurants serve French food, and the architecture is European.

The wide roads and shimmering, blue-green coasts of Pondicherry make it a vacationer's Eden. Sanctuary can be found in many places here, although the most popular spot is the auspicious Aurobindo Ashram established in 1926. The French artist Mirra Alfassa (later known as "the Mother") helped the Bengali mystic Sri Aurobindo Ghose popularize his spiritual teachings among thousands of devotees worldwide. The fruits of their efforts are apparent today: the ashram occupies a sizeable chunk of real estate in Pondy, and at the Mother's request, followers have established the experimental community of Auroville 12km north of the city. Like everything else in Pondicherry, the Aurobindo Ashram is a multifaceted entity. For many locals, the Mother emerges as "The French God," complementing "The Muslim God," "The Hindu God," and other powers in the local pantheon. For the several thousand non-Indians who now call Pondicherry home, Auroville is a rural haven where The Mother's research into scientific yoga and the inner-cellular evolutionary passage to the next species can be continued. The ashram and its devotees strike many tourists as anachronistic remnants of the 1960s. Alongside the colonial buildings, the Sri Aurobindo legacy stands as a monument to grandiose Western visions lost to the ravages of time.

The streets of this promenader's paradise are populated from early morning until late evening with magistrates in flowing robes, barefoot bourgeois joggers, and hip wayfarers holidaying in the sun. Most of the elaborate architecture in the city can be attributed to its former French occupation, which was established in 1673 by Francois Martin, who hoped to gain a commercial advantage for his country over the roving Dutch and English mercenaries. Over the next two centuries, the French ruled their South Asian colonial enclaves from Pondicherry. In 1954, the French handed over their scattered territories to India, which became the semi-autonomous Union Territories with Pondicherry as their capital. Lingering French influence has molded Pondy into a chic and decidedly pricier city.

⯅ TRANSPORTATION

Trains: The **railway station** (tel. 36684) is a sleepy, little-used place on South Blvd. Four trains leave daily for nearby **Villupuram** (*Pondicherry-Villupuram Passenger*, 1hr., Rs7) with frequent connections to the Chennai-Rameswaram line.

Buses: Pondy's two bus stations are located 500m apart on Lal Bahadur Shastri, 600m west of Anna Salai. Buses depart from the massive U-shaped **State Bus Stand** to: **Chidambaram** (every 15-30min., 2hr., Rs16); **Chennai** (every 15-30min., 4hr., Rs29); **Mahabalipuram** (every hr., 2hr., Rs22). The one semi-organized operation working out of this zoo, the **Tamil Nadu State Transport Corporation (TSTC)** has a booking office at the far end of the station (at the center of the base of the U) and reserves seats for some trips. Reservations office open daily 5am-12:30pm and 2-9:30pm. To: **Bangalore** (8:30am and 10pm, 7hr., Rs75); **Chennai** (every hr.); **Kanchipuram** (7:30, 11:25am, 3:40, and 8:12pm; 4hr.; Rs18); **Kumbakonam** (every hr., 4hr., Rs35); **Tirupati** (9:30pm, 6hr., Rs53); **Tiruchirappalli** (#315; 4:45, 6:09, 10:10am, and 10pm; 5hr.; Rs34). 500m east is the computerized-but-comatose **State Express Transport Corporation (SETC)** stand. SETC buses go to **Madurai** (9:30pm, 8hr., Rs60) and **Coimbatore** (#842; 8, 8:45, 9, and 10pm; 12hr.; Rs75).

Local Transportation: Auto-rickshaws line up at the stand on Capt. Xavier St., and they also wait in packs outside every major tourist spot. Pay no more than Rs20 for a trip between the bus stands and the French side of town. **Tempos** are overcrowded, often unsafe, and best avoided.

ORIENTATION

Pondy is a remarkably well-planned city. Bordered on the east by the **Bay of Bengal**, it is divided into eastern and western sections by a covered canal. Its streets are laid out in a simple grid. Three major commercial thoroughfares (from north to south), **Jawaharlal Nehru (JN)**, **Rangapillai**, and **Lal Bahadur Shastri Streets**, run east-west. Lal Bahadur Shastri leads west the **bus stand**. West of the canal, the major north-south avenue is **Mahatma Gandhi (MG) Road**. East of the canal, the major north-south thoroughfares are **Rue Suffren** and **Romain Roland Street**, both of which end at the centrally located **Government Place**. Beach Road (**Goubert Salai**) runs along the shore and hooks west as it heads south, becoming **South Boulevard** (Subbaiyah Salai). The rarely utilized **railway station** is off Subbaiyah Salai. As Subbaiyah Salai heads north, it passes the Botanical Gardens and becomes **West Boulevard** (Anna Salai). To the north, **North Boulevard** (Sardar Vallabhai Patel Salai) completes Pondy's circumference and links West Blvd. and Beach Rd.

PRACTICAL INFORMATION

Tourist Office: Pondicherry Tourism and Transport Development Corporation (PTTDC), 40 Goubert Salai (tel. 334978), north of Lal Bahadur Shastri St., dispenses an excellent map of the city and several glossy brochures advertising possible activities. They also conduct a 4hr. tour that covers the Aurobindo Ashram, Auroville, the Government Museum, and the Chunnambar Boat House. **Tours** (2pm; Rs42, A/C bus Rs50) depart from the tourist office. Make reservations by 1pm. Open daily 8:45am-1pm and 2-5pm.

Diplomatic Missions: The **French Consulate**, Compagnie St. (tel. 334174), at Marine St. near the beach, in the light yellow building. Open for information and visas M and W 7:30am-12:45pm; Tu, Th, and F 7:30-11:45am.

Currency Exchange: Banks are sprinkled throughout the city. **State Bank of India,** Surcouf St. (tel. 36208), at Rue Suffren. Open M-F 10am-2pm and Sa 10am-noon. On the western side of town, **Souvenir,** on Mission St. above the Bennetton store, changes all currencies and traveler's checks for a Rs5 fee. Open M-Sa 9am-1pm and 3-7pm.

Cultural Centers: Alliance Française, 38 Rue Suffren (tel. 334351), has French classes and a French library. It also sponsors cultural events and periodically hosts art displays in the gallery. Open M-F 8:30am-12:30pm and 2-8pm; Sa 8:30am-noon. Library open M-F 8:30am-noon and 4-7pm. **Romain Roland** (a French Public Library), Rangapillai St. Open T-Su 7:30am-8:30pm.

Bookstore: Higginbothams, Gingy St. (tel. 333836), just north of Rangapillai St., is heavy on academic texts and light on fiction. **French Bookshop,** Rue Suffren (tel.

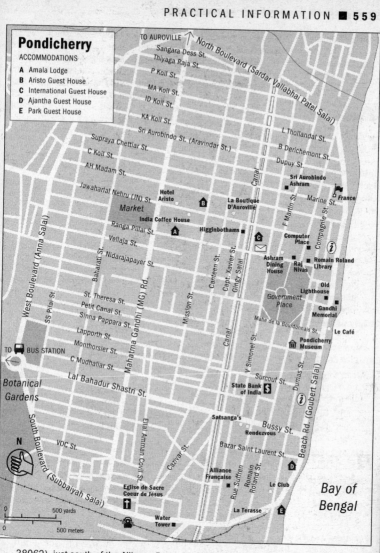

Pondicherry

ACCOMMODATIONS
- **A** Amala Lodge
- **B** Aristo Guest House
- **C** International Guest House
- **D** Ajantha Guest House
- **E** Park Guest House

TO AUROVILLE

North Boulevard (Sardar Vallabhai Patel Salai)

Sangara Dess St.
Thiyaga Raja St.
P Koil St.
MA Koil St.
iD Koil St.
KA Koil St.
Sri Aurobindo St. (Aravindar St.)
Supraya Chettiar St.
C Koil St.
AH Madam St.
Jawaharlal Nehru (JN) St.
Market
Ranga Pillai St.
Vellaja St.
Nidarajapayer St.
Bharat St.
St. Theresa St.
Petit Canal St.
Sinna Pappara St.
Lapporth St.
Monthorsier St.
C Mudhaliar St.
Lal Bahadur Shastri St.
VOC St.
SS Pillai St.
West Boulevard (Anna Salai)
Mahatma Gandhi (MG) Rd.
Mission St.
Canteen St.
Capt. Xavier St.
Gingy Salai
Canal
V Simonel St.
Surcouf St.
Dumas St.
Beach Rd. (Goubert Salai)
South Boulevard (Subbaiyah Salai)
Ellai Amman Coril St.
Cazivar St.
Rue Suffren
Romain Roland St.
Bussy St.
Bazar Saint Laurent St.
Satsanga's
Rendezvous
Alliance Française
Le Club
Eglise de Sacre Coeur de Jésus
Water Tower ■

L. Thollandat St.
B Derichemont St.
Dupuy St.
Sri Aurobindo Ashram
France
Marine St.
F Martin St.
Compagnie St.
Computer Place
Ashram Dining House
Raj Nivas
Romain Roland Library
Old Lighthouse
Government Place
Gandhi Memorial
Mahe de la Bourdonnais St.
Le Café
Pondicherry Museum
State Bank of India
La Terasse

Hotel Aristo
India Coffee House
La Boutique D'Auroville
Higginbothams

TO BUS STATION
Botanical Gardens

N

0   500 yards
0   500 meters

Bay of Bengal

TAMIL NADU

38062), just south of the Alliance Française. Both open M-Sa 9am-12:30pm and 3:30-7:30pm. **Sabda Ashram Bookstore,** Marine St., across from the ashram. Everything relating to Sri Aurobindo in most Indian and many European languages. Open M-Sa 8:30-11:45am and 2:45-5:15pm.

Pharmacy: National Medicals, JN St. (tel. 333073), east of MG Rd. Open daily 7am-10pm.

Hospital/Medical Services: The best place to go for medical concerns is **Jawaharlal Institute of Medical and Educational Research (JIMER)** (tel. 72389), a few km north of town; take NH 45 straight. **General Hospital,** Victor Simonel St. (tel. 336050), just south of Government Place. **St. Joseph's Hospital,** 16 Romain Roland (tel. 339513), is open daily 3am-12:30pm and 4-7:30pm.

Police: 14 Goubert Ave. (tel. 36790). **Emergency,** tel. 100.

Post Office: GPO, Rangapillai St. (tel. 33050), maintains a well-organized *Poste Restante* service. Open M-Sa 10am-7:30pm. **Postal Code:** 605001.

Internet: Computer Place, Saint Louis St. Rs1 per min. to browse the net; Rs10 to check mail; Rs20 to send. Open M-Sa 9am-1pm and 3-7:30pm.

Telephones: STD/ISD booths are located west of the canal, with high concentrations on JN St. and MG Rd. There is also a string of booths on Bussy St. The communications megaplex next to the GPO is open 24hr. Rs5 per min. for callbacks in Pondy.

PHONE CODE	0413

ACCOMMODATIONS

Apart from a couple of over-priced "luxury" hotels, accommodations in Pondy fall into two basic categories: standard Indian lodges and ashram guest houses. If you can get a room, the ashrams are by far the most appealing options in town. Run by the followers of Sri Aurobindo, ostensibly for devotees, the ashram guest houses, all on the French side of town, offer serene, immaculate rooms. The guest houses abide by a curfew and prohibit smoking, drinking, and drug-taking.

Park Guest House, Goubert Salai (tel. 334412; email parkgh@auroville.org.in). You may think you're dreaming, but this hotel really *is* paradise. Lush gardens surround the building, and balconies afford stunning views of the ocean crashing against the rocks. Cleaned daily, rooms have couch, desk, comfy bed, mosquito net, and bureau. Attached baths with seat toilet, towels, soap, and shower head. Complimentary filtered water and bike rental (Rs20 per day). Check-out 24hr. Singles Rs300; doubles Rs400.

International Guest House, 17 Gingy St. (tel. 336699). A sense of purity and calm reigns in the spacious white rooms. Small "dressing rooms" lead into gleaming bathrooms. Communal meditation room and indoor garden. Check-out noon. One single Rs70; doubles Rs150, with A/C Rs350; suites Rs150-250. Often full, so call ahead.

Aristo Guest House, 50A Mission St. (tel. 336728), just north of JN St. Management is up a flight of stairs. Pink painted rooms are cool and clean. Stroll on the upper balcony for fresh air. Check-out 24hr. Singles Rs100, with A/C Rs550; doubles Rs150/650.

Ajantha Guest House, 22 Goubert Salai (tel. 38898), south of the tourist office. Musty rooms could use some light, but the morning breeze compensates. Attached baths with clean seat toilets. Check-out 24hr. Singles Rs250; doubles Rs300, with A/C Rs450.

Amala Lodge, 92 Rangapillai St. (tel. 38910), between MG Rd. and Mission St. Simple rooms with attached baths are reasonably clean, with yellow walls that sparkle amid the dinginess. Squat toilets and showers—hot water by the bucket in the morning. Check-out 24hr. Singles Rs60-70; doubles Rs120.

FOOD

For those weary travelers who'd rather make a bodily sacrifice to Shiva than down another *dosa*, eating out in Pondicherry is a welcome change of pace. Pondy's colonial legacy includes a handful of glitzy Continental restaurants featuring gourmet French fare and ample drink menus. Both sides of the canal also offer better-than-average Indian cuisine at inflated prices.

Satsanga's, 13 Bussy St., around the corner from Rendezvous Restaurant. Quite the lovers' nest at night, with its high arches, lush potted jungle plants, and candlelight. Try the organic Italian salad with homemade cheese (Rs45), pizza (Rs55-75), and *café au lait* (Rs10). Check out the gallery while you wait for your food. Open T-Su 8am-2pm (breakfast 'til noon) and 5-10pm. Tea salon open 8am-noon and 3-7pm.

La Terasse, 5 South Blvd., a short jaunt westwards from the southern end of Goubert Salai. Relax in a small courtyard beneath a thatched roof as the musty scent of the wood-fire oven wafts into the dining area. European-style thin crust pizza (from Rs50) is tasty, but you'll have to bat away the flies. Fresh fruit juices (Rs20) and fried banana (Rs22) satisfy the sweet tooth. Open Th-Tu 8:30am-2:30pm and 6-10pm.

Le Café, on the Goubert Salai promenade. The ocean mist and a sea-salty scent pervade the small ring of tables that front the ocean. Food is simple but hearty; eat an omelette (Rs18) or *dosa* (Rs16) while your coffee (Rs10) is being brewed, then sip it with the waves lapping at your feet. Open daily 24hr.

Rendezvous, 30 Rue Suffren, just south of Lal Bahadur Shastri St., east of the canal. Dine amid tuxedoed waiters and elegantly folded *serviettes* either downstairs or on the rooftop. Continental dishes are priced a bit higher than your Indian faves (pasta with sauce Rs60-100). The rich mousse (Rs25) will satisfy your chocolate craving. Open W-M 8-10:30am, 11:30am-3pm, and 6-10:30pm.

Ajantha Sea View Restaurant, 22 Goubert Salai, upstairs from the hotel of the same name. Although only a few tables actually enjoy an ocean vista, this spacious restaurant remains immensely popular with locals. Savory chicken *biryani* Rs32. Indian and Continental dishes Rs50-150. Attached bar (beer Rs35-40). Open daily 10am-11pm.

Hotel Aristo, 714 JN St., between Mission St. and MG Rd., west of the canal. A hot favorite, this rooftop restaurant will transport you from the chaos of Nehru St. to a peaceful palace of culinary pleasure, where birds chirp and vines dangle overhead. A variety of salads (Rs30) and fish dishes (Rs65-75). The mango "juice" (Rs23) is more like a thick puree but is quite refreshing and squishy. Open daily 9-10:30am and 6-10pm.

Le Club, 33 Dumas St. French open-terrace restaurant with a lush foyer and gracious service *en français ou en anglais.* Try *brochette de crevettes* (grilled shrimp, Rs190), or one of the other seafood entrees. Tea served with scalded milk. European desserts include chocolate mousse and apple fritters (Rs70-85). Excellent Continental breakfasts (Rs100-150). Open Tu-Th 8-10am, noon-2pm, and 7-10pm. AmEx, Visa.

Ashram Dining House, on Ranga Pillai St., right before the post office. Yet another perk of staying at one of the Ashram guest houses: for Rs20 you get a voucher entitling you to 3 meals here. Piles of luscious *basmati* rice and fresh fruits will be heaped upon your metal platter. Daily serving times: 11:30am-12:30pm, 5:45-6pm, and 8-8:30pm.

ENTERTAINMENT

By Tamil Nadu's conservative standards, alcohol flows quite freely in this town, and bars are relatively common in the French side. Many teenage boys from neighboring towns come here to procure cheep beer. Most of the bars attached to hotels—including the **Ajantha Bar** and the **Bar Qualithé Hotel,** located on the southern edge of Government Place—are dominated by local men, and are not the most comfortable place for foreigners, especially women. Many tourists spend the evening at any of the waterfront restaurants that serve alcohol, including the **Ajantha Sea View Restaurant,** the **Blue Dragon,** and **Le Café.**

Chunnamber Boat House, 10km out of town on the backwaters of the Bay of Bengal, offers boat rentals (kayak, paddle, sail, water scooter Rs10-75). Take in some murky green water and open sky, but don't go too far out or you'll find yourself in the ocean. From February to September it is also possible to take dolphin-watching **sea cruise.** Contact the tourist office (tel. 339497) for more information.

SIGHTS

SRI AUROBINDO ASHRAM

Marine St. Open daily 8am-noon and 2-6pm. Free. Photography allowed only with prior permission. Children under 3 not permitted.

A Bengali mystic named **Sri Aurobindo Ghose** created the method of "internal yoga" as a way of mingling the principles of yoga with the findings of modern science. Born in Kolkata in 1872, he left for schooling in England at the age of seven and eventually earned a degree in Classics from King's College, Cambridge. As a young adult, he headed up an Indian nationalist newspaper, and his staunch opposition to British rule led to his incarceration in 1908. In the confines of the prison cell he underwent a spiritual evolution, and in 1910 he gave up political activities and headed for French-ruled Pondicherry to found an ashram in 1926. Here, Sri Aurobindo met **"the Mother,"** French artist **Mirra Alfassa,** who had come to India to further her spiritual development. The Mother gradually became involved in the activities of the ashram, and she was Sri Aurobindo's constant companion until his death in 1950. After he died, she dominated the spiritual life of Pondicherry, lending her energy and charisma to "internal yoga" until her death in 1973. Under the Mother's leadership, the ashram witnessed remarkable growth, drawing about 2000 people to Pondicherry to work in this spiritual community. After her death, the ashram faced tumultuous times, as internal struggles developed over the direction the ashram would take, particularly in regard to the fate of Auroville, the ashram's experimental community (see **Near Pondicherry,** p. 562). These days, the ashram houses an exquisite **rock garden** and the flower-strewn **samadhis** (mausoleums) of Sri Aurobindo and the Mother. At any time of the day, devotees can be seen around the perimeter of the *samadhis* bowing their heads in silent prayer. The ashram teems with international devotees who have chosen to follow the teachings of Sri Aurobindo. Non-devotees may have a hard time understanding the goings-on here—it is best to learn about the ashram before visiting.

OTHER SIGHTS

Aside from the ashram, most of Pondicherry's attractions are clustered around **Goubert Salai,** the pleasant promenade where Pondicherriens go to see and be seen in the evening hours. During the day, the street is peacefully desolate, disturbed only by tourists and the occasional ice cream vendor. The 1500m rocky beach is pretty to look at but not safe for swimming. Along the beach is a 4m statue of a striding Mahatma Gandhi surrounded by eight elaborately sculpted monoliths, as well as some splendid French architecture, including a monument built in memory of Indians who died fighting on the French side during World War I.

About 1km north of the Alliance Française and just west of Goubert Salai is the **Government Place,** a pleasant park with a grassy quadrangle framing a solemn, neoclassical monument dating from the time of Napoleon III. On the northern edge of the park is the elegant, French-built **Raj Nivas,** once the home of Governor Dupleix and now the plush residence of Pondicherry's Lieutenant Governor. At the southern edge of Government Place is the **Pondicherry Museum,** which displays dusty 19th-century French furniture and an assortment of pottery and other objects dug up at the nearby site of Arikamedu. Among the museum's most interesting pieces are a small collection of Chola bronze sculpture and some remarkable Thanjavur paintings. There is also an exhibition of vintage black and white photographs of colonial buildings in Pondicherry. (*Museum open Tu-Su 10am-5pm. Rs1.*)

If shady pleasures and greener pastures are on your agenda, follow Goubert Salai to South Blvd. to reach the **Botanical Gardens.** Planted by the French in 1826, the gardens are home to exotic species from around the world. (*Open daily 9am-5:30pm.*) On your way to the gardens, have a peek at the absolutely mammoth Gothic **Eglise de Sacre Coeur de Jésus,** whose altar is flanked by three stunning stained-glass panels depicting the life of Christ.

NEAR PONDICHERRY: AUROVILLE ஆரோவல்

Here stands an entire community built upon a dream, literally. The ethereal "aura" of Auroville can be attributed to Sri Aurobindo's disciple—the Mother—who, in a dream, envisioned a crystalline sanctum where it would be possible to achieve ultimate levels of meditation. Her dream was realized with the construction of Auroville's temple, the **Matrimandir,** which symbolizes the spiritual goals of the Mother and her followers: the integration of science and meditation, and the peaceful coexistence of an international community. Soil from 126 countries was placed in an urn at the community's opening in 1968, and the town built up around the temple now consists of about 70 rural settlements inhabited by 500 families from all over the world, many living in eccentric houses they designed themselves. Each settlement focuses on one of the town's principal developmental goals. A large number are devoted to improvements in agricultural technology and methods. Another sector focuses on education and community development. Perhaps best-known are Auroville's industrial and entrepreneurial settlements, which include **Aurelec,** the town's very own computer company. The community leadership hopes that, as these settlements continue to grow, Auroville will eventually reach its target population of 50,000.

INFORMATION AND ACCOMMODATIONS. Visits to Auroville are hindered both by the inaccessibility of the town and by the discouragement of residents unappreciative of tourists who lack sincere interest in their way of life. If you're interested in a brief visit to Auroville, consider joining the **tour** (Rs42) sponsored by the tourist office in Pondicherry (see p. 557). As part of a group, you'll avoid the hassles of transportation and the bureaucracy of getting to see the Matrimandir. To get to Auroville on your own, you can employ one of the many eager rickshaw-*wallahs* in Pondy (Rs100 plus waiting charges) or, if you are in good physical condition, you can brave the Indian streets on a **bike**. You can rent one from the Park Guest House in Pondicherry and pedal the 12km to Auroville. One advantage to visiting the community on your own is that you'll have a better chance of actually meeting Aurovilians and seeing their interesting homes. The tour office's brief excursions are limited to the temple and visitors' office. **Accommodations** for visitors to Auroville are limited to guest houses in each of the settlements, which range from under Rs100 to Rs400. Many of the accommodations include kitchen facilities, bath, laundry services, and breakfast. The Visitors' Information Centre will gladly provide a list and make arrangements.

THE TOUR. Once you've actually gotten into Auroville, your first stop will be the **Visitor's Information Centre,** a tan brick building surrounded by carefully landscaped gardens. The Centre sells various brochures and displays photos and exhibits detailing Auroville's mission and development, including a model of the proposed town with its fractal-like design. An 11-minute video about the community is shown at 10:30am and 3:30pm every day except Sunday. Just across the way from the exhibits is a larger version of the Boutique d'Auroville, selling all things New Age (boutique open M-Sa 9am-1pm and 2-5:30pm), and a **cafeteria** with fresh veggie offerings (*thalis* Rs53 and cakes Rs15). Before leaving the Visitor's Information Centre, be sure to pick up a pass to see the **Matrimandir** (passes are available 3:30-4:30pm; make sure to get there early, especially on weekends). Battalions of butterflies flutter over the gigantic dome of the Matrimandir and its exquisite surrounding **gardens** (open daily 8am-3:30pm). The sound of their gently flapping wings don't break the strict code of silence enforced by the city volunteers who stand guard at the temple. The temple has been a source of tension in the striving-to-be-harmonious community, as some residents feel the considerable money and energy funneled into the project has been misdirected. Some may find the rocky gravel path tough on bare feet; wear socks. Inside, a winding ramp leads past the construction work to the other-worldly meditation chamber, which houses a large crystal ball surrounded by a ring of slender white columns. The crystal is illuminated by sunlight deflected from a mirror atop the dome; when the sky is overcast, lamps lit by solar power provide the necessary light. In fact, everything in the Matrimandir is powered by the sun, including the frigid A/C air of the meditation chamber (we told you to wear socks!). This is not unlike entering another dimension—don't be surprised if this short experience leaves you dazed. Work is currently underway to drape the entire dome in a shimmering golden coat. At present, the structure remains an unfinished reminder of the 1960s and the Mother's unrealized vision of a world without religion. (Matrimandir open daily 4-4:45pm.)

FOR LONGER STAYS. If you are intrigued by Auroville, then you might consider a longer stay, which will allow you to tap into the town's prime source of information: its inhabitants. For more information, contact **La Boutique d'Auroville,** 12 Jawaharlal Nehru St. (tel. 37264), Pondicherry. Alternatively, you can contact the **Visitor's Information Centre** in Auroville directly (tel. 62239; fax 62274; open daily

9:30am-5:30pm). If you'd like to plan your trip before you leave for India, contact **Auroville Guest Programme**, Visitor's Centre, Auroville 605101 (email guests@auroville.org.in). Information regarding **joining Auroville permanently** can be garnered from Entry Group, Auroville Secretariat, Bharat Nivas 605101, Auroville, Tamil Nadu, India (tel. 413 62191; fax 413 62274; email entry@auroville.org.in). Be advised that there is currently a housing shortage in Auroville for newcomers.

CHIDAMBARAM சிதம்பரம்

History has heaped affection on Chidambaram, entwining its past in legend and lore. According to belief, it was here that Shiva descended from the divine firmament as Nataraja ("King of Dance") and performed the *ananda tandavam* ("Cosmic Dance"). The forested clearing where Nataraja danced became sacred ground; the town that grew around it was dubbed "Chit Ambaram," or "wisdom-suffused sky." Choosing Nataraja as their patron deity, the ascendant Cholas made Chidambaram their capital in AD 907, and from the time of Koluttanga (AD 1070-1120), the history of the Cholas merged with that of Chidambaram. The Cholas built a grand temple, Sabhanayaka Nataraja, and enlarged and embellished it over the centuries.

Today, the temple and its four resplendent *gopurams* dominate the center of town, drawing thousands of Shaivite and Vaishnavite pilgrims to its sacred grounds, one of the holiest sites in India. Many tourists feel compelled to visit the temple for its superb examples of pre-modern architecture and sculpture, but Chidambaram and its magnificent temple merit little more than a short trip from Pondicherry or Thanjavur. The bi-annual "car festivals" (when ritual chariots glide through the four streets bearing their names) attract revelers in mid-January and June, as does the Tamil New Year (April 14th every year). Every February, prominent dancers from throughout the country converge in Chidambaram to present dance-offerings to Nataraja in the Natyanjali Festival. This year, the Natyanjali Festival will be extended from the normal five-day celebration to 20 days, due to the change of the millennium. The festival will begin in January.

ⓘ ORIENTATION AND PRACTICAL INFORMATION

Chidambaram is small and easy to navigate. **North Car Street, East Car Street, South Car Street,** and **West Car Street** form a rectangular border around the temple. To reach them from the bus stand, turn right (north) as you exit, then take your immediate left onto Venugopal, a.k.a **VGP Street.** After three main intersections, VGP St. turns into S. Car St. To get to the **Tourist Office** from the bus stand, take a left and then another left about 200m later onto **Pillaiyar Koil Street.** You will cross over the **Khan Sahib Canal** before making your first right onto **Railway Feeder Road.** Here you will find the office, many hotels, and, at the end of the street, the railway station.

Trains: The small station is uncommonly quiet. Most travelers opt for buses to avoid the longer, more roundabout train routes. Fares listed are 2nd/1st Class. To: **Chennai** (6714, 1:18am, 6hr; 6702, 11:57pm, 5hr., Rs62/313); **Kumbakonam** (*Cholan Exp.* 6153, 2pm, 2hr., Rs27/140); **Thanjavur** (611, 4:36pm, 2hr.; 627, 5:03am, 2hr., Rs34/184); **Tiruchirappalli** (*Cholan Exp.* 6153, 2:18pm; 6799, 1am, 5hr., Rs64/322); **Tirupati** (*Maduri-Tirupati Exp.* 6800, 5:45pm, 10½hr., Rs82/410).

Buses: The typically chaotic **bus stand,** just off the eastern end of S. Car St., services all parts of Tamil Nadu. To: **Chennai** (4:30am, 1:30, and 7:00pm; 5hr.; Rs43); **Madurai** (8hr., Rs65); **Pondicherry** (every 30min., 1½hr., Rs12); **Thanjavur** (every 30min., 3hr., Rs18); **Tiruchirappalli** (3hr., Rs35).

Local Transportation: Rickshaws are an unnecessary extravagance in a town where everything can be reached by foot in under 15min. Still, the little buggers are everywhere—primarily in front of the bus stand, hospital, and East Temple Gate.

Tourist Office: TTDC (tel. 38739), at the beginning of Railway Feeder Rd., next to Hotel Tamil Nadu on the way to the railway station. Open daily 10am-5:45pm.

Currency Exchange: The nearest place to change currency is in Pondicherry.

Hospital: The **Kamaray Government Hospital** (tel. 23099), 100m west of the canal on Pillaiyar Koil St., has an attached 24hr. pharmacy. The **Vani Pharmacy,** W. Car St. (tel. 22252), is open 9am-11pm.

Police Station: Chidambaram Police Station, W. Car St. (tel. 22201), is open 24hr.

Post Office: A tall, cream colored building covered by a patchwork of orange squares on the western end of N. Car St. Open M-F 10am-5pm. **Postal Code:** 608001.

Telephones: STD/ISD booths, most 24hr., are attached to many hotels. There is also a booth outside of Hotel Palace and another at the end of VGP St.

PHONE CODE	04144

ACCOMMODATIONS

Hotels-a-plenty surround the temple—finding mid-range accommodations should be no problem.

Hotel Palace, Railway Station Rd. (tel. 38639). Clean, blue-green rooms have extremely large attached baths with squat toilets. Breezy patios off each hallway, attached restaurant, and STD service. Padlocks on doors. Check-in 24hr. Singles Rs70; doubles Rs90.

Hotel Tamil Nadu, Railway Station Rd. (tel. 38056), in the multi-level white building a few hundred meters north of the train depot. Slightly run-down rooms with seat or squat toilets. Attached restaurant. Singles Rs135; doubles Rs195, with A/C and TV Rs550.

Ganesha Bhavan Hotel, 115 W. Car St. (tel. 22985). Spic & span rooms with lots of cubby space. Bathrooms are a bit musty. Padlocks on doors. Attached restaurant. Singles Rs55; doubles Rs90.

Hotal Akshaya, 17-18 East Car St. (tel 20191). Somewhat upscale decor at a reasonable price. Basic attached baths with seat or squat toilets. All rooms have telephones. Rooftop terrace offers a spectacular aerial view of the temple. Excellent attached restaurant. Singles Rs160; doubles Rs195, with A/C Rs480; quads Rs396. Extra beds Rs50.

FOOD

True to the town's predominantly tourist-oriented structure, most eateries are attached to hotels—almost every one has its own restaurant.

The Regency, on 2 VGP St. in one of India's ritziest hotels, The Hotel Afsan Plaza. Indulge in a full range of Indian and Chinese cuisine. *Tandoori* chicken is superb (Rs55 for a half), and the *ghee naan* (Rs8) is lip-smacking. Open 24hr.

Aswini Restaurant, 17-18 East Car St., in the Hotel Akshaya. Quiet dining in regal, cushioned chairs, with smooth soul and jazz music piped in. Fluffy, golden *dosas* are wonderful—Indian food at its best. Open daily 7-10am, 11am-3pm, and 6-10pm.

WHAT GOES AROUND... The depiction of Ganesh (also known as Vinayakar) on the east side of the Sabhanayaka Nataraja Temple in Chidambaram is taken from a story in which Lord Shiva held a contest between his two sons, Ganesh and Kartikkeya. A delicious *mambazha* (mango) was to be given to the son who could go around the universe and return first. Kartikkeya immediately mounted his peacock and set off, confident of victory. The short, plump Ganesh had only a little mouse for a mount. He thought for a while and then rode around his parents, Shiva and Parvati. When Shiva asked his son what he was up to, the clever Ganesh replied: "Going around the supreme Lord Shiva and Goddess Parvati who create and contain the universe is equivalent to going around the universe." Shiva smiled in satisfaction and presented the mango to his slow-footed but quick-witted son.

Hotel Saradharam, opposite the bus stand. Four different restaurants, each with its own distinct flavor. Up front, **Pallavi** creates gargantuan *thalis* and other veg. delights. Open 24hr. **Annu Pallavi,** in back, serves up very spicy, meaty meals for the adventurous. Open daily 11am-11pm. **Moon Shadow** is a barbecue grill during summer only. Open Mar.-July daily 6-10pm. **After Hours** serves coffee. Open daily 10am-6pm.

👁 SIGHTS

SABHANAYAKA NATARAJA TEMPLE

Open daily 6am-noon and 4-10pm. Puja at 7, 9, 11am, noon, 6, 8, and 10pm.

Distinctive not only as an amazing architectural achievement, the Sabhanayaka Nataraja Temple draws daily crowds of thousands because it is one of the few temples where Shiva and Vishnu are enshrined together. It was here that the dance duel between Kali and Shiva, the Nataraja, took place.

Covering more than 54 hectares, the temple dominates central Chidambaram. Though scholars believe that work on the temple began in the 10th century, local tradition holds that there has been a temple at this site for thousands of years. The modern Nataraja Temple, it is said, was built starting in the 6th century, when the Kashmiri monarch Simhavarman II (r. 550-575) made a pilgrimage to Chidambaram in the hope that bathing in the tank of the ancient Nataraja Temple would cure his leprosy. Speedily recovering after his bath, the king (thereafter known as Hiranyavarman, or the "golden-bodied one") was gleeful, and he ordered the temple enlarged and modernized. In addition, Hiranyavarman decreed that the holy entourage of 3000 *brahmin* priests (*Dikshitars*) who had accompanied him from Kashmir should remain behind at Chidambaram to serve the temple. Descendants of the *Dikshitars* still live in Chidambaram; they can be recognized by the knot of hair at the front of their heads. Regardless of the leper-king legend's veracity, it is built around at least a kernel of truth—the Nataraja Temple was not built all at once, but in stages; its architecture mingles ancient and modern elements.

THE OUTERMOST EDGE. Most visitors enter through either the eastern or western *gopuram* (gateway), where **guides** immediately accost any foreign-looking person. Their level of knowledge varies tremendously, so hiring one is something of a crap-shoot. Also beware of English-speaking individuals who try to usher you to a priest to anoint you with *kumkum* for a "voluntary" donation. To avoid most of the general hassle, enter instead through the northern-most gate.

The temple's four massive, pyramidal **gopurams** are painted every 50 years in a rainbow of pastel tones and reflect the fragmented construction patterns characteristic of the entire complex. The 42m northern *gopuram*, erected in the 14th century, bears an inscription claiming that it was built by a 16th-century Vijayanagar king. Its interior is embellished with carvings of the 108 dance poses associated with *bharat natyam*. The southern *gopuram*, raised in the 12th century, contains a set of impressive carvings of the goddess Lakshmi. Each of the four *gopurams* retains its original granite base, although the brick towers have been replaced numerous times, often falling victim to the winter monsoon. Across the front of each base are carvings of Shiva and Parvati.

As you enter through the western gate, the **Shivaganga Tank** is diagonally to the left. This is where King Simhavarman bathed, emerging with golden-hued skin. Across from the tank is the **Shivakumarasundari Temple,** dedicated to Shiva's consort Parvati. On the other side of the tank, in the northeast corner of the temple grounds, stands the 103m-long **Raja Sabha,** the temple's "1000-pillared corridor" where the victory processions of the Pandavas, Cholas, and other local powers were held. The corridor has only 999 pillars; Shiva's leg serves as the 1000th.

THE INNER CHAMBERS. The inner chambers are accessible from the north and south. On the eastern side of the enclosure, look out for the **Devasabha,** the "Hall of the Gods," where images of deities are stored when not being used and where temple meetings are held. In the southwest corner of the second enclosure, the **Nritta Sabha** (Dance Hall) marks the spot where Shiva and Kali had their famous dance duel. The hall is adorned with 56 pillars representing various dance poses.

The holy **Inner Sanctum,** accessible from the southern side of the second enclosure, is off-limits to non-Hindus. However, it is possible to get a glimpse of the gold-led **Chit Sabha** and **Kanaka Sabha** from the outside. Five silver-plated stone steps ead to the Chit Sabha; they are said to represent the five Sanskrit letters that comprise the famous Hindu Panchakshara mantra, "Nama Shivaya." The Chit Sabha ouses small images of Nataraja and Parvati. To the right, behind a string of vilva aves, is the Chidambara Rahasyam ("Secret of Chidambaram"): the **Akasa Linga,** epresenting the elusive and invisible element *akasa* (ether). In the passageway ading to the sanctum sanctorum is a hallway which leads to the **Govindaraja Tem-** le, dedicated to Vishnu. This uncommon juxtaposition of the images of Vishnu and hiva explains why both Vaishnavites and Shaivites worship at the Nataraja Temple.

KUMBAKONAM கும்பகோணம்

he name of this 2000 year-old town is derived from the holiday for which it is med, the **Kumbh Mela.** Hindus from across India descend upon the town's Maha-akham Tank into which the waters of nine sacred rivers are said to flow every 12 ears. Besides the tank, Kumbakonam has an abundance of holy sites that cludes five major temples within the city and two others in the nearby towns of arasuram and Gangaikondacholapuram. When not inundated by pilgrims or cred streams, Kumbakonam's significance as a religious center takes a back seat its role as an emerging center of silk production and small-scale industry.

ORIENTATION AND PRACTICAL INFORMATION

avigating Kumbakonam is somewhat confusing; every street seems to end at a mple gate. To get from the train station to the center of town, take your first left Kamaraj Road and walk straight 1km. Once in town, familiarize yourself with the ree principal roads where you'll find food and lodging: the two east-west thor-ughfares are **TSR Big Street** and another major street, which is called **Thanjavur** oad at the town's eastern end, **Nageswaran Road** in the middle, and then finally yikulam Road in the west. **Head Post Office (HPO) Road** runs north-south, intersect-g Ayikulam Rd. at its northern end and the famed **Mahamakham Tank** to the south. arrow cross streets merge with these main streets, making navigation difficult.

Trains: The **railway reservations counter** (tel. 20052 or 131) is open daily 10am-2pm and 4-7pm. Fares listed are for 2nd/1st class. To: **Madurai** via **Trichy** (*Trichy Pass.* 109, 6:05am, 3hr., Rs65/158; *Rameswaram Exp.* 6701, 4:50am, 2½hr., Rs104/198; *Cholan Exp.* 6853, 3:55pm, 3hr., 2nd class Rs70); **Chennai** (*Chennai Pass.* 110, 7:45pm, 11hr.; *Chennai Fast Pass.* 628, 6:30pm, 9hr., Rs88/354); **Rameswaram** (*Rameswaram Exp.* 6701, 4:50am; *Sadhu Exp.* 6713, 9pm, 10hr., Rs151/466); **Thanjavur** (*Saidu Exp.* 6713, 9pm, 1½hr., Rs84/198); **Tirupati** (*Tirupati Exp.,* 4:10pm, 13½hr., Rs168/524); **Villupuram** (*Cholan Exp.* 6854, 10:12am, 4hr., Rs61/176.)

Buses: Follow Ayikulam Rd. to its end, take a left and you will be at Kumbakonam's **bus stand.** Buses leave for **Thanjavur** (frequent, 1hr., Rs15); **Tiruchirappalli** (frequent, 2½hr., Rs22); **Karaikal** (every 45min., 2hr., Rs13); **Chennai** (every hr. 4-9pm, 6hr., Rs70); **Bangalore** (7pm, 10hr., Rs120).

Currency Exchange: City Union bank Ltd., 140 TSR Big St. (tel. 432322), close to several other banks on the same road, happily exchanges foreign currency.

Hospital: ST Hospital, HPO Rd., south of Ayikulam Rd.

Police Station: West Police Station, Thanjavur Rd. (tel. 421450), by VPR lodge.

Post Office: The **Head Post Office** is located farther south, on HPO Rd., next to Hotel Rayas. Open M-F 6am-6pm, Sa 6am-1pm. **Postal code:** 612001.

Telephones: STD/ISD booths are plentiful on TSR Big St. and HPO Rd. Many open 24hr.

PHONE CODE	0435

TAMIL NADU

ACCOMMODATIONS

Femina Lodge, up two flights of narrow stairs in the red-tiled building across from Hotel Kaya. Large beds dominate small, modest rooms, all with spotless, tiled bathrooms (squat or seat toilets). Doubles Rs150; quads Rs250.

VPR Lodge, 102/3 TSR Big St. (tel. 421949), at the very end of the road. Older lodge offers functional accommodations. The one drawback is the dank bathrooms that adjoin every room. Singles Rs60, with A/C Rs90; doubles Rs100/Rs120; triples Rs150; 5-bed family room with 2 showers and 3 fans Rs195.

Hotel ARR, TRS Big St., opposite City Union Bank Ltd. A parade of nine colored flags and glittering bronze candelabras greets you at the reception desk. Rooms have color TVs, sofas, and seat or squat toilets. Attached bar. Check-out 24hr. Prices include 20% luxury tax. Double deluxe Rs360; Family (4 bed) Rs600; extra beds Rs50.

Hotel Athityaa (tel. 421794), south of Sarangapani Temple on the "Thanjavur" end of Ayikulam Rd. A breezy staircase with multi-colored glazed panels leads to well-furnished rooms complete with towels, televisions, and floor lighting. Seat and squat toilets available. Friendly management, attached restaurant and bar. Singles Rs325, with A/C Rs500; doubles Rs350/500. 20% luxury tax.

Hotel Rayas, 28/29 HPO Rd. (tel. 423170), north of the post office and clock tower. Carved doors open to nice looking rooms with the firmest beds in town. Attached baths have seat or squat toilets, 24hr. hot water, and classy metal wash basins. Color TV with music channels provides entertainment, and the downstairs **Sathars** restaurant (see below) offers extravagant culinary options. Doubles Rs450-630. Extra bed Rs75-100.

FOOD

Eating in Kumbakonam is about basic biological survival, not tastebud titillation. Most local restaurants serve food-stand style, and few offer seated dining.

Arul. From the bank on TSR Big St., go right down the small sidestreet, then take your first left. *Thalis* (Rs16) are served up on the dimly lit faux wood tables, with generous second-helpings of rice and ladles full of rich *sambar*. Open daily 8am-10pm.

Hotel Athityaa, 11/12 Thanjavur Rd., Veg. staples such as *poori* (Rs12), North and South Indian snacks and Chinese dishes (Rs15-60) the hotel's restaurant, **Arogya.** Alcoholic delights served at the **Nattiya** permit room. Open daily 11am-11pm.

Sathars, inside Hotel Rayas on HPO Rd. Chicken, mutton, seafood, and beef dishes from across India (Rs30-115). Attached bar. Count on delicious *naan* (Rs8-15), *basmati* rice (Rs15), elaborate *thalis* (Rs25-36, 11am-4pm only), and excellent *dal* garnished with cilantro. Open daily 11am-11pm.

Pandiyar Hotel, across from Arul. Ground-floor cafeteria teems with hungry pilgrims. If you can find a seat, a banana leaf will be slapped down before you as your *thali* (Rs15) is constructed one heaping spoonful at a time. Open daily 11:30am-2pm and 4-10pm.

SIGHTS

KUMBESHWARA TEMPLE. The Kumbeshwara Temple faces east, with its elaborately sculpted main *gopuram* rising to a height of 128 ft. Most people enter on this side, through a crowded market area. From the outer entrance, a hallway with painted columns leads to the portals of the main *gopuram*. The *linga* enshrined in this temple is said to have been shaped by the hands of Shiva himself. According to legend, Lord Brahma placed a pot containing sacred nectar and the seed of creation atop Mount Meru. A potent flood carried the pot from the Himalayas to Kumbakonam, where it was discovered by Shiva, who was passing through disguised as a hunter. Shiva aimed an arrow at the pot and let loose, destroying the pot and spilling the nectar in all directions. Shiva then fashioned a *linga* from the pieces of the broken pot, or *kumbh*, and the nectar eventually spread to the five locales

TAMIL NADU

within a 10-mile radius of Kumbakonam. Traditionally, modern pilgrims visit these shrines before coming to Kumbeshwara. Some drops of nectar also trickled to the present day site of the Mahamakham Tank. The inner sanctum, which is closed to non-Hindus, opens with a figure of Nandi, Shiva's vehicle. The *prakarams* (corridors) surrounding the sanctum sanctorum contain shrines to many lesser deities as well as resplendent sculptures of the 63 Nayanmar poet-saints. *(Western end of Thanjavur Rd. Open daily 6am-12:30pm and 4-10pm. Puja at 7, 9am, noon, and 5pm.)*

ARANGAPANI TEMPLE. Sarangapani is one of the three most sacred Vishnu shrines in India, along with Srirangam near Tiruchirappalli (see p. 576) and Tirupati in Andhra Pradesh (see p. 610). On the right, as you enter the courtyard, is a sacred shrine to Lakshmi, the goddess of prosperity. Legend holds that the Sage Hema discovered the goddess seated upon a thousand-petaled lotus in a tank thereafter referred to as the Golden Lotus Tank) within the temple grounds. It was only later that Vishnu came to Kumbakonam to wed Lakshmi. It is customary for visitors to stop at the goddess' shrine before proceeding to the **inner sanctum** through either the north or south entrance. During certain holidays, devotees are required to use the southern entrance; it was from here that Vishnu and Lakshmi merged after their marriage. The area around the sanctum is dark and best visited in the morning or early afternoon. It is believed that some drops of nectar from the pot broken by Shiva's arrow ended up at the **Golden Lotus Tank.** Bathing in the tank is seen to cleanse the body and soul of sins or ailments, leading to *moksha. (Take a left at the end of TSR Big St. Open daily 6am-noon and 4-8pm. Puja on the hour.)*

NAGESHWARA TEMPLE. The Nageshwara Temple, dedicated to Shiva, was built sometime during the 10th century and is thought to be the oldest temple in Kumbakonam. The sculpted figures that adorn the *gopurams* are some of the best examples of early Chola workmanship. Many of the temple's finest sculptures lie within the sanctum itself; surrounding the sanctum sanctorum are niches containing carvings of Shiva and Parvati. The temple has been constructed in such a way that sunlight passes through the opening in the *gopuram* three times a year and illuminates the shrine image. It is believed that Lord Surya (the sun god) worships Shiva at these times. *(From the bottom of HPO Rd., take your first left and then your first right. Open daily 6am-noon and 4:30-8pm. Puja on the hour.)*

MAHAMAKHAM TANK. A multi-functional, man-made pond where people go to swim, do laundry, or worship. The sacred nectar of Brahma's *kumbh*, broken by Shiva, is said to have collected here. Every 12 years, the tank's tranquility is disrupted by the **Kumbh Mela** (see p. 213), when thousands of pilgrims descend on Kumbakonam to bathe in the murky waters. It is said that when Jupiter passes Leo, the waters of the Ganga and eight other sacred Indian rivers (the Yamuna, Kaveri, Godavari, Narmada, Krishna, Saraswati, Sarayu, and Tungabhadra) flow into the tank, making it a *tirtha* (sacred river crossing). During the 1992 festival, over one million devotees came to Kumbakonam for a purification bath. During a chaotic stampede to see the political leader, Jayalalitha, take her purifying dip, 60 pilgrims were trampled to death. *(At the bottom of HPO Rd. Open 24hr.)*

NEAR KUMBAKONAM

A short 4km from Kumbakonam, **Darasuram** is famed for its **Airavateshwara Temple,** a modestly sized but stunning example of 12th-century Chola architecture. The grande temple received its name from Airavata, the white elephant mount of Indra; the pious pachyderm is said to have worshipped Shiva here in hopes of changing his skin, turned black by an angry god, back to white. Near the base of the temple's inside wall are some remarkably well-preserved carvings, depicting supple gymnasts, *bharat natyam* dancers, and even a woman giving birth. Carvings along the corridor and those on the fabulously intricate *vimana* (temple tower), are being refurbished by the Archaeological Survey of India. From Kumbakonam, **buses** bound for Thanjavur will let you off at Darasuram (20min., Rs20).

THE ANTI-BEAUTY MARK If it's your first time in India, you might be wondering why so many small Indian children seem to have identical black birthmarks—one on the forehead, the other on the left cheek. Actually, it's no genetic similarity (nor an obscure skin condition) that causes these marks—they are, in fact, dots of charcoal placed on the child by its mother. This practice of *drishti* is performed in order to protect the beautiful baby from the envy of others. Jealousy, it is feared, could jinx the child and bring misfortune upon it, so the mother **uglifies** her offspring with these black smudges in an attempt to thwart the "green-eyed monster."

The legacy of King Rajendra I (r. 1012-1044), son of Raja Raja (builder of the Brihadishwara Temple in Tanjore) lives on at **Gangaikondacholapuram,** some 35km north of Kumbakonam. The town, whose name means "the city of the Chola who conquered the Ganga," was built by Rajendra when he defeated the kingdoms to the north. To commemorate his victory, the king had water from the Ganga transported south and dumped into the tank at this temple. The temple is dedicated to Shiva—a sizeable Nandi guards the entrance—and among the most impressive carvings is a frieze that depicts Shiva and Parvati crowning King Rajendra. **Buses** leave from Kumbakonam (frequent, 1hr., Rs6-10). Don't worry, bus attendants will eagerly help as you stumble through the name: *Gangai-konda-chola-puram.*

KARAIKAL காரைக்கால் AND VELANKANNI வேலாங்கண்ணி

This medium-sized town of **Karaikal** is always in a state of pandemonium, thanks to its proximity to several neighboring holy cities. Impatient pilgrims jostle you on the streets and at the bus stand, flooding vehicles as they arrive, leaving less aggressive travellers with standing room only. The few who haven't come to Karaikal in transit are Hindus paying homage to the female Shaivite saint Punithavathi, in either the **Darbanyeswar** or **Ammaiyar** temples, on Bharathiar Rd. The **Tourist Office,** Nehru St., is about nine sidestreets west of Hotel Paris (open daily 9am-1pm and 2-5:30pm). The **bus stand** services Chennai (every hr., 6hr. Rs76); Chidambaram (every 10min., 1½hr., Rs45); and Mylar (for train connections; every 45min., 1hr, Rs20). The **State Bank of India,** 14 Thirumallar Rd. (tel. 22524), changes money (open M-F 10am-2pm, Sa 10am-noon). For lodging, you best bet is **Hotel Paris** (tel. 20304), a marble tiled building with reasonably priced rooms (singles Rs175; doubles Rs225). The attached **Tasty Restaurant** is probably the cleanest place to eat and serves six-inch long egg rolls for Rs22 (open daily 6-11:30am and 4:30-8:30pm). **Telephone Code:** 04368.

The gleaming white spires of the **Roman Catholic Church of our Lady of Good Health** in **Vellankani** twinkle a shining answer to the question, "Why did I go to Karaikal?" Thousands of pilgrims visit the church and adjoining **tank** daily, drawn by the site's legendary curative powers. It is said that the Virgin Mary, to whom the church is dedicated, and the infant Jesus appeared to a boy selling buttermilk at this exact spot and cured his lame leg. In the **Museum of Offerings,** located behind the church offerings of golden necklaces, rings, and body parts are displayed alongside note explaining their significance. (Church and museum open daily 5am-9pm.) From Karaikal, you will have to first take a **bus** to Nagapattinam (every 5min., 45min. Rs3). From there buses go to Velankanni (every 5min., 20min., Rs3).

THANJAVUR (TANJORE) தஞ்சாவூர்

Though only an hour from the burgeoning urban center of Tiruchirappalli, Thanjavur remains laid back and provincial. Evident in the thatched farming huts and plowed fields that surround the town, Thanjavur's strong agricultural focus and its bronze handicraft trade are both remnants of the Chola Empire, who ruled the area between the 10th and 14th centuries. The spectacular architecture of the Brihadishwara Temple, along with Chola bronzes and paintings on display at local museums, are sure to delight. For the humble visitor, Thanjavur offers stretches of open space, fresh air to fill the lungs, and kind, hospitable people.

TAMIL NADU

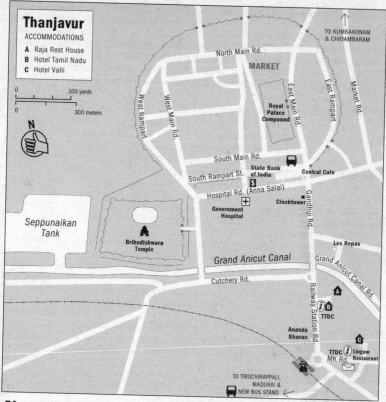

Thanjavur
ACCOMMODATIONS
A Raja Rest House
B Hotel Tamil Nadu
C Hotel Valli

Z PRACTICAL INFORMATION. The **railway station** is on Railway Station Rd., 600m south of the canal (rickshaw to the center of town Rs15-30). To: **Chennai** (*Cholan Exp.* 6154, 9:20am, 9hr., Rs84/283); **Chidambaram** (*Cholan Exp.* 6154, 9:20am, 2½ hr., Rs34/209; *Tirupathy Exp.* 6800, 2:40pm, 3hr., Rs34/205); **Madurai** (*Vaigai Exp.* 2365, 6:55pm, 3hr., Rs67) via **Chidambaram**; **Rameswaram** (*Rameswaram Exp.* 6701, 5:45am, 8½ hr., Rs79/440); and **Tiruchirappalli** (*Tirupathy Exp.* 6799, 4:05am, 1hr., Rs22/198). The **Old Bus Stand** is in the city center where Gandhiji Rd. turns into East Main Rd., and the **New Bus Stand** is 4km southwest of the city center. Buses arriving from Tiruchirappalli and other points south and west terminate at the new stand. Local buses #74, 74A, 74B, 74D, 41, and 60 travel between the two stands. From the new stand to: **Chidambaram** (1hr., Rs25); **Kumbakonam** (1hr., Rs8); and **Tiruchirappalli** (1½hr., Rs10). The #323 bus runs to **Chennai** (every 30min., Rs75). **TTC** runs to **Pondicherry** (10am and 4pm, 5hr., Rs45).

Thanjavur is divided into northern and southern sections by the **Grand Anicut Canal.** From the station, **Railway Station Road** curves slightly as it heads north, passing a branch of the tourist office and several hotels before reaching the canal. As it crosses the canal, Railway Station Rd. becomes **Gandhiji Road,** which is dominated by upscale silk shops. The busiest part of town and the entrance to the bus stands is located immediately north of the intersection of Gandhiji and **Hospital Road.** Gandhiji Rd. becomes **East Main Road,** which leads to the Royal Palace and museum. **Kutchery Road,** just south of the bridge is the main east-west thoroughfare south of the canal. The cross street **West Rampart** leads right up to the **Brihadishwara Temple.** The **TTDC office,** Railway Station Rd. (tel. 30984), in front of the Hotel Tamil Nadu complex has an English-speaking staff (open daily 10am-2pm, 4-8pm).

The **State Bank of India,** Hospital Rd. (tel. 30082), is opposite the Government Hospital (open M-F 10am-2pm, Sa 10am-noon). The **Thanjavur Medical College Hospital,** Medical College Rd. (tel. 22459), is a 15min. rickshaw ride from the station to toward Tamil University. There is a government hospital on Hospital Rd. The **East Police Station** is in the Palace Complex, East Main St. (tel. 21450). The post office, MK Rd. (tel. 31022), is off Railway Station Rd. in the southern part of town (open M-Sa 7:30am-7pm, Su noon-4pm). **Postal Code:** 613001. **Telephone Code:** 04362.

■■ **ACCOMMODATIONS AND FOOD.** Accommodations south of the canal are likely to be quieter than those that overlook the bus stand. All hotels have a 24-hour checkout policy. **Hotel Valli,** 2948 MK Rd. (tel. 31580), east from the railway station, past the tourist office, is shaded by lumbering trees and a variety of tropical plants. Slightly dusty and musty rooms have attached baths (squat and seat toilets). It also has a reasonably priced attached restaurant. (Singles Rs165; doubles Rs195, with A/C Rs480.) **Hotel Tamil Nadu** (tel. 31421), in the large white complex on Gandhiji Rd., has rooms with phones, wall hangings, comfy beds, and attached bathrooms with seat toilets. There is a restaurant and bar downstairs. (Doubles Rs300, with TV Rs420, with A/C Rs600.) The **Raja Rest House** (tel. 30515), off Gandhiji Rd., directly on the left of Hotel Tamil Nadu as you come from the train station. Tucked away from the main street, the Raja House is secluded and noise-free. Its ring of rooms surrounds a courtyard overgrown with weeds. Squat toilets and hot water by the bucket (Rs4). Singles Rs60; doubles Rs100; triples Rs150.

Most of the food in Thanjavur is the same wherever you go. There are hordes of seemingly indistinguishable vegetarian restaurants around the bus stand that cater to locals. Carnivores will find slim pickings in this Hindu town. **Sathars Restaurant,** 167 Gandhiji Rd., is north of the canal. Woven reed matting encloses the lower sitting area, while the upstairs terrace sports a Western-style decor. Garnished chicken, beef, and seafood delicacies are Rs26-105. (Open daily noon-11:30pm.) **Ananda Bhavan,** Railway Station Rd., up the street from the railway station, serves good old-fashioned South Indian *masala dosa* (Rs10) on banana leaves. Its location makes it a key stop for locals on their way to work, so expect morning crowds. Open daily 6:30-10:30am and 11:30am-10pm.

⬛ **SIGHTS.** The **Brihadishwara Temple** is the pride of Thanjavur, and acclaimed by many as one of the most spectacular temples in all of India. At over 64m tall, the *vimana* stands as the highest point in the city. The temple heralds distant memories of the city's former splendor and opulence under the Chola king Raja Raja I (r. 985-1013) who constructed the monument over the course of 12 years. Legend has it that he built the temple to save his own life. Unable to find a cure for his leprosy, Raja Raja turned to his religious tutor for guidance, who advised him to build a temple to Shiva using a *linga* from the Narmada River. Raja Raja rushed off to the river and pulled a *linga* from the water; as he pulled, the *linga* grew and grew, and Raja Raja had no choice but to build a massive temple to enclose it.

The *vimana* itself is fourteen stories tall and soars over the *gopurams* in an inversion of the traditional South Indian architectural order (*gopurams* are usually taller than *vimanas*). On the eastern face of the *vimana*, an exquisite carving depicts Shiva and Parvati atop a mountain in the Himalayas. On the eastern parapet is an image of the Buddha. The *vimana* is capped with an octagonal *stupa*, atop which a 4m golden *kalasa* juts skyward. Aside from the *linga* housed in the central *vimana*, there are over 252 other *lingas* in the surrounding courtyard shrines.

Shrines and *linga* are guarded by a giant sculpture of Nandi, the bull who protects and carries Shiva. This monolithic sculpture is 6m long, 2.6m wide, and 3.7m high, weighing in at 25 tons and making it the second largest Nandi in India. Vivid 16th-century frescoes depicting Nandi and other characters from Hindu scriptures brighten the courtyard walls. They were recently restored by the Archaeological Survey of India and record major events in Shiva's life. Outside the temple, a pathway on the left leads to the **Shivaganga Tank** and garden, where visitors can take a stroll or relax on the grass. *(Open daily roughly 6am-12:30pm and 4-9pm. Donations accepted in Temple office. Fourth Maha Kumbhabhishekam performed Su 7:30am.)*

The large **Royal Palace** built as a residence by the Nayaks in the 16th century and subsequently refurbished by the Marathas. These days, the palace has been colonized by a number of incongruous outfits, including a secondary school, an agricultural office, and a martial arts academy. If you are persistent, you might be able to locate the half-dozen museums which have been carved out of the remains of the royal residence. Among the more interesting museums is the **Durbar Hall Art Museum,** which displays an excellent collection of Chola bronzes and stone sculptures *(open daily 9am-1pm and 3-6pm; Rs3)*. Also inside the palace is the **Tamil University Museum** which displays antique musical instruments. Be sure to ask the curator to show you the wooden revolving chair—its maker would probably be shocked to see his design operating in modern office buildings. *(Open M-F 10:30am-1pm and 2:30-5pm. Rs1.)* The palace houses the **Saraswati Mahal Library,** famous for its collection of ancient palm leaf manuscripts. With 33,433 holdings (24,627 in Sanskrit, 953 in Marathi, 1206 in Tamil, 816 in Telugu, and 5831 others—we counted), the collection is considered one of the world's finest. The stacks are not open to the public, but a **museum** provides a sample of the collection. *(Open Th-Tu 10am-1pm and 2-5pm.)*

TIRUCHIRAPPALLI திருச்சிராப்பள்ளி

For a growing industrial center of 700,000, Tiruchirappalli (commonly called Trichy or Tiruchi) remains remarkably clean and relatively tranquil. The city has been continuously occupied for over 2000 years, ruled at various times by the Cholas, Pandyas, Pallavas, and Nayaks, whose prosperous reign brought about the creation of the imposing Rock Fort. Since the late 19th century, when British-designed railroads brought industry to South India, Trichy has been ruled by manufacturing—today, the city is home to a large working-class population that helps produce staggering quantities of *bidis* and costume jewelry. Trichy's greatest attraction is the temple city of Srirangam, 4km north of town across the Kaveri River. For those en route to destinations farther south, Trichy is a convenient stop, with the railway station, bus stand, and a slew of hotels all within comfortable walking distance of each other.

▛ TRANSPORTATION

Airport: 8km south of the city, 25min. by direct "airport" buses (every 15min., Rs2) or taxi (Rs100). **Indian Airlines,** Dindigul Rd. (tel. 462233), 500m southwest of its intersection with Junction Rd., has flights to Chennai (3 per week, 1hr., US$70). If you can pass for under 30, ask for the 25% youth discount. **Air Lanka,** Williams Rd. (tel. 460844), Hotel Femina Complex, has flights to **Colombo, Sri Lanka** (3 per week, 45min., US$62). Open M-Sa 9am-5:30pm.

Trains: The user-friendly **Trichy Junction Railway Station** in the south of town, off the intersection of Junction and Madurai Rd. The **Reservations Building** (tel. 461461) is the small white structure to your left as you approach the main building. Open M-Sa 8am-8pm, Su 8am-2pm. Fares listed are 2nd/1st class. To: **Chennai** (*Vaigai Exp.* 2636, 9am; *Pallava Exp.* 2606, 6am, 5½hr., Rs206/302; *Rockfort Exp.* 6878, 9:45pm, 7hr., Rs146/612); **Chidambaram** (*Cholan Exp.* 6854, 8am; *Tiruphan Exp.* 6800, 2pm, 4½hr, Rs62/176); **Kollam** (*Quilon Exp.* 6161, 4:15pm, 12hr., Rs174/545); **Madurai** (*Vaigai Exp.* 2635, 6pm, 3hr., Rs58/212); **Rameswaram** (*Rameswaram Passenger* 791, 6:50am, 6½hr., Rs135/179); **Tirupati** (*Tirupati Exp.* 6800, 2pm, 15hr., Rs194/630) via **Thanjavur** (1½hr., Rs57/156).

Buses: The **State Bus Stand** at the intersection of Rockins and Royal Rd. To: **Bangalore** (4 per night, 10hr., Rs150); **Chennai** (every hr., 7hr., Rs100); **Coimbatore** (every 30min., 6hr., Rs60); **Madurai** (every 15min., 3hr., Rs27); **Pondicherry** via **Villupuram** (every hr., 5hr., Rs40); **Thanjavur** (every 10min., 1½hr., Rs15).

Local Transportation: Even the tourist office raves about Trichy's **local bus** system, probably the most efficient in all of Tamil Nadu. A fleet of brand-new, shiny silver buses, each equipped with a deafening sound system, shuttles passengers around the city. The **#1 bus** is every tourist's best friend; it passes the railway station, the State Bank of India, and the Head Post Office on its way to the Rock Fort (Rs2) and the Srirangam Temple (Rs4). Buses depart every few minutes from the State Bus Stand. As a result, Trichy has hordes of hardly-used **rickshaws** congregating in the bus stand/tourist office area. They aren't really necessary, unless you need to get to the airport (Rs50).

✴ ORIENTATION

With the **Kaveri River** forming its northern border, Tiruchirappalli is split into two segments by the **Woyakondan Channel.** The northernmost portion (nearest to the Kaveri River) is Trichy's industrial area, hoarding a wealth of textile shops, in addition to the **Rock Fort** and the town's **railway station.** To the south of the channel is a calmer, hotel-dominated area and the busy **Trichy Junction Railway Station,** where most trains arrive and depart. The streets around the railway station are peppered with hotel and banks, and the area also contains the GPO, the tourist office, and the town's two **bus stands.** From the station, **Madurai Road** runs northeast, forming a "V" with the northwest-bound **Lawson's Road,** which, in turn, leads to the **bus stands. Dindigul Road** connects to Lawson's Rd., looping around the western streets all the way up to the eastern side of the Woyakondon Channel, where it intersects with **Big Bazaar Road,** northern Trichy's main street.

Tourist Office: TTDC, 1 Williams Rd., Cantonment (tel. 460136), diagonally opposite the central bus stand. The knowledgeable staff dispenses a decent map of the city (Rs10). Open M-F 10am-5:45pm.

Currency Exchange: State Bank of India (tel. 460172 or 462654), off a courtyard on Dindigul Rd., around the corner from Jenney's Residency. Open M-F 10am-2pm, Sa 10am-noon.

Pharmacy: Subasree Medicals (tel. 410228), near the central bus stand. Open M-Sa 9am-10:30pm.

Hospital: Government Hospital, Puthur High Rd. (tel. 771465). Open 24hr. The best private hospital is the 24hr. **Sea Horse Hospital,** 6 Royal Rd. (tel. 771920).

Post Office: Head Post Office, Dindigul St. (tel. 460575). Open M-Sa 10am-6pm. **Postal Code:** 620001.

Internet: Star Vision, 1 Dindigul Rd. (tel. 410856; email starvisions@vsnl.com), attached to Hotel Vignesh (neon sign visible), near the bus stand. Internet access Rs1 per min. Open M-Sa 9am-9pm.

Telephones: 24hr. **STD/ISD** booths opposite the bus stand on McDonald's Rd.

PHONE CODE	0431

▐ ACCOMMODATIONS

The Trichy Junction area has plenty of hotels, all with 24-hour check-out.

Ashby Hotel, 17-A Junction Rd. (tel. 460652 or 460653), near the intersection with State Bank Rd., bursts with personality. Aged paintings, a tank full of guppies, and wooden floors impart a homey feel. Rooms are dim but spacious, and the leafy courtyards keep things cool. Attached restaurant and bar. Singles Rs175, with A/C Rs480; doubles Rs300/630.

Hotel Gajapriya, 2 Royal Rd. (tel. 414411). Look for the sign in the sky. Spacious rooms have modern furnishings, TVs, and attached bathrooms with seat toilets and hot water. A laid-back place with an equally laid-back staff. Room service. Attached Chinese restaurant and bar. Singles Rs190, with A/C Rs450; doubles Rs330/600. 20% luxury tax. Diner's Club, MC, Visa.

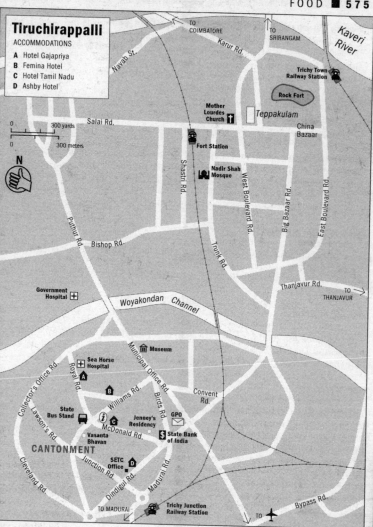

Tiruchirappalli

ACCOMMODATIONS

A Hotel Gajapriya
B Femina Hotel
C Hotel Tamil Nadu
D Ashby Hotel

Femina Hotel, 14-C Williams Rd., Cantonment (tel. 414501). The cavernous lobby sparkles, and every inch of space oozes with decadence: plush carpets, balcony views of the Rock Fort, and bathtubs to boot! Singles Rs225, with A/C Rs600; doubles Rs400/900. 20% luxury tax. MC, Visa.

Hotel Tamil Nadu, McDonald's Rd. (tel. 414346), next to the tourist office. A notch above most TTDC offerings, its well-kept rooms are covered with amber tiles and dressed with gleaming white sheets and dark, billowy curtains. Singles with A/C Rs300; doubles Rs225-275, with A/C Rs500-600. 20% luxury tax.

FOOD

Trichy's restaurants fall squarely into two categories: hotel restaurants and South Indian "meals" joints. You won't have to venture far to find food, and even the swankiest hotel restaurants are reasonably priced.

Vasanta Bhavan, on the ground floor of Hotel Abhirami, opposite the bus stand. Enjoy a filling banana-leaf *thali* (Rs20), or choose from a number of typical options, including delicious coconut rice (Rs10) and *gobi masala* (Rs16). Open daily 6am-11pm.

Amaravathi Restaurant, Ramyas Hotel, near the tourist office. The dim, cool setting complements your tasty meal. *Biryani* (Rs35-45), chicken *masala* (Rs55), and veg. fried rice (Rs35). Open daily 11am-3:30pm and 7-11pm.

Golden Rock, Femina Hotel. With window shades closed and A/C in overdrive, this little cafe certainly helps you chill out, serving *idlis* (Rs9), heavenly *masala dosas* (Rs22) and a selection of international soups—hot and sour (Rs30), cream of mushroom (Rs50), and others. Open 24hr.

Jenney's Residency, 3/14 McDonald's Rd. Recently bought out by the Park Sheraton group, this posh hotel is home to two restaurants. The South Indian **Suvia** has a break-fast buffet and serves a sumptuous lunchtime *thali* (Rs60). Open daily 6am-11pm. The **Peaks of Kunlun,** a Chinese and Continental restaurant, has good soups (Rs20-35) and rice and noodles (Rs30). Open daily 11am-3pm and 7pm-midnight.

🎵 ENTERTAINMENT

For a refreshing **swim,** head over to **Jenney's Residency,** where you can do laps in the not-quite-Olympic-sized pool (open daily 7am-7pm; Rs100). Jenney's also houses the most original watering hole in town, the **Wild West Bar,** an old-fashioned saloon complete with swinging doors and an intoxicated cowboy clutching an economy-size bottle of liquor (open daily 11am-11pm). If you fancy yourself an anthropologist and don't mind being a trifle conspicuous, head to the banks of the **Kaveri River** between 7 and 11am to witness a series of ceremonies and rituals by the river, as pilgrims bathe for good fortune, priests pray for childbirth, and mourners spread fresh ashes. Take the #1 bus and ask to be let off at Amma Mandapam (Rs4). For a more detailed explanation of the goings-on, see **Srirangam,** p. 576.

👁 SIGHTS

THE ROCK FORT. The massive monolith upon which the fort stands, overlooking the city from its perch 85m above, is believed to be one of the planet's oldest geological specimens—a rock some 3.8 billion years in the making. The site was developed as a citadel by the Pallavas and later by the Nayaks. Today, most people who reach the summit are Hindu pilgrims visiting its shrine or camera-wielding tourists hoping to capture views. Four hundred numbered, rock-cut steps lead to the summit. At the foot of the staircase is a small shrine to Ganesha; remove your shoes before you ascend the staircase. A little way up is the official entrance where you can deposit your shoes. Most of the shrines along the side of the staircase are off-limits to non-Hindus. At the top (whew!) from the northwest corner of the rock, the view is just spectacular—the *gopurams* of the Sri Ranganathaswamy and Jambukeshwara Temples in nearby Srirangam are visible. A final crooked staircase leads to the whitewashed Vinayaka (Ganesh) temple at the very top. This temple is closed to non-Hindus. *(Take bus #1 for Rs2 and get off when you see the towering Saint John's Cathedral; turn right at St. John's, and follow the street for about 3min. up to the crowded overhang entrance to the Rock Fort. Open daily 6am-8pm. Rs1; camera fee Rs10.)*

OTHER SIGHTS. Saint John's Cathedral, a Catholic church modeled after France's Lourdes Basilica, is worth a stop on your way to the Rock Fort. Also on your way, the **China Bazaar** is marked by an arched entrance and is chock full of stalls vending flowers, *chappals*, silk fabrics, and locally produced handicrafts.

NEAR TIRUCHIRAPPALLI

Five kilometers to the north of Trichy lies **Srirangam,** home of the **Sri Ranganathaswamy Temple.** This Vishnu temple, situated on a 600-acre island straddled by the Kaveri River and its tributary, the Kollidam, is by far the most fully developed of all the temples in South India. It was built over many centuries, starting in the 12th century during the Pandya period, and was expanded greatly during the Vijayanagar period. Construction has continued into the modern era; the largest of the temple's 21 *gopurams*, rising to a height of 72m, was completed only in 1987. The sheer expanse of the temple makes it unique; the seven concentric walls of the complex contain nearly 700 sq. km of land and an entire town. The entrance to the temple is to the south, where a gargantuan *gopuram* greets guests with its resplendent hues. Vendors in the courtyards hawk *puja* offerings such as fruit, coconuts, and sweet-smelling garlands along with all sorts of religious parapher-nalia. Visitors need not remove their shoes until reaching the fourth wall, beyond which are housed the oldest and most elaborate sculptures in the complex. On the eastern side of the fourth enclosure is a "1000-pillared hall," containing 936 col-umns carved in the shape of horsemen riding rearing steeds. The famous sculp-tures of Krishna frolicking with *gopis* (milkmaids) in the Venugopala shrine are visible on the southern side of the courtyard. The inner courtyards are inaccessi-ble to non-Hindus. It takes hours to traipse through the massive complex, but the sheer number of *gopurams*, the magnificent collection of jewels, and the marvel-ous stone pillars of this masterpiece make the trip rewarding. To get the best aerial view of the temple, be certain to take advantage of the staircase to the roof (Rs3), immediately inside on the left as you enter. The **Vaikunta Ekadasi Festival** (Dec.-Jan.) draws thousands of pilgrims to the site; during the festival, a procession enters through a doorway called the "Gateway of Heaven" to ensure everlasting afterlife. The sanctuary is closed to non-Hindus. Depending on your budget and time frame, you might hire one of the government-licensed **tour guides** who make this temple their base. Contact S. Murali (tel. 434095 or 431741), 43C Ragavendra-puram, Srirangam, a knowledgeable guide who offers tours in French, Italian, and English. (Bus #1 leaves from Trichy's bus stand. Temple open daily 6am-9pm.)

The **Sri Jambukeshwara Temple,** shrine of the submerged *linga*, lies 2km east of Srirangam. One of the oldest and largest Shiva temples in Tamil Nadu, it is named after a legendary elephant who worshipped the *linga*. Fashioned by Parvati as an act of penance, the *linga* is called Jambukeswara, after the holy *jambu* (black-berry) tree that shades it. The temple, with five enclosures, contains an 800-pillar *mandapam* and a serene tank fed by a natural spring. Try to make it to the temple between noon and 12:30pm, when a special ceremony is performed by a priest, clad in a *sari* and crown, said to represent the goddess Parvati. After the *puja* offering, the priest proceeds to the goddess's sanctuary with an elephant in tow. (Buses leave from Trichy's bus stand. Temple open daily 7am-8pm.)

MADURAI மதுரை

It's said that Shiva himself once stood over Madurai to dry his matted hair; the aus-picious nectar that fell from his holy locks sopped the city and gave it its name, derived from the Tamil word *madhuram* (sweetness). The sugar buzz is still going strong in modern Madurai, a temple town both holy and wholly modern, cra-zily chaotic but small enough to energize the thousands who visit it daily. Since it was founded more than 2500 years ago, Madurai has thrived for years as a cultural center. Madurai was the flourishing capital of the Pandya kingdom, which ruled central South India as far back as the 4th century BC. The powerful Vijayanagar Kingdom reigned throughout the 15th and early 16th centuries, when the temples and towers of the city's famous Meenakshi Amman Temple were built. From 1559 onward, Madurai was ruled by the Nayak dynasty, which built the modern city's attractions—the Teppakkulam and the Raya Gopuram. The Nayak Empire lost power in 1736 when the East India Company bought and de-fortified the city, tear-ing down its walls and filling in its moat where the Veli streets now run today.

Still damp from its original good-luck drenching, Madurai has survived to become an important commercial center with a population of 1.2 million. Huge electronic signboards illuminate the night sky, and large volumes of traffic (both automobile and bovine) surge through the streets, giving the town the feel of an ancient city entering the modern era in a whir of undirected enthusiasm. For all its vibrant clamor, though, Madurai still sways to the rhythm of the temple's activities, and the festival season sees the traditional procession through town of deities followed by throngs of residents and visiting pilgrims.

▐ TRANSPORTATION

Airport: (tel. 670433), 15km south of the city center. A taxi into town costs upwards of Rs170. Hourly buses leave near the exit. **Indian Airlines,** 7A W. Veli St. (tel. 741234 or 741236), opposite the railway station. Open daily 10am-5pm. To: **Chennai** (1 per day, 1hr., US$80); **Mumbai** (4 per week, 2hr., US$170). 25% youth discount.

Trains: Madurai Junction Railway Station, W. Veli St. (tel. 743131). Reservations counter open M-Sa 8am-1:30pm and 2-8pm, Su 8am-2pm. Fares listed are 2nd/1st class. To: **Bangalore** (*Bangalore Exp.* 6731, 8pm, 12hr., Rs202/871); **Chennai** (*Madurai-Chennai Exp.* 6718, 7:50pm, 11hr.; *Pearl City* 6704, 8:20pm, 11hr., Rs186/587); **Tirupati, Chidambaram,** and **Thanjavur** via **Trichy** (*Vaigai Exp.* 2636, 6:10am, 2½hr., Rs72/212); **Coimbatore** (*Coimbatore Exp.* 6716, 6:10am, 4½hr., Rs115/346); **Kanyakumari** (*Kanyakumari Exp.* 6121, 3:50am, 6hr., Rs170/351); **Rameswaram** (*Rameswaram Exp.* 6715, 6am, 5hr., Rs65/222).

Buses: Madurai has consolidated its 5 bus stands into one station to help clear traffic from the congested roads. 7km northeast of the city center, the gargantuan **Mattu Thavani** bus stand services all destinations in Tamil Nadu and beyond. All buses run under the Government Express Transport Operation. Rickshaws (Rs50) or local buses #3, 75, and 703 (Rs2) from the **Periyar Stand** (see below) get you there. To: **Bangalore** (6 per day 6-9am and 8-10:30pm, 9hr., Rs120); **Chennai** (every 30min., 10hr., Rs118); **Coimbatore** (every 30min., 5hr., Rs27); **Kanyakumari** (every hr., 6hr., Rs50); **Kodaikanal** (5 per day 5:40am-5pm, 4hr., Rs25); **Mangalore** (4pm, 17hr., Rs174); **Pondicherry** (8:45pm, 8hr., Rs73); **Rameswaram** (every hr., 4hr., Rs25); **Thanjavur** (every 30min., 4hr., Rs25); **Tiruchirappalli** (every hr. 5:30am-9pm, 4hr., Rs26); **Thiruvananthapuram** (8:30am and 10:30pm, 8hr., Rs88); **Tirupati** via **Vellore** (4 per night 7:30-10:30pm, 9hr., Rs110); **Trivandrum** (every hr., 8hr., Rs75).

Local Transportation: Local **buses** leave from the **Periyar Bus Stand** on W. Veli St., a 2min. walk south from the railway station. The stand is so congested that a small overflow lot has been set up east of the bus stand between W. Veli and W. Perumal Maistry St. Auto- and cycle-**rickshaws** are abundant; the main stand is right outside the railway station. A pre-paid rickshaw booth opens when trains arrive.

▐ ORIENTATION AND PRACTICAL INFORMATION

Madurai sprawls north and south of the **Vaigai River.** South of the river, the city is bordered on the west and south by railway tracks and is dominated by the **Meenakshi Temple.** The **Periyar Bus Stand** and the busy **Madurai Junction Railway Station** are located off **West Veli Street,** 1km west of the temple. To reach the city center from the railway station, follow **Town Hall Road** east; from the **TTC Bus Stand,** follow **Dindigul Road.** In the vicinity of the temple, streets are arranged concentrically around the temple, forming an irregular grid. Closest to the temple are North, East, South, and West **Chittrai Streets.** A bit farther from the temple are North, East, South, and West **Avani Moola Streets.** North, East, South, and West **Masi Streets** are encircled by North, East, South, and West **Veli Streets.** To cross the Vaigai River, head 1km northeast of the temple and across **Victor Bridge.** The road leading northeast from the bridge, **Alagar Koil Road,** is intersected by the north-west **Tamukkam Road.**

Tourist Office: Tamil Nadu Tourism Development Corporation (TTDC), 180 TB Complex, W. Veli St. (tel. 734757). Exit the main bus stand to the south; it's on the opposite side of the street to the right. Extremely friendly staff answers questions about the city and excursions from it. Open M-F 10am-5:30pm, Sa 10am-2pm. Offices at the airport (open irregularly) and railway station (tel. 542888; open daily 8am-8pm).

TAM

Madurai

ACCOMMODATIONS

A Hotel Keerthi
B Hotel Santosh
C Hotel Ravi Towers
D Hotel Alavai
E Hotel Aarathy

Tamukkam
Palace

Dr. SVKS Thangaraj Rd.

Gandhi Museum

TO ALAGARKOIL

Anna Bus Stand

Anna Nagar Main Rd.

Central
Telegraph
Office

Tamukkum
Rd.

Kuruvikaran Salai

TO MATTU THAVANI BUS STATION

Panagal Rd.

Kamarajar Rd.

New Ramanad Rd.

Alagar Koil Rd.

Vaigai River

Chairman
Muthuramaiyer Rd.

TO KODAIKANAL

Kalpalam Rd.

Victor Bridge

Munichalai Rd.

Madurai East Railway Station Rd.

Madurai East
Railway Station

Mariamman
Teppakkulam

E. Veli St.

E. Market St.

E. Masi St.

Palace Rd.

Old Kosavar Palayam Rd.

Workshop Rd.

Tamil Sangam Rd.

N. Veli St.

N. Masi St.

E. Avani Moola St.

E. Chitrai

N. Chitrai

W. Chitrai

S. Chitrai

S. Masi St.

Meenakshi
Temple

Tirumalai
Nayak Palace

MADURAI
MAIN
MARKET

GPO

TO MADURAI
BRIDGE STATION

Hotel
Mahal
Rest.

Town Hall Rd.

New Arya
Bhavan

Dindigul Rd.

W. Perumal Maistry St.

Priya
Surya

Ruby

W. Vadampokki St.

S. Vel St.

Kudal
Azhagar
Temple

TTDC

TO (15km)

300 yards

300 meters

Madurai Railway
Station

Periyar
Bus Stand

W. Veli St.

TO TUTICORIN AND
KANYAKUMARI

TO BODINAYAKKANUR

TPK Rd.

N

Currency Exchange: State Bank of India, 6 W. Veli St. (tel. 741650, foreign exchange tel. 742127), Sangam Towers, north of the railway station and across the street. Exchanges Thomas Cook traveler's checks in U.S. and U.K. currencies and AmEx traveler's checks in U.S. currency only. Open M-F 10am-2pm, Sa 10am-noon.

Market: The chaotic **Central Market,** on N. Avani Moola St., sells food.

Bookstore: Malligai Book Centre, 11 W. Veli St. (tel. 740534), opposite the railway station, sells an assortment of Indian and English novels and guidebooks on Madurai. Open M-Sa 9:30am-1pm and 3:30-9pm.

Pharmacy: Suresh Medicals, 63 Town Hall Rd. (tel. 541625). Open M-Sa 7:30am-10:30pm.

Hospital: Government Hospital, Panagal Rd. (tel. 532535), across the Vaigai River. The private **Jawahar Hospital,** 14 Main Rd., KK Nagar (tel. 650021 or 650022), also on the northern bank of Vaigai, is better. Both have 24hr. pharmacies.

Police: The main station (tel. 538015) is on the north bank, on the road to Natham.

Post Office: Head Post Office (tel. 743894), on N. Veli St. The main entrance is around the corner on Scott St., labeled *Poste Restante.* Open M-Sa 9am-7pm, Su 9am-4pm. **Postal Code:** 625001.

Internet: Uni Internet Club, 10 TPK Rd., 1st fl. Keep your eyes peeled for the narrow steps under a sign marked "Dunlop Sports." Rs 85 per hr. Open M-Sa 10am-9pm.

Telephones: Modern Tourism, 29 W. Perumal Maistry St. Callbacks Rs5 per 10min.

PHONE CODE	0452

ACCOMMODATIONS

Nearly all of Madurai's hotels are within walking distance of the Meenakshi Temple and the city's transportation hubs. Good budget options do exist, though rooms under Rs150 are an endangered species.

Hotel Aarathy, 9 Perumal Koil, W. Mada St. (tel. 731571), down the small road on the right after W. Perumal Maistry St. as you walk east on S. Masi St. A well-maintained establishment with rooms overlooking the nearby Kudal Azhagar temple. Room service and attached restaurant. Pine-fresh attached bathrooms with seat or squat toilets. Check-out 24hr. Singles Rs195, with A/C Rs300; doubles Rs300/450; triples Rs550.

Hotel Ravi Towers, 9 Town Hall Rd. (tel. 741961; fax 743405), 2 blocks east of W. Perumal Maistry St. Neat, tiled, cool rooms with clean sheets. Rooms have 24hr. hot water, reality-numbing TV (if you can hum the Star TV theme song, it's time to ask for help), and STD/ISD phone service. Clean attached baths with seat toilets available on request. Room service. Check-out 24hr. Singles Rs125; doubles Rs195.

Hotel Keerthi, 40 W. Perumal Maistry St. (tel. 741501), 1½ blocks north of Town Hall Rd., has tiny whitewashed rooms with spotless sheets, ample lighting, TVs, and phones. Clean attached baths with tepid water and squat toilets. Attached restaurant. Singles Rs175; doubles Rs220, with A/C Rs300. 20% tax.

Hotel Alavai, 86 W. Perumal Maistry St. (tel. 740551). Simple rooms offer the basic bed, plastic chair, and attached bathroom with squat toilet. Could use a little cleaning, but it's cheap. Singles Rs60; doubles Rs100; triples Rs150.

Hotel Santosh, 7 Town Hall Rd. (tel. 743692), next to Hotel Ravi Towers. Dim corridors lead to moss-green rooms whose ascetic decor sharply contrasts with the huge TVs. All rooms have baths with oft-scrubbed squat toilets. Doubles Rs135, with TV Rs170.

FOOD

The best restaurants in Madurai are in and around the hotels on W. Perumal Maistry St. and Town Hall Rd. Many of the hotels offer rooftop dining, which usually means quiet surroundings, cool breezes, and, great temple views.

Priya, 102 W. Perumal Maistry St., in Hotel Prem Nivas. Small eatery offers phenomenally cheap and yummy Indian dishes: huge *masala dosa* (Rs8) and delicious *thalis* (Rs25-30). Quick service. Open daily 6:30am-10pm.

New Arya Bhavan, 241-A W. Masi St., at Dindigul Rd. A hot favorite among Madurai residents, despite the incessant rumble of bus traffic. Try the *pakoras* (Rs10) and butter roast *dosa* (Rs12). The sweet shop has *jangiri, laddus,* and milk sweets, but their *kalkand burfi* (Rs125 per kg) takes the cake. Open daily 6am-10pm.

Hotel Mahal, 13 Town Hall Rd., next to the Taj Restaurant. The most varied dining options in town are served amid tanks of tropical fish. North Indian *thali* (Rs35), *tandoori* (Rs30-40), pasta (Rs65), and lamb (Rs60). Open daily 7am-11pm.

Ruby Restaurant, W. Perumal Maistry St. next to Hotel Alavalai. This chic little patio is one of Madurai's prime foreigner hubs, serving Indian, Continental, and Chinese dishes. Spring rolls (Rs40) and tomato omelettes (Rs15). Open daily 11am-11pm.

Surya, 110 W. Perumal Maistry St., on the roof of Hotel Supreme, with a great view of Madurai and the *gopurams* of the Meenakshi Temple. Extensive veg. menu has Indian, Chinese, and Continental faves (Rs30-40). If you can't handle the great outdoors, head to the 1st fl. restaurant (same menu). Restaurant open daily 6am-11pm. Rooftop open daily 5pm-midnight.

🎵 🛍 ENTERTAINMENT AND SHOPPING

There are a few **cinemas** near the Periyar Bus Stand. *The Hindu* has the latest listings for English-language films. Check with the tourist office for **cultural programs** such as classical dancing and music in Lakshmi Sundaram Hall, Tallakulam (tel. 530858). Madurai is filled with **textile shops** and *sari* showrooms. You will undoubtedly be accosted by tailors who will offer to sew an exact copy of the pants you're wearing for a nominal cost. As always, beware of auto-rickshaw drivers who force you to check out a particular handicraft store—they're just after the commission. Even if you don't plan on buying anything, you may find yourself drinking a free 7-Up as a smooth-talking salesman convinces you to buy that Rs500 parakeet-embroidered pillowcase you never knew you wanted. **Parameswari Stores,** 21 E. Chittrai St., just outside the southern *gopuram* of the Meenakshi Temple, is well-known for its silk-cotton blends. **Cooptex Sales Emporium,** W. Chittrai St., sells fabric as well as *saris*. **Khadi Emporium,** Town Hall Rd., is a good place to buy gifts and wooden carvings. Handicraft enthusiasts should visit the **Madurai Gallery,** Cottage Expo Crafts, 19 N. Chittrai St. (tel. 627851).

👁 SIGHTS

MEENAKSHI AMMAN TEMPLE

Entrance to the temple complex from E. Chitrai St., just south of the eastern gopuram. Open daily 5am-10pm. Sanctum closed 12:30-3pm. Free; camera fee Rs30.

Though everyone has a personal favorite, the Meenakshi Amman Temple, which draws more than 10,000 tourists and devotees every day, is probably the most splendid in all of Tamil Nadu. Besides dazzling visitors with the vibrant hues of the 30 million sculptures adorning the complex, the temple impresses with its sheer size—the complex covers an incredible 65,000 square meters, and the tallest of the temple's twelve *gopurams* reaches 49m.

HISTORY. Originally built by the Pandyas as a humble shrine, the temple was embellished later by the Vijayanagar kings. The Nayaks came to power in the 16th century, continuing this work by further expanding the complex and building the temple's massive *gopurams*. The temple was opened to Untouchables after Gandhi initiated a boycott, and the Mahatma made a crucial visit here in 1946. The temple is dedicated both to the goddess Meenakshi and to Shiva. Legend has it that the Pandya King Malayadwaja was childless and desperately sought a male heir. The king appealed to the gods by performing a series of *yagnas* (fire sacrifices).

POLLY WANT A FUTURE?

In these modern times, the hand-cast horoscope is going the ill-starred way of, well, the dodo. Thanks to computers, one can now have one's *jadhagam* (horoscope) plotted just by specifying a date of birth, to be checked against a database of the stars' and planets' positions. The result is unceremoniously printed out in barely-legible dot matrix. In some parts of India, though, one's fortune can still be told the old-fashioned way: by *kili josyam* (parrot astrology). The human astrologer has a number of cards with pictures of deities placed face down. To determine a client's fortune, he releases a trained parrot from its cage, and the bird grabs one of the cards in its beak. Each deity corresponds to a chapter in the *Agastya Arudal*, an ancient treatise written by the sage Agastya. The astrologer then divines one's fortune from the designated chapter. The prognosticating polly is re-caged, but the game continues, as the same astrologer is usually also a palmist and has a myriad methods to clarify or elaborate upon the parrot's prediction.

To his great surprise, during one such ceremony, a three-year-old girl emerged from the sacred flames. Named Meenakshi, the "fish-eyed" goddess (fish-like eyes being considered a mark of beauty), the child was born with three breasts and a lot of divine attitude. The king was a little troubled by his daughter's physical excesses, but a voice from above assured him that her third breast would disappear as soon as she met her future husband. After growing up to become a beautiful princess, Meenakshi set out to conquer the world, which she did promptly by defeating the other gods and demons, until only Shiva was left. When Meenakshi confronted Shiva (known in Madurai as Sundareswar, the "good-lookin' lord"), however, her heart turned to *ghee*, her third breast disappeared, and she was easily domesticated. It is said that Meenakshi and Sundareswar were wed in Madurai, where they jointly ruled the Pandya kingdom. A grand festival, the **Meenakshi Kalyanam,** commemorates the wedding.

ASHTA SHAKTI AND MEENAKSHI NAYAKKAR MANDAPAMS. In the southeast corner is the brightly painted **Ashta Shakti Mandapam** (Eight Shakti Corridor), where hawkers peddle postcards, curios, and *puja* offerings. The passage was named from the eight avatars of the goddess Shakti carved on its pillars. Other sculptures and paintings depict the *tiruvilayadals* (miracles) of Shiva. The spacious **Meenakshi Nayakkar Mandapam** has six rows of pillars, carved with images of the *yali*, mythological beasts with the body of a lion and the head of an elephant.

POTRAMARAI KULAM. The corridors that surround the serene Potramarai Kulam (Golden Lotus Tank) are often crowded by devotees relaxing in the shade or taking in the spectacular view of the temple's southern *gopuram*. The tank itself is frequented by pilgrims seeking a purifying bath in its light green waters, following the tradition of Indra, who is said to have bathed here. In ancient times, the Tamil Sangam (Academy of Poets) met in the area around the tank. Locals claim that the Sangam judged the merit of literary works by tossing submissions into the tank. If a work sank, the aspiring writer's hopes went along with it. If the work floated, however, it was deemed worthy of the Sangam's attention. Particularly beautiful is the surreal reflection of moonlight in the pool's waters.

KILIKOOTU MANDAPAM. The northwest corner of the tank leads directly to the **Meenakshi Shrine,** which is closed to non-Hindus; the corridor surrounding the shrine, however, is accessible to all. Called the Kilikootu Mandapam, or Parrot Cage Corridor, the space was once used to keep cages of lucky green parrots (trained to repeat Meenakshi's name) to be used as offerings to the goddess. The *mandapam's* 28 pillars are expertly carved with images from Hindu mythology.

OONJAL MANDAPAM. In the neighboring 16th-century Oonjal Mandapam (Swing Corridor), the golden images of Meenakshi and Sundareswar are carried in, placed on a swing, and sung to every Friday at about 5:30pm. The shrine has a three-story *gopuram* guarded by two stern *dwarapalakas* (watchmen) and is supported by rectangular golden columns that bear the mark of a lotus. Along the perimeter of the chamber, black granite panels of Shiva and Meenakshi overlook the crowds of *darshan*-seekers. It is said that as a mother-fish need only look upon her spawn to bring them to life, worshipers' spirituality is stirred to life when the fish-eyed Meenakshi casts her gaze upon them.

KAMBATHADI MANDAPAM. North of the Oonjal Mandapam is the **Sundareswar Shrine** (also closed to non-Hindus), with its eight-foot image of Ganesha (Mukku-runi Vinayakar), discovered in the 17th century when King Tirumalai Nayak began digging the Mariamman Teppakulam in the southeastern corner of the city. Even the iron gratings along the top of the outer walls, where a bit of sunlight filters in, have been fashioned in the shape of Nandi and a *linga*. In the northeast corner of the enclosure (accessible to all) is the Kambathadi Mandapam, adorned with elegant pillars, each of which bears a sculpture of Meenakshi or Shiva. Sculptures of Shiva and Kali trying to out-dance one another are pelted with balls of *ghee* by devotees who hope to soothe their competitiveness. The second enclosure houses shrines to various gods, including Durga and Siddhar. The inner chamber contains the image of Sundareswar as well as an image of Nataraja, unique for having his *right* foot raised. Apparently, King Rajasekhara Pandya, a great devotee of Shiva, set out to learn the dance performed by Nataraja. While practicing, the king realized the great strain placed upon Nataraja's leg and felt a change was necessary.

AYIRAKKAL MANDAPAM. East of the Kambathadi Mandapam is a lively market, where vendors sell necklaces, postcards, and religious trifles. These stands surround the Ayirakkal Mandapam (Thousand Pillar Hall), which boasts 985 carved pillars (no word on the other 15). It has been converted into a **museum** displaying a substantial collection. The *mandapam* also has a set of pillars which plays seven notes when tapped. *(Open daily 7am-7:30pm. Rs2; camera fee Rs10.)*

OTHER SIGHTS

TIRUMALAI NAYAK PALACE. What remains of Tirumalai's grand 17th-century palace is the cavernous **Swargavilasam** (Celestial Pavilion), an arcaded courtyard where the Nayak rulers held public audiences. Though heroic efforts are being made to renovate the courtyard, there is no undoing the damage wrought by Tirumalai's grandson, who looted the palace to outfit his own in Tiruchirappalli. However, parts of the interior have been fully restored; the deep crimson hue, along with the cream-colored carvings and figures in relief, hints at the palace's former grandeur. The daily **sound and light show** blares out an unintelligible narration of the Tamil epic *Sillapadigaram*. *(1.5km southeast of the Meenakshi Temple. Open daily 9am-1pm and 2-5pm. Rs1. Sound and light show in English daily 6:45-7:30pm. Purchase tickets starting at 6:30pm; Rs2-5.)*

VANDIYUR MARIAMMAN TEPPAKULAM. This squarish water tank has a tree-surrounded **shrine** in the center. The tank was built in 1646 by Tirumalai Nayak, who retired with his harem to the central shrine. These days, the tank is usually dry, and the only activity in the area is the occasional family picnic. When full, the tank uses water from the Vaigai via a network of underground channels. Every year, a colorful float festival (Jan.-Feb.) commemorates the birth of its builder. *(Kamarajar Rd., 5km southeast of the railway station. Bus #4 or 4A.)*

THIRUPPARANKUNDRAM. Though not as awe-inspiring as Meenakshi Amman, Thirupparankundram is an impressive cave-temple dedicated to Lord Subramanya, which currently houses several Sanskrit writing schools. The **inner sanctum** is carved right out of the rock in the side of a mountain. Guides will eagerly take you through the cavernous shrine. *(8km south of town. Guides Rs50.)*

TAMIL NADU

RAMESWARAM இராமேசுவரம்

The setting of the epic *Ramayana* (see p. 586), Rameswaram is said to be the venerated spot where Rama, the epic's hero, launched an attack on Ravana's fortress in Lanka. According to a later myth, Rama, after defeating Ravana in their cosmic battle, made a *linga* of sand here to honor Shiva and expiate the sin of murder. This remote island off the country's southeasterb coast draws thousands of Hindu pilgrims from all over India; the shores lapping the famous Ramanathaswamy temple throng with worshippers who ritually immerse themselves in the Bay of Bengal. The train ride to Rameswaram from the mainland is one of the most spectacular in India. Rameswaram also marks the southern holy *dham* (abode), one of India's four sacred places marking the cardinal directions. (The others are Dwarka in the west, Badrinath in the north, and Puri in the east.) A number of festivals are held in Rameswaram, including Thai Amavasai (Jan.), Masi Sivarathiri (Feb.-Mar.), Thirkalyanam (July-Aug.), and Mahalaya Amavasai (Sept.).

ORIENTATION AND PRACTICAL INFORMATION

Navigating Rameswaram consists of circling the four **Car Streets**—North, East, South, and West—which box in the **Ramanathaswamy Temple.** Most hotels, restaurants, and shops are located on these four streets and on **Sannadhi Street,** which runs east from the middle of E. Car St. to the Bay of Bengal. To reach the temple from the railway station, walk out the main entrance and follow the road for about 300m, as it curves slightly, then turn left (north) when you hit the principal north-south thoroughfare. Proceed north for 500m until you reach **Middle Street,** which leads east to the middle of W. Car St. and the western entrance of the temple.

Trains: Rameswaram Station, 1km southwest of the temple. Reservations counter open M-Sa 8am-2pm and 2:15-8pm, Su 8am-2pm. Tourists are encouraged to contact the Station Master directly for bookings. Fares listed are 2nd/1st class. To **Chennai** (*Saidu Exp.* 6114, 3:30pm, 14hr., Rs 120/450; *Madras Mail* 6102, noon, 14hr., Rs120/450); **Coimbatore** (*Coimbatore Exp.* 6116, 4pm, 13hr., Rs65/350).

Buses: The **bus stand** is on Bazaar Rd., 2km west of the temple, a short auto-rickshaw (Rs10) or bus (Rs1) ride from the temple. **SETC** runs buses to **Chennai** via **Tiruchirappalli** (every hr., 6hr., Rs45); **Coimbatore** (8am and 2pm, 12hr., Rs90); **Kanyakumari** (4 per day, 10hr., Rs80); **Madurai** (every 10 min., 4hr., Rs35).

Local Transportation: Unmetered **auto-rickshaws** circulate though Rameswaram, and silver-and-red **local buses** shuttle between the bus stand and E. Car St. Shops on the Car Streets rent **bikes** for about Rs3 per hr.

Tourist Office: 14 E. Car St. (tel. 21371), gives out a rudimentary map of Rameswaram. Open M-F 10am-5:45pm. The **Tourist Information Centre** (tel. 21373), inside the train station, and the **Temple Information Center,** inside the temple, are helpful.

Currency Exhange: The nearest place to change currency is Madurai.

Pharmacy: Shekhar Medical, Bazaar St. Open M-F 7am-10pm.

Hospital: Government Hospital (tel. 21233), near the railway station; toward the temple and left off Bazaar St. before the Township Office. Open daily 8am-7:30pm. You can also try the **Temple Trust Ayurvedic Dispensary,** near the temple police station.

Police station: (tel. 21227), in a red brick building at the junction of E. and N. Car St.

Post office: One branch on Middle St., toward the bus stand. Smaller office on E. Car St.

PHONE CODE	04573

ACCOMMODATIONS AND FOOD

Except for the TTDC Rest House, most hotels are located in the immediate vicinity of the Ramanathaswamy Temple. Accommodations are very basic, catering to pil grims looking for a cheap place to crash for the night. Rameswaram's tap water can be salty, and showers are extremely rare, so test the plumbing before checking in. Reserve ahead during the pilgrimage season (July-Aug.). Dining options are extremely limited, but *thali* restaurants abound in the streets around the temple.

Sant Shri Bajrangdas Bapa Annachetra (tel. 21021), at the edge of S. Car St., is unquestionably the best deal in town. The swastika-ed building has fresh, huge rooms with views of the glimmering ocean just meters away. Constructed for *sadhus'* use, it is often full, so call ahead. Check-out 24hr. Singles Rs75; doubles Rs100.

Hotel Maharaja's, 7 Middle St. (tel. 21271), has peachy, well-maintained rooms with cable TV. Attached squat toilets are the cleanest you'll get; hot water available upon request. Check-out 24hr. Singles Rs120; doubles Rs195, with A/C Rs420.

Hotel Abirami, on Sannadhi St., serving up piping-hot *chapatis* (Rs8) and vegetable *sabjis* (Rs10), is the best of Rameswaram's restaurant picks. Open daily 6am-10pm.

Hotel Tamil Nadu, on the beachfront 250m from the temple, has the town's only permit room. Those who crave a beer can sip it in a cane chair overlooking the sea. Tends to get crowded around mid-day with pilgrims on day tours. Meals Rs20-45. Open daily 7:30-10am, 12:30-2:30pm, and 7:30-9:30pm.

SIGHTS

THE RAMANATHASWAMY TEMPLE. The center around which Rameswaram revolves, the Ramanathaswamy Temple sees thousands of Hindu pilgrims pass through its *gopurams* every day. Its construction began in the 12th century under the direction of the architecturally prolific Chola empire; the temple was last altered significantly in the mid-18th century by the Raja of Ramnathapuram, Muthuramalinga Sethupathi. Since then, construction has been slow; the eastern *gopuram* was just completed earlier this century.

The temple registers as one of the most sacred sites for Hindus, as it is believed the inner sanctum houses a *linga* fashioned out of sand by Rama. According to a later version of the *Ramayana*, after Rama killed Ravana in Lanka and rescued Sita, he returned to Rameswaram, only to discover that Ravana had been a *brahmin*—his murder was thus a grave sin. Rama sent Hanuman to bring back a *linga* with which Rama could worship Shiva and expiate his guilt, but the monkey was late, and Rama had to make do with a *linga* of sand. When Hanuman finally returned, Rama suggested that they replace the sand *linga* with the new one. When Hanuman tried to pull out the makeshift *linga*, it would not budge, so the new *linga* was installed to the left of it. It was decreed that all pilgrims should worship Hanuman's installation first.

The inner sanctum of the temple (inaccessible to non-Hindus) houses both *lingas* in a smoky central chamber. Facing the main shrine is a huge sculpture of Shiva's bull, Nandi. Before having *darshan* of the resident deities, visitors normally bathe in the waters of 22 *tirthas* (tanks). To expedite the process, temple employees are on hand to dump buckets of holy water on the devotees. Taking part in the ritual is a once-in-a-lifetime experience. Interested parties should contact a tour guide to avoid the bureaucratic hassle of gaining entrance to the inner sanctums. Aside from its spiritual importance, the Ramanathaswamy Temple is also famous for its sculpted pillars, which form corridors measuring 264m from east to west and 200m from north to south. The 1200 soft stone pillars in the outer corridor harmoniously unite form with function. *(Temple gates open daily 4am-8pm; Rs2. Inner sanctum closed noon-4pm. Contact M. Selvam, 25 N. Car St., tel. 21353 or 21501, for more information on immersion rituals; full ritual Rs250.)*

OTHER SIGHTS. Dedicated to Rama, the **Kothandaramar Temple** is said to mark the site where Ravana's brother Vibhishana was crowned king of Lanka after Ravana's death. *(20km along the precarious road towards Sri Lanka. Open daily 8am-5pm.)* The **Gandamadana Paravtham**, a simple, white-washed temple atop the highest hill

TAMIL NADU

THE RAMAYANA Arguably the most culturally influential work of literature in India, the *Ramayana* (ra-MA-yahn-uh) has inspired thousands of dances, paintings, shadow puppet shows, inter-religious riots, and even its own TV mini-series. The
epic Sanskrit poem's main characters, Rama and Sita, are revered as archetypes of
those who unwaveringly follow their *dharma* (duty or fate). It is believed that the poet
Valmiki composed the *Ramayana* (literally, "the romance of Rama") around 400 BC,
basing it on events that took place between 1000 and 700 BC.

   Act I, Scene 1: Rama is born to King Dasaratha's wife Kausalya in Ayodhya, capital
of Kosala. Dasaratha's other wives, Kaikeyi and Sumithra, bear him Bharata and the
twins Lakshmana and Shatrugna, respectively. **Scene 2:** Rama journeys with his guru
Viswamitra to the kingdom of Mithila, where he falls in love at first sight with King Janaka's beautiful daughter Sita. But winning her hand is not an easy task. Fearing he will
lose his daughter to an unworthy man, Janaka declares that only he who is able to
break Shiva's divine bow can have her hand in marriage. **Scene 3:** Rama successfully
breaks the bow, and the two kingdoms delight in the wedding of Rama and Sita. **Scene
4:** Dasaratha, growing old, names Rama as his successor and king of Kosala. But his
wife Kaikeyi refuses to accept Rama as king and forces Dasaratha to banish Rama to
the forest for 14 years. Kaikeyi's son Bharata is crowned king instead.

   Act II, Scene 1: Rama, Sita, and Rama's faithful brother Lakshmana leave Ayodhya
for the forest. The sorrowful Dasaratha soon dies, and Bharata rushes to the forest,
begging Rama to return to claim the throne. Unwilling to break his promise to his
father, Rama stays in the forest for the next 14 years. **Scene 2:** Ravana, chief of the
asuras (demons), abducts Sita to his island kingdom of Lanka. **Scene 3:** The two
brothers journey in search of Sita, encountering en route the clever monkey Hanuman,
son of the wind god. Rama sends Hanuman to Lanka to appraise the situation and
deliver a token to his beloved wife. Hanuman sets fire to the entire capital of Lanka
before he leaves. **Scene 4:** With the help of a Lankan spy, Rama and his army of monkeys advance on Ayodhya. The valiant monkeys build a bridge to Lanka, and a celestial
battle ensues. Rama emerges victorious, vanquishing Ravana and winning back Sita.
Scene 5: 14 years are up, and Rama, Lakshmana, Sita, and Hanuman return to Kosala. Rama is crowned king, and Ayodhya erupts in celebration upon the revelation that
Rama is an avatar of Vishnu. **Scene 6:** Sita's fidelity during Rama's absence is ques-
tioned. Subordinating his trust of Sita to his princely duty, Rama subjects her to an
ordeal of fire, from which she emerges unscathed and vindicated.

in town, houses an imprint of Lord Rama's feet and commands splendid views of
the sandy island terrain. *(3km north of the Ramanathaswamy Temple.)* The southeastern end of the island forms a great finger of sand pointing towards Sri Lanka.
Because the railway line to **Dhanushkodi**, at the tip, was destroyed by a cyclone in
1964, the only access is by auto-rickshaw, hired jeep or on foot. There is no trace
of human habitation here, but those who make the chilly pre-dawn trek are
rewarded with a stunning sunrise. *(6km walk. Auto-rickshaw Rs150. Jeep with driver
Rs500. Local buses also make the trip.)* For the aquatically inclined, **boats** can be hired
at **Sangumal,** 2.5km northeast of the temple. A guide (also the navigator of the
boat) will strap a mask onto your face and take you snorkelling in the beautiful
coral reef, about 2km from the shore. *(Boats Rs300 for 4hr.)*

KANYAKUMARI கன்னியாகுமரி

Kanyakumari (Cape Comorin) marks the southernmost tip of the Indian subcontinent. In keeping with the Hindu belief in the auspicious nature of physical confluence, this meeting place of three bodies of water—the Arabian Ocean, the Bay of
Bengal, and the Indian Ocean—is a particularly holy site. Hindu pilgrims of all
types, from dredded *babus* to giggling families, come in droves to sacred Kanyakumari, to watch the sun set into one ocean and rise from another. Stories tell of the
goddess Kanya Devi, an incarnation of Parvati, who did heavy penance here in

order to win Lord Shiva's hand in marriage. Shiva consented and set off for the midnight wedding ceremony. The other gods, wanting Kanya Devi to retain her divine *shakti* by remaining a virgin, schemed to spoil the wedding. The sage Narada assumed the form of a crowing rooster to falsely herald the dawn and make Shiva think he was late for the ceremony. Shiva fell for the trick and went home, leaving poor, heartbroken Kanya Devi an eternal virgin. The Kumari Amman Temple in Kanyakumari celebrates her penance and loss.

The prestige lent to Kanyakumari by this myth fades by day, however, as tour buses parked along the seafront disgorge masses of pilgrims into the waiting arms of beach vendors hawking cheap souvenirs and "shell art." The gaudy buildings pockmarking the southernmost tip of the city come into view, making Kanyakumari seem less-than-pure. But when the booths light up by night, the temple takes on a carnival air that manages to mitigate some of the town's grimness.

TRANSPORTATION

Trains: The **railway station,** on Main Rd., is a 15min. walk from the sea. Fares listed are for 2nd/1st class. To: **Bangalore** (*Bangalore Exp.* 6525, 6:20am, 20hr., Rs162/797); **Chennai** (*Kanyakumari-Chennai Exp.* 6120, 3:15pm, 17hr., Rs174/862); **Ernakulam** (4:30 and 6:20am, 10hr., Rs77/370); **Mumbai** (*Kanyakumari-Mumbai Exp.* 1082, 4:30am, 48hr., Rs264/1576); **Trivandrum** (4:30 and 6:20am, 2½hr., Rs30/159).

Buses: The **bus stand** posts schedules in English and has a helpful information desk. The tourist office also has up-to-date bus schedules and rates. Buses are prone to last-minute cancellations. To: **Chennai** (11 per day 9:30am-8:30pm, 16hr., Rs146); **Coimbatore** (7pm, 11hr., Rs97); **Ernakulam** (7:15 and 9am, 9hr., Rs89); **Kodaikanal** (8:45pm, 10hr., Rs82); **Kovalam** (6:30am, 1:15, 2, and 9:15pm; 2½hr.; Rs19); **Madurai** (frequent 9:30am-8:45pm, 6hr., Rs64); **Trivandrum** (12 per day 5:45am-9:15pm, 2½hr., Rs20). Buses also go to **Nagercoil** (every 20min., 30min., Rs4), which offers frequent connections to many cities. **Tamil Nadu Government Express** (tel. 71019) runs daily buses to Bangalore, Coimbatore, Kodaikanal, Madurai, Chennai, Ooty, Pondicherry, Rameswaram, and Tirupati.

Local Transportation: Kanyakumari is small enough to navigate on foot, but you won't have difficulty finding a **rickshaw** if you want one.

ORIENTATION AND PRACTICAL INFORMATION

Buses from Trivandrum and Madurai head south down **Main Road** past the **railway station.** Buses turn west onto **Bus Stand Road** at the Main Rd. Junction, pass the square-towered **lighthouse,** and stop at the **bus stand.** Main Rd. continues south past this junction to the **tourist office** and peters out at the seafront **Gandhi Memorial.** Running east from Main Rd. Junction, the road crosses **Sannadhi Street** before ending at the **ferry service station.** Sannadhi St. heads south through the souvenir stalls to the Kumari Amman Temple, situated at the very tip of the subcontinent.

Tourist Office: Main Rd. (tel. 71276), in a circular building north of the Gandhi Memorial on the right. Knowledgeable staff doles out pamphlets, brochures, and info. Open M-F 10am-5:45pm.

Budget Travel: Several small offices north of the temple sell private bus and train tickets.

Currency Exchange: Canara Bank, Main Rd., a 5-10min. walk north of Main Rd. Junction on the left. Changes AmEx and Thomas Cook traveler's checks. Gives cash advances on Visa, MC, and AmEx. Allow at least 1hr. Open M-F 10am-2pm, Sa 10am-noon.

Bookstore: Shamus Book Centre, Sannadhi St., near Hotel Saravana. Carries maps and travel guides. Open F-W 8:30am-9pm.

Pharmacy: Sastha Pharmacy, Main Rd. (tel. 71455), halfway between the railway station and the tourist office. Open daily 8:30am-9:30pm.

Hospital: Government Hospital, off Main Rd., close to the police station. Since it has no phone, tourists might want to call **Dr. Arumugam's** clinic, E. Car St. (tel. 71349), between hotels Manickham and Maadhini.

Police Station: Main Rd. (tel. 71224), next to the GPO.

Post Office: GPO, Main Rd., just south of Canara Bank. Stamps and *Poste Restante*. Open M-Sa 8am-noon and 1:30-4:30pm. **Postal Code:** 629702.

PHONE CODE	04652

🏔 ACCOMMODATIONS

Judging from Kanyakumari, it might seem that the phenomenon of pilgrimage was invented by the hotel industry—every second building provides lodging of some kind. Prices begin to soar in August, peaking from October to February.

Hotel Maadhini, E. Car St. (tel. 71787), on the shore 200m north of the temple. Brand new, with all the amenities of a Western hotel. Carpeted rooms have bright lighting and large disinfected baths with soap and towels. The Discovery Channel and breathtaking balcony views of the ocean and coastal fishing village vie for your attention. 24hr. hot water. Doubles Rs200-450, with A/C Rs800.

Kerala House (tel. 71229), on the seaward side of Bus Stand Rd. near the bus stand. A sort of upscale government guest house, with dining room tables, separate dressing rooms, and enormous ocean views. Slightly faded, but still an elegant option. Singles Rs400, with A/C Rs600; doubles Rs500/750.

Manickam Tourist House, Car St. (tel. 71387), near Hotel Maadhini. Most of the amenities of Hotel Maadhini, but the views aren't quite as good and the facilities are a little tired, so it's cheaper. Clean rooms with attached bathrooms and balconies. Buckets of hot water upon request. Doubles Rs250-350; triples Rs450, with A/C from Rs650.

Hotel Sangam, Main Rd. (tel. 71351), across the street from the GPO. Less-than-tranquil location, but clean, well-lit rooms have spotless baths with seat toilets. All rooms have sea views. 24hr. room service. Deluxe A/C rooms have TVs. Rooms Rs450; deluxe Rs520, with A/C Rs850-1200.

Hotel Narmadha, Bus Stand Rd. (tel. 71365), close to Main Rd. Junction. Clean, spacious doubles have baths with squat toilets and hot water. Rooms Rs200-250.

🍽 FOOD

Since people come to Kanyakumari to attend to spiritual affairs, one shouldn't be too surprised that material matters, like food, are neglected.

Hotel Saravana has two branches—one on Sannadhi St., 50m in front of the temple, and another around the corner towards Main Rd. Junction. South Indian breakfasts (*masala dosa* Rs13), as well as Gujarati, Rajasthani, Punjabi, and South Indian veg. *thalis* (Rs18). Open daily 6am-10pm.

Hotel Sangam, Main Rd., opposite the GPO. Your best, possibly only, bet for Chinese and non-veg. fare. A wide range of slightly misspelled tasties (most dishes Rs25-70) are supposedly available 24hr.

Bhagavath Amman Canteen, right next to the temple entrance, serves up basic fare (*masala dosa* Rs12, veg. meal Rs15) to satisfied punters. Open daily 6am-9pm.

Anila Restaurant, Bus Stand Rd., in Hotel Narmadha close to Main Rd. Junction. Decent, if basic, source for North Indian veg. dishes (*alu gobi* Rs12). Open daily 7am-10:30pm.

👁 🎵 SIGHTS AND ENTERTAINMENT

KUMARI AMMAN TEMPLE. The seaside Kumari Amman Temple is right on the tip of India, unmistakable with its red-and-white vertical temple stripes. Dedicated to

Kanya Devi, the temple celebrates the penance she did in hopes of winning Shiva's hand in marriage. All visitors must doff their shoes to enter, and men must also shed their shirts. *(Open daily 4am-noon and 4-8:30pm.)*

GANDHI MANDAPAM. This unusual interpretation of Orissan architectural style overlooks the southernmost bit of the subcontinent's land mass. A black marble box marks the spot where the ashes of Mahatma Gandhi were briefly stored before being scattered seaward. The *mandapam* rises 79 ft. (23m), one for each year of Gandhi's life. It is engineered so that it is hit by rays of sunlight at noon every year on his birthday (October 2). Though the "guard" might hit you up for some cash, it is worth taking his advice and climbing the spires for an inspirational photo-op. *(At the seaward end of Main Rd. Open daily 6:30am-noon and 3-7:30pm.)*

VIVEKANANDA MEMORIAL. Accessible only by ferry, the two rocks marking the Vivekananda Memorial sit in the Bay of Bengal east of Kanyakumari. The Hindu reformer Swami Vivekananda swam here and meditated atop the rocks for several days in 1892 before heading to Chicago for the 1893 World Religions Conference (see **Modern Hinduism,** p. 85). The glossy Vivekananda Memorial temple commemorates the event. Arrows mark a path around the island, which also houses a temple built around one of Parvati's footprints. The notice board at the ferry terminal on the mainland gives information on sunrise times. *(Ferries daily 7:45am-4pm. Rs6.)*

FISHING VILLAGE. Although the sections of Kanyakumari near the temple and the cape overflow with cheap lacquered seashells, Ray-Ban-*wallahs*, and nondescript hotels, the village on the east coast north of the hotel district has many charms—bright, lavender and yellow houses, small church-shrines, and a thriving catamaran fishing business. The elegant and imposing **St. Mary's Church,** with its impressive facade, towers over the southern edge of the village. The church's interior contains only a few bright plastic flowers and gaudy gold-foil-edged portraits of a milky-white Jesus and Mary.

FESTIVALS. Kanyakumari's **Pongal Festival** (Jan. 14-15) celebrates the end of the rice harvest with South India's beloved, sweet, sticky rice. The **Cape Festival** (last week of Nov.) celebrates Tamil culture, especially *bharat natyam* dance. Finally, **World Tourism Day** (Sept. 27) is celebrated with free cultural shows, free food, and free garlands for foreign tourists (see **Holidays and Festivals,** p. 806).

NEAR KANYAKUMARI

The **Suchindram Temple,** 13km from Kanyakumari, is dedicated to the holy trinity of Hinduism—Shiva, Vishnu, and Brahma—and contains many sculptural odds and ends, including India's only depiction of a female Ganesha. Also of note are a 2500-year-old tree and a limestone Nandi which, according to local lore, is actually growing. (Open daily 4:30am-noon and 4:30-8:45pm.) Rickshaws, taxis, and tour buses make the trip from Kanyakumari. **Padmanabhapuram,** 45km from Kanyakumari on the way to Trivandrum, was the capital of Travancore until 1798. Inside Padmanabhapuram's **fort** is a grand **palace** spanning 2.5 hectares (open Tu-Su 9am-5pm; Rs6). Many tour buses from Trivandrum stop here en route to Kanyakumari.

KODAIKANAL கொடைக்கானல்

Set apart from major cities by a stretch of nearly 160km of arid plain, green, grand Kodaikanal rises above the flatlands as one of Tamil Nadu's most popular hill stations. The heady scent of eucalyptus mingles with fresh breezes, wafting over Kodai's mountainside covered in blue-gums and *kurinji* blossoms. During the hottest months of the year (Apr.-June), the town swarms with foreigners and middle class Indian tourists who descend on the town en masse to take languid strolls on its gentle slopes and to breathe in the crisp air. It was the British who began this trend in the 1840s, when they founded Kodai as an antidote to the sweltering, malaria-infested plains. Today, Kodai remains free of noise and pollution, and its surroundings are arguably the most beautiful of any hill station. Kodai can get a bit nippy at night, and the daily temperature is usually 10-20°C cooler than in Chennai.

TAMIL NADU

⌐ TRANSPORTATION

Trains: Kodaikanal Road Station (tel. (4543) 38226) is a 3hr. bus ride from town. Fares listed are 2nd/1st class. From Kodaikanal Rd. to: **Chennai** via **Tiruchirappalli** (*Pandian Exp.* 6718, 8pm, 14hr., 2nd class Rs102; *Muthunagar Exp.* 6704, 9:15pm, 17hr., Rs102/561); **Madurai** (*Madurai Passenger* 711, 8am, 1hr., Rs18/103; *Kanyakumari Exp.* 6121, 3am, 1hr., Rs21/136).

Buses: The **bus stand** is a dirt lot just off Anna Salai, on Wood Will Rd. Reservations booth open 9:30am-5:30pm. To: **Bangalore** (6pm, 12hr., Rs152); **Chennai** (6:30pm, 12hr., Rs105); **Coimbatore** (8:30am and 4:30pm, 6hr., Rs32); **Kankyakumari** (8:30am, 9hr., Rs65); **Madurai** (every 30min. 7:30am-4:30pm, 4hr., Rs35); **Ooty** (8:30am and 4:30pm, 8hr., Rs55); **Trichy** (1:30, 3:30, and 5:45pm; 5hr.; Rs38). A number of **private bus** operators with offices on Anna Salai offer deluxe bus service to Chennai, Madurai, Ooty, and Coimbatore (Rs150-700).

Local Transportation: The best way to get around is on foot or bike. **Bike rental** available in the lake area (Rs10 per hr.). For the weak-kneed, however, **taxis** might be helpful in traversing Kodai's hilly roads. Taxis are available outside the bus stand (min. Rs40).

◪ ORIENTATION AND PRACTICAL INFORMATION

Getting around in Kodai is a snap. Buses pull into a lot just south of **Anna Salai (Bazaar Road)**, the town's major east-west thoroughfare. Anna Salai leads west to the **Seven Road Junction,** where (at last count) six roads meet at a traffic circle. At the junction, **Club Road** and the restaurant-laden **PT Road (Hospital Road)** head north. PT Rd. connects Anna Salai with **Law's Ghat Road,** which runs roughly parallel to it. Taking an immediate left at the junction takes you to **Bryant's Park** and **Coaker's Walk,** while west of the junction sits Kodai's artificial lake. **Observatory Road** leads west past the lake and out of town.

Tourist Office: (tel. 41675), on the northern side of Anna Salai, a 2min. walk east of the bus stand; look for the glut of tourist vans. Open daily 10am-5:45pm.

Budget Travel: For bus, train, and airline bookings, try the travel agency adjacent to **Hilltop Towers Hotel,** Club Rd. Open M-Sa 9am-1pm and 2-5pm, Su 2-5pm.

Currency Exchange: State Bank of India (tel. 41068), next to the tourist office, changes traveler's checks in U.S. and U.K. currencies. Open M-F 10am-2pm, Sa 10am-noon.

Bookstore: CLS Bookstore (tel. 40465), opposite the tourist office, has miscellaneous books and some tourist information. Open M-Sa 9am-1pm and 2-6pm.

Market and Pharmacy: Kurunji Mini Super Market, next to the post office. Stock up on peanut butter, Kotex, and mineral water. Pharmacies also line Anna Salai.

Hospital: Government Hospital (tel. 41292). From the Seven Road Junction, follow PT Rd. north for about 250m; the hospital is on the right, before Law's Ghat Rd. **Van Allen** (tel. 40273) is a reputable private hospital near Coaker's Walk.

Police: (tel. 40262), diagonally opposite the post office on Anna Salai.

Post Office: (tel. 41267), a huge yellow building on Anna Salai, opposite Snooze Inn. Open M-F 9:30am-5pm. *Poste Restante.* **Postal Code:** 624101.

PHONE CODE	04542

⌐ ACCOMMODATIONS

Kodai is rapidly becoming infested with budget tourist traps. The cheapest lodgings along Anna Salai and, as you move away from the town center, quality and prices increase exponentially. The high season runs from April to June.

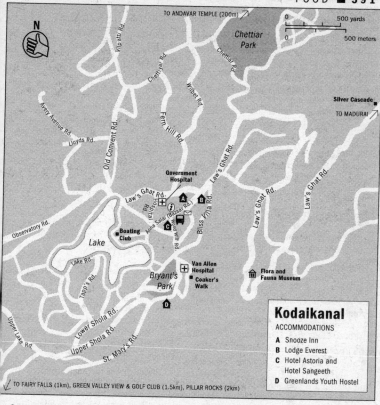

Kodaikanal

ACCOMMODATIONS

A Snooze Inn
B Lodge Everest
C Hotel Astoria and
   Hotel Sangeeth
D Greenlands Youth Hostel

Snooze Inn, Anna Salai (tel. 40837). Cozy beds with cushioned headrests, surrounded by soft red carpets and ethnic *objets d'art*. Pint-sized TVs in all rooms. Ultra-clean bathrooms have marble tiles, seat toilets, and hot water. Heater Rs30, extra blanket Rs7. Doubles Rs575; quads Rs690. Off-season: Rs300/450. 20% luxury tax.

Greenlands Youth Hostel, St. Mary's Rd. (tel. 40899), near Coaker's Walk. Take a left at Hotel Astoria; walk down 5min. Situated near a cliff, your front patio has an absolutely stunning view of the plains below. Dorms escape the cell-block feel that characterizes most hostels. Cozy private rooms with attached baths (hot water!) and working fireplaces. Dorm beds Rs55; doubles Rs300. Off-season: doubles Rs195.

Lodge Everest, Anna Salai (tel. 40100), a small lodge on the eastern end of Anna Salai before it makes a steep descent. Rustic, wood-paneled lobby and pleasant staff. Simple, cozy rooms have baths and seat toilets. Dorm beds Rs50; doubles Rs150. Off-season: Rs30/100.

Hotel Astoria (tel. 40524), at the intersection of Wood Will Rd. and Anna Salai. Upscale place somehow retains a homey feel. Large beds, seat toilets, and satellite TV. Doubles Rs650; quads Rs900. Off-season: Rs350/500. 20% luxury tax.

FOOD

Kodai's restaurant scene caters to the culinary tastes of its cosmopolitan visitors. If you don't leave town a kilo or two heavier, you've probably missed out. Many excellent restaurants line Hospital Rd., north of the Seven Road Junction.

Tibetan Brothers Restaurant, PT Rd., 2nd fl. on the left. Mouth-watering cuisine served by the Tibetan family that owns the place. Crispy vegetable *momos* (Rs35), lemon tea

(Rs25), Tibetan bread (Rs10), and steaming hot chocolate (Rs12) are perfect munchies for a cool day in Kodai. Open daily noon-4pm and 5:30-10pm.

Hotel Astoria (see **Accommodations,** above). The restaurant in the bowels of the popular hotel is famous for a wide variety of North Indian favorites. Rajana curry (Rs25), *channa patura* (Rs24), and onion *oothapam* (Rs15). Open daily 7am-9:30pm.

Chef Master, Hospital Rd., just past Tibetan Brothers. Gratifyingly grease-free Chinese, Continental, and Keralan food draws locals and foreigners alike. Assortment of chow mein (Rs30-40) and soups (Rs18-35). Open daily 9am-10pm.

Hotel Punjab, Hospital Rd., just north of the Seven Road Junction. Classy restaurant serving lip-smackin' delicious *tandoori* dishes: chicken *tikka* kebab (Rs60), Punjabi chicken (Rs80), and cucumber *raita* (Rs18). Open daily 10am-10pm.

Eco-Nut, Hospital Rd., up a flight from Hot Breads. A crunchy health foods and natural products shop loaded with the most ecologically sound food options: almonds, walnuts (Rs45 per 100g), whole grain muffins (Rs12), and dried fruits (Rs60 per 100g).

👁️ 🏔️ SIGHTS AND SCENERY

Quite naturally, Kodai's main attractions are its scenic spots—walks in the hills lead to breathtaking views of the surrounding Western Ghats.

THE LAKE AND ENVIRONS. Tourist activity centers on and around the man-made lake—the 5km path that encircles it is dotted with bicycle rental stands *(bikes Rs10 per hr.).* The **Kodaikanal Boating Club** rents boats *(open daily 9:30am-5:30pm; Rs15 per 30min.).* Just south of the lake is **Bryant's Park** with a fragrant **botanical garden** founded in 1902. Expertly trimmed and clipped by a staff of 45, the gardens are ablaze with a cornucopia of flowers, trees, and cacti. *(Open daily 8:30am-6:15pm. Rs5; camera fee Rs25. Plant a tree for Rs1000.)*

COAKER'S WALK. Kodai's most famous scenic promenade is Coaker's Walk, a 10-minute stroll along a paved precipice that traces an arc from Taj Lodge to Greenland's Youth Hostel. On clear mornings, the views of the surrounding hills and plains are amazing—you can see as far as Madurai. Most days, though, it's tough to see much of anything because of the mist. A small **telescope house** near Coaker's western end allows a technologically enhanced peek at the surrounding countryside. *(Head left through the gardens toward the painted tree stumps and exit Bryant's Park. Open daily 6:30am-7:30pm. Rs2; camera fee Rs5. Telescope house Rs1.)*

PILLAR ROCKS AND GREEN VALLEY VIEW. Get a taste of Kodai's best scenery at **Pillar Rocks,** an assemblage of boulders soaring upto 122m. Also in the area are the **Fairy Falls** on your way to the entrance to **Green Valley View,** which allows grand views of the surrounding countryside on only the clearest of days *(open daily 8am-8pm).* The roadside promontory nearby offers superb views of the Pillar Rocks on clear mornings. About 40m beyond the promontory, several unmarked paths thread their way into the forest, which swarms with loud vacationers during the high season. No matter—the woods here are lovely, dark, and deep, and there are many chances to see the hulking Pillar Rocks up close. *(Follow Upper Shola Rd. south, walk 8km from the town bus stand toward Pillar Rocks. To Fairy Falls and Green Valley View, head left at the fork in the road. Walk west 15min. to the roadside promontory.)*

CHETTIAR PARK. A secluded spot, Chettiar Park renews its fame every 12 years when the chronically shy *kurinji* plant springs into colorful bloom; blossoms are next scheduled for 2006. Don't blink twice if you see some flowers, though—there are a few plants whose biological clocks are off kilter. Also in Chettiar Park is the **Kurinji Andavar Temple** (dedicated to Muruga), with a splendid panoramic view. *(3km northeast of the bus stand.)*

OTHER SIGHTS. The **Flora and Fauna Museum,** on the grounds of the Sacred Heart College, features a fine orchid house *(follow Law's Ghat Rd. southeast and out of town for 3km; open M-Sa 9:30am-noon and 3-6pm; Rs1).* About 800m past the museum is **Silver Cascade,** a small waterfall along the road to Madurai—you may have caught a glimpse of it on your way into town.

COIMBATORE கோயம்புத்தூர்

Coimbatore is a pulsating industrial center full of modern hotels and cybercafes. Although it has no real tourist attractions aside from a handful of picturesque lakes, the city's bus and railway stations teem with travelers, most of them en route to or from Ooty, Kerala, or Karnataka. You too will probably only spend the night and maybe check your email, leaving most of Coimbatore unexplored.

⚐ ORIENTATION AND PRACTICAL INFORMATION. Though Coimbatore's city limits expand daily with the influx of new residents, the area of interest to travelers transiting through remains fairly self-contained. The north-south thoroughfare of **Bank Road** is home to a number of tourist services. Bank Rd. heads north from the bank; 200m before it hits **Mill Road** (called **Avinashi Road** farther east), it forks: the right fork feeds into Avinashi Rd., while the left fork hits Mill Rd. and continues north as **Dr. Nanjappa Road,** Coimbatore's chaotic main drag.

Coimbatore's **airport** is 10km northeast of the city center. Indian Airlines (tel. 309821) has flights to **Calicut, Chennai,** and **Mumbai. Coimbatore Junction Railway Station** (reservations tel. 131) is in the southern part of the city on Bank Rd. (open M-Sa 8am-8pm, Su 8am-2pm). Fares listed are 2nd/1st class. To: **Bangalore** (*Island Exp.* 6525, 7:45pm, 8½hr., Rs158/490); **Chennai** (*Nilgiri Exp.* 6606, 8:35pm, 9½hr.; *Cheran Exp.* 6674, 10:30pm, 9hr., Rs186/587); **Delhi** (*Kerala Exp.* 2625, 8:20pm, 20hr., Rs572/2246); **Kanyakumari** via Trivandrum (*Trivandrum Superfast* 2625, 5am, Rs96/484); **Madurai** (6707, 4pm, 6hr., Rs115/346); **Mumbai** (*Mumbai Exp.* 1082, 6:05pm, 23hr., Rs332/1391); and **Ooty** (*Nilgiri Exp.* 6605, 5:30am, Rs40).

Three of the city's four **bus stands** are on the northern end of Dr. Nanjappa Rd., 1.5km from the railway station. The northernmost is the **TSTC** and **Karnataka Regional Transport Corp. (KRTC)** stand (tel. 434969), on Cross Cut Rd. just east of the intersection with Bharatiyar Rd. (reservations center open daily 7am-10pm). Buses go to: **Chennai** (every hr. 5:30am-10pm, 12hr., Rs128); **Madurai** (every hr., 6hr., Rs42); **Mysore** (4:30am, 2, and 3pm; 6hr.; Rs50); and **Trichy** (9:30 and 11am, 5½hr., Rs44). Diagonally across the street is the **Town Bus Stand** (known to locals as **Gandhipuram**), providing local service. From here you can catch buses which shuttle between the bus stand area and the railway station (#55, 57, or 24; Rs1). A five-minute walk south on Dr. Nanjappa Rd. will bring you to the well-organized **State (Central) Bus Stand,** with departures to: **Bangalore** (morning and evening departures, 9hr., Rs76); **Mysore** (3 per day, 6hr., Rs29); and **Ooty** (every 30min., 3hr., Rs21). A fourth stand, **Ukkadam,** 1.5km south of the other three, services smaller towns to the south. Buses from Kerala and other southern destinations arrive here. Take bus #38B from Ukkadam to the railway station or a rickshaw (Rs20-300).

State Bank of India, Bank Rd. (tel. 213251) exchanges currency (open M-F 10am-2pm, Sa 10am-noon). **Pharmacies** dot the bus stand and train station area. The 24-hour **KG Hospital** (tel. 212121) is near the Railway station on Art College Rd. There is a **police station** (tel. 216749) on Bank Rd. The **Head Post Office** is on Railway Feeder Rd.; from the intersection of Mill and Dr. Nanjappa Rd., head west and make the first left after Hotel Sri Thevar (open M-F 9am-5:30pm). Access the **Internet** at **Krisan Business Center,** 1 Art College Rd. (tel. 214716), 300m to the right as you face the hospital (Rs40 per 30min.). **Postal Code:** 641001. **Telephone Code:** 0422.

⌂ ACCOMMODATIONS AND FOOD. Coimbatore's best hotels and restaurants are around the bus stands, but there are a few hotels near the railway station. The best option for those who need to catch a train may be the **railway retiring rooms,** upstairs in the station building across from the computerized reservation area. Immaculate and often full, the enormous blue rooms with attached baths are set along a shiny hallway; the only drawback is the noise. (Rooms Rs250-300, with A/C Rs300-350.) A small path directly across the street from the railway station entrance leads to **Hotel Anand Vihar** (tel. 300580). This friendly establishment has basic rooms with baths and squat toilets. (Singles Rs60; doubles Rs110. Extra person Rs20.) **Hotel Tamil Nadu** (tel. 236311), down the street from the main bus terminals on Dr. Nanjappa Rd., has standard rooms (singles Rs195; doubles Rs320, with A/C Rs600; 20% luxury tax). There are also plenty of high-rise hotels in the same price range on Nehru St. and Sastri Rd., opposite the central bus stand. Dining options run the gamut from typically proletarian eateries to gourmet buffets. For the former, head to **Sree Annapoorna,** just south of the State Bus Stand on Dr. Nanjappa Rd. It'll seem like every itinerant traveler in town is here, slurping *sambar* by the bucket. (Meals Rs21. Open daily 7:30am-10pm.) For the gourmet, **Cloud Nine,** at the Hotel City Tower, tosses up Indian, Chinese, and Continental dishes ranging from Rs60 to Rs105 (open daily 11am-3pm and 7-11:45pm). Next door, the **Heritage Inn** has an excellent breakfast buffet for Rs97 (open daily 7:30am-10:30pm).

OOTY (UDHAGAMANDALAM) உஊட்டி

Wrapped in layers of movie legend, the lofty hill station of Ooty provides not only a sublime backdrop for Indian cinematographers but also a paradise for the common vacationer. Established in 1821 by an enterprising collector with the East India Company, John Sullivan, Ooty quickly earned a reputation as an exclusive getaway. The town lost its aura when the film industry began popularizing Ooty's panoramic wealth. No longer the elite retreat Sullivan founded, Ooty is now considered a tourist trap: exhaust fumes sully the crisp mountain air, rubbish defiles the once-pristine valley, and the booming hotel-and-package-tour-industries detract from Ooty's quaint charms. For years, the town has served hordes of middle class Indian tourists as well as the rich and famous.

With a little assiduous exploring, you can discover the friendly, laid-back locals; the lush tea, potato, and carrot plantations; and the mighty Mt. Doddabetta, which, at 2638m, is the closest you can get to heaven in South India. Ooty's season runs from April to mid-June, when temperatures hover around a dry 25°C during the day and nights can be chilly. Monsoon season runs from July to August. Ooty's cold, relatively dry winter stretches from November to March.

▐▀ TRANSPORTATION

Trains: Railway Station, North Lake Rd. Reservations counter open daily 10am-2pm and 3:30-4:30pm. The Blue Mountain Railway (the "toy train") chugs through tea and potato plantations and past waterfalls; like the rest of Ooty, it is often crowded. Fares listed are 2nd/1st class. The steam-powered mini-trains head to **Coonoor** (9:30am, 12:15 and 3pm; return 8, 11am, and 1:30pm; Rs5/53); **Mettupalayam** (3pm, return 7:50am; 4hr.; Rs23/90).

Buses: The **bus stand** is 100m south of the railway station. Regular and private buses operate out of one dusty lot. The departure bays are labeled in English (wow!), and the buses actually use them, most of the time. The **State Transport Company** reservations counter (tel. 494969) is open daily 9:30am-1pm and 1:30-5pm. Make reservations for long-distance buses 2 days in advance. To: **Bangalore** (every 2hr. 6:30am-8pm, 8hr., Rs116); **Chennai** (5:45pm, 8hr., Rs111); **Coimbatore** (every 10min., 3hr., Rs17); **Erode** and **Salem** (10:30am and 5:15pm, 10hr., Rs160); **Mysore** (8am and 3:30pm 5hr., Rs38); **Thanjavur** via **Trichy** (8:15am and 6:15pm, 10hr., Rs80); **Tirupati** (6pm, 12hr.). **Karnataka State Road Transport Corporation (KSRTC)** has a reservations counter open daily 6:30am-10:30pm. To: **Bangalore** (9:45, 10:30am and 10:45pm); **Coonoor** (every 10min. 5:30am-11pm, 30min., Rs4); **Mettupalayam** (every 15min 5:30am-8:30pm, Rs11); **Mysore** (11:30am); **Pykara** (every 15min. 5:30-11pm, Rs5).

Local Transportation: Unmetered **auto-rickshaws** charge at least Rs15 for a ride from the railway station to Charing Cross.

▐ ORIENTATION AND PRACTICAL INFORMATION

Because its streets snake about the valley and surrounding mountainsides, getting around in Ooty can be disorienting. Not to worry: the town is fairly small, and

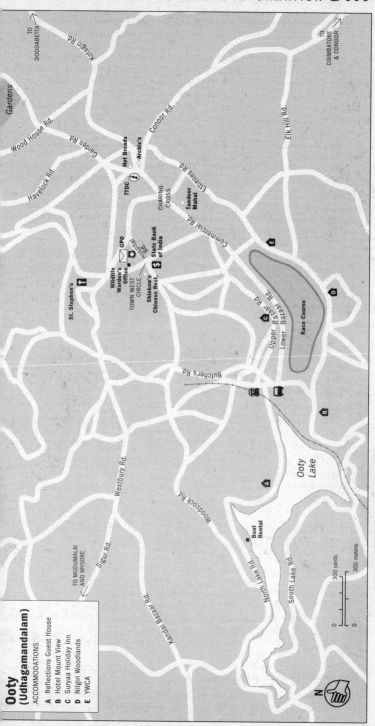

Ooty
(Udhagamandalam)

ACCOMMODATIONS

A Reflections Guest House
B Hotel Mount View
C Suryaa Holiday Inn
D Nilgiri Woodlands
E YWCA

TAMIL NADU

TO DODDABETTA

Kotagiri Rd.

Wood House Rd.

Gardens

Havelock Rd.

Garden Rd.

Hot Breads
Archie's

TTDC

Conoor Rd.

TO COIMBATORE & CONOOR

Elk Hill Rd.

CHARING CROSS

Ettines Rd.

Tandoor Mahal

GPO
Hospital
Wildlife Warden's Office
TOWN WEST CIRCLE

Commercial Rd.

State Bank of India

Shinkow's Chinese Rest.

St. Stephen's

Upper Bazaar Rd.

Lower Bazaar Rd.

Race Course

E

C

D

Butcher's Rd.

B

Westbury Rd.

Woodcock Rd.

Ooty Lake

A

Boat Rental

TO MUDUMALAI AND MYSORE

Sigur Rd.

Kandal Bazaar Rd.

North Lake Rd.

South Lake Rd.

300 yards
300 meters

0

N

locals are accustomed to directing tourists. Ooty's expansive **lake** is in the southwestern part of town, a 200m walk west from the **railway station** and the **bus stand** along **North Lake Road.** From the railway station, walk northeast along **Upper Bazaar Road** for 1.5km to get to **Charing Cross** in the town center. From the bus stand, you can reach Charing Cross by skirting the fruit market via **Lower Bazaar Road,** which becomes **Commercial Road** 750m before hitting Charing Cross. From Charing Cross, follow **Garden Road** 1km north to reach the **Botanical Gardens.** Climb the hill 500m behind Charing Cross to reach **Town West Circle.** From there, **Hospital Road** makes a steep and lengthy westward descent to the railway station area.

Tourist Office: TTDC, Commercial Rd. (tel. 43977), 200m from Charing Cross, provides information and maps. Open M-F 10am-5:45pm. For trekking information and reservations for government accommodations at **Mudumalai Wildlife Sanctuary** (see p. 599), contact the Wildlife Warden (tel. 44098), Town West Circle, next to the police station. Open M-F 10am-5:45pm.

Budget Travel: Tourist agencies are as numerous as *paan* stalls, and they all offer the same unimaginative tours of Ooty and environs. **Thomson Tours and Travels** (tel. 43111), in the strip of stores at Hotel Charing Cross, books plane tickets and bus tours (from Rs75) to nearby cities. Open daily 9am-5:30pm.

Currency Exchange: State Bank of India, Town West Circle (tel. 44099). Changes AmEx and Thomas Cook traveler's checks in U.S. and U.K. currencies. Open M-F 10am-2pm and 3-5:50pm, Sa 10am-noon.

Market: K. Chellaram's, Commercial Rd., has cheddar cheese, toilet paper, eucalyptus oil, and Nilgiri tea. Open daily 9:30am-1:30pm and 3-7:30pm.

Bookstore: Higginbothams, Commercial Rd. (tel. 43736), next to the tourist office. Stocked with *Hobson-Jobson's,* current paperbacks, and the latest installment of the *X-Files* reader. Open Th-Tu 9:30am-1pm and 3:30-7:30pm.

Pharmacy: Commercial Rd. is lined with pharmacies, most of which close at 9pm.

Hospital: Government Hospital, Jail Hill, Hospital Rd. (tel. 42212). **Vijaya Hospital,** Etiennes Rd. (tel. 42500), behind Alankar Theatres. 24hr. ambulance.

Police: Town West Circle (tel. 43973), near the collector's office.

Post Office: Town West Circle (tel. 43791). From the traffic circle, head northwest up the steep staircase on the side of the hill. Post office open M-Sa 9am-5pm. *Poste Restante* and special services M-F 9am-5pm, Sa 9am-2pm. Telegraph Office open M-F 8am-10pm. **Postal Code:** 643001.

PHONE CODE	0423

ACCOMMODATIONS

Seeing that this *is* a resort town, it should come as no surprise that most of Ooty's buildings are hotels. The lake area has more spacious and quieter lodging options.

Hotel Mount View, Etiennes Rd. (tel. 43307). Charming colonial house turned hotel has spacious rooms and pine-wood floors and is strangely reminiscent of the Raj. Seat toilets and hot water in the morning. Doubles Rs300; deluxe Rs800. Off-season: Rs199/400. 20% luxury tax.

The Reflections Guest House, North Lake Rd. (tel. 43834), 500m west of the bus stand. Proprietress Mrs. Dique is legendary in backpacker circles for her scrumptious, home-cooked meals and maternal disposition. Soft beds and woolly flannel bedcovers, wild-flowers, and a lake view make this place sublime. Clean bathrooms with seat toilets. Heat in the winter; hot water 6-11am. Check-out noon. Rooms Rs400-450. Off-season Rs200-250. Reserve 14 days ahead in season.

Surya Holiday Inn, Upper Bazaar (tel. 42567). One of the few decent hotels in the Bazaar and Commercial Rd. area. The cheapest deal within acceptable living standards. 24hr hot water and squat toilets. Check-out noon. Singles Rs125; doubles Rs250. Off-season: Rs75/175.

YWCA, Etiennes Rd., 500m from the racetrack. Sparkling cottages have wicker chairs and seat toilets. Sunlit sitting rooms in the main building offer TV and a piano. Grungy dorms are best avoided. Attached restaurant. Check-out 11:30am. Dorm beds Rs77; cottages Rs300-1040. Off-season: Rs66/195-655.

Nilgiri Woodlands, Etiennes Rd. (tel. 42551), on the southern side of the racetrack, perched on the hill. A mounted bull's head welcomes you to the reception area. Spacious rooms have high ceilings, soft carpets, and antique furniture. Clean attached baths with seat toilets have 24hr. hot water. Rooms Rs450-1150; cottages Rs600. Off season: Rs300-900/500. MC, AmEx, Visa.

FOOD

For a town that's sold its soul to the tourist deities, Ooty has a surprising paucity of top-notch restaurants. Luckily, the few good ones are true culinary gems; you might even find yourself stocking up on goodies to take with you.

Shinkow's Chinese Restaurant, 42 Commissioners Rd., across from the State Bank of India, Town West Circle. Serving mouthwatering, authentic stir-fry to locals and tourists since 1954. The wide range of far-eastern grub includes sliced beef (shhhh!) with broccoli (Rs45/60) and cashew chicken (Rs35/50). Open daily 9am-4pm and 6-10pm.

Hot Breads, Charing Cross, near the international school. Warm, freshly baked breads, pizzas, and pastries. Delectable butter rolls (Rs8), chicken burgers (Rs20), and exquisite slices of chocolate truffle cake (Rs16). Open daily 10am-8:30pm.

King Star, The English Confectionery, Commercial Rd., a few hundred meters from Charing Cross. You'll want to shower the owner with kisses after he offers you free samples (yes, FREE samples) of the deliciously decadent options. The milk chocolate walnut, the fudge, and the mango-flavored chocolate (Rs 30-45 per 100g) are all simply divine. Open daily 11:30am-8:30pm.

Tandoor Mahal, 69 Commercial Rd. The interior is classier than the generic yellow sign suggests. Efficient service. Perfectly polished silver pitchers, but don't drink the water. Serves *tandoori* and Chinese cuisine (veg. Rs20-40, non-veg. Rs50-100). Open daily 9:30am-3:30pm and 6:30pm-midnight.

Archie's Fast Foods, Charing Cross. A hole in the wall (literally) near the intersection of Commerical and Coonoor Rd. Spicy "frankies" (chicken, mutton, or vegetable curries wrapped up in *parathas* (Rs25), vegetable and mutton burgers, pizza (Rs25), and shakes (Rs15). Open daily 10:30am-7:30pm.

ENTERTAINMENT AND SHOPPING

If at all occupied, **bars** in Ooty usually have just a few men in the corner. A somewhat cheerful watering hole is the bar at **Hotel Charing Cross** (tel. 44387), where you can drain a Kingfisher for Rs40 (open daily 11am-11pm).

Atari-era refugees might one of several **arcades** along Commercial Rd. **Moodmaker's** is near the Charing Cross Hotel, beyond the brandy shop (open daily 10am-9:30pm). A bit farther down the street, at 49 Commercial Rd., is the subterranean **Missing Link**, where denizens dish out Rs1 for a game of Pac-Man, Super Mario Bros., or Tetris (open daily 10am-6pm). About 750m up from Moodmaker's on Garden Rd. is **Assembly Movie Theater**, which screens dated American flicks (2:30 and 6:30pm; Sa 2:30, 6, and 8:30pm; Rs2-12). The **Race Course**, near the bus stand, is a 1¼-mile loop where jodhpured jockeys run their horses to the delight of riotous but low-betting crowds. Races are held from April to June.

Shopping in Ooty focuses upon locally made body oils and textiles. **The Big Shop** (tel. 44136), halfway between Charing Cross and the Lower Bazaar on Commercial Rd., sells Toda tribal shawls (Rs200-300), silver jewelry, and handicrafts. They

A WILD LIFE Covered in dense deciduous forest and rolling hills, the **Mudumalai Wildlife Sanctuary** is home to nearly 800 wild elephants and 25 tigers, as well as panthers, leopards, bears, hyenas, parakeets, and eagles—and one renegade, cop-killing gentleman-poacher, the infamous **Veerappan.** Although Mudumalai was closed for much of 1998 officially due to drought and monsoon, informed locals from Ooty to Bangalore gladly divulge the real story behind the sanctuary's closing.

Veerappan "the Bandit" is said to have roamed the park since childhood, emerging as a poacher or a sandalwood smuggler, and most recently as a well-connected criminal with a cadre of assistants. One of his favorite activities, when he and his crew aren't killing police officers sent to capture them, is hijacking tour buses. After commandeering a busload of nature-lovers, he serves everyone tea and biscuits (so that they can enjoy his hospitality), refuses any offers of jewelry or money, and releases almost everyone except for government officials. This tendency is naturally rather irksome to law-and-order types, who have tried arresting and bargaining with Veerappan's friends and relatives, all to no avail—the bandit remains at large, though lately his nefarious activities have become less frequent. Still, a mention of the name "Veerappan" is sure to elicit a few amused smiles and the latest scoop on his antics.

accept traveler's checks, MC, Visa, and AmEx. (Open daily 8am-9pm.) A **Tibetan Refugees' Market,** along Garden Rd. near the Botanical Gardens, has many stands selling mohair sweaters and all the colorful wool blankets you'll need to brave Ooty's freezing winter nights (open daily 6am-8:30pm).

👁 SIGHTS

BOTANICAL GARDENS. Ooty's Botanical Gardens, a 22-acre oasis of flora to please landscaper and layperson alike, were originally established in 1847 and then spruced up in 1995. A century and a half after their inception, they are as green as ever. With more than 2000 species on display, the gardens have come a long way from their original purpose of producing "English vegetables at reasonable cost." From the vivid colors of the rose garden (India's largest), to the many quiet, well-sculpted knolls surrounding the park, the whole serene area is gorgeous. A **flower show** during the third week of May is a veritable carnival of flowers. *(Open daily 8:30am-6:30pm. Rs5; camera fee Rs25, video Rs500.)*

OTHER SIGHTS. Just west of the railway station and bus stand is Ooty's lily-filled **lake,** constructed in the 1820s by the ever-enterprising John Sullivan *(rowboats and pedal boats Rs40 per 30min.; boat house admission Rs2, camera fee Rs5).* Near the boat house is a miniature train *(Rs5 for a whirl).* Horse rentals near the lake are officially Rs100 per hour, but if you feign indifference they might come down to Rs50. On the way to the boathouse you'll pass a **children's playground** with jungle gyms and topiaries *(Rs1, camera fee Rs3).*

NEAR OOTY: COONOOR குன்னூர்

Separated from Ooty by only 18km, this sister hill station is easily accessible from the city (see **Ooty: Practical Information,** p. 594); it's getting to the sights that's a little. The railway station and bus stand are in Lower Coonoor, the town's center of commerce (and traffic). There are a few inexpensive accommodations here, but most of the attractions are in the posher Upper Coonoor. Local buses go to most sights, but it might be easier to hire a taxi so you can take your time and not be at the mercy of mass transport. Coonoor's response to Ooty's Botanical Gardens is **Sim's Park,** located high on a hill on the road to Kotagiri, 3km from the Coonoor bus stand. Set in a small ravine, the park displays a variety of flora not found in Ooty. (Open daily 8am-6:30pm. Rs5, Rs2 for children; camera fee Rs5, video Rs25.) Eight kilometers from Lower Coonoor is **Dolphin's Nose,** a rock formation affording views of a gaping, waterfall filled gorge. Buses depart from Coonoor to Dolphin's Nose (7 per day 7am-4:15pm). **Lamb's Rock,** 12km from Lower Coonoor, overlooks the Coimbatore plains far below. Buses run to Lamb's Rock (4:45 and 6:45pm). Travel around Coonoor invariably involves traversing tea plantations; for those with piqued pekoe passions, several **tea factories** in the area offer tours, and in January there's a week-long **Tea and Tourism Festival.** For more information, contact the Public Relations Department of the United Planters' Association of South India (tel. 30270), in Upper Coonoor.

NEAR OOTY: PYKARA டைகாரா

Twenty kilometers west of Ooty lies the tranquil village of **Pykara,** the perfect place for those who long for the hills. A small boathouse on Pykara's lake rents out boats and sells snacks for visitors to munch on while floating on the placid water (boats Rs50-100 per 30min.). Near the lake is the **Pykara Dam,** 2.5 km downstream, with an attractive series of rocky **waterfalls** which gush most impressively in July and August. All buses to Gudalur from Ooty pass through Pykara (every 30min. 6:30am-9pm). If you're up for the climb, the 9km hike up **Mt. Doddabetta** offers a level of detail you won't get from an aisle seat of a tour bus (trail open daily 8:30am-5:30pm, 2hr. long). No visit to Ooty's surrounds would be complete without a **Filmy Chakkar** ("Film Trip"), a tour of scenic spots where romantic pairs have frolicked before Bollywood's cameras. The recently re-opened **Mudumalai Wildlife Sanctuary,** of Veerappan fame (see **A Wild Life**), is worth the slow-moving bus ride; who knows, you might just spot a wild elephant while you're there (Rs25).

TAMIL NADU

ANDHRA PRADESH

ఆంధ్రదేశము

The state of Andhra Pradesh occupies a large portion of southeastern India, from the dry Deccan Plateau to the coast of the Bay of Bengal, where the Krishna and Godavari Rivers feed into rich, cyclone-drenched deltas. Inland lies Telangana, the poorer region of Andhra Pradesh. The state is named for the kingdom of the Andhras, also known as the Satavahanas, who ruled most of the Deccan from the 2nd century BC until the 3rd century AD. As part of Emperor Ashoka's vast kingdom, the region was also a major Buddhist center. Beginning in the 16th century, Andhra Pradesh was ruled by Muslims, first under the Golconda Sultanate, then as part of the Mughal Empire, and finally under the Nizams, who ruled from Hyderabad under British protection from 1723 until 1948. In spite of religious differences that might separate them, the people of Andhra are bound together by their language, Telugu. In 1956, Andhra Pradesh became the first state in India to have its boundaries drawn along linguistic lines. When India gained Independence in 1947, the Nizam of Hyderabad refused to cede his lands to the new nation. After a year-long standoff, the Indian government forcibly annexed the territory, which was later merged with other Telugu-speaking areas to form Andhra Pradesh. Though one of the least touristed destinations in India, the state is home to a number of superb attractions worth visiting.

HIGHLIGHTS OF ANDHRA PRADESH

■ Unpretentious **Hyderabad's** bazaars and monuments (p. 608) complement the spooky ruins of **Golconda Fort** (p. 606), west of town, and the gorgeous marble **Birla Mandir** (p. 607) atop Naubat Pahar hill.

■ A visit to **Tirupati's** hilltop temple frenzy (p. 610) reveals an interesting facet of contemporary Hinduism and then thrills with a harrowing bus ride down to calmer climes.

HYDERABAD హైదరాబాదు

Let millions of men and women of all castes, creeds, and religions make it their abode, like fish in the ocean.
—Muhammad Quli Qutb Shah, upon laying Hyderabad's foundation

The story of Hyderabad's origins stands as a testament to the overwhelming power of love across boundaries in a country plagued by religious strife. The city was founded in the late 16th century by Muhammad Quli Qutb Shah, Sultan of Golconda. Though he was to ascend to the throne of one of the great kingdoms in India, the young Muhammad had fallen in love too hard and too fast to heed religious and social barriers; his love, Bhagmati, was a beautiful Hindu dancer and singer. Muhammad risked his life and inheritance making midnight horseback journeys from Golconda to a village on the banks of the Musi River to tryst with the beautiful Bhagmati. Upon discovering his son's infatuation, Muhammad's father relented, allowing his son to marry the common Hindu girl. The boy became king and founded a new city on the banks of the Musi and christened it Bhagnaga

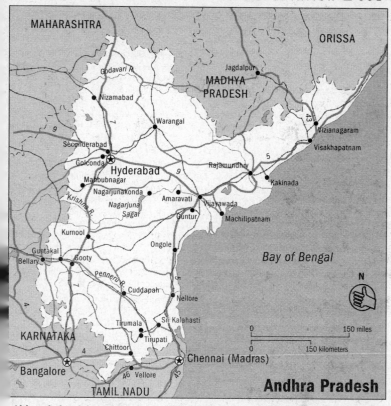

MAHARASHTRA

ORISSA

Godavari R.

Jagdalpur

MADHYA
PRADESH

Nizamabad

Warangal

Vizianagaram

Visakhapatnam

Secunderabad

Golconda

Hyderabad

Rajamundhry

Mahbubnagar

Kakinada

Nagarjunakonda

Amaravati

Vijayawada

Krishna R.

*Nagarjuna
Sagar*

Guntur

Machilipatnam

Kurnool

Ongole

Bay of Bengal

Guntakal

Bellary

Gooty

N

Penner R.

Cuddapah

Nellore

0   150 miles

Tirumala

Sri Kalahasti

0   150 kilometers

KARNATAKA

Tirupati

Chittoor

Vellore

Chennai (Madras)

Bangalore

Andhra Pradesh

TAMIL NADU

Although the city was later renamed Hyderabad and Golconda is now in shambles,
the city's syncretist tendencies remain legendary.

Today, this sparkling metropolis of five million has the highest proportion of
Muslims of any city in the south; ironically, it was one of the few urban centers
that did not erupt in riots following the 1992 destruction of the Babri Masjid in
Ayodhya. The Muslim Nizam of Hyderabad ruled over a Hindu-majority state until
his death in the 1950s. The city's architecture is not only impressive (the last
Nizam was reputedly the wealthiest man in the world, and he liked to show it), but
also a masterful embodiment of Indo-Saracenic character. While Hyderabad used
to be noted for its relatively clean streets and mellow pace, recent years have seen
increasing congestion and urbanization, with all the related benefits and problems. A huge new bus station and plans for an international airport have solidified
the city's status as the travel and tourism hub of Andhra Pradesh—you won't need
to take a midnight horseback ride to get here—but the increased traffic has quick-
ened drivers' tempers and dirtied the streets. Nevertheless, the beautiful Muslim
monuments and traditional bazaars of the Old City rightly make Hyderabad a popular tourist destination.

TRANSPORTATION

Airport: Begumpet Airport (enquiry tel. 140, recorded flight information tel. 142), on the
north side of Husain Sagar, off Sardar Patel Rd. 8km north of Abids. Auto-rickshaws go
to Abids (Rs65 fixed). Taxis cost twice as much. **Airline offices: Air Canada, Air France**
(tel. 230947), **Gulf Air** (tel. 240870), **Kuwait Airways** (tel. 234344), **Royal Jordanian,**
and **TWA** (tel. 598774), all in the same building, 500m north of Basheer Bagh. **Bang-**

ladesh Biman (tel. 598775), Flat 202 Gupta Estate, Basheer Bagh. **Lufthansa,** 3-5-823 Hyderguda Rd. (tel. 235537), to the right off Basheer Bagh Circle. **Delta Airlines, Jet Airways** (tel. 330 1222), **Singapore Airlines** (tel. 331 1144), and **Swissair** all in the Navbharet Chambers, Raj Bhavan Rd. **KLM Royal Dutch Airlines,** 3-6-284 Hyderguda Rd. (tel. 322 7351). All open M-F 9:30am-5:30pm, Sa 9:30am-1:30pm. **Air India,** 5-9-193 HACA Bhavan (tel. 237243), opposite the Public Gardens. Open M-Sa 9:30am-1pm and 1:45-5:30pm. **Indian Airlines,** Secretariat Rd. (tel. 236902 or 141), opposite Assembly Saifabad. Open daily 10am-1pm and 2-5:15pm. 25% discount for travelers under 30. Flights to: **Ahmedabad** (3 per week, 1½hr., US$150); **Bangalore** (3 per day, 1hr., US$95); **Bhubaneswar** (M, W, and F; 1½hr.; US$145); **Calcutta** (2 per day, 2½hr., US$190); **Chennai** (3 per day, 1hr., US$95); **Delhi** (3 per day, 2hr., US$185); **Mumbai** (5 per day, 1hr., US$105); **Tirupati** (Tu and Th, 1hr., US$75).

Trains: There are tourist quotas at each of Hyderabad's three **stations** (centralized enquiry tel. 7833541): **Secunderabad, Nampally** (in Abids) and **Kachiguda** (east side of Sultan Bazaar). Trains stop at multiple stations. Enquiry counters at the stations open 24hr. Reservations (tel. 135) open M-Sa 8am-8pm, Su 8am-2pm. Fares listed are 2nd/1st class. To: **Bangalore** (*Secunderabad-Bangalore Exp.* 7085, 7:15pm (Secunderabad) and 7:48pm (Kachiguda), 11½hr.; Rs220); **Chennai** (*Hyderabad-Chennai Exp.* 2760; 7pm (Nampally) and 7:30pm (Secunderabad), 13½hr., 2nd class Rs275); **Delhi** (*Andhra Pradesh Exp.* 2723, 6:45am (Nampally) and 7:15am (Secunderabad), 37hr., Rs200/965); **Mumbai** (*Hussainagar Exp.* 7001, 2:30pm (Nampally), 23hr., Rs406/1280); **Tirupati** (*Krishna Exp.* 7406, 5:30am (Nampally) and 6am (Secunderabad), Rs145/700; *Narayandri Exp.* 7424, 6:10pm (Secunderabad), 14hr., Rs245/787).

Buses: The new **Imlibun Central Bus Stand** (enquiry tel. 461 4406), across the Musi River from the old station, proclaims itself to be Asia's largest. You'll believe it as you wander its 73 platforms. Open 24hr. Deluxe to: **Bangalore** (every 30min. 4:30am-9:15pm, 12hr., Rs220); **Chennai** (4:30pm, 14hr., Rs276); **Hospet** (every 3hr., 8hr., Rs154); **Mumbai** (7pm, 16hr., Rs362); **Nagarjunakonda** (every hr., 4hr., Rs60); **Tirupati** (9 per day 2:30-8pm, 14hr., Rs220).

Local Transportation: Buses are typically packed until overflowing—you'll need turbo-*chappals* to catch one. Terminals located at Nampally, Nurkhan Bazaar, near the Charminar, and Secunderabad Railway Station. From Secunderabad Station to Nampally: #2 and 8A. From Nampally to Golconda Fort: #119 and 142N. **Auto-rickshaw** *wallahs* are disarmingly civil; most use the meter without even trying to milk you (Rs6 for 1km, Rs3 per km thereafter). **Taxis** are unmetered and twice as expensive.

✳ ORIENTATION

The **Musi River** divides the **Old City**—containing the Charminar, Mecca Masjid, and bazaars—from the **New City** of government offices, glitzy downtown shops, and glimmering Birla-commissioned landmarks to the north. The **Abids** area forms the heart of the New City, about 1.5km south of the gargantuan, Gautama-guarded **Husain Sagar,** the artificial lake built during the Golconda empire, and it contains **Hyderabad (Nampally) Station,** one of the area's transport hubs. The other hub is in **Secunderabad,** to the northeast of Husain Sagar, where the **railway station** sends travelers in and out of the city.

🛈 PRACTICAL INFORMATION

Tourist Office: Government of India Tourist Office, 2nd fl. Sandozi Building, Himayatnagar (tel. 763 0037); from Basheer Bagh, the office is 750m down the road, on the left. A useful source for information and advice regarding travel throughout India. Free Hyderabad city map. Open M-F 9:30am-5:30pm. The **Andhra Pradesh Tourism Development Corporation Ltd.** (tel. 781 6375), adjacent to Lumbini Park Tank, Bund Rd. Open daily 10:30am-6pm.

Budget Travel: Sita World Travel, 3-5-874 Hyderguda Rd. (tel. 233629; fax 234223) next to Apollo Hospital. Coming from Abids Circle to Basheer Bagh, take a right. Open

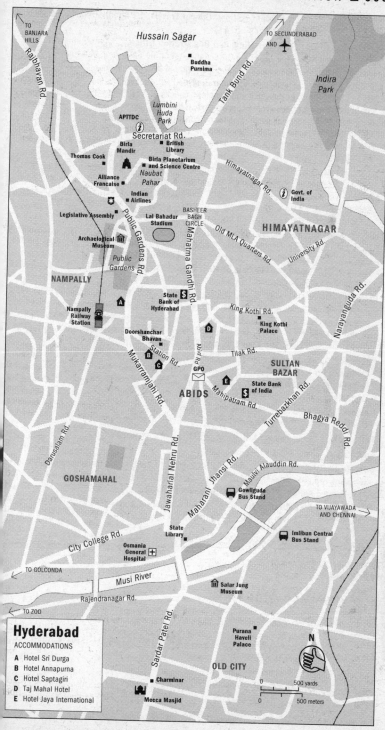

TO BANJARA HILLS

Raibhavan Rd.

Hussain Sagar

TO SECUNDERABAD AND

Buddha Purnima

Indira Park

Lumbini Huda Park

Tank Bund Rd.

APTTDC

Secretariat Rd.

Birla Mandir

British Library

Thomas Cook

Birla Planetarium and Science Centre

Himayatnagar Rd.

Govt. of India

Alliance Francaise

Naubat Pahar

Indian Airlines

HIMAYATNAGAR

Legislative Assembly

Public Gardens Rd.

Lal Bahadur Stadium

BASHEER BAGH CIRCLE

Old MLA Quarters Rd.

University Rd.

Archaeological Museum

NAMPALLY

Public Gardens

A

State Bank of Hyderabad

King Kothi Rd.

King Kothi Palace

Narayanguda Rd.

Nampally Railway Station

Doorshanchar Bhavan

Mahatma Gandhi Rd.

D

Station Rd.

B

C

Abid Rd.

GPO

Tilak Rd.

SULTAN BAZAR

ABIDS

E

State Bank of India

Mukarramjahi Rd.

Mahipatram Rd.

Turrebazkhan Rd.

Bhagya Reddi Rd.

Danusalam Rd.

GOSHAMAHAL

Jawaharlal Nehru Rd.

Maharani Jhansi Rd.

Maulvi Alauddin Rd.

Gowliguda Bus Stand

TO VIJAYAWADA AND CHENNAI

City College Rd.

State Library

Imlibun Central Bus Stand

Osmania General Hospital

TO GOLCONDA

Musi River

Sardar Patel Rd.

Rajendranagar Rd.

Salar Jung Museum

TO ZOO

Purana Haveli Palace

N

Hyderabad

ACCOMMODATIONS

A Hotel Sri Durga
B Hotel Annapurna
C Hotel Saptagiri
D Taj Mahal Hotel
E Hotel Jaya International

Charminar

Mecca Masjid

OLD CITY

0   500 yards

0   500 meters

ANDHRA PRADESH

M-F 9:30am-6pm, Sa 9:30am-1:30pm. **Omega Travels,** 13 Buddha Bhavan Complex, MG Rd., Secunderabad (tel. 782 5111).

Immigration Office: Foreigners Regional Registration Office, Commissioner of Police, Purana Haveli Rd. (tel. 809715), 500m southeast of the Salar Jung Museum. Registration fee Rs150. Visa extensions US$5-100. Open M-Sa 10am-5pm. Closed 2nd Sa.

Currency Exchange: State Bank of Hyderabad, MG Rd. (tel. 320 1594), 700m north of Abids Circle. Changes currency and traveler's checks M-F 10:30am-2:30pm, Sa 10am-noon. In Secunderabad, **Synergy Forexpress,** 62 Sarojini Devi Rd. (tel. 780 6854), near Gangaram's. Changes all currencies for no commission. Guaranteed 5min. exchange or your money back. Open daily 9am-7:30pm. **Thomas Cook,** 6-1-57 Saifabad (tel. 329 6521), near the junction of Secretariat and Public Gardens Rd. Changes 30 currencies and traveler's checks. Rs20 charge per exchange. Open M-Sa 9:30am-5:30pm.

Bookstore: AA Hussain & Co., 5-8-551 Arastu Trust Building, Abid Rd., Abids (tel. 320 3724). An international paperback collection, including copies of the book you now hold in your hands. Open M-Sa 10am-8:30pm. **Walden,** 6-3-871 Greenlands Rd., Begumpet (tel. 331 3434), between Abids and the airport, in the Vivekananda Hospital complex. One of the best-stocked bookstores in South India. Open W-M 9am-8:30pm.

Library: State Central Library, Turrebaz Khan Rd. (tel. 500107), near Osmania General Hospital. Open daily 8am-8pm. **British Library,** 5-9-22 Sarovar Centre, Secretariat Rd. (tel. 230774). Members-only, but policy is don't ask/don't tell. Open Tu-Sa 11am-7pm. **Henry Martyn Institute of Islamic Studies Library,** Chirag Ali Lane (tel. 201134). Open M-F 9:30am-4:30pm.

Cultural Centers: Bharatiya Vindya Bhavati, 5-9-1105 King Kothi Rd. (tel. 237825), off Basheer Bagh Circle. Holds classical and popular dance and music concerts, often for free. Check *Channel 6* for details. **Alliance Francaise,** Adarshnagar (tel. 236646), next to the Birla Science Centre. Two weekly movies, plus cultural events and short-term French courses. Open M-F 9am-1pm and 3-6pm, Sa 9am-1pm.

Pharmacy: Apollo Pharmacy, in the Apollo Hospital Complex. Open 24hr. **Medwin Hospital Pharmacy** (tel. 320 3820), off Station Rd. on Chirag Ali Ln., in a tall building visible even from the Nampally Railway Station. The pharmacy is inside the lobby to your left. Open daily 24hr.

Hospital: Apollo Hospital Medical Center, Jubilee Hills (tel. 360777), north of Abids. Open daily 24hr. **Gandhi Hospital** (tel. 770 1089), near Secunderabad RS.

Police: Abids Circle Police Station (tel. 230191), to the right as you face the GPO.

Emergency: Police, tel. 100. **Ambulance,** tel. 102.

Post Office: GPO, Abids Circle (tel. 474 5978). *Poste Restante* in the back left corner of the main room. Stamps upstairs on the right. Open M-Sa 8am-8:30pm. *Poste Restante* M-F 10am-3pm, Sa 10am-1pm. **Postal Code:** 500001.

Internet: Zen Computerdrome, Bluechip Arcade, Himayangar (tel. 322 6631; email rajesh@hd1.vsnl.net.in), 100m east of the tourist office, on the right. Rs80 per hr. Open daily 7:30am-10:30pm.

Telephones: Telegraph Office, Abids Circle, adjoins the GPO on the left. Open 24hr.

PHONE CODE	040

▸ ACCOMMODATIONS

Budget dives are 10-paise-a-dozen in the upscale Abids area. There are a few lodges around the Secunderabad Railway Station, but the area is grungy and there's no reason to stay there unless you have a morning train to catch. Almost all hotels have attached restaurants.

ABIDS

Hotel Jaya International, 4-1-37/A&B Reddy Hostel Rd. (tel. 475 2929). Facing the GPO in Abids Circle, bear left along Mahipatram Rd., then make a left at the Dhanalakshmi

Bank. The best value for its price, with huge windows, seat toilets, and showers. Check-out 24hr. Singles Rs240, with A/C Rs525; doubles Rs300-350/630. Visa, MC, AmEx.

Taj Mahal Hotel, 4-1-999 King Kothi Rd. (tel. 237988). Walk away from the GPO in Abids Circle and veer right after 200m. One of Hyderabad's most popular hotels. Large, well-kept rooms have gleaming mirrors and polished floors. TVs, direct-dial phones, seat or squat toilets, 24hr. hot water. Check-out 24hr. Singles Rs300, with A/C Rs500; doubles Rs400-425/750. 5% luxury tax. Visa, MC, AmEx.

Hotel Saptagiri, 5-4-651 Nampally Station Rd. (tel. 460 3601), down a narrow dirt road opposite the CLS Bookshop. Scrubbed and polished through and through. Well-lit rooms have TVs, too. Is this good enough for you? Balconies, telephones, seat toilets. Check-out 24hr. Singles Rs170; doubles Rs215.

Hotel Annapurna, 5-4-730 Nampally Station Rd. (tel. 473 2612), near Hotel Saptagiri, sandwiched between a slew of electronics stores. Overwhelmingly pink (but otherwise unexciting) place has TVs, direct-dial phones, and towels. Star-shaped rooms have faux-leather couches and seat toilets. Check-out 24hr. Singles Rs220-240; doubles Rs300, with A/C Rs530. 5% luxury tax.

Hotel Sri Durga, Public Garden Rd. (tel. 202286), on the left corner up the street from the rail station. Friendly staff tries to make up for the slightly unsavory location. Groovy green walls enclose slightly dirty rooms. Cheap, and it shows. Squat toilets. Hot water 6-9am. Check-out 24hr. Singles Rs100; doubles Rs165.

SECUNDERABAD

Hotel Sitara, 7-1-2, SPG Church Complex (tel. 770 0308). From the Secunderabad station, veer diagonally left. By far the cleanest and friendliest hotel in the area. Broad, well-lit hallways, tiled bathrooms with flush squat toilets, balconies, and spacious rooms. 24hr. hot water. Singles Rs165; doubles Rs225, with air-cooling Rs270.

National Lodge, 9-4-48 Syed Abdulla St. (tel. 770 2622), opposite the Secunderabad station. Basic rooms have narrow beds, tube lighting, and no hot water, but rooms and bathrooms are relatively clean, and the management is polite. Check-out 24hr. Doubles with bath Rs100.

◖ FOOD

Traditional Andhra cuisine demands iron taste buds or stubborn stoicism. Either way, you'll never have clogged sinuses in Hyderabad. To ease your pain, delve into one of the ubiquitous bakeries that have popped up in the past few years or gorge at one of the many four-star cosmopolitan restaurants in the Abids area.

Taj Mahal, King Kothi Rd. off MG Rd., is a Hyderabad legend for good reason: it's cheap, comfortable, and generous with portions of South and North Indian favorites. *Masala dosa* costs Rs12 in the regular section and Rs18 in the cushy, hygienic, A/C section. No smoking or alcohol. Tiffin 7am-9:30pm. Open daily 11am-3:30pm and 7-10:30pm.

Palace Heights, 8th fl., Triveni Complex, Abids Rd., 500m north of the GPO, just before King Kothi Rd.; look for the blue neon sign. Opulent decor suits the paintings of past maharajas on the walls. Fabulous city views and an elaborate array of gourmet Chinese, Indian, and Continental entrees (Rs70-125). Open daily 11:30am-3pm and 7-11pm.

Blue Diamond, 100m south of Basheer Bagh circle. Chinese food as authentic as it gets here. Wide selection includes Manchurian prawns (Rs100), Hong Kong chicken (Rs90), and sweet-and-sour pork (Rs80). Open daily 10:30am-3:30pm and 6:30-10:30pm.

The Terrace, adjoined to the Birla Science Museum. Outdoor dining patio and elegant enclosed area (if outside gets too rowdy) and an impressive array of Chinese and Indian cuisine. Garlic kebab (Rs115), Cantonese chicken (Rs125). Open daily 12:30-11pm.

Minerva Coffee Shop, 3-6-199/1 Himayat Nagar, from MG Rd., on the right. A chi-chi veg. joint where *dosas* come in avatars such as veg. cheese (Rs23). Huge *puris* (Rs18). Prompt servers weave between the rows of potted plants as locals gossip away. Minerva Special Ice Cream Rs45. *Thalis* 11am-2:30pm and 7-9:30pm. Open daily 7am-11pm.

🎵 ENTERTAINMENT

Hyderabad is justly proud of its myriad cultural events, including dance programs, *ghazal* sessions, and plays. **Ravindra Bharati** (tel. 233672), in the Public Gardens, stages about four events per week. Hyderabad unofficially claims more than 100 **cinemas.** The best English theaters are **Sangeet,** 23 Sardar Patel Rd., Secunderabad (tel. 770 3864), and **Skyline,** 3-6-64 Basheer Bagh Rd., Hyderabad (tel. 231633). There are usually three shows per day, and balcony seats cost Rs25. The **Alliance Francaise** (tel. 236646), screens two flicks per week: one French, the other German or English. The **Hyderabad Film Club** (tel. 290265), has weekly screenings at the Sarathi Studio Preview Theatre in Ameerpet, north of Banjara Hills. *Channel 6,* a weekly publication, is the best source of information for upcoming events.

As Hyderabad only recently repealed its prohibition law, the **bar scene** is just getting off the ground. **One Flight Down** (tel. 320 4060), in the Residency on Public Garden Rd., is fairly popular, and many other five-star hotels are planning their own watering holes. For a different kind of liquid refreshment, try the **Ritz Hotel,** Hill Fort St., Basheer Bagh (tel. 233570), where you can swim in the same **pool** as the Nizam's privileged guests (open daily 3-7pm, Rs60 per hr.). If you can't handle the sultry mid-mornings, there is also a pool at the **Taj Residency,** Rd. No.1, Banjara Hills (tel. 339 9999; Rs150 per hr.; open daily 7am-7pm).

👁 SIGHTS

GOLCONDA FORT

8km west of the city. Open daily 7am-8pm. Sa-F Rs2, Su free; video fee Rs25. 1hr. sound and light show in the central courtyard daily 7pm, Nov.-Feb. 6:30pm; adults Rs25, children Rs15. English show on W and Su.

The erstwhile headquarters of the Qutb Shahi kingdom from 1512 to 1687, the fort is Hyderabad's most popular attraction. In its heyday, the Golconda empire stretched to the Bay of Bengal; now the circumference of the fort is a mere 7km. Crushed and annexed after two sieges by the Mughal emperor Aurangzeb, the kingdom was, at its zenith, a thriving center for arts and learning, as well as a bastion of religious tolerance. At dusk, the crumbling ruins, shrieking bats, and sheer drops marking the path to **Durbar Hall** make you look over your shoulder, half expecting to see specters of the Qutb Shahi Kings. Durbar Hall is a 1000-step climb that takes a mere half-hour. At the top there is a panoramic view of the ramparts below and Hyderabad's other landmarks: you can make out the Birla Mandir and the Charminar in the distance to the east, near the horizon (squint hard).

The fort is best toured counter-clockwise. On the way up, visitors follow the path used by the common people during the fort's heyday; the steep descent leads down a route once used exclusively by the king and his pallbearers. Visitors first pass through the heavily studded **Balahisar Gate,** which served as the first line of defense against invaders. Just ahead, past some small exhibits, lies the **Grand Portico,** where guides are often seen clapping to demonstrate the fort's acoustics: Golconda was engineered so that a clap at the summit of Durbar Hall would reverberate at five places along the inside perimeter of the fortress wall. A clap at the center of the Grand Portico can be heard at the summit, 1km away. This built-in communication system was used to notify the king of any visitors even though they were still far off. Continuing straight ahead leads to the covered **bodyguard barracks.** Ahead and to the right is the **Nagina Bagh,** a royal garden. From the gardens, a stone staircase begins the ascent to the summit. At the foot of the steps, on the right, one can see the 12m deep **water tank,** one of three within the fort. The water came from a natural spring and was transported by a complex system of limestone pipes, the stumps of which can still be seen today.

Durbar Hall commands spectacular views of Hyderabad and Secunderabad. Unfortunately, much of the interior has been defaced by visitors' carving their names into the walls. The summit is also home to the 12th century Hindu **Sri Jagad-**

ANDHRA PRADESH

PISCINE PLACEBO Every year in early June, thousands of asthmatics flock to the outskirts of Hyderabad to the home of the Battina Gowd brothers. The reason: they dispense an ancient ayurvedic cure that involves ingesting a live fish wrapped in herbs. According to a loose interpretation of Vedic texts, the live fish squirms around inside the body, clearing up breathing passages. But there's an added benefit: the fish is said to be a heat-generating agent and a preventive measure for the coughs and colds that accompany the beginning of the monsoon season in early June. To accommodate the demand for this treatment, the Indian government has arranged extra trains to Hyderabad during the fish camp season. It's difficult to gauge the fish's effectiveness, but many patients report a decrease in attacks and return annually to have the slimy little suckers shoved down their throats. The treatment is free, so the masses will probably continue to come.

amba Temple (the garish paint is a more recent addition). From Durbar Hall, one must descend the king's staircase almost entirely before reaching the next sight. At the foot of the hill there is a water tank, and around the corner are the **Rani Mahals,** a series of buildings once occupied by the king's harem and their bodyguards. A somewhat functional fountain graces the central courtyard, where the daily sound and light show is held. Once upon a time, these buildings were decorated with curtains, mirrored glass, and jewels. Now, a colony of bats occupies the main building, and the once-lush gardens have been overtaken by weeds. Passing through the Rani Mahals takes you by the **Taramati Mosque** to the three-story arched **arsenal.** There are only a few dusty guns and cannonballs inside, but authorities are in the process of converting the building into a museum that will doubtless feature, well, dusty guns and cannonballs.

OTHER SIGHTS

QUTB SHAHI TOMBS. Housing the remains of seven of the dynasty's patriarchs (each of whom supervised his own tomb's construction), the Qutb Shahi tombs play an undeserved second fiddle to the more frequently visited Golconda Fort. They are magnificent architectural specimens in amazingly good condition. Locals frequent the area to stroll among the elaborate structures or picnic in the gardens. Each tomb is built on a square base and capped with a Muslim-style onion dome, but adorned with Hindu motifs like lotus friezes and leaves. The synthesis of styles testifies to the empire's religious tolerance and cultural syncretism. The cenotaph in the center of the tomb draped in a sheer cloth, covers the real crypt below. Labels in English describe the history of the king buried within each and some of the structural attributes of his tomb. Though the tombs have a similar shape, each bears the distinctive mark of its designer. The grandest tomb is that of **Sultan Muhammed Quli Qutb Shah,** which is surrounded by gardens criss-crossed by waterways. Farthest from the entrance, the tall, thin tomb of **Jamshid Qutb Shah** commands views of Golconda and other ruins from its terrace. The complex also contains a mortuary bath, where bodies were ritually cleansed before being buried. Next door, a small **museum** contains a variety of artifacts from Qutb Shahi times: ceramics, weapons, and beautiful hand-written texts. The portraits of the Qutb Shahi kings allow you to finally place names with faces. (1km north of Golconda Fort. *Open 9am-4:30pm. Rs2. Museum open Sa-Th 9am-1pm and 2-4:30pm; Rs2, camera fee Rs5, video Rs25.)*

ALL THINGS BIRLA. The **B.M. Birla Science Centre and Archaeological Museum** atop Naubat Pahar hill offers enough activities for many a rainy (or sunny) day. Upstairs is the technologically advanced **Science Center,** with hands-on experiments for the curious kid in you. Downstairs is an impressive archaeological section, with excavations from Vaddamanu dated between 100 BC and 200 AD, wood and stone sculptures, and miniature paintings. *(Open daily 10:30am-8:15pm, closed last Tu. Rs8.)* Exit to the right and climb the stairs leading to the domed **Birla Planetar-**

ium, where you can learn all about stars and aliens *(Tel. 241067; 3 English shows per day; closed last Th. Rs12; combined ticket to the planetarium and the museum Rs18).* Across the street from the planetarium is the spectacular **Birla Mandir,** dedicated to Lord Venkateshwara. Commissioned by the industrial kings of India and built over 10 years, it affords awesome views of Hyderabad and Secunderabad. The temple's elevation and the pure white Rajasthani marble against the blue of Husain Sagar paint a sublime picture, and the serenity is unmarred by shoe-touts or alms-driven priests. At night, the whole structure is illuminated. *(Open daily 7am-noon and 2-9pm.)*

CHARMINAR. The four-minaret Charminar is Hyderabad's most enduring and recognizable landmark. The edifice was built by Muhammed Quli Qutb Shah in 1591 to celebrate the end of an epidemic which had been plaguing the city. An image of the four towers graces every packet of Charminar cigarettes—it's said that the last Nizam of Hyderabad refused to smoke any other brand. There's not much to see in the building, since you're no longer allowed to climb the 149 steps to the small mosque on top, but a prime bazaar area surrounds it.

MECCA MASJID. Like the Charminar, the Mecca Masjid was built during the sultanate of Muhammad Quli Qutb Shah, but after Golconda's fall, completion of the mosque was left to Aurangzeb. Fourteen hundred bullocks were supposedly needed to haul the granite slabs that form the colonnaded entrance from a quarry 11km away. Named for the few bricks from Mecca embedded in its central arch, the mosque is the largest in Hyderabad, accommodating up to 10,000 people at Friday prayers. Before entering the Mecca Masjid, check your *chappals* at the podium on the left (Rs5) and walk through a pavilion containing the tombs of various Hyderabad nizams. *(2km south of the Musi River on Sardar Patel Rd.)*

SALAR JUNG MUSEUM. The imposing white Salar Jung Museum is touted as one of the world's largest collections amassed by a single individual but is actually the work of three generations of Salar Jungs, each of whom served as the nizam's *wazir* (prime minister). The museum is huge and well-stocked with everything from gorgeous Chola sculptures to mediocre European oil paintings. Room 14, the Ivory Room, displays a solid ivory chair given to Tipu Sultan by Louis XV. Room 17 has some marvelous modern paintings by premier Indian artists including Ravi Varma and K. Hebbar. In Room 18, next door, you can trace the chronological and regional evolution of Indian miniature painting. *(CL Badari Malakpet, south of the Musi River. Tel. 523211. Open Sa-Th 10am-5pm. Rs6. Free guided tours depart from the office on the right as you enter.)*

OLD CITY. The back streets of the Old City, with their distinctly Muslim flavor, are arguably the most "Hyderabadi" part of Hyderabad. Along these streets are some of the most sacred pilgrimage sites for Shi'a Muslims, each housing a revered *alam*, a heavy banner into which gold, gemstones, and precious objects are woven. Ask a local to show you to the **Biha ka alawa,** which protects a bright green shrine within its whitewashed walls. The *alam* is said to contain pieces of a wooden plank upon which the Prophet Muhammad's daughter bathed. Not far away is the **Sar tauq ka alawa,** which houses an *alam* containing portions of the shackles and chains in which the fourth *imam* was bound.

HUSAIN SAGAR. Visitors to Hyderabad cannot escape noticing Husain Sagar, the 6.5km by 800m tank whose blue waters provide a pleasant backdrop to the city's landscape. Historians say that the tank was constructed during the Golconda Empire, but some believe that the tank's origin is far less mundane. Legend has it that the tank was promised hundreds of years ago by a *sadhu* who collected large sums of money from the thirsty population. Weeks passed and no construction had begun, prompting the people to confront the *sadhu*, who then promised to undertake the project or return their money. The next morning, a shimmering tank was in place, and the *sadhu* had disappeared. The magic continued in the 1980s, when a monolithic **Buddha statue** was built (amid a lot of hype) and then placed on a barge for transport across the artificial lake. It promptly sank into the water, dragging down seven people with it. Several years ago, the statue was retrieved from the bottom intact, no damage having been inflicted by the accident. The only real park on the lake is **Lumbini Huda Park**. Though small, it is nicely landscaped and well-maintained. Boats are available for tours or do-it-yourself jaunts. A musical fountain chimes away on three separate occasions every night. *(Just off Secretariat Rd., near Public Gardens Rd. Open Tu-Sa 9am-9pm. Rs2. Boats available Tu-Su 9am-6pm; 4-person motorboat with driver Rs70, paddle boats Rs10.)*

 SHOPPING

The bazaars around the Charminar in the Old City are the best places to hone your bargaining skills. The **Laad Bazaar,** extending west from the Charminar, is renowned for its bangles and exquisite wedding fashions. Step into a shop and take a look at the heavily embroidered *kamdani* dresses for women or the regal, sultan-esque caps for men. People from all over India make a trip here for pre-nuptial purchases. If you're not into buying jewelry (strands of imperfect pearls for Rs100-500) and armfuls of bangles (around Rs25 per set), then just stroll around and look into the stalls where craftsmen hand-pound sheets of silver foil. Most of the shops in the Old City are open from 10am to 7pm; some observe Friday as a holiday. Emporia line the roads in the Abids area. **Kalanjali Arts and Crafts,** Hill Fort Rd. (tel. 231147), across from the Air India office, is not too expensive (open daily 9:30am-8:30pm).

NAGARJUNAKONDA (NAGARJUNASAGAR) నాగార్జునకొండ

The ruins of one of the largest Buddhist monasteries and learning centers in South India lie 150km southeast of Hyderabad and about 20m underwater. Excavations in 1926 first revealed evidence of *stupas*, *chaityas*, and other artifacts dating back to the 2nd century BC. Much later, in the 1950s, plans to build a dam on the Krishna River adjacent to the site spurred government archaeologists to resume digging. The most important ruins were evacuated, brick-by-brick, to a nearby hill before the dam was finished in 1966. Today, a lake occupies the original site, and the island of Nagarjunakonda now supports both the rebuilt structures and a museum. Nagarjuna, a first-century Buddhist scholar, had no problem meditating in the sleepy village nearby, and neither would you, but don't expect to find much else to do. Visitors typically head from the ferry straight to the **museum,** which features a range of sculpture, friezes, and other artifacts, all accompanied by detailed description in several languages (open Sa-Th 9am-4pm). The rebuilt **ruins** are somewhat anticlimactic, but each has a sign describing the purpose of the original structure. Nearby is the **Ethipothala Waterfall,** a popular picnic spot.

The **Nagarjunasagar Dam** is the axis around which the village revolves. The lake is to the west, and the **Krishna River** runs to the east. To the north lies **Hill Colony,** home to the better tourist hotels and the **bus stand.** The nearest **train station** is in Macherla, 13km east of the dam, but Vijayawada is better serviced. **Buses** depart from Nagarjunasagar (14km from the ruins in Nagarjunakonda) to Hyderabad (every hr., 4hr., Rs60); Tirupati (7:30am and 1:30pm, 13hr., Rs150); and Vijayawada (7am and 1pm, 4hr., Rs60). The **boat launch** is on the opposite end of the dam at Vijayapuri South (ferries Sa-Th 9:30am and 1:30pm, 45min., Rs20; returns 12:15 and 4:15pm). Buses are your best bet for getting back to Hill Colony. The APTDC **tourist office** (tel. 76634; open Sa-Th 9am-6pm) is opposite the bus stand in Project House (Sagara Paryataka Vihar). The **police station** (tel. 76533) and **post office** are nearby. **Postal Code:** 508202. About 6km south of Hill Colony, just before the dam, is Pylon Colony, with a number of **STD/ISD** booths. **Telephone Code:** 08680. The best rooms in town are those in Hill Colony run by the APTDC. **Project House** (tel. 76540) has clean double rooms with squat toilets (Rs150). The **Vijay Vihar** complex (tel. 76633), 2km north, has more spacious doubles with A/C, attached baths, and seat toilets (Rs300-400). Both have 24-hour check-out and dining halls.

TIRUPATI తిుపటీ AND TIRUMALA తిుమల

Red rock hills covered with lush greenery form the backdrop to the temple of the Sri Venkateshwara at Tirumala, the most popular pilgrimage site in South India. Built in the 11th century by the founder of the Sri Vaishnava sect, the temple constantly swarms with thousands upon thousands of Hindu pilgrims, each of whom must be housed, fed, and herded around—a task relegated to Tirupati, the town located 20km down the hill. Thriving off the economic activity provided by its divine neighbor, the town's shops sell flowers and trinkets and its lodges and restaurants compete for customers. Although Sri Venkateshwara is one of the few temples in India that allow non-Hindus into the inner sanctum, it is not visited by many foreigners. Aside from the temple, there's little to do or see, and battling the crowds for *darshan* of the image can be nerve-racking and physically exhausting. If you're not a devout Hindu, make your trip on a weekday, preferably Tuesday, in order to escape the weekend rush; avoid the months of June and September, and any public holidays.

🗷 **ORIENTATION AND PRACTICAL INFORMATION.** Tirupati's **airport** is 12km from the city. **Indian Airlines** (tel. 25349; open daily 10am-5pm), in the Hotel Vishnupriya complex opposite the Tirumala bus stand, flies to **Chennai** (Tu, Th, and Sa 1:30pm; 20min.; US$35) and continues to **Hyderabad** (1hr., US$75). The **railway station** (enquiry tel. 131) is in the heart of town, near the Govindaraja Temple. The reservations counter (tel. 25850) is across from the station, next to the bus stand (open M-Sa 8am-8pm, Su 8am-2pm). Fares listed are for 2nd/1st class. Trains to: **Chennai** (*Saptagiri Exp.* 6054, 9:30am and 5:30pm, 3hr., 2nd class Rs176); **Chidambaram** (*Meenakshi Exp.* 6799, 3:40pm, 10hr., Rs148/465); **Hyderabad** (*Rayalaseema Exp.* 7430, 7pm, 12hr., Rs245/787); **Mumbai** (*Balaji Exp.* 7494, Th and Su 9:40pm, 24hr., 2nd class Rs321); **Thanjavur** (*Meenakshi Exp.* 6799, 3:40pm, 12½hr., Rs182/571); and **Tiruchirapalli** (*Meenakshi Exp.* 6799, 3:40pm, 14hr., Rs194/680). The **APSRTC bus station** (tel. 22333) is 500m from the center of Tirupati. Buses travel to: **Bangalore** (every 30min., 5½hr., Rs180); **Chennai** (every 15min., 4hr., Rs55); **Hyderabad** (4 per day, 12hr., Rs240); **Nagarjunakonda** (6pm, 12hr., Rs165); **Pondicherry** (3pm, 6hr., Rs56); and **Vijayawada** (4 per day, 10hr., Rs142). The **Tirumala bus stand**, 250m from the railway station, sends a constant stream of buses up the hilltop along Alipiri Rd. (Rs15). Be prepared for a long wait, and buy a round-trip ticket to avoid waiting again on the way back. The bus ride to Tirumala takes 45 minutes on curvy roads (57 hairpin turns) with insane driving—you might consider taking a taxi (Rs50 shared). The **tourist office** (tel. 23208), near the bus stand, offers daily tours of the area (open daily 10am-5pm; tours Rs200, not including admission fees). The **State Bank of India** (tel. 20699) accepts major traveler's checks. Follow the road opposite the Bhimas Deluxe Hotel, and take the first right. (Open M-F 10am-2pm, Sa 10am-noon.) Gandhi Rd. fronts the **police station** (tel. 20352) and the **post office** (tel. 22103; open M-F 10am-5pm, Sa 10am-2pm). **Telephone Code:** 08574.

🗷🗷 **ACCOMMODATIONS AND FOOD.** All of the good hotels are in Tirupati. The only option in Tirumala is the Devasthanam dormitory rooms, which offer the barest minimum. Rooms are free but usually full; if they are, then you'd best head back to town. The **Bhimas Hotel**, 42 G Car St. (tel. 25744), about a block from the railway station, is popular with Indian pilgrims because of its reasonable price and prime location. The rooms aren't spectacular, but the place is generally clean and fans make sure things stay cool in the dry Andhra heat. The attached baths have thoroughly disinfected squat toilets. (Singles Rs75, deluxe Rs150; doubles Rs175 with A/C Rs550.) One kilometer away are the white towers of **Hotel Bliss**, Renigunta Rd. (tel. 21650), the town's most luxurious hotel, with four-star accommodations for an unexpectedly low price: singles Rs425, with A/C Rs700; doubles Rs495-850; deluxe Rs1150 (5% luxury tax; MC, Visa, AmEx). Aside from some grubby *dhabas*, the best **restaurants** are attached to hotels in Tirupati. Dining in Tirumala only for those eager to wait in line with thousands of others to eat questionably hygienic (but free) food slapped onto a banana leaf. In Tirupati, the **Bhimas Deluxe** has a popular, subterranean restaurant that offers the usual North and South Indian fare. It has odd hours to accommodate pilgrims returning from Tirumala. **Surya,** Hotel Mayura's vegetarian restaurant, serves fresh North and South Indian food (Rs20-45; open daily 9am-10pm).

█ SIGHTS. Receiving the *darshan* of Lord Venkateshwara (Balaji) at the **Sri Venkateshwara Temple** in Tirumala is something that most devout Hindus hope to experience at least once during their lifetime. It is believed that any wish made at the temple will be granted by Lord Venkateshwara. For this reason, pilgrims flock here by the thousands each day, many expending their scant resources for the lengthy trip to this tiny town. Visits to the temple begin in Tirupati, where buses shuttle passengers along a winding mountainside road to Tirumala and deposit them at the top of the hill; you'll have to follow the crowds past vendor stalls, bathing areas, and pilgrims' quarters to reach the vicinity of the temple. Don't be surprised to find a large number of people with shaved heads, as pilgrims to Tirupati commonly make a sort of barber-barter agreement with God: hair in exchange for some favor. If you're willing to lose your locks, tonsuring stations will gladly do the job in assembly-line fashion. (Not surprisingly, the area around Tirupati is home to a flourishing wig industry.)

Near the temple grounds, large billboards proclaim the different types of *darshan* available. Regular *darshan* comes at no cost, but often entails a wait of 12 hours or more. The "special *darshan*" queue (Rs30) will reduce your waiting time to two to four hours, depending on the crowds; follow the signs for **Sarvadarsham.** Do not rely on middlemen to purchase your tickets, as scams are common; head directly to the appropriate temple office. Before entering the temple grounds, you'll have to leave your shoes with a shop owner for a few rupees. The wait to enter the temple—even in the "special *darshan*" line—involves passing through a network of narrow wire cages. You'll be pressed into constricted passageways with hundreds of other pilgrims. Once you've entered the line, you'll have little idea of where you're going or how much farther you have to inch along. Just rest assured that a few hours later, you'll round the corner to the home stretch.

Although it's hard to appreciate the temple's structural attributes while you're being jostled on all sides, the interior contains some impressive sculpted columns. The *vimana* is fully covered with gold, and its dazzling brilliance is testimony to the wealth of the temple. After the long wait in line, *darshan* will seem exceptionally short. Temple workers will yell at you in Telugu as they yank your arm to force your exit. If they recognize you as a (wealthy) foreigner, the workers may pull you aside, giving you extra *darshan* time in exchange for *baksheesh*. The impressive image wears a gold crown and is covered with flowers so that not much is visible, save for the mask of Vishnu drawn clearly on its forehead. The last leg of the visit takes you to the *prasad* line, where workers dish out free food consecrated by Lord Venkateshwara. Opposite the temple is a small, unremarkable **museum** (open M-F 8am-8pm; Rs3). If you feel rather like an amusement park patron after all the waiting in line, the roller-coaster bus descent will not disappoint. But there's no need to fear for loss of life or limb; you've got Lord Venkateshwara on your side. Temple open daily 24hr.

ORISSA ଓଡ଼ିଶା

The sea has had a major influence on Orissan history and continues to play a central role in the lives of almost all who live here. The Bay of Bengal licks the state's coastline for 482km, nearly all of Orissa's urban residents live within rock-throwing distance of the Mahanadi River Delta, and most of its rural population toils in half-submerged rice paddies. Every morning, fishing fleets fight the pounding surf in their narrow wooden boats—a far cry from images of the maritime prowess of the Kalingas and other local dynasties that once ruled these high seas and sent colonists as far as Java. In the hills of the Eastern Ghats, thick forest cover has allowed *adivasis* (tribal peoples) to survive relatively undisturbed.

Although unequivocally a part of modern India, Orissans have defended their independence for thousands of years. The Kalingas held out against the expanding Mauryan Empire in the 3rd century BC, capitulating only after a battle so bloody that it convinced Emperor Ashoka to renounce violence and convert to Buddhism. Orissa also withstood Muslim rule until 1568, almost 400 years after surrounding regions had been conquered. Orissa's cultural autonomy throughout the centuries has led to the development of the distinctive art forms for which it is hailed, including its style of Hindu temple architecture and the *odissi* form of dance.

Today Orissa is one of India's most uniformly Hindu states, with over 95% of the population professing the religion (and worshipping first and foremost Lord Jagannath, a local version of Krishna whose primary temple is in Puri). Prone to cyclones and heavy monsoons that wreak havoc on crops, the state is also one of India's poorest. The poverty, however, can be difficult to detect amid the fertile greens that color the countryside.

HIGHLIGHTS OF ORISSA

■ Edged by the Bay of Bengal, **Puri** (p. 621) gracefully juggles dual roles as religious center and beach-side resort.
■ Temple-packed **Bhubaneswar** (below) showcases the unique beauty of the region's varied and intricate Hindu architecture.
■ **Konark** (p. 619), the third point of Orissa's "Golden Triangle" of tourism, is the site of the spectacular **Sun Temple** and a wonderfully tranquil beach.

BHUBANESWAR ଭୁବନେଶ୍ୱର

Promoted for good reason as "the temple city," Bhubaneswar has Hindu temples comprise the finest such assemblage anywhere. As the capital of powerful maritime dynasties that ruled the Bay of Bengal's coast, Bhubaneswar was the center of trade and commerce for over a thousand years in the area now known as Orissa. Members of the Hindu ruling classes erected the finest devotional structures money could buy; with their patronage, temple architecture became a highly developed art form. Under Muslim and British rule, however, neglect reduced many of the monuments to rubble. Reborn as the new capital of Orissa in 1950, Bhubaneswar grew a modern appendage—urban planners built monumental bureaucratic warrens along wide, shaded avenues, and the preservation of the old town's remaining temples became not only a religious, but also a civic imperative. Today, Bhubaneswar exhibits both the outward characteristics of a modern state capital and the enduring spirit of the majestic kingdom that was classical Orissa.

⊟ TRANSPORTATION

Airport: Bhubaneswar Airport (tel. 406472 or 401084), northwest of the temples in the Old Town. Cycle- and auto-rickshaws Rs50. **Indian Airlines** (tel. 400533 or 400544

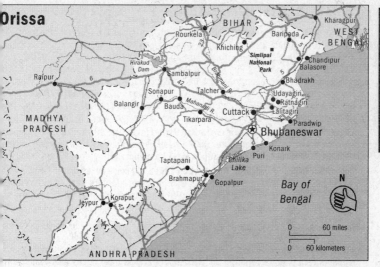

across the street from Capital Market. Open daily 10am-1pm and 2-4pm. Flights to: **Kolkata** (6 per week 8:30 and 9am, 1hr., US$75); **Chennai** (Tu, Th, and Sa 1:30pm; 2hr.; US$180); **Delhi** (10:30am, 2hr., US$195); **Hyderabad** (M, W, and F; 2hr.; US$145); **Mumbai** (M, W, and F 4:35pm; Tu and Th 2:35pm; 2hr.; US$225).

Trains: Bhubaneswar Railway Station, Station Sq. (reservations tel. 502042). Make enquiries at the 2nd-class booking counter (tel. 402233). Tourist quota available. Fares listed are 2nd/1st class. To: **Kolkata** (*Dhauli Exp.* 2822, 2:20pm; *Puri-Howrah Exp.* 8008, 9pm, Rs209/1043; *Sri Jagannath Exp.* 8410, 11pm, 9hr., Rs90/490); **Chennai** (*Coromandel Exp.* 2841, 8:45pm, 20hr., Rs339; *Chennai Mail* 6003, 4am, 25hr., Rs285); **Delhi** (*Purshottam Exp.* 2801, 9:55pm, 32hr., Rs157/767); **Hyderabad** (*East Coast Exp.* 8045, 7pm; *Falaknuma Exp.* 7703, Tu, F, and Su 2:50pm, 19hr., Rs263/960). Frequent trains to **Puri** (1½hr.).

Buses: Baramunda New Bus Station, NH5 (tel. 526977), 9km from Raj Mahal Sq. Buses to: **Balasore** (every 10min. 4:30am-10pm, 4hr., Rs55); **Berhampur** (6 per day 5-11am and 3pm; 4hr.; Rs50, deluxe Rs55); **Kolkata** (4:15, 6, and 6:30pm; 13hr.; Rs120); **Cuttack** (every 15min., 1½hr., Rs6.50); **Konark** (every 30min. 6am-5pm, 2hr., Rs14); **Puri** (every 15min.; 1½hr.; Rs13, express Rs14). Buses also depart from **Kalpana Sq.**

Local Transportation: Minibuses cover all the major streets (Rs2-3). A useful route runs from the front of the Kalinga Ashok Hotel to the Baramunda Bus Stand, passing the bank and airline office on the way. Most **cycle-rickshaw** *wallahs* will settle for 50% of the price first quoted. **Auto-rickshaws** are unmetered—*wallahs* will grudgingly take Rs5 per km. **Taxis** in front of larger hotels and the OTCD office Rs25 per km in town.

ORIENTATION

Bhubaneswar consists of the well-planned and spaced-out **New Town** to the north and the temple-packed **Old Town** to the south. Large roads like the north-south **Jan Path** and **Sachivalaya Marg** and the east-west **Raj Path** cut the New Town into neat squares called **nagars**, or **units**. Units have numbers, while *nagars* have names. **Station Square,** in front of the railway station with a horse statue in its roundabout, is the closest thing to a city center in Bhubaneswar. To the west and north of Station Sq. are **Ashok** (Unit 2) and **Kharavela Nagar** (Unit 3), containing most shops and services. Many hotels are located around Station Sq., but the cheaper ones are at **Kalpana Square,** located at the junction of **Cuttack Road** and Raj Path, to the south. The haphazardly laid out Old Town, south of Kalpana Sq., has no main road. The **Bindu Sagar** tank is in its center and the tall **Lingaraj Temple** lies south of it.

ORISSA

🛈 PRACTICAL INFORMATION

Tourist Office: Government of Orissa Tourist Office, 5 Jayadev Nagar (tel. 431299), off Puri Rd. to the south; it's 50m down on the left. Open M-Sa 10am-5pm. Counters at the airport (tel. 404006) and railway station (tel. 530715) open 24hr. **OTDC** (tel. 432282), on the corner of Puri Rd. and Jayadev Nagar, behind the Panthanivas Tourist Bungalow, arranges cheap, rushed tours of Bhubaneswar, Puri, and Konark. Contact Transport Unit Panthanivas (tel. 431515). **Government of India Tourist Office,** B-21 Kalpana Sq. (tel. 432203). From the railway station, take the last left before the fork that leads to Puri Rd.; it's on a side road 750m on the right. Open M-F 9am-6pm.

Budget Travel: Swosti Travels, 103 Jan Path (tel. 508526; fax 520796; email swost@cal.vsnl.net.in), next to the Hotel Swosti. From Station Sq., walk north on Jan Path. Reputable and professional. Open M-Sa 7am-7pm.

Immigration Office: Foreigners Registration Office, District Intelligence Bureau, Sahid Nagar (tel. 403399). From Station Sq., 3km north on Jan Path to the Jan Path-NH5 intersection. The FRO is on the left inside the police station. Open M-Sa 10am-5pm.

Currency Exchange: State Bank of India, Main Branch, Raj Path (foreign exchange tel. 403810 or 404994). A short walk from Raj Mahal Sq., on Raj Path, across from Capital Market. No commission. Open M-F 10am-3:30pm, Sa 10am-12:30pm.

Market: Capital Market, Unit 2, Raj Path, across from Indian Airlines. Handicrafts, clothing, and fresh produce. Open Tu-Su 10am-8pm. TLC and other necessities available at the **Mom and Pop** store, past Panthanivas on the right. Open daily 7:30am-10:30pm.

Library: Harekrishna Mahtab State Library and **Bhubaneswar Public Library,** Sachivalaya Marg (tel. 404315). From Station Sq., head northwest on MG Marg to Sachivalaya Marg. Turn right; the library complex is 300m on the left, across from Keshari Talkies. Open M-F and alternate Sa 9am-8pm.

Bookstore: Modern Book Depot (tel. 502373), on the right side of Station Sq. Wide selection of maps and books about Orissan history and culture presided over by a knowledgeable owner. Open M-Sa 9am-1pm and 4-9pm.

Pharmacy: Iswar Medical, Ashok Nagar (tel. 400359), half a block north of Raj Mahal Sq. Open daily 9am-10pm. **Capital Hospital's** pharmacy is open 24hr.

Hospital: Capital Hospital, Unit 6 (tel. 400688 or 401983). From Raj Mahal Sq., go south on Jan Path. After 1 long block, turn right and head west on Udyan Marg past its intersection with Sachivalaya Marg. A wee bit to the left is the 24hr. **government hospital** with English-speaking staff. **Ayurvedic Hospital,** Malisha Sq. (tel. 432347), east of Vivekananda Marg, across from the Brahmeswar Temple.

Post Office: GPO, PMG Sq. (tel. 406340), on the corner of MG and Sachivalaya Marg. Head from the horse statue in Station Sq. across Jan Path. Inside the courtyard, on the right. *Poste Restante* at window #6. Open daily 10am-5pm. **Postal Code:** 751001.

Internet: Com-Cyber Tech, Ashoka Market (tel. 425180), on the southeast corner of Station Sq. Internet access (Rs2 per min., 10min. minimum) and email (send only, Rs20 per page). Open M-Sa 9am-6:30pm.

Telephones: The railway station's **STD/ISD** booth is open 4am-midnight. **Central Telegraph Office,** inside the GPO. Open daily 8am-8pm.

PHONE CODE	0674

🛏 ACCOMMODATIONS

Bhubaneswar—and Orissa in general—has become a hip destination, and hotels have evolved to meet the demands of foreign travelers with deep pockets.

🏨 **Hotel Raj Mahal,** Raj Mahal Sq. (tel. 532448), at the corner of Jan and Raj Path. Centrally located. Airy hallways lead to clean, cool rooms with balconies and attached baths. Singles Rs110; doubles Rs170-200. Extra person Rs20.

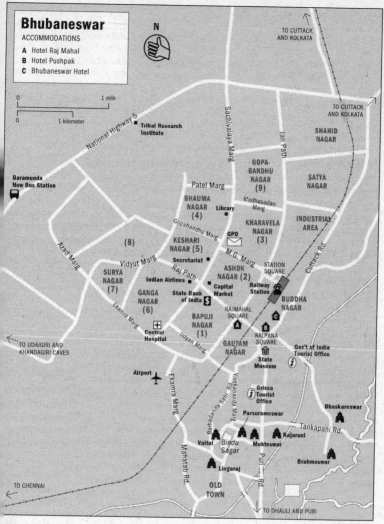

Bhubaneswar

ACCOMMODATIONS

A Hotel Raj Mahal
B Hotel Pushpak
C Bhubaneswar Hotel

ORISSA

Hotel Swagat, Cuttack Rd. (tel. 416686 or 425879). Exit the east side of the railway station (not the main exit facing Station Sq.), turn right, and walk 5min. Clean rooms, affordable prices. Restaurant inside. No visitors after 10pm. Singles Rs125; doubles with bath Rs200, with TV Rs250-300, with A/C Rs550; triples with TV Rs300.

Hotel Pushpak, Kalpana Sq. (tel. 415545 or 415943). At the corner of Raj Path and Cuttack Rd. Parties sometimes spill out into the hallway from large, clean, and well-ventilated rooms. Restaurant and full bar downstairs, complete with color TV blaring Hindi hits (open 11am-11pm). Room service brings drinks until midnight. Singles with bath Rs100; doubles with bath Rs150, with A/C and TV Rs350.

Bhubaneswar Hotel, Cuttack Rd. (tel. 416977), past Swagat. This deservedly popular hotel won Bhubaneswar's best budget accommodation award in 1997. Small, well-appointed rooms. Mosquito nets available. Attached restaurant (*thalis* Rs40-60) and travel counter (air and train bookings). Singles with bath Rs125, with TV Rs300; doubles Rs175-200, deluxe with A/C Rs550; triples Rs250-275. 8% service charge.

FOOD

Bhubaneswar is the perfect place to sample traditional Orissan cuisine, served in small *ginas* arranged on a large *thali*. This toned-down version of South Indian food is lightly spiced. The entirety of Jan and Raj Path, culminating in the Kalpana Sq. area, offers delicious veg. and non-veg. choices for under Rs50.

Hotel Suruchi, Market Building, Capital Market, several blocks northwest of Raj Mahal Sq., across from the State Bank of India. The perfect place to refuel after browsing the wares of the daily market. Stuff your stomach with the Suruchi Special (Rs24)—a scoop of rice with *puri* and *ginas* swimming in spicy, strictly veg. South Indian sauces. Speedy service and highly recommended by locals who know. Open daily 7am-10:30pm.

Hare Krishna Restaurant, Lalch and Market Complex, Master Canteen, across from Hotel Jajati. From the railway station, head towards Station Sq. and turn right. Run by adherents to the faith whose name it bears, this is reputedly the best veg. deal in town. Full veg. *thalis* Rs20-40. No alcohol. Open daily 11am-3pm and 7-10pm.

Cook's Kitchen/Restaurant, 260 Bapuji Nagar. South on Jan Path from Station Sq.; take the third left past Raj Mahal Sq. Street-side "take away" kitchen offers full-flavored curries (from Rs18) and vividly clean, A/C restaurant (1st fl. of Blue Heaven Hotel) has savory *navartana* curry (Rs25). Open daily 10:30am-10:30pm.

Shanti Restaurant, 50 Ashok Nagar, Jan Path (tel. 531041), one flight up. A quiet, A/C family restaurant as peaceful as its name. Bar upstairs. A huge menu with a variety of soups (Rs20-40), *dal* fry (Rs12), and tasty kebabs (from Rs60), as well as Chinese and Continental selections. Open daily 10:30am-11pm.

SIGHTS

It is said that there are more ancient **temples** in Orissa than in the rest of North India combined. While more famous and monumental temples stand in Puri and Konark, Bhubaneswar has Orissa's most extensive collection. The temples' sculptures, carved between the 7th and 12th centuries under several Hindu dynasties, tell the story of Hinduism's resurgence—the frequent depiction of a lion pouncing on an elephant represents Hinduism's triumph over Buddhism. Lakulisa, a 5th-century Shaivite saint who converted many Orissans, also appears frequently on temple walls. Most of Bhubaneswar's temples are dedicated to Shiva, whose cult remains an important part of the lives of most in the region. The densest concentration of temples, around the center of the Old Town, can be explored in a few hours. Guides roam the temple circuit soliciting customers, but they are of little use. Certified **guides** can be hired from the state tourism office. Be wary of the men with a "temple register" listing contributions made by foreign visitors—it's a scam.

The temples are in the Old Town, south of the Railway Station; most of the major temples are in the area around the Bindu Sagar. All are open from dawn to dusk. Many temples officially have an entrance fee of Rs2, but it is rarely collected.

LINGARAJ TEMPLE. Bhubaneswar's biggest bunch of flags flies atop the Lingaraj Temple, to the south of the Bindu Sagar. The Lingaraj is one of Orissa's great temples, notable especially for the balanced placement of sculpture on its 45m spire. Built around AD 1100, it has a full four-chambered temple structure: a sanctum (under the spire), a porch, a dance hall, and an offering hall. Shiva is worshipped here in the form of Tribhubaneswar (Lord of Three Worlds), Bhubaneswar's namesake. The temple's name, however, is derived from an earlier name for Shiva. The temple compound contains a jungle of ornate stonework—more than 50 smaller temples are strewn around the main one. The second-largest temple in the compound, in front of the main temple to the right, is devoted to Shiva's consort Parvati. The entire compound is closed to non-Hindus, but the British built a **viewing platform** right next to the wall, providing tourists with a peek inside.

PARSURAMESWAR TEMPLE. The oldest and best-preserved of the early group of Orissan temples, the boxy 7th-century Parsurameswar Temple exhibits many of the common features of early temples, including a small, squat *shikhara* and an uncarved roof over the porch. The window-like shapes that frame many of its sculptures derive from an even earlier artistic element used in Buddhist temple architecture. Standing sentinel at the back of the temple, on the left side of the rear entrance, is a *linga* with 1000 tiny *lingas* carved into it. *(From the New Town, turn down the road to the left just before the Bindu Sagar; the temple is not far on the left.)*

MUKTESWAR TEMPLE. The Mukteswar Temple was built 300 years after the Parsurameswar Temple. Here, in contrast to the Parsurameswar's single building, a whole landscape of small monuments rises from the complex, which has a bold, U-shaped archway in front and a lotus carved into the porch's ceiling. The Mukteswar is considered one of the finest Orissan temples, both for its carvings and its well-preserved condition. *(A short walk down the road from the Parsurameswar Temple.)* From the Mukteswar Temple, turn left past the trinket stands and cold drink shops to reach the whitewashed and very active **Kedareswar Temple.**

RAJARANI TEMPLE. Originally named for the *raja* (red) and *rani* (yellow) stones from which it was constructed, this 11th-century, now-defunct temple is administered by the Archaeological Survey. The *shikhara* is multiplied in the *shekhari* style, with miniature *shikharas* projecting from it on all sides. Though common in other parts of India, this type of tower is rare in Orissa. The carvings of the *dikpalas*, the guardians of the eight points of the compass, are the best around. These ancient Vedic gods stand stiffly holding flags, thunderbolts, and nooses. *(Up the road behind the Mukteswar Temple, after a right on Tankapani Rd.; after a 5min. walk, you'll see the temple on the right, at the back of a rectangular park.)*

BHASKARESWAR AND BRAHMESWAR TEMPLES. The chunky **Bhaskareswar Temple** is no artistic triumph but it contains a 3m-high *linga* encased in what is thought to be a 3rd-century BC Ashokan column. Wander down a cow-trampled lane to the right after the Bhaskareswar Temple to the 9th-century **Brahmeswar Temple,** unfortunately closed to non-Hindus. The temple has smaller Shiva shrines at the four corners of its compound. Some of the carvings depict temple dancers who were "married" to the deity here; they worked in the temple, often having to perform "favors" for local men in exchange for contributions to the temple. *(A short rickshaw ride down Tankapani Rd., past the sewage canal.)*

VAITAL TEMPLE. The Vaital Temple, sunk in the ground at a crossroads on the western side of the Bindu Sagar, differs stylistically from Bhubaneswar's other temples. Its oblong, rounded *shikhara* was adapted from principles of Buddhist temple design that had become obsolete by the time the other temples were built. Take a flashlight with you to illuminate the gory carvings inside, depicting scenes of human sacrifice and the skull-clad goddess Chamunda with her attendant owl

---

ORISSAN TEMPLE ARCHITECTURE

Orissa's Kalinga kings staved off temple-razing Muslim invasions until 1568, allowing the development of a distinctive style of architecture. Orissa boasts some of the most exquisite examples of old stone Hindu temple design in northern India.

The most important part of the temple, the *deul* (inner sanctum) housed an image of the deity. It was crowned by a huge, pyramidal *shikhara* (spire) and, above that, a lotus-shaped stone called an *amlaka*. On top was a small pot and the deity's weapon—a trident for Shiva temples and a discus for Vishnu. Adjoining the *deul* was a rectangular *jagamohana* (assembly hall). Bigger temples added more rooms in single file behind the *jagamohana*: first a *nata mandir* (dance hall), then a *bhoga mandir* (offering hall). Aside from the consecrated images in the sanctum, the symbols depicted in temple sculpture were either relevant to the temple itself (as with images of guardian figures) or illustrations of legends.

ORISSA

and jackal. Chamunda is a popular form of Durga these days, but in the 8th century, when the Vaital Temple was built, she was worshipped by Tantric cults. Beside the Vaital Temple is the **Sisireswar Temple.** At first sight, it appears to be a small replica of Vaital, but in fact, it's a near-duplicate of the nearby **Markandeswar Temple.** In both twin temples, images were carved directly into the temple walls, a technique which was later discontinued.

BINDU SAGAR. An important landmark in the Old Town, this large green tank at the foot of Vivekananda Marg plays a central role in the city's religious life. The waters of the Bindu Sagar (Ocean-Drop Tank) contain drops from all of India's holy pools and streams. Early-morning bathers take advantage of the blessings the waters bestow, that is, when the tank isn't bone-dry on account of a tardy monsoon. An image of Lord Tribhubaneswar takes a dip in the tank during the local **Cart Festival,** held in March or April.

MUSEUMS. The **State Museum** houses a small collection of illuminated palm leaf manuscripts, a room full of traditional Orissan musical instruments, ethnographic exhibits on the region's tribal people, and heaps of orphaned temple sculptures and friezes *(Puri Rd., a short walk from Kalpana Sq.; tel. 430870; open Tu-Su 10am-1pm and 2-5pm; Rs1).* At the **Tribal Research Institute,** rooms full of bureaucrats sort papers in the front building, while *adivasi* experts put the finishing touches on replicas of traditional tribal buildings in the jungly garden behind *(NH5, 2km east of the Baramunda Bus Station; tel. 403649; open M-Sa 10am-5pm; free).*

NEAR BHUBANESWAR: DHAULI ଧଉଳି

The hill of Dhauli (also known as **Dhauligiri**), 8km south of Bhubaneswar on the Puri road, marks Orissa's claim to fame in world history and reflects the Buddhist influence in this predominantly Hindu region. The Mauryan emperor Ashoka the Terrible defeated the Kalingas in a horrific battle here in 261 BC. He was so appalled by the bloodshed that he subsequently converted to nonviolent Buddhism and thus became Ashoka the Righteous. A long-winded **rock edict** in Brahmi script at the foot of Dhauli Hill explains Ashoka's theory of governance according to the principle of *dharma* (an English translation is posted near these inscriptions). Coming out of the rock above is one of the earliest stone carvings from embryonic Buddhist India—a gently and elegantly sculpted head and forepart of an **elephant** commemorating the emperor's conversion. On the summit of Dhauli hill, affording fantastic views of Bhubaneswar and the sandy River Durga, sits the **Shanti Stupa** (Peace Pagoda), built by Japanese Buddhists who also erected a similar structure in Rajgir, Bihar. (You can visit Dhauli as part of a guided bus **tour**—see p. 614. **Auto-rickshaws** cost Rs100 round-trip, and **buses** drop you off 3km from the hill for Rs4. Sites open daily 5am-8pm. Free.)

NEAR BHUBANESWAR:
UDAIGIRI ଉଦୟଗିରି AND KHANDAGIRI ଖଣ୍ଡଗିରି CAVES

More vestiges of antiquity can be found at the Udaigiri and Khandagiri Caves, 6km west of Bhubaneswar, less than 1km off National Highway 5 past Baramunda Bus Station. Cut into these twin hills are 33 small niches which functioned as sacred retreats for Jain ascetics in the first and 2nd centuries BC. A road now divides the Udaigiri caves (on the right) from the Khandagiri caves (on the left). An explanation of the various carvings and paintings decorating the caves can be found in the "Inscription of Kharavela" at Udaigiri, near Cave 12.

The best sculptures are found in and around Cave 1 at Udaigiri, the two-storied **Rani Gumpha** (Queen's Cave), with its faceless guardians. Cave 12 is carved as the gaping mouth of a tiger, Cave 13 is a cobra, and Cave 14, the **Hathi Gumpha** (Elephant Cave), has an inscription on its ceiling from King Kharavela of the Chedi Dynasty, perhaps the greatest of Kalinga kings and the patron of the caves. Images from Jain legends, mythology, and iconography decorate **Rani Nur** and **Ganesh Gumpha** (Cave 10). The top of the hill, directly above Ganesh Gumpha, has the foundation of an old building that was probably a Jain hall of worship.

The caves of Khandagiri are not as well-carved, though an active **Jain temple** sits at the top of the hill. From here, there's a great view of Bhubaneswar, including the Lingaraj Temple and Dhauli Hill in the distance. The best preserved carvings at Khandagiri are in **Cave 3.** Crawl into the caves at your own risk—they are home to hundreds of hanging bats! If you don't bring peanuts, be prepared to face down the tiny, hungry baby monkeys, many of whom are as persistent at pursuing hand-outs as the "priests" and *chai-wallahs.* (**Auto-rickshaws** from Bhubaneswar Rs80. Caves open daily 8am-6pm. Rs2 for Udaigiri, free for Khandagiri.)

NEAR BHUBANESWAR: NANDANKAN ZOOLOGICAL PARK

Part zoo and part wildlife park, Nandankan, situated in a vast expanse of the Chandaka forest, draws tourists from all over India with its famed collection of animals in a quasi-natural setting. The crown jewel of its extensive collection of native animals is the rare **white tiger.** Most animals are on display in cages and artificial ponds, or in the park's indoor aquarium (Rs1), but some lions and white tigers can be viewed via **bus safari** (Rs10) through the park's fenced-off game preserve. It's not exactly "Wild Kingdom"—these "vicious predators" actually look rather bored. **Paddle-boats** (Rs10) take you around the large, man-made lake; a **toy train** (Rs22) runs through the park; and **cable cars** (Rs10) ride high above it. (**Buses** from Bhubaneswar Rs5 for the 1½hr. trip; **auto-rickshaws** Rs90 round-trip. Open daily 8am-5pm. Admission Rs20, vehicles Rs20.)

KONARK ଚକାଶାର୍କ

Konark, named for the god who was "sun of the corner," sits along an isolated stretch of Orissa's coast. While little is known about the town's ancient history, its Sun Temple is hailed throughout India as one of the country's greatest architectural marvels. Even in ruins, the Sun Temple is magnificent, and it is completely accessible to non-Hindus. Since the temple's excavation and restoration in the early 20th century, Konark has become a much-frequented tourist spot. Small hotels have sprung up nearby, and touts abound, but Konark and its deserted beaches still manage to provide a more peaceful retreat than neighboring Puri.

⚡ ORIENTATION AND PRACTICAL INFORMATION

Konark's street plan resembles a "Z." The diagonal stroke is the main street with the temple entrance and a bevy of small shops; the top stroke is the road to Bhubaneswar; the bottom stroke is the road to Puri, passing beautiful deserted beaches along the way. The **Orissa State Tourism Office** (tel. 35821) is inside the Yatri Nivas Hotel (open M-Sa 10am-5pm). **Buses** depart from the middle of the intersection before Yatri Nivas to Bhubaneswar (every hr. 5am-6pm, 3hr., Rs15) and Puri (every 15min. 8am-8pm, 1hr., Rs9). Labanya Lodge rents **mopeds** (Rs150) and **bikes** (Rs20), and the tourist office arranges **taxis.** The **post office** is just past the Archaeological Museum, on the right (open M-Sa 9:30am-5pm). Labanya Lodge offers **STD/ISD** services (open 24hr. for guests, 6am-11pm for non-guests). **Canara Bank** (tel. 35828), past the post office, changes traveler's checks (open M-F 10am-2pm, Sa 10am-noon). **Police:** tel. 35825. **Postal Code:** 75211. **Telephone Code:** 06758.

🏠🍴 ACCOMMODATIONS AND FOOD

Labanya Lodge (tel. 35824; fax 35860), a few minutes out of town on the road to Puri, is a tasteful salmon-colored box framed by palm trees (singles Rs50; doubles with bath Rs75-150; extra person Rs10). The state-run **Yatri Nivas** (tel. 35820), next to the museum on the road to Bhubaneswar, offers small, clean rooms around green courtyards (doubles Rs100, with A/C Rs250; quads Rs120). **Konark Lodge** (tel. 75221), on the right just as you enter town from Puri, has dark, basic rooms. It's cheap, and you get what you pay for. (Doubles with bath Rs70.) Konark's food is nothing to write home about, but the **Geetanjali Restaurant,** next to the Pantha

Nivas and set back in the trees, has great breakfasts (scrambled eggs Rs18, french toast Rs13; open daily 6am-10pm). **Sharma Marwad Restaurant,** next door to Geetanjali, is a popular veg. restaurant with various *thalis* (Rs20-50; Open daily 6:30am-10:30pm). The **Sun Temple Hotel,** on the right, just past Pantha Nivas, has the longest, most wide-ranging menu (including veg. curry Rs15) in town, but achingly slow service (open daily 8am-10pm).

 SIGHTS

THE SUN TEMPLE

Temple open dawn-dusk. Rs5, free on F.

Konark's Sun Temple, dedicated to **Surya** (the sun god), is designed in the form of his huge chariot. It once stood along the shore and was used as a navigational aid by European sailors on the way to Kolkata who called it the "Black Temple" to distinguish it from the "White Pagoda"—the Jagannath Temple at Puri. An earlier Surya temple existed in Konark as long ago as the 9th century, but most of the existing structure dates from about 400 years later. Over time, the shoreline has receded more than 3km, and today, a wall of tall pines stretching to the beach conceals the Sun Temple from sea-going vessels. Though worn and collapsed in places, the temple remains the central feature in the geographic—and economic—landscape of the area. Half the town, it seems, freelances as "guides" to the temple's racy iconography, while the other half aggressively hawks trinkets from street-side stalls surrounding the **temple entrance;** the ticket booth is up to the left of the gated entrance. Another entrance to the grounds, the next left after the Archaeological Museum, brings you to the outer wall of the complex, but you still have to walk around to the booth to pay.

JAGAMOHANA. Whatever your angle of approach, the *jagamohana* (porch, or audience hall), a step pyramid rising up in the middle of the compound, is the ruined temple's most prominent feature. Originally, the eastward-facing door caught the light of the morning sun, transmitting it to the sanctuary, which stood behind the porch. The sanctuary is now in ruins, and the doorway and interior of the porch have been filled in to support the crumbling structure.

PLATFORM AND PORCH. The sanctuary and the porch are mounted on an ornate **platform** carved with 24 giant wheels and seven horses, simulating Surya's chariot riding across the sky. The clock-like spokes of the chariot wheels represent the hours of the day, and in some cases the images carved on them follow this logic. On one wheel, toward the front of the porch on the south side, the first six spokes are decorated with images of a woman bathing and performing housework, while the last six spokes—the nighttime hours—show her making love to her husband.

The **porch** itself is also carved with erotic images, some tiny and intricate, others blocky and larger-than-life. Behind the porch, steps lead up to three images of Surya in chlorite stone on the south, north, and west sides. Two modern staircases lead from the three statues to the remains of the sanctuary itself. Before the temple was ruined, the sanctuary could only be reached through the porch, but engineers created the alternate route when the porch was filled in.

SANCTUARY. Considering the breathtaking appearance of the Sun Temple as a whole, the sanctuary by itself is rather plain. The Surya statue that once presided here is no more, and archaeologists can only speculate about its design. Some tour guides claim that the statue floated in the air, suspended by powerful magnets lodged in each corner of the sanctuary. It more likely rested on the highly ornate pedestal still extant. The frieze on the east side of the pedestal shows King Narasimha, the temple's patron, and his queen. The north and south faces depict the retinues of the queen and king, respectively.

ORISSA

OTHER SIGHTS

MAYADEVI TEMPLE. Behind the sanctuary of the Sun Temple and to the south-west are the remains of a **Mayadevi Temple.** Once thought to be dedicated to one of Surya's wives, it is now believed to be an older Surya temple. Erotic images decorate the exterior. In front of the main sanctuary is a huge **platform** with four columns rising up in the corners, each decorated with carvings. Some say it was a dancing hall, but it was more likely used for ritual banquets in honor of the deity.

ARCHAEOLOGICAL MUSEUM. Various sculptures from the temple have been scattered about the site by plunderers and collectors. Some of the finest fragments, cleaned and polished, now reside in the Archaeological Museum. (Other fragments from the temple's sculptures are kept in the Indian Museum in Kolkata and the Victoria and Albert Museum in London.) Well worth a visit, the museum sells the Archaeological Survey's informative guide to the Sun Temple for Rs15. *(On the road to Bhubaneswar, down from Yatri Nivas. Tel. 35822. Open Tu-Su 10am-5pm.)*

PURI ପୁରୀ

Despite the multitudes that have descended upon Puri over the years, this tranquil seaside town has managed to age gracefully. Since the 12th century, the cityscape has been dominated by the immense temple of Lord Jagannath which rises above the crowded old town, but it is Puri's placid, white sand beaches that have long drawn vacationers and sun worshippers from landlocked Indian cities. In the 1960s and 1970s, Puri's permissive attitude towards (and plentiful supply of) drugs increased its popularity as a stop along India's well-established hippie trail. Today, three distinct categories of visitors can be found here almost year-round. There is little interaction between the groups, though—Hindu pilgrims tend to occupy the area around the Jagannath Temple (closed to non-Hindus) and the eight *dharamshalas* that line Grand Avenue, Indian tourists populate the busy downtown boardwalk area, and international tourists seek refuge in the expat resort community lining the quieter beach east of town. With the constant influx of travelers, it is easy to forget that Puri is also a place where people live and work. East of the international commune area lies a friendly and vibrant fishing village whose residents still farm the seas in boats from a bygone era.

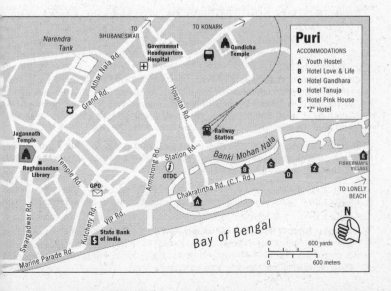

■ TRANSPORTATION

Trains: Puri Railway Station, Station Rd., at the intersection with Hospital Rd. 2nd class booking office is open 24hr. Tourist quota tickets available at the reservation counter (tel. 131). Open M-Sa 8am-8pm, Su 8am-1pm. Foreign non-reserved tickets at window #7. Fares listed are for 2nd/1st class. To: **Kolkata** (*Puri-Howrah Exp.* 8008, 6:45pm; *Jagannath Exp.* 8410, 9:15pm, 12hr., Rs112/546); **Delhi** (*Purushottam Exp.* 2801, 8:10pm; *Utkal Exp.* 8477, 4:40pm; *Neelachal Exp.* 8475 and 2815, Su-F 9:15am, 33hr., Rs1385/270). Regular trains to **Bhubaneswar,** but the bus is more convenient.

Buses: New Bus Stand, Grand Rd., past Canara Bank. Buses to **Konark** (every 15min. 7am-7pm, 1hr., Rs10). Numerous **private companies** operate interstate buses; tour agencies and hotel desks make arrangements. To: **Bhubaneswar** (every 5min., 2hr., Rs13); **Kolkata** (7am, 16hr., Rs140); **Cuttack** (frequent, 2½hr., Rs20).

Local Transportation: Cycle- and **auto-rickshaws** ride from one corner of Puri to another for under Rs20—the going rate for Indians is Rs5 per km; foreigners are charged more. Unmetered **taxis** can be arranged by your hotel or travel agent. **Local buses** (under Rs5) rarely run properly, if at all. One convenient route runs from the New Bus Stand to the Jagannath Temple, to the beach, and back (Rs3). **Aju's,** east on CT Rd. across from the Holiday Home, has **bikes** (Rs20 per day), **scooters** (Rs200 per day), medium-sized **motorcycles** (Rs250-300 per day), and attractive Enfield Bullets for the motorcycle-experienced (Rs300 per day). Passport required for rentals. Open daily 7am-8pm.

■ ORIENTATION AND PRACTICAL INFORMATION

Puri's busiest area is **Grand Avenue,** which runs east-west through the northern (inland) part of town, arching southwest near the **Jagannath Temple** to become **Swargardwar Road.** On its southern side, Puri is washed by the Bay of Bengal. Along the shore runs **Chakratirtha (CT) Road,** lined with a number of budget hotels. As it runs west, CT Rd. intersects with **VIP** and **Marine Parade Road.**

Tourist Office: Government of Orissa Tourist Office, Station Rd. (tel. 22664). From the railway station, follow Station Rd. west 500m. The office is on the right just before VIP Rd. Upstairs, a tiny branch of the State Museum displays local handicrafts and photos of the Rath Yatra. Both open M-Sa 10am-5pm.

Budget Travel: Om Travels, CT Rd. This ashram, travel agency, and religious bookshop offers standard tours run by Orissa Tourism. Open daily 6am-10pm. MC, Visa. **Gandhara International** (tel. 24623; fax 25909), in front of Hotel Gandhara, provides a wide variety of services including train and international flight booking. Open M-Sa 8am-8pm, Su 8am-1pm. AmEx, MC, Visa.

Currency Exchange: State Bank of India, VIP Rd. (tel. 23995 or 23682). From the train station, head west on Station Rd., turn left onto Armstrong Rd., left again onto VIP Rd., and follow it south past the Bose statue. No commission. Open M-F 10am-2pm, Sa 10am-noon. **Hotel Gandhara** changes traveler's checks for a small fee. Open M-Sa 8am-8pm, Su 8am-1pm.

Market: Laxmi Market, west on Grand Rd. The best and priciest of Puri's markets sells fresh produce, fish, and more. Farther east on Grand Rd. is the smaller **Municipality Market.** Both open daily 10am-10pm.

Library: Raghunandan Library, Grand Rd. (tel. 22252), opposite the Jagannath Temple. Historically a monastery and library, it houses books and palm-leaf manuscripts on the 1st fl. Open daily 8am-noon and 4-7pm.

Bookstore: Loknath Bookshop and Library, CT Rd., toward the fisherman's village, next door to Raju's Restaurant. Books can be rented (Rs10 per day, with a Rs300 deposit) or purchased (Rs200-900). Passport photos (Rs20 for 3) and stamps are also sold. Open daily 9am-9pm; May-Aug. 8am-noon and 3-8pm.

Hospital: Government Headquarters Hospital, Grand Rd. (tel. 23742). An old and dilapidated facility that is best avoided. English is hardly spoken, but the **ambulance service** (tel. 102) is decently run. **Emergency:** tel. 22094.

Police: Town Police Station, Grand Rd. (tel. 24059), near Jagannath Temple. The control room is open 24hr. **CT Rd.** area police station (tel. 25208). Contact **City Beach Police** (tel. 22025, emergency tel. 100) in case of a beach emergency.

Post Office: GPO, Kutchery Rd. (tel. 22051). From CT Rd., walk west past the Bose statue and turn right after the State Bank of India; proceed north on Kutchery Rd., and the GPO will be visible down the first street to the left. *Poste Restante.* Stamps sold M-Sa 9am-6pm, Su 3-5pm. **Postal Code:** 752001.

Internet: Harry's Cafe (tel. 23852 or 27032; open daily 8am-10pm) and **Gandhara International** (tel. 24623; open M-Sa 8am-8pm, Su 8am-1pm) both offer full Internet access (Rs3 per min.). **"Z" Hotel** has cheaper service (Rs100 per hr.) daily 9am-5pm.

Telephones: Most **STD/ISD** booths open 24hr. in season. **Telegraph Office,** Chandan Hazuri Ln. (tel. 22806), opposite the mission. Open M-Sa 7am-10pm, Su 8am-3:30pm.

PHONE CODE	06752

ACCOMMODATIONS

Budget accommodations are concentrated around CT Rd., a small stretch of beach accessed most easily by rickshaw.

> **! WARNING.** Ricksha-*wallahs* play a commission game with some hotel owners who kick back up to 50% of the rent—ignore their claims that the hotel you are looking for is "closed," "full," "very expensive," or "has changed its name."

 Hotel Gandhara (tel. 24117), at the end of CT Rd., opposite a path to the beach. The 19th-century bungalow in front contains dorm and budget rooms; the 5-story building behind it offers pricier accommodations. Friendly and expertly run, with a travel agency and restaurant serving great Japanese specialties (Rs100; make reservations by noon). Collect calls (Rs10 per min.) from the attached rooms. Check-out 9am. Dorm beds Rs30; singles Rs110; doubles Rs100-550, with A/C Rs750. AmEx, MC, Visa.

"Z" Hotel (tel. 22554), east of Hotel Gandhara past Restaurant Peace draws many tourists with its sea-view rooms, garden, and direct beach access. Once home to the maharaja of Puri, "Z" (pronounced "zed" by everyone but the Americans) is now run by a member of India's Parliament. Excellent cook, 24hr. room service, and accommodating staff. Dorm beds (women only) Rs50; singles Rs150; doubles Rs250, with bath Rs450.

Hotel Pink House (tel. 22253), 5min. south of CT Rd. A bit run down from constant sea winds, this ultra-budget cottage offers the open Bay of Bengal for next to nothing. Rooms that open directly onto the beach make for beautiful sunrises, but sandy floors. Mosquito nets, coils, and bug spray available. Road-weary Suny cycles await rental (Rs100-175). Doubles Rs100-120; triples Rs180-250; quads Rs180-250.

Hotel Love & Life (tel. 24433; fax 26093), next to Hotel Gandhara. A perennial favorite with travelers but less romantic than the name suggests. Dorm beds Rs30. Singles Rs80-125; doubles Rs100-250; cottages (double occupancy) Rs200-250.

Hotel Tanuja (tel. 24823 or 24974), across from Harry's Cafe and the Mickey Mouse Restaurant. Alcohol, smoking, and visitors are allowed in the rooms. Mosquito nets, a common TV room, laundry service, in-house postal service, and attendant Tanuja Tribe Tour agency complete the offerings. Singles Rs70; doubles Rs70-300.

Youth Hostel (tel. 22424), closer to town. Popular, clean, and frequented by both Indians and foreigners. Check-out 8am. Dorm beds only Rs20, non-members Rs40.

FOOD

Food in Puri is cheap and tailor-made for foreign tourists, with a wide array of non-Indian fare on CT Rd. Fish is as fresh as anywhere in coastal India.

"Z" Hotel Restaurant. The kitchen staff does a superlative job cooking up a spicy fish curry (Rs35) with the day's catch. The veg. *navaratan* (Rs25) and *alu dum* (Rs14) stand out, and the beer (Rs60) is always chilled. Open daily 7am-3pm and 6-10:30pm.

Mickey Mouse Restaurant, diagonally across the street from the "Z" Hotel. A reggae-playin', international-copyright-violatin' hippie holdover. Try 11 different *lassis* (Rs10-30), 18 varieties of custard (Rs10-30), or one of 46 pancake permutations (Rs10-40). Coffee and honey combo (Rs12) is a must. Complete *thalis* Rs12-52. Alcohol not sold here but may be brought in. Open daily 6am-11pm.

Harry's Cafe, near the "Z" Hotel. Perhaps Puri's best-known and most popular tourist trap. Better for dessert than for dinner, with coconut milkshakes (Rs15) and chocolate pancakes (Rs20). No alcohol. Open daily 8am-10pm.

Chung Wah, VIP Rd., west on CT Rd. then right on VIP Rd.; less than 1km down on the left. One of the cleanest and coolest spots in Puri. Sink into the squishy chairs and choose from an array of authentic flavors of the Middle Kingdom. Veg. dishes Rs20-25. Garlic fish (Rs52) by request. Open daily 11am-3pm and 6-10:30pm.

Wild Grass, VIP Rd., around the corner from Chung Wah. An extraordinary garden setting with ordinary South Indian fare at non-local prices (*thalis* Rs40). Thatched roofs and tribal drawings evoke Orissa's "primitives." Cheap snacks (veggie burger Rs15) available for students daily 4-6pm. Open daily 11:30am-10:30pm.

ENTERTAINMENT

In a pilgrim city like Puri, festivals are abundant throughout the year, although most locals don't always make them well-known. The grand-daddy of these is the **Rama Yatra Fetsival,** when Lord Jagannath, his brother Balabhadra, and his sister Subhadra are paraded through the city on large chariots (see below). Puri's **Beach Festival** (late Mar. or early Apr.), showcases the best of Orissan folk dancing, music, and handicrafts. The Government of Orissa Tourist Office also arranges **dance and theatrical programs** (check their bulletin board for current information). You can even take an evening stroll along Marine Parade through the Swargadwar area and the **night market** in western Puri. *Saris* color the market landscape, and the bright lights from Puri's burning *ghats* glow in the distance.

SIGHTS

JAGANNATH TEMPLE. Constructed in the early 12th century by the Ganga king Anantavaram Chodaganga, the Jagannath Temple is a stunning example of Orissan temple architecture. Every pilgrim's entrance into Puri is initiated by a short devotional stop in front of the main **simhadwara** (lion gate)—the eastern and most important entrance to the spectacular Jagannath Temple—which rises to 65m. It's *the* feature of the Puri skyline, symbolizing the power that the charcoal-faced Jagannath, the "Lord of the Universe," continues to wield over the town below.

The three roughly hewn but divine inhabitants of the temple are abstractly depicted: dense, rectangular wooden blocks represent the bodies of **Jagannath,** his brother **Balabhadra,** and his sister **Subhadra.** Tiny arms extend from stumpy legless abdomens and enormous, unblinking eyes glare out from disproportionately sized, perfectly round heads. It is said that Lord Jagannath has no eyelids so that he can continually look after the well-being of the world—some say he never sleeps. His small arms project outwards in a gesture of unconditional love. Temple priests cite ancient myths to explain the peculiarly shaped forms, while many academics suggest that the deities' forms have tribal origins.

GODS ON WHEELS Sweating, singing, shouting, and praying, exuberant crowds move en masse to enact an event of cosmic proportions. The **Rath Yatra** (Cart Festival) of Puri is celebrated two days after the new moon in the month of Ashadh (June-July). The festival day begins with the Gajapati (the King of Puri) making a gesture of *chhera paharna*, ritually "sweeping" the *rathas* (chariots) to symbolize humanity humbling itself in preparation for the mercy and goodwill of Jagannath. As the mesmerizing chants of the *sadhus* and the ecstatic shouts of "Jai Jagannath" fill the frenzied air, Jagannath arrives on the scene to take the yellow-and-red-draped seat of pomp in his 13m, 18-wheeled, gold-domed chariot, otherwise known as Nandigosha. Once Balabhadra and Subhadra, the other members of the divine family, are placed in their respective chariots, movement can begin. On the day of the festival, each of the three deities is pulled by some 4000 devotees from the main gate of the temple east along Grand Ave. As if propelled by divine force, the *ratha* carriers proceed forward on a 3km journey, dragging the newly constructed chariots. The three gods spend nine days at **Gundicha Ghar** (Garden House), where they are dressed anew each day and eat specially prepared rice cakes. Their symbolic tour of the universe, as erratic and intensely delirious as the trip to Gundicha Ghar, is completed with a repeat processional performance back to the temple. Nineteenth-century British observers reported that ecstatic devotees would sometimes throw themselves under the wheels of the carts to obtain instant *moksha*. The word "juggernaut" (meaning an object that crushes everything in its path) comes from the god's name.

Patterned on the same architectural principles as the older Lingaraj Temple in Bhubaneswar (see p. 616), the abode of Jagannath is structurally aligned from east to west. The *bhoga mandir* (offering hall) and *nata mandir* (dance hall) nearest to the entrance were 15th- and 16th-century additions to the original *jagamohana* (assembly hall). The *deul* (inner sanctuary), crowned by a 65m pyramidal roof, signifies the presence of the divine trio. Surrounded by a 6m-high wall, the massive temple compound hosts action-packed days of *darshan* and treats worshippers to devotionals and sacred dances at night. The complex employs approximately 6000 specially trained temple priests who care for the deities (waking, cleaning, feeding, and dressing them). Communities of artists work to produce ritual materials, and thousands prepare *prasad* daily for Jagannath himself. The kitchen to the left of the temple, claimed to be the world's largest, serves unique meals of **mahaprasad** to 10,000 people daily and up to 25,000 during festival times, such as the Rath Yatra. (The temple is strictly closed to non-Hindus—Prime Minister Indira Gandhi herself was denied access because of her marriage to a Parsi.)

OTHER SIGHTS. A full view of the eastern gate, the Jagannath Temple, and the surrounding smaller temples can be had from atop the roof of the **Raghunandan Library,** across the street. Travelers are ushered in by a palm leaf manuscript expert and a capricious congregation of temple monkeys. (*Open daily 8am-noon and 4-7pm.*) The **Lokanath Temple** is a bit of a "poor man's" Jagannath: smaller, less beautiful, and farther out of town. Still, it merits a look since its Hindus-only rules are not strictly enforced. (*1km away. Open dawn to dusk.*)

BEACHES

WARNING. The beaches of Puri are generally free of violent crime, but locals advise against going alone at night. Leaving your valuables in the hotel.

Puri's white sand beaches are reputed to be the most beautiful in Eastern India, but much like a pointillist painting, they show their spots when viewed up close. If it's brown and it floats, it isn't a horseshoe crab! Still, for those who successfully dodge the debris, the beaches are all the entertainment most travelers need. A short walk away from the hotels will reward you with cleaner sand and fewer sweaty, middle-aged massage-*wallahs* offering their oily services. At the main beach near the town center, mobs of Indian tourists wade in their customary, fully clothed style, while east of CT Rd., friendly and enterprising children selling coral necklaces abound. For a few rupees, fishermen can often be talked into providing a boat ride or angling excursion—the sometimes rough waters and tricky tides make this a risky, though thrilling, endeavor.

CUTTACK କଟକ

Cuttack may occupy the top of the Mahanadi River Delta, but it occupies the bottom of the barrel of Orissa's most attractive and exciting destinations. Here, the inland waters fan out before making their way to the Bay of Bengal, but not much else happens in this crowded metropolis of a quarter-million people. Cuttack had an inauspicious beginning—not long after King Anangabhima Deva III of the Ganga dynasty founded the city, Muslim invaders sacked it. The Marathas and British eventually followed suit, but Cuttack's most recent sacker has been Orissa's government, which erased Cuttack's one distinguishing feature by moving the state capital to Bhubaneswar, 35km away. Nowadays, tourists seldom stay in Cuttack for long, usually just passing through on their way to Orissa's Buddhist sites at Lalitagiri, Udayagiri, and Ratnagiri.

◪ **ORIENTATION AND PRACTICAL INFORMATION.** Cuttack is crammed onto a skinny finger of a peninsula that points northwest. **National Highway (NH) 5** and the railway line cut across the southeast; the fort-like **railway station** lies east of the **Badambadi Bus Stand.** The center of town houses Cuttack's main **bazaars;** the fort and **dock** to Dhabaleshwar lie in the less crowded northwest. Passenger **trains** run to: **Bhubaneswar** (1:54pm, 1½hr., Rs14); **Kolkata** (6 per day, 8hr., Rs95/471 for 2nd/1st class); and **Puri** (8am, 4:20, and 7:30pm; 3hr.; Rs30). You might also catch one of the many trains on the Kolkata-Chennai line that swing by the coast, but you'll pay more (Rs81 for 2nd class to Puri or Bhubaneswar). **Buses** run from the Badambadi Bus Stand to **Bhubaneswar** (every 15min. 6:15am-10:30pm, 1hr., Rs11). Private buses to **Puri** (frequent, 2½hr., Rs20) leave from **private bus stands,** most of which are opposite the Badambadi. **Cycle-rickshaws** go almost anywhere (under Rs10) and harder-to-find **auto-rickshaws** cost about twice that. The **Tourist Office,** Link Rd. (tel. 612225), 1km from the bus stand, at the left front of the Arunodag Market complex (open M-Sa 10am-5pm), also has an outpost at the railway station (tel. 610507; open daily 10am-5pm). The **State Bank of India** (tel. 618235), west of Choudhury Bazaar, is next to the High Court; foreign exchange is upstairs (open M-F 10am-2pm, Sa 10am-noon). The **GPO** (tel. 620150) is 50m off of Buxi Bazaar's main intersection (open M-Sa 10am-5pm). The **Cuttack Medical College Hospital** (tel. 614499 or 614622) is 20 minutes down the road past the GPO; its **pharmacy** is open 24 hours. **Cyber Zone,** Dolmundai Square (tel. 611207), offers full Internet access (Rs3 per min.; open daily 6am-11pm). There is an **STD/ISD** booth in the railway station, opposite the tourist office (open 5am-11pm). **Police:** Control room (tel. 621477). **Postal Code:** 753001. **Telephone Code:** 0671.

◪◪ **ACCOMMODATIONS AND FOOD.** Seedy hotels surround the bus stations and a few more are hidden in the bazaars. **Hotel Adarsh,** Choudhury Bazaar (tel. 619201), halfway between the mosque and the jewelers, has tiny cubicles with ceiling fans and hot water in the winter months (singles Rs50, with bath Rs60; doubles with bath Rs70). That famous smile greets you at the **Hotel Mona Lisa** (tel. 621109), rising high over Badambadi Bus Stand. The hotel has hot water buckets and 24-hour check-out. The courtyard decorations, reminiscent of IM Pei's, are the closest you'll get to the Louvre in Cuttack. (Singles Rs120; doubles Rs150, with A/C Rs300.) **Panthanivas** (tel. 621916 or 621867), in the middle of Buxi Bazaar, is Orissa Tourism's clean, well-maintained hotel with large rooms overlooking a courtyard. The 8am check-out, however, is a bit outrageous. (Rooms Rs300, with A/C Rs500, deluxe with A/C and cable Rs575.) The A/C **Panthanivas Hotel Restaurant** (tel.

521916) dishes up a thick, rich vegetable *korma* (Rs20). Though their official policy is to serve only guests of the hotel, it's enforced with a "don't ask, don't tell" vigilance. (Open daily 7am-11pm, though they claim to serve guests at any time.) **Hotel City Light,** across from the GPO, makes its rolls (veg. Rs8, chicken Rs12) in front of an open window to entice passersby. Sit back in the crowded, stylin' dining room and watch the cows come home, which, in this country, may happen sooner than you think. (Open daily 4pm-midnight.)

🖿 SIGHTS. Even the tourist office admits that Cuttack's blessings do not include must-see historical monuments or spectacular natural wonders. **Dhabaleshwar,** the most prominent feature in the State Tourism's pitch, is an island on the Mahanadi River. A Shiva temple, a state-run hotel, and an excuse to get out of the house make it a popular outing for locals. (Take a town bus to Bidanasi, where small private launches at Cuttack Ghat cross the river to Dhabaleshwar.) The road to the *ghat* passes small, leafy **Deer Park,** where a herd of spotted deer can be seen grazing. The ruins of the **Barbati Fort** are near a park in the northwest of town. Demolished by the British, the fort is now only a small pile of stones, marred by graffiti, remains from what was once a nine-story palace, complete with moat and gate.

NEAR CUTTACK

LALITAGIRI ଲଳିତଗିରି, UDAYAGIRI ଉଦୟଗିରି, & RATNAGIRI ରନ୍ଗିରି

Although Orissa's "Golden Triangle" of tourism is shaped by the towering temples of Bhubaneswar, Konark, and Puri, the state boasts a fascinating Buddhist heritage as well. Forming their own triangle of sorts, Udayagiri, Lalitagiri, and Ratnagiri stand as monuments to a religious culture steeped in art and learning. **Lalitagiri's** first-century ruins include a large brick monastery, several *stupas*, and numerous other artifacts in various stages of discovery and recovery. The ruins at **Udayagiri,** several centuries younger than their counterparts in Ratnagiri and Lalitagiri, comprise Orissa's largest Buddhist site, replete with *stupa*, brick monastery, stone step-well, and some splendid hilltop Bodhisattva and Dhyani Buddha sculptures. Like its be-*giri*'d neighbors, **Ratnagiri** too features monasteries, *stupas*, shrines, sculpture and a sizeable Siddhartha statue. All three locations are still active excavation sites, providing great opportunities to view ancient relics au naturel. All three sites can be visited on a day-trip from Cuttack. From the **private bus** yard, take the 60km (1hr.) ride to **Chandikol,** which is 7, 9, and 12km from Lalitagiri, Udayagiri, and Ratnagiri, respectively. **Tempos** by the bus stand make the journey to Ratnagiri and stop at Udayagiri on the way back (Rs250 round-trip, add Rs100 for Lalitagiri). You can also board a tempo ferrying locals to villages near the sites (the entire circuit can be completed this way for under Rs20). The surrounding countryside has some of the most beautiful natural scenery in India. However you travel, bring plenty of water—*dhabas* are ubiquitous in Chandikol, but mineral water is scarce. (All sites open daily dawn-dusk. Free.)

FORGOTTEN GANDHI After his assassination in Delhi on January 30, 1948, Mohandas K. Gandhi was cremated on a pyre next to the Yamuna River. His ashes were divided into two dozen lots, each sealed in a ceremonial wooden coffin. These were then sent to India's holiest places, where they were scattered over the sacred rivers and revered *ghats*. Remarkably, one batch of Gandhi's ashes were overlooked, and for nearly 50 years it remained locked in a safe deposit box at the State Bank of India office in Cuttack, Orissa. One of Gandhi's great-grandchildren attempted to claim them, but without a receipt State Bank officials were unwilling to give up the goods. After drawn-out legal proceedings, the Supreme Court affirmed the authenticity of the ashes in 1996 and ordered that they be turned over to the Gandhi family. Bank officials, still fretting over the missing receipt, dug the ashes out of the vault and turned them over to a heavily armed military unit for delivery by train to Allahabad, where Gandhi's great-grandson poured them into the Ganga.

BIHAR बिहार

Bihar is justly proud of its past. Some of India's most formative events took place in its once-thick forests. The Ganga Valley's eastern region gets its name from the word *vihara* (monastery), referring to the secluded centers of Buddhist learning that flourished here during the first millennium. The Buddha gained enlightenment under a tree in Bodh Gaya, and the Mauryan and Gupta Empires both grew from the city of Pataliputra (modern-day Patna).

However, few tangible traces are left of Bihar's past glories—Bihar is now the least urbanized and poorest state in India. Bihari politics have seen an unending stream of controversy and periodic outbreaks of caste-based violence over the years. In July 1997, Bihar's Chief Minister, Laloo Prasad Yadav, stepped down after a series of corruption scandals; in his place, he appointed his illiterate wife Rabri Devi and promised to continue his rule via mobile phone from his prison cell. India's fragile ruling coalition has tried several times to remove the cow-herder's daughter from office, but without success. Much of the Bihari countryside is effectively ruled by *goondas* (thugs) with under-the-table connections to politicians, and *dacoits* (bandits) are still part of Bihari life, but foreign visitors are unlikely to encounter anything worse than persistent curiosity.

HIGHLIGHTS OF BIHAR

■ The so-called **Lotus Circuit** traces the Buddha's steps through eight of Bihar's towns—**Bodh Gaya** (p. 637), where the Buddha achieved enlightenment; **Rajgir** (p. 633), where his teachings were compiled; **Nalanda** (p. 635), where he studied philosophy; **Vaishali** (p. 642), where some of his ashes are interred; and **Patna** (p. 628), which was a bloated transit hub even then.

Traveling in Bihar can be a frustrating business; conditions are the most basic, electricity cuts are frequent, and journeys of just a few kilometers can take most of the day. Partly because of these logistical inconveniences and the state's general lawlessness, Bihar draws few Western tourists. Some come to visit its important Buddhist sites, and many simply pass through on their way to Nepal, but it is worth putting up with Bihar's many hassles for the insight it offers into an India outside the big-*baksheesh* cocoon of the major tourist circuit.

PATNA पटना

Most travelers visit Patna, the capital of the much-maligned Bihar, on their way to or from Nepal or while they're on the Buddhist pilgrim circuit, and many find its essence captured in the name of one of its major streets: Boring Road. There is little to see here and less to do; most travelers opt quite sensibly to stay in this energy-sapping, swampy sump of a city for as short a time as possible. All this is in spite of Patna's illustrious past—Patna was, in a way, the first capital city of India. The Mauryan Empire was seated here, and the Guptas, too, made it their capital. But Pataliputra, as it was called in antiquity, was abandoned after the decline of the Guptas and was only refounded as Patna in 1541 by Sher Shah Suri, a rival of the Mughals. Patna became a regional center for the Mughals and the British—the

...ast India Company's largest opium warehouses are here, now converted (vice for ...ice) into a state government printing office. But Patna's glory days are long gone ...ow. Though the city continues to serve Bihar and northeast India as a major ...dustrial center, there is nothing much here to attract visitors and no reason to ...ant to get stuck here any longer than is absolutely necessary.

■ TRANSPORTATION

Airport: Patna Airport, 6km from the railway station (taxi Rs150, auto-rickshaw Rs50, cycle-rickshaw Rs25). To: **Kolkata** (2 per day, 1hr., US$90); **Delhi** (3 per day, 2-3hr., US$130); **Lucknow** (1 per day, 1hr., US$90); **Mumbai** (3 per day, 3hr., US$195); **Kathmandu** (M, W, and Sa; US$75). **Indian Airlines,** S. Gandhi Maidan (tel. 222554).

Trains: Patna Junction Station is a major hub. Fares listed are 2nd/AC class. To: **Kolkata** (*Howrah Exp.* 5050, Th 1:40am, 10hr.; *Rajdhani Exp.* 2306, 5:30am, 7½hr.; *Poorva*

Exp. 2304, 7:45am, 8½hr., Rs117/552); **Gaya** (*Palamau Exp.* 3348, 8:15pm, 2hr., Rs31/161); **Lucknow** (*Amritsar Mail* 3005, 5:02am, 11hr.; *Himgiri Exp.* 3073, Tu, F, and Sa 10:15am, 9hr.; *Howrah-Amritsar Exp.* 30, 2am, 13hr., Rs123/577); **New Jalpaiguri** (*Mahananda Exp./A Link Exp.* 4084, 1am, 14hr.; *Rajdhani Exp.* 2424, 5:17am, 8½hr.; *Northeast Exp.* 5622, 10pm, 12hr., Rs117/619); **Varanasi** (*Amritsar Mail* 3005, 5:02am, 5hr.; *Himgiri Exp.* 3073, W, Sa, and Su 10:25am, 4hr.; *Howrah Exp.* 5049, F 10:25am, 4hr.; *Shramjeevi Exp.* 2401, 11:20am, 3hr., Rs61/330).

Buses: The **bus stand**, Station Rd., is 500m west of Patna Junction. To: **Hajipur** (frequent, Rs9; for connections to **Vaishali** and **Sonepur** at Hajipur); **Raxaul** (frequent, 6hr., Rs70). From Gandhi Maidan to **Siliguri** (4:30pm, Rs139).

Local Transportation: Tempos to many other places in the city. Large numbers of tempos and **rickshaws** also congregate in the area around the **Gandhi Maidan**.

② ORIENTATION AND PRACTICAL INFORMATION

Patna sprawls along the south bank of the mighty Ganga. Getting from east to west across the city is a road trip in itself. **Ashok Raj Path** is the main thoroughfare, sticking close to the river the whole way, while **Kankar Bagh Road (Old Bypass Road)** covers the same distance on the southern side of the city, just south of the railroad tracks. The east end of town is Old Patna. Most trains stop at the west end's **Patna Junction Station. Fraser Road,** where Patna's hotels, restaurants, and other conveniences are concentrated, runs straight north from the station. The **Gandhi Maidan,** a large park north of Fraser Rd. (touching Ashok Raj Path), is a major landmark and local transportation hub. Next to the railway station, **Station Road** leads west to the **bus station** and various government buildings.

Tourist Office: State Government Tourist Office, Fraser Rd. (tel. 225295), 300m up on the right on the 2nd fl. of the Silver Oak bar and restaurant building. Open M-Sa 10am-5pm. **Government of India Tourist Office,** Sudama Palace Complex, 3rd fl., Kankarbagh Rd. (tel. 345776), near the Jasmine Hotel. Tall building on the right by the petrol pump; no sign on the street, only on the 3rd fl. balcony. Open M-F 9am-6pm, Sa 9am-1pm.

Budget Travel: Royal Nepal Airlines, Dunlop Compound, Fraser Rd. (tel. 231946), just before the road makes a right hook. Ultra-knowledgeable staff.

Currency Exchange: State Bank of India, Gandhi Maidan (tel. 226134). Tempo from the railway station (Rs3). The bank—a squat, white concrete bunker at the beginning of the circle—is on the left. Open M-F 10:30am-2:30pm, Sa 10:30am-12:30pm.

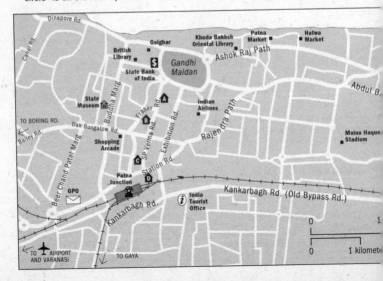

Luggage Storage: On the right as you exit the railway station. Rs5 per piece, per day.

Market: Maurya Lok, Dak Bungalow Rd., is a major shopping center, with clothing stores, hair salons, and fast-food joints. There are several **fruit markets,** including **New Patna Market,** in front of the railway station, and **Patna** and **Hatwa Markets,** on Ashok Raj Path near Gandhi Maidan and the Ganga.

Library: British Library, Bank Rd. (tel. 24198). Open Tu-Sa 10am-7pm.

Bookstore: Tricel, Fraser Rd. (tel. 221412), opposite the Satkar International Hotel. Small but varied selection. Open M-Sa 10am-8:30pm.

Pharmacy: Popular Pharmacy (tel. 226393), on the left of the railway station, across from the mosque on the far side. Open daily 8:30am-10pm.

Hospital: Raj Lakshmi Nursing Home, Kankarbagh Rd. (tel. 352225 or 354320), 4km east of the Government of India Tourist Office.

Police: Control Room (tel. 223131), on N. Gandhi Maidan, next to the white-domed Shri Krishna Memorial Hall, opposite the Maurya Patna Motel. **Emergency:** tel. 111.

Post Office: GPO, Station Rd. (tel. 225019 or 224150), to the left, opposite the railway station. Open M-Sa 10am-8:30pm, Su 10am-1pm. **Postal Code:** 800001.

Internet: Cyberzone, SP Verma Road (tel. 224717), before the intersection with Fraser Rd., on the right; opposite the Ruby Hotel. Internet and email access Rs100 per hr. Open M-Sa 9:30am-8:30pm.

PHONE CODE	0612

■ ACCOMMODATIONS

Many cheaper hotels don't have the paperwork needed to register foreigners, and mid-range hotels are often full. Still, it's possible to find bargains around Fraser Rd., particularly on Hotel Ln., an alley opposite the Satkar International Hotel.

Hotel Anand Lok, Station Rd. (tel. 223960), is a large white building towering over the railway station. A gate by the luggage office leads right to the door. Excellent service. Generator protects against power cuts. Restaurant/bar downstairs open until 10pm. Despite the noise, this is your best bet for a hassle-free night's sleep. Spacious rooms have attached baths. Check-out 24hr. Singles Rs200/300; doubles Rs300/400.

Patna Youth Hostel, Fraser Rd., after it jogs right, then left. The best bargain in town by far, with beds in 2- and 4-person rooms with attached baths. Max. 7-day stay. Open 24hr. Rooms Rs40; Rs20 for HI members.

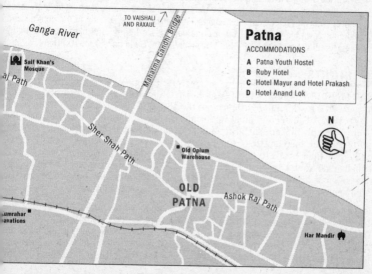

Hotel Mayur (tel. 224142). From the railway station, 500m up Fraser Rd. on the right. Classical statuettes and a great wooden peacock are the tasteful *objets d'art* arranged around the Mayur's reception lobby, where busy fans clack like castanets competing with the around-the-clock entertainment of the hotel's favorite TV. Pleasant rooms with attached baths. Singles Rs200; doubles Rs300, with air-cooling Rs350.

Ruby Hotel, S.P. Verma Rd. A little elusive; take a rickshaw up to SP Verma Rd., and the hotel is on the left before the 2nd big intersection. Small, dark rooms are bearable with the fan working overtime but can become stuffy during frequent power cuts. All rooms have attached bath. Check-out 24hr. Singles Rs50; doubles Rs80.

🍴 FOOD

Most of the restaurants are on Fraser Rd., though there are a few fast food places in the shopping arcade at Maurya Lok. There are several **bars** tied to restaurants and hotels, where you and the locals can daydream about being somewhere else.

Mamta Restaurant and Bar, Fraser Rd., next to Mayfair Ice Cream Parlor. A friendly, well-cooled oasis in which to recuperate after a day spent struggling in the smog and noise. Fish bubble away in the bar-side aquarium, and a welcome air of calm and quiet pervades. Good food at decent prices (*kashmiri korma* Rs40). Open daily 10am-10:30pm.

Anarkali Restaurant, Fraser Rd., upstairs in the Mamta Hotel farther up past the Mayfair on the right. From the subdued lighting and unrestrained sitar music to the shiny chintz mirrored mosaics and the fish tanks filled with spinning-wheel novelties and plastic fish, everything here should help make you feel indulgent. Excellent food, full blast A/C, and ice-cold Kingfisher lager. Open daily 7am-10:30pm.

The Silver Oak Restaurant and Bar, Fraser Rd. On the right towards Gandhi Maidan, just before the road veers right and merges with SP Verma Rd. From finger chips and fried *chapatis* to peanuts and *paneer pakora,* the Silver Oak packs in the locals on a nightly basis for beer and bar snacks to the background hum of American light rock. Wooden tables set close together make for a snug and smoky atmosphere. Open daily 10am-10:30pm.

Rajasthan Hotel Restaurant, Fraser Rd., on the right, north of the intersection of Fraser and Dak Bungalow Rd. If repeated consumption of Indian food has waged war on your mouth (and stomach), try these subtly spiced, if predictable, veg. dishes and soups. *Navratan kofta* Rs50, *paneer masala* Rs60. Open daily 8am-10:30pm.

Mayfair Ice Cream Parlor and Restaurant, Fraser Rd., across from the Bansi Vihar, 5min. from the railway station. With all the dark, subterranean charm of an aging army mess hall, the Mayfair is packed most nights with young people sucking in the cool air and slurping down ice cream (flavors include vanilla, strawberry, and blind love). Lengthy veg. (Rs18-42) and non-veg. (Rs22-60) menus too. Open daily 9am-10:30pm.

👁 SIGHTS

HAR MANDIR. In the twisting lanes of Old Patna is Har Mandir, a Sikh *gurudwara* marking the birthplace of the 10th and last Sikh guru, Gobind Singh (born 1666). The second-most important throne of the Sikh religion (after the Golden Temple in Amritsar), Har Mandir is an impressive, white-domed building, set among the busy bustle of the old town's *chowk*. Visitors must remove shoes and cover their heads to enter (scarves are provided). The present building was constructed after a 1954 earthquake destroyed the original temple. You can climb a set of steps inside the temple up to the roof, which offers a good view of the city. A museum honoring Gobind Singh holds a few relics and pictures.

PATNA MUSEUM. The Patna Museum houses an excellent collection of stone and bronze sculpture, some of it dating from the Mauryan (3rd century BC) and Gupta (4th-6th centuries AD) periods. An extensive menagerie of stuffed animals contains pieces that range from tiger and bison to little cats and a rather grumpy-losoking hedgehog; all are in various stages of neglected decomposition. Upstairs is a collection of terra-cotta figures and Buddha heads, as well as a large selection of Tibetan *thankas. (Buddha Marg. Open Tu-Sa 10:30am-4:40pm. Rs2.)*

GOLGHAR. One of Patna's most bizarre but also most popular landmarks is the Golghar, an egg-shaped grain storage bin near Gandhi Maidan. Built by the British in 1786 to protect against famine, it was never used and now sits like a great stone space helmet just to the left of Gandhi Maidan. Two staircases spiral 29m above the street and offer one of the quickest ways for people to get up out of the smog and dirt at ground level. The smoke-blue corners of the city and the mud-brown Ganga can be seen from the top.

KUMRAHAR EXCAVATION PARK. Although archaeologists have unearthed bits of Patna's past, most of the city's history remains concealed beneath its flaking concrete and dirt. Remains of Ashoka's ancient capital Pataliputra have been excavated in Kumrahar, south of Patna. *(5km out of town. Take a Rs4 tempo from the railway station along Kankarbagh Rd. Open Tu-Sa 9am-5pm. Rs5.)*

KHUDA BAKHSH ORIENTAL LIBRARY. The library houses a vast and esoteric collection of Islamic literature and relics, but there is little on display for the browsing tourist. In the lobby, display cases show off a few illuminated manuscripts, 19th-century astronomical and astrological equipment, and a manuscript copy of a poem by Rabindranath Tagore. *(Ashok Raj Path. Open Sa-Th 9:30am-5pm.)*

RAJGIR राजगृह

The collection of rocks and ruins that is Rajgir was capital of the powerful Magadha kingdom, whose rulers built grandly—the faintest outlines of their palaces and the great 40km wall with which they fortified their city lie in the middle of a well-trodden tourist path. Because Rajgir figured prominently in the Buddha's life, pilgrims flock here during the winter months. A chair lift takes them to Gridhrakuta, or "Vulture's Peak," a secluded mountain retreat where the Buddha gathered his disciples to unfold the Four Noble Truths. The first Buddhist Council took place at Rajgir, and the extensive nearby ruins of the university at Nalanda convey a sense of the success and scale of Buddhist learning that thrived here for nearly a thousand years. Jain influence in Rajgir was also strong, and Jain temples dot the low hills around the city center, commemorating the 14 seasons that Mahavira spent in this tranquil valley. Apart from a messy stretch of hotels and restaurants that has sprung up around the bus station and is often loud and choked with fumes, Rajgir remains a peaceful place to spend a day or two surrounded by the silence of history and hills.

🗹 **ORIENTATION AND PRACTICAL INFORMATION. Buses** from Bihar Sharif pass Nalanda and then, 15km later, arrive at the bus stand in Rajgir. From here, frequent buses run to **Gaya** (every 30min. 5:30am-6pm, 3hr., Rs18); **Nalanda** (every 20min., Rs4); and **Patna** (3 and 6pm, 4hr., Rs28). There are also frequent buses to Bihar Sharif, from where there is more regular service to and from Patna. The road continues as a new bypass, but the left turn just opposite the bus stand leads down the muddy, rutted strip that makes up the **center of town.** The markets, post office, hospital, telephone exchange, and the Burmese and Bengali temples can all be found here, along this smoggy, muddy mile-long stretch of road designed to test the patience of all but the most mellow and detached of pilgrims. After the **Burmese Temple,** this road reunites with the bypass just before the line of shops containing the tourist office. Farther on, a well-marked road to the left leads to the base of **Mt. Ratnagiri** and the lift to the top. The state-run **tourist office** has a detailed and imaginative map on its walls, but not much else (open M-Sa 10am-5pm). Rajgir's tiny **railway station** is set back 1km on the left of the main intersection on the way to Nalanda. Passenger trains leave for **Patna** (5:50am and 4pm, Rs16). There is no place for **currency exchange. New Popular Pharmacy,** next to the post office, has a decent stock of medicines (open daily 6am-9pm). The **police station** (tel. 5228; open

24hr.) is 200m past the **post office,** which is on the main road just after it turns right towards the Burmese Temple. **Postal Code:** 803116. There are plenty of **STD/ISD** booths all along the main road, including a couple of late-night places attached to hotels. **Telephone Code:** 06119.

⬛⬛ ACCOMMODATIONS AND FOOD. The hotels and restaurants that line the main road are uniformly ugly and uninspiring, but alternatives do exist. The **Burmese Buddhist Temple** (tel. 5024), towards the end of the old road just before the bypass, is a good, friendly place away from the noise with views from the top out over the fields and hills. Plaques attesting to the karma-improving effects of the place adorn everything from the fridge to the ceiling fans to the crockery. The temple has comfortable mosquito-netted beds and a large dining hall (dorm beds, doubles, and triples with common bath for a donation, usually Rs50). The **Bengali Buddhist Society Temple,** next to the Burmese temple, provides clean and comfortable rooms for a donation. There are no fewer than three government-run tourist bungalows in Rajgir. The **Hotel Gautam Vihar** (tel. 5273), also known as Government Bungalow #1, on the main road between the bus stand and the railway station, has large, high-ceilinged rooms set around a pleasant garden (dorm beds Rs50; doubles Rs321; A/C rooms Rs535; off-season: Rs25/214). Most visitors to Rajgir come on high-volume package tours and eat where they live. *Dhabas* and basic hotel restaurants around the bus stand serve cheap *thalis* and *chapatis.* **Green Hotel Restaurant** (tel. 5352), at the other end of the shopping strip containing the tourist office, has a wide selection of cheap, unremarkable fare (Rs15-40; open daily 7am-10pm). In the evenings, the **Blue Beer Bar,** on the main road opposite the all-singing, all-dancing Raj hotel, offers a lively environment for the mostly mustached crowd to engage in drinking and spitting competitions. Particularly atmospheric during power cuts. Extra-strength beer and whisky are the local favorites.

⬛ SIGHTS. Rajgir's sights are spread out over a fair distance and are best covered by tonga, which should cost around Rs35-50 for a half-day. The sights on and around **Mt. Ratnagiri** are the main focus of Buddhist interest in Rajgir. A creaking **chair lift**—the "pride of Rajgir"—leads up to the top (open 8am-1pm and 2-5pm; Rs15), where the huge new Japanese-built **Viswa Shanti** peace *stupa* casts its shadow over the valley below. Drums banging and voices chanting the lotus *sutra* echo out over the hills from the small temple next door. From the *stupa,* a small bridle path winds around the side of the mountain back down to the road; take the first left onto a series of stony steps that leads up and down until it arrives at **Gridhrakuta,** or "Vulture's Peak." Once a favorite rainy season retreat of the Buddha, Gridhrakuta marks the site of two caves where the Buddha gave sermons and where the remains of a monastery from the Gupta period lie. At the foot of Mt. Ratnagiri are the remains of **Jivakamra Vana,** an early monastery built in the mango garden that was another of the Buddha's favorite spots. Off the main road to the right as you approach Ratnagiri are two chambers carved out of the cliff-face known as the **Swarna Bhandar.** Said to be the location of Buddhist-convert King Bimbisara's treasury, a "secret" doorway is supposed to lead from the cave and through the rock into the still-intact treasure trove. The site of **Bimbisara's jail,** where he was imprisoned and eventually executed by his son and successor, Ajatasatru, is also on the way out to Ratnagiri. The king is supposed to have chosen the site of his own incarceration; from here he could look out from his cell and watch the Buddha as he meditated and taught up on the mountain tops.

Just outside of town on Vaibhara Hill is the **Saptaparni Cave.** Shortly after the Buddha's death, the first Buddhist Council of 500 monks gathered here to compile in written form the Buddha's teachings. Nearby is **Pippala Cave,** a rectangular rock once used as a watch tower, which later became a revered abode of hermits. At the foot of Vaibhara Hill are the half-dozen **hot springs,** incorporated into the design of a Hindu temple. Known as **Lakshmi Narim,** they constitute the main draw for local tourists. Some of the springs, directed through the temple sculptures, gush from the mouths of lions. Mornings are busiest, when locals and pilgrims crowd the baths to perform ablutions or just to have a warm wash in the lower pools. A sign at the temple entrance warns non-Hindus not to enter, but this rule is not always rigidly enforced. Be on guard for "priests" looking for "contributions."

NEAR RAJGIR: NALANDA नलन्दा

Nalanda is the site of one of the oldest universities in the world. Built by the Guptas in the 5th century, it has a reputation as a center of learning dating back to the first millennium BC. By the time the Buddha made his visits to Nalanda, it was already a teeming and prosperous population center. Jainism's founder Mahavira spent 14 rainy seasons in retreat here, and Sariputra, one of the Buddha's earliest disciples, was born and also died in Nalanda. The great Chinese traveler Hiuen Tsang, whose detailed accounts of the places he visited during his *sutra*-collecting journeys around India are the best source of information on the period today, stayed and studied here during the 7th century; by this time, the university was home to as many as 4000 students, studying everything from Buddhist and Vedic philosophy to logic, grammar, chemistry, metallurgy, and medicine. As Nalanda's fame and fortune increased in subsequent centuries, so did its size. New buildings soared to the height of nine stories, and with the aid of King Harsha of Kannauj, Nalanda amassed a **library** of over nine million manuscripts. Nalanda continued to prosper as a center of learning into the 12th century, but by the 13th, successive waves of Muslim invaders had chased out all the students and reduced the library collection to cinders. Today it is possible to walk through the excavated remains of a dozen monastery buildings, all situated within a peaceful, evocative, and well-kept park run by the Archaeological Society of India.

The remains of an impressive **main temple** are at the south entrance. From the top, the view extends northward, where the monasteries on the right face the temples on the left. A **smaller temple** to the right of the monasteries is plastered with 6th-century wall paintings. A **museum** there houses a collection of Buddhist images and other archaeological finds unearthed nearby (open Sa-Th 10am-5pm; Rs2). Frequent **buses** leave for Nalanda from the bus stand at Rajgir (Rs3). From Nalanda's bus stand, you can take a **tonga** (Rs25) or walk the 2km to the site.

GAYA गया

According to folklore, the name Gaya derives from the demon Gayasura, who purified himself through rigorous yoga and received as a reward this sacred tract of land along the River Phalgu. As a further reward, Gaya was imbued with the power to absolve ancestral sins—it is said that one *shraddha* (funeral rite) in Gaya is equivalent to 11 *shraddhas* at any other place. Hindu pilgrims visit each of the 45 shrines in Gaya (including the Bodhi Tree in Bodh Gaya), offering prayers for the dead and rupees for the *gayaval* (attending priests). The high season comes in September when the Phalgu swells up with monsoon rains and thousands of pilgrims descend the *ghats* to perform their ritual ablutions. Gaya is almost as important to devout Hindus as its sister city is to Buddhists. Unfortunately, Gaya keeps most of its holiness well hidden from foreign eyes. Many of the most important sites are closed to non-Hindus, and the town itself has next-to-nothing to recommend it as anything more than a quick staging post en route to somewhere more interesting. Thirty-six kilometers north of Gaya are the **Barabar Caves,** a series of rock-hewn Jain temples dating from the 3rd century BC, that were featured as the "Marabar Caves" in E.M. Forster's *A Passage to India*.

⊏ TRANSPORTATION

Trains: Trains leave from **Gaya Junction Station.** Fares listed are 2nd/1st class. To: **Bela** (10 per day, 1hr., 2nd class Rs17; from Bela to the Barabar Caves, 12km tempo or tonga ride for Rs20-25 plus a 5km walk); **Kolkata** (*Radhani Exp.* 2302, 4:35am, 6hr., Rs765/1070; *New Delhi-Howrah Poorva Exp.* 2382, 8:48am, 7½hr.; *Kalka-Howrah Mail*

2312, 9:20pm, 9½hr., Rs104/510); **Patna** (*Palamau Exp.* 3347, 2:17am, 2½hr; *Hatia-Patna Exp.* 8624, 3:40pm, 2½hr., Rs31/161; *Sealdah-Jammu Tawi Exp.* 3151, 9:05pm, 5½hr., Rs61/268); **Varanasi** (*Doon Exp.* 3009, 5:32am, 5½hr., Rs61/294).

Buses: Panchayati Akara Bus Stand, 4km from Gaya Junction near Ram Shila Hill, has buses to locations in southern Bihar. **Bihar State Road Transport,** near Gandhi Maidan (Rs5 rickshaw ride from Gaya Junction). To: **Jamshedpur** (5 per day 6am-9pm, 11hr., Rs102); **Ranchi** (5 per day 7am-9pm, 7hr., Rs60). The **Manpur Bus Stand,** across the Phalgu River near the bridge, has buses to **Nalanda** and **Rajgir** (every hr. 6am-6pm, 2hr., Rs18). The **Zila School Bus Stand,** near the Kachahari area, has buses to **Bodh Gaya** (frequent, Rs4). Buses also go to **Patna** and **Varanasi.**

Local Transportation: Rickshaws (Rs5) go to the Zila School Bus Stand, where there are buses and tempos to Bodh Gaya; to the Vishnupad Temple or Shaktipith, Rs10.

🛈 ORIENTATION AND PRACTICAL INFORMATION

Gaya's boundaries are marked by the **railway station** on the northwest bank of the River Phalgu in the northeast and the base of **Brahmyoni Hill** in the southwest. **Station Road** goes right from the railway station and then takes a sharp left turning into **Civil Lines,** the administrative center of the city; here you will find the post office, police station, bus stands, and banks. Continuing east, the broad lanes of Civil Lines dissolve into the cluttered streets of the **Kachahari Road Bazaar,** approach the river and disperse north and south into narrow brick paths dotted with shrines and small shops. The spiritual center of the city is built around the **Vishnupad Temple** and the *ghats* of the Phalgu River.

Tourist Office: Inside the railway station. Has a wall map of Gaya. Open M-Sa 6am-8pm.

Currency Exchange: The nearest banks that change currency are in Bodh Gaya, but the **Siddharth International Hotel** (tel. 436243) will change major currencies and traveler's checks at criminally low rates. **Bank of Baroda** (tel. 22884) gives advances on major credit cards. Right on Station Rd., left at the bend, and the first right.

Luggage Storage: Platform 1, Gaya Junction Station. Rs5 per day. Open 24hr.

Market: Fruit market at **Purani Godam,** Tekari Rd., between Gaya Junction and the river.

Pharmacy: Many pharmacies are located along Station Rd. Most open 8am-9pm.

Hospital: The **Magadh Medical College** (tel. 22410) is a government hospital. Bihar's government services being what they are, Gaya is an awful place to be sick.

Police: Control Room (tel. 223131 or 223132). **Emergency:** tel. 20999.

Post Office: GPO, Kachahari Rd. (tel. 20660). Rs10 rickshaw ride from the railway station, right along Station Rd., and then left through the main fruit market. Open M-Sa 7am-6pm. There is a smaller post office on Station Rd., 200m or so right of the station on the left-hand side. **Postal Code:** 823001.

Telephones: A 24hr. **STD/ISD** booth is located inside the railway station.

PHONE CODE	0631

🏨🍴 ACCOMMODATIONS AND FOOD

Cheap hotels have accumulated across from the railway station and to the right along Station Rd., though they tend to be quite noisy. The hotel restaurants along Station Rd. offer the usual range of cheap Indian and Chinese food; more upscale is the expensive restaurant in the Siddharth International Hotel.

Hotel Buddha, Laxman Sahay Ln. (tel. 23428), straight back from the railway station, at the end of a long road perpendicular to Station Rd. Much quieter than the hotels along Station Rd. Small, sunny, clean doubles have comfortable mattresses, TVs, and attached baths with decent showers. Singles Rs150; doubles Rs180.

Ajatsatru Hotel, Station Rd. (tel. 21514 or 23714), across from the railway station on the left side. One of the largest hotels along the crowded Station Rd. strip, and probably the least spartan in terms of facilities. Also has one of the best restaurants around. Check-out 24hr. Singles from Rs160; doubles from Rs175, with A/C Rs595.

Pal Rest House, Station Rd. (tel. 436753). Turn right out of the station; the hotel is 250m down on the left-hand side, after the post office. Simple rooms around a central stairwell. This is an unremarkable little place, but it passes the all-important "clean, cheap, and friendly" test. Singles Rs60, with bath Rs80; doubles Rs100/110.

Station View Hotel, Station Rd. (tel. 20512), several hundred meters to the right of the station, past the Ajatsatru Hotel on the left side of the street. Don't be misled by the hotel's name: among its assets is the *lack* of a station view. A creaking and crumbling old oblong building, Station View is the place to come if you're looking to save Rs40 for your bus fare. All rooms have attached bath. Singles Rs50; doubles Rs60.

Siddharth International Restaurant, Station Rd. From the railway station, walk right 500m; it's on the left. Heavy curtains block out the outside world, industrial-strength fans whirr and buzz from all 4 corners of the room, and the stereo cranks out ornately orchestrated movie soundtracks. Fewer flies and more fresh air here than at other places on Station Rd. Most dishes Rs40-60; beer Rs150. Open daily 7am-11:30pm.

👁 SIGHTS

Gaya is one of Hinduism's most sacred cities, though its temples lack the splendor and atmosphere of those in other large pilgrimage centers.

VISHNUPAD TEMPLE. Towering over the bank of the Phalgu River, this golden-spired temple is said to house the 2m footprint of Vishnu in the form of the Buddha, enshrined in a silver basin. Non-Hindus may not enter the main shrine, but they can try to get a closer look at the sanctum (but not the print) by climbing the stairs at the back of the first shop to the left of the temple entrance.

BRAHMYONI HILL. One-thousand steep stones twist up to the Shiv Mandir at the top of this hill, where you are rewarded by the rare lungful of fresh air and views over Gaya, Bodh Gaya, and the surrounding countryside. There is also a small goddess temple with an image of Shiva's foot at the door. The hill is sacred to Buddhists, as it is associated with Gayasirsan (the Head of Gaya), the mountain where the Buddha is said to have delivered several important sermons. (*One km southwest of the Vishnupad Temple.*)

DURGA TEMPLE. In this rather mundane temple, non-Hindus can observe and even participate in the *shraddha*. Pilgrims who wish to perform the *shraddha* at Gaya must first circle their own village five times. Once in Gaya, a *gayaval* (priest trained in the *shraddha*) guides them in a complicated ritual involving Sanskrit prayers and offerings of *pinda* (water and rice kneaded into a ball). The pilgrims usually repay the *gayaval* for his services with a hefty donation. (*One km east of the Vishnupad Temple.*)

SHAKTIPITH. Sati's breast is said to have fallen here after she was cut to pieces (see **Divine Dismemberment,** p. 687). Images of the goddess are housed in a squat, cavernous mausoleum, inscribed on the front with the epic verse of Sati's destruction. (*Open daily 6am-noon and 1pm-midnight.*)

BODH GAYA बोध गया

Of all the holy Buddhist sites scattered around Northern India, Bodh Gaya is the holiest by far. One of the most significant events in the history of Asia took place here in the 6th century BC, when Prince Siddhartha Gautama gained enlightenment after prolonged meditation under the famous pipal tree, a descendent of which still stands on the same spot today. For Buddhists, this is the most impor-

THIS DOESN'T BODH WELL Though most of the Buddhists in Bodh Gaya hail from countries elsewhere in Asia, a few Indian Buddhists also live here. Recently, Indian Buddhists began a campaign to wrest control of the trust that oversees Bodh Gaya's religious matters from the Hindus who dominate its board of directors. Local Hindus protest that they too are Buddhists, as they worship the Buddha as an incarnation of Vishnu, and thus are suited to administer Bodh Gaya. It is countered that, except for at the town's temples, images of the Enlightened One are generally not a fixture of Hindu temples. Given Bihar's often hysterical political scene and Bodh Gaya's international presence, the dispute may have widespread consequences.

tant pilgrimage site in the world, and Bihar's other Buddhist sites, most of which consist of little more than piles of rubble, pale in comparison.

The Buddhist presence in Bodh Gaya, however, is quite new and mostly foreign. Although Buddhist monasteries thrived here long ago, they were left to sink into the mud after Buddhism faded out of India in the 12th century. It wasn't until the 19th century that Bodh Gaya was reborn as an important religious center, when British-led archaeological teams persuaded monks from Sri Lanka and Burma to raise the funds necessary to restore the Mahabodhi Temple to its former glory.

The winter (Dec.-Feb.) is the busiest and most vibrant time to visit, when monks, pilgrims, and students from around the world (the Dalai Lama included) congregate here. The monasteries quietly fill up, visiting teachers offer meditation courses, tent restaurants spring up to see to the pilgrims' more secular needs, and monks from around the world intone *sutras* in monasteries and temples built in their own national styles. By April, however, the crowds thin out, many of the restaurants and hotels close down, and the streets of Bodh Gaya again take on the air of meditative quietude that has reigned here for thousands of years.

♀ ORIENTATION AND PRACTICAL INFORMATION

It would require real effort to get lost in Bodh Gaya. The main road from Gaya runs through town, linking all the major sights and hotels, and stops by the **market** just in front of the **Mahabodhi Temple.** The area immediately in front of the temple has recently been converted into a paved pedestrian zone closed to traffic. Rickshaw-*wallahs* and postcard sellers congregate to the right of the temple, where the main road resumes again in front of the Tibetan monastery. This road turns left at the **Chinese Temple** and passes the **museum** and the **Thai Temple,** on either side of which smaller roads lead down to many of the other monasteries. The main road continues past the **Root Institute** and on to the future site of the new Maitreya statue.

Buses: Buses leave for **Gaya** from the stand near the Burmese Temple (every 30min. 5am-6pm, Rs5), with the bus stopping every 10m for passengers to embark, disembark, and sometimes just bark. Shared tempos are well worth the added nominal expense. Buses to **Patna** (7am and 2pm, 4½hr., Rs35) depart from the tourist bungalows, and a bus to **Varanasi** (5:30am, Rs60) stops in front of the Mahabodhi Society.

Local Transportation: Rickshaws (Rs5-10) go anywhere within Bodh Gaya.

Tourist Office: (tel. 400672), in the tourist bungalow compound just after the Thai Temple on the main road out of town. There's no real reason to come here, unless you're keen on adding to your collection of tourist pamphlets. Open M-Sa 10am-5pm.

Budget Travel: Middle Way Travels (tel. 400648), opposite the main temple, next to Weston Shoes. Extremely helpful and well-informed, this the best place in the area to arrange your tickets out of town. Offers all-inclusive tours of Buddhist sites in Northern India and can also arrange meditation courses at the nearby Vipassana Meditation Center. Buddhist bookstore and Internet facilities scheduled to open late summer/early fall 1999. Major credit cards accepted. Open daily 9am-9pm.

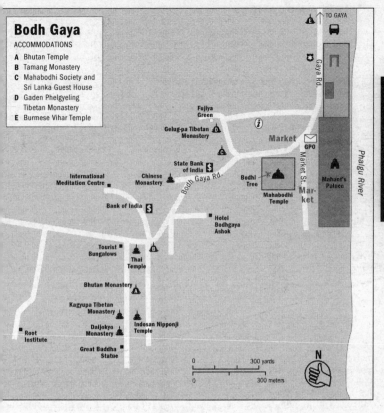

Bodh Gaya

ACCOMMODATIONS

A Bhutan Temple
B Tamang Monastery
C Mahabodhi Society and
  Sri Lanka Guest House
D Gaden Phelgyeling
  Tibetan Monastery
E Burmese Vihar Temple

BIHAR

Currency Exchange: State Bank of India, Gaya Rd. (tel. 400746), opposite the Hotel Bodh Gaya Ashok, 200m from the Mahabodhi Temple. Changes currency and traveler's checks. **Bank of India** (tel. 400750), opposite the Thai Temple, on a small path. Both banks open M-F 10:30am-2:30pm, Sa 10:30am-12:30pm.

Market: At the intersection of Gaya and Bodh Gaya Rd., a small lane to the left leads to a bazaar where you can buy fruit, handicrafts, and umbrellas.

Library: Temple Management Committee of Bodh Gaya and Library (tel. 400735), at the end of the pedestrian precinct. Collection includes daily newspapers as well as a comprehensive range of Buddhist texts and periodicals. Open daily 9am-5pm.

Hospital: Conditions at the **government hospital,** on the left on the way into town, are far from ideal. Doctors at the **Japanese temple's** clinic will see tourists in an emergency.

Police: (tel. 400741), 200m past the Burmese Temple.

Post Office: Gaya Rd. (tel. 400472), as you enter town, on the left. Open M-Sa 10:30am-5pm. **Postal Code:** 842231.

Telephones: STD/ISD booths opposite the Mahabodhi Temple and behind the Mahabodhi Society. Open 24hr.; off-season: 7am-9:30pm. The Burmese Vihar's booth is open 24hr. year-round.

PHONE CODE	0631

ACCOMMODATIONS

Bodh Gaya is full of hotels, but the temple- and monastery-run guest houses are the best options. Always remember to respect the norms of the religious community—drinking, smoking, and "improper sexual conduct" are not allowed.

Mahabodhi Society and Sri Lanka Guest House (tel. 400742), set back from the road across the street from the Mahabodhi Temple. Spotlessly clean and conscientiously managed place offers accommodations ranging from dorm beds to deluxe doubles with attached baths. Often full during peak season. The hostel is run on donations, which go towards running the society's various schools and charities. Check-out 24hr.

Bhutan Temple, Temple Rd. (tel. 400710), near the Great Buddha image. Situated in beautifully maintained garden grounds dominated by a colorful Bhutanese-style temple, rooms are clean and spacious and have mosquito nets. Rooms from Rs100.

Gaden Phelgyeling Tibetan Monastery, next to the Mahabodhi Society. Another popular place, built around a Tibetan-style quadrangle. The monastery gates close at 9:30pm. Tiny singles Rs50; larger rooms with bath Rs100.

Burmese Vihar Temple, Gaya Rd. (tel. 400721), on the right as you enter town; across from the bus station. Simple rooms with mosquito coils and nets look out onto quiet fields and rice paddies. During high season (Nov.-Jan.), 35 students from Antioch College transform the usually serene temple into an American university dormitory. Gates close at 9:30pm. Dorm beds Rs40; rooms from Rs40; large doubles with bath Rs250.

Tamang Monastery, Bodh Gaya Rd. (tel. 400802), on the left side of the main road, down the dirt path across from the International Meditation Centre. Clean, cramped rooms fill this charming little temple. Advanced booking is essential in season. Bed Rs100, with bath Rs150. Off-season: Rs50/100.

FOOD

Restaurants in Bodh Gaya are highly seasonal. During the winter, the gourmand can stray from the middle path and pig out on anything from chocolate chip cookies at the **Original Pole-Pole**, across from the Burmese Temple, to the famed chocolate cake at the popular **Om Cafe.** During off-season, most of the restaurants and food tents close or disappear—the places listed below are open all year.

Sujata Restaurant, inside Hotel Bodh Gaya Ashok, next to the museum. The best by far of the few perennial places, but also the most expensive. Offers the standard antiseptic, A/C atmosphere with Indian veg. and non-veg. dishes (Rs125-145). To ditch the asceticism, indulge in the in-season all-you-can-eat lunch and dinner buffets (Rs300).

Fujiya Green, near the Tibetan Temple. Leaving the pedestrian precinct with the Mahabodhi Temple to your left, make a right and follow the signs around to the left. This cozy little shack serves up cheap dishes in a comfortable atmosphere among the fields behind the Tibetan monastery. Veg. chop suey Rs25, ginger chicken Rs65. Open daily 7am-9pm.

Kalyan Restaurant, opposite the main temple, 70m down a small lane on the left-hand side. Simple, open-air place serves the usual range of dishes as well as vegetable *gyoza* for Rs25. Open daily 7am-10pm.

SIGHTS

MAHABODHI TEMPLE. The main point of interest in Bodh Gaya is the Mahabodhi Temple, referred to simply as "the *stupa*" by most Buddhists. Built right next to the site of the Buddha's Enlightenment, the temple rises up from peaceful flowery gardens to tower above the sacred Bodhi Tree that marks the spot where Siddhartha Gautama meditated through the night and awoke to Buddhahood. Smaller shrines throughout the grounds mark different stages in the Buddha's meditations; he is supposed to have spent a total of 49 days here deep in thought after deciding that the practice of extreme asceticism was getting him no closer to a true under-

THE TREE OF KNOWLEDGE As with any object of religious veneration worth its offering of flowers and gold leaf, the pipal tree at Bodh Gaya has been the subject of countless legends and stories over the years. Central to the mystique and holiness of the tree that today stands in Bodh Gaya is the belief that it is a direct descendent of the one under which the Buddha meditated over 2500 years ago. Some believe that the original tree was cut down by Emperor Ashoka himself before his famous conversion to Buddhism. The tree was miraculously restored to life, only to be hacked down again by Ashoka's wife, newly jealous of the attention and respect her husband had started to bestow upon the tree since its remarkable recovery. But the tree once again sprung up from its roots. Suitably impressed by its hardiness, Ashoka and his wife sent a sapling from the original tree to Sri Lanka, where it is believed to still prosper today. The centuries to come were to witness a series of attacks on the tree at Bodh Gaya, which weakened it to such an extent that it finally fell in a storm in 1876. The incarnation that is the object of such veneration today was grown from a seedling taken from the original tree's offspring in Sri Lanka.

standing of life's suffering. Emperor Ashoka built the first temple on this site in the 3rd century BC, but the present temple, which has been through layers and layers of restorations, probably dates from the 6th century AD. Much of the rescue work was initiated in 1882 by Burmese monks after the temple was found neglected and overrun by squatters. Over the last 30 years, many statues have been stolen from the temple's circular niches. The oldest structure left on the site is a stone railing built in the first century AD to keep out wild animals; a good quarter of it, however, has been removed and whisked away to museums in London and Kolkata.

At the back of the temple is the sacred **Bodhi Tree** (see below), a direct descendent of the tree under which the Buddha attained enlightenment *(open daily 6-8am and 6-8pm)*. The **Vajrasana**, or "diamond throne," between the tree and the temple, is thought to be the precise spot where the Buddha sat. A large gilded image of the Buddha is kept behind glass in the temple, and another is on the first floor, which is only open in the evenings for meditation. A part of the first floor is permanently closed off, due to one man's recent attempt to saw off a branch of the sacred tree as a souvenir. *(Open daily 5am-9pm. Free; camera fee Rs10.)*

OTHER TEMPLES AND MONASTERIES. The **Thai Temple**, Bodh Gaya's second-most prominent landmark, is located 500m after the main road takes a sharp left. A large *wat* with the classic claw-like tips on its orange roof, the temple opened in 1957 (year 2500 in the Buddhist calendar). Side-roads branch off the main road on either side of the Thai Temple. To the left are the **Bhutan Monastery** and the Japanese **Indosan Nipponji Temple**. The Indosan Nipponji's peace bell rings with a swinging cadence throughout the morning. The lane on the right side of the Thai Temple leads to the **Kagyu-pa Tibetan Monastery**, which contains brightly-colored, larger-than-life murals depicting the life of the Buddha. Next door is the **Daijokyo Temple**, another Japanese construction with an oppressive modern concrete exterior. Just up the road from the Daijokyo Temple, the 25m **Giant Buddha Statue**, which was built by Japanese monks and inaugurated by the Dalai Lama in 1989, sits on a lotus, the Buddha's robe rippling out of the red sandstone blocks. Statues of the Buddha's first disciples surround the main image. The chapel walls of the **Gelug-pa Tibetan Monastery**, next to the Mahabodhi Society, are painted with *thanka*-style clouds, wheels, and *bodhisattvas*. Visitors are invited to turn the massive silo of a prayer wheel downstairs. And don't neglect the **Mahant's Palace**, on the left just before you reach the center of town. Now a working Hindu temple, its rear views of the Neranghana River and the Sujata Mountain beyond make it a great spot for meditation, contemplation, or just plain chillin' out. *(Most temples open daily dawn-noon and 2pm-dusk.)* The Archaeological Society of India has a small **museum**, just off the main road, which contains images unearthed nearby *(open Sa-Th 10am-5pm; free)*.

BUDDHISM AND COMMUNITY SERVICE

During the high season, meditation courses are a major industry in Bodh Gaya. Teachers from all over the world jet (or rickshaw) in to provide training to Buddhists and aspiring Buddhists in the *dharma*-rich atmosphere of this temple town. A few permanent institutions in Bodh Gaya dedicated to spreading the word of the Buddha also conduct courses, and though the peak season runs only from October to March, a couple of places remain open and active throughout the summer. The **Root Institute for Wisdom Culture** (tel. 400714; fax 400548), at the edge of town down a dirt path to the left, offers 10-day courses in the winter with guest *lamas* and Western teachers in a quiet, intimate setting (Rs2900-4600, including room and board). Room and board is also available for non-meditators and, although they don't provide instruction in the off-season, visitors are welcome all year. The **International Meditation Center,** across from the Thai monastery, offers courses in the Vipassana Method year-round. The 10-day course is free, but a donation of Rs70-100 per day will defray the costs of a dorm bed in a double or triple and three meals. Shorter courses are also available. The **Vipassana Meditation Center** (tel. 400437), behind the university, has 10-day courses every month except July. They house and feed you for a donation. A branch of Goenha, the **Dhamana Bodhi Meditation Center** (tel. 400437), 1km past the big Japanese Buddha, also holds classes in season, as does the **Burmese Vihar** (see **Accommodations,** above).

There are a number of charitable organizations in Bodh Gaya. The **Root Institute,** which sponsors tree planting, in addition to year-round leprosy and polio projects, is always looking for volunteers and donations. The Mahabodhi Society runs a number of charitable programs, including a free pharmacy, a primary school, an ambulance service, and a rehabilitation center. They also have information on the many charitable organizations which pop up during peak season.

VAISHALI वैशाली

Fifty-five kilometers from Patna, Vaishali is a tiny, one-cow town surrounded by rice paddies and home to a handful of farming families, a scattering of small street stalls, and the ruined remains of the world's first republic. As the capital of the Lichavis during the 6th century BC, Vaishali was renowned as far away as Tibet for its peace and prosperity and for its elected system of government. Birthplace and hometown of Jainism's founder Mahavira, Vaishali also featured prominently in the life of the Buddha. He is thought to have preached one last sermon here before announcing his approaching *parinirvana.* Also mentioned in the *Ramayana* as the place where the gods and demons pow-wowed before churning the ocean, Vaishali today is a quiet, friendly place off the well-trodden tourist path. During the high season (Oct.-Feb.), Vaishali attracts tourists of Bihar's Buddhist sites; off season, you will almost certainly have the place to yourself.

A gate to the left just after the tourist lodge leads back to most of the ruins and to the Youth Hostel. Fifty meters farther down the highway is another fork which leads left through fields and villages to the walled compound containing the **Ashokan Pillar** and **stupa,** 4km away. Direct **buses** go to Vaishali from the main bus stand in Patna (5:30, 10:30, and 11:30am; 2hr.; Rs20). Alternatively, after crossing the M Bridge on one of the frequent buses to Hajipur (Rs8), get on another bus to Lagang (Rs7), where many shared **taxis** (Rs6) ply the road passing through Vaishali. Ask to be let off at the **Government's Tourist Lodge.** Direct buses from Vaishali to Patna (6:45, 8:30am, 12:30, and 3pm; Rs20) pass by the Tourist Lodge, and there are regular jeeps and trucks to Lalgang, where connections to Patna are frequent. A combination of jeeps, buses, tempos, and flying pigs can also get you from here to Raxaul, on the border with Nepal. Take a **jeep** going north from Vaishali to Muzaffarpur (Rs10), and then take a bus straight through to Raxaul (Rs40). The **Tourist Lodge** on the main road has simple rooms, with fan and attached bath (singles Rs50; doubles Rs75), and a restaurant (open Oct.-Feb.). The **Youth Hostel** is c

...e main road (dorm beds Rs20; doubles with bath Rs75). Their restaurant is also ...osed off season, when the only place to eat is at one of the small *dhabas*.

SIGHTS. Through a gateway to the left just after the Tourist Lodge is the large ...ctangular pond known as the **Coronation Tank,** once used to anoint the town's ...aders during inaugural ceremonies. Today it's the favorite soaking spot for local ...rmers and their buffalo. A small **museum** on the right side of the tank showcases ...me of the stone and terra-cotta pieces retrieved from nearby sites (open Sa-Th ...am-5pm; free). Down a small lane to the back of the museum, a small garden ...closes the **stupa** thought to contain a portion of the Buddha's ashes, which were ...vided up after his cremation and distributed among the leaders of the eight ...ajor kingdoms of Northern India. Today, a shallow circle of stones is all that ...mains of the *stupa* covered by a conical green tin roof. (Open dawn-dusk.) The ...her side of the tank is dominated by the **Japanese Temple** and the great crowned ...hite dome of the new **Vishwa Shanti Peace Stupa** consecrated here in 1996.

The Tourist Lodge rents bikes (Rs20) for the 4km ride through the fields to the ...hokan Pillar. Circled by a pinkish brick wall and clearly visible from the road that ...ts left off the highway, the well-preserved pillar and its lion capital, cut from a ...ngle piece of limestone, dominate the remains of this major monastic complex. ...he lion faces Kushinagar where the Buddha died. An age-withered **stupa** stands in ...e pillar's shadow, and an air of quietude surrounds the compound. The small ...nk is said to be the spot where a monkey once presented honey to the Buddha.

AXAUL रक्सौल

...ith all the dirt but none of the charm you'll find elsewhere in India, Raxaul, ...6km north of Patna, is a particularly nasty town, and you should aim to be stuck ...re for no longer than absolutely necessary. Transportation is easy to come by— ...ckshaws go to the Nepalese border town of **Birganj** (less unpleasant than Raxaul; ...e p. 781), and buses go to **Patna,** with its train connections to Kolkata and Delhi.

Raxaul's main street leads straight over the bridge into Nepal, cutting through ...e market area with a tangle of alleyways to the east and west. Coming from ...epal, you'll have to stop at Indian **customs,** right after the bridge, then at the **immi-** **ation office,** a little farther down on the right (open daily 5am-8pm; Nepalese ...migration closes at 7pm). **Buses** leave from the bus park on the north side of ...wn, just off the main road near the railway tracks (6-9am and 6-11pm). During ...e rest of the day, buses leave from Laxmipur, 3km south of Raxaul (IRs10 by ...ckshaw), with service to Patna (every hr., 8hr., IRs70). **There are no facilities for** **anging money in Raxaul**—Birganj and Patna are the closest places to do so. The ...st office is on the west side of the main street (open M-Sa 9am-4pm). **Postal Code:** ...5305. **Pharmacies** and **STD/ISD** booths line the main road. **Telephone Code:** 06255.

WARNING. Crossing the border into Nepal requires four steps: Indian Immigration, Indian Customs, Nepalese Immigration, and Nepalese Customs. You'll need a photo and US$15 to pay for your visa. **No other currencies are accepted, and there are no currency exchange facilities at the border.** Exact change is best, and the closest place to buy U.S. dollars is in Patna. Also, remember to **get your passport stamped** to say that you left India, or you'll have trouble entering Nepal. The Indian **immigration office** is easy to miss; some rickshaw-*wallahs* don't know where it is since Indians and Nepalis don't have to go there.

If you're stuck here overnight, then you're either woefully unlucky or recklessly ...nprepared. **Hotel Ajanta,** Ashram Rd. (tel. 61019), down a lane east of the main ...ad, is a tolerable enough place. All the rooms have fans, but only those with ...tached baths have mosquito nets. The hotel has its own generator and an ...tached **restaurant.** (Singles Rs77; doubles Rs103, with bath Rs157, with bath and ...r-cooling Rs321.)

WEST BENGAL

পশ্চিম বঙ্গ

West Bengal is India's most densely populated state, with 777 people per sq. km of its 88,752 sq. km area. With this crush of humanity comes a history and a cultur that has dominated India for hundreds of years; it continues to thrive today. In th 19th century, Bengal was the fulcrum of literary and religious revival and a hotbe for national activism—the Bengali Renaissance produced India's finest writer: thinkers, and social reformers, including Rabindranath Tagore, India's first Nobe laureate for literature, and Swami Vivekananda, a spiritual leader who attempte to infuse Hinduism with Western ideas of material progress. As the state's capita Kolkata still maintains its position as India's artistic and intellectual epicenter.

West Bengal's location, spanning the Gangetic delta, made it a rich agricultura and commercial region which attracted European plunderers in the 17th and 18t centuries. After the Battle of Plassey in 1757, when Robert Clive defeated Nawa Siraj-ud-Daula and the French to claim Bengal for Britain, the province began it rise to prominence. Although the British made Kolkata their capital and sought t use Bengal as a base, they found themselves unable to subdue the region's tena cious cultural identity. For centuries, Bengalis have spoken their own languag and maintained unique religious traditions. The year 1905 witnessed the infamou Partition of Bengal, which divided the state along religious lines: East Benga (later East Pakistan, then Bangladesh in 1971) and Assam held a strong Musli population, and West Bengal, together with Bihar and Orissa, was largely Hind The partition was tragic and bloody and directly paved the way for the even bigge bloodier partition of the subcontinent in 1947 into India and Pakistan. Today, Be gal revels in its enlightened Marxist traditions—the Communist Party of India ha ruled since the 1960s. The state continues to face the problem of a huge refuge influx from its neighbor Bangladesh, and many Bengalis display an admirab social conscience, funneling much of their income into refugee charities.

West Bengal is home to a collage of landscapes and cultures. At its northern en is Darjeeling, India's most famous hill station, lying at the foothills of the Himal yas. The southern end of the state drops right down to sea level at the swamp mangrove forests of the Sunderbans, home of the Royal Bengal Tiger. One hu dred kilometers inland from the Bay of Bengal lies 309-year-old Kolkata, a choke crowded, and yet captivating city embodying both the glories of the past and th hopes for the future of the nation.

HIGHLIGHTS OF WEST BENGAL

■ India's most famous hill station, **Darjeeling** (p. 663) seduces heat-weary travelers with tea plantations, toy trains, and superb Himalayan views.

■ **Kolkata's** temples, monuments, museums, and parks (p. 655) are rivaled only by the unchecked exuberance of the city's denizens.

KOLKATA (CALCUTTA) কলিকাতা

Oh Kolkata! Bursting at the seams with 13 million people, Kolkata is India's larges city, encompassing an area of a mind-boggling 853 sq. km. Even to its own res dents, Kolkata sometimes seems like a human cyclone. You can't just walk dow the street in Kolkata—you must step into, over, and around it, and you can't avoi breathing in layers of snot-blackening soot. Old men trot with the traffic by da

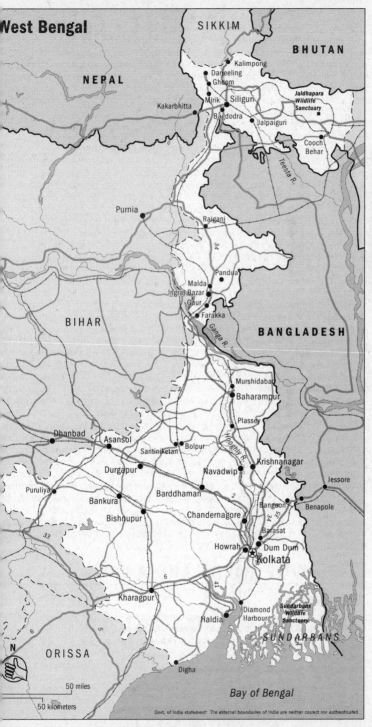

WEST BENGAL

hauling the world's last fleet of hand-pulled rickshaws; families, by the thousands, sleep on the pavement at night. Yet the same Kolkatans who lament their city's overpopulation and pollution also sing of their hometown as a "City of Joy" (the name of Kolkata's most famous slum). For years the city has enjoyed a position at the vanguard of Indian culture, dictating fashions and intellectual trends for the entire country. The city churns out poets, painters, and saints and exhibits magnificent parks and palaces; its citizens exude a vitality not found in any other Indian city. A recent return to its Bengali name "Kolkata," derived from the word "Kalikshetra" ("Ground of Goddess Kali"), betrays the spirit behind its residents' exuberance and follows the nation-wide return to Indian city names, as did Bombay and Madras. The worship of Kali is an essential facet of the city's character, and the annual Durga Puja in October is the highlight of any Kolkata experience.

Though the city is well-endowed with scores of Indian temples scattered around the River Hooghly, its streets still smell strongly of the Raj. Competing with the temples for attention are the many monuments to British monarchs, governors-general, and martyrs. In 1690, East India Company agent Job Charnock bought up the fertile land, combining it into a rapidly developing trading-post and industrial base. Though captured in 1756 by Bengal's Nawab, Siraj-ud-Daula, the fortified city became the centerpiece of British India soon after Robert Clive's victory at Plassey—Kolkata officially became the Raj's capital in 1773. Under the first governor-general, Warren Hastings (r. 1774-1785), Bengalis began to get their first taste of English education. Yet the new literati remained too proud to submit to assimilation by a foreign power, and the 19th century witnessed the elite-led Bengal Renaissance. Ram Mohan Roy (1774-1833) started the movement by pushing for social and religious reform with his Brahmo Samaj, a theistic movement that called for reform within Hinduism. Kolkata's upper-class salons hosted a revolution in literature, music, dance, and painting that culminated in the work of the Nobel Prize-winning poet Rabindranath Tagore. Kolkata also became a center for virulent anti-British politics. Tagore renounced his knightship after the Jallianwallah Bagh massacre at Amritsar. Realizing their power was waning, the British quickly created a new capital, Delhi, to quell Kolkata's influence. When the British tried to partition Bengal in 1905, their efforts were met with bombs and boycotts.

By the end of the 19th century, however, Kolkata had its critics, even among the British colonialists who built her. A series of blows, beginning with the 1911 transfer of the capital to Delhi, continuing with the opening of the Suez Canal (rendering Bombay a far more prosperous port), and culminating in the bloody 1947 Partition, established the city's reputation for squalor. Increasing urban migration from Bangladesh and the rest of India, combined with the silting of the increasingly unnavigable Hooghly, has only exacerbated the problems. The Communist government has worked wonders in the countryside but has failed to rid the city of all its problems. In 1984 Kolkata inaugurated its Metro, the first of its kind in India, and the government is currently developing Salt Lake to the east as a "second Kolkata." Untroubled by the rioting that has plagued other Indian cities, Kolkatans appear unified in their unmatched love for their hometown. Three centuries after its founding, the city plods forward, tracking its past behind it.

▐ GETTING THERE AND AWAY

FLIGHTS

Officially called Netaji Subhas Chandra Bose Airport (tel. 511 8070 or 511 8079), **Dum Dum Airport** is 2km northeast of the city. The **pre-paid taxi** stand in the domestic terminal is the best bet for a ride into downtown Kolkata (40min., Rs150). City buses #303, 46, and 510 (Rs4) and the less direct E3 (Rs5) all run between the Esplanade and the airport. Minibus #151 (Rs18) goes from BBD Bagh to the airport. The airport has a **currency exchange counter** (to the left in the international terminal), a **post office,** West Bengal and India **tourist offices,** and the carriers **Indian Airlines, Jet Airlines,** and **Sahara India Airlines** (domestic terminal). The **train ticket**

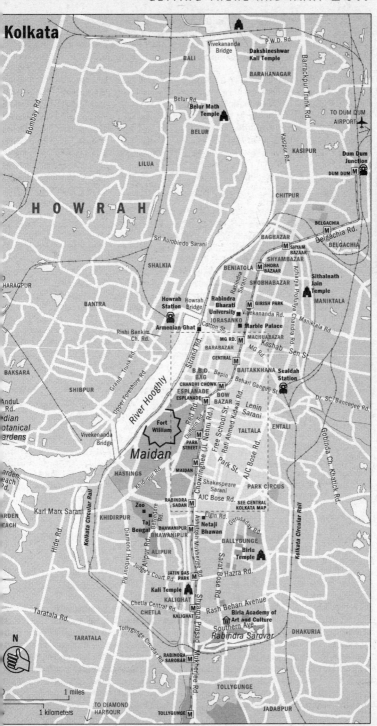

Kolkata

WEST BENGAL

P.W.D. Rd.

Vivekananda Bridge

Dakshineshwar Kali Temple

BALI

BARAHANAGAR

Bombay Rd.

Belur Rd.

Belur Math Temple

BELUR

LILUA

Barrackpur Trunk Rd.

Kasipur Rd.

KASIPUR

TO DUM DUM AIRPORT

Dum Dum Junction

DUM DUM

H O W R A H

Sri Aurobindo Sarani

SHALKIA

CHITPUR

BELGACHIA

Belgachia Rd.

BELGACHIA

BAGBAZAR

BENIATOLA

SHYAM BAZAAR

SHYAMBAZAR

SHOBA BAZAR

SHOBHABAZAR

Rabindra Sarani

Acharya Profulla Chandra Rd.

Sithalnath Jain Temple

MANIKTALA

HARAGPUR

BANTRA

Howrah Station

Howrah Bridge

Rabindra Bharati University

JORASANKO

Armenian Ghat

Cotton St.

GIRISH PARK

Vivekananda Rd.

Marble Palace

Maniktala Rd.

Rishi Bankim Ch. Rd.

MG RD.

MACHUABAZAR

BARABAZAR

Kashab Sen St.

BAKSARA

SHIBPUR

Grand Trunk Rd.

Upper Foreshore Rd.

CENTRAL

MG Rd.

B.B.D. BAG

Bepin Behari Ganguli St.

BAITAKKHANA

Sealdah Station

Andul Rd.

dian otanical ardens

River Hooghly

CHANDNI CHOWK

ESPLANADE
ESPLANADE

BOW BAZAR

Lenin Sarani

Dr. SC Bannerjee Rd.

Gobinda Ch. Khatick Rd.

Vivekananda Bridge

Fort William

Red Rd.

Dufferin Rd.

Chowringhee (JL Nehru Rd.)

Free School St.

Rafi Ahmed Kidwai Rd.

TALTALA

ENTALI

PARK STREET

Maidan

MAIDAN

Park St.

AJC Bose Rd.

Shakespeare Sarani

arden each d.

ARDEN EACH

HASTINGS

Khidirpur Rd.

PARK CIRCUS

SEE CENTRAL KOLKATA MAP

Karl Marx Sarani

RABINDRA SADAN

AJC Bose Rd.

Elgin Rd.

Netaji Bhavan

Kolkata Circular Rail

KHIDIRPUR

Zoo

Taj Bengal

BHAWANIPUR

BHAWANIPUR

ALIPUR

Ashutosh Mukherjee Rd.

Purusuttip Rd.

BALLYGUNGE

Birla Temple

Hide Rd.

Diamond Harbour Rd.

Judge's Court Rd.

JATIN DAS PARK

Sarat Bose Rd.

Hazra Rd.

DHAKURIA

Kali Temple

KALIGHAT

Chetla Central Rd.

CHETLA

KALIGHAT

Rash Behari Avenue

Southern Ave.

Birla Academy of Art and Culture

Rabindra Sarovar

Taratala Rd.

TARATALA

Tollygunge Circular Rd.

Shyama Prasad Mukherjee Rd.

RABINDRA SAROBAR

Shyama Prasad Mukherjee Rd.

N

TOLLYGUNGE

JADABPUR

1 miles

1 kilometers

TO DIAMOND HARBOUR

TOLLYGUNGE

counter serves Delhi, Bombay, and Madras only. The Airport Manager in the Domestic Terminal can arrange beds for tired travelers with a layover of 24 hours or less. There is a counter at the domestic terminal where you can make hotel reservations, but most budget accommodations aren't on their list.

INTERNATIONAL AIRLINES. All carriers have offices at the airport as well as in Kolkata proper. **AeroFlot,** 58 Chowringhee Rd. (tel. 242 1617). Open M-F 10am-1pm and 2-5:30pm, Sa 10am-1pm. **Air France,** 41 Chowringhee Rd. (tel. 226 6161). Open M-Sa 9am-5:30pm. **Air India,** 50 Chowringhee Rd. (tel. 242 2356 or 242 1187). Open daily 9:30am-5:30pm. **Alitalia,** 230A AJC Bose Rd. (tel. 247 7394). Open daily 9:30am-5:30pm. **American Airlines,** 2-7 Sarat Bose Rd. (tel. 747622). Open M-F 9am-1pm and 1:30-5:30pm, Sa 9am-1:30pm. **Air Canada, Gulf Air,** and **TWA,** 230A AJC Bose Rd. (tel. 247 7783). Open M-F 9am-1pm and 1:30-5:30pm, Sa 9am-1:30pm. **Bangladesh Biman,** 33C Chowringhee Rd. (tel. 293709). **British Airways,** 41 Chowringhee Road (tel. 226 3453). Open M-Sa 9:30am-5:30pm. **Canadian, SAS, South African,** and **United Airlines,** 2-7 Sarat Bose Rd. (tel. 747623). Open M-F 9:30am-1pm and 2-5:30pm, Sa 9:30am-1pm. **Cathay Pacific,** 1 Middleton St. (tel. 240 3211). Open M-F 9:30am-1pm and 2-5:30pm, Sa 9:30am-1:30pm. **Delta,** 13D Russell St. (tel. 246 3873 or 246 3826). Open M-F 9am-5:30pm. **Japan Airlines,** 35A Chowringhee Rd. (tel. 226 7920). Open M-F 9am-1pm and 1:30-5:30pm, Sa 9am-1pm. **KLM and Northwest,** 1 Middleton St., Jeevan Deep (tel. 247 4593). Open M-F 9am-5pm, Sa 9am-1pm. **Lufthansa,** 30A/B Chowringhee Rd. (tel. 249 5777; fax 246 4010). Open M-F 9am-1pm and 1:30-5:30pm. **RNAC,** 41 Chowringhee Rd. (tel. 246 8534). Open M-F 9am-1pm and 2-4pm, Sa 9am-1pm. **Thai Airways,** 18G Park St. (tel. 229 9846). Open 24hr.; tourist window (#12) open M-F 9am-1pm and 2-5pm.

DOMESTIC AIRLINES. Indian Airlines, 39 Chittaranjan Ave. (tel. 236 0870 or 236 4433; fax 236 5391). Open 24hr. Great Eastern Hotel branch, 1-3 Old Court House St., 2nd fl. (tel. 248 0073 or 248 8009). Open M-Sa 10am-1:30pm and 2-5pm. **Jet Airways,** 18D Park St. (tel. 229 2660). Open daily 9am-7pm. **Sahara,** 2A Shakespeare Sarani (tel. 282 8969 or 282 7686). Open M-Sa 10:30am-5pm.

To: **Agartala** (1-2 per day, 1hr., US$40); **Ahmedabad** (M-Sa, 2½hr., US$160); **Aizawl** (M, W, and F; 1hr.; US$65); **Bagdogra** (M, W, F, and Su; 1hr.; US$70); **Bangalore** (1 per day, 3½hr., US$185); **Bhubaneswar** (M-Sa, 1hr., US$60); **Chennai** (2 per day, 2hr., US$160); **Delhi** (3 per day, 2hr., US$140); **Dibugarh** (M, W, F, and Su; 1½hr.; US$85); **Dimapur** (4 per week, 2hr., US$85); **Guwahati** (1 per day, 1hr., US$50); **Hyderabad** (1 per day, 3hr., US$150); **Imphal** (1 per day, 2hr., US$65); **Jaipur** (3 per week, 2½hr., US$160); **Jorhat** (Tu and Sa, 1½hr., US$85); **Lucknow** (1 per day, 2½hr., US$100); **Mumbai** (2 per day, 3hr., US$205); **Nagpur** (3 per week, 1½hr., US$100); **Patna** (1 per day, 1hr., US$70); **Port Blair** (5 per week, 2hr., US$195); **Dhaka, Bangladesh** (M-W and F-Sa, 1hr., US$50); and **Kathmandu, Nepal** (M-W and F-Sa, 1½hr., US$100).

TRAINS

Kolkata has two stations, **Sealdah Station,** northeast on AJC Bose Rd., with trains going north, and **Howrah Station,** across the Hooghly River from Kolkata, with trains going to the rest of India. The best way to get to or from Howrah Station is by **bus.** If you're going to the Sudder St. area, take a bus to the Esplanade (Rs2) and walk five minutes. There is a **pre-paid taxi** stand at the station (Rs40 to downtown Kolkata). There is a **West Bengal Tourist Office** at the station (open M-Sa 7am-1am, Su 7am-12:30pm). Tickets can be purchased at the **Railway Booking Office,** 6 Fairlie Pl. (tel. 220 3496), near BBD Bagh. The **Foreign Tourist Office,** on the first floor, has a helpful staff but long lines. There are train offices scattered around the city, but this is the only one that sells from the tourist quota. Foreign currency or rupees with an encashment certificate are accepted. (Open daily 9am-1pm and 1:30-4pm.)

Fares listed are 2nd class sleeper/3-tier A/C. From **Sealdah Station** to: **New Jalpaiguri** (*Darjeeling Mail* 3143, 7:15pm, 13hr.; *Kanchenjunga Exp.* 5657, 6:25am, 12hr., Rs213/1046); **Patna** (*Lal Quila Exp.* 3111, 8:15pm, 10hr., Rs183/804). From **Howrah Station** to: **Bhubaneswar** (*Rajdhani Exp.* 2422, 8hr., Rs283/860); **Chennai**

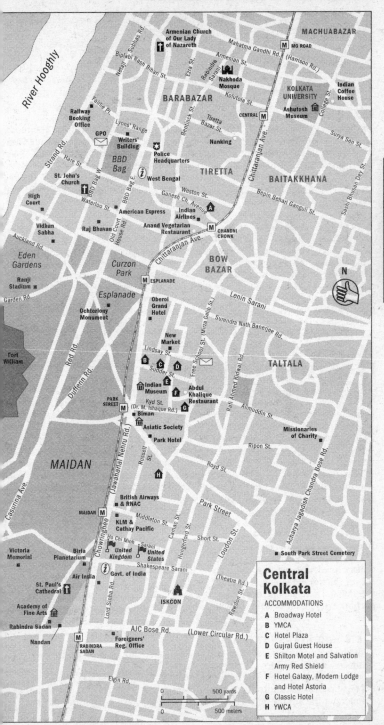

WEST BENGAL

Central Kolkata

ACCOMMODATIONS

A Broadway Hotel
B YMCA
C Hotel Plaza
D Gujral Guest House
E Shilton Motel and Salvation Army Red Shield
F Hotel Galaxy, Modern Lodge and Hotel Astoria
G Classic Hotel
H YWCA

(*Madras Mail* 6003, 8:15pm, 32hr.; *Coromandel Exp.* 2841, 2pm, 28hr., Rs317/
878); **Delhi** (*Rajdhani Exp.* 2301, 5pm, 18hr., 3-tier A/C Rs1500; *Poorva Exp.* 2381,
9:15am, 23hr., Rs309/791); **Mumbai** (*Howrah-Mumbai Mail* 8002, 7:20pm, 36hr.,
Rs4201; *Geetanjali Exp.* 2860, 12:25pm, 32hr., Rs350/964); **Patna** (*Rajdhani Exp.*
2305, 1:45pm, 7hr., Rs915, 3-tier A/C only); **Puri** (*Howrah-Puri Exp.* 8007, 10pm,
10½hr.; *Sri Jagannath Exp.* 8409, 7:20pm, 11hr., Rs178/684); and **Varanasi** (*Howrah-Amritsar Mail* 3005, 7:20pm, 15hr., Rs236).

BUSES

Private buses go to Siliguri (12hr.), a departure point for Darjeeling. The most
direct bus is run by West Bengal Tourism, departing Kolkata at 6pm, reaching **Siliguri** at 6am and **Jalpaiguri** at 6:15am (Rs195). Buses also run to **Dingha** (7am, 6hr.,
Rs55) and **Jaigon** (6pm, 19hr., Rs235). Tickets must be purchased in advance at the
booth at the Esplanade: to get there, take a left off Chowringhee Rd. on SN Banerjee Rd.; the booth is on the right just before the tram tracks. Other private bus
company booths are to the left (follow the tracks).

BOATS

Two to three ships sail to **Port Blair** in the Andaman Islands each month, but their
schedule depends on the weather. Tickets and a tentative schedule for the month
are available at the **Shipping Corporation Office,** 13 Strand Rd. (tel. 246 2354), two
blocks south of the Railway Booking Office; enter through the mail entrance, go
through the back door and up one floor (open M-F 10:30am-1pm). Arrivals and
departures are announced on the radio and in local daily newspapers a week in
advance. Ticket sales begin seven days before the scheduled departure and often
sell out in the first couple of days. Bring three passport photos to purchase tickets.
(3-4 days. Bunk Rs955; 2nd class Rs2243; 1st class Rs2852. Food per day costs
Rs50 in bunk; Rs100 in 1st and 2nd classes.)

▣ GETTING AROUND

BUSES

Buses in Kolkata are cheap, ubiquitous, and crowded. However, it's important to
let go of the "bus stop" concept: you can get on just about anywhere—just put your
hand out and the driver will slow down. If it's moving too fast for you to feel comfortable running alongside and jumping aboard, politely shout *"asthe!"* The key to
finding your bus is identifying a major destination that's in the same direction.
Women can usually find a designated "Ladies" seat, and if you can't get an official
one, most men are happy to stand if asked. When the ticket-*wallah* comes, tell him
where you're going—he'll tell you how much you owe and, if you ask, when to get
off. Make sure you get a ticket, or he may ask you to pay again. (Fares are Rs2-5.)

TRAMS AND SUBWAYS

Trams depart from the central Esplanade to major destinations throughout South
Kolkata and to Sealdah and Howrah Bridges (Rs1-2). They are slow and sometimes crowded. A list of routes can be purchased at any bookstand. India's first
subway (metro) extends in a virtually straight line from Tollygunge, up Chowringhee Rd., to Dum Dum Station. From this station, a taxi or auto-rickshaw to the airport takes 45 minutes, with traffic (Rs70). The metro is relatively uncrowded and
rapid. (Rs3-7; open M-Sa 8am-9:30pm, Su 2-9:30pm.)

TAXIS AND RICKSHAWS

Though expensive and isolating, **taxis** are the most convenient way to cover long
distances in Kolkata. Drivers must use the meters; don't ride in a cab if the driver
won't turn on the meter. The meter begins at Rs5, and the fare is double the displayed fare (to take into account the rising cost of petrol). The prepaid taxi
counters at the airport may have long lines, but they are worth the wait (Rs150).

Kolkata's **hand-pulled rickshaws** fight for space on the congested roads. In most cases, you can walk faster than they can pull. **Auto-rickshaws,** though quite efficient, leave you open to breathe all the exhaust fumes. They are cheaper than taxis but aren't metered; negotiate beforehand.

✈ ORIENTATION

Though the city is expansive and sprawling, Kolkata's layout is relatively straightforward; a little time in the city should be enough to get your bearings. The **River Hooghly** cuts through town, separating Kolkata proper from **Howrah;** these areas are linked by one of the world's most heavily used bridges, **Howrah Bridge,** and, farther south, by the **Vivekananda Bridge.** Howrah's centerpiece is the frenetic **Howrah Station,** easily accessed from Kolkata by the Howrah Bridge. The main road in Howrah, running parallel to the river, is the **Grand Trunk Road,** which connects the Botanical Gardens in the south with the Belur Math up north.

Flanking the river's east bank is the sizable **maidan,** a grassy field cut through by streets and sprinkled with monuments. The central city hugs the maidan, while **Strand Road** cuts between it and the river. At the maidan's northeast corner is the **Esplanade** (rhymes with lemonade), the central bus and train terminus. A couple of blocks north is **BBD Bagh,** around which are clustered the tourist office, GPO, railway and shipping companies, and several banks. To the east of BBD Bagh is **Old Court House Road,** which continues north to become Netaji Subhas Rd. Along with Chittaranjan Ave. to its east, it is the major thoroughfare leading to North Kolkata.

Running up the maidan's east side is **Chowringhee Road** (renamed Jawaharlal Nehru Rd.). Several smaller streets wend their way east from Chowringhee: these include Park St., with fancier restaurants, hotels, and shopping areas, and (two blocks north of Park St.) **Sudder Street,** home to the vast majority of budget accommodations. At Sudder St.'s eastern end is the north-south **Free School Street** (now Mirza Ghalib St.), with a range of eating and shopping facilities. Even farther east is **Acharya Jagadish Chandra (AJC) Bose Road,** which used to circle the city—to the south it curves back westward in a semicircular pattern and leads to St. Paul's Cathedral and the Victoria Memorial, both located at the maidan's southeast corner. East of it all is the clean and efficient **Eastern Metropolitan Bypass.** This is the route taxi drivers should take to bring you into town.

In the south, Chowringhee Rd. becomes **Ashutosh Mukherjee Road,** which continues into southern Kolkata. To the west is the posh area of **Alipur,** which also houses the zoo and the National Library; south of Alipur is the Kalighat Temple.

♂ PRACTICAL INFORMATION

TOURIST AND FINANCIAL SERVICES

Tourist Office: Government of India Tourist Office, 4 Shakespeare Sarani (tel. 242 1402 or 242 5318; fax 242 3521). The best source of info, this office provides an excellent map of Kolkata and a free pamphlet detailing cultural events, *Kolkata This Fortnight.* *Kolkata: Gateway to the East* (Rs25), published by the West Bengal Chamber of Commerce, is a smart, honest, and comprehensive introduction to the city and its sights. The office also provides a list of host families and *dharamshalas* for those seeking alternative accommodations. Open M-F 9am-6pm, Sa 9am-5pm. **Airport Branch** (tel. 511 8299) in the domestic terminal of Dum Dum Airport. **West Bengal Tourist Bureau,** 3/2 BBD Bagh E. (tel. 248 8271). Provides city tours (full day, Rs100), information and tours for all of West Bengal, and passes for wildlife parks and the Marble Palace. Open M-Sa 10:30am-1pm, Su and holidays 7am-1pm. Counters at the airport and Howrah Station (tel. 660 2518) both open daily 7am-1pm. The Government of India Tourist Office can direct you to tourist offices for most of the 26 Indian states.

Diplomatic Missions: Bangladesh, 9 Circus Ave. (tel. 247 5208). Open M-Sa 10am-5pm. **Bhutan,** contact **Bhutan Tourism,** 35A Chowringhee Rd. (tel. 246 8370). Open M-F 10am-5pm. **Nepal,** 19 National Library Ave. (tel. 479 1224). Open M-F 9:30am-

12:30pm and 1:30-4:30pm. **Sri Lanka,** Nicco House, 2 Hare St. (tel. 248 5102). Open M-F 10am-5:30pm. **Thailand,** 18B Mandville Gardens (tel. 440 7836). Open M-F 9am-noon. **U.K.,** 1 Ho Chi Minh Sarani (tel. 242 5171). Open M-F 9am-noon. **U.S.,** 5/1 Ho Chi Minh Sarani (tel. 242 3611). Open M-F 8:30am-12:30pm and 2-4pm.

Immigration Office: Foreigners Registration Office, 237 AJC Bose Rd. (tel. 247 3301). Provides visa extensions and work visas only. Open M-F 9am-1pm and 2-4pm.

Currency Exchange: 24hr. **ATMs** can be found all over Calcutta and all major banks have attached ATMs unless noted. **Banque National de Paris,** 4A BBD Bagh E. (tel. 248 2166 or 248 0197). Open M-F 10am-5pm, Sa 10am-2pm. **Citibank,** 43 Chowringhee Rd. (tel. 249 2484). Open M-F 10am-2pm, Sa 10am-noon. **ANZ Grindlays,** 41 Chowringhee Rd. (tel. 248 3371). Open M-F 10am-3pm, Sa 10am-12:30pm. **State Bank of India,** Dum Dum Airport, international terminal. Open 24hr. **HSBC,** 8 Netaji Subhas Rd. (tel. 248 6363), also holds mail. Open M-F 9am-4pm. **American Express,** 21 Old Court House St. (tel. 248 2133 or 248 9555; fax 248 8096), has travel services and currency exchange. Open M-Sa 9:30am-6:30pm. **Thomas Cook,** 230A AJC Bose Rd. (tel. 247 4560; fax 247 5854), Chitrakut Bldg., 2nd fl., side entrance, offers travel services and currency exchange. No ATM. Open M-Sa 9:30am-1pm and 1:45-6pm.

LOCAL SERVICES

Luggage Storage: Howrah Station cloak room, track 12. Rs5-8 per day. Luggage must be locked. Note "Beware of Rats" sign. Most **hotels** store guests' luggage.

Market: New Market, north of Lindsay St., sells everything from Kashmiri carvings and *filmi* cassettes to fruit, vegetables, and even animals. Open dawn-dusk. Don't miss the **flower market,** just before Howrah bridge, on the left. Open M-Sa 8-11am.

Library: National Library, Alipur Rd., near the zoo. India's largest library—2 million books in all of India's official languages. Ask for access as a casual visitor. Open M-Sa 9am-8pm, Su 10am-6pm. **Asiatic Society of Bengal,** 1 Park St. (tel. 226 0355). A Kolkata institution dating back to 1784 and the best place to go to study Persian manuscripts and 19th-century academic tomes. Adjacent museum contains paintings by Rubens and Reynolds. Open M-F 10am-6pm. **British Council,** 5 Shakespeare Sarani (tel. 282 5378). Membership Rs400. Open Tu-Sa 10:30am-6:30pm.

Cultural Centers: Alliance Francaise, 24 Park Mansions, Park St. (tel. 282 8793). **British Council,** 5 Shakespeare Sarani (tel. 242 5378). Open Tu-Sa 10:30am-6:30pm. **Academy of Fine Arts,** Cathedral Rd. (tel. 248 4302). **Rabindra Sadan,** corner of Cathedral Rd. and AJC Bose Rd. **Birla Academy of Art and Culture,** Southern Rd.

Bookstore: Oxford Book Store, Park St. (tel. 297662). Carries everything from Clive Cussler to James Joyce. Open M-Sa 10am-8:30pm. The **Modern Book Depot,** 15A Chowringhee Rd. (tel. 249 3102), just west of New Market across the street from Light House cinemas at the entrance to Shreeram Arcade. Open M-F 10am-7:30pm, Sa 10am-4:30pm. **College Street** is lined with book stalls. **Survey of India Map Sales Office,** 13 Wood St., has a good selection of trekking maps. Sign in: the guard will point the way. Open M-F 10:30am-1pm and 2:30-5pm. Nationwide English publications can be found in newsstands. *The Statesman* and *The Telegraph* are dailies that focus on Kolkata. *The Asian Age* (daily) has informative entertainment and sports sections.

EMERGENCY AND COMMUNICATIONS

Pharmacy: Common throughout the city. **Dey's Medical Store, Ltd.,** 6A Nell Sengupta Sarani (tel. 249 9810), on the left where Madge St. intersects New Market. Particularly large and well-stocked. Open M-F 8:30am-9pm, Sa 8:30am-5pm.

Hospital: Kothari Medical Centre, 8/3 Alipur Rd. (tel. 456 7049). Highly recommended English-speaking doctors. Ambulance service available.

Police: Police Headquarters (tel. 479 1311-5), Lal Bazaar.

Emergency: Police, tel. 100 or 215 5000.

Post Office: GPO, BBD Bagh (tel. 248 2574), has *Poste Restante.* Let the people outside in the "guide" booths help you avoid lines. Open M-Sa 7am-8:30pm. **Branch post**

offices: Airport, Russell St., Park St., and Mirza Ghalib St. **New Market Post Office,** Free School St., opposite Sudder St. **Postal Code:** 700001.

Internet: Oxford Book Store and the **New Empire Cinema,** behind New Market, offer web access at Rs50 per 30min. Many other Internet centers are popping up around the city.

Telephones: Most **STD/ISD** booths throughout the city also have fax services. **Central Telegraph Office,** 8 Red Cross Pl. has free callbacks. Open 24hr.

PHONE CODE	033

ACCOMMODATIONS

Prices in Kolkata tend to be slightly inflated. Most of the budget accommodations in town are concentrated around the **Sudder Street** area. The location is central, and the prices reasonable, but the hotels are a little shabby. A few other cheap hotels are located off Chittaranjan Rd., south of the Indian Airlines office, and to the northeast of New Market. Hotels generally receive at any hour but often fill up before noon; most have a noon check-out policy. Contact the Government of India Tourist Office for a comprehensive list of host families willing to take in **paying guests** (Rs200-400 a night, including breakfast). The office can also supply a list of *dharamshalas* that accept foreign visitors for free or for a small donation.

Classic Hotel, 6/1A Kyd St. (tel. 290256), just off Mirza Ghalib St., next to Mehfil restaurant. Walking barefoot in its cool marble interior is a welcome respite from the hot city streets. Generator in case of power cuts. Room service with a smile (tip generously). Singles Rs175; doubles with bath Rs300, with bath and A/C Rs500-650.

YMCA, 25 Chowringhee Rd. (tel. 249 2192; fax 249 2234). From Sudder St., turn right; it's immediately on the right. Enormous, clean rooms each have spacious attached bath; dorm rooms are also quite clean. Breakfast is included. No drinking or gambling (including card playing) allowed. Church service Su. Luggage storage Rs5 per piece per day. Dorm beds Rs110, with a less-than-great dinner Rs220; singles Rs325, with A/C Rs565; doubles Rs460/730. Reserve 10 days ahead.

Modern Lodge, 1 Stuart Ln. (tel. 244 4960). From the east end of Sudder St., across from Astoria Hotel and down a street on the left; 2nd fl. Popular with Missionaries of Charity volunteers. Clean bathrooms. Moderately sized rooms have desks and tables. Lockers Rs2 per day. Check-out 10am. Singles Rs85; doubles with bath Rs120-300.

Gujral Guest House, Lindsay St. (tel. 244 0392 or 245 6066). Circle around the right side of Lindsay Hotel and turn left on an alley behind it; look for the painted signs. Enormous, comfortable rooms await on the third floor; some doubles have Star TV. Potted plants, nature paintings, telephones. Common TV room; tea and breakfast available. Singles Rs220; doubles with bath Rs450-650.

Salvation Army Red Shield Guest House, 2 Sudder St. (tel. 245 0599). Walking towards the maidan, look for the large building on your left. One of the most popular hotels with the backpacker set, it has large (if grungy) dorm rooms. The bathrooms are not exactly gleaming, but the lounge is spacious and the staff friendly. Small lockers Rs2 per day; luggage storage Rs5 per item per day. Lights-out 10pm; gate closes at midnight. Check-out 10am. Dorm beds Rs60; doubles with bath Rs100-300. Reservations not accepted, but rooms are usually available.

Hotel Galaxy, 3 Stuart Ln. (tel. 246 4565), opposite the Modern Lodge. Only slightly more expensive than other budget digs, Galaxy is a steal. The staff is very friendly and huge rooms have color TV, A/C, and wood furniture. Singles Rs420; doubles Rs520.

Hotel Astoria, 612 Sudder St. (tel 2449679 or 2449361), in the middle of Sudder St. Large clean rooms with surprisingly modern interiors. Doubles have sparkling clean bathrooms. Singles Rs200; doubles Rs300, with TV and A/C Rs450.

Hotel Plaza, 10 Sudder St. (tel 2446411 or 2492435), on its western end. Medium-sized rooms, all with attached bath, have strong doors and solid furniture. All rooms

WEST BENGAL

have clean beds, baths, and adequately cleaned carpets. Sweet tea and toast make for a scrumptious breakfast. Singles Rs300; doubles Rs450.

Shilton Hotel, 5A Sudder St. (tel. 245 1512 or 245 1527). Set back away from the bustle on Sudder St.; look for signs. Huge rooms have spotless bathrooms, good lighting, and desks. Dark but friendly TV room. Singles Rs200; doubles Rs300; triples Rs325.

YWCA, 1 Middleton Rd. (tel. 297033; fax 292494), right off Park St. Simple but spacious and clean rooms. Meals are included, as is access to table tennis and badminton tables (lawn tennis Rs20 extra). The staff is quite friendly and keeps the place safe and secure for women. Singles Rs325, with bath Rs570; doubles Rs600/800. Reserve at least a week in advance.

🍴 FOOD

Good food is not difficult to find. In addition to the standard Chinese and Indian fare that most restaurants serve, **Bengali cuisine** is hot on the scene with its mix of mustard-seasoned rice and fish (avoid seafood in monsoon season). Those whose stomachs are strong enough for street food may want to peruse the stands that dot the city, particularly on **Park Street.** The highest concentration of restaurants is also here, many dating from the jazz scene of the 1960s and 70s. For excellent, cheap, and authentic Chinese food, jump in a cab and head to **Tangra,** 20 minutes west of the city center. Pick any restaurant, but watch your wallet grow slim. Bengalis adore their government, but gentle Marxism doesn't come free—watch for taxes up to 30%. Good service merits at least 10% gratuity; bad service merits none.

■ **Abdul Khalique and Sons Restaurant,** 32 Marique Amir St., a block south of Sudder St. near Jamuna Movie Theatre. You can watch your food being cooked at this popular, hectic eatery. Find a place on a bench and enjoy the pungent local flavors. Beef stew (Rs9), mutton *masala* (Rs16), fish curry (Rs10). Open daily 5am-11:30pm.

■ **Anand Vegetarian Restaurant,** 19 Chittaranjan Ave., between the Indian Airlines office and Chowringhee Rd. Excellent South and North Indian food on 2 floors behind tinted glass. Popular with bourgeois Kolkatans for post-cinema jaunts. Try the fresh *pakoras* (Rs15). Entrees Rs20-40.

Khalsa Restaurant, Madge Ln., just north of the Salvation Army Guest House, serves the best economy meals around. Thick *dal* (Rs10) goes well with *paratha* (Rs7) and mixed vegetables (Rs20). Open daily 4:30am-10pm.

Mehfil Restaurant, 54 Mirza Ghalib St., 2 blocks south of Sudder St. on the right. The sunken room at the corner is popular for quick-serve Bengali food. Very busy during peak hours. Mutton *kofta* (Rs22), Lucknow chicken (Rs25). Open daily 7am-11:30pm.

Indian Coffee House, 15 Bankim Chatterjee St., 1st fl., just off College St. near Kolkata University. Popular haunt for students and Kolkata's intelligentsia. A portrait of Rabindranath Tagore presides over the scene. Spectacular South Indian coffee (Rs7), chicken *hakka* (Rs25).

How Hua, Mirza Ghalib St. Across from Hotel Paramount, south of Sudder St. People from northern China lovingly prepare their native cuisine in a classy, quiet, and dark A/C dining hall. Their specialty is *chimney* soup, which can be made with chicken, crab, or bean curd (bowl for 8 Rs200, bowl for 3-4 Rs160, for a loner Rs45). Freshly made noodles are scrumptious. Open W-M 11am-11pm.

Bar B-Q, 43/47 Park St. (tel. 299916). This elegant, spacious restaurant with extensive Chinese and Indian (dinner only) menus rewards the weary backpacker with an escape from the grime. Don't order your food spicy unless you've got coolant in your belly. Szechuan chili chicken Rs70. Open noon-3pm and 7-10:30pm. Major credit cards accepted. Reserve ahead on weekends.

Flurys, 18 Park St., large white building on the corner. A Kolkata landmark. Relaxed cafe has an enormous pastry and sweets shop. They specialize in sweet buns and chocolate pastries. Ask for a pastry assortment (Rs9) with your tea while you decide what to take home. Open daily 7am-8pm.

Nizam's, 22/25 New Market (tel. 245 2665), northeast of New Market, just southwest of the large red municipal building. Ask for directions—everyone knows where it is. The "pioneer of kebab rolls in India" sells their specialty in chicken, mutton, and beef for Rs15-25. Delivery available.

Tulika's Ice Cream Parlor, Russell St., next to the post office across the street from the Royal Kolkata Turf Club. Possibly the best ice cream in Kolkata. Feel like a kid on 2ft.-tall butterscotch and chocolate benches. Snacks, *idlis, dosas,* and pizzas (Rs30-60). Popular with the office crowd for its sweet lunches. Open daily 8am-11pm.

Hare Krishna Bakery, at the corner of Russell and Middleton St., 2 blocks west of the U.S. consulate. Toned down a little bit recently, the bakery no longer features *sadhus* and shaved heads; only the background music serves as a reminder that the profits go to ISKCON, the International Society for Krishna Consciousness. All the food—breads, pastries, *samosas* (Rs10-15)—is *prasad* (blessed), so don't leave any on your plate. Open daily 10:30am-8pm.

Haldiram Bhujiawala, AJC Bose Rd. at the corner of Chowringhee Rd. next to the AeroFlot office. A neon sign advertises this eat-and-run sweet and snack shop that's popular with Kolkata's middle class. Fried food abounds in this establishment, try the cutlets (Rs15) and puffs (Rs10-20). The *kulfi* (Rs20), which comes with *faluda,* is famous.

🎵 ENTERTAINMENT

Kolkata supports a thriving tradition of **performing arts.** Bengali music, dance, and drama are staged at several venues throughout the city. The Drama Theater at the back of the **Academy of Fine Arts** (tel. 223 4302) has performances daily (6:30pm, Sa 10am and 3pm; Rs10-25). On the corner of Cathedral and AJC Bose Rd. sits **Rabindra Sadan** (tel. 223 9936 or 223 9917), an important concert hall dedicated to Tagore and mobbed by well-to-do Kolkatans in the evenings. Other playhouses, like the **Kala Mandir,** are also found along AJC Bose Rd. Although Kolkata is home to India's artsiest film industry, its **cinemas,** such as **Globe Theater** on the corner of Madge and Lindsay St., typically show Indian and Western bilge. The gigantic **New Empire** and **Light House Cinema** movie theaters, located side by side just west of New Market, both favor recent Western hits. **Nandan Theater,** just south of the Academy of Fine Arts, has both English and Bengali productions (shows 2, 4, and 6pm; Rs5-12). Check newspapers for listings and go early for tickets. The **Kolkata Information Centre** (tel. 248 1451), in the same complex as the Nandan, provides information on theater, film, and other cultural events (open M-F 1-8pm).

Although Kolkata has numerous bars, most of the city's **nightlife** is not particularly welcoming to foreigners, especially women. All of the five-star hotels feature nightclubs, but most are open only to guests. Those that are more welcoming are often ludicrously expensive. Your best bet is probably **Someplace Else,** at the Park Hotel on Park St. (open Th-Sa 7pm-2am; Rs300 cover).

👁 SIGHTS

Kolkata's monuments are not simply "sights," but rather a fundamental part of the city. The best introduction to the city is probably West Bengal Tourism's day tour (Rs100). While they rush you around the city in just ten hours, it's a good way to catch a glimpse of everything and decide what to return to.

MAIDAN, PARK STREET, AND NEW MARKET AREA

VICTORIA MEMORIAL. The south end of the maidan is the domain of the Victoria Memorial, Kolkata's greatest flower of imperialism. The British spent 15 years (1906-21) building this tombless Taj Mahal for the self-proclaimed "Empress of India." Four minarets surround a central dome of white marble, lugged at great expense from the same Rajasthani quarries that furnished the material for Shah Jahan's project. But unlike Agra's great white monument, the "VM" is shaped by the angles and spheres of the Italian Renaissance, with a bronze winged statue of Victory on top of it. A statue of an aging Queen Victoria waits at the entrance to the complex, greeting the crowds who come to wander through her gardens and pools. A much younger Victoria stands inside the building, now a **museum** chock full of British war memorabilia and state portraits. Much of the colonialist artwork and finery on display still provokes resentment among Bengali tourists, but their malice doesn't extend to the ever-popular queen, whose name has remained affixed to the building despite decades of political efforts to change it. The most impressive exhibit is undoubtedly the cool **Calcutta Gallery,** a timeline chronicling the city's history and featuring examples of artwork, literature, and craftsmanship by leading Bengali figures. Be sure to check out the letter written by Rabindranath Tagore, asking for his knightship to be revoked after the Jallianwallah Bagh Massacre (see p. 660). The entire monument is beautifully illuminated at night. *(Museum open Tu-Su 10am-5pm; Nov.-Feb. 10am-4pm. Rs2; photography not permitted. Sound and Light Show Tu-Su 8:15pm. Rs10. Garden open 24hr.)*

ST. PAUL'S CATHEDRAL. St. Paul's Cathedral is the cavernous and friendly center of Anglican Kolkata. The British moved their center of worship to this white Gothic building in 1847. *(At the south end of Chowringhee, on Cathedral Rd., opposite the Victoria Memorial. Open M-Sa 9am-noon and 3-6pm; services Su 7:30, 8:30, 11am, and 6pm.)*

BIRLA PLANETARIUM AND ACADEMY OF FINE ARTS. For celestial viewing, head to the **Birla Planetarium,** a *stupa*-esque edifice just south of St. Paul's Cathedral *(English shows at 2:30 and 8:30pm; Rs10).* The **Academy of Fine Arts** is part of Kolkata's ongoing cultural buzz, holding exhibitions of local artists' work. The permanent collection here features many works by Rabindranath Tagore and the Bengal School of painters. *(South of St. Paul's. Permanent collection open Tu-Sa noon-6:45pm. Rs2. Local artists' exhibition open M-Sa 3-8pm. Free)*

INDIAN MUSEUM. The nation's largest and oldest museum houses an impressive collection of sculpture from around India in an Italian-style building. Though the museum's collection is poorly organized and displayed, the patient tourist is rewarded with an enormous collection of stuffed fauna from all over India, a strong geology collection, and a neat display on the evolution of man in the anthropology wing. Many of the greatest works of Indian art have been transported here, including several Mauryan and Shunga capitals and a large section of railing from the *stupa* at Bharhut in Madhya Pradesh. The painting collection upstairs is usually closed to visitors, but persuasion and a little *baksheesh* can work wonders. The central courtyard, adorned with flowers and fountains, is a welcome refreshment spot. *(At the corner of Sudder St. and Chowringhee Rd. Open Tu-Sa 10am-5pm; Dec.-Feb. Tu-Sa 10am-4:30pm. Rs50.)*

PARK STREET CEMETERY. The final resting place of British colonialists since 1767, the cemetery is one of the city's most serene spots. The desolate area allows solitude; the surrounding walls block out most street noise. Famous Brits are buried here; the epitaphs make interesting reading. Ask for the guidebook (Rs30) at the gate. *(Southeast end of Cemetery Rd., near AJC Bose Rd. Open daily 7am-4pm. Free.)*

THE MAIDAN. Unquestionably the best spot for a taste of Kolkata's public life, the maidan is a mix of unkempt nature and splendid greens and gardens. Robert Clive cleared this vast field to give his soldiers a clear shot, and the old cannons that dot the ground hint at the maidan's military past. Unfortunately its *raison d'etre*, **Fort William,** is strictly closed to the public. During the Raj period, the maidan was the site of a posh, year-round whites-only cocktail party/cricket-pitch hybrid, but these days it belongs to the masses. Tram and bus lines run straight through the maidan, and it is also the site of daily community rallies of workers announcing various grievances and *bandhs* (strikes). At the northwest corner of the maidan, near the river, lie the **Eden Gardens,** site of soccer and *kabaddi* matches; these take place in the shadow of the enormous Ranji Stadium, which has a capacity of over 100,000. The maidan is often the site of local festivals and parades. Near the maidan's northern edge is the **Shahid Minar** (Martyrs' Tower), built by the British in

THE BLACK HOLE OF KOLKATA

Rumor has it that the silver-domed General Post Office, in BBD Bagh, is built over the site of Kolkata's best-kept secret. The original Fort William once stood at the very spot, its past shadowed with grim misdeeds and suffering. In 1756, the Nawab of West Bengal Siraj-ud-Daula attacked Kolkata when the city's patron, the East India Company, neglected to protect the city during the Seven Years' War. The nawab imprisoned city council member John Holwell along with several other Europeans in the local penitentiary, dubbed the "Black Hole"—it was a room 18 feet long and 14 feet wide, with two small windows. According to Holwell, 146 were imprisoned and only 23 emerged alive; he was one of the lucky few not to have been suffocated. Later, researchers attested that Holwell must have been exaggerating, since a room of such small dimensions could not have held that many people. Further research indicated that the death toll was significantly less, and that any casualties were due purely to the nawab's negligence. The topic is still controversial; it's one of the few colonial incidents where the Brits were not the bad guys.

1817 and named **Ochterlony Monument.** Originally designed as a tribute to David Ochterlony, who led royal forces against Nepal in 1814-16, the obelisk—renamed in 1969—is now a symbol of fierce Bengali pride. To climb its 224 steps, you have to obtain a free permit from the police headquarters in Lal Bazaar (near BBD Bagh). No one is allowed in after dusk.

BBD BAGH (DALHOUSIE SQUARE) AREA

Most of Kolkata's historic buildings are located near its center, north of the maidan. **BBD Bagh,** the hub of this area, previously known as Dalhousie Sq., was renamed for Benoy, Badal, and Dinesh, three freedom fighters hanged by the British during protests following the 1905 partition of Bengal. The misty Lal Digha ("Red Tank"), a big square tank, sits in the center. Up Netaji Subhas Rd. to the left side of the Writers' Building is Kolkata's financial district. On **Lyons Range,** *bakdawallahs* sell stocks in the street, but only Indians can buy. To the southwest of the Writer's Building is the GPO, alleged site of the infamous Black Hole of Kolkata incident (see graybox below).

WRITER'S BUILDING. Spanning the north side of BBD Bagh is the red-brick caterpillar of the Writer's Building. No great literary figures toiled here, other than the clerks of the East India Company, for whom it was built in 1780. It's now the lair of the West Bengal state government, containing Kafkaesque tunnels of bureaucracy. The elevators recently got a full makeover after the West Bengal Chief Minister got stuck in one, and, upon his rescue, ordered wholescale upgrades.

ST. JOHN'S CHURCH. With its clumsy-looking spire, St. John's is the oldest British church in Kolkata. The octagonal mausoleum of Job Charnock, founder of Kolkata, is tucked away in the sometimes groomed yard. Some belongings of Warren Hastings, the first governor-general of India, are kept inside the church. *(Down Government Place W. Open M-F 9am-noon and 4-6pm. Weekday services 9am, Su 8am.)*

RAJ BHAVAN AND HIGH COURT. The vast grounds of **Raj Bhavan** (Government House) are the West Bengal governor's official residence, formerly home to British governors-general and viceroys. The furnishings inside are suitably palatial, but it's not open to the public, so enjoy the walk in the shade of the barbed wire. Nearby, on the other side of Government Place W., are the State Legislature and the cheerful tricolor Gothic **High Court.** *(Diagonally opposite St. John's.)*

NORTH KOLKATA

MARBLE PALACE. Built in 1835 as a mansion for the *zamindar* Raja Rajendro Mullick Bahadur, the Marble Palace features works by Rubens and Titian, as well as many displays of pseudo-Mughal lavishness. The Mullick family still lives here but they hide while you see their stuff. Get a free pass from the West Bengal

Tourist Office, on BBD Bagh, or the Government of India Tourism Office, on Shakespeare Sarani, but a little *baksheesh* works just as well. (*Muktaram Babu Dr., off Chittaranjan Ave. Open Tu-W and F-Su 10am-4pm. Free.*)

RABINDRA BHARATI UNIVERSITY. One of several universities founded by Bengal's most famous son, Rabindranath Tagore, this one is the site of his lifetime home. The old mansion of the prolific Tagore family has been expanded and turned into an arts college, and the house itself has been preserved as the Rabindra Bharati **museum.** Beginning with the room where Rabindranath Tagore died, the museum traces the story of the Tagores and the Bengal Renaissance with a large collection of art and memorabilia. There is an entire section devoted to paintings by Rabindranath himself. (*Dwarakanath Tagore Ln., near the Marble Palace. Museum open M-F 10am-5pm, Sa 10am-1pm. Free.*)

PARASNATH JAIN TEMPLE. Built by a jeweler in 1867, this exquisite shimmering palace is dedicated to Sithalnath, the tenth Jain *tirthankara* (spiritual leader). The building itself features colored glass and mirrors everywhere, set with sparkling and intricate designs. In one corner is an "ethereal lamp" that has been burning since the temple's founding. Chandeliers from the likes of Belgium and the Czech Republic adorn the ceiling. (*Open daily 6am-noon and 3-7pm. Free.*)

DAKSHINESHWAR TEMPLE. It was here that the Hindu spiritual leader Sri Ramakrishna had his vision of the unity of all religions. One day, a brash, urbane young agnostic walked into the compound and asked for proof of God. Promising revelation, Ramakrishna led him into an adjacent chamber, where the young follower was shown God—in his heart. Later, he came to be known as Swami Vivekananda, a spiritual leader who traveled around the world spreading the message of spiritual unity. The temple consists of three parts: the smallest chamber is devoted to Vishnu; the more impressive building nearby is dedicated to Shakti, adjacent to the sacrificial platform; directly opposite, built in traditional Bengali style, are five domes, each of which houses a Shiva *linga*. (*10km from the city center. Bus #32 from the Esplanade, Rs5. Open daily 6am-9pm. Free.*)

NICCO PARK AND SCIENCE PARK. Amuse yourself at Nicco Park with all your thrill-seeking Indian friends—a collection of amusement park rides could be a good jolt out of India and into a fantasy land. The Science Park is a large complex with several large buildings and exhibits. From space travel to dinosaurs, enjoy the hands-on experience in one of India's finest science museums. Don't get scared by the 50ft. dinosaurs on display. (*Off the East Metropolitan Bypass; Nicco Park is 2km from Science Park. Buses from BBD Bagh Rs5, taxis from BBD Bagh Rs40. Both open daily 9am-9pm. Science Park Rs15; Nicco Park Rs25. Nicco admission includes 10 ride tickets.*)

THE BIG CATS OF BENGAL
Catching a glimpse of the Bengal tiger, a majestic beast with a deep reddish tan, black stripes, and white-furred belly, is a somewhat rare event. Although most tigers in West Bengal are found only in the swampy mangrove forests of the Sunderbans, occasionally they can stray. In 1974, a tiger made it all the way to a village 50 miles from Kolkata, where he killed a local woman. Only about 4% of tigers are "man-eaters," but all big cats will attack if disturbed. Forest guards wear fiberglass head and neck protectors since these are the parts most vulnerable to attack. Honey-gatherers wear masks on the back of their heads since tigers tend to attack only when people are looking away. Researchers are trying to train tigers to stay away from humans by positioning electrified dummies in the forest—a 300V shock is administered if the tiger attacks. The experiment has been successful so far, but some people still look to the gods for protection. Many wood-cutters and honey-farmers refuse to enter the Sunderbans without being escorted by *fakirs*, religious men who have the power to ward off tiger attacks. (West Bengal Tourism conducts tours to the Sunderbans; the best season to visit is Nov.-Feb.)

HOWRAH

BELUR MATH. As the center of the movement founded in 1897 by Ramakrishna's disciple Swami Vivekananda to unite all religions, Belur Math features several shrines devoted to Hindu saints and their wives. While the soaring temple dominates the grounds, the most peaceful spot on the compound is at the end of the field, in a small cottage where Vivekananda spent his last days. His bedroom has been preserved, and an attached museum contains some of his belongings. Make sure to take in the view of the temple from all four faces: each one is in the form of a different place of worship—church, temple, mosque, and *gurudwara*. *(Taxis from BBD Bagh Rs50. Open Tu-Su 7-11am and 4-7pm; Oct.-Mar. 7-11am and 4-6pm. Free.)*

BOTANICAL GARDENS. The Botanical Gardens are one of Kolkata's more relaxing spots—if you go during the week, you'll have few companions other than the storks, cranes, insects, and plants that constitute the gardens' astonishing array of flora—there are plants here from every continent. Picnic underneath the **Great Banyan Tree,** claimed to be the largest in the world, with roots stretching out nearly a mile from the treetop. A series of storms destroyed the trunk decades ago, but its standing roots still survive and flourish under the expansive canopy. *(20min. by taxi from Howrah Station. Ferries from Armenian Ghat Rs3. Open dusk-dawn. Free.)*

SOUTH KOLKATA

KALI TEMPLE AT KALIGHAT. Kolkata's most important temple, Kalighat, is where the goddess Sati's little toe is said to have fallen to earth after being hacked off by Vishnu (see **Divine Dismemberment,** p. 687). Though pilgrims have streamed in and out of the structure since its construction in 1809, authorities have recently decided to close it to foreigners. Nevertheless, a bit of charisma and *baksheesh* might be enough to get you into the impressive building, built in the medieval Bengali style. Inside you can gaze into the goddess's wise and terrifying red eyes, which are reproduced on dashboards and refrigerators all over West Bengal. During Durga Puja and Kali Puja in October, goats are sacrificed on the compound. *Open daily 6am-10pm. Free.)*

NETAJI BHAVAN. For many, the non-violent tactics of Gandhi are seen as anathema to real progress. Their hero is Subhas Chandra Bose, erstwhile leader of the Indian National Army, which sought to wrest control of the country from the British by force. Netaji Bhavan is the home of Bose, who, along with the Japanese, led troops against the British during WWII. It features a museum with Bose's belongings (including letters) and a history of his achievements. Every January 23rd, his birthday is celebrated here. *(Elgin St., near Chowringhee. Open Tu-Sa noon-4pm. Rs2.)*

ZOOLOGICAL GARDENS. Kolkata's zoo boasts India's foremost collection of predatory felines; the centerpiece is a large island home to the zoo's Bengal Tigers. Although sightings are rare during the hot season, don't fret—the lions and tigers are also on display in cages, where they laze in the open one more frequently. Avoid the weekends when it bursts at the seams with young visitors. Skip the aquarium across the street—it's small and mostly houses small fish. *(Near the Taj Bengal. Rs25 by taxi from Park St. Open F-W 9am-5pm. Zoo Rs5, camera fee Rs250. Aquarium Rs2.)*

VOLUNTEER OPPORTUNITIES

Even after her passing, Mother Teresa's organization continues to care for the destitute and dying. Now headed by Sister Nirmala, the **Sisters of Charity** have bases around the city. Their **Mother House,** 54 AJC Bose Rd., is the place to go if you're interested in learning more about volunteering. While the Sisters always welcome those willing to help, they expect a certain degree of dedication, commitment, and fortitude. They are also notoriously difficult to get a hold of—go late in the afternoon, before 6pm, for the best chance of talking to someone in charge.

RABINDRANATH TAGORE The Bengali poet Rabindranath Tagore (1861-1941) towers over modern Indian literature and Bengali life. The youngest son in the large family of the prominent *zamindar* and Brahmo Samaj leader Debendranath Tagore, Rabindranath dropped out of school at an early age to educate himself in English and Sanskrit. Rabindranath began writing poetry while still a boy, and before long his poems broke new ground, introducing English forms previously unknown in Bengali. He traveled around Bengal looking after his family's estates; many of his poems and stories concern the lives of villagers in Bengal, and his songs draw from the melodies of Bengali folk music. Tagore translated many of his verses into rhythmic English prose, catching the attention of Western readers. In 1913 he received the Nobel Prize for *Gitanjali* (Song Offerings), a collection of poems expressing his wish to become one with God. Tagore was knighted by the British in 1915, but he renounced his title following the 1919 Jallianwallah Bagh massacre in Amritsar. In his later years Tagore experimented with novels, plays, and elaborate songs; near the end of his life he took up painting as well. Gandhi and other political leaders considered Tagore an inspiration and frequently visited him at Shantiniketan, the school he founded in 1901. Verses by Tagore now constitute the national anthems of both India and Bangladesh. His plays are widely produced, and his songs, known as *Rabindrasangit,* have become a genre of their own. The filmmaker Satyajit Ray has produced interpretations of several of Tagore's novels.

SHANTINIKETAN শান্তিনিকেতন

Shantiniketan is the living legacy of India's foremost poet and intellectual Rabindranath Tagore. The town was originally the site of an ashram founded by Tagore's father. Tagore himself founded a school here, **Visva Bharati,** to respond to the roteness and rigidity of his own primary education. His curriculum emphasized creative expression and spontaneity and promoted scholarship on Indian and Eastern civilizations. At the peaceful, sprawling campus outside the town of Bolpur circles of saffron *kurta*'d children sit beneath trees to learn and discuss their daily lessons in their mother tongue, while Bengali doctoral students on bicycles debate Indian philosophy and musicians tune up their sitars.

The **museum** inside **Rabindranath Bhavan** on the right side of the main Campus Rd. is a small but excellent tribute to Tagore. With pictures and paraphernalia, the museum tells Tagore's inspiring story: his childhood, his art, his experiments in education, his engagement in politics, his work in rural development, and his vision for a prouder, freer India and a better relationship with the West. (Museum open Th-M 10am-4pm, Tu 10:30am-1pm. Rs5, students Rs1.) Most of the guides roaming around, including the "authorized" ones outside of Rabindra Bhavan, are a rip-off. If you would like to sit in on lectures (the university is English medium) or meet with professors, the staff in Rabindranath Bhavan can direct you to the appropriate department. Visva Bharati offers one-year **Foreigner Casual Course,** which can be taken in any subject—painting, Indian philosophy, music, and Indian languages are the most popular (Rs50 per month). Contact Pritam Ray, Advisor to Foreign Students, Visva Bharati University, Shantiniketan, W.B. 731235 (tel. (03463) 52751, ext. 362; fax (03463) 52672; email pritam@vbharat.ernet.in). The university kitchen also serves basic meals (Rs12). Ask to reserve **accommodations** at the West Bengal Tourism Office, BBD Bagh.

Shantiniketan is accessible from Kolkata by **train** to Bolpur (*Rampurhat Exp.* 6:45am; *Shantiniketan Exp.,* 9:55am, 3hr., reserved 2nd class Rs77). From the train station, it's a Rs20 cycle-rickshaw ride to Shantiniketan's campus. The *Rampurhat Express* returns to Kolkata in the evening, stopping at Bolpur at 6:30pm

SILIGURI শিলিগুড়ি AND NEW JALPAIGURI

Because Siliguri and New Jalpaiguri function as the main transit point to Nepal, Sikkim and the Northeast, most travelers come here out of necessity. Linked by urban sprawl, these two indistinguishable cities have managed to capture all the congestion, noise, and filth of urban India with none of the beautiful scenery or fresh air that their remote location might seem to suggest. Due to the low elevation of Siliguri and New Jalpaiguri (114m), their climate is much more akin to Kolkata's scorching heat than to the cooler temperatures of nearby Darjeeling (80km). This self-proclaimed "gateway to the Indian Himalayas" offers nary a hint of the natural splendor to be found just up the road. The best advice is to treat your stay here as a layover—make the most of it, but get a move on to bigger and better things.

▟ TRANSPORTATION

Airport: Bagdogra Airport, 16km west of Siliguri. Take the Hill Cart Rd. bus, which leaves from NJP Station, stopping in front of Tenzing Norgay Bus Terminal before arriving in Bagdogra (Rs3); then hop on a rickshaw to the airport (Rs10). The trip takes 1hr. To: **Kolkata** (M, T, Th, and F; 1hr.; US$80); **Delhi** (M, T, Th, and F; 3hr.; US$185); **Guwahati** (M, W, and F; 45min.; US$50). Check schedules and make reservations at **Indian Airlines,** 2nd fl., Mainak Hotel, Hill Cart Rd. (tel. 431495), a 5min. walk north from the bus station. Open M-F 10am-4:30pm. Also check with **Jet Airways,** Hotel Vinayak, Hill Cart Rd. (tel. 450589), about 100m south of the West Bengal Tourist Office, for flights to Delhi and Kolkata. Open M-F 10am-5pm.

Trains: All trains to this area stop at **New Jalpaiguri Station,** Hill Cart Rd., before continuing on to the Northeastern States. The **Central Rail Booking Office** (tel. 423333; reservations tel. 431493) is near the police traffic booth north of Siliguri Town Station, immediately on the right. Open daily 8am-8pm. Fares listed are 2nd/1st class. To: **Kolkata-Sealdah** (*Darjeeling Mail* 3144, 7pm; *Teesta Torsha Exp.* 3142, 3:45pm; *Kanchan Jungha Exp.* 5658, 8am, 12hr., Rs124/611); **Kolkata-Howrah** (*Kamrup Exp.* 5660, 4:45pm, 12hr., Rs172/480); **Delhi** (*Mahananda Exp.* 4083, 12:15pm, Rs290/790; *Brahmaputra Mail* 4055, 10:50pm, 33hr., Rs340/887; *Rajdhani Exp.* 2424, 3 per week 12:40pm, 33hr., A/C 3-tier Rs1225).

Buses: Government buses leave **Tenzing Norgay Bus Terminal,** next to the Siliguri Junction Station at the north end of Siliguri. **Private buses** congregate on Hill Cart Rd. next to the main bus station and are slightly more expensive, more frequent, and faster than their public counterparts. Fares listed are for private coaches and change frequently. To: **Kolkata** (3 per day, 12hr., Rs170); **Darjeeling** (every 30min. 5:30am-10:30pm, 3½hr., Rs45); **Kalimpong** (every 30min. 6:15am-4:35pm, 4hr., Rs40); **Kurseong** (every hr. 7am-5pm, 1hr., Rs30); **Mirik** (every hr. 7am-4pm, 3hr., Rs45). **Sikkim Nation Transportation (SNT) Centre** is located on Hill Cart Rd., a 2min. walk south from the bus station. To: **Gangtok** (every ½hr. 7am-3pm, 4hr., Rs47/Rs80 deluxe); **Mangan** (1pm, 5hr., Rs60); **Pelling** (1pm, 5hr., Rs60). Buses for **Kathmandu** leave from Kakarbhitta, Nepal. Take a city bus north along Hill Cart Rd. to the Nepali border town of Panitanki (1hr., Rs6), where cycle-rickshaws cross the border to Kakarbhitta (Rs10). **Private jeeps,** which fit up to 11 passengers and leave across the street from Tenzing Norgay Bus Terminal, are the fastest but most expensive means of transportation. To: **Darjeeling** (every 20min. 5:40am-4pm, 3hr., Rs50); **Kurseong** (every hr. 7am-5pm, 1hr., Rs40).

▟ ORIENTATION AND PRACTICAL INFORMATION

The bustling termini of these conjoined cities are Siliguri's Tenzing Norgay Bus Terminus (named for Edmund Hillary's Everest-climbing partner) and, 6km south (cycle-rickshaw Rs20), the New Jalpaiguri Railway Station. For the most part, the entire area is oriented along the north-south axis defined by Hill Cart Road (also known as Tenzing Norgay Road), a bustling "miracle mile" that connects the cities. There are two useful landmarks: the now-defunct Siliguri Town Station, where trains cross Hill Cart Rd., and the Mahananda River Bridge farther north. Most of

the shops and bazaars are around the town station area, while budget accommo
dations cluster north of the bridge near the bus terminal.

Tourist Office: West Bengal Tourism (tel. 431974; fax 431979), just beyond the 2n
police box at the major intersection north of Siliguri Town Station, tucked away in a
alley on the right. Open M-F 10am-5pm. There's a smaller branch at the NJP Railwa
Station (tel. 561118). The West Bengal Tourism **Manager's Office** (tel. 433891)
located in the Hill Cart Rd., just north of the Mahananda River Bridge, is sometimes nec
essary for booking tours or hotel rooms at future destinations. **Sikkim Tourist Offic**
(tel. 432646), SNT Centre, across from the bus station, has information and free **pe**
mits (bring a passport-sized photo) for those heading to Sikkim. Open M-Sa 10am
4pm, closed 2nd Sa. Private jeeps can also be booked here.

Currency Exchange: State Bank of India, next to the West Bengal Tourism office. Ope
M-F 10am-2pm, Sa 10am-noon. Many banks and hotels on Hill Cart Rd. change money

Luggage Storage: Tenzing Norgay Bus Terminal, on the right as you enter; or **NJP Sta**
tion, on track 4. Both charge Rs3 per day.

Market: Hong Kong Market, a 5min. walk north of the West Bengal Tourism Office, i
where locals gander at local produce, Indian-made goods, and the latest in Nepales
exports, including cameras, calculators, and fake name brands.

Pharmacy: Medical booths dot the city. Ask around. Or just look around.

Emergency: Police, tel. 100.

Post Office: GPO (tel. 421965). Turn right at first police traffic booth north of Siligu
Town Station, then walk up Hospital Rd. on the right. *Poste Restante.* Open M-Sa 7am
7pm. **Postal code:** 734401.

Internet: Moulik Informatics (tel. 432312), in the backside basement of the Hote
Vinayah building, on Hill Cart Rd. Internet use: Rs90 (student) and Rs100 (profes
sional) per 30min. for non-members. Open M-Sa 9am-8pm.

Telephones: Most **STD/ISD** booths close by 11pm.

PHONE CODE	0353

■ ACCOMMODATIONS AND FOOD

The friendly **Hotel Mount View,** Hill Cart Rd. (tel. 425919 or 531598), lets large, inst
tutional rooms (most with TV) and has a good attached restaurant. The buildin
may be prone to power outages. MC and Visa are accepted, and reservations ar
recommended. (Check-out noon. Singles Rs175-250; doubles Rs250-350; triple
Rs300-350; quads Rs375.) The 11-room **Siliguri Lodge** (tel. 533290), across the mai
street from the bus station and set back to the right, offers a collegial atmospher
lush (by Siliguri standards) garden, and impressive lobby art. Rooms are les
attractive than Mount View, and most don't have attached baths. Reservations a
recommended. (Check-out noon. Singles Rs100; doubles Rs140; quads Rs200, wit
bath Rs350.) The **Rajasthan Guest House** (tel. 525163), 50m north of Siliguri Tow
Station, left off Hill Cart Rd., offers spacious, though grim, rooms. (Singles Rs6
with bath Rs80; doubles Rs110/140; triples Rs200; quads Rs250.)

There are **fruit markets** at each of the railway stations, but locals prefer the **Hon**
Kong Market, where the fruit is cheaper. The **Sharaz Restaurant** at the **Ranjit Hote**
Hill Cart Rd. (tel. 431539 or 431680), a few minutes south of the West Bengal Tou
ist Office, is popular with locals and serves pan-Indian and quasi-Continental cu
sine (entrees Rs24-120; open daily 6am-10:30pm).

■ JALDAPARA WILDLIFE SANCTUARY

Jaldapara is truly a site fit for kings—or so the kings of Bhutan and Coochbhea
(now part of West Bengal) believed some 100 years ago, when each jealously co
eted the land as a royal rhinoceros hunting ground. Along came the British to "se

ANIMAL HOUSE Tourists aren't the only ones starved for nightlife in early-to-bed, early-to-rise Northeast India. The natives are apparently getting restless as well. In fact, in recent years drunken gallivanting and late-night carousing are on the rise among local populations...of elephants. Last call at many of the popular pachyderm watering-holes occurs in late November when Jaldapara's streams fall victim to the winter dry season. Rather than resort to a winter on the wagon, wild elephants have been hitting the human hot spots (usually people's huts) in search of Hariya, a locally micro-brewed rice wine. But the hedonism does not stop there. With their booze-fed libidos primed, the male wild elephants, or tuskers, cruise for chicks at the make-shift brothel which hosts domesticated, female touring elephants. After having their way, the tuskers stagger back to the jungle—presumably to sleep the bender off.

tle the dispute" in true imperial fashion, by claiming the entire Dooras ("gateway") region as their own and gradually converting thousands of acres of lush jungle into vast tea plantations. This ecological upheaval left only a few large pockets of dense forest; Jaldapara Wildlife Sanctuary has preserved one.

Jaldapara offers the best, if only, reason not to flee straight into the hills from Siliguri. Officially designated a sanctuary in 1985, Jaldapara is one of a handful of parks left in India with a sizable population of rhinos, and it contains over 100 species of birds. Jaldapara's well-run services ensure a comfortable, safari-like experience. Best of all, the park is still relatively undiscovered by the tourists that flock to India's other wildlife sanctuaries. (High season Oct.-Apr., closed June15-Sept. 15. Rs20. Camera fee Rs20. Jeep transportation Rs150, plus driver's entrance fee.)

Jaldapara is located about 125km east of Siliguri, which provides the only major access point to the park. Fortunately, the journey is picturesque, as road and rail wind their way through lush foothills and expansive tea fields. Buses and trains stop in a town called **Madarihat,** which is 7km from the park and within walking distance from the tourist lodge. **Trains** depart from the Siliguri Jct. Station to Madarihat (6pm) and run from Madarihat to Siliguri (7am, 3½hr., Rs22). **Buses** also run daily between Siliguri and Madarihat (every 30min. 6am-7pm, 4hr., Rs30). There is an overnight bus from Madarihat to Guwahati (9pm, 8hr., Rs200).

There are only two lodgings in the area, but both are excellent. Rooms should be booked in advance from the tourist office in Siliguri or from one of its many private travel agencies. Located at the edge of Madarihat, the **Jaldapara Tourist Lodge** (tel. 03563 or 62230) is very plush, with large, comfy rooms and a huge yard. Prices are reasonable, considering that all meals (excellent Indian fare) are included. The staff is friendly and attentive. (Dorm beds Rs250; singles Rs595; doubles Rs850.) Another appealing option is the **Hollong Lodge** (tel. 62228), located within the confines of the park. Its prime location and well-maintained garden make this a pricier pick, and meals are not included. (Doubles Rs1000.)

Though it's one of India's smaller wildlife sanctuaries, Jaldapara is home to an impressive community of wildlife including rhinos, monkeys, deer, and elephants. One way to view the park's wonders is via an **elephant ride** (Rs120). Other options include a drive (Rs200) and trek to the **tiger reserve,** where you'll be lucky to see a tiger. Jeeps (Rs90) tour the area's **tea gardens,** which include a few monasteries and well-preserved British colonial forts. You can also arrange tours (Rs100) to **Bhutan,** though visas may be difficult to secure (see p. 13).

DARJEELING দার্জিলিং दार्लिन্

As the road from Siliguri winds up through forested hills, the temperature drops, signs in Bengali begin to disappear, and the people begin to take on a distinctly Nepalese look. This is Gorkhaland, a semi-autonomous area within West Bengal whose proud and kind inhabitants battled long and hard for independence. Their urban center throbs with an electric pulse worthy of the name Darjeeling, "the Place of the Thunderbolt." When the British chanced upon this wooded ridge in

1828, they were so enraptured with the cool climate and majestic mountain views that they cornered the king of Sikkim into letting them use it as a health resort. Darjeeling's popularity as a getaway for heatstruck colonials grew and grew; by 1861 Sikkim was forced to cede this great playground of colonial India to the British. Today, Darjeeling is as famous as the staging point for the earliest Everest expeditions and as a center for tea production as it is for the spectacular scenery; its infrastructure is under constant strain to meet tourists' demands for electricity, water, and transportation. The region's Gorkha inhabitants, most of them brought over from Nepal as laborers, never abandoned their language, dress, or blend of Hinduism and Buddhism. The Gorkha National Liberation Front's war for secession culminated in the 1958 formation of the Gorkha Hill Council, which now governs the area. Tensions persist, and the Council occasionally holds *bandhs* (strikes), during which the entire town and the road to Siliguri are closed for a day.

▐ TRANSPORTATION

Trains: The **Reservation Booth** (tel. 52555) at the **railway station** issues quota tickets for major trains leaving NJP (Siliguri) Station. Open 10am-4pm. The station also services the **Toy Train,** which traverses the route between Siliguri and Darjeeling (from Darjeeling 8:25am, from Siliguri 6:30am; Rs20/90 for 2nd/1st class).

Buses and Jeeps: Virtually all rides out of Darjeeling leave from the main bus stand at the bazaar on Hill Cart Rd., including private buses. Buses to: **Siliguri** (frequent 6am-5pm, 3½hr., Rs38); **Gangtok** (8:30am, 5hr., Rs75). Jeeps to: **Kalimpong** (frequent 7am-4:30pm, 2½hr., Rs50); **Jorethane** (1½hr., Rs40), where service is available to points farther north. Do not accept passage on vehicles with white numbers on black license plates; **they are not authorized to carry passengers** and may be detained by the police.

✦ ORIENTATION

Darjeeling is draped like a blanket on a clothesline over either side of a narrow, north-south ridge, and its steep, tangled streets, alleys, and stairways will strain both your legs and your sense of direction. Fortunately, locals are very knowledgeable and helpful with directions. Few streets are within range of cars, and staircases are as important as streets. The town's belly is **Hill Cart Road,** on the west side near the bottom. The **railway** and **bus stations** are here, as is the motor entrance to town. It's quite a climb from Hill Cart Rd. to **Chowrasta,** the town center near the top of the ridge. The Chowrasta intersection has a bandstand at one end and a fountain and tourist office at the other. To the right of the fountain is **Nehru Road** (also called the **Mall**), one of the town's main avenues for shops and restaurants. **Laden La Road** runs right below, between Nehru Rd. and Hill Cart Rd. The road to the left of the fountain (past the ponies) leads to the TV tower area, where many of the cheap hotels are. A major landmark on the north side of town (on west Mall Rd., left of the bandstand) is **St. Andrew's Church,** a yellow Gothic edifice that sits where the road to Chowrasta meets the series of roads leading to the bus stand.

▐ PRACTICAL INFORMATION

Tourist Office: West Bengal Tourist Office, Chowrasta (tel. 54050), just above the Indian Airlines office; enter around to the right, up the ramp. Friendly, English-speaking staff provides hiking maps, luggage storage, and good transportation information. Runs a bus to Bagdogra Airport (3½hr., Rs65) if there are enough passengers. **Trekkers** should check out the free and helpful "Himalayan Treks" brochure. Reports from trekkers written in tourist logs at the Youth Hostel, Aliment Hotel, and Tower View Lodge are also helpful. Open M-F 10am-4:30pm. Transport desk open daily during tourist season.

Immigration Office: The process of securing a **Sikkim permit** is a bureaucratic hassle that may take hours (it's much easier at the office in **Siliguri**—see p. 662). First go to the **District Magistrate's Office,** 7min. down Hill Cart Rd., north of the bus stands; look for

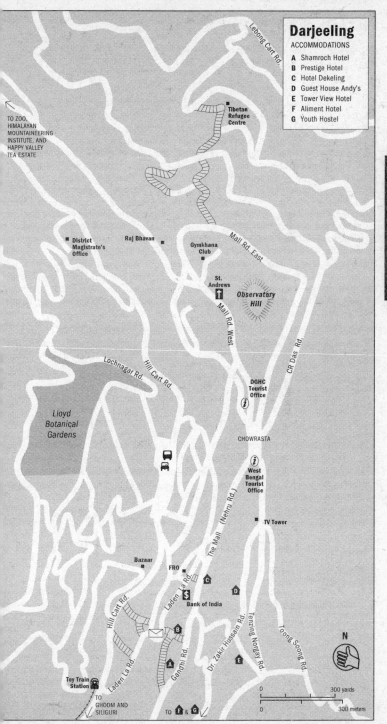

Darjeeling
ACCOMMODATIONS

A Shamroch Hotel
B Prestige Hotel
C Hotel Dekeling
D Guest House Andy's
E Tower View Hotel
F Aliment Hotel
G Youth Hostel

Lebong Cart Rd.

Tibetan Refugee Centre

TO ZOO, HIMALAYAN MOUNTAINEERING INSTITUTE, AND HAPPY VALLEY TEA ESTATE

District Magistrate's Office

Raj Bhavan

Gymkhana Club

Mall Rd. East

St. Andrews

Observatory Hill

Mall Rd. West

CR Das Rd.

Lochnagar Rd.

Hill Cart Rd.

DGHC Tourist Office

Lloyd Botanical Gardens

CHOWRASTA

West Bengal Tourist Office

TV Tower

The Mall (Nehru Rd.)

Bazaar

FRO

C

Laden La Rd.

Bank of India

D

B

Gandhi Rd.

Dr. Zakir Hussain Rd.

Tenzing Norgay Rd.

Toong Soong Rd.

A

E

N

Toy Train Station

TO GHOOM AND SILIGURI

Laden La Rd.

TO F & G

0   300 yards

0   300 meters

DISORIENT EXPRESS Ninety kilometers in nine hours? Sounds like a fast-paced trek, but the toy train uses every minute to lug some 80 passengers up more than 2000m of vertical ascent from Siliguri to Darjeeling. This little engine that can (most of the time) hauls three cars and manages the climb (and descent) by traversing the main auto road at least 100 times. Service is sporadic, due to seasonal weather variations and constant mechanical problems. However, if the train is running, the breathtaking views and unique experience make the toy train an attraction that should not be missed. The two time-saving alternatives are to ride the train to Kurseong, roughly the mid-point, and then catch a bus (2hr., Rs20) or a jeep (1½hr., Rs30) the rest of the way; or experience the train for the one-hour ride between Darjeeling and Shoom (although this may be the most boring part of the trip). And don't worry should part of the train slip from its 60cm tracks (this has been known to happen), locals will emerge from the woods bearing poles to lever the carriage back on course!

the "Sikkim Pass" sign. Office is on 1st fl. of central building. Open M-F 10:30am-4:30pm. With the stamped form, go to the **Foreigners' Registration Office,** Laden La Rd. (tel. 54203), next to ANZ Grindlays Bank, for a police signature (or stamp). Open M-F 10am-4pm. Then return to the District Magistrate's Office for the official permit. It's worth the effort, though; the permit is free and valid for 15 days.

Currency Exchange: ANZ Grindlays Bank, Laden La Rd. (tel. 54551), just down from the Nehru Rd. intersection. Changes traveler's checks, cash, and gives cash advances on Visa. Open M-F 10am-3pm, Sa 10am-12:30pm; traveler's checks only M-F 10:30am-1pm. Rs100 fee. **Bank of India,** Laden La Rd., changes traveler's checks M-Sa 10am-1pm. Rs100 fee. Open M-F 10am-2pm, Sa 9am-noon.

Luggage Storage: Free at the tourist office, most hotels, and trekking companies.

Cultural Center: The **Manjushree Center of Tibetan Culture,** 8 Burdwan Rd. (tel. 54159; fax 53298), organizes intensive 3-, 6-, and 9-month language courses ($150/$230/$280). It also holds seminars, lectures, and cultural programs concerning Tibetan culture and Tibetan Buddhism. Contact Norbu Dekevas.

Bookstore: Oxford Bookshop, Chowrasta (tel. 54325), overlooking town. Serving English (and English-speaking) customers since the time of the Raj, this well-stocked shop has an ample collection of regional travel books and English literary classics. Open M-F 9:30am-7pm, Sa 9:30am-2:30pm, Su in season. MC, Visa.

Pharmacy: Economic Pharmacy, Laden La Rd. (tel. 52174), across the street from the GPO at the bend. Open daily 8am-7:30pm.

Hospital: (tel. 54077), above the main bus stand. **Emergency:** tel. 100.

Post Office: GPO, Laden La Rd. (tel. 52076), halfway down, just after sharp bend. Open M-F 9am-3pm, Sa 9am-noon. **Postal Code:** 734101.

Internet: Cybercafe at Udayan Communication, 37 Laden La Rd. (tel. 53950), about 300m south of the GPO, upstairs in the Hotel Red Rose. Full Internet access Rs3 per minute. Open daily 9am-8pm.

Telephones: Most **STD/ISD** booths close around 11pm.

PHONE CODE	0354

ACCOMMODATIONS

Darjeeling is home to a wide array of high quality, cheap hotels; there's no need to settle for the wrong place or price. Offseason (mid-June to Aug.) discounts of up to 40% are often available; in season (Oct., Nov., Mar.-May), you may have to hunt a bit for a room.

Aliment, 40 Dr. Zakir Hussain Rd. (tel. 55068). From Chowrasta, take the road to the left of the Indian Airlines office and bear right when the road splits into three. After the TV tower (on right), bear right up the hill, and follow Dr. Z's around to the left. An unassuming but expertly run hotel with an excellent restaurant. The owner's tips and the detailed tourist log are helpful in planning treks. Laundry service. Hot water Rs5 extra. Dorm beds Rs35; singles Rs60-70; doubles Rs100. Off-season: Rs30/50/80.

Tower View, 8/1 Dr. Zakir Hussain Rd. (tel. 54452; fax 54330) It is actually just off Dr. Z's Rd. The outgoing owner welcomes foreigners, sharing his regional knowledge and the tourist log, which has good trekking tips. Rooms look out over Kanchenjunga, facing the sunrise. Backpacker-filled restaurant serves breakfast. STD service. Dorm beds Rs35; singles Rs50, with bath Rs70; doubles Rs100-120.

Guest House Andy's, 102 Dr. Zakir Hussain Rd. (tel. 53125). Close to Chowrasta, 150m past the *puri* stalls. Huge doubles with great views. Quiet and spotlessly clean, with large seat toilets (don't fall in!). Top priced rooms have hot shower. Same rate all seasons. Doubles Rs200-300.

Hotel Shamroch (tel. 56387), located in an alley off the main staircase between Laden La and Gandhi Rd. The Shamroch's cozy living room (with TV) and fantastic dinners (Rs40) feel like home, but the views attest otherwise. Free buckets of hot water. Dorm beds Rs65; singles Rs80; doubles Rs160.

Prestige Hotel (tel. 53199), on the steps between Laden La and Gandhi Rd. No views, but clean, inexpensive rooms with 24hr. hot water. Kerosene heat and color cable TV (both Rs80 per night) available on request. A la carte breakfast. Dorm beds Rs250 per 4 people; singles Rs88-132; doubles Rs132-165.

Hotel Dekeling, 51 Gandhi Rd., right before Chowrasta, coming from train station. Prime location in the center of town and a quality restaurant downstairs (see below). Hot showers, hot water bottles, and extra blankets free of charge. Singles Rs150/300; doubles Rs450/1000.

FOOD

Restaurants abound in Darjeeling, with **Aliment** being the best of the hotel variety. Numerous quasi-fast-food joints are in Chowrasta and along Nehru Rd.

The Park Restaurant, Laden La Rd. The consensus among locals and tourists alike is that the Park serves the best Indian food in town. Savory Chicken *tikka masala* (Rs66). Open daily 8am-9pm. Visa, MC.

Hasty Tasty Restaurant, 13 Nehru Rd. Darjeeling's widest selection of all-veg. Indian, Chinese, and Continental options (Rs25-80). Open daily 8am-9pm.

Glenary's Bakery, Nehru Rd. The self-proclaimed master baker lives up to his own billing. Request a window seat for great mountain views. If only the service were as good as the food. Pastries run Rs10-40. Open daily 6:30am-7pm.

Keventer's Restaurant, 9 Nehru Rd. Though a bit dumpy looking, "Kev's" is famous for its hearty English breakfasts (Rs40), served from 7:30-11:30am. Also serves snacks (Rs15-25) until 7:30pm.

Nimto Snacks, at the intersection of Nehru and Laden La Rd., across from the police booth. The all-veg. snacks and sweets are clean, cheap, and yummy. Excellent Tibetan *momo* (4 pieces with hot soup Rs6).

Dekevas, Gandhi Rd., across the street from Kev's. Classy venue serves excellent food. Traditional Tibetan dishes like *thukpa* (veg. noodle soup) and Tibetan bread, in addition to Indian, Continental, and Chinese food. Service is slow when crowded, but they keep a fire going in the winter. Entrees Rs30-50.

Greenwood, Dr. Zakir Hussain Rd. (tel. 52663), just before Aliment. Dinesh and Sarita prepare exquisite Nepalese and Tibetan cuisine. Choose between a 5-course Nepalese meal, 2 kinds of traditional Tibetan meals, and the organic green and fruit salads. Rs60 per meal. Open daily 7am-1pm and 6-9:30pm.

ENTERTAINMENT

As for nightlife, Darjeeling is essentially dead after 8pm. One exception is **Joey's Pub,** an oasis of familiarity for bar-starved Westerners. Joey, a Darjeelingite who spent two years in London in the '70s, has succeeded in recreating the British pub scene—Indian style. Relax with a cold pint of your favorite...OK, they only have Indian beers, but the music (classic American and British rock) and ambience (bar stools and Guinness posters) are a great cure for homesickness. They even serve traditional pub fare, including fish and chips for Rs30. (Open daily 10am-10pm.) The Gorkha Hill Council holds **cultural programs** almost every evening in season. They also conduct **rafting expeditions.** Contact their tourist office for more information. (3m from Chowrasta to the left, past the bandstand.)

SIGHTS AND SCENERY

MOUNTAIN VIEWS. Darjeeling's most popular sight is **Kanchenjunga,** the world's third-highest mountain. Located on the border between Nepal and Sikkim, some 70km from Darjeeling, its 8586m cone can be seen on a clear day. For Kanchenjunga views, nothing beats the sunrise on **Tiger Hill,** which has become something of a pilgrimage site for Indian tourists. An observation tower on top of the 2590m rise offers views stretching from the flood plains of the Ganga delta to the snowcaps of the Himalayas, each peak lighting up in turn as the sunlight inches west. Everest and its neighbors are occasionally visible. Beginning in June, however, such views become elusive, and you may end up taking pictures of fellow backpackers among the clouds. There's nowhere to stay on the hill unless you camp, and most sunrise spectators come right back down once it gets bright. *(11km out of Darjeeling. Jeeps leave 4-5am on clear days, Rs50.)* While **Observatory Hill** is known for its excellent mountain views, it's also a sacred site for Hindus and Buddhists—it has a shrine to Shiva as Mahakali, and colorful Buddhist prayer flags flap around the temple complex. Watch out for the monkeys.

ZOOLOGICAL PARK. Darjeeling has more to offer than just mountains. At the north end of Darjeeling's ridge) is a complex containing both Darjeeling's zoo, the Padmaja Naidu Himalayan Zoological Park, and the Himalayan Mountaineering Institute (see below). Though pitifully small, this park gives its animals much leafier spaces than most Indian zoos, and it has species rarely seen elsewhere, including Siberian tigers and red pandas. Animal lovers may be upset by the conditions. *(20min. walk from Chowrasta, straight along the road to the left of the bandstand.)* A few restless snow leopards are being coaxed into breeding in the **Snow Leopard Breeding Center** on the other side of the hill from the zoo *(open F-W; Rs10).*

HIMALAYAN MOUNTAINEERING INSTITUTE (HMI). Above the zoo's Siberian tigers is the cenotaph of **Tenzing Norgay,** a Sherpa from Darjeeling who co-conquered Everest with Sir Edmund Hillary in 1953. Tenzing was the long-time director of the HMI, which is adjacent to the zoo. HMI offers climbing courses to Indians only; its main function is to instruct Indian Army soldiers. Darjeeling has had a long connection with mountaineering; when Nepal was a closed country, the earliest Everest trips took off from Darjeeling. HMI's **Everest Museum** is full of relics. The displays in the affiliated **Mountaineering Museum** range from butterflies to ice picks to relief models of the Himalayas. Around the corner, a telescope is set up to catch views of Kanchenjunga; it was given to one of Nepal's Rana prime ministers by Adolf Hitler. *(Museums open F-W 9am-4pm. Rs6.)*

RANGEET VALLEY PASSENGER ROPEWAY. Clockwise around the ridge from the HMI is the starting point for the Rangeet Valley Passenger Ropeway. The cable car no longer makes the full trip to Singla Bazaar north of Darjeeling, but it does go for a scenic half-hour dip over the tea shrubs. They won't operate the cars until full (10-20 people), so service can be erratic. *(Cars run daily 9am-5pm. Round-trip Rs45.)*

GHOOM MONASTERY. The region's most famous monastery, Yiga Choling Ghoom, was founded in 1850. The Ghoom Monastery's large shrine contains a 5m golden statue of the Maitreya Buddha (the future Buddha). The murals inside have just been refurbished and appear beautifully reborn. Don't confuse this with the new and not terribly interesting Samten Choling Ghoom Monastery below the road to Ghoom. (In Ghoom, 8km from Darjeeling. Toy Train runs here twice daily.)

HAPPY VALLEY TEA ESTATE. This is the best place to see a Darjeeling tea plantation, where pickers work through the shrubs on the hills around you, and the "factory" is open to visitors. Except during the off season (late June-Aug.), a worker will guide you through four days in the life of a tea leaf as it is processed by various machines; don't forget to give him a small tip. (Hill Cart Rd., past the District Magistrate's Office, down a rocky road. Open Tu-Sa 8am-4pm, Su 8:30am-noon.)

OTHER SIGHTS. The **Gymkhana Club,** a dilapidated Raj-era time warp complete with butlers, snooker tables, and Chesterfield cigars allows visitors to tour the cane furniture and tiled fireplaces of the regime. (Below Observatory Hill on the town side. Open daily 8am-8pm. Day membership Rs30, 1-week membership Rs150. Additional activities Rs10.) Below the Gymkhana Club is the **Bengal Natural History Museum,** which has an extensive collection of stuffed creatures, particularly birds (open F-W 10am-4pm; Rs2). Below the bus stand are the **Lloyd Botanical Gardens,** which specialize in alpine foliage (open daily 6am-5pm).

🛍 SHOPPING

Darjeeling's main product is its excellent **tea,** available in shops and stalls all over town. For the best stuff, head to Nehru Rd., which is lined with tea shops. **Hayden Hall,** Laden La Rd. (tel. 53228), across from the Bank of India, is a women's cooperative that sells locally made handmade blankets, rugs, bags, and sweaters. Proceeds go to needy women in Darjeeling. (Open M-Sa 9am-5pm.) A larger collection of handmade goods is available at the **Tibetan Refugee Self-Help Centre,** located beyond and below Observatory Hill. Follow Mall Rd. to the left of the bandstand and around to the other side of the hill; it's down the path and steps. Established by Tibetans who fled here in 1959, the workshop produces carpets, sweaters, woodcarvings, and other crafts. (Open to visitors M-Sa 9am-4pm.)

🏔 TREKKING AROUND DARJEELING

Trekking is the best way to get around the Darjeeling region and Western Sikkim from October to early December and from March to early June. Treks consist of six- or seven-hour day hikes between villages, where small hotels (usually Rs35) and food are available. On the trail itself, water and snacks are usually unavailable and should be packed, along with a sleeping bag, warm clothes, and rain gear. If you bring your own purification system, you can drink stream water. The routes are often old jeep roads with trails bypassing large sections of the winding road. For the most recent and detailed information, consult **West Bengal Tourism** (see p. 664) and tourist logs at the Youth Hostel, Tower View, and Aliment Hotel.

Rimbik is the most common starting and finishing point for treks and has the best accommodations, food, and transportation. **Buses** run from Darjeeling to Rimbik (7am, 12:30, and 1pm) and back (6am and noon, 4½hr., Rs42). **A popular loop** is from Rimbik to Gorkhey, Phalut, Sandakphu, and back to Rimbik—each leg takes a day. The direct trail from Sandakphu to Rimbik has many bifurcations and it's easy to get lost; it's better to go from Sandakphu to Rimbik via Gurdum and Srikola, which has a nice trekkers' hut. **For a longer trek,** it's best to start in Manabhanjan (buses from Darjeeling 7am, 12:30, and 1pm; 1½hr.; Rs18) and hike north up the Singalila Ridge, pass through Sandakphu and Phalut, and end in Rimbik. North of Phalut, the ridge forms the border between Nepal and Sikkim and leads up to the peak of Kanchenjunga. Perhaps **the most popular trek** in this area runs Darjeeling-Maneybhanjang-Tonglu-Sandakphu and back. This 118km route, studded with fabulous views of Kanchenjunga, can be covered in four days by a combination of jeep and foot. Check the tourist office for details.

THE RAJ IS DEAD, LONG LIVE THE RAJ

Though the sun has set on the Indian portion of the British empire, Darjeeling, perhaps more than any other Indian city, still bears the stamp of colonial life. In fact, without leaving the city limits, it is possible to plan a day that more or less approximates a day in the life of a British colonialist. Kick off the top-o'-the morning with a full English breakfast at either Kev's ar Glenary's, complete with such favorites as sausage, omelettes, and beans. Then proceed to oversee the operation of the British-built Happy Valley Tea Estate. While you're there, enjoy a spot of tea before moving on to the Oxford Book Shop, at Chowrasta, where you can browse the large collection of English literary favorites. After pickin' your Dickens, tally ho to the Windamere Hotel for high tea, complete with cucumber finger sandwiches. Before the sun goes down, make haste to the Gymkhana Club for some tennis, squash, or snooker before dinner. Finally, for the nightcap, have a pint or two or more at Joey's pub. There you have it: a full day in London-East, circa 1930. All that is missing are the double-decker buses.

KALIMPONG কালিমপং কালিম্প

Largely neglected by tourists, Kalimpong (1250m) is the black sheep of the family of Indian Himalayan towns. However, this small but lively center of the Gorkha independence movement has grown in recent years, in population as well as popularity among travelers. For many, the breathtaking ride from Darjeeling to Kalimpong makes this often-overlooked town worth the trip. The road to Kalimpong borders a deep precipice to the Teesta River which cuts a narrow, green swath through the mountains, and then makes a steep, winding climb up to the town. In many ways, Kalimpong's future lies in its location as a crossroads between kingdoms. As Sikkim increasingly opens to tourism and rumors fly of new connections with the formerly impenetrable Tibet, Kalimpong no longer seems content to play second fiddle to its much-visited sibling Darjeeling. The close of this century just might offer travelers one last chance to savor Kalimpong's cool climate and relaxed pace before the city is reborn as a bustling metropolis.

🛈 ORIENTATION AND PRACTICAL INFORMATION

The **bus stand** consumes most of **Market Square** in the center of town. On the east of Market Square is Hotel Cosy Nook; on the west is a corrugated-roofed building. **Sikkim Nation Transport (SNT)** is located just to the left of this building, and the Himilashree Lodge is to the right. Just south of Market Square is the old **football field**, also known as the **Mela Grounds. Ongen Road** crosses the square at the west end. Parallel to Ongen Rd. is **Main Road,** the town's major thoroughfare and primary axis, extending from **Gompu's Restaurant** and the central bank to the post office, telephone exchange, police station, and Foreigners Registration Office (all just beyond the south end of the football field). On either end, Main Rd. becomes **Rishi Road,** leading north to Deki Lodge and south past Hotel Silver Oaks.

Trains: The closest station is NJP in Siliguri, but there is a **booking office** (tel. 55643) in Kalimpong, 2nd alley on the right as you exit Market Sq. toward Gompu's. Quota seats are available on major trains, but reservations must be made a few days in advance. Open M-Sa 10am-1pm and 4-5pm, Su 10am-1pm.

Buses: Buses depart from Market Sq., with booking offices along the perimeter, particularly by the football field. To: **Darjeeling** (12:30pm, 3hr., Rs38); **Gangtok** (7:30 and 8am, 3hr., Rs38); **Siliguri** (every 30min. 6am–5pm, 2hr., Rs35). **SNT** runs a crowded bus to **Gangtok** (8:30am, 3½hr., Rs37). Reserve in advance. Open M-Sa 7:30am-2pm.

Tourist Information: The best information is found at local hotels. The **Deki Lodge** has maps and information about the area (see below). A guide to Kalimpong is also available at the West Bengal Tourist Office in Darjeeling (see p. 664).

Worldwide Calling Made Easy

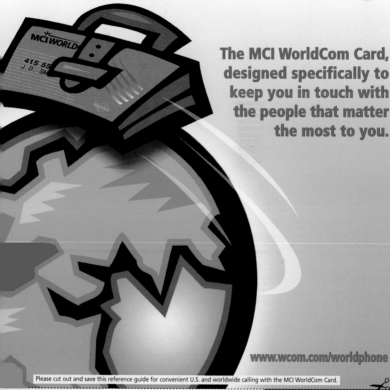

The MCI WorldCom Card, designed specifically to keep you in touch with the people that matter the most to you.

www.wcom.com/worldphone

Please cut out and save this reference guide for convenient U.S. and worldwide calling with the MCI WorldCom Card.

✂

nd, it's simple
call home or to
her countires.

the WorldPhone toll-free
ss number of the country
re calling from (listed inside).

w the easy voice instructions
old for a WorldPhone
ator. Enter or give the
ator your MCI WorldCom
number or call collect.

or give the WorldPhone
ator your home number.

e your adventures with
family!

COUNTRY		WORLDPHONE TOLL-FREE ACCESS #
St. Lucia ÷		1-800-888-8000
Sweden (CC) ◆		020-795-922
Switzerland (CC) ◆		0800-89-0222
Taiwan (CC) ◆		0080-13-4567
Thailand ★		001-999-1-2001
Turkey (CC) ◆		00-8001-1177
United Kingdom	(CC) To call using BT ■	0800-89-0222
	To call using CWC ■	0500-89-0222
United States (CC)		1-800-888-8000
U.S. Virgin Islands (CC)		1-800-888-8000
Vatican City (CC)		172-1022
Venezuela (CC) ÷ ◆		800-1114-0
Vietnam ●		1201-1022

(CC)	Country-to-country calling available to/from most international locations.
÷	Limited availability.
▼	Wait for second dial tone.
▲	When calling from public phones, use phones marked LADATEL.
■	International communications carrier.
★	Not available from public pay phones.
◆	Public phones may require deposit of coin or phone card for dial tone.
●	Local service fee in U.S. currency required to complete call.
▶	Regulation does not permit Intra-Japan calls.
❖	Available from most major cities

MCI WorldCom Worldphone Access Numbers

MCI WORLDCOM℠

The MCI WorldCom Card

The easy way to call when traveling worldwide

The MCI WorldCom Card gives you…

- Access to the US and other countries worldwide.
- Customer Service 24 hours a day
- Operators who speak your language
- Great MCI WorldCom rates and no sign-up fees

For more information or to apply for a Card call:

1-800-955-0925

Outside the U.S., call MCI WorldCom collect (reverse charge) at:

1-712-943-6839

COUNTRY	WORLDPHONE TOLL-FREE ACCESS #
Argentina (CC)	
To call using Telefonica ■	0800-222-6249
To call using Telecom ■	0800-555-1002
Australia (CC) ◆	
To call using AAPT ■	1-800-730-014
To call using OPTUS ■	1-800-551-111
To call using TELSTRA ■	1-800-881-100
Austria (CC) ◆	0800-200-235
Bahamas	1-800-888-8000
Belgium (CC) ◆	0800-10012
Bermuda ÷	1-800-888-8000
Bolivia (CC) ◆	0-800-2222
Brazil (CC)	000-8012
British Virgin Islands ÷	1-800-888-8000
Canada (CC)	1-800-888-8000
Cayman Islands	1-800-888-8000
Chile (CC)	
To call using CTC ■	800-207-300
To call using ENTEL ■	800-360-180
China ÷	108-12
For a Mandarin-speaking Operator	108-17
Colombia (CC) ◆	980-9-16-0001
Collect Access in Spanish	980-9-16-1111
Costa Rica ◆	0800-012-2222
Czech Republic (CC) ◆	00-42-000112
Denmark (CC) ◆	8001-0022
Dominican Republic	
Collect Access	1-800-888-8000
Collect Access in Spanish	1121
Ecuador (CC) ÷	999-170
El Salvador	800-1767

COUNTRY	WORLDPHONE TOLL-FREE ACCESS #
Finland (CC) ◆	08001-102-80
France (CC) ◆	0800-99-0019
French Guiana (CC)	0-800-99-0019
Guatemala (CC) ◆	99-99-189
Germany (CC)	0-800-888-8000
Greece (CC) ◆	00-800-1211
Guam (CC)	1-800-888-8000
Haiti ÷	193
Collect Access in French/Creole	190
Honduras ÷	8000-122
Hong Kong (CC)	800-96-1121
Hungary (CC) ◆	00▼800-01411
India (CC) ÷	000-127
Collect Access	000-126
Ireland (CC)	1-800-55-1001
Israel (CC)	
BEZEQ International	1-800-940-2727
BARAK	1-800-930-2727
Italy (CC) ◆	172-1022
Jamaica ÷	Collect Access 1-800-888-8000
(From Special Hotels only)	873
(From public phones)	#2
Japan (CC) ◆	To call using KDD ■ 00539-121▶
To call using IDC ■	0066-55-121
To call using JT ■	0044-11-121
Korea (CC)	To call using KT ■ 00729-14
To call using DACOM ■	00309-12
To call using ONSE ■	00369-14
Phone Booths÷	Press red button, 03, then ∗
Military Bases	550-2255
Lebanon	Collect Access 600-MCI (600-624)

COUNTRY	WORLDPHONE TOLL-FRE
Luxembourg (CC)	
Malaysia (CC) ◆	1-8
To call using Time Telekom ■	1-8
Mexico (CC) Avantel	01-8(
Telmex ▲	001-8(
Collect Access in Spanish	01-8(
Monaco (CC) ◆	
Netherlands (CC) ◆	080
New Zealand (CC)	
Nicaragua (CC) Collect Access in Spanis	
(Outside of Managua, (	
Norway (CC) ◆	
Panama	
Military Bases	
Philippines (CC) ◆ To call using PLDT	
To call using PHILCO	
To call using Bayante	
To call using ETP	
Poland (CC) ÷	00-80
Portugal (CC) ÷	8
Puerto Rico (CC)	1-8
Romania (CC) ÷	(
Russia (CC) ◆ ÷	
To call using ROSTELCOM ■	
(For Russian speaking operator	
To call using SOVINTEL ■	
Saudi Arabia (CC) ÷	
Singapore	8
Slovak Republic	(CC) 0
South Africa (CC)	08
Spain (CC)	

Budget Travel: Mintri Transport, Main Rd. (tel. 55741 or 55697), books airline tickets and runs daily buses to Bagdogra Airport (7:15am, Rs100) and NJP Station (time changes daily, Rs45). Open M-Sa 8am-7pm, Su 9am-5pm. **Shangri-La Services,** Rishi Rd. (tel. 55109), is an authorized agent for Jet Airways, Blue Dart Express, and Sita World Travels and also rents cars. Open daily 8am-5pm.

Immigration Office: Because Kalimpong is so close to the Chinese border, foreigners are required to register their arrival and departure at the **Foreigners Registration Office** (tel. 55312), next to the post office. No visa extensions given here. Open daily 9:30am-6pm.

Currency Exchange: None of Kalimpong's banks changes currency. **Silver Oaks Hotel,** Rishi Rd., on the left after the post office, changes currency for guests only. Mintri Transport will change it for one and all, but at a horrible rate.

Pharmacy: Shree Tibet Stores, Main Rd. (tel. 55459), across from Snow White Fashion near Gompu's Restaurant. Open daily 8:30am-8:30pm. Doctor available 9:30am-6pm. If it's an after-hours emergency, knock loudly on the door.

Post Office: GPO, Main Rd. (tel. 55990), at the end of the football field. Open M-Sa 10am-4pm. *Poste Restante.* **Postal Code:** 734301.

Internet: Delta Communications, Main Rd. (tel. 55911). Full Internet access Rs50 for first 15min., Rs3 each additional min. Open M-Sa 8:30am-7pm.

Telephones: Most **STD/ISD** booths are open 6am-11pm.

PHONE CODE	03552

WEST BENGAL

ACCOMMODATIONS

Himalshree Lodge, Market Sq. (tel. 55070), just to the right of the corrugated-roofed building. It's worth the walk up several flights of stairs. Six cozy rooms are often full, but no reservations are taken. The noise outside starts early. Meals available on advance order. Hot water buckets Rs5. Doors lock at 9pm. Singles Rs60; doubles Rs120.

Gompu's Hotel (tel. 55818), just west of Market Sq. Immaculate rooms, the best mountain views in town, and a quality restaurant downstairs. All rooms have attached baths. Singles Rs150; doubles Rs300.

Deki Lodge, Tripai Rd. (tel. 55095), right at Gompu's Restaurant and up the hill to Rishi Rd. Branch left off Rishi Rd.; it's just up the hill on the left. Peaceful location, perpetually smiling staff, and relaxed backpacker atmosphere set Deki apart. Spacious rooms and hot showers. Set off armed with the owner's extensive local knowledge. Singles Rs100-150; doubles with bath Rs150-650. Off-season (Jun.-Sept.): 10% discount.

Cosy Nook, Market Sq. (tel. 55541). The *betel*-chewing owner offers advice on seeing the sights. Rooms are small and basic, but all have attached bath (bucket hot water Rs4). Dorm beds; singles Rs150; doubles Rs250.

Bethlehem Lodge, Rishi Rd. (tel. 55185), just beyond the movie theater on the right. Large, immaculate rooms and bathrooms. The location is peaceful and yet close to Market Sq. Doubles Rs350; triples Rs450. Off-season: Rs200/400. 10% service charge.

FOOD

Kalimpong has a scant selection of good restaurants, but some Chinese eateries have popped up around Market Square. Main Rd. is lined with veggie snack stalls.

Kelsang Restaurant, by the football stadium. Follow the path towards the field, then go down some steps into a kind Tibetan family's home. No menus, but cheap, non-veg. Tibetan food—all you have to do is ask. *Momos* Rs10, beef chow mein Rs25. Open daily 7am-7:30pm.

Gompu's Restaurant, Main Rd. (tel. 55818), west of Market Sq. Centrally located and hopping. Dim lighting, fast service. Chinese (Rs25-40) and chicken (Rs50-60) entrees. Order ahead for large, well-prepared *momos*. Beer Rs50. Open daily 7am-8:30pm.

Kalash Vegetarian Snacketeria, Main Rd. The best of a growing number of veg. snack bars in town. Specializes in North and South Indian as well as Continental favorites. Great *dosas* for Rs40. Open daily 8am-8pm.

👁🎵 SIGHTS AND ENTERTAINMENT

Kalimpong offers a bountiful bouquet of orchids, amaryllises, roses, gladiolus, and dahlias, most impressive from March to June. **Ganesh Mani Pradhan Nursery,** past the monastery, specializes in orchids; calling ahead is recommended (12th Mile Rishi Rd.; tel. 57217; open daily 9am-5pm.) Also on the premises are beautiful but expensive guest cottages (doubles Rs1500). **Tharpa Choling Gompa Monastery,** a Gelug-pa (Yellow Hat) monastery, was founded in 1892 and has just completed renovations; visitors are likely to see wood carvers and other artisans at work (a 40min. walk uphill east of town beyond the Deki Lodge, off DM Moktan Rd.). The complex of **Dr. Graham's Home** was built in 1900 when a Scottish minister set up a home for six orphaned students. The school eventually acquired the whole hilltop and became largely self-sufficient. Almost entirely funded by alumni donations, it now has over 1200 students from as far away as Kolkata and is the model for many schools for poor and handicapped children. (Farther up Deolo Hill from the monastery.) The brilliant yellow **Bhutanese Monastery,** also called Thongsa Gompa, was established in 1692 (at the bottom of Deolo Hill). Another popular attraction is the **Samco Ropeway,** a modified ski lift installed by the Swedish to help villagers cross the Teesta. The rope, which hangs about 30m above the river in spots, is not for the faint of heart. (Halfway between Kalimpong and Siliguri. 2hr. bus from Kalimpong Rs25.) The **Kanchan Cinema Hall** often shows somewhat stale Hollywood films to go along with the standard Hindi attractions (on Rishi Rd. between Tripai Rd. and Market Sq.; showings 11am, 2pm, and 5pm; Rs4-12).

SIKKIM सिक्किम

Aesthetically and geographically, Sikkim is the cherry on top of India's Northeast. Bordered by Nepal, Tibet, Bhutan, and West Bengal, the state is trustee to some of the most inspiring natural scenery anywhere: a countryside full of peacefully grazing sheep, lush hills, leaping waterfalls, thundering rivers, and placid lakes. Maintaining a tradition of communal intermingling, Sikkimese society remains among the most peaceful in the world (indeed, the state once appeared in the *Guiness Book of World Records* for going 10 years without a single criminal case).

The earliest known inhabitants of Sikkim were the Lepchas, who arrived in the 13th century. In the 15th and 16th centuries, following conflicts between Buddhist sects in Tibet, many Tibetans immigrated to North India. The first *chogyal* (king) of Sikkim was appointed in the 17th century. Under the British protectorate, which began in 1861, Hindu Nepalese were brought to Sikkim by the British to work on tea plantations, and they soon came to outnumber the Lepchas and Tibetans. In Sikkim, people from the flatlands to the south are "Indian," while those who grew up in the mountains identify themselves according to their ancestry: Nepalese, Bhutanese, Tibetan, or Lepcha. The Hindu Nepalese currently represent 75% of the population, although Sikkim is historically a Buddhist kingdom, closely linked to Tibet and home to over 250 monasteries. The result of all this ethnic diversity is a remarkably friendly confluence of cultures. When India became inde-

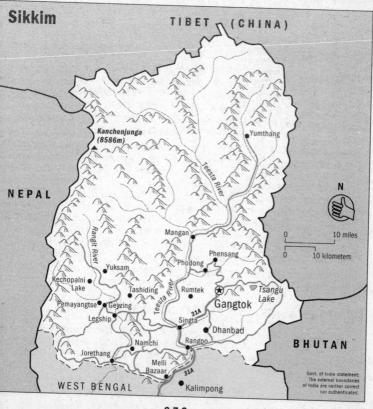

pendent in 1947, Sikkim was made a semi-independent Indian protectorate. In 1975, 97% of the Sikkim's electorate voted to join India, and the territory became the country's 22nd state. Sikkim has managed to maintain a degree of regional distinctiveness since joining the Indian union. Though it has gradually begun to open its borders to tourists, the people of Sikkim take its new status as a tourist destination in stride; travelers can expect a refreshingly hassle-free and tranquil stay.

The best times to visit Sikkim are from late March to May, when the flowers are in bloom, and October to November, when clear views are guaranteed. **Visitors to Sikkim must first obtain permits** (see **Special Permits**, p. 11).

HIGHLIGHT OF SIKKIM

■ **Western Sikkim's** treks (p. 679) wind from **Geyzing and Pelling** (p. 678) through clouded hills past Buddhist monasteries and pristine lakes.

GANGTOK गातोक

Carved out of the hillside, Sikkim's capital is dwarfed both in altitude and scenic beauty by its spectacular surroundings. Still, Gangtok has its own appeal with friendly, helpful people, relatively clean streets, and easy travel connections to Sikkim's most picturesque spots. The mighty tourist infrastructure dominates the town's activity, and Gangtok is the state's best bet for store-bought goods and supplies, as well as practical services. In order to extend Sikkim permits or obtain the appropriate documentation for trekking north of Yuksam or Phodong, travelers must deal with red tape and a Delhi-esque bureaucracy. However, several worthwhile sights remain tucked away in the surrounding hills, and Gangtok is an altogether pleasant hub from which to make daytrips and deeper forays into the hills.

☞ TRANSPORTATION

Flights: The nearest airport is **Bagdogra**, near Siliguri. **Josse and Josse**, MG Rd. (tel. 24682), next to Raj Enterprise, are authorized agents for Jet Airways, Sahara, and Skyline NEPC. Open daily 9am-7pm. The proprietor of the **Green Hotel**, MG Rd. (tel. 24049; fax 23354), is a sub-agent for Indian Airlines and Jet Airways.

Trains: The **railway reservations window**, at the far end of the SNT Bus Terminal, has quota tickets on major trains leaving New Jalpaiguri. Open M-Sa 8am-2pm, Su 8-11am.

Buses: Sikkim Nation Transport (SNT) Bus Terminal (tel. 22016), located down from the National Highway at the north end of town. Book tickets early at the far left window. Open daily 6:30am-3pm. The crowded, subsidized buses are the cheapest, although slowest, mode of transport. To: **Darjeeling** (7am, 5hr., Rs75); **Geyzing** (7am, 5hr., Rs45); **Jorethang** (7am and 2pm, 3hr., Rs35); **Kalimpong** (8:15am, 3hr., Rs37); **Mangan** (8am and 3pm, 5hr., Rs44); **Namchi** (7:30am and 2pm, 5hr., Rs46); **Rumtek** (4pm, 1hr., Rs11); **Siliguri** (6 per day 6am-12:15pm, 4hr., Rs47). **Private buses** gather along the highway around Naya Bazaar. **Shared Jeeps**, available below Lal Bazaar just below the highway, are faster and costlier than SNT buses (to Siliguri, Rs80). Make sure you are sharing a jeep and not paying for the whole thing (over Rs1000).

Local Transportation: Taxis run up and down the National Highway. Prices are negotiated first. It shouldn't cost more than Rs25 for the length of the city.

☷ ORIENTATION AND PRACTICAL INFORMATION

The **National Highway** cuts up the hill diagonally northeast, with roads branching off horizontally above and below. The **SNT Bus Terminal** is 100m off the highway at the northern end of town. **Mahatma Gandhi (MG) Road** branches up off the highway 30m south of the intersection that leads to the SNT Terminal. The tourist center dominates this intersection. Farther south MG Rd. becomes **Naya Bazaar**, below which, on the highway, is **Lal Bazaar**, where shared jeeps and private buses await.

Tourist Office: National Tourist Centre (tel. 23425 or 22064), on the corner of MG Rd. and the highway. Useful maps of Gangtok and Sikkim. Open M-Sa 10am-4pm.

Tours: Tour companies provide comprehensive trek services, including permits, guides, and equipment. Tours cost around US$25 per day, but they are necessary in order to get a permit for any trek beyond Yuksam. **Modern Central Hotel,** Tibet Rd. (tel. 24670), is somewhat affordable, as are agencies closer to the trails like **Bumchu Tours and Travels,** Tashiding Bazaar, P.O. Sinek, West Sikkim 737111. **River rafting** in the Teesta river is becoming popular. Tour agencies, including several along MG Rd., organize trips. Overnight adventures cost about US$40 per person, less if the group is large.

Currency Exchange: State Bank of India, National Highway (tel. 23326), behind the tourist center. Located on the 1st fl.; enter through the right side entrance. Cashes AmEx traveler's checks. Open M-F 10am-2pm, Sa 10am-noon.

Pharmacy: Many along MG Rd. and Naya Bazaar. Locals like **Chiranjilal Lalchand Pharmacy,** MG Rd., across from the Green Hotel. Open daily 8am-8pm.

Hospital: Sir Thutab Namgyal Memorial (STNM) Hospital (tel. 22059), located above the National Highway above the tourist center.

Police: tel. 22033.

Post Office: (tel. 23085), halfway up the street from SNT Terminal and National Highway. On the left as you descend. *Poste Restante.* Open M-Sa 9:30am–5pm.

Internet: Gokul Communications, Yama Building, MG Rd. Web access Rs25 per 15min., Rs45 per 30min. Open daily 9am-7:30pm. **Green Hotel,** MG Rd. Rs3 per min. Open daily 9am-7pm.

Telephones: STD/ISD booths are in tourist offices along the road on which the GPO stands. Most are open until 11pm.

PHONE CODE	03592

ACCOMMODATIONS

Many of Gangtok's hotels are sparkling new but tend to be oriented toward wealthier Indian tourists. The few places that have kept their prices low are usually crowded. Always ask for a discount—many managers take pity on well-behaved travelers. Consider staying near the **Rumtek Monastery** (see p. 676), 24km across the river valley. Prime seasons are September-December and March-May.

Green Hotel, MG Rd. (tel. 24049 or 25057; fax 23354), on the right just beyond the tourist center. The clean rooms in this popular and established hotel are usually filled. Restaurant on main floor. STD, fax, Internet access, and travel agency. Singles Rs150; doubles Rs250-450. Off-season: up to 50% discount.

Modern Central Hotel, Tibet Rd. (tel. 24670). Go up the hill off MG Rd. at the tourist center and turn left on Tibet Rd.; it's around the bend. TV room upstairs. Common bath has a delightfully hot shower. Travel agency at the front desk run by the tremendously helpful manager/owner. Dorm beds Rs40; doubles with bath Rs120-200.

Travel Lodge, Tibet Rd. (tel. 23858), one block from Modern Central, closer to MG Rd. Huge rooms have balconies and hot showers. Star TV in all rooms. Worth the added expense. Doubles Rs300-350. Off-season: 20% discount.

FOOD

Food can be expensive in Gangtok. Bulk foods for hiking are available along Naya Bazaar, which offers the best selection in Sikkim. The restaurant in the **Green Hotel** (entrees Rs20-40) is popular with locals, as is the one in the **Modern Central Lodge** great *momos,* Rs20).

KEEPING SIKKIM GREEN With the central government understandably preoccupied with pervasive poverty, disputed borders, and inter-ethnic conflict, it is little wonder that India's environmental health is often overlooked. Token clean-up efforts such as the "Keep India Green" postering campaign in India's urban centers have proven unsuccessful as the mounds of refuse keep growing. In Sikkim, however, environmental action is no joke. In 1999, the state's Chief Minister Pawan Kumar Chamling was honored by environmentalists as India's most green-friendly state head for his instituting a complete ban on the use of plastic and polyethylene bags in Sikkim. In recognizing Chamling, the non-governmental organization Centre for Science and Environment expressed its hope that the rest of India might soon follow suit.

Sagar, Daigha, and **Laxmi Sweets,** MG Rd., across from the Green Hotel and to the south. A popular trio of side-by-side snack shops. Open daily 6:30am-8pm.

Hungry Jack Restaurant, National Highway, south of the lower taxi/private bus stand, just beyond the gas pumps. Clean, spacious, westernized restaurant and bar. North Indian, Chinese, and sandwiches (Rs35-65 plus 10% service charge). Sikkim-brewed Dansberg beer Rs33. Open daily 7:30am-8:30pm.

Tripti's Bakery Confectionery, National Highway, below Hungry Jack. Enter from highway side. Mouth-watering assortment of desserts, breads, and ice cream. The aroma alone should last you at least half a trek. Most pastries Rs10-25. Open daily 6:30am-7pm.

Khampie Restaurant, Tibet Rd., in the Mig-Tin Hotel. Try Khampie for a little bit of everything: North Indian, Chinese, excellent Italian (lasagna Rs50), and even, for the brave, Mexican (tacos Rs45). Open daily 7am-8:30pm.

SIGHTS AND SHOPPING

Though not much of a destination in itself, Gangtok is surrounded by lakes, parks, and gardens that make ideal daytrips. Taking Sikkim Tourism's **sight-seeing trips** is one way to take in everything. You can also book tours at one of the local travel agencies (Rs250-500). Contact the Tourist Department for more information.

The **Enchey Monastery** is perched on the landing spot of Lama Druptob Karpo, who is said to have flown over from Maenam Hill over 200 years ago. The building itself dates from 1909 and has beautiful views of Kanchenjunga (a 40min. hike from Gangtok). The mural-covered walls of the **Tsuglakhang,** or Royal Chapel, enclose huge collections of scriptures. Officially, the monastery and chapel are closed to tourists, but you may be able to charm your way in as long as you're not toting a camera or an especially large gun. (Farther south and closer to town.)

The **Research Institute of Tibetology** was founded by the Dalai Lama in 1957 and now holds approximately 30,000 volumes of old Tibetan documents (mostly wooden boards called xylographs). Its collection of ornate *thankas* is quite impressive. Though it is billed as the world's foremost center for Tibetology, there are now only a few researchers here; the center in Darjeeling seems to have more to offer. (1km south and downhill from Naya Bazaar along a large road. Tel. 22525 or 24822. Open M-Sa 10am-4pm. Rs2.)

The **Government Institute of Cottage Industries** serves as a "factory" for handicrafts and furniture and a display center where colorful crafts are sold (20min. north of the tourist center on the National Highway, on the left; open M-Sa 10am-5pm). For additional shopping, the **Kunphenling Tibetan Co-operative Society Handicraft Emporium,** is located just below the highway on the way to the SNT terminal.

NEAR GANGTOK: RUMTEK रुम्तेक

Rumtek is a large and beautiful hillside monastery only 24km away, on the oppo site side of the Valley from Gangtok (40 min., Rs25 in a shared jeep). It is the head of the Karma-pa (Black Hat) sect of the Kargyu-pa order of Tibetan Buddhism. The **Rumtek Monastery,** built in the 1960s, is modeled on the main Kargyu-pa monastery in Chhofuk, Tibet. Located in a back room is an impressive collection of golden statues of the 16th Gwalpa who fled Tibet when China invaded. Turn on the charm, and a monk might let you have a peek. A 45-minute walk downhill is the impressive **Old Monastery,** which is visible from behind the Kunga Delek; ask a young monk to show you the path. The not-to-miss sight here is the collection of sometimes-uplifting, sometimes-horrifying (think disembowelment) wall paintings. Two days before Losar, the Tibetan New Year (in February), and on the 10th day of the 5th month of the Tibetan calendar (in July), Rumtek is the site of celebratory dances called *chaams*.

Accommodations around Rumtek are a less convenient, but cheaper high-season alternatives to the crowds in Gangtok. The **Sangay Hotel** (tel. 52238) is located just up the hill beyond the checkpoint for the monastery. A friendly family runs the hotel and serves good, cheap food. (Singles Rs50; doubles Rs75-100.) **Kunga Delek** (tel. 52246), is farther up the hill, close to the monastery. All rooms have great views and attached baths with hot showers. Another option is the **Sun-gay Guest House** (tel. 52221), near the checkpoint. Beautiful, spacious rooms with attached bath are a great value. (Singles Rs100; doubles Rs120 in the front with hot water, Rs100 in the back with cold water.) Finally, tucked away behind the Kunga Deleh (and without a sign) is the **Hotel 93** (tel. 52250), named for the year of its founding. Four rooms, all with hard wood floors. (Doubles with hot water Rs120, with cold water Rs100.) If you plan to return to Gangtok in the evening, you'll need a taxi from the city (Rs250 round-trip), as jeeps leave Rumtek only in the morning.

NEAR GANGTOK: TSONGA LAKE

Cradled at the top of some of Eastern Sikkim's highest peaks, Tsonga Lake (3700m) feels like the top of the world. Just a two-hour jeep ride east (and straight up, at times) from Gangtok, this sacred site is jaw-droppingly beautiful. The lake is frozen Dec. and Jan., ringed with snow until late March, and surrounded by wildflowers in the warmer seasons. The jeep tour to get there (round-trip US$12; book with any local travel agent) may hurt the wallet a bit, but the trip is well worth it. For the energetic, a short but steep hike up to the ridge overlooking the lake (4000m, 1hr. up, 20min. down) gives a spectacular, 360° panorama which includes (in clockwise order) the lake, the Kanchen-junga range, the mountains of Tibet, and those of Bhutan. Tsonga lake may be above the treeline, but it's not above the snack-bar line (*momos* Rs10 at any of the cafeterias).

WESTERN SIKKIM

Everything seems bigger in Western Sikkim, except the prices and crowds. The hills are more rugged, the lakes more expansive, and the monasteries truly exhilarating. The ancient soul of Sikkim remains in the West—the first Sikkimese capital was at Yuksam, in the north of Western Sikkim, and the ruins of the second palace of Sikkim's *chogyals* (kings) lies near Pemayangtse Monastery. To this day, the people exhibit a pride in their land and culture that they are eager to share with visitors.

This once tightly restricted area has opened up considerably in the past few years. Nowadays most general Sikkim permits are stamped with extensions for Western attractions like Yuksam, Pemayangtse, and Khechopalri Lake. To secure a permit to trek in Northern Sikkim or north of Yuksam, get paperwork processed in Gangtok. The easiest and most common way to enter Western Sikkim is to take a jeep or bus from Gangtok or Darjeeling. Transportation to the region will usually stop in Geyzing or Pelling, ideal transit points for treks or rides to the rest of Western Sikkim. Most towns are five or six hours apart on foot, and only slightly less if you travel over the winding roads by bus or jeep.

GEYZING गेज़िन्ग AND PELLING पेल्लिनग

Judging by its location high up in the clouds, one might expect Geyzing to be peaceful and relaxing. Yet as a bustling marketplace and transportation hub, it proves less than ideal for those wishing to "get away from it all." Pelling, a hamlet above Geyzing, is a better bet for those seeking peace and relaxation. The starting point for paths to Yuksam, Tashiding, and Khechopalri Lake, the town caters to foreign trekkers; its accommodations are excellent sources for hiking information. Pelling is also within easy walking distance of **Pemayangtse Monastery** (25min.) and numerous other sacred spots (inquire at any of the hotels).

7 ORIENTATION AND PRACTICAL INFORMATION. Geyzing's **SNT Bus Terminal** is down the main road from the central square at the bend in the road. To: **Gangtok** (7am, 5hr., Rs50); **Jorethang** (7, 9:30am, and 1pm; 2½hr., Rs20); **Pelling** (M-Sa 2:30 and 3:30pm, Su 2:30pm, 30 min., Rs5; the 2:30pm bus continues on to Khechopalri Lake, 3hr.); **Siliguri** (7am, 5hr., Rs50); **Tashiding** (1:30pm, 3hr., Rs15); and **Yuksam** (Rs25). Jeeps run frequently to **Pelling** (20min., Rs10) from the small gazebo next to the field near the bus station. Jeeps are available in season but are more difficult to find off season. Given the irregularities in the transportation schedule, walking from town to town is often more convenient than taking buses or jeeps. **Currency exchange** is not available. The **post office** is located on the side of the Sikkim Tourist Centre building in Pelling (open M-F 9am-4pm, Sa 9am-2pm) and just off of central square in Geyzing (same hours). Only the service window and sign are visible. **STD/ISD** services are available in the booth next to the No Name Hotel in the Geyzing central square (open 6am-9pm) and at **Hotel Window Park,** next to Hotel Garuda in Pelling. **Telephone Code:** 03595.

⌂⌂ ACCOMMODATIONS AND FOOD. Accommodations in Geyzing are limited. Most hotels are in the central square area. The best bet is **Hotel No Name** (tel. 50722 or 50768), located on the end of the square closest to the SNT bus station. The attached restaurant serves decent Indian fare (chicken curry Rs30). Rooms are large and clean, but hot water comes only in buckets. (Dorm beds Rs30; doubles Rs60; triples Rs120.)

Pelling, on the other hand, is budding with new accommodations, but the majority are expensive. A few places maintain low prices, but don't expect them to be particularly clean or bug-free. The family at **Hotel Garuda** (tel. 50614), right in front of the jeep stand (look for the sign), gives out a helpful map of Pelling and surrounding areas and keeps a tourist log with extensive firsthand information on trekking. An attached restaurant serves up Sikkimese, Chinese, and Continental fare (entrees Rs20-40). They allow luggage storage and will even make you a bag lunch. (Dorm beds Rs70-80; singles Rs80-180; doubles Rs100-120.) If they're full, the owner will direct you to the nearby and nearly identical **Sister Guest House** (tel. 50569). **Hotel Kabur** (tel. 50685), just uphill from the tourist office, has similar offerings. One of the children there might join you for a walk to Pemayangtse. (Dorm beds Rs50; singles Rs200; doubles Rs350.) Both Kabur and Garuda serve meals (entrees Rs18-45). For a great meal outside of a hotel, try the **Alpine Restaurant**, located on the road behind and below the Hotel Garuda. Enjoy the intimate, family setting and outstanding North Indian and Chinese specialities, if you don't mind the one-hour wait. (Chow mein Rs20, beer Rs35; open daily 6:30am-9pm.)

NEAR PELLING: PEMAYANGTSE पमयान्नाटसे

Founded in 1705 during the reign of Chadov Namgyal, the third king of Sikkim, the *gompa* of **Pemayangtse** (The Sublime Perfect Lotus) is currently the principal Nyingma-pa (Red Hat) monastery, with over 100 monks. In the top room at the monastery is the **Sang Thog Palri**, a massive wooden representation of Maha Guru's Paradise. Despite the Legoland feel of the brightly-colored, intricate figures, the explicit sex scenes and gruesome depictions of Hell banish any childlike thoughts. You may have to wait for a young monk to retrieve a key before showing you the way. Behind the white Buddhist *stupa* at the first bend in the road up to the monastery is the **Cheshay Gang,** an old seat for the three-trunked tree. (Monastery open daily 7am-5pm, Rs10.)

The **Rangdentse Palace ruins** are located past the entrance to Pemayangtse towards Geyzing. From the main road, take a left onto a small path just before the 3km marker. The path crosses a small meadow before it climbs to the main ruins. Sikkim's second king, Tensung Namgyal, built the palace in 1670 in a move to shift the capital from Yuksam. On the right as you climb through the ruins are the remnants of the stable and military headquarters; on the left is the site of the main throne. The view from here captures the holiest areas of Western Sikkim, including Yuksam and Tashiding.

The Monastery also runs the **Denjong Padma Choeling Academy,** a 30-minute walk from Pelling toward Pemayangtse and Geyzing—take the stairs on the right. A school for destitute Sikkimese children, the Academy lets foreign tourists stay for a small donation. Visitors here find few comforts but get a chance to bond with the schoolchildren who are eager to practice their English. The children are all from Sikkimese families, and some are orphans. The headmaster is actively recruiting Westerners who are willing to tutor or aid in the renovation of the school building. Contact Yapo S. Yongda (at DPC Academy, Yongda Hill, Drakchong Dzong - 737113, West Sikkim, India; tel. (03595) 50656; fax (03592) 24802) for more information. He may be able to help with permit extensions for volunteers.

Pemayangtse isn't the only major *gompa* in the area. A scenic 45-minute walk up the hill to the west of Pelling is the **Sarga Choeling Monastery.** Even older than the Pemayangtse Monastery (1697), this monastery also contains beautiful murals.

TREKKING IN WESTERN SIKKIM

The best way to take in the culture and natural beauty of Western Sikkim is on foot. Though the most popular sites are connected by road, the more enjoyable and most challenging routes are the unmarked "short-cuts." These trails have many branches, but there are plenty of farmers around who will help you find your way. Keep in mind that while finding dinner and a place to sleep is rarely a problem, there is almost never lunch or bottled water available along the trail. Many hotels will provide trekkers with a bag lunch (Rs20-30). Also keep in mind that there is no phone service in Western Sikkim north of Pelling.

There are two extremely popular trekking routes in Western Sikkim which differ greatly in duration, difficulty, price, and degree of advanced planning required. The **Local Trek** (3-4 days) hits many of Western Sikkim's top destinations. It is not too difficult, requires no advance booking or additional permits, and should cost roughly Rs150-250 per day. It begins with a hike (5hr.) from Pelling to **Kechopalri Lake** (see below). The shortcut trail starts at the Mondol Lodge in Lower Pelling and descends to the Rimbi River (1½hr.). After traversing the river, the trail leads up to the road, following it to **Yuksam** (see below)—ask locals for shortcuts along the way. The five- to six-hour walk to **Tashiding** (see below) can be made by shortcut, but the walk along the road is gorgeous, taking hikers past the Bhamrong Waterfall (1½hr.), through the village of Garadhang (2½-3hr.), where snacks and water are available, and eventually along a ridge where the hilltop monastery is visible. At this point there is a choice between a 16km (4hr.) hike along the road to **Legship** (see below), where transportation is available to most destinations, or the shortcut back to Pelling (5-6hr.). If you plan to return to Pelling, it may be wise to leave your main pack at the hotel and take only a daypack on the circular trek.

For serious trekkers seeking the more challenging (and more costly) **High Altitude Trek** (6-9 days) leaves from Yuksam, and ascends well above 4000m. It must be booked ahead of time in Gangtok, and can cost anywhere from US$15 per day (roughing it) to US$80 per day (bring your hair dryer, a porter will carry it for you). The trek goes from **Yuksam** (1780m) to **Dzongri** (4024m) over a period of four days. Some trips continue on to **Goeche La** (4940m) for three more days before returning to the "lowlands." Although most of these treks are guided and should be relatively safe, read up on Acute Mountain Sickness (AMS) before you go (see p. 40).

KHECHOPALRI LAKE. Located 30km from Pelling, Khechopalri is the holiest lake in Sikkim (make your wish wisely), and legend has it that a sacred bird removes the leaves from its surface as soon as they land in the water. No swimming is allowed. There is a festival here on the 15th and 16th of the first month of the lunar calendar (Feb. or Mar.). Just before the monastery, on the left side, there is a privatized **trekkers' hut** (dorm beds Rs30, doubles Rs100). Home-cooked meals (*dal* and rice Rs40) and biscuits for the next day's lunch are available. There is also a **pilgrims' hut** at the monastery (Rs40; the only toilet is the public one outside). Basic food is available at nearby stalls (biscuits Rs10). Among the sites accessible by a day hike around the lake are the **Chubuk** and **Dupuk** caves, where religious ceremonies are performed by local monks, and the **"footprint rock,"** where legend has it that a monk's foot was printed when he stepped on it. Ask at the trekker's hut for directions to these attractions. **Buses** for Geyzing leave in the morning (7am, 2hr., Rs10).

YUKSAM. The historic town of Yuksam is a three-hour bus ride or five-hour walk (via shortcut) from Pelling and slightly shorter from Khechopalri Lake. According to some accounts, Yuksam became the first capital of Sikkim when, in 1641, its king was consecrated by three Tibetan Lamas—hence the name Yuksam, "three Lamas" in the Lepcha language. The white stone throne in front of the monastery is called Norbugang Chorten. The **Dubdi Monastery,** the oldest in Sikkim, is a one-hour walk up the hill. Founded by Gyalwa Lhabchen Chenpo in 1701, it currently houses about 60 monks.

Permits for the **forest lodge** (above the road on the left side; follow the sign) must be obtained from the Forestry Department in Gangtok (Rs60 per person). The **Wild Orchid** hotel, on the right side of the road just before the town's bazaar, offers information on the area and home-cooked breakfast for Rs30 (in-season singles Rs75; doubles Rs100; triples Rs150). For meals outside of the hotel, the two best options are the snack-bar-like **Gupta Restaurant** (*momos* and beer Rs45) and, for an aprés-trek treat, the restaurant at the luxurious **Hotel Tashi Gang.** While it may be too expensive to stay here, meals are excellent and reasonably priced (Rs50-75). There are also accommodations in the village, home mostly to Bhutanese farmers. Treks to **Dzongri** leave from here, but the tour companies in town are of little use to foreigners, who must process their paperwork in Gangtok. **Buses** and **jeeps** for Geyzing (3hr.; bus Rs30, jeep Rs75) and Tashiding (1½-2hr.; bus Rs20, jeep Rs50) leave only in the morning.

TASHIDING MONASTERY. An unreliable two-hour bus ride or a six-hour walk (via shortcut) from Yuksam, the Tashiding Monastery is located on a *stupa*-dotted hill between the Rangeet and Ralhong Rivers, up from the main town. The monastery dates from 1716 and now houses about 50 monks and the **Bhumchu,** a sacred water vase at the center of a local festival every March. At the festival, the water vase, which was sealed empty one year prior, is opened to reveal a bounty of fresh water—a miracle! Climbing up the hill, the path to the cave is on the left just before the first major *stupa*. The **Hotel Blue Bird,** on the right side of the road as you walk into Tashiding Bazaar, is simple but familial (dorm beds Rs30; singles Rs50; doubles Rs60).

LEGSHIP. Though not a major tourist destination, Legship makes a convenient terminus for treks because of its location on the road from Geyzing to Gangtok or Siliguri. The only real option for overnight stays is the **Hotel Trishna** (tel. 50887), located just up the street from the SNT bus terminal (doubles Rs100, with bath Rs200). **Buses** out of town leave from the terminal for Gangtok (7:30am, 4½hr. Rs42); Siliguri (6:30 and 7:30am, 4½hr., Rs45); and Geyzing (11am and 12pm, 45min., Rs8). Most bus routes originate elsewhere, so seating may be limited. Ask at the hotel for directions to the **hot springs** located half-hour walk from town.

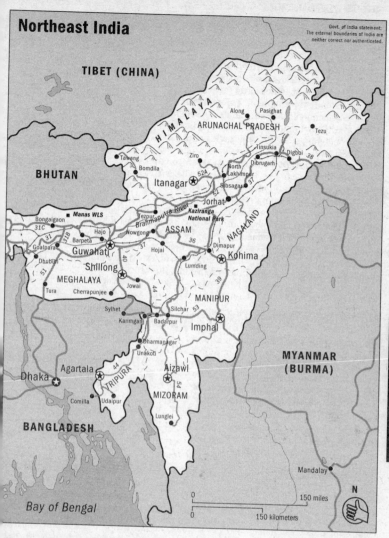

Northeast India

Govt. of India statement: The external boundaries of India are neither correct nor authenticated.

TIBET (CHINA)

HIMALAYA

ARUNACHAL PRADESH

Along Pasighat Tezu

Tinsukia Digboi 38

Tawang Ziro North Lakhimpur Dibrugarh 37

Bomdila 52A Sibsagar

BHUTAN

Itanagar

Jorhat

Bongaigaon Manas WLS Tezpur Brahmaputra River Kaziranga National Park

31C 31B Hajo Nowgong ASSAM NAGALAND

Barpeta Guwahati 31 Hojai 36 Dimapur

Goalpara 40 Kohima

Dhubri 51 Shillong Lumding

MEGHALAYA Jowai 39

Tura Cherrapunjee 44 MANIPUR

Sylhet Silchar 53

Karimganj Badarpur Imphal

Dharmanagar

Unakoti

MYANMAR (BURMA)

Dhaka Agartala 44 Aizawl

Comilla TRIPURA 54

Udaipur MIZORAM

BANGLADESH

Lunglei

Mandalay

Bay of Bengal

0   150 miles
0   150 kilometers

N

NORTHEAST INDIA

Northeast India consists of seven states connected to the rest of the country by a narrow isthmus and an even narrower thread of cultural similarity. Forming the heart of the region is the Brahmaputra Valley state of Assam, which until recently encompassed the entire region. The Northeast is largely inhabited by *adivasis* (tribal peoples) who have had little or no exposure to modernization. In 1963, these diverse tribes' struggles for autonomy led to the splintering of Assam and the creation of six new states: Arunachal Pradesh, Nagaland, Manipur, Mizoram, Tripura, and Meghalaya, which together comprise the hilly regions bordering China, Burma, and Bangladesh. Turmoil and bureaucratic difficulties accompanied the changes, and instability threatens many areas to this day. The capital of

Assam (formerly Shillong) was officially moved to Guwahati in 1974, two years *after* Meghalaya became a separate state. Until 1981, Assam, Nagaland, Manipur, Tripura, and Meghalaya were administered by one governor.

The legacy of armed insurrection in Mizoram, Nagaland, and Assam continues only partially abated, and political violence is still common in the Northeast. Dissidents claim that India takes advantage of the region's rich natural resources while ignoring its underdevelopment. Political instability, coupled with Indian fears of a Chinese invasion (China still claims Arunachal Pradesh), kept the entire region closed to foreigners until 1995. However, the long-promised easing of restrictions is finally becoming a reality, and travel in the region has never been easier. Assam, Meghalaya, and Tripura are now open to unrestricted tourism. Permits, which must be obtained in Delhi or secured when you apply for a visa, are required for the other states (see p. 11). They take anywhere from two hours to two months to attain, due to the erratic pace of bureaucratic processing. The best advice is to come up with a convincing reason why you want to go and then be persistent.

The Northeast offers the traveler virgin natural beauty and a glimpse of tribal culture. Assam and Meghalaya are the most popular destinations, as their cities offer a cosmopolitan introduction to the Northeast as well as a mellower climate than is found in much of the rest of India. Arunachal Pradesh, Nagaland, and Mizoram remain spectacular, pristine natural paradises, while Manipur and Tripura offer less exotic scenery but boasts a proud cultural legacy. Finally, not entirely unrelated to its appeal is the Northeast's lack of infrastructure, which makes exploration that much more exciting but, alas, more expensive.

HIGHLIGHTS OF NORTHEAST INDIA

■ Assam's **Kaziranga National Park** (p. 687) teems with wildlife, including a large population of protected rhinos.
■ One of the wettest places on earth, **Meghalaya** (p. 691) showers visitors with hospitality, sublime scenery, and well-watered greenery.
■ Less-traveled states like **Manipur** (p. 697) and **Mizoram** (p. 696) are renowned for their natural beauty and distinctive cultural heritage.

ASSAM असम

Stretching 800km through the low-lying Brahmaputra Valley, Assam is the largest state in Northeast India. It did not enter recorded history until the 13th century, when the Ahoms, a Buddhist tribe from Thailand, conquered the area's indigenous peoples and established a capital at Sibsagar. The cultural victory, however, belonged to the Hindus, who quickly converted their conquerors. Today, Assamese-speaking and East-Asian-looking pilgrims perform *puja* alongside Hindi-speaking Aryan Indian pilgrims. A weak central government allowed control of Assam to shift during the 19th century from the Ahoms to the Burmese to the Brits, with each new leadership trying unsuccessfully to unite the dissolute tribes and, in the last case, to annex Assam to Bengal. The British built huge tea plantations (Assam now grows over half of India's tea) and Asia's first oil refinery at Digboi. Assam's resources and economy, however, have languished since they left.

An influx of migrants from West Bengal and illegal immigrants from Bangladesh has added a substantial Bengali-speaking Muslim population to Assam and has fomented tension between the new arrivals and indigenous tribes. Anti-Bengali sentiment brought the now-entrenched Ahom Gana Parishad (AGP) party to power in the early 1980s, but Bengali-Assamese tensions have supposedly improved in recent years. Frustration over the poor economy, the increasing illegal immigration of Bangladeshis, and the central government's neglect have led to the formation of Assamese separatist organizations such as the United Liberation Front of Assam (ULFA), whose tactics include train bombings and kidnappings.

Fed by rains from the Bay of Bengal, Assam is heavily forested and has two major wildlife preserves, one of which is closed indefinitely due to political violence. Assam's capital, Guwahati, is an inescapable gateway to the other northeastern states because of its air and rail connections. Bumpy rides on rickety buses lead from Guwahati to outlying towns rich in tribal culture. At Majuli, the largest river island in the world, tourists can visit *satras* (monasteries) to see traditional Assamese drama, art, music, and dance.

 WARNING. For the past few years, there have been occasional terrorist attacks on trains and buses in Assam. In June 1998, explosions temporarily severed all road and rail links between the Northeast and West Bengal, and since then there have been sporadic clashes between the ULFA and government forces. Travelers are advised to keep abreast of the news and avoid traveling at night.

GUWAHATI ওয়াহাটি

Though often referred to in ancient Indian texts as Pragjyotishpur, meaning "City of Astrology," Guwahati (pop. 632,000) derives its present name from its much more earthly function as a betel-nut (*guwa*) market (*hatt*). While the city itself is not particularly attractive, it is bounded by the natural splendor of lush green hills and the mighty Brahmaputra River. Rifle-toting soldiers are ubiquitous, but so are the friendly and welcoming citizens. Although Guwahati may seem much like India's other urban centers, it is distinct as the gateway to the nation's northeast, one of India's most culturally unique and isolated regions.

Most visitors would agree that the city makes a pleasant stopover on the way to the Northeast's even less-visited destinations. A few interesting sights, including the Kamakhya Temple, line the edges of the modern city. In the west, Nilachal Hill casts its shadow over the Brahmaputra River and portends of the mountainous regions to the north and south of Assam.

⌐ TRANSPORTATION

Airport: Gopinath Bordelai Airport (tel. 840221), 24km from town in Borjhar. **Buses** go from Judge Field, adjacent to Nehru Park, to **VIP Point** (every 30min., Rs3), 2km from the airport, where you can pick up an auto-rickshaw (Rs10-20). To get to Judge Field from the front of the railway station, take a rickshaw (Rs5) or city bus or walk straight through 2 major traffic circles. You can share a cab directly to the airport (Rs60 per person) or hire the whole car (Rs300). To: **Agartala** (Tu, Th, and Sa; 40min.; US$30); **Bagdogra** (1 per day, 45min., US$50); **Kolkata** (2-3 per day, 1hr., US$50); **Delhi** (1 per day, 2½hr., US$160); **Imphal** (Th and Su, 1hr., US$30).

Trains: The main railway station, **Guwahati Junction,** is centrally located between Pan and Paltan Bazaars. For problems, go to the main office at the **North Eastern Railways Reservation Building** (tel. 541799), 200m in front of the railway station on the right. Open M-Sa 8am-8pm, Su 8am-2pm. There is no train service to most of the other northeastern states, but there are trains to outlying cities in Assam, from which buses go to the capital cities of other states. Fares listed are 2nd class sleeper/3-tier A/C. To: **Kolkata** (*Kamrup Exp.* 5960, 7am, 24hr., Rs265/700; *Sarai Ghat Exp.* 3046; M, Th, and F 10am; 18½hr.; Rs265); **Delhi** (*Rajdhani Exp.* 2423; M, W, Th, F, and Su 6am; 28hr.; A/C 3-tier Rs906, 2-tier, Rs1650; *Northeast Exp.* 5621, 8:30am, 36hr., Rs380/1053); **Dimapur** (for buses to Kohima and Imphal, *Delhi-Dimapur Brahmaputra Mail* 4050, 12:30pm, 7hr., Rs97/260); **Harmoti** (for buses to Itanagar, first take a train to Rangia, 7am, 3hr., Rs21/109; then *Arunachal Exp.* 5813, 7:30pm, Rs118/300); **Silchar** (for buses to Tripura and Mizoram, take *Delhi-Dimapur Brahmaputra Mail* 4055 to Lamding, 12:30pm, 4hr., Rs47/185; then *Cachar Exp.* 5801 to Silchar, 7:30pm, 11½hr., Rs134/613).

Buses: The **Kacheri Bus Stand** is behind the railway station; **Assam State Transport** and **Meghalaya State Transport** buses depart from here. Reservation booths open daily 6am-6:30pm. Departures for most of the major cities in the northeast are between 6 and 8am. To: **Agartala** (3:30pm, 24hr., Rs300); **Dimapur** (10-12hr., Rs100); **Imphal** (Rs220); **Kaziranga** (every 30min. 6:30-10am, Rs84; 11:30am, 12:30, and 2pm, 5hr., Rs79); **Silchar** (6am and 5pm, 12hr., Rs170); **Tura** (8hr., Rs84). Private buses leave from Paltan Bazaar; tickets are sold at Blue Hills Travels or Network Travels. Government buses go to Shillong (if demand is sufficient, every hr. 6am-4pm, 3hr., Rs30/40). Private buses go to Shillong every hr. and to other major northeastern cities; fares are 10% more, but government buses are generally more reliable.

Local Transportation: Cycle-rickshaws and **auto-rickshaws** whiz about. City **buses** run on M.G., AT, Shillong, and GS Rd. (Rs1-3 within the city). You can catch a bus going west along MG Rd. to the base of Nilachal Hill and the Kamakhya Temple. **Ferries** to Umananda (Rs5 per person or Rs100 per boat) run unless the river's too high. Government-run river cruises also leave from the ferry landing (daily 11am and 4pm, Rs35).

◤ ORIENTATION AND PRACTICAL INFORMATION

The city center is small. The bazaars, bus and railway stations, and important public offices are all within walking distance of one another. The Guwahati Junction railway station and the Kacheri bus stand are adjacent; Paltan Bazaar is just behind these, to the south. Pan Bazaar (with more expensive lodgings) and Fancy Bazaar are a 15-minute walk to the northwest. Mahatma Gandhi (MG) Road runs behind Pan Bazaar along the river's edge; government buses ply this route to the Kamakhya Temple, 8km to the west, and the Navagraha Temple, 1km to the east.

Tourist Office: Government of India Tourist Office, Dr. BK Kakoti Rd. (tel. 547407), Ulubari. Turn right at a police point onto BK Kakoti Rd.; it's on the right, through a little gate. Open M-F 9:30am-5:30pm, Sa 10am-1pm. **Assam State Tourist Office** (tel. 544475), inside the tourist lodge, on the left side of the road leading to the front of the railway station. Open M-Sa 10am-5pm, closed 2nd and 4th Sa. Runs a 2-day, 1-night tour to Kaziranga Wildlife Sanctuary (Rs750) that leaves every day when at least 7 people sign up. Also runs a Guwahati City Tour (W and Sa 9am, Rs70).

Immigration Office: Superintendent of Police (tel. 544475), near District Court, extends visas. Open M-Sa 10am-4:30pm.

Currency Exchange: **State Bank of India,** MG Rd. (tel. 544264), near District Court. Open M-F 10am-2pm, Sa 10am-noon. **ANZ Grindlays Bank** (tel. 540597), across from Assam State Museum, cashes traveler's checks and gives credit card advances. Open for exchange M-F 10am-2pm.

Hospital: Guwahati Medical College (GMC), GS Rd. (tel. 569161 or 562521), Bhangagarh, specializes in trauma and common gastrointestinal complaints. **Downtown Hospital,** Dispur (tel. 560824 or 562741), near Capitol Complex, has fluent English speakers on staff and is the best place for extended stays.

Police: Stations in Pan Bazaar (tel. 540106) and Paltan Bazaar (tel. 540126).

Post Office: GPO, Meghdoot Bhawan (tel. 543588), near Pan Bazaar. Open M-Sa 10am-6pm. **Postal Code:** 781001.

Internet: Sangita Communications (tel. 550292), at the Anuranda Cinema Complex, Bamunimaiden (rickshaw from downtown Rs30). Full Internet access Rs2 per min.

Telephones: Central Telegraph Office (CTO), Pan Bazaar (tel. 540209), allows free callbacks. Open 24hr.

PHONE CODE	0361

ACCOMMODATIONS

In general, Guwahati's accommodations are either cheap and extremely unsanitary or expensive and luxurious. Either way, most are overpriced. The proximity of Paltan Bazaar to the railway and bus stations does not make up for its nastiness; there are good options in Pan Bazaar, Fancy Bazaar, and near the riverside. They fill up quickly, so book in advance.

Mayur Hotel (tel. 541115 or 541116), behind the bus station and next to the Vandana on MG Road. This modern, well maintained hotel is surprisingly inexpensive, and the veg. restaurant on the ground floor serves tasty Assamese specialties (*thaal* Rs30). Singles Rs99; doubles Rs154-176.

Broadway, MG Rd. (tel. 548604), Machkhowa, Riverside. From the railway station, a Rs15 rickshaw ride to the river. Combines the lowest prices in Guwahati with a serene riverside location. Airy rooms have attached baths with shower and mosquito nets. Restaurant inside. Call in advance, but be patient—the management speaks little English. Curfew 10pm. Check-out noon. Singles Rs85; doubles Rs120-140.

Hotel Vandana, GS Rd. (tel. 543475), Paltan Bazaar. From behind the railway station, turn right onto GS Rd.; it's set back on the left before the Mayur Hotel. Rarely full and somewhat dingy, the Vandana has a large lobby/lounge area and an STD/ISD booth open until midnight. Large rooms and beds with foam rubber mattresses. Singles Rs100-150; doubles Rs120-280; triples Rs180-650; 10-person dorm Rs550.

Assam Tourist Lodge (tel. 544475), same building as the Assam Tourist Office, in front of the railway station. Convenient location and spacious, comfortable rooms. Singles Rs90; doubles Rs150.

◉ FOOD

Assamese cuisine, which consists of fish, rice, and heavy mustard seasoning, is readily available but of greatly varying quality. Chinese food is plentiful and good—some of the restaurants along Rajgarh Rd., far to the east near the Gandhi Memorial, are run by Chinese immigrants.

Paradise, Moniram Dewan Rd. (tel. 546904), Silpukuri. From the front of the railway station, take a rickshaw or city bus toward Silpukuri. Excellent Assamese dishes in a soothing environment. The *thali* (Rs55) has 11 different varieties, including fried fish and chili chicken; the veg. version (Rs50) is equally eclectic. Beer Rs55. Open daily 10am-3:30pm and 6-9:30pm.

Madras Cabin, GS Rd., Paltan Bazaar. From the back of the railway station, turn right; the Cabin is on the left, by the Vandana Hotel. Popular with locals for (what else?) South Indian snacks. *Masala dosa* Rs14. Open daily 5am-10pm.

Motu Halwa, just off SS Road near the Dynasty Hotel. This bakery/sweet shop is a local favorite. Delicious fresh-baked pastries Rs10-35. Open daily 7am-7pm.

Chopsticks Restaurant, on SS Road, in the Dynasty Hotel. A bit pricey, but well worth it. Large portions of outstanding Chinese and Continental dishes. Entrees Rs50-80. Open daily 7-10:30am, noon-2:30pm, and 7:30-11pm.

◉ SIGHTS

The best way to see all the sights is with the Assam State Tourist office's full-day tour (see p. 685).

KAMAKHYA TEMPLE. Devout pilgrims approach the Kamakhya Temple from the footpaths leading up from the road. Designated by the Government of India Tourism Department as one of the 10 most important pilgrim tourist sites in the country, the temple is the most sacred *shakti pitha* for Hindus—it is said that the goddess Sati's *yoni* (vulva) fell on this spot when she was cut into pieces by Vishnu (see **Divine Dismemberment,** below). After it was burned down by a *brahmin* priest who converted to Islam, the temple, with its beehive-shaped spire, was rebuilt in 1665 by King Naranarayana. The king is said to have inaugurated his new temple by offering the goddess Kamakhya 140 human heads. Inside, the Mother-Goddess is worshipped in the form of a crevice in a rock, rather than as a sculpted image. The ancient stone bleachers that rise up from the base of the temple seat spectators eager to see animal sacrifices—male goats tied to the posts at the main temple gate each morning are decapitated by evening. The shrine inside the temple is open to non-Hindus, but hour-long queues are normal. *(From MG Rd., it's a 5km bus ride west to the temple, which is on Nilachal Hill. Open daily 10am-6pm.)*

BRAHMAPUTRA RIVER. The mighty Brahmaputra ("Son of Brahma") surges past the city in the north, often overrunning its banks in the rainy season and flooding the riverside settlements. From its banks, or from any of the adjacent hills, the river (incidentally, the only river classified in Hindi as a male) might look serene or even sluggish, but its undercurrents are swift. The river's vast hydroelectric potential has not yet been exploited (building dams in an earthquake-prone area is extremely costly), but engineers claim that the Brahmaputra could satisfy 30% of India's energy needs. Ferries run regularly from Umananda Ghat, near the Brahmaputra Ashok Hotel, to the **Umananda Temple,** which sits on a small island in the middle of the river. The temple is unimpressive, but it offers the best possible view of the river. En route to the temple is the **Urbashi Kharti,** a yard stick that measures the level of the water during the monsoon; according to legend, it is, in fact, a beautiful woman that has been transformed into a rock.

NAVAGRAHA TEMPLE. The small Navagraha ("Nine Planets") Temple serves as a reminder that Guwahati was once a great center of astronomy and astrology. An echo chamber holds nine *lingas* dedicated to the nine heavenly bodies that

DIVINE DISMEMBERMENT

Legend has it that the beautiful goddess Sati fell in love with an uncouth ascetic who actually dared to marry her. Her disapproving father, Daksha, decided to hold a sacrifice and invite every god except for the vagabond bridegroom, Shiva. Incensed by her father's snub of her husband, Sati flung herself on the sacrificial pyre (incidentally lighting the way for generations of Indian women to commit ritual suicide, a practice banned by the British). When Shiva learned of his wife's demise, he tenderly lifted up her blackened body and began to sob convulsively, perilously shaking the entire universe. In the interest of saving the cosmos, Vishnu stepped in and began hacking off bits of the charred corpse with his *chakra* (discus-like weapon). Strangely enough, this action seemed to soothe Shiva, who ceased his sobbing. The places where fragments of Sati's body fell to earth became *shakti pithas*. These sacred sites, which number 4, 51, or 108 by various accounts, began as independent goddess shrines, but the myth of Sati's dismemberment provides a unifying thread. The most important *shakti pithas* are those which came from the most potent parts of Sati—which is why the **Kamakhya Temple** in Guwahati is the greatest of all (see above).

ancient Indians identified without the aid of astronomical equipment: the sun, the moon, the ascending and descending nodes of the moon, Mercury, Venus, Mars, Jupiter, and Saturn. The dark, dank temple now seems more abandoned than mysterious. *(On a hill in east Guwahati. Open daily 10am-6pm.)*

OTHER SIGHTS. The **Assam State Museum**, Dighali Pukhi, has a large collection of Assamese cultural artifacts, as well as a fascinating photography exhibit on the independence movement *(next to the library and across from the lake; open in summer Tu-Sa 10am-5pm, winter 10am-4:15pm, closed 2nd and 4th Sa; Rs2).* A new cultural center, the **Sarkardev Kalashetra Complex,** recently opened on 6th mile *(Rs60 by auto-rickshaw from the train station).* Named for a famous Assamese artisan who devoted his life to the promotion of regional culture, the center is a veritable theme park of all that is Assamese, complete with reconstructions of temples, an open air amphitheater, and a beautifully landscaped "Heritage Park" which contains sculptures, paintings, and mosaics depicting scenes from rural Assamese life. *(Open daily 10am-7pm. Rs5, children ages 5-15 Rs3.)*

NATIONAL PARKS & WILDLIFE SANCTUARIES

With three national parks, two of which are UNESCO World Heritage sites, and several wildlife sanctuaries, Assam is home to an exceptional and diverse array of protected wildlife. The responsible, conservation-minded approach of the parks' staffs is a model for the rest of India and beyond. The bad news: government-imposed prices for all of Assam's parks are exorbitant. Standard entry fees (Rs175) and camera charges (Rs175, telephoto Rs210, video Rs525) are a strain on budget travelers. The most frustrating aspect of these charges is that the profits are almost entirely swallowed up by the Assamese government while the parks make the most of insufficient funding and the employees work long hours for meager wages. Still, if your budget allows, Assam's wildlife parks should not be missed. Even at a premium, they will not disappoint. All of Assam's parks are closed for the monsoon (June-Sept.).

🐾 KAZIRANGA NATIONAL PARK

The Kaziranga National Park, located in tea country 217km from Guwahati, is Assam's top tourist attraction and the undisputed heavyweight champion of wildlife parks in the Northeast. Most visitors come to see the Indian one-horned rhinoceros—Kaziranga boasts 65% of the world's population of this endangered species. Since 1966, the park's rhino population has increased threefold, despite the best efforts of horny horn poachers (the phallic proboscis is a much-coveted aphrodisiac). While rhinos are the top box office draw, Kaziranga's cast of supporting characters is equally impressive. Your chances of seeing a tiger are close to nil, but Asiatic wild buffalo (or *gaur*), equipped with mammoth horns, abound. The park also boasts four kinds of deer and a multitude of wild elephants. For bird lovers, the treetops call out with the cries of fishing eagles, grey-headed pelicans, and even the rare, and much sought after, bengal florican.

The 430 sq. km sanctuary, only a small part of which is open to human traffic, is a hodgepodge of habitats. Swampland gives way to jungle, which rises up to deciduous forests and eventually to the evergreen slopes of the Karbi Anglong Hills. The best view of the animals is from the back of an elephant—each seats up to four humans—since they are able to get much closer to the animals than the jeeps can. The sanctuary is open from late October to late April; during the monsoon, animals flee the flooded marshland for the muddy roads, making passage through the park dangerous or impossible.

GETTING TO THE PARK. Kaziranga is 217km from Guwahati and 96km from Jorhat, the closest airport. The most common way to visit the park is on the ATDC's **package tour,** a two-day trip including transportation in a luxury coach, one night's accommodation, and a one-hour elephant ride into the park on the morning of the second day (Rs750). The bus departs from the **Assam Tourist Office,** located just down the road from the railway station in Guwahati. Unfortunately, this two-day tour involves a lot of waiting around and only one trip into the park. For those wishing to arrange their own ride, **buses** from Guwahati are frequent (every 30min. 6:30-10am, 11:30am, 12:30, and 2pm, 5hr., Rs79-84). **Blues Hills Travel,** located behind the bus station, runs a private deluxe bus each morning (7am, Rs90). All of these buses continue on to other Eastern Assam destinations and can be joined on their way through Kaziranga. Similarly, all westbound buses stop on their way to Guwahati (6am-12:30pm).

Local buses and the tourist stop at **Kohora,** a small group of tea stalls and government lodges at the edge of the sanctuary. The road into the park diverges into three main routes: the eastern, central, and western Regions (see below). Details and maps of each can be obtained at the Directorate of Tourism. All currency should be exchanged in Guwahati. Five kilometers from Kohora is a small village called Bokakhad, and National Highway 37 continues on to Jorhat and Sibsagar.

LODGES AND FOOD. All of the lodges are located in the Kohora villages near the entrance to the park's central region. Most travelers eat where they sleep, but you can certainly mix and match. The **Aranya Tourist Lodge** has expensive rooms (singles Rs350, with A/C Rs450; doubles Rs450/550) and a Continental restaurant-bar. **Bonani** has slightly less expensive rooms (doubles Rs175) and a restaurant (meals Rs25-65). The recently opened **Soil Conservation Rest House** has the largest available rooms (singles Rs200, doubles Rs350), and the **Forest Rest House** offers the best park information (doubles Rs120). Finally, **Bonoshree** has basic doubles with attached bath (Rs170). The cheapest option is the dormitory in **Kunjuban,** but you get what you pay for (beds Rs15-30, no linen). There is also a beautiful private resort called **Wild Grass** (tel. 03766 62437), located 5km from the park (doubles Rs850, prices negotiable for budget travelers). Reservations at any of the lodges can be booked through Assam Tourism either at Kaziranga (tel. 03766 6423) or in Guwahati (tel. 544475).

REGIONS OF THE PARK. There are three regions of the park open to tourists and two modes of transport used to access them (jeep and elephant). The rates for **elephant rides,** which only operate in the central region, are Rs525 for one hour rental of the elephant, plus Rs175 for the park **entrance fee.** For **jeep safaris**, rates are Rs10 per km. The **central region** is the most popular and frequently visited part of the park, largely because it is the only region that offers elephant rides. A jeep tour here is also an option, especially in the afternoon, as elephant rides are only available at 5:30 or 6:30am. The jeep route extends 45km through lush terrain loaded with rhinos and wild elephants. This region also contains several excellent watchtowers; there's a nice photo opportunity at the tower marked with the record monsoon flood levels. The **eastern region** is the area of the park farthest from the tourist lodges. The road taken by jeep safaris winds through 70km of remarkably varied terrain: lakes, forests, and river beds are all en route. While rhinos are relatively scarce here, in comparison to their numbers in the rest of the park, the eastern region does have a large population of elephants, as well as a pelican colony. An extra Rs50 can convince the jeep driver to extend the tour to include the sometimes off-limits Tiger Project. The **western region** is the least frequently visited—a pity because it contains the park's highest concentration of rhinos. A 45km jeep ride will all but guarantee multiple sightings of the rare and spectacular beast.

🏞 OTHER PARKS

MANAS NATIONAL PARK. Manas is reputedly one of the most beautiful wildlife parks in all of Asia. This UNESCO World Heritage Site located 176km west of Guwahati is home to rhinos, elephants, an astonishing array of birds, and Assam's only major Tiger Project. Unfortunately, in recent years it has also become the primary stomping ground of a particularly violent faction of BODO rebels, who have battled the Assamese government for years to assert an independent, autonomous state. The bottom line is that, for the time being, foreign tourists are banned from the park without police escort; the police, understandably, are generally unwilling to take tourists in. This volatile situation could possibly improve in the near future. To check the status, call the Tourist Information Office (tel. 03666 32749), at Barpeta Road, the railhead for the park.

NAMERI NATIONAL PARK. Assam's newest national park, Nameri, is rarely visited but is well worth a trip. Managed jointly by the Assamese government and the Bhorelli Angler's Association, Nameri offers a diversity of wildlife and a riverside location that has led it to be dubbed a mini-Manas. It was named a National Park in 1998 soon after the discovery of a family of extremely rare white winged wood ducks; the area turned out to be home to 50 of the 650 surviving members of this endangered species. Nameri is located 30km north of **Tezpur**, at the intersection of the Bordikarai and Bhareli Rivers, which form its southeastern and southwestern boundaries. To the north, it is bounded by the border with Arunachal Pradesh, but the park is actually contiguous with the 800 sq. km Pakhni Sanctuary in Arunachal; together, the park and sanctuary form a vast protected area. **Buses** between Tezpur and Balipara stop at the park's entrance (frequent, Rs10). Staying at the park isn't cheap, so daytrips from Tezpur (see below) are recommended. The only accommodations available are at the **Eco Lodge,** located 1km from the Bhareli River (booking through Bhorelli Angler's Association, tel. 037142 4246). The lodge has large "luxury tents" (doubles Rs650-800) and a dorm (beds Rs105). It also has an attached restaurant (meals Rs80-120). Because it is part of the Angler's Club, and not a hotel per se, they welcome all nature lovers but expect that the grounds will be treated accordingly.

Nameri offers an array of activities: guided **bird-watching walks** (Rs100 per person) and **rafting trips** (Rs650 for a three 3-person raft all day) are among the most popular. Also, as the only sanctuary in India to allow **fishing,** Nameri can arrange licenses if booked in advance (equipment is not provided) for Rs25 per day. They keep records of the largest Mahseer caught in the river each year (28kg in 1996). The **entrance fee,** as with all Assam's parks, is an additional Rs175.

ORANG WILDLIFE SANCTUARY. Like Nameri, Orang Wildlife Sanctuary has been pegged as a miniature version of a larger and more famous counterpart. This "mini-Kaziranga" packs rhinos, elephants, a small population of tigers, and rare birds (including the rare bengal florican) into just 76 sq. km. Located at the edge of a tribal village of Bangledeshi Muslims, remote, quiet Orang makes a great one night getaway. Orang is 150km from Guwahati and 32km from Tezpur, on the North bank of the Brahmaputra. From Tezpur, there are frequent **buses** (Rs5) to the town of Orang, 18km from the park. From here, another bus takes visitors to Silbari, a 2km walk from the park. Alternatively, a **car** can be hired in Tezpur for the drive to the park (Rs200). Accommodations consist of two basic **forest bunga-lows,** the better of which is located within the confines of the park (for booking call 03713 22065; doubles Rs120). If you bring food, the ranger can help you cook.

TEZPUR

Tezpur, the "city of blood," is a pleasant town with a grim mythological past. Sight of the legendary battle between Hari (Krishna) and Hara (Shiva, in the form of Banasura), Tezpur was drenched in blood by the vicious conflict. The red stains have been washed away, but many relics of Tezpur's ancient past remain, drawing tourists and missionaries in steadily increasing numbers. Tezpur's most notewor-thy sights are **Da-Parbatia,** where an astonishingly small gate is all that remains of one of the oldest temples in Assam; **Agnigrgh,** the ruins of a rampart located 5km outside of town on a hillside facing the river; and the **Mahabhairab Temple,** on a site frequented by religious missionaries. A new attraction is the beautifully land-scaped and recently renovated **Cole Park,** a lake and green across the street from the tourist office (open daily 7:30am-8pm, Rs5). It is also possible to make daytrips to Kaziranga, Orang, and Nameri parks (see above).

Located 180km from Guwahati, Tezpur lies on the opposite (north) bank of the Brahmaputra River from Assam's capital. The town itself lacks any distinct center or main road, but most of the action goes on in the area between the bus stand and the police point where the roads leading to Guwahati, Nameri, and Kaziranga intersect. Tezpur is most easily reached via one of five daily **buses** from Guwahati (3½ hr., Rs70). **Trains** heading east from the capital also stop at Rangapara station, 26km north of Tezpur, where a connecting train goes into town. Saloni **Airport,** 10km from town, has infrequent flights to and from Guwahati (1 per week, 40 min, US$40). The **tourist office** (tel. 21016) is located near the bus stand, as is the **post office. Postal Code:** 784001. There is no **currency exchange** available in town. **Tele-phone Code:** 3712. The tourist office has a **lodge** with six double rooms (Rs170) and a dorm (beds Rs30). Slightly more expensive but much nicer, the **Hotel Luit,** Ranu Singh Road (tel. 21220), has large, clean rooms with cable TV and some with A/C (doubles Rs175-750). The hotel restaurant is the best in town (veg. curry Rs50).

JORHAT AND MAJULI

Though it's not much of a destination in and of itself, you'll probably have to spend a night in the town of Jorhat on your way to Majuli, a huge island and the site of several prominent **satras** (Hindu Vaishnava monasteries). Jorhat is relatively devoid of sights, but it does have a Raj-era **Gymkhana Club,** Na Ali (tel. 320030), where guests can play golf (if they have clubs) or snooker (Rs10). As the world's largest river island, Majuli is itself a sight. However, far more interesting (espe-cially considering Majuli annually forfeits its title temporarily due to monsoon ero-sion) are the island's *satras*, sites of Hindu worship and spectacular dance performances. Among the main *satras*, accessible on foot or by bus or taxi, are **Garamurh,** with a display of ancient cannons called "Bortop;" **Anniati,** famous for its Aspara dance performances; and **Kamalabari,** which has sent performers through-out India and abroad.

Jorhat is located 80km east of Kaziranga on the South bank of the Brahmaputra. The town centers on a quadrant defined by **AT Road** and **KB Road,** running east-west, and MG Rd. and Gar Ali, running north-south. The **bus stand** is located on MG Rd. between AT Rd. and KB Rd. Majuli is a river island 20km from Jorhat. Rowriah **Airport,** located 5km from Jorhat, has flights to Kolkata (1 per day, 1½hr., US$50) and Dimapur (1 per week, 1½hr., US$65). **Trains** to Guwahati leave in the evening (8:30 and 9:30pm, Rs30). **Buses** between Jorhat and Guwahati run every day (6:30-11:30am, 7hr., Rs115). Buses also go to: Neamati (the Majuli Ferry launching point, 8:30-9:15am, Rs4, 1hr.), and Sibsagar (1½hr., Rs20). In Majuli, there is a bus from the ferry landing to the town of Garamurh (20min., Rs2). **Ferries** run to Majuli (depart 10:30am, return 1:30-3pm; 1hr.; Rs4). Upon arrival in Majuli, you mus**t** report to the police station in Gurhmur. The **Tourist Office** is located on MG Rd. (tel. 321045). There are several **pharmacies** along AT Rd. The **post office** (tel. 320045) is located near the bus stand (open M-Sa 10am-5pm). **Postal Code:** 785001. Both the **police station** (tel. 320022) and an **STD/ISD** booth are located near the Tourist Lodge. **Telephone Code:** 0376.

Jorhat has an **Assam Tourist Lodge** in the same building as the Tourist Office (tel. 321045; singles Rs100, doubles Rs170). Slightly more money gets you a significantly better room in the **Paradise Hotel,** AT Rd. (tel. 33521; singles Rs175, doubles Rs250). The **Food Hut** (tel. 323465), near the Tourist Office on MG Rd., serves good, cheap Indian, Chinese, and Continental food (open daily 9:30am- 9:30pm, entrees Rs25-50). On Majuli, there is only one real lodge, the **Circuit House** in Garamurh (tel. 74439; rooms Rs100). Basic meals are available in town, but travelers are advised to bring their own. It is also possible to stay at one of the **satras,** such as one in Kamalabari (tel. 73392), for a minimal donation (Rs50). The **Kaziranga Safari Travel Agency** (tel. 325468) in Jorhat can also assist with booking a spot there.

MEGHALAYA

Travelers who take the hilly roads from Assam into Meghalaya soon discover why the region is called the "Abode of Clouds." The state's seven ranges of hills seem perpetually swathed in a cool, cumulonimbus mist, which occasionally bursts into violent action, dousing the valley areas and swelling the Brahmaputra. Meghalaya is home to Cherrapunjee and Mawsyn, two of the wettest places on earth, and the state boasts a wealth of flora and fauna.

The state is inhabited by two distinct ethnic groups: the Proto-Australoid Hynniewtrep people, most of whom live in the east; and the Tibeto-Burmese Achiks, or Garos, in the Garo Hills to the West. Welsh missionaries settled here during the 19th century, spreading Christianity throughout the region (75% of Meghalayans remain Christian). With little regard for the indigenous peoples, British government officials built an 18-hole golf course in Shillong and made it the capital of Assam. The British were also unpopular for their discouragement of human sacrifice. To this day, Meghalayans remember the Welsh with fondness, while they resent the British. Meghalaya gained independence from Assam and became India's 21st state in 1972. Democratic values have much deeper roots here, though. Regional *syiem* (kings) have long allowed and encouraged popular self-government through public discourse and referendums. Gender egalitarianism, too, is a long-standing value in Meghalaya, sustained in part by institutions of matrilineal descent and property inheritance.

Meghalaya was opened to unrestricted tourism only in 1995, and though Indians on holiday have long come here in droves, foreign tourists are now just beginning to discover its charms. Most people come to Meghalaya to enjoy the cool weather of Shillong and neighboring spots in the Khasi Hills or else to visit the several wildlife sanctuaries in West Meghalaya that can be approached from Shillong.

SHILLONG

As a cosmopolitan hill station, Shillong draws inevitable comparisons with Darjeeling, its West Bengali counterpart. While the Meghalayan capital lacks the snow-capped Himalayan backdrop, the two towns do have a lot in common—both were favorite British retreats, both are blessed with gorgeous surroundings, and both radiate a sense of prosperity and well-being—but Shillong has yet to draw the throngs of Western tourists that Darjeeling long has. Although its name derives from an incarnation of the Khasi Creator, the hill station's identity, most conspicuously its rise to prominence in the state, is bound up in its history as the erstwhile capital of British Assam; to this day, English remains the town's *lingua franca*.

The town does exhibit a few signs of modern fraying around the edges: ubiquitous signs warn against the dangers of AIDS, drugs, and extortion, while scattered graffiti—e.g., "Khasi by birth, Indian by accident"—expresses repressed anger and frustration. Still, Shillong exudes an exhilarating energy that extends from its fanciest shops to the bustling and tangled Bara Bazaar.

TRANSPORTATION

Trains: Shillong has no train service, but reservations for trains elsewhere can be made at the booth in the MTC building (tel. 221303; open daily 8am-1:30pm and 2-5pm). Tickets for trains leaving **Guwahati** (see p. 683) should be reserved a week in advance. Tourist quota tickets not available.

Buses: Government buses depart from the **MTC bus stand** in Police Bazaar; tickets can be purchased and reserved in the MTC building. To: **Guwahati** (every hr. 6am-5pm, 4hr., Rs34/46); **Siliguri** (1pm, Rs150); **Tura** and **Williamnagar Wildlife Preserve** (4:30pm, 12hr., Rs147). Government buses also go to **Ranikor**; you can jump off en route and then walk 2km to **Mawsyn.** Taking the MTDC tour of **Cherrapunjee** is the only practical way to go (see **Sights,** p. 694). **Private buses** to cities in other northeastern states leave from the Polo Ground (Rs10 taxi from Police Bazaar). Tickets can be booked at any of the travel agents near the MTC bus stand. For buses to **Agartala, Aizawl,** and **Imphal,** first take a bus to Silchar (7am-7pm, 10hr., Rs110).

Local Transportation: Shared taxis, Rs5 per head, barrel through the city streets without even coming to a complete stop to pick up passengers. Try to flag down a taxi that already has passengers, or the driver might think you want it all to yourself. Taxis can be hired for trips to more remote tourist spots for about twice the local rate.

ORIENTATION AND PRACTICAL INFORMATION

Situated on a plateau, Shillong has a remarkably flat terrain for a hill station. The town's streets resemble a network of varicose veins. Many tiny, nameless roads snake out around the MTC bus stand in **Police Bazaar. Guwahati-Shillong (GS) Road,** lined with many budget hotels, twists westward and eventually leads to **Bara Bazaar** (Big Bazaar), a web of narrow lanes littered with pineapple tops and animal fat. **MG Road** (Kacheri Rd.), winding away from Police Bazaar to the southeast, fronts many government offices. Along this wide, tree-lined boulevard you'll find the Shillong Club, the State Bank of India, and at its southern tip, the State Museum. Aside from **Ward Lake,** adjacent to one curve of IGP Point, most of Shillong's natural wonders—waterfalls and parks—sit on the outskirts of town.

Tourist Office: Government of India Tourist Office, GS Rd. (tel. 225632), near Police Bazaar. Friendly staff. Open M-F 9:30am-5:30pm, Sa 9:30am-2pm. **Meghalaya Tourist Information** (tel. 226220), at the bus stand, Police Bazaar, right across from the MTC building. Open M-Sa 7:30am-4:30pm, Su 7:30-11am.

Budget Travel: Network Travels, Quinton Rd. (tel. 221863), just down from the central police point and not far from the MTC bus stand. Open daily 6am-8pm. **Sheba Travels** (tel. 221834), by the police point, runs a daily bus to Guwahati Airport (6:30am, Rs125). Open M-Sa 10am-5pm, Su 10am-noon.

Immigration Office: Foreigners Registration Office, MG Rd. (tel. 224137), across from the main office of the YMCA, near the State Museum. Foreigners are technically supposed to report their arrival and departure. Open M-F 10am-4pm. Visa extension applications (rarely granted) can be filed at the **Secretariat** (tel. 224201), a big white sore thumb (with a clock tower) 2 doors down to the right. Open M-F 10am-5pm.

Currency Exchange: State Bank of India, MG Rd. (tel. 223520), accepts AmEx travelers checks in US$ only. Open M-F 10am-5pm, Sa 10am-2pm.

Market: The outdoor **Bara Bazaar** in West Shillong carries everything from pineapples and star fruit to cow hooves and electronic equipment. Open daily 9am-7pm.

Library: State Library, MG Rd., next to the State Museum. Open M-Sa 10am-5pm. Closed 2nd and 4th Sa.

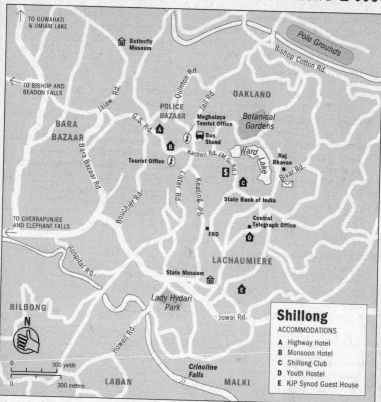

Pharmacy: Assam Pharmacy, Police Bazaar. Open daily 7am-7pm.

Hospital: Woodlands Nursing Home, Dhanketi, South Shillong (tel. 225240 or 224885), is a private hospital with the most up-to-date equipment.

Police: Superintendent's Office, IGP Rd. (tel. 223801 or 224150), adjacent to the Foreigners Registration Office. Open M-Sa 10am-4:30pm. **Emergency:** tel. 100.

Post Office: GPO (tel. 222768), across from Raj Bhawan. Open M-F 10am-6:30pm, Sa 10am-1pm. **Postal Code:** 793001.

Telephones: Central Telegraph Office, Vivekananda Marg, European Ward (tel. 226288), opposite the hostel. Free callbacks. Open daily 7am-midnight, holidays 8am-6pm.

PHONE CODE	0364

ACCOMMODATIONS

Most of the old British hotels are now in disrepair, but budget dives and family hotels are popping up like toadstools along the shadowy lanes of Police Bazaar. Slightly better places are on GS, Thana, or Quinton Rd. (towards Cherrapunjee).

Youth Hostel (HI-AYH), Vivekananda Marg (tel. 222246). Possibly the least hostile hostel in India. Enormous 6-bed dorm rooms, wonderfully spotless and spacious bathrooms. 9pm curfew, 10pm "lights out." Breakfast included. Dorm beds Rs60, HI members Rs40; doubles Rs200. Discounts for extended stays.

🛏 **KJP Synod Guest House,** MG Rd. (tel 228611), opposite the State Museum. Run by a tiny Khasi woman called "Auntie" who speaks little English. Comfortable dorm beds in spacious rooms with fireplaces. Common kitchen and complimentary breakfast. Weekly services are held in a central chapel, and most of the guests are Christians from Mizoram and Manipur. Check-out noon. Dorm beds Rs85; triples Rs140.

Highway Hotel, GS Rd. (tel. 223681). It might not be pretty, but it's got character, even though the Elvis and Janis Joplin posters in the lobby seem out of place. Moderately sized rooms with several common bathrooms. Singles Rs60; doubles Rs130.

Shillong Club, Kacheri Rd. (tel. 225533; fax 221840). Though it has suffered since the British pulled out, the club is still pretty classy. Huge rooms with TVs, fireplaces, and phones. "Temporary membership" (singles Rs10, doubles Rs12) includes access to the club's billiard tables and library. Singles Rs240; doubles Rs425/525. Reservations required; call, or write to Shillong Club Ltd., Residential, P.O. Box 45, Shillong 793001.

Monsoon Hotel, GS Rd. (tel. 223316), across from Govt. of India Tourist Office. The least claustrophobic of the GS Rd. hotels. Large, recently renovated rooms with wooden furniture. Singles with bath Rs200-250; doubles Rs350-400; triples Rs450.

🍴 FOOD

Decent Chinese food can be found in Police Bazaar, and Khasi food at many small shops in Bara Bazaar, though one glance at its meat market might dissuade you.

Pizza (Fast Food), Jail Rd., Police Bazaar, on the right before the bus stand. American food with an Indian flair that makes it better than the original. Veggie burger (Rs20) is fat, filling, and flavorful. Popular with locals. Open daily 9am-7:30pm.

Broadway Restaurant, GS Rd., in the overpriced Broadway Hotel; the restaurant is a far better value. Chicken curry Rs50. Open daily 10am-9pm.

Abba Restaurant, GS Rd., by Monsoon Hotel. Authentic Chinese food including veg. chow mein (Rs50). There is another branch in South Shillong. Open daily 10am-7:30pm.

Host Restaurant, GS Road. Large portions of cheap, excellent Chinese and Indian cuisine (Rs20-50). Open daily 7am-8:30pm.

👁 SIGHTS

The cheapest and most convenient way to see the city's major sights is to take the MTDC's half-day **tour** (8:30am, Rs70). It includes visits to **Shillong Peak** (1965m), the highest point in Meghalaya; **Elephant Falls,** a set of pools and falls where an elephant came to die; **Ward's Lake,** a beautiful park and lake (4-person paddle boats Rs15-20; open daily 9:30am-5pm); **Lady Hydari Park** and zoo (Rs2); and the unexciting **State Museum** (open M-Sa 10am-4pm, free).

Crinoline Falls, near Lady Hydari Park within the city limits, has a swimming hole (take a local bus toward IGP Point, Rs2). **Sweet Falls,** 8km from Police Bazaar, has unspectacular cascades but plenty of explorable paths and picnicable spots. Beetle (if not Beatle) fans will love the **Butterfly Museum.** The vast collection of exotic bugs includes 30cm-long poisonous stick bugs and the world's heaviest beetle. Started by a Mr. Wankhar in the 1930s, the collection was passed down to his son in the 1960s, and now *his* son is being groomed for the job of caretaker. (GS Rd. Walk past the Grand Hotel on your right; take the first soft right onto Umsohsun Rd.; at the fork, go left and follow the curving residential street for 500m. The museum is on the right and the sign is difficult to see. Tel. 223411. Open M-F 10:30am-4pm, Sa 10:30am-1pm. Rs5.)

NEAR SHILLONG

Until recently, the town of **Cherrapunjee,** 56km south of Shillong, held the world record for the most rainfall within a 24-hour period. An unbelievable 104cm of rain fell here on June 16, 1876. The only real way to see Cherrapunjee, which has no

THE COOK, THE THIEF, HIS WIFE, AND THEIR VISITOR

All of the lips, teeth, and gums in Meghalaya are stained orange. Everyone—men, women, and children—chews *paan*. Here, it is made not from the processed, shredded *supari* of the plains, but from the unadulterated, locally grown betel nut. A Meghalayan myth that connects the ingredients of *paan* with the characters of a dastardly drama steeps the spittle of *paan* in social significance.

The story goes that a poor couple was visited by a guest and had no food to offer him. Unable to bear the shame, the husband and wife said to their guest, "Please sit down, just a moment," then went into the kitchen and killed themselves. The guest, after waiting and waiting, became alarmed and wandered into the kitchen to find his friends dead. Feeling that he was responsible, he also killed himself. When a thief showed up soon afterward, he was shocked to find, instead of loot, three dead bodies. Overcome with panic, he mopped up the blood and hid inside the house.

Now, *paan* consists of three parts: *kwai* (betel nut), *shun* (lime paste), and *tympew* (leaf). *Kwai* is masculine, and represents the husband. *Paan*-eaters chew *kwai* first, as it was the husband's blood that was first shed. *Shun* is feminine and represents the wife. *Tympew*, again masculine, stands for the guest, whose arrival wraps the house in disaster. The robber, finally, is represented by the masculine *dumasha*, or tobacco leaf, which Khasi women use to wipe the red stains from their teeth. It is said that Meghalayan hosts will never again have to commit suicide because even the poorest can afford to offer their guests *kwai tympew shun*. *Paan* exceeds even *chai* as the standard offering in Meghalayan households. If your host tempts you to orange your mouth, sit down first—Meghalayan *paan* packs a punch that'll float the unaccustomed sky-high.

local transportation and no accommodations, is by guided **tour.** One rickety tour bus goes to Cherrapunjee from the MTDC office in Shillong (departs 8am, returns 4:30pm; Rs90). Cherrapunjee's watery sights are spread out over several kilometers on the outskirts, but the MTDC tour covers all the major spots, stopping first at the **Nohkalikai Falls** (*Noh*: jumping; *Kalikai*: the name of a woman who plunged to her death here), India's second-highest waterfall, which plummets into a lush valley. The deserted flood plains of Bangladesh are visible on a clear day. The next stop is **Mawsmai Caves,** which are flooded during the monsoon—some of the more adventurous guides will let you strip down and wade through the water to the jungle on the other side. The caves are not for the claustrophobic or those with difficulty climbing. Bring a flashlight so you don't have to rent one (Rs10). Around 1pm, the bus pulls up to the cusp of a deep valley and stops at the Tourist Bungalow for lunch and a view of the **Seven Sisters Falls** before returning to Shillong.

During July, the Jaintas of the town of **Jowai**, 64km from Shillong, celebrate a festival by dancing in a pool of muddy water to stomp out epidemics and pray for a healthy crop. Buses (Rs40) and jeeps (Rs350, or Rs50 per person) leave from the private bus stand across from Anjalee Cinema Hall, near Bara Bazaar. For more information on festivals in Meghalaya, contact the Shillong branch of the Government of India Tourist Office or the MTDC.

Meghalaya is also a popular spot for **spelunking.** The best information and tours are provided by the hardy members of the Meghalaya Adventurers Association (tel. 243059), near the Synod Complex in Mission Compound, Shillong. (Contact B.O. Kharpran Daly (general secretary), c/o Hotel Centre Point, Police Bazaar, Shillong.) MTDC distributes a brochure called *Discover the Caves of Meghalaya.*

TRIPURA

The tiny state of Tripura comprises a finger of land poking into Bangladesh. At the southwestern corner of Northeast India, the region is rather distinct from its neighboring states. The Manikya, the historical ruling people of Tripura, submitted to the Mughals, but they regained and retained direct control of the state throughout the Raj. Tripura was a princely state until 1949, when it joined the Indian Union. While several ethnic groups continue to inhabit the state, the majority of the population is Bengali; ethnic demography is a point of contention for such insurgent groups as the National Liberation Front of Tripura and the Tripura Resurrection Army. Tripura has several prominent forests and wildlife sanctuaries, but expansive development is threatening these precious ecological preserves. Today the few who visit Tripura are drawn by its cultural attractions, which are all in close proximity to one another.

Agartala is the sleepy capital of Tripura. Though there's little to do in this small administrative center, some travelers have been charmed by its relaxed pace, and a few have been known to stay for weeks. The town is dominated by the **Ujjayant Palace** at its center. The sprawling white structure was built in 1901 by Radhakishore Manikya; it now houses the State Legislature. Go around to the back for the **Tripura Tourist Office** (tel. 225930 or 223893; fax 224013). This is the place for inquiries regarding accommodations and food. The staff can also direct you to **currency exchange** facilities and the Bangladesh **visa** office. (Open M-Sa 10am-4pm.) **Buses** connect Agartala with Silchar in Assam. There are also a few buses that run directly to Guwahati. For safety, consider flying directly to the city, which is connected directly to Kolkata and Guwahati. You can also reach the town by bus from **Dhaka,** Bangladesh (6hr.). **Telephone Code:** 0381.

The famed **Water Palace** at Neermahal lies 53km south of Agartala. Built in 1930 as a summer resort for Bir Bikram Kishore Manikya, the palace is an exquisite example of Indo-Saracenic architecture. The red-and-white structure lies in the middle of a large lake. A **tourist lodge** and a few restaurants dot the shore: the area is left blissfully deserted at night. Neermahal is 1km from **Melaghar,** which is connected by **bus** to Agartala (2hr., Rs50).

MIZORAM

The southernmost state of this corner of India, Mizoram is known for its peaceful hill stations and lush valleys, as well as for its residents' hospitality. Bound by a code of ethics known as *tlawmgaina*, the Mizos tend to be very welcoming and have traditionally not discriminated on the basis of class or sex. Originally from northwestern China, the Mizos fought a 21-year war of independence before finally acceding to the Indian Union in 1987. Today, they remain overwhelmingly Christian and maintain one of the highest literacy rates in India.

Although Mizoram attracts tourists with its natural splendor, its ecological story sadly parallels that of much of the region. Mizos practice "*jhum* cultivation," essentially slash-and-burn agriculture. Politically troubled and only superficially prosperous, the state is constantly threatened by resource depletion. In addition, because the Indian government considers Mizoram a strategically important region, foreign tourists are required to band together in groups of at least four and obtain a **Restricted Area Permit** (see p. 11) to visit. Fortunately, these permits are relatively easy to procure and should not deter travelers in the least.

Cool and placid **Aizwal** (EYES-wall) is perched over 1000m above sea level. To the east of the ridge on which it hangs flows the river Tuiral; on the west is the Tlawang. The scenery from the city is nothing short of overwhelming. Despite supporting a population of just 200,000, Aizwal has a substantial number of parks, gardens, and museums. Information regarding these and accommodations can be obtained from the **Mizoram Tourist Office** (tel. 21226). Aizwal is connected by **bus** to **Silchar,** in Assam (6hr.), and **Shillong,** in Meghalaya. It is also accessible by **air** from Kolkata and Guwahati. **Telephone Code:** 0389.

MANIPUR

Despite a long history of foreign invasions and domestic insurgency, Manipur has only recently begun to break away from its "at least we're not as boring as Tripura" tourism campaign. The predominantly Hindu state draws visitors to **Moirnag**, the site of yearly folk festivals, and **Loktak Lake**, the largest body of fresh water in the Northeast and home to the world's only **floating national park.** Manipuri martial arts and dances, including the *jagoi* form of dance, are known throughout India, and the state claims to be the birthplace of modern polo. Despite these distinctions, Manipur has never been much of a tourist destination, and its infrastructure is correspondingly underdeveloped.

The principal inhabitants of Manipur are the Meities; other tribal groups include the Naga and Kuki-Chin-Mizo. While these people have lived together peacefully for centuries, in recent times there has been some tension between them, occasionally building to the point of violence. Travelers are advised to contact the Government of India Tourist Office for the latest details. While Indians do not need permits to visit Manipur, those arriving by road must obtain an Inner Line Permit to pass through Nagaland. Foreigners need **Restricted Area Permits** (see p. 11).

At 790m, **Imphal,** the capital of the state, is a pleasant, moderately sized city set amid a rich landscape of green hills and lakes. Wildlife and foliage are the main attractions, but the town also has a number of notable monuments and temples. Most prominent is the Vaishnavite **Shree Govindjee Temple,** where religious significance overshadows architectural distinction. Manipur's struggle against the British is immortalized in the **Shaheed Minar** and **War Cemetery.** For information on these sights, as well as excursions to nearby destinations and accommodations in Manipur, contact **Manipur Tourism** (tel. 224603), which has a small branch at the airport. **Flights** arrive in Imphal from Kolkata and Guwahati. **Bus** service runs from Guwahati and Shillong. **Telephone Code:** 0385.

NAGALAND

Historically one of India's least accessible areas, Nagaland is slowly opening up to tourism. The state's precarious position between Assam and Burma has often resulted in crackdowns by the Indian Army on Naga nationalists, who continue their struggle for autonomy (which they enjoyed under the British) and, someday, perhaps independence. The fiercest fighting was incited by the Nagaland National Council, with support from China. One of the largest factions of these militants laid down their arms in 1974, bringing a degree of peace to the region.

Today, Nagaland promotes itself as an outdoor recreation destination and scenic getaway. There is good trekking in the Dzukou Valley, 30km from the capital **Kohima,** and around Mt. Saramati, 269km from Kohima. The best way to experience the region is probably to arrange a guided tour or trek with **Naga Tourism,** in Kohima (tel. 22214 or 21607; open M-F 10am-4pm). **Telephone Code:** 0370.

Dimapur is home to impressive monoliths and the state's only **airport.** Kohima is connected to Dimapur by road (3hr., Rs70). Foreigners must travel in groups of four or more and obtain a **Restricted Area Permit** (see p. 11), which is considerably more difficult to obtain than permits to visit other states.

NORTHEAST INDIA

THE ANDAMAN ISLANDS

अंडमान द्वीपसमूह

Beautiful isolated beaches, luscious rainforests, mangrove swamps, and unique marine and bird life paint the idyll that is the Andaman Islands, an area only recently opened to tourism and still largely untouched by commerce. The *Ramayana* identifies the monkey-god Hanuman (from which "Andaman" is derived) as the first visitor to the islands—he used them as stepping stones to hop across to Burma. If the story is true, Hanuman was also the first to trample on the territorial rights of the islands' indigenous inhabitants. In turn, the British would arrive to build a penal colony to imprison agitators for Indian Independence. Since Independence, the Indian government has tempered further efforts to colonize the islands with an anthropological interest in the island tribes, but natives have still been forced to watch their land succumb to settlement and deforestation. Tourism, however, has brought with it money for improvements in infrastructure and standard of living. Port Blair, on South Andaman, is the main transportation hub, connected to Chennai and Kolkata by boat and plane. Despite recent advances, the islands still have poor commercial and transportation infrastructures—the neighboring Nicobar Islands are off-limits to foreign tourists altogether—and getting around (or getting what you need) requires a lot of energy and patience. Your efforts at dealing with the islands' limitations will be rewarded, however, with some of the most secluded beaches in the world. The temperature remains tropical throughout the year, although a lot of rain (sometimes accompanied by cyclones) falls from June to mid-September and from November to December.

> **!** **WARNING.** The relationship between the Andaman and Nicobar Islands' indigenous peoples and outsiders has been soured in many cases by deforestation, poaching, and government blunders. Understandably, some tribes are unfriendly to visitors, even to the point of violence. **Do not attempt to come into contact with indigenous peoples here.**

PORT BLAIR पोर्ट ब्लैर

Port Blair hasn't come that far since its days as a British penal colony where political activists who took part in the Mutiny of 1857 were sent. Although its hilly streets are filled with exceptionally friendly people, mopeds, and lots of coconut water stands, there's not much to see or do. However, as the Andamans' major city, and a hub for air and water transport, it has good tourist offices and plentiful hotels, and is really the only access point for the rest of the islands.

TRANSPORTATION

Airport: Junglighat Rd., past the Government of India Tourism Office on the left. Public buses leave every 30min. from the bus stand (5am-8:30pm, Rs3). Taxis to the airport run from downtown (Rs50). **Indian Airlines** (tel. 33744) is downhill from the tourist office, on the right side of the road. Open M-Sa 9am-1pm and 2-4pm. Flights to: **Kolkata** (Sa-Tu and Th, US$195) and **Chennai** (M, W, F, and Su; US$195).

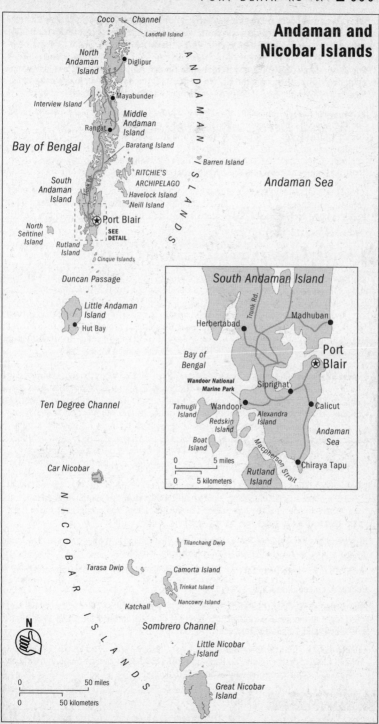

Andaman and Nicobar Islands

Coco — Channel
Landfall Island

North Andaman Island

Diglipur

ANDAMAN

Mayabunder

Interview Island

Middle Andaman Island

Rangat

Bay of Bengal

Baratang Island

ISLANDS

Barren Island

RITCHIE'S ARCHIPELAGO

Andaman Sea

South Andaman Island

Havelock Island
Neill Island

North Sentinel Island

Port Blair
SEE DETAIL

Rutland Island

Cinque Islands

Duncan Passage

Little Andaman Island

Hut Bay

Ten Degree Channel

Car Nicobar

N
I
C
O
B
A
R

Tarasa Dwip

Tilanchang Dwip

Camorta Island

Trinkat Island

Katchall

Nancowry Island

Sombrero Channel

I
S
L
A
N
D
S

Little Nicobar Island

N

0   50 miles
0   50 kilometers

Great Nicobar Island

Detail: South Andaman Island

South Andaman Island

Trunk Rd.

Madhuban

Herbertabad

Bay of Bengal

Port Blair

Wandoor National Marine Park

Siprighat

Tamugli Island

Wandoor

Alexandra Island

Calicut

Redskin Island

Boat Island

Andaman Sea

Macpherson Strait

0   5 miles
0   5 kilometers

Rutland Island

Chiraya Tapu

ANDAMAN ISLANDS

Ships: The ticket booth at **Phoenix Bay Jetty**, a 5min. walk north past Lighthouse Cinema. Open 9am-noon. Tickets are available 1 day in advance. Ships sail to: **Diglipur** via **Mayabunder** (3 per week 6:30am, 16hr., Rs75); **Havelock** via **Neil Island** (3-4 per week 6:15am, 4hr., Rs16); **Rangat** (4 per week 6:15am, 9hr., Rs35); **Ross Island** (Th-Tu 4 per day, 20min., Rs16). Boats to **Mahatma Gandhi National Marine Park** leave from **Wandoor Jetty,** 30km from the city (Tu-Su 10am, 24hr., Rs32). Port Blair's newspaper, the *Daily Telegraph,* has updates on frequently changing ship schedules.

Buses: Leave from the bus stand in Aberdeen Bazaar (tel. 32278). Ask the ticket-*wallahs* on the buses for route information. To: **airport** (every 30min. 5am-8:30pm, 10min., Rs3); **Chiriya Tapu** via **Corbyn's Cove** (approx. every hr. 5am-6pm, 1½hr., Rs8); **Diglipur** (6am, 12hr., Rs75); **Mayabunder** (5:30am, 8hr., Rs70; deluxe 5am, Rs143); **Rangat** (6am, 5hr., Rs53; deluxe 5am, Rs105); **Wandoor** (6 per day, 1½hr., Rs9). Buses returning from northern towns depart at the same times.

Local Transport: Most distances are walkable, though the terrain is hilly. **Taxis** don't use meters and charge Rs50 every ride. **Jagganath Guest House** rents **motorbikes** (Rs20 per day) and **cycles** (Rs35). **TSG Autos** (tel. 32787), Jungle Ghat Rd., rents motorbikes (Rs75 per ½day, Rs120 per day; Rs500 deposit).

7 ORIENTATION AND PRACTICAL INFORMATION

Port Blair is quite small, and almost everything is within walking distance. The **bus stand** is at one end of **Aberdeen Bazaar** at the center of town. Uphill and east from the bus stand is the **clock tower.** From there, the road to the youth hostel and, eventually, **Corbyn's Cove,** heads east and then south. If you walk in the other direction from the bus stand, you'll come to **Lighthouse Cinema.** The road straight ahead from here leads to Jagganath Guest House; the road to the right leads to **Phoenix Bay Jetty,** and uphill to the left sits the Andaman Islands' **tourist office.**

Tourist Office: The **Andaman Islands Tourism Office** (tel. 32747) is the tall, spiffy-looking building at the top of a hill. The helpful staff provides thorough information, and they can make reservations for Dolphin Guest House, the only place to stay on Havelock Island, as well as for other government-run hotels farther north. Open M-F 8:30am-4:45pm, Sa 8:30am-12:30pm. The *Daily Telegraph* has a "Today for Tourists" section.

Currency Exchange: State Bank of India is across from the bus stand. Open M-F 10am-2pm, Sa 10am-noon. **Island Travels** (tel. 33358), 110m east of the clock tower, is a better bet. Open daily 9am-6:30pm. Off-season: 3-4pm.

Library: Post Office Rd., next to the Telegraph Office. Open M-Sa 12:30-7:45pm. Closed 2nd Sa. There's a decent library upstairs in the **Zonal Anthropological Museum,** but you'll have to convince the head office (on the left, 100m down Junglighat Jetty on the left) that you're a "researcher."

Pharmacy: Devraj Medical Store, Hospital Rd. (tel. 34344), in the bazaar across from the stadium, is trustworthy. Open daily 8am-1pm and 2-8pm.

Hospital: G.B. Panth Hospital (tel. 32102, emergency tel. 100) has ambulance service.

Police: Aberdeen Bazaar (tel. 33077).

Post Office: GPO, Post Office Rd. (tel. 32226). From the tourist office, go downhill and turn right at the second intersection; the post office is on the right. Open M-Sa 9am-12:30pm and 1-5pm. **Postal Code:** 744101.

Telephones: The **Central Telegraph Office,** Post Office Rd. (tel. 32551), next to the post office. Open M-Sa 8am-8pm, Su 8am-1pm. **STD/ISD** booths can be found in Aberdeen Bazaar, but connections are spotty and often muffled.

ANDAMAN ISLANDS

| PHONE CODE | 03192 |

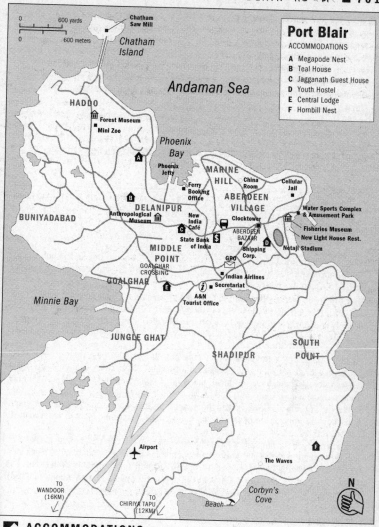

ACCOMMODATIONS

Central Lodge (tel. 33632 or 33634), downhill from the tourist office near Goalghar; ask around for the specific location. Retired professor R.K. Sharma was inspired by his army barracks to build this ultimate budget guest house. Bare, uncarpeted rooms offer little sensory stimulation but are clean and comfortable enough. Camp on the lawn or in the jungle-like "garden." Often packed during high season. Camping Rs20; singles Rs40; doubles Rs70, with bath Rs90. Extra person Rs20.

Youth Hostel, Aberdeen Bazaar (tel. 32459), by the ocean, across from the stadium. Great location, floral surroundings, and clean bathrooms with showers. As the temporary home of lots of young mainlanders and islanders on tour, it has a friendly, collegial environment. No alcohol. Check-out 10am. Dorm beds Rs20, for non-members Rs40; doubles Rs40/80.

Jagganath Guest House, Moulana Azad Rd. (tel. 33140). Well-kept by a kind, thoughtful manager. Rooms have windows, private balconies, sometimes-hot showers, tiled bathrooms, and 24hr. water. Free bottles of filtered water. Snorkeling equipment (Rs50 per day), bicycles (Rs35 per day), and motor bikes (Rs120 per day) for rent. Singles Rs80; doubles Rs125.

Teal House (tel. 34060 or 340611), down Moulana Azad Rd., away from the center of town; look for the signs. Sweet-smelling, carpeted rooms with a wonderful hilltop view. Telephones, bamboo furniture, mosquito nets, and big bathrooms with hot showers. Call the tourist office 1 month in advance for in-season (Sept.-May) bookings. Check-out 7am. Doubles with bath Rs250, with A/C Rs400. Off-season: 25% discount.

Megapode Nest (tel. 32207), towards Haddo past the Phoenix Bay Jetty. The tourist office will direct you here. Air-conditioned rooms with attached bath, hot showers, TVs, and a stunning bay view. Doubles Rs500; cottages Rs800.

Hornbill Nest (tel. 33018), a short walk towards Corbyn's Cove on the east coast. With its open-air, spider-shaped atrium, Hornbill appears to have been teleported straight out of the 1950s. A bit out of the way, but the cheapest place near the beach. Clean, bland rooms. Doubles Rs250; quads Rs300. Off-season: 25% discount.

◔ FOOD

Soil on the Andaman Islands is not very fertile, so most fruits and vegetables must be imported from the mainland. Seafood, as you might expect, is everywhere and usually very fresh. Prawns are especially plentiful and delicious. The *dhabas* between the bus stand and the clock tower also serve sumptuous food.

Lighthouse Restaurant. The youth hostel's canteen has simple, delicious, cheap food. The atmosphere is brotherly and, at times, a little raucous. Veg. and non-veg. *thalis* Rs10-15. Open daily 5:30am-9:30pm.

China Room, on Marine Hill. From the bus stand, walk north 1km and turn right up the hill; it's on the left, lit with a red sign. A dizzying selection of gourmet seafood—daily specials include cashew prawns (Rs120) and barracuda fillet (Rs90). With a day's notice, roast duck (Rs250) or *szechuan* lobster (Rs300) may be available. Open daily noon-2pm and 5:30-10:30pm.

New India Cafe, below Hotel Jai Mathi, 20m from Jagganath Guest House. A surf-style cafeteria with delicious, no-frills dishes and excellent butter *naan*. Great service and a welcome break from Hindi pop make this a great place to pretend you're in California and not India. Fish *thali* (Rs20) and prawn coconut curry (Rs45).

The Waves, at Corbyn's Cove, across the street from the beach. Lounge around in bamboo chairs in front of the ocean at this full bar and restaurant. Snacks (sandwiches, *papad*) Rs5-12, prawn *pakora* Rs55, beer Rs65. Open daily 6am-10pm.

Ananda, Aberdeen Bazaar, below Kavita hotel. Walk from the bus stand to the clock tower and turn right; it's on the left. A wide variety of Indian dishes is available. The chicken is served in a million different ways with a million different spices. Popular with locals. Eat in A/C comfort for Rs1 extra. Chicken 65 (that's 65 spices and seasonings; Rs50) tastes great with butter *naan* (Rs10). Snacks Rs7-13.

◉ SIGHTS

CELLULAR JAIL AND MUSEUM. With their infinite capacity to divide and conquer, British colonials used the Andamans to isolate and imprison freedom fighters, their rationale being that rebel activists were less of a threat if they couldn't rile up fellow prisoners on the mainland. The Cellular Jail, which once served such purposes, has become a monument to India's freedom struggle. The museum's two ground floor galleries chart the history and inhumane conditions of the prison and document the broad base of Indian resistance to colonialism. One room upstairs is devoted to the life and work of Subhash Chandra Bose, who was imprisoned here. The portaits of revolutionaries are wonderfully done. *(From the clock tower, go down toward the ocean and bear left and uphill. Tel. 30117. Jail open daily 9am-5pm. Museum open Tu-Su 9am-noon and 2-5pm. Sound and light show Tu-Su 7:15pm, weather permitting.)*

OTHER SIGHTS. The **Zonal Anthropological Museum** is one of the few places where you can find photos and relics of the islands' wide variety of indigenous peoples. Unfortunately, there isn't a great deal of information displayed. A better bet for getting information about the tribal cultures of the Andaman and Nicobar Islands would be to attend one of the tourism department's **free documentary screenings** (M-F 5:30pm; M and Th at the Teal House, W and F at the Megapode Nest, and Tu at the Hornbill Nest). A 15-minute coastal bike ride from the museum takes you to **Corbyn's Cove,** an idyllic white sand beach surrounded by green palms that will introduce you to the stupendous beauty of the rest of the Andamans (from the clock tower, go downhill, turn right, and follow the road and the coastline). Finally, the **Water Sports Complex and Amusement Park** offers evening fun (open M-Sa 4pm-8pm, Su 8am-noon and 2-8pm).

NEAR PORT BLAIR

Ross Island, on the northeast side of South Andaman, houses the ruins of the British penal colony for which it was once the center of operations. It's a great (and surreal) place to wander around for the day. **Ferries** leave from Phoenix Bay Jetty (8:30am, 10am, and 12:30pm; 2hr.; Rs15). The last ferry back to Port Blair is at 5:30pm. **Viper Island,** like Ross Island, features the hauntingly overgrown ruins of the British penal project. You can reach Viper on the general Harbour Cruise, which leaves daily from Phoenix Bay Jetty (3pm, 2hr., Rs25). **Chiriya Tapu** is a tiny village on the south end of South Andaman, 30km from Port Blair. The road is rough at times, but the trip is made worthwhile by Tapu's long strip of beach, decent snorkeling, and excellent camping.

The water at **Mahatma Gandhi National Marine Park** is a mysterious world of living **coral** structures that are home to millions of wildly colored, elegantly and oddly shaped marine life including angelfish, clown fish, starfish, silver jacks, yellow butterfly fish, green parrot-fish, sea anemones, and even the occasional hammerhead shark. The park makes for a nice day-trip from Port Blair.

The 8:30am bus to Wandoor from the Port Blair bus stand connects with the 10am boat to either **Jolly Buoy** or **Red Skin Island** (Rs60). A **park permit** costs Rs15, and renting snorkel **equipment** is Rs50, but equipment gets scarce during season—you should bring your own or rent from it from a Port Blair hotel. The boat there will take you to a **glass-bottomed boat,** where you can catch glimpses of the expanse of underwater beauty that is this park's treasure. Many visitors choose to explore the underwater world on their own. **Coral and shell collecting is forbidden.** **Bharat Hotel,** a shack 50m from the boat dock, rents snorkels, serves excellent fish curry (Rs8) and *chapati* (Rs2), and may rent you one of its tiny rooms (Rs50-80). The road leads a few kilometers past the boat dock to a beautiful beach with driftlogs perfect for setting up a tarp. Beer (Rs65) and basic food can be had at the government-run restaurant a few yards away.

OTHER ISLANDS

RITCHIE'S ARCHIPELAGO

Although Havelock Island is the most popular tourist getaway on Ritchie's Archipelago, **Neil Island, Long Island,** and **North Passage** are also open for overnight stays (camping is probably the best option). Ships leaving Phoenix Bay Jetty stop at Neil (3-4 per week 6:15am, Rs8) and Long (2 per week 6:15am, Rs13).

HAVELOCK ISLAND. Havelock Island has white sand, white sand, more white sand, and an occasional dolphin leaping out of the sapphire blue water. You won't want to do anything here but lie on the beach, sun-bathing the day away and gazing up at the heavens at night. Havelock does not have many tourist sights, but that is precisely what draws the crowds. Located only 38km from Port Blair, it is the most popular island among foreign visitors. No special permits are required to stay on Havelock Island; your Andaman and Nicobar permit suffices.

Boats leave Port Blair for Havelock Island from the **Phoenix Bay Jetty** (3-4 per week 6:15am, 4hr., Rs16) and return from Havelock the next day. It's a bumpy ride, so have those motion sickness pills handy. Once you arrive, a government bus will shuttle you to your accommodations.

TRIBES OF THE ANDAMAN AND NICOBAR ISLANDS

Outside of the bustle of Port Blair, the Andaman Islands seem beautifully and peacefully underpopulated. But there is a sizable (though still precariously small) indigenous population here, and their recent history has been far from peaceful. Troubles began with the British penal colony established on Viper Island. Western diseases, deforestation, and armed skirmishes (spears vs. rifles) initiated a decimation of the Andaman and Nicobar tribal populations that began to level off only in the 1980s. By then, the entire Andamanese population, which has now been relegated to Strait Island, had been reduced to just 28 survivors. With the exception of the Nicobarese, who have fared better by "integrating" themselves in government development programs, other tribes have suffered declines of similar magnitude.

Since Independence, the Indian government, in shifting its tribal policy from colonize-or-bust to colonize-with-scientific-curiosity, has set aside indigenous reserves. Still, quite understandably, some tribes have opted for zero communication with the disastrously bungling invaders. The Sentinelese of North Sentinel Island (64km southwest of Port Blair) have been a target of government anthropological excursions since 1967. Government boats would pull up to the island, leave gifts of plastic buckets, roast pigs, and sacks of coconuts in an attempt to establish contact with the tribe. The Sentinelese would take the gifts—and then fire arrows at the anthropologists. The Jarawa, who occupy much of the busier Middle Andaman, have had a more contentious time resisting, and many have been shot while trying to deter poachers and loggers (in one case by chopping off the offenders' hands). Buses plying Trunk Rd., which runs directly through "reserve" land, now carry armed guards—an arrow or two still occasionally crashes through the windows.

For more information on the Andaman and Nicobar tribes, see the exhibits at the Zonal Anthropological Museum (see p. 700).

The island is thinly inhabited and the villages are named only by numbers. Beaches lining most of the coast have remained pristine. **Coral and shell collecting is strictly forbidden**—it hurts the environment, so don't do it. These items can be purchased in Port Blair if you must have them. It's best to bring or rent a bike to get around the island since there is no other transportation except for your feet and one local bus which runs erratically (Rs2). **Bikes** are available for rent in villages #1 and #3 for Rs50 per day from the huts labeled "Bicycles for Hire." A hybrid post office/police depot is located near the jetty (open M-F 10am-5pm). You won't probably won't need either of these: it is highly unlikely that crime will be a problem here, and to save time, you're better off holding onto your **mail** until you return to the mainland. There is no STD/ISD phone on the island nor is there a facility for currency exchange.

Usually only government accommodations are available, but they are well-kept and fairly inexpensive. The best experience can be had staying in one of the **Tent Resorts** located at either end of the island on beaches #5 and 7. Each tent has a double bed with common bathroom (Rs125), and a maximum stay of four nights is enforced in season. More posh digs can be found at the **Dolphin Yatri Niwas** (tel. 30933) complex on beach #5 (doubles Rs300 -1500). Reservations for both of these accommodations must be made in Port Blair at the state government tourist office. The only other options are located away from the beach. The **MS Guest House** and **Guaranga Lodge**, both near the dock, have doubles for Rs110 and Rs55, respectively. For fresh food prepared in a clean kitchen, head to the **Dolphin Yatri Niwas.** Fried prawns (Rs20), coconut prawn curry (Rs35), and seafood bisque (Rs15) are tasty treats.

NORTH AND MIDDLE ANDAMANS

Baratang, Middle Andaman, and **North Andaman** are accessible by buses which head up the Grand Trunk Rd. or by ferry from Phoenix Bay Jetty. Because the road has been built through reserves set aside for the indigenous Jarawa, travel on it is generally limited to government buses (which carry armed guards to deter attacks). The only places to stay on Middle and North Andaman are the main towns of **Mayabunder** (Middle) and **Diglipur** (North). The Tourism Office has recently opened **Swiftlet Nest** in Mayabunder (doubles Rs275) and **Turtle Nest** in Diglipur (doubles Rs350). Reservations must be made at the tourist office in Pt. Blair.

NEPAL नेपाल

LAND AND BIODIVERSITY

Nepal is home to some of the most rugged and difficult mountain terrain in the world. With eight of the world's ten highest peaks packed within its 140,797 sq. km, Nepal is nearly 75% mountain. Once completely submerged, the mountainous region was thrust up some 50-60 million years ago in the tectonic collision between India and Asia. The mountains continue to grow at the rate of a few centimeters per year.

The **Terai,** the northernmost reach of the Indo-Gangetic Plain, is fertile, low-lying (200m), hot, and humid. Once covered with dense, malarial forest that supported only wildlife, recent years have seen vast deforestation, and today it is the hub of Nepal's growing population. Rising abruptly from the Terai plain to altitudes in excess of 1500m, the forested **Chure Hills** run parallel to the 3000m Mahabharat Range farther north. The broad basins of the **Inner Terai** form the region between the Chure and the **Mahabarat Hills.** With steep escarpments to the south offering natural fortification and arable land for terrace farming, the Mahabharat is moderately settled but, except for its passes, cut off from human traffic. The region is cut by the deep, north-south river gorges of Nepal's three major river systems—the Karnali, Narayani, and Kosi. At altitudes of 500 to 2000m, the **Pahar** region, north of the Mahabarat, holds flat, fertile valleys, including the Kathmandu, Banepa, and Pokhara Valleys. The Pahar has been inhabited and cultivated for centuries, and today it supports nearly 40% of Nepal's population.

Nepal's most famous geographic feature, the **Himalayas** are inhabited only in scattered mountain pockets, valleys, and elevated plateaus. Human settlements become sparse at about 4000m, where pervasive mist and clouds inhibit crop cultivation. Here, dense forest yields to alpine pasture, which yields in turn to snowline (4900m), beyond which nothing but mountains grow. Ten Nepalese peaks rise higher than 8000m, including **Mount Everest** (8848m), the highest point on earth. North of these peaks is the high desert plateau of the **Trans-Himalaya.**

Nepal's plant life grows scant as altitudes increase, with the timber forests (home to the *khair, sissoo, sal,* and pine) giving way to spruce, birch, rhododendron, and finally grasslands just below the snowline. The Terai is inhabited by tigers, leopards, *gaur* (wild oxen), elephants, and several species of deer, and the Lesser Rapti Valley is one of the last homes of the Indian rhinoceros.

PEOPLE AND LANGUAGE

Nepal supports a population of 20.6 million people representing over 60 ethnic, linguistic, and caste groups. Much of its cultural heterogeneity is derived from its rugged and sometimes impassable terrain, which has kept different areas of the country isolated. Only over the past few centuries has the word "Nepal" come to represent the land as a whole (formerly, a "Nepali" was an inhabitant of the Kathmandu Valley), and it is still customary for people to identify themselves regionally as *pahari, madeshi,* or *bhotia* (hills, plains, or northern-border dwellers).

Forming a nation of villages, about 90% of Nepalis live in small market centers and rural settlements. In this predominantly agricultural economy, with most people dependent on subsistence farming, Nepal's population density is a function of agricultural productivity. The fertile Terai supports Nepal's densest population and has become the country's bread-basket and a booming industrial region. The highlands and Trans-Himalayan valleys, with less than 1% of land under cultivation, remain sparsely populated, with the majority of people leading a nomadic way of life.

The official language of Nepal is **Nepali,** also called Gorkhali. The mother tongue of 50% of the population, Nepali is spoken and understood by nearly everyone. As a descendent of Sanskrit, like the languages of North India, it uses the Devanagari script. (For basic Nepali vocabulary, see the **Phrasebook,** p. 811.)

While most Nepalis are Hindu and trace Indo-Aryan ancestry, many are equally influenced by the Buddhist tradition. The **Newaris,** the earliest known arrivals to Nepal and the original settlers of the Kathmandu Valley, practice a synthesis of Buddhism and Hinduism. The Newari language is of Tibetan origin, although it has borrowed its Devanagari script and half of its vocabulary from Sanskrit. Accounting for only 4% of the current population, they produce some of the country's most celebrated art. The Eastern mid-hills are inhabited by **Rais, Limbus,** and **Sunwars,** and the Terai is populated by **Tharus, Yadavas, Safars, Rajvanshis,** and **Dhimlas,** who speak dialects of Hindi such as Bhojpuri and Maithili. In west-central Nepal, the **Gurungs** and **Magars** are also thought to be among Nepal's earliest inhabitants.

Recent large-scale migrations from Tibet brought Tibeto-Burmese languages and Tibetan Buddhist culture to Nepal. Today, 45% of the population claims Tibeto-Burmese descent. While Indo-Aryans settled mostly in southern regions and lower altitudes, where Hindus are a majority (although there are also groups of Muslims and aboriginal tribes here), the Tibeto-Burmese settled mostly in the higher altitudes of the north, where Buddhist culture predominates. Among the most recent immigrants from Tibet are the **Tamangs,** the most populous of Tibeto-Burmese ethnic groups, and the **Sherpas,** some of the inhabitants of the northern-most Himalayas. Tibetan refugees continue to seek asylum in Nepal, so the use of Tibetan, which uses a Sanskrit-based script, is not uncommon. Some English is also spoken in Nepal, and it's not too hard to get around knowing no more than "*namaste,*" a Sanskrit term than translates literally as "I salute the God in you."

GOVERNMENT AND POLITICS

Nepal became a constitutional monarchy with a parliamentary system of government on Nov. 9, 1990. The power of the Sovereign, a position held since 1972 by **King Birendra Bir Bikram Shah,** is limited, although His Majesty is vested with certain powers, such as the ability to pass bills. Real executive power is in the hands of the Prime Minister (currently **Krishna Prasad Bhattarai**), who is chosen by a majority in the 205-member House of Representatives. Members of the House are elected by universal suffrage for a term of up to five years. An upper house, the 60-seat National Assembly, consists of appointed and elected positions. Nepal's judiciary branch purports to be politically impartial.

The main political parties in Nepal are the moderate Nepali Congress (NC), the Communist Party of Nepal/United Marxist-Leninist (CPN-UML), and the younger right-wing National Democratic Party (NDP). Though the NDP lacks the wide base of support of the NC and the Communist Party, it has played king in the nation's coalition politics. Also on the scene is the Nepal Sadhbhavana Party (NSP), a regionalist party from the Terai.

ECONOMICS

With 90% of its population depending on subsistence agriculture, Nepal ranks as one of the least developed countries in the world. Hillsides are used for terrace farming, but landslides and erosion make it difficult to cultivate. In the Terai, where farming is potentially more lucrative, high population growth makes even subsistence farming difficult. The geography of Nepal presents two hurdles to economic development—a lack of mineral resources and a rugged terrain that snags cultivation. The pearl in the economic oyster is the hydroelectric potential of Nepal's raging rivers, but its development stands at odds with the bankable tourist appeal of pristine valleys for rafting and hiking. Meanwhile, roads are expensive to build and maintain, and the Indian border is the only easily negotiable channel of trade. Large industry is therefore concentrated in the Terai, with most of its manufactured goods and machinery imported from India.

Nepal

N

SIKKIM

WEST BENGAL

TIBET (CHINA)

100 miles

100 kilometers

Sagarmatha
(Mt. Everest) 8848m
Lhotse 8516m
Cho Oyu 8201m
Makalu 8463m
Kanchenjunga 8586m

Sagarmatha
National
Park

Makalu-Barun
National Park

Gauri Shankar
7134m

Nyalam

Langtang
National
Park

Manaslu
8163m

Annapurna
Conservation
Area

Annapurna I
8091m

Dhaulagiri I
8167m

Shey-Phoksundo
National Park

Bardia
National
Park

Sukla
Phanta
WLR

Chitwan
National Park

Koshi-
Tappu WLR

Kodari
Chautara
Lamosangu
Jiri
Charikot
Dhulkhel
Bhaktapur
Kathmandu
Patan
Godavari
Daman
Hetauda

Lukla
Namche
Bazar

Bhojpur

Dhankar

Sindhulimadi

Janakpur

Jaleswar

Birganj

Raxaul

Trisuli
Dhunche

Gorkha
Dumre
Mugling
Narayanghat
Bharatpur

Besisahar
Damauli

Pokhara
Kusma
Baglung

Jomsom

Simikot

Jumla

Birendranagar

Dipayal

Dadeldhura

Mahendranagar

Dhangadhi

Kohalpur
Nepalganj

Tulsipur
Pyuthan

Lamahi

Tansen
Butwal
Bhairawa
Taulihawa
Lumbini

Sonauli

Bhairawa

Gorakhpur

Faizabad

Lucknow

UTTAR PRADESH

INDIA

BIHAR

Tumlingtar
Basantapur
Taplejung
Ilam
Kakarbhitta
Bhadrapur

Dharan
Dhankuta
Itahari
Dharan

Rajbiraj
Biratnagar

Hile

Dhalkebar

Tamur R.
Arun R.
Dudh Kosi R.
Sun Kosi R.
Tama Kosi R.
Bagmati R.
Kosi R.
Rapti R.
Kali Gandaki R.
Marsyangdi R.
Budhi Gandaki R.
Trisuli R.
Bheri R.
Karnali R.
Seti R.
Mahakali R.

Siddhartha Hwy
Prithvi Hwy
Tribhuvan Hwy
Mahendra Hwy

Charkhot

NEPAL

Govt. of India statement:
The external boundaries of India are
neither correct nor authenticated.

Nepal's biggest source of foreign exchange is the export of woolen goods and international aid. While it has been a boost to the Nepali economy, foreign assistance over the past four decades has, in fact, intoduced several complications. Nepal's donors have been responsible for many mistakes, such as development programs unsuited to the region, uneven distribution of aid, corrupt and unregulated rural NGOs (non-governmental organizations), and assistance for blatantly political ends. Environmentalists raise the question of whether industrial "development" is a good idea at all in a country which has maintained a way of life that does not require sustenance by floods of consumer goods.

HISTORY

Despite the religions, languages and traditions that it has borrowed from its neighbors, India and China, the tiny Himalayan kingdom has maintained a history and culture that are as unique and diverse as the land itself. Nepal's proximity to India has led to Indian influence in the Terai, while the central hills and mountain valleys, including Kathmandu, have tended towards independence but not isolation. In the heart of the mountains, life has progressed without much outside influence at all.

ORIGINS AND EARLY DYNASTIES (200,000 BC-AD 1200)

Much of Nepal's early history is shrouded in myth and mystery. Stone Age settlers are thought to have arrived around 200,000 BC, and written references to the region appear as early as the first millennium BC. The **Kiratis,** a Mongoloid people who migrated into Nepal during the 8th century BC, were the first known rulers of the Kathmandu Valley. Small kingdoms began to develop in the Terai region around 500 BC in response to the growth of powerful Aryan kingdoms to the south. **Siddhartha Gautama,** the man who would become the Buddha, was born into one of these early tribal confederations, the Sakya clan. Three centuries later, the Buddhist emperor **Ashoka** came to the land that spawned the man who spawned his faith, installing one of his famed pillars at **Lumbini** (see p. 774). Although it is not clear whether or not Nepal was ever included in the territories of the Mauryan Empire, the region was greatly influenced by the Mauryas, both politically and culturally. Buddhism was established throughout much of Nepal during Ashoka's reign, and the concept of the king as upholder of *dharma*, which was borrowed from the Mauryas, began to play a major role in Nepal. The early kingdoms, however, content to guard their strategic positions and control the closest adjacent lands, never expanded far. Most of what is known of Nepal's early history comes from the Kathmandu Valley, the historical heartland of Nepal and the source of its greatest cultural contributions.

Between the 4th and 5th centuries AD, the **Licchavis,** Nepal's first dynasty from the Indian plains, overthrew the Kiratis. The Licchavis brought with them Hinduism and the caste system, and established a tradition of Hindu upper classes ruling over Buddhist commoners. Under the Licchavis, the Kathmandu Valley enjoyed an era of economic prosperity and artistic flourishing which continued despite the petty wars and poor administration of the **Thakuris,** who rose to power in the 9th century.

MALLA KINGDOMS (1200-1742)

A new dynasty emerged from the Kathmandu Valley in 1200, when the **Mallas** came to power. Despite shaky beginnings, they ushered in the best years of Kathmandu Valley culture and ruled for over 500 years. Although the Mallas imposed Hindu laws on the valley, their tolerance of Buddhism allowed Tantrism to flourish. After the death of Yaksha Malla, the greatest of the Malla kings, in 1482, the kingdom he had ruled from Bhaktapur was split among his three children. Kathmandu, Patan, and Bhaktapur became rival city-states, and internal competition sharpened the Malla family's political acumen. Despite constant feuding over trade with Tibet, all three kingdoms reached new heights in urban planning and art—the great wood-screened temples and cobbled **Durbar Squares** of the valley date from this time.

THE ABOMINABLE SNOWMAN If you spot a couple of footprints in the snow that seem a trifle too large to be made even by a size 18 shoe, you might be on the trail of the *Yeti*, the Himalayas' own Bigfoot. Local legend has it that a Sherpa girl was grazing her yaks in the Himalayas when an ape-like creature attacked, breaking the necks of the yaks by grabbing the horns. The footprints may be the work of fallen lumps of snow, or they may be made by bears' feet, an artifact of the animals' placing their hindfoot partially over the impression of the forefoot, thus creating the impression of an unusually large pawprint. Though nobody has ever seen this shaggy beast face to face, the legend of the mountain giant lives on.

UNIFICATION AND THE SHAH DYNASTY (1742-1816)

The Mallas were unprepared for the force that would hit them in the 18th century and expand their dominion into a proper Kingdom of Nepal. The small hill-state of Gorkha, 50km west of Kathmandu, was under the rule of the **Shahs,** the most ambitious of the many immigrant Rajput clans that came to western and southern Nepal between the 14th and 16th centuries, driven out of India by Muslim invaders. In 1742 King Prithvi Narayan Shah ascended to the throne of Gorkha, and within two years he set out to conquer Nepal's richest region, the Kathmandu Valley. After a 25-year war of attrition, the three cities of Kathmandu, Patan, and Bhaktapur surrendered. When Prithvi Narayan Shah invaded Kathmandu, King Jaya Prakash Malla asked the English East India Company for help, but to no avail. If the company had acquiesced, the British might have ruled Nepal. Instead, the victorious Shah became the founder of the modern nation of Nepal, and his Gorkha army proceeded to conquer the eastern Terai and hills. Prithvi Narayan implemented a closed-door policy that would keep Nepal isolated until the 1950s. An astute ruler, he set up an exemplary government. Calling his kingdom a "garden of many flowers," he respected the country's local institutions and rewarded his officials according to their merit. After his death in 1775, however, Prithvi Narayan's kingdom deteriorated. The throne passed to a series of infant Shahs, and members of the nobility battled one another to act as regent.

Eventually the shrewd chief minister **Bhim Sen Thapa** took control, finding that he could unite Nepal by launching a war against the west, annexing the Garwhal and Kumaon regions (now part of India's Uttar Pradesh state) as well as Himachal Pradesh. But Nepal mishandled its new lands and got into trouble with foreign powers. From 1788-92 it fought a war with Tibet and China, and in 1814 its expansion into the Terai provoked the hostility of the East India Company.

Although Nepal did not defeat Britain, the Anglo-Nepalese War was not the easy victory the British expected. In spite of superior numbers and weaponry, the British were routed by Nepalese soldiers, who held their hilltop forts and charged at the redcoats with *khukuri* knives. It was two years before the British were able to break through and defeat Nepal in 1816. The **Treaty of Segauli** stripped Nepal of Himachal Pradesh, Garhwal, Kumaon, and the Terai lands and fixed its eastern and western borders where they remain today. The prospect of another insurrection led the British to a more sensitive stance towards Nepal; it became the only country in South Asia to remain independent of colonial power. Eventually, the British began recruiting Nepalese soldiers for their new **Gorkha** (or Gurkha) regiments.

STAGNATION AND COUP D'ETAT (1816-46)

Prime Minister Bhim Sen Thapa kept the country stable by strengthening its army, but chaos ensued when he fell from grace in 1837, and various palace factions struggled for power. On September 14, 1846 a powerful minister was murdered, and the queen assembled the entire royal court to find the culprit. The personal guards of **General Jung Bahadur,** the cabinet minister for the army, surrounded the Kot and opened fire, killing 32 of Kathmandu's most powerful nobles. During the next few hours, the queen appointed Jung Bahadur prime minister in a secret agreement.

NEPAL

THE RANA REGIME (1846-1951)

Jung Bahadur took the title of **Rana,** and under this name his family would keep its iron hold on Nepal for 105 years, amidst family feuds and nepotism. Jung Bahadur usurped the king, Rajendra, and took total control for himself. Encouraged by a visit to London in 1850 during which he saw the efficacy of Britain's institutions, he instituted a series of reforms. Jung began to thoroughly bureaucratize the Nepalese government—he did away with patronage and kept strict track of spending. In a victory for the common peasants, land tenure was registered, and landlords could no longer arbitrarily evict their tenants. In 1856, Jung Bahadur promoted himself to the title of super-Minister as well as "Maharaja of Kaski and Lamjung," a position which held the power to overrule the king. The title was made hereditary, and the Shah dynasty kings thereafter became mere figureheads.

The Indian **Mutiny of 1857** provided an opportunity for Nepal to flex its muscles and win British support. Jung Bahadur sent 10,000 men to aid the British, and, in return, the British gave back the Terai lands they had taken in 1816. The British gave Nepal "guidance" on its foreign policy, but Nepal remained independent, scoffing at British demands for trading rights and limiting Gorkha recruitment. The Rana prime ministers, however, were as interested in advancing their family fortunes as they were in helping the country. Jung Bahadur Rana ruled Nepal until his death in 1877, and his successors turned out to be just as venal but less competent. In the late 19th century, halfhearted public works projects were undertaken, in an effort to impress the British.

Chandra Shamsher Rana, who ruled from 1901-29, was a better administrator than the other Ranas, but his motivation—whether one of social conscience or egotism—remains a controversial point. He began his reign by building the enormous Singha Durbar palace for himself, consuming all of the national public works budget for the first three years of his rule. During WWI, Chandra Shamsher started implementing changes in order to appease the 100,000 Nepalese Gorkha soldiers who had gone to fight overseas or in India and returned with new ideas from around the world. The introduction of a mechanized system of transportation and a slate of social reforms, such as the banning of slavery and *sati*, were among the first of the changes. Soon after, Nepal's first college, Tri Chandra College, was founded, and tenant farmers were made the owners of the lands they had rented for centuries. The Treaty of Friendship with Britain formally recognized Nepal's independence in 1923. However, fewer trade restrictions made Nepal more economically dependent on imported British and Japanese goods. Prime Minister Judha Shamsher Rana (r.1932-45) returned Nepal to military rule, and dissatisfaction became rampant.

Indian Independence in 1947 gave Nepal a new neighbor to deal with, and Prime Minister Jawaharlal Nehru disapproved of the Rana regime. In 1947 the **Nepali Congress** was formed in the tradition of the Congress that had led India to freedom. Unable to deal with these forces, some Rana family members who favored democratization went to India and joined the growing anti-Rana resistance. The turning point came in 1950 when **King Tribhuvan,** a palace figurehead since 1911, also fled to India. By this time, he had captured popular support. The king, the prime minister, and Congress leaders met in Delhi, where Nehru engineered the **Delhi Compromise of 1951,** effectively ending the Rana regime. The king would now preside over a government of Ranas as well as popularly elected leaders.

NEPAL AFTER THE RANAS (1951-1990)

After the Rana defeat, Nepal's foreign policies underwent a dramatic change for the better. The Delhi Compromise was replaced in 1959 by a new constitution which called for a democratically elected assembly. The Nepali Congress won a large majority in the elections, and its leader, **B.P. Koirala,** became prime minister. But this state of affairs was fragile. King Tribhuvan had died in 1955, and his son **Mahendra,** who succeeded him, was less enthusiastic about political reforms, believing Nepal wasn't developed enough to handle them. He dismissed the Congress government almost as soon as it took power and threw its leaders in jail. In

962 a new constitution replaced the national assembly with a system of *pan-
hayats* (village councils) to elect members to district councils, which, in turn,
ected a National Panchayat. Political parties were banned, and the new system,
upposedly a democracy custom suited to Nepalese traditions, was effectively a
eturn to absolute monarchy. Mahendra opened Nepal to foreign aid and started
e controversial process of development that is transforming Nepal today.

King Birendra, who came to power in 1972 (although for astrological reasons he
asn't crowned until 1975) fully supported the *panchayat* system. Early in his
areer Birendra declared Nepal a "Zone of Peace" (a declaration of neutrality
hich angered India) and tightened visa restrictions for foreigners. The *pan-
hayat* system was highly contested, however, and resistance came to a head in
979 with riots in Kathmandu and Patan. In response, Birendra called for a
ational referendum between *panchayats* and multiparty democracy. The *pan-
hayats* won by the narrow margin of 10 percent, and monarchy hung on for ten
ore years, assisted by censorship and police brutality.

EMOCRACY RESTORED (1991-PRESENT)

nspired by the previous years' revolutions in Eastern Europe and provoked by an
conomic blockade by India, the outlawed opposition parties banded together in
990, and protests for democracy filled the streets of Kathmandu. When King
irendra realized that mass arrests would not quell the uprising, he gave in and
fted the ban on political parties on April 8. A week later the major parties formed
n interim government and wrote a new constitution. A parliamentary system of
emocracy came into effect, and Birendra became a constitutional monarch.

The May 1991 elections gave a majority to the Nepali Congress, which had led the
emocracy movement. The **Communist Party of Nepal–United Marxist-Leninist (CPN-UML)**
ecame the main opposition. The prime minister was now **G.P. Koirala,** the brother of
e late B.P. Koirala. Although G.P. Koirala's government stabilized Nepal's democ-
cy, most people were disappointed by his leadership. Rising inflation caused general
scontent, and an agreement with India over the Mahakali Dam project on Nepal's
estern frontier brought accusations of selling out to India. Unimaginative and stub-
orn, Koirala alienated much of his own party, and he was forced to resign in 1994.

The ensuing elections brought the Communists to power in a minority govern-
ent. Prime Minister **Man Mohan Adhikari** quickly launched a series of populist
chemes, including the "build-your-own-village" program, which gave large cash
rants to local governments. Adhikary then resigned, hoping to improve his gov-
rnment's standing through another election. While the king approved Adhikari's
ll for elections, the Supreme Court ruled against this manoeuver in 1995. No
ections were held, and the Congress party took power by allying itself with the
ght-wing **National Democratic Party (NDP).**

New Congress Prime Minister **Sher Bahadur Deuba's** efforts to bolster ties with the
DP were waylaid by intra-party dissentions, and a March 1997 no-confidence motion
efeated the party. The breakaway NDP faction led by **Lokendra Bahadur Chand** formed
coalition government with the CPN-UML, pushing Nepal into a new era of instability.
lthough democracy appears fairly well-established, several years of little or no sub-
antial legislation has resulted in the *panchayat* system. In 1998, Guerillas from the
ommunist Party of Nepal-Maoist turned violent, slaying some non-governmental
rganization (NGO) employees, alleging that they mishandled funds. The assassina-
on of an opposition party parliamentarian brought on strikes and widespread unrest.

HIS YEAR'S NEWS

fter former Prime Minister **Girija Prasad Koirala's** denied appeal for fresh elections
December, the King finally dissolved parliament in January, calling for elections
pon the request of the CPN-UML coalition. In April 1999, former prime minister
nd Nepali communist leader Man Mohan Adhikary died at the age of 78. In the
ouse of Representative elections of May 1999, the Nepali Congress won 110 seats
the Communist Party's 68. The Congress Party candidate in the Kathmandu dis-

CLIMB (ALMOST) EVERY MOUNTAIN

Since large-scale mountaineering began in the Himalayas in the 1950s, many climbers have come close enough to see the summits and returned to the bottom without actually standing on top, in deference to the deities and sacred powers that dwell there. The mythical Mt. Meru is believed by Hindus to be the center of the universe and the axis of all power. Mt. Kailash in Tibet is considered Shiva's stomping ground, and the Gauri-Shankar and Annapurna mountains in Nepal are both named after gods. Most of the Himalayan peaks, including those with more mundane names—such as Macchapuchare, which means "fish tail," and Kanchenjunga, which means "five treasures"—are considered sacred. In fact, the Himalayan range itself is said to be the father of Shiva's consort, Parvati. Soaring to heights of over 8000 meters, the Nepalese Himalayas contain eight of the world's top ten highest peaks. It's not difficult to understand how they came to be seen as the abode of the gods.

trict **Krishna Prasad Bhattarai** is the current prime minister. Maoist insurgence that was threatened all throughout the elections increased after polling, and by June the Maoist rebels were responsible for more than 20 deaths in their protest to se up a communist "people's party" government. Nepal and neighboring Bhutan hav come into conflict over the latter's effectively exiling 100,000 Nepalese-speakin Bhutanese by tightening citizenship requirements. The displaced people are cur rently living in refugee camps in southeastern Nepal. Bhutan maintains that the exiles are mostly Nepalese who emigrated illegally to Bhutan for its greater pros perity. Multiple rounds of negotiations have failed to resolve the repatriation dis pute, and India has declined Nepal's request to intervene.

RELIGION

Nepal's religious diversity reflects its position at the cultural crossroads betwee India and Tibet. Nepal is 89.5% Hindu, 5.3% Buddhist, 2.7% Muslim, and 0.24% Christian, Jain, and others. However, strict divisions do not belie the syncretism which characterizes the nation's faith—although theirs is the only country in th world with Hinduism as its state religion, most Nepalis follow some combinatio of Hinduism and Buddhism, with plenty of local traditions thrown in for good mea sure. Asked if they are Hindu or Buddhist, many Nepalis will say they don't know or that they're "both." The fact that the Nepalese can at once follow a religion of 3 million gods and a religion that originally recognized no gods at all baffles man visitors, but it seems to work nonetheless.

In general, the mountainous northern regions of Nepal close to Tibet tend to b Buddhist, while the Terai lands close to India are Hindu. The hilly areas in betwee (including the Kathmandu Valley) have gone the furthest in blending the two.

HINDUISM

Hinduism first came to the Kathmandu Valley and other parts of the Nepalese hill with the Licchavi dynasty during the 4th and 5th centuries AD. Introduced to the hill by conquerors, it has long been Nepal's religion of status—**brahmins** (the priestly caste and **chhetris** (Nepalese *kshatriyas*) traditionally rank at the top of the social hierarchy Various Nepali Hindu legal reforms long ago tried to force the lower-class Buddhist into an occupational caste system; the practice has taken hold socially, although fe Buddhists truly recognize the legitimacy of the caste system.

Shiva is perhaps the most popular Hindu god in Nepal; he is a fitting lord for thi mountainous land, since he began his career as a Himalayan wanderer. He com monly appears in Nepal as Bhairava or "Bhairab," a terrible ghoulish figure wh chases away demons, but he is also referred to as the compassionate Mahadev an worshipped out of love and devotion. In his form as Pashupatinath, the benevolen Lord of Animals, Shiva is Nepal's patron deity, and Nepal is often referred to a

ashupatinath Bhumi (Land of Pashupatinath). The temple of Pashupatinath near
Kathmandu is the most important Hindu site in Nepal (see p. 738).

Vishnu, the cosmic "preserver," is also the object of a large devotional cult. In
Nepal he is often called Narayan, a name which comes from his role in the Hindu
creation myth—he sleeps on the cosmic ocean while the creator god, Brahma,
sprouts from his navel. As in India, goddesses are also worshipped, and Nepal's
grandest festival, Dasain, is held in honor of **Durga.** Nepal also holds a special place
for **Annapurna,** goddess of abundance and distributor of food. The goddesses are
all considered separate individuals but are also seen as consorts of the male deities, embodying the female aspect (*shakti*) of each god. In the Nepalese religious
treatises, the *Tantras*, this *shakti* is considered the most powerful and active
force in the cosmos. (For a more detailed introduction to **Hinduism,** see p. 81.)

BUDDHISM

The Buddha was born around 560 BC, in Lumbini, which is within the borders of
present-day Nepal. Although he left Lumbini and spent most of his time in India,
his doctrines eventually returned to the land of his birth, spreading much further
in the mountains than in the Terai where he was born.

Buddhists in Nepal follow the **Mahayana** (Great Vehicle) school, which differs in
many ways from the **Theravada** (Way of the Elders) school. Mahayana Buddhism
developed as a popular new sect around the first century AD and came to predominate in India, Tibet, China, and other parts of East Asia. The more orthodox Theravada school persisted in Sri Lanka and most of Southeast Asia. While Buddhism
in India was subsumed by Hinduism, a particularly Indian-influenced Mahayana
Buddhism remained in Nepal, where it is still practiced today.

Mahayana Buddhism initially developed after a disagreement over the *vinaya*
(monastic rules) in the Buddhist communities. The Mahayana doctrines de-
emphasized the individual quest for *nirvana* and stressed instead the need for
acquiring compassion for all beings. The Buddha became more than just an
enlightened human being in the Mahayana tradition—he is a cosmic *bodhisattva*
with many incarnations. The concept of a *bodhisattva*, one who vows to put off
his enlightenment for the sake of saving all sentient beings, is very important in the
Mahayana tradition, and a number of *bodhisattvas* are worshipped alongside the
Buddha. (For a more detailed introduction to **Buddhism,** see p. 89.)

TIBETAN BUDDHISM

In Tibet, a unique form of Buddhism developed when the Mahayana and Vajrayana
(Thunderbolt Vehicle) Buddhist traditions blended with the indigenous religion,
Bön. Even though Buddhism was brought to Tibet through Nepal, the tradition
developed in Tibet has had a great influence on Nepal. Due to the Chinese occupation of Tibet, many Tibetan Buddhists have immigrated here, and prayer wheels
and prayer flags blow the mantra *Om Mani Padme Hum* ("Hail to the jewel in
the lotus") all across Nepal's mountains and hills. The beliefs of Tibetan Buddhism are not very different from those of Mahayana Buddhism, though different
rituals and imagery are used. The Buddha is divided into five "aspects," reflected
in each of the five elements (earth, water, air, fire, and space). Tibetan Buddhism
is also noted for its monastic tradition—it is estimated that before the Chinese
invasion, 25% of Tibetans belonged to a religious order. Of the 6000 Tibetan monasteries that were in existence at the time of the original occupation, only about
five remain. The rest were destroyed in by the Chinese. **Tibetan monasteries** are
headed by teachers called *lamas*, addressed by the title *rimpoche* (precious one),
who are believed to have cultivated wisdom over many lifetimes, transmitting
their knowledge to each reincarnation. The reincarnated *lama* is identified
through a combination of using astrology, consulting the Tibetan oracle, and having the young candidates identify the former *lama*'s possessions.

THE YOGA OF PLEASURE The system of Tantra, which means "liberation through extension" in Sanskrit, emphasizes five basic truths—the creation of the world, the absorption of the world, the worship of gods, the attainment of desires, and union with the divine. The last of these, the **Yoga Tantra,** has shot into the Western limelight due to its blatant sexuality and obsession with sex as the source of life and release of energy. So popular is this form of yoga that Western websites offering "e-sensuals" are not uncommon. Viewing the body as a temple, Tantra aims to unite the *manas* (the mental energy), *prana* (the breath energy), and *virya* (the sexual energy). This practice of sacred sex is used in conjunction with *yantras* (symbolic images) and *mantras* (Sanskrit chants).

TANTRA

Tantra holds that polar opposites are actually dual manifestations of the same consciousness. Therefore, the true nature of the mind can be realized by transcending opposites. Acts which are typically condemned, such as the eating of meat, fish and parched grain, and the drinking of alcohol are prescribed as means of transcending dualities. The rituals of Tantra also involve the harnessing and release of different energies in the body through sexual intercourse.

There is much that Tantra has in common with the Hindu traditions of *shakti* and yoga. From the 7th through the 9th centuries, Tantra became quite popular throughout India as part of both Hinduism and Buddhism, and while it eventually died out in India, its influence can still be seen in Tibetan Buddhism. Some forms of Tibetan Buddhism can be classified as **Vajrayana** (Thunderbolt Vehicle), a separate sect from the Mahayana and Theravada schools. Vajrayana has inherited much of this symbology from the tradition of Tantra—the major symbols of Vajrayana are the *vajra* or *dorje* (thunderbolt) and the *ghanti* (bell), which represent the male element of compassion and the female element of wisdom respectively. The conscious release of bodily energy, achieved by visualization meditations upon goddess figures, is also prominent. Vajrayana couples the *dhyani* Buddhas and the major *bodhisattvas* with *taras*, female consorts who have much more power and strength. These figures are often depicted engaged in sexual intercourse, symbolic of the reconciliation of dual energies.

INDIGENOUS TRADITIONS

Nepal has its own pantheon of indigenous deities, and most Nepalis worship these local heroes, regardless of the religion they follow. Common in the Kathmandu Valley is the worship of the **Kumari,** a young girl recognized as an incarnation of the Hindu goddess Durga. The living goddess, who is chosen from the community, stays secluded in a palace for her entire childhood until she reaches puberty or sheds blood, at which point she reverts to the status of a mortal. The Newaris also worship **Macchendranath,** the god born of a fish who is identified both with Lokesvara, Shiva's form as "Lord of the World," and the *bodhisattva* of compassion, Avalokitesvara. Macchendranath's towering chariot makes his festivals easy to identify. The Newar craftsmen of the Kathmandu Valley have also turned **Bhima** (or Bhimsen), the hero from *Mahabharata* epic, into their patron deity. Also prominent in the valley is **Manjushri,** the valley's creator god, who is associated with Saraswati, the Hindu goddess of learning. Manjushri used his sword to cut into the valley wall and drain its primordial lake, and he continues to use it to slice through ignorance.

Outside the Kathmandu Valley various ethnic groups preserve many of their local beliefs in spite of the arrival of Buddhism and Hinduism. The local gods are worshipped in return for good harvests and healthy children, and animal sacrifices to the gods are common. Many of Nepal's local religions are led by shamans, who mediate between the human and supernatural worlds.

THE ARTS

In art, as in many things, Nepal has long stood at the confluence of various styles. Absorbing elements of Indian and Tibetan aesthetics as it has, the art of the Newari artisan castes of the Kathmandu Valley has nevertheless managed to take on a unique form of its own. Unfortunately, much of the older works, made of wood and other ephemeral materials, have disappeared. But many of the valley's masterpieces remain in their original settings. Much like in India, Nepalese art has generally been inspired by religion, funded by kings, and executed by anonymous craftsmen.

THE VISUAL ARTS

ARCHITECTURE

The oldest remaining structures in the Kathmandu Valley are **stupas,** sacred mounds of earth layered with centuries of plaster. *Stupas* take the shape of large hemispherical domes and usually mark Buddhist holy places or enclose relics. Nepalese *stupas,* typified by the Kathmandu Valley's gargantuan Boudha Stupa (see p. 747), display distinctive symbols on the square, golden spire at their top; these **chakus** are usually painted with the eyes of the Buddha surveying the four cardinal directions, and a number one (?) to represent universal unity. *Stupas* are often accompanied by **chaityas,** small stone shrines containing written *mantras* or pieces of scripture.

The Kathmandu Valley's greatest architectural achievements, however, are the wood and brick **pagodas** which resemble elaborate *chakus*; it is thought that they may have evolved from this early architectural form. Nepal is considered the birthplace of the pagoda—a 13th-century architect named Arniko is said to have exported the pagoda to Kublai Khan's China, and it was later adopted by the rest of Asia. Most of Nepal's pagodas function as Hindu temples, built around a central sanctum housing the temple's deity. The sanctum is made of brick, with intricately carved wooden doors, window frames, and pillars. The pillars and struts on the outside support the tiered, sloping clay-tile roof. The upper portions of the temple are not separate stories as they appear; they are left deliberately empty, since there is to be nothing above the deity except the roof. The whole structure usually sits on a terraced stone base which resembles a step pyramid.

The Newaris also planned and built **bahals,** blocks of rooms surrounding a rectangular courtyard. These compact community units were used either as monasteries or blocks of houses. *Bahals* are designed to be perfectly symmetrical, and the main doors and windows usually appear along the group's central axis.

Despite their xenophobic foreign policy, the Rana prime ministers, who reigned from 1846 to 1951, embraced a European Neoclassical style of architecture—parts of Kathmandu's Durbar Square seem like they belong in Trafalgar Square. Though the Ranas never popularized this style, their change of taste adversely affected patronage for many of the Kathmandu Valley's traditional crafts. Modern architecture in Nepal is mainly utilitarian, using brick and concrete block.

SCULPTURE

Early sculpture in the Kathmandu Valley was highly influenced by North Indian styles of stone sculpture. Newari artisans of the Licchavi period made devotional images of Vishnu and the Buddha that strongly resembled the work of the Mathura school, although they gave it a distinctly Nepalese flavor. Written accounts indicate that wood sculpture also flourished at this time, but none of it has survived.

Stone sculpture in Nepal reached its zenith in the 7th, 8th, and 9th centuries but virtually disappeared after the 10th century. Metal became the medium of choice for medieval Nepalese sculpture under the influence of eastern and southern India. In the 7th and 18th centuries, Nepalese sculpture became highly influenced by Tibet. Newari artisans made bronze images of Tantric aspects of the Buddha which were exported to

Tibetan monasteries. Many bronze sculptures usually identified as "Tibetan" were actually made in Nepal. Nepalese artists of the Malla period also created fantastic wood sculptures as architectural ornaments. Temple roof struts and window grilles were made of wood that was ornately carved with plant and animal forms.

In the last two centuries, the crafts of bronze-casting and wood-carving have declined due to lack of patronage. Foreign-funded restoration projects have recently given sculptors some business, and the demand created by tourism has encouraged the mass production of consumer-oriented crafts. Although just about anything made in Nepal can be bought in Kathmandu, certain crafts can be found cheaper and in better selection in their places of origin. For woodcarving and pottery, head to Bhaktapur; for papier mache masks and puppets, Thimi; for metalwork, Patan; and for Tibetan crafts like *thankas*, Boudha.

PAINTING

The earliest paintings from the Kathmandu Valley appear on palm leaf manuscripts. A few samples from as far back as the 10th century have survived, but most are badly decayed. More common in Nepal today are Tibetan *thankas* (intricate scroll-paintings of deities) and *mandalas* (meditation aids that represent theological ideas. During the medieval period there emerged a Newari style of *thanka* called a *paubha*, which was painted on coarser cloth and without the landscape background of a traditional Tibetan *thanka*. Later paintings in Nepal were heavily influenced by the detailed miniatures of the Indian Mughal and Rajasthani styles.

MUSIC

Music in Nepal is not simply relegated to professional performances and cultural festivals; it is a part of everyday life. Styles and occasions for performance are as numerous as its ethnic, religious, regional, caste, and tribal identities. The **gaine,** a caste of musician-storytellers, once actively wandered the hills, accompanying themselves on the *sarangi* (a four-stringed fiddle). Music of a traditional *panchai baja* (five-instrument) ensemble is often played for weddings, processions, and temple rituals. Though the women of Indo-Nepalese castes are usually excluded from music-making, they are permitted to sing in public during rice-transplanting and at the *teej*, an annual women's festival.

Several traditional styles of hill music still exist. Most popular is the *maadal*-based (double-sided drum held horizontally) *jhyaure* music of the western hills. The Jyapu farming caste developed an upbeat rhythmic style involving many percussion instruments, including the *dhime* (a large two-sided drum) and the use of woodwinds to accompany nasal singing. The *selo* style, developed by the Tamangs but shared by others, keeps rhythm with the *damphu* (a flat one-sided drum).

Music is vital to many occasions within Hindu and Buddhist rituals. In traditional Newari communities, most young men complete a musical apprenticeship which enables them to participate in festival processions. Newari Buddhist priests chant ancient Tantric verses as part of meditation exercises, and, on sacred occasions, ritual dancing accompanies such hymns. The music of the Sherpas derives much of its character from the ancient rituals of Tibetan Buddhism.

The continued presence and influence of Indian classical music in Nepal harkens back to the days when it was the rage in the courts of Malla kings. The Rana prime ministers were such fervent patrons of Indian classical musicians that they banned Nepalese folk performers from their courts.

DANCE

Nepalese dance, be it folk or classical, usually concerns the dramatic retelling of sacred Buddhist and Hindu stories. The Newaris of the Kathmandu Valley are the chief exponents of **classical dance.** Newari performers enter into a trance to become vessels for the embodiment of gods. Sporting elaborate costumes and ornately painted papier mache masks, they gyrate and gesture with emotion and precision. On the tenth day of

ARE YOU A TEA SNOB? Knowing and distinguishing the different varieties of tea can set your average tea-drinker apart from the connoisseur. In Nepal, the manufacture and consumption of tea has become an art, available to both the masses as well an elite group of tea fans.

The Basics: The two types of black tea grown in Nepal and India are known as **orthodox tea** (or leaf tea), from the Ilam tea estate, and **Cut-Tear-Curl (CTC) tea,** which is grown in the lowlands of the Jhapa district. The strongly flavored and inexpensive **lowland tea** is used in *chiya*, the omnipresent milk tea. The high altitudes ensure slower growth, which limits production but enhances the quality—**highland teas** are hailed as top notch for their lighter orange-colored liquors and delicious aroma.

Manufacture: Green leaves are **withered** for 16 hours to extract moisture. Next, the dried leaves are **rolled** for 45 minutes on a large rolling machine. **Fermentation** follows for a couple of hours as the rolled leaves are laid out on aluminum trays or ceramic tiles. Then the leaves are **dried** at 220°F in a large oven for over 20 minutes. Finally, they are sorted according to grade, and the stalks are removed.

Tea terms: Unscrambling the acronyms of once-British tea industries can be confusing. Strictly speaking, there are four grades of black tea. The first is denoted as **FTG-FOP,** for "Fine Tippy Golden Flowery Orange Pekoe." The second is **TGBOP,** for "Tippy Golden Broken Orange Pekoe." The third and fourth, dust-like teas are used in tea bags for speedier brewing: **GOF,** for "Golden Orange Fannings" and **PD,** for "Pekoe Dust."

the Dasain festival (in Sept. or Oct.), *nawa* Durga dancers of Bhaktapur perform the vigorous dance-drama of the goddess Durga's victory over the buffalo demon.

The pulse of Tibetan Buddhism also engages music, dance, and dramatic forms in festivals, ceremonies, and sacred rites. Performances often involve intricate hand gestures, ritual objects, and the contributions of many unusual and symbolic musical instruments. **Cham** is a dance-drama specific to Tibetans and Bhotiyas in which monks don masks and costumes to enact various Buddhist tales.

THE MEDIA

The Nepalese press is dominated by the Nepali daily, *Gorkha Patra*, and a few English-language **newspapers**—*The Rising Nepal* and the *Kathmandu Post* are both dailies published in English. *The Rising Nepal* is essentially a government mouthpiece that comes out in a Nepali edition as well, but the *Post* is independent and focuses more on business. The monthly magazine *Himal* covers South Asian issues intelligently and thoroughly. The *International Herald-Tribune*, *Time*, and *Newsweek* are widely available in English-language bookshops in Kathmandu, as are several Indian papers.

Nepal has been infected with the same **satellite TV** craze currently ravaging India. Star TV beams in the BBC and/or CNN, along with rock videos, Hindi films, and American drivel. Nepal has one brand new **radio** station, 100 FM, which broadcasts mostly English (classic and modern rock) and a little Nepalese and Hindi music from 7am to midnight.

FOOD AND DRINK

Dal bhat tarkari (lentils, rice, and curried vegetables) is the staple dish for most Nepalis, as it is for people in large parts of North India. Indeed, *bhat*, the word for cooked rice, is often used as a synonym for *khana* (food). Food in Nepal differs little from Indian food, with the exception of some Tibetan dishes which have made their way onto the Nepalese dining table. Ravioli-like **momo** and **thukpa,** a soup made with noodles, are popular dishes. Newari food is based largely on buffalo meat and radishes. **Choyala** is buffalo fried with spices and vegetables.

The most popular breads in Nepal are **chapati,** identical to their Indian counterpart. Nepalis don't really eat breakfast, but it is commonly served in tourist restaurants and hotels. As in India, vegetarians should have no trouble finding delicacies to their taste. Due to Hindu religious beliefs, buffalo meat is commonly served instead of beef.

Milk, or **dudh**, is an important staple of the Nepalese diet that is often served hot, making it safe to drink. **Chiya** (tea) is served hot with milk and lots of sugar. Yogurt (*dahi*) is popular and forms the basis for **lassis**, which are the same as in India, and for the Newari delicacy **juju**, made from yogurt, cardamom, and cinnamon. Most sweets, including **burfi** and **peda**, are milk-based.

Alcohol is consumed in Nepal primarily in the form of beer, which is locally produced and quite tasty (especially when cold), and *chang*, a homemade Himalayan brew. *Raksi* is a stronger version of *chang* that bears a resemblance to tequila in both taste and potency. *Tong-ba* is a Tibetan alcoholic brew that is made from fermented millet and sipped through a straw.

FURTHER SOURCES

GENERAL

Nepal: Profile of a Himalayan Kingdom, by Leo E. Rose and John T. Scholz (1980). Covers the history, politics, culture, and economics of Nepal. Very sensibly written, if somewhat out of date.

Culture Shock! Nepal, by Jon Burbank (1992). A guide to Nepali customs and etiquette especially aimed at those planning to live and work in Nepal. Advice for all sorts of social situations and business hassles.

TRAVEL AND CULTURE

Trekking in the Nepal Himalaya, by Stan Armington (1997). The most comprehensive trekking guidebook available. It includes maps, day-by-day descriptions, and altitude charts for the most popular treks.

Trekking in Nepal, by Stephen Bezrucha (1997). Detailed route descriptions and a comprehensive section on planning and health concerns. Especially rich on historical, cultural, and biological commentary on Nepal's trekking routes.

The Snow Leopard, by Peter Mathiessen (1978). Travelogue interspersed with contemplations of the existential variety. Sold ubiquitously in Nepal, The Snow Leopard sums up a lot of the soul-searching and nature-gazing that draw many to Nepal.

Into Thin Air: A Personal Account of the Mount Everest Disaster, by Jon Krakauer (1998). This first-hand account of the highly publicized May 1996 Everest expeditions, in which 12 lives were tragically lost, presents an intimate and thought-provoking look at the tragedy.

HISTORY AND POLITICS

Nepal: Growth of a Nation, by Ludwig Stiller (1993). An account of the period from the unification of Nepal until 1950. One of the few histories of Nepal that doesn't slobber all over the Shah dynasty.

Politics in Nepal: 1980-1990, by Rishikesh Shah (1990). Once banned by the government, these essays take a look at the country's more recent political history.

RELIGION

Short Description of Gods, Goddesses, and Ritual Objects of Buddhism and Hinduism in Nepal. Published by the Handicraft Association of Nepal, this short but comprehensive book includes illustrations and is a valuable (and portable) reference. Available in Kathmandu bookstores (Rs80-100).

The Festivals of Nepal, by Mary M. Anderson (1988). A month-by-month description of the legends and practices surrounding Nepal's major festivals; you'll be in the right place at the right time.

LITERATURE

Himalayan Voices: An Introduction to Modern Nepali Literature, by Michael Hutt (1991). The best of the limited number of English translations of Nepali poetry and prose.

Nepali Visions, Nepali Dreams: The Poetry of Laxmiprasad Davkota, translated by David Rubin (1980). A good introduction to Nepal's most prominent modern poet.

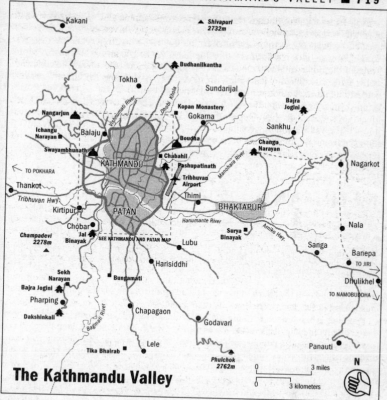

The Kathmandu Valley

THE KATHMANDU VALLEY

He may have been a goofy-looking brute with a staggering case of halitosis, but Prithvi Narayan Shah knew a good thing when he saw it. So enamored was he with the Kathmandu Valley's green and rust-colored slopes, the two-step of light on the rough edges of its terraces, and its aura of sanctity that he bid so long to the fun-loving maidens of Gorkha and lived out of his rucksack for ten long years, channeling his waxing libido into the conquest of the Malla trinity that ruled the region to eventually amass a kingdom of diverse states. Since Shah's choosing Kathmandu to be his capital in 1769, the valley has developed into a landscape of remarkable contrasts—bovines yield to exhaust-belching cars, and concrete structures stretch farther and farther uphill as an increasing number of people seek long-term refuge in the swelling valley, but the area outside the city retains its graceful beauty.

HIGHLIGHTS OF THE KATHMANDU VALLEY

■ Though most cities in Nepal have a **Durbar Square, Patan's** (p. 752), with its temples, palaces, and pavilions, sets the standard by which all others are judged.
■ **Bhaktapur's** cobbled streets and restored temples (p. 748) are a window into valley life before backpackers and brownie sundaes arrived.
■ The great stupa at **Boudha** (p. 746) graces so many postcards for a reason—a visit to the monument provides a glimpse of Tibetan Buddhism in Nepal.

NEPAL

While Nepal's long-termers lament the changes wrought upon their erstwhile Eden-at-1300m, and though many newer visitors will stay only long enough to get a trekking permit, the hills that surround Kathmandu are home to an impressive seven UNESCO World Heritage Sites complemented by the backdrop of green hills and awe-inspiring peaks of the Himalayas. Kathmandu, Patan, and Bhaktapur were once individual city-states vying for control of the valley. Today, each boasts its own Durbar Square filled with brick and wood temples and the unrivaled metalwork of the indigenous Newari people, who are among South Asia's foremost artisans. Between the cities, the red-brick towns set amid lush farmland are surprisingly urban, with tightly packed, multi-storied houses. The valley's hilltops command terrific views and a pollution-free serenity far removed from city commotion only a bus stop away. The Kathmandu Valley is guaranteed to be as captivating for visitors as it was for the pugnacious Gorkha godfather who fell in love with it over two centuries ago.

KATHMANDU काठमाण्डु

Thirty-eight years after Nepal opened its borders to the world, Kathmandu has become a mecca for trekkers, a hippie haven, and a thriving cosmopolitan center. It is home to Newaris, aspiring businessmen, Tibetan refugees, *sadhus*, and several ethnic groups. But defying the frustrations of rapid industrialization, the honking buses, whistling rickshaw-*wallahs*, casinos, and Khukuri shops shout back that this city is *alive*—never mind the World Heritage Sites. Experiencing the city requires a sense of humor and some humility—all the savvy in the world won't prepare you for the pungent smells of incense ash, hash, and trash.

Founded as Manju-Patan around AD 723, Kathmandu was not always the valley's pre-eminent city. In Malla days, when it was also known as Kantipur, Kathmandu stood on par with Patan and Bhaktapur, although it was more successful than the others at controlling trade with Tibet. King Prithvi Narayan Shah made Kathmandu his capital when he unified Nepal in the 18th century, and it has been the hub of the valley ever since. Bursting into the 1990s as the fast-growing capital of a very poor country, present-day Kathmandu bears the scars and trophies of economic growth and rapid Westernization. The trophies include an array of imported goods, arts, and institutions; a plethora of diplomatic missions and foreign aid agencies; and of course, tourists. But in spite of such bounty, and the optimism inspired here by the 1990 movement for democracy, Kathmandu faces many problems. The city suffers from oppressive pollution, resource shortages, and a lack of infrastructure as it despairs under corrupt politicians.

Even so, Kathmandu is a fascinating old city, where pagodas crowd the traffic into narrow cobbled lanes and people gaze from their carved wood balconies at ancient courtyards as neighborhood boys kick soccer balls around dusty stone shrines. As in the other cities of the Kathmandu Valley, myth and history mingle at every corner, in the forms of glazed-over Ganesh shrines and old shops that have sunk into the street as the ground level has risen. However, not everything in Kathmandu is remote or mysterious; much of it is very mundane, and some of it smells very bad. But it's all part of the package—one which is guaranteed to leave jaws gaping, eyes bulging, and neurons stinging. Grin and let it overwhelm you.

⊏ GETTING THERE AND AWAY

INTERNATIONAL AND DOMESTIC FLIGHTS

If you're flying into Kathmandu from the east, try to sit on the right side of the plane to get a good view of the mountains. Flights land at **Tribhuvan International Airport,** 5km east of the center of town. Planes are small, the number of passengers limited, and facilities are so basic that even slightly bad weather invariably delays flights, so bring a book. The cheapest way into town is by **bus;** the stop is right down the hill. Bus #1 goes to Ratna Park (frequent, 30min., Rs5) but may be prohibitively crowded. To get to Thamel from Ratna Park, turn right after exiting the bus park, walk north along Durbar Marg all the way to the end, turn left and walk three blocks. The walk takes 20 minutes without luggage. Alternatively, **pre-paid taxis** (to Thamel, Rs200) can be arranged at a counter just before the exit or at a booth outside.

Visas are issued upon arrival to those with a passport and hard currency (available from the exchange counter). For more information, see **Visas: Nepal**, p. 12. Flying out, there is a **departure tax** of Rs600 to South Asian countries and Rs700 to all others. **RNAC** and **Indian Airlines** fly to **India.** International flights to: **Delhi** (3-4 per day, 1½hr., US$142); **Kolkata** (1 per day, 1hr., US$96); **Mumbai** (W, 2hr., US$257); **Varanasi** (1 per day, 40min., US$71). If you're under 30, you can get a 25% discount on international flight tickets to India purchased in Kathmandu.

Fares on domestic flights are virtually identical across airlines. **RNAC**, Kantipath (tel. 220757 or 214640), at New Rd. Open daily 9:30am-1pm and 2-5pm. **Necon Air**, Khicha Pokhari (tel. 242507, reservations tel. 480565), south of New Rd., offers 25% student discounts on domestic flights; student ID required. Open daily 9am-1:30pm and 2-5pm. To: **Bharatpur** (3-4 per day, 30min., US$40); **Bhadrapur** (W and Sa, 1hr., US$99); **Biratnagar** (10 per day, 1hr., US$77); **Janakpur** (1 per day, 35min., US$55); **Jomsom** (4 per day, 55min., US$101); **Lukla** (1-15 per day in season, 40min., US$83); **Nepalganj** (1 per day, 1½hr., US$99); **Pokhara** (15 per day, 30min., US$61). Mountain-viewing flights from Kathmandu cost US$99.

BUSES

Most buses to destinations outside the Kathmandu Valley leave from **New Bus Park,** Ring Rd., in Gongabu, quite far from central Kathmandu. Almost all city buses make a stop at the New Bus Park. Bus #23 from Ratna Park takes one of the most direct routes; it also stops along Kantipath, north of Rani Pokhari (every 5min. 5am-8pm, 30min., Rs3-6). You can also take a taxi (Rs58 from Thamel, Rs65 from New Rd.). The departure bays are not labeled in English, but the staff of the 24-hour "Police Room" will direct you to the right counter; most of the ticket vendors speak English.

There are no express or deluxe distinctions here, and even tourist buses have been known to pick up locals along the way. Buses that leave after noon are night buses—for these you should book 1-2 days in advance during high season. Unless otherwise noted, prices are for morning/night buses. To: **Bhairawa** (frequent 6am-7pm, 10hr., Rs128/155); **Birganj** (7 per day 6-8pm, 8hr., Rs120/150); **Butwal** (all buses to Bhairawa and Lumbini, 9hr.); **Dharan** (10 per day, 16hr., Rs298); **Hetauda** (direct 7am, others until 12:25pm; 7hr.; Rs100/125) or hop on any bus to Birganj, Dharan, Janakpur, and Kakarbhitta; **Janakpur** (4 per day, 12hr., Rs157/206); **Kakarbhitta** (10 per day 3-5pm, 16hr., Rs337); **Lumbini** (7pm, 11hr.; Rs162); **Pokhara** (every 30min. 6am-4pm, 7hr., Rs93/113); **Narayanghat** (frequent 6:30am-2:10pm, 6hr., Rs80); **Tansen** (5:30pm, 12hr., Rs170); **Tardi Bazaar** for **Sauraha** (frequent 7:45am-1:45pm, 7hr., Rs90).

GOVERNMENT BUSES.
Sajha, the government bus corporation, runs day buses; reserve 2 days in advance. Blue Sajha buses are 5% cheaper and faster than other buses. To: **Birganj** (3 per day, 9hr., Rs114); **Bhairawa** (7, 7:45, and 9am; 9hr.; Rs148); **Hetauda** departing from Tribhuvan Highway Rd. (7am, 6hr., Rs67); **Janakpur** (6:30 and 7am, 9hr., Rs158); **Narayanghat** (5 per day 6:30am-2pm, 5hr., Rs68); **Pokhara** (6:30, 6:45, and 7:30am, 7½hr., Rs93; night bus 7pm, Rs107); **Tansen** (7:30am, 9hr., Rs131).

TOURIST BUSES.
Tourist buses are slightly more expensive minibuses with clear aisles and more comfortable seats. They leave from counter #25 to **Pokhara** (7 per day 7am-2pm, 7hr., Rs119). Tickets for tourist buses to **Chitwan, Pokhara,** and **Nagarkot** can also be booked through travel agencies in Thamel. Fares include a commission, but the stops are much more conveniently located across from the Nepal Grindlay's Bank on Kantipath at the intersection with Tridevi Marg. **Greenline Buses** (tel. 253885 or 257544) leave at 7 and 8am from the corner of Tridevi Marg and Kantipath. Air-conditioned coaches offer service to **Pokhara** (9hr., Rs600) and **Chitwan** (5hr., Rs480), with breakfast included. Tickets should be purchased one day in advance (MC, Visa, AmEx).

NEPAL

Kathmandu and Patan

ACCOMMODATIONS

A Mahendra Youth Hostel
B Mountain View Guest House
C Cafe de Patan

TO BUDHANILKANTHA

Australia
Bangladesh

TO BOUDHA

Gujeshwari

Pashupatinath

Chabahil

BALUWATAR

HARIGAU

MAHARAJGANJ

United States

PANI POKHARI

India

GYANESWAR

Lazimpath

LAZIMPATH

Police
Headquarters

American Center

GYANESWAR

NAXAL

KAMAL
POKHARI

DILLI

Ram Sha

Kamaladi

United Kingdom

Ring Rd

New Kathmandu
Bus Terminal

BALAJU

Lekhnath Marg

Royal
Palace

Tridevi Marg

Durbar
Marg

THAMEL

KATHMANDU

NAYA
BAZAR

SEE CENTRAL
KATHMANDU MAP

Kathmandu
Guest House

CHHETRAPATI

Vishnumati River

Swayambhunath

Ring Rd

Ring

Khola

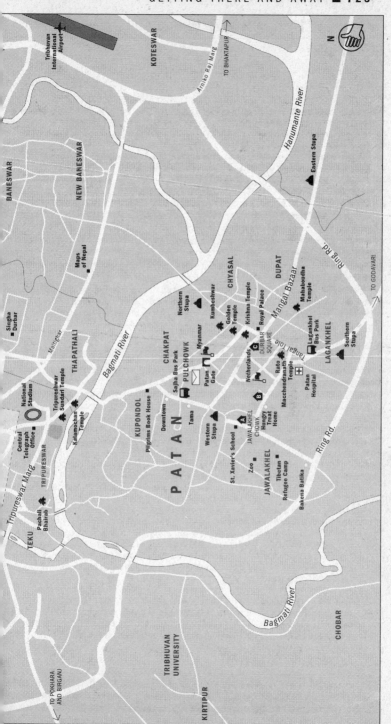

⊟ GETTING AROUND

LOCAL BUSES

By far the cheapest means of getting around the Kathmandu Valley, the bus ensures that you rub shoulders with locals—just when you thought another wailing child couldn't possibly squeeze in, five more people and seven roosters climb on board. Despite their appearance, Kathmandu buses do function; many are now painted with route numbers. **Always confirm that the bus is going to your destination.** The valley bus station is known as **Ratna Park** (named for the park across the street); Nepalis also call it *purano* (old) bus park. Bus #23 leaves from Rani Pokhari. Buses generally leave as soon as they're full.

#	Destination	Length	Cost	#	Destination	Length	Cost
1	Pashupatinath Airport	40min.	Rs4	12	Dhulikhel	2hr.	Rs15
2	Boudhanath	1hr.	Rs6	14	Patan and Jawlakhel	20min.	Rs4
2	Pashupatinath	30min.	Rs4	19	Swayamblau	45min.	Rs4
4	Sankhu	2hr.	Rs10	21	Kirtipur	1hr.	Rs4
5	Budhanilkantha	1hr.	Rs6	22	Dakshinkali	1½hr.	Rs12
7	Bhaktapur	45min.	Rs6	23	New Bus Park	30min.	Rs3
9	Old Thimi	30min.	Rs5	23	Balaju	30min.	Rs3
9	Bahaka Bazaar	1hr.	Rs6	26	Patan	30min.	Rs4

TROLLEYBUSES

Haggard, Chinese-built electric trolleybuses creak between Kathmandu and Bhaktapur (frequent, 45min., Rs5). The first stop is on **Tripureswar Marg,** just south of the National Stadium. Trolleybuses tend to be less crowded than buses, and they are a far more pleasant (and environmentally friendly) ride.

TAXIS AND RICKSHAWS

Shiny new red, green, or yellow **taxis** are all metered, as are the older ones (identifiable by their black license plates). If the driver refuses to use the meter, get out and find another taxi. Rates typically start at Rs5-7. Fares within the city should be less than Rs150; Rani Pokhari to Swayambhu or Pashupathi runs about Rs75; and shorter jaunts like Thamel to New Road will cost around Rs40. An all-day sight-seeing tour around the valley costs about Rs600. Round up to the nearest rupee, but don't tip. At night, rates go up by over 50%, and drivers may be unwilling to go to some destinations. Taxis queue on Tridevi Marg near the entrance to Thamel. If you can persuade the driver to use his outdated meter, **auto-rickshaws** are cheaper than taxis. Aggressive **cycle-rickshaw** drivers drive a hard bargain, charging almost as much as auto-rickshaws. The high seats and smooth pace make them a great way to observe Kathmandu's less polluted back streets, but be aware that rickshaws are not allowed on some major streets (e.g. Durbar Marg).

TEMPOS

Larger, sturdier versions of auto-rickshaws, tempos can be flagged down anywhere along their routes; to request a stop, bang on the metal ceiling. Tempos use the same route numbers as buses but leave from different places. The tempos leave from **Sundhara,** just outside the GPO: #2 to **Boudhanath** via **Pashupatinath** (30min., Rs6). Others depart from just north of **Rani Pokhari:** #5 to **Budhanilkantha** via **Lazimpath** (45min., Rs6) and #23 to **Balaju** (40min., Rs3).

BICYCLES

Bicycles can be rented from numerous shops in Thamel, especially around Thamel Chowk. Mountain bikes (Rs150 per day) are better for trips outside the city; heavier, bell-equipped one-speeders (Rs60 per day) are more suitable for getting around the city.

✵ ORIENTATION

Kathmandu is rather small; neighborhoods, major temples, and main thoroughfares make navigation pretty straightforward. The shrines of **Swayambhunath** and **Pashupatinath** anchor the western and eastern edges of the city. Almost exactly halfway between

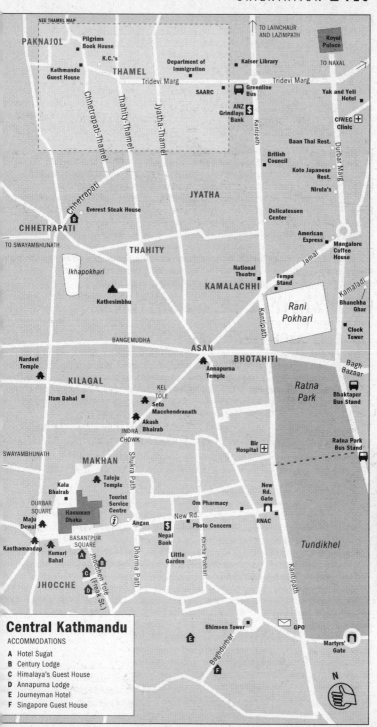

SEE THAMEL MAP

TO LAINCHAUR
AND LAZIMPATH

Royal
Palace

PAKNAJOL

Pilgrims
Book House

K.C.'s

TO NAXAL

Kathmandu
Guest House

THAMEL

Department of
Immigration

Kaiser Library

Tridevi Marg

Tridevi Marg

Chhetrapati-Thamel

Thahity-Thamel

Jyatha-Thamel

SAARC

Greenline
Bus

Yak and Yeti
Hotel

ANZ
Grindlays
Bank

CIWEC
Clinic

Baan Thai Rest.

Durbar Marg

British
Council

Chhetrapati

JYATHA

Koto Japanese
Rest.

Nirula's

CHHETRAPATI

Everest Steak House

Delicatessen
Center

TO SWAYAMBHUNATH

THAHITY

American
Express

Mangalore
Coffee
House

Ikhapokhari

Jamal

Kamaladi

National
Theatre

Bhanchha
Ghar

Kathesimbhu

KAMALACHHI

Tempo
Stand

Rani
Pokhari

Clock
Tower

BANGEMUDHA

ASAN

BHOTAHITI

Kantipath

Bagh
Bazaar

Nardevi
Temple

Annapurna
Temple

Ratna
Park

KILAGAL

KEL
TOLE

Bhaktapur
Bus Stand

Itum Bahal

Seto
Macchendranath

Akash
Bhairab

INDRA
CHOWK

Ratna Park
Bus Stand

SWAYAMBHUNATH

MAKHAN

Shukra Path

Bir
Hospital

Kala
Bhairab

Taleju
Temple

New
Rd.
Gate

DURBAR
SQUARE

Hanuman
Dhoka

Tourist
Service
Centre

Om Pharmacy

Maju
Dewal

Angan

New Rd.

Photo Concern

RNAC

Kasthamandap

Nepal
Bank

BASANTPUR
SQUARE

Kumari
Bahal

A

B

Little
Garden

Tundikhel

Dharma Path

Khicha Pokhari

JHOCCHE

C

D

Jhochen Tole
(Freak St.)

Bhimsen Tower

GPO

E

Kantipath

Martyrs'
Gate

Central Kathmandu

ACCOMMODATIONS

A Hotel Sugat
B Century Lodge
C Himalaya's Guest House
D Annapurna Lodge
E Journeyman Hotel
F Singapore Guest House

Baghdurbar

F

N

them, the two main roads of **Kantipath** and **Durbar Marg,** run parallel to each other, north to south. Kantipath, on the west, is home to the post office and plenty of banks; Durbar Marg, on the east, has its share of airline offices, trekking agencies, luxury hotels, and restaurants, as well as the **Royal Palace** at its north end. Between the two streets farther south is the **Tundikhel** parade ground, around which Kantipath and Durbar Marg become one-way streets.

Kantipath and Durbar Marg divide Kathmandu into two halves—west of Kantipath are the older, more interesting parts of the city, while the area east of Durbar Marg consists mainly of new neighborhoods. The year-round tourist carnival that is **Thamel** is west of Kantipath, at the northwestern end of town. Thamel is joined to Kantipath and Durbar Marg by the wide **Tridevi Marg.** The area just south of Thamel is **Chhetrapati,** centered on a six-way crossing with a bandstand in the middle. Kathmandu's old center, **Durbar Square,** filled with magnificent architecture, is also west of Kantipath, south of Thamel and Chhetrapati, and close to the banks of the **Vishnumati River. New Road,** built in 1934 out of the rubble of a great earthquake, runs east from Durbar Square to Kantipath. New Rd. is the city's top commercial district, with rows of jewelers and electronics sellers. A nameless narrow lane that sprouts northeast from Durbar Square used to be the main trading center. It cuts through **Indra Chowk,** one of Kathmandu's most interesting neighborhoods, and **Asan Tol,** the seething center of Kathmandu's main bazaar.

Tripureswar Marg is the biggest road in the southern half of town, running east-west and leading to the **Patan Bridge.** Kathmandu's twin city, Patan, lies across the **Bagmati River,** the southern limit of Kathmandu. **Ring Road** encircles Kathmandu and Patan, connecting them with the new suburbs that have grown around them.

🔢 PRACTICAL INFORMATION

TOURIST AND FINANCIAL SERVICES

Tourist Office: There are 2 government-run **Tourist Information Centers,** one at Basantapur Sq., New Rd. (tel. 220818) and the other at Tribhuvan Airport (tel. 470537). Both open Su-Th 9am-6pm, F 9am-4pm. During the monsoon season: open Su-F 10am-2pm. **Tourist Service Center** (tel. 256232 or 256230; fax 227281; email tourism@mos.com.np), south of Ratna Bus Park, just east of Durbar Marg. The staff is friendly and speaks English. Open Su-Th 10am-5pm, F 10am-3pm.

Trekking Information: Himalayan Rescue Association (HRA), P.O. Box 4944 (tel. 262746; email hra@aidpost.mos.com.np), Thamel Mall at Jyatha-Thamel. Focuses on mountain safety, providing information on altitude sickness and free safety talks in the spring and fall. Talks Su-F 2pm. HRA also runs 2 clinics in Manang (Annapurna circuit) and Pheriche (Everest trek); they appreciate donations—both medicine and money. **Kathmandu Environmental Education Project (KEEP),** P.O. Box 9178 (tel. 259275; fax 411533; email tour@keep.wlink.com.np), Thamel Mall, in the same building as HRA, has slide show presentations twice a week (Sept.-Nov. and Feb.-Mar. 3pm). Fill out an embassy registration form at one of these offices (or at your embassy) before you go trekking. Both open Su-F 10am-5pm.

Budget Travel: Visit one of the well-established agencies on Durbar Marg: **Annapurna Travels, Everest Express,** or **Yeti Travels.** For bookings on tourist buses to places like Pokhara and Chitwan, most agencies offer comparable prices—check out a few to make sure you're getting the going rate. For plane tickets, go directly to the airline offices, usually located on Kantipath; travel agencies might take a commission on flights (see **Getting There and Away,** p. 720).

Diplomatic Missions: Australia, Bansbari (tel. 371678; fax 371533), on Maharajgunj, just past Ring Rd. Open M-Th 8:30am-5pm, F 8:30am-1:15pm. Consular services 24hr. **Bangladesh,** Maharajgunj (tel. 372843; fax 373265), on Chakrapath near Hotel Karnali. 2 photographs and US$45 in Nepali currency required for U.S. citizens seeking a 15-day tourist/transit visa. Open Su-Th 9am-5pm. Apply for visa Su-Th 9:30-noon and pick it up the next day after 4pm. **Canada,** Lazimpath (tel. 415193), down the lane opposite Navin Books stationery shop. Open M-F 9am-4pm. **China,** Baluwatar (tel. 411740, visa services tel. 419053). Visas Rs2000 for U.S. citizens; bring your passport and 1 photo. Allow 4 days for processing. Visas to **Tibet** available only to organized groups of 5 and can only be obtained through a travel agency; 4 days to process. Open M-F 10am-5pm. Visa dept. open M, W, and F 10am-noon. **India,** Lainchaur (tel. 410900; fax 413132). Walk north up Lazimpath and veer left before Hotel Ambassador. Obtaining a visa can take up to a week. 2 photos required; 3-month Rs1200, 6-month Rs2300; additional Rs1220 for U.S. citizens. Apply for visa M-F 9:30-11am. Transit visas require 1 photo and Rs300; valid for 15 days from date of issue and ready the same day after 4:30pm. Apply at counter A, M-F 9:30am-noon. **Malaysia:** Visas to Malaysia administered through the U.K.'s consular services (tel. 410583). 3-month tourist visa (Rs2400) requires 2 photographs, traveler's checks, plane ticket, and occasionally a hotel reservation slip; processing takes 2 days. **Myanmar** (Burma), Chakupat, Patan (tel. 521788; fax 523402), near Patan Gate. Visas M-F 9:30am-1pm and 2-4:30pm. Visas ready in 1hr.; 3 photos required. Tourist visa US$20. **Pakistan,** Chakrapath (tel. 374024; fax 374012), near the intersection of Ring Rd. and Maharajgunj, northwest quadrant. Passports and 2 photos necessary; Rs3543 for 3-month tourist visa for U.S. citizens. Apply M-F 10-11am and pick up the next day 10am-noon. **Sri Lanka,** Baluwatar (tel. 413623), near the Russian embassy. Visa applications (2 photos required) Su-F 9am-12:30pm. **Thailand,** Bansbari (tel. 371410; fax 371408). Turn east just north of the Australian Embassy. 2 photos required; 1-month tourist visa Rs450, 2-month Rs700. Apply M-F 9:30am-12:30pm; visas ready in 24hr. **U.K.,** Lainchaur (tel. 414588; fax 411789). Open M-F 8:15am-12:30pm and 1:30-5pm. Consular services 9am-noon. **U.S.,** Pani Pokhari, Maharajgunj (tel. 411179; fax 419963). Open M-F 8am-5pm.

Immigration Office: Department of Immigration (tel. 470950 or 494273), north side of Tridevi Marg where it narrows and enters Thamel. **Trekking permits** for Kanchenjunga and Dolpa (US$10 per week for the 1st month, US$20 per week thereafter); Mustang and Upper Dolpa (US$700 for the first 10 days, US$70 per day thereafter); Manaslu (Sept.-Nov. US$90 per week, Dec.-Aug. US$75 per week); Humla (US$90 for the first week, US$15 per day thereafter); all other areas (US$5 per week for the 1st 4 weeks, US$10 per week thereafter). 2 photos and passport required. Apply Su-Th 10am-2pm, pick-up 1-5pm; apply F 10am-noon, pick-up noon-3pm. Payment accepted in rupees only. You can complete the process in 1 day, but at the height of the trekking season, long lines can extend the process to 2 or even 3 days—get there early. The office closes for a couple of days during the Dasain holiday in late-Sept. Permit officials may make a fuss if all the members of the group seeking permits aren't present. Additional fee for treks entering a national park or a conservation area: Rs1000 for conservation areas and Makalu-Baran National Park, Rs650 for other national parks. The **Entry Fee Collection Centre** (tel. 233088, ext. 363), across the street in the basement of the Himalayan Bank Building, to the right, collects entry fees. Open Su-Th 10am-5pm, F 10am-3pm.

Currency Exchange: Nepal Bank Ltd., New Rd. (tel. 221185), offering the lowest commission around for traveler's checks (0.5%); bring your Nepalese visa as well as your passport. Open daily 8am-1pm and 1:30-6pm. **ANZ Grindlays,** Kantipath, just south of Tridevi Marg, gives credit card cash advances and sells MC, Visa, and AmEx traveler's checks. The foreign exchange department, around the back of the building, is open Su-Th 9:45am-3:30pm, F 9:45am-12:45pm. The several official exchange counters around Thamel generally charge 2% commission. **Western Union,** at Annapurna Travel and Tours, Durbar Marg (tel. 222339; fax 222966), on the east side of the street. Money can be wired here within 10min. Open daily 9:30am-8pm. **American Express: Yeti Travels,** Hotel Mayalu, Jamal, P.O. Box 76 (tel. 226172 or 227635; fax 226152 or 226153). Mail and faxes held for traveler's check and card holders. Open Su-Th 10am-1pm and 2-5pm, F 10am-1pm and 2-4:45pm.

LOCAL SERVICES

Luggage Storage: Available at most guest houses for free or a few rupees per day.

Laundry Service: Almost all guest houses have laundry service, but independent establishments often charge less. **The 1 Hour Laundry,** next door to the Khukuri House, has low rates and the quickest service around. Open daily 9am-5pm.

Market: Asan Tol, in front of the Annapurna Temple, has fresh fruits and vegetables **Open Market** (also called Hong Kong Market), south of Ratna bus park down the stairs A large tarpaulin congregation of shoe sellers and "Levi's" hawkers popular with locals Picnic and trekking supplies can be found at the **Best Shopping Centre,** Tridevi Mar (tel. 410986), right where it narrows into Thamel. Open daily 8am-8pm. AmEx.

Library: Kaiser Library, Ministry of Education compound (tel. 411318), on the corner c Tridevi Marg and Kantipath. 35,000-volume, non-circulating library housed in a charm ingly decrepit Rana palace. Open Su-Th 10am-5pm, F 10am-3pm. Closed governmer holidays. **American Center,** Gyaneswar (tel. 415845). Open M-F 11am-6pm.

Bookstore: Pilgrims Book House, Thamel (tel. 424942; fax 424943; www.gfas.com/pi grims), houses a big selection of used books. Open daily 8am-10pm.

EMERGENCY AND COMMUNICATIONS

Pharmacy: Om Pharmacy, New Rd. (tel. 244658), across from RNAC, is recommended b local medical experts, but it might be difficult to find an English speaker there. Ope daily 8am-9pm. Several pharmacies are across from Bir Hospital.

Hospital/Medical Services: Kathmandu has numerous reliable **clinics** geared towar Westerners. In case of illness, visit one of these first. If you are too ill to go to a clini ask your guest house to arrange a house call. If you need more care than the clinic phy sician can provide, you'll be sent to the appropriate hospital. **CIWEC Clinic** (te 228531 or 241732), off Durbar Marg, behind the Yak and Yeti sign, to the right. Staffe by Western doctors. US$50 per consultation. Open M-F 9am-noon and 1-3:30pm. Ope Sa-Su for emergencies and vaccinations. Emergency call 24hr. MC, Visa, Amex. **Nepa International Clinic** (tel. 412842), across from the Royal Palace, 3min. east of th main gates, down a lane to the right. Western-educated Nepalese doctors. Consultatio US$40. Open Su-F 9:30am-1pm and 2-5pm, Sa 3-5pm. On-call 24hr. for emergencie MC, Visa, Amex. **Himalayan Internal Clinic,** Jyatha-Thamel (tel. 225455; fax 226980 Western-educated doctors. Consultation US$20 (US$40 housecall), follow-up US$1(Discounts available for students with financial need. Open Su-F 9am-5pm, Sa 9an 1pm. **Patan Hospital,** Lagankhel, Patan (tel. 522295), has a better reputation than th government hospital in Kathmandu proper, **Bir Hospital.**

Police: (tel. 100 or 226999). **Tourist Police,** Basantapur Tourist Information Center (te 220818), handle petty thefts and rip-offs and speak English. Contact the city police fc more serious issues.

Emergency: Fire, tel. 101. **Ambulance,** tel. 228094 (Red Cross). No English spoken any of these numbers. **CIWEC** (tel. 228531 or 241732) has 24hr. emergency service

Post Office: GPO, near Bhimsen Tower, entrance just off Kantipath. Self-service *Post Restante* is behind the counter on the left. Open Su-Th 10:30am-4pm (winter 10:30ar 3pm), F 10:30am-2pm. Stamps sold and cancelled Su-F 7am-6pm, Sa 11am-3pn Mail letters at stamp cancellation window #1. **Express Mail Service (EMS),** at the GP(delivers within 3 days to Australia, New Zealand, Canada, Denmark, Italy, Germany, an the United States, as well as to most Asian countries. Open Su-Th 10am-5pm, F 10an 3pm. The entrance to the **Foreign Parcel Office** is around the corner on Kantipath. Brin your open parcel to be checked by customs. Open Su-Th 10:15am-1:30pm. **FedE UPS,** and **Airborne Express** offer services in Thamel.

Internet: Easy Link Cybercafe (tel. 425933; email easylink@visitnepal.com), 2 block north of Tridevi Marg on Thahiti-Thamel.

Telephones: Central Telegraph Office, on Kantipath, west of the National Stadium, ha the best international rates and free callbacks. Open 24hr. Most have the same rate on outgoing calls but have different deals on callbacks—shop around. **Global Commur cations,** Tridevi Marg (tel. 228143; fax 220143; email glocom@mos.com.np), in th shopping center across from Immigration, also offers good rates and charges a fl Rs25 for callbacks; local calls Rs4 per 3min.; email Rs10 per Kb; web access Rs7 p min. Open Su-F 8am-8pm, Sa 11am-5pm. The **GPO** (fax 225145) has great fax rate (Rs10 per page). Open Su-Th 10am-5pm, F 10am-3pm. **Directory Assistance:** 197.

PHONE CODE	01

⌐ ACCOMMODATIONS

increased competition in Thamel has led to a general standardization of prices for similar accommodations. While this means there are fewer "finds," it by no means spells the death of budget travel. The prices listed are for high season and do not include the 0% government tax, but these are usually negotiable, depending on the season and the length of your stay. Ask for **student discounts;** many establishments will at least discount the 10% tax. As in India, **beware of touts:** don't let anyone lead you to his "friend's hotel;" is commission will appear on your bill.

Freak Street is Kathmandu's original tourist district. Having hit its peak back in the 0s, Freak Street is cheaper, less hectic, and less populated than Thamel; most of its otels have been around for the last 25 years, growing musty as lodges in Thamel real all their business. **Sundhara** is popular with Indian tourists; its ccommodations—cheap, unassuming, and conveniently located just south of New d.—are not quite the bargains found in Thamel, but they are wise selections if you ant to "find" the city before it finds you. The places below, unless otherwise noted, ave hot water, seat toilets, laundry service, luggage storage, and a noon check-out, it no towels or toilet paper.

HAMEL

Kathmandu Guest House (tel. 413632 or 418733; fax 417133; email kgh@thamel.mos.com.mp). All directions in Thamel are given in relation to this place, so you'd better figure out where Kathmandu's original "budget hotel" is. The singles in the old wing have best access to the guest house's communication center, swank lobby with satellite TV, ticket booking, bike rental, and barber shop. Old wing: Singles with sink US$6-8, with bath US$10; doubles US$8-10/12. New wing: Singles US$17-25; doubles US$20-30; triples US$25-35. 10% discount for stays of over a week, 30% for over a month. Visa, MC, AmEx. Reserve ahead Sept.-Nov. and Feb.-Apr.

Hotel Potala (tel. 419159; fax 416680), across from K.C.'s, at the center of Thamel. Clean showers and toilets on each floor. Well-ventilated rooms allow for easy eavesdropping, whether you like it or not. Clean rooms (some with fans) have shared balconies that create a nice neighborhood feel. Plants on the roof terrace and in the lobby. Singles Rs125; doubles Rs175-250.

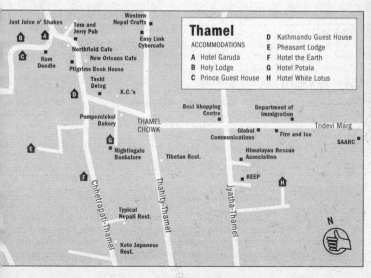

NEPAL

Hotel The Earth, Chhetrapati-Thamel (tel. 260039 or 260312). South of Kathmandu Guest House on the west side of the street. Large, clean, and generously furnished rooms with YMCA-style setup, offering Western amenities at economy prices. Discount for students, volunteers, and long-term guests. Singles Rs150, with bath Rs400; doubles Rs250/RS650.

Holy Lodge, Satghumti (tel. 416265 or 413441), north of Kathmandu Guest House—turn left at the intersection. Spotless rooms off a quiet courtyard with phones and fans. Singles US$4, with bath US$7; doubles US$12; triples with bath US$15.

Hotel Garuda (tel. 416340 or 414766; fax 413614), just around the curve north of the Kathmandu Guest House. Elaborate facilities and 5-star service at really low prices. It also boasts one of the few "rooftop gardens" in Thamel that is actually a garden. Free 24hr. callbacks. All rooms have carpets and attached baths with towels and toilet paper. 25% student discount. Singles US$9-25; doubles US$13-25. MC, Visa, AmEx.

Prince Guest House, Satghumti-Thamel (tel. 414456; fax 220143), across from Holy Lodge. The Artist Formerly Known As would die for this pink 'n' purple decor with wall-to-wall carpeting. Brand-new, spotless rooms with fans, phones, and attached baths complete with seat toilets and shower curtains. Rooftop garden and restaurant. Staff is very friendly and helpful. Singles US$5; doubles US$10.

Hotel White Lotus, Jyatha Thamel (tel. 249842; fax 220143). Sits beside the parking lot just south of Tridevi Marg, opposite the immigration office. Rooms vary in amenities and price, but all are clean. A dizzying spiral staircase leads to the roof garden; every floor has a balcony with rattan furniture. Towels, ISD phones, safe deposit available. Singles US$3-4, with bath US$10; doubles US$6-8, with bath US$14; triples US$8, with bath US$17. 20% student discount in season.

Pheasant Lodge, (tel. 417415), down a short alleyway off Chhetrapati-Thamel just south of Pub Maya. Cheap and smack dab in the middle of things. Basic rooms from the folks who brought you the Restaurant at the End of the Universe (see p. 757). Bamboo walls, clean sheets, and a choice of common toilets—squat or sit as you please. The hotel is often full—try right at the noon check-out time. Singles Rs100; doubles Rs150.

FREAK STREET

Hotel Sugat (tel. 246454; fax 221824), along the southern edge of Basantapur Sq. (facing the royal palace). A few wrinkles suggest that this place eroded slightly during Freak Street's turbulent adolescence, but its location, prices, and mellow demeanor more than compensate for a lack of dazzle. Large, carpeted rooms overlook Durbar Sq.; some have tubs and balconies. Fans, toilet paper, towels provided. Singles Rs150, with bath Rs300; doubles Rs300/350-400. Long-term, off-season, and student discounts.

Annapurna Lodge (tel. 247684), on the right as you walk from Durbar Sq. Angled stairway leads to quiet, basic rooms off a balcony. Seat toilets in attached baths; squat and seat toilets in common bath. Attached restaurant shows movies. Singles Rs175, with bath Rs250; doubles Rs225/300.

Himalaya's Guest House, Basantapur, Jhochhen (tel. 246555). From Durbar Square, head down a quiet lane filled with butcher shops on the right off of Freak St. Rooms are bright and clean, with fans and free international callbacks. Singles Rs150; doubles Rs250, with bath Rs300. TV Rs30 extra. Long-term discounts.

Century Lodge, Freak St., near Basantapur Sq. Diminutive quarters give the place an *Alice in Wonderland* feel. Well-worn rooms are furnished conventionally with squat toilets on each floor. Two hot showers on ground floor courtyard. Singles Rs85; doubles with bath Rs250, with private garden balcony Rs275; quads Rs300.

SUNDHARA

Journeyman Hotel, Ganabahal, Pipalbot (tel. 253438; fax 22644), along the paved road leading southwest from Bhimsen Tower; continue west past the pipal tree and it's on your right. Large, carpeted rooms with phones and fans are old but well-maintained. Friendly, accommodating management. Attached restaurant. Singles Rs150, with bath Rs250; doubles Rs250/350. TV Rs100 extra. Student and long-term group discounts.

Singapore Guest House, Baghdurbar (tel. 244105), south of Bhimsen Tower, towards the end of the street on the left. Large, quiet rooms with carpets, fans, and attached bath. Attached restaurant. Singles Rs225; doubles Rs250; triple Rs450. Visa, MC.

⬡ FOOD

Kathmandu has achieved mythic status as an oasis of displaced delicacies, from the 1954 founding of Kathmandu's first luxury hotel by a charismatic Russian entrepreneur who had chandeliers and fresh fish carried in by porters, to the advent of "Pie Alley," where 1960s overlanders gathered for apple pie and hash brownies. Today, mostly Western favorites are de rigueur on tourist menus; much of this fare tastes blandly similar, borrowing most of its flavor from the *ghee* in which it was baptized. The Japanese, Thai, Tibetan, and Indian restaurants that elbow for room in neighborhoods frequented by foreigners and wealthy Nepalis generally offer more appetizing and less contrived fare. Try out the set Nepali meals offered at many restaurants or, for the most authentic experience possible, get yourself invited to someone's home for a meal.

THAMEL

Typical Nepali Restaurant, Chhetrapati-Thamel, south of Kathmandu Guest House down an alley on the left. Singing servers persistently refill clay bowls of *raksi* (rice wine), while live Nepali music plays in the background. Complimentary bananas and popcorn provided to accompany all-you-can eat regional plates (Rs80-130), including *dal bhat taraari, roti, momos,* and *achaar.* Open daily 8:30am-10pm. MC, Visa, Amex.

Tibetan Restaurant, Thahiti-Thamel, 1st fl. next to the sandwich shop with the Hebrew lettering, serves Chinese and Tibetan dishes (Rs13-35). Open daily 9am-9:30pm.

Fire and Ice, in the shopping center on Tridevi Marg across from the Immigration Office. Wafting pizzeria smells will lure you in, and the opera music and yummy food will keep you (and plenty of other tourists) there. Fantastic pizza (Rs160-270), minestrone soup (Rs110), salad, delicate crepes (Rs65-110), and imported soft-serve ice cream (Rs50-90) provide a taste of Naples in Nepal. Wine Rs160 per glass. Open daily 11am-11pm.

Pumpernickel Bakery, across from K.C.'s. A Thamel institution. At breakfast time, the line to order freshly baked croissants, cakes, and cinnamon rolls (Rs8-25) spills onto the street. The pleasant garden patio and wicker furniture in the back make it a nice place to linger and watch the tourists. Open daily 8am-6pm.

Just Juice 'n' Shakes, down a lane to the right, just past Redrock Restaurant, north of Kathmandu Guest House. Friendly place has gained quite a reputation for their thick, frozen smoothies and shakes (Rs50-80), hot espresso (Rs50), cappuccino (Rs50), and yummy cakes (Rs30). Check out the amusing visitors log. Open daily 6am-midnight.

Koto Japanese Restaurant, Chhetrapati-Thamel, next to Greenleaves Restaurant, near the Chhetrapati intersection (with another branch in Durbar Marg). Impeccable service compliments the austere simplicity of the bamboo furnishings. Refills and *yakis* will enliven the pizza-weary. Noodles, soups, meat, fish, and Japanese curries (Rs150-350). Open daily 11am-9pm. 10% tax.

New Orleans Cafe, just north of the Kathmandu Guest House. Deliver yourself to the bayou in the bustling but low-key candle-lit patio as you enjoy jambalaya, creole chicken, and other delicacies. Veg. dishes Rs80-165, non-veg. Rs80-250. Live jazz on the outdoor patio Sa 6-9pm. Open daily 6:30am-midnight.

The Northfield Cafe, a few doors north of Pilgrims Book House. This offspring of the legendary Mike's Breakfast is a great place for homesick gringos to down chips and salsa (Rs90) and gnaw on spicy chicken wings (Rs100). After appetizers and huge burritos (Rs110–125), quesadillas (Rs120), and meat dishes (up to Rs205), the blaring classical, jazz, and blues will likely entice you to stay for dessert (brownie sundaes Rs100). The breakfast menu is one of the best around. Open daily 7:30am-11pm

K.C.'s, Tridevi Marg, across the street from the Maya Cocktail Bar. The 3rd. floor terrace is especially lovely in the candle-lit evening. Veg. rice, pasta, and meat dishes Rs65-250. Open daily 7am-10pm. MC.

Delicatessen Center, Kantipath, stocks an awesome variety of imported cheeses and meats, sold by the ounce. The bakery produces an equally impressive array of breads and pastries. Hot dishes include goulash (Rs95), onion rings (Rs35), and fish'n'chips (Rs120). Open daily 9am-9pm.

DURBAR MARG

Mangalore Coffee House, Jamal Tol, just off Durbar Marg above American Express. South Indian cheap eats: *masala dosa* (Rs30) and *thalis* (Rs80). *Momos* and chow mein (Rs25-65) available too. Open daily 11am-9pm.

Bhanchha Ghar, Kamaladi. From Durbar Marg, turn left at the clock tower; it's on the right. The name is Nepali for "kitchen," but there's no *dal bhat* in this elegant restaurant—this is Nepalese *haute cuisine*. Specialties (Rs140-200) include wild boar and curried high-altitude mushrooms. The enormous set menu is pricey (Rs640), but it includes a cultural show at night. Open daily noon-10pm. MC, Visa, Amex. 10% tax.

Baan Thai Restaurant. Authentic Thai food in a swank, A/C setting. Watch Durbar Marg through lace curtains while you enjoy *pad thai* (Rs130-150) and seafood (Rs325-395). Open daily noon-3pm and 6-9:30pm. Visa, MC.

NEW ROAD

Little Garden, Khicha Pokhari. From New Rd., walk south down Kicha Pokhari; the restaurant is down the second lane to the right, behind the Little Home Supermarket. Ample portions of cheap and tasty standbys: *momos, thukpa, pakauda,* and chow mein (Rs25-50); burger and fries (Rs35-55). Open daily 8:30am-8:30pm.

Angan Sweet Namkeens and Vegetarian Fast Food, at the intersection of New Rd. and Dharma Path. Serves ice cream (Rs20-45), Indian sweets, *dosas* (Rs25-50), and other veg. treats (Rs12-50) to Nepalis on the go. Pay in front and shoulder your way into the back room to find a table. Free mineral water. Open daily 8:30am-9pm.

▣ ▨ ENTERTAINMENT AND NIGHTLIFE

Hotel de l'Annapurna, Durbar Marg (tel. 228787), has dance shows (daily 7pm, Rs250). **Himachali Cultural Group,** Durbar Marg (tel. 415280), also has shows daily; call for reservations (6:30pm, Rs300). At least half a dozen restaurants—among them **Lotus Restaurant, Margarita Restaurant, Everest Steakhouse,** and **Paradise Pizzeria**—keep Video Nights in Kathmandu, showing videos of recent releases.

When it comes to nightlife in Nepal, Kathmandu is where it's at—options include bars that close by midnight, several casinos, and a few nightclubs. Kathmandu now boasts the only four casinos on the subcontinent. **Casino Royal** is at the Yak & Yeti, **Casino Everest** is at Hotel Everest, **Casino Anna** is at the Hotel de l'Annapurna, and the **Royal Nepal Casino** is at the Soaltee Holiday Inn. All but the Casino Royal are open 24 hours. In addition to the following pubs and discos, check out the **New Orleans Cafe** (see p. 731).

Maya Cocktail Bar and **Maya Pub,** Thamel. The cocktail bar is upstairs from the Pumpernickel Bakery; the pub is at the intersection. Both offer free popcorn, pop music, and 2-for-1 cocktails 4-7pm. The dark, eccentrically decorated pub is strange enough to be interesting; the cocktail bar is bigger and more swingin'. Both open daily 3pm-midnight.

The Tunnel Club, Thamel; follow the sign across from K.C.'s. This back-alley, all-night bar/pool hall is popular with night-owl Westerners and expats. On Friday nights local bands play American rock hits until late at night—a must see event. Pool and snooker tables Rs100 per 30min. Open (like its says) "Dusk 'til Dawn."

The Rum Doodle 40,000½-Feet Bar and Restaurant (tel. 414336), Thamel. Follow the turn in the road north of the Kathmandu Guest House; it's on the left. The bar's namesake is a 1956 literary spoof about a mountaineering expedition; the book is sold at the bar. Exotic cocktails and beer (Rs140). Open daily 10am-11pm. MC, Visa.

Club Dynasty, halfway down Durbar Marg on the right. By far the most popular nightclub among local Nepalis. DJs really spin a mix, blending hip hop with old rock for a unique

NEPAL

sonic experience. The bar serves a range of Western drinks found no where else in Nepal and the crowd is super-friendly. Cover: men Rs400, women Rs200.

Jolly Blues, Thamel, across from Global Communications. Caters to the tourist crowd with a no-cover-for-tourists policy and a distinctly Western setup with multi-tier dance floors, bouncers, and a hi-tech lighting system. Hoppin' during the high months.

◉ SIGHTS

There are so many temples in Kathmandu that the word "templescape" has been coined to describe the city's skyline. The city's main attractions lie in **Durbar Square, Indra Chowk,** and **Asan Tol.** The best way to tour Kathmandu is on foot.

DURBAR SQUARE

Durbar (Palace) Square is the heart of the old city. The royal family is gone from the palace here, having moved late last century to the north end of town, but that hasn't diminished Durbar Square's religious, social, or commercial importance. Many of Kathmandu's most interesting temples and historic buildings are located here, and the wide open space is infused with a bustling energy.

HANUMAN DHOKA DURBAR. The old royal palace takes its name from the statue of Hanuman guarding the entrance—the monkey-god lounges under a parasol, his face disfigured by all the *sindur* rubbed on it. Although the palace has been uninhabited for over a century, it is still used for royal ceremonies including King Birendra's coronation in 1975. Although the building has evolved steadily since the time of the Licchavi kings of the 13th century, its art and architecture were influenced mainly by the patronage of King Pratap Malla (r. 1641-74). No Licchavi buildings remain, though, and the palace now has plenty of Shah-era whitewashing. Just inside the palace entrance is **Nasal Chowk,** a courtyard where the nobles of the kingdom used to assemble. It was here that in 1673 Pratap Malla danced in a costume of Narasimha, Vishnu's man-lion incarnation. Afraid that Vishnu would be angry about the stunt, he installed a Narasimha statue just inside the palace out of remorse. The main section of the palace open to the public is the **Tribhuvan Memorial Museum.** King Tribhuvan (r. 1911-55), who overthrew the Ranas in 1951 and restored Nepal's monarchy, is eulogized here in a display of personal belongings. The display cases of ceremonial outfits, newspaper clippings, watches—even Tribhuvan's desk and fish tank—make you feel like you know the guy. At the southern end of Nasal Chowk stands **Basantapur Tower,** a nine-story lookout erected by Prithvi Narayan Shah after he conquered the valley. It offers great views of Durbar Square from above. The circuit around Nasal Chowk next leads to the **Mahendra Memorial Museum,** which isn't quite as impressive as Tribhuvan's, but a walk-through diorama simulating one of the king's hunts is worth your attention. Outside the palace, along the wall past the Hanuman statue, is a **stone inscription** erected by Pratap Malla, which uses words from 15 different languages (including English and French). It's said that if anyone manages to read the whole text—a poem

NEPAL

THE LEGEND OF THE KATHMANDU VALLEY

According to local mythology, the Kathmandu Valley was once a huge lake inhabited by snakes called *nagas.* A lotus grew out of the lake and was called *swayambhu,* or "self-created." When the *bodhisattva* of knowledge, Manjushri, went on a pilgrimage to the lotus, he was dismayed to find it overflowing with snakes and inaccessible to human pilgrims. He sliced his sword into the valley, creating Chobar Gorge; the lake's water drained, taking the *nagas* with it. Then, to appease the *naga* king Krakatoa, Manjushri allowed him to live in Taudaha Lake as guardian of the monsoon. The fertile valley was now ready for its first civilization, and a shrine—the *stupa* of Swayambhunath—was built on the hill from which the lotus had grown. According to geology, the valley was indeed once filled with water, Swayambhu was an island, and the Chobar Gorge was created by an earthquake—but there's no mention of snakes.

dedicated to the goddess Kali—milk will gush from the spout. *(Near the Jagannath Temple. Open Sa-M and W-Th 10:30am-4pm, F 10:30am-2pm. Winter: Sa-M and W-Th 10:30am-4pm, F 10:30-2pm. Rs250. Cameras prohibited.)*

KASTHAMANDAP. Kathmandu is said to have taken its name from this gorgeous temple. The wooden pavilion (supposedly built from the wood of a single tree) may be Kathmandu's oldest existing building. Dating from the 14th century, it has been substantially altered over the centuries. Originally a *dharamshala*, it was made into a temple, but a feeling of transience remains, and loitering porters give the place a train-platform feel. The Kasthamandap is a sacred space, with a central image of Gorakhnath, the deified Hindu saint who watches over the Shah dynasty. A small Ganesh shrine sits in each corner; one of the idols' golden mouse-mount points its nose at another Ganesh shrine in its own metal-flagged enclosure. This **Maru Ganesh** (also known as **Ashok Binayak**) is frequently worshipped—as the remover of obstacles, Ganesh is a good god to visit before traveling. *(Southwest of Durbar Sq.)*

TALEJU MANDIR. The Taleju Temple's three-tiered golden pagoda towers over everything else in the square. King Mahendra Malla built the temple in 1564 to honor Taleju, his dynasty's patron goddess. At 37m, the Taleju Temple was, for a long time, the tallest building in Kathmandu, a distinction preserved by building codes; but the city, eager to modernize, has dispensed with this tradition. Ordinarily, the temple is open only to the king and a few priests, but on the ninth day of the festival of Dasain, lay Hindus are allowed to enter. *(Northeast of the Hanuman Dhoka Durbar. Non-Hindus not allowed inside.)*

KUMARI BAHAL. A traditional-looking 18th-century Kathmandu palace, the Kumari Bahal has beautiful carved window frames—some are shaped like peacocks, and the central one is covered in gold. This is where the living, earthly, human goddess of Kathmandu, the **Kumari,** resides, sometimes appearing at one of the windows in the courtyard. If she doesn't appear, plenty of touts in the square will offer their services in summoning her appearance. Soft drinks and film are sold inside the courtyard. *(Across from the neo-classical columns on the other side of the Trailokya Mohan temple, on the right. Photography is prohibited.)*

MAJU DEWAL. The Maju Dewal Shiva temple takes up the prime location in the main Durbar Square, towering over everything on its great step-pyramid. The temple was built in 1690, and it makes a well-placed observation deck for Durbar Square—its height, however, does nothing to isolate it from the fray below. You could sit here for hours watching the square, but you're bound to be hassled by "guides," "English students," and kids asking, "Do you have one coin from your country?" *(Across from and to the left of the Trailokya Mohan temple.)*

TRAILOKYA MOHAN TEMPLE. This temple is a shrine to Vishnu, with a dusty-black statue of Garuda (Vishnu's man-bird mount) kneeling before the image. On the other side of the temple, great white columns bear down on the square. Prime Minister Chandra Shamsher Rana added this wing to the main royal palace in 1908. *(From Maru Ganesh, turn right past the row of stalls.)*

OTHER SIGHTS. The **Temple of Shiva and Parvati** rests on a skewed platform, and an image of the divine couple can be seen by the window above the door *(next to the Maju Dewal)*. The **Big (Taleju) Bell** that rings for worship in the Degutaleju Temple, and is similar to the big bells found in the other valley cities of Patan and Bhaktapur *(next to the Shiva Parvati temple)*. The figure of **Sweta Bhairab** (White Bhairab), with a big, fanged, and golden face, sits behind a wooden screen. At the Indra Jatra festival (Aug.-Sept.), the screen comes off and beer issues from the mouth of this fearsome form of Shiva as devotees crowd in for a drink. *(To the right of the Taleju Bell.)* The road widens ahead at the column of King Pratap Malla, the architect of many of the buildings in this area. His statue at the top of the column prays toward his personal shrine in the **Degutaleju Temple**. *(East of Durbar Sq.)* The huge, garish monolith of **Kala Bhairab** (Black Bhairab) threatens that anyone who dares to tell a lie in front of this raging destroyer of evil will supposedly vomit blood and die *(back down the road to the main sq.)*. The octagonal **Krishna Temple** houses images of Krishna and two goddesses that bear a curious resemblance to Pratap

Malla and his wives *(just beyond Kala Bhairab)*. The **Jagannath Temple** is the oldest temple in the northern part of the square, dating from 1563 *(on Pratap Malla's left)*. The **Mahendreshwar Temple** is a popular Shiva temple *(across the street from the Taleju temple)*. The police compound to the west is the site of the **Kot Massacre** (see **History**, p. 710), where Jung Bahadur Rana murdered most of Nepal's nobility in 1846, inaugurating 105 years of Rana rule *(west of Durbar Sq.)*.

NORTH OF DURBAR SQUARE

Kathmandu's most interesting street runs northeast from Durbar Square. Without a name of its own, this funny diagonal street takes the title of whatever area it's running through. In earlier times, it was the beginning of the trade route from Kathmandu to Tibet, and it was Kathmandu's main commercial area until New Rd. was built after the earthquake of 1934.

INDRA CHOWK. The second-story temple of **Akash Bhairab** is unmistakable with its garish metal gargoyles. Akash Bhairab's image, a large silver mask, is barely visible. During the Indra Jatra festival it is displayed in the middle of the chowk, along with a *linga* specially erected next to it. *(The first crossroads on the diagonal street away from Durbar Sq. is called Indra Chowk. Akash Bhairab is on the left side at this corner.)*

KEL TOL. The **Temple of Seto Machhendranath** is one of the most widely revered shrines in the valley, where Hindus and Buddhists pay homage to Machhendra, the Valley's guardian and the most compassionate of the gods. The white-faced image is paraded around during the Machhendranath festival in April. *(In a passageway behind Kel Tol.)* The pagoda in the middle of Kel Tol is dedicated to **Lunchun Lun Bun Ajima.** This goddess' bathroom-tiled sanctuary is now sunk beneath street level because the road has been repaved so many times. *(Kel Tol is the second crossing after Durbar Square, marked by a short pillar capped with a meditating Buddha on the left.)*

ASAN TOL. At Asan Tol, the next crossing, the road widens and is lined with stacks of vegetables. The **Temple of Annapurna** is on the right, draped with broad brass ribbons. The goddess of plentiful food, Annapurna is depicted here simply as a silver pot. *(Asan Tol is the third crossing north of Durbar Square.)*

BANGEMUDHA. Bangemudha means "Twisted Wood"—in one of the southern corners is a twisted lump of wood stuck to the wall, with an armor of coins nailed into it. The wood is dedicated to the god of toothaches, **Vaisya Dev,** and nailing a coin here is supposed to relieve dental pain. On the road north from Bangemudha you'll be greeted by jawfuls of grinning teeth. This is the dentists' quarter, and their signs bear this happy symbol. On the left side of this road a lane leads to **Kathesimbhu,** a miniature model of the Swayambhunath *stupa* west of Kathmandu. Kathesimbhu is said to have been built with leftover earth from Swayambhunath, so it shares some of Swayambhunath's power. The elderly and those too weak to climb the hill to Swayambhunath can obtain an equal blessing here. Children seem to be the most devoted visitors to Kathesimbhu, however, holding endless soccer games around its *chaityas*. *(The Bangemudha crossing is near the diagonal road, west of Asan Tol.)*

SOUTH ASIAN SEDER With 95% of Nepal's 20 million citizens claiming Hinduism, Buddhism, or both, as their religion, you'd hardly expect Kathmandu to host the largest *seder* (ritual Jewish Passover meal) in the world. In some ways it seems fitting that this Hindu kingdom which has taken religious syncretism to such impressive heights should pay tribute to another of the world's oldest religions. Each year the Israeli Embassy houses a *seder* for over 1000 young Jews who find themselves in Nepal during the week of Passover. Most of them have come to roam the Nepali wilderness following completion of their national military service, but at the *seder,* the trekking diaspora ditches *chapatis* and *dal bhat* in favor of *matzos* and *maror,* in remembrance of the ancient Israelite exodus from Egypt. In 2000, Passover is April 21-22. For more information, contact the Israeli Embassy (tel. 411811).

OTHER SIGHTS. The **Rani Pokhari** tank and the temple in its center were built by King Pratap Malla to console his wife over the death of their son. Unfortunately the green-and-yellow fence around it is locked all year except on Diwali (Oct. 26, 2000), the festival of light. *(On Kantipath, east of Asan Tol.)* The current **Royal Palace** is hard to miss—built in the 1960s, the grand mansion is capped by a pagoda roof The building is open to the public only on the 10th day of Dasain, when the king and queen offer blessings to their subjects. *(At the top of Durbar Marg.)*

SOUTH OF DURBAR SQUARE

SINGHA DURBAR. Singha Durbar was once the greatest of the Rana palaces; alas, most of it was burned down in a fire one night in July 1974. The off-white building, which was meant to rival the palaces of Europe, was built in a few frantic years from 1901 to 1904 by Prime Minister Chandra Shamsher Jung Bahadur Rana—his monogram decorates all the railings. The prime minister's household and entire administration fit into this complex, which, with 1700 rooms, claims to be the largest building in Asia. Ministries and departments are lodged in what's left of the palace, and their offices are off-limits to the public. *(East of Tundikhel.)*

BHIMSEN TEMPLE. The Bhimsen Temple is dedicated to the hero-god of Newari craftsmen—its bottom floor has been entirely taken over by shops. Next to it is a hiti (water tap) in a cellar-like depression, where jugs are filled from an elephant-shaped spout. *(On the lane that runs southwest of the Kasthamandap.)*

JAISI DEWAL TEMPLE. The Jaisi Dewal Temple is a Shiva temple of the step-pyramid sort. Painted with flowers and leopard-skin patterns, the temple is graced with a smooth figure of Shiva's mount, Nandi, at the base of the steps. Across the street from the entrance, a 2m-high, uncarved *linga* rises up from a *yoni*. *(Continue to the end of the road from the Bhimsen Temple, turn left and go up the hill.)*

BHIMSEN TOWER. The 59m-high Bhimsen Tower is a useful landmark by which to navigate Kathmandu's streets. It looks like a lighthouse with portholes, though Bhimsen Thapa, the prime minister who built it in 1832, was probably trying to imitate the Ochterlony Monument in Calcutta—ironic, since the British erected that monument to commemorate the defeat of Nepal in 1816. *(At a crossroads in southern Kathmandu, close to Kantipath. The tower is closed to the public.)*

TUNDIKHEL AND MARTYR'S GATE. The **Tundikhel**, or parade ground, is occasionally used for military marches and equestrian displays (e.g., the Ghora Jatra Horse Festival in late March). Kathmandu's newer neighborhoods are located to the east of the Tundikhel. *(On the other side of Kantipath.)* **Martyrs' Gate** is a monument to four accused conspirators who were executed after a 1940 coup attempt. *(On a circle in the middle of the road, south of the Tundikhel.)*

PACHALI BHAIRAB. Though the area by Tripureswar Marg is wet and dirty, and the wind whips past some of Kathmandu's worst slums, the temples make it very interesting and worth exploring. The shrine of Pachali Bhairab is home to the image of Bhairab, garlanded with coins, under the spreading roots of a great pipal tree. Music from the nearby monastery jangles down into Bhairab's courtyard, where a golden human figure lies peacefully dead: this is a *betal*, a representation of death meant to guard against death. *(Farther downstream from the other temples, just before the footbridge across the river, slightly inland.)*

KALAMOCHAN TEMPLE. The Kalamochan Temple is hard to miss with its onion dome evocative of Mughal mausolea. Its dragons and doorways are Nepali, however, and on the exterior, Jung Bahadur Rana's figure rises from a shaft protruding from a turtle's back. This Machiavellian prime minister built the temple in the mid-19th century. The ashes of the 32 noblemen he slaughtered in the Kot Massacre are supposed to be buried in the foundations. *(In the cluster of temples on the other side of Tripureswar Marg by the banks of the Bagmati River. Kalamochan is visible from Tripureswar Marg, close to the Patan Bridge.)*

THE LIVING GODDESS: KUMARI A Newari Buddhist girl considered to be the living embodiment of the Hindu goddess Durga, the Kumari is a perfect example of the religious syncretism of the Kathmandu Valley. Kathmandu's Kumari, the most important of the 11 in the valley, is selected at the age of four or five from the Buddhist clan of the Newari *shakya* (goldsmith) caste. The Kumari-to-be must satisfy 32 physical requirements, including having thighs like a deer's, a chest like a lion's, eyelashes like a cow's, and a body shaped like a banyan tree. She must remain calm in a dark room full of buffalo heads, frightening masks, and loud noises. Finally, her astrological chart must not conflict with the king's. If all these conditions are met, the Kumari is installed in the Kumari Bahal in Durbar Square, where she leads the privileged, secluded life of a goddess until she reaches puberty. Several times a year she is paraded about on a palanquin (the Kumari's feet must not touch the ground). As soon as the Kumari menstruates, or sheds blood any other way, her goddess-spirit is said to leave her body, and she must return to her parents' home, where the transition to mere mortality can be difficult. Former goddesses often have difficulty finding a husband, since men who marry them are said to die young.

TEKU. The junction of the Bagmati and Vishnumati Rivers at Teku is a sacred place often used for cremations. The wailing of families echoes around the temples and *chaityas*, and a tall brick *shikhara* stands over the confluence. The riverbanks might frame a pastoral idyll with buffalo munching hay in the shade, but closer inspection tells you that the buffalo are in fact about to be slaughtered. *(In the southwest corner of the city. Be sensitive about photography.)*

WEST OF THE CITY

The west bank of the Vishnumati River is beyond Kathmandu's traditional city limits, but it has been brought into the metropolis by Ring Rd.

SWAYAMBHUNATH. The most prominent feature of the west bank is the hilltop *stupa* of Swayambhunath, over 2000 years old. Swayambhunath is the holiest place for Newari Buddhists and the focus of the Kathmandu Valley's creation myth (see p. 733). The road from Kathmandu to Swayambhunath certainly has a bit of a red-carpet feel to it, with the shrine looming on the hilltop ahead. At the base of the hill is a large rectangular gateway, and after that the long crooked steps start to work their way through the trees and Buddha-icons to the top. You'll be catching your breath, but right at the top of the steps is an enormous *vajra*, the Tibetan thunderbolt symbol. And then there's the **stupa,** white-washed and flattened on top like other Nepali *stupas*. From the golden cube on top of the *stupa*, the Buddha's all-seeing eyes gaze out in each direction; the views are indeed splendid. What looks like a nose is actually a number "1" representing the unity of all things.

Nine golden shrines surround the *stupa*, four of them at the cardinal points of the compass, plus one at an angle. They enclose images of the *dhyani* Buddhas, who represent the Buddha's different aspects through the elements of earth, water, fire, air, and space. The four Buddhas also have female elements (*taras*) who occupy the shrines at the secondary points. Rhesus macaques slide down*stupa's* dome using the fallen prayer flag as a tie-line. *(3km from the city. A 30min. walk or bus #19 from Ratna Park leads you to Ring Rd., just west of Swayambhunath. Stupa Rs50.)*

BUDDHIST MUSEUM. The Buddhist Museum is small and dark, but it has a good assortment of Buddhist and Hindu images in its sculpture collection. Next to the museum is a small monastery that welcomes visitors and their donations. The small temple in front of the monastery is dedicated to Harati, the goddess of smallpox, who can either protect or infect. It's not clear what she does now that smallpox is eradicated, although she is generally responsible for looking after children. *(On a platform west of the stupa. Open W-F and Su-M 10am-5pm. Free.)*

NATIONAL MUSEUM. Nepal's National Museum has an art gallery with a good collection of wood, stone, and metalwork. Equally excellent carvings can be seen in their places on the Kathmandu Valley's houses and temples, but the museum allows for a closer look. The Historical Museum Building is at least as interesting as (and certainly more eclectic than) the Art Gallery. Its natural history section sports the pelt of a two-headed calf, a set of mandibular bones from a blue whale, and an unusual abundance of stuffed deer heads. The Nepalese history section is an amusing tribute to rulers and their playthings. The museum grounds are pleasant, and the roof terrace of the art gallery has a good view of the surrounding valley. *(1km south of Swayambhunath, on the road coming from the riverside. Open W-Th and Sa-M 10:30am-4pm; winter Sa-M 10:30am-3pm, F 10:30am-2:30pm. Tickets sold 10:30am-2pm. Rs50; camera fee Rs100.)*

NATURAL HISTORY MUSEUM. The Natural History Museum houses a 14,000-piece collection of high-altitude flora and fauna. *(Follow the motor road down the hill south of Swayambhunath. Tel. 271899. Open Su-F 10am-4pm. Rs10; camera fee Rs10.)*

🛍 SHOPPING

In Thamel or Durbar Square, roving merchants aggressively hawk items as diverse as flutes, chess sets, and Tiger Balm. Bargain good-naturedly, and hope that the merchant does the same. Although just about anything made in Nepal can be bought in Kathmandu, certain crafts can be found cheaper and in better selection in their places of origin. For woodcarving and pottery, head to Bhaktapur; for papier mache masks and puppets, Thimi; for metalwork, Patan; and for Tibetan crafts like *thankas*, Boudha. A lot of Indian crafts are sold in Kathmandu too. Bagh Bazaar is the best place for *saris*; cloth and beads can be found north of Indra Chowk.

The **Khukuri House** in Thamel, at the zig-zag north of the Kathmandu Guest House, near Rum Doodle's, deserves special mention. This well-reputed knife shop is owned by a former Gorkha officer. (Open Su-F 10am-7pm.) **Western Nepal Crafts,** on Thahiti-Thamel, has a wide selection of handmade paper products with fixed prices (about US$3-5 for stationery, US$10-20 for photo albums). **Didi's Boutique** and **Didi-daju,** both on Chhetrapati, east of Everest Steak House, carry a wide selection of distinctive items, most of which are produced by the Janakpur Women's Development Centre. (Both open daily 10am-9pm. Visa, MC.)

VOLUNTEER OPPORTUNITIES

Expat prisoners in the central jail at **Sundhara,** near the GPO, appreciate visitors who'll talk to them for a little while. The **Sisters of Charity of Nazareth** (tel. 426453 or 419965), Navjyoti Center, Baluwatar, perform prison ministry including assisting former women prisoners. **St. Xavier's School** (tel. 521050 or 521150), Jawalakhel, and **The Missionaries of Charity** (tel. 471810), Mitra Park, work with the destitute.

PASHUPATINATH पशुपती नाथ

The temple complex of Pashupatinath, east of Kathmandu, is the holiest Hindu site in Nepal. It is dedicated to Shiva's incarnation as Pashupati, the kind and gentle Lord of Animals and the guardian deity of Nepal. Thronged by devotees of Shiva, Pashupatinath is the heart of Nepali Hinduism—the king himself often comes to worship here. At the Shivaratri festival, which occurs in March, thousands come here to bathe and celebrate the deity's birthday (Mar. 4, 2000). Also auspicious for bathing in the Bagmati are full-moon nights and the eleventh day after them.

The **Pashupati Temple,** built in 1696, sits right on the Bagmati. A road leads directly up to it, though non-Hindus may not enter. The brass Nandi is visible through the entrance, but the rest of the temple is obscured. Other viewpoints in the area afford over-the-wall glimpses of the wood and marble pagoda. Backtrack away from the river, turn left and left again until another, bigger road leads back to the river; on the right side of this road is a group of five temples known as **Panch Dewal;** its compound has become a social welfare center. **Biddha Ashram,** operated here by Mother Teresa's Missionaries of Charity, welcomes walk-in volunteers. Ahead, stone walls and *ghats* squeeze the river, making it look more like a canal. Two footbridges are laid across it here, and right between them on the near (west) bank is the 6th-century **Bacchareswari Temple.** The **ghats** downstream are used for cremations. If there are cremations in progress, be sensitive about taking pictures.

Across the footbridges on the east bank of the Bagmati is a row of 11 small Shiva shrines. From here it's possible to see into the entire Pashupati Temple compound. The *ghats* immediately below are sometimes used for VIP cremations, including those of members of the royal family. The steps up the hill on the east bank of the river eventually level out at a small wooded village of Shiva temples; Nandi figures line the main street. At the end of it is a temple of Gorakhnath, an 11th-century saint who is revered as a form of Shiva. The steps continue downhill to the **Gujeshwari Temple,** which is locally considered to be the place where the Sati's *yoni* fell when she was cut into pieces by Vishnu (the Kamakhya Temple in Guwahati, India is more widely recognized as this site—see **Divine Dismemberment,** p. 687). Buddhist lore, however, interprets the sacred well in the temple as a bottomless hollow left by the root of the lotus which blossomed atop Swayambhu and inspired the creation of the Kathmandu Valley (see **The Legend of the Kathmandu Valley,** p. 733). Non-Hindus may not enter. The road downstream in front of the temple leads to a bridge; to the left, a set of broken stone steps leads over the hill and back to the Pashupati Temple. The road to the right heads to **Boudha,** a pleasant 45-minute walk north through fields and small neighborhoods.

Pashupatinath is only nominally outside of Kathmandu, and it's simple to get there by **bike**—follow Tridevi Marg away from Thamel, and turn right at the first road after Durbar Marg. At the Marco Polo Business Hotel, turn left and follow the zig-zagging road east across a bridge. Eventually, signs will appear showing maps of Pashupatinath. **Bus** #1 from Ratna Park (frequent, 45min., Rs3) stops along Ring Rd. at the turnoff to Pashupathi; follow the signs from there. The #2 **tempo** from Sundhara (via Rani Pokhari) stops across the street, just inside Ring Rd. (frequent, 30min., Rs6). **Taxis** from Thamel cost about Rs50.

PATAN पाटन

With only the Bagmati River lying between Kathmandu and its temple-dotted neighbor Patan (PAH-tan), the two cities have practically merged. The legacy of their development as independent kingdoms persists, however, and Patan has managed to maintain its own distinct character. Wander through Patan's temple-lined streets for hours without the racket of rickshaws, the hassle of hash dealers, or the trouble of touts. Well established as the valley's center of Newari crafts production, Patan is the place to stroll through alleys to observe artisans at work. Also a spiritual center, the city is graced with many small *stupas, shikharas,* and onion-domed temples. While some of these shrines languish in disuse and are invaded by weeds, many host daily *puja* for Patan's residents.

⚡ ORIENTATION AND PRACTICAL INFORMATION

Patan is linked to Kathmandu by a bridge over the **Bagmati River** and bounded to the south by the same **Ring Road** that encircles Kathmandu. Patan's main road, which runs from Kathmandu, goes by the name of whatever neighborhood it is passing through: from the bridge south to Ring Rd. it is called **Kopundol,** then **Pulchowk,** and finally **Jawalakhel.** The old city, east of the main road, is loosely bounded by four **stupas** (purportedly built by Ashoka in the 3rd century BC), one in each direction. The eastern *stupa* lies beyond Ring Rd.; the western *stupa* sits along the main road, across from the turn-off to **Durbar Square,** the center of the oldest part of town. Several branches lead east from the main road. From north to south, the first leads to **Patan Dhoka** (Patan Gate), north of Durbar Square The second becomes **Mangal Bazaar,** the road that runs along the south end of Durbar Square Finally, at **Jawalakhel Chowk,** the road leads toward **Lagankhel** and the **bus park.**

Local Transportation: Bus #14 runs frequently from Ratna Park in Kathmandu along the main road to the bus park in Lagankhel (30min., Rs5). Buses depart for Kathmandu from Patan Gate. **Tempos** (frequent, 20min., Rs10) leave from Kathmandu's GPO. Most head to Jawalakhel and then Lagankhel, but some go to Mangal Bazaar—ask the driver. Tempos leave for Kathmandu from Durbar Square on Mangal Bazaar. **Taxis** from Thamel to Patan's Durbar Sq. about Rs75, auto-rickshaws Rs50.

Currency Exchange: Nepal Grindlays, Jawalakhel Chowk (tel. 522490), charges a 1% commission on traveler's checks. Open Su-Th 10am-5pm, F 10am-1pm.

Market: Fruit, spices, and cheap fabric are sold in Lagankhel, near the bus park. A huge vegetable market is just south of the bus park. **Namaste Supermarket,** along the main road in Pulchowk, offers a range of pre-packaged goods. Open daily 9am-8pm.

Bookstore: Pilgrims Book House has a huge branch on the main road in Kopundole. Open daily 9am-8pm. Visa, MC.

Pharmacy: Many can be found on Mangal Bazaar, right below Durbar Sq. **Alka Pharmacy** (tel. 535146), on the main road in Jawalakhel, north of St. Xavier's School, hosts a variety of specialist clinics and can arrange house calls. Open daily 7am-10pm.

Hospital: Patan Hospital, Lagankhel (tel. 522295), has a good reputation.

Post Office: Outside Patan Gate, on the west side. Open Su-F 10:30am-2:30pm.

Internet: Available at several booths around Jawalakhel Chowk. Rs5-10 per min., email Rs15-20 per kb.

PHONE CODE	01

■ ACCOMMODATIONS

Thamel's tourist explosion has put the squeeze on Patan's budget accommodations. Today most people just ride into Patan for the day and return to Kathmandu at night. However, a night or two in Patan means freedom from the tourist ghettos of Thamel and the promise of a quiet respite from the early morning racket of Kathmandu.

Cafe de Patan, Mangal Bazaar (tel. 537599), just southwest of Durbar Sq. Clean, comfortable, quiet rooms are available above this restaurant. Balconies, abundant furnishings, and spotless tiled bathrooms with seat toilets. Doubles Rs300, with bath Rs500.

Mountain View Guest House, Kumaripati (tel. 538168). Walk west 10min. from Lagankhel bus park; it's on the right behind the Campion Academy. A little removed from the older section of town. Above the restaurant behind a stained-glass door are new, clean rooms and facilities. STD/ISD available. Singles Rs250; doubles Rs350, with attached bath Rs400.

Hungry Treat Home (tel. 534792 or 533568), a few minutes' walk east of Jawalakhel Chowk. The ample rooms with large windows, fans, and Astroturf carpeting don't win prizes for aesthetics, but they are clean and equipped with all the necessities. Tiled bathrooms with seat toilets and toilet paper. Attached restaurant. Doubles Rs200, with bath Rs300; triples Rs350.

Mahendra Youth Hostel, Pulchowk Rd. (tel. 521003), north of Jawalakhel Chowk. Down the second lane to the right, next to the Dept. of Irrigation across from St. Xaviers. No smoking and no hot water. Check-in 6am-10pm. Check-out noon. Dorm beds Rs50-75; doubles with bath Rs200. 10% tax, but 10% discounts for HI/IYHF members.

■ FOOD

Patan's food selection is less varied than Kathmandu's, but it's also less tourist-centered, with more *tarkari* (veg. curry) than teriyaki. Fast-food *tandoori* joints line the main road. More expensive tourist places serve the same fare in more pleasant settings. For the breakfast-seeking Westerner, **Hot Breads** and **The Bakery Cafe** on Jawalakhel Chowk both offer a wide range of pastries. For extra-yummy cake, loaves of bread (Rs25-30), and other baked goods, head for the **German Bakery,** north of J1nsawalakhel Chowk.

Tama Restaurant and Bar, Pulchowk, across the street and south of the Sajha bus garage, set back from the road. Cheap Indian menu (Rs75-200) and pricier Japanese entrees (Rs155-300) served in a tidy, peaceful dining area. Open daily 11am-9:30pm.

Downtown Restaurant, Pulchowk. Lace curtains screen the sights but not the sounds of the busy street. Deservedly popular with the expat community for its extensive menu and low prices. Chicken *tikka masala* (Rs75) is rich and flavorful, and *naan* (Rs12) sops up the sauce nicely. Open Su-F 10am-9pm.

Cafe de Patan, Mangal Bazaar, southwest of Durbar Sq. Walk through the souvenir and music shop to the ground floor dining area or the garden rooftop. Cheap, authentic Newari menu (snacks Rs10-40, meals Rs70-90) available M-Sa. Open daily 8am-9pm.

Bakena Batika, Jawalakhel, just inside Ring Rd. south of the Tibetan Refugee Camp. Beautifully renovated Nepali house and tranquil courtyard make the perfect setting for light meals (Rs70-100), traditional Nepali courses (Rs150-190), and *risotto* (Rs190). Open daily noon-8:30pm.

The Third World Restaurant, Durbar Sq., opposite the Patan Museum, directly upstairs from the craft boutique. Despite its name, there aren't any relief aid staples on this menu. Continental fare (Rs70-150), sandwiches (Rs50-100). Open daily 8am-9pm.

SIGHTS

As in the other cities of the valley, Durbar Square is sight-seeing central. Exhaustive renovations have made it the perfect place to indulge in quixotic visions of kingdoms past, but Patan's narrow streets offer glimpses of daily life that will coax you back into the present.

DURBAR SQUARE

One tactic for exploring Durbar Square is to start at the southern end of the **Royal Palace,** which makes up the eastern side of the square, then continue north and circle around counter-clockwise. The southern courtyard, **Sundari Chowk,** is not open to the public, but **Mul Chowk,** dating from the mid-17th century, can be entered between the two stone lions. On the southern wall, gilded statues of the Indian river goddesses Ganga (on a tortoise) and Yamuna (on a *makara*, a mythical snouted sea creature) guard the locked doorway to the **Taleju Shrine.** Dedicated to the patron goddess of Nepal's royal families, the shrine is open to Hindus one day per year during the Dasain festival. The other pagodas that rise around Mul Chowk are the **Taleju Bhawani Mandir,** an octagonal tower in the northeast corner, and, on the north side, the **Degu Talle Temple,** the tallest in the square.

The new **Patan Museum** is housed in **Keshav Narayan Chowk,** the northernmost section of the palace; the entrance is an elaborate golden doorway. The whitewashed shrine inside is dedicated to Narayan. Beautifully restored with the help of the Austrian government and the Smithsonian Institution, the museum houses metal, wood, and stone sculptures with extensive and informative labels. Wide, cushioned window seats provide lookouts onto the square below, and a cafe in the manicured courtyard serves snacks. (Museum open W-M 10:30am-4:30pm. Rs120 for foreigners.) Around the corner from the palace to the north is the sunken water tank known as **Manga Hiti;** its mythical crocodile-like statues have been spouting water since the sixth century. The northern adjacent pavilion, **Mani Mandap,** was once used for coronations.

Diagonally across the way, the northernmost temple in the square is the three-tiered **Bhimsen Mandir,** with a lion-topped pillar in front of its recently added marble facade. Merchants toss coins onto the older, gilded first floor of this temple dedicated to the god of trade. The next temple to the left is the **Vishwanath Mandir,** a double-roofed Shiva temple guarded by two stone elephants, originally dating from 1627. The temple collapsed in 1990, but it has since been restored. The *linga* inside is said to replicate the Vishwanath *linga* in Varanasi (see p. 206). A Nandi faces the other side of the temple. As you continue south, the next temple is the stone, Indian *shikhara*-style **Krishna Mandir.** This temple stands out because of its foreign design and because it is one of the few temples in Durbar Square still in active use. In the evenings, devotees set the build-

NEPAL

ing aglow with oil lamps. The upper floors, carved with friezes depicting scenes from the *Mahabharata* and *Ramayana*, are closed to non-Hindus.

Vishnu is the patron god of the next temple, the **Jagan Narayan Mandir.** Stone lions flank the front of this more Nepalese pagoda-style temple, complete with wildly erotic roof struts. Built in 1565, this is the square's oldest temple. The **Bhai Deval Mandir** lies to the southwest corner of the square, and if you continue around clockwise, you'll pass a fountain before arriving at the octagonal stone **Chyasin Deval**, which, like the other Krishna temple in the square, was built in an Indian style. Its construction is linked with the death of one of the Malla kings, but whether it spontaneously appeared, or was built to honor his eight wives who committed *sati*, is now a matter of controversy. The **Taleju Bell** next door was the first of the valley's three big bells, cast in 1736. The next temple to the north is the **Hari Shankar Mandir,** an elaborately carved three-tiered pagoda from the 18th century. The temple is jointly dedicated to Vishnu (called Hari here) and Shiva (Shankar). Circling back into the square, you can see the stone pillar topped by a golden statue of **King Yoganarendra Malla,** a monument with legends of its own. The king kneels under the protection of a cobra's hood, and it is said that as long as the figure of a bird perched on the cobra's head remains there, the king may return. A door and window to his palace remain open, and his *hookah* waits inside. If the bird flies away, the elephants that guard the Vishwanath Mandir will leave their posts to drink from the Manga Hiti.

SOUTH OF DURBAR SQUARE

Continuing along Mangal Bazaar east of Durbar Square, you'll see signs for the **Mahaboudha Temple;** the right-hand turn-off is a short walk from the square. Inside the courtyard that houses this "temple of a thousand Buddhas," painted arrows point the way to walk around it, and even the prayer wheels are labeled. The temple's architect was inspired by the Mahabodhi Temple in Bodh Gaya, India, where the Buddha achieved enlightenment (see p. 637). The foreign influence is obvious: the *shikhara*-style temple is covered with terra cotta tiles, each of which is painted with an image of the Buddha. As you turn right from the Mahaboudha, the **Uka Bahal (Rudravarna Mahabihar),** the oldest monastery in Patan, is on the left at the next intersection. A pair of stone lions guards this former Buddhist monastery, while an ark full of brass beasts stands watch in the courtyard.

Tinker Street is on the left as you exit Uka Bahal. The sound of metal being hammered into form fills the street, which ends at the wide market street that runs south from Durbar Square At the intersection of the two streets stands the **Ibaha Bahal,** a recently renovated monastery dating from 1427. Farther south along the same street, but on the other side behind a water tank, is the **Minnath Mandir,** with its garishly painted details. Minnath is often called *sanno* ("little") Machhendranath, in reference to the deity who inhabits the temple down a short lane across the street. This temple, the **Rato Machhendranath Mandir,** a 17th-century pagoda with an intricate, colorful, three-tiered roof, stands in the center of a big, grassy compound. A collection of brass animals, each representing a month of the Tibetan calendar, is perched on posts facing the temple. The *rato* ("red") image of Machhendranath gets to ride in a towering chariot that makes its rounds of Patan during late April. Machhendranath is a multi-purpose deity: he's the *bodhisattva* of compassion, as a Newari god he controls the rains, and he's also revered as the guru of a 7th-century saint.

NORTH OF DURBAR SQUARE

GOLDEN TEMPLE. The Golden Temple, one of Patan's most famous structures, is a five-minute walk up the first northern lane west of Durbar Square. Also known as **Hiranyavarna Mahavihar,** this ornate, gilded temple makes up the west side of the **Kwa Bahal,** a 12th-century Buddhist monastery whose courtyard is decorated by a golden shrine. **No leather is allowed beyond the walkway around the edge of the courtyard.** The temple's facade is elaborately worked in *repoussé* with images of Buddhas, *taras*, and mythological creatures. Gods are supposed to be able to slide down the *patakas*, the golden belts that hang from the roofs. Upstairs, in the northeast corner of the *bahal*, is a collection of Tibetan-style murals. A pair of stone tortoises stands on the south side of the courtyard. *(Rs25 for foreigners.)*

UMBESHWAR MAHADEV. If you continue another minute north, the five-tiered pagoda of the Kumbeshwar Mahadev comes into view. The oldest temple in Patan, it had only two tiers when it was built in 1392. The three stories added later have made it one of two free-standing five-roofed pagodas in the Kathmandu Valley (the other is the Nyatapola Temple in Bhaktapur). The deity-in-residence is Shiva, as indicated by the Nandi outside the temple. The water tank next to the temple inside the compound is believed to be connected to the holy Himalayan lake of Gosainkund. A pilgrim is said to have dropped a *kumbh* (pot) in the lake, which then emerged in the tank in Patan, giving the temple its name. Thousands of devotees come to bathe in the tank during the **Jana Purnima festival** (held in August), when high-caste Hindus change their sacred threads. One block east of the temple, the road to the right leads straight back to the northern end of Durbar Square.

JAWALAKHEL

The Jawalakhel neighborhood is notable for its foreign residents, mostly expats working for aid organizations and Tibetan refugees.

CENTRAL ZOO. Just west of Jawalakhel Chowk is the Central Zoo with a pond in the middle of the landscaped grounds. You can see that tiger (as well as the showcased guinea pigs) that eluded you at Chitwan. *(Open Tu-Su 10am-6pm. Tickets sold until 5pm. Rs50 for foreigners; proceeds go toward renovations; camera fee Rs10, video Rs50.)*

JAWALAKHEL HANDICRAFT CENTRE. A part of the Tibetan Refugee Camp, Jawalakhel Handicraft Centre was established by the Red Cross and the Nepalese government in 1960. The center employs Tibetans who fled their country after 1959. Visitors are free to wander freely observing the carpet-making processes with no pressure to buy. Proceeds from the souvenir shop go to the workers. *(5-10min. walk south of Jawalkhel Chowk. Tel. 521305. Open Su-F 8am-5pm.)*

■ SHOPPING

A lower-pressure sales atmosphere than Kathmandu and an equally wide selection make Patan an ideal place for souvenir shopping. Because most of the items sold in Patan were actually produced there, prices and selection tend to be even better than in Kathmandu. This is especially true for carpets, metal work, wooden toys (like model auto-rickshaws), and puppets. Patan is full of non-profit craft outlets that sell crafts from all over the country at fixed prices. Many of them benefit underprivileged workers—especially women—and ensure fair wages. They can be found in the old Royal Palace on Durbar Square, and in Kopundol. **Sana Hastakala** (tel. 522628), opposite Hotel Himalaya, is sponsored by UNICEF and has a good selection (open Su-F 9:30am-5pm, Sa 10am-5pm; MC, Visa, AmEx).

NEAR PATAN: GODAVARI गोदावरी

A horticultural haven, Godavari is home to the peaceful, expertly landscaped Royal Botanical Garden, the National Herbarium, a bee-keeping workshop, a marble quarry, and the nurseries that supply florists in Patan. The **Botanical Garden** is a 10-minute walk from the bus park, which is the last stop; continue until the paved road terminates at the garden's entrance. The **quarry,** five minutes up the hill past St. Xavier's School from the bus park, offers an interesting view of the mining and polishing of the marble, and marble chunks picked up along the way make great souvenirs. From Langankhel bus park, **buses** #13 and 14 continue up the hills to Godavari (1hr., Rs4), with spellbinding, misty views of rice paddies along the way. A **Jesuit ashram** (tel. 522219 or 290558; fax 535620; email supreg@njs.mos.com.np), just beyond the bus park, will provide pleasant lodgings for guests given a week's notice (Rs350 per day for stays under 5 days, includes 3 veg. meals and 2 teas). Basic **restaurants** can be found near the Botanical Garden.

KIRTIPUR कितींपुु

The citizens of Kirtipur are proud of their gallant 18th-century stand against Prithv
Narayan Shah's encroaching Gorkha forces (see **History**, p. 708). When Shah firs
attacked in 1757, neighboring towns came to Kirtipur's aid and handily defeated th
invading army. During a second battle in 1764, Shah's brother was shot in the ey
with an arrow, and the Gorkhas again retreated. But the Gorkhas' superior weap
onry turned the tide two years later, when, after a six-month siege of the town, Kir
tipur finally surrendered. The Gorkhas punished the city's men by slicing off thei
noses, ears, and lips so that throughout the country folks would recognize them a
troublemakers from Kirtipur. Today, Kirtipur offers a taste of Newari life away from
the hustle of Kathmandu. Young, uniformed children hurry along narrow, windin
streets on their way to school while women wash their laundry and men head out t
work in the terraced fields. Kirtipur is also home to a number of ornate temples
and Nepal's largest university; **Tribhuvan University's** campus lies below the town o
land once cultivated by Kirtipur farmers.

⁊ ORIENTATION AND PRACTICAL INFORMATION. To reach Kirtipur from
Kathmandu take a **taxi** (Rs200) or **bus #21** (frequent departures, 40min., Rs3) from
the Ratna Park bus station. Stay on the bus until it stops at a bus park just down th
hill from Kirtipur. From the bus park, the paved road goes uphill into town. At th
top of the hill is a partially rusted but still legible city map. Facing the map, the roa
extends to the left into the **Naya Bazaar** (New Market). The bazaar is a mix of stree
vendors peddling fresh produce and small shops (catering to locals) selling cloth
ing, toiletries, and pre-packaged items. The bazaar is also home to several smal
shops offering **STD** and **Internet** services. Along the road through the bazaar, a few
steps down on the left is the **Shree Kirti Vihara**. Further down the road, a few yard
past a huge dead tree on your right, a steep stone path extends uphill to the right. A
the end of this path a narrow walkway extends uphill to the **Chilandeo Stupa**; to th
left, the road leads to the town square and the **Bagh Bhairab Mandir.**

◉ SIGHTS. The first thing one sees upon ascending the hill into Kirtipur is a
immaculately kept Thai Buddhist Temple. The **Shree Kirti Vihara** was built in 197
and is tended by monks clad in saffron-colored robes. The red-, yellow-, and green
roofed temple houses gilded statues of the Buddha. The building on the sid
encases a larger-than-life sized Buddha in *parinirvana* guarded by a series of lio
statues. The 1400-year-old **Chilandeo Stupa** is well worth the short, steep walk lead
ing up to it. To its left is a path leading to the **Bagh Bhairab Mandir,** a temple dedi
cated to Shiva the destroyer (Bhairab) in the form of a *bagh* (tiger), but significan
to Hindus and Buddhists alike. Look for the Gorkhali swords and uniforms mounte
on the upper facade, commemorating Kirtipur's defeat by the Gorkhas. Worshi
pers and musicians visit Bagh Bhairab every morning and evening, and there ar
chicken or buffalo sacrifices on Tuesdays and Saturdays. Bagh Bhairab is also th
center of Kirtipur's December festival for the goddess Indrani, an offshoot of Kath
mandu's Indrani festival. A separate monument commemorates Rama's birth wit
Brahma, Vishnu, and Shiva looking on.

Facing the Bagh Bhairab Mandir, the road to the left leads to the **Uma-Maheshwa
Mandir.** Two stone elephants guard the temple, where intricately carved woode
images of Shiva and his consort Parvati are housed; the divine pair is of special sig
nificance to married couples. More noteworthy than the temple itself, however is it
superb panoramic view. To the southwest looms one of the highest points of th
Kathmandu Valley's rim, and to the northeast sprawls Kathmandu (look fo
Swayambhunath, the Monkey Temple, and Bhimsen Tower for orientation). On
clear day, the towering peak of Mt. Everest is visible. For a view of gorgeous moun
tain scenery and a glimpse of locals working on terraced fields, walk along the mai
road of Kirtipur past the bazaar. The road opposite the large dead tree on the mai
road leads out of town for 2km until the terraces appear on the left.

CHOBAR चोभार

When Manjushri released the waters of the Bhagmati river from the Kathmandu Valley's surrounding mountains with one swing of his sword, it was here that his blow is said to have landed. Whether the **Chobar Gorge** was formed by Manjushri's sword or by an earthquake, as geologists suggest, the legend has made tales of Chobar an important part of Nepalese lore. Spanning the gorge is a narrow **suspension bridge,** which was built in 1903 to provide a walking route to Patan. The long stairway up to the village also leads to the eclectic **Adinath Lokeshwar Mandir,** atop its summit. The half-Hindu, half-Buddhist temple is covered with pots and pans—contributions of kitchenware to the temple are said to enhance the culinary skills of new brides. Just down the hill from the ridge on the banks of the river sits the three-tiered **Jal Binayak,** a temple dedicated to Ganesh. The deity is represented here in the form of a large rock protruding from the back of the temple. Around the temple a stylized Shiva *linga* dances with Parvati before a statue of a rabbit.

Bus #22 (frequent, 45 min., Rs5) heads to Chobar from Ratna Park in Kathmandu. Get off when the bus turns west into the gates of Tribhuvan University, and continue along the main road passing the **Himalayan Bee Concern** on the right and a **cold store** on the left, the last one on the way to Patan; it's a good idea to stock up here. The stone stairs leading uphill to Chobar are a few yards past the cold store on the right. From Kirtipur, Chobar is half an hour away. Follow the main road through the Naya Bazaar (see p. 744); with the Buddhist temple on your left, turn left at Ratna's Beauty Parlor, take the next possible left and follow the path until it meets a main road near a small temple with a gate. Turn left onto the main road and follow the stairway leading uphill to Chobar. To reach Chobar Gorge from Chobar, head down the hill towards the cement factory until you reach the Gorge (it's hard to miss). From the Gorge it's about an hour to Patan; cross the bridge and head straight along the uphill path.

NAGARJUN नागर्जुन AND BALAJU बालाजु

Many believe that the Buddha once meditated atop Nagarjun; others maintain that the first *bodhisattva*, Viswapa, stood on the peak to throw the lotus seed that would blossom into *swayambhu* (see **The Legend of the Kathmandu Valley,** p. 733). After you complete the strenuous two-hour walk to the summit and look out over the valley, you will see that both claims are tenable. Crowned by an old *stupa* draped in a virtual canopy of colored prayer flags, Nagarjun (also called "Jamacho") is convincingly holy. As the closest summit to Kathmandu, it offers a breathtaking vista of the valley in clear weather (Rs5). Camping is permitted, but finding a place to camp can be problematic (Rs90 per tent).

The #23 **tempo** (every 30min., Rs4) leaves from Rani Pokhari and stops by **Balaju Water Garden.** The water garden is marked by the ticket window and gate with turnstiles. One of the few well-maintained public spaces in the area, the garden has fountains, painstakingly pruned hedges, and shaded benches, all unified by their pastel scheme. (On the left. Open daily 7am-7:30pm. Rs3; camera fee Rs2.) During festival season, worshippers bathe in the water coursing from the 22 carved crocodiles of the **Baais Dhara,** to the right. Midway through the park on the right is the small **Bala Nilkantha,** a 7th-century contemporary of the more elaborate sleeping Vishnu, northeast of the valley in Budhanilkantha. The **swimming pool** within the garden is a big, noisy place to keep cool. (Open daily 9am-12:30pm and 1-4pm. Women only Th. Rs35; students Rs30.)

To reach Nagarjun, turn left after exiting the water garden and continue north for about 10 minutes. Nagarjun sits in **Rani Ban** (also called Nagarjun Royal Forest), a sizable chunk of forest protected by the government. The Rani Ban entrance is on the left as you walk up the hill. If you continue a few meters past the entrance, you will come to a short dirt trail on the left leading up to a 15m-long cave that holds a Buddhist shrine. A natural stone image of Buddha was supposedly found near the back of the cave, and a man-made image sits near the front on the left (bring a flashlight). Back down the road by the entrance to Rani Ban, a well-marked trail on your right leads to Nagarjun's summit (5km, 2hr.). The steep trail winds through the forest preserve. At the top is the Buddhist shrine **Jamacho.** Though rarely visited on ordinary days, Jamacho is the center of April's full moon festival, **Balaju Jatra.** During this festival, worshippers hold an all-night vigil at the summit and descend to Balaju the next day for a ritual bath in Baais Dhara.

BOUDHA (BOUDHANATH) बौद्धनाथ

Dominated by the whitewashed dome of Nepal's largest *stupa* and dotted with *gompas* representing all four sects of Tibetan Buddhism (Nyingma, Kagyupu, Sakyapa, and Gelupa), Boudha is one of the best places outside Tibet to get some exposure to Buddhist culture. Nearly everyone who circumambulates Boudha's massive *stupa* claims origins elsewhere. Many have fled Tibet since the Chinese crackdown in 1959; others have migrated from Nepal's northern peaks, either to spend years or just to wait out the winter; and others are Buddhists from the rest of the world who have cashed in their life savings to make the pilgrimage to the *stupa*. The monasteries that surround it offer not only schooling for children and training for monks but also respite for an increasing number of Westerners. A prevailing attitude of celebration and contemplation, informed by worldly realism, reflects the faith that is a common denominator for this complex community. For the casual visitor, Boudha's atmosphere is a proper tonic for the frenetic business of travel, and the simplicity of its *stupa* relieves eyes weary of jumbled alleys and carved temple struts.

☀ ORIENTATION AND PRACTICAL INFORMATION

While Boudha has expanded far beyond the confines of the **stupa compound**, the *stupa* remains its symbolic center and is the reference point for all other geographical directions. Five kilometers east of Kathmandu, the *stupa* compound is entered through a **gate** on the north side of the main east-west road. Directions to places on the **main road** are given locally as either "right" (west) or "left" (east) of the gate. The sprawling community north of the *stupa*, where you will find most of Boudha's monasteries, is accessed by two parallel lanes leading north out of the *stupa* compound. One, referred to here as the **northern lane**, begins directly north of the *stupa*, just beside the **Original Stupa View Restaurant.** Small east-west lanes connect these two. Always walk clockwise around the stupa.

Buses: Bus #2 from **Ratna Park** (about every 30min., 35min., Rs5) is crowded. Beware of pickpockets. The bus will drop you off a few yards before the gate. Blue **tempos** (#2, Rs6) leave from **Rani Pokhari. Taxis** from **Thamel** cost a reasonable Rs100.

Local Transportation: Mountain bikes can be rented from a small stand on the left hand side of the main lane (Rs60 per day).

Currency Exchange: Mandala Money Changer, inside the southern gates on the left, uses bank rates. Charges 1% fee for traveler's checks, 2% for cash. Open daily 8:30am-6pm.

Market: Fruit sellers gather on the main road to the left of the *stupa* gate and in the lanes north of the *stupa*. Across the main road, a few minutes' walk to the left, the **Gemini Grocer** is well-stocked with Western treats and toiletries and takes credit cards. Open daily 8am-8pm. Within the *stupa* compound is **Khashyor Bazaar,** which has shelves of packaged goodies. Open daily 8:30am-8:30pm.

Internet and Telephones: High Himalaya (tel. 472051), in the *stupa*, has **STD/ISD** with private booths and good rates, **email** (Rs10 per Kb to send or receive), **Internet** (Rs6 per min.), and **fax** services (Rs80 per min.). Open daily 7am-9:30pm.

PHONE CODE	01

♖ ACCOMMODATIONS

Most visitors to Boudha spend either a few hours or a few months, but the many clean and peaceful lodgings might make you want to stay a few nights. Cheap places line the main road, but the ones in the back lanes are sheltered from exhaust and only slightly harder to find. Be warned that the neighboring *gompas* begin clanging and nagging at 4:30am. Check-out is noon at all guest houses.

Lotus Guest House (tel. 472432 or 472320), beside the colorful Dobsang Monastery. Follow signs from the Original Stupa View Rest. Motel-style layout, clean, sparsely furnished rooms, and a beautiful garden courtyard. Reservations recommended Oct.-Nov., especially for longer stays. Singles Rs220, with bath Rs260; doubles Rs300/350.

Dragon Guest House (tel./fax 479562), a 10min. walk down the *other* northern lane. Follow signs past the Khentse monastery. Remote but clean, with sparkling bathrooms and a large Western clientele. Free 7am tea, a small library, and attached veg. **restaurant** (breakfast Rs20-60, entrees Rs15-60; open daily 7am-10pm). Singles Rs220; doubles Rs340, with kitchenette Rs440. Discounts for longer stays.

Kailash Guest House (tel. 480741), 5min. down the main lane on the right. Simple rooms furnished with mirrored bureau. Pleasant terraces on each floor. Hot water, seat toilets, and discounts for students and longer stays. In-season: singles Rs200; doubles Rs250, with bath Rs300. Off-season: Rs50 and under.

Peace Guest House, just inside the southern *stupa* gates on the right, has a double, a triple, and a quad, all filled for Rs80 per bed. Large rooms have carpet and fans but no hot water. Check-in 7:30am-9pm. Austere but friendly communal feel. Padlocks with shared keys. Attached restaurant has separate Chinese and English menus. Guess which one's cheaper. Open daily 7:30am-9pm.

🍴 FOOD

The Original Stupa View Restaurant, next to the *stupa* where the northern lane begins. Not to be confused with its neighbor of a similar name, the Original Stupa View boasts an original menu melding together local and Middle Eastern flavors. Small but appetizing selection of veg. entrees Rs120-200.

Om Shanti Restaurant and Cafe, on the western side of the *stupa*. This enthusiastically decorated place seats you right next to the *stupa*, plays good music, and serves cheap Tibetan (Rs35-50) and Indian (Rs25-80) specialties. Open daily 7am-9pm.

Tashi Delek Restaurant, on the corner of the *stupa* compound where the main lane begins. A blue-and-white curtain marks this 3-table, low-profile eatery. Wide selection of entrees Rs15-70. The portions aren't huge, but they're yummy, and at Rs15 a plate, you can afford seconds. Open daily 6am-8pm.

Double Dorjee Restaurant, just past the Karmapa Service Society Nepal on the right off the main lane. A favorite with monks and ex-pats. Low tables, floral upholstery, paper lanterns, and "inspirational" posters. Blackboard menu offers Tibetan, Chinese, Japanese, and Continental entrees (Rs40-110). A Tibetan family provides slow and friendly service, so you'll have plenty of time to chat with the regulars while you wait for your food. Open daily 7:30am-9:30pm.

🛕 SIGHTS

THE STUPA

Boudha's is not only Nepal's most imposing stupa, but also one of the world's largest. Various legends detail the *stupa's* origins, and the 5th-century date assigned by historians is only a guess. A Tibetan myth tells of a poultry farmer's daughter who wanted to build a *stupa*. The king granted her the area that could be covered by a buffalo skin. Not content to build so small a *stupa*, the girl cut the skin into enough strips to trace the perimeter of the huge lot on which the *stupa* now stands. The Newari version relates a story of a king who constructed taps from which no water would flow. Convinced that only the sacrifice of a great man would bring water, he tricked his son into patricide by ordering him to go to the spouts and behead the shrouded man he found lying there. This, of course, turned out to be the king, and, horrified by his deed, the remorseful prince built the *stupa* in the hope of redeeming himself.

Whatever its origins, the *stupa* has inspired awe and reverence since ancient times, when its location along the Kathmandu-Lhasa trade route made it a popular pilgrimage site (people still pray at Boudha for safe passage through the Himalayas). Each segment of its structure is said to correspond to one of the five elements: the three-leveled *mandala*-shaped base represents earth; the dome, water; the spire (with its 13 steps corresponding to the 13 steps to nirvana), fire; the parasol, air; and the pinnacle, ether. The red-rimmed blue Buddha-eyes that gaze out from each of the four sides of the golden spire are unique to Nepali *stupas*, and the "nose" in between them is actually the number "1" in Nepali script. The *stupa* is whitewashed and splashed with stripes of rust-colored wash to resemble the lotus shape. Its wall is inset with niches containing prayer wheels and 108 images of the Buddha. At the entrance to the *stupa* itself is a shrine to the Newari goddess Ajima, protectress of children and goddess of smallpox. The *stupa* affords a view punctuated by prayer flags and the golden roofs of *gompas*.

Visitors are usually welcome in the **gompas**—there is one right off the *stupa* compound and many more farther afield—as long as they observe the necessary etiquette (usually posted on signs outside the *gompas*). Dress modestly, take your shoes off before entering the *lhakang* (main hall), walk around clockwise inside, and always ask before taking photos. As monasteries have traditionally relied on contributions from visitors and pilgrims passing through, donations are greatly appreciated. If you visit a *lama*, present him with a white *khata* (prayer scarf). These are inexpensive and available at many shops around Boudha, where someone can show you how to fold them properly. In the *lhakang*, you'll find intricate wall paintings in overwhelmingly vivid colors. Gold statues of the Buddha, other *bodhisattvas*, and the *gompa* sect's founder are surrounded by offerings of food, incense, and butter-lamps.

The year's largest celebrations happen in February. Thousands come to Boudha and reunite with friends and family for **Losar,** the Tibetan New Year. The **Festival of Lights,** held the night of February's full moon, is a more sober occasion commemorating the completion of the *stupa* hundreds of years ago. Beginning at dusk, worshippers circle the *stupa*, praying and chanting in penance and thanksgiving.

The *stupa* is surrounded by shops. You don't need to come all the way to Boudha to buy the standard tourist junk, but it is *the* place for Tibetan antiques and cheap souvenirs like Tibetan head- and foot-gear and Buddhist prayer flags.

STUDY AND VOLUNTEER OPPORTUNITIES

The **Ka-Nying Shedrup Ling Monastery** (tel. 470993), known as the white monastery or *seto gompa*, is located between the two northern lanes and is particularly welcoming of Westerners. Its charming and charismatic leader, Chyoki Nyima Rinpoche, meets with visitors (daily 10am-noon) and holds a teaching session in English (Sa 11:30am-12:30pm). To speak to him, walk around to the right of the main hall and climb the stairs to the top floor. **Kopan Monastery** (tel. 481268; fax 481267), located atop a hill 2km north of Boudha, offers several meditation courses throughout the year and welcomes volunteers to work in their **library** (Su-F 1-3pm) or clinic. It offers accommodations (dorm beds Rs80; rooms Rs190 per bed with bath; breakfast included) throughout the year and welcomes visitors for meditation and English discussion sessions (Su-F 10am). Kopan is a 45-minute walk from Boudha. From the northern lane, head northwest from the *stupa* and turn right onto the taxi road that leads north and winds up the hill. A large map sits just inside Kopan's entrance, and a shop on the left sells refreshments and postcards. The reception is behind you as you face the map. (Office open daily 9am-noon and 1-5pm.) Finally, the **Vajra Center** (tel. 481562 or 478978) is a great place for English-speakers to teach Tibetans English for either short or long-term periods. Tibetan classes are offered in exchange. (Classes run from 7:30-9:30am and 3:30-5:30pm.) The Center is up the *other* northern lane on the right from the *stupa*, minute's walk before the white monastery.

BHAKTAPUR भक्तपु

On the eastern rim of the Kathmandu valley lies an idyllic, though anachronistic town. A 1934 earthquake leveled most of Bhaktapur's famous temples and landmarks. Soon after, plans were set in motion to restore the city to its 15th century splendor and give a boost to local craftsmanship. Excellent civic planning has made Bhaktapur the clean est, most attractive city in the Kathmandu Valley. Entering the neatly-paved pedestrian-only area for a Rs300 fee might evoke the feeling of being at a theme park, but Bhaktapur is no fairy town. The entry fee continues to finance restoration projects and civic programs such as trash pickup.

Founded in the 9th century, Bhaktapur (also called Bhadgaon) was the capital of the Kathmandu Valley until the region was divided into three kingdoms in 1482. The town's prominence faded when the Gorkhas conquered it in 1768 and established the capital in Kathmandu (see **History**, p. 708). Many of its buildings are reconstructed versions of temples built in the 15th to 17th centuries. Restoration and rebuilding continue, encouraged by a German development project in the 1970s, as the municipality is well aware of the value of its treasures. Attracted by its famous temples and museums (whose artifacts are of religious significance to Hindus and Buddhists alike), as well as by the town's strong sense of community, Nepali tourists constitute a large portion of Bhaktapur's non-resident population.

> **WARNING.** Visitors of Bhaktapur will be followed relentlessly by young boys who claim to be practicing their English. Extremely well-informed about Bhaktapur's history, they will inevitably ask for money directly, promote a *thanka* painting shop, or beg you to buy them a school book or school clothes. These they will later return to the store for a portion of the price.

ORIENTATION

Bhaktapur is bordered to the north and south by main paved roads running to and from Kathmandu, 14km to the east. The southern half of the city is characterized by residential streets, fields, and multiple *ghats* (platforms for religious worship) along the **Hanumante River.** Bhaktapur's main sights are in the northern half of the city, in three squares strung together by a curving main street. Anchoring the city's northwest edge, **Durbar Square** is connected in its southeast corner to **Taumadhi Tol** by a short lane. From the northeast corner of Taumadhi Tol, the connecting street widens into Bhaktapur's commercial area, **Sukuldhoka,** and makes a right-angle turn about a quarter of the way to **Tachapal Tol** (also called **Dattatraya Square**), which is about ten minutes away by foot. Alleyways twist north and south of this main artery. Minibuses from Kathmandu arrive near a large water tank called **Navpokhu Pokhari,** which is to your left when coming from Durbar Square Gate. The **trolleybus** stops at the southern edge of town, 15 minutes from Durbar Square.

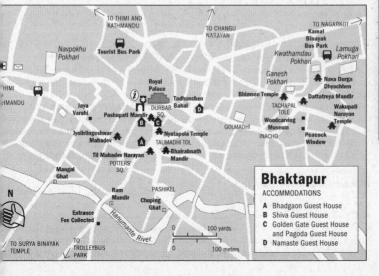

Bhaktapur

ACCOMMODATIONS

A Bhadgaon Guest House
B Shiva Guest House
C Golden Gate Guest House and Pagoda Guest House
D Namaste Guest House

Tourists must pay Rs300 or US$5 at **Durbar Square Gate** or at the other checkpoints that secure access to the city. If you get into town by another route and avoid these booths, you may still be asked for your ticket inside. The ticket can be used for multiple entries and days as long as you notify the **Tourist Service Centre.**

🛈 PRACTICAL INFORMATION

Buses: Minibus Park, near Navpokhu Pokhari (a large water tank). Express bus to Kathmandu's **Bagh Bazaar,** east of Durbar Marg (#7, frequent, 45min., Rs6). **Trolleybus Park,** south of Bhaktapur. Walk south from Durbar Square to the main paved road. Less crowded than buses, **trollies** head to Kathmandu's **Tripureswar,** near the **National Stadium** (frequent, 1hr., Rs4). **Kamal Binayak,** in the northeast edge of Bhaktapur. Turn left after the pottery square east of Dattatraya Square, and head north to the edge of town. To: **Nagarkot** (every hr., 1½hr., Rs10-25).

Local Transportation: Buses: Bus #7 runs along the northern edge of town from the hospital to Kamal Binayak. **Taxis** wait at the **Tourist Bus Park** just outside the main gate leading into Durbar Square. **Bicycles** are available on the road connecting Navpokhu Pokhari and Durbar Square. **Cycle Repair Center,** on the south side of the road, rents out standard one-speed bikes for Rs10 per hr., Rs50 per day. Open daily 7am-7pm.

Tourist Office: Tourist Service Centre and Information Hall, Durbar Square Gate (tel. 612249). Run by the Bhaktapur Municipality, this is where you can pay the Rs300 or US$5 entrance fee and get a brochure and a useful map. Keep your ticket and have it certified to re-enter if you leave. Public toilets with toilet paper. Open daily 6am-8pm.

Currency Exchange: Layaku Money Exchange Counter (tel. 612208), down the alley to the right of Durbar Square Gate. Commission 1.5%. Open daily 10am-5pm.

Market: Sukuldhoka, the main street that connects Tamadhi Tol and Tachapal Tol. Fruit, vegetable, and material sellers line the street from roughly 6am-6pm.

Pharmacy: Several across from the hospital, including **Sewa Medicine Store** (tel. 613773). Open daily; 24hr. pharmacist.

Hospital: Government Hospital (tel. 610676), west of the Navpokhu Pokhari Minibus Park, on the north side of the street. Not the cleanest, most up-to-date of medical clinics—if you're really ill you might consider heading to Kathmandu for treatment. Staffed by specialists 9am-2pm; physicians and paramedic on call 24hr.

Police: (tel. 612204), just inside Durbar Square Gate on the left, all the way in the rear of the courtyard. Manned 24hr.

Post Office: Across from the Navpokhu Pokhari Minibus Park. No *Poste Restante*. No English either. Open Su-Th 10am-5pm, F 10am-3pm.

Internet: Dhaubhadel Handicraft and Communication Center, Bahatal (tel. 611320; fax 612780; email dhaubdel@mos.com.np), connecting Durbar Square to Taumadhi Tol, across the street from Marco Polo Restaurant. **Email** (Rs20 per Kb) and **web access** (Rs10 per min.). Open daily 8:30am-6pm. A number of other shops in Durbar Square have also begun offering Internet services.

Telephones: STD/ISD offices dot the town. **Laiku Worldwide Communications** (tel./fax 610258), near the corner on the right, facing the outside of Durbar Square Gate. Free callbacks and a private booth. Open daily 7am-7pm. **World Wide Hello Service,** Tibukchhen (tel. 613342 or 613473; fax 612607), past Namaste Guest House on the left, towards Dattatraya Square. Callbacks Rs10 per min. Open daily 8am-8:30pm.

PHONE CODE	01

🏠 ACCOMMODATIONS

For many visitors to the Kathmandu Valley, Bhaktapur is just a daytrip from Kathmandu. Bhaktapur's guest houses are either very nice or very cheap. But even the most luxurious hotels are moderately priced, and all accommodations have hot showers, laundry, convenient temple-side locations, ultra-accommodating owners, and rooftop gardens with magnificent views. Once you determine your price range, deciding which temple you want outside your window might be your greatest dilemma. Rates are always negotiable, especially for groups, students, and travelers planning longer stays. During the off-season (May-Aug.), bargain hard. Reservations are recommended in high season. Noon check-out is standard everywhere, and most places lock up at 10pm. Prices listed here are high season.

Pagoda Guest House, Taumadhi Tol (tel. 613248; fax 612685), right behind the Nyatapola temple, to the left. Bed and breakfast atmosphere and a unique location (practically on top of a 5-story temple) make this an inviting place to stay. Squat and seat toilets. Singles Rs350, with bath Rs800; doubles Rs400/Rs1000. Group discounts available.

Namaste Guest House, Sakotha Tol (tel. 610500), on the corner where Tibukchhen meets Sakotha, leading into the northeast corner of Durbar Square. Clean, spacious rooms with wildly decorated bedsheets and friendly, helpful staff. Guests receive a discount at the affiliated **Sunny Restaurant** (see below). Singles Rs250, with bath Rs450; doubles Rs400/600. MC, Visa.

Shiva Guest House (tel. 613912; fax 610740; email bisket@wlink.com.np), on the road connecting Durbar Square to Taumadhi Tol, next door to Dhaubhadel Handicraft and Communication Center. Clean rooms, email service, in-house travel agency, and attached bar. Rs400, with bath Rs1000; doubles Rs550/1400.

Bhadgaon Guest House, Taumadhi Tol (tel. 610488; fax 610481), on the left just as you enter Taumadhi Tol from Potters' Square, before Cafe Nyatapola. Marble stairs and carefully kept garden courtyard make this Bhaktapur's swankiest hotel. Rooftop restaurant with terrific views (entrees Rs100-180). Nine rooms, all with attached bath—toilet paper, towels, and slippers, too. Singles Rs600; doubles Rs800.

Golden Gate Guest House, Bahatal (tel. 610534; fax 611081), on the left side of the street as you approach Taumadhi Tol from Durbar Square. Duck through the doorway to reach the Golden Gate, two courtyards removed from Durbar Square. 9 rooms with common bath, 6 with attached bath. Nicest rooms are at the top. Singles Rs250, with bath Rs550; doubles Rs400/1000. MC, Visa, AmEx.

FOOD

While most of Bhaktapur's restaurants whip up the standard Nepali-Continental-Indian-Chinese fare, some do stand out because of their settings. Many guest houses have rooftop restaurants whose elevation is more alluring than their copycat menus. Less touristy restaurants, providing Nepali cuisine for half the price and twice the excitement, are clustered in the older, more residential areas of town, easily distinguished by their dirt roads. Most any place with tables, benches, and a stove will make a mean *dal bhat* for under a buck. *Ju dhau* (king of curds), a creamy, sweet yogurt, is a local specialty that can be found almost anywhere.

Sunny Restaurant, Taumadhi Tol, located in a typical old house, just to the right facing Nyatapola Temple. Clay floors, low ceilings, canvas-painted walls, knee-high tables, and rooftop kitchen enhance the basic fare. Continental (Rs75-160), Newari (Rs65-110), and Nepali (Rs100-225) meals. Beer (Rs85-110) is the cheapest around.

Marco Polo Restaurant, Taumadhi Tol immediately to the left facing Nyatapola Temple. With its green shutters and plaid tablecloths, Marco Polo is a less sexy, but cheaper alternative to other tourist restaurants. Rub elbows, shoulders, and knees with other budget travelers on the tiny balcony overlooking the northwest corner of the square. Fairly extensive menu with dishes (lasagna, burgers, Indian, and Nepali) from Rs60-100. Open daily 7am-8pm.

Cafe de Temple Town Restaurant, Durbar Square (tel. 612432). Walking from Durbar Square Gate, turn right. A small garden screens the patio tables from the noise of the square without obscuring the sights. Enjoy familiar fare during the day, or hang with the locals at night over grilled chicken, goat, and water buffalo. Vegetable dishes Rs75-100, entrees Rs90-250. Open daily 8am-9pm.

Cafe de Peacock and Somo Bar, Tachapal Tol, facing Dattatraya Temple. 2nd floor on the left. Indoor and outdoor seating make for great people-watching. Mexican, Italian, and Nepalese plates (Rs150-300). Hard liquor (Rs30-120) and beer (Rs90-120). MC, Visa, AmEx. 10% European Traveler's Network discount. Open daily 9am-9pm.

👁 SIGHTS

DURBAR SQUARE

Bhaktapur's is the oldest and least cluttered Durbar Square in the valley. Thinned out by a 1934 earthquake, the wide-open pedestrian area hosts just enough architectural wonders to be imposing but not overwhelming. The **Royal Palace** encloses the north side of the square. The current buildings date from the 16th and 17th centuries when, under Malla rule, Bhaktapur was the heart of valley life. Paintings, statues, and tapestries from this era still decorate the west wing of the palace, which now houses the **National Art Gallery.** The gallery displays incredibly intricate Newari *paubha* and Tibetan *thanka* paintings; its oldest objects are stone sculptures from as early as the 11th century. The gallery affords the best view of the palace's courtyards, most of which are closed to visitors. Next door is the famous Garuda-crested **Golden Gate,** built in the early 18th century by King Bhupatindra Malla. The king's image caps a stone pillar facing the gate. To the east of the larger palace building sits the **Palace of 55 Windows.** The carved wooden windows are less flashy but more impressive than the gate itself—each window took a craftsman about 100 days to construct.

Like the palace, Durbar Square's temples exemplify the remarkable craftsmanship of the Malla era. The westernmost temple in the Square, **Bansi Narayan** is dedicated to Krishna, and its roof struts depict various incarnations of Vishnu. Behind the king's pillar is the elephant-flanked stone **Vatsala Durga Temple.** Built in the mid-18th century in the *shikhara* style, this temple boasts an impressive display of stone carving, metalwork, and wood carving. To the left is the **Chyasilin Mandap** (Eight-Cornered Pavilion), a 1990 reconstruction incorporating fragments of the 18th-century original. Using a 100-year old photograph of the *mandap,* the German Agency for Technical Cooperation and local craftsmen built on the ruins to restore the structure to its past grandeur. They reinforced the building with steel to protect against future earthquake damage. Upstairs is where tourists and teenagers congregate, the former to take in the view and the latter just to hang out. In the eastern section of the square, around the corner of the palace, there are several more temples and temple foundations. The most interesting is the 17th-century stone **Siddhi Lakshmi Temple,** with its procession of animals and people on either side of the stairs. The souvenir shops that surround this part of the square were once *dharam-shalas* (pilgrims' resthouses). Back in the southeast corner of the main part of the square, the **Pashupatinath Mandir,** the most active of the Durbar Square temples, contains a 17th-century reproduction of the *linga* at Pashupatinath. Check out the especially creative contortions of the couples on the roof struts, the only parts of the building that survive from the original 15th-century structure. *(Mandir open W-Th and Sa-M 10:15am-4:30pm, F 10am-2:30pm. Rs20. No cameras allowed inside. English information pamphlet available.)*

TAUMADHI TOL

Connected to Durbar Square by a short, shop-lined street, Taumadhi Tol is Bhaktapur at its best, a place where architectural masterpieces and religious ceremony mingle with daily life. Musicians and daily worshippers converge on the square during the **Bisket Jatra,** Bhaktapur's renowned celebration of the new year in April. Nepal's tallest pagoda, **Nyatapola Temple,** dominates the square and all of Bhaktapur. The newly renovated five-story red pagoda was originally built in 1702 by King Bhupatindra Malla. Five pairs of stone creatures flank the stairs to the temple. Each pair is said to be ten times stronger than the one below, starting with a pair of Malla wrestlers who seem ten times stronger than the average man. Next are a pair of elephants, followed by lions, giraffes, and finally the goddesses Bahini (the Tigress)

THANKAS FOR THE MEMORIES Hanging in shop windows, peering out at you from glass frames with their gold-painted eyes, *thankas* are everywhere in the Kathmandu Valley. Traditional *thankas* (pronounced THANG-ka, or "something rolled up") are religious scroll paintings that serve as aids for meditation in temples or family altars. Colorful and elaborate, they are painted to comply with strict rules that dictate style and subject matter. Most *thankas* depict the lives of the Buddha, *bodhisattvas*, saints, or *lamas*; the wheel of life; and the *mandala*, or the Tibetan calendar. In representations of the Buddha's life, pictures start in the top left-hand corner and continue counter-clockwise. The wheel of life *thanka* reveals mankind's various states, from sin (at the bottom) to enlightenment (on top). The *mandala*, which depicts the steps to enlightenment, is the most popular. A good *thanka* could take a week or six months to create; the outlines of the images are drawn, then colors are added in layers. In a workshop, layers are worked by increasingly skilled artists: first large blocks of color, then the setting, then any gold details, and finally the faces of the figures. A *thanka* cannot be used, however, until it has been consecrated by a *lama*, who makes an inscription on the back. Most *thankas* that are sold have not been consecrated and many don't comply with guidelines. If you're interested in buying a *thanka*, shop around first. As with any fine art, the range in prices (Rs100-10,000) reflects the range of quality, though a high price does not necessarily mean high quality.

and Singhini (the Lioness). The image of **Siddhi Lakshmi**, the goddess to whom the temple is devoted, is locked inside and accessible only to priests.

The eastern side of the square is dominated by the comparably solid **Bhairavnath Mandir**, which was built as a single-story temple in the 18th century. A second story was later added, and the entire structure was rebuilt with the existing three stories after the 1934 earthquake. The golden image that peers down from the third story of the temple is that of Lord Bhairav, god of Terror; his head is supposedly locked inside. A doorway in the building at the south side of the square leads to a courtyard filled by the **Til Mahadev Narayan Mandir,** a 17th-century temple (on an 11th-century temple site) reminiscent of Changu Narayan with its pillar-mounted golden Garuda, *chakra*, and *sankha*.

TACHAPAL TOL (DATTATRAYA SQUARE)

A wide, curving street of shops catering to locals rather than tourists (although some of their wares make great souvenirs) links Taumadhi Tol to Bhaktapur's oldest square, Tachapal Tol. The wooden buildings that enclose the square were once *maths* (priests' residences). The **Dattatraya Mandir** presides over the square from the eastern end. Built in 1427, it is the oldest surviving building in Bhaktapur, and like other famous structures in the Kathmandu Valley, it is said to have been built from the trunk of just one tree—from the looks of it, one *mammoth* tree. A pair of Malla wrestlers, gaudily painted during festivals, guards the entrance; they contrast starkly with the monochrome of the temple's beautiful wood carvings. Dattatraya appeals to both Hindus and Buddhists since he is considered an avatar of Vishnu, a guru of Shiva and a cousin of the Buddha. At the other end of the square is the rectangular **Bhimsen Temple,** honoring the favorite god of Newari merchants.

Behind the Dattatraya Temple are two museums housed in *maths*. To the left, the **Brass and Bronze Museum** displays a collection of 300-year-old functional objects such as lamps, cooking pots, hookahs, spittoons, and carved ritual paraphernalia. In the **Pujari Math** is the **National Art Gallery Woodcarving Museum,** worth visiting more for its magnificent courtyard than for its collection. Halfway down the street around the corner from the Woodcarving Museum is the famous **Peacock Window,** dating from the 17th century. (*Admission to any one of the three museums allows entry to the other two. Open Sa-M and W-Th 10am-5pm, F 10am-3pm. Rs20; camera fee Rs20.*)

NEPAL

OTHER SIGHTS

In the squares just east and south of Taumadhi Tol, both known as **Potters' Square,** you can see hundreds of pots lined up to dry in the sun or stacked up to be sold. Stroll south toward the river to see *ghats*, fields, and temples which, in contrast to their northern counterparts, are more functional than they are decorative. Amble through the Kamal Binayak market to avoid tourists, even if it means tripping over playing children or having refuse hurled at you from the windows; the Bhaktapur experience is singularly unpredictable.

 SHOPPING

Bhaktapur is home to some of the finest **pottery** in the valley and, while similar items are also available in Kathmandu, it's infinitely more satisfying to purchase directly from the artisans here in Bhaktapur. The best place to meet up with potters and their collections of bowls, masks, and icons is **Potter's Square.** Bhaktapur also has a long-standing reputation for fine **wooden handicrafts,** which are sold in Durbar and Tachapal Squares. While the painted wooden toys are actually made in Patan, the miniature carved windows are all produced in Bhaktapur. You'll also see **papier maché masks** and marionettes—any of the handmade paper products are made at the UNICEF factory in Bhaktapur.

CHANGU NARAYAN चाँगु नारायण

After you've seen your 27th Nepali temple, the prospect of making a trip out to Changu Narayan to see yet another temple might not seem too enticing, but in this case it should. 7km north of Bhaktapur atop the "shaking hill" of Changu, the temple of Changu Narayan is Nepal's oldest and most sacred. Worshippers have visited, adorned, restored, and revered the Vishnu shrine on this site since the 4th century. Eclectically patched and elaborated over the intervening centuries, it is a living time capsule revealing more than a millennium's worth of stylistic and artistic developments. Equally impressive are the large sculptures and polished black relief panels that cluster around it. These works are considered among Nepal's greatest treasures. The town that surrounds this marvellous site is an idyllic spot for peaceful respite and breathtaking panoramic views. The town now charges a Rs60 **entrance fee** payable at a small shack to the left of the city gates (open 6am-6pm). In return for the fee you receive an informative brochure guide filled with historical information on the temple and environs.

◪ **ORIENTATION AND PRACTICAL INFORMATION.** A **taxi** ride is the fastest, but most expensive way to reach Changu Narayan (Rs500 from Kathmandu, Rs200 from Bhaktapur). **Buses** depart from and arrive at Bhaktapur's bus park, across from the hospital (every hr., 30min., Rs5; last bus to Bhaktapur 6pm). For those looking to forego four-wheeled transportation, Changu Narayan is a 45-minute bike ride from Bhaktapur. Just follow the signs from the Mini Bus Park. The town can also be reached via a two-hour hike from the mountain viewpoint of Nagarkot to the east. Getting off the Nagarkot bus at Telkot (#7, 30min., Rs5) and walking straight along the ridge will get you there in about an hour and a half. Another approach is from the north side, off the road between Boudha and Sankhu, but it is trekkable only in the dry season when the Manohara River is low enough to be forded. The main road into Changu Narayan leads into the new Changu Narayan bus park. The **temple** is up the steps from the city gates.

◪▢ **ACCOMMODATIONS AND FOOD.** At the back of the Changu Narayan bus park sits the **Binyak Restaurant.** Offering standard Continental (Rs50-200) and Indian (Rs50-120) fare as well as a range of alcoholic beverages (Rs80-120), it's a good place to catch a light meal while waiting for your bus. Next to the main gate (where you paid the Rs60 fee) sits the lovely **Coffee House.** Not nearly as lovely as its view, this cold store with seating still makes for a pleasant place to sit and enjoy the surroundings. Valued for its location, if not its cuisine, the **Champak Restaurant,** located right inside the Changu Narayan Temple complex, offers a light breakfast or lunch (Rs5-25) as well as a range of beverages. For those looking to spend the night, posible accommodations are anything but posh. The **Changu Narayan Bed and Breakfast,** ocated right before the temple entrance, and the **Changu Narayan New Hill Resort,** ten minutes down the main road from the bus park, offer basic backpacker-style accommodations (singles Rs100; doubles Rs200).

SIGHTS. Entering the courtyard of the **Changu Narayan Temple** from town puts ou behind the temple with two stone gryphons facing you. Stone lions guard the temple, and a spreading copper doorway embossed with flower designs frames the entrance. The temple, with its 7th-century golden image of Vishnu, is open only to *rahmins*. On either side of the temple, pillars bear the symbols of Vishnu: a life-wheel and a stone staff on the left represent *brahmins* and *chettris* respectively, and a conch shell and lotus flower on the right represent the occupational and business castes. The **inscription** at the base of the pillar is the oldest in the valley, dating from AD 454 and relating the victories of King Manadeva. The statue of Vishnu's man-bird vehicle, Garuda, kneeling at the door with a cobra around his neck, was carved at about the same time. His face is said to be a likeness of King Manadeva himself, who reputedly said that he too was a vehicle for Vishnu. In the birdcage over Garuda's shoulder are two more recent figures, Bupathindra Malla and Bubana Lakshmi, the 17th-century king and queen of Bhaktapur who introduced metalwork to the temple by financing the ornate copper doorway.

The best **sculptures** are beside the main temple, past the right pillar on the brick pavilion of the **Lakshmi Narayan Temple** (with black wooden columns). In the central relief, Vishnu as Narasimha, half-man and half-lion, tears a hole in the chest of a demon. To the left of this, a relief shows the story of Vishnu as Vikrantha, the dwarf who grew to celestial size and crossed the earth and the heavens in three steps. The heavens swirl around him, and people clutch at his toes while his legs span the whole scene. On the platform next to the Lakshmi Narayan Temple is an image of Vishnu as Narayan, sleeping on a knotted snake. The ten-headed, ten-armed figure above Narayan depicts the universal face of Vishnu, showing each of his ten avatars. Across the courtyard is the sculpture of Vishnu riding Garuda that appears on 0-rupee notes. All of these sculptures date from the Licchavi period, before the Mallas took over in 1200, when stone sculpture in the valley was at its height (see **Malla Kingdoms,** p. 708).

DHULIKHEL धुलिखेल

Bursting with mountain views, and hemmed in by terraced valleys and jagged peaks, Dhulikhel is a veritable paradise at 1550m. Less touristed than neighboring Nagarkot, the town promises Himalayan sunrises to beat them all. If the panoramic views have as you craving even more natural beauty, the many short treks into the surrounding area can surely satisfy. Hikers and bikers throng to this eastern mountain town to wander into the wilderness beyond. The multitude of signs written only in Nepali script belies Dhulikhel's local importance as an important market town on the Nepal-China trade route.

ORIENTATION AND PRACTICAL INFORMATION. Dhulikhel is just off the Arniko Highway, 32km southeast of Kathmandu. The road to Dhulikhel runs past the **bus park** on the right and past a sign for the hospital, also on the right. The road then curves past the **Rastriya Banijya Bank,** uphill to the **town center,** where a bust of King Mahendra stands next to a water tank. To the right of the statue, the road leads northwest into the main square and the old town. From Kathmandu, take the **#12 bus** (every 20min., 1½hr., Rs20), which also makes stops near Bhaktapur's trolley-bus park and Banepa's bus park. **Rastriya Banijya Bank** charges a 1.5% commission on currency exchange (open Su-Th 10:30am-2:30pm, F 10:30am-noon). The best **pharmacy,** with an English-speaking staff, is down the road on the right (open Su-F 8am-7pm, Sa 7am-1pm). The **hospital** (tel. 61497) is 10min. away from the bus park—follow the sign. General practitioners staff the amazingly well-kept clinic daily 8am-5pm (on call after 5pm), except for W and Sa, when it offers emergency care only.

Its in-house **pharmacy** opens at 9am. Broad inventory makes it the best place to get prescriptions filled. The **post office** is downhill from town center, on the right (open Su-Th 10am-5pm, F 10am-3pm). The town center is dotted with businesses offering **Internet access** (average rate Rs10 per min. or Rs20 per Kb). **Sunrise Travels** (tel. 62025; fax 64014), centrally located across the street and downhill from Raju's Store, provides full Internet access (open daily 7am-9pm). **Raju's Store** (tel. 61472), past the post office and volleyball courts, has **STD/ISD** and callbacks for Rs3 per min (open Su-F 7am-6pm).

▓▓ ACCOMMODATIONS AND FOOD. **Panorama View Lodge** (tel. 62085), can be reached by following the road to the left of the Mahendra statue, then taking the road that veers right up the hill. Large doubles with balconies, clean bathrooms with hot showers and seat toilets. (In season: singles Rs600; doubles Rs1000. Off-season discounts available. Reservations recommended. MC, Visa.) **Nawaranga Guest House** (tel. 61226), a five-minute walk up the road. Backpacker haven has rooms with low ceilings, concrete floors, and good rooftop views. Clean, common squat toilets. Hot water Rs10 per bucket. Superb restaurant (entrees Rs20-100) and art gallery. (Dorm beds Rs75; singles Rs100; doubles Rs150.) **Dhulikhel Lodge** (tel. 61753), across the street from the bus park, has 20 large rooms with common bath (seat or squat toilets). Restaurant offers Nepali and Italian meals (Rs100-200) and a 10% student discount. (In-season: singles Rs1000; doubles Rs1300. 25% discount off-season. MC, Visa, Amex.) **Dhulikhel Royal Guest House** (tel. 64059), on the right past the sign to the hospital, was once called the Royal East Inn, though the place now has only average cleanliness and general appeal. Attached restaurant has a good selection of continental entrees for Rs60-130. (Singles Rs270, with bath Rs540; doubles Rs470/1000. 25% student discount. Reservations recommended.) Alternatively, you can pick up a quick snack at any of the cold stores in town.

▣ SIGHTS AND SUNRISES. The beautiful sunrise over the mountains is the main draw to Dhulikhel, and the most popular vista for watching the spectacle is the **Kali Shrine.** To reach the shrine, walk to the Panorama View Lodge, and continue uphill; the shrine is at the summit. The hike takes a little over an hour from the center of town, so plan ahead to catch the sunrise. Dhulikhel's cobblestoned main square is also worth exploring. The square's two temples honor two different forms of Vishnu: the small, brightly tiled temple is dedicated to Harisiddhi and the even smaller one facing it, to Narayan. They are guarded by two Garudas. Further northwest, at the high point of the town, the pagoda-like **Bhagwati Mandir** is of more interest as a lookout than as a temple.

NEAR DHULIKHEL

Dhulikhel is the starting point for a number of short, one-day treks. Most worthwhile among these are the treks to **Namobuddha** and **Panauti.** *Namobuddha* means hail to the Buddha—it is the place where he supposedly offered his body as food to a starving tigress. Around this area are a number of actively used *stupas* as well as a Buddhist retreat center and a small tea shop, making this an ideal place to break and observe the daily rituals of the local Buddhist monks. Namobuddha is three hours from Dhulikhel with two paths running to and from, allowing for a full loop. Panauti, home to the **Indreshwar Mahadev Temple,** is a small Newari village famous for its wood carvings. The hike to Panauti takes about four hours and can be combined with the Namobuddha trek to form an all day excursion. **Buses** run from Panauti to Dhulikhel (frequent, Rs10), so a one-way trek is possible. (Maps for these treks can be obtained for free from any of the major guest houses.)

The road along the pastoral hillside from Dhulikhel to Bhaktapur is ideal for **mountain biking.** Leaving from the bus park, follow the main highway away from town and then follow the signs to Bhaktapur. There are no bike rental facilities in Dhulikhel, so it is best to rent in Kathmandu. You can bring your bike on the bus (the driver will attach it to the roof for you) or put it in the back of a taxi.

NAGARKOT नगरकोट

Teetering at 2175m on the eastern rim of the Kathmandu Valley 32km from the capital, Nagarkot is the popular Himalayan viewpoint from which, in clear weather, one can see Mt. Everest. Tourism has spurred the development of Nagarkot from its origins as a military base. Daytrippers (actually, more like one-nighters) come to any of the dozen guest houses to catch the Himalayan sunrise. There are several day treks down to neighboring mountain villages that offer glimpses of the Nepalese village life you'll never see in foreigner-packed Nagarkot. On the bus ride up, if you can peek out of the window as the bus careens around a hairpin turn, you'll see patterned rice and corn plots etched into the hillside next to uncultivated hills draped in lush vegetation. Monsoon season is exactly the wrong time to visit unless you're seeking cold air and not mountain views. Nagarkot gets quite chilly at night; bring warm clothes.

◪ **ORIENTATION AND PRACTICAL INFORMATION.** Nagarkot consists of an ever-growing cluster of guest houses along a verdant **ridge.** The road from Bhaktapur continues north past the bus stop and forks at the base of a hill, where a large **map** on the left charts Nagarkot's guest houses. The road that curves to the right leads to **The Tea House** and **Club Himalaya**, both of which sit on top of the hill. The road that curves north around the left side of the hill leads to the bank, the rest of Nagarkot's guest houses, and the high point on the ridge marked by the tiny **Mahakal Shrine. Local buses** leave from Kamal Binayak bus stop in the northeast of Bhaktapur (every hr., 1hr., Rs15; last bus leaves Nagarkot 5pm). **Tourist buses** leave from Kantipath in Kathmandu (1:30pm, 2½hr., Rs80) and return from Nagarkot the next morning (10am, 2½hr., Rs80). Tickets can be purchased at any agency in Thamel. **Taxis** leave from Bhaktapur (Rs400) and Kathmandu (Rs500). **Himalayan Bank Ltd.** (tel. 290885), just below the Tea House, **exchanges currency** for Rs150 or 1.5% fee (open Su-Th 10am-2pm, F 10am-noon). The nearest **hospital** is in Bhaktapur. **Club Himalaya** (tel. 290883) has email services for Rs10 per Kb, Internet services for Rs15 per min., and international telephone services with free callbacks.

▨ **ACCOMMODATIONS AND FOOD.** As the hotel strip above the clouds expands, true budget lodges are becoming an endangered species. Prices are negotiable (especially off season), and many hotel managers offer student discounts up to 15%. The following hotels cling to the ridge below the Mahakal Shrine. **The Resort at the End of the Universe** (tel. 290709) is one of Nagarkot's originals. Rustic, wooded, and remote, the brick and bamboo bungalows are simple but comfortable. (Singles Rs300; doubles with bath Rs500. 10-15% student discount on food and lodging. Reservations, recommended in high season, can be made directly or through the New Orleans Cafe in Thamel.) **The Hotel Madhuban Village** (tel. 290709) is a collection of A-frame bamboo cottages with big windows and not much room for anything but two single beds and a common squat toilet (no hot water). The glassed-in dining room (curries Rs200-250) affords good views. Doubles Rs300, with bath Rs600. 30% student discount.)

   The Tea House, just below Club Himalaya, is Nagarkot's most elegant place to eat, with tablecloths and plate-glass windows offering terrific views on all sides. It's a super-clean place to get some fresh air after the bus ride. Uniformed waiters serve Continental (Rs125-250) and Indian and Nepali dishes (Rs60-150). **The Restaurant at the End of the Universe**, attached to the similarly titled resort, offers the typical Continental variety of entrees, served in a pleasant space with cushioned platform seating. (Burgers, chicken, and rice Rs50-200.) Despite its name, there is nothing French about the **Cafe du Mont,** attached to the Peaceful Cottage. But it serves good standard tourist fare (veg. Rs90-175, non-veg. Rs110-250).

▧ **SIGHTS.** The hip thing to do in Nagarkot is watch the sun rise above the hills and set behind the valley, washing the mountain peaks in pink light. While all guest houses have great views, you can also walk up to the **Mahakal Shrine,** right next to the **End of the Universe,** or find out if the **lookout tower,** an leisurely hour-long walk south from the bus stop past the army base, is open. Lodge owners enthusiastically offer directions for walks to **Changu Narayan** (2hr.), **Sankhu** (2hr.), **Dhulikel** (5hr.), and **Shivapuri** (2-3 days).

NEPAL

GETTING SOUSED IN SHANGRI-LA Sure, you can stick to imported liquors or settle for whatever brand of red wine the Western supermarket happens to have in stock—neither of these practices will cause a dent in your booze budget. But braver, stingier souls consume domestic beer. The price (Rs60-90 for 650mL) is guaranteed to please, but the libations themselves are of varying quality. **Turborg** is tasty, while **Star** is palatable only if chilled to absolute zero. If your buck stops at the local brewery, though, you'll miss the fantastic opportunity to indulge in the fruits of the vanishing art of moonshining. **Chang** is your basic rice- or millet-based home brew, enjoyed by the masses and also appreciated by *lamas* in the high mountains. Perhaps the most elusive brew for foreigners is **tong-ba,** a Tibetan millet concoction that is by far the mellowest of the alcoholic trinity. Begin with fermented millet in the bottom of your vessel. Add hot water (make sure it's been boiled!), let it steep, and sip from a special straw that catches the grains. Kick back and enjoy the refills—the grains are good through several servings. Finally, **raksi** (rhymes with foxy) is Nepal's proudest and most potent offering. A distilled alcohol that resembles tequila, it's a sweet swallow that packs a serious punch. *Raksi* figures prominently in essential drinking vocabulary: *"malaai raksi laagyo"* literally means, "I am stricken by alcohol."

SANKHU सँखु

Surrounded by farmland, Sankhu sits at the end of the eastern road from Boudha. While it lacks the charm and community feel that would make it an interesting destination on its own (those looking for the typical Newari town experience would be better served by a journey to Kirtipur), Sankhu is popular as a starting point for those headed to the **Bajra Jogini Mandir** (Vajra Yogini). Built on an ancient Buddhist holy site, this 17th-century temple stands as a testament to Nepal's unique fusion of Hinduism and Buddhism. Buddhists have long revered the goddess as a protectress. Some say Bajra Jogini convinced Manjushri to drain the water-filled Kathmandu Valley. Another legend suggests that she requested the construction of the Boudhanath *stupa* and sent a white crane to select its location. She has since been adopted as a Tantric goddess, representing for Newari Buddhists the powerful female characteristics of Buddha, while Hindus in the valley worship her as a form of Durga. The temple has three gilded roofs and an elaborate door shielding the goddess's image from the public. The small two-tiered temple enshrines a replica of the Swayambhunath *stupa*.

The 2km walk from town starts through the cement archway to the left of the bus stop. The dirt road leads through town; about halfway to the temple, it continues to the right, while a stone-paved footpath leads straight ahead. The two meet up again at the base of the long, steep stairway to the top of the hill. From the base of the stairs, it's a 15-minute walk to the top. Giving Swayambunath a run for its money, the stairs to the temple are swarming with exceedingly playful monkeys—don't leave your possessions unattended.

Bus #4 (1½hr., Rs10) departs Ratna Park in Kathmandu for Sankhu as soon as it is full. It also stops east of Boudha. Sankhu is also accessible by **bicycle** (the road from Kathmandu is flat and, beyond Boudha, fairly pollution-free) or by **foot,** down from Nagarkot along a northwest trail. It is also possible to walk between Sankhu and Changu Narayan in the dry season. There are a few **cold stores** along the way.

DAKSHINKALI दक्षिण काली

While "Southern Kali" looks like an average quiet town on the fringe of the Kathmandu Valley, it takes on a different personality every Tuesday and Saturday morning, between 7-10am. The town hosts the famous Dakshinkali animal sacrifices, bloody offerings to propitiate the patron goddess Durga. Brightly clad women, men with roosters, goats, sheep, and ducks queue up to offer their animals at the shrine. At the western end of the compound sits a small black image of Kali perched in vic-

ry atop a corpse, hardly visible to tourists who are allowed only on the walkways
ove. It was installed in the 17th century by King Pratap Malla, purportedly on the
ders of the goddess herself, though Durga worship has taken place at the site long
fore that. Devotees wash their feet and animal offerings in the stream behind the
rine before making the sacrifice. If the animals do not attempt to shake off the
ater poured over their heads, they cannot be sacrificed. It's believed that animals
lled in sacrifice will enjoy the reward of higher incarnation. Those offered during
e eighth and ninth days of the festival of **Dasain,** the October celebration of the tri-
mph of good over evil, are relieved from burdensome animal life and reincarnated
 humans. When man and beast reach the image of Kali, the animal's throat is cut,
d its blood spatters on the idols. The animal's head is given as payment to the
tchers—the body is considered *prasad* (blessed) and becomes the main course
r a family picnic in the surrounding hills.

Bus #22 runs from Ratna Park in Kathmandu to Dakshinkali (Tu, Sa, 2hr., Rs10).
owever, huge crowds and small numbers of buses mean you'll have to get to the
s station very early if you want to see the sacrifices. Alternatively, the journey
n be made by **taxi** (Rs500, round trip) or **motorcycle** (Rs400, round trip). Either
ay, the tortuous ride up through hillside homes and fields offers stunning views of
e valley. Stay on the bus past Pharping, past the deceptive Dakshinkali Cold
ore, past the "Welcome to Dakshinkali" sign. Wait until the bus turns in to a park-
g lot filled with about 100 motorcycles and other sundry vehicles. When the belea-
ered busload of folks and fowl get off, you know you've arrived. Stands selling
acks, garlands, bangles, and *sindur* line the walkway to the staircase down to the
mple, which sits in a valley at the junction of two muddy streams.

EAR DAKSHINKALI

nder the shadow of a forbidding cliff and in the shade of big leafy trees, the **Sekh
arayan Temple,** with its clear pools teeming with large colorful fish is a road-side oasis
st an hour's hike outside of Dakshinkali. Built during the 17th century to honor
mana (the dwarfish 5th incarnation of Vishnu) the temple has been dutifully main-
ined, and its bold, bright colors give it an almost surreal appearance. A short walk
om the temple is a Buddhist Monastery built in the 20th century, whose modern
sign reminds the viewer that despite its age, the Sekh Narayan Temple is still an
tive place of worship.

To reach the Sekh Narayan Temple from Dakshinkali, walk down the main road
wards the Dakshinkali Temple until the green gate leading down to the temple is on
ur left. Follow the uphill stairway to the right until it turns into a dirt path. Continue
raight along the path for half a mile until it comes out to a main road next to a soccer
ld in the village of Pharping. Continue downhill on the main road for a half mile until
e Sekh Narayan Temple appears on your left.

THE WESTERN HILLS

odern-day Nepal was conceived in the hills west of Kathmandu, where 250 years ago
ng Prithvi Narayan Shah of Gorkha had a vision of a unified country. The magnificent
ntral Himalayas, dominated by Machhapuchhare and the Annapurna range provide a
agnificent backdrop to one of the most popular regions of Nepal.

NEPAL

HIGHLIGHTS OF THE WESTERN HILLS

■ Nepal's second-most visited city, lakeside **Pokhara** (p. 765) lies in a beautiful subtropical valley.

■ The hill towns of **Tansen** (p. 762) and **Gorkha** (below) offer scenic respite from
Nepal's tourist mainstream.

■ The ridge-top **Manakamana Temple** (p. 761) boasts the country's first and only
cable car and one of Nepal's most ancient religious practices, animal sacrifice.

GORKHA गोर्खा

Spectacularly positioned on a hillside halfway between Pokhara and Kathmandu, Gorkh was under the control of many small kingdom-states until Prithvi Narayan Shah, a dire ancestor of the present King of Nepal, initiated the military rampage that eventually gav rise to modern Nepal. In 1744, Prithvi Narayan set off to conquer the Kathmandu Valley; took him 24 years, but he got there in the end, and he even appended a chunk of the Ter to his kingdom as an afterthought. Shah's mighty soldiers were originally given the nam "Gorkha," but all Nepalese soldiers eventually became known as Gorkhas (or Gurkhas They were recruited by the British army and now comprise a significant minority in th Indian army. Currently, Gorkhas are popular among Hong Kong's business elite as top-o the-line bodyguards. Gorkha's history is enshrined in the hilltop Gorkha Durbar, birt place of Prithvi Narayan. As the terminus of a paved road to the Kathmandu-Pokhar highway, Gorkha is now the link between many sleepy mountain villages and the outsic world and a starting point for treks in the Annapurnas (see p. 792).

🛈 ORIENTATION AND PRACTICAL INFORMATION

Gorkha has evolved into three distinct sections. The newest part of town, only 15 yea old, centers on the **bus park** and trickles downhill. The second area, about a century ol winds uphill past three small shrines and into the main street. The oldest section is a hour's walk up to the ridge-top; the **Gorkha Durbar** presides over the town from one sic and the sparkling peaks of the Himalayas from the other.

Buses: Prithi Rajmarga Bus Syndicate, at the bus park, marked by a red sign. Open dai 6am-7pm. All buses from Gorkha go through **Anbu Khaireni,** a few kilometers west Mugling, where the Gorkha road intersects the Kathmandu-Pokhara highway. To: **Anb Khaireni** (frequent 6am-6pm, 1hr., Rs22); **Bhairawa/Sunauli** (7am, 7hr., Rs110); **Bi ganj** (4 per day 6:30-11:20am, 7hr., Rs105); **Kathmandu** (8 per day 6:15am-3:40pr 6hr., Rs65/85); **Narayanghat** (12 per day 6:30am-3:30pm, 3hr., Rs36/55); **Pokha** (6 and 9:15am, 4hr., Rs60); **Tardi,** for **Chitwan National Park** (5 per day 6:30ar 3:30pm, 4hr., Rs45). **Sahja Yatayat** (tel. 20106), next to the bus park, sends buses Kathmandu (6:45am and 1:30pm, 5hr., Rs63).

Currency Exchange: Rastriya Banijya Bank (tel. 20155), at the end of the older part town; walk to the end of the narrow street just below the post office. Changes cash ar traveler's checks in CDN$, US$, and UK£. Open Su-Th 10am-5pm, F 10am-1:15pm.

Pharmacy: Gorakha Medical Center (tel. 20116), across from Hotel Gorkha Princ Open Su-F 7am-8pm, Sa 7am-1pm.

Hospital: (tel. 20208), walk 5min. downhill on the main road from the bus park; take left at the first paved road after the police station and walk 5min. uphill to a dirt roa The hospital is yellow with red stripes.

Police: To get to the **police station** (tel. 20199) from the bus park, walk downhill f 5min., turn right at the blue sign down the unpaved road, and take another right; th police station is the white building straight ahead.

Post Office: (tel. 20112), a white-walled building at the end of the older section Gorkha. No *Poste Restante.* Open Su-Th 10am-5pm, F 10am-3pm.

Internet and Telephones: Hello Gorkha (tel. 20226), 50m down the main road from th bus park, has good rates (callbacks Rs5 per min.) and **email** service. Open daily 7ar 7:30pm. **Hotel Gorkha Prince** has free callbacks.

PHONE CODE	064

🏠🍴 ACCOMMODATIONS AND FOOD

Hotel Gorkha Prince (tel. 20131), 100m from the bus park; the hotel, marked by a re signboard, is on the left. Spacious rooms around a courtyard, friendly staff, STD/IS service, rooftop restaurant, and a tidy common room with Star TV. Rooms with squat to let Rs150; with TV, seat toilet, and toilet paper Rs200.

Hotel Gorkha Bisauni (tel. 20107), down the main road 250m below the bus park. More impressive outside than in, Bisauni has rooms with quiet hill-view balconies, brightly tiled bathrooms, and hot showers. Friendly, helpful staff facilitates comfort and repose. Some rooms are decidedly gloomy—ask to see several. Check-out noon. Singles Rs300; doubles Rs200-300, with bath Rs400, with seat toilet Rs500. Extra bed Rs100. Off-season: 25-40% discount.

Fulpati Restaurant, Gurkha Inn, 120m down the main road from the bus park; it's on the right. Great views, a beautiful garden, and tasty food make this Gorkha's premier eating establishment. Breakfast Rs86-160, Nepalese/Indian/Chinese fare Rs20-120. The potatoes chili (Rs38) will bring tears to your eyes. Open daily 6am-9pm.

Hill Top Restaurant, at the bus park. Sit at an outdoor table under an umbrella, sip beer, and watch the hubbub of the bus park. Hearty breakfasts Rs60-80; Chinese, Italian, Tibetan, and Indian entrees Rs30-70. Open daily 7am-8:30pm.

Gorkha Prince Rooftop Restaurant, down the road from the bus park. Rooftop with rock-bottom prices. *Dal bhat* (Rs70), veg. chow mein (Rs30), and Indian, Italian, and Continental fare. Open daily 7am-10pm.

⚑ SIGHTS

GORKHA DURBAR. This grand palace is where Prithvi Narayan Shah was born in 1722, following a dream his mother had in which she swallowed the sun. He was crowned 20 years later. After the Gorkhali army set out from Durbar to capture the Kathmandu Valley, Prithvi Narayan never returned to the place of his birth. The palace is thought to have been built eight generations earlier, in 1609. The city of Gorkha was ignored by the Shah Dynasty until King Mahendra, father of the present King Birendra, returned here in 1958. In the more than 200 years of royal absence, the same families of Hindu priests had continued to perform religious functions at the temples in the Durbar; the palace's present priests are direct descendants of those who served during and before Prithvi Narayan's rule. Prithvi Narayan's **throne** is visible through a tiny window. Since you cannot wear shoes here, consider bringing a pair of flip flops as the Durbar tends to be a little sticky underfoot—frequent sacrifices were once made here. The Himalayas dominate the horizon, and you see more of the mountains from the palace than you can from Pokhara, but there's an even better view from the top of the hill Upalkot, another 30 minutes up the stone stairway. *(Walk uphill 1hr. through the older section of Gorkha and up the stone stairway. Open daily 6am-6pm. Cameras and leather articles, including belts and shoes, are not allowed inside the compound. There is no repository for these items; leave them behind in Gorkha. Main temple and palace closed to the public. Some parts of the compound closed to non-Hindus; ask the policeman on duty.)*

OTHER SIGHTS. The **Rani Pokhari** (Queen's Pond), a terrace with a sunken pool, has an elevated statue of Prithvi Pati Shah, Prithvi Narayan's father. The three temples on the right of the pond honor Mahadev, Vishnu, and Ganesh. *(100m uphill from the bus park.)* Continuing on the stone road past the temples leads to an open square. On the left is the **Bhimsen Mandir,** which draws crowds of pilgrims for the Janai Purnima festival in August. The brown gateway leads to the magnificent **Tallo Durbar Palace,** built between 1835 and 1839 by King Rajendra in a failed attempt to lure his older son away from Kathmandu and succession to the throne. A **museum park** honoring Prithvi Narayan has been under construction for years, and promised opening dates come and go regularly. Ask to be shown the interior courtyard of the palace, which is full of exquisite woodcarving. The streets in the older part of the city merit a gentle wander. They're pleasantly clean, thanks to the Gorkha Youth Movement for the Environment's strategic distribution of trash cans marked "Give me Dust."

NEAR GORKHA: MANAKAMANA मनकामना

Getting to Manakamana Temple, one of Nepal's most frequented pilgrimage sites, used to involve an arduous 45-minute hike from Anbu Khaireni, a nearby town. It was claimed that the goddess Manakamana's choice of a remote, rugged hilltop for an

NEPAL

earthly abode was her way of testing her devotees' resolve. Her plan, however, has bee somewhat undermined by the arrival of Nepal's first and only cable car system, runnin from Cheres, 5km east of Mugling on the road to Kathmandu, right up to the temple' perch atop a 1300m ridge.

The story goes that the wife of a Gorkha king Rama Shah (1614-1636) had divin powers that she concealed from all but one devotee, Lakhan Thapa. Mr. Thapa wa understandably distraught when she committed *sati* on the funeral pyre of her hus band, but she had promised him that she would reappear shortly in fulfilment of hi wishes. When, months later, a farmer came across a split stone oozing both milk an blood, Lakhan Thapa took this to be the promised reappearance. The stone is at th shrine of the **Devi of Manakamana** temple, and its current attendant is a 17th generatio descendant of Lakhan Thapa. Because Manakamana Devi is known as the wish fulfilling goddess, it's not surprising that she is particularly popular. Half a million vis tors come here annually, sacrificing goats and chickens to the goddess with a bruta lack of ceremony. Cable car employees supply pilgrims lugging their dead offering home with plastic sacking to help keep the blood off the shiny new floors. (Inner sanc tum closed to non-Hindus.)

Hilltop accommodations are mainly geared to the local market, so most hote names are not even written in English; they line the busy lane running down from th temple. If you're in a pinch, try **Hotel Satkar** (tel. (064) 20176), with pleasantly airy room (doubles with squat toilet Rs250); friendly **Hotel Minar** (tel. 29300), with basic double (Rs100, with bath Rs150); or the **Alpine Hotel** (tel. 29302), with bigger rooms (double with bath Rs300). The latter has a passable, if faintly derelict rooftop restaurant (eg fried rice Rs45; open daily 6am-10pm).

A visit to Manakamana could be a daytrip on your way between Kathmandu an Pokhara; just ask the bus driver to drop you at the cable car. **Buses** running to Kath mandu from **Pokhara's Lakeside** (daily 6:30am, Rs200) should reach Cheres at 10am After completing your pilgrimage to the shrine, hop on any east-bound vehicle to get t Kathmandu. Opened in November 1998, the **cable car** cost US$6 million to install and i chock full of safety systems. The ride to the top is positively surreal, with views of th Trisuli river and terraced greenery dotted with hamlets untouched by the space-ag incursion overhead. (Open M-Sa 7am-noon and 1:30-5pm, Sa 7am-5pm. Round-tri Rs250, one-way Rs200; signs in the ticket office demanding payment in "convertible cu rency" are cheerfully ignored.)

TANSEN (PALPA) तानसेन

It is hard to believe that a scenic and architectural jewel like Tansen could remain rela tively untouched by the traffic between Pokhara and Sunauli. Perched at 1370m in th Mahabarat range, this bustling town of near-perfect clime, steep cobblestone streets small storefronts, and delicate architecture sees few Westerners. Beginning its growt under the 16th-century Sen kings, the mighty Kingdom of Palpa is said to have extende from Mustang to the Terai. From its assimilation into the kingdom of Nepal in the earl 19th century until the fall of the Ranas of 1951, Tansen served as an honorable place o exile for troublesome, power-hungry royal relatives; more recently, foreign aid organ zations have funded a new rash of development-inspired castles on the terraced hil sides. As a result, Tansen is one of Nepal's tidiest and most endearing hill towns, wit exquisite views of the valleys and the Chure hills to the south and the great Himalaya to the north.

🛈 ORIENTATION AND PRACTICAL INFORMATION

The **bus park** is just south of Tansen, and the main road heading into town swings lef past the **tourist office** and university campus; 500m later, it reaches a junction. Gau Shankar Guest House is to the left; continuing right, you pass Hotel the White Lak before reaching an intersection marked by a **police post** and the **post office.** A stee unmotorable flagstone road leads downhill from here to the bus park. The main roa continues north becoming **Bank Road,** with the entrance to **Durbar Square** on the left. A he end of Bank Rd., another flagstone lane takes off downhill, this one to **Amar Narayan Temple,** while the main road curves around to a major intersection, **Shital Pati,** marked by a white gazebo-esque structure. There is another entrance to Durbar Sq. here, as well as access to **Bhagwati Temple.** The paved road continues uphill towards **Srinagar Hotel** and a viewpoint.

Buses: A counter at the northeast corner of the bus park sells tickets to: **Butwal** (every 30min. 6am-6pm, 2hr., Rs24); **Kathmandu** (6am, 8hr., Rs130; 5:30pm, 11hr., Rs170); **Pokhara** (6 and 9am, 6hr., Rs70). **Sajha Buses** has a ticket office in Bishan Bazaar, southwest of the telegraph office. Open daily 5:30am-5:30pm. Bus to **Kathmandu** (6:15am, Rs130).

Local transportation: Hotel Proprietoire has **jeeps** for hire (to Srinagar Rs100-150).

Tourist Office: The **Tourist Information Center,** just north of the bus park. Open Su-Th 11am-1pm. Check out the map signboards located in the bus park and Shital Pati.

Currency Exchange: Nepal Bank (tel. 20130), cashes traveler's checks Su-F 10am-2pm.

Pharmacy: Sajha Swasta Sewa pharmacy (tel. 20464), opposite the post office, has a pharmacist on call 24hr.

Hospital: Skip the district hospital west of Tansen in favor of the **United Mission to Nepal Hospital** (tel. 20111, ambulance tel. 20600), a short walk northeast of town.

Police: The **main police station** (tel. 20255) is in Durbar Sq. Police **booths** along the western edge of the bus park and in front of the post office.

Post Office: At the southern end of Bank Rd. Open Su-Th 10am-5pm, F 10am-3pm.

Internet: Pooja Computer (tel. 20462; email pooja@pcc.starcomp.wlink.com.np). Send email for Rs50 per Kb. Open Su-F 8am-7pm.

Telephones: Telegraph office, west of the post office. Take the first right, continue up a dirt lane, and turn right; it's at the end of the lane. Cheapest **STD/ISD** and fax services in Tansen and free callbacks. Open daily 7am-7pm.

PHONE CODE	075

ACCOMMODATIONS AND FOOD

Nanglo West, Shital Pati, in a handsomely refurbished traditional building. Comfortable dining in the shady courtyard or on cushions in the elegant, traditional upstairs dining room. The bakery out front has freshly made croissants (5 for Rs20) and cinnamon danish (Rs12); restaurant at the back has local exotica—*sukuti* (dried buffalo meat with garlic and ginger Rs50)—and international non-exotica—hamburger (Rs50). Open daily 10:30am-8:30pm.

Gauri Shankar Guest House, Silkhan Tol (tel. 20150). Walk 10min. north from the bus park and turn left, continuing past the university campus; it's on your right. The best deal with its bright, well-maintained rooms; baths have hot water and toilet paper. Attached restaurant serves Nepali, Indian, Chinese, and some Continental items for Rs50-100 (open daily 7am-10pm). Singles Rs125, with bath Rs200; doubles Rs175/300-400; triples Rs250/400.

Hotel the White Lake (tel. 20291; fax 20502). Rooms have carpeting, fans, and thick beds, and attached baths with seat toilets, towels, and toilet paper. Attached restaurant serves one of the broadest menus in town—set breakfasts (Rs50-100), pizzas (Rs75-110), Continental non-veg. dishes (Rs100-150), and beer (Rs75 per can, Rs90 per bottle). Singles US$12; doubles US$16, but you should be able to get the Nepali rate of Rs400/600. 25% student discount.

Hotel the Bajra (tel. 20443), north of the bus park, is a bit older than the others, but its clean, linoleum-floored rooms have large windows. Attached baths and hot water buckets. Attached restaurant. Dorm beds Rs50; singles Rs150; doubles Rs250-320.

Hotel Srinagar, northwest of town. Serves standard tourist fare: chicken chili (Rs110); up-market *dal bhat* (Rs150), with meat (Rs250). Meals are a little more expensive here, but on a clear day it's money well spent—the patio dining area, perched on the ridge just west of Srinagar peak, has excellent views of the Himalayas to the north and terraced hills to the south. Open daily 7am-10pm.

SIGHTS

AMAR NARAYAN TEMPLE. One of Tansen's oldest structures, the Amar Narayan Temple serves as a stopover for pilgrims, and especially *sadhus*, on their way to Muktinath. After annexing the city in 1804, Amar Singh Thapa imported Newari craftsmen and artisans and began to Kathmandu-ize Tansen. The grandest of his accomplishments, the Amar Narayan complex encloses an image of Vishnu; it is surrounded by the 1m-wide **Great Wall of Palpa** (not, in fact, visible from the moon), a water tank with spouts fed by a natural spring, and a garden as popular with bats as it is with worshippers. *(Exit Durbar Sq. through Baggi Dhoka; turn right and follow a steep flagstone lane down through the old bazaar.)*

DURBAR SQUARE. Located at its center is Tansen's Durbar Square, entered from Shital Pati through **Baggi Dhoka,** a large whitewashed gate built by Palpa's first exile Khadga Shumshere, who came here in 1891. Said to be the largest gate in Nepal, it was made to measure for Shumshere *and* his elephant—dismounting can be such a hassle. Shumshere also erected the square's first palace, but the present blue-and-pumpkin colored structure was built by General Pratap Shumshere in 1927. The 65-room **Tansen Durbar** currently houses Palpa's district secretariat.

BHAGWATI TEMPLE. The Bhagwati Temple commemorates an 1815 victory over the British. It is the center of Tansen's largest festival, **Bhagwati Jatra,** held in late August. An all-night celebration precedes the festival; in the morning, a chariot holding an image of Bhagwati is led through town. *(Northwest of Tansen Durbar.)*

SRINAGAR HILL. From the Ganesh temple, the flagstone path continues up the hill to Srinagar, Tansen's vigorously promoted viewpoint. The pleasant hilltop park commands one of the longest mountain views in Nepal, from India's peaks to those of Tibet, including the Dhaulagiri range, Annapurna's Machhapuchhare, and Ganesh Himal. The park gets most of its wear on Saturdays, when Tansen denizens make the trek up to enjoy a bit of familial quality-time. Sunrises and sunsets during the week are usually staged for just a handful of hardy souls. If the pre-dawn hike up the hill doesn't appeal, consider spending the night in the park—there's an open-sided shelter and water spigot. Make a round trip up Srinagar by returning to town via the concrete steps which lead down from the shrine at the eastern end of the ridge. At the bottom of the steps, pick up the broad trail to the right and follow it as it hugs the hill for the couple of kilometers back to Tansen. *(The hilltop is a 15min. sweat up from the temple; an easier 20min. walk along the ridge from Hotel Srinagar, northwest of town; or a 10min. ride up the road.)*

OTHER SIGHTS. A few minutes south of Amar Narayan, the **Tundikhel** marks the southeast edge of town. Next to it, the rose-filled **Birendra Park** is in constant use. The town also has several less conspicuous temples—of special note are the **Mahachaitya Bihar** and a **Ganesh Temple** (across from each other, a 5min. walk west of Shital Pati). The road running directly north of Shital Pati leads to another **Ganesh Temple,** set into the hillside. A short, steep flagstone path leads to the small red-and-white temple, which affords good views of the city below. (15min. walk north of town.) The minarets of Tansen's **Jama Masjid** are visible just south of the temple.

SHOPPING

A few locally produced goods deserve special mention. Palpa's Newari craftsmen employ the lost wax method in their remarkable **metalworks;** the Palpali *kuruwa,* a bronze water jar, is particularly well-known. Palpali *dhaka,* woven by women in Tansen and the surrounding hills, is also noteworthy; several handicraft associations in town (especially along Bank Rd.) sell shawls, *topis* (hats), and handbags produced from this cloth.

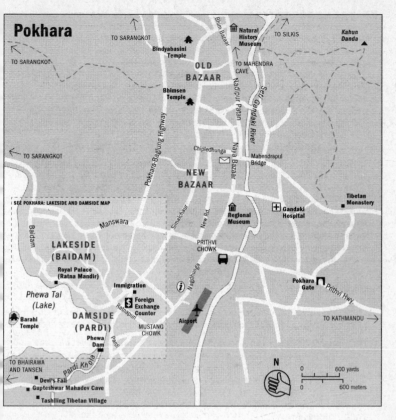

POKHARA पोखरा

Nepal's biggest tourist destination outside the Kathmandu Valley, Pokhara is sunk in a subtropical valley surrounded by lofty peaks, forming some of the world's most impressive vistas. Nowhere else in Nepal is there such an abrupt change in altitude—the tip of Annapurna I (the world's 10th highest mountain), only 48km away, is 7.2km higher than Pokhara. But Pokhara isn't only about mountains: its name derives from the Nepali word for "pond," *pokhari*. Pokhara Valley, like the Kathmandu Valley, was once a single huge lake. Today, only three lakes—Phewa, Begnas, and Rupa—remain. The Gurungs, the true "natives" of the region, lived on the hilltops surrounding the valley. Only when Newari traders—traffickers of salt between Kathmandu, Bandipur, and Dhankuta—settled in Pokhara, did a city begin to rise on the banks of the Seti ("Milk") River. These traders built the Bindyabasini Temple in the 16th century, by far the oldest structure in Pokhara. More recent development began with the construction of two highways in the 1970s—one connecting Pokhara to Kathmandu, the other linking it to India. Originally something of a hippie hideaway, Pokhara is now prominent on the global tourism map. The banks of Phewa Tal, Nepal's second-largest lake, are now a concrete jungle of hotels, restaurants, and souvenir shops; their garish signs compete with the mountains for attention. An important commercial and administrative center, Pokhara is the launchpad for some of Nepal's most popular treks and the heart of Nepal's river rafting industry. Pokhara bristles with activity in season, but the city is also worth a visit off season (May-Sept.), when it feels more like a small town.

⌐ TRANSPORTATION

Airport: The **airport** is between the bus park and the lake. Taxi fares from the airport to Lakeside are fixed (Rs80-100), but bargaining is expected for rides to the airport (Rs40-50). The airport has minimal facilities. **Buddha Air** (tel. 28997), **Cosmic Air** (tel. 21846), **Gorkha Airlines** (tel. 25971), **Lumbini Air** (tel. 27233), and **Yeti Airlines** (tel. 300016) all have offices close to the airport. **Necon Air**, Naya Bazaar (tel. 25311). Most offices open daily 8am-6pm. **RNAC** (tel. 21021), near the airport. Open Su-F 10am-5pm, Sa 10am-noon. To: **Kathmandu** (frequent 8:10am-5pm, US$61); **Jomsom** (4 per day 6:30-7:50am, US$50-55); **Manang** (3 per week 7:30am, US$50). Flights are added or canceled according to demand.

Buses: The **bus park** is a muddy hell-hole when it's wet and a dusty hell-hole when it's dry. It's a 20-25min. bike ride from Lakeside. Taxi Rs60. The **day bus office** (tel. 20272), in the center of the muck, has one blue and one red window. Open daily 5am-6pm. The **night bus office,** facing into the bus park, is on the right and up a set of stairs, under a white sign with a flag. Open daily 8:30am-8:30pm. **Day buses** to: **Besisahar** (7:25 and 8:30am, 6hr., Rs70-100); **Bhairawa/Sunauli** (10 per day 5am-noon, 8hr., Rs126); **Birganj** (5 per day 5:40-10:15am, 8hr., Rs120); **Gorkha** (7 and 9:30am, 4hr., Rs60); **Kathmandu** (8 per day 5am-noon, 8hr., Rs100); **Narayanghat** (every 30min. 5:30am-9:30am, 5hr., Rs65); **Tansen** (7am, 7hr., Rs80). **Night buses** to: **Bhairawa/Sunauli** (6, 7:45, and 8pm; 8½hr.; Rs150); **Birganj** (7, 7:30, and 8pm; 8hr.; Rs140); **Butwal** (4 per day 6-8:30pm, 8hr., Rs102-150 depending on route); **Kathmandu** (9 per night 6:30-8:45pm, 8hr., Rs113); **Narayanghat** (4 per day 6pm-8:30pm, 5hr., Rs75). Buses heading out on the road to Baglung depart from the **Baglung Bus Stand,** across the town from Prithvi Chowk. There is no such thing as a "tourist fare," no matter how much touts try to convince you there is. To: **Baglung** (every hr. 5:30am-6pm, 54hr., Rs45), via **Dhampus Phadi** (30min., Rs15) and **Nayapul** (2hr., Rs26); **Beni** (7, 9:30am, and noon; 5hr.; Rs70). Travel agencies at Lakeside/Damside operate pricier and more comfortable coaches with morning departures (6-10am) from hotels. To: **Kathmandu** (Rs200-250); **Narayanghat** (Rs170); **Sunauli** (Rs200). Buses added or canceled according to demand. **Green Line Tours** (tel. 26562), Lakeside, operates luxury services (including complimentary breakfast) to: **Kathmandu** (7 and 8am, Rs500-600); **Chitwan** (8am, Rs480).

Local Transportation: **Bikes** are probably the best way to get around when it isn't raining. Shops in Lakeside/Damside rent bikes (Rs8-15 per hr., Rs30-50 per day). **Taxi** fares rise in season; fares are higher Sa and double after 7pm. Destinations such as the bus park, airport, and Mahendra Pul from Lakeside/Damside cost Rs60 or Rs12 shared. A **local bus** leaves Bahrai Chowk, the huge tree next to Moondance and Hotel Hungry-Eye, for major locations in the city (every 30min., under Rs5). Ask locals for specifics.

✦ ORIENTATION

For all of its rustic feel, is, Pokhara is actually a huge, sprawling city. **Phewa Tal** (the lake) and **Pardi** (the dam) are the two major points of orientation—many travelers never get beyond **Lakeside (Baidam)** or **Damside (Pardi)**. The residential section of town is to the north, away from the lake. The **Siddhartha Highway,** linking Pokhara to India, forms a great north-south arc through the city. It meets the **Prithvi Highway** from Kathmandu at **Prithvi Chowk,** the city center, where you'll also find the **bus station.** Farther north, the main road comes to the **Mahendra Pul** area, the historical heart of the city and the center of the **Pokhara Bazaar.**

Lakeside now overshadows **Damside** both in size and popularity. Lakeside's two main sections extend south from the campground to the Hotel Hungry-Eye and east from the Royal Palace to Fish Tail Lodge—it's a 30-minute walk from one end to the other. Damside reaches south from the intersection with the main Lakeside thoroughfare along **Pardi Road.** The **maps** posted at some of Pokhara's *chowks* and intersections can be helpful.

⚡ PRACTICAL INFORMATION

Tourist Office: (tel. 20028), a short walk from the airport entrance or a 20min. bike ride from Lakeside. Open Su-Th 10am-5pm, F 10am-3pm; Nov.-Feb.: Su-Th 10am-4pm, F 10am-3pm.

Immigration Office: (tel. 21167), where the roads to Lakeside and Damside meet. Extends visas. Open for applications Su-Th 10:30am-1pm, F 10am-noon; Nov. 17-Feb. 13: Su-Th 10:30am-12:30pm, F 10am-noon. Also issues **trekking permits** for the Annapurna region (US$5 per week for the first 4 weeks, US$10 each additional week). Bring your passport and 2 photos; shops in Lakeside take "instant" visa photos (4 photos Rs150), as does a photo booth outside the immigration office (Rs200). Permits can be picked up Su-Th 4-5pm; F 2-3pm; Nov.17-Feb.13: Su-Th 3-4pm, F 2-3pm. **Annapurna Conservation Area** entry fees (Rs1000) can be paid at a small office 100m from the Immigration Office. From Immigration, head towards Damside and right down a narrow dead-end street; it's on your left. Open Su-Th 10am-5pm, F 10am-3pm.

Budget Travel: Local **trekking agencies** can arrange **visa extensions** (service charge Rs100) and **trekking permits** (service charge Rs200). For same-day service go to the agencies before 9am. Some agencies will attempt to "expedite" the process; for Rs250-350 you might obtain your permit by noon. **Encounter Overland** (tel. 21963), in Lakeside offers comprehensive local transport services. Open daily 7am-8pm.

Trekking Information: Annapurna Conservation Area Project (tel. 21102), in the Natural History Museum, Prithvi Narayan Campus in north Pokhara. The most authoritative source of information on the Annapurna region provides free, impartial information on ACAP and general advice on trekking. Good maps and books for sale; several free pamphlets. Open Su-F 9am-12:30pm and 1:30-5pm. Nov.-Feb.: closes 4pm.

Currency Exchange: Lakeside and Damside each have half a dozen authorized currency exchange counters and a bank. Most accept major currencies and AmEx, Visa, and Thomas Cook traveler's checks. **Nepal Grindlays Bank** (tel. 20102), in northern Lakeside just south of the campground, gives cash advances on Visa and MC and cashes traveler's checks. Open Su-Th 9:45am-4:15pm, F 9:45am-1:15pm.

Market: The Lakeside/Damside area markets vend clothes, trekking equipment, pharmaceuticals, and souvenirs. Locals shop at the less expensive **Mahendra Pul** area (taxi Rs60-70 one-way, but worth it). **Saleways**, in Mahendra Pul, has cheap trekkers' food. Open Su-F 8am-7:45pm, Sa 10am-7:45pm.

Pharmacy: The half-dozen small pharmacies in Lakeside and Damside carry first-aid supplies for trekking; many have doctors on call. Many of Lakeside's supermarkets also stock the components of a trekking first aid kit.

Hospital: Most hotels and lodges can recommend a doctor or clinic. The clinic in the **International Nepal Fellowship Compound** (tel. 20111) has a nurse on duty daily 10:30am-12:30pm. Popular with the expat community. **Barahi Medical Hall** (tel. 22862), in the center of Lakeside, has a doctor in season Su-F 5-7pm; he's on call off season. Open daily 7am-9pm. **Mahishi Medical Hall** (tel. 25650), Damside, has Dr. Prakash Mishra on call 24hr. Open daily 7am-9:30pm. **Gandaki Hospital** (tel. 20066), a 15min. taxi ride (Rs100) from Lakeside, has Western doctors.

Police: The **police station** (tel. 21087), a 10min. bike ride from the center of Lakeside; it's on the right just before the Immigration Office. The small **police post** at the entrance to the camping grounds at the end of Lakeside is open 24hr. in season. There is also a 24hr. **Tourist Police Booth** located in front of the Hungry-Eye.

Post Office: The **main post office** (tel. 22014), on the main street in Mahendra Pul, (30min. by bike; taxi Rs50-60). *Poste Restante.* Another post office is nearer Lakeside—head out of Lakeside and turn left immediately after the Immigration Office; it's on your left after 200m. Both open Su-Th 10am-5pm, F 10am-3pm; registered mail Su-Th 10am-2:30pm, F 10am-12:30pm. Most bookstores in Lakeside and Damside vend stamps and post letters.

Internet: Internet access providers in Pokhara have formed cartels to prevent competition—the going rate is a brutal Rs9 per min. or Rs15 per Kb. **CyberWorld** (tel. 24618), above the As You Like It store near the Hungry-Eye, has several terminals and enough battery back-up to face the worst of power cuts. Open daily 8am-10pm.

PHONE CODE	061

ACCOMMODATIONS

Lakeside bursts with travel agents, bookstores, money changers, supermarkets, and entertainment, while Damside, a half-hour away, is quieter and smaller. Off season, Lakeside mellows out and Damside dries up. All hotels listed have luggage storage, laundry service, fans, seat toilets, STD/ISD facilities, noon check-out and mosquito coils on request. Expect off-season discounts of up to 50%.

LAKESIDE AREA

 Sacred Valley Inn, on the Damside side of the Hungry-Eye, behind Ratna Mandir. Excellent location—it's a brief stroll to the hoppin' heart of Lakeside. Brand new hotel run by a Nepali-American couple, it has huge, white slabs of marble everywhere. Big, airy rooms with rattan furniture on the balconies, and 24hr. hot water. Breakfast (eggs, toast, and hash browns) is worth the wait. Doubles Rs200-250, with bath Rs300-700.

Hotel Nirvana (tel. 23332), close to the Ratna Mandir a little farther towards Damside. Peaceful, but close to the action. Recently opened by a Nepali-Western couple. Big, breezy rooms, many with views of the lake and mountains. Solar and geyser hot water. Doubles with bath US$6-15. Off-season discounts.

Hotel Avocado (tel. 23617), behind Once Upon a Time, in the center of Lakeside but away from the noisy street. Helpful management, sparkling clean rooms, and an attractive little garden (no avocado tree). Water is both solar and geyser-heated 24hr. Doubles with bath Rs300-400.

Hotel the Trans-Himalaya (tel. 20917). Heading north away from Damside, turn right at Pyramid Restaurant; continue 100m to your right. Older but spic-and-span and well-run. All rooms have attached bath, green carpets, and blue bathroom tiles. Singles Rs200; doubles Rs250, deluxe with bath tub Rs400.

Butterfly Lodge (tel. 22892), on the same road as Trans-Himalaya but farther from the main street. Quiet garden lodge with lots of open space. Fresh coffee (Rs15). Doubles US$5, with sparkling-tiled bath US$15. Student and long-term discounts available.

Alka Guest House (tel. 21478), in the center of Lakeside, right on the main drag. Bright, shiny building with fancy wooden handrails and marble floors. STD/ISD phones in the rooms. No smoking. Foreigners must pay in "convertible currency." Singles US$6, with bath US$12; doubles US$8/16. Extra bed US$3/5. Visa, MC.

Camping Ground (tel. 21688), north end of Lakeside; make a left turn at the police booth and it's on the right. Bordering the lake, with unobstructed mountain views, Pokhara's only campground is ideal in dry weather but sloppy during the monsoon. Squat toilets. Check-out 6pm. Hot showers Rs30, cold showers free. Tents Rs40, vehicles Rs60.

DAMSIDE AREA

Hotel Himali (tel 25385), on the main road of Damside. Older than other Lakeside digs, but the rooms are in good shape and well-kept. Also operates a trekking agency, **Fewa Treks** (tel. 25804). Singles Rs150; doubles Rs300. Extra bed Rs50.

Hotel Super Lodge (tel. 21861), left off the main road in Damside, has old but well-maintained blue rooms. Singles Rs150, with bath Rs290; doubles Rs290/540.

New Hotel Cosmos (tel. 21964), behind the main road in Damside. If you're hell-bent on being on the water, this small hotel is a good option. Try to get one of the 3 rooms with a view. Friendly, familial feel. All rooms have attached bath. Singles US$10; doubles US$15. Off-season: US$5/7.

Hotel Bharat (tel. 24021), opposite Super Lodge, just off Damside's main drag, is one of the area's newer establishments. Grand and faintly antiseptic, it gets an 'A' for comfort and value. Singles with bath Rs250; doubles with bath Rs350. TV Rs200 extra.

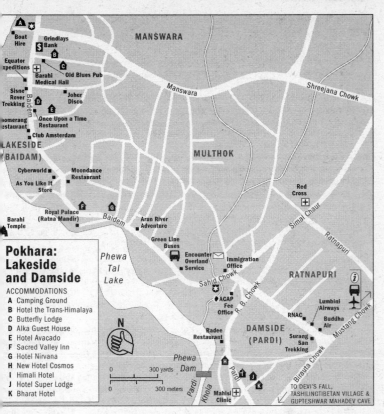

Pokhara: Lakeside and Damside

ACCOMMODATIONS
A Camping Ground
B Hotel the Trans-Himalaya
C Butterfly Lodge
D Alka Guest House
E Hotel Avacado
F Sacred Valley Inn
G Hotel Nirvana
H New Hotel Cosmos
I Himali Hotel
J Hotel Super Lodge
K Bharat Hotel

Map labels: Boat Hire, Grindlays Bank, Equator Expeditions, Barahi Medical Hall, Old Blues Pub, Sisne Rover Trekking, Joher Disco, Boomerang Restaurant, Once Upon a Time Restaurant, Club Amsterdam, LAKESIDE (BAIDAM), Cyberworld, Moondance Restaurant, As You Like It Store, Barahi Temple, Royal Palace (Ratna Mandir), Baidem, Arun River Adventure, Green Line Buses, Encounter Overland Service, Immigration Office, Phewa Tal Lake, ACAP Fee Office, Radee Restaurant, Sahid Chowk, R. B. Chowk, Phewa Dam, Pardi Khola, Mahisi Clinic, DAMSIDE (PARDI), Surang San Trekking, RNAC, Buddha Air, Lumbini Airways, RATNAPURI, Red Cross, Simal Chaur, Ratnapuri, Mustang Chowk, Birauta Chowk, Pardi, MANSWARA, MULTHOK, Manswara, Shreejana Chowk

TO DEVI'S FALL, TASHILINGTIBETAN VILLAGE & GUPTESHWAR MAHADEV CAVE

0   300 yards
0   300 meters

FOOD

True, you won't find a lot of Nepalese food here—but with cinnamon buns, Swiss chocolate, garlic pizza, and steak *au poivre*, who's whining for *dal bhat*? Indian and local meals abound in Mahendra Pul, where the food, the price tag, and the service are much more palatable. **Bars** are prominent along the main drags, and they have successfully cross-bred with international restaurants. **Musical entertainment** runs the gamut from Nepali dances to Indian pop bands; there's even a piano bar. Food prices remain high all year, and it's easy to while away the hours sipping coffee *lassis* (Rs50), which give their biggest jolt when the bill arrives.

LAKESIDE AREA

Boomerang, central Lakeside. Probably the premier restaurant in Lakeside, Boomerang enhances its 8-page menu with an attached German bakery (great for breakfast) and lakefront seating in private pagodas, from where you can watch water buffalo. If this turns you off to the buffalo items on the menu, chow down on veg. *mousaka* (Rs140), chicken tacos (Rs165), grilled lake fish (Rs215-235). Open daily 6am-10pm.

Sheela Bakery is some way into Lakeside, close to Grindlays Bank, but on the other side of the street. Mainly serves sandwiches. Well-garnished "cheese and tomato" sandwich Rs30, bowl of muesli Rs25, and apple strudel Rs10. Open daily 6am-9pm.

Moondance, central Lakeside, next to Hotel Hungry-Eye. Named for the Van Morrison song, Moondance is reputed to play the best and most diverse music in Lakeside—they'll honor requests Sa-W in season with their live R&B band. Comfortable, dark, and *au naturel,* from the hay roof to the decorative yak tails. Board games in the afternoons. Make your own pizza (from Rs105) or enchilada (chicken Rs115). Entrees Rs85-160, side dishes Rs45-70. Open daily 7:30am-10pm.

Once Upon A Time, central Lakeside. Among the most popular restaurants in Lakeside. Bamboo hut with bamboo furniture, even bamboo curtains. Pleasant ambience and so so food. Entrees Rs75-170, beer Rs99, cocktails Rs89-149. Happy hour (5-8pm) is little more than a handful of popcorn with your beer order. Open daily 8:30am-10pm.

Maya Pub, central Lakeside, plays your requests (loudly) and serves 2-for-1 cocktails (Rs150) during happy hour (5-9pm). Packed, even during low-season. Chicken mushroom enchilada Rs150, beer Rs95-110. Open daily 7am-10pm.

MAHENDRA PUL

🔖 **Marwadi Sewa Bhojanalaya.** Veg. Indian restaurant serving sublime *baingan bharta* (Rs30) and *masala dosa* (Rs30). Top it off with *ras malai* (Rs20) for dessert. Pleasant upstairs dining room is home to the local business set at lunch. Open daily 6am-9pm.

🔖 **Kohinoor Punjabi Restaurant,** in an alley behind Saleways; look for the "Club Ten" sign. The best in its gastronomic home territory (North India), it also serves Chinese and Continental dishes. The chicken butter *masala* (Rs80) will have you scrambling to buy a Punjabi cookbook. *Alu gobi* (Rs30). Open daily 7:30am-10pm.

Nepali Khona, to the right as you stand facing Saleways; it's a hole-in-the-wall, and the name is written only in Devanagari. Amazing *thakali* proprietress dishes up the best *da bhat* in Pokhara (Rs45, with meat Rs70). Open daily 9am-9pm.

🎵 ENTERTAINMENT

Entertainment in Pokhara primarily consists of eating, drinking, listening to music, and taking in the views from within Lakeside restaurants. Many restaurants feature **Nepali cultural shows** (e.g. **The Hungry-Eye, Boomerang**) or **movies** (e.g. **Once Upon a Time, Laxman**) during the evenings. Look for announcements posted on their signboards daily. Pokhara has a few good places to hear music, imbibe, and dance. **Club Amsterdam** in central Lakeside has live music, food including a brunch menu, booze, a pool table, a TV, an outdoor sitting area, and "the cleanest toilet in Lakeside." (Beer Rs110-125. Open daily 11am to 11pm, later if the crowd is jumpin'. Live music Tu, F, and Sa.) For those wishing to catch a glimpse of Pokhara's hippie past or just a piece of small town USA that re-emerged in Pokhara, head to **Old Blue's Night Pub,** at the center of Lakeside. Pool tables, dart boards, TV sports, and wallspace shared by Marilyn Monroe, U2, Ganesh, Jimi Hendrix, Count Basie, and a yak head make for a kind of manic grooviness. (Soft drinks Rs15-25, beer Rs110-120. Open daily noon-midnight, later in season.) **The Joker Dance Place,** 100m from the right turn at Nirula's, is the only place in Pokhara where you can bust a move on a sunken dance floor under the glare of disco lights (open daily 6pm-late). Several restaurants across the lake also have **special parties,** advertised around town on hard-to-miss signs. Most begin around 10pm and rage until the wee hours of the morning (a boat there and back Rs40-70).

🔭 SIGHTS

A large portion of the old bazaar of Pokhara burned down in 1949 in a fire that spread from a *puja* at Bindyabasini Temple, so most of the architecture is very recent. Taxis will take you on a three-hour tour of all sights within Pokhara for Rs450-650—contact any travel agent to make arrangements. Alternatively, some lakeside agents (try **Encounter Overland,** tel. 21963) will book a mini-bus tour of the valley and its attractions (9:30am-1pm Rs110; 9:30am-5pm Rs150, with Begnas Tal as the added afternoon attraction.)

REGIONAL MUSEUM. The farmhouse-like Regional Museum showcases plenty of interesting information about Nepal's Central Western region, like the huge **La Phewa** festival held every 12 years in the Thak Khola. The last one was in 1992. Check out the photo of a Gurung shaman being consecrated—halfway up a tree, he's blindfolded and has the heart of a ram in his mouth. (To the right on the road between Prithvi Chowk and Mahendra Pul. Taxi from lakeside Rs60; bike ride 30min. Tel. 20413. *Open Sa-M and W-Th 10am-5pm, F 10am-3pm. Rs5; camera fee Rs10.)*

THE LAKE. Secluded on an island in the middle of the lake is the **Barahi Temple**—rent one of the colorful boats from Barahi Ghat near central Lakeside to get there. *(Rs120 for the first hour, Rs150 for 2hr., Rs300 for the whole day; with guide Rs150 per hr., Rs250 for 2hr.).* Across the lake, the **Peace Pagoda** (still under construction) is atop the hill. Row to the pink Hotel Fewa and take the trail behind it to the top *(1hr. hike).*

DEVI'S FALL. The lake's water flows out at the south end into the Pardi Khola, a stream which suddenly shoots down into a hole at Devi's Fall (known locally as **Patale Chhango** or Hell's Fall, it goes by several names—it's also called Devin's or David's, for a legendary trekker or two washed away here), 1km out of Pokhara down the road toward the Indian border. Around to the left and behind the falls, there is a pool suitable for pre-monsoon swimming. Women should beware, however; groups of young men will insist on following. *(1km from Pokhara. Taxis from Lakeside Rs100 round-trip, 25min. by bike. Open daily 9am-6pm. Rs5.)*

GUPTESHWOR MAHADEV CAVE. Just discovered in 1992, this cave houses many ancient carvings and extends 3km into the earth. March is the best time to explore the cave; bring a flashlight. It is filled with water the rest of the year, but it's still worth the walk down to the mouth of the cave, where a large *linga* stands under an umbrella of cobra heads. The statue is old, the cobras are not. *(Across the street from Devi's Fall. Cave open daily 6am-6pm. 8-10hr. to explore the entire cave. Rs20. No photos.)*

BINDYABASINI TEMPLE. A long flight of steps leads up to Bindyabasini Temple, built in the 16th century by Newari traders who had just settled in the Pokhara Valley. The fire that engulfed Pokhara in 1949 started here. The main shrine, dedicated to Kali, is accompanied by a new Shiva temple. The small Buddhist monastery at the base of the steps hints at Nepal's synthesis of Buddhist and Hindu styles. *(In a park at the north end of town, on the highway to Baglung. Taxis from Lakeside Rs90; 45min. uphill bike ride.)*

NATURAL HISTORY MUSEUM. The museum is home to the Annapurna Conservation Area Project's public exhibits; it's sometimes known as the Annapurna Museum. The ACAP side of the museum is strong on the ethnography of the Annapurna region and definitely merits a pre-trek visit. The natural history collections are biased towards the predilections of the museum's staff, particularly those of resident lepidopterist Colin Smith—there's a superb collection of Nepal's 600 plus butterfly species. *(At the north end of Pokhara on the Prithvi Narayan Campus. Open Su-F 10am-12:30pm and 1:30-5pm; Sept.-Feb.: 10am-12:30pm and 1:30-4pm. Free.)*

OTHER SIGHTS. The refugees at the **Tashling Tibetan Village** sell an array of jewelry and souvenirs. Farther into the village there is a shed where wool is dyed and spun for carpets, as well as a Tibetan Children's Village for orphaned Tibetan children in Nepal *(across the road from Devi's Fall).* The hilltop **Tibetan Monastery** has excellent views of the valley. Below the bridge, the river rushes through the 46m-deep Seti gorge. *(Ask for it by its Tibetan name, "Madepani Gompa." Follow the road to the regional museum, turn right at Mahendra Pul Bridge, and cross the Seti Gandaki River. Taxi from Lakeside Rs80 one-way. 1hr. by bike.)* North of Pokhara, outside the city limits, is a cave, **Mahendra Gupha.** Tunnels inside the cave allow a good half-hour of exploration; some parts of the cave have electricity, but take a flashlight anyway. *(Taxi Rs150. Rs10.)*

🔺 RAFTING AND TREKKING

More than 40 travel agencies are based in Lakeside and Damside, many of them associated with hotels. Agents usually specialize in rafting or trekking. Most accept major credit cards. The established **rafting** companies include **Himalayan Encounters** (tel. 22682; open daily 8:30am-7pm), **Ultimate Descents** (open daily 9am-7pm), **Equator Expeditions** (tel. 20688; open daily 8am-8pm), and **Sisne Rover Trekking** (tel. 20893; open daily 8:30am-9pm). The first two are open only September to May. All four charge between US$35 and US$60 per person per day. Rates usually include equipment rental, guides, instruc-

NEPAL

tion, food, and transportation. The rafting permit fee (2-day trip Rs80) should be covered by the company. Some companies (including Ultimate Descents and Equator Expeditions) provide one or two safety kayakers who accompany every trip. Other companies have cheaper packages; check up on their reputations before signing up. Routes on the challenging **Kaligandaki** (Class 4) and manic **Marsyangdi** (Class 5) run only in season—monsoon rains make them unnnavigable. The **Seti Khola** and **Trisuli** (Class 3-4) are more fun during the high water level from June to August. Some companies combine a Trisuli trip to Narayanghat with a visit to **Chitwan National Park** (see p. 777).

Trekking agencies provide everything from equipment rental to individual guides to fully planned treks. Expect to pay US$12-15 per day for an English-speaking guide. Reputable agents include **Equator Expeditions; Sisne Rover; Sa-Rang San Tours** (tel. 30031) close to the airport (open daily 8:30am-6pm); **Pokhara Tours and Travels** (tel. 22976), on Simal Chaur as it heads north towards town; it's a 15-minute bike ride from Lakeside (open daily 8am-6pm); and **Himalayan Journeys** (tel. 21720), opposite the airport (open Su-F 7am-8pm). Women trekkers should check out **3 Sisters Adventure Trekking** (tel. 24066), which provides female guides and porter services. Follow the road round towards Sarangkot; it's on your right. (Open daily 8am-8pm.) For where and when to trek, see **Treks in the Annapurna Region**, p. 792.

NEAR POKHARA

Phewa, Begnas, and **Rupa Lakes** were all part of the body of water that once filled the Pokhara Valley. Phewa bears the burden of tourist traffic; Begnas and Rupa remain untouched. **Begnas Bazaar**, 15km from Mahendra Pul, is serviced by **local buses** departing from of the entrance to the main Prithvi Chowk bus park in Pokhara (every 15min. 6am-6pm, 30min., Rs15). The two-and-a-half hour **bike ride** to Begnas will certainly loosen up your legs before the trek. **Taxis** charge Rs500-600 round-trip and will wait for your return. By renting a **boat** (Rs200 per hr.) and rowing to the other end of Begnas you can hike the trail to Rupa over Panchabhaiya Danda from Begnas (20min.).

Sarangkot (1592m) is one of the best places to view the mountains above and the lakes below. There are several ways to get there. If you're feeling lazy, take a **taxi** up the road that runs most of the way to the top and walk up for another half hour (Rs500-600 round-trip, Rs100 per hr. waiting time; price includes Rs30 toll). You can walk up the road—turn left off the Baglung road as you head north at the "Sarangkot" sign, 1km north of the Baglung bus park. Much nicer and longer is the walk up from Lakeside (3hr.). Because it's easy to lose your way among the myriad trails that crisscross the hillside, don't hesitate to get the services of one of the many guides who appear as soon as you start heading up the hill (Rs25). Dawn is the best time for mountain-viewing from Sarangkot, so consider staying overnight in one of the lodges just below the top. Accommodations options are **Lake View Lodge** (doubles Rs100) and **Didi Lodge** (doubles Rs60). Lake View does a "small breakfast" of two eggs, hash browns, tea, and toast (Rs80).

THE TERAI तराई

The most maligned of Nepal's geographic regions, the Terai is the flat bit of Nepal to the south dipping into the Gangetic plain. Its flatness has fostered the construction of many of Nepal's best roads, but travelers continue to see the Terai as a sweaty, mosquito-infested purgatory between India and Nepal's mountains, meriting no more than a few hours' transit. For Nepalis, however, these fertile flatlands are more than a just tedious passage—the Terai produces the vast majority of the country's rice and hosts most of its industry, construction, and transportation infrastructure. The Terai was covered with impregnable malarial jungle until the 1950s and 1960s; eradication efforts prompted massive migrations from Nepal's hills and the bordering Indian states. Fortunately, large chunks of land like the Royal Chitwan National Park have been set aside to preserve some of the original abundance of flora and fauna. Still, there continues to be conflict between wildlife needs, the demands of a growing population, and now, a bur geoning tourism industry. The neighboring towns of Narayanghat and Bharatpur form the gateway from the hills. Hetauda is an important transportation hub to the east, as is Butwal to the west. The Mahendra Rajmarg Highway, running east-west from one corner of Nepal to another, connects these cities with the whole Terai. Lumbini, in the near-west, and Janakpur, in the near-east, are two of Nepal's main religious sites.

HIGHLIGHTS OF THE TERAI

■ The jungles, swamps, and plains of **Chitwan National Park** (p. 777) are proof that even the flatter parts of Nepal can be pretty darn beautiful.

■ **Janakpur's** temples (p.782) offer a look at heavily Indian-influenced culture and architecture, without the headache of a **border crossing** (p.773, 781, and 785).

BHAIRAWA (SIDDHARTHANAGAR) भैरहवा

Where the road to Lumbini parts company with the Sunauli-Pokhara road stands Bhairawa, a town where residents exude an old-fashioned hospitality and courteousness. What the town lacks in the way of sights it makes up for with pleasant accommodations; it's a popular stop en route to or from the border, or for daytrips to Lumbini. The **Siddhartha Ramjarg Highway** runs north-south through town. **Bank Road** heads west from **Bus Chowk** (Bhairawa's center) to the main bazaar. A 15-minute walk north of Bus Chowk toward Butwal leads to **Lumbini Chowk,** where the Lumbini road splits from the highway and heads west to the **airport,** 5km farther.

Necon Air (tel. 21244) is just north of the Bus Chowk (open daily 8am-1pm and 2pm-6:30pm). **Buddha Air** (tel.21893) is just east of Bus Chowk (open daily 8am-6pm). Both have flights to Kathmandu (Buddha Air 3:30pm, Necon Air 6:10pm; 45min.; US$72). The **bus counter** (tel. 20350) is at Bus Chowk (open daily 4am-8:30pm). Buses to Sunauli (frequent, 10min., Rs3) and Butwal (frequent, 1hr., Rs11) leave from Bus Chowk; buses to Lumbini (every 30min. 6:50am-6:40pm, 1¼hr., Rs12) leave from Lumbini Chowk. A **rickshaw** from Lumbini Chowk to Bus Chowk costs Rs10, and to Sunauli Rs20. **Private jeeps** haul passengers to the **airport** (Rs100), Sunauli (Rs70), and Lumbini (Rs400-500 roundtrip, depending on waiting time) and can be rented at Bus Chowk (Open 4am-9pm). There are frequent **public jeeps** to Sunauli (Rs3), but passengers must wait until these fill up. **Lumbini Exchange,** Bank Rd., can handle your banking needs (cash only; open daily 7am-6pm). **Bhim Hospital,** Bank Rd. (tel. 20193), 150m from Bus Chowk, and **Siddhartha Medical Hall** (tel. 22707), just east of the westernmost entrance to the hospital, are both open 24 hours. The main **police station** (tel. 20199) is on Barmeli Tole; follow Bank Rd. from Bus Chowk to the next major intersection, and make a right. The **GPO,** Bank Rd., 200m west of Bus Chowk, has *Poste Restante* (open Su-Th 10am-5pm, F 10am-3pm). Send **email** at Roopchaya Photo Studio (tel. 21243; Rs25 per Kb; open daily 8am-8pm). **Postal Code:** 32901. **Telephone Code:** 071.

Sayapatri Guest House, Bank Rd. (tel. 21236), to the left, is the best deal. Rooms are small but clean and bright, and they come with fans and flip-flops for the bathroom. (Singles Rs125, with bath and hot water Rs300; doubles Rs250/500.) **Hotel Everest** (tel 20317), next door and under the same management, is newer and grander but probably not worth the extra money. Bathrooms come with towels and flush squat toilets. (Singles Rs550; doubles Rs700.) A few minutes' walk west on Bank Road, signs indicate a turn-off for **Kasturi Restaurant** (tel. 21580), serving inexpensive and tasty Indian food on dark wooden tables surrounded by comfy throne-like chairs (entrees Rs30-48; open daily 8am-9pm).

SUNAULI सौली

The most generous thing one can say about Sunauli is that it isn't as miserable as the other hypertrophied bus stops that link India and Nepal. The second-most popular entry point to Nepal (after Tribhuvan International Airport in Kathmandu), Sunauli has all the inevitable frontier grime (including touts) but is far less of a hassle than Birganj and significantly less dismal than Kakarbhitta. The location is central; it is a stone's throw away from a number of towns in Nepal.

⚄ ORIENTATION AND PRACTICAL INFORMATION. The **bus park** on the Indian side is about 500m south of the border. Tickets are purchased on board. Buses leave frequently for: **Delhi** (4:30am-6:30pm, 22hr., IRs288) via **Lucknow** (10hr., IRs105); **Gorakhpur** (4am-9pm, 2-3hr., IRs33); and **Varanasi** (7 per day 4:30am-7pm, 9hr., IRs106). The **bus park** (main ticket counter tel. 20194), on the Nepal side, is about 100m from the border. Buses run to: **Kathmandu** (6 per day 4:30am-1:30pm, 11hr., NRs128; 6 per night 4:30-8pm, 11hr., NRs160); **Pokhara** (frequent 4am-8pm, 10hr., NRs128-156); **Bhairawa** (frequent 5am-7pm, 10min., NRs3). The Kathmandu and Pokhara buses pass through **Butwal,** where there are connections to other Nepalese destinations. You can walk across the border or, if your luggage looms large, you can take a **rickshaw** (NRs30). The requisite stops at both Indian and Nepali customs and immigration should take under an hour. Nepalese visas can be obtained on the spot, but citizens of any country other than India or Nepal will need to have a visa already in order to enter India. The border, as well as both Nepalese and Indian immigration offices, is open 24 hours. The Nepali **tourist office** (tel. 20304), between the Immigration Office and the border, has free brochures about Nepal's tourist attractions and little else (open Su-Th 10am-5pm, F 10am-3pm). Several authorized **currency exchangers** on the Nepal side exchange foreign currencies and cash traveler's checks (most open 7am-8pm; 1% commission for traveler's checks, 2% for cash). The only bank on the Indian side does not change foreign currencies. **Telephone Codes:** Sunauli (India) 05522; Sunauli (Nepal) 071.

⚄⚄ ACCOMMODATIONS AND FOOD. The best place to stay in Sunauli is the government-run **Hotel Niranjana** (tel. 38201), on the Indian side, just north of the bus park. A distinctive white fort-like structure, the hotel has a great location that blocks out most of the traffic noise. Decent rooms have balconies, attached bath, and hot water. (Dorm beds IRs40; singles IRs200, with air-cooling IRs341; doubles IRs240/394.) The only remotely recommendable place on the Nepali side is **Hotel Paradise** (tel. 22777), next to the noisy bus station. The large, clean rooms with thick mattresses and tiled attached baths are leagues above the others offered in Sunauli. (Singles NRs300; doubles NRs400.) Their restaurant dishes up Indian and Chinese standards (NRs12-85) as well as pizza (NRs55-140; open 6am-10:30pm). The restaurant in Hotel Niranjana is the best bet on the Indian side, serving Indian, Continental, Chinese, and Japanese dishes (*thalis* IRs35, other entrees IRs 20-40; open daily 7am-10:30pm). **Mandro,** 150m from the border on the Nepal side, serves tasty Indian and Chinese standards (NRs30-90) as well as burgers (NRs80-150) and pizzas (Rs55-100) on a dimly lit patio (open daily 5am-10pm).

LUMBINI त्लुबीनी

According to legend, Siddhartha Gautama, a prince in the Sakya royal family, was born at Lumbini in 623 BC, when the site was merely a forest grove near a water tank. Siddhartha's mother, Mayadevi, was on her way back from her husband's palace when she stopped for a bath in the water tank and then gave birth, holding the branch of a sal tree for support. Siddhartha's birth was unusual not only because he exited his mother through the rib cage, but because he was born with the ability to speak. Upon entering the world, he said "I am the foremost of all the creatures to cross the riddle of the ocean of existence. I have come to the world to show the path of emancipation. This is my last birth and hereafter I will not be born again." Today, the Sacred Garden marks the spot of this event; it also contains the pillar erected by the Indian Emperor Ashoka as a token of his visit to Lumbini. The pillar cites Lumbini as Buddha's birthplace, lending legitimacy to the location, if not the parturition particulars. Further evidence comes from remains of monasteries and *stupas* that date from as far back as the 3rd century BC and from accounts of early visitors. By the 15th century, however, Lumbini's claim to fame had been forgotten, and it wasn't until 1896 that Ashoka's pillar was unearthed. The current half-hearted drive to raise the town's status from just an obscure spot in the Terai began in 1967 with a visit by U. Thant of Burma, then secretary general of the U.N., and continued with unsuccessful attempts by Japanese architect Kenzo Tange. Various countries are constructing monasteries and study centers in the "International Monastery Zone"; followers of Mahayana occupy one side of the dividing canal, follow-rs of Theravada the other. Lumbini may not yet have become the "peace-oriented, igh-quality meditation place" envisioned by the planners, but, in its sleepy Terai way, 's as peaceful as it could ever hope to be.

■ ORIENTATION AND PRACTICAL INFORMATION. The **Sacred Garden** is a 10-inute walk from the **bus stop.** Walk west past the tourist information booth, keep left : the bunch of sign posts, and continue to the Lumbini Garden Restaurant. Opposite e garden are the monasteries and rest house. To the north is the **Eternal Flame** (a)min. walk), the half-finished monasteries and temples of various Buddhist countries, nd farther north across the main east-west road from Bhairawa, Lumbini's only **tourist ccommodations.** There is no local transportation in Lumbini, which means both soles nd souls get a good work out here. Take the **bus** to Bhairawa (every hr. 7am-7pm, ⁄hr., Rs12) from the bus stop at the intersection of the main road with the road lead-g to the garden, or walk 2km. En route you can visit the scruffy village of Lumbini Iehalbar, which dispatches three buses per hour to Lumbini. **Jeeps** go to Bhairawa's umbini Chowk (Rs300-500 round-trip, including waiting time). Information is available om the **Lumbini Development Trust** (tel. 80194), in one of the administrative buildings)uth of the garden. There is a very basic, free **first aid clinic** in the pilgrims' home across om the Sacred Garden, but head to Bhairawa for serious medical care. The **police sta-on** (tel. 80171) is a few minutes southwest of the Sacred Garden. **Telephone Code:** 071.

▐ ACCOMMODATIONS AND FOOD. Most people make daytrips to Lumbini nd then head back to hotels in Bhairawa. Lumbini's best option is **Sri Lanka Pilgrims est** (tel. 80109), a 3km walk north of the Sacred Garden (rickshaw Rs50). Walk to the ternal Flame, keep going along the canal, past all the temples and the Korean-funded ≥search center, make a left on the main road, and take the next right. Built for Sri Lan-an pilgrims, it houses 196 people in simple red-brick rooms ranging from doubles to ormitories. Beds cost Rs258 for non-SAARC citizens, but you should be able to sweet-lk the management into winking at that rule (Rs77 on the ground floor, Rs143 1st oor). The building's circular design is centered around the dining hall, which isn't ncy but serves good Chinese (chow mein Rs35), Continental, and Indian food (*aloo* auliflower Rs30; open 7am-10pm, 24hr. service available for guests). The monastery omplex across from the Sacred Garden provides spartan but conveniently located ccommodations. The white building is a **pilgrims' rest house** (tel. 80172), with rooms at are little more than empty cubicles with hard straw mats, no bedding, and a single ght bulb. The outside toilets and (cold water) shower room could use a cleaning. here is no fixed price, but donations are expected (Rs50-200 per night). Small **food ands** in front of the rest house serve snacks and basic Nepali meals. Lumbini's only al restaurant, **Lumbini Garden Restaurant,** on the main road south of the turn to the acred Garden, serves a decent selection of Chinese, Indian, Nepali, and Continental od at exorbitant prices (entrees Rs100-205; open daily 7am-10pm).

▐ SIGHTS. Lumbini's **Sacred Garden** is dominated by the **Mayadevi Temple,** which is cur-ntly under renovation and, for now, swathed in an unsightly yellow tarp. The main **May-devi sculpture** (3rd-4th century AD), which has long been worshipped by Hindus as a presentation of a fertility goddess, was moved to the building at the entrance of the gar-en three years ago and will not be moved back to the temple until renovations are com-ete. The sculpture has been worn down from centuries of devoted caresses. There is nother statue beside it with a detailed depiction of the Buddha's birth. Behind the May-levi Temple is Nepal's oldest monument, the **Ashokan Pillar,** erected in 249 BC when shoka came to Lumbini to mark the 20th anniversary of his coronation. The emperor imself is believed to have written the script at the bottom. South of the Ashokan Pillar is e sacred **water tank** where Mayadevi bathed before giving birth to Siddhartha. To the outheast of the Ashokan Pillar are the remains of monasteries, temples, and *stupas* dat-g from the 3rd century BC to the 9th century AD. By the huge tree next to the water ink, the sleeping Buddha and child Buddha statues bear the red-and-yellow coloring of aditional Hindu worship. The large yellow temple opposite the Sacred Garden was con-tructed by King Mahendra in 1953 and contains statues from Burma, Thailand, and

NEPAL

Nepal, including a large, gold Buddha at the main altar. Wall paintings depict the wheel c
life, four *bodhisattvas*, and the major Hindu gods welcoming Siddhartha back to Nepa
after he had become the Enlightened One. A 10-minute walk north of the Sacred Garden
the **Eternal Flame** commemorates the 1986 International Year of Peace. The road fork
here; each branch continues north (enclosing what will soon be a reflecting pool) to tem
ples and monasteries under construction by the 15 member nations of the Internationa
Lumbini Development Committee. Each country plans to send monks to live at its templ
and represent its particular approach to Buddhism.

NARAYANGHAT नारायणगढ़
AND BHARATPUR भरतपु

The twin cities of Narayanghat and Bharatpur, on the Mahendra Rajmarg Highway i
the center of Nepal, together constitute one of the nation's largest urban areas. Naray
anghat hosts most of the area's businesses, shops, hotels, and tourists, while Bharatpu
provides a semi-rural respite from traffic, just 15 minutes on foot down the Mahendr
Highway away from the Narayani River. An hour's walk up the river from Narayangha
is the *sadhu* community of sacred and sublime Devghat, where the Kali Gandaki an
Trisuli Rivers merge into one, becoming the Narayani.

⊞ ORIENTATION AND PRACTICAL INFORMATION. Narayanghat revolve
around the junction of the Narayanghat Mugling Highway and the Mahendra Rajmar
Highway. **Pulchowk Bus Park** is at the intersection, while **Sangam Chowk,** the center o
Narayanghat, lies about 120m away from Pulchowk on the Mahendra Highway toward
Bharatpur. The **Pokhara Bus Park,** 15 minutes north of Pulchowk towards Mugling, send
buses to and from Pokhara, Gorkha, and Devghat.

Cosmic Air (tel. 24218), Gorkha Air (tel. 21093 or 21096), Lumbini Air (tel. 23858), and RNA
(tel. 21881 or 20326) all have offices in Bharatpur's airport or across the road from it (al
open daily 7am-5pm). There are flights to **Kathmandu** (4 per day 11:10am-1pm, US$50)
Buses leave from the Pulchowk bus park to: **Birganj** (every 30 min., 4hr., Rs75); **Butwa**
(every 45min., 3hr., Rs55); and **Kathmandu** (every 30min., 6hr., Rs85). From Pokhara bu
park, buses go to: **Pokhara** (every 30min. 6am-2:45pm, 5hr., Rs65) and **Gorkha** (every h
6:45am-4:30pm, 3hr., Rs36). Minibuses to **Bharatpur** and **Tardi Bazaar** (every 10min. 6am
7pm, 25min., Rs7) leave from the Sangam Chowk area. **Rickshaws** service the two bu
parks (Rs10). **Tempos** also leave from west of Sangam Chowk for Bharatpur (Rs5).

Chitwan Sauraha Tours and Travels (tel. 21890), at the southwest edge of the bus park a
Pulchowk, sells tickets for tourist buses to Kathmandu (open daily 7am-10pm). **Nepa
Bank** (tel. 20170), 500m northeast of Pulchowk on the road to Mugling, changes major for
eign currencies and traveler's checks (open Su-Th 10am-3pm, F 10am-1:30pm). Sangam
Chowk is home to about half a dozen **medical stores** (most open 6am-8pm). There is a hos
pital (tel. 20111) north of the main square in Bharatpur. The **post office** is on the road to
Mugling, not far from the Pokhara bus park (open Su-Th 10am-5pm, F 10am-3pm). **Hell
Chitwan** (tel. 22715), just beyond Sangam Chowk towards Bharatpur, has email (Rs10 pe
Kb) and web access (Rs10 per min.; open daily 8am-7pm). **Telephone Code:** 056.

⊞⊞ ACCOMMODATIONS AND FOOD. There are accommodations in Narayang
hat, a stone's throw from the noisy Pulchowk Bus Park. **Regal Rest House** (tel. 20755)
across from the Gulf gas station at Pulchowk Bus Station, has clean rooms with lur
green walls, fans, attached baths with hot water, and air-cooling (singles with batl
Rs250; doubles Rs350; triples Rs400; TV Rs100 extra). **Hotel River View** (tel. 21151), jus
behind Pokhara bus stand, has a river view from the upper floors. It's friendly, messy
and somewhat like a trekking lodge. Rooms have mosquito nets and attached bath
with squat toilets. (Doubles Rs100, with bath Rs150.) **Quality Guest House** (tel. 20939)
100m northeast of Pulchowk bus park, has a somewhat isolated location. The room
don't sparkle, but they're not filthy either. Bathrooms have seat toilets and hot water
(Singles Rs100, with bath Rs175; doubles Rs250/300; triples with bath Rs300.) Jus
beyond Sangam Chowk on the road to Bharatpur is the **Roof Top Restaurant,** whicl

boasts a *tass*—a large open-air clay barbecue pit. Set meals (Rs35) consist of grilled mutton, *bhuja* (puffed rice), and pickles. (Open daily 8am-10pm.)

🔆 SIGHTS. Devghat, a short taxi ride through towering forests towards Mugling, exists to honor the confluence of the Trisuli and Kali Gandaki Rivers, and is therefore a popular *sadhu* hangout. Don't miss the 4m-high pink statue of the monkey king Hanuman. Across the bridge there are many shrines to various deities and saints, most prominently Mahadevi and Durga (non-Hindus should refrain from entering the small temples). Every morning, the devout strike a delicate balance between hypothermia and ritual purity as they go about their ablutions. The real action, however, comes around January 15 when thousands make a pilgrimage here. (Round-trip taxi ride plus 1hr. waiting time, Rs250.)

CHITWAN NATIONAL PARK चिटवान

Until recently, Chitwan was the playground for Nepal's elite—and the sport was hunting big game. Nepalese history books conscientiously contain photos of ranas and foreign dignitaries posing on elephants behind the day's kill—tigers, black bears, and deer. As of 1846, hunting rights in Chitwan were reserved for royalty and their guests. But things have moved on since, and Royal Chitwan National Park is now the most protected wildlife reserve in Nepal. In fact, the real threat to the wildlife came not from aristocratic rifles but from the area's successful malaria eradication program in the 1950s, which indirectly resulted in total habitat destruction as people moved down from the hills to take advantage of the fertile flatlands. People who had settled in Chitwan began to be resettled in 1964, and the area was declared a national park in 1973. Eleven years later, UNESCO designated Royal Chitwan National Park a Natural World Heritage Site.

The wildlife is extremely well-protected, but visitors can still experience some real live jungle. Guests at the more expensive hotels inside the park are led through a standard two- or three-day safari program and treated to facilities and services that strive (often successfully) to provide luxury au naturel. Outside the park, the most popular and most developed tourist base is the village of Sauraha. Lodges with varying facilities and prices have planted themselves here just outside the entrance to the park. Regardless of where you stay or how much you pay, herds of tourists don't obscure the wildlife, although in season, demand can exceed supply of some jungle-related activities. If you can handle the rain and humidity, consider visiting the wild between May and October.

🚌 TRANSPORTATION

Buses: The **bus counter** (tel. 60134), in Tardi, just east of the turn to Sauraha, is marked "Prithvi Rajmarg Bus Syndicate." Open daily 7am-9:30pm. To: **Kathmandu** (10 and 11am, 5hr., Rs100-150); **Pokhara** (9 and 10am, 5hr., Rs100-150). Prices may vary with service charges. **Green Line** sends A/C buses to **Kathmandu** and **Pokhara** (both 9:30am; Rs480 including complimentary breakfast). Reserve ahead with the hotels in Sauraha or the travel agents in Tardi. A **mini-bus** (every 10min. 6am-7pm, 25min., Rs7) to Narayanghat allows you to connect to other towns.

Local Transportation: Transportation between Tardi and Sauraha is a hassle. **Jeeps** (Rs300 for 10 people) go between the two towns. If you don't already have a pre-paid package (including Tardi-Sauraha transfers) avoid the offers of a free ride in exchange for a stay in a cheap hotel. There may be no jeeps off season; it's a good idea to reserve a night's accommodation to ensure that a vehicle will be awaiting you. The pleasant 1½hr. walk affords a first-hand glimpse of life in Tardi. Sauraha has plenty of **bicycle** rental opportunities (mountain bikes Rs10-25 per hr., Rs90 per day).

🛈 ORIENTATION AND PRACTICAL INFORMATION

Chitwan National Park is at the center of Nepal, bordering India to the south. Narayanghat and Bharatpur form the gateway area. The **Mahendra Rajmarg Highway** runs almost parallel to the northern boundary of the park. Roads head south to each of the park

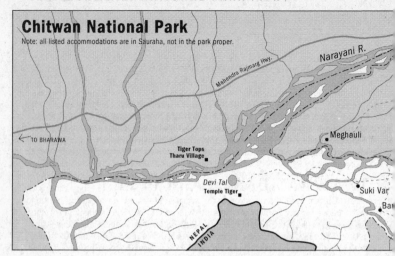

Chitwan National Park

Note: all listed accommodations are in Sauraha, not in the park proper.

Narayani R.

Mahendra Rajmarg Hwy.

← TO BHARAWA

Tiger Tops
Tharu Village

Meghauli

Devi Tal
Temple Tiger

Suki Var

Ba

NEPAL
INDIA

hotels and to the few villages outside the park. **Tardi Bazaar,** 35 minutes east of Naray anghat on the highway, is the closest bus stop to Sauraha and the entrance to the park both of which are 7km away from Tardi. There are two ways to the park entrance fron **Sauraha Bazaar.** One is to follow the main gravel road when it veers left in front of th Jungle View Restaurant, past the **Tharu Village,** and make two right turns. The other is t go right and follow the line of the river, partly on the beach, partly on trails. Canoe depart from the riverbank next to the entrance and elephants depart from the speciall constructed elephant boarding tower, a two-minute walk beyond the park office.

Tourist Office: The **ticket office** at the park entrance offers elephant rides (8am an 4pm). Open daily 6:30-9am and 1-3:30pm. The National Park **entry fee** (Rs650, vali for 2 full days) covers general entry and river canoeing rights. **Steep fines** await thos caught in the park without a valid permit. **No one may enter the park at night.** In sea son, the wait to get park entry permits can be 3-4hr. For an additional Rs50-100, a tou from a guide service or your hotel may be able to get the permit for you.

Currency Exchange: Sauraka Money Changer changes both cash and traveler's checks a reasonable rates. 2% commission. Open daily 7am-7pm. **Himalayan Bank,** Tardi Bazaa 200m east of the Sauraha turn-off, exchanges money and gives cash advances on Visa (1% commission, Rs50 "telecommunication fee"). Open Su-Th 10am-3pm, F 10am-1pm

Bookstores: Jungle Books, near Jungle View Restaurant. Open daily 7am-9pm.

Pharmacy: Raj Medical Hall, Tharu Village Rd., near the center of Sauraha. Open dail 7am-9pm. The pharmacist doubles as a "health assistant," but the nearest hospita (tel. 20111) is in Bharatpur.

Police: The **main police station** is a 20min. walk east of Sauraha. For the police statio in Tardi, walk 300m east on the main highway from the turn to Sauraha.

Internet: Web World Computers (tel. 60309), right at the Sauraha turn-off in Tardi. Emai Rs15 per Kb, web access Rs15 per min. Open Su-F 7am-8pm.

PHONE CODE   056

ACCOMMODATIONS AND FOOD

Many tourists came to Chitwan on pre-paid package deals arranged in Kathmandu o Pokhara, but if you arrive in Tardi without a reservation, head to Sauraha. Standar accommodations take the form of free-standing cottages in garden compounds wit solar-heated water (i.e. hot shower before bed, not before breakfast). All hotels offe

NEPAL

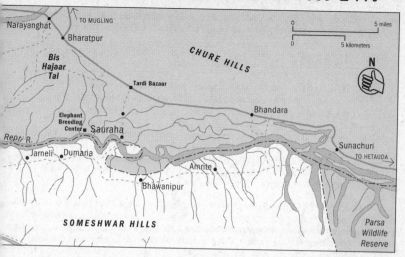

basically the same three-day, two-night package consisting of a jeep or elephant ride, half-day jungle walk, canoe trip, stick dance, lodgings, meals, and bus transportation from Kathmandu or Pokhara to any return city in Nepal. Be wary of bogus budget "deals," and ask to see a park permit. Prices plummet off season; bargain hard, although realize that some of the costs (park entry fee, elephant ride) are fixed by the park.

Hotel Wildlife Camp (tel. 29363—messages only), north of Sauraha Bazaar. The garden is almost as pretty as the campfire, which blazes from a permanent embankment. The attractive brick houses have carpeted, well-furnished rooms with fans. All bathrooms have hot water. Doubles with bath Rs500-600. Off-season: Rs200-400.

Chitwan Resort Camp (tel. 29363—messages only), on the main road north of Sauraha Bazaar. Fairly large, attractive, and well-furnished rooms have sparkling, tiled bathrooms. If you want to be lulled to sleep by jungle breezes, check out the mosquito-net-equipped bamboo observation tower. The dining room is a goodie—spaghetti bolognese Rs100. Bamboo tower Rs100. Rooms Rs500. Off-season: Rs200-400.

Jungle Tourist Camp (tel. 29363—messages only), north of Sauraha Bazaar, comes with a less-exquisite garden. Attached baths. Restaurant open 6am-8pm. Mud houses with mud floors and thatched roof Rs100; linoleum-floored cabins Rs250-300.

Eden Guest House (tel. 29371), at the end of Sauraha, a 10min. hike east from the park entrance. The isolation makes the hike here worth it, especially in season. The beds and lighting are better in the newer huts, which have clean attached bathrooms; the older mud houses have doubles with common bath. Attached restaurant. Rooms Rs100-300.

Jungle Adventure World (tel. 29364), popularly known as JAW, is best approached from the beach; follow the main road south to the beach and take a left at the sign. Comfortable, carpeted cottages set in a sylvan glade overlooking the river and the park on the other side—Sauraha's best hotel location. Prices negotiable. Doubles US$20.

Jungle View Restaurant and Bar, Sauraha Bazaar, specializes in Italian food, including exceptional lasagna (Rs70-90). Gorgeous rooftop views of the river, especially in the evenings. Happy hour 4-8pm (beer and snacks Rs80-90). With a German bakery downstairs—apple strudel Rs40, cinnamon roll Rs25—and culinary ambitions extending in every direction, it's not surprising the menu is 12 pages of dense text. Most entrees Rs80-110. Open daily 6:00am-10pm.

K.C.'s Restaurant and Bar, Sauraha Bazaar. The bamboo hut rooftop has good views and a good selection of English music. Its menu features an A-Z of all known food, but Mexican is the chef's choice of cuisine. Friendly and knowledgeable staff help arrange budget deals on jungle activities. Happy hour 4-8pm (beer and snacks Rs80-90), and two for-one cocktails (Bloody Mary Rs140). Entrees Rs90-150. Open daily 6am-11pm.

THE PARK

> ❗ **WARNING.** Due mainly to rhino risk, visitors to Chitwan National Park must be accompanied by a guide at all times. **Let's Go does not recommend being bitten, gored, or trampled.**

Chitwan National Park's mammalian highlights include the one-horned rhinoceros, Bengal tiger, leopard, sloth bear, and wild bison. There are estimated to be 470 mammal species, over 500 species of birds, 9 species of amphibians, 126 species of fish, 150 species of butterflies, and 47 species of reptiles in the park. A 1995 study places 107 of Nepal's 300 tigers in Chitwan. (Open 6:30-9am and 1-1:30pm.)

TOURS AND GUIDES. Package tours organize everything from jungle activities to return transportation for any destination in Nepal. One money-saving alternative is to arrange individualized itineraries by booking activities, a la carte, through a hotel *(service charge of about Rs50 per activity)*. This can make life easier as hotel guests get priority in space-limited activities, especially during the high season. **Guide companies** provide guides for every activity in Chitwan and generally charge less than hotels for bookings. The newer **United Jungle Guide Service** is under K.C.'s Restaurant in the Jungle Guide Office *(open daily 6am-10pm)*. When looking for a guide, ask other tourists for referrals; the number of years' experience should also be on the guide's permit certificate. Be sure to tip the guide at the end of a good trip.

THROUGH THE JUNGLE. Elephant rides are the most popular activity at Chitwan. They offer an opportunity to see the jungle animals up close—if you're lucky, you could end up literally 2m away from a rhino—in ways that walking and jeep tours can't afford. Not all elephant rides take you into the park itself, so make sure to ask. *(8am and 4pm. About 1hr. Rs650, service charge Rs50-100. Reserve through a guide company or hotel, or queue up before the park's opening times.)* The **jungle drive** comes in a close second to the elephant ride in popularity. Because jeep rides are long, they cover more of the jungle, including the park headquarters at Kasara and the Gharial Conservation Project. But jeeps, unlike elephants, can't leave the road to follow animals or go through tall grass, although rhino sightings are practically guaranteed on any jungle drive. As the grass grows tall from June to the annual grass-cutting in January or February, animal spotting becomes increasingly difficult. Each jeep should come with a driver and a separate wildlife spotter. *(7am and 1pm. 4-6hr. Rs350-650, depending on season. Jeep rental Rs5000 per vehicle per day.)* Most **canoe rides** involve an hour of floating down the river followed by a two- to three-hour guided walk back. The canoe ride and walk may be billed separately but should be part of the same package. *(8am and 2pm. 3-4hr. Rs300-350 per person. Rs50-100 service charge for hotel or agency booking.)* **Jungle walks** are ideal for jungle immersion, photography, and animal sightings, but since walkers are unarmed and have no easy getaway, rampant rhinos can pose a real threat. A guide takes a maximum of eight people. There is only one walking path in some sections of the jungle, so you may end up spotting a lot of Homo sapiens. *(6-7am. 3hr. walk Rs250; full-day walk Rs500.)*

OTHER EXCURSIONS. There is a two-day jungle walk to **Kasara**, the park headquarters and the site of the museum and the Gharial Conservation Project. From Kasara, walk back to Sauraha, or get a ride via Bharatpur. Guides charge about Rs500 per person, with discounts for large groups. Some guides offer one- to two-hour bird watches (Rs150), but much of that time is spent walking to and from the lookouts. Another option is a **bicycle ride** to **Bis Hajaar Tai** (Twenty Thousand Lakes), outside the park to the northwest of Sauraha. It's best to leave early in the morning to see gharials, birds, and rhinos at the lakes. Bicycles need to be reserved the night before. Note that being outside the park does not make the rhinos any less dangerous. *(Guides charge Rs200-300. Jeep shared between 6 people costs Rs1500 for 3hr. round-trip to Bis Hijaar.)*

CHITWAN'S PONDEROUS PACHYDERMS

Besides its rhino and tiger denizens, Chitwan is also populated by elephants. Just about every elephant in Chitwan is from India, where wild elephants still roam despite a millennium-old trade of capturing and training them. With elephant stomping grounds receding and trapping on the wane, elephant prices have sky-rocketed—they can cost up to one million Indian rupees. Chitwan has responded with its Elephant Breeding Centre, established in 1987. Training begins when an elephant turns two; both a human and a "role model" senior elephant are teachers. Each elephant has 3 attendants; the *mahout* is elephant companion numero uno. However, when they're giving tourists rides, elephants are driven by the second guy in charge, the *phanet*. The elephant stables, which hold between 17 and 22 elephants throughout the year, are a 10-minute walk east from the park entrance. At feeding time, the elephants chomp on the main course—*kuchii* grass balls stuffed with rice grains, salt, and molasses, knocking back between 80 and 90 of these delicacies a day.

The **Tharu,** the indigenous people of Chitwan, have the dubious privilege of serving as an additional "attraction" alongside the tigers and the rhinos. A **guided walk** through the Tharu village along the road to the park entrance covers the culture, history, and religion of the people *(2hr., Rs75 per person).* Tharu stick dances exuberantly invite participation. Dance troupes perform regularly at hotels and every evening at the Tharu Culture Program on the main drag north of Sauraha Bazaar. *(Programs start 7:30-8:30pm depending on season; check in advance. Rs50 per person.)*

HETAUDA ह्टौडा

Hetauda is home to heavy industries and the first stop for cargo shuttling between Kathmandu and the Terai. Vehicles from the Indian border also speed through the town, which is unfortunately treated as a half-hour pit stop; but the hills by the Rapti River, and the broad, tree-lined streets offer pleasant strolls, and **Makwanpur Gudi** affords superb views along a three-hour hike.

The north-south **Tribhuvan Highway** cuts right through town; Mahendra Vira Vikram Shah's **statue** marks the intersection with the town's main east-west street. The **bus park** is southwest of the statue, along an east-west road just south of the main street. All Birganj buses pass through Hetauda, and other frequent buses and trucks run between the two (2hr., Rs40). The pink **post office** is readily recognizable by the red letterbox in front; it's five minutes down the western branch from the intersection (open Su-F 10am-5pm). The **police** headquarters is next door. Across the street is the **hospital** (tel. 20305), which has out-patient care, a **pharmacy** (open Su-Th noon, F 9-11am), 24-hour **emergency** care, and Red Cross ambulance service. The **Community Health Center** is well-stocked (open daily 7am to 7pm). The **Nepal Bank,** along the highway south of the statue, will exchange traveler's checks (open Su-F 10am-3pm). The only English that marks it is an "NB" on the gate; look for a three-story building a few doors south of Hotel Seema. **Telephone Code:** 057.

Off-season rates in Hetauda are negotiable. **Motel Avocado** (tel. 20429), just north of town on the highway, is a ten-minute walk from the bus park. All rooms have attached baths with towels and toilet paper, screened windows, fans, and mosquito mats. The most expensive rooms have A/C, color TV, and phones. (Singles Rs350-1500; doubles Rs550-2000. Student discounts up to 25%. Attached restaurant: entrees Rs35-125.) The **Lido Inn** (tel. 20937, fax 20655), on the highway south of Hotel Seema, is new and clean. All rooms have attached baths with towels and toilet paper, TVs, fans, and firm beds. (Singles Rs350-450; doubles Rs450-600.)

BIRGANJ बिरगञ्ज

Birganj is the funnel through which traffic to India passes, narrowing at the border into a pot-holed, exhaust-filled artery clogged with trucks, rickshaws, bullock-carts, and tongas. Nepalis are the first to declare that Birganj is a miserable place for tourists; the

> **WARNING.** Crossing the border from Nepal to India requires four steps (see p. 643). Also remember that although the Indian immigration office is always open, **Indian visas are not available at the border.** The Indian embassy in Kathmandu is the only place in Nepal that issues them. The Nepali immigration office at the border is open daily from 6am to 7pm. If you don't already have a Nepalese visa when you arrive at the border (from India), you'll need a photo and US$15 in cash. **There are no exchange facilities at the border giving out U.S. dollars.** For more information see **Visas,** p. 11.

only reason to come is to cross the border. If you're heading to India, Birganj will relieve any separation anxiety and make you glad to leave Nepal. If you're coming from India, perhaps you'll appreciate that Birganj is at least a little more bearable than **Raxaul** (p. 643), India's border town.

⚐ ORIENTATION AND PRACTICAL INFORMATION. Birganj sprawls for miles along the main road that leads over the Indian border. Buses bypass the main road and stop at the **bus park** directly east of the **clock tower,** Birganj's main landmark, at the north end of town. **Buses** mercifully run from Birganj to virtually every major city in the Terai; day buses (7am-noon, 8hr., NRs150) and night buses (6-8pm, 8hr., NRs150) head to **Kathmandu.** Private buses also run from the many tour operators that line the street of Birganj. Unless there's a real disaster, you should be in and out of Birganj within a couple of hours. **Local transport** consists of rickshaws and tongas. Both cross the border into India, but only rickshaws will wait while you stop at immigration. A rickshaw from Birganj to Raxaul takes from 40 minutes to two hours, depending on traffic (NRs35). The **Nepal Indo-Suez Bank** (tel. 22733 or 75277) exchanges traveler's checks and most currencies. Turn left immediately after the Hotel Kailas, and head west along Adarsha Nagar; the bank is on the left-hand side, after about 500m. (Open Su-Th 10am-2:30pm, F 10am-12:30pm.) The hotels will also change money, and they accept Indian rupees. **Pharmacies** are plentiful along the main street at the southern end of town. **Telephone Code:** 051.

🛏🍴 ACCOMMODATIONS AND FOOD. The two best places to stay are next door to one another, along the north-south road one block west of the main road and well south of the clock tower. The **Hotel Kailas** (tel. 23084) has a range of clean, concrete rooms. The most basic have fans and mosquito nets; the more expensive have private baths, A/C, and TVs, but still no hot water. (Singles NRs100, with bath NRs200; doubles Rs430/600; triples Rs265/430.) The **Hotel Diyalo** (tel. 22370; fax 25375) is more expensive and no less dank or old than the Kailas, but it has more perks—a 24-hour international communications center, a rooftop beer garden, and rooms with attached bath, TVs, phones, and mosquito nets. Cheaper rooms have fans and cold water; more expensive rooms have A/C and hot water. (Singles NRs500-1500; doubles NRs600-1800.) Although both hotels have restaurants, the Kailas' is by far the better, with a wide range of Indian and Chinese dishes and a good selection of foreign beers.

JANAKPUR (JANAKPURDHAM) जनकपु

Janakpur was once the capital of the mythical kingdom of Mithila, which supposedly flourished in the 10th to 3rd centuries BC. Most visitors to Janakpur are Indians making their pilgrimage to the birthplace of the famous *Ramayana* heroine Sita, whose father Janaka gave his name to the city. Despite the ancient associations, however, none of the buildings is particularly old, and roads here are often obstructed by vagrant cows and goats. The cityscape is dominated by the flaking onion domes and triangular roofs of its many *kutis* (pilgrims' hostels) and is filled with *sagars* (artificial ponds) used for ritual baths. The pastel-colored buildings glow at dawn and dusk, when the sounds of cymbals and drums from the temples fill the air. The city truly comes to life during its festivals, particularly **Vivaha Panchami** (Nov.-Dec.), which features a re-enactment of Rama and Sita's wedding.

⊞ ORIENTATION AND PRACTICAL INFORMATION. Janakpur's network of curving alleyways makes it easy for someone to get disoriented, but the city is small enough that a recognizable landmark is never far away. The **railway station** sits at the northeast corner of town. Janakpur's main thoroughfare, **Station Road,** runs southwest from the railway station through **Bhanu Chowk** (named for the Nepalese poet whose bust tops a pillar in the middle of the intersection) and then bears south past **Dhanush Sagar** and **Kuna Village.** The road continues south to the **airport,** 2km from town. Necon runs **flights** to Kathmandu (1pm, 30min., US$55). Their office (tel. 21900) is on Station Rd., south of Bhanu Chowk (open daily 8am-6pm). **Bus** tickets are sold at the bus park, but the several English-speaking agents who cluster just south of the railway station usually charge comparable rates. Buses go to numerous destinations, including **Kathmandu** (7am-9pm, 10-12hr., Rs140), but catching a local bus from a major intersection— Dhalkebar to Janakpur from Hetauda, or Itahari to Dharan, Hile, and other points north—is often the best way to get where you're going. There are **cycle-rickshaws** for intra-city travel (Rs30), but you can get around easily on foot. The **Ram Mandir,** across from Dhanush Sagar, on the west side of Station Rd., is another useful landmark. The road that runs northeast of the Mandir leads through Janakpur's old bazaar area to **Janaki Mandir.** The major road that heads west (and then southwest), south of Ram Mandir, leads to the **bus park,** which sits at the southwest corner of town, just south of a tall tele-communications **tower.** The **tourist office** (tel. 20755) is on Station Rd., north of Bhanu Chowk (open Su-Th 10am-5pm, F 10am-3pm). The **Nepal Rastraya Bank** is also on Station Rd. (open Su-F 10am-5pm). There is a **hospital** just west of the Janaki Mandir, and **pharmacies** line Station Rd. The **haat bazaar** (Su and W) is held west of Ram Mandir. The **post office,** southwest of Dhanush Sagar, is difficult to find, so ask for directions or take a rickshaw (open Su-Th 10am-4:30pm, F 10am-2pm). **Telephone Code:** 041.

▟▛ ACCOMMODATIONS AND FOOD. Kathmandu Guest House (tel. 21753), right at Bhanu Chowk, is a friendly and simple place with open atriums, screened windows, ceiling fans, mosquito nets, and attached bathrooms with squat toilets (singles Rs150; doubles Rs300; triples Rs350). At the north end of Station Rd., near the railway station, is the **Aanand Hotel** (tel. 20562), which is run by a group of young men and features crowded rooms with good ceiling fans, mosquito nets, and attached baths with hot water. (Singles Rs100, with bath Rs150; doubles with bath, air-cooling, and TV Rs250.) **Hotel Welcome,** Station Rd. (tel. 20646), northeast of Dhanush Sagar, has bright rooms that run the amenities gamut. Private baths have hot water and squat toilets. (Singles Rs50, with bath Rs75, and A/C Rs600; doubles Rs150/300/1000-1500. Additional 10% tax.) The restaurant below, thanks to friendly proprietors, is the town's most popular, serving North Indian food (veg. Rs20-50; non-veg. Rs70-90). As for the rest of Janakpur's dining scene, it's North Indian, North Indian, or North Indian, but some of it is so tasty that you'll hardly notice that there's no other choice. **Ramilo Restaurant** and **Eight Restaurant,** just southwest of Bhanu Chowk, are both good and cheap and serve almost identical menus, though Ramilo has more of a sports bar atmosphere, while Eight feels like a tavern.

◎ SIGHTS. None of Janakpur's temples are very old, but all are in use. The **Janaki Mandir,** a huge wedding cake of a construction, was built in 1911 on the spot where an image of Sita was found in 1657, also where the infant Sita is said to have been discovered by her father. Her silver image is uncovered twice a day, once in the early morning and again in the evening. Next door is the **Ram Janaki Vivaha Mandap,** built a decade ago to mark the place where Rama and Sita were married (Rs5, camera fee Rs5). During the **Vivaha Panchami Festival** in December, *sadhus* and *brahmin* priests re-enact the wedding ceremony of Ram and Sita. Southeast of the Janaki Mandir is the **Ram Mandir,** Janakpur's oldest (built in 1882) and most typically Nepalese temple. Built under a big banyan tree, the temple hosts the **Ram Navami Festival** the first week of April, celebrating Ram's incarnation on earth. To the east of the Ram Mandir are Janakpur's largest and holiest ponds, **Dhanush Sagar** and **Ganga Sagar.** Across from Ramanand Chowk on the main highway is a brick path that leads to the peaceful **Bihara Kund,** surrounded by temples. South of

MITHILA PAINTING Maithili women (from the area of southern Nepal and northern India that was once the Mithila kingdom) have developed a painting tradition handed down from mother to daughter for generations. The art form originated with the bright designs that women paint on the walls of their houses (mud-covered bamboo huts with thatched roofs) and has become known as **Madhubani.** These paintings often serve a ritual purpose as part of a festival or wedding—a woman may create paintings for her future husband as part of their courtship, for instance. The paintings are characterized by bold outlines filled in with bright colors; subjects vary from abstract geometric designs to scenes from daily life. Images have different symbolic significance; pregnant elephants, parrots, bamboo, turtles, and fish represent fertility and marriage, while peacocks and (non-pregnant) elephants are good-luck symbols. The process and the purpose of the paintings are more important than the product, which may be destroyed. Nowadays, they're sold to tourists at hefty prices.

Ramanand Chowk on the main highway is **Hanuman Durbar,** a small temple which, until recently, housed the world's largest monkey, thought to be an incarnation of Hanuman and known to be a victim of stomach cancer.

There are a few other things to do in Janakpur aside from temple-hopping. The **Janakpur Women's Development Centre** (tel. 21080) is a must for anyone interested in art or economic development. Almost an hour's walk south of Janakpur, the center is best reached by rickshaw (Rs25); ask to be taken to the "development store." Signs along the road to the airport indicate an eastern turn-off into the village of Kuwa. From a temple at the western edge of Kuwa, a 10-minute walk southeast leads to the center. Wandering back through the village, you'll see Mithila paintings in place on the walls of the houses. The artists use the traditional motifs of Mithila paintings on handmade paper, paper-mâché, ceramics, and textiles (see **Mithila Painting,** above). The products are for sale here and at various non-profit outlets in Kathmandu and Patan. The center also trains women in literacy, mathematics, and business management. (Open Su-Th 10am-5pm, F 10am-4pm.)

Janakpur is also the point of departure for Nepal's only **steam railway,** a good way to see the surrounding countryside. Trains service Bijalpur, to the west (7am and 3pm, 1hr.) **Get off the train before the border; you may not be able to re-enter Nepal.**

DHARAN धरान

At the point where the landscape rises from the plains to meet the hills lies the bazaar town of Dharan, where people from both come to buy everything from cloth to electronics. Despite efforts to increase tourism, the few visitors who come here tend not to stay for long. While Dharan is a far more pleasant overnight than many of the Terai's transportation hubs, there isn't much to do unless you head for the surrounding hills. **Chatara,** where river rafters on the Sun Kosi pull out, is 15km west, and **Hile** (p. 786) and **Basantapur** (p. 786) are trekking trailheads to the north. Once home to one of the British Army's Gorkha training camps, Dharan still hosts a number of Nepal's *khukuri*-smiths who now make knives for tourists.

Two long blocks uphill from the main north-south road is **Bhanu Chowk,** the major intersection of **Chata Chowk. Nepal Bank Ltd.** (tel. 20084) is just north of Chata Chowk (open Su-Th 10am-3pm, F 10am-noon). The closest **airport** is in Biratnagar; Necon Air and RNAC have several daily flights to Kathmandu. **Buses** go to Hile (every 30min., 4hr., Rs55) via Dhankuta, continuing on to Basantapur (Rs80) and Biratnagar (frequent, 2hr., Rs20). There is a bus to Kathmandu (4pm, 17hr., Rs300). Other bus connections can be made at Itahari (frequent, 30min., Rs14) at the junction of the area's two highways. **Telephone Code:** 025. **Shisti Guest House** (tel. 20569), down Chatra Line, left from Chata Chowk, has well-maintained, large rooms with fans (singles Rs125; doubles Rs150, with bath Rs250). The **Bamboo House** (tel. 21309), just east of Bhanu Chowk, on the left, serves veg. (Rs20-50) and non-veg. (Rs35-65) curries in a dark setting (open daily 7am-9:30pm).

KAKARBHITTA काकर भित्ता

Kakarbhitta is a small trading town on the India-Nepal border; spanning atop the flood plain of the Mechi River, Kakarbhitta's **bridge** sees almost no traffic. Kakarbhitta is essentially a large, dusty bazaar centered on the **bus station,** which sits about 100m from the border on the northern side of the **east-west highway.** Many of Kakarbhitta's establishments—hotels, restaurants, and banks—line the highway east of the bus station. From the west side of the bus station, alleys that run parallel to the highway constitute the **market area.**

Several **buses** leave for Kathmandu (1:40-6:40pm, 18hr., NRs340). **Rickshaws** run from the border to Panitanki in India (IRs5/NRs8), where there are buses to Siliguri (1hr., IRs8; IRs30 for taxi). The **tourist office** (tel. 29035), on the northern side of the highway, to the right of Hotel Kathmandu, disseminates bus information (open Su-Th 10am-5pm, F 10am-2pm; closes 1hr. earlier in winter). **Travel agencies** around the bus station charge NRs30 commission, which can be avoided by buying tickets at the white building near the center of the bus park. At the border, a Nepali visa is available to those with a passport photo (US$50 for 60 days). Nepali **immigration** is open daily from 6am to 6pm. Indian immigration is open 24 hours. **Entry visas,** however, must be obtained from the Indian embassy in Kathmandu. **Nepal Rastra Bank,** across the highway from the tourist information center, buys foreign currency and traveler's checks at 1% commission and sells Indian and Nepali rupees. It is also one of the last places that will exchange Nepali rupees if you are headed into India. (Open daily 7:30am-6pm for foreign exchange.) **Telephone Code:** 023.

Hotels surround the bus stand; at the far left corner of the bus park is the **Hotel Rajat** (tel. 29033), with the cleanest dining area in town. Old rooms are clean, with fans, mosquito nets, hot water, and squat toilets across the yard. Rooms in the new building have immaculate attached baths with seat toilets (some have tubs), fans, TVs, phones, hot water, and mosquito mats; one room has A/C. (Old rooms: singles Rs100; doubles Rs150. New rooms: singles IRs400, with A/C IRs1000; doubles IRs600/1500; triples IRs800. 10% service charge. Discounts available.) The attached garden restaurant—sporting the only grass in Kakarbhitta—serves an impressive array of entrees (Rs25-90; open daily 7am-9pm). The somewhat dingier **ABC Lodge** (tel. 29025), down the second alley north of the highway from the bus station, next to the vegetable market, has bright rooms with ceiling fans, mosquito mats, and common bath with squat toilets (singles IRs100; doubles IRs120).

THE EASTERN HILLS

Eastern Nepal's soaring peaks are no match for mere mortals, but don't let that deter you. These mammoths are merciless, and visitors grow to love the challenge they present. Almost 9km above sea level, Everest is a staggering prospect to even the most experienced mountaineers. The less well-known landscape farther east, which includes some of Nepal's most jagged and otherworldly peaks, similarly pulls no punches. Casual trekkers, marveling at the serendipity that brings them face-to-face with these peaks, usually stagger back to Kathmandu with wise and satisfied Cheshire grins, not to mention tauter leg muscles. But a trip to the east is not all fireworks and adrenaline. While the mountains are truly awesome, the hills are also sublime. If the pinnacles are imperious, the humble rolling landscape below is gentle and accommodating. And both the hills and the giants, including the oft-trodden Everest (see p. 802), greet guests with a refreshing natural grace.

Everest (see p. 802)

HIGHLIGHT OF THE EASTERN HILLS

■ Steeped in cool mists, the hills and tea fields of **Ilam** (p.787) are resplendent and serene, offering a little-touristed option for those interested in more than distant peaks.

NEPAL

JIRI जीरी

The one-road town of Jiri (1935m), the main trailhead for the Everest trek, provides travelers the rest, comfort, and sustenance necessary for recovery from the grueling ride from Kathmandu. **Buses** leave **Kathmandu** (5:30, 6:30, 8, and 9:30am; 11hr.; Rs145) from the Old Ratna bus park in the rear of the lot. Tickets can be purchased at any time prior to departure, it's best to get them early if you want a window seat—you do. There is also an express bus from Jiri to Kathmandu (7, 9, and 11am; 8hr.; Rs170), but not vice versa. Tickets must be purchased the night before, and you are expected to arrive at the bus park half an hour before departure.

On Saturdays, a **market** is held on the hilltop of **Naya Bazaar**, a 30-minute walk from the bus park. **Jiri Medical Mall,** at the bus park, has basic services (open daily 5:30am-7pm). The poorly marked **hospita**l is a five-minute walk from the bus park on the unpaved path (open daily 9am-2:30pm). The Jiri Helminth Project, just down the hill from Naya Bazaar, is staffed by two doctors; it administers free services and drugs (when available) and provides ambulance service to Kathmandu (open M, Tu, Th, and F 8:30am-noon). The **police station** is 4km away on the road to Kathmandu. The only **telephone** in Jiri is outside Cherdung Lodge (tel. (049) 20190; open daily 6am-8pm); it is sometimes functional (calls to Kathmandu Rs7 per min.; other countries Rs500-700 first 3min., Rs150 each additional; free callbacks).

Most lodges are within 100m of the bus park; they are clean and government-registered: **Cherdung Lodge** (doubles Rs110; triples Rs150); **Sagarmatha Guide Lodge** (doubles Rs60; triples Rs100); and **Hotel Jiri** (doubles Rs100; triples Rs150). **Hotel Gauri Himal** has a decent rooftop restaurant and a great view of the Jiri Valley, as well as the cleanest bathrooms in all of Jiri (doubles Rs200).

HILE हीले

Perched above the Arun Valley at a cool, misty 1900m, Hile has spectacular mountain views and a unique ethnic mix of Bhotiyas, Rais, Newaris, and Indians. A trailhead for treks into the world's deepest valley, Hile hosts a colorful, bustling market—shops stacked with shiny plastic buckets and heaps of flip-flops and salt—but the terraced villages below offset the bartering frenzy. Piles of *doka* (the conical, head-strapped baskets that porters use) wait to be filled and carried off into the hills. Most of Hile's visitors soon head for higher ground, but the town merits a visit even for non-trekkers, with several small *gompas* and a tea estate on the way up to Basantapur, but the attention-grabber is the Himalayan range—there are great views from the hilltop north of town, a 45-minute walk away.

The **bus stand** is at the northern end of town facing south. Tickets are sold at a small booth set back on the left side of the street. Buses to and from Dharan leave every hour (4hr., Rs62), and there is a direct night bus to **Kathmandu** (1pm, 18hr., Rs335). South of the bus stop are several trekking-style lodges which have electricity, showers, hot water on request, and restaurants. **Himali Hotel** (tel. 20340), a few minutes south of the bus stop on the left, has large, bright rooms (singles Rs50; doubles Rs80; triples Rs120; attached restaurant: entrees Rs20-45; open daily 7am-10pm). North of Himali, **Hotel Gajur** (tel. 20339) has **international phone** service and a nice garden and restaurant (singles Rs55; doubles Rs100; triples Rs150). The friendly **Doma Hotel** (tel. 20574), across from Himali, has cheap and pleasant rooms (doubles Rs60; triples Rs80). The **post office** is down the hill from Hotel Doma on the same side of the street. It isn't marked—ask around. **Telephone Code:** 026.

BASANTAPUR बसन्तपु

Looking down from an elevation of 2200m, Basantapur is blessed with a beauty mitigated only by impertinent diesel roosters intent on rousing slumberers at 4am. This is the end of the road for buses but only the beginning for trekkers in the Eastern Hills. The **bus** ride (every hr., 2hr., Rs35) from Hile terminates at Basantapur's southern tip, near the **police post**. A five-minute walk along the rutted road brings you to the other end of town, where the road continues east to **Therathum** and, in clear weather, great mountain views. All of Basantapur's lodges offer similar tea-house accommodation: beds in wooden rooms, common squat-toilets, and cozy restaurants where you can spend the evening sipping *tong-ba* (Rs10-20) and watching people stare at you. **Hotel Yak** (tel. 69047), a few minutes past the bus park along the main road has such luxuries as electricity, a shower room with hot water, and **STD/ISD** service, also available to non-guests from 7am to 10pm (singles Rs55; doubles Rs100; triples Rs130; quads Rs150; attached restaurant open daily 7am-10pm). **Laxmi Hotel** (tel. 69022), just past the bus park, provides less aesthetically pleasing accommodations at lower prices. There are no showers, but the rooms have electricity; the TV-equipped restaurant hosts most of Basantapur's after-dark action. (Singles Rs35; doubles Rs70; triples Rs80.) Across the street from the Laxmi, **Birat Hotel and Lodge** (tel. 69043) is the only place around to devour *dal bhat* under the watchful eyes of V.I. Lenin. Birat does not have electricity, but there is a shower facility and rooms are tidy. (Singles Rs40; doubles Rs60; quads Rs120.) Basantapur's **post office** is just past Hotel Yak (toward Therathum). It isn't marked in English, so look for a red-and-white sign and stairs leading to a letter box. (Open Su-F 10am-5pm, Sa 10am-1pm.) **Telephone Code**: 026.

ILAM इलाम

Safely removed from the rest of civilization by a 16-hour bus ride, Ilam is one of Nepal's most under-appreciated gems. Its few stalwart visitors are rewarded for trip with the calm provided by the cool air, pleasant strolls among tea hills, and amazing views of lush hills and vales. Curious tourists can have an unintelligible, impromptu guided tour of the factory of Ilam's **tea estate,** which stretches over the hills above the bus park. The **haat bazaar,** held outside the town square by the post office every Sunday, may be less risque, but it promises some action. Ilam is also one starting point for treks through the **Kanchenjunga** region, although daytrips in the surrounding countryside can be just as rewarding. The four- to six-hour walk to the pilgrimage site of **Mai Pokhari,** 12km to the north, winds past tea gardens and forests to the top of a ridge, crowned by a temple and sacred lake. To the northwest, a three-hour walk leads to the bazaar town of **Mangalbare.** Descending to the scenic **Mai Khola** is another breathtaking journey of just a few hours on foot.

Getting a seat on the **bus** that winds its way up to Ilam can be difficult. Your chances are best from Birtamod, accessible by local bus from Kakarbhitta (frequent, 25min., Rs9). Night buses from Kathmandu reach Birtamod (every hr. 6:30-11:30am, 12hr., Rs300) and continue to Ilam (4hr., Rs80). Return buses leave for Charali and Birtamod in the morning (every hr., Rs80) and for Kathmandu (noon, 24hr., Rs340). Private jeeps and trucks can be entreated to take passengers south. The Ilam bus park is at the bottom of the hill, a short walk from the town square. Lodges and **pharmacies** cluster along the main street, from the bus park up to the **town square. Mechi Tours and Travels** (tel. 20113), on the left side of the square, provides bus and domestic plane tickets, private vehicles and drivers, **STD/ISD** and **fax** service, and **currency exchange** (no travelers checks). The proprietor is a good source of information about the surrounding areas. (Open Su-F 9am-5pm, Sa 9am-1pm.) Two lanes diverge from the square opposite the main street. The one to the right leads to the **post office** (open Su-Th 10am-5pm, F 10am-3pm) and the **haat bazaar** (Sa and Th). The rudimentary **hospital** is at the end of the path. **Telephone Code:** 027. **Bhattarai Hotel and Lodge** (tel. 20139), next to the bus park, compensates for the noise with electricity and large, clean doubles (Rs80-100); some have attached baths with squat toilets and cold showers (Rs150). The **Himalayan Restaurant** downstairs is one of the few places to eat.

TREKKING IN NEPAL

For many years only the **Annapurna, Langtang,** and **Everest** regions were open to foreigners, but recently there has been an explosive growth in trekking routes all over Nepal. However, most trekkers stick to the original three areas. Fabulous treks in their own right, these have the benefit of a good trekking infrastructure—you can stay in tea houses and eat locally prepared food and not worry about the tents and freeze-dried stuff that has blighted many a backpacking trip. The facilities also help keep costs down since fewer guides and porters are needed, and trekking permits for the "Classic Three" are cheaper than for elsewhere in Nepal.

NEPAL

CHOOSING YOUR ROUTE

ANNAPURNA

The Annapurna trek is the most popular in Nepal for good reason. The terrain ranges from magnificent snow-covered peaks to lush valleys; barren, high-altitude desert to river-fed tropical lowlands. Even during the snowy winter and monsoon-drenched summer, trekkers make their way up to or around Annapurna, named for the Hindu goddess of the harvest. There are three main treks in the Annapurna region, and it's possible to mix and match segments of these routes to generate treks of just a few days out of Pokhara.

The **Annapurna Circuit** (see p. 793) has long been synonymous with trekking in Nepal. 150 miles long and typically taking about three weeks, this is one of the few trekking routes on which you never have to re-trace your steps, since it's exactly that: a circuit around the entire Annapurna massif. Because it involves traveling north of the Himalaya, beyond the reach of the monsoon, you traverse several ecological and ethnic zones—from the monsoonal lowlands to the high-altitude desert of the Trans-Himalaya, from Nepal's Hindu valleys to the Tibet-influenced Buddhist highlands. The "big day" on the circuit is crossing the **Thorung-La** pass (5416m). If done in its entirety, the circuit takes 18-21 days. As with all high altitude treks, proper equipment and acclimatization are necessary.

A popular alternative to the circuit, and one that avoids the high pass, is the so-called **Jomsom Trek** (see p. 795). This trek along the north-south valley of the **Kali Gandaki,** the deepest gorge in the world, is actually the final third of the circuit and passes between **Dhaulagiri** and **Annapurna,** the planet's 7th- and 11th-highest peaks respectively. This trek can be done in two weeks, as a straight there-and-back, or in seven to ten days, with a flight between Jomsom and Pokhara.

A third popular route in the Annapurna region leads to the **Annapurna Sanctuary** (see p. 797), an extraordinary area in the middle of the massif surrounded by Himalayan peaks. It's possible to vary the lower parts of the route, but this is largely a there-and-back trip. From Pokhara, the sanctuary trek normally takes between seven and ten days.

LANGTANG

Legend has it that the Langtang Valley was discovered by a *lama* who stumbled into it while chasing a renegade yak. While, this story may be true, another oft-repeated bit of mountain lore—that Annapurna and Everest are Nepal's only real treks—is certainly not. The **Langtang** (see p. 799), **Helambu** (see p. 800), and **Gosainkund treks** (see p. 801) represent some of the best year-round trekking Nepal has to offer. The first expedition to the Langtang region was led by H.W. Tilman in 1949, and the area was declared Nepal's first Himalayan National Park in 1971. The least frequented of the Classic Three, the Langtang region is situated in the central Himalayas, with a border on Tibet to the north and east, and a southern border not too far north of Kathmandu. In fact, it's possible to start a trek into Helambu from **Sundarijal,** on the Northern edge of the Kathmandu Valley. A number of routes in Helambu can provide a pleasant introduction to life on the trail without the high altitude. Most people, however, choose to combine Helambu with a visit to the holy lakes at **Gosainkund** (4380m) and a trip up the Langtang Valley to **Kyangjn Gomba** (3900m), which serves as a base for admiring and exploring the peaks and glaciers of the Langtang Himalaya. You can get back to Kathmandu by bus from **Dhunche** (3-4 days walk back down the Langtang Valley). Depending on whether you choose to combine Helambu and Langtang or limit yourself to one or the other, this region provides anything from a few days to several weeks of trekking.

EVEREST

The **Everest trek** (see p. 802) is a pilgrimage to the famous viewpoint from where every hair-raising detail of the original Norgay-Hillary route can be made out. A road extends from Kathmandu to **Jiri,** but from there Everest is still 10 days to two weeks away, and it's a tough walk. Because you're walking against the grain of the land—up from one river, over a ridge, and down to the next—most people either fly one or both ways to the airstrip at **Lukla.** From Lukla, it's two short days to **Namche Bazaar,** the fabled capital of the Sherpas, and from there four days to a week (depending on acclimatization) to **Kala Pattar** (5623m). The stark black pyramid of Everest's southwest face dominates this magnificent viewpoint on the flank of **Pumori.** It's a half-day trip farther up the Khumbu glacier from **Gorak Shep,** at the base of Kala Pattar, to basecamp, which becomes a tent metropolis in the peak climbing season of April to March. There are plenty of **side-trips** you can take in and around the Everest area. One of the best and most popular is a trip to the **Gokyo Lakes** (4791m; 2-4 days from Kala Pattar), situated in the lateral moraine of the great **Ngozumpa Glacier** that drains **Cho Oyo** (8201m). Although it's possible to make a relatively short trek of Everest by flying in and out of Lukla, the high altitude of its most impressive routes requires that parties take it slowly, allowing plenty of time to acclimatize.

SUGGESTED ROUTES

Treks can range in duration from three hours to a month, and many variations are possible. The following suggestions represent just a few of the trekking options in the Annapurna, Langtang, and Everest regions.

Less than a week. 1: Short routes north of Pokhara (e.g. Birethanti-Ghorepani-Gandruk-Birethanti). 2: Helambu trek.

One to two weeks. 1: Annapurna Sanctuary. 2: Fly to Jomsom and walk back. 3: Everest, flying to and from Lukla. 4: Langtang trek.

Two to three weeks. 1: Everest, flying to Lukla one way. 2: Jomsom trek, walking both ways. 3: Fly to Jomsom, and walk back with a detour to Annapurna Sanctuary. 4: Langtang with Helambu and Gosainkund.

More than three weeks. 1: Annapurna Circuit, possibly including the sanctuary. 2: Everest, there and back on foot from Jiri.

TREKKING IN OTHER REGIONS OF NEPAL

If you're interested in traveling in regions beyond the Classic Three, then you've gone beyond this book, and you should speak with a trekking company in Nepal or in your home country. Some of the more popular non-Classic Three treks include:

Lamjung. Starting in Gorkha, this route takes trekkers up a minor peak, Rambrong (4400m), for fantastic views of the east end of the Annapurna massif.

Manaslu Circuit. The high point and highlight of this major trip, also starting in Gorkha, is the Larkya La Pass (5153m).

Dhaulagiri Circuit. This trip around the world's 7th-highest peak takes you over not one, but two 5000m+ passes.

Dolpo and Mustang. An exploration of 2 remote and rugged regions where the awesome mountain scenery competes for attention with living vestiges of ancient cultures.

Kanchenjunga Base Camp. Kanchenjunga is not only the world's 3rd-highest peak; it may be the biggest single lump of mountain anywhere. Kanchenjunga's south face is the centerpiece of one of the planet's most awesome mountain vistas.

Simikhot to Kailas. Trek into the far northwest of Nepal, and cross the border into Tibet to join pilgrims paying their respects to holy Mt. Kailas and the Mansorovar Lakes.

PREPARATIONS

Trekking permits (see p. 726) and **park entry fees** must be acquired prior to departure. Permits for all regions are issued by the immigration office in Kathmandu (in New Baneswar), while the office in Pokhara issues permits only for the Annapurna region. The Kathmandu office can be a crowded nightmare in season, so, if you're planning on

NEPAL

spending time in Pokhara prior to heading into the Annapurna region, it's best to get your permits there. You might also consider paying the Rs200 that it costs to have a trekking agency do it for you.

GEAR

Gear requirements are pretty minimal as you'll essentially be walking from lodge to lodge. However, bringing a **sleeping bag** will save you from the brutal, in-season competition for a lodge's few blankets. If you're going high (over 3500m or so), you need decent **warm clothing**; if you skimp in order to lighten your load, you could end up cold and miserable at the most spectacular part of your trek. Mountaineering equipment *per se* is not necessary on the Classic Three routes, but you should have a proper pair of **boots** if you're going high and perhaps also a pair of **snow gaiters**; check with people who've done your route recently to see what the snow conditions are like.

Everything you need can be either bought or rented in Nepal. Backpacks and sleeping bags, for example, rent for Rs15-20 per day, depending on size and quality. You will be expected to leave a hefty deposit (e.g. US$100 in traveler's checks) with the rental shop. A lot of rental equipment is manufactured in Nepal and emblazoned with fake Gortex, North Face, or Patagonia labels, so choose carefully, especially when it comes to a vital piece of equipment like a backpack—that's something you really don't want falling to pieces when you're halfway up the Thorung-La. Remember that an old piece of expedition equipment that looks kind of grimy and tired might also be tried and tested. Kathmandu is the best place to rent or buy (and sell) stuff, with Pokhara coming in a respectable second. You can also rent equipment in Namche Bazaar (en route to Everest) and Chomrong (en route to Annapurna Sanctuary). You can buy gear in Chame, Manang, and Jomsom on the Annapurna Circuit, but the rental opportunities are limited because most people are heading on, never to return there. Prices for rental and purchase are pretty comparable in Kathmandu and Pokhara but higher elsewhere.

WATER

Although it is now possible to buy bottled water even in the higher and more remote villages on the major routes, treating your own water is both cheaper and more environmentally friendly. If each of the Annapurna region's 50,000 trekkers per year consumes three liters of bottled water per day in the course of a trek that lasts an average of two weeks, it makes for a total of more than two million trashed plastic bottles in the Annapurna region alone, *every year*. **Boiling** is usually impractical (and ineffective at high altitudes where water boils at a lower temperature), so most people opt for water that has been chemically treated in some way. **Iodine** is the way to go—it's the only stuff that'll kill off some of the nastier nasties like giardia. Bottles of iodine solution are available in pharmacies in Kathmandu and Pokhara (Rs25); add 5 drops per liter. A pricey, but much less messy, alternative is iodine tablets (e.g. **Potable Aqua**), available in bottles of 50; add two tablets per liter. Tablets are available in Kathmandu from Kathmandu Environmental Education Project (KEEP) for Rs450 or from Himalayan Rescue Association (HRA) for Rs500 (see p. 726). They are also available for Rs500 on the trail at ACAP checkpoints (in Annapurna) and HRA offices (in Manang, Annapurna and Pheriche, Everest).

BOOKS AND MAPS

Let's Go: India & Nepal is not a detailed trekking guide, and we recommend supplementing it with an additional reference. Two books dominate the market: Stan Armington's *Trekking in the Nepal Himalaya* (7th Ed., 1997 Lonely Planet) and Stephen Bezrucha's *Trekking in Nepal* (7th Ed., 1997 The Mountaineers, Seattle). Both books contain detailed route descriptions along with comprehensive sections on planning and health, and are usually available in used book stores in Kathmandu and Pokhara. Consider photocopying the section on your route to lighten your load, but remember to photocopy the health sections as well.

It's easy to find **maps** of the main trekking areas, and they are an important part of your pre-trek shopping list. Be warned, however, that most maps produced in Nepal are, at best, "approximate," and their information should be treated with skepticism. Still, these maps (such as those produced by Nepa Maps) are useful for letting you know vaguely where you are and where you're headed. More accurate and expensive maps, generally known as "Schneider maps," are also available in Kathmandu, but these are more likely to be out-of-date. The *National Geographic Society's* map of Everest is a great trekking aid for those headed in that direction. KEEP and HRA in Kathmandu (see p. 726) are good sources of current information on trekking routes. Their bulletin boards may also be helpful if you're looking for trekking partners.

PORTERS AND GUIDES

Even though "tea-house" trekking (see **Accommodations,** below) requires that you carry relatively little, that sleeping bag, that copy of *War and Peace,* and that set of fleece long johns can seem outrageously heavy when you're laboring up a hill at 5000m. Porters can be hired just about anywhere in Nepal, but be careful not to get ripped off. Paying the **surcharge** associated with hiring a porter through a hotel, lodge, or trekking agency is probably a good investment from the peace-of-mind perspective—your porter is less likely to abscond if he or she has to answer to a boss. You may also consider hiring a guide: someone who speaks English and can fill you in on what you're walking through. Guides are basically unnecessary, though, on the major routes. Bezrucha's book (see above), for example, is packed with *more* than you could want to know about each region, and most porters speak some English and can serve as porters-cum-guides.

Porters are hired at a **daily rate** and are expected to pay for their own accommodation and food (rates vary, but US$3-10 is standard). Guides, on the other hand, are paid less but expect to have their food and accommodation bought for them; this can get pricey if your guide has a penchant for beer. When you hire someone, **negotiate** the terms of your arrangement in advance. Outline exactly what is expected of them and be sensitive about the conditions to which you're about to subject them. As their employer, you are responsible for their well-being. Consider buying or renting essential equipment like sturdy footwear and sunglasses for them if you're going high, but make sure, in the case of a rental, it is understood that the equipment is *not* a gift.

Having a porter and/or guide does a lot more than take a burden off your shoulders; they provide you with an entry into local culture. They are probably familiar figures on the trail and often have many friends along the way. If you're lucky, you might even end up as a guest for a night in their home village. And you'll probably end up learning much more Nepali than you would otherwise. There is, however, a downside: they set the agenda. You go at their pace and end up staying at a lodge of their choice, either because it's owned by their sister-in-law or because the owner supplies them with a hefty commission for bringing you in. Either way, this might not be exactly what you had in mind on the accommodation front. Also, women trekking alone or in all-female groups have occasionally had problems with guides (not usually porters) overly inclined to uninvited familiarity. Women trekking in the Annapurna region might consider hiring female porters/guides from Pokhara's all-female trekking agency, **3 Sisters Adventure Trekking** (see p. 771).

ON THE TRAIL

Instead of sticking to a strict schedule, such as one prescribed in Armington's book or by the rubric on many of the locally available maps, we suggest that you simply take as long or as short a time over the trek as is comfortable. Some people enjoy hurtling along the trail while others like to stop every 30 seconds to scrutinize yet another wildflower. Most people get up early and hike for five or six hours total. This makes for plenty of time at the end of the day to wash your socks, take a shower, and hang out around your lodge's dining table. The social scene in lodges is often of good value and may also be a source of trekking companions for days to come.

ROUTE-FINDING

Route-finding on the major routes is straightforward; you are following the mountain equivalent of a highway. Since you are essentially walking from village to village, when in doubt, simply ask in what direction the next village lies. It's not always a good idea to ask lodge employees, even though their English may be good, because they've been known to exaggerate the distance to the next place in the hope that you'll give up for the day and stay at their lodge. In general, a desire not to offend may impair the directions given to you by passersby. For example, if you ask whether village X lies to the north, you might get a polite "yes" even though it is in fact to the south; the person you asked may not want to upset you by telling you that you're wrong. Therefore, try to formulate your question in as non-leading a way as possible.

ACCOMMODATIONS AND FOOD

In the Classic Three trekking areas, entrepreneurs have long since converted their villages into dense constellations of lodges. These were once the **tea houses** of "tea-house trek" fame but are now fancy neo-hotels, complete with single or double rooms (some even with *en suite* facilities), solar heated shower systems, and extensive menus. Some of the fancier establishments even boast Western-style toilets. However, there remain plenty of places—usually a village or two off the beaten track—where you can still stay in the simplest of accommodations.

Food on the trail used to consist uniformly of *dal bhat*, but it's now quite easy to avoid it altogether if you so choose. Common food options include oatmeal, pizza, fried rice, apple pie, and chocolate cake. Bear in mind that food in mountain villages tends to be prepared with reckless disregard for even rudimentary standards of hygiene. A full range of bottled drinks, from Coke to Carlsberg, is also generally available, though prices skyrocket the farther away you are from a roadhead.

Though trekking costs can add up, it's difficult to spend more than Rs500 a day, and you could probably make do at lower altitudes on Rs200 a day, as everything gets more expensive as you ascend. Lodge and restaurant rates are generally regulated by each town, which means that prices are effectively fixed. Make sure to over-budget for those knick-knacks you can pick up along the way.

LOCAL SERVICES

There are a few **banks** on the major routes (in Chame, Tatopani, and Jomsom in Annapurna, and in Namche in Everest), but they offer poor exchange rates, and they *do not* deal with credit cards. Change can be a problem, so take a considerable proportion of your cash in small denomination bills. Some of the ritzier lodges will change U.S. currency, though at abysmal rates. On the major routes, you'll be amazed at what you can buy in even the most impoverished-looking of villages. **Film** and **batteries**, for example, are widely available, and you may even be able to pick up a disposable camera. **Pharmacies**, however, are few and far between, and you should not expect to find medications en route.

 WARNING: There have been occasional reports of robberies and rapes on the trails. Trekkers (especially women) should think twice before going alone, particularly during low-season, when the trails are less crowded.

THE ANNAPURNA REGION अन्नपु

There are three main treks in the Annapurna region: the Annapurna Circuit, the Jomsom trek, and the Annapurna Sanctuary. They can be done separately or combined into a single mega-trek. In addition, it's possible to pare down any one of these treks if you've only got only a few days. If you've only got a few days, it's easy to get a good taste of trekking by connecting some of the routes out of Pokhara. A popular option is

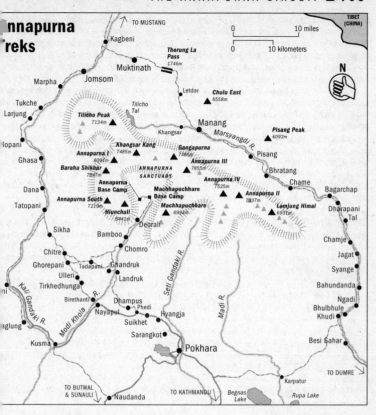

the 4- to 5-day loop from Pokhara to Ghorepani to Ghandruk and back. This supplies fine views (from **Poon Hill** above Ghorepani) and a chance to spend some time in some handsome Gurung villages. Alternatively, you can trek through Birethanti, Ghandruk, Landruk, then Dampus. Both of these routes involve cobbling together parts of the Jomsom (see p. 795) and Sanctuary (see p. 797) treks.

◤ THE ANNAPURNA CIRCUIT

This is Nepal's classic trek. The circuit's combination of remarkable cultural and ecological diversity, superb mountain scenery, and physical challenge (the Thorung-La Pass at 5416m) guarantees an exhilarating hike. Its 150 miles are deceptively long, and the tough terrain and the need to acclimatize will occupy you for about **three weeks.** Almost everybody walks it in the same direction, crossing the pass *from* Manang *to* Muktinath; the pass is easier to cross in this direction and there's accommodation higher up on the Manang side than on the Muktinath side. But there's an additional advantage to this uni-directionality: it makes the route seem much less crowded since there's no traffic coming towards you.

BESISAHAR TO TAL. The circuit starts at **Besisahar** (823m), located at the end of a road heading north from Dumre on the Kathmandu-Pokhara road. Dumre (5hr. from Kathmandu, 2hr. from Pokhara) is not a standard stop on the **bus** route between Kathmandu and Pokhara, but any driver can be induced to stop here. The trip from Dumre to Besisahar (about 40km) is a headache. Since the road is unfinished in places, the ongoing construction can delay traffic for hours, and heavy rain can render the road impassable. Irregular buses (3hr., Rs35) ply the route, but if you arrive in Dumre on one of the early morning "tourist" buses from Pokhara Lakeside, you may be able to round up Cir cuiters to rent a jeep (Rs2000, 10 people max.). Besisahar is a typical Nepali end-of-the road town with plenty of accommodations and electricity and phone service.

From Besisahar, the trail leads to **Khudi** and then heads north beside the Marsy angdi, criss-crossing the river on suspension bridges. **Bhubhule,** which boasts an ACAP office, and **Ngadi** are next. The first real climb of the trek up to **Bahundanda** (1311m), situated at a notch in the ridge high above the river, serves as a reminder that you are, in fact, hiking among the highest mountains on the planet. You'll still be high above the river after the steep descent beyond Bahundanda, and you follow a magnificent trail literally hewn out of the valley's rock walls. Of the many water falls along this trip, the most scenic is the one that comes crashing down the west wall of the valley close to **Shyange** (1136m), where a suspension bridge takes traffic across the river. Beyond Chamje (1380m), a steep climb up through the rubble of a huge landslide brings you to **Tal** (1664m), a paradise on the dry lake bed left when that landslide dammed the river. There's an ACAP office here.

TAL TO CHAME. There are three river crossings between Tal and **Dharapani** (1884m), where you'll find a police check-post, post office, and, in the Muktinath Hotel, a tele phone. Beyond Dharapani, the Marsyangdi and the route take a left turn to take you around to the north of the main Annapurna massif. Tibetanization of the villages and an increasing climatic aridity becomes apparent as the country gradually evades the mon soon. Next, you'll pass through **Bagarchap** (2103m), a town swept away in a 1995 land slide, and **Danaque** (2176m), the town of grand lodges that has sprung up in its stead. Beyond Danaque the trail splits into high and low routes. **Lattemarang** (2353m), the main settlement on the lower route, possesses few lodges, but does have its own hot spring. **Kotho** (2530m) straggles over a quarter mile or so, and the center of town, along with the police check post, is some way beyond the first cluster of lodges. **Chame** (2615m), no far from Kotho, is the seat of government for the Manang district. It's the closest thing to a metropolis since leaving Besisahar's dusty streets. Chame has everything: its own hospital, a bank, a post office, the district police headquarters, the last telephones before Manang, and stores where you can stock up on just about anything, including cold weather gear. Beyond Chame, altitude sickness is a serious issue.

CHAME TO MANANG. The route from Chame to **Pisang** (3133m), via the two small settlements of Bhratang and Dhukur Pokari, is dominated to the north by the "Great Wall of Pisang," a huge smooth slab of slate that rises 1200m above the valley floor—to the native Gurung, it is the gateway to the land of the dead. New Pisang, on the south side of the river, is a slew of enormous lodges; Old Pisang, up the hill on the north side, is a dense tangle of flat-roofed stone buildings clustered around a *gompa* that's surely not changed much in the past 500 years.

From Pisang, you have a choice of routes to Manang. The low walk is a short day's hike, while the high route takes a couple of hours longer. The **low route** from Lower Pisang is the main drag along the valley floor, past the airstrip at **Hongde** (flights to Pokhara: 3-5 per week 7:30am, US$50; check departure details at the RNAC office oppo site the airstrip) and on to **Braga** and **Manang.** Much more spectacular (and much harder work) is the **high route,** which begins with a short sharp ascent to old Pisang and then continues on for a relatively flat first few kilometers before heading steeply uphill to **Ghyaru** (3673m), where the views of the Annapurnas to the south are unbeatable. From Ghyaru, the road stays high, contouring along the valley wall to a promontory just above the ruined fort at Tiwol Danda ("Red Fort on the Hill") before arriving at pictur esque **Ngawal** (3650m).

From Ngawal, the route heads back down to join the low route in the main valley. Route-finding can be a little tricky here: pick up the trail dropping down the minor val ley just beyond Ngawal, but avoid the major left fork (which leads to the airstrip). The high route follows the north bank of the river until the main trail—the low route— crosses the river to join it at **Mungje** (3482m). **Braga** (3490m), a mere half-hour farther, i an extraordinary village crowned with the region's oldest *gompa*, well worth a visi (open daily 7-10am and 1-5pm).

MULE TRAIN SPOTTING A feature of both the Kali Gandaki and Marsyangdi Valley routes is the mule traffic: beasts of burden with distinctive carpet saddles and colorful ornamental plumes. The sound of mule bells, along with the whoops and yells of their drivers, is part of the trail experience. Mule transport has long been a fixture in these valleys, especially the Kali Gandaki: salt from Tibet came south and rice headed north. The closing of the Chinese border in the 1950s had a severe impact on the trade, but mules have remained the most efficient way to transport goods into the hills. The relationship between trekking and trading has been quite close: the settlements in these areas were once trading towns, so they adapted easily to the new form of traffic. In the Kali Gandaki, locals have long been professional innkeepers catering to traders. What you see here—even if it involves solar showers and chocolate cake—is merely the continuation of an ancient way of life.

Manang (3499m) is, in some sense, the main destination of the Circuit trek—it's very name brings to mind the desolate and remote stretches of mountain country north of the Annapurnas. Despite the recent trekking-associated accretions, Manang looks as medieval as many of the Tibetan-style villages in the area, but its inhabitants are, in fact, extraordinarily worldly. Because the region has long had special trading privileges, today's Manangba is likely to be just as much at home in Hong Kong as in Manang itself. This is your last chance to make sure that your gloves are warm enough for the Thorung-La. Manang's HRA clinic has a free talk on altitude sickness at 3pm during high season (Sept.-Dec.; Mar.-May; 30min.). The HRA shop sells iodine, vitamin C, diamox, and T-shirts. There's also an ACAP office and a post office in town. Because people often spend a day or two in and around Manang, there's plenty to do here, and the immediate vicinity is home to a number of *gompas*. **Khangsar** (3712m) is a popular destination for day-hikers heading out of Manang to acclimatize, an easy two-hour walk away. There are lodges here that can serve as a first step en route to the great high altitude lake, **Tilicho Tal** (5000m), first explored by Herzog's 1950 expedition; in addition, there's a seasonal lodge between Khansar and the lake.

MANANG TO MUKTINATH. Beyond Manang, thoughts turn to the **Thorung-La.** Although local traders will do the crossing from Manang to Muktinath in one day, the rest of the world prefers to take two or three days in their approach to the pass, all the while keeping an eye open for the first signs of altitude sickness. Stops can include **Tengi** (3642m), a mere 30 minutes beyond Manang, **Ghunsang** (3879m), and **Yak Kharka/Letdar** (4100m). There are plenty of opportunities for hikes up the flanks of **Chulu,** north of Ghunsang and Letdar.

The final pre-Thorung destination is the rather desolate little settlement of **Thorung Phedi** (4468m), literally "foot of Thorung." The throngs gather here prior to the big push over the pass. There are currently two routes from Letdar to Phedi. The lower one, which on paper looks to be the easier of the two, is inadvisable. It is actually very landslide- and avalanche-prone—people have been killed here. Set out from Thorung Phedi at first light. Severe conditions are common on the pass, and plenty of trekkers have departed to the Thorung-La with frostbite as a souvenir. Be properly prepared, and be willing to sit out bad weather in a hut rather than pressing on if conditions are not ideal. There are three stone huts above Phedi, including one on the pass itself. If everything goes well, crossing the pass can be a marvelous experience. It's a long, steep descent to **Muktinath** (3798m), and the only settlement along the way is the lodge at **Chatar Puk** (4115m), not far above it. Once you've made it to Muktinath, the only remaining challenge is following the route description for the Jomsom Trek *backwards*.

◪ JOMSOM TREK जोमसोम

This there-and-back route can be converted into a "there" *or* "back" by flying one way between Jomsom (2713m) and Pokhara. Flying directly to high altitudes entails spending a day or two acclimatizing upon arrival.

NEPAL

BIRETHANTI TO GHOREPANI. Trekkers typically start at **Birethanti** (1097m), which can be reached by road from Pokhara (2hr. away). Take a bus to **Naya Pul** from the Baglung Bus Park (every hr. 5:30am-6pm, Rs26), or hire a car from Lakeside (Rs600, 4 passengers max.); Birethanti is a 20-minute walk from the road. Situated at the confluence of the Bhurungdi and Modi Khola Rivers, Birethanti is a picturesque spot boasting plenty of lodges, a bank, a post office, its own art gallery, and an ACAP checkpost where you should show your trekking permit.

The trail follows the Bhurungdi Khola to **Hille** and another dense cluster of lodges at **Tirkedhunga** (1577m). Now the climbing starts in earnest: it's basically up all the way to Ghorepani. The first and steepest section brings you through intricately terraced hillsides to the straggling village of **Ulleri.** Beyond Ulleri, you move into the increasingly dense montane forest. If you're trekking in the pre-monsoon season (Mar.-May), this area will likely reward you with spectacular floral displays of the arboreal rhododendrons characteristic of the Himalaya.

Ghorepani (2819m), or the pass (**Deorali**) just beyond it, is something of a tourist must, and the surrounding area thus bears the ugly scars of deforestation. There's an ACAP office here and, in a phone in the Nice View Lodge. Ghorepani itself, a creation of the trekking business, looks like a bizarre hybrid of resort and shanty town. There are a number of side trails through the nearby forests, and Ghorepani commands a magnificent panorama of Dhaulagiri and the entire Annapurna massif—the view is best seen at dawn from **Poon Hill** (3194m), an hour behind Ghorepani. It is possible to connect to **Ghandruk** via a forest path from Ghorepani.

GHOREPANI TO DANA. From Ghorepani, the main trail heads gently downhill through Chitre, Phalate, Sikha, and Ghara to **Tatopani** (1189m), and the Kali Gandaki Valley. From Chitre, there are trails via Tadapani to Ghandruk and Chomro en route to the Annapurna Sanctuary. Long famed for its hot springs, Tatopani has hosted hippies and trekkers since the original routes were opened, and still serves its traditional role as a staging post on the trade routes up and down the Kali Gandaki. Tatopani has everything to meet your needs, including a shoe-repair shop, post office, bank, public phone, booksellers, fresh tangerines, and a police check post. The main hot springs are beside the river right in town; follow the footpath from the Trekkers Lodge. Check at the enormous landslide that obliterated part of the trail close to Tatopani in 1998.

While most people heading south through Tatopani choose to head up towards Ghorepani, an alternative low-level route following the river to **Beni** (823m) and **Baglung** offers the quickest passage between Pokhara and Tatopani. Beni marks the current endpoint of the road out of Pokhara and is within a day's walk from Tatopani. Because part of the road is unfinished, you may need to take two buses from Beni to Pokhara (5hr., Rs70). A private vehicle will set you back Rs2500—contact the Yeti Hotel in Beni for jeep service.

Heading north out of Tatopani, start your journey through the Himalayas with Dhaulagiri to your left and the Annapurnas to your right. Houses range from the scattered thatched homes of the Nepalese hinterland to the flat-roofed stone houses of the higher altitudes, which are often tightly clustered into dense, claustrophobic villages for protection against the brutal upland winds. Hindu shrines and iconography never disappear entirely, but the prayer flags, wheels, and stones become the dominant religious motifs as you head north. Make sure to pass all shrines with them *on your right*—to do the reverse is a sign of deep disrespect. Ecologically, too, the shift is abrupt: from the lichen- and moss-encrusted trees of the forests to the naked geology of the gaunt desert hills of Trans-Himalaya.

The first major settlement north of Tatopani, **Dana** (1402m) once thrived on salt trade taxation, as its grand, handsomely carved houses attest. From here to **Ghasa** (2040m), keep an eye open for langur monkeys. **Lete** and **Kalopani** (2530m), the next major settlements, have effectively fused into one and are linked by a beautifully laid flagstone trail. As you head north from Kalopani, you are immediately below the immense eastern buttresses of Dhaulagiri. Its magnificent ice fall dominates the view; a trail out of the valley will take you on a daytrip to the base of the ice fall. Navigation south of **Tukche** (2591m) can be a little tricky in the dry season because the route heads to the stony valley floor, crossing the river on wobbly temporary bridges. If you overshoot, do not attempt to ford the river, but head back to the bridges—the river is unexpectedly deep and the current vicious.

DANA TO MUKTINATH. The next town north, **Marpha** (2667m) is a favorite. Its neatly clustered stone homes and elegantly paved main street make it almost too perfect. Beyond Marpha lies the high altitude desert of Trans-Himalaya. This area (and everywhere north) is blasted every afternoon by brutal winds that can whip the grit of the river valley into a blinding, flesh-stinging frenzy, so it's best to be indoors by mid-day, especially if you're heading south *into* the wind.

Jomsom (2713m), the regional administration center, is a weird mix of traditional highland trading town, trekking mecca, and unpopular posting for bureaucrats. With its well-serviced airstrip, it's also the beginning or end of many treks. Don't be misled, however, by the Jomsom trek's name: Jomsom is not the goal of the trek; it's merely the biggest town on the route. If you're flying out of Jomsom, you can choose from RNAC, Cosmic, Yeti, and Lumbini airlines (all flights 7am, weather permitting; RNAC US$50, others US$55). Jomsom has all the facilities you'd expect of an administrative center. Many of the services, including the post office and the government telecommunication center, are located on the east bank of the river across the new suspension bridge. The bank offers better rates than the money changers. The District Administration Office is the only place in the whole region to extend trekking permits. Jomsom also has a police check post.

Beyond Jomsom, as you head up the broad valley past desolate brown hills, politically you may still be in Nepal, but geographically, climatically, and ethnically, you are essentially in Tibet. Keep going north (you need special and expensive permits to do this) and you will enter the ancient Buddhist kingdom of **Mustang**, a finger of Nepal that juts northwards into Tibetan territory. It was this area that Kampa guerillas from western Tibet made their own during the 60s as they waged war against the occupying Chinese. A regular trekking permit prevents you from venturing north of **Kagbeni** (2804m), a dusty cluster of Tibetan houses around an ancient *gompa* set in its own small patch of irrigated green.

The real goal of the Jomsom trek is **Muktinath** (3802m), situated at the head of a side valley to the east of the main Kali Gandaki Valley. It can be approached from Kagbeni, or more directly from Jomsom. Muktinath is a holy site for both Hindus and Buddhists, drawing pilgrims from all over Asia. While following the stony riverbed of the Kali Gandaki north of Jomsom, keep an eye open for fossil ammonites, those distinctively coiled long-dead mollusks which symbolize Vishnu. It's partly the abundance of these fossils, known locally as *shaligram*, that accounts for Muktinath's importance to Hindus.

The Muktinath Valley is one of the most beautiful places on the planet, and should not be regarded as merely an appendage of the Jomsom trek, but rather as the trek's primary destination. The brown, ochre, and gray desert hills, the snow-capped peaks to the south, the deep blue sky, the little patches of irrigated green in the valley floor, and the Tibetan villages scattered about the valley make Muktinath worth every drop of sweat and every aching joint. There is also an ACAP office and a police office here. If Muktinath is your final destination, budget a couple of days here. Wandering up the trail towards the Thorung-La makes for an excellent day hike. Then it's time to retrace your steps to Jomsom and, from there, to head back by air or on foot to Pokhara.

THE ANNAPURNA SANCTUARY

Pioneered by British climbing expeditions in the late 50s, the route into the Annapurna Sanctuary up the Modi Khola Valley offers the quickest and easiest route from Pokhara to the Himalayan giants. The sanctuary is a surprisingly benign strip of country right in the midst of the Annapurna massif.

BIRETHANTI TO DEORALI. The trek begins at **Birethanti** (also the starting point for the Jomsom trek, see above) and goes north up the west bank of the Modi Khola. This pleasant riverside amble turns serious at **Syauli Bazar** (1150m), when the trail turns uphill to **Kimche** (1760m) and, many stone steps later, **Ghandruk** (2012m). For many years, the source of this well-heeled Gurung village's wealth was the British army, which recruited heavily here for its famed Gorkha fighters. Now, however, the village is riding the crest of a major trekking wave, as its several grand concrete hotels attest. Ignore the signs for Jhinu hot springs—they're a *long* walk away. ACAP is headquartered here and there is a "Gurung Museum." Hotel Everest has a public phone.

From Ghandruk, the route heads up to **Kimrong Danda** (2255m) before descending steeply to a river crossing and ascending painfully to **Upper Chomro** (2182m). There are plenty of lodges, but try to resist the temptation to call it a day here, and go down to **Chomro proper** (2050m), another large, handsome Gurung village which boasts a beautifully engineered stone staircase. Chomro is your last chance to stock up on supplies for the sanctuary; you can both buy and rent gear here for non-negotiable rates. ◨ **The Chhomrong Guest House** wins the prize for "Best Lodge in the Annapurnas." It's friendly, efficient, and comfortable, and the chocolate cake is unforgettable. Route-finding through Chomro can be tricky. Keep left, heading down to the river crossing and up towards **Sinuwa** (2324m), past the Sherpa Guest House. It is in Sinuwa, at the Hilltop Lodge, that the route returns to the river, and beside the river it will stay all the way into the sanctuary.

The first settlement after Sinuwa marked on the map, Kuldhighar, no longer exists. **Bamboo** (2347m), a mere cluster of lodges, is the first sign of civilization in the forest, and **Dovan** (2606m) is the next. Ten minutes beyond Dovan, a pool 50m upstream from a creek crossing provides the best rinse you're likely to have for several days—lodges up the higher reaches of the Modi Khola Valley are not as amenity-rich as those lower down. Himalaya Hotel (2873m) is an hour or so beyond Dovan. The last stop-off in the valley proper is at **Deorali** (3231m), just beyond **Hinko** (3139m), a huge over-hanging boulder which has provided shelter for many a weather-beset party. Note that rate of altitude gain should now be a serious consideration, especially if you've come straight up from Pokhara.

DEORALI TO ANNAPURNA BASE CAMP. The section between Deorali and **Machhapuchhare Base Camp** (3703m), or **MBC**, on the lip of the sanctuary, can be dangerous. It basically serves as a repository for avalanches coming off the upper slopes of Hiunchuli to the west; this means that it's not a good place to be after heavy snowfall. At times, avalanche danger will close down the trail at this point. Take note of the conditions and seek local advice—trekkers have died in avalanches here. The views gradually spool out as you emerge from the narrow gorge of the Modi Khola and enter the sanctuary. The first cluster of lodges is at what is inaccurately called Machhapuchhare Base Camp—the mountain is sacred and is off-limits. The best views are a couple of hours farther into the sanctuary at the **Annapurna Base Camp** (4130m), or **ABC**. If you've come up from Pokhara and altitude sickness is a potential problem, consider spending two nights at MBC and doing an early start there-and-back trip to ABC. Originally established by Chris Bonington's Annapurna South Face Expedition of 1970, ABC now consists of several lodges crouched, rather forlornly, in a very desolate, windblown spot (if you're trekking Jan.-Feb. check to see if the lodges are open). The view from ABC includes a whole series of Himalayan walls; clockwise from the south are: Hiunchuli, Annapurna South, Baraha Shikhar (Fang), Annapurna I, Singu Chuli (Fluted Peak), Tharpu Chuli (Tent Peak), Annapurna III, and Machhapuchhare.

ABC TO DHAMPUS. The return trip involves straight back-tracking to Chomro, from where it's possible to vary the route back to Pokhara. From Upper Chomro, drop down steeply **Jhinu Danda** (1725m), where there are hot springs to soothe the stresses of trekking. Continue to cross the Modi Khola on the now-quite-old bridge at **New Bridge** (1653m), which also boasts a small cluster of lodges. Then, it's a matter of following the river until the ascent to the big bustling village of **Landruk** (1628m). The contours south from Landruk among the terraces, high above the river, with the monstrous south face of Annapurna South as a backdrop. **Tolka** (1725m) is strung out over 2km. A final reminder of the rigors of uphill hiking brings you to **Bhichok Deorali** (2097m). It's then a pleasant walk along the ridge to **Potana** (1969m). If you're heading up towards Landruk from Potana, keep right at both the forks that come up shortly after Potana. If you're heading down from Potana, keep left at the fork ten minutes after Potana. **Dhampus** (1695m) is the final settlement on the route. A big village stretching out along a ridge for a couple of kilometers, Dhampus used to have something of a reputation among trekkers as a den of thieves, but that dubious claim to fame seems to have been based on only a handful of incidents that occurred 20 years ago. The final descent from Dhampus to **Dhampus Phedi** (1143m) on the Pokhara-Baglung Rd. is long, steep, hot, and dusty. Buses into Pokhara's Baglung bus park run at least every hour (6am-6pm, Rs15). In season, there will also probably be something of a taxi rank at Dhampus Phedi (to Lakeside Rs250, 4-passenger max.).

THE LANGTANG REGION लाङटान

Langtang National Park is sandwiched between the Tibetan border and the Helambu region due north of Kathmandu. "Langtang" is actually trekking shorthand for three distinct regions, **Langtang** itself, **Gosainkund,** and **Helambu.** It's possible to limit your trek to any one of these three, but the most popular routes in the area traverse them all. Because of their proximity to Kathmandu and their relatively low altitude, these areas have long been popular with trekkers. Lacking the glamor of Annapurna or Everest, the region is also considerably less crowded.

▲ THE LANGTANG TREK

It takes five or six days to walk up the Langtang valley to Kyangjin Gompa, depending on how quickly you acclimatize. Then you can either head back down in as few as two days, strike out on other routes, or just get high for a few days on the peaks and glaciers around Kyangjin Gompa.

DHUNCHE TO PAIRO. Dhunche (1966m) is the traditional starting point for treks in the Langtang region. **Buses** depart Kathmandu's New Bus Park daily (7 and 7:45am, 9hr., Rs100); tickets go on sale 8am the day before. If you're heading back to Kathmandu from Dhunche, you can purchase bus tickets a day in advance from the counter in the Thakali Hotel. Dhunche is a major regional administrative center and has all the facilities you'd expect. At the headquarters of the Langtang National Park, you can pay your park entry fee (Rs650) if you didn't already when getting a trekking permit in Kathmandu. The trail starts about 6km farther along the road at **Thulo Bharku** (1844m)—it's a little tricky to find the path, so it's best to ask for the route to Brabal or Syabru. It's a pleasant walk through forest to **Brabal** (2304m), where the **Shedup Cheling Gompa** is definitely worth checking out. You'll soon have your first views up the Langtang Valley, eccentric (by Himalayan standards) for running east-west instead of north-south. **Syabru** (2240m) is a large, handsome village spread along a ridge with superb mountain views. The local people are an interesting hybrid of lowland and highland stock who speak Tamang but sing in Sherpa. The route descends towards the Langtang Khola and heads into the Langtang Valley. This is wet country, highly prone to landslides, and the trail tends to make many brief detours to avoid the worst of the recent slides. In **Pairo** (1676m), literally meaning "Landslide," the alternative trail from Syabrubensi joins the up-valley route from Syabru.

BAMBU TO KYANGJIN GOMPA. The first settlement in the Langtang gorge is the cluster of lodges in the forest at **Bambu** (1975m). Keep an eye open for wildlife as you head on up the valley to **Rimche** (2390m) and farther on to **Lama Hotel** (2481m), named for the original lodge built there. Beyond **Gumnachowk** (2774m) and **Ghora Tabela** (3005m), altitude sickness becomes an issue; you should watch for symptoms and adjust your rate of ascent accordingly. Your National Park permit will be checked at the army base in Ghora Tabela. As the route continues to head east and up, the forests thin out and the valley is transformed from the sharp "V" of river-erosion to the flat-bottomed "U" of an upland glacial valley.

Beyond the *gompa* at **Kangtansa** lies the region's oldest settlement, the village of **Langtang** (3420m), a town that still retains much of its Tibetan charm despite its invasion by trekking entrepreneurs. Even over the relatively short distance up the Langtang valley, there is a wholesale architectural shift from Nepali (Hindu) to Tibetan Buddhist style. **Kyangjin Gompa** (3900m), situated high among the glacial moraines, is essentially the end of the road. These days it's a major agglomeration of lodges. Spend a couple of days here exploring the high country and enjoying the produce of the local yak cheese factory. There are plenty of short hikes in the area, many of them—like the trip up the prayer-flag-festooned summit of the small hill behind the *gompa*—yielding unforgettable views of peaks including Dorje Lapka (6966m), Gangchenpo (6388m), and Langtang Lirung (7246m). It should be possible to hire guides (and/or tents and other equipment) in Kyangjin Gompa.

THE RETURN. There are plenty of ways to head back from Kyangjin Gompa. You can retrace your steps to Dhunche or turn off at Syabru and connect up to **Gosainkund** (see p. 801). You can also follow a trail to **Syabrubensi** (1417m), an hour beyond Dhunche on the road, which is served by a **bus** from Kathmandu (7am, 10hr., Rs135). Shortly after Pairo, head down, take a right fork in the trail, and follow the river down to **Domin** (1640m) and, two hours later, to Syabrubensi, at the confluence of the Langtang Khola and the Bhote Kosi. The **Ganga-La** pass (5122m), typically open May to November, connects the area at the head of the Langtang valley with Helambu and allows a direct return to the Kathmandu Valley via Helambu. This challenging pass requires mountaineering skills to cross; it should not be attempted without an experienced guide.

◪ THE HELAMBU TREK ह्माम्बु

Helambu is the area immediately behind Siva Puri, the forested hill that forms the northern rampart of the Kathmandu Valley. It is a great spot to experience life on the trail and enjoy the fine mountain views without having to endure an interminable bus journey. Nice treks can be made in under a week; you can also connect with Gosainkund and go on to Langtang.

SUNDARIJAL TO MANGEGOTH. Treks start at **Sundarijal** (1390m), on the northern edge of the Kathmandu Valley. **Buses** leave from Ratna Park (every hr. 6am-6:30pm, 1½hr., Rs12). Alternatively, take one of the frequent buses from Boudha. **Taxis** from the center of Kathmandu shouldn't cost more than Rs550. It's possible to avoid much of the initial ascent by taking a **jeep** from Sundarijal to Pati Bhanjyang, but the walk out of the valley is worth it for the fantastic views.

The first part of the trek is hard work. Initially up stone steps beside an enormous water pipe, the trail leads up and over the eastern shoulder of Siva Puri via **Mulkhark** (1896m) to **Burlang Bhanjyang** (2438m), where there are views north to the main range. Then it's down, via **Chisapani** (2194m), to **Pati Bhanjyang** (1768m), a major village with a police checkpost.

The route continues north along terraced ridges and ascends to **Chipling** (2165m) before descending to **Gulphu Bhanjyang** (2141m). The ups and downs continue to **Khutumsang** (2469m), where you'll have to either show or buy a Langtang National Park permit. The route then passes out of agricultural areas into sparsely inhabited country. Tall pines give way to rhododendron forest, and wildlife, most notably the troops of black-faced, silver-furred langur monkeys, becomes more prevalent as you move beyond the agricultural lowlands. **Mangegoth** (3285m), four hours farther on, is the first cluster of lodges beyond Khutumsang.

THAREPATI TO MALEMCHI PUL BAZAAR. Two hours more along the forested ridge is **Tharepati** (3633m), the highest point on the Helambu routes, with plenty of accommodations and great early-morning views. Tharepati is a trail junction—one route heads northwest to Gosainkund and ultimately to Langtang (see below), while the Helambu trail continues due east and down through the forest to **Malemchiga** (2560m), a burgeoning highland metropolis fully equipped with telephone facilities and hydroelectricity.

Tarke Ghyang (2560m), an attractive cluster of homes, seems close to Malemchigaon, but it's a ways on foot. The trip between the two villages involves descending

iver crossing at 1890m. Some of the navigation—especially as you sweat up
vards Tarke Ghyang—is tricky; a guide (even an obliging local kid) will be very
pful. From Tarke Ghyang, it's possible to connect, via Thimbu, Talamarang, and
bre, back to Pati Bhanjyang; from there, you can retrace your outward steps to
ndarijal. However, there have been some reports of crime on the trail here and the
ute is little used. **Do not attempt this if you are traveling alone.** The standard route
es on to Malemchi Pul Bazaar.

The route heads from Tarke Ghyang to **Gangal** (2615m) before reaching **Sherman-
ng** (2603m), situated at a notch in the ridge three to four hours from Tarke Ghyang.
llow the ridge to **Kakani** (1969m), from where it's again possible to join the direct
ute back to Pati Bhanjyang. Navigation becomes a little tricky here, and a guide
y be helpful as you continue down the ridge to Dubhachaur (1603m). Your goal,
lemchi Pul Bazaar (828m), is now below you. Descend steeply to the town that
rks the confluence of the Malemchi and Indrawati Khola Rivers and the roadhead.
oss the Malemchi Khola on the suspension bridge, and the walking is done. **Buses
m Malemchi Pul Bazaar (last bus 3pm) go directly to Kathmandu or Banepa, which
easy connections to Kathmandu.

THE GOSAINKUND TREK गोशाईकुण्ड

sainkund ("Priest Lake") has given its name to the whole area between Helambu and
ngtang. There's a series of high-altitude lakes, the most sacred being Gosainkund
elf, where Shiva is supposed to have slaked his thirst during one of his more trying
ercations with his divine colleagues. A major pilgrimage destination, the area draws
wds as large as 50,000 annually for **Janai Purnima,** during the July-August full moon.
hough it's possible to do a week-long there-and-back trek starting in Dhunche, most
kkers incorporate Gosainkund as the link between Langtang and Helambu.

If you're approaching Gosainkund from Helambu, you should follow the Helambu
ute to **Tharepati** (3633m) and head northwest on the trail through dense rhododen-
on forest to the small clump of lodges at **Gopte** (3408m). **Phedi** (3780m) is the last set-
ment before the ascent to the **Laurebina Pass** (4609m). The pass and the route up to it
en't particularly difficult, but in snowy conditions, it's easy to get lost. Bear in mind
at altitude sickness can be a serious factor up here, too. If you're planning to spend
e night in a lodge by the lakes, then you should ensure that you are already well accli-
atized. The first of the holy lakes is not far below the pass, and there is accommoda-
n at **Gosainkunda Lake** (4381m).

From the lakes, you can head down to Dhunche or the Langtang Valley. Follow the
ge down to **Laurebinayak** (3901m) and on to **Cholang Pati** (3669m), where there is a
nction. Take a right to head down to Syabru and the route up the Langtang valley, or
ep straight on towards Sing Gompa and Dhunche. Views from here include the
napurnas to the west and Langtang Himal to the east. The major settlement at **Sing
mpa** (3304m) also has a side trail down to Syabru. From here, it's downhill all the way
Dhunche (1966m).

LANGTANG/GOSAINKUND/HELAMBU COMBINATIONS

e Helambu-Gosainkund-Langtang route supplies several kinds of topographic fla-
rs: the intensively farmed Nepalese hinterland of Helambu, the forested gorges of
ngtang, and the bare, high-altitude landscape of the upper Langtang Valley. You will
so witness the religious activities along an important pilgrimage route to Gosainkund
d the rapid cultural transition from Nepal to Tibet in Langtang. The route is best done
the direction of Helambu to Langtang (rather than the reverse), because the higher
lambu side makes it more likely that you'll be altitude-acclimatized prior to crossing
e Laurebina Pass. The typical route would be as follows: Kathmandu—Sundarijal—
arepati—Phedi—Laurebina Pass—Gosainkunda—Cholang Pati—Syabru—Kyangjin
mpa; the return to Kathmandu is made via either Dhunche or Syabrubensi. The
ole trip should take two to three weeks. Those lacking the time to go up the Lang-
ng Valley can head to Dhunche via Sing Gompa from Cholang Pati.

NEPAL

THE EVEREST REGION

The Everest trek isn't only about paying homage to the highest point on the planet; the trek also exposes you to one of the most engaging and enterprising of Nepal's ethnic groups, the Sherpas. Originally Tibetan, the Sherpas migrated to the Solu Khumbu region south of Everest within the past several centuries, and they retain many Tibetan characteristics in their language, religion, and dress. The Sherpa capital, Namche Bazaar, long famous from accounts of expeditions to the region, is one of the most vibrant of all of Nepal's towns

A trip to Everest used to involve setting out on foot from Kathmandu, several hundred kilometers to the west. The route crossed the grain of the land established by rivers draining the Himalayas to the north, making for a sequence of arduous ascents and descents of up to 2000m at a time. Now, however, a road extends approximately half of the way, to Jiri, which is connected by bus to the capital. From Jiri, it still takes a good 10days to walk to Namche Bazaar, which itself is several days shy of Everest. Thus, a trip to Everest by bus and on foot is a month-long undertaking. Most people shorten things by flying at least one way. Lukla, a two-day walk south of Namche, has an airstrip. However, because the landing strip is short, conditions have to be pretty good for flights to get in and out. If you prefer to hike one way, rather than flying both in and out of Lukla, the logical choice is to walk in: the going will be easier, and you'll arrive in Namche already acclimatized. Many people do the reverse, walking from Namche to Jiri, because waiting for a flight out—particularly if you've got fixed international connections to make—can be extremely frustrating.

⚠ THE EVEREST TREK

LUKLA TO NAMCHE BAZAAR. Flights to **Lukla** (2860m) can be booked directly through the airlines or through a travel agency in Kathmandu. Lumbini and RNAC both have two flights a day in season (early morning departures, 45min., US$83). If you're flying back from Lukla, you should reconfirm your flight with the appropriate airline office as soon as you get into town. Lukla has developed into a major trekking center, and many people choose to spend the night. For those flying in altitude sickness can be a real problem, and taking an easy first few days is recommended, with limited altitude gain each day.

Choplung (2692m) is the first village beyond Lukla, and it is here that the traffic from Lukla joins the main trail from Jiri. Next is **Phakding** (2652m), down beside the river, a village grown fat on years of the trekking trade. The route dips occasionally into the rhododendron forest of the Dudh Kosi Valley as it criss-crosses the river between frequent villages. After Benkar (2905m) comes **Mondzo** (2835m), where you enter the **Sagarmatha** (the Nepali name for Everest) National Park for an Rs650 entry fee (if you didn't pay it when getting your trekking permit). Just beyond **Jorsale** (2774m), the trail crosses the river on a suspension bridge over a mini-gorge, and the first serious climb of the trek begins—the hike to **Namche Bazaar** (3446m). The trail zig-zags up through the pine forest, yielding occasional fine views of the Dudh Kosi valley.

The capital of the Sherpas, Namche is a monument to Sherpa enterprise and business flair. These days, it is dominated by the trekking and climbing industries, but it nevertheless retains some of its traditional character, especially in the big Saturday market. Tucked into a small bowl in the hills, Namche looks out on the vast, forbidding Kwangde Massif. Make sure that you stroll up the hills to the back of town to admire the views.

Namche has everything an administrative center should, including telephones and electricity. There's a bank, post office, dentist, police checkpost, and even a national park museum. There's a good hospital (tel. 038 21113) in the nearby village of Kunde (3841m), established by Sir Edmund Hillary's Himalayan Trust.

If you've flown into Lukla, it's best to spend at least a couple of nights in Namche for acclimatization purposes. There are plenty of interesting daytrips to keep you busy while your body adjusts. A sharp climb up the hills behind Namche brings you to the two large villages of **Kunde** and **Khumjung** (3780m), from where most Sherpa guides are

Everest Treks

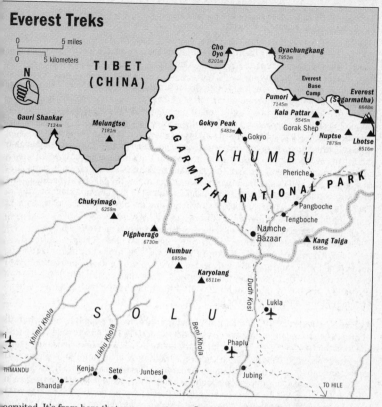

0 ___ 5 miles
0 ___ 5 kilometers

N

TIBET (CHINA)

Cho Oyo
8201m

Gyachungkang
7952m

Everest Base Camp

Pumori
7145m

Everest (Sagarmatha)
8848m

Gauri Shankar
7134m

Melungtse
7181m

Gokyo Peak
5483m

Kala Pattar
5545m

Gokyo

Gorak Shep

Nuptse
7879m

Lhotse
8516m

S A G A R M A T H A

K H U M B U

Pheriche

N A T I O N A L   P A R K

Chukyimago
6259m

Pangboche

Tengboche

Pigpherago
6730m

Numbur
6959m

Namche Bazaar

Kang Taiga
6685m

Karyolang
6511m

S   O   L   U

Dudh Kosi

Lukla

Khimti Khola

Likhu Khola

Beni Khola

Phaplu

KATHMANDU

Kenja

Sete

Junbesi

Jubing

TO HILE

Bhandar

recruited. It's from here that you can get your first views up the valley towards Everest, nearly obscured by the great wall of Lhotse. Another excellent daytrip from Namche is to the large village of **Thami** (3780m), birthplace of Tenzing Norgay, where a fine old monastery has been carved out of the cliff face.

NAMCHE TO EVEREST BASE CAMP. You are now entering some serious high country, and plenty of trekkers have died up here because they ignored the symptoms of **Acute Mountain Sickness** (see p. 40). Watch your rate of ascent carefully, and stop going up if any member of your party starts experiencing symptoms.

You can pick up the main route through the valley from Kunde and Khumjung, or from Namche; the two trails converge at **Sangnasa** (3597m) from where the route descends to **Pungo Tenga** (3247m) on the Dudh Kosi. After crossing the river, it's a steep ascent through the forest to the fabled monastery of **Tengboche** (3867m). The monastery was destroyed by fire in 1989, and the current one is a bigger and better incarnation.

Continue down through forest draped in sheets of lichen, past the nunnery at Deboche (3757m), across the river, and on to **Pangboche** (3901m), the highest permanent settlement in the Khumbu and home to the region's oldest *gompa*, about 300 years old. The trail heads on towards the great Lhotse wall, with Ama Dablam on the right, until it reaches **Pheriche** (4252m). This is high, glacial country—the valleys have a broad, open, and scraped by glaciers. The most notable peak is Taboche, opposite Pheriche. (Everest hides behind the twin bulks of Nupse and Lhotse.) The town is the last hint of civilization before Everest. Its **trekkers' aid post,** run by the Himalayan Rescue Association, provides a free talk on AMS (in season daily 3pm). Pheriche is good for a two-night stop-off, with acclimatizing daytrips up the valley towards Everest or east to Dingboche on the Imja Khola.

A couple of kilometers beyond Pheriche brings you to the terminal moraine of the Khumbu Glacier. Halfway up, nestled among the boulders, are the lodges at **Dughla** (4593m). The rest of the route to the final stop at Gorak Shep follows the glacier, typically picking its way among the rocks of the lateral moraine on the western side. As you crest the terminal moraine, there's a small cemetery with monuments to those who have died in the mountains ahead.

You have arrived in one of the world's greatest mountain amphitheaters. Nupse is to the right and the rounded lump of Pumori is in front of you. **Lobuche** (4930m) offers a few simple lodges, and then it's the end of the road at **Gorak Shep** (5184m). There are simple lodges here, but many people prefer to sleep at the slightly lower altitude of Lobuche, visiting Gorak Shep and all that lies beyond on a dayhike.

From Gorak Shep, there are just two stops to go. **Kala Pattar** (5623m), the hill behind the lodges at Gorak Shep, offers superb views of the area, particularly of Everest's southwest face. It was from here that the Tilman/Shipton reconnaissance party first viewed Everest and determined that the South Col route (the one used by Hillary and Tenzing) would be a good bet. The **Khumbu Ice Fall**—the glacier equivalent of Niagara Falls—is a nearly vertical jumble of slowly moving ice blocks the size of apartment buildings. It's possible to find routes through it, but they change every time a major ice block moves. Many people have died here, crushed instantly under tons of ice.

The other destination from Gorak Shep is **Everest Base Camp.** Getting there involves hiking across the Khumbu Glacier itself and should therefore be approached with caution, especially as the route is often unclear. The best indicator of the route may be the trail of yak droppings. Base camp is situated at the head of the valley, just below the forbidding wall of the Khumbu Ice Fall, and there are no accommodations for trekkers here.

EVEREST BASE CAMP. Instead of returning directly to Namche, many people choose to make a detour past the lakes at Gokyo (4791m), in the next valley over from the Khumbu Glacier. There are several routes between the two valleys, including a high glaciated pass, the **Cho-La** (5420m), which should only be attempted by those with guides and mountaineering experience. This route takes between four and six days.

The route starts from Upper Pangboche and follows a trail high above the river on its western bank; much of the time you overlook Tengboche on the other side of the river. At the large village of **Phortse** (3700m), the route takes a right and heads northwest up the Ngozumpa Valley. The trail again takes the high road as you travels past the lodges at **Konar** (4092m) and **Thare** (4343m) to **Na** (4400m), wedged below the snout of the Ngozumpa Glacier. Here the route crosses the valley beneath the tongue of the glacier and picks up the main Namche-Gokyo route up the western side of the valley. It's not far from the terminal moraine to the lakes, which are tucked in beside the lateral moraine of the glacier. The sparkling blue lakes perfectly offset the immense gray crags that come crashing down behind them. The lodges are beside the third lake. The enormous Ngozumpa glacier drains **Cho Oyu** (8153m) to the north. The best views are from the top of **Gokyo Ri** (5483m), from where Everest is but one of an ocean of peaks.

To return to Namche from Gokyo, follow the route along the western side of the valley. This is a major trail and there are several settlements with lodges: Pangka (4548m) Maccherma (4465m), Dole (4084m), and Phortse Tenga (3643m). From here, it's a uphill slog to **Mong La** (3962m), down again to join the main Namche-Tengboche trail close to **Sangnasa** (3597m), and on to Namche.

JIRI TO LUKLA. Although the heavy-duty mountain action of the Everest trek lies north of Namche, the hike in from Jiri provides many other rewards. The trek takes you through a great swath of central eastern Nepal and introduces you to a range of Nepal ethnic groups and lifestyles.

Jiri (1905m) is very much a typical Nepali roadhead town. **Buses** depart Kathmandu Ratna Park (5:30, 6:30, 8, and 9:30am, 11hr., Rs145; express 7am, 8hr, Rs170); buy you ticket a day in advance. They all head back from Jiri early in the morning (first depar ture 5am). From Jiri, the route climbs to a minor pass (2400m) before descending to river crossing and the village of **Shivalaya** (1800m), site of a police checkpost. The rou goes up again to **Sangabanda** (2240m), and on to a pass (2713m) that leads into a han some open valley. The largest town, **Bhandar** (2194m), has several lodge offerings. The valley closes suddenly to a narrow gorge as you descend to the Likhu Khola, which you follow upstream on its east bank to **Kenja** (1634m). The first major ascent of the trek is up to the **Lamjura Pass** (3530m) via **Sete** (2575m). In keeping with the Everest trek's roller-coaster reputation, it's now time for a long descent, via Tagdobuk (2860m), to **Junbesi** (2675m), a wealthy Sherpa town with many attractive houses. A couple of hours north of Junbesi—and definitely worth a side trip—is the **Thubten Chholing Gompa**, a large and active Tibetan Buddhist monastery.

Ascend out of Junbesi through a pretty pine forest to the next ridge crest and the attractive town of **Sallung** (2953m), where you will catch your first (and rather distant) glimpse of Everest. Descend to cross the Ringmo Khola and up to **Ringmo** (2805m), where a trail leads south to **Phaplu**, which has a scheduled air service. The next pass is the **Tragshindo-La** (3071m), and then it's down, down, through the forest and then the terraces, to the Dudh Kosi, the river that drains the Everest region. En route is the big Sherpa town of **Manidingma** (2194m). Having reached the Dudh Kosi valley, the route turns to head north towards Namche; the arduous east-west phase is over.

Jubing (1676m) is the first settlement on the route in the valley, followed by **Karikhola** (2004m), another village whose grand homes attest to Sherpa economic prosperity. The route up the Dudh Khola valley is very steep. The trail to **Bupsa** (2347m) and **Poiyan** (2796m) heads into the forest before descending to **Surkhe** (2293m), a cluster of hospitable lodges. It's only when you reach **Chaumrikharka** (2713m), another handsome village boasting a plethora of *mani* walls, that the country starts to flatten out a bit. From here, there's no major climb until the haul up to Namche. **Choplung** (2674m), close to Chaumrikharka, is where you'll meet the fresh-off-the-plane Lukla traffic.

NEPAL

APPENDIX

HOLIDAYS AND FESTIVALS

Hindu, Sikh, Buddhist, and Jain festivals correspond to the Indian lunar calendar, so the dates vary from year to year with respect to the Gregorian calendar. The Muslim lunar calendar is made up of a year of 12 lunar cycles, meaning that festivals rotate throughout the solar year; the dates given are approximate. The secular holidays in India are dated according to the Gregorian calendar, and in Nepal they follow the official Vikram Sambat calendar. The dates given here are for 2000.

DATE	HOLIDAYS AND FESTIVALS
January 1	**New Year's Day** of the Gregorian calendar, celebrated in both India and Nepal.
January 9	**Eid-ul-Fitr,** a three-day feast celebrating the Prophet's recording of the word of God in the Holy Qur'an; marks the end of **Ramadan.**
January 11	**Prithvi Narayan Shah's Birthday,** the festival honors the king who united Nepal.
January 14-16	**Pongal** is a three-day festival celebrating the end of the harvest in Tamil Nadu.
January 26	**Republic Day,** one of India's four national public holidays; highlights include a military parade in New Delhi.
February	**Lhosar,** the Tibetan New Year, is a three-day festival celebrated by thousands of Tibetans and Sherpas who flock to Boudhanath Stupa in Nepal and to Dharamsala.
February 1	**Vasant Panchami** honors Saraswati, the Hindu goddess of learning.
March 4	**Maha Shivaratri,** an all-day, all-night Hindu festival dedicated to Shiva, whose creation dance took place on this day.
March 17	**Eid-ul-Zuha,** when Muslims commemorate Abraham's intended sacrifice of his son Isaac, celebrated with the slaughtering of lamb for feasts.
March 20	**Holi,** a rowdy Hindu festival during which revelers from both India and Nepal throw colored water and powder at each other.
April	**New Year's Day** of the Vikram Sambat Year 2056, celebrated in Nepal.
April 12	**Ramanavami** celebrates Rama's birth, with readings of the *Ramayana* in Hindu temples all over India and Nepal.
April 14	**Vaisaki,** the Sikh festival celebrating the day Guru Gobind Singh founded the Khalsa; features readings of the Guru Granth Sahib, besides major feasting.
April 16	**Mahavira Jayanti,** Jainism's major festival that celebrates the birthday of its founder.
April 16	**Muharram** commemorates the martyrdom of the Prophet Muhammad's grandson; especially important for Lucknow Muslims.
April/May	**Machhendranath Rath Yatra,** a popular festival, during which a massive chariot holding Lokesvar, a patron deity of Kathmandu, is pulled through the streets of Nepal by hundreds of worshippers.
May 18	**Buddha Jayanti** honors the Buddha's birthday and his subsequent attainment of *nirvana.*
May	**Meenakshi Kalyanam** celebrates the goddess Meenakshi in Madurai.
July 2	**Rath Yatra,** commemorates the journey Krishna made to Mathura; Hindus throng the Jagannath Temple in Puri and cities in the South.
June 26	**Milad-un-Nabi (Eid-ul-Mulad),** the Prophet Muhammad's birthday.
August 15	**Independence Day,** India's biggest national holiday.
August 15	**Raksha Bandhan** celebrates the Hindu sea god Varuna; the holiday is associated with brother and sisters.
August 22	**Zoroastrian New Year's Day,** celebrated by Parsis in India.
September 1	**Ganesh Chaturthi** is when Hindus venerate the god of obstacles with spectacular processions, especially in Bombay and Rajasthan.
September/October	**Indra Jatra,** when Kathmandu celebrates the capture of the King of Gods, Indra, in the Kathmandu Valley; processions and the annual blessing of the King of Nepal by the Living Goddess Kumari.

DATE	HOLIDAYS AND FESTIVALS
October 7	**Dussehra,** a 10-day festival, celebrates the vanquishing of demons and honors Durga, the demon-slaying goddess. Known as **Dasain** in Nepal and **Durga Puja** in West Bengal.
October 26	**Diwali** (Deepavali), a five-day festival of lights celebrating Rama and Sita's home-coming as per the *Ramayana*.
October/November	**Tihar,** the Festival of Lights, an important five-day holiday in Nepal.
November	**Pushkar Camel Fair,** one of India's most famous camel fairs held at the sacred lake at Pushkar, Rajasthan.
November 11	**Guru Nanak Jayanti,** the founder of Sikhism's birthday.
December 11	**Ramadan,** a 28-day period when Muslims fast, a celebration ending with **Eid-ul-Fitr.**
December 25	**Guru Gobind Singh's Birthday,** celebrated by Sikhs everywhere, particularly important in the Punjab.
December 28	**King's Birthday,** a Nepalese public holiday declared by the monarch.

GLOSSARY

aarti: Hindu floating lights ceremony
adivasi: aboriginal, tribal people of India
Agni: Hindu god of fire, messenger of the gods
ahimsa: non-violence
AIADMK: All-India Anna Dravida Munnetra Kazhagam, regional party in Tamil Nadu
AIR: All-India Radio
air-cooling: low-budget air-conditioning—a fan blows air over the surface of water
Allah: literally, "the God," to Muslims
alu: potato
am: mango
AMS: Acute Mountain Sickness
appam: South Indian rice pancake
arrak: drink made from fermented barley
artha: material wealth, one of the four goals of Hindu life
ashram: hermitage for Hindu sages and their students
ASI: Archaeological Survey of India
atman: Hindu concept of individual soul, the breath of Brahman
attar: alcohol-free perfume
auto-rickshaw: three-wheeled, semi-enclosed vehicle with the engine of a scooter
Avalokitesvara: the popular *bodhisattva* of compassion
avatar: descent of a Hindu god (usually Vishnu) to earth; an incarnation
ayurveda: ancient Indian system of medicine
azan: Muslim call to prayer, usually given from a minaret
badam: almond
bahal: Newari houses or monasteries forming a quadrangle with a central courtyard
baingan: eggplant
baksheesh: tip, donation, bribe, or all of these at once
bagh: garden
ban: forest
bandh: general strike; often involves shop closings and transportation difficulties
barfi: milk- and sugar-based Indian sweet
basti: Jain temple
bazaar: market area of a town
betel: red nut with mild narcotic properties when chewed; key ingredient in *paan.*

Bhagavad Gita: Hindu philosophical scripture sung to the hero Arjuna by the god Krishna
bhajan: Hindu devotional song
bhaji: vegetables dipped in batter and fried
bhakti: personal, emotional devotion to a Hindu deity
bhang: dried leaves and shoots of the male cannabis plant
bhangra: Punjabi folk music
Bharat: the Sanskrit word for India
bhat: cooked rice
bhavan: office or building
bhindi: okra (lady's fingers)
bidi: small cigarette made from a rolled-up tobacco leaf
bindi: forehead mark, worn mostly by Hindu women; symbolizes the third, all-seeing eye
biryani: rice cooked with spices and vegetables or meat
BJP: Bharatiya Janata Party (Indian People's Party); the major Hindu nationalist party, symbolized by a lotus
bodhisattva: would-be Buddha who postpones his own enlightenment to help others
Bön: pre-Buddhist, animist religion of Tibet
Brahma: The Creator in the Hindu trinity, no longer commonly worshipped
Brahman: the universal soul or spirit, embodied by Brahma
brahmin: member of the hereditary priesthood; highest of the four Hindu *varnas*
Buddha: Enlightened One
bugyal: high meadow above the treeline
cantonment: former British military district
capsicum: bell pepper
caste: Hindu group that practices a hereditary occupation, has a definite ritual status, and marries within the group
chaat: snack
chador: shawl
chai (chiya): tea, generally boiled with milk and sugar
chaitya: Buddhist prayer hall or miniature *stupa*
chakra: Wheel of the Law in Buddhism; Vishnu's discus weapon in Hinduism
chalo: let's go
chang: Himalayan rice wine
channa: chickpeas

chappals: leather sandals
chapati: unleavened, griddle-cooked bread
charbagh: traditional Mughal garden form, used particularly in tombs.
cheeni: sugar
chhattri: cenotaph; cremation monument
chikki: peanut brittle
chillum: mouthpiece of a *hookah,* or a pipe use to smoke *ganja*
chorten: Tibetan Buddhist memorial shrine
chowk (chauk): market area or square
chowkidar: watchman
coir: woven coconut fibers
communalism: religious prejudice, especially between Hindus and Muslims
Congress (I): party that grew from Indian National Congress that pushed for Indian Independence; party of Jawaharlal Nehru, Indira Gandhi; "I" is for "Indira"
CPM, CPI(M): Communist Party of India (Marxist), based in West Bengal, symbolized by a hammer and sickle
CPN-UML: Communist Party of Nepal-United Marxist-Leninist, symbolized by a sun
crore: ten million, written 1,00,00,000
cutlet: meat or vegetable patty
dahi: yogurt
dal: lentil soup; staple dish eaten with rice
dacoit: armed bandit
Dalit: currently preferred term for former "Untouchables"
darshan: "seeing" a Hindu deity through his or her image
deodar: tall Indian cedar tree
dhaba: roadside food stand
dham: place, often a sacred site
dharamshala: resthouse for Hindu pilgrims
dharma: system of morality and way of life or religion (Hindu or Buddhist); one's duty and station in life
dhobi: washerman or -woman
dhoti: *lungi* with folds of cloth between the wearer's legs
dhow: boat of Arab origins
diwan-i-am: hall of public audience
diwan-i-khas: hall of private audience
DMK: Dravida Munnetra Kazhagam, regional party in Tamil Nadu
dorje: Tibetan Buddhist thunderbolt symbol
dosa: South Indian rice-flour pancake
dowry: money or gifts given by a bride's parents to the son-in-law's as part of a marriage agreement; officially illegal but still practiced
dudh: milk
dum: steamed
dun: valley
dupatta: scarf worn as part of the *salwar-kameez* costume
durbar: royal palace or court
Durga: Hindu goddess who slayed the buffalo demon Mahisha
eve-teasing: cat-calling, sexual harassment
fakir: Muslim ascetic
feni: Goan drink made from fermented coconuts or cashews
FRO: Foreigners' Registration Office
ganj: market
ganja: dried leaves and flowering tops of female cannabis plant, used for smoking
garam: hot
Garuda: Vishnu's half-man, half-bird vehicle
ghat: riverbank used for bathing, often paved with steps

Ghats: the name of the ranges of hills on the east and west coasts of the Indian peninsula
ghazal: Urdu love song
ghee: clarified butter
godown: factory warehouse
gompa: Tibetan Buddhist monastery
gopis: Krishna's milkmaids
gopuram: trapezoidal entrance tower of a South Indian Hindu temple
gosht: mutton or goat
GPO: General Post Office
gulab jamun: dry milk balls in sweet syrup
guru: religious teacher; in Sikhism, one of the ten founding leaders of the Sikh faith
gurudwara: Sikh temple
Guru Granth Sahib: Sikh holy book
Haj: the pilgrimage to Mecca that all Muslims are required to make once in their lifetime if physically and financially able
halal: food prepared according to Islamic dietary rules
Hanuman: monkey god, helper of Rama in the *Ramayana*
harmonium: air-powered keyboard instrument
harijan: literally, "child of God"; Mahatma Gandhi's name for the Untouchables
hartal: general strike
haveli: Rajasthani mansion, traditionally painted with murals
hijra: eunuch; transvestite
hookah: elaborate smoking apparatus in which the smoke is drawn through a long pipe and a container of water
howdah: seat for an elephant rider
idli: South Indian steamed rice-flour cakes
imam: prayer leader of mosque, or Shi'a Muslim leader descended from Muhammad
imambara: tomb of a Shi'a Muslim imam, or a replica of one
Indo-Saracenic: architecture merging Indian style with Islamic style from the Middle East
Indra: early Hindu god of thunder, king of the Vedic gods
jagamohana: audience hall or "porch" of a Hindu temple
jalebis: deep fried, orange, syrup-filled sweet
jali: geometric latticework pattern in Islamic architecture
Janata Dal: political party based in U.P. and Bihar, supported by low-caste Hindus, symbolized by a wheel
Jat: large North Indian agricultural caste
jati: sub-division within the four Hindu castes
jauhar: Rajput custom of mass *sati*
-ji: suffix added to names as a mark of respect
JKLF: Jammu and Kashmir Liberation Front, militant group seeking independence for Kashmir
juggernaut: corruption of the deity Jagannath's name; refers to large ceremonial carts used to transport the deity
kaju: cashew nut
Kali: black-skinned Hindu goddess with lolling tongue who wears snakes and skulls
kama: physical love, one of the four goals of a Hindu's life
kameez: loose-fitting woman's shirt
karma: what goes around, comes around
kata: silk prayer shawl, usually presented to a lama when visiting a monastery
khadi: homespun, handwoven cotton cloth

Khalistan: "Land of the Pure"; name of independent Punjab desired by Sikh separatists

khalsa: Punjabi for "pure"; a "baptized" Sikh

kheer: rice cooked in sweetened milk, raisins, and almonds

khukuri: machete-like Nepalese "Gurkha" knife

kofta: meat- or vegetable-balls

korma: creamy curry

Krishna: Hindu god; plays flute and frolics with milkmaids; Arjuna's charioteer in *Mahabharata* who sang *Bhagavad Gita;* considered an avatar of Vishnu

kshatriya: member of the warrior/ruler caste, second highest of the four *varnas* of the Hindu caste system

kulfi: thick pistachio-flavored ice cream

kumbh: pitcher or pot

kurta: long men's shirt

lakh: one hundred thousand (usually rupees or people), written 1,00,000

Lakshmi: Goddess of fortune and wealth, often considered the consort of Vishnu

lama: Tibetan-Buddhist priest or holy man

lassi: yogurt and ice-water drink

lila: Hindu concept of divine "play:" a god (usually Krishna) sporting with human worshippers, or theatrical production depicting a myth (usually *Ramayana*).

linga: also *lingam;* stone shaft that symbolizes Shiva; while originally a phallic symbol, it has lost that meaning for most Hindus

Lok Sabha: lower house of Indian parliament

lungi: sarong tied around a man's waist

Macchendranath: Newari rain god

machli: fish

maha: great

Mahabharata: Sanskrit epic about the five Pandava brothers' struggle to regain their kingdom

mahal: palace

mahout: elephant trainer

mandala: circle symbolizing universe in Hindu and Buddhist art, used in meditation

mandapam: colonnaded hall leading up to a Hindu or Jain temple sanctum

mandir: Hindu or Jain temple

mani: stone wall with Tibetan inscriptions

mantra: sacred word or chant used by Hindus and Buddhists to aid in meditation

marg: road

masala: a mix of spices, usually containing cumin, coriander, and cardamom

masjid: mosque; Muslim place of worship

math: residence for Hindu priests or sadhus

maya: the illusory world of everyday life

mehendi: painting of intricate, semi-permanent henna designs on the hands or feet

mela: fair or festival

mirch: hot pepper

moksha: Hindu salvation; liberation from *samsara*

momo: Tibetan stuffed pastry similar to wontons or ravioli

monsoon: season of extremely heavy rains

muezzin: crier who calls Muslims to prayer from the minaret of a mosque

mullah: Muslim scholar or leader

murgh: chicken

mutter: green peas

naan: unleavened bread cooked in a tandoor

nadi: river

naga: Hindu aquatic snake deity

nagar: city

Nandi: Shiva's bull vehicle

Narayan: Vishnu sleeping on the cosmic ocean

naryal: coconut

nawab: Muslim governor or landowner

NDP: National Democratic Party, right-wing party in Nepal

neem: plant product used as an insecticide

Nepali Congress: centrist party that led the movement for democracy in Nepal, symbolized by a tree

nirvana: nothingness, a blissful void, the goal of Buddhists

Om: ॐ; sacred invocation; mantra used by Hindus and Buddhists.

paan: betel leaf stuffed with areca nut

paise: 1/100 of a rupee

pagoda: Nepalese Hindu temple with tiered roofs

pakoras: cheese or other foods deep-fried in chick-pea batter

palak: spinach

palanquin: hand-carried carriage

panchayat: traditional five-member village

pandit: honored or wise person; Hindu priest

paneer: homemade cheese

pani: water

papad: crispy lentil wafer

paratha: multi-layered, whole-wheat bread cooked on a griddle

Parsi: "Persian"; Zoroastrians who migrated to India after Muslim conversion of Iran

Partition: 1947 division of British India along religious lines to create India and Pakistan

Parvati: mountain goddess; consort of Shiva through whom his power is expressed

peon: low-level worker

phal: fruit

pipal: bodhi tree

pitha: Hindu holy place associated with the goddess Sati

pongal: rice item garnished with black peppers and chilies, often sweet

prasad: food consecrated by a Hindu deity and given out to worshipers

puja: prayers and offerings of food and flowers to a Hindu deity

pujari: Hindu priest conducting ceremonies in a temple

pukkah: finished, ripe, complete

pulao: fried rice with nuts or fruit

Puranas: Hindu mythological poems

purdah: Muslim practice of secluding women

puri: small, deep-fried bread

qawwali: Sufi devotional or love song

qila: fort

Qur'an: Muslim holy book containing Muhammad's Arabic divine revelations

Radha: milkmaid consort of Krishna

raga: melodic structure, the base for lengthy musical improvisations

raita: spicy salad of vegetables and yogurt

raksi: strong Himalayan liquor

raj: government or sovereignty

Raj: the British Empire in India

raja: king

Rajputs: medieval Hindu warrior-princes of central India and Rajasthan

Rama: Hindu hero-god of the *Ramayana* who defeats the demon Ravana; avatar of Vishnu

Ramadan: holiest month in the Islamic calendar, when Muslims fast from dawn to dusk

Ramayana: epic "romance of Rama" telling of Rama's rescue of wife Sita from Ravana

rani: queen

rath: cart, particularly one used in Hindu religious festivals

Ravana: villain of the epic *Ramayana*

RNAC: Royal Nepal Airlines Corporation

roti: bread

RSS: Rashtriya Swayamsevak Sangh (National Volunteer Corps), Hindu nationalist paramilitary organization

saag: pureed spinach or other greens

sabji: vegetables

sadhu: ascetic Hindu holy man

sagar: sea or lake

sahib: "master," title given to English colonial bosses and still used for Europeans

salwar: women's baggy pants worn with kameez

sambar: large, dark brown deer

sambar: South Indian lentil soup

samosa: deep-fried vegetable or meat pastry

samsara: the endless cycle of life, death and rebirth in Buddhism and Hinduism

sangam: meeting point of two rivers; also name of early gatherings of Tamil poets

sankha: Vishnu's conch shell

sannyasin: "renouncer," Hindu ascetic wanderer who has given up worldly life

sant: saint, holy man

sari: six (sometimes nine) yards of cloth, usually silk or cotton, draped around a woman's body, worn with a matching blouse

sati: custom that widows burned themselves on their husbands' funeral pyres

Sati: Hindu goddess who landed in pieces all over India, forming *shakti* pithas; considered Shiva's consort

satyagraha: "truth force," Mahatma Gandhi's protest by non-violent non-cooperation

scheduled castes: official name for the former "Untouchable" groups, whose castes are listed in a "schedule" in the constitution

scheduled tribes: aboriginal groups recognized under the Indian constitution

sepoy: Indian serving in British Indian army under the Raj

Shaivite: follower of Shiva

shakti: divine feminine power in Hinduism

Shankara: Shiva

shanti: peace

Shi'a: Muslim sect which split from the Sunnis in the 8th century AD in a succession dispute; Shi'as look to imams in Iran as their spiritual leaders

shikhara: pyramid-shaped spire on a Hindu temple

Shitala: "cool" goddess of smallpox and other fever diseases in North India

Shiva: great god of Hinduism, known as the Destroyer in the Hindu trinity; usually depicted as an ascetic holy man

Shiv Sena: regional Hindu nationalist party in Maharashtra

shudra: member of the laborer caste, lowest of the four Hindu *varnas*

sindur: vermilion paste used as an offering to Hindu deities

Sita: Rama's wife in the *Ramayana*, kidnapped by Ravana

sitar: 20-stringed instrument made from a gourd with a teakwood bridge

Sri: title of respect and veneration

STD/ISD: standard trunk dialing/international subscriber dialing

stupa: large hemispherical mound of earth, usually containing a Buddhist relic

Sufi: member of Islamic devotional, mystical movement

Sunni: largest Muslim sect; believes in elected leaders for the Islamic community

swadeshi: domestic goods; the Indian freedom movement called for their use rather than British imports

swaraj: self-rule; what the Indian freedom movement demanded

sweeper: low-caste or Untouchable Hindu whose vocation is sweeping streets or cleaning latrines

tabla: two-piece drum set

tal: lake

tandoor: clay, funnel-shaped oven

tara: Tantric female companion to a *dhyani* Buddha

Terai: foothills at the base of the Himalayas

tempo: three-wheeled motor vehicle

thali: complete meal served on steel plate with small dishes of condiments

thanka: Tibetan scroll-painting of a *mandala*, used as an aid in meditation

thukpa: Tibetan noodle soup

tiffin: snack or light meal

tirtha: "crossing" between earth and heaven

tirthankara: one of 24 Jain "crossing-makers," a series of saints culminating with Mahavira, the founder of Jainism

toddy: unrefined coconut liquor

tong-ba: Nepali grain liquor

tonga: two-wheeled carriage drawn by a horse or pony

topi: cap

trishul: trident; symbol of Shiva and originally a symbol of the Goddess

Untouchables: casteless Hindus, formerly shunned by high-caste Hindus because their touch was considered polluting; now known as scheduled castes, Dalits, or Harijans

Upanishads: speculative, philosophical Sanskrit Hindu hymns composed around 800 BC

utthapam: thick dosa made with onion

vadai: doughnut-shaped rice cake dipped in curd or sambar

Vaishnavite: follower of Vishnu

vaishya: member of the merchant caste, third-highest of the four Hindu *varnas*

vajra: Nepalese Buddhist thunderbolt symbol

varna: broad group of Hindu castes; *brahmins, kshatriyas, vaishyas,* and *shudras* are the four *varnas*

Vedas: sacred Sanskrit hymns composed between 1500 and 800 BC, forming the basis of the Hindu religion

vindaloo: very hot South Indian curry

Vishnu: one of the Great Gods of Hinduism, known as the Preserver in the Hindu trinity; frequently appears on earth as an *avatar* to save earth from demons

VHP: Vishwa Hindu Parishad (World Hindu Society); Hindu nationalist organization

wallah: occupational suffix, e.g. rickshaw-*wallah*

yaksha/yakshi: early Hindu nature deity

Yama: early Hindu god of death

zakat: almsgiving required of Muslims

zamindar: tax collector or landlord in Mughal India

PHRASEBOOK

ENGLISH	HINDI	ENGLISH	HINDI
	Hindi is understood in most of North India.		
Hello.	Namaste.	How are you?	Kaisehain?
Sorry/Forgive me.	Maaf kijiyega.	Yes/No	Ha/Na.
Thank you.	Shukriya.	No thanks.	Nahin, shukriya.
Good-bye.	Phir milenge.	No problem.	Koi baat nahin.
When (what time)?	Kab?	What?	Kya?
OK.	Thik hai.	Why?	Kyon?
Who?	Kaun?	Help!	Bachao!
How much does this cost?	Iska dam kya hai?	Go away/Leave me alone.	Chale jao/Mujhe tang mat karo.
Stop/enough.	Bas.	Is...available?	Yaha...milta hai?
Please repeat.	Phir se kahiye.	What's this called in Hindi?	Hindi mein ise kya kehte hain?
Please speak slowly.	Zara dhire boliye.	I don't understand.	Samajha nahin.
What is your name?	Apka nam kya nai?	My name is...	Mera nam...hai.
I like...	Mujhe...acha lagta hai.	I don't like...	Mujhe...acha nahin lagta.
My country is...	Mera desh...hai.		

Directions			
(to the) right	dayne hath	(to the) left	bayan hath
How do I get to...?	...ka rasta kya hai?	How far is...?	...kitna dur hai?
near	pas mein	far	dur
Where is...?	...kahaan?	out	bahar
below	niche	at the back of	piche
above	upar	in front of	samne

Food and Drink			
bread	dabal roti	rice	chawal
meat	maans	water	pani
vegetables	sabzi	sweets	mitthai

Times and Hours			
open	khula	closed	band
What time is it?	Kitne baje hain?	morning	subah
afternoon	dopahar	evening	shaam
night	raat	yesterday	kal
today	aaj	tomorrow	kal

Other Words			
alone	akela	friend	dost
good	accha	bad	bura
hot	garam	cold	thanda
medicine	dawaii	doctor	daaktar

Numbers					
one	ek	१	ten	das	१०
two	do	२	eleven	gyaarah	११
three	teen	३	twelve	baarah	१२
four	char	४	fifteen	pandraah	१५
five	panch	५	twenty	bees	२०
six	chei	६	twenty-five	pachees	२५
seven	saat	७	fifty	pachaas	५०
eight	aath	८	one hundred	ek sau	१००
nine	naun	९	one thousand	ek hazar	१०००

ENGLISH	BENGALI	ENGLISH	BENGALI
	Bengali is spoken in West Bengal and Bangladesh.		
Hello.	Nomoshkar.	How are you?	Kemon achen?
Sorry/Forgive me.	Maf korben.	No problem.	Hoye jabe.
Thank you.	Dhonyobad.	Yes/No.	Ha/Na.
Goodbye/ See you later.	Bidayo/Abar dakha hobe.	OK.	Achha/Thik.
Why?	Kano?	When?	Kata?
Who?	Ke?	What?	Ki?
What is your name?	Apnar nam ki?	Stop/enough.	Bas.
How much does this cost?	Koto taka?	Go away/leave me alone.	Chede bin/Birakt korben na.
Is...available?	...ase?	What's this called in Bengali?	Banglay eta ke ki bole?
Help!	Bachao!	Please repeat.	Aabar bolun.
My name is...	Amar nam...	Please speak slowly	Aste aste bolun.
I like...	Amar...bhalo lage.	I don't like...	Amar...bhalo lage na.
I don't understand.	Bujhi na.	My name is...	Amar nam...

Directions			
(to the) right	dan dike	(to the) left	bam dike
How do I get to...?	...kothayo bolben ki?	How far is...?	...koto door?
near	kache	far	door
Where is...?	...kothai?	across	opar

Food			
bread	paoruti	rice	bhat
meat	mansho	water	jol/pani
vegetables	shobji	fish	maachh

Times and Hours			
open	khola	closed	bandho
What time is it?	Koita baje?	morning	shokal
afternoon	bikel	evening	sondhya
night	rat	yesterday	gotokal
today	aj	tomorrow	agamikal

Other Words			
alone	aka	friend (M/F)	bondhu/banhobi
good	bhalo	bad	kharap
happy	khushi	sad	dukkhi/mon mora
hot	gorom	cold	thandha
office	doftor	backpack	bojha
condoms	nirodh	pain	byatha

Numbers					
one	ak	১	twenty	bish	২০
two	dui	২	thirty	tirish	৩০
three	tin	৩	forty	chollish	৪০
four	char	৪	fifty	ponchash	৫০
five	panch	৫	sixty	saat	৬০
six	choi	৬	seventy	sattar	৭০
seven	shat	৭	eighty	aashi	৮০
eight	at	৮	ninety	nabbai	৯০
nine	noi	৯	one hundred	ek sho	১০০
ten	dosh	১০	one thousand	ek hajar	১০০০

ENGLISH	TAMIL	ENGLISH	TAMIL
		Tamil is spoken in Tamil Nadu.	
Hello.	Namaskaram.	How are you?	Yep padi irukkai?
Sorry/Forgive me.	Mannikkavum.	No problem.	Kavalai illai.
Thank you.	Nanri.	No thanks.	Illai, véndam.
Yes/No.	Amam/Illai.	OK.	Se ri.
Good-bye.	Poittu Varén.	When (what time)?	Yeppo?
Why?	Yén?	What?	Yenna?
Who?	Yaru?	Is...available?	...irukka?
How much does this cost?	Yenna vélai?	Go away/leave me alone.	Yenna vidu.
Please speak slowly.	Medhoova pésungo.	What's this called in Tamil?	...Tamilla yenna?
I don't understand.	Puriyalai.	Help!	Kaa-paathu!
Please repeat.	Thiruppi.	Stop/enough.	Porum.
I like...	Ennaku...pidikkum.	I don't like...	Ennaku...pidikkaathu.
What is your name?	Unga péyar ennai?	My name is...	En peyar...

Directions

(to the) right	valadu pakkam	(to the) left	idadhu pakkam
How do I get to...?	...eppadi poradu?	How far is...?	...evvalavu dooram?
near	pakkam	far	dooram
at the back of...	...kku pinnadi	above...	...kku melai
in front of...	...kku munnadi	below...	...kku kirai

Food and Drink

vegetables	kari kai	rice	saadam
meat	maamsam	water	thanni
mango	maampazham	bread	roddi

Time and Hours

open	tharandhu	closed	moodi
What time is it?	Yenna néram?	morning	kaathaalai
afternoon	madyaanam	evening	saayankaalam
night	raatri	yesterday	néthikki
today	innikki	tomorrow	nalai

Other Words

alone	thaniya	friend	nanban
good	nalladhu	bad	kettadhu
hot	soodu	cold	aarinadhu
temple	kovil	doctor	maruthuvar
hospital	aaspathri	medicine	marunthu

Numbers

one	onrru	1	twenty	erupathu	20
two	eranndu	2	thirty	muppathu	30
three	moonrru	3	forty	naapathu	40
four	naanru	4	fifty	aiympathu	50
five	aiynthu	5	sixty	arrupathu	60
six	aarru	6	seventy	yerupathu	70
seven	yeru	7	eighty	annpathu	80
eight	yettu	8	ninety	thonnoorru	90
nine	onpathu	9	one hundred	noorru	100
ten	paththu	10	one thousand	aayeram	1000

ENGLISH	MARATHI	ENGLISH	MARATHI
		Marathi is spoken in Maharashtra.	
Hello.	Namaste/Namaskaar.	How are you?	Kasa kaya aahey?
Sorry/Forgive me.	Maaf karaa.	OK.	Achha/Thik aahey.
Thank you.	Dhanyawad.	No thanks.	Nako.
Who?	Kuon?	When (what time)?	Kehva?/Kadhi?
Why?	Kaa?	What?	Kaaya?
Please.	Krupa.	I want a room.	Mala ek kholi pahije.
I don't understand.	Mala samasta hani.	Yes/No.	Ho/Naahi.
Please speak slowly.	Sowkash bolaa.	Is...available?	...aahey kaa?
What's this called in Maratheet?		Please repeat.	Parat Sangaa.
Go away/Leave me alone.	Ikerdun zaa.	How much does this cost?	Hey kiti aahey?
My name is...	Maaza nau...aahey.	Wait a little	Jara thamb.
I like...	Mala...avad ta.	I don't like...	Mala...awardat naahi.
Help!	Madat laraa!	My country is...	Maza gay...ahey.
Directions			
(to the) right	uz ni kar dey	(to the) left	daa vi kar dey
How do I get to...?	Mala kaa zaitsa...?	How far is...?	Kiti dur...?
near	zawal	far	dur
right	ujvi baju	left	davi baju
up	var	down	khali
in front of	samor	behind	mage
inside	at	around	bhovti
Food and Drink			
bread	chapati/bhakri	rice	bhat
vegetables	bhaji	water	pani
meat	mans	fruit	phal
Times and Hours			
What time is it?	Kiti waazle?	closed	band
night	ratri	morning	sakaali
today	kal	yesterday	kal
tomorrow	aazudya	open	ughad
Other Words			
alone	ekta	friend (M/F)	mitra/maitrin
hot	garam	cold	thandha
good	changla	bad	vait
medicine	ausadh	doctor	vaidya
road	rasta	restaurant	upahargriha
museum	padarthasangrahalay	bathroom	snangriha
student	vidyarthi	library	granthalay
Numbers					
one	ek	१	twenty	vis	२०
two	don	२	thirty	tis	३०
three	tin	३	forty	chalis	४०
four	char	४	fifty	pannas	५०
five	pach	५	sixty	sath	६०
six	saha	६	seventy	sattar	७०
seven	sat	७	eighty	ainsi	८०
eight	ath	८	ninety	navvad	९०
nine	nau	९	one hundred	sambhar	१००
ten	daha	१०	one thousand	ek hajar	१०००

ENGLISH	NEPALI	ENGLISH	NEPALI
		Nepali is spoken in Nepal.	
Hello.	Namaste/ Namaskar.	How are you?	Kasto chha?
Sorry/Forgive me.	Sorry (maph garnus).	No problem./I'm fine.	Thik chha.
Thank you.	Danyabad.	No thanks.	Pardaina, danyabad.
Yes/No.	Ho/Hoina.	Good-bye.	Namaste.
When(what time)?	Kahile?	What?	Ke?
Who?	Ko?	Is...available?	...paincha?
Why?	Kina?	OK.	Huncha./La.
How much does this cost?	Kati ho?	Go away. (polite/ impolite)	Tapai januus ta./Jau!
I don't understand.	Bujina.	Please repeat.	Feri bhannus.
Please speak slowly.	Bistarai bolnus.	What's this called in Nepali?	Nepali ma ke bhanchha?
What is your name?	Tapai ko naam ke ho?	My name is...	Mero naam...ho.
Help!	Guhar!	My country is...	Mero desh...ho.
I like...	... man parcha.	I don't like...	... mar par dai na.
Stop/enough.	Pugyo.	Please give me..	Kripa garera malai...
Does anyone here speak English?	Yahan angreji bolne kohi chha?	I have a reservation.	Mero yahan reservation chha.
		Directions	
(to the) right	daya, dahurie.	(to the) left	baya, debre.
How do I get to...?	...kosari janne?	How far is...?	...kati tada cha?
near	najik	far	tada
east	purba	west	paschima
		Food and Drink	
bread	pauroti	rice	bhat
meat	masu	water	pani
vegetables	tarkari	food/meal	khana
		Time and Hours	
open	khulcha	closed	bandha
What time is it?	Kati bajyo?	morning	bihana
afternoon	diooso	evening	sanjha
night	rati	yesterday	hijo
today	aaja	tomorrow	bholi
		Other Words	
alone	eklai	friend	sathi
good	ramro	bad	naramro
happy	kushi	sad	dukhi
hot	garmi (weather)/tato	cold	jaado (weather)/chiso
newspaper	akhbar	magazine	patrika

		Numbers			
one	ek	१	twenty	biss	२०
two	dui	२	thirty	tees	३०
three	teen	३	forty	chaliss	४०
four	char	४	fifty	pachass	५०
five	panch	५	sixty	saathi	६०
six	chha	६	seventy	sattari	७०
seven	saat	७	eighty	asi	८०
eight	aathh	८	ninety	nabbe	९०
nine	nau	९	one hundred	ek saya	१००

ENGLISH	GUJARATI	ENGLISH	GUJARATI
Gujarati is spoken in Gujarat.			
Hello.	Namaste.	How are you?	Kem cho?
Sorry/Forgive me.	Maaf karo.	Yes/No.	Ha/Na.
Thank you.	Aabhar.	I am fine.	Hu majama chu.
Good-bye.	Avjo.	No problem.	Kaye vandhon nathi.
When?	Kyare?	I like...	Mane...gameche.
Is...available?	...maleche?	Stop/enough.	Bas.
What is your name?	Tamaru nam su che?	Help!	Bachao!
My name is...	Maru nam...che.	My country is...	Maro desh...che.
Go away/Leave me alone.	Jatore.	I don't like...	Mane...gamtu nathi.
Directions			
to the right	jamani baju	to the left	dabi baju
How do I get to...?	...no rasto kayo che?	How far is...?	...ketlu dur che?
Time and Hours			
open	khulu	closed	band
night	raat	yesterday	kale (gay kale)
today	aaje	tomorrow	kale (avti kale)
Numbers					
one	ek	૧	six	chah	૬
two	be	૨	seven	sat	૭
three	tran	૩	eight	aath	૮
four	char	૪	nine	nav	૯
five	pach	૫	ten	das	૧૦

ENGLISH	KANNADA	ENGLISH	KANNADA
Kannada is spoken Karnataka.			
Hello.	Ain samachar.	Good-bye.	Namaskara.
What is your name?	Ni nna he sa ru?	My name is...	Na nna he sa ru...
Please excuse me.	Da ya ma di na nna ksha mi si ri.	How much is this?	...nsu he ge?
Give me...	Ardha...	newspaper	varthapatrike
room	kone	address	vilasa
Directions			
to the right	jamani baju	to the left	dabi baju
How do I get to...?	...no rasto kayo che?	How far is...?	...ketlu dur che?
front	munde	back	hinde
Time and Hours			
open	khulu	closed	band
evening	sayankala	night	rathri
noon	hagalu	early morning	...ketlu dur che?
Food and Drink			
bread	rotti	rice	akki
meat	mamsa	fruit	hannu
vegetables	tharakarl	water	niru
curd	mosaru	dal	thovve
Numbers					
one	ondu	೧	six	aru	೬
two	eradu	೨	seven	elu	೭
three	muru	೩	eight	entu	೮
four	nalku	೪	nine	ombathu	೯
five	aidu	೫	ten	haththu	೧೦

ENGLISH	MALAYALAM	ENGLISH	MALAYALAM
	Malayalam is spoken in Kerala.		
Hello.	Namaste.	How are you?	Enngane irikkunnu?
Sorry/Forgive me.	Kshemikkuga.	Yes/No	Ade/alla
Thank you.	Valara upakaram.	No thanks.	Véndá.
Good-bye.	Pogetté.	No problem.	Sárawilla.
When/What time?	Eppoyá/eppam?	OK.	Seri.
Who?	Árá?	I like...	Enikka ... istamá.
Go away/Leave me alone.	Pó, salyappadade.	Stop/enough.	Madi.
I don't understand.	Samajha nahin.	Use the meter!	Míteru kanakkáyitta!
What is your name?	Ninngade pér endá?	Help!	Onnu saháyikkámó?
My name is...	Enda péru ...	My country is...	Enda támassam ... ilá.
	Directions		
How do I get to...?	... édu vazhiyá?	How far is...?	... ettara dúramá?
Where is...?	Ewidá?	above...	... ende molil
below...	... ende thara	in front of...	... munbil
behind...	... pinnil	inside	aahathe
outside	purethe		
	Food and Drink		
bread	rotti	rice	córa
meat	eracci	water	vellam
meal	batchanam		
	Time and Hours		
open	torannu	closed	adaccu
What time is it?	Ettara maniyá?	yesterday	innala
today	innu	tomorrow	nále

	Numbers				
one	onnu	൧	six	aaru	൬
two	rendu	൨	seven	eru	൭
three	moonu	൩	eight	ettu	൮
four	naalu	൪	nine	onpathu	൯
five	anju	൫	ten	pathu	൰

ENGLISH	TELUGU	ENGLISH	TELUGU
	Telugu is spoken in Andhra Pradesh.		
Hello.	Emandi	How are you?	Meeru ela unnaru?
Sorry/Forgive me.	Kshaminchandi.	No problem.	Paravaledu.
Thank you.	Krithagnatalu	No thanks.	Vaddandi.
Yes/No.	Avunu/Kaadu	OK.	Sare.
Good-bye.	Poyesta.	When(what time)?	Eppudu (time entha)?
What is your name?	Mee peru emiti?	My name is...	Naa peru ...
	Directions		
How do I get to...?	... ki poye daniki dari emiti?	How far is...?	... entha duramu?
near	daggara	far	dooramu
	Food		
vegetables	kooragayalu	rice	annamu
meat	mamsamu	water	neeru

	Numbers				
one	okati	1	six	aaru	6
two	rendu	2	seven	eedu	7
three	moodu	3	eight	enimidi	8
four	naalugu	4	nine	tommidi	9
five	aidu	5	ten	padi	10

INDEX

Next time, make your *own* hotel arrangements.

Yahoo! Travel

READER QUESTIONNAIRE

Name: _____

Address: _____

City: _____ State: _____ Country: _____

ZIP/Postal Code:_____ E-mail: _____ How old are you?____

And you're...? in high school in college in graduate school

employed retired between jobs

Which book(s) have you used? _____

Where have you gone with Let's Go? _____

Have you traveled extensively before? yes no

Had you used Let's Go before? yes no **Would you use it again?** yes no

How did you hear about Let's Go? friend store clerk television

review bookstore display

ad/promotion internet other: _____

Why did you choose Let's Go? reputation budget focus annual updating

wit & incision price other: _____

Which guides have you used? Fodor's Footprint Handbooks Frommer's $-a-day

Lonely Planet Moon Guides Rick Steve's

Rough Guides UpClose other: _____

Which guide do you prefer? Why? _____

Please rank the following in your Let's Go guide: (1=needs improvement, 5=perfect)

packaging/cover	1 2 3 4 5	food	1 2 3 4 5	maps	1 2 3 4 5
cultural introduction	1 2 3 4 5	sights	1 2 3 4 5	directions	1 2 3 4 5
"Essentials"	1 2 3 4 5	entertainment	1 2 3 4 5	writing style	1 2 3 4 5
practical info	1 2 3 4 5	gay/lesbian info	1 2 3 4 5	budget resources	1 2 3 4 5
accommodations	1 2 3 4 5	up-to-date info	1 2 3 4 5	other: _____	1 2 3 4 5

How long was your trip? one week two wks. three wks. a month 2+ months

Why did you go? sightseeing adventure travel study abroad other: _____

What was your average daily budget, not including flights? _____

Do you buy a separate map when you visit a foreign city? yes no

Have you used a Let's Go Map Guide? yes no If you have, which one? _____

Would you recommend them to others? yes no

Have you visited Let's Go's website? yes no

What would you like to see included on Let's Go's website? _____

What percentage of your trip planning did you do on the web? _____

What kind of Let's Go guide would you like to see? recreation (e.g., skiing) phrasebook

spring break adventure/trekking first-time travel info Europe altas

Which of the following destinations would you like to see Let's Go cover?

Argentina Brazil Canada Caribbean Chile Costa Rica Cuba

Morocco Nepal Russia Scandinavia Southwest USA other: _____

Where did you buy your guidebook? independent bookstore college bookstore

travel store Internet chain bookstore gift other: _____

Please fill this out and return it to **Let's Go, St. Martin's Press,** 175 Fifth Ave., New York, NY 10010-7848. All respondents will receive a free subscription to **The Yellow-jacket**, the Let's Go Newsletter. You can find a more extensive version of this survey on the web at http://www.letsgo.com.